Readings for Diversity and Social Justice

Fourth Edition

For nearly 20 years, *Readings for Diversity and Social Justice* has been the trusted, leading anthology to cover a wide range of social oppressions from a social justice standpoint. With full sections dedicated to racism, religious oppression, classism, ableism, youth and elder oppression, as well as an integrative section dedicated to sexism, heterosexism, and transgender oppression, this bestselling text goes far beyond the range of traditional readers. New essay selections in each section of this fourth edition have been carefully chosen to keep topic coverage timely and readings accessible and engaging for students. The interactions among these topics are highlighted throughout to stress the interconnections among oppressions in everyday life. A Table of Intersections leads you to selections not in the section dedicated to an issue.

Retaining the key features and organization that has made *Readings for Diversity and Social Justice* an indispensable text for teaching issues of social justice while simultaneously updating and expanding its coverage, this new edition features:

- Over 40 new selections considering current topics and events such as the Black Lives Matter movement, workplace immigration raids, gentrification, wealth inequality, the disability rights of prisoners and inmates, and the Keystone XL pipeline protests.
- An updated companion website with additional resources and short classroom-friendly videos that further complement the readings in each section.
- A holistic approach to sexism, gay, lesbian, trans and gender-queer oppression that challenges widely held assumptions about the usual practice of separating analyses of sex and gender binaries.
- A more optimistic focus on the role of social justice at all levels of society, whether personal, institutional, local, or global, and the intersections among them.

Offering over 140 selections from some of the foremost scholars in a wide range of fields, *Readings for Diversity and Social Justice* is the indispensable volume for every student, teacher, and social justice advocate.

Readings for Diversity and Social Justice, First Edition, 2000
Edited by Maurianne Adams, Warren J. Blumenfeld, Carmelita (Rosie) Castañeda, Heather W. Hackman, Madeline L. Peters, and Ximena Zúñiga

Readings for Diversity and Social Justice, Second Edition, 2010
Edited by Maurianne Adams, Warren J. Blumenfeld, Carmelita (Rosie) Castañeda, Heather W. Hackman, Madeline L. Peters, and Ximena Zúñiga

Readings for Diversity and Social Justice, Third Edition, 2013
Edited by Maurianne Adams, Warren J. Blumenfeld, Carmelita (Rosie) Castañeda, Heather W. Hackman, Madeline L. Peters, and Ximena Zúñiga

Readings for Diversity and Social Justice

Fourth Edition

Edited by

Maurianne Adams, Warren J. Blumenfeld,
D. Chase J. Catalano, Keri "Safire" DeJong,
Heather W. Hackman, Larissa E. Hopkins,
Barbara J. Love, Madeline L. Peters,
Davey Shlasko, and Ximena Zúñiga

Routledge
Taylor & Francis Group

NEW YORK AND LONDON

Fourth edition published 2018
by Routledge
711 Third Avenue, New York, NY 10017

and by Routledge
2 Park Square, Milton Park, Abingdon, Oxon, OX14 4RN

Routledge is an imprint of the Taylor & Francis Group, an informa business

© 2018 Taylor & Francis

First edition published by Routledge 2000

Third edition published by Routledge 2013

Library of Congress Cataloging-in-Publication Data
A catalog record for this book has been requested

ISBN: 978-1-138-05527-8 (hbk)
ISBN: 978-1-138-05528-5 (pbk)

Typeset in Swiss 721 and Classical Garamond
by Swales & Willis Ltd, Exeter, Devon, UK

Visit the companion website: www.routledge.com/cw/readingsfordiversity

Contents

Table of Intersections

The tables on the following pages will enable readers to see at a glance the multiple issues that are taken up in each one of the selections. This Table of Intersections follows the sequence of the Contents, but it is laid out to show the multiple interconnections discussed in each of the selections. Column indicators are as follows:

R	Racism
Cl	Classism
RO	Religious Oppression
S	Sexism
H	Heterosexism
TG	Transgender Oppression
Ab	Ableism
Y&E	Youth Oppression and Elder Oppression
Global Issues	Discussion of issues outside of US borders
Language Issues	Non-English or English as second language speakers, or use of American Sign Language rather than vocal speech

Selection number	Author and title	R	RO	S	H	TG	CI	Ab	Y&E	Global Issues	Language Issues
Getting Started: Core Concepts for Social Justice Education											
1	Tatum, "The Complexity of Identity"	X									
2	Kirk and Okazawa-Rey, "Identities and Social Locations"	X		X			X		X		X
3	Johnson, "The Social Construction of Difference"	X		X	X			X			
4	Sue, "Microaggressions, Marginality, and Oppression"	X	X	X	X		X	X			
5	Harro, "The Cycle of Socialization"	X	X	X	X		X	X	X		
6	Bell, "Theoretical Foundations for Social Justice Education"; Adams and Zuniga, "Core Concepts for Social Justice Education"	X		X			X	X			X
7	Young, "Five Faces of Oppression"	X		X			X	X	X		
8	Collins and Bilge, "Intersectionality Revisited"	X		X			X			X	
Racism											
CONTEXT											
9	Tatum, "Defining Racism"	X	X	X	X		X		X		
10	Takaki, "A Different Mirror"	X	X	X	X		X			X	
11	Dunbar-Ortiz, "This Land"	X									
12	Lipsitz, "The Possessive Investment in Whiteness"	X					X				
13	Smith, "Heteropatriarchy and the Three Pillars of White Supremacy"	X								X	
14	Anzaldúa, "La conciencia de la mestiza"	X		X	X		X				X
15	Dalmage, "Patrolling Racial Borders"	X	X	X	X		X		X		X
16	NNIRR Reports	X	X	X	X		X	X			
VOICES											
17	Chung, "Finding My Eye-dentity"	X		X							
18	Gansworth, "Identification Pleas"	X									X
19	Gomaa, "American Hijab"	X		X							
20	Aviles, "My Tongue Is Divided into Two"	X									
21	Coates, "Letter to My Son"	X		X							
22	DiAngelo, "My Class Didn't Trump My Race"	X									

Selection number	Author and title	R	RO	S	H	TG	CI	Ab	Y&E	Global Issues	Language Issues
43	NDWA, "Home Economics"	X		X			X				X
44	Charts from United for a Fair Economy	X		X			X				
Religious Oppression CONTEXT											
45	Pew, "America's Changing Religious Landscape"		X								
46	Killerman, "Examples of Christian Privilege"		X								
47	Blumenfeld, "Christian Privilege and the Promotion…"	X	X								
48	Bayoumi, "Racing Religion"	X	X							X	
49	Hilberg, "Precedents"	X	X								
50	Gilbert, "Maps"	X	X							X	
51	Eck, "Working it Out" and "See You in Court"	X	X								
52	Echo-Hawk, "Native American Religious Liberty"	X	X								
53	Dallas, "Religious Freedom Advocates…"		X		X	X					
54	Williams, "From Pearl Harbor to 9/11"	X	X							X	
55	Semple, "A Somali Influx Unsettles Latino Meatpackers"	X	X							X	
VOICES											
56	Kaye/Kantrowitz, "Jews in the U.S."	X	X	X			X			X	
57	Ahmad, "Oral History of Adam Fattah" and Zawam, "Oral History of Hagar Omram"	X	X	X							
58	Nowicki, "Modesto-Area…"		X								
59	Christina, "Why Are You Atheists So Angry?"	X	X	X	X						
NEXT STEPS											
60	Nasir and Al-Amin, "Creating Identity-Safe Spaces…"	X	X	X							
61	Kivel, "Guidelines for Christian Allies"		X								
62	Edwards, "Critical Reflections on the Interfaith Movement"	X	X								

Selection number	Author and title	R	RO	S	H	TG	CI	Ab	Y&E	Global Issues	Language Issues
84	Blow, "Real Men and Pink Suits"		X	X	X						
85	Martinez, "*Mestiza/o Gender*"	X		X	X	X				X	X
86	Green, "Look! No, Don't!"			X		X					
87	Gessen, "My Life as an Out Gay Person in Russia"				X						
NEXT STEPS											
88	LaDuke, "Grassroots"	X		X							
89	National Latina Institute for Reproductive Health report	X		X						X	
90	Evans and Washington, "Becoming an Ally"	X		X	X	X					
91	Chestnut, "Transgender Day of Remembrance"	X		X	X	X					
92	Maathai, "Unbowed"			X						X	
93	Chess et al., "Calling All Restroom Revolutionaries!"	X		X		X		X			
94	Sen, "Why I Marched on Washington"			X							
95	Utt, "Getting to Why"			X							
Ableism											
CONTEXT											
96	Bryan, "Struggle for Freedom"	X		X				X			
97	Schweik, "Immigration, Ethnicity, and the Ugly Law"	X						X			
98	Ferton, "Disability Does Not Discriminate"	X						X			
99	Murphy, "Post-Traumatic Stress Disorder…"						X	X		X	
100	Erevelles, "Disability in the New World Order"	X		X			X	X	X	X	
101	Vallas, "Disabled Behind Bars"	X		X			X	X	X		
102	Wilson, "The Silent Victims"						X	X			
103	Davis, "Go to the Margins of the Class"	X		X	X		X	x			
104	Colligan, "Why the Intersexed Shouldn't Be Fixed"			X	X		X	X	X		
105	Grasgreen, "Students with Disabilities…"							X			

Selection number	Author and title	R	RO	S	H	TG	CI	Ab	Y&E	Global Issues	Language Issues
NEXT STEPS											
125	Mock et al., "An Immediate End…"	X		X	X	X	X		X		X
126	Sazama, "Allies to Young People"								X		
127	Gullette, "Taking a Stand Against Ageism at All Ages"			X				X	X		
128	Markee, "What Allies of Elders Can Do"								X		
129	DeJong and Love, "Youth Oppression as a Technology of Colonialism"								X		
Working for Social Justice											
CONTEXT											
130	Pharr, "Reflections on Liberation"	X		X	X		X		X		
131	Love, "Developing a Liberatory Consciousness"	X		X	X		X				
132	Collins, "Toward a New Vision"	X		X	X		X	X			
133	Johnson, "What Can We Do?"	X		X	X		X	X			
134	Harro, "The Cycle of Liberation"	X		X	X						
VOICES											
135	West, "Courage"	X		X	X		X				
136	Anzaldúa, "Allies"	X		X	X		X			X	X
NEXT STEPS											
137	Smith, "Social Struggle"	X		X	X		X			X	
138	Zúñiga et al., "Intergroup Dialogue"	X		X							
139	Mohanty, "Decolonizing Theory, Practicing Solidarity"										
140	Wong, "The Renaissance of Student Activism"										

Key: R = Racism, RO = Religious Oppression, S = Sexism, H = Heterosexism, TG = Transgender Oppression, CI = Classism, Ab = Ableism, Y & E = Youth and Elder Oppression, Global Issues = discussions of issues outside of US borders. Language issues = non-English or English as second language speakers, or use of American Sign Language rather than vocal speech

Acknowledgments

The editing team for this fourth edition of *Readings for Diversity and Social Justice* brings together multiple and intersecting perspectives on the social justice issues presented in this book—we are male, female, transgender, and genderqueer; gay, lesbian, bisexual, heterosexual, and queer; African American, Latina and Latino, South Asian and White; Jewish, Christian, and atheist; US-born and born outside the US from diasporas of various immigrant generations and statuses. Some of us have learning disabilities and physical disabilities; are young adults, middle-aged, and elders; were born poor, working class, and middle class. Our academic specializations include ableism, classism, heterosexism, racism, religious oppression, sexism, transgender oppression, and youth and elder oppression. We include college faculty, administrators, program directors, and consultants—we are Social Justice Education faculty and doctoral alums who have, cumulatively among us, many decades of experience teaching middle and high school, college undergraduates and graduate students; facilitating faculty, professional development, and community seminars and workshops; collaborating with grassroots and activist organizations; and speaking at professional conferences on all of these social justice issues, as single and intersectional, local and global.

We have worked together on this volume (as on its predecessors) as a collaborative editorial team, valuing the different gifts and perspectives each one of us brings to this work, and achieving consensus on the overall scope, organization, and content of each of our editions of this volume as times have changed and the contents of each edition have changed as well.

As a collegial writing team in which all co-editors have equally contributed to each of the sections, we have resisted the tendency of libraries, reviewers, and scholars to cite our work by first author only. We are all too aware that this practice of convenience discourages collaborative work in academe, insofar as colleagues presume incorrectly that first authors are senior or primary. We search for ways to accurately represent our collaborative interactions as a writing team and the synergistic emergence of ideas and sharing of resources. The possibility of linking our names in a circle, while intriguing and eye-catching, has proven too challenging for typesetters and production teams. We regret that we have not yet found a manageable alternative to the convention of alphabetical order in listing editors and contributors, an ordering that affirms equity if only because it is "merely" alphabetical. In order to draw attention to our collaborative contributions, we have placed a statement at the beginning of each multiply-authored section that honors the nature and value of our collaborative work with a request that people who cite us include the full names of *all* listed authors. We have followed our own preferred practice by including *all* names of multiply-authored works in the works we cite in our reference lists.

While working as an overall collaborative editorial team, we delegate specific areas of primary editorial responsibility for each section of this volume. The editors whose names are identified in the Contents and the section-introduction title pages have primary responsibility for choosing the reading selections, writing the introductions, and developing section websites based upon their primary areas of expertise and experience. Agreement among section co-editors and co-authors of section introductions is not always easy—especially as we communicate by email, telephone conference calls, computer-supported conferences, or video conference technology—but this process has only increased our mutual respect and appreciation for the knowledge and insight, the dedication, energy, and goodwill that each of us continues to bring to this project.

It is especially important for us to acknowledge the contributions of our many generous, knowledgeable and supportive colleagues, families, friends, and students. We have drawn upon suggestions made by Social Justice Education course instructors and colleagues at the University of Massachusetts Amherst and at the many other places where we teach, conduct workshops, and consult, as well as the insights and practice of the graduate and undergraduate students who work with us in classrooms, residence halls, multicultural and diversity programs, and community organizations. We appreciate the feedback from those readers who have used earlier editions and shared their wisdom and ideas in preparation of this fourth edition.

We consider ourselves tremendously fortunate to have Catherine Bernard as our editor at Routledge, and her gracious, expert editorial team, who cheer us on and provide critical logistical and editorial support. This new edition has benefited immeasurably from Catherine's unwavering commitment, her support and enthusiasm for this project, her careful reading of many iterations of the text, her knowledge of the literature of social justice, her expert and helpful judgment calls on numerous challenges of substance and logistics in preparing this volume, and her tactful but firm guidance in helping us make hard choices—especially when it comes to cutting text. Her own astute social consciousness and awareness of societal challenges faced by our readership have informed our choices and our work at every stage.

Seventeen years ago, we first came together as an editorial team in Amherst, Massachusetts, a group of faculty colleagues and advanced doctoral students, to prepare the first edition of this book of readings in Maurianne's living room. But now we live and work in far-flung, professional roles and geographical locations, relying upon virtual rather than face-to-face communication from various points in California, Iowa, Illinois, Massachusetts, Minnesota, New York, Wyoming, and Santiago, Chile. But in doing this work we continue to feel as if we were still in the same room—well, almost.

We appreciate and acknowledge the many ways in which our long-time Social Justice Education program colleagues and mentors Lee Bell, Pat Griffin, Rita Hardiman, Bailey Jackson, Linda Marchesani, and Matt Ouellett, together with generations of social diversity and Social Justice Education course instructors, workshop facilitators, and students from the 1970s through to the present day, have enriched the vision of social justice education that underpins this volume. We have built upon each other's instructional practice in the growing international community of Social Justice Education educators. Our readers will find the fruits of this collaborative work in the many pedagogical designs, activities and resources published in the three editions, CD and websites of *Teaching for Diversity and Social Justice* (now in its third edition) whose work we continue to draw upon for inspiration and guidance in this companion volume of readings.

Maurianne Adams, Warren J. Blumenfeld, D. Chase J. Catalano,
Keri "Safire" DeJong, Mike Funk, Heather W. Hackman, Larissa E. Hopkins,
Barbara J. Love, Christopher MacDonald-Dennis, Madeline L. Peters,
Davey Shlasko, Rani Varghese, Ximena Zúñiga
September 2017

Readings for Diversity and Social Justice

A General Introduction

OUR APPROACH TO SOCIAL JUSTICE

This fourth edition of *Readings for Diversity and Social Justice* reflects an approach to social justice education that examines multiple instances of contemporary injustice and oppression while also affirming opportunities for achieving a socially just society. This volume has current-day topical introductions and selected readings that explore the historical roots and present-day dynamics of privilege and disadvantage rooted in racism, sexism, classism, and other forms of social oppression. We present examples of inequality, social hierarchy, and systemic oppression as described by people who benefit or are harmed by these conditions and we offer inspiring examples of individuals and groups who have taken action to achieve positive and sustained social change. We pay attention to the ways in which marginalized social groups contest their social inequality by renaming themselves and working together (often in alliance with privileged groups) to achieve empowerment and equality.

Social diversity and *social justice* are intertwined, in that members of different social identity groups experience social advantage or disadvantage on the basis of their race, gender, class, or other social group identities. Thus, the readings in this volume acknowledge and appreciate social and cultural differences, but also illustrate how these social and cultural differences are too often used to justify and maintain ongoing inequality. Although we understand social and cultural *difference* to be important in its own right, we want to emphasize how it also often serves as the basis for *inequality*, especially when differences rationalize privilege for social groups who are part of the accepted social "norms"—and when those norms are assumed to be available to everybody, while in practice are not available to marginalized or disadvantaged social groups. The overarching social system that maintains and reproduces these inequities is the system we call *oppression* and throughout this volume we explore this system from perspectives of personal experience, social institutions, and overarching social and cultural systems that operate nationally and globally.

This approach to social difference, social identity, social location, and social inequity has characterized our work since our first edition of this volume in 2000. At the same time, our understanding has deepened as we are repeatedly reminded of the intersections among our multiple, complex, fluid, and cross-cutting social identities and the ways they are heightened or diminished by different social settings. In the years during which we've presented four editions of this work, much has changed locally, nationally, and globally— for good and for ill. We have celebrated victories for social justice—marriage equality, the election of a black president, the visibility of women in national and local politics—and we have been disheartened by racist and sexist backlash, and the misuse of claims to free religious exercise as an excuse for homophobia and transphobia. In this volume, as in previous volumes, we maintain an undiminished optimism that socially just communities and society can be achieved and we also acknowledge the many challenges that confront all of our efforts to create more socially just relationships and institutions.

As in our earlier volumes, this fourth edition is organized in sections that foreground specific social justice "isms" while noting in the background the intersections among them. We believe "There is no hierarchy of oppressions" (Audre Lorde, 1983) and are aware that different forms of oppression affect people in different ways; that they vary in their intensity or virulence in different historical periods or geographical locations; that their duration and impact differs by time, place, and situation. It is not useful to argue competitive victim status or to ask who has suffered more or longer from different forms of oppression. It is far more useful to understand that all forms of oppression affect all of us, although in different ways and to different degrees.

This and other "core" points are made by authors throughout this volume. It is one of the several core social justice concepts that we present in the first section of this volume— "Getting Started: Core Concepts for Social Justice Education"—that serves as a preface to the other selections in this volume. For example, we take a complex "both/and" approach that acknowledges the differences among forms of oppression as well as the parallels and similarities in their dynamics, including the ways in which assumptions about domination and subordination become internalized and influence individual behavior, relationships, social institutions, and the "norms" of the larger society.

DISTINCTIVE FEATURES OF THIS FOURTH EDITION

This fourth edition of *Readings for Diversity and Social Justice* pays close attention to the many dramatic changes for better and worse since we wrote our earlier editions—on the negative side, we've been disheartened by abrupt reversals in immigration and educational policy and direction within national and local politics, efforts to reverse marriage equality and transgender rights, and misguided claims that US national identity is linked to one dominant religious affiliation; on the positive side, we've been moved by the vigorous youth activism and alliances, the national movement for Black Lives Matter, organizations that offer sanctuary to undocumented immigrants, and religious institutions that have welcomed gender-non-conforming parishioners. It feels as if the world has shifted under our feet in the past few years and that it is our responsibility, as editors and authors as well as social justice educators and practitioners, to rethink our approach; to offer the best examples we can to enhance our readers' understanding of current struggles; and to suggest ways to build creative alliances and networks that will sustain resistance to injustice and lead to lasting change.

In response to the changing social climate, we have shifted our theory and practice from a primary emphasis on anti-oppression work to a more optimistic focus on imagining what social justice might look like at different "levels" of society, including our relationships and local communities, and how we can achieve these visions of social justice personally, locally, and where possible systemically. This emphasis has been explained in *Teaching for Diversity and Social Justice*, third edition (Routledge, 2016), a book for which this volume of selected readings is the companion piece and which explores at greater depth many of the issues noted more briefly in the introductions to the sections of this volume.

Both *Teaching* (third edition) and *Readings* (fourth edition) take a newly holistic approach to sexism, gay, lesbian, trans, and gender-queer oppression through an analysis that explores them as interrelated manifestations of the same misguided gender binary. Recent writing on these interrelated oppressions challenges widely held assumptions about sex and gender binaries and highlights the role of medical science—and science more generally—in constructing our assumptions about "normal" human identities while pathologizing identities and experiences outside the normative boundaries.

Similarly, rather than having separate sections on different manifestations of religious oppressions (antisemitism or Islamophobia, for example), we propose an approach to Religious Oppression (in Christian-dominant nations of the West) that focuses on Christian hegemony, while noting that other dominant religions elsewhere in the world can be similarly hegemonic. We are well aware of the different manifestations of the various US "racisms" against Native peoples, Blacks, Latinx peoples, Asians, Arabs—all of them peoples with their own identity and culture who become "racialized" by Whites as different from and thereby inferior—and at the same time we believe that racism in all its different forms remains a self-perpetuating historical and current day force in the United States that requires coherent unified analysis.

In the same vein, we take a unitary approach to youth and elder oppression at the two ends of the human lifespan and note how together they illustrate the intersections among all forms of oppression. We have gained new appreciation for the ways in which various forms of privilege or disadvantage—classed, raced, gendered—intersect and complicate each other in local as well as global settings and life experiences. These new understandings inform this fourth edition of *Readings for Diversity and Social Justice*, having already reshaped our approach to the third edition of *Teaching for Diversity and Social Justice* (2016). We urge readers of this new edition of *Readings* to read the companion volume *Teaching* as well, to enrich their understanding and analysis of the kaleidoscopic interactions of the many ways in which hierarchical structures of advantage and disadvantage, privilege and marginalization, shift and change in local and global contexts.

As in our earlier editions, this fourth edition is organized in sections focused upon specific forms of social identity and oppression (namely Racism; Classism; Religious Oppression; Sexism, Heterosexism, and Trans* Oppression; Ableism; Youth and Elder Oppression) that foreground the issue itself without losing sight of the many intersections among all of these social group identities and their kaleidoscopic manifestations of privilege or disadvantage. We know that each one of us is raced, gendered with sexual identities, classed, identified with a religious or non-religious affiliation, able-bodied/minded or disabled, with memories of youth oppression carried in our movement along the age continuum.

We thus understand that each one of us combines privilege with marginalization, in different proportions, according to our different social identities and social locations, and that these proportions of advantage and disadvantage inevitably shift according to time, place, and situation.

These complexities lead to seeming contradictions or paradoxes in our work as social justice educators. We know that we must pay attention to the privileges accorded to and normalized by advantaged social groups and inaccessible to disadvantaged social groups. We tend to assume and thus ignore our experiences of privilege or social advantage, while often focusing on instances in which we are targeted or disadvantaged. We hope that the selections in this volume will illustrate how every one of us is differently "privileged" or "disadvantaged" by our intersections of social identities as well as by the social situations in which one identity may have greater salience than another, or visibility or invisibility.

The current controversies concerning immigration and the re-emergence of America-first "nativism" in US national politics have led us to reframe our discussions of historical and contemporary racism(s), ethnocentrism, nationalism, and the intersections among them with renewed urgency. These intersections have included the undeniable racialization of religious "others" while obscuring the degree to which US racism shapes our attitudes toward religious difference. More than an "intersection," the simultaneity of prejudices or hatreds based on both religion and race in current politics makes the two "categories" of religion and race appear indistinguishable. At the same time, it has been encouraging to see the push-back to resist those who would use religion to rationalize their heterosexism, transgender oppression, and sexism as well as their racism. Social relations change, but also seem to stay the same.

The 2016 US election—as well as similar election tensions throughout Britain and Europe—forced a rethinking of local and global economic systems as well as class and classism, because of the radical, socialist, populist, and conservative clashes and coalitions that resurfaced after a period of seeming quiescence and shared prosperity. It now seems obvious to almost everyone that global financial markets favor only the few while harming and leaving behind the many, so that politicians and citizens are forced to grapple with the consequences of global financial interconnectedness on local communities as well as national Gross Domestic Product (GDP) together with economic consequences for other forms of social inequality and injustice. While we have not addressed the consequence of climate change explicitly in this volume, we consider it a deeply troubling result of resource- and economic-driven inattention to the interdependence of life on this earth.

In this new edition, we have selected readings to provide context, hear contemporary voices, and suggest ways to foster change, given these recent challenges—many of which mirror earlier historical challenges. We drew upon the recommendations of many users and reviewers of our previous third edition to help us decide which readings to keep from the earlier edition and where updates and new selections were needed. The readings were chosen to do the dual job of "foregrounding" the subject of each section while clearly "backgrounding" other intersecting identities and forms of oppression. These intersections are noted in a Table of Intersections that is located immediately following the Contents. This Table of Intersections provides a checklist of sorts, to help readers identify all selections that treat issues of race, religion, gender, sexuality, disability, class, and age, beyond those in designated topical sections.

Not only has our approach to each social justice issue grown more intersectional over the years; we also take a more global, less US-centric approach through our introductions and through our selection of some readings. The economy itself is global, and issues of class, race, gender, sexuality, language, youth and age are increasingly shaped by immigrant and native-born communities newly living side by side. Given the multiple zigzag diasporas of peoples crossing oceans and moving across national boundaries, it is no longer useful (if it ever was) to think in terms of domestic as distinct from "foreign" international racial or ethnic identities, especially as communities of color in the United States and elsewhere frame and reframe their own racial, ethnic, national self-awareness on current and/or more distant racial, ethnic, national, or religious legacies. Examination of religious oppression in the United States, to offer another example, brings us face-to-face with peoples who may be first-generation US citizens and also the progeny of intergenerational diasporas, so that in this case as well, domestic and international dimensions of religious difference or conflict cannot be neatly separated from each other, may reiterate conflicts in nations or regions of origin, and thus reflect complex class-based or ethnic/race-based group conflicts. The internet creates instantaneous networks and propels conflict as well as constructive social activism across thousands of miles.

As section editors, we are always faced with significant space constraints in preparing a manageable book covering multiple manifestations of oppression book-ended by Core Concepts and Working for Social Justice. We cannot presume to be exhaustive either in the number of topics we cover or in the depth and completeness of our inquiry into each. Our website adds a few additional resources, including short classroom-friendly videos geared to each of the section topics that provide additional perspectives. We hope to stimulate interest and curiosity and we trust that readers will carry ideas and approaches from these readings into everyday life.

OUR USE OF TERMINOLOGY AND LANGUAGE

We capitalize but do not hyphenate specific ethnicities (African American, Asian American) and capitalize racial designations when used as proper nouns (Blacks, Latinx, Whites) but not when used as adjectives (black communities, white settlers) although ethnic "proper names" are capitalized when used as adjectives as well as nouns (Native American, Native peoples; Latinx or Latino/a workers). We note that racial and racialized group identity designations such as Black, Latino/a, Native American, Asian/Pacific Islander, White are not really parallel terms in that they conflate race, ethnicity, and pan-ethnicity from different historical, geographical, and diasporic legacies. They are "socially constructed" as we explain throughout this volume and because they are socially constructed, they change. Hispanics, Latinos/as, Latinx, Chicanos/as are politically and ideologically different although they refer to many of the same peoples. *Latinx* is becoming a preferred term because it degenders while avoiding the awkward Latino/a or Latin@ and is both a singular and plural adjective/noun.

In discussions of peoples who experience global diasporas, race-based or ethnic or religious descriptors become even more problematic. Whenever possible, we use terms that refer to national/geographic origin (people of South Asian descent, for example). We note that Arab, Asian, and African, for example, are "pan-ethnic" terms that reflect whole continents and collapse the specific identities of peoples from Jordan, Palestine, or Saudi Arabia; from China, Japan, Korea, or Vietnam; and peoples whose ancestry includes tribal or national identities within Africa.

We capitalize religions because they are names (Christians, Muslims, Jews) and we acknowledge our inconsistency in following current usage by not capitalizing antisemitism, capitalizing Islamophobia, and thus obscuring the origins of *Semitic* as a linguistic group that includes Arabic, Aramaic, and Hebrew languages.

We encourage the use of gender-inclusive pronouns in order to acknowledge the complexity of gender identities that have been erased by gender binaries, and we urge honoring personal pronoun preferences and change with the understanding that gender identification is not fixed. Some prefer the terms "ze, hiz, hir" and/or "they" used as a singular or plural pronoun that avoids the awkward "he/she" or "s/he" construction while also degendering.

Our guiding principle is to adopt terms preferred by people from targeted groups who have named themselves: "people of color" rather than "nonwhite"; "gay, lesbian, bisexual, pansexual" rather than "homosexual"; "people with disabilities" rather than "handicapped." Some of the reading selections will also draw on language used by targeted communities to reclaim previously negative terms such as "queer," "crip," "girl," "tranny," in order to reframe slurs into terms of pride and ownership. We know that naming is a necessarily fluid, sometimes situational and at times contradictory and confusing process, by which peoples/groups/communities rightly insist on defining themselves rather than acquiescing to names imposed by others. We encourage people to recognize that such terms will continue to evolve and change and to appreciate the significance of the power to name oneself as an important aspect of group identity and resistance. The authors of each section of readings address considerations of language usage as appropriate to the issues raised in their respective sections and, within selected readings, we retain the usage of the original author.

We want to notice how the terms used to describe the roles people play within the dynamics of oppression can be problematic. We propose terms that signal not the social location of individual actors but rather the social roles and outcomes created by an oppressive system. The binary terms "oppressor" and "oppressed" for example, that we used in earlier editions, no longer work for us in expressing the complex and nuanced intersections of privilege or disadvantage across different identities and different social locations or positions. We continue to struggle to frame language that doesn't trivialize the power or the damage from the oppressive system we want to expose. We use various terms to emphasize different dimensions of the binaries—terms such as *privileged, targeted, minoritized, racialized, gendered, marginalized, advantaged, disadvantaged, dominant, subordinate*—to convey the relative positions of groups of people within a system of social hierarchies.

As already noted in the Acknowledgments, we have also struggled over many years—and now in this fourth edition—to find ways to publicly reflect our own collaboration in a way that does not play into the dynamics of academic power and privilege fostered by the tendency of libraries, reviewers, booksellers, and scholars to cite multiply-authored work by the first author and reducing co-authors as "et al." We want to acknowledge our own collaborative work and encourage that of others in ways that do not maintain the presumed seniority and power dynamics accorded the first name listed. We have searched for ways of naming all of the authors in our collaborative work in order to contest assumptions of greater or lesser professional power or relative status that follow from the listing of names. We are well aware that the strictly alphabetical approach we have adopted is also unsatisfactory, in that any line of names, however arranged, suggests a ranking order—and we hope that alphabetizing our names levels the playing field and sends a clear message that we present ourselves and each other as having equivalent authority, expertise, and status.

To emphasize our shared authority, we intentionally place a statement at the beginning of each section to honor the nature and value of our collaborative work with a request that people who cite us *always* include the full names of *all* authors named as equally responsible for a given section, a practice we have followed in all editions of *Teaching for Diversity and Social Justice* in the second edition of which we used the following footnote: "We ask that those who cite this work always acknowledge by name all of the authors listed rather than either only citing the first author or using 'et al' to indicate coauthors. All authors listed on a section collaborated equitably on the conceptualization, development, and writing of this section." We have followed our own preferred practice by including the names of all co-authors of the works we cite within our own section introductions and permissions citations. The importance we attach to this challenge to professional practice is clear from the fact that we have already made this point in the Acknowledgments, repeat it here in the General Introduction and again in the footnotes to all of our multiply authored sections.

SUGGESTIONS ON HOW TO USE THIS BOOK

This volume offers examples of theory and historical context, voices of real people in real situations of advantage or disadvantage, and options for change that have emerged in the relatively new field of social justice education. In our own practice in our own communities we link the readings in this volume with a social justice practice that is experiential, student-centered, interactive, dialogic, question-probing rather than answer-providing—an approach that is more fully described and spelled out in our companion volume for teachers, facilitators, and everyone interested in pedagogical process, noted above.

Our focus is on specific manifestations of oppression (racism, classism, religious oppression, for example) as experienced by specific social identity groups, those privileged as well as those disadvantaged by each of the manifestations of oppression. The key themes and principles are illustrated by selections in Section 1, "Getting Started: Core Concepts for Social Justice Education," a section that readers should use to help theorize and shed light on approaches that will illuminate the selections throughout the entire volume. We combine a section-by-section focus on specific topics of social diversity and oppression, yet we also call attention to the intersections among social identities and experiences of oppression. Each section introduction highlights contemporary manifestations as well as intersections and the Table of Intersections identifies all selections that shed light on these topics, wherever they may be located in the volume. We urge readers to use the "Getting Started: Core Concepts for Social Justice Education" section and the section introductions for key definitions, historical contexts, and current topics as well as an overview of the goals served by each section's reading selections. We encourage course instructors to assign these introductions among their selected readings. We also urge that all readers use the Table of Intersections to find readings about specific social justice topics in different sections.

Our approach to social diversity and oppression also shapes the overall organization for each separate topic section into the three areas of "Context," "Voices," and "Next Steps." Each topical section starts with "Contexts" that offer historical background and overviews of relevant issues, followed by personal descriptions or narratives in "Voices." The "Next Steps" sections emphasize the extraordinary efforts that individuals and groups of people have made, and continue to make, to challenge privilege and disadvantage in order to create social change. Thus each section concludes with selections that describe pathways for empowerment, action, and change at the individual/interpersonal, institutional, and systemic levels.

The selections in the final section, "Working for Social Justice: Visions and Strategies for Change," build on the ideas and actions described in the "Next Steps" sections. We encourage readers to be aware of the many opportunities they can create or join to effect positive social change and to express that hope through individual and everyday actions, or through community, grassroots, or national coalitions and organizations. As educators, we believe that if we are to present information about systemic inequities, disadvantage, and oppression—and to expect that we become responsible for these inequities once we know about them—then as educators we must also present pathways of hope by acknowledging the role of social movements in US history as well as emerging networks and social movements.

This fourth edition is supplemented by a website that identifies videos for classroom or supplementary use, and lists discussion questions linked to the selected readings. The alphabetically organized Permission Acknowledgments and Citations at the rear of the book is the only bibliographical citation provided for all of the reading selections. Readers wanting to track citations, notes, and references that were cut from the reading selections due to space constraints—or to read the entire selections—should use this to locate the selections in their entirety.

We offer this book for use by different readers in many settings and situations. We use these readings in our own general education and graduate diversity classes; in graduate and undergraduate weekend seminars; as supplementary material for consultations, workshops, seminars, or presentations at conferences; in teacher education classes; and in multicultural education classes on our own campuses and communities in California, Illinois, Iowa, Massachusetts, Michigan, Minnesota, New Jersey, New York, and Wyoming and our consultations with communities, organizations, and campuses nationally. We know that earlier editions of this volume have been used in other settings—in ethnic studies; women's, queer, and gender studies; history; social studies; sociology and psychology courses; in social work and management; and in centers for teaching excellence—wherever there is an interest in the broad range of human experiences that have been shaped by social difference and by privilege or disadvantage. We anticipate that these reading selections will provide bridges among readers differently situated in their life experiences and who as readers themselves have had similar or dissimilar experiences. Our intention and hope is that they will provide opportunities for personal thought and reflection, empathy, connection, and discussion and, ultimately, liberation for all.

Reference

Lorde, A. (1983). There is no hierarchy of oppressions. *Interracial Books for Children Bulletin*, 14(3–4), 9.

SECTION 1

GETTING STARTED
CORE CONCEPTS FOR SOCIAL JUSTICE EDUCATION

Introduction

Maurianne Adams

This chapter introduces the core concepts frameworks that will help readers take a social justice approach to the sections that follow. We do not claim that these core concepts are the only foundations for social justice education or even that the authors and editors in this volume think about and use these concepts in the same ways. However, we encourage readers to keep these concepts in mind as they read other selections throughout this volume on specific social justice "isms" and the intersections among them, in order to understand our emphasis in this book. These social justice concepts will help readers recognize social injustices that crop up in every-day life and take a more thoughtful social justice approach to their own observations of fairness and unfairness.

The concepts that we think of as "core" include understanding (1) the differences between a diversity and a social justice approach; (2) the social construction of social group identities which are the result of inherited historical inequalities and allow for the maintenance of oppression; (3) the socialization processes by which everyone learns, reinforces and reproduces oppressive relationships and social structures; (4) the individual and group identities that people act on in different social contexts, which operate to maintain unequal privilege and advantage, or marginalization and disadvantage; (5) the pervasiveness of systems of oppression at all levels of social organization; (6) the intersections that play out among all social identities which are more or less unequal and more or less salient in different social settings; and (7) the importance of critical awareness, knowledge and skills to challenge, resist and take effective action for change.

Although there is not a one-to-one relationship between the eight reading selections presented in this section of the book and the seven concepts listed above, it will prove helpful to refer to these concepts in reading all of the selections that follow (see Adams and Zúñiga, 2016, for greater detail).

(1) SOCIAL DIVERSITY DIFFERS FROM SOCIAL JUSTICE

Social diversity and *social justice* are too often used interchangeably, since both are thought to refer to *cultural differences* as well as to *unequal social status*. While it is true that these two terms are closely related they are not interchangeable. By *social diversity,* we are referring to the differences among social identity groups based on race and ethnicity, gender and sexuality, class, religion, ability or disability, and age (youth and elders). These differences are expressed through cultural traditions and practices, language or accent, style of dress, values or worldviews that characterize the cohesion and experiences of social identity groups within the larger society that are assumed to be correct by "insiders" but are often stereotyped or misunderstood by "outsiders." This "diversity" among social identity groups is thought of as mere "differences" that need to be understood and respected by everyone and if so understood and respected, would lead to social justice for all. These issues are explored in Bell and by Adams and Zúñiga (both parts of selection 6).

In contrast, it is the view taken by many social justice educators that respectful acknowledgment of differences (emphasized in a "diversity" approach) offers a necessary but not sufficient step toward social justice. *Social justice* requires not only the recognition of social group differences, but also an understanding of how social differences (which are valued and necessary) are connected to *social group inequality* (which is unnecessary and calls for change). Too often, social differences are the rationale and justification for economic, political and social inequality, based on the historical reluctance of socially privileged groups to include and value socially marginalized or devalued groups. The philosopher John Rawls wrote that "Justice is the first virtue of social institutions, or more exactly, the way in which the major social institutions distribute fundamental rights and duties and determine the division of advantages from social cooperation" (1999 [1971], p. 7) while acknowledging the reality of the opposite – that social structures rarely accord with principles of justice and that people occupy unequal social positions and experience political, economic, and social advantages and obstacles. These "deep inequalities" in the social system, he wrote, are "not an unchangeable order beyond human control but a pattern of human action" (1999 [1971], p. 102) – and in this, unexpectedly, he echoed a similar claim from another of the primary philosophers of social justice, Paulo Freire, who urged that people who experience oppression "must perceive [that reality] not as a closed world from which there is no exit, but as a limiting situation which they can transform" (Freire, 1994 [1971], p. 31).

In order to achieve *Justice as fairness* (2001), Rawls wrote that all people must "agree to share one another's fate" through participation in a social system that has been designed without favoritism or privilege for anyone's expected social status or class position (pp. 7, 102). Such "fairness" is key to the notion of social justice; fairness allows neither advantage nor disadvantage based on one's social group identity.

If one thinks of oneself as a "normal" member of one's larger society, it may be difficult to see one's own "normality" as part a larger pattern of overall advantage and disadvantage, leading to social injustice. Instead, the norm shapes one's devaluation of "differences" or "otherness" which get marginalized because of their deviation from norms. In this sense, it is clear why *diversity* ("differences") shape group advantages for "normalized" identities in relation to the disadvantages for all the "others" whose *social inequalities* are rationalized on the basis of social norms. We use the term *oppression* to name structural and systemic inequality. Although it's more comfortable to talk about *diversity* than *inequality, oppression* or *social injustice*, we need to understand *social justice* if we are ever to dismantle the unequal and oppressive institutions and policies in order to reconstruct institutions and policies based on principles of fairness, equity and justice. All eight selections in this section take this approach, most notably Bell, Adams, Zúñiga (selection 6) and Young (selection 7).

(2) SOCIAL GROUP IDENTITIES ARE ROOTED IN HISTORICAL LEGACIES THAT HAVE BEEN SOCIALLY CONSTRUCTED

The second conceptual framework presented in this section examines social diversity based on differences in social identity and social location. Tatum (selection 1) explores social identity in a complex, multifaceted way that captures the tensions between dominant and subordinate identities (those privileged or disadvantaged on the basis of social group memberships) and gives examples of the tensions between them in present-day interactions. She explains the development of social identity in the context of identity development more generally, and describes the ways in which one's identity comes about through the interaction between one's internal sense of who one is (based upon one's social group identities) and the often stereotyped and inaccurate views of oneself and one's group that can be reflected back by others in the broader society.

Kirk and Okazawa-Rey (selection 2) note how one's own (and one's group's) social identity combine self-perception on the one hand, with misleading or damaging attributions made by others on the other hand. The balance between self-perception and attribution by others will likely differ in various contexts and different contexts may also highlight different dimensions of one's intersecting identities, so that one may be alert to one's racial identity in one context, gender or sexual or class identity in other contexts, and also the degree to which that identity is privileged or devalued in specific situations. Kirk and Okazawa-Rey also draw our attention to the *history* behind unequal social interaction and status in the present day, at the *micro* level (between individuals), at the *meso* level (within communities or social institutions) and at the *macro* level (the overarching society and culture). The authors in the second part of selection 6 (Adams and Zúñiga) discuss the need for an historical perspective on current-day oppression, to avoid guilt over inherited legacies of privilege or shame over inherited legacies of disadvantage. A historical perspective provides examples of social change movement and, because inequality comes to us from the past, it can be changed for the future.

Since the world of the present day is rooted in the world of the past, we need to examine the past if we are to understand why things are the way they are. If we pay attention, for example, to the *social, economic, legal and political construction of racism* in the United States, we can point to specific historical situations in which elites subordinated others on the basis of race to retain their group's advantages or ensure that other groups marked by race were disadvantaged. In this way, social identities can be understood as social creations and one's assumptions of superiority or inferiority, related to privilege and disadvantage, that one may have thought "natural" or "immutable" are instead understood to be social constructions within specific historical moments. As Johnson explains through the concept of *privilege* (selection 3) and Sue takes further in noting the cumulative impact of *microaggressions* (selection 4), most of what we experience in personal and social life is itself a social creation – and the social differences we consider so significant, so natural or so theologically sanctioned, are in fact based on unexamined cultural constructions and not on essential qualities of groups or persons.

The implications of the fact that social constructions of inequality linger in the form of unquestioned historical legacies, provides a momentous insight. Once we grasp how specific historical and cultural conditions have given rise to instances of privilege and to disadvantage, we can then see more clearly that these inequities can be changed. Paulo Freire's writing helps us understand how important it is for people to locate conditions of oppression within history, rather than fatalistically as inevitable – that "humans, in their permanent relations with reality, produce not only material goods . . . but also social institutions, ideas, and concepts . . . create history and become historical-social beings" (1994 [1971], p. 82). Freire recommends a problem-posing approach to education that takes "the people's historicity as their starting point" (1994 [1971], p. 65).

(3) PEOPLE ARE SOCIALIZED WITHIN SOCIETAL INSTITUTIONS THROUGH WHICH OPPRESSION GETS LEARNED, REINFORCED OVER TIME, AND REPRODUCED IN DIFFERENT SOCIAL SETTINGS

The importance of historical legacies for the perpetuation of present-day practices serves as a backdrop for Harro's "Cycle of Socialization" (selection 5), which presents an accessible snapshot of the socialization processes of everyday life. If one links these two frameworks – historical legacies and present-day socialization – one better understands the mechanisms by which the past is perpetuated in the present. Harro reminds us of our early and later experiences within social institutions – the family, schools, our peers, the workplace – where socialization (or "normalization") takes place without anyone thinking about what it is that is being perpetuated. Harro's discussion of "institutional and cultural socialization" and "enforcements" are key to the role of meso (institutional or small group) and macro (societal) levels where social norms, roles and norms of privilege or marginalization are learned in early childhood and reinforced during adulthood within trusted and familiar contexts – in families, schools, playgrounds, neighborhoods, the workplace and the media.

Later, in Section 8, "Working for Social Justice: Visions and Strategies for Change" (selection 134 titled "The Cycle of Liberation"), Harro's elaboration on her suggestion in selection 5 for "choosing the direction for change" becomes the starting point for how to question and resist socialization based on inequality and generate creative ways to work in coalition with others toward social change.

(4) THE INDIVIDUAL AND GROUP IDENTITIES THAT PEOPLE ACT ON IN DIFFERENT SOCIAL CONTEXTS OPERATE AS UNEQUAL SOCIALLY CONSTRUCTED POSITIONS OF PRIVILEGE AND ADVANTAGE, OR MARGINALIZATION AND DISADVANTAGE

It is challenging to discover that skin color, accented speech, perceived gender or sexual differences from norms of gender and sexuality, or the presence or absence of a physical or mental disability, are all *socially constructed* categories and are, therefore, useless as real-world indicators of talent, character, intelligence or morality. The readings throughout this volume identify many stereotypes we have been led to believe about "others" and place this misinformation within its original historical and cultural context by emphasizing the fact that our assumptions about what it means to be female or male or transgender; gay or straight or queer; white, Latino or black; young or old; learning disabled or able-bodied; Christian or atheist or Jewish, Hindu or Muslim, have been *constructed within historical conditions* that established advantage for some relative to disadvantage for others (examples include selections 10, 57, 66, 91, 111, 112, 129 and 132). As noted above, Harro's selection (selection 5) shows how we continue, from one generation to the next, to absorb stereotypes and prejudices as an unconscious part of our heritage.

Two selections focus specifically on the "flip sides" of privilege and oppression based on race, gender, sexuality and disability. Johnson (selection 3) gives concrete examples of "what privilege looks like in everyday life" and Sue (selection 4) gives concrete examples of the "microaggressions" which pile up daily on people who are marginalized by race, gender and sexuality, disability, religious and class oppression. This concrete and individual approach, noting specific instances of privilege or disadvantage, can be applied to all forms of oppression treated throughout this book. Many other selections point out the daily reproductions of privilege or disadvantage on the basis of identity and positionality. As Sue writes, these "microaggressions" are cumulative, through actions of well-intentioned people who are unaware of their role in excluding, silencing, ignoring and repeating stereotypes that marginalize and psychologically damage members of disadvantaged groups.

(5) OPPRESSION IS PERVASIVE AT ALL LEVELS OF SOCIAL ORGANIZATION

Social justice needs a theory of *oppression* to understand the dynamics of social inequality in a pluralistic US society founded on concepts of equality of opportunity and fairness in life's rewards. Thus, we need to move beyond the individual (or "micro") level of the socialization process that is described by Tatum (selection 1), Johnson (selection 3) and Harro (selection 5) to analyze how oppression is enacted and reproduced at the institutional level ("meso") and the societal/cultural ("macro") level. As Harro shows, the "micro" examples of privilege and oppression take place on an everyday basis in larger institutional settings such as our extended families, neighborhoods, schools, places of worship. Similarly, our socializing experiences in these social institutions are daily reinforced by the broader, overarching societal and cultural messages we simultaneously pick up from the media and accept without question in our normative culture.

In the two parts of selection 6, Bell, and then Adams and Zúñiga, describe the broadly structural features of oppression, with a major focus on the *levels* at which the dynamics of social identity advantage or disadvantage take place: enacted by the *individual* (as it is internalized) or played out between individuals; reproduced by the *institutional* (small groups such as classrooms or work-groups, larger institutions such as schools or corporations); and pervasive throughout the *societal* (overall social dynamics, as seen in the culture or the media).

Often these levels overlap, as in the case of a Christian college coach who leads prayer groups as pre-game motivation and team-building for a baseball team that includes Jewish, Muslim and atheist teammates, or a high-school counselor who assumes that a working-class student from an immigrant family is "not college material." Both the coach and the counselor are individuals who reproduce through their behavior their institution's normative values that reflect societal norms – and in these cases, students are excluded and devalued on the basis of their marginalized religious, class and ethnic social identities.

Kirk and Okazawa-Rey (selection 2) are also interested in the complex and overlapping ways by which personal and social group identities (as Tatum had presented them, in selection 1) overlap at what they term *micro-, meso-* and *macro-* levels of society. Their terminology may differ from the language of interpersonal, institutional and societal/cultural dimensions of oppression used by Bell, Adams and Zúñiga, but their analyses are similar. Young's (selection 7) analysis of the different dimensions of oppression also emphasizes the institutional and the societal/cultural levels, but she focuses instead on "faces" or facets of oppression, as if it were a kaleidoscope whose shape shifts as one turns the outer lens. Young describes five "faces" or facets of oppression that often interact, but are analytically distinguishable as *exploitation, powerlessness*, and *marginalization* of oppressed groups and their experiences of *cultural imperialism* and *violence*.

(6) SOCIAL IDENTITIES PLAY OUT INTERSECTIONALLY ALTHOUGH THEY HAVE DIFFERENT SALIENCE IN DIFFERENT SOCIAL SETTINGS

Most of the selections in Section 1 and throughout this entire volume combine a single "ism" approach (focusing on racism, classism and other forms of oppression) while noting the intersections among them. But if we were to examine our own personal experiences in everyday life, it would be obvious that our advantages or disadvantages on the basis of race, gender, sexuality, class, ability, religion and age interact at all times although with different degrees of visibility or salience, depending on the setting. There is therefore a tension in how best to analyze these phenomena – whether to focus on each form of oppression (the specific advantages relative to disadvantages) for the purposes of clarity and understanding, as in the selections by Tatum, Johnson or Sue, or to focus instead on their complex, dynamic interactions, as in Collins and Bilge (selection 8).

In this volume, we generally foreground the specific "isms" to better understand them, but we do not ignore the background of their interactions. To make the intersectional backgrounds more visible to our readers, we present a "Table of Intersections" immediately following the Contents, to identify and highlight the intersecting issues within each selection in this volume.

At the same time, we emphasize the importance of grappling with the strengths and challenges of taking an intentionally *intersectional* approach. In this section, Collins and Bilge (selection 8) pay close attention to the *relationships* among forms of oppression, the *social contexts* within which one or another social identity might seem most salient, as well as the shifting of balances between one's sense of advantage or disadvantage depending on the privilege or marginalization through which each of the intersecting identities has been experienced. Collins and Bilge write about *relationality* as their challenge to the habits of describing social identity categories as if they were separate, and instead stress that these social identity categories are interconnected not only in experience, but in one's practice – as a workshop facilitator, classroom teacher or grassroots community organizer. Every human interaction or setting has all social categories present, in that we are all raced, gendered, classed, with differing relationships of advantage or disadvantage in each of the categories. (See Adams, Bell, Goodman and Joshi, 2016, for discussions of how *intersectionality* is essential to effective social justice education practice.)

Collins and Bilge thus link *relationality* to *social context* in order to examine institutional contexts, national or international contexts, and historical contexts. Their examples of these three different kinds of *social context* lead them to a provocative analysis of *power relations, social inequality* and *social justice.* For example, they ask about the intersections of racism and sexism *across domains of power* – structural, disciplinary (in academe), cultural and personal (in relationships). They note that an intersectional critique of social inequality is not the same as an intersectional activism toward social justice, although both engage intersectional analyses and engagement.

(7) CRITICAL AWARENESS, KNOWLEDGE AND SKILLS ARE NEEDED TO CHALLENGE, RESIST AND TAKE EFFECTIVE ACTION FOR CHANGE

All selections in this first section and throughout this volume hold implications for a view of society characterized instead by fairness and justice. Readers of these selections might challenge themselves to imagine what a non-oppressive society might look like, in the absence of each and all of the five faces of oppression (Young, selection 7), or the reversal of the examples of privilege or microaggressions (Johnson and Sue, selections 3 and 4) – as Harro changes direction from a "Cycle of Socialization" (selection 5) to a "Cycle of Liberation" (selection 134). How might one actually describe actions to take or collaborative projects to plan toward social change, in order to achieve relationships, institutions and an overarching social system and culture that do not enforce or reproduce oppression? That is the question that should challenge readers of this volume. It is a challenge that this volume accepts, with possibilities and examples offered in the "Next Steps" selections in each of the "ism" sections and in Section 8, "Working for Social Justice: Visions and Strategies for Change."

References

Adams, M., Bell, L.A., Goodman, D.J. and Joshi, K.Y. (Eds.) (2016). *Teaching for diversity and social justice,* 3rd edition. New York: Routledge.

Adams, M. and Zúñiga, X. (2016). Getting started: Core concepts for social justice education. In Adams, M., Bell, L.A., Goodman, D.J. and Joshi, K.Y. (Eds.). *Teaching for diversity and social justice,* 3rd edition, pp. 95–130. New York: Routledge.

Freire, P. (1994 [1971]). *Pedagogy of the oppressed* (new revised edition). New York: Continuum.

Rawls, J. (1999 [1971]). *A theory of justice.* Cambridge, MA: Harvard University Press.

Rawls, J. (2001). *Justice as fairness: A restatement.* Cambridge, MA: Harvard University Press.

1

The Complexity of Identity

"Who Am I?"

Beverly Daniel Tatum

The concept of identity is a complex one, shaped by individual characteristics, family dynamics, historical factors, and social and political contexts. Who am I? The answer depends in large part on who the world around me says I am. Who do my parents say I am? Who do my peers say I am? What message is reflected back to me in the faces and voices of my teachers, my neighbors, store clerks? What do I learn from the media about myself? How am I represented in the cultural images around me? Or am I missing from the picture altogether? As social scientist Charles Cooley pointed out long ago, other people are the mirror in which we see ourselves.

This "looking-glass self" is not a flat, one-dimensional reflection but a multidimensional one. . . . Yet how one's racial identity is experienced will be mediated by other dimensions of oneself: male, female, or transgender, young or old; wealthy, middle-class, or poor; gay, lesbian, bisexual, or heterosexual; able-bodied or with disabilities; Christian, Muslim, Jewish, Buddhist, Hindu, or atheist. . . .

Who I am (or say I am) is a product of these and many other factors. Erik Erikson, the psychoanalytic theorist who coined the term *identity crisis*, introduced the notion that the social, cultural, and historical context is the ground in which individual identity is embedded. Acknowledging the complexity of identity as a concept, Erikson writes,

> We deal with a process "located" *in the core of the individuals and yet also in the core of his [her, their] communal culture.* In psychological terms, identity formation employs a process of simultaneous reflection and observation, a process taking place on all levels of mental functioning, by which the individual judges himself in the light of what he perceives to be the way in which others judge him in comparison to themselves and to a typology significant to them; while he judges their way of judging him in the light of how he perceives himself in comparison to them and to types that have become relevant to him. This process is, luckily, and necessarily, for the most part unconscious expect where inner conditions and outer circumstances combine to aggravate a painful, or elated, "identity-consciousness.". . .

WHO AM I? MULTIPLE IDENTITIES

Integrating one's past, present, and future into a cohesive, unified sense of self is a complex task that begins in adolescence and continues for a lifetime. . . .The salience of particular aspects of our identity varies at different moments in our lives. The process of integrating the component parts of our self-definition is indeed a lifelong journey.

Which parts of our identity capture our attention first? While there are surely idiosyncratic responses to this question, a classroom exercise I regularly use with students and other adult audiences reveals a telling pattern. I ask them to complete the sentence. "I am ....," using as many descriptors as they can think of in sixty seconds.

All kinds of trait descriptions are used—friendly, shy, assertive, intelligent, honest, and so on—but over the years I have noticed something else. Students of color usually mention their racial or ethnic group: for instance, I am Black, Puerto Rican, Korean American. White students who have grown up in strong ethnic enclaves occasionally mention being Irish or Italian. But in general, White students rarely mention being White. When I use this exercise in coeducational settings, I notice a similar pattern in terms of gender, religion, and sexuality. Women usually mention being female, while men don't usually mention their maleness. Jewish students often say they are Jewish, while mainline Protestants rarely mention their religious identification. A student who is comfortable revealing it publicly may mention being gay, lesbian, or bisexual. Though I know usually most of my participants are heterosexual, it is very unusual for anyone to include their heterosexuality on their list.

Common across these examples is that in the areas where a person is a member of the dominant or advantaged social group, the category is usually not mentioned. That element of the person's identity is so taken for granted that it goes without comment. It is taken for granted because the dominant culture takes it for granted. In Eriksonian terms, the person's inner experience and outer circumstance are in harmony with one another, and the image reflected by others is similar to the image within. In the absence of dissonance, this dimension of identity escapes conscious attention.

The parts of our identity that *do* capture our attention are those that other people notice, and that reflect back to us. The aspect of identity that is the target of others' attention, and subsequently of our own, often is that which sets us apart as exceptional or "other" in their eyes. In my life I have been perceived as both. A precocious child who began to read at age three. I stood out among my peers because of my reading ability. This "gifted" dimension of my identity was regularly commented upon by teachers and classmates alike and quickly became part of my self-definition. But I was also distinguished by being the only Black student in the class, an "other," a fact I grew increasingly aware of as I got older.

While there may be countless ways one might be defined as exceptional, there are at least seven categories of "otherness" commonly experienced in US society. People are commonly defined as other on the basis of race or ethnicity, gender (including gender expression), religion, sexual orientation, socioeconomic status, age, and physical or mental ability. Each of these categories has a form of oppression associated with it: racism, sexism, religious oppression/anti-Semitism, heterosexism, classism, ageism, and ableism, respectively. In each case there is a group considered dominant (systematically advantaged by the society because of group membership) and a group considered subordinate or targeted (systematically disadvantaged). When we think about our multiple identities, most of us will find that we are both dominant and targeted at the same time. But it is the targeted identities that hold our attention and the dominant identities that often go unexamined. . . .

DOMINATION AND SUBORDINATION

Dominant groups, by definition, set the parameters within which the subordinates operate. The dominant group holds the power and authority in society relative to the subordinates and determines how that power and authority may be acceptable used. Whether it is reflected in determining who gets the best jobs, whose history will be taught in school, or whose relationships will be validated by society, the dominant group has the greatest influence in determining the structure of the society.

The relationship of the dominants to the subordinates is often one in which the targeted group is labelled as defective or substandard in significant ways. For example, Blacks have historically been characterized as less intelligent than Whites, and women have been viewed as less emotionally stable than men. The dominant group assigns roles to the subordinates that reflect the latter's devalued status, reserving the most highly valued roles in the society for themselves. Subordinates are usually said to be innately incapable of being able to perform the preferred roles. To the extent that the targeted group internalizes the images that the dominant group reflects back to them, they may find it difficult to believe in their own ability. . . .

The dominant group is seen as the norm for humanity. . . . Consequently, it remains perfectly acceptable in many circles to tell jokes that denigrate a particular group, to exclude subordinates from one's neighborhood or work setting, or to oppose initiatives that might change the power balance.

In a situation of unequal power, a subordinate group has to focus on survival. It becomes very important for the subordinates to become highly attuned to the dominants as a way of protecting themselves from them. For example, women who have been battered by men often talk about the heightened sensitivity they developed to their partner's moods. Being able to anticipate and avoid the men's rage was important to survival.

Survival sometimes means not responding to oppressive behavior directly. To do so could result in physical harm to oneself, even death.

The use of either strategy, attending very closely to the dominants or not attending at all, is costly to members of the targeted group. Not-learning may mean there are needed skills that are not acquired. Attending closely to the dominant group may leave little time or energy to attend to one's self. Worse yet, the negative messages of the dominant group about the subordinates may be internalized, leading to self-doubt or, in its extreme form, self-hate. There are many examples of subordinates attempting to make themselves over in the image of the dominant group—Jewish people who want to change the Semitic look of their noses, Asians who have cosmetic surgery to alter the shape of their eyes, Blacks who seek to lighten their skin with bleaching creams. Whether one succumbs to the devaluing pressures of the dominant culture or successfully resists them, the fact is that dealing with oppressive systems from the underside, regardless of the strategy, is physically and psychologically taxing. . . .

The history of subordinate groups is filled with so-called troublemakers, yet their names are often unknown. Preserving the record of those subordinates and their dominant allies who have challenged the status quo is usually of little interest to the dominant culture, but it is of great interest to subordinates who search for an empowering reflection in the societal mirror.

Many of us are both dominant and subordinate. Clearly racism and racial identity are at the center of discussion in this book, but as Audre Lorde said, from her vantage point as a Black lesbian, "There is no hierarchy of oppression." The thread and threat of violence runs through all of the isms. There is a need to acknowledge each other's pain, even as we attend to our own.

For those readers who are in the dominant racial category, it may sometimes be difficult to take in what is being said by and about those who are targeted by racism. When the perspective of the subordinate is shared directly, an image is reflected to members of the dominant group that is disconcerting. To the extent that one can draw on one's own experience of subordination—as a young person, as a person with a disability, as someone who grew up poor, as a woman—it may be easier to make meaning of another targeted group's experience. For those readers who are targeted by racism and are angered by the obliviousness of Whites sometimes described in these pages, it may be useful to attend to your experience of dominance where you may find it—as a heterosexual, as an able-bodied person, as a Christian, as a man—and consider what systems of privilege you may be overlooking. The task of resisting our own oppression does not relieve us of the responsibility of acknowledging our complicity in the oppression of others.

Our ongoing examination of who we are in our full humanity, embracing all of our identities, creates the possibility of building alliances that may ultimately free us all.

2

Identities and Social Locations

Who Am I? Who Are My People?

Gwyn Kirk and Margo Okazawa-Rey

Identity formation is the result of a complex interplay among a range of factors: individual decisions and choices, particular life events, community recognition and expectations, societal categorization, classification and socialization, and key national or international incidents. It is an ongoing process that involves several key questions:

Who am I? Who do I want to be?
Who do others think I am and want me to be?
Who and what do societal and community Institutions, such as schools, religious institu-
    tions, the media, and the law, say I am?
Where/what /who are my "home" and "community"?
Which social groups(s) do I want to affiliate with?
Who decides the answers to these questions, and on what basis?

The *American Heritage Dictionary* (1993) defines *identity* as

the collective aspect of the set of characteristics by which a thing is definitely known or
    recognizable;
a set of behavioral or personal characteristics by which an individual is recognizable as a
    member of a group;

. . . .

These definitions point to the connections between us as individuals and how we are perceived by other people and classified by societal institutions. They also involve a sense of individual agency and choice regarding affiliations with others. Gender, race, ethnicity, class, nationality, sexuality, age, religion, dis/ability, culture, and language are all significant social categories by which people are recognized by others. Indeed, on the basis of these categories alone, others often think they know who we are and how we should behave. Personal deci- sions about our affiliations, culture, and loyalties to specific groups are also shaped by these categories. For example, in communities of color women may struggle over the question of race versus gender. Is race a more important factor than gender in shaping their lives? If a Latina speaks out publicly about sexism within the Latino community, is she betraying her people? This separation of categories tends to set up false dichotomies in which people often feel that they have to choose one aspect of their identity over another. It also presents particular difficulties for mixed-race, bisexual, or transgender people who do not fit neatly into such narrow categories. . . .

BEING MYSELF: THE MICRO LEVEL

At the micro level, individuals usually feel the most comfortable as themselves. Here one can say, for example, "I am a woman, heterosexual, middle class, African American,

Buddhist, with a movement disability; but I am also much more than those categories." At this level we define ourselves and structure our daily activities according to our needs and preferences. At the micro level we can best feel and experience the process of identity formation, which includes naming specific forces and events that shape our identities. At this level we also seem to have more control of the process, although there are always interconnections between events and experiences at this and the other levels.

Critical life events, such as entering kindergarten, losing a parent through death or divorce, or the onset of puberty, may all serve as catalysts for a shift in how we think about ourselves. A five-year-old Vietnamese American child of immigrants may experience the first challenge to her sense of identity when her kindergarten teacher admonishes her to speak only in English. A white, middle-class professional woman who thinks of herself as "a person" and a "competent attorney" may begin to give more weight to the significance of gender if she witnesses younger, less experienced male colleagues in her law office passing her by for promotions. A woman who has been raped who attends her first meeting of a women's campus support group feels the power of connection with other rape survivors and their allies. An eighty-year-old woman, whose partner of fifty years has died, must face the loss of her lifetime companion, friend, and lover. Such experiences shape each person's ongoing formulation of self, whether or not the process is conscious, deliberate, reflective, or even voluntary.

Identity formation is a lifelong process that includes discovery of the new; recovery of the old, forgotten, or appropriated; and synthesis of the new and old, as illustrated by several writers in this chapter who reflect on how their sense of identity has developed over the course of their lives. At especially important junctures during the process, individuals mark an identity change in tangible ways. An African American woman may change her name from the anglicized Susan to Aisha, with roots in Islamic and African cultures. A Chinese immigrant woman, on the other hand, may adopt an anglicized name, exchanging Nu Lu for Yvonne Lu as part of becoming a U.S. citizen. Another way of marking and effecting a shift in identity is by altering your physical appearances; changing your wardrobe or makeup; cutting your hair very short, wearing it natural rather than permed or pressed, dyeing it purple, or letting the gray show after years of using hair coloring. . . .

COMMUNITY RECOGNITION, EXPECTATIONS, AND INTERACTIONS: THE MESO LEVEL

It is at meso level—at school, in the workplace, or on the street—that people most frequently ask "Who are you?" or "Where are you from?" in an attempt to categorize us and determine their relationship to us. Moreover, it is here that people experience the complexities, conflicts, and contradictions of multiple identities, which we consider later.

The single most visible signifier of identity is physical appearance. How we look to others affects their perceptions, judgements, and treatment of us. Questions such as "Where do you come from?" and questioning behaviors, such as feeling the texture of your hair or asking if you speak a particular language, are commonly used to interrogate people whose physical appearances or behaviors do not match the characteristics designated as belonging to established categories. At root, we are being asked, "Are you one of us or not?" These questioners usually expect simple and straightforward answers, assuming that everyone will fit existing social categories, which are conceived of as undifferentiated and unambiguous. Among people with disabilities, for example, people wanting to identify each other may expect to hear details of another's disability rather than fact that the person being questioned also identifies equally strongly as, say, a woman who is white, working class, and bisexual.

Community, like home, may be geographic and emotional, or both, and provides a way for people to express group affiliations. "Where are you from?" is a commonplace question in the United States among strangers, a way to break the ice and start a conversation, expecting answers like "I'm from Tallahassee, Florida," "I'm from the Bronx." Community might also be an organized group like Alcoholics Anonymous, a religious group, or a political organization like the African American civil rights organization, the National Association for the Advancement of Colored People (NAACP). Community may be something much more abstract, as in "the women's community" or "the queer community," where there is presumed to be an identifiable group. Increasingly these communities may be virtual as the Internet links people worldwide. In these examples there is an assumption of shared values, interests, culture, or language sometimes thought of as essential qualities that define group membership and belonging. This can lead to essentialism, where complex identities get reduced to specific qualities deemed to be essential for membership of a particular group: being Muslim or gay, for example.

At the community level, individual identities and needs meet group standards, expectations, obligations, responsibilities, and demands. You compare yourself with others and are subtly compared. Others size up your clothing, accent, personal style, and knowledge of the group's history and culture. You may be challenged directly, "You say you're Latina. How come you don't speak Spanish?" "You say you're working class. What are you doing in a professional job?" These experiences may both affirm our identities and create or highlight inconsistencies and contradictions in who we believe we are, how we are viewed by others, our role and status in the community, and our sense of belonging. . . .

SOCIAL CATEGORIES, CLASSIFICATIONS, AND STRUCTURAL INEQUALITY: MACRO AND GLOBAL LEVELS

Classifying and labelling human beings, often according to real or assumed physical, biological, or genetic differences, is a way to distinguish who is included and who is excluded from a group, to ascribe particular characteristics, to prescribe social roles, and to assign status, power, and privilege. People are to know their places. Thus social categories such as gender, race, and class are used to establish and maintain a particular kind of social order. The classifications and their specific features, meanings, and significance are socially constructed through history, politics, and culture. The specific meanings and significance were often imputed to justify the conquest, colonization, domination, and exploitation of entire groups of people, and although the specifics may have changed over time, this system of categorizing and classifying remains intact. For example, Native American people were described as brutal, uncivilized, and ungovernable savages in the writings of early colonizers on this continent. This justified the near-genocide of Native Americans by white settlers, public officials, and the U.S. military, as well as the breaking of treaties between the U.S. government and Native American tribes. Today, Native Americans are no longer called savages but are often thought of as a vanishing species, or a nonexistent people already wiped out, thereby rationalizing their neglect by the dominant culture and erasing their long-standing and continuing resistance. . . .

These social categories are the foundation of the structural inequalities present in our society. Those in dominant positions are deemed superior and legitimate and those relegated—whether explicitly or implicitly—to subordinate positions are deemed inferior and illegitimate. Of course, individuals are not simply in dominant or subordinate positions. A college-educated, Arab American heterosexual man has privilege in terms of gender, class, and sexuality, but is considered subordinate in terms of race and culture. Depending on context, these aspects of his identity will contribute to his experience of privilege or disadvantage. Self-awareness involves recognizing and understanding the significance of our identities. For white people descended from European immigrants to this country, the advantages of being white are not always fully recognized or acknowledged. . . . As a result, white people in the United States tend to think of all identities as equal: "I'm Italian American, you're Polish American. I'm Irish American, you're African American." This assumed equivalence ignores the very big differences between an individualist symbolic identity and a socially enforced and imposed racial identity. Note that all Europeans were not considered equal when they immigrated to the United States in the nineteenth and early twentieth centuries. Germans, English, Scots, Irish, French, Italian, Polish, and Russian Jewish people, for, example, were differentiated in a hierarchy based on skin color, culture, language, and their histories in Europe. . . .

MAINTAINING SYSTEMS OF STRUCTURAL INEQUALITY

Maintaining systems of inequality requires ongoing objectification and dehumanization of subordinated peoples. Appropriating their identities is a particularly effective method of doing this, for it defines who the subordinated group/person is or ought to be. This happens in several ways:

Using the values, characteristics, features of the dominant group as the supposedly neutral standard against which all others should be evaluated. For example, men of a particular racial/ethnic group are generally physically larger and stronger than women of that group. Many of the clinical trials for new pharmaceutical drugs have been conducted using men's bodies and activities as the standard. The results, however, have been applied equally to both men and women. Women are often prescribed the same dosage of a medication as men are even though their physical makeup is not the same. Thus women, as a distinct group, do not exist in this research.

Using terms that distinguish the subordinate from the dominant group. Terms such as "non-white" and "minority" connote a relationship to another group, white in the former case and majority in the later. A non-white person is the negative of the white person; a minority person is less than a majority person. Neither has an identity on her or his own terms.

Stereotyping. Stereotyping involves making a simple generalization about a group and claiming that all members of the group conform to it. Stereotypes are behavioural and psychological attributes; they are commonly held beliefs about groups rather than individual beliefs about individuals; and they persist in spite of contradictory evidence. Lesbians hate men. Latinas are dominated by macho Latinos. Women with physical disabilities are asexual. Fat women are good-humored but not healthy. As philosopher Judith Andre (1988) asserted, "A 'stereotype' is pejorative; there is always something objectionable in the beliefs and images to which the word refers."

Exoticizing and romanticizing. These two forms of appropriation are particularly insidious because on the surface there is an appearance of appreciation. For example, Asian American women may be described as personifying the "mysterious Orient", Native American women as "earth mothers" and the epitome of spirituality, and Black women as perpetual towers of strength.

In all three cases, seemingly positive traits and cultural practices are identified and exalted. This "positive" stereotyping prevents people from seeing the truth and complexity of who these women are.

Another aspect of romanticization may be cultural appropriation, where, for example, white people wear nose studs or dreadlocks, have their hands decorated with henna, or claim to have been Native American in a former life. Fashion is always seeking something new. Typically, consumers do not think too much about the culture or history of the people who created the styles that are now commodified and sold in the global market place. Thus, objects and styles are lifted out of their original cultural context and become "cool stuff" for other people to buy. . . .

Given the significance of identity appropriation as an aspect of oppression, it is not surprising that many liberation struggles have included projects and efforts aimed at changing identities and taking control of the process of positive identity formation and representation. Oppressed people often use the same terminology to name themselves as the dominant group uses to label them. One crucial aspect of liberation struggles is to get rid of pejorative labels and use names that express, in their own terms, who they are in all their humanity. Thus, groups may change the name they use to refer to themselves to fit their evolving consciousness. As with individual identity, naming ourselves collectively is an important act of empowerment. One example of this is the evolution of the names African Americans have used to identify themselves, moving from Colored to Negro to Black to Afro-American, and African American. Similarly, Chinese Americans gradually rejected the derogatory label "Chink" preferring to be called Orientals and now Chinese Americans or Asian Americans. These terms are used unevenly, perhaps according to the age and political orientation of the person or the geographic region, where one usage may be more popular than another. Among the very diverse group of people connected historically, culturally, and linguistically to Spain, Portugal, and their former colonies (parts of the United Stated, Mexico, the Caribbean, and Central and South America), some use more inclusive terms such as Latino or Hispanic; others prefer more specific names such as Chicano, Puerto Rican, Nicaraguan, Cuban, and so on. Also, many transgendered people now use the broad term "trans" rather than medical terminology developed by doctors and psychotherapists that suggests abnormality and pathology.

COLONIZATION, IMMIGRATION, AND THE U.S. LANDSCAPE OF RACE AND CLASS

Global-level factors affecting people's identities include colonization and immigration. Popular folk lore would have us believe that the United States has welcomed "the tired, huddled masses yearning to breathe free." This ideology that the United States is "a land of immigrants" obscures several important issues excluded from much mainstream debate about immigration: Not all Americans came to this country voluntarily. Native American peoples and Mexicans were already here on this continent, but the former experienced near-genocide and the latter were made foreigners in their own land. African peoples were captured, enslaved, imported to this country, and forced to labor and bear children. All were brutally exploited and violated—physically, psychologically, culturally, and spiritually—to serve the interests of those in power. The relationships between these groups and this nation and their experiences in the United States are fundamentally different from the experiences of those who chose to immigrate here, though this is not to negate the hardships the latter may have faced. These differences profoundly shaped the social, cultural, political, and economic realities faced by these groups throughout U.S. history and continue to do so today.

Robert Blauner (1972) makes a useful analytical distinction between colonized minorities, whose original presence in this nation was involuntary, and all of whom are people of color, and immigrant minorities, whose presence was voluntary. According to Blauner, colonized minorities faced insurmountable structural inequalities, based primarily on race, that have prevented their full participation in social, economic, political, and cultural arenas of U.S. life. Early in the history of this country, for example, the Naturalization Law of 1790 (which was only repealed in 1952) prohibited peoples of color from becoming U.S. citizens, and the Slave Codes restricted every aspect of life for enslaved African peoples. These laws made race into an indelible line that separated "insiders" from "outsiders." White people were designated insiders and granted many privileges while all others were confined to systematic disadvantage. . . . The role of labor unions, community organizations, and political parties, as well as the crucial importance of racism, is usually left out of these accounts, which emphasize individual effort and hard work. . . .

On coming to the United States, immigrants are drawn in to the racial landscape of this country. In media debates and official statistics, this is still dominated by a Black/white polarization, with the addition of "Hispanics" as a non-white third category. Demographically, the population is much more diverse but often characterized in binary terms: people of color or white people. Immigrants generally identify themselves according to nationality—for example, as Cambodian or Guatemalan. Once in the United States, they may adopt the term *people of color* as an aspect of their identity here. Chandra Talpade Mohanty notes her transition from "foreign student" to "student of color" in the United States. "Racial and sexist experiences in graduate school and after made it imperative that I understand the U.S. in terms of its history of racism, imperialism, and patriarchal relations, specifically in relation to Third World immigrants."

This emphasis on race tends to mask differences based on class, an important distinction among immigrant groups. For example, the Chinese and Japanese people who came in the nineteenth century and early twentieth century to work on plantations in Hawaii, as loggers in Oregon, or building roads and railroads in several western states were poor and from rural areas of China and Japan. The 1965 immigration law made way for "the second wave" of Asian immigration. It set preferences for professionals, highly skilled workers, and members of the middle and upper middle classes. The first wave of Vietnamese refugees who immigrated between the mid-1970s and 1980 were from the middle and upper classes, including many professionals; by contrast, the second wave of immigrants from Vietnam was composed of poor and rural people. The class backgrounds of immigrants affect not only their sense of themselves and their expectations but also how they can succeed as strangers in a foreign land. For example, a poor woman who arrives with no literacy skills in her own language will have a more difficult time learning to become literate in English than one who has formal schooling in her country of origin that may have included basic English. . . .

MULTIPLE IDENTITIES, SOCIAL LOCATION, AND CONTRADICTIONS

The social features of one's identity incorporate individual, community, social, and global factors. Social location is a concept used to express the core of a person's existence in the social and political world. It places us in particular relationships to others, to the dominant culture of the United States, and to the rest of the world. It determines the kinds of power and privilege we have access to and can exercise, as well as situations in which we have less power and privilege.

Because social location is where all the aspects of one's identity meet, our experience of our own complex identities is both enriching and contradictory, and pushes us to confront questions of loyalty to individuals and groups. It is through the complexity of social location that we are forced to differentiate our inclinations, behaviors, self definition, and politics from how we are classified by larger societal institutions.

3

The Social Construction of Difference

Allan G. Johnson

The late African American novelist James Baldwin once offered the provocative idea that there is no such thing as whiteness or, for that matter, blackness or, more generally, race. "No one is white before he/she came to America," he wrote. "It took generations and a vast amount of coercion, before this became a white country."

. . .

Baldwin isn't denying the reality that skin pigmentation varies from one person to another. What he is saying is that unless you live in a culture that recognizes such differences as significant, they are socially irrelevant and therefore, in a way, do not exist. A "black woman" in Africa, therefore, who has not experienced white racism, does not *think* of herself as black or experience herself as black, nor do the people around her. African, yes, a woman, yes. But not a *black* woman.

When she comes to the United States, however, where privilege is organized according to race, suddenly she becomes black because people assign her to a social category that bears that name, and they treat her differently as a result. . . .

So Baldwin is telling us that race and all its categories have no significance outside systems of privilege and oppression in which they were created in the first place. This is what sociologists call the "social construction" of reality.

. . .

The same is true with the definition of what is considered "normal." While it may come as a surprise to many who think of themselves as nondisabled, disability and nondisability are socially constructed. This doesn't mean that the difference between having or not having full use of your legs is somehow "made up" without any objective reality. It does mean, however, that how people notice and label and think about such differences and how they treat other people as a result depend entirely on ideas contained in a system's culture.

Human beings, for example, come in a variety of heights, and many of those considered "normal" are unable to reach high places such as kitchen shelves without the assistance of physical aids—chairs and step-stools. In spite of their inability to do this simple task without special aids, they are not defined as disabled. Nor are the roughly 100 million people in the United States who cannot see properly without the aid of eyeglasses. . . .

Disability and nondisability are . . . constructed through the language used to describe people. When someone who cannot see is labeled a "blind person," for example, it creates the impression that not being able to see sums up the entire person. In other words, blind becomes what they *are*. The same thing happens when people are described as "brain damaged" or "crippled" or "retarded" or "deaf"—the person becomes the disability and nothing more. Reducing people to a single dimension of who they are separates and excludes them, marks them as "other," as different from "normal" (white, heterosexual, male, nondisabled) people and therefore as inferior. . . .

There is a world of difference between using a wheelchair and being treated as a normal human being (who happens to use a wheelchair to get around) and using a wheelchair and being treated as invisible, inferior, unintelligent, asexual, frightening, passive, dependent, and nothing more than your disability. And that difference is not a matter of the disability itself but of how it is constructed in society and how we then make use of that construction in our minds to shape how we think about ourselves and other people and how we treat them as a result.

What makes socially constructed reality so powerful is that we rarely if ever experience it as that. We think the way our culture defines something like race or gender is simply the way things are in some objective sense. . . . In the 19th century, for example, U.S. law identified those having *any* African ancestry as black, a standard known as the "one-drop rule," which defined "white" as a state of absolute purity in relation to "black." Native American status, in contrast, required at *least* one-eighth Native American ancestry in order to qualify. Why the different standards? . . . Native Americans could claim financial benefits from the federal government, making it to whites' advantage to make it hard for anyone to be considered Native American. Designating someone as black, however, took *away* power and *denied* the right to make claims against whites, including white families of origin. In both cases, racial classification has had little to do with objective characteristics and everything to do with preserving white power and wealth.

This fact has also been true of the use of race to tag various ethnic groups. When the Chinese were imported as cheap laborers during the 19th century, the California Supreme Court declared them not white. Mexicans, however, many of whom owned large amounts of land in California and did business with whites, were considered white. Today, as Paul Kivel points out, Mexicans are no longer considered white and the Chinese are "conditionally white at times."

. . .

WHAT IS PRIVILEGE?

No matter what privileged group you belong to, if you want to understand the problem of privilege and difference, the first stumbling block is usually the idea of privilege itself. When people hear that they belong to a privileged group or benefit from something like "white privilege" or "male privilege," they don't get it, or they feel angry and defensive about what they do get. *Privilege* has become one of those loaded words we need to reclaim so that we can use it to name and illuminate the truth. . . .

Privilege exists when one group has something of value that is denied to others simply because of the groups they belong to, rather than because of anything they've done or failed to do. If people take me more seriously when I give a speech than they would someone of color saying the same things in the same way, then I'm benefiting from white privilege. That a heterosexual black woman can feel free to talk about her life in ways that reveal the fact that she's married to a man is a form of heterosexual privilege because lesbians and gay men cannot casually reveal their sexual orientation without putting themselves at risk.

. . .

WHAT PRIVILEGE LOOKS LIKE IN EVERYDAY LIFE

. . . Privilege shows up in the daily details of people's lives in almost every social setting. Consider the following examples of race privilege. . . .

- Whites are less likely than blacks to be arrested; once arrested, they are less likely to be convicted and, once convicted, less likely to go to prison, regardless of the crime or circumstances. Whites, for example, constitute 85 percent of those who use illegal drugs, but less than half of those in prison on drug-use charges are white.

. . .

- Whites are more likely than comparable blacks to have loan applications approved and less likely to be given poor information or the runaround during the application process.
- Whites are charged lower prices for new and used cars than are people of color, and residential segregation gives whites access to higher-quality goods of all kinds at cheaper prices.

. . .

- Whites are more likely to control conversations and be allowed to get away with it and to have their ideas and contributions taken seriously, including those that were suggested previously by a person of color and ignored or dismissed.
- Whites can usually assume that national heroes, success models, and other figures held up for general admiration will be of their race.

. . .

- Whites can assume that when they go shopping, they'll be treated as serious customers not as potential shoplifters or people without the money to make a purchase. When they try to cash a check or use a credit card, they can assume they won't be hassled for additional identification and will be given the benefit of the doubt.

. . .

- Most whites are not segregated into communities that isolate them from the best job opportunities, schools, and community services.
- Whites have greater access to quality education and health care.

. . .

- Whites can succeed without other people being surprised.
- Whites don't have to deal with an endless and exhausting stream of attention to their race. They can simply take their race for granted as unremarkable to the extent of experiencing themselves as not even having a race. Unlike some of my African American students, for example, I don't have people coming up to me and treating me as if I were some exotic "other," gushing about how "cool" or different I am, wanting to know where I'm "from," and reaching out to touch my hair.
- Whites don't find themselves slotted into occupations identified with their race, as blacks are often slotted into support positions or Asians into technical jobs.

. . .

- Whites can reasonably expect that if they work hard and "play by the rules," they'll get what they deserve, and they feel justified in complaining if they don't. It is something other racial groups cannot realistically expect.

In the following list for male privilege, note how some items repeat from the list on race but other items do not.

- In most professions and upper-level occupations, men are held to a lower standard than women. It is easier for a "good but not great" male lawyer to make partner than it is for a comparable woman.
- Men are charged lower prices for new and used cars.
- If men do poorly at something or make a mistake or commit a crime, they can generally assume that people won't attribute the failure to their gender. The kids who shoot teachers and schoolmates are almost always boys, but rarely is the fact that all this violence is being done by males raised as an important issue.

. . .

- Men can generally assume that when they go out in public, they won't be sexually harassed or assaulted just because they're male, and if they are victimized, they won't be asked to explain what they were doing there.

- Male representation in government and the ruling circles of corporations and other organizations is disproportionately high.

. . .

- Men are more likely than women are to control conversations and be allowed to get away with it and to have their ideas and contributions taken seriously, even those that were suggested previously by a woman and dismissed or ignored.
- Most men can assume that their gender won't be used to determine whether they'll fit in at work or whether teammates will feel comfortable working with them.
- Men can succeed without other people being surprised.
- Men don't have to deal with an endless and exhausting stream of attention drawn to their gender (for example, to how sexually attractive they are).
- Men don't find themselves slotted into a narrow range of occupations identified with their gender as women are slotted into community relations, human resources, social work, elementary school teaching, librarianship, nursing, and clerical, and secretarial positions.

. . .

- The standards used to evaluate men as *men* are consistent with the standards used to evaluate them in other roles such as occupations. Standards used to evaluate women as women are often different from those used to evaluate them in other roles. For example, a man can be both a "real man" and a successful and aggressive lawyer, while an aggressive woman lawyer may succeed as a lawyer but be judged as not measuring up as a woman.

In the following list regarding sexual orientation, note again items in common with the other two lists and items peculiar to this form of privilege.

- Heterosexuals are free to reveal and live their intimate relationships openly—by referring to their partners by name, recounting experiences, going out in public together, displaying pictures on their desks at work—without being accused of "flaunting" their sexuality or risking discrimination.
- Heterosexuals can marry as a way to commit to long-term relationships that are socially recognized, supported, and legitimated. This fact confers basic rights such as spousal health benefits, the ability to adopt children, inheritance, joint filing of income tax returns, and the power to make decisions for a spouse who is incapacitated in a medical emergency.

. . .

- Heterosexuals can move about in public without fear of being harassed or physically attacked because of their sexual orientation.
- Heterosexuals don't run the risk of being reduced to a single aspect of their lives, as if being heterosexual summed up the kind of person they are. Instead, they can be viewed and treated as complex human beings who happen to be heterosexual.
- Heterosexuals can usually assume that national heroes, success models, and other figures held up for general admiration will be assumed to be heterosexual.
- Most heterosexuals can assume that their sexual orientation won't be used to determine whether they'll fit in at work or whether teammates will feel comfortable working with them.
- Heterosexuals don't have to worry that their sexual orientation will be used as a weapon against them, to undermine their achievements or power.

. . .

- Heterosexuals can live where they want without having to worry about neighbors who disapprove of their sexual orientation.
- Heterosexuals can live in the comfort of knowing that other people's assumptions about their sexual orientation are correct.

In the following list regarding disability status, note again items in common with the other lists and items peculiar to this form of privilege.

- Nondisabled people can choose whether to be conscious of their disability status or to ignore it and regard themselves simply as human beings.
- Nondisabled people can live secure in other people's assumption that they are sexual beings capable of an active sex life, including the potential to have children and be parents.

. . .

- Nondisabled people can assume that they will fit in at work and in other settings without having to worry about being evaluated and judged according to preconceived notions and stereotypes about people with disabilities.

. . .

- Nondisabled people don't have to deal with an endless and exhausting stream of attention to their disability status. They can simply take their disability status for granted as unremarkable to the extent of experiencing themselves as not even having one.
- Nondisabled people can ask for help without having to worry that people will assume they need help with everything.
- Nondisabled people can succeed without people being surprised because of low expectations of their ability to contribute to society.
- Nondisabled people can expect to pay lower prices for cars because they are assumed to be mentally unimpaired and less likely to allow themselves to be misled and exploited.

. . .

- Nondisabled people are more likely to control conversations and be allowed to get away with it and have their ideas and contributions taken seriously, including those that were suggested before by a person with disabilities and then dismissed or ignored.
- Nondisabled people can assume that national heroes, success models, and other figures held up for general admiration will share their disability status.

. . .

- Nondisabled people can generally assume that when they go out in public, they won't be looked at as odd or out of place or not belonging. They can also assume that most buildings and other structures will not be designed in ways that limit their access.
- Nondisabled people can assume that when they need to travel from one place to another, they will have access to buses, trains, airplanes, and other means of transportation.
- Nondisabled people can count on being taken seriously and not treated as children.
- Nondisabled people are less likely to be segregated into living situations—such as nursing homes and special schools and sports programs—that isolate them from job opportunities, schools, community services, and the everyday workings of life in a society.

. . .

Regardless of which group we're talking about, privilege generally allows people to assume a certain level of acceptance, inclusion, and respect in the world, to operate within a relatively wide comfort zone. Privilege increases the odds of having things your own way, of being able to set the agenda in a social situation and determine the rules and standards and how they're applied. Privilege grants the cultural authority to make judgments about others and to have those judgements stick. It allows people to define reality and to have prevailing definitions of reality fit their experience. Privilege means being able to decide who gets taken seriously, who receives attention, who is accountable to whom and for what. And it grants a presumption of superiority and social permission to act on that presumption without having to worry about being challenged.

To have privilege is to be allowed to move through your life without being marked in ways that identify you as an outsider, as exceptional or "other" to be excluded, or to be included but always with conditions. . . .

OPPRESSION: THE FLIP SIDE OF PRIVILEGE

For every social category that is privileged, one or more other categories are oppressed in relation to it. . . . Just as privilege tends to open doors of opportunity, oppression tends to slam them shut.

Like privilege, oppression results from the social relationship between privileged and oppressed categories, which makes it possible for individuals to vary in their personal experience of being oppressed ("I've never been oppressed as a woman"). This also means, however, that in order to have the experience of being oppressed, it is necessary to belong to an oppressed category. In other words, men cannot be oppressed *as men*, just as whites cannot be oppressed as whites or heterosexuals as heterosexuals, because a group can be oppressed only if there exists another group with the power to oppress them.

As we saw earlier, people in privileged categories can certainly feel bad in ways that can feel oppressive. Men, for example, can feel burdened by what they take to be their responsibility to provide for their families. Or they can feel limited and even damaged by the requirement that "real men" must avoid expressing feelings other than anger. But although access to privilege costs them something that may *feel* oppressive, to call it oppression distorts the nature of what is happening to them and why.

. . .

The complexity of systems of privilege makes it possible, of course, for men to experience oppression if they also happen to be of color or gay or disabled or in a lower social class, but not simply because they are male. In the same way, whites can experience oppression for many reasons, but not because they're white.

. . .

Finally, being in a privileged category that has an oppressive relationship with another isn't the same as being an oppressive *person* who behaves in oppressive ways. That males as a social category oppress females as a social category, for example, is a social fact. That doesn't, however, tell us how a particular man thinks or feels about particular women or behaves toward them. This can be a subtle distinction to hang on to, but hang on to it we must if we're going to maintain a clear idea of what oppression is and how it works in defense of privilege.

. . .

4

Microaggressions, Marginality, and Oppression

An Introduction

Derald Wing Sue

Microaggressions are the everyday verbal, nonverbal, and environmental slights, snubs, or insults, whether intentional or unintentional, that communicate hostile, derogatory, or negative messages to target persons based soley upon their marginalized group membership. In many cases, these hidden messages may invalidate the group identity or experiential reality of target persons, demean them on a personal or group level, communicate they are lesser human beings, suggest they do not belong with the majority group, threaten and intimidate, or relegate them to inferior status and treatment. Any marginalized group in our society may become targets: people of color, women, lesbian/ gay/ bisexual/transgendered people, those with disabilities, religious minorities, and so on.

The most detrimental forms of microaggressions are usually delivered by well-intentioned individuals who are unaware that they have engaged in harmful conduct toward a socially devalued group. These everyday occurrences may on the surface appear quite harmless, trivial, or be described as "small slights," but research indicates they have a powerful impact upon the psychological well-being of marginalized groups and affect their standard of living by creating inequalities in health care, education, and employment.

RACIAL MICROAGGRESSIONS

- A White man or woman clutches her purse or checks his wallet as a Black or Latino man approaches or passes them. (Hidden message: You and your group are criminals.)
- An Asian American born and raised in the United States, is complimented for speaking "good English." (Hidden message: You are not a true American. You are a perpetual foreigner in your own country.)
- A Black couple is seated at a table in the restaurant next to the kitchen despite there being other empty and more desirable tables located at the front. (Hidden message: You are a second-class citizen and undeserving of first-class treatment.)

GENDER MICROAGGRESSIONS

- An assertive female manager is labelled as a "bitch," while her male counterpart is described as "a forceful leader." (Hidden message: Women should be passive and allow men to be the decision makers.)
- A female physician wearing a stethoscope is mistaken for a nurse. (Hidden message: Women should occupy nurturing and not decision-making roles. Women are less capable than men.)

- Whistles or catcalls are heard from men as a woman walks down the street. (Hidden message: Your body/appearance is for the enjoyment of men. You are a sex object.)

SEXUAL ORIENTATION MICROAGGRESSIONS

- Students use the term "gay" to describe a fellow student who is socially ostracized. (Hidden message: People who are weird, strange, deviant, different are "gay".)
- A lesbian client in therapy reluctantly discloses her sexual orientation to a straight therapist by stating she is "into women." The therapist indicates he is not shocked by the disclosure because he once had a client who was "into dogs." (Hidden message: Same-sex attraction is abnormal and deviant.)
- Two gay men hold hands in public and are told not to flaunt their sexuality. (Hidden message: Homosexual displays of affection are abnormal and offensive. Keep it private and to yourselves.)

As indicated previously, microaggressions can be based upon any group that is marginalized in this society. Religion, disability, and social class may also reflect the manifestation of microaggressions. Some of these examples include the following.

- When bargaining over the price of an item, a store owner says to a customer, "Don't try to Jew me down." (Hidden message: Jews are stingy and money grubbing.)
- A blind man reports that people often raise their voices when speaking to him. He responds by saying, "Please don't raise your voice; I can hear you perfectly well." (Hidden message: A person with a disability is defined as lesser in all aspects of physical and mental functioning.)
- The outfit worn by a TV reality-show mom is described as "classless and trashy." (Hidden message: Lower-class people are tasteless and unsophisticated.)

MARGINALITY AND OPPRESSION

. . . .

Microaggressions reflect the active manifestation of oppressive world views that create, foster, and enforce marginalization. To be confined to the margins of existence in mainstream life is to be oppressed, persecuted, and subjugated; denied full rights of citizenship; imprisoned or trapped to a lower standard of living; stripped of one's experiential reality; and restricted or limited as to life choices. Oppression can occur through imposition or deprivation. In both cases, they span a continuum from its direct/concrete nature to those with more symbolic or psychological manifestations and from being consciously perpetrated to being unintentional, indirect, and subtle.

IMPOSITION

Oppression by imposition, force, coercion, and duress . . . can be anything from bullet, a bludgeon, shackles, or fists, to a penis, unhealthy food, or abusive messages designed to cause or sustain pain, low self-efficacy, reduced self determination, and so forth. . . .

Most of us can immediately recognize the horror and heinous nature of overt and concrete acts of rape (imposition of physical and psychological abuse), murder (taking away life), and unjust imprisonment as obvious forms of injustice and unfairness visited upon individuals and groups. . . . Good, moral, and decent folks do not condone such actions. Yet, acts of oppression by imposition or force *through microaggressions* can be many times more harmful to racial/ethnic minorities than hate crimes.

The power of microaggressions lies in their invisibility to perpetrators and oftentimes the recipients. The definition of oppression includes imposing "abusive messages" (microaggressions) that both reflect and perpetuate false beliefs. Those beliefs cause humiliation and pain, reduce self-determination, confine them to lesser job roles and status in society, and deny them equal access and opportunities in education, employment, and deny them equal access and opportunities in education, employment, and health care. Most of the pain and detrimental impact comes from ordinary, normal, decent people who believe in life, liberty, and the pursuit of justice for all. They are unaware of their biases and prejudices but act them out in the form of microaggressions.

DEPRIVATION

Oppression can also take a second form—that of deprivation. It can be seen as the flip-side of imposition and involves depriving people of desired jobs, and education, health care, or living conditions necessary for physical and mental well-being. Food, clothing, shelter, love, respect, social support, or self-dignity can be wrested from any marginalized group. In our history, we once banned the Sioux nation from practicing their spiritual and religious traditions, deprived them of their lands, and took away their dignity as Indigenous people in their own country. Taking away a group's humanity and integrity through forced compliance is a very common practice directed toward marginalized groups. . . . When nursing home attendants address their elderly residents as "sweetie" and "dear," they are unaware of how these microaggressive terms belittle and infantilize the elderly and how they deprive them of their roles as capable and competent adults. "Elderspeak" has been identified as a very harmful and humiliating form of microaggression and can result in a downward spiral for older persons, low self-esteem, withdrawal, and depression.

FORMS OF MICROAGGRESSIONS

Microaggressions may take three forms: (1) microassault, (2) microinsult, and (3) microinvalidation. . . .

MICROASSULTS

Microassaults are conscious biased beliefs or attitudes that are held by individuals and intentionally expressed or acted out overtly or covertly toward a marginalized person or socially devalued group. They differ from the other two forms of microaggressions (to be discussed shortly) in that the perpetrator harbors conscious bias toward an indentified and socially devalued group. This bias may be directly and publicly expressed through racist, sexist, or heterosexist statement (using racial epithets or making catcalls toward women, for example) or acted out in any number of ways (preventing a son and daughter from dating or marrying outside of their race, giving second-class service to a woman, and so on). In extreme forms of microassaults, LGBTs may experience teasing and bullying in schools, isolation, physical violence, hate speech, and anti-LGBT legislation. . . .

MICROINSULTS

Microinsults are also forms of microaggressions, but they differ significantly from microassaults in that they likely occur outside the level of conscious awareness of the perpetrator. These are either interpersonal interactions (verbal/nonverbal) or environmental cues that communicate rudeness, insensitivity, slights, and insults that demean a person's racial, gender, sexual orientation, or group identity and heritage. Microinsults are subtle snubs often unconsciously disguised as a compliment or positive statement directed towards the target person or group. The contradictory communication starts with what appears to be a positive statement but is undermined with an insulting or negative metacommunication.

For example, an African American student who has done outstanding work in his economics class is told by the professor, "You are a credit to your race." On the conscious level, the professor appears to be complimenting the Black student; while on the other hand, the metacommunication contains an insulting message: "Blacks are generally not as intelligent as Whites. You are an exception to your people." This type of microinsult does several things: (1) it disguises a racial bias or prejudicial worldview of the perpetrator; (2) it allows the perpetrator to cling to the belief in racial interiority, albeit unconsciously; and (3) it oppresses and denigrates in a guilt-free manner.

Microinsults can take many other forms. For example, they can occur environmentally. Men who display nude pictures of women from *Hustler* or *Playboy* magazines in their places of employment (offices, desks, locker rooms, etc.) may be unknowingly contributing to sexual objectification. The hidden message is that women's bodies are not their own and they exist to service the sexual fantasies of men. The impact is to strip women of their humanity and the totality of their human essence (intelligence, emotions, personal attributes, and aspirations) and to relegate them to being only sexual beings. Environmental microaggressions are generally invisible to those in the majority group but quite visible to those groups most disempowered. . . .

MICROINVALIDATIONS

Microinvalidations are similar to microinsults in that they generally occur outside the level of conscious awareness of perpetrators. However, this form of microaggression is perhaps the most insidious, damaging, and harmful form, because microinvalidations directly attack or deny the experiential realities of socially devalued groups. They accomplish this goal through interpersonal and environmental cues that exclude, negate, or nullify the psychological thoughts, feelings, beliefs, and experiences of the target group.

Color blindness, for example, is one of the most frequently delivered microinvalidations directed toward people of color. It can be defined as an unwillingness to acknowledge or admit to seeing race or a person's color. Such an orientation is predicated on the mistaken belief by many Whites that "not seeing color" means they are unbiased and free of racism. As a result, many Whites engage in defensive maneuvers not to appear racist by either pretending not to see color or by actively avoiding any discussions associated with race. Despite studies indicating that race and gender are two of the most easily identifiable qualities seen by people, color blindness and gender blindness inundate our everyday interactions. "There is only one race: the human race." "When I look at you, I don't see color." "We are all Americans." "Regardless of your gender or race, I believe the most qualified person should get the job." Such statements and their orientation serve to deny the racial, gender, or sexual orientation reality and experiences of these groups. . . .

THE CATCH-22 OF RESPONDING TO MICROAGGRESSIONS

Microaggressions, especially microinsults and microinvalidations, place socially devalued group members in an unenviable position of (1) trying to ascertain the motivations behind the actions of perpetrators and (2) deciding whether and how to respond. Since many microaggressions are likely to be delivered unintentionally and their real motives are not conscious to the perpetrator, they are usually filled with double meanings and/or are very ambiguous. On a conscious level, dominant group members who engage in unconscious microaggressions believe they are acting in an unbiased manner, complimenting the target, or making a rational decision. When a statement such as "I believe the most qualified person should get the job" is made to a female job candidate, the job seeker is caught in a double bind: On the one hand, the statement is valid and reasonable, but the other hand, experience has shown the woman job hunter that it can be used to justify not hiring women and offering such positions to male candidates. When students of color are seldom called upon by a White professor to answer questions, is this a random act, or is the professor operating from an unconscious assumption that minorities are less likely to have intelligent comments or answers to class problems? The term "attributional ambiguity" has been given to motivational uncertainty in that the motives and meanings of a person's action are unclear and hazy. Studies suggest that attributional ambiguity depletes psychological energy by diverting attention away from other important tasks (problem solving in classrooms and work productivity in the workplace).

Second, a catch-22 is often induced in the recipient of microaggressions. The conflict involves how to respond to the person when a remark or action conveys a demeaning insult of offense.

In the face of an offensive group-specific comment, the target is placed in a "damned if you do and damned if you don't" situation. That is if the person does nothing, he or she may suffer from a sense of low self-esteem, a feeling of not being true to the self, and a loss of self-integrity. Yet, to confront the perpetrator or to raise the issue may result in negative consequences. . . .

Ever present in the awareness of marginalized group members is the power differential that generally exists between perpetrators and targets. Should a Latina/o student who is the target of microaggressions from fellow White students or even from the professor raise the issue? In this case, the Latina/o student may be outnumbered in the class by fellow White students who will be unable to see the microaggressions; they may become defensive, or they may see the Latina/o student as oversensitive. Additionally, the power differential becomes especially clear if a White professor is involved. Questions and thoughts likely to race through the mind of the student include: "Will the professor be offended?" "Will the professor think less of me?" "Will I get a poor grade in his or her class?" "Maybe I should just do nothing and let it go."

5

The Cycle of Socialization

Bobbie Harro

INTRODUCTION AND CONTEXT

Often, when people begin to study the phenomenon of oppression, they start with recognizing that human beings are different from each other in many ways based upon gender, ethnicity, skin color, first language, age, ability status, religion, sexual orientation, and economic class. The obvious first leap that people make is the assumption that if we just began to *appreciate differences,* and *treat each other with respect,* then everything would be all right, and there would be no oppression. This view is represented beautifully by the now famous quote from Rodney King in response to the riots following his beating and the release of the police officers who were filmed beating him: "Why can't we all just get along?" It should be that simple, but it isn't.

Instead, we are each born into a specific set of *social identities,* related to the categories of difference mentioned above, and these social identities predispose us to unequal *roles* in the dynamic system of oppression. We're then socialized by powerful sources in our worlds to play the roles prescribed by an inequitable social system. This socialization process is *pervasive* (coming from all sides and sources), *consistent* (patterned and predictable), *circular* (self-supporting), *self-perpetuating* (intradependent) and often *unrecognizable* (unconscious and unnamed). All of these characteristics will be clarified in the description of the *Cycle of Socialization* that follows.

In struggling to understand what roles we have been socialized to play, how we are affected by issues of oppression in our lives, and how we participate in maintaining them, we must begin by making an inventory of our own social identities with relationship to each issue of oppression. An excellent first learning activity is to make a personal inventory of our various social identities relating to the categories listed above—gender, race, age, sexual orientation, religion, economic class, and ability/disability status. The results of this inventory make up the mosaic of social identities (our *social identity profile)* that shape(s) our socialization.

We get systematic training in "how to be" each of our social identities throughout our lives. The Cycle of Socialization that follows is one way of representing how the socialization process happens, from what sources it comes, how it affects our lives, and how it perpetuates itself. The "Directions for Change" that conclude this chapter suggest ways for interrupting the Cycle of Socialization and taking charge of our own lives. For purposes of learning, it is often useful to choose only *one* of our social identities, and trace it through the Cycle of Socialization, since it can be quite overwhelming to explore multiple identities at once.

THE BEGINNING (CIRCLE NO. 1)

Our socialization begins before we are born, with no choice on our part. No one brings us a survey, in the womb, inquiring into which gender, class, religion, sexual orientation, cultural group, ability status, or age we might want to be born. These identities are ascribed

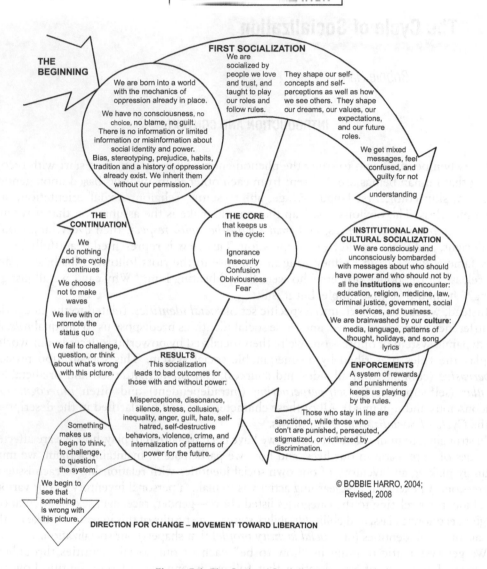

CYCLE OF SOCIALIZATION

FIRST SOCIALIZATION
We are socialized by people we love and trust, and taught to play our roles and follow rules.

They shape our self-concepts and self-perceptions as well as how we see others. They shape our dreams, our values, our expectations, and our future roles.

We get mixed messages, feel confused, and guilty for not understanding

THE BEGINNING

We are born into a world with the mechanics of oppression already in place.

We have no consciousness, no choice, no blame, no guilt. There is no information or limited information or misinformation about social identity and power. Bias, stereotyping, prejudice, habits, tradition and a history of oppression already exist. We inherit them without our permission.

THE CONTINUATION

We do nothing and the cycle continues

We choose not to make waves

We live with or promote the status quo

We fail to challenge, question, or think about what's wrong with this picture.

Something makes us begin to think, to challenge, to question the system.

We begin to see that something is wrong with this picture.

THE CORE
that keeps us in the cycle:
Ignorance
Insecurity
Confusion
Obliviousness
Fear

RESULTS
This socialization leads to bad outcomes for those with and without power:

Misperceptions, dissonance, silence, stress, collusion, inequality, anger, guilt, hate, self-hatred, self-destructive behaviors, violence, crime, and internalization of patterns of power for the future.

INSTITUTIONAL AND CULTURAL SOCIALIZATION
We are consciously and unconsciously bombarded with messages about who should have power and who should not by all the **institutions** we encounter: education, religion, medicine, law, criminal justice, government, social services, and business.
We are brainwashed by our **culture**: media, language, patterns of thought, holidays, and song lyrics

ENFORCEMENTS
A system of rewards and punishments keeps us playing by the rules.

Those who stay in line are sanctioned, while those who don't are punished, persecuted, stigmatized, or victimized by discrimination.

© BOBBIE HARRO, 2004; Revised, 2008

DIRECTION FOR CHANGE – MOVEMENT TOWARD LIBERATION

Figure 5.1 The Cycle of Socialization

to us at birth through no effort or decision or choice of our own; there is, therefore, no reason to blame each other or hold each other responsible for the identities we have. This first step in the socialization process is outside our control. In addition to having no choice, we also have no initial consciousness about who we are. We don't question our identities at this point. We just *are* who we are.

On top of these givens, we are born into a world where all of the mechanics, assumptions, rules, roles, and structures of oppression are already in place and functioning; we have had nothing to do with constructing them. There is no reason for any of us to feel guilty or responsible for the world into which we are born. We are innocents, falling into an already established system.

The characteristics of this system were built long before we existed, based upon history, habit, tradition, patterns of belief, prejudices, stereotypes, and myths. *Dominant* or *agent* groups are considered the "norm" around which assumptions are built, and these groups receive attention and recognition. Agents have relatively more social power, and can "name" others. They are privileged and ascribed access to options and opportunities, often without realizing it. We are "lucky" to be born into these groups and rarely question it. Agent groups include men, white people, middle- and upper-class people, abled people, middle-aged people, heterosexuals, and gentiles.

On the other hand, there are many social identity groups about which little or nothing is known because they have not been considered important enough to study. These are referred to as *subordinate* groups or *target* groups. Some target groups are virtually ignored while others are defined by misinformation or very limited information. Targets are disenfranchised, exploited, and victimized by prejudice, discrimination, and other structural obstacles. Target groups include women; racially oppressed groups; gay, lesbian, bisexual and transgendered people; disabled people; Jews; elders; youth; and people living in poverty. We are "unlucky" to be born into target groups and therefore devalued by the existing society. Both groups are dehumanized by being socialized into prescribed roles without consciousness or permission.

FIRST SOCIALIZATION (ARROW NO. 1)

Immediately upon our births we begin to be socialized by the people we know, love, and trust the most, our families or the adults who are raising us. They shape our self-concepts and self-perceptions, the norms and rules we must follow, the roles we are taught to play, our expectations for the future, and our dreams. These people serve as role models for us, and they teach us how to behave. This socialization happens both intrapersonally (how we think about ourselves), and interpersonally (how we relate to others). We are told things like, "Boys don't cry"; "They're better than we are. Stay in your place"; "Don't worry if you break the toy. We can always buy another one"; "Christianity is the true religion"; "Children should be seen and not heard"; "Don't tell anyone that your aunt is mentally retarded. It's embarrassing"; and "Don't kiss other girls. You're supposed to like boys." These messages are an automatic part of our early socialization, and we don't initially question them. We are too dependent on our parents or those raising us, so we unconsciously conform to their views.

It is important to observe that they, too, are not to be blamed. They are doing the best they can to raise us, and they only have their own backgrounds from which to draw. They may not have thought critically about what they are teaching us, and may be unconsciously passing on what was taught to them. Some of us may have been raised by parents who *have* thought critically about the messages that they are giving us, but they are still not in the majority. This could be good or bad, as well, depending on what their views are. A consciously racist parent may intentionally pass on racist beliefs to his children, and a consciously feminist parent may intentionally pass on non-stereotypical roles to her children, so it can go either way.

Regardless of the content of the teaching, we have been exposed, without initial question, to a strong set of rules, roles, and assumptions that cannot help but shape our sense of ourselves and the world. They influence what we take with us when we venture out into the larger world of other institutions.

A powerful way to check out the accuracy of these assertions is to choose one of our social identities and write down at least ten examples of what we learned about being that identity. It's helpful to consider whether we chose an agent or a target identity. We may find that we have thought more about our target identities, and therefore they are easier to inventory. We might also consider doing it for an agent group identity, like males, white people, heterosexuals, gentiles, adults, middle-class people, able-bodied or able-minded people. Most likely, we will find it easier to list learnings for targeted groups than for agent groups.

INSTITUTIONAL AND CULTURAL SOCIALIZATION (CIRCLE NO. 2)

Once we begin to attend school, go to a place of worship, visit a medical facility, play on a sports team, work with a social worker, seek services or products from a business, or learn about laws and the legal system, our socialization sources are rapidly multiplied based on how many institutions with which we have contact. Most of the messages we receive about how to be, whom to "look up to" and "look down on," what rules to follow, what roles to play, what assumptions to make, what to believe, and what to think will probably reinforce or contradict what we have learned.

We might learn at school that girls shouldn't be interested in a woodworking shop class, that only white students go out for the tennis team, that kids who learn differently or think independently get put in special education, that it's okay for wealthy kids to miss classes for a family vacation, that it's okay to harass the boy who walks and talks like a girl, that most of the kids who drop out are from the south side of town, that "jocks" don't have to do the same work that "nerds" do to pass, or that kids who belong to another religious group are "weird." We learn who gets preferential treatment and who gets picked on. We are exposed to rules, roles, and assumptions that are not fair to everyone.

If we are members of the groups that benefit from the rules, we may not notice that they aren't fair. If we are members of the groups that are penalized by the rules, we may have a constant feeling of scrutiny. We learn that these rules, roles, and assumptions are part of a structure that is larger than just our families. We get consistent similar messages from religion, the family doctor, the social worker, the local store, or the police officer, and so it is hard to not believe what we are learning. We learn that black people are more likely to steal, so store detectives follow them in stores. Boys are expected to fight and use violence, so they are encouraged to learn how. We shouldn't stare at or ask questions about disabled people; it isn't polite. Gay and lesbian people are sick and perverted. Kids who live in certain sections of town are probably on welfare, taking our hard-earned tax dollars. Money talks. White means good; black means bad. Girls are responsible for birth control. It's a man's world. Jews are cheap. Arabs are terrorists. And so on.

We are inundated with unquestioned and stereotypical messages that shape how we think and what we believe about ourselves and others. What makes this "brainwashing" even more insidious is the fact that it is woven into every structural thread of the fabric of our culture. The media (television, the Internet, advertising, newspapers, and radio), our language patterns, the lyrics to songs, our cultural practices and holidays, and the very assumptions on which our society is built all contribute to the reinforcement of the biased messages and stereotypes we receive. We could identify thousands of examples to illustrate the oppressive messages that bombard us daily from various institutions and aspects of our culture, reinforcing our divisions and "justifying" discrimination and prejudice.

ENFORCEMENTS (ARROW NO. 2)

It might seem logical to ask why people don't just begin to think differently if they don't like what they are seeing around them. Why don't we ignore these messages if we are uncomfortable with them, or if they are hurting us? Largely, we don't ignore the messages, rules, roles, structures, and assumptions because there are enforcements in place to maintain them. People who try to contradict the "norm" pay a price for their different thinking, and people who conform (consciously or unconsciously) minimally receive the benefit of being left alone for not making waves, such as acceptance in their designated roles, being considered normal or "a team player," or being allowed to stay in their places. Maximally, they receive rewards and privileges for maintaining the status quo such as access to higher places; attention and recognition for having "made it" or being the model member of their group; or the privilege that brings them money, connections, or power.

People who go against the grain of conventional societal messages are accused of being troublemakers, of making waves, or of being "the cause of the problem." If they are members of target groups, they are held up as examples of why this group is inferior to the agent group. Examples of this include the significantly higher numbers of people of color who are targeted by the criminal justice system. Although the number of white people who are committing crimes is just as high, whites are much less likely to be arrested, charged, tried, convicted, or sentenced to jail than are people of color. Do different laws apply depending on a person's skin color? Battering statistics are rising as more women assert their equal rights with men, and the number one suspect for the murder of women in the United States is the husband or boyfriend. Should women who try to be equal with men be killed? The rationale given by some racists for the burning of black churches was that "they were getting too strong." Does religious freedom and the freedom to assemble apply only to white citizens? Two men walking together in a southeastern U.S. city were beaten, and one died, because "they were walking so close, they must be gay." Are two men who refuse to abide by the "keep your distance" rule for men so threatening that they must be attacked and killed? These examples of differential punishment being given to members or *perceived* members of target groups are only half of the picture.

If members of agent groups break the rules, they too are punished. White people who support their colleagues of color may be called "n—lover." Heterosexual men who take on primary child-care responsibilities, cry easily, or hug their male friends are accused of being dominated by their spouses, of being "sissies," or being gay. Middle-class people who work as advocates on economic issues are accused of being do-gooders or self-righteous liberals. Heterosexuals who work for the rights of gay, lesbian, bisexual, or transgendered people are immediately suspected of being "in the closet" themselves.

RESULTS (CIRCLE NO. 3)

It is not surprising that the results of this systematic learning are devastating to all involved. If we are examining our target identities, we may experience anger, a sense of being silenced, dissonance between what the United States stands for and what we experience, low self-esteem, high levels of stress, a sense of hopelessness and disempowerment that can lead to crime and self-destructive behavior, frustration, mistrust, and dehumanization. By participating in our roles as targets we reinforce stereotypes, collude in our own demise, and perpetuate the system of oppression. This learned helplessness is often called *internalized oppression* because we have learned to become our own oppressors from within.

If we are examining our agent identities, we may experience guilt from unearned privilege or oppressive acts, fear of payback, tendency to collude in the system to be self-protective, high levels of stress, ignorance of and loss of contact with the target groups, a sense of distorted reality about how the world is, fear of rising crime and violence levels, limited worldview, obliviousness to the damage we do, and dehumanization. By participating in our roles as agents, and remaining unconscious of or being unwilling to interrupt the Cycle, we perpetuate the system of oppression.

These results are often cited as the problems facing our society today: high drop-out rates, crime, poverty, drugs, and so on. Ironically, the root causes of them are inherent in the very assumptions on which the society is built: dualism, hierarchy, competition, individualism, domination, colonialism, and the scarcity principle. To the extent that we fail to interrupt this cycle we keep the assumptions, the problems, and the oppression alive.

A way that we might personally explore this model is to take one of the societal problems and trace its root causes back through the Cycle to the core belief systems or patterns in U.S. society that feed and play host to it. It is not a coincidence that the United States is suffering from these results today; rather, it is a logical outcome of our embracing the status quo, without thinking or challenging.

ACTIONS (ARROW NO. 3)

When we arrive at the results of this terrible cycle, we face the decision of what to do next. It is easiest to do nothing, and simply to allow the perpetuation of the status quo. We may choose not to make waves, to stay in our familiar patterns. We may say, "Oh well, it's been that way for hundreds of years. What can I do to change it? It is a huge phenomenon, and my small efforts won't count for much." Many of us choose to do nothing because it is (for a while) easier to stay with what is familiar. Besides, it is frightening to try to interrupt something so large. "What does it have to do with me, anyway?" say many agents. "This isn't my problem." We fail to realize that we have become participants just by doing nothing. This cycle has a life of its own. It doesn't need our active support because it has its own centrifugal force. It goes on, and unless we choose to interrupt it, it will continue to go on. Our silence is consent. Until our discomfort becomes larger than our comfort, we will probably stay in this cycle.

Some of us who are targets have been so beaten down by the relentless messages of the Cycle that we have given up and resigned ourselves to survive it or to self-destruct. We are victimized by the Cycle, and are playing our roles as victims to keep the Cycle alive. We will probably go around a few more times before we die. It hurts too much to fight such a big cycle. We need the help of our targeted comrades and our agent allies to try for change.

THE CORE OF THE CYCLE

As we begin to examine this decision, we may ask, "What has kept me in this cycle for so long?" Most answers are related to the themes listed in the core of the Cycle: fear, ignorance, confusion, insecurity, power or powerlessness.

Fear— For targets, fear of interrupting the system reminds us of what happens to targets who challenge the existing power structure: being labeled as "trouble-makers," experiencing discrimination, being deported, raped, beaten, institutionalized, imprisoned, or killed. There are far too many examples like these. Some targets may decide not to take the risk.

For agents, the fear of interrupting the system is different. We fear losing our privilege if we interrupt the status quo. Will I be targeted with the targets? Will I have to face my own guilt for the years when I did nothing? Will I experience "pay-back" from targets if I acknowledge my role as an agent? Agent privilege sometimes allows us to avoid action, and the Cycle continues.

Ignorance—For both targets and agents, lack of understanding about how oppression and socialization work makes it difficult to initiate change. Agents struggle more from our ignorance because we have not been forced to examine our roles. Because most of us have some agent and some target identities, we may be able to transfer what we learned in our target identities to educate ourselves in our agent identities. For example, a white lesbian may be able to translate her own experiences as a woman and a lesbian to understanding racism. This inability to see the connections may prevent us from interrupting the system.

Targets and agents both struggle with not seeing the big picture, and in our target identities, we may get caught in our own pain to the point that we cannot see the connections to other "isms." For example, a heterosexual Black man may have experienced so much racism that he cannot identify with gay people or women in the U.S. This may prevent him from interrupting the systems of heterosexism and sexism.

Confusion— Oppression is very complex. It is difficult to know how to interrupt the system. That confusion sometimes prevents both targets and agents from taking action. "What if I use the wrong word when taking a stand on ableism? What if I don't know what to say when someone tells an offensive joke? What if I think I know more than I actually do?" Will I do more harm than good? Targets may know how to deal with their own category of oppression, but not categories in which they are agents. It's easy to make a mistake, and that confusion often prevents action.

Insecurity—Rarely have we been prepared for interrupting oppression, unless we went to a progressive school or worked in a progressive organization that has provided skill-building sessions. Most targets and agents feel somewhat insecure about resistance against oppression.

Power or Powerlessness— People with power have gained it through the existing system. It is difficult to risk losing it by challenging that same system. People without power may think they can't make a difference. As long as we are "living" in the Cycle of Socialization with the core themes holding us there, it will be difficult to break out of it, but people do it every day.

CHOOSING THE DIRECTION FOR CHANGE

How do people make the decision to interrupt the Cycle and stand up for change? Sometimes the decision is triggered by a critical incident that makes oppression impossible to ignore. Perhaps a loved one is affected by some type of injustice or inequity, and we become motivated to do something about it. Heterosexual parents of gay and lesbian children report that they became activists when they saw what their children were experiencing.

Perhaps we have a "last straw" experience, where things have become so intolerable that one last incident pushes us into action. Our discomfort becomes more powerful than our fear or insecurity, and we are compelled to take some action. Women who file sex discrimination suits after years of being overlooked professionally report this example; so do women who leave abusive relationships once and for all.

Sometimes it might be some new awareness or consciousness that we gain. Perhaps a friend from a different identity group shows us a different perspective, or we read a book that makes us think differently, or we enroll in a course that introduces new possibilities. We begin to see the big picture that groups all over the world are working on these same issues. Change movements are filled with people who made decisions to interrupt the Cycle of Socialization and the system of oppression. Once you know something, you can't *not* know it anymore, and knowing it eventually translates into action. In the words of Malcolm X, "Don't be in a hurry to condemn because [someone] doesn't do what you do or think as you think or as fast. There was a time when you didn't know what you know today."

People often share qualities that have developed as a result of uniting for change. We share a sense of hope and optimism that we can dismantle oppression. We share a sense of our own efficacy that we can make a difference in the world. We empower ourselves and we support each other. We share an authentic human connection across our differences rather than fear because of our differences. We are humanized through action; not dehumanized by oppression. We listen to one another. We take one another's perspectives into account. We learn to love and trust each other. This is how the world changes.

6

Theoretical Foundations for Social Justice Education

Lee Anne Bell

WHAT IS SOCIAL JUSTICE?

Social justice is both a goal and a process. The *goal* of social justice is full and equitable participation of people from all social identity groups in a society that is mutually shaped to meet their needs. The *process* for attaining the goal of social justice should also be democratic and participatory, respectful of human diversity and group differences, and inclusive and affirming of human agency and capacity for working collaboratively with others to create change. . . .

Our *vision* for social justice is a world in which the distribution of resources is equitable and ecologically sustainable, and all members are physically and psychologically safe and secure, recognized, and treated with respect. We envision a world in which individuals are both self-determining (able to develop their full capacities) and interdependent (capable of interacting democratically with others). Social justice involves social actors who have a sense of their own agency as well as a sense of social responsibility toward and with others, their society, the environment, and the broader world in which we live. These are conditions we not only wish for ourselves but for all people in our interdependent global community.

WHAT IS JUSTICE?

Philosophers and others have long debated the question, "What constitutes justice?" Our definition of social justice draws on theories that describe justice as a fair and equitable *distribution of resources* with the imperative to address those who are least advantaged. We also draw on theories that affirm the importance of fair and equitable *social processes*, including recognition and respect for marginalized or subjugated cultures and groups. We see these two aspects as intertwining, acknowledging that social justice must address *both* resources and recognition. . . .

Social *justice* refers to reconstructing society in accordance with principles of equity, recognition, and inclusion. It involves eliminating the *injustice* created when differences are sorted and ranked in a hierarchy that unequally confers power, social, and economic advantages, and institutional and cultural validity to social groups based on their location in that hierarchy. . . . Without truly valuing diversity, we cannot effectively address issues of injustice. Without addressing issues of injustice, we cannot truly value diversity. . . .

UNDERSTANDING OPPRESSION

Oppression is the term we use to embody the interlocking forces that create and sustain injustice. In this book, we focus on how oppression is manifested through racism, classism, sexism, heterosexism, transgender oppression, religious oppression, ableism, and youth and elder oppression. In order to work toward a vision of justice, it is essential to understand how oppression operates institutionally and personally in everyday life. The features of oppression that social justice educational strategies are intended to expose, analyze, and challenge can be seen as interwoven strands in a social fabric that renders oppression durable, flexible, and resilient, as shown in Fig. 6.1. In order to work against oppression effectively, we need to understand the component strands and how they weave together to reinforce and strengthen each other in maintaining an oppressive system.

The dictionary definition of oppression includes such terms as domination, coercion, cruelty, tyranny, subjugation, persecution, harassment, and repression. These terms describe important overt features of oppression but do not capture the more subtle and convert aspects of how oppression is normalized in everyday life. Below we define and discuss both overt and subtle features that characterize oppression as restrictive, pervasive, and cumulative; socially constructed, categorizing, and group-based; hierarchical, normalized, and hegemonic; intersectional and internalized; and mutable. These features are illustrated with examples that show how they interlock with one another to sustain the overall system. While presented as separate terms, these features in fact interweave and mutually reinforce each other in ways that are not as simple to tease apart as a list of discrete terms might suggest. Rather, they should be understood as interlocking constituent parts of a dynamic process.

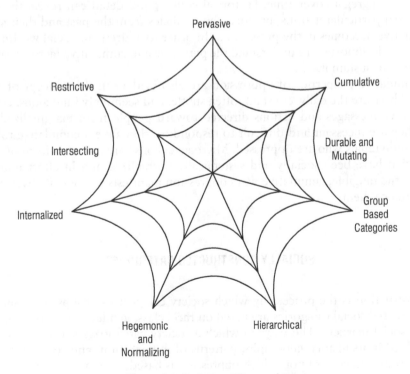

Figure 6.1 Features of Oppression

RESTRICTIVE

On the most general level, oppression denotes structural and material constraints that significantly shape life opportunities and sense of possibility. Oppression restricts both self-development and self-determination, delimiting the person one can imagine becoming as well as the power to act in support of one's rights and aspirations. It encapsulates the fusion of institutional/systemic discrimination with personal bias, bigotry, and social prejudice through a complex web of relationships and structures that saturate everyday life. . . .

PERVASIVE

Oppression is institutionalized through pervasive practices grounded in history, law, economic policy, social custom, and education that rationalize and maintain hierarchies among individuals and groups. Individuals are socialized into this system and internalize the dynamics that sustain it. Woven together through time and reinforced in the present, these individual, interpersonal, and institutional practices interact to create and mutually reinforce an all-encompassing, pervasive system. . . .

CUMULATIVE

Oppression accumulates through institutional and social patterns, grounded in history, whose effects aggregate over time. Historical context and detail can reveal the relationships between particular actions, practices, and policies from the past and their structural and cumulative outcomes in the present. . . . In order to address the racial wealth gap that exists today, it is important to understand the pervasive and cumulative factors that created and continue to sustain it. . . .

The cumulative properties of oppression are also evident in the concept of microaggressions. These are the daily, constant, often subtle, and seemingly innocuous, covert and overt negative messages and actions directed toward people from marginalized groups. Because they are incessant and difficult to respond to, they take a cumulative toll on the psyche of individuals who are oppressed. Microaggessions "are in fact, a form of everyday suffering that have been socially and systemically normalized and in effect minimized". They show the tangible, cumulative ways oppression manifests in the daily lives of people who experience them.

SOCIALLY CONSTRUCTED CATEGORIES

Social construction is the process by which society categorizes groups of people. In the U.S., constructed social categories are based on race, class, gender, sexuality, age, religion, and other social markers. The ways in which a society categorizes social identity groups are embedded in its history, geography, patterns of immigration, and social-political context. The group categories upon which oppression is based, such as gender roles or racial designations, are not "real," but through implicit beliefs and social practices that operate as of real, they become so in practice. Social constructions are used to rationalize differential treatment or allocation of resources and to explain social reality in ways that make inequitable outcomes seem inevitable.

For example, the construction of distinct racial groups was produced to justify particular social, economic, and political practices that justified the enslavement, extermination, segregation, and exploitation of other "races." The meaning-making system of race gained force and power through its reproduction in the material practices of the society across historical eras. Anti-miscegenation laws and segregation in housing, employment, schooling, and other areas of social life reproduced and reinforced race as a social category. Thus, using, and continuing to use, race to allocate resources and opportunities made race real in practice. Today, the idea of race is so taken for granted that it is difficult to see the apparatus that created it in the first place.

The social construction of gender provides another example. Gender divides humans into categories of male and female with dichotomous masculine or feminine identities, traits, and social roles. A socialization process that treats presumed gender differences as innate reinforces these constructs and makes them appear "natural"(i.e., that there are only two genders—male and female; or that boys are naturally active and rambunctious, while girls are passive and sweet). Such assumptions are supported and reinforced through social norms, roles, and interpersonal and organizational practices that regard and treat males and females accordingly. . . .

Social constructions presented as natural and inevitable are difficult to question and challenge. Once their provenance comes into question, however, imagining alternative scenarios becomes possible. Part of the work of social justice education and social justice movements is to expose and take apart oppressive constructs, understand how they have been created and maintained, and then reconstruct more just ways to organize social life. . . .

History, geography, patterns of immigration, and socio-political context are important to how identities are categorized and constructed. For example, the group labeled "Hispanic" in the United States is extremely diverse, comprised of people from many different countries of origin who speak various languages; they are from divergent racial, ethnic, and socio-economic groups and arrive in the United States under widely different conditions of immigration, colonization, or slavery, and over different time periods. The category may include a Spanish-speaking, upper-class white man from Cuba as well as a dark-skinned, Mayan speaking, Indian woman from Guatemala. The dominant society lumps them together in a group labeled "Hispanic" to which certain attributions, assumptions, and stereotypes are applied. . . .

In actual practice, neither individual identities nor social groups are homogeneous or stable. Identity categories interact with and co-constitute one another in different geographic and historical contexts to create unique social locations. Essentialist notions of group identity as fixed ignore the fluid and changing ways that people experience themselves, both as individuals and as members of different social groups, over the course of a lifetime. . . .

POWER HIERARCHIES

Social groups are sorted into a hierarchy that confers advantages, status, resources, access, and privilege that are denied or rationed to those lower in the hierarchy. Social groups are not simply different, but ranked in a hierarchy. Thus, individuals are positioned as *dominant* or *advantaged* in relation to other groups that are *subordinated* or *disadvantaged*. Power hierarchies create and maintain a system of advantage and disadvantage based on social group membership.

Dominant groups hold the power and authority to control, in their own interests, the important institutions in society, determine how resources are allocated, and define what is natural, good and true. They are seen as superior, more capable and more credible—as normal—compared to those who are differently situated. People in dominant groups are socialized to accept their group's socially advantaged status as normal and deserved, rather than recognizing how it has been conferred through systems of inequality. Thus, one of the privileges of dominant group status is the luxury to see oneself as simply an individual. . . .

Subordinated or marginalized groups are represented as less than, inferior, and/or deviant. People who are oppressed are not seen as individuals but as representatives or members of social groups. For people in subordinated groups, social group membership trumps individuality. They can never fully escape being defined by their social group memberships and the ascriptions the dominant society applies to their group. . . .

Young (1990) developed the concept of five faces of oppression to distinguish families of concepts or conditions that constitute oppression differently in the lives of different groups. The five faces are: exploitation, marginalization, powerlessness, cultural imperialism, and violence. In our teaching, we often use these five terms as a heuristic device to illustrate the shared and different ways oppression plays out and is experienced among different groups of people. In some of the ism chapters in this book, the five faces are used as a tool to examine how oppression operates for that oppression (see Section 4, Religious Oppression, and Section 6, Ableism, for examples).

HEGEMONIC AND NORMALIZED

The concept of hegemony was developed by Gramsci to explain how domination and control are maintained not only through coercion but also through the voluntary consent of both those who are dominated and those who gain advantage because of the oppression of others. Through hegemony, the reproduction of advantage and disadvantage come to be assumed as natural, normal, "business as usual," even by those who are disempowered.

Woven so effectively into the social fabric, the processes and effects of oppression become normalized, thus making it difficult to step outside of the system to discern how it operates—like fish trying to understand the water in which they swim. For example, the exclusion of people with disabilities from many jobs does not require overt discrimination against them. Business as usual is sufficient to prevent change. Physical barriers to access go unnoticed by those who can walk up the stairs, reach elevator buttons and telephones, use furniture and tools that fit their passage, and thus support and maintain policies that seem perfectly natural and fair from the privileged vantage point of those not affected.

In hegemonic systems, power is relational and dynamic, something that circulates within a web of relationships in which we all participate, rather than something imposed from top down. Power operates not simply through persons or groups unilaterally imposing their will on others, but through ongoing systems that are mediated by well-internationed people acting, usually unconsciously, as agents of oppression by merely going about their daily lives. Hegemony and structural injustice are thus produced and reproduced by "thousands or millions of persons usually acting within institutional rules and according to practices that most people regard morally acceptable." In such a system, responsibility for oppression often cannot be isolated to individual or institutional agents but is rather more indirect, collective, and cumulative. . . . Through hegemony, the roles and rules, institutional norms, historical accounts, and social practices of dominant groups come to be accepted as the natural order. The advantages of dominant groups and the disadvantages of marginalized groups are normalized through language, ideology, and cultural/material practices. . . .

INTERNALIZED

Through the process of socialization, members of society appropriate and internalize social norms and beliefs to make meaning of their experiences and to fit in, conform, and survive. As part of this process, people learn and incorporate oppressive stereotypes and beliefs reflected in the broader society. Such stereotypes and beliefs circulate through everyday language and cultural scripts that frame their assumptions and interactions with others. In this way, oppression is internalized so that it operates not only through external social institutions and norms, but also through discourse and practice. The processes of socialization and internalization illustrate how an unjust status quo comes to be accepted and replicated by those who benefit as well as by those who suffer from oppressive norms. Attribution and internalization are thus reciprocal and mutually reinforcing processes. . . .

INTERSECTIONAL

Each form of oppression has distinctive qualities and historical/social legacies that distinguish it from other forms of oppression, and we believe that learning about the specific legacies and historical trajectories of different groups is critical for understanding the specific ways different forms of oppression operate. At the same time, we recognize that different forms of oppression interact with and co-constitute one another as interlocking systems that overlap and reinforce each other, at both the systemic/institutional level and at the individual/interpersonal level.

Telescoping in on a single form of oppression can provide valuable information for understanding the particular historical contexts and contemporary manifestations of that oppression. Panning out to focus on the broader pattern of interlocking systems yields important knowledge about general features of oppression that cut across specific forms and about how different forms mutually reinforce each other. Focusing on the intersections where different forms of oppression meet in the lives of particular individuals can reveal the differential impacts of varying locations within the overall system of oppression. . . . Such an intersectional approach to gender violence can reveal how strategies predicated on the experiences of white, middle class, heterosexual, and cisgender women may not address the particular problems and obstacles faced by poor women, women of color, lesbian, bisexual, or transgender women because of their different locations within intersecting form of oppression.

For each form of oppression, we can be purposeful in looking at how it intersects with other forms:

We challenge individuals to see interconnections by "Asking the other question." When I see something that looks racist, I ask, "Where is the patriarchy in this?" When I see something that looks sexist, I ask, "Where is the hetereosexism in this?" When I see something that looks homophobic, I ask, "Where are the class interests in this?"

Intersectionality operates at the level of identity, as well as the level of institutions and the overall system, in ways that are multiplicative, and simultaneous. Individuals experience their lives based on their location along all dimensions of identity and thus may occupy positions of dominance and subordination at the same time. For example, an upper-class professional man who is African American (still a very small percentage of African Americans overall) may enjoy economic success and professional status conferred through being male, and class privilege and perhaps dominant language and citizenship privilege as an English-speaking native-born citizen, yet face limitations not endured by co-workers who are white. Despite economic and professional status and success, he may be threatened by police, unable to hail a taxi, and endure hateful epithets as he walks down the street. The constellation of identities that shape his consciousness and experience as an African American man, and his varying access to privilege, may fluctuate if he is light or dark skinned; Ivy League educated or a high school dropout; heterosexual, gay, or transgender; incarcerated or unemployed; or a tourist in South Africa, Brazil, or Europe, where his racial status will be differently defined.

From our perspective, no single form of oppression is the base for all others; all are connected and mutually constituted in a system that makes them possible. . . . In our approach, we argue for the explanatory and political value of identifying the particular histories, geographies, and characteristics of specific forms of oppression as well as the intersections across isms that mutually reinforce them at both the systemic and individual levels. Focusing on one facet of a prism does not remove it from its broader context, but provides a way to highlight and focus in order to ground learning at a particular point in time.

DURABLE AND MUTABLE

A final feature of oppression in its resilience and ability to shape-shift into new forms to prevail against challenges to it. The civil rights movement was successful in eliminating de jure segregation, but the system of racism evolved to create new ways to segregate and discriminate while calling itself "post racial." Obviously, overt discrimination still exists, but racism has also become more subtle and insidious. . . .

CONSEQUENCES FOR ALL

Oppression has consequences for everyone. People in both marginalized and advantaged groups are dehumanized by oppression. Thus, a goal of social justice education is to engage all people in recognizing the terrible costs of maintaining systems of oppression. For example, when millions of Americans are homeless and hungry, those who are comfortable pay a social and moral price. The cost of enjoying plenty while others starve is the inability to view our society as just and see ourselves as decent people. Just as important, it also prevents a clear view of underlying structural problems in the economic system that ultimately make all people vulnerable in a changing international economy that disregards national boundaries or allegiances. The productive and creative contributions of people who are shut out of the system are lost to everyone. Rising violence and urban decay make it increasingly difficult for anyone to feel safe. Reduced social supports, limited affordable housing, and scarcities of food and potable water loom as a possible future for all who are not independently wealthy, particularly as people reach old age.

The impetus for change more often comes from those on the margins, since they tend to see more clearly the contradictions between myths and reality and usually have the most incentive to change. . . . Those advantaged by the system also have an important role to play in joining with others to challenge oppression. They can expose the way advantage works from the inside and articulate the social, moral, and personal costs of maintaining privilege. Those in dominant groups can learn to see that they have an investment in changing the system by which they benefit, by recognizing they also pay a price.

6 (CONTINUED)

Core Concepts for Social Justice Education

Maurianne Adams and Ximena Zúñiga

DIFFERENCES BETWEEN DIVERSITY AND SOCIAL JUSTICE APPROACHES

A *diversity* approach generally emphasizes the social, cultural, and other differences and commonalities among social identity groups based on the ethnic, racial, religious, gender, class, or other "social categories" generally recognized within the U.S. (These will differ transnationally as well as historically.) The goals of a diversity approach include appreciation of differences among and within groups in a pluralistic society.

A diversity approach does not necessarily include issues of inequality as fundamental to the ways in which diversity is experienced in the U.S. It is also unlikely to address the ways in which social group differences have been used historically and in the present day to rationalize and justify the damage done by inequality and injustice within the larger society, or the ways in which privileges and disadvantages are situated within a larger context of systemic inequality and oppression.

For example, a diversity approach might focus on understanding the cultural values, religious affiliations, educational experiences, families, national and language origins for specific ethnic groups, like Puerto Rican or Mexican Latinos/as, or U.S.-born African Americans, or Afro-Caribbeans (Cubans, Dominicans, Haitians). Yet this approach often remains silent on the biases and daily microaggressions people from these groups encounter, the pervasive discrimination in employment and educational tracking, and the systemic disadvantages these groups face within the system of U.S. racism. . . .

In contrast, *social justice education* focuses attention on the ways in which social group differences of race and ethnicity, national origins, language, religion, gender, sexuality, class, disability, and age interact with systems of domination and subordination to privilege or disadvantage difference social group members relative to each other. We use the term *social justice education* as distinct from diversity education to capture an emphasis upon unequal social structures, supremacist ideologies, and oppressive politics and practices by which members of dominant social groups, whether knowingly or unconsciously, perpetuate their own social and cultural privilege to the disadvantage of marginalized or subordinated social groups.

An SJE approach is based on a vision of society organized upon principles of social justice, and draws on a theory of oppression to analyze the ways in which societies fall short of such a vision. The goals of an SJE approach include awareness and understanding of oppression, acknowledgement of one's role in that system (as a privileged or disadvantaged social group member), and a commitment to develop the skills, resources, and coalitions needed to create lasting change.

STRUCTURAL INEQUALITY OCCURS AT EVERY LEVEL OF SOCIETY: INDIVIDUAL, INSTITUTIONAL, AND SOCIETAL/CULTURAL

Structural inequality plays out and can be analyzed at every of social organization from the most individual and personal, to the most abstract and societal. The terms that we use in this book—individual, institutional, and societal/cultural—refer to the levels of social organization at which inequality is maintained and reproduced.

The individual level refers to persons in themselves and in relationship with others; it includes "internalized" understandings of privilege or inequality within a person's individual consciousness as well as attitudes and behaviours that play out interpersonally.

The institutional level refers to social institutions such as schooling, banking and finance, and criminal justice institutions that enforce the law and political institutions that create the law. The institutional level can also refer to smaller units within larger institutions or organizations, such as a particular school district, a particular classroom within a school system, or a police department or prison within the larger legal system.

The cultural and societal levels refer to the broad abstract understandings that pervade a social system. At the cultural level, we examine prevailing norms and values that govern communication style, gender roles, family structure, expectations of physical and mental capacities, relationship to time and place, aesthetic standards, and more. The term *norm* means that certain ways of being are viewed as correct and *normal* while differences are defined as wrong, unhealthy, or *abnormal*. Culture is not one thing, but an aggregate of many norms, expectations, attitudes, and behaviors that are expressed by individuals and institutions. Likewise, society is an aggregate of institutions that reproduce attitudes and values from the dominant culture, and in their cumulative interactions convey the feeling that one is living within a cohesive system that can be described as *society*.

We find the three levels—individual, institutional, and societal/cultural—useful for drawing general distinctions among levels of social organization, and for describing interactions among them. For some groups of participants, these terms may not seem sufficiently nuanced. They may want additional terms to differentiate between the intrapersonal (within the self) and interpersonal (between several individuals), or to describe the dynamics within groups of people (such as a working group, a club, or a family) that are too small or informal to be "institutional" and yet often are the groupings within which the policies and practices of an institution get understood, carried out, and rewarded. Similarly, it may seem difficult to grasp the meaning of "the culture" or "the society" except through the interplay of specific institutional players such as the media, the rhetoric deployed by politicians running for public office, or the policies and practices that provide or prevent access to health care or school systems or safe neighborhoods. . . .

OPPRESSION IS SOCIALLY CONSTRUCTED BY HISTORICAL LEGACIES EMBEDDED IN INSTITUTIONS AND BELIEF SYSTEMS

Today's oppression grows out of the legacy of yesterday's accumulated and persistent inequality. Many contemporary manifestations of oppression gain strength from the assumption that something "has always been done this way." When we examine historical legacies, we better understand how different manifestations of oppression evolved as they did, and why they have persisted. We can also begin to imagine how things might have turned out differently. Novelist William Faulkner's famous statement, "The past is never dead. It's not even past" conveys this sense of the continuity of history and why we must dig deep into the past if we are to build a better future.

The term *social construction* refers to the idea that norms, ideas, and institutions that may now seem natural or inevitable actually grew out of specific historical and social processes. When, as children, we learn norms around respectful communication between children and adults, acceptable behaviour in public and private spaces, and expectations of men and women, these norms seem absolute. But in fact they vary across cultures and shift over time within cultures. Abstract ideas like democracy, peace, and romantic love are socially constructed, as are the very concepts on which social identity categories are based—race, ethnicity, sex, gender, sexual orientation, disability, childhood, and adulthood. . . .

Institutions tend to perpetuate themselves and often outlive their original intentions. For example, long-term incarceration of criminals began in the late 18th century as a well-intentioned alternative to the public humiliation of whipping and hanging, and was the first penal system in the Western world intended to rehabilitate as well as punish. Within less than 100 years, strong evidence showed that incarceration, especially solitary confinement, was in fact more damaging than rehabilitative. But by that time, other institutions had grown up around incarceration that had their own interests to protect and all of these institutions are more entrenched today. Private prisons contract with states to fill prison beds for profit, unions for prison guards protect their members' job security, outside companies hire prisoners at extremely low wages, and policitians cite incarceration as proof that they are "tough on crime." Questions about whether incarceration diminishes crime, or is appropriate for a particular crime, or is cruel and unusual, or is racially biased, bump up against established institutions and accepted ideas that perpetuate the status quo. Thus, consideration of the historical legacies of social institutions—in connection with why they were established and who now benefits—enables participants to understand how historical and cultural forces shape the manifestations of oppression we see today.

It is often challenging to think about how social identity categories are also social constructions with tangled historical roots. For example, "race" is a complicated social construction that was created and used to subordinate people with darker skin color for the purposes of enslavement, economic exploitation, and /or colonization and conquest. The fluidity and instrumental nature of racial categories is captured by the term "racialization"—*the extension of racial meaning to a previously racially unclassified relationship, social practice, or group.*" The process of racialization helps explain how the U.S. has racialized geographically and historically diverse migrants through a shifting color line that sorts people into a racially stratified workforce. Rather than a biological or even purely cultural fact, race is a social fact constructed through legal, economic, cultural, and other forces in the service of creating and maintaining inequality. . . .

Historical legacies are transnational as well as U.S. centered, and it is important to understand the interconnections among global and U.S. instances of oppression and resistances. For example, the 20th century Black Consciousness and anti-apartheid movements in South Africa were linked to the civil rights and racial consciousness movements in the U.S. Likewise, 19th and 20th century anti-colonial nationalist movements in Africa, Arabia, and the Americas were inspired in part by the American Revolution and the anti-monarchy ideas from the French Revolution. . . .

THE ROLE OF SOCIALIZATION AND HEGEMONY IN MAINTAINING SYSTEMS OF OPPRESSION

Socialization refers to the lifelong process by which we inherit and replicate the dominant norms and frameworks of our society, and learn to accept them as "common sense." In particular, we learn to think of social identity categories as essential and natural, and of social hierarchies as inevitable. Our socialization processes rarely point out that our norms perpetuate a world view based upon the maintenance of advantage for some, relative to disadvantage for others.

"The internalization of socially rooted and historically developed activities is the distinguishing feature of human psychology," in that external events and interpersonal processes are transformed into intrapersonal ones (Vygotsky). This general principle of socialization which is the ongoing process by which external activities and processes become reconstituted as part of an interior self applies to the internalization of oppressive activities and processes.

Oppression depends on the internalization and acceptance of advantaged and disadvantaged social group relationships within the social hierarchy of the larger society. Disadvantaged social groups can live within a system of oppression that injures them or deprives them of certain rights without having the language or consciousness (Freire used the term "conscientizcao") to name the oppression or to understand their situation as an effect of oppression, rather than the natural order of things. Memmi described this as "psychological colonization" whereby disadvantaged groups internalize their oppressed condition and collude with the oppressive ideology and social system, a process Freire referred to as "playing host to the oppressor." . . .

The dominant norms we are socialized to accept can be described as *hegemonic*. Hegemonic norms wield power, because most people behave in accordance with social norms without being told or forced to do so and judge harshly those who behave otherwise. For those who benefit from the norms by virtue of their membership in privileged social groups, going along with business as usual provides unquestioned access to social advantages. One of the subtlest advantages is the ability to see oneself and be seen as "normal," in contrast with those considered different, strange, alien, or "other." . . .

For example, heterosexuality is an enforced norm. People who are heterosexual don't need to "come out" because it is the assumed default. Individuals and couples who are heterosexual (or perceived as heterosexual) can experience themselves as normal and unremarkable, and encounter institutions designed to meet their needs (at least on the dimension of sexual orientation). . . . The pervasive cultural, institutional, and individual reinforcement of heterosexuality as the norm means that most people across identity categories go through life with a more or less conscious understanding that heterosexuals fit the norm while queer, bisexual, lesbian, and gay people do not. Norms form part of a pervasive hegemonic system that can seem enormously difficult to change.

INDIVIDUALS EXPERIENCE PRIVILEGE AND DISADVANTAGE RELATIVE TO HOW THEY HAVE BEEN CATEGORIZED INTO SOCIAL IDENTITY GROUPS

Each of us has multiple *social group identities* that are based on our *social group memberships*. Both are based on *categories* that are socially constructed and have long roots in established historical legacies, as described above. These categories represent ways of sorting people and establishing privileges or exclusions based solely on their social group memberships. There is almost always a history of injustice behind the establishment of these social categories.

Participants who are not familiar with the idea of *social categories, social group memberships,* and *social identities* may confuse these with specific *social roles* (such as parent-child, teacher-student, doctor-patient). Although social roles are also constructed and often are attached to power differences, they are not essentialized to the same extent as social group memberships.

Social group memberships are also not the same as *voluntary club* or *team memberships* (Republican-Democrat, hockey player-Little League member, volunteer for Big Brothers Big Sisters). One key difference is that we are free to join and leave such groups without feeling or being perceived as a "different person" as a result of the change (unlike when someone undergoes religious conversion or gender transition, for example). There may be overlaps and interactions among one's social group memberships and identity (e.g., as a Latina), social roles (e.g., as a mother, a wife, and a college teacher) and voluntary memberships (e.g., on a Board of Directors for an Upward Bound program). Nevertheless, the distinction is important because of the strength of socially constructed hegemonic meaning attached to social group memberships and identities.

Social categories, social group memberships and social identities. The core concepts of social category and social identity are closely related but not the same. Social categories are socially constructed, with historical legacies, enforced hegemonic meanings, and widespread unquestioned acceptance. Although socially constructed and therefore potentially changeable, social categories and the meaning attached to them tend to remain relatively stable. Thus, we tend to experience our social group memberships as fixed, natural, and inevitable, and accordingly our social identities—how we "identify with" our social group memberships—feel like inherent traits.

Some social group memberships are inherited from our families (such as race and ethnicity) or from the group we are assigned to at birth (such as class and sex). Some are relatively fixed, while others may emerge or change over time. Our social class or terms for ethnic self-identification may change with economic circumstances, migration, political organizing, and other life events that impact our access to resources. People born with no disabilities may acquire a disability through accident, illness, or aging; and all of us start off as children, move as we age into the category of adult, and if we're lucky eventually become elders. Although we often talk about one social identity at a time, in actuality we experience them simultaneously. One is not separately a white person, an elder, and male; one is an old white man. Each unique combination of social identities carries its own social meanings and its own combinations of advantages and disadvantages. . . .

Border identities. Social group categories are often constructed as binary, but the reality of how identities play out, especially across different contexts and settings, is far more complex. Sometimes identities do not fall clearly on one side of an advantaged/disadvantaged binary. We acknowledge this nuance with the idea of border *identities,* identities that border but do not fully fit either category. Examples of border identities include people of mixed racial backgrounds, children adopted and raised by parents of a different race than their own, and young adults who are over the age of legal majority but still treated as young or immature. . . .

Advantage and disadvantage attached to social group membership. In this volume, we present six forms of oppression, each of them based on social categories of advantage and disadvantage—racism; classism; religious oppression; ableism; youth/age oppression; and sexism and transgender oppression (considered together). These isms are rooted in U.S.

and global categories of domination and subordination. A central task for instructors and students in justice education courses is to understand, explore, and compare how people are privileged and/or marginalized on the basis of both particular social group memberships and intersecting group memberships.

Almost everyone has some identities that confer advantage (privilege) and others that confer disadvantage. People are often less aware of their advantaged identities and more aware of their disadvantaged identities. The salience of particular identities may also vary depending on context and other factors, but they all matter. For example, Barack Obama is widely referred to as the first black president of the U.S. In addition to being black, he is also male, heterosexual, and Christian; benefits from considerable financial and educational privilege as a lawyer and college professor; and is the biracial son of a white mother. His blackness is salient in public discourse because his success as a leader contradicts many of the dominant associations with blackness, while his privileged identities may seem unremarkable because they are shared with most other political leaders. Yet those privileged identities probably played an important role in securing voters' confidence in him, even though the privileges they confer are less secure than they would be for a politician who is white. Thus, it is rarely useful to categorize someone simply as advantaged or disadvantaged; instead, we encourage consideration of *how* someone is advantaged and/or disadvantaged by particular social group memberships and combinations of social group memberships.

Privilege. People are often unaware of privileges accorded to them based on dominant social group memberships, because those privileges have been *normalized* to be expected. By contrast, people who are denied the same privileges are often painfully aware of them. Advantaged groups sometimes oppose social justice change efforts because they fear losing privileges that they assume to be their "rights" even though those so-called rights are not enjoyed by everyone. *Privileges* are benefits based on social group membership that are available to some people and not others, and sometimes at the expense of others. Some privileges are material—such as access to adequate health care—while others are nonmaterial—such as the ability to experience oneself as normal and central in society. The concept of privilege reminds us that such benefits are not earned, but rather result from social advantage relative to others' disadvantage.

Some examples of privileges include:

- White men can count on being perceived as professional and their expertise as legitimate.
- Heterosexual couples, especially those who conform to norms of gender expression, can count on their relationships being seen as natural.
- Owning-class and professional middle-class young people can make decisions about which career paths to pursue without worrying about supporting themselves or their family members financially.

Many further examples or privilege can be found in each ism section.

SOCIAL GROUP MEMBERSHIPS, IDENTITIES, AND FORMS OF OPPRESSION ARE INTERSECTIONAL AT ALL LEVELS

Intersectionality suggests that our various advantaged and disadvantaged social group memberships do not act independent of one another, or in a simply additive way. Rather, they interrelate to create specific experiences of oppression that are not reducible to one or another identity. For example, people of color who experience racial microaggressions are complicated by gender (for women and for men alike, as well as those whose gender expression is outside the norm), by religion (given the ways that religions associated with the Arab or Asian diaspora are racialized or the Black Church historically kept outside of white Christianity), by class (given the ways in which economic advantage or disadvantage are linked to racial classification), and so on.

Patricia Hill Collins proposes that "a system of interlocking race, class, and gender oppression" for any historical or contemporary context will offer a more accurate and inclusive framework that focuses attention on both the core and the intersecting systems of oppression. Collins further proposes a "paradigmatic shift" that asks that we think inclusively about other structures of oppression (age, sexual orientation, religion, ethnicity) and conceptualize all such oppression, and resistance, at all three levels "of personal biography; the group or community level of the cultural context created by race, class, and gender; and the systemic level of social institutions."

The paradigmatic shift replaces additive or binary models of oppression through models of intersecting axes of race, gender, social class, and other social categories that operate at all three levels of social organization (the individual, cultural, and institutional)—each representing sites of domination as well as potential sites for resistance. But there is a limit to the generalizability of this approach (as in Fig. 6.2), which is "centered" at the core of intersecting axes. Although this "center" conveys the centrality of any one system of oppression, it generates further inquiry, whether the "center" implies some core identity, a "fixity or status" that "does not adequately represent the fluidity of identities" for a "self" that is always in process [and] "the *simultaneous process of identity, institutional and social practices,* which operate concurrently and together to construct people's identities and shape their experiences, opportunities, and constraints." . . .

Thus, it becomes clear that intersections occur at the same moment not only within personal experience, but also at institutional, systemic, and cultural levels that have impacts in the moment and also across time, affecting individuals and social groups. . . .

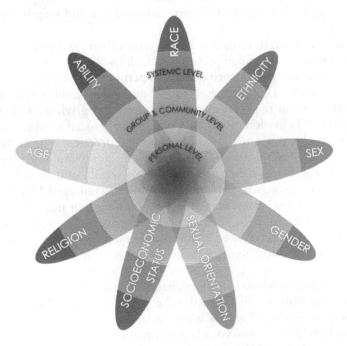

Figure 6.2 Matrix of Interlocking Systems and Levels of Oppression and Resistance Adapted by Zúñiga, X. & Lee, E. Y. (2015).

THE IMPORTANCE OF CRITICAL AWARENESS, KNOWLEDGE, AND SKILLS TO
CHALLENGE, RESIST, AND TAKE EFFECTIVE ACTION FOR CHANGE

Important goals of SJE include helping us recognize oppressive situations when we encounter them, and developing the knowledge and skills to take action when possible using the questions in the cycle of socialization as openings for change. Instead of feeling hopeless and overwhelmed by the pervasive and damaging impacts of oppression on entire groups of people, we want to help turn attention to places they can take action to create change, both as individuals and through coalitions and networks with others. . . .

Barbara Love has framed individual preparation as "developing a liberatory consciousness" (in homage to Freire), and she identifies awareness, analysis, action, and accountability/allyship as key ingredients for individual action. Awareness and analysis involve identifying places where the normalization of systems of privilege and disadvantage should be questioned, resisted, and changed at all levels—social, cultural, institutional, and personal. As noted earlier, these often overlap.

Learning to question oneself and others, and to resist and transform hegemonic norms and oppressive practices, can take many forms. Historical accounts of past and recent people's struggles for human and civil rights, and for equity and justice, provide powerful illustrations of how members of different social groups have struggled—for basic human rights to food, safety, shelter, minimal wage—as well as for civil rights, educational equity, immigration reform, redistribution of wealth, and against different forms of violence including hate crimes, violence against women, and police brutality against men and women of color. One important lesson from reading and studying people's struggles is that we must not despair. As Zinn puts it, through the study of history, "we can find not only war but resistance to war, not only injustice but rebellion against injustice, not only selfishness but self-sacrifice, not only silence in the face of tyranny but defiance, not only callousness but compassion." Things do change as the result of such struggle. The study of history can motivate and inspire people to create and sustain change.

Individuals also can learn to recognize and interrupt their own complicity in the reproduction of systems of privilege and oppression. As Collins observes, we often fail to see how our own values, ideas, and behaviors contribute to perpetuate someone else's mistreatment or disadvantaged location. Thus, increased knowledge and awareness of how we have been socialized to participate in the reproduction of systems of privilege and oppression is a critical first step toward envisioning and working towards social justice. . . .

It is often the case, however, that unjust policies and practices require more than a single individual to create and sustain change. Institutions are complex entities, and change calls for assets from multiple members of coalitions within and outside the institution or community, as well as across advantanged and disadvantaged identity groups. The process of "action planning" stresses intentional planning that includes critical analysis, collaboration, seeking multiple perspectives and information sources, and building dialogue and networks across divides. Effective change plans take into account step-by-step timelines, resources, considerations, obstacles, spheres of influence, and risk levels for participants. . . .

Activists use a range of terms to talk about change at the individual or institutional levels. *Allies* are people who work in alliance with others toward a shared goal of change. *Allies* might be members of privileged groups who are ready to leverage their privilege toward change. They might be people who have transformed disadvantage into empowerment to work on their own behalf and those of others. Other terms include *activists*, *advocates*, and *change agents*, all of whom are likely to be individuals working within *coalitions* or *networks* within communities or organizations. Change at the cultural and societal level calls for broad-based social movements.

There are countless opportunities in our personal lives to question oppressive beliefs and discriminatory practices and policies, and to work in alliance with others to change them. For example:

- People can interrupt offensive jokes and educate about the impact of microaggressions.
- A teacher can incorporate social justice issues into courses not ordinarily focused on social justice.
- A community organizer can create networks of school administrators and service providers to create continuity of support for the children of migrant workers or homeless youth.
- Men can choose to do their fair share of childcare and housework even though sexism would let them get away with not doing it, and make themselves accountable to women in their lives.
- A person with financial resources can make micro-loans to people in need, and donate money to organizations led by poor people.
- People of all ages can make commitments to practice awareness, analysis, action, and accountability in their relationships and interactions.

While the tools for creating change at the personal and interpersonal level may include our own growing awareness, knowledge, commitments, passions, and skills for interrupting oppression and the increased capacity to leverage support for social justice actions in our own sphere of influence, these tools may not be sufficient to challenge hegemonic forces at the institutional and cultural level. We can certainly take active roles in organizations and institutions to change policies and practices impacting people's lives, but we are likely to be more effective to promote change beyond personal and interpersonal contexts by engaging in collective action. Forging pathways for collective action may require understanding the role of social movements in contributing to the most durable instances of change. Social movement methods such as protests, strikes, sit-ins, boycotts, and informing the public of specific discriminatory policies have been historically effective in advancing social justice goals. Along with historical examples, instructors and participants should be aware of current-day alliances, coalitions, and networks that are taking effective action towards legal, structural, and economic changes.

7

Five Faces of Oppression

Iris Marion Young

. . .

In this chapter I offer some explanation of the concept of oppression as I understand its use by new social movements in the United States since the 1960s. My starting point is reflection on the conditions of the groups said by these movements to be oppressed: among others, women, Blacks, Chicanos, Puerto Ricans and other Spanish-speaking Americans, American Indians, Jews, lesbians and gay men, Arabs, Asians, old people, working-class people, and the physically and mentally disabled. I aim to systematize the meaning of the concept of oppression as used by these diverse political movements, and to provide normative argument to clarify the wrongs the term names.

Obviously the above-named groups are not oppressed to the same extent or in the same ways. In the most general sense, all oppressed people suffer some inhibition of their ability to develop and exercise their capacities and express their needs, thoughts, and feelings. In that abstract sense all oppressed people face a common condition. Beyond that, in any more specific sense, it is not possible to define a single set of criteria that describe the condition of oppression of the above groups. Consequently, attempts by theorists and activists to discover a common description or the essential causes of the oppression of all these groups have frequently led to fruitless disputes about whose oppression is more fundamental or more grave. The contexts in which members of these groups use the term *oppression* to describe the injustices of their situation suggest that oppression names in fact a family of concepts and conditions, which I divide into five categories: exploitation, marginalization, powerlessness, cultural imperialism, and violence.

. . .

OPPRESSION AS A STRUCTURAL CONCEPT

. . . In its traditional usage, oppression means the exercise of tyranny by a ruling group. Oppression also traditionally carries a strong connotation of conquest and colonial domination. The Hebrews were oppressed in Egypt, and many uses of the term oppression in the West invoke this paradigm. . . . New left social movements of the 1960s and 1970s, however, shifted the meaning of the concept of oppression. In its new usage, oppression designates the disadvantage and injustice some people suffer not because a tyrannical power coerces them, but because of the everyday practices of a well-intentioned liberal society. . . .

. . . Oppression in this sense is structural, rather than the result of a few people's choices or policies. Its causes are embedded in unquestioned norms, habits, and symbols, in the assumptions underlying institutional rules and the collective consequences of following those rules. . . . In this extended structural sense, oppression refers to the vast and deep injustices some groups suffer as a consequence of often unconscious assumptions and reactions of well meaning people in ordinary interactions, media and cultural stereotypes, and structural features of bureaucratic hierarchies and market mechanisms—in short, the normal processes of everyday life. . . .

I do not mean to suggest that within a system of oppression individual persons do not intentionally harm others in oppressed groups. The raped woman, the beaten Black youth, the locked-out worker, the gay man harassed on the street, are victims of intentional actions by identifiable agents. I also do not mean to deny that specific groups are beneficiaries of the oppression of other groups, and thus have an interest in their continued oppression. Indeed, for every oppressed group there is a group that is privileged in relation to that group. . . .

Racism, sexism, ageism, homophobia, some social movements asserted, are distinct forms of oppression with their own dynamics apart from those of class, even though they may interact with class oppression. From often heated discussions among socialists, feminists, and antiracism activists in the last ten years, a consensus is emerging that many different groups must be said to be oppressed in our society, and that no single form of oppression can be assigned causal or moral primacy. The same discussion has also led to the recognition that group differences cut across individual lines in a multiplicity of ways that can entail privilege and oppression for the same person in different respects. Only a plural explication of the concept of oppression can adequately capture these insights.

Accordingly, I offer below an explication of five faces of oppression as a useful set of categories and distinctions which I believe is comprehensive in the sense that it covers all the groups said by new left social movements to be oppressed, and all the ways they are oppressed. I derive the five faces of oppression from reflection on the condition of these groups. Because different factors, or combinations of factors, constitute the oppression of different groups, making their oppression irreducible, I believe it is not possible to give one essential definition of oppression. The five categories articulated in this chapter, however, are adequate to describe the oppression of any group, as well as its similarities with and differences from the oppression of other groups. But first we must ask what a "group" is.

THE CONCEPT OF A SOCIAL GROUP

. . . A social group is a collective of persons differentiated from at least one other group by cultural forms, practices, or way of life. Members of a group have a specific affinity with one another because of their similar experience (or way of life), which prompts them to associate with one another more than with those not identified with the group. Groups are an expression of social relations; a group exists only in relation to at least one other group. . . .

A social group is defined not primarily by a set of shared attributes, but by a sense of identity. What defines Black Americans as a social group is not primarily their skin color; some persons whose skin color is fairly light, for example, identify themselves as black. Though sometimes objective attributes are a necessary condition for classifying oneself or others as belonging to a certain social group, it is identification with a certain social status, the common history that social status produces, and self-identification that define the group as a group. . . .

Groups constitute individuals. A person's particular sense of history, affinity, and separateness—even the person's mode of reasoning, evaluating, and expressing feeling—are constituted partly by her or his group affinities. This does not mean that persons have no individual styles, or are unable to transcend or reject a group identity. Nor does it preclude persons from having many aspects that are independent of these group identities. . . .

While I agree that individuals should be free to pursue life plans in their own ways, it is foolish to deny the reality of groups. . . . Even when they belong to oppressed groups, people's group identifications are often important to them, and they often feel a special affinity for others in their group. I believe that group differentiation is both an inevitable and a desirable aspect of modern social processes. Social justice requires not the melting away of differences, but institutions that promote reproduction of and respect for group differences without oppression.

. . .

THE FACES OF OPPRESSION

EXPLOITATION

The central insight expressed in the concept of exploitation is that this oppression occurs through a steady process of the transfer of the results of the labor of one social group to benefit another. The injustice of class division does not consist only in the distributive fact that some people have great wealth while most people have little. Exploitation enacts a structural relation between social groups. Social rules about what work is, who does what for whom, how work is compensated, and the social processes by which the results of work are appropriated operate to enact relations of power and inequality. These relations are produced and reproduced through a systematic process in which the energies of the have-nots are continuously expended to maintain and augment the power, status, and wealth of the haves. . . .

Feminists have had little difficulty showing that women's oppression consists partly in a systematic and unreciprocated transfer of powers from women to men. Women's oppression consists not merely in an inequality of status, power, and wealth resulting from men's excluding them from privileged activities. The freedom, power, status, and self-realization of men is possible precisely because women work for them. Gender exploitation has two aspects: transfer of the fruits of material labor to men, and the transfer of nurturing and sexual energies to men. . . . Thus, for example, in most systems of agriculture production in the world, men take to market the goods women have produced, and more often than not men receive the status and often the entire income from this labor.

. . . Women provide men and children with emotional care and provide men with sexual satisfaction, and as a group receive relatively little of either from men. The gender social- ization of women makes us tend to be more attentive to interactive dynamics than men, and makes women good at providing empathy and support for people's feelings and at smoothing over interactive tensions. Both men and women look to women as nurturers of their personal lives, and women frequently complain that when they look to men for emotional support they do not receive it. The norms of heterosexuality, moreover, are oriented around male pleasure, and consequently, many women receive little satisfaction from their sexual interactions with men.

. . .

Is it possible to conceptualize a form of exploitation that is racially specific on anal- ogy with the gender-specific forms just discussed? I suggest that the category of *menial* labor might supply a means for such conceptualization. In its derivation, "menial" des- ignates the labor of servants. Wherever there is racism, there is the assumption, more or less enforced, that members of the oppressed racial groups are or ought to be servants of those, or some of those, in the privileged group. In most white racist societies this means that many white people have dark- or yellow-skinned domestic servants, and in the United States today there remains significant racial structuring of private household service. But in the United States today much service labor has gone public: anyone who goes to a good hotel or a good restaurant can have servants. Servants often attend the daily—and nightly—activities of business executives, government officials, and other high-status professionals. In our society there remains strong cultural pressure to fill servant jobs—bellhop, porter, chambermaid, busboy, and so on—with Black and Latino workers. These jobs entail a transfer of energies whereby the servers enhance the status of the served.

Menial labor usually refers not only to service, however, but also to any servile, unskilled, low-paying work lacking in autonomy, in which a person is subject to taking orders from many people. Menial work tends to be auxiliary work, instrumental to the work of others, where those others receive primary recognition for doing the job. Laborers on a construc- tion site, for example, are at the beck and call of welders, electricians, carpenters, and other skilled workers, who receive recognition for the job done. In the United States explicit racial discrimination once reserved menial work for Blacks, Chicanos, American Indians, and Chinese, and menial work still tends to be linked to Black and Latino workers. I offer this category of menial labor as a form of racially specific exploitation, as a provisional category in need of exploration. . . .

The injustice of exploitation consists in social processes that bring about a transfer of energies from one group to another to produce unequal distributions, and in the way in which social institutions enable a few to accumulate while they constrain many more. The injustices of exploitation cannot be eliminated by the redistribution of goods, for as long as institutionalized practices and structural relations remain unaltered, the process of transfer will re-create an unequal distribution of benefits. Bringing about justice where there is exploitation requires reorganization of institutions and practices of decision making, alteration of the division of labor, and similar measures of institutional, structural, and cultural change.

MARGINALIZATION

Increasingly in the United States, racial oppression occurs in the form of marginalization rather than exploitation. *Marginals* are people the system of labor cannot or will not use. Not only in Third World capitalist countries, but also in most Western capitalist societies, there is a growing underclass of people permanently confined to lives of social marginality, most of whom are racially marked—Blacks or Indians in Latin America, and Blacks, East Indians, Eastern Europeans, or North Africans in Europe.

Marginalization is by no means the fate only of racially marked groups, however. In the United States a shamefully large proportion of the population is marginal: old people, and increasingly people who are not very old but get laid off from their jobs and cannot find new work; young people, especially Black or Latino, who cannot find first or second jobs; many single mothers and their children; other people involuntarily unemployed; many mentally and physically disabled people; American Indians (especially those on reservations).

Marginalization is perhaps the most dangerous form of oppression. A whole category of people is expelled from useful participation in social life and thus potentially subjected to severe material deprivation and even extermination. The material deprivation marginalization often causes is certainly unjust, especially in a society where others have plenty. Contemporary advanced capitalist societies have in principle acknowledged the injustice of material deprivation caused by marginalization, and have taken some steps to address it by providing welfare payments and services. The continuance of this welfare state is by no means assured, and in most welfare state societies, especially the United States, welfare redistributions do not eliminate large-scale suffering and deprivation.

Material deprivation, which can be addressed by redistributive social policies, is not, however, the extent of the harm caused by marginalization. Two categories of injustice beyond distribution are associated with marginality in advanced capitalist societies. First, the provision of welfare itself produces new injustice by depriving those dependent on it of rights and freedoms that others have. Second, even when material deprivation is somewhat mitigated by the welfare state, marginalization is unjust because it blocks the opportunity to exercise capacities in socially defined and recognized ways. I shall explicate each of these in turn.

. . .

Today the exclusion of dependent persons from equal citizenship rights is only barely hidden beneath the surface. Because they depend on bureaucratic institutions for support or services, the old, the poor, and the mentally or physically disabled are subject to patronizing, punitive, demeaning, and arbitrary treatment by the policies and people associated with welfare bureaucracies. Being a "dependent" in our society implies being legitimately subject to the often arbitrary and invasive authority of social service providers and other public and private administrators who enforce rules with which the marginal must comply, and otherwise exercise power over the conditions of their lives. In meeting the needs of the marginalized, often with the aid of social scientific disciplines, welfare agencies also construct the needs themselves. Medical and social service professionals know what is good for those they serve, and the marginals and dependents themselves do not have the right to claim to know what is good for them. Dependency in our society thus implies, as it has in all liberal societies, a sufficient warrant to suspend basic rights to privacy, respect, and individual choice.

Although dependency produces conditions of injustice in our society, dependency in itself need not be oppressive. One cannot imagine a society in which some people would not need to be dependent on others at least some of the time: children, sick people, women recovering from childbirth, old people who have become frail, depressed or otherwise emotionally needy persons have the moral right to depend on others for subsistence and support.

An important contribution of feminist moral theory has been to question the deeply held assumption that moral agency and full citizenship require that a person be autonomous and independent. Feminists have exposed this assumption as inappropriately individualistic and derived from a specifically male experience of social relations, which values competition and solitary achievement. Female experience of social relations, arising both from women's typical domestic care responsibilities and from the kinds of paid work that many women do, tends to recognize dependence as a basic human condition. Whereas on the autonomy model a just society would, as much as possible, give people the opportunity to be independent, the feminist model envisions justice as according respect and participation in decision making to those who are dependent as well as to those who are independent. Dependency should not be a reason to be deprived of choice and respect, and much of the oppression many marginals experience would be lessened if a less individualistic model of rights prevailed.

Marginalization does not cease to be oppressive when one has shelter and food. Many old people, for example, have sufficient means to live comfortably but remain oppressed in their marginal status. Even if marginals were provided a comfortable material life within institutions that respected their freedom and dignity, injustices of marginality would remain in the form of uselessness, boredom, and lack of self-respect. Most of our society's productive and recognized activities take place in contexts of organized social cooperation, and social structures and processes that close persons out of such social cooperation are unjust. . . .

POWERLESSNESS

As I have indicated, the Marxist idea of class is important because it helps reveal the structure of exploitation: that some people have their power and wealth because they profit from the labor of others. For this reason I reject the claim some make that a traditional class exploitation model fails to capture the structure of contemporary society. It remains the case that the labor of most people in the society augments the power of relatively few. Despite their differences from nonprofessional workers, most professional workers are still not members of the capitalist class. Professional labor either involves exploitative transfers to capitalists or supplies important conditions for such transfers. Professional workers are in an ambiguous class position, it is true, because they also benefit from the exploitation of nonprofessional workers.

While it is false to claim that a division between capitalist and working classes no longer describes our society, it is also false to say that class relations have remained unaltered since the nineteenth century. An adequate conception of oppression cannot ignore the experience of social division reflected in the colloquial distinction between the "middle class" and the "working class," a division structured by the social division of labor between professionals and nonprofessionals. Professionals are privileged in relation to nonprofessionals by virtue of their position in the division of labor and the status it carries. Nonprofessionals suffer a form of oppression in addition to exploitation, which I call *powerlessness*.

. . . [D]omination in modern society is enacted through the widely dispersed powers of many agents mediating the decisions of others. To that extent many people have some power in relation to others, even though they lack the power to decide policies or results. The powerless are those who lack authority or power even in this mediated sense, those over whom power is exercised without their exercising it; the powerless are situated so that they must take orders and rarely have the right to give them. Powerlessness also designates a position in the division of labor and the concomitant social position that allows persons little opportunity to develop and exercise skills. The powerless have little or no work autonomy; exercise little creativity or judgment in their work; have no technical expertise or authority; express themselves awkwardly, especially in public or bureaucratic settings; and do not command respect. Powerlessness names the oppressive situations Sennett and Cobb describe in their famous study of working-class men.

This powerless status is perhaps best described negatively: the powerless lack the authority, status, and sense of self that professionals tend to have. The status privilege of professionals has three aspects, the lack of which produces oppression for nonprofessionals.

First, acquiring and practicing a profession has an expansive, progressive character. Being professional usually requires a college education and the acquisition of a specialized knowledge that entails working with symbols and concepts. Professionals experience progress first in acquiring the expertise, and then in the course of professional advancement and rise in status. The life of the nonprofessional by comparison is powerless in the sense that it lacks this orientation toward the progressive development of capacities and avenues for recognition.

Second, while many professionals have supervisors and cannot directly influence many decisions or the actions of many people, most nevertheless have considerable day-to-day work autonomy. Professionals usually have some authority over others, moreover—either over workers they supervise, or over auxiliaries or clients. Nonprofessionals, on the other hand, lack autonomy, and in both their working and their consumer/client lives often stand under the authority of professionals.

Though based on a division of labor between "mental" and "manual" work, the distinction between "middle class" and "working class" designates a division not only in working life, but also in nearly all aspects of social life. Professionals and nonprofessionals belong to different cultures in the United States. The two groups tend to live in segregated neighborhoods or even different towns, a process itself mediated by planners, zoning officials, and real estate people. The groups tend to have different tastes in food, decor, clothes, music, and vacations, and often different health and educational needs. Members of each group socialize for the most part with others in the same status group. While there is some intergroup mobility between generations, for the most part the children of professionals become professionals and the children of nonprofessionals do not.

Thus, the privileges of the professional extend beyond the workplace to a whole way of life. I call this way of life *respectability*. To treat people with respect is to be prepared to listen to what they have to say or to do what they request because they have some authority, expertise, or influence. The norms of respectability in our society are associated specifically with professional culture. Professional dress, speech, tastes, demeanor all connote respectability. Generally professionals expect and receive respect from others. In restaurants, banks, hotels, real estate offices, and many other such public places, as well as in the media, professionals typically receive more respectful treatment than nonprofessionals. For this reason nonprofessionals seeking a loan or a job, or to buy a house or a car, will often try to look "professional" and "respectable" in those settings.

The privilege of this professional respectability appears starkly in the dynamics of racism and sexism. In daily interchange, women and men of color must prove their respectability. At first they are often not treated by strangers with respectful distance or deference. Once people discover that this woman or that Puerto Rican man is a college teacher or a business executive, however, they often behave more respectfully toward her or him.

CULTURAL IMPERIALISM

Exploitation, marginalization, and powerlessness all refer to relations of power and oppression that occur by virtue of the social division of labor—who works for whom, who does not work, and how the content of work defines one institutional position relative to others. These three categories refer to structural and institutional relations that delimit people's material lives, including but not restricted to the resources they have access to and the concrete opportunities they have or do not have to develop and exercise their capacities. These kinds of oppression are a matter of concrete power in relation to others—of who benefits from whom, and who is dispensable.

Recent theorists of movements of group liberation, notably feminist and Black liberation theorists, have also given prominence to a rather different form of oppression, which following Lugones and Spelman I shall call *cultural imperialism*. To experience cultural imperialism means to experience how the dominant meanings of a society render the particular perspective of one's own group invisible at the same time as they stereotype one's group and mark it as the Other.

Cultural imperialism involves the universalization of a dominant group's experience and culture, and its establishment as the norm. . . . Often without noticing they do so, dominant groups project their own experience as representative of humanity as such. Cultural products also express the dominant group's perspective on and interpretation of events and elements in the society, including other groups in the society, insofar as they attain cultural status at all.

An encounter with other groups, however, can challenge the dominant group's claim to universality. The dominant group reinforces its position by bringing the other groups under the measure of its dominant norms. Consequently, the difference of women from men, American Indians or Africans from Europeans, Jews from Christians, homosexuals from heterosexuals, workers from professionals becomes reconstructed largely as deviance and inferiority. Since only the dominant group's cultural expressions receive wide dissemination, their cultural expressions become the normal, or the universal, and thereby the unremarkable. Given the normality of its own cultural expressions and identity, the dominant group constructs the differences which some groups exhibit as lack and negation. These groups become marked as Other.

The culturally dominated undergo a paradoxical oppression in that they are both marked out by stereotypes and at the same time rendered invisible. As remarkable, deviant beings, the culturally imperialized are stamped with an essence. The stereotypes confine them to a nature which is often attached in some way to their bodies, and which thus cannot easily be denied. These stereotypes so permeate the society that they are not noticed as contestable. Just as everyone knows that the earth goes around the sun, so everyone knows that gay people are promiscuous, that American Indians are alcoholics, and that women are good with children. White males, on the other hand, insofar as they escape group marking, can be individuals.

Those living under cultural imperialism find themselves defined from the outside, positioned, placed, by a network of dominant meanings they experience as arising from elsewhere, from those with whom they do not identify and who do not identify with them. Consequently, the dominant culture's stereotyped and inferiorized images of the group must be internalized by group members at least to the extent that they are forced to react to the behavior of others influenced by those images. This creates for the culturally oppressed the experience that W. E. B. Du Bois called "double consciousness"—"this sense of always looking at one's self through the eyes of others, of measuring one's soul by the tape of a world that looks on in amused contempt and pity." Double consciousness arises when the oppressed subject refuses to coincide with these devalued, objectified, stereotyped visions of herself or himself. While the subject desires recognition as human—capable of activity, full of hope and possibility—she receives from the dominant culture only the judgment that she is different, marked, or inferior.

The group defined by the dominant culture as deviant, as a stereotyped Other, is culturally different from the dominant group, because the status of Otherness creates specific experiences not shared by the dominant group, and because culturally oppressed groups also are often socially segregated and occupy specific positions in the social division of labor. Members of such groups express their specific group experiences and interpretations of the world to one another, developing and perpetuating their own culture. Double consciousness, then, occurs because one finds one's being defined by two cultures: a dominant and a subordinate culture. Because they can affirm and recognize one another as sharing similar experiences and perspectives on social life, people in culturally imperialized groups can often maintain a sense of positive subjectivity.

Cultural imperialism involves the paradox of experiencing oneself as invisible at the same time that one is marked out as different. The invisibility comes about when dominant groups fail to recognize the perspective embodied in their cultural expressions as a perspective. These dominant cultural expressions often simply have little place for the experience of other groups, at most only mentioning or referring to them in stereotyped or marginalized ways. This, then, is the injustice of cultural imperialism: that the oppressed group's own experience and interpretation of social life finds little expression that touches the dominant culture, while that same culture imposes on the oppressed group its experience and interpretation of social life. . . .

VIOLENCE

Finally, many groups suffer the oppression of systematic violence. Members of some groups live with the knowledge that they must fear random, unprovoked attacks on their persons or property, which have no motive but to damage, humiliate, or destroy the person. In American society women, Blacks, Asians, Arabs, gay men, and lesbians live under such threats of violence, and in at least some regions Jews, Puerto Ricans, Chicanos, and other Spanish-speaking Americans must fear such violence as well. Physical violence against these groups is shockingly frequent. Rape crisis center networks estimate that more than one-third of all American women experience an attempted or successful sexual assault in their lifetimes. Manning Marable catalogs a large number of incidents of racist violence and terror against Blacks in the United States between 1980 and 1982. He cites dozens of incidents of the severe beating, killing, or rape of Blacks by police officers on duty, in which the police involved were acquitted of any wrongdoing. In 1981, moreover, there were at least five hundred documented cases of random white teenage violence against Blacks. Violence against gay men and lesbians is not only common, but has been increasing. While the frequency of physical attack on members of these and other racially or sexually marked groups is very disturbing, I also include in this category less severe incidents of harassment, intimidation, or ridicule simply for the purpose of degrading, humiliating, or stigmatizing group members.

. . .

What makes violence a face of oppression is less the particular acts themselves—though these are often utterly horrible—than the social context surrounding them, which makes them possible and even acceptable. What makes violence a phenomenon of social injustice, and not merely an individual moral wrong, is its systemic character, its existence as a social practice.

Violence is systemic because it is directed at members of a group simply because they are members of that group. Any woman, for example, has a reason to fear rape. Regardless of what a Black man has done to escape the oppressions of marginality or powerlessness, he lives knowing he is subject to attack or harassment. The oppression of violence consists not only in direct victimization, but in the daily knowledge shared by all members of oppressed groups that they are *liable* to violation, solely on account of their group identity. Just living under such a threat of attack on oneself or family or friends deprives the oppressed of freedom and dignity, and needlessly expends their energy.

Violence is a social practice. It is a social given that everyone knows happens and will happen again. It is always at the horizon of social imagination, even for those who do not perpetrate it. According to the prevailing social logic, some circumstances make such violence more "called for" than others. The idea of rape will occur to many men who pick up a hitch-hiking woman; the idea of hounding or teasing a gay man on their dorm floor will occur to many straight male college students. Often several persons inflict the violence together, especially in all-male groupings. Sometimes violators set out looking for people to beat up, rape, or taunt. This rule-bound, social, and often premeditated character makes violence against groups a social practice.

Group violence approaches legitimacy, moreover, in the sense that it is tolerated. Often, third parties find it unsurprising because it happens frequently and lies as a constant possibility at the horizon of the social imagination. Even when they are caught, those who perpetrate acts of group-directed violence or harassment often receive light or no punishment. To that extent society renders their acts acceptable.

. . .

[T]he violation of rape, beating, killing, and harassment of women, people of color, gays, and other marked groups is motivated by fear or hatred of those groups. Sometimes the motive may be a simple will to power, to victimize those marked as vulnerable by the very social fact that they are subject to violence. If so, this motive is secondary in the sense that it depends on a social practice of group violence. Violence-causing fear or hatred of the other at least partly involves insecurities on the part of the violators; its irrationality suggests that unconscious processes are at work.

Cultural imperialism, moreover, itself intersects with violence. The culturally imperialized may reject the dominant meanings and attempt to assert their own subjectivity, or the fact of the cultural difference may put the lie to the dominant culture's implicit claim to universality. The dissonance generated by such a challenge to the hegemonic cultural meanings can also be a source of irrational violence.

. . . I have argued that group-directed violence is institutionalized and systemic. To the degree that institutions and social practices encourage, tolerate, or enable the perpetration of violence against members of specific groups, those institutions and practices are unjust and should be reformed. Such reform may require the redistribution of resources or positions, but in large part can come only through a change in cultural images, stereotypes, and the mundane reproduction of relations of dominance and aversion in the gestures of everyday life.

APPLYING THE CRITERIA

. . .

I have arrived at the five faces of oppression—exploitation, marginalization, powerlessness, cultural imperialism, and violence—as the best way to avoid such exclusions and reductions. They function as criteria for determining whether individuals and groups are oppressed, rather than as a full theory of oppression. I believe that these criteria are objective. They provide a means of refuting some people's beliefs that their group is oppressed when it is not, as well as a means of persuading others that a group is oppressed when they doubt it. Each criterion can be operationalized; each can be applied through the assessment of observable behavior, status relationships, distributions, texts, and other cultural artifacts. I have no illusions that such assessments can be value-neutral. But these criteria can nevertheless serve as means of evaluating claims that a group is oppressed, or adjudicating disputes about whether or how a group is oppressed.

The presence of any of these five conditions is sufficient for calling a group oppressed. But different group oppressions exhibit different combinations of these forms, as do different individuals in the groups. Nearly all, if not all, groups said by contemporary social movements to be oppressed suffer cultural imperialism. The other oppressions they experience vary. Working-class people are exploited and powerless, for example, but if employed and white do not experience marginalization and violence. Gay men, on the other hand, are not qua gay exploited or powerless, but they experience severe cultural imperialism and violence. Similarly, Jews and Arabs as groups are victims of cultural imperialism and violence, though many members of these groups also suffer exploitation or powerlessness. Old people are oppressed by marginalization and cultural imperialism, and this is also true of physically and mentally disabled people. As a group, women are subject to gender-based exploitation, powerlessness, cultural imperialism, and violence. Racism in the United States condemns many Blacks and Latinos to marginalization, and puts many more at risk, even though many members of these groups escape that condition; members of these groups often suffer all five forms of oppression.

Applying these five criteria to the situation of groups makes it possible to compare the oppressions without reducing them to a common essence or claiming that one is more fundamental than another. One can compare the ways in which a particular form of oppression appears in different groups. For example, while the operations of cultural imperialism are often experienced in similar fashion by different groups, there are also important differences. One can compare the combinations of oppressions groups experience, or the intensity of those oppressions. . . .

8

Intersectionality Revisited

Patricia Hill Collins and Sirma Bilge

RELATIONALITY

The theme of *relationality* that reappears in various forms across intersectional scholarship and practice has had an important impact on both. This insight that the connections among entities that had been seen as separate and often oppositional constitute a major contribution of intersectionality to all types of projects. . . . Entities that are typically treated as separate may actually be interconnected. For intersectionality, this interconnectedness lies in the relationships between systems of race, class, gender, sexuality, age, ability, and citizenship spaces. An intersectionality framework counsels that these entities, in various combinations or in total, can all be accommodated under the umbrella of intersectionality.

Scholars and activists alike have found the concept useful, generating endless new questions and avenues of investigation. For example, the either/or binary thinking that has been so central to Eurocentric social thought is less relevant for intersectionality. Instead, intersectional projects look at the relationships among seemingly different phenomena. For example, interdisciplinary fields concerned with social justice are often informed by intersectional frameworks. Such fields strive to go beyond oppositional thinking carried out by Eurocentric binaries and attempt to forge a complex and interactive understanding of the relationships between history, social organization, and forms of consciousness, both personal and collective in short, *relational* thinking.

We have also been attentive to how this idea of relationality informs praxis. For example, we have criticized versions of intersectionality that reduce identity to an apolitical, individualistic category, drawing on the theme of relationality to show the complexities of collective identity politics. We also present an argument about the centrality of relationality to coalition politics, investigating how what seem to be scattered social movements may in actuality be interrelated phenomena in response to a global world order. The case of the Afro Brazilian women's movement in Brazil provides a sketch of how coalitions that took both similarities and differences into account were crucial to the creation and maintenance of a vibrant social movement.

We have spent less time examining intersectionality's relationship with similar discourses, such as critical race theory, feminism, ethnic studies, or the intellectual debates in which these areas participate. We think that intersectionality would benefit by thinking through how dialogs among forms of inquiry and expressions of critical praxis that resemble its own might unfold. Intersectionality's interconnectedness with other similar knowledge projects might draw inspiration from Freire's dialogical pedagogy or education for critical consciousness.

When engaging discourse, intersectionality must be wary of annexing other perspectives, such as decolonial and transnational approaches, under its wide tent umbrella. When intersectionality enters these contexts via humanitarian, developmental frameworks, and projects from the North, it can erase local resistant knowledges and praxis and silence local knowledge producers (which might also be true in northern contexts, for instance France and Germany). There is an enormous difference between cases where disenfranchised groups *themselves* claim versions of intersectionality, for example, black women in Brazil forming an independent black feminist movement, and where some national or supranational instance imposes a top-down, watered-down diversity *qua* intersectionality agenda upon historically disenfranchised people.

We wish that we could have . . . incorporated multiple knowledge projects and points of view from various regions of the globe and within a more expansive time period than the late twentieth and early-twenty-first centuries. We want to see more people involved in the kind of dialogical intellectual and political work that doing interesectionality entails. This openness would encourage a dialogical methodology for intersectionality that would advance a more democratic construction of knowledge itself.

The analysis of intersectionality may. . . be universally applicable, yet there is no way of knowing so without greater and different participation of scholars, activists, practitioners, policy makers, and teachers from the Global South. We have included the ideas and experiences of social actors from disenfranchised groups within the Global North as well as social actors in the Global South whenever possible, taking care to do so in ways that do not reduce their experiences to data that reinforce frameworks of the Global North. For example, case studies of the black women's movement in Brazil and their successful project of Latinidades and the increasing visibility of the anti-sweatshop movement following the Rana Plaza collapse illustrate the significance of starting analysis in the Global South, Brazil and Bangladesh respectively. We also reject trying to fix problems of exclusion by simply adding in missing people and experiences into intersectionality as a preconceived entity. Instead, intersectionality requires a rethinking of these approaches in ways that democratize the social construction of knowledge.

Incorporating the global is not enough. Attending to global phenomena means that intersectionality must take a critical stance concerning its own social location both as a legitimated discourse within the Global North, and as a set of ideas and practices that only a small segment of educated, well-off people in the Global South can access. Because being able to read books such as this one elevates those with literacy above those who lack it, literacy articulates with individual and collective exclusion. But as we have also discussed throughout this book, people find innovative ways to access and do intellectual work, to develop multiple forms of literacy, for example, by using the media in global hip hop culture or digital activism. At maximum, intersectionality would be a much more inclusive dialogical process than is currently the case

SOCIAL CONTEXT

The theme of social *context* has many interpretations. We have examined the relationship between intersectionality and the social institutions that are part of its social context whenever possible. We have highlighted the academy as an important institutional context of intersectionality: our analysis of shifting meanings of intersectionality within social movements and incorporation into the academy contrasts the effects of these two institutional environments on intersectionality; our analysis of neoliberal state power, its discourse of securitization, and how institutional structures are shaped by these ideas is a primary theme. . . .

We have expressed our concern that the growth, acceptance, and legitimation of intersectionality within the academy and some public policy venues necessarily changes its composition and purpose, often for the better, but also for the worse. For example, we explore the politics of intersectionality's naming and incorporation into the academy as a bona fide discourse. Is intersectionality the victim of its own success? Contemporary trends that reduce intersectionality to a theory of identity also reflect the challenges of absorption. Within US higher education, the splitting of intersectionality into an academic component of scholarship and diversity initiatives of institutional service signals an attack on intersectionality's critical perspective. Via these concerns, we raised the question of who benefits from intersectionality's legitimation. The answers to this questions are far from clear, and may vary from one situation to the next. It is not enough to simply bury oneself in one's own work, claiming intersectionality as a set of stimulating ideas while ignoring the conditions that make that work possible.

The tongue-in-cheek phrase "saving intersectionality from intersectionality studies" reminds all scholars to be self-reflexive regarding our own practices in the context of intersectionality's newfound visibility and legitimation. Saving intersectionality might involve reclaiming intersectionality from people who often have little or no commitment to intersectionaliy's social justice ethos. This may also mean saving intersectionality from ourselves if few practice intersectionality as "business as usual", namely, as just another scholarly discourse or content specialization without implicating our work within the power relations that shape the field and academy at large. Such practices often follow prevailing canonical rules of identifying some key figures within the field whose ideas become proxy for the field itself, then moving on to use these straw-women figures as coterminous with intersectionality itself.

We also recognize the significance of how politics shapes the way in which physical and geographic space is understood and organized. Contextualizing intersectional categories that define space, for example, matters whether one is a citizen of Syria or Germany, or whether one plays soccer in South Africa or Spain. Intersectionality as a form of critical inquiry and praxis gains it meaning within specific social contexts. Placing greater emphasis on the specifics of social context of local, regional, and national geography would provide a more nuanced discussion of global processes.

Then there is the issue of historic context. Intersectionality appears at a specific historical moment and is an intervention in that moment. While it speaks to contemporary issues, it is also simultaneously formed and transformed by them. . . . For current debates inflected by the growing influence of intersectionality within United Nations venues, juxtaposed with increasingly verbal critiques of intersectionality within the European academy, intersectionality seems to represent both a promise and a threat. Accordingly, we reflect upon the specificities of historical events in which intersectionality is embedded, with the aim of understanding and describing how different historical conjunctures frame different theoretical and political moments of intersectionality. . . .

POWER RELATIONS, SOCIAL INEQUALITY, AND SOCIAL JUSTICE

Power, another core idea of intersectionality, is complex and contested. We have tried to situate intersectionality within contemporary power relations and analyze the significance of that positioning.

We have argued that power relations are to be analyzed both *via their intersections*, for example, of racism and sexism, as well as *across domains of power*, namely, structural, disciplinary, cultural, and interpersonal. How does intersectionality critically assess power relations of race, class, gender, sexuality, age, ethnicity, nationality, and ability? How might intersectionality better understand how intersecting power relations shape its own praxis? These questions must repeatedly be asked and answered under changing power relations themselves.

We have also criticized intersectionality when it seemed to be veering away from what we see as its core concern areas that are clearly associated with power relations. For example, because we have been especially troubled by the decreasing focus on *social inequality* within intersectionality's scholarship, we emphasize this theme. The hollowing-out of meanings of rich scholarly traditions that have long been associated with processes and systems of social inequalities—for example, capitalism, colonialism, racism, patriarchy, and nationalism—and replacing them with shortcut terms of race, gender, and nation may appear to be a benign substitution, but much is lost when systems of power compete for space under some versions of intersectionality. The terms themselves may appear to be equivalent and easily substituted for one another, yet the social relations that these shorthand terms reference are far more complicated. For example, sexism, racism, and heterosexism contain the "ism" that makes them recognizable as unjust systems of power, nuance that is lost when gender, race, and sexuality become redefined as identify categories. In contrast, the term "class" performs a different kind of reduction. By reducing the complex economic relations of capitalism to class, the complexities and sophistication of Marxist social thought and other serious analyses of capitalism are minimized. The rich traditions of nationalism, both celebratory and critical, simply don't fit comfortably under the signifier of nation. So replacement terms such as "citizenship status" or "undocumented migrants" take up the slack by referencing selected populations that are penalized by nationalist ideologies and nation state policies. They are referencing similar phenomena but are not readily reducible to one another.

This strategy of using shortcut language to make intersectionality's task of rethinking social inequality easier seemingly solves one set of problems, yet creates others. Over time, these terms no longer invoke the original meanings of racism, sexism, and capitalism, for example, but instead become recast as floating signifiers that, unmoored from specific scholarly traditions, can be assembled and reassembled far more easily than would be the case if one seriously tried to place the actual traditions in dialog with one another. This reduction of intersectionality to an assemblage of shortcut terms does appear to be more democratic in that it encompasses more categories than before. Yet the mantra of "race, class, and gender" has been so often repeated that it can become meaningless. The phrase serves as an unexamined litmus test for scholars who can claim that their work is better than race-only or class-only analyses, primarily because it references more terms of social inequality.

We have similar concerns with versions of intersectionality that may pay lip service to *social justice*, yet seem unaware of its significance. People who claim intersectionality as a field of *critical* inquiry and praxis often hold an implicit and often explicit commitment to an ethics of social justice as part of their analytical lens. For a form of inquiry that grapples with complex social inequalities, its *raison d'etre* is not simply to provide more complex and comprehensive analyses of how and why social inequalities persist—critical engagement has been a strong theme within intersectionality as a field of inquiry—but also to engage questions of social justice. Social inequality and social injustice are not the same, although these ideas are often used interchangeably. The work of practitioners not only shows how social justice is critical, but also how social justice work challenges the borders between academic and activist work.

We have been careful to point out that intersectionality is not a simple substitute for social justice. Each project must be interrogated for its connections to social justice, not just assuming that because intersectional scholarship examines some facet of social inequality, it is by default furthering social justice. We raised a similar argument concerning diversity initiative within higher education as a case where intersectionality may invoke earlier social justice traditions, yet where actual programs have been pressured to relinquish traditional emphasis on access and equity.

INTERSECTIONALITY'S COMPLEXITY

Overall, these core ideas of relationality, social context, power, inequality, and social justice highlight intersectionality's complexity. Because each of these core ideas interact with one another, collectively they contribute to intersectionality's complexity. Thinking about social inequalities and power relations within an ethos of social justice, and doing so not in abstract generalizations but in their specific contexts, brings complexity. Attending to how intersecting power relations shape identities, social practices, institutional arrangements, and cultural representations and ideologies in ways that are contextualized and historicized introduces a level of complexity into everything. Moreover, the creative tension linking intersectionality as a form of critical inquiry and critical praxis introduces complexity into intersectional projects.

This creative tension raises important questions about which understandings of intersectionality will prevail. When we focus on intersectionality as a form of critical inquiry, we find a rich tapestry of scholarship produced by people who use intersectionality as an analytic tool in new and creative ways. Not all scholarship is like this, and not all people who claim intersectionality share this vision. But, overall, intersectionality's scholarship record thus far has been impressive. When we broaden our lens to include intersectionality as critical praxis, both its initial expression within social movements as well as its global dispersion beyond the academy, the practices and ideas of diverse people past and present, in the Global North and in the Global South, come into view.

We think that it is imperative that intersectionality remain open to the element of our prise. Our efforts to provide a useful but not final definition of intersectionality speak to the impetus to invite others into the conversation. We see the impetus toward intersectionality as more connected to the puzzles presented by the social world that we live in, rather than the concerns of established disciplinary endeavours. . . .

Telling the story of intersectionality does a certain kind of political work in terms of authenticating and legitimizing particular schools of thought and subjects, privileging particular genealogies and national locations at the expense of others. Particular histories that chart intersectionality as a field of study in particular ways might be rightly viewed as acts of closure, be they temporary. These histories pursue in their own ways scientific recognition, authority, and legitimacy and settle intersectionality within the Euro-American scientific archive in particular ways. As such, they participate in the establishment of intersectionality as a legitimate field of knowledge, which might be at odds with the pursuit of social justice. Our history of intersectionality has emphasized praxis, a dimension of intersectionality that does not routinely appear in these legitimated histories although a critical praxis does permeate intersectionality.

What ideas and experiences are *not* here? In what ways is our interpretation of intersectionality limited by these omissions? More importantly, how might we go about expanding the breadth of intersectionality to encompass the heterogeneity of ideas and experiences that are global without flattering their differences? Intersectionality can't engage these expansive questions if it chooses the narrow pathway of defining itself as a "feminist theory of identity," or, worse yet, if it severs its critical inquiry from its critical praxis. These questions have no straightforward answers, certainly none that can easily be resolved. Rather, they call out for more people working on them, in essence, an expansion of global conversations.

The central challenge facing intersectionality is to move into the politics of the not-yet. Thus far, intersectionality has managed to sustain intellectual and political dynamism that grows from its heterogeneity. This is immensely difficult to achieve when faced with the kinds of intellectual and political challenges that we have explored. But just because something is difficult does not mean that it's not worth doing. We see intersectionality's heterogeneity not as a weakness but rather as a source of tremendous potential. Intersectionality is a tool that we can all use in moving toward a more just future.

See Chapter 5 in *Teaching for Diversity and Social Justice* for corresponding teaching materials.

SECTION 2

RACISM

Introduction

Mike Funk, Rani Varghese, and Ximena Zúñiga[1][2]

Nearly a decade ago, the candidacy and election of the first black president of the United States, Barack Hussein Obama, offered hope for a more racially and economically just society at a time when racial and class disparities were exacerbated by the effects of the 2008 economic crisis. Despite this historic and symbolic breakthrough in political representation, the cumulative and durable manifestations of racial inequality have remained "locked in" place (Roithmayr, 2014, p. 5). Racial disparities continue to persist in education, criminal sentencing, employment, and political representation even as important gains have accrued in the last fifty years (Bell, Funk, Joshi, & Valdivia, 2016).

Racism can be defined as a system of advantage based on race (Tatum, 1997). Contemporary manifestations of racism have grown out of a historical legacy of accumulated and persistent racial inequality that has privileged some racial/ethnic groups and disadvantaged others based on socially constructed and shifting racial categories. As a system of inequality, racism is enacted at multiple levels simultaneously: institutional, cultural, interpersonal, and individual. For example, at the institutional level, Indigenous people were forced into reservations and others have been racially segregated into under-resourced schools by laws, policies and practices; at the cultural level, the norms and preferences of the white dominant group viewed as superior or "normal"; at the interpersonal level, discriminatory practices built into systems, such as the criminal justice system, have been enacted by federal agents and police officers; and negative attitudes and beliefs about different minoritized racial groups have operated at the individual level to promote acceptance of all of these discriminatory practices. As a result, everyday actions within socially, economically, and racially segregated systems reinforce and reproduce white advantage in employment, housing, and education, while people of color continue to experience higher rates of poverty, unemployment, and underemployment (Roithmayr, 2014).

This system of advantages based on race has not gone unchallenged. Resistance to the institution of slavery led to abolition in 1865, and Jim Crow laws enforcing racial segregation in public education were declared unconstitutional in 1954 after much local and national struggle. Similarly, the passage of the Civil Rights Act of 1964 and the Voting Rights Act of 1965 resulted from years of concerted collective action, advocacy, and court challenges. Individuals from different racial/ethnic immigrant groups have continually challenged racial restrictions on citizenship, which, at the inception of the nation, was limited to immigrants who were "free white persons of good character"

(Haney-López, 2006). As a result of these challenges, racial restrictions on naturalization were ended in 1952. As with other issues related to race, however, enduring beliefs about what it means to be "American" continue to shape public perceptions and policy decisions (Takaki, 1993) and are reflected in contemporary struggles for refugee and immigrant human and civil rights.

Yet one important lesson from reading and studying historical accounts of past and recent people's struggles is that we must not despair (Adams & Zúñiga, 2016). The election of an African American president, which may have been unthinkable fifty years ago, reflects changing attitudes about race and is now part of the nation's history. Past and present struggles for Indigenous land rights, civil rights, educational equity, fair housing laws and policies, immigration rights, affordable health care, and a livable minimum wage all provide powerful illustrations of how people can resist, challenge and change laws and institutional practices. Finally, movements such as Black Lives Matter, DACA (Deferred Action for Childhood Arrivals Program), Refugee and Immigrant Sanctuary Movement, and the 2017 Women's March in Washington DC, illustrate how people organize themselves at the grassroots and national level to challenge current racist policies and practices and other forms of injustice, locally and nationally.

Our main objective for this chapter is to provide foundational frameworks and definitions for examining our historical legacies in an inclusive and nuanced way. We introduce readers to key concepts informing our approach to race, racism, and white supremacy and highlight salient contemporary manifestations of racism and white supremacy and resistance movements. We then provide an overview of the readings we selected to illustrate theoretical, conceptual, and personal ways to understand, critically analyze, and challenge the realities of race relations in the United States.

RACE, RACISM, AND WHITE SUPREMACY: KEY CONCEPTS

Race is a socio-political, not a biological construct, one that is created and reinforced by social and institutional norms and practices and by individual attitudes and behaviors. Like other constructed social identities addressed throughout this book, race emerged historically in the United States to justify the dominance of peoples defined as "white" (colonists/settlers) over other peoples defined as racially different or inferior, such as Native Americans and enslaved Africans and later, Mexicans, Chinese, Puerto Ricans, South Asians, Arab Americans, and other marginalized racial groups. Motivated by economic interests and entrenched through law and public policy, we see this process of racialization of subordinate groups as a process that has its roots in historical legacies and is continually reinvented in response to current social, political, and economic circumstances to perpetuate social advantages for peoples racialized as white. We call this process and the system it sustains *white supremacy* (Bonilla-Silva, 2001; Haney-López, 2006).

Racism is the set of institutional, cultural, and interpersonal patterns and practices that create advantages for people legally defined and socially constructed as "white," and the corollary disadvantages for people defined as belonging to racial groups that were not considered white by the dominant power structure that shaped the rules and laws that were considered essential to the formation of the United States. While the construction of disadvantage and subordination of different communities of color has been enacted in historically specific ways for differently racialized groups, we call attention to the overarching patterns and practices that illustrate racism across groups and the distinctive ways that racism plays out for particular peoples of color at different points in US history. Thus, the frequently unstated assumption that race is a matter of black/white relationships obscures a far more complex, historically rooted, racial *system* that impacts differently racialized peoples in historically and regionally distinctive ways. Indeed, we talk about *racism(s)* to connote the many different forms racism has taken throughout US history. A critical analysis of racism(s) should thus include how perceived racial phenotype, ethnicity, language, class, sexuality, age, gender identity, immigration status, religion, and culture impact a people's experience of racism. Further, the analysis of racisms becomes intersectional when we acknowledge that people from all racialized groups—whether advantaged or disadvantaged by racism—are also differently gendered, classed, sexualized, and aged and that these intersections differentially shape their experiences and the impact of racism on their life chances and opportunities.

Systems of white supremacy and racism rationalize inequality (as if natural and given), and compress social diversity into binaries, dividing racialized groups into artificial hierarchies. The one-drop rule that defined as "black" any person with blood quantum of a certain percentage (that varied by state and region) exemplifies this binary system. Established during the period of legal slavery, the one-drop rule ensured that anyone who had a remote relative of African descent, even if this heritage was not visible, could be *kept* in slavery (and later segregated under Jim Crow laws). This not only protected the interests of a small group of propertied Whites who reaped the benefits of the economic system in place but contributed to create a relatively large pool of surplus cheap labor. Conversely, federal standards for who could be considered Native American used "blood quantum" rules to *eliminate* most "mixed-bloods" from tribal nationality rolls as a device to decrease Indians' claims for tribal land rights. In both cases of "making up people" (Omi & Winant, 2015, p. 105), the goal was to perpetuate a system of advantages benefiting white wealth and ownership. The realities of people's lives under this system are far more complex than a racialized binary suggests. While multiracial people have historically identified as belonging to more than one race, it was not until the 2000 Census (Johnston-Guerrero, 2010) that they were *officially* recognized as having more than one race.

As long as patterns of racial inequality continue to persist, despite some changing features, "transcending race" should not be our goal. Instead, we should account for past and current practices of dominance, economic exploitation, and marginalization, and work assiduously to eradicate the disproportional life circumstances created by racism and white supremacy. We should devise reparation for its effects in contemporary life, and transform our society into an inclusive and just democracy in which differences are respected and valued, and people from all groups are treated fairly and equitably. In the next to the last section of this chapter, we discuss some concrete ways people resist and work toward transforming racism and systems of white advantage.

HISTORY OF RACISM: A BRIEF SNAPSHOT

The history of racism in the United States reaches back to before our origins as a nation: through settler colonialism, the colonization and attempted extermination of the Indigenous peoples whose land was stolen by conquest, broken treaties, and deception; the enslavement of First Nations peoples and then kidnapped Africans to provide coerced and unpaid labor to develop agricultural and capital wealth for the early European settlers; the displacement of Mexican and Indigenous people, appropriation of their land, and redefining them as "foreign," as borders moved through war and conquest. It continued with the recruitment and then abuse and exploitation of Chinese, Japanese, and Filipino laborers who worked the mines and built the railroads that enabled the expansion of US wealth and power to other parts of the globe (Takaki, 1993). Rationalized by Manifest Destiny and a "civilizing" mission, people of European Christian descent determined who could attain citizenship and its corresponding benefits in the United States (Haney-López, 2006).

Migrants racialized as "white" in the context of the United States expanded and then consolidated a system of racial advantages based on "whiteness" to eventually include successive waves of European immigrants. Some northern Europeans were absorbed easily, while others considered "not quite white" (e.g., Italians, Irish, Jews) took longer but were assimilated as "white" over time (Brodkin Sacko, 1004; Gaultieri, 2001; Guglielmo, 2003; Roediger, 1991). Those who could claim whiteness reaped the benefits of an economic and political system consolidated under white supremacy. Other advantages flowed from the attainment of citizenship and incorporation as Whites, such as property and voting rights, that enabled them to further accumulate wealth, to control the political system, and to write a version of history that glorified and normalized their dominance as legitimate and natural. This "colonization of the mind" enabled a portrayal of Latino/a/x[3] and Indigenous peoples as "immigrants" and "foreigners" with no claim to the Americas, while "European Americans were constructed as the natural owners and inheritors of these lands" (Villenas & Deyhle, 1999, p. 421). Non-elite Whites illustrated another form of colonization of the mind—trading the potential of cross-race class alliances against elite Whites for the benefits of belonging to the "superior" white group, often against their own economic interests.

Nativism, a recurrent phenomenon in US history, particularly during times of economic crisis, supporting the interests of "native-born" people over "foreign-born" people, combined with racial animus toward migrants of color to shape restrictive anti-immigration laws and populist white sentiments (Spickard, 2007). Immigration laws of the 1800s restricted immigration as rising nativist sentiments combined racism with the traditional hostility of US-born, white, Anglo-Saxon Protestants toward newer immigrants from Catholic Ireland and Southern Europe and Jews from Eastern Europe. Immigration laws tightly restricted immigration from China, Japan, the Philippines, and later on to Arab-speaking people from Greater Syria, Lebanon, and Palestine due to the US Congress Immigration Quota Act of 1921 (Jaradat, 2017). Nativism intermingled with race, religion, and class interests to sustain the dominance of white, Anglo-Saxon, Protestant elites, while restricting access for other groups. These policies continued to shape political and social life across the United States and to entrench and increase white economic and political advantage until the Immigration and Nationality Act (1965) relaxed barriers to immigration, and the Civil Rights Act (1964) opened political and civil rights to people of African, Asian, Latino/a/x, and Indigenous descent.

Nativism sentiments have resurged during the past decade reinforced by new legislations. Politicians and legislators have exploited a general anti-immigrant public sentiment to propose and pass anti-immigration laws in a number of states, including Alabama, Arizona, Georgia, Indiana, South Carolina, and Utah. Arizona's prototypical legislation was passed in 2010 (SB 1070), mandating police officers to stop and question people about immigration status if they suspect they may be in this country illegally, criminalizing undocumented workers who do not possess an "alien registration document," allowing US citizens to file suits against government agencies that do not enforce the law, and criminalizing employers who transport or hire undocumented workers (Sinha & Faithful, 2012). In 2013, the Immigration and Customs Enforcement (ICE) agency prioritized the Secure Communities initiative, a program that brings together the FBI, ICE, and local law enforcement agencies to identify and deport undocumented individuals who are arrested. This initiative was temporarily suspended in 2014 but restarted through Trump's Executive Order 13768 (U.S. ICE, n.d.). We continue to see a resurgence of nativism, reinforced by the call to build a wall between the US and Mexico, executive orders attempting to ban immigration from six Muslim countries, and increased funding for border militarization (Domonoske, 2017).

CONTEMPORARY AND INTERSECTING MANIFESTATIONS OF RACISM AND WHITE SUPREMACY

The web of racism and white supremacy is wide and deep in its scope and influence, drawing upon many individuals, institutions, and practices that on first glance appear to be "color blind," "race neutral," and benign. This web is "systematic and comprehensive," existing at many levels, involving both informal and formal practices (Miller & Garran, 2017, p. 77). Although there have been periods in US history when race-based policies and practices have seemed to reduce prejudice, discrimination, and marginalization of minoritized racial groups (i.e., the 1960s Civil Rights Movements and the laws passed in their wake), racist practices endure. For example, the criminal justice system disproportionally targets black men and other men of color, hindering their right to participate in civic life (Alexander, 2011; Taylor, 2016). Racist practices are also reproduced through pervasive gaps in wealth and income between white people and people of color. In 2013, households headed by Whites had median net worth (a measure of value of what a household owns minus what it owes) thirteen times higher than those headed by Blacks and eleven times higher than those headed by Latino/a/x (Pew Research Center Social Demographics Trends, n.d.). Racism and nativism also manifests in the relentless criminalization of refugees and immigrants due to their immigration status and incarceration in detention centers awaiting deportation (see NNIRR, selection 16). National borders have become war-like zones where thousands of unaccompanied minors risk their lives in an effort to escape violence and poverty. The Customs and Border protection 100-mile rule is in direct violation of constitutional rights (ACLU, 2017); therefore, individuals located in major cities are increasingly at risk for interrogation or warrantless searches.

These policies manifest in the incarceration in detention centers without evidence or legal warrant (under the Patriot Act, 2001) of Arab Americans following the terrorist attacks of September 11, 2001. Racism is at work in racial and religious profiling of immigrants of Africa, Asia, Latin America, and the Middle East in the widespread raids in homes and workplaces and the poor working conditions of undocumented workers who labor in rural and urban centers.

In alignment with the rhetoric of the "Birther" movement that promotes a more recent form of nativism that privileges the election of natural-born officials, the current administration is driving a nationalist agenda that promises to build a wall on the Mexican border in an effort to protect our citizens from "bad hombres" (Salama, 2017) and remove "carnage" from inner-cities by reinstating the war on drugs (Rosenthal, 2017). The bolstered support for military, law enforcement, ICE, and the Office of Homeland Security has left many people of color in urban and rural communities feeling disconcerted and vulnerable.

CONTEMPORARY RESISTANCE TO INSTITUTIONAL MANIFESTATION OF RACISM AND WHITE SUPREMACY

Learning about the long and persistent history of racism and white supremacy in this country can bring forth hopelessness and despair. As important as it is to have an understanding of the deleterious impact the web of oppression has across institutions, it is equally important to acknowledge the web of resistance that has forged alliances and efforts toward solidarity among various racial and ethnic groups (Bell et al., 2016; Miller & Garran, 2017). The Black Lives Matter (BLM) movement, founded by three black women, was driven by a collective effort to cease the dehumanization of black communities, in an effort to stop police brutality and other forms of violence. Unlike the 1960s Civil Rights Movement, BLM provides an intersectional framework that resists a single-issue struggle toward liberation and, instead, includes black queer, trans*, undocumented, and people with disabilities (Black Lives Matter, n.d.; Taylor, 2016).

While much of the BLM grassroots mobilization initially permeated within cities, kicking off in Ferguson, MO, protests quickly expanded to college campuses throughout the United States. As a result, the development of multiracial alliances and organizing efforts gained significant momentum. New technologies and the use of social and mass media provide highlights of solidarity among students manifesting in Anti-Ban, Anti-Wall, and Say No DAPL (Dakota Access Pipeline Protest) (NNIRR, n.d.). Simultaneously, in response to the failure of the DREAM Act bill (Development, Relief and Education for Alien Minors), new initiatives, such as DEEP (DREAM for Educational Empowerment Program), a non-partisan organization, comprised largely of immigrant youth, is working to create tuition equity for undocumented students on college and university campuses nationwide (United We Dream, n.d.).

Pervasive historical legacies and deeply entrenched economic, political, and social factors continue to shape the experiences of people of color from diverse racial/ethnic groups in both shared and unique ways, as the readings in this section delineate. We hope this introduction and the selected readings that follow will encourage readers to develop a sophisticated and complex understanding of race and racism, and facilitate the development of strong, multiracial coalitions for racial justice. It is up to us to transform historical legacies and current manifestations of racism and white supremacy to create a society with justice for all. Given this, it is equally important to understand how diverse racial/ethnic groups experience, resist, and organize to dismantle racism and other forms of intersecting oppression in particular contexts.

CONTEXTS

The authors of our Contexts selections conceptualize and trace some of the enduring and changing features of racism and white supremacy and demonstrate how racism functions on multiple levels and in different ways for different racial/ethnic groups. In the first essay, Beverly Daniel Tatum (selection 9) provides a definition of racism as a phenomenon rooted in a system of advantage based on race. Tatum examines how white privilege conveys social influence and power to Whites as a group and corollary disadvantages to people of color. She also highlights the price we pay for inequality and injustice.

Ronald Takaki (selection 10) reveals the complexity of the racialization process, describing the historical trajectories, similarities, and differences in the experiences of Native Americans, African Americans, Chicanos, and Asian Americans as the nation developed. He explores the divergent experiences of immigrants, such as the Irish and Jews, whose assimilation as white over time allowed them entrance into the advantaged white group.

Roxanne Dunbar-Ortiz's introduction to *An Indigenous People's History of the United States,* "This Land," (selection 11) argues that the history of the United States is shaped by a particular form of colonialism—settler colonialism. She condemns the "doctrine of discovery" that justifies the usurpation of land on the part of Anglo-American settlers and the system of colonialism imposed by the US government that has devastated Indigenous nations. She traces our national legacy of theft, dispossession, and genocide to policies that are well documented in the literature and in the oral histories of Indigenous communities.

George Lipsitz (selection 12) further unpacks the unacknowledged but ever present cumulative effects of racism by examining the "possessive investment in whiteness" that shapes public and private life in our society. He explores how white hegemony has been developed and preserved, influenced by the legacies of slavery and segregation, Indigenous peoples' extermination and immigrant restriction, conquest, and settler colonialism. He argues that only an explicitly antiracist, interethnic movement that acknowledges and challenges the power of white supremacy will be powerful enough to break the hold of the possessive investment in whiteness.

Such a movement requires the kind of sophisticated thinking and analysis offered by Andrea Smith in her piece on the three pillars of white supremacy (selection 13): one based on the logic of slavery, a second, on the logic of genocide and colonialism, and a third, on the logic of Orientalism and war. Understanding these pillars, Smith argues, helps explain the divergent experiences of African Americans, Native Americans, Asian Americans, Latino/a/x, and Arab Americans, all of whom experience racism but not quite in the same ways.

Next, Gloria Anzaldúa (selection 14) develops her concept of "*mestiza* consciousness," one that embraces the complexity of multiple perspectives, learns to tolerate ambiguities, and breaks down dualistic paradigms to enable imagining a new way of thinking about the intersections of race, culture, language, and identity. She argues that *mestiza* consciousness provides a way to value the complex racial experiences of our hybrid nation and more creatively address the individual and collective challenges we face.

Next, Heather Dalmage (selection 15) discusses how questions of citizenship and resource distribution impacted the development of binary racial thinking in the United States, which was, in turn, reinforced by anti-miscegenation laws that discriminated and marginalized multiracial families and individuals culturally, institutionally, and interpersonally. While the Civil Rights Movement paved the way for the legal acceptance of multiraciality, she argues, racial policing practices, holding that racial borders are static, continue to push multiracial families, youth, and children to claim only one race using various "border enforcing" methods.

Finally, five reports by the National Network on Immigrant and Refugee Rights (NNIRR) (selection 16) illustrates how the US government, over the last 10 years, has put in place a relentless policing system to patrol national borders and to criminalize immigrants. These policies and practices increasingly support the criminalization of undocumented immigrants, normalizes the separation of families regardless of their immigration history or status, and the destabilization of border, rural, and urban communities. The rise of this policing regime propagates widespread human rights violations and contributes to the increase of racial discrimination and hate crimes against immigrants, particularly immigrants of color, who are perceived to be foreign born or "illegal." Taken together, the readings in the Context section help us think about racism systematically and analytically so that we will be prepared for new forms it may take as white supremacy, as it has in the past, shapeshifts to maintain its hold on society.

VOICES

This section honors that reading and learning from the personal experiences of individuals who belong to different social identity groups can be a powerful and often transformative experience. Olivia Chung in "Finding My Eye-dentity" (selection 17) remembers her struggle as an Asian American female in trying to let go of white dominant definitions of beauty and physical appearance; she comes to embrace a broader definition of beauty.

In "Identification Pleas," Eric Gansworth (selection 18), a member of the Onondaga Nation, describes his experience when the US border patrol mistakenly assumed he was Latino/a/x and rejected his tribal ID card as valid US identification. History shows how the erasure of individual and group experience through stereotyping and minoritization deprives people of their humanity and can help justify colonization, exploitations, marginalization, and multiple forms of discrimination. Mariam Gomaa in "American Hijab: Why My Scarf Is a Sociopolitical Statement, Not a Symbol of Religiosity" (selection 19) describes her decision to wear hijab, highlighting the ways in which it has particular meaning for her within the US context. It represents a rejection of her white-passing experiences and a marked solidarity with people of color.

In "My Tongue Is Divided into Two," Quique Aviles (selection 20) describes his journey of learning the English language and using it as a source of empowerment and liberation. In "Letter to My Son," Ta-Nehisi Coates (selection 21) describes the legacies of racism and white supremacy, which have resulted in different lived experiences for Blacks compared to Whites in the United States. He encourages his son to develop a critical awareness of these legacies that are enacted daily on his body and the bodies of other black males. Finally, Robin DiAngelo's "My Class Didn't Trump My Race" (selection 22) shares her own experience of learning about racism through the lens of class. She invites Whites to examine the ways they have internalized racial dominance and to consider the pervasive impact of white privilege and whiteness in their lives.

NEXT STEPS

In this last section, we highlight concrete action steps we can take to challenge the causes and effects of racism and white supremacy and to work toward transforming historical legacies through individual actions, dialogues across racial divides, and multiracial coalitions for change. In the first selection, Andrea Ayvazian and Beverly Daniel Tatum (selection 23) illustrate the power of sustained dialogue to explore, validate, and critically examine peoples' experiences and perspectives across race and other social identities to foster meaningful understanding and a strong sense of relational connection, even in the midst of conflict in order to forge strong ally relations.

Analouise Keating (selection 24) offers a set of premises for changing ourselves and changing the world that may be helpful to anyone who tries to do so at home, in the written word, and in the classrooms. At home, Keating strives to engage in spiritual interconnectedness with everyone in order to remain open and permeable. In the classroom, she troubles "race" as a category of difference and strives to historicize and denaturalize its usage. Lastly, Keating invites us to take risks, to transform the walls that divide us and take action in the everyday world.

We close with Chip Smith's "The Personal is Political" (selection 25). This selection helps us think about how we each can strengthen our engagement in the struggle against white supremacy through becoming aware of privilege and internalized oppression; building intentional relationships based on equality; studying the history of people of color; questioning and challenging the evidence of white supremacy at work, schools, and in communities; taking inventory of activism in one's community; and examining other aspects of one's community that may bring people together to actively address racial inequality.

Notes

1 We ask that those who cite this work always acknowledge by name all of the authors listed rather than only citing the first author or using "et al." to indicate coauthors. All authors listed on a section collaborated equitably on the conceptualization, development, and writing of this section.

2 We want to acknowledge the valuable contributions made to the second edition and third edition of this introduction and reading selections by Lee Ann Bell and Carmelita (Rosie) Castañeda.

3 We use the term Latino/a/x to refer to people from Latin American or Hispanic descent of different genders—men, women, trans*, gender non-conforming.

References

Adams, M., & Zúñiga, X. (2016). Getting started: Core concepts for social justice education. In M. Adams, L. Bell, D. Goodman, & K. Joshi (Eds.), *Teachings for diversity and social justice (3rd ed.)* (pp. 95–130). New York, NY: Routledge.

Alexander, M. (2011). *The new Jim Crow*. New York, NY: The New Press.

American Civil Liberties Union (ACLU). (2017). FactSheet on customs and border protection's 100-mile zone. Retrieved from www.aclu.org/other/aclu-factsheet-customs-and-border-protections-100-mile-zone?redirect=immigrants-rights/aclu-fact-sheet-customs-and-border-protections-100-mile-zone.

Arizona Senate Bill 1070. (2010). The support our law enforcement and safe neighborhoods act.

Bell, L., Funk, M., Joshi, K., & Valdivia, M. (2016). Racism and white privilege. In M. Adams, L. Bell, D. Goodman, & K. Joshi (Eds.), *Teachings for diversity and social justice (3rd ed.)* (pp. 133–182). New York, NY: Routledge.

Black Lives Matter. (n.d.). Retrieved from http://blacklivesmatter.com/herstory/.

Bonilla-Silva, E. (2001). *White supremacy and racism in the post civil rights era*. Boulder, CO: Rienner.

Brodkin Sacks, K. (1994). How did Jews become white folks? In S. Gregory & R. Sanjek (Eds.), *Race* (pp. 78–102). New Brunswick, NJ: Rutgers University Press.

Civil Rights Act of 1964. (1964). P.L. No. 88–352, 78 Stat. 241.

Domonoske, C. (2017). Trump signs new order blocking arrivals from 6 majority-Muslim countries. Retrieved from www.npr.org/sections/thetwo-way/2017/03/06/516408650/trump-signs-new-order-blocking-arrivals-from-6 majority-muslim-countries.

Gaultieri, S. (2001). Becoming "White": Race, religion and the foundations of Syrian/Lebanese ethnicity in the United States. *Journal of American Ethnic History, 20*(4), 29–59.

Guglielmo, T. A. (2003). Rethinking whiteness historiography: The case of Italians in Chicago, 1890–1945. In A. W. Doane & E. Bonilla-Silva (Eds.), *White out: The continuing significance of racism* (pp. 49–61). New York, NY: Routledge.

Haney-López, I. F. (2006). *White by law*. New York, NY: New York University Press.

Immigration and Nationality Act of 1965. (1968). Pub. L. No. 89–236, 79 Stat. 911.

Jaradat, A. R. (2017). Factors that shape Arab American college student identity. *Doctoral Dissertations 2014-current* 1018. http://scholarworks.umass.edu/dissertations_2/101.

Johnston-Guerrero, M. (2010). Multiracial microaggressions: Exposing monoracism in everyday life and clinical practice. In D. W. Sue (Ed.), *Microaggressions and marginality: Manifestion, dynamics and impact* (p. 123–144). New York, NY: Wiley.

Miller, J. L., & Garran, A. M. (2017). *Racism in the United States: Implications for the helping professions*. New York, NY: Springer.

National Network for Immigrant and Refugee Rights (NNIRR). (n.d.). Border militarization policy. Retrieved from www.nnirr.org/drupal/border-militarization.

Omi, M., & Winant, H. (2015). *Racial formation in the United States*. New York, NY: Routledge.

Patriot Act. (2001). The USA PATRIOT Act: Preserving Life and Liberty. P. L. No. 107-56, 115 Stat. 272.

Pew Research Center Social Demographic Trends. (n.d.). A growing wealth gap between black and whites. Retrieved from www.pewsocialtrends.org/2016/06/27/1-demographic-trends-and-economic-well-being/.

Roediger, D. R. (1991). *The wages of whiteness: Race and the making of the American working class*. London: Verso.

Roithmayr, D. (2014). *Reproducing racism: How everyday choices lock in white advantage*. New York, NY: New York University Press.

Rosenthal, A. (2017). Trump gives us "American carnage." *New York Times*. Retrieved from www.nytimes.com/interactive/projects/cp/opinion/presidential-inauguration-2017/trump-gives-us-american-carnage.

Salama, V. (2017). Trump to Mexico: Take care of "bad hombres" or US might. *AP News*. Retrieved from https://apnews.com/0b3f5db59b2e4aa78cdbbf008f27fb49.

Sinha, A., & Faithful, R. (2012). State battles over immigration: The forecast for 2012. Retrieved from www.advancementproject.org/sites/default/files/publications/Immigrant%20Rights%202012%20Legislative%20Battles_FINAL%20Feb%201%202012_0.pdf.

Spickard, P. (2007). *Almost all aliens: Immigration, race and colonialism in American history and identity*. New York, NY: Routledge.

Takaki, R. (1993). *A different mirror: A history of multicultural America*. Boston, MA: Little, Brown.

Tatum, B. T. (1997). *Why are all the black kids sitting together in the cafeteria: And other conversations about race*. New York, NY: Basic Books.

Taylor, K.-Y. (2016). *From #Blacks Lives Matter to black liberation*. Chicago, IL: Haymarket Books.

United We Dream. (n.d.). DEEP. Retrieved from https://unitedwedream.org/about/projects/education-deep/.

U.S. Immigration and Customs Enforcement (ICE). (n.d.). Secure communities. Retrieved from www.ice.gov/secure-communities.

Villenas, S., & Deyhle, D. (1999). Critical race theory and ethnographies challenging stereotypes: Latino families, schooling, resilience and resistance. *Curriculum Inquiry, 29*, 413–445.

9

Defining Racism

"Can We Talk?"

Beverly Daniel Tatum

. . .

The impact of racism begins early. Even in our preschool years, we are exposed to misinformation about people different from ourselves. Many of us grew up in neighborhoods where we had limited opportunities to interact with people different from our own families. When I ask my college students, "How many of you grew up in neighborhoods where most of the people were from the same racial group as your own?" almost every hand goes up. There is still a great deal of social segregation in our communities. Consequently, most of the early information we receive about "others"—people racially, religiously, or socioeconomically different from ourselves—does not come as the result of firsthand experience. The secondhand information we do receive has often been distorted, shaped by cultural stereotypes, and left incomplete.

. . .

Sometimes the assumptions we make about others come not from what we have been told or what we have seen on television or in books, but rather from what we have *not* been told. The distortion of historical information about people of color leads young people (and older people, too) to make assumptions that may go unchallenged for a long time. . . .

. . .

Omitted information can have similar effects. For example, another young woman, preparing to be a high school English teacher, expressed her dismay that she had never learned about any Black authors in any of her English courses. How was she to teach about them to her future students when she hadn't learned about them herself? A White male student in the class responded to this discussion with frustration in his response journal, writing "It's not my fault that Blacks don't write books." Had one of his elementary, high school, or college teachers ever told him that there were no Black writers? Probably not. Yet because he had never been exposed to Black authors, he had drawn his own conclusion that there were none.

Stereotypes, omissions, and distortions all contribute to the development of prejudice. *Prejudice* is a preconceived judgment or opinion, usually based on limited information. I assume that we all have prejudices, not because we want them, but simply because we are so continually exposed to misinformation about others. Though I have often heard students or workshop participants describe someone as not having "a prejudiced bone in his body," I usually suggest that they look again. Prejudice is one of the inescapable consequences of living in a racist society. Cultural racism—the cultural images and messages that affirm the assumed superiority of Whites and the assumed inferiority of people of color—is like smog in the air. Sometimes it is so thick it is visible, other times it is less apparent, but always, day in and day out, we are breathing it in. None of us would introduce ourselves as "smog-breathers" (and most of us don't want to be described as prejudiced), but if we live in a smoggy place, how can we avoid breathing the air? If we live in an environment in which we are bombarded with stereotypical images in the media, are frequently exposed to the ethnic jokes of friends and family members, and are rarely informed of the accomplishments of oppressed groups, we will develop the negative categorizations of those groups that form the basis of prejudice.

People of color as well as Whites develop these categorizations. Even a member of the stereotyped group may internalize the stereotypical categories about his or her own group to some degree. In fact, this process happens so frequently that it has a name, *internalized oppression*. . . .

. . .

To say that it is not our fault does not relieve us of responsibility, however. We may not have polluted the air, but we need to take responsibility, along with others, for cleaning it up. Each of us needs to look at our own behavior. Am I perpetuating and reinforcing the negative messages so pervasive in our culture, or am I seeking to challenge them? If I have not been exposed to positive images of marginalized groups, am I seeking them out, expanding my own knowledge base for myself and my children? Am I acknowledging and examining my own prejudices, my own rigid categorizations of others, thereby minimizing the adverse impact they might have on my interactions with those I have categorized? Unless we engage in these and other conscious acts of reflection and reeducation, we easily repeat the process with our children. We teach what we were taught. The unexamined prejudices of the parents are passed on to the children. It is not our fault, but it is our responsibility to interrupt this cycle.

RACISM: A SYSTEM OF ADVANTAGE BASED ON RACE

Many people use the terms *prejudice* and *racism* interchangeably. I do not, and I think it is important to make a distinction. In his book *Portraits of White Racism*, David Wellman argues convincingly that limiting our understanding of racism to prejudice does not offer a sufficient explanation for the persistence of racism. He defines racism as a system of advantage based on race. In illustrating this definition, he provides example after example of how Whites defend their racial advantage—access to better schools, housing, jobs—even when they do not embrace overtly prejudicial thinking. Racism cannot be fully explained as an expression of prejudice alone.

This definition of racism is useful because it allows us to see that racism, like other forms of oppression, is not only a personal ideology based on racial prejudice, but a *system* involving cultural messages and institutional policies and practices as well as the beliefs and actions of individuals. In the context of the United States, this system clearly operates to the advantage of Whites and to the disadvantage of people of color. Another related definition of racism, commonly used by antiracist educators and consultants, is "prejudice plus power." Racial prejudice when combined with social power—access to social, cultural, and economic resources and decision-making—leads to the institutionalization of racist policies and practices. While I think this definition also captures the idea that racism is more than individual beliefs and attitudes, I prefer Wellman's definition because the idea of systematic advantage and disadvantage is critical to an understanding of how racism operates in American society.

. . .

The systematic advantages of being White are often referred to as White privilege. In a now well-known article, "White Privilege: Unpacking the Invisible Knapsack," Peggy McIntosh, a White feminist scholar, identified a long list of societal privileges that she received simply because she was White. She did not ask for them, and it is important to note that she hadn't always noticed that she was receiving them. They included major and minor advantages. Of course she enjoyed greater access to jobs and housing. But she also was able to shop in department stores without being followed by suspicious sales-people and could always find appropriate hair care products and makeup in any drugstore. She could send her child to school confident that the teacher would not discriminate against him on the basis of race. She could also be late for meetings, and talk with her mouth full, fairly confident that these behaviors would not be attributed to the fact that she was White. She could express an opinion in a meeting or in print and not have it labeled the "White" viewpoint. In other words, she was more often than not viewed as an individual, rather than as a member of a racial group.

. . .

Understanding racism as a system of advantage based on race is antithetical to traditional notions of an American meritocracy. For those who have internalized this myth, this definition generates considerable discomfort. It is more comfortable simply to think of racism as a particular form of prejudice. Notions of power or privilege do not have to be addressed when our understanding of racism is constructed in that way.

. . .

RACISM: FOR WHITES ONLY?

. . .

I sometimes visualize the ongoing cycle of racism as a moving walkway at the airport. Active racist behavior is equivalent to walking fast on the conveyor belt. The person engaged in active racist behavior has identified with the ideology of White supremacy and is moving with it. Passive racist behavior is equivalent to standing still on the walkway. No overt effort is being made, but the conveyor belt moves the bystanders along to the same destination as those who are actively walking. Some of the bystanders may feel the motion of the conveyor belt, see the active racists ahead of them, and choose to turn around, unwilling to go to the same destination as the White supremacists. But unless they are walking actively in the opposite direction at a speed faster than the conveyor belt—unless they are actively antiracist—they will find themselves carried along with the others.

. . .

It is important to acknowledge that while all Whites benefit from racism, they do not all benefit equally. Other factors, such as socio-economic status, gender, age, religious affiliation, sexual orientation, mental and physical ability, also play a role in our access to social influence and power. A White woman on welfare is not privileged to the same extent as a wealthy White heterosexual man. In her case, the systematic disadvantages of sexism and classism intersect with her White privilege, but the privilege is still there. This point was brought home to me in a 1994 study conducted by a Mount Holyoke graduate student, Phyllis Wentworth. Wentworth interviewed a group of female college students, who were both older than their peers and were the first members of their families to attend college, about the pathways that led them to college. All of the women interviewed were White, from working-class backgrounds, from families where women were expected to graduate from high school and get married or get a job. Several had experienced abusive relationships and other personal difficulties prior to coming to college. Yet their experiences were punctuated by "good luck" stories of apartments obtained without a deposit, good jobs offered without experience or extensive reference checks, and encouragement provided by willing mentors. While the women acknowledged their good fortune, none of them discussed their Whiteness. They had not considered the possibility that being White had worked in their favor and helped give them the benefit of the doubt at critical junctures. This study clearly showed that even under difficult circumstances, White privilege was still operating.

It is also true that not all people of color are equally targeted by racism. We all have multiple identities that shape our experience. I can describe myself as a light-skinned, well-educated, heterosexual, able-bodied, Christian African American woman raised in a middle-class suburb. As an African American woman, I am systematically disadvantaged by race and by gender, but I systematically receive benefits in the other categories, which then mediate my experience of racism and sexism. When one is targeted by multiple isms—racism, sexism, classism, heterosexism, ableism, anti-Semitism, ageism—in whatever combination, the effect is intensified. The particular combination of racism and classism in many communities of color is life-threatening. Nonetheless, when I, the middle-class Black mother of two sons, read another story about a Black man's unlucky encounter with a White police officer's deadly force, I am reminded that racism by itself can kill.

THE COST OF RACISM

. . . Why should Whites who are advantaged by racism *want* to end that system of advantage? What are the *costs* of that system to them?

A *Money* magazine article called "Race and Money" chronicled the many ways the American economy was hindered by institutional racism. Whether one looks at productivity lowered by racial tensions in the workplace, or real estate equity lost through housing discrimination, or the tax revenue lost in underemployed communities of color, or the high cost of warehousing human talent in prison, the economic costs of racism are real and measurable.

As a psychologist, I often hear about the less easily measured costs. When I ask White men and women how racism hurts them, they frequently talk about their fears of people of color, the social incompetence they feel in racially mixed situations, the alienation they have experienced between parents and children when a child marries into a family of color, and the interracial friendships they had as children that were lost in adolescence or young adulthood without their ever understanding why. White people are paying a significant price for the system of advantage. The cost is not as high for Whites as it is for people of color, but a price is being paid. . . .

The dismantling of racism is in the best interests of everyone.

. . .

10

A Different Mirror

Ronald Takaki

I had flown from San Francisco to Norfolk and was riding in a taxi to my hotel to attend a conference on multiculturalism. Hundreds of educators from across the country were meeting to discuss the need for greater cultural diversity in the curriculum. My driver and I chatted about the weather and the tourists. The sky was cloudy, and Virginia Beach was twenty minutes away. The rearview mirror reflected a white man in his forties. "How long have you been in this country?" he asked. "All my life," I replied, wincing. "I was born in the United States." With a strong southern drawl, he remarked: "I was wondering because your English is excellent!" Then, as I had many times before, I explained: "My grandfather came here from Japan in the 1880s. My family has been here, in America, for over a hundred years." He glanced at me in the mirror. Somehow I did not look "American" to him; my eyes and complexion looked foreign.

. . .

Questions like the one my taxi driver asked me are always jarring, but I can understand why he could not see me as American. He had a narrow but widely shared sense of the past—a history that has viewed American as European in ancestry. "Race," Toni Morrison explained, has functioned as a "metaphor" necessary to the "construction of Americanness": in the creation of our national identity, "American" has been defined as "white."

. . .

But how should "we" be defined? Who are the people "stuck here" in America? One of the lessons of the Los Angeles explosion is the recognition of the fact that we are a multiracial society and that race can no longer be defined in the binary terms of white and black. "We" will have to include Hispanics and Asians. While blacks currently constitute 13 percent of the Los Angeles population, Hispanics represent 40 percent. The 1990 census revealed that South Central Los Angeles, which was predominantly black in 1965 when the Watts rebellion occurred, is now 45 percent Hispanic. A majority of the first 5,438 people arrested were Hispanic, while 37 percent were black. Of the fifty-eight people who died in the riot, more than a third were Hispanic, and about 40 percent of the businesses destroyed were Hispanic-owned. Most of the other shops and stores were Korean-owned. The dreams of many Korean immigrants went up in smoke during the riot: two thousand Korean-owned businesses were damaged or demolished, totaling about $400 million in losses. There is evidence indicating they were targeted. "After all," explained a black gang member, "we didn't burn our community, just *their* stores."

. . .

African Americans have been the central minority throughout our country's history. They were initially brought here on a slave ship in 1619. Actually, these first twenty Africans might not have been slaves; rather, like most of the white laborers, they were probably indentured servants. The transformation of Africans into slaves is the story of the "hidden" origins of slavery. How and when was it decided to institute a system of bonded black labor? What happened, while freighted with racial significance, was actually conditioned by class conflicts within white society. Once established, the "peculiar institution" would have consequences for centuries to come. During the nineteenth century, the political storm over slavery almost destroyed the nation. Since the Civil War and emancipation, race has continued to be largely defined in relation to African Americans—segregation, civil rights, the underclass, and affirmative action. Constituting the largest minority group in our society, they have been at the cutting edge of the Civil Rights Movement. Indeed, their struggle has been a constant reminder of America's moral vision as a country committed to the principle of liberty. Martin Luther King clearly understood this truth when he wrote from a jail cell: "We will reach the goal of freedom in Birmingham and all over the nation, because the goal of America is freedom. Abused and scorned though we may be, our destiny is tied up with America's destiny."

Asian Americans have been here for over one hundred and fifty years, before many European immigrant groups. But as "strangers" coming from a "different shore," they have been stereotyped as "heathen," exotic, and unassimilable. Seeking "Gold Mountain," the Chinese arrived first, and what happened to them influenced the reception of the Japanese, Koreans, Filipinos, and Asian Indians as well as the Southeast Asian refugees like the Vietnamese and the Hmong. The 1882 Chinese Exclusion Act was the first law that prohibited the entry of immigrants on the basis of nationality. The Chinese condemned this restriction as racist and tyrannical. "They call us 'Chink,'" complained a Chinese immigrant, cursing the "white demons." "They think we no good! America cuts us off. No more come now, too bad!" This precedent later provided a basis for the restriction of European immigrant groups such as Italians, Russians, Poles, and Greeks. The Japanese painfully discovered that their accomplishments in America did not lead to acceptance, for during World War II, unlike Italian Americans and German Americans, they were placed in internment camps. Two-thirds of them were citizens by birth. "How could I as a 6-month-old child born in this country," asked Congressman Robert Matsui years later, "be declared by my own Government to be an enemy alien?" Today, Asian Americans represent the fastest-growing ethnic group. They have also become the focus of much mass media attention as "the Model Minority" not only for blacks and Chicanos, but also for whites on welfare and even middle-class whites experiencing economic difficulties.

Chicanos represent the largest group among the Hispanic population, which is projected to outnumber African Americans. They have been in the United States for a long time, initially incorporated by the war against Mexico. The treaty had moved the border between the two countries, and the people of "occupied" Mexico suddenly found themselves "foreigners" in their "native land." As historian Albert Camarillo pointed out, the Chicano past is an integral part of America's westward expansion, also known as "manifest destiny." But while the early Chicanos were a colonized people, most of them today have immigrant roots. Many began the trek to El Norte in the early twentieth century. "As I had heard a lot about the United States," Jesus Garza recalled, "it was my dream to come here." "We came to know families from Chihuahua, Sonora, Jalisco, and Durango," stated Ernesto Galarza. "Like ourselves, our Mexican neighbors had come this far moving step by step, working and waiting, as if they were feeling their way up a ladder." Nevertheless, the Chicano experience has been unique, for most of them have lived close to their homeland—a proximity that has helped reinforce their language, identity, and culture. This migration to El Norte has continued to the present. Los Angeles has more people of Mexican origin than any other city in the world, except Mexico City. A mostly mestizo people of Indian as well as African and Spanish ancestries, Chicanos currently represent the largest minority group in the Southwest, where they have been visibly transforming culture and society.

The Irish came here in greater numbers than most immigrant groups. Their history has been tied to America's past from the very beginning. Ireland represented the earliest English frontier: the conquest of Ireland occurred before the colonization of America, and the Irish were the first group that the English called "savages." In this context, the Irish past foreshadowed the Indian future. During the nineteenth century, the Irish, like the Chinese, were victims of British colonialism. While the Chinese fled from the ravages of the Opium Wars, the Irish were pushed from their homeland by "English tyranny." Here they became construction workers and factory operatives as well as the "maids" of America. Representing a Catholic group seeking to settle in a fiercely Protestant society, the Irish immigrants were targets of American nativist hostility. They were also what historian Lawrence J. McCaffrey called "the pioneers of the American urban ghetto," "previewing" experiences that would later be shared by the Italians, Poles, and other groups from southern and eastern Europe. Furthermore, they offer contrast to the immigrants from Asia. The Irish came about the same time as the Chinese, but they had a distinct advantage: the Naturalization Law of 1790 had reserved citizenship for "whites" only. Their compatible complexion allowed them to assimilate by blending into American society. In making their journey successfully into the mainstream, however, these immigrants from Erin pursued an Irish "ethnic" strategy: they promoted "Irish" solidarity in order to gain political power and also to dominate the skilled blue-collar occupations, often at the expense of the Chinese and blacks.

Fleeing pogroms and religious persecution in Russia, the Jews were driven from what John Cuddihy described as the "Middle Ages into the Anglo-American world of the *goyim* 'beyond the pale.'" To them, America represented the Promised Land. This vision led Jews to struggle not only for themselves but also for other oppressed groups, especially blacks. After the 1917 East St. Louis race riot, the Yiddish *Forward* of New York compared this anti-black violence to a 1903 pogrom in Russia: "Kishinev and St. Louis—the same soil, the same people." Jews cheered when Jackie Robinson broke into the Brooklyn Dodgers in 1947. "He was adopted as the surrogate hero by many of us growing up at the time," recalled Jack Greenberg of the NAACP Legal Defense Fund. "He was the way we saw ourselves triumphing against the forces of bigotry and ignorance." Jews stood shoulder to shoulder with blacks in the Civil Rights Movement: two-thirds of the white volunteers who went south during the 1964 Freedom Summer were Jewish. Today Jews are considered a highly successful "ethnic" group. How did they make such great socioeconomic strides? This question is often reframed by neoconservative intellectuals like Irving Kristol and Nathan Glazer to read: if Jewish immigrants were able to lift themselves from poverty into the mainstream through self-help and education without welfare and affirmative action, why can't blacks? But what this thinking overlooks is the unique history of Jewish immigrants, especially the initial advantages of many of them as literate and skilled. Moreover, it minimizes the virulence of racial prejudice rooted in American slavery.

Indians represent a critical contrast, for theirs was not an immigrant experience. The Wampanoags were on the shore as the first English strangers arrived in what would be called "New England." The encounters between Indians and whites not only shaped the course of race relations, but also influenced the very culture and identity of the general society. The architect of Indian removal, President Andrew Jackson told Congress: "Our conduct toward these people is deeply interesting to the national character." Frederick Jackson Turner understood the meaning of this observation when he identified the frontier as our transforming crucible. At first, the European newcomers had to wear Indian moccasins and shout the war cry. "Little by little," as they subdued the wilderness, the pioneers became "a new product" that was "American." But Indians have had a different view of this entire process. "The white man," Luther Standing Bear of the Sioux explained, "does not understand the Indian for the reason that he does not understand American." Continuing to be "troubled with primitive fears," he has "in his consciousness the perils of this frontier continent. . . . The man from Europe is still a foreigner and an alien. And he still hates the man who questioned his path across the continent." Indians questioned what Jackson and Turner trumpeted as "progress." For them, the frontier had a different "significance": their history was how the West was lost. But their story has also been one of resistance. As Vine Deloria declared, "Custer died for your sins."

By looking at these groups from a multicultural perspective, we can comparatively analyze their experiences in order to develop an understanding of their differences and similarities. Race, we will see, has been a social construction that has historically set apart racial minorities from European immigrant groups. Contrary to the notions of scholars like Nathan Glazer and Thomas Sowell, race in America has not been the same as ethnicity. A broad comparative focus also allows us to see how the varied experiences of different racial and ethnic groups occurred within shared contexts.

During the nineteenth century, for example, the Market Revolution employed Irish immigrant laborers in New England factories as it expanded cotton fields worked by enslaved blacks across Indian lands toward Mexico. Like blacks, the Irish newcomers were stereotyped as "savages," ruled by passions rather than "civilized" virtues such as self-control and hard work. The Irish saw themselves as the "slaves" of British oppressors, and during a visit to Ireland in the 1840s, Frederick Douglass found that the "wailing notes" of the Irish ballads reminded him of the "wild notes" of slave songs. The United States annexation of California, while incorporating Mexicans, led to trade with Asia and the migration of "strangers" from Pacific shores. In 1870, Chinese immigrant laborers were transported to Massachusetts as scabs to break an Irish immigrant strike; in response, the Irish recognized the need for interethnic working-class solidarity and tried to organize a Chinese lodge of the Knights of St. Crispin. After the Civil War, Mississippi planters recruited Chinese immigrants to discipline the newly freed blacks. During the debate over an immigration exclusion bill in 1882, a senator asked: If Indians could be located on reservations, why not the Chinese?

Other instances of our connectedness abound. In 1903, Mexican and Japanese farm laborers went on strike together in California: their union officers had names like Yamaguchi and Lizarras, and strike meetings were conducted in Japanese and Spanish. The Mexican strikers declared that they were standing in solidarity with their "Japanese brothers" because the two groups had toiled together in the fields and were now fighting together for a fair wage. Speaking in impassioned Yiddish during the 1909 "uprising of twenty thousand" strikers in New York, the charismatic Clara Lemlich compared the abuse of Jewish female garment workers to the experience of blacks: "[The bosses] yell at the girls and 'call them down' even worse than I imagine the Negro slaves were in the South." During the 1920s, elite universities like Harvard worried about the increasing numbers of Jewish students, and new admissions criteria were instituted to curb their enrollment. Jewish students were scorned for their studiousness and criticized for their "clannishness." Recently, Asian-American students have been the targets of similar complaints: they have been called "nerds" and told there are "too many" of them on campus.

Indians were already here, while blacks were forcibly transported to America, and Mexicans were initially enclosed by America's expanding border. The other groups came here as immigrants: for them, America represented liminality—a new world where they could pursue extravagant urges and do things they had thought beyond their capabilities. Like the land itself, they found themselves "betwixt and between all fixed points of classification." No longer fastened as fiercely to their old countries, they felt a stirring to become new people in a society still being defined and formed.

. . .

. . . Through their stories, the people who have lived America's history can help all of us, including my taxi driver, understand that Americans originated from many shores, and that all of us are entitled to dignity. "I hope this survey do a lot of good for Chinese people," an immigrant told an interviewer from Stanford University in the 1920s. "Make American people realize that Chinese people are humans. I think very few American people really know anything about Chinese." But the remembering is also for the sake of the children. "This story is dedicated to the descendants of Lazar and Goldie Glauberman," Jewish immigrant Minnie Miller wrote in her autobiography. "My history is bound up in their history and the generations that follow should know where they came from to know better who they are." Similarly, Tomo Shoji, an elderly Nisei woman, urged Asian Americans to learn more about their roots: "We got such good, fantastic stories to tell. All our stories are different." Seeking to know how they fit into America, many young people have become listeners; they are eager to learn about the hardships and humiliations experienced by their parents and grandparents. They want to hear their stories, unwilling to remain ignorant or ashamed of their identity and past.

. . .

Through their narratives about their lives and circumstances, the people of America's diverse groups are able to see themselves and each other in our common past. They celebrate what Ishmael Reed has described as a society "unique" in the world because "the world is here"—a place "where the cultures of the world crisscross." Much of America's past, they point out, has been riddled with racism. At the same time, these people offer hope, affirming the struggle for equality as a central theme in our country's history. At its conception, our nation was dedicated to the proposition of equality. What has given concreteness to this powerful national principle has been our coming together in the creation of a new society. "Stuck here" together, workers of different backgrounds have attempted to get along with each other.

> *People harvesting*
> *Work together unaware*
> *Of racial problems,*

wrote a Japanese immigrant describing a lesson learned by Mexican and Asian farm laborers in California.

. . .

11

This Land

Roxanne Dunbar-Ortiz

. . . US policies and actions related to Indigenous peoples, though often termed "racist" or "discriminatory" are rarely depicted as what they are: classic cases of imperialism and a particular form of colonialism—settler colonialism. As anthropologist Patrick Wolfe writes, "The question of genocide is never far from discussions of settler colonialism. Land is life—or, at least, land is necessary for life."

The history of the United States is a history of settler colonialism—the founding of a state based on the ideology of white supremacy, the widespread practice of African slavery, and a policy of genocide and land theft. Those who seek history with an upbeat ending, a history of redemption and reconciliation, may look around and observe that such a conclusion is not visible, not even in utopian dreams of a better society.

Writing US history from an Indigenous peoples' perspective requires rethinking the consensual national narrative. That narrative is wrong or deficient, not in its facts, dates, or details but rather in its essence. Inherent in the myth we've been taught is an embrace of settler colonialism and genocide. The myth persists, not for a lack of free speech or poverty of information but rather for an absence of motivation to ask questions that challenge the core of the scripted narrative of the origin story. How might acknowledging the reality of US history work to transform society? That is the central question this [article] pursues.

Teaching Native American studies, I always begin with a simple exercise. I ask students to quickly draw a rough outline of the United States at the time it gained independence from Britain. Invariably most draw the approximate present shape of the United States from the Atlantic to the Pacific—the continental territory not fully appropriated until a century after independence. What became independent in 1783 were the thirteen British colonies hugging the Atlantic shore. When called on this, students are embarrassed because they know better. I assure them that they are not alone. I call this a Rorschach test of unconscious "manifest destiny," embedded in the minds of nearly everyone in the United States and around the world. This test reflects the seeming inevitability of US extent and power, its destiny, which an implication that the continent had previously been *terra nullius*, a land without people.

Woody Guthrie's "This Land Is Your Land" celebrates that the land belongs to everyone, reflecting the unconscious manifest destiny we live with. But the extension of the United States from sea to shining sea was the intention and design of the country's founders. "Free" land was the magnet that attracted European settlers. Many were slave owners who desired limitless land for lucrative cash crops. After the war for independence but preceding the writing of the US Constitution, the Continental Congress produced the Northwest Ordinance. This was the first law of the incipient republic, revealing the motive for those desiring independence. It was the blueprint for gobbling up the British-protected Indian Territory ("Ohio Country") on the other side of the Appalachians and Alleghenies. Britain had made settlement there illegal with the Proclamation of 1763.

In 1801, President Jefferson aptly described the new settler-state's intentions for horizontal and vertical continental expansion, stating: "However our present interests may restrain us within our own limits, it is impossible not to look forward to distant times, when our rapid multiplication will expand itself beyond those limits and cover the whole northern, if not the southern continent, with a people speaking the same language, governed in similar form by similar laws." This vision of manifest destiny found form a few years later in the Monroe Doctrine, signaling the intention of annexing or dominating former Spanish colonial territories in the Americas and the Pacific, which would be put into practice during the rest of the century.

Origin narratives form the vital core of a people's unifying identity and of the values that guide them. In the United States, the founding and development of the Anglo-American settler-state involves a narrative about Puritan settlers who had a covenant with God to take the land. That part of the origin story is supported and reinforced by the Columbus myth and the "Doctrine of Discovery." According to a series of late-fifteenth-century papal bulls, European nations acquired title to the lands they "discovered" and Indigenous inhabitants lost their natural right to that land after Europeans arrived and claimed it. . . .

The Columbus myth suggests that from US independence onward, colonial settlers saw themselves as part of a world system of colonization. "Columbia," the poetic, Latinate name used in reference to the United States from its founding throughout the nineteenth century, was based on the name of Christopher Columbus. The "Land of Columbus" was—and still is—represented by the image of a woman in sculpture and paintings, by institutions such as Columbia University, and by countless place names, including that of the national capital, the District of Columbia. The 1798 hymn "Hail, Columbia" was the early national anthem and is now used whenever the vice president of the United States makes a public appearance, and Columbus Day is still a federal holiday despite Columbus never having set foot on the continent claimed by the United States. . . .

Awareness of the settler-colonialist context of US history writing is essential if one is to avoid the laziness of the default position and the trap of a mythological unconscious belief in manifest destiny. The form of colonialism that the Indigenous peoples of North America have experienced was modern from the beginning: the expansion of European corporations, backed by government armies, into foreign areas, with subsequent expropriation of lands and resources. Settler colonialism is a genocidal policy. Native nations and communities, while struggling to maintain fundamental values and collectivity, have from the beginning resisted modern colonialism using both defensive and offensive techniques, including the modern forms of armed resistance of national liberation movements and what now is called terrorism. In every instance they have fought for survival as peoples. The objective of US colonialist authorities was to terminate their existence as peoples—not as random individuals. This is the very definition of modern genocide as contrasted with premodern instances of extreme violence that did not have the goal of extinction.

The United States as a socioeconomic and political entity is a result of this centuries-long and ongoing colonial process. Modern Indigenous nations and communities are societies formed by their resistance of colonialism, through which they have carried their practices and histories. It is breathtaking, but no miracle, that they have survived as peoples.

To say that the United States is a colonialist settler-state is not to make an accusation but rather to face historical reality, without which consideration not much in US history makes sense, unless Indigenous peoples are erased. But Indigenous nations, through resistance, have survived and bear witness to this history. In the era of worldwide decolonization in the second half of the twentieth century, the former colonial powers and their intellectual apologists mounted a counterforce, often called neocolonialism, from which multiculturalism and postmodernism emerged. Although much revisionist US history reflects neocolonialist strategy—an attempt to accommodate new realities in order to retain the dominance—neocolonialist methods signal victory for the colonized. Such approaches pry off a lid long kept tightly fastened. One result has been the presence of significant numbers of Indigenous scholars in US universities who are changing the terms of analysis. The main challenge for scholars in revising US history in the context of colonialism is not lack of information, nor is it one of methodology. Certainly difficulties with documentation are no more problematic than they are in any other area of research. Rather, the source of the problems has been the refusal or inability of US historians to comprehend the nature of their own history, US history. The fundamental problem is the absence of the colonial framework.

Through economic penetration of Indigenous societies, the European and Euro-American colonial powers created economic dependency and imbalance of trade, then incorporated the Indigenous nations into spheres of influence and controlled them indirectly or as protectorates, with indispensable use of Christian missionaries and alcohol. In the case of US settler colonialism, land was the primary commodity. With such obvious indicators of colonialism at work, why should so many interpretations of US political-economic development be convoluted and obscure, avoiding the obvious? To some extent, the twentieth-century emergence of the field of "US West" or "Borderlands" history has been forced into an incomplete and flawed settler-colonialist framework. The father of that field of history, Frederick Jackson Turner, confessed as much in 1901: "Our colonial system did not start with the Spanish War (1898); the U.S. had had a colonial history and policy from the beginning of the Republic; but they have been hidden under the phraseology of 'inter-state migration' and 'territorial organization.'"

Settler colonialism, as an institution or system, requires violence or the threat of violence to attain its goals. People do not hand over their land, resources, children, and futures without a fight, and that fight is met with violence. In employing the force necessary to accomplish its expansionist goals, a colonizing regime institutionalizes violence. The notion that settler-Indigenous conflict is an inevitable product of cultural differences and misunderstandings, or that violence was committed equally by the colonized and the colonizer, blurs the nature of the historical processes. Euro-American colonialism, an aspect of the capitalist economic globalization, had from its beginnings a genocidal tendency.

The term "genocide" was coined following the Shoah, or Holocaust, and its prohibition was enshrined in the United Nations conventions adopted in 1948: the UN Convention on the Prevention and Punishment of the Crime of Genocide. The convention is not retroactive but is applicable to US-Indigenous relations since 1988, when the US Senate ratified it. The terms of the genocide convention are also useful tools for historical analysis of the effects of colonialism in any era. In the convention, any one of five acts is considered genocide if "committed with intent to destroy, in whole or in part, a national, ethnical, racial or religious group":

killing members of the group;

causing serious bodily or mental harm to members of the group;

deliberately inflicting on the group conditions of life calculated to bring about its physical
    destruction in whole or in part;

imposing measures intended to prevent births within the group;

forcibly transferring children of the group to another group.

In the 1990s, the term "ethnic cleansing" became a useful descriptive term for genocide.

US history, as well as inherited Indigenous trauma, cannot be understood without dealing with the genocide that the United States committed against Indigenous peoples. From the colonial period through the founding of the United States and continuing in the twenty-first century, this has entailed torture, terror, sexual abuse, massacres, systematic military occupations, removals of Indigenous peoples from their ancestral territories, and removals of Indigenous children to military-like boarding schools. The absence of even the slightest note of regret or tragedy in the annual celebration of the US independence betrays a deep disconnect in the consciousness of US Americans.

Settler colonialism is inherently genocidal in terms of the genocide convention. In the case of the British North American colonies and the United States, not only extermination and removal were practiced but also the disappearing of the prior existence of Indigenous people—and this continues to be perpetuated in local histories. Anishinaabe (Ojibwe) historian Jean O'Brien names this practice of writing Indians out of existence "firsting and lasting." All over the continent, local histories, monuments, and signage narrate the story of first settlement: the founder(s), the first school, first dwelling, first everything, as if there had never been occupants who thrived in those places before Euro-Americans. On the other hand, the national narrative tells of "last" Indians or last tribes, such as "the last of the Mohicans," "Ishi, the last Indian," and *End of the Trail*, as a famous sculpture by James Earle Fraser is titled.

Documented policies of genocide on the part of US administration can be identified in at least four distinct periods: the Jacksonian era of forced removal; the California gold rush in Northern California; the post-Civil War era of the so-called Indian wars in the Great Plains; and the 1950s termination period. Cases of genocide carried out as policy may be found in historical documents as well as in the oral histories of Indigenous communities. An example from 1873 is typical, with General William T. Sherman writing, "We must act with vindictive earnestness against the Sioux, even to their extermination, men, women and children . . . during an assault, the soldiers cannot pause to distinguish between male and female, or even discriminate as to age." As Patrick Wolfe has noted, the peculiarity of settler colonialism is that the goal is elimination of Indigenous populations in order to make land available to settlers. That project is not limited to government policy, but rather involves all kinds of agencies, voluntary militias, and the settlers themselves acting on their own.

In the wake of the US 1950s termination and relocation policies, a pan-Indigenous movement arose in tandem with the powerful African American civil rights movement and the broad-based social justice and antiwar movements of the 1960s. The Indigenous rights movement succeeded in reversing the US termination policy. However, repression, armed attacks, and legislative attempts to undo treaty rights began again in the late 1970s, giving rise to the international Indigenous movement, which greatly broadened the support for Indigenous sovereignty and territorial rights in the United States.

The early twenty-first century has seen increased exploitation of energy resources begetting new pressures on Indigenous lands. Exploitation by the largest corporations, often in collusion with politicians at local, state, and federal levels, and even within some Indigenous governments, could spell a final demise for Indigenous land bases and resources. Strengthening Indigenous sovereignty and self-determination to prevent that result will take general public outrage and demand, which in turn will require that the general population, those descended from settlers and immigrants, know their history and assume responsibility. Resistance to these powerful corporate forces continues to have profound implications for US socioeconomic and political development and the future.

These are more than five hundred federally recognized Indigenous communities and nations, comprising nearly three million people in the United States. These are the descendants of the fifteen million original inhabitants of the land, the majority of whom were farmers who lived in towns. The US establishment of a system of Indian reservations stemmed from a long British colonial practice in the Americas. In the era of US treaty-making from independence to 1871, the concept of the reservation was one of the Indigenous nation reserving a narrowed land base from a much larger one in exchange for US government protection from settlers and the provision of social service. In the late nineteenth century, as Indigenous resistance was weakened, the concept of the reservation changed to one of land being carved out of the public domain of the United States as a benevolent gesture, a "gift" to the Indigenous peoples. Rhetoric changed so that reservations were said to have been "given" or "created" for Indians. With this shift, Indian reservations came to be seen as enclaves within state boundaries. Despite the political and economic reality, the impression to many was that Indigenous people were taking a free ride on public domain.

Beyond the land bases within the limits of the 310 federally recognized reservations—among 554 Indigenous groups—Indigenous land, water, and resource rights extend to all federally acknowledged Indigenous communities within the borders of the United States. This is the case whether "within the original or subsequently acquired territory thereof, and whether within or without the limits of a state," and includes all allotments as well as rights-of-way running to and from them. Not all the federally recognized Indigenous nations have land bases beyond government buildings, and the lands of some Native nations, including those of the Sioux in the Dakotas and Minnesota and the Ojibwes in Minnesota, have been parcelled into multiple reservations, while some fifty Indigenous nations that had been removed to Oklahoma were entirely allotted—divided by the federal government into individual Native-owned parcels. . . .

As a result of federal land sales, seizures, and allotments, most reservations are severely fragmented. Each parcel of tribal, trust, and privately held land is a separate enclave under multiple laws and jurisdictions. The Diné (Navajo) Nation has the largest contemporary contiguous land base among Native nations: nearly sixteen million acres, or nearly twenty-five thousand square miles, the size of West Virginia. Each of twelve other reservations is larger than Rhode Island, which comprises nearly eight hundred thousand acres, or twelve hundred square miles, and each of nine other reservations is larger than Delaware, which covers nearly a million and a half acres, or two thousand square miles. Other reservations have land bases of fewer than thirty-two thousand acres, or fifty square miles. A number of independent nations-states with seats in the United Nations have less territory and smaller populations than some Indigenous nations of North America.

Following World War II, the United States was at war with much of the world, just as it was at war with the Indigenous peoples of North America in the nineteenth century. This was total war, demanding that the enemy surrender unconditionally or face annihilation. Perhaps it was inevitable that the earlier wars against Indigenous people, if not acknowledged and repudiated, ultimately would include the world. According to the origin narrative, the United States was born of rebellion against oppression—against empire—and thus is the product of the first anticolonial revolution for national liberation. The narrative flows from that fallacy: the broadening and deepening of democracy; the Civil War and the ensuing "second revolution," which ended slavery; the twentieth-century mission to save Europe from itself—twice; and the ultimately triumphant fight against the scourge of communism, with the United States inheriting the difficult and burdensome task of keeping order in the world. It's a narrative of progress. The 1960s social revolutions, ignited by the African American liberation movement, complicated the origin narrative, but its structure and periodization have been left intact. . . .

The provincialism and national chauvinism of US history production make it difficult for effective revisions to gain authority. Scholars, both Indigenous and a few non-Indigenous, who attempt to rectify the distortions, are labelled advocates, and their findings are rejected for publication on that basis. Indigenous scholars look to research and thinking that has emerged in the rest of the European-colonized world. To understand the historical and current experiences of Indigenous peoples in the United States, these thinkers and writers draw upon and creatively apply the historical materialism of Marxism, the liberation theology of Latin America, Frantz Fanon's psychosocial analyses of the effects of colonialism on the colonizer and the colonized, and other approaches, including development theory and postmodern theory. While not abandoning insights gained from those sources, due to the "exceptional" nature of US colonialism among nineteenth-century colonial powers, Indigenous scholars and activists are engaged in exploring new approaches. . . .

12

The Possessive Investment in Whiteness

George Lipsitz

. . .

Whiteness is everywhere in U.S. culture, but it is very hard to see. As Richard Dyer suggests, "[W]hite power secures its dominance by seeming not to be anything in particular." As the unmarked category against which difference is constructed, whiteness never has to speak its name, never has to acknowledge its role as an organizing principle in social and cultural relations. To identify, analyze, and oppose the destructive consequences of whiteness, . . . requires an understanding of the existence and the destructive consequences of the possessive investment in whiteness that surreptitiously shapes so much of our public and private lives.

Race is a cultural construct, but one with sinister structural causes and consequences. Conscious and deliberate actions have institutionalized group identity in the United States, not just through the dissemination of cultural stories, but also through systematic efforts from colonial times to the present to create economic advantages through a possessive investment in whiteness for European Americans. Studies of culture too far removed from studies of social structure leave us with inadequate explanations for understanding racism and inadequate remedies for combating it.

Desire for slave labor encouraged European settlers in North America to view, first, Native Americans and, later, African Americans as racially inferior people suited "by nature" for the humiliating subordination of involuntary servitude. The long history of the possessive investment in whiteness stems in no small measure from the fact that all subsequent immigrants to North America have come to an already racialized society. From the start, European settlers in North America established structures encouraging a possessive investment in whiteness. The colonial and early national legal systems authorized attacks on Native Americans and encouraged the appropriation of their lands. They legitimated racialized chattel slavery, limited naturalized citizenship to "white" immigrants, identified Asian immigrants as expressly unwelcome (through legislation aimed at immigrants from China in 1882, from India in 1917, from Japan in 1924, and from the Philippines in 1934), and provided pretexts for restricting the voting, exploiting the labor, and seizing the property of Asian Americans, Mexican Americans, Native Americans, and African Americans.

The possessive investment in whiteness is not a simple matter of black and white; all racialized minority groups have suffered from it, albeit to different degrees and in different ways. The African slave trade began in earnest only after large-scale Native American slavery proved impractical in North America. The abolition of slavery led to the importation of low-wage labor from Asia. Legislation banning immigration from Asia set the stage for the recruitment of low-wage labor from Mexico. The new racial categories that emerged in each of these eras all revolved around applying racial labels to "nonwhite" groups in order to stigmatize and exploit them while at the same time preserving the value of whiteness.

Although reproduced in new form in every era, the possessive investment in whiteness has always been influenced by its origins in the racialized history of the United States—by its legacy of slavery and segregation, of "Indian" extermination and immigrant restriction, of conquest and colonialism. Although slavery has existed in many countries without any particular racial dimensions to it, the slave system that emerged in North America soon took on distinctly racial forms. Africans enslaved in North America faced a racialized system of power that reserved permanent, hereditary, chattel slavery for black people. White settlers institutionalized a possessive investment in whiteness by making blackness synonymous with slavery and whiteness synonymous with freedom, but also by pitting people of color against one another. Fearful of alliances between Native Americans and African Americans that might challenge the prerogatives of whiteness, white settlers prohibited slaves and free blacks from traveling in "Indian country." European Americans used diplomacy and force to compel Native Americans to return runaway slaves to their white masters. During the Stono Rebellion of 1739, colonial authorities offered Native Americans a bounty for every rebellious slave they captured or killed. At the same time, British settlers recruited black slaves to fight against Native Americans within colonial militias. The power of whiteness depended not only on white hegemony over separate racialized groups, but also on manipulating racial outsiders to fight against one another, to compete with each other for white approval, and to seek the rewards and privileges of whiteness for themselves at the expense of other racialized populations.

. . .

Yet today the possessive investment is not simply the residue of conquest and colonialism, of slavery and segregation, of immigrant exclusion and "Indian" extermination. Contemporary whiteness and its rewards have been created and recreated by policies adopted long after the emancipation of slaves in the 1860s and even after the outlawing of *de jure* segregation in the 1960s. There has always been racism in the United States, but it has not always been the same racism. Political and cultural struggles over power have shaped the contours and dimensions of racism differently in different eras. Antiracist mobilizations during the Civil War and civil rights eras meaningfully curtailed the reach and scope of white supremacy, but in each case reactionary forces engineered a renewal of racism, albeit in new forms, during succeeding decades. Racism has changed over time, taking on different forms and serving different social purposes in each time period.

Contemporary racism has been created anew in many ways over the past five decades, but most dramatically by the putatively race-neutral, liberal, social democratic reforms of the New Deal Era and by the more overtly race-conscious neoconservative reactions against liberalism since the Nixon years. It is a mistake to posit a gradual and inevitable trajectory of evolutionary progress in race relations; on the contrary, our history shows that battles won at one moment can later be lost. Despite hard-fought battles for change that secured important concessions during the 1960s in the form of civil rights legislation, the racialized nature of social policy in the United States since the Great Depression has actually increased the possessive investment in whiteness among European Americans over the past half century.

During the New Deal Era of the 1930s and 1940s, both the Wagner Act and the Social Security Act excluded farm workers and domestics from coverage, effectively denying those disproportionately minority sectors of the work force protections and benefits routinely afforded whites. The Federal Housing Act of 1934 brought home ownership within reach of millions of citizens by placing the credit of the federal government behind private lending to home buyers, but overtly racist categories in the Federal Housing Agency's (FHA) "confidential" city surveys and appraisers' manuals channeled almost all of the loan money toward whites and away from communities of color. In the post-World War II era, trade unions negotiated contract provisions giving private medical insurance, pensions, and job security largely to the white workers who formed the overwhelming majority of the unionized work force in mass production industries, rather than fighting for full employment, medical care, and old-age pensions for all, or even for an end to discriminatory hiring and promotion practices by employers in those industries.

Each of these policies widened the gap between the resources available to whites and those available to aggrieved racial communities. Federal housing policy offers an important illustration of the broader principles at work in the possessive investment in whiteness. By channeling loans away from older inner-city neighborhoods and toward white home buyers moving into segregated suburbs, the FHA and private lenders after World War II aided and abetted segregation in U.S. residential neighborhoods. . . .

The federal government has played a major role in augmenting the possessive investment in whiteness. For years, the General Services Administration routinely channeled the government's own rental and leasing business to realtors who engaged in racial discrimination, while federally subsidized urban renewal plans reduced the already limited supply of housing for communities of color through "slum clearance" programs. In concert with FHA support for segregation in the suburbs, federal and state tax monies routinely funded the construction of water supplies and sewage facilities for racially exclusive suburban communities in the 1940s and 1950s. . . .

At the same time that FHA loans and federal highway building projects subsidized the growth of segregated suburbs, urban renewal programs in cities throughout the country devastated minority neighborhoods. During the 1950s and 1960s, federally assisted urban renewal projects destroyed 20 percent of the central-city housing units occupied by blacks, as opposed to only 10 percent of those inhabited by whites. More than 60 percent of those displaced by urban renewal were African Americans, Puerto Ricans, Mexican Americans, or members of other minority racial groups. The Federal Housing Administration and the Veterans Administration financed more than $120 billion worth of new housing between 1934 and 1962, but less than 2 percent of this real estate was available to nonwhite families—and most of that small amount was located in segregated areas.

Even in the 1970s, after most major urban renewal programs had been completed, black central-city residents continued to lose housing units at a rate equal to 80 percent of what had been lost in the 1960s. Yet white displacement declined to the relatively low levels of the 1950s. In addition, the refusal first to pass, then to enforce, fair housing laws has enabled realtors, buyers, and sellers to profit from racist collusion against minorities largely without fear of legal retribution. During the decades following World War II, urban renewal helped construct a new "white" identity in the suburbs by helping to destroy ethnically specific European American urban inner-city neighborhoods. Wrecking balls and bulldozers eliminated some of these sites, while others were transformed by an influx of minority residents desperately competing for a declining supply of affordable housing units. As increasing numbers of racial minorities moved into cities, increasing numbers of European American ethnics moved out. Consequently, ethnic differences among whites became a less important dividing line in U.S. culture, while race became more important. The suburbs helped turn Euro-Americans into "whites" who could live near each other and intermarry with relatively little difficulty. But this "white" unity rested on residential segregation, on shared access to housing and life chances largely unavailable to communities of color.

. . .

In 1968, lobbyists for the banking industry helped draft the Housing and Urban Development Act, which allowed private lenders to shift the risks of financing low-income housing to the government, creating a lucrative and thoroughly unregulated market for themselves. One section of the 1968 bill authorized FHA mortgages for inner-city areas that did not meet the usual eligibility criteria, and another section subsidized interest payments by low-income families. If administered wisely, these provisions might have promoted fair housing goals, but FHA administrators deployed them in ways that actually promoted segregation in order to provide banks, brokers, lenders, developers, realtors, and speculators with windfall profits. As a U.S. Commission on Civil Rights investigation later revealed, FHA officials collaborated with blockbusters in financing the flight of low-income whites out of inner-city neighborhoods, and then aided unscrupulous realtors and speculators by arranging purchases of substandard housing by minorities desperate to own their own homes. The resulting sales and mortgage foreclosures brought great profits to lenders (almost all of them white), but their actions led to price fixing and a subsequent inflation of housing costs in the inner city by more than 200 percent between 1968 and 1972. Bankers then foreclosed on the mortgages of thousands of these uninspected and substandard homes, ruining many inner-city neighborhoods. In response, the Department of Housing and Urban Development essentially red-lined inner cities, making them ineligible for future loans, a decision that destroyed the value of inner-city housing for generations to come.

Federally funded highways designed to connect suburban commuters with downtown places of employment also destroyed already scarce housing in minority communities and often disrupted neighborhood life as well. Construction of the Harbor Freeway in Los Angeles, the Gulf Freeway in Houston, and the Mark Twain Freeway in St. Louis displaced thousands of residents and bisected neighborhoods, shopping districts, and political precincts. The processes of urban renewal and highway construction set in motion a vicious cycle: population loss led to decreased political power, which made minority neighborhoods more vulnerable to further urban renewal and freeway construction, not to mention more susceptible to the placement of prisons, incinerators, toxic waste dumps, and other projects that further depopulated these areas.

. . .

Minorities are less likely than whites to receive preventive medical care or costly operations from Medicare. Eligible members of minority communities are also less likely than European Americans to apply for food stamps. The labor of migrant farm workers from aggrieved racialized groups plays a vital role in providing adequate nutrition for others, but the farm workers and their children suffer disproportionately from health disorders caused by malnutrition. In her important research on health policy and ethnic diversity, Linda Wray concludes that "the lower life expectancies for many ethnic minority groups and subgroups stem largely from their disproportionately higher rates of poverty, malnutrition, and poor health care."

Just as residential segregation and urban renewal make minority communities disproportionately susceptible to health hazards, their physical and social location gives these communities a different relationship to the criminal justice system. A 1990 study by the National Institute on Drug Abuse revealed that while only 15 percent of the thirteen million habitual drug users in the United States were black and 77 percent were white, African Americans were four times more likely to be arrested on drug charges than whites in the nation as a whole, and seven to nine times more likely in Pennsylvania, Michigan, Illinois, Florida, Massachusetts, and New Jersey. A 1989 study by the Parents' Resource Institute for Drug Education discovered that African American high school students consistently showed lower levels of drug and alcohol use than their European American counterparts, even in high schools populated by residents of low-income housing projects. Yet, while comprising about 12 percent of the U.S. population, blacks accounted for 10 percent of drug arrests in 1984, 40 percent in 1988, and 42 percent in 1990. In addition, white drug defendants receive considerably shorter average prison terms than African Americans convicted of comparable crimes. A U.S. Sentencing Commission study found in 1992 that half of the federal court districts that handled cases involving crack cocaine prosecuted minority defendants *exclusively*. A *Los Angeles Times* article in 1995 revealed that "black and Latino crack dealers are hammered with 10-year mandatory federal sentences while whites prosecuted in state court face a minimum of five years and often receive no more than a year in jail." Alexander Lichtenstein and Michael A. Kroll point out that sentences for African Americans in the federal prison system are 20 percent longer than those given to whites who commit the same crimes. They observe that if blacks received the same sentences as whites for these offenses, the federal prison system would require three thousand fewer prison cells, enough to close completely six of the new five-hundred bed institutions.

Racial animus on the part of police officers, prosecutors, and judges accounts for only a small portion of the distinctive experience that racial minorities have with the criminal justice system. Economic devastation makes the drug trade appealing to some people in the inner city, while the dearth of capital in minority neighborhoods curtails opportunities for other kinds of employment. Deindustrialization, unemployment, and lack of intergenerational transfers of wealth undermine parental and adult authority in many neighborhoods. The complex factors that cause people to turn to drugs are no more prevalent in minority communities than elsewhere, but these communities and their inhabitants face more stress while having fewer opportunities to receive private counseling and treatment for their problems.

The structural weaknesses of minority neighborhoods caused by discrimination in housing, education, and hiring also play a crucial role in relations between inner-city residents and the criminal justice system. Cocaine dealing, which initially skyrocketed among white suburban residents, was driven into the inner city by escalating enforcement pressures in wealthy white communities. Ghettos and barrios became distribution centers for the sale of drugs to white suburbanites. Former New York and Houston police commissioner Lee Brown, head of the federal government's antidrug efforts during the early years of the Clinton presidency and later mayor of Houston, noted, "There are those who bring drugs into the country. That's not the black community. Then you have wholesalers, those who distribute them once they get here, and as a rule that's not the black community. Where you find the blacks is in the street dealing."

You also find blacks and other minorities in prison. Police officers in large cities, pressured to show results in the drive against drugs, lack the resources to effectively enforce the law everywhere (in part because of the social costs of deindustrialization and the tax limitation initiatives designed to shrink the size of government). These officers know that it is easier to make arrests and to secure convictions by confronting drug users in areas that have conspicuous street corner sales, that have more people out on the street with no place to go, and that have residents more likely to plead guilty and less likely to secure the services of attorneys who can get the charges against them dropped, reduced, or wiped off the books with subsequent successful counseling and rehabilitation. In addition, politicians supported by the public relations efforts of neoconservative foundations often portray themselves to suburban voters as opponents of the "dangerous classes" in the inner cities.

Minority disadvantages craft advantages for others. Urban renewal failed to provide new housing for the poor, but it played an important role in transforming the U.S. urban economy from one that relied on factory production to one driven by producer services. Urban renewal projects subsidized the development of downtown office centers on previously residential land, and they frequently created buffer zones of empty blocks dividing poor neighborhoods from new shopping centers designed for affluent commuters. To help cities compete for corporate investment by making them appealing to high-level executives, federal urban aid favored construction of luxury housing units and cultural centers like symphony halls and art museums over affordable housing for workers. Tax abatements granted to these producer services centers further aggravated the fiscal crisis that cities faced, leading to tax increases on existing industries, businesses, and residences.

. . .

When housing prices increased dramatically during the 1970s, white homeowners who had been able to take advantage of discriminatory FHA financing policies in the past realized increased equity in their homes, while those excluded from the housing market by earlier policies found themselves facing even higher costs of entry into the market in addition to the traditional obstacles presented by the discriminatory practices of sellers, realtors, and lenders. The contrast between European Americans and African Americans is instructive in this regard. Because whites have access to broader housing choices than blacks, whites pay 15 percent less than blacks for similar housing in the same neighborhood. White neighborhoods typically experience housing costs 25 percent lower than would be the case if the residents were black.

. . .

When confronted with evidence of systematic racial bias in home lending, defenders of the possessive investment in whiteness argue that the disproportionate share of loan denials to members of minority groups stems not from discrimination, but from the low net worth of minority applicants, even those who have high incomes. This might seem a reasonable position, but net worth is almost totally determined by past opportunities for asset accumulation, and therefore is the one figure most likely to reflect the history of discrimination. Minorities are told, in essence, "We can't give you a loan today because we've discriminated against members of your race so effectively in the past that you have not been able to accumulate any equity from housing and to pass it down through the generations."

Most white families have acquired their net worth from the appreciation of property that they secured under conditions of special privilege in a discriminatory housing market. In their prize-winning book *Black Wealth/White Wealth*, Melvin Oliver and Thomas Shapiro demonstrate how the history of housing discrimination makes white parents more able to borrow funds for their children's college education or to loan money to their children to enter the housing market. In addition, much discrimination in home lending is not based on considerations of net worth; it stems from decisions made by white banking officials based on their stereotypes about minority communities. The Federal Reserve Bank of Boston study showed that black and Latino mortgage applicants are 60 percent more likely to be turned down for loans than whites, even after controlling for employment, financial, and neighborhood characteristics. . . .

Yet bankers also make money from the ways in which discrimination creates artificial scarcities in the market. Minorities have to pay more for housing because much of the market is off limits to them. Blockbusters profit from exploiting white fears and provoking them into panic selling. Minority home owners denied loans in mainstream banks often turn to exploitative lenders who make "low end" loans at enormously high interest rates. If they fail to pay back these loans, regular banks can acquire the property cheaply and charge someone else exorbitant interest for a loan on the same property.

. . .

The policies of neoconservatives in the Reagan and Bush administrations during the 1980s and 1990s greatly exacerbated the racialized aspects of more than fifty years of these social welfare policies. Regressive policies that cut federal aid to education and refused to challenge segregated education, housing, and hiring, as well as the cynical cultivation of an antiblack consensus through attacks on affirmative action and voting rights legislation clearly reinforced possessive investments in whiteness. In the U.S. economy, where 86 percent of available jobs do not appear in classified ads and where personal connections prove the most important factor in securing employment, attacks on affirmative action guarantee that whites will be rewarded for their historical advantage in the labor market rather than for their individual abilities or efforts.

. . .

Yet even seemingly race-neutral policies supported by both neoconservatives and liberals in the 1980s and 1990s have increased the absolute value of being white. In the 1980s, changes in federal tax laws decreased the value of wage income and increased the value of investment income—a move harmful to minorities, who suffer from a gap between their total wealth and that of whites even greater than the disparity between their income and white income. The failure to raise the minimum wage between 1981 and 1989 and the decline of more than one-third in the value of Aid to Families with Dependent Children (AFDC) payments injured all poor people, but they exacted special costs on nonwhites, who faced even more constricted markets for employment, housing, and education than poor whites.

Similarly, the "tax reforms" of the 1980s made the effective rate of taxation higher on investment in actual goods and services than on profits from speculative enterprises. This change encouraged the flight of capital from industrial production with its many employment opportunities toward investments that can be turned over quickly to allow the greatest possible tax write-offs. Government policies thus discouraged investments that might produce high-paying jobs and encouraged investors to strip companies of their assets to make rapid short-term profits. These policies hurt almost all workers, but they fell particularly heavily on minority workers, who because of employment discrimination in the retail and small business sectors were overrepresented in blue-collar industrial jobs.

. . .

Subsidies to the private sector by government agencies also tend to enhance the rewards of past discrimination. Throughout the country, tax increment financing for redevelopment programs offers tax-free and low-interest loans to developers whose projects use public services, often without having to pay taxes to local school boards or country governments. In St. Louis, for example, tax abatements for wealthy corporations deprive the city's schools (and their majority African American population) of $17 million a year. Even if these redevelopment projects eventually succeed in increasing municipal revenues through sales and earnings taxes, their proceeds go to funds that pay for the increased services these developments demand (fire and police protection, roads, sewers, electricity, lighting, etc.) rather than to school funds, which are dependent upon property tax revenues. Nationwide, industrial development bonds resulted in a $7.4 billion tax loss in 1983, which ordinary taxpayers had to make up through increased payroll taxes. Compared to white Americans, people of color, more likely to be poor or working class, suffer disproportionately from these changes as taxpayers, as workers, and as tenants. A study by the Citizens for Tax Justice found that wealthy Californians spend less than eleven cents in taxes for every dollar earned, while poor residents of the state pay fourteen cents out of every dollar in taxes. As groups overrepresented among the poor, minorities have been forced to subsidize the tax breaks given to the wealthy. While holding property tax assessments for businesses and some home owners to about half of their market value, California's Proposition 13 deprived cities and counties of $13 billion a year in taxes. Businesses alone avoided $3.3 billion to $8.6 billion in taxes per year under this statute.

Because they are ignorant of even the recent history of the possessive investment in whiteness—generated by slavery and segregation, immigrant exclusion and Native American policy, conquest and colonialism, but augmented by liberal and conservative social policies as well—Americans produce largely cultural explanations for structural social problems. The increased possessive investment in whiteness generated by disinvestment in U.S. cities, factories, and schools since the 1970s disguises as *racial* problems the general social problems posed by deindustrialization, economic restructuring, and neoconservative attacks on the welfare state. It fuels a discourse that demonizes people of color for being victimized by these changes, while hiding the privileges of whiteness by attributing the economic advantages enjoyed by whites to their family values, faith in fatherhood, and foresight—rather than to the favoritism they enjoy through their possessive investment in whiteness.

. . .

Yet public opinion polls of white Americans reflect little recognition of these devastating changes. Seventy percent of whites in one poll said that African Americans "have the same opportunities to live a middle-class life as whites," and nearly three-fourths of white respondents to a 1989 poll believed that opportunities for blacks had improved under Reagan. If such optimism about the opportunities available to African Americans does not demonstrate ignorance of the dire conditions facing black communities, it indicates that many whites believe that blacks suffer deservedly, because they do not take advantage of the opportunities offered them. In opinion polls, favorable assessments of black chances for success often accompanied extremely negative judgments about the abilities, work habits, and character of black people. A National Opinion Research Report in 1990 disclosed that more than 50 percent of U.S. whites viewed blacks as innately lazy and less intelligent and less patriotic than whites. More than 60 percent said that they believed that blacks suffer from poor housing and employment opportunities because of their own lack of will power. Some 56.3 percent said that blacks preferred welfare to employment, while 44.6 percent contended that blacks tended toward laziness. Even more important, research by Mary Edsall and Thomas Byrne Edsall indicates that many whites structure nearly all of their decisions about housing, education, and politics in response to their aversions to black people.

. . .

. . . As long as we define social life as the sum total of conscious and deliberative individual activities, we will be able to discern as racist only *individual* manifestations of personal prejudice and hostility. Systemic, collective, and coordinated group behavior consequently drops out of sight. Collective exercises of power that relentlessly channel rewards, resources, and opportunities from one group to another will not appear "racist" from this perspective, because they rarely announce their intention to discriminate against individuals. Yet they nonetheless give racial identities their sinister social meaning by giving people from different races vastly different life chances.

The gap between white perception and minority experience can have explosive consequences. Little more than a year after the 1992 Los Angeles rebellion, a sixteen-year-old high school junior shared her opinions with a reporter from the *Los Angeles Times*. "I don't think white people owe anything to black people," she explained. "We didn't sell them into slavery, it was our ancestors. What they did was wrong, but we've done our best to make up for it." A seventeen-year-old senior echoed those comments, telling the reporter, "I feel we spend more time in my history class talking about what whites owe blacks than just about anything else when the issue of slavery comes up. I often received dirty looks. This seems strange given that I wasn't even alive then. And the few members of my family from that time didn't have the luxury of owning much, let alone slaves. So why, I ask you, am I constantly made to feel guilty?"

More ominously, after pleading guilty to bombing two homes and one car, vandalizing a synagogue, and attempting to start a race war by planning the murder of Rodney King and the bombing of Los Angeles's First African Methodist Episcopal Church, twenty-year-old Christopher David Fisher explained that "sometimes whites were picked on because of the color of their skin. . . . Maybe we're blamed for slavery." Fisher's actions were certainly extreme, but his justification of them drew knowingly and precisely on a broadly shared narrative about the victimization of "innocent" whites by irrational and ungrateful minorities.

The comments and questions raised about the legacy of slavery by these young whites illuminate broader currents in our culture, with enormous implications for understanding the enduring significance of race in our country. These young people associate black grievances solely with slavery, and they express irritation at what they perceive as efforts to make them feel guilty or unduly privileged because of things that happened in the distant past. The claim that one's own family did not own any slaves is frequently voiced in our culture. It is almost never followed with a statement to the effect that of course some people's families did own slaves and we will not rest until we track them down and make them pay reparations. This view never acknowledges how the existence of slavery and the exploitation of black labor after emancipation created opportunities from which immigrants and others benefited, even if they did not personally own slaves. Rather, it seems to hold that, because not all white people owned slaves, no white people can be held accountable or inconvenienced by the legacy of slavery. More important, having dispensed with slavery, they feel no need to address the histories of Jim Crow segregation, racialized social policies, urban renewal, or the revived racism of contemporary neoconservatism. On the contrary, Fisher felt that his discomfort with being "picked on" and "blamed" for slavery gave him good reason to bomb homes, deface synagogues, and plot to kill black people.

Unfortunately for our society, these young whites accurately reflect the logic of the language of liberal individualism and its ideological predispositions in discussions of race. In their apparent ignorance of the disciplined, systemic, and collective *group* activity that has structured white identities in U.S. history, they are in good company. In a 1979 law journal article, future Supreme Court justice Antonin Scalia argued that affirmative action "is based upon concepts of racial indebtedness and racial entitlement rather than individual worth and individual need" and is thus "racist." Yet liberal individualism is not completely color-blind on this issue. As Cheryl I. Harris demonstrates, the legacy of liberal individualism has not prevented the Supreme Court from recognizing and protecting the group interests of *whites* in the Bakke, Croson, and Wygant cases. In each case, the Court nullified affirmative action programs because they judged efforts to help blacks as harmful to whites: to white expectations of entitlement, expectations based on the possessive investment in whiteness they held as members of a group. In the Bakke case, for instance, where the plaintiff argued that medical school affirmative action programs disadvantaged white applicants like himself, neither Bakke nor the Court contested the legitimacy of medical school admissions standards that reserved five seats in each class for children of wealthy donors to the university or that penalized Bakke for being older than most of the other applicants. . . . But they did challenge and reject a policy designed to offset the effects of past and present discrimination when they could construe the medical school admission policies as detrimental to the interests of whites as a group—and as a consequence they applied the "strict scrutiny" standard to protect whites while denying that protection to people of color. In this case, as in so many others, the language of liberal individualism serves as a cover for co-ordinated collective group interests.

. . .

. . . But an explicitly antiracist interethnic movement that acknowledges the existence
and power of whiteness might make some important changes. Antiracist coalitions also
have a long history in the United States—in the political activism of John Brown, Sojourner
Truth, and the Magon brothers among others, but also in our rich cultural tradition of
interethnic antiracism connected to civil rights activism. . . . These all too infrequent but
nonetheless important efforts by whites to fight racism, not out of sympathy for someone
else but out of a sense of self-respect and simple justice, have never completely disappeared; they remain available as models for the present.

. . .

13

Heteropatriarchy and the Three Pillars
of White Supremacy

Rethinking Women of Color Organizing

Andrea Smith

Scenario #1

A group of women of color come together to organize. An argument ensues about whether
or not Arab women should be included. Some argue that Arab women are "white" since
they have been classified as such in the US census. Another argument erupts over whether
or not Latinas qualify as "women of color," since some may be classified as "white" in their
Latin American countries of origin and/or "pass" as white in the United States.

Scenario #2

In a discussion on racism, some people argue that Native peoples suffer from less racism
than other people of color because they generally do not reside in segregated neighborhoods within the United States. In addition, some argue that since tribes now have gaming,
Native peoples are no longer "oppressed."

Scenario #3

A multiracial campaign develops involving diverse communities of color in which some
participants charge that we must stop the black/white binary, and end Black hegemony
over people of color politics to develop a more "multicultural" framework. However, this
campaign continues to rely on strategies and cultural motifs developed by the Black Civil
Rights struggle in the United States.

These incidents, which happen quite frequently in "women of color" or "people of color"
political organizing struggles, are often explained as a consequence of "oppression olympics." . . . In this essay, I want to argue that these incidents are not so much the result of
"oppression olympics" but are more about how we have inadequately framed "women of

color" or "people of color" politics. . . . [T]he premise behind much "women of color" organizing is that women from communities victimized by white supremacy should unite together around their shared oppression. . . .

This framework has proven to be limited for women of color and people of color organizing. First, it tends to presume that our communities have been impacted by white supremacy in the same way. Consequently, we often assume that all of our communities will share similar strategies for liberation. In fact, however, our strategies often run into conflict. For example, one strategy that many people in US-born communities of color adopt, in order to advance economically out of impoverished communities, is to join the military. We then become complicit in oppressing and colonizing communities from other countries. Meanwhile, people from other countries often adopt the strategy of moving to the United States to advance economically, without considering their complicity in settling on the lands of indigenous peoples that are being colonized by the United States.

Consequently, it may be more helpful to adopt an alternative framework for women of color and people of color organizing. I call one such framework the "Three Pillars of White Supremacy." This framework does not assume that racism and white supremacy is enacted in a singular fashion; rather, white supremacy is constituted by separate and distinct, but still interrelated, logics. . . .

SLAVERY/CAPITALISM

One pillar of white supremacy is the logic of slavery. As Sora Han, Jared Sexton, and Angela P. Harris note, this logic renders Black people as inherently slaveable—as nothing more than property. That is, in this logic of white supremacy Blackness becomes equated with slaveability. The forms of slavery may change—whether it is through the formal system of slavery, sharecropping, or through the current prison industrial complex—but the logic itself has remained consistent.

This logic is the anchor of capitalism. . . . To keep this capitalist system in place—which ultimately commodifies most people—the logic of slavery applies a racial hierarchy to this system. . . . This helps people who are not Black to accept their lot in life, because they can feel that at least they are not at the very bottom of the racial hierarchy—at least they are not property; at least they are not slaveable.

The logic of slavery can be seen clearly in the current prison industrial complex (PIC). While the PIC generally incarcerates communities of color, it seems to be structured primarily on an anti-Black racism. . . . [P]rior to the Civil War, most people in prison were white. However, after the thirteenth amendment was passed—which banned slavery, except for those in prison—Black people previously enslaved through the slavery system were reenslaved through the prison system. Black people who had been the property of slave owners became state property, through the . . . [convict] leasing system. Thus, we can actually look at the criminalization of Blackness as a logical extension of Blackness as property.

GENOCIDE/COLONIALISM

A second pillar of white supremacy is the logic of genocide. This logic holds that indigenous peoples must disappear. In fact, they must *always* be disappearing, in order to allow non-indigenous peoples rightful claim over this land. Through this logic of genocide, non-Native peoples then become the rightful inheritors of all that was indigenous—land, resources, indigenous spirituality, or culture. As Kare Shanley notes, Native peoples are a permanent "present absence" in the US colonial imagination, an "absence" that reinforces, at every turn, the conviction that Native peoples are indeed vanishing and that the conquest of Native lands is justified. Ella Shoat and Robert Stam describe this absence as "an ambivalently repressive mechanism [which] dispels the anxiety in the face of the Indian, whose very presence is a reminder of the initially precarious grounding of the American nation state itself. . . . In a temporal paradox, living Indians were induced to 'play dead,' as it were, in order to perform a narrative of manifest destiny in which their role, ultimately, was to disappear."

Rayna Green further elaborates . . . "The living performance of 'playing Indian' by non-Indian peoples depends upon the physical and psychological removal, even the death, of real Indians. In that sense, the performance, purportedly often done out of a stated and implicit love for Indians, is really the obverse of another well-known cultural phenomenon, 'Indian hating,' as most often expressed in another, deadly performance genre called 'genocide'" (Green, 1988). After all, why would non-Native peoples need to play Indian—which often includes acts of spiritual appropriation and land theft—if they thought Indians were still alive and perfectly capable of being Indian themselves? The pillar of genocide serves as the anchor for colonialism—it is what allows non-Native peoples to feel they can rightfully own indigenous peoples' land. It is okay to take land from indigenous peoples, because indigenous peoples have disappeared.

ORIENTALISM/WAR

A third pillar of white supremacy is the logic of Orientalism. Orientalism was defined by Edward Said as the process of the West defining itself as a superior civilization by constructing itself in opposition to an "exotic" but inferior "Orient." . . . The logic of Orientalism marks certain peoples or nations as inferior and as posing a constant threat to the well-being of empire. These peoples are still seen as "civilizations"—they are not property or "disappeared"—however, they will always be imaged as permanent foreign threats to empire. This logic is evident in the anti-immigration movements within the United States that target immigrants of color. It does not matter how long immigrants of color reside in the United States, they generally become targeted as foreign threats, particularly during war time. Consequently, Orientalism serves as the anchor for war, because it allows the United States to justify being in a constant state of war to protect itself from its enemies.

For example, the United States feels entitled to use Orientalist logic to justify racial profiling of Arab Americans so that it can be strong enough to fight the "war on terror." Orientalism also allows the United States to defend the logics of slavery and genocide, as these practices enable the United States to stay "strong enough" to fight these constant wars. . . . For the system of white supremacy to stay in place, the United States must always be at war.

Because we are situated within different logics of white supremacy, we may misunderstand a racial dynamic if we simplistically try to explain one logic of white supremacy with another logic. For instance, think about the first scenario that opens this essay: if we simply dismiss Latino/as or Arab peoples as "white," we fail to understand how a racial logic of Orientalism is in operation. . . . Latino/as and Arabs are often situated in a racial hierarchy that privileges them over Black people. However, while Orientalist logic may bestow them some racial privilege, they are still cast as inferior yet threatening "civilizations" in the United States. Their privilege is not a signal that they will be assimilated, but that they will be marked as perpetual foreign threats to the US world order.

ORGANIZING IMPLICATIONS

Under the old but still potent and dominant model, people of color organizing was based on the notion of organizing around shared victimhood. In this model, however, we see that we are victims of white supremacy, but complicit in it as well. Our survival strategies and resistance to white supremacy are set by the system of white supremacy itself. What keeps us trapped within our particular pillars of white supremacy is that we are seduced with the prospect of being able to participate in the other pillars. For example, all non-Native peoples are promised the ability to join in the colonial project of settling indigenous lands. All non-Black peoples are promised that if they comply, they will not be at the bottom of the racial hierarchy. And Black, Native, Latino, and Asian peoples are promised that they will economically and politically advance if they join US wars to spread "democracy." Thus, people of color organizing must be premised on making strategic alliances with each other, based on where we are situated within the larger political economy. . . . [F]or example, Native peoples who are organizing against the colonial and genocidal practices committed by the US government will be more effective in their struggle if they also organize against US militarism, particularly the military recruitment of indigenous peoples to support US imperial wars. If we try to end US colonial practices at home, but support US empire by joining the military, we are strengthening the state's ability to carry out genocidal policies against people of color here and all over the world.

. . . These approaches might help us to develop resistance strategies that do not inadvertently keep the system in place for all of us, and keep all of us accountable. In all of these cases, we would check our aspirations against the aspirations of other communities to ensure that our model of liberation does not become the model of oppression for others.

These practices require us to be more vigilant in how we may have internalized some of these logics in our own organizing practice. For instance, much racial justice organizing within the United States has rested on a civil rights framework that fights for equality under the law. An assumption behind this organizing is that the United States is a democracy with some flaws, but is otherwise admirable. Despite the fact that it rendered slaves three-fifths of a person, the US Constitution is presented as the model document from which to build a flourishing democracy. However, as Luana Ross notes, it has never been against US law to commit genocide against indigenous peoples—in fact, genocide *is* the law of the country. The United States could not exist without it. In the United States, democracy is actually the alibi for genocide—it is the practice that covers up United States colonial control over indigenous lands.

Our organizing can also reflect anti-Black racism. Recently, with the outgrowth of "multiculturalism" there have been calls to "go beyond the black/white binary" and include other communities of color in our analysis, as presented in the third scenario. There are a number of flaws with this analysis. First, it replaces an analysis of white supremacy with a politics of multicultural representation; if we just *include* more people, then our practice will be less racist. Not true. This model does not address the nuanced structure of white supremacy, such as through these distinct logics of slavery, genocide, and Orientalism. Second, it obscures the centrality of the slavery logic in the system of white supremacy, which is *based on a black/white binary*. The black/white binary is not the *only* binary which characterizes white supremacy, but it is still a central one that we cannot "go beyond" in our racial justice organizing efforts.

If we do not look at how the logic of slaveability inflects our society and our thinking, it will be evident in our work as well. For example, other communities of color often appropriate the cultural work and organizing strategies of African American civil rights or Black Power movements without corresponding assumptions that we should also be in solidarity with Black communities. We assume that this work is the common "property" of all oppressed groups, and we can appropriate it without being accountable

. . .

. . . Simply saying we need to move beyond the black/white binary (or perhaps, the "black/non-black" binary) in US racism obfuscates the racializing logic of slavery, and prevents us from seeing that this binary constitutes Blackness as the bottom of a color hierarchy. However, this is not the *only* binary that fundamentally constitutes white supremacy. There is also an indigenous/settler binary, where Native genocide is central to the logic of white supremacy and other non-indigenous people of color also form "a subsidiary" role. We also face another Orientalist logic that fundamentally constitutes Asians, Arabs, and Latino/as as foreign threats, requiring the United States to be at permanent war with these peoples. In this construction, Black and Native peoples play subsidiary roles.

Clearly the black/white binary is central to racial and political thought and practice in the United States, and any understanding of white supremacy must take it into consideration. However, if we look at only this binary, we may misread the dynamics of white supremacy in different contexts. . . . [C]ritical race theorist Cheryl Harris's analysis of whiteness as property reveals this weakness. In *Critical Race Theory*, Harris contends that whites have a property interest in the preservation of whiteness, and seek to deprive those who are "tainted" by Black or Indian blood from these same white property interests. Harris simply assumes that the positions of African Americans and American Indians are the same, failing to consider US policies of forced assimilation and forced whiteness on American Indians. These policies have become so entrenched that when Native peoples make political claims, they have been accused of being white. When Andrew Jackson removed the Cherokee along the Trail of Tears, he argued that those who did not want removal were really white. In contemporary times, when I was a non-violent witness for the Chippewa spearfishers in the late 1980s, one of the more frequent slurs whites hurled when the Chippewa attempted to exercise their treaty-protected right to fish was that they had white parents, or they were really white.

Status differences between Blacks and Natives are informed by the different economic positions African Americans and American Indians have in US society. African Americans have been traditionally valued for their labor, hence it is in the interest of the dominant society to have as many people marked "Black," as possible, thereby maintaining a cheap labor pool; by contrast, American Indians have been valued for the land base they occupy, so it is in the interest of dominant society to have as few people marked "Indian" as possible, facilitating access to Native lands. "Whiteness" operates differently under a logic of genocide than it does from a logic of slavery.

Another failure of US-based people of color in organizing is that we often fall back on a "US-centricism," believing that what is happening "over there" is less important than what is happening here. We fail to see how the United States maintains the system of oppression here precisely by tying our allegiances to the interests of US empire "over there."

HETEROPATRIARCHY AND WHITE SUPREMACY

Heteropatriarchy is the building block of US empire. In fact, it is the building block of the nation-state form of governance. . . . Christian Right activist and founder of Prison Fellowship Charles Colson makes the connection between homosexuality and the nation-state in his analysis of the war on terror, explaining that one of the causes of terrorism is same-sex marriage:

> Marriage is the traditional building block of human society, intended both to unite couples and bring children into the world . . . There is a natural moral order for the family . . . the family, led by a married mother and father, is the best available structure for both child-rearing and cultural health. Marriage is not a private institution designed solely for the individual gratification of its participants. If we fail to enact a Federal Marriage Amendment, we can expect not just more family breakdown, but also more criminals behind bars and more chaos in our streets.

Colson is linking the well-being of US empire to the well-being of the heteropatriarchal family. He continues:

> When radical Islamists see American women abusing Muslim men, as they did in the Abu Ghraib prison, and when they see news coverage of same-sex couples being "married" in US towns, we make this kind of freedom abhorrent—the kind they see as a blot on Allah's creation. We must preserve traditional marriage in order to protect the United States from those who would use our depravity to destroy us.

As Ann Burlein argues in *Lift High the Cross*, it may be a mistake to argue that the goal of Christian Right politics is to create a theocracy in the United States. Rather, Christian Right politics work through the private family (which is coded as white, patriarchal, and middle class) to create a "Christian America." She notes that the investment in the private family makes it difficult for people to invest in more public forms of social connection. In addition, investment in the suburban private family serves to mask the public disinvestment in urban areas that makes the suburban lifestyle possible. The social decay in urban areas that results from this disinvestment is then construed as the result of deviance from the Christian family ideal rather than as the result of political and economic forces. As former head of the Christian Coalition, Ralph Reed, states: "The only true solution to crime is to restore the family" (Reed, 1990). . . .

As I have argued elsewhere, in order to colonize peoples whose societies are not based on social hierarchy, colonizers must first naturalize hierarchy through instituting patriarchy. In turn, patriarchy rests on a gender binary system in which only two genders exist, one dominating the other. . . . Just as the patriarchs rule the family, the elites of the nation-state rule their citizens. Any liberation struggle that does not challenge heteronormativity cannot substantially challenge colonialism or white supremacy. . . . [S]uch struggles will maintain colonialism based on a politics of secondary marginalization where the most elite class of these groups will further their aspirations on the backs of those most marginalized within the community.

. . . [N]ational liberation politics become less vulnerable to being coopted by the Right when we base them on a model of liberation that fundamentally challenges right-wing conceptions of the nation. We need a model based on community relationships and on mutual respect.

CONCLUSION

Women of color–centered organizing points to the centrality of gender politics within antiracist, anticolonial struggles. Unfortunately, in our efforts to organize against white, Christian America, racial justice struggles often articulate an equally heteropatriarchal racial nationalism. This model of organizing either hopes to assimilate into white America, or to replicate it within an equally hierarchical and oppressive racial nationalism in which the elites of the community rule everyone else. Such struggles often call on the importance of preserving the "Black family" or the "Native family" as the bulwark of this nationalist project, the family being conceived of in capitalist and heteropatriarchal terms. The response is often increased homophobia, with lesbian and gay community members construed as "threats" to the family. . . . Perhaps, instead, we can reconstitute alternative ways of living together in which "families" are not seen as islands on their own. . . .

14

La conciencia de la mestiza

Towards a New Consciousness

Gloria Anzaldúa

Por la mujer de mi raza
bablará el espíritu.

José Vasconcelos, Mexican philosopher, envisaged *una raza mestiza, una mezcla de razas afines, una raza de color—la primera raza síntesis del globo*. He called it a cosmic race, *la raza cósmica*, a fifth race embracing the four major races of the world. Opposite to the theory of the pure Aryan, and to the policy of racial purity that white America practices, his theory is one of inclusivity. At the confluence of two or more genetic streams, with chromosomes constantly "crossing over," this mixture of races, rather than resulting in an inferior being, provides hybrid progeny, a mutable, more malleable species with a rich gene pool. From this racial, ideological, cultural and biological cross-pollinization, an "alien" consciousness is presently in the making—a new *mestiza* consciousness, *una conciencia de mujer*. It is a consciousness of the Borderlands.

UNA LUCHA DE FRONTERAS/A STRUGGLE OF BORDERS

Because I, a *mestiza*,
continually walk out of one culture
and into another,
because I am in all cultures at the same time,
alma entre dos mundos, tres, cuatro,
me zumba la cabeza con lo contradictorio.
Estoy norteada por todas las voces que me hablan
simultáneamente.

The ambivalence from the clash of voices results in mental and emotional states of perplexity. Internal strife results in insecurity and indecisiveness. The *mestiza*'s dual or multiple personality is plagued by psychic restlessness.

In a constant state of mental nepantilism, an Aztec word meaning torn between ways, *la mestiza* is a product of the transfer of the cultural and spiritual values of one group to another. Being tricultural, monolingual, bilingual, or multilingual, speaking a patois, and in a state of perpetual transition, the *mestiza* faces the dilemma of the mixed breed: which collectivity does the daughter of a darkskinned mother listen to?

El choque de un alma atrapado entre el mundo del espíritu y el mundo de la técnica a veces la deja entullada. Cradled in one culture, sandwiched between two cultures, straddling all three cultures and their value systems, *la mestiza* undergoes a struggle of flesh, a struggle of borders, an inner war. Like all people, we perceive the version of reality that our culture communicates. Like others having or living in more than one culture, we get multiple, often opposing messages. The coming together of two self-consistent but habitually incompatible frames of reference causes *un choque*, a cultural collision.

Within us and within *la cultura chicana*, commonly held beliefs of the white culture attack commonly held beliefs of the Mexican culture, and both attack commonly held beliefs of the indigenous culture. Subconsciously, we see an attack on ourselves and our beliefs as a threat and we attempt to block with a counterstance.

But it is not enough to stand on the opposite river bank, shouting questions, challenging patriarchal, white conventions. A counterstance locks one into a duel of oppressor and oppressed; locked in mortal combat, like the cop and the criminal, both are reduced to a common denominator of violence. The counterstance refutes the dominant culture's views and beliefs, and, for this, it is proudly defiant. All reaction is limited by, and dependent on, what it is reacting against. Because the counterstance stems from a problem with authority—outer as well as inner—it's a step towards liberation from cultural domination. But it is not a way of life. At some point, on our way to a new consciousness, we will have to leave the opposite bank, the split between the two mortal combatants somehow healed so that we are on both shores at once and, at once, see through serpent and eagle eyes. Or perhaps we will decide to disengage from the dominant culture, write it off altogether as a lost cause, and cross the border into a wholly new and separate territory. Or we might go another route. The possibilities are numerous once we decide to act and not react.

A TOLERANCE FOR AMBIGUITY

These numerous possibilities leave *la mestiza* floundering in uncharted seas. In perceiving conflicting information and points of view, she is subjected to a swamping of her psychological borders. She has discovered that she can't hold concepts or ideas in rigid boundaries. The borders and walls that are supposed to keep the undesirable ideas out are entrenched habits and patterns of behavior; these habits and patterns are the enemy within. Rigidity means death. Only by remaining flexible is she able to stretch the psyche horizontally and vertically. *La mestiza* constantly has to shift out of habitual formations; from convergent thinking, analytical reasoning that tends to use rationality to move toward a single goal (a Western mode), to divergent thinking, characterized by movement away from set patterns and goals and toward a more whole perspective, one that includes rather than excludes.

The new *mestiza* copes by developing a tolerance for contradictions, a tolerance for ambiguity. She learns to be an Indian in Mexican culture, to be Mexican from an Anglo point of view. She learns to juggle cultures. She has a plural personality, she operates in a pluralistic mode—nothing is thrust out, the good the bad and the ugly, nothing rejected, nothing abandoned. Not only does she sustain contradictions, she turns the ambivalence into something else.

She can be jarred out of ambivalence by an intense, and often painful, emotional event which inverts or resolves the ambivalence. I'm not sure exactly how. The work takes place underground—subconsciously. It is work that the soul performs. That focal point or fulcrum, that juncture where the *mestiza* stands, is where phenomena tend to collide. It is where the possibility of uniting all that is separate occurs. This assembly is not one where severed or separated pieces merely come together. Nor is it a balancing of opposing powers. In attempting to work out a synthesis, the self has added a third element which is greater than the sum of its severed parts. That third element is a new consciousness—a *mestiza* consciousness—and though it is a source of intense pain, its energy comes from continual creative motion that keeps breaking down the unitary aspect of each new paradigm.

En unas pocas centurias, the future will belong to the *mestiza*. Because the future depends on the breaking down of paradigms, it depends on the straddling of two or more cultures. By creating a new mythos—that is, a change in the way we perceive reality, the way we see ourselves, and the ways we behave—*la mestiza* creates a new consciousness.

The work of *mestiza* consciousness is to break down the subject-object duality that keeps her a prisoner and to show in the flesh and through the images in her work how duality is transcended. The answer to the problem between the white race and the colored, between males and females, lies in healing the split that originates in the very foundation of our lives, our culture, our languages, our thoughts. A massive uprooting of dualistic thinking in the individual and collective consciousness is the beginning of a long struggle, but one that could, in our best hopes, bring us to the end of rape, of violence, of war.

LA ENCRUCIJADA/THE CROSSROADS

A chicken is being sacrificed
    at a crossroads, a simple mound of earth
a mud shrine for *Eshu*,
    Yoruba god of indeterminacy,
who blesses her choice of path.
    She begins her journey.

Su cuerpo es una bocacalle. La mestiza has gone from being the sacrificial goat to becoming the officiating priestess at the crossroads.

As a mestiza I have no country, my homeland cast me out; yet all countries are mine because I am every woman's sister or potential lover. (As a lesbian I have no race, my own people disclaim me; but I am all races because there is the queer of me in all races.) I am cultureless because, as a feminist, I challenge the collective cultural/religious male-derived beliefs of Indo-Hispanics and Anglos; yet I am cultured because I am participating in the creation of yet another culture, a new story to explain the world and our participation in it, a new value system with images and symbols that connect us to each other and to the planet. *Soy un amasamiento*, I am an act of kneading, of uniting and joining that not only has produced both a creature of darkness and a creature of light, but also a creature that questions the definitions of light and dark and gives them new meanings.

We are the people who leap in the dark, we are the people on the knees of the gods. In our very flesh, (r)evolution works out the clash of cultures. It makes us crazy constantly, but if the center holds, we've made some kind of evolutionary step forward. *Nuestra alma el trabajo*, the opus, the great alchemical work; spiritual *mestizaje*, a "morphogenesis," an inevitable unfolding. We have become the quickening serpent movement.

C
O
N
T
E
X
T

Indigenous like corn, like corn, the *mestiza* is a product of crossbreeding, designed for preservation under a variety of conditions. Like an ear of corn—a female seed-bearing organ—the *mestiza* is tenacious, tightly wrapped in the husks of her culture. Like kernels she clings to the cob; with thick stalks and strong brace roots, she holds tight to the earth—she will survive the crossroads.

Lavando y remojando el maíz en agua de cal, despojando el pellejo. Moliendo, mixteando, amasando, haciendo tortillas de masa. She steeps the corn in lime, it swells, softens. With stone roller on *metate*, she grinds the corn, then grinds again. She kneads and moulds the dough, pats the round balls into *tortillas*.

> We are the porous rock in the stone *metate*
> squatting on the ground.
> We are the rolling pin, *el maíz y agua,*
> *la masa harina. Somos el amasijo.*
> *Somos lo molido en el metate.*
> We are the *comal* sizzling hot,
> the hot *tortilla*, the hungry mouth.
> We are the coarse rock.
> We are the grinding motion,
> the mixed potion, *somos el molcajete.*
> We are the pestle, the *comino, ajo, pimienta,*
> We are the *chile colorado,*
> the green shoot that cracks the rock.
> We will abide.

. . .

SOMOS UNA GENTE

> *Hay tantísimas fronteras*
> *que dividen a la gente,*
> *pero por cada frontera*
> *existe también un puente.*
>
> Gina Valdés

Divided Loyalties. Many women and men of color do not want to have any dealings with white people. It takes too much time and energy to explain to the downwardly mobile, white middle-class women that it's okay for us to want to own "possessions," never having had any nice furniture on our dirt floors or "luxuries" like washing machines. Many feel that whites should help their own people rid themselves of race hatred and fear first. I, for one, choose to use some of my energy to serve as mediator. I think we need to allow whites to be our allies. Through our literature, art, *corridos*, and folktales we must share our history with them so when they set up committees to help Big Mountain Navajos or the Chicano farmworkers or *los Nicaragüenses* they won't turn people away because of their racial fears and ignorances. They will come to see that they are not helping us but following our lead.

Individually, but also as a racial entity, we need to voice our needs. We need to say to white society: We need you to accept the fact that Chicanos are different, to acknowledge your rejection and negation of us. We need you to own the fact that you looked upon us as less than human, that you stole our lands, our personhood, our self-respect. We need you to make public restitution: to say that, to compensate for your own sense of defectiveness, you strive for power over us, you erase our history and our experience because it makes you feel guilty—you'd rather forget your brutish acts. To say you've split yourself from minority groups, that you disown us, that your dual consciousness splits off parts of yourself, transferring the "negative" parts onto us. (Where there is persecution of minorities, there is shadow projection. Where there is violence and war, there is repression of shadow.) To say that you are afraid of us, that to put distance between us, you wear the mask of contempt. Admit that Mexico is your double, that she exists in the shadow of this country, that we are irrevocably tied to her. Gringo, accept the doppelganger in your psyche. By taking back your collective shadow the intra-cultural split will heal. And finally, tell us what you need from us.

. . .

15

Patrolling Racial Borders

Discrimination Against Mixed Race People

Heather Dalmage

"Is she part Black?" asked the imposing woman ahead of us in line at the Dollar Store. "Yes," I responded, not wanting to continue this conversation in an impersonal and public arena in front of my two-year-old daughter for whom the word race still meant, "last one to the porch is a rotten egg."

Raising her voice, the Black woman bent down toward my daughter's face and proclaimed, "We call that mulatto. Yes, indeed, you're a mulatto."

I felt strongly compelled to respond but was uncertain which piece should be addressed and how. Should I have begun to talk with this woman about the ugly origins of the term mulatto? Should I have addressed the dehumanizing and degrading aspects of categorizing other people (especially children)? I knew I was not going to let someone else impose the context of a race debate in front of my two-year-old. I left the store.

While such intrusions are not uncommon, more often they remain in the realm of the silent stare. A multiracial woman once said to me that being stared at was such a part of her existence that when it came time for her to perform in front of an audience she was very comfortable. Historically, in academic research and beyond, much emphasis has been placed on the ways multiracial people adjust to race in society. The assumption underlying much of the analysis is that race is a concrete, objective, and static phenomenon. I propose that if we want to more fully understand multiracial experiences we need to "flip the script" and analyze why racial categories have been created in particular ways and why people who identify themselves with a single racial category feel the need and right to intrude upon, pass judgement on, and discriminate against multiracial people and their families.

GROUP BOUNDARIES AND DISCRIMINATION

Race thinking developed in the U.S. around and through questions of citizenship and resource distribution. The history of U.S. immigration and citizenship reflects a system deeply embedded in the protection of White privilege and the denial of rights to people of color. Colonization, slavery, genocide of indigenous people, the Chinese Immigration Exclusion Acts of the 1800s, the Bracero Program, internment camps, Jim Crow laws, and numerous other legally sanctioned forms of discrimination have been used to define and defend Whiteness by creating clear distinctions between White people and all others. When the distinctions seemed threatened, anti-miscegenation laws—those that denied people the right to marry across race lines—were enforced through penalties that included imprisonment, enslavement, and death. The primary threat was not the marriage itself but rather the fact that in the U.S. marriage legitimizes the offspring. If multiracial children were deemed legitimate, then all laws based on the separation of "the races" would be delegitimized. After three centuries of anti-miscegenation laws, in 1967, buttressed by the strength of the Civil Rights Movement, the Supreme Court ruled that interracial marriages must be recognized in every state. Unfortunately, multiracial families still face discrimination, and the children of these marriages are still expected to claim only one race.

While the Civil Rights Movement paved the way for the legal acceptance of multi-racial families, it also created a new set of struggles for these families. The Civil Rights Movement included various groups struggling for liberation and self-definition such as the Young Lords, the Chicano Movement, the Black Power Movement, the Asian American Movement, and the American Indian Movement. Through these struggles, groups of color that had previously been on the defensive against White supremacist abuses began to define themselves for themselves. This meant that the distinction between insider and outsider was defined from *within* each of these groups rather than predominantly imposed from the outside by Whites. However, the way lines were drawn caused many problems for those who found themselves on the borders of racial groups, particularly those who were racially mixed. Moreover, the struggle for civil rights led to the passing of legislation meant to address and redress racism. The government needed a way to track compliance and by 1977 had agreed on four discrete racial categories; every U.S. citizen was required to check one. The census became a vehicle for protecting people of color against White supremacist abuse, *and* it strengthened the distinctions between racial categories. As a result, multiracial people, already discriminated against in a White supremacist society, became more susceptible to discrimination from all sides.

How "sides" are defined is a matter of history. Those people with whom we identify most closely, those with whom we share a history, a collective memory, and a collective way of knowing are generally considered our in-group, our side. For instance, a quick trip to the Gaza Strip makes the point clear. Stone-throwing Palestinians do not have a natural or inherent disdain for the Jews at whom they throw the stones. Likewise the tank-driving Israelis are not genetically driven to violence toward Palestinians. This particular conflict is driven by historical circumstances in which children are raised and through which they understand themselves and their world. The collective memories on each side are used to define the boundaries of in-groups. Often, as is the case in the Middle East, in-group cohesion is strengthened through the hatred of an out-group, those against whom in-group members define themselves. Moreover, each side knows itself in the negation of the other; for it is at the boundaries that identities are framed. In such a construction, little room exists for someone to be both Palestinian and Israeli.

The history of Whiteness and various forms of racism directed at groups of color has meant that in the U.S. being a member of one race—or one side—has immediately placed an individual as an out-group of the other. The greater the power imbalance between groups, the greater the emphasis on maintaining boundaries between sides. The boundaries are maintained on both the institutional and individual levels through various forms of discrimination. On an institutional level, discrimination occurs as an outcome of laws and the way society functions. For example, many children of color are denied equal access to education as a result of years of housing discrimination in a society in which a large portion of school funding is tied to property values through taxes. The segregated housing market ensures that children of color, particularly African Americans and Latinos, are disproportionately receiving an inferior education relative to White children. Discrimination and racism also play out between individuals. For instance, one student refuses to speak to another because she sat at the wrong lunchroom table. In this case, the discriminatory act is clear; the individual discriminator can be identified. Given that institutional mechanisms, from the housing market to the census, have functioned to keep lines between racial and ethnic groups clear and defined, multiracial children are facing unending demands to choose a side and stake a claim. In other words, demands are made that they adhere to the larger rules of race that guide U.S. racial thinking.

On all sides, border patrollers, or the race police, believe the color line is static and immutable, and thus they think they can distinguish between "us" and "them." Border patrollers claim that race is a simple concept, demand that others comply, and make their presence felt through various actions. The most common action, by far, is the stare. Other forms of border patrolling include probing and inappropriate questions. "What are you?" is one of the most common questions faced by multiracial people. Many times, however, people will not ask: instead they will begin to label a multiracial person. A friend of mine once told me that cab drivers assume she is whatever they are. Because border patrollers think they can determine "authentic" behaviors they also think they have the right to grant or withhold acceptance. Even when acceptance is not granted, individuals are expected to act in ways deemed appropriate; to do otherwise will provoke further patrolling.

All racial groups patrol the borders; thus, in addition to facing White racist abuse, multiracial people also face discrimination from their communities of color. Here I identify five broad areas of everyday life in which multiracial children are patrolled and face discrimination and demands to comply with existing racial rules.

1.   PATROLLING OF THE CHILD'S PHYSICALITY

All children tend to be conscious of appearance; however, not all children have to give conscious thought to the racial implications of their choice of hairstyle, make-up, weight and body shape, clothes, shoes, bags, and hats. Multiracial children do—they must because border patrollers on each side are watching and commenting. This form of discrimination can be very hurtful to multiracial children who must expend an inordinate amount of energy negotiating their appearance. For example, a Black-White multiracial woman I interviewed spoke of the devastation she felt as a child because her White mother did not learn to do "Black hair." As a result she faced relentless teasing from Black girls at school. Unfortunately, many parents, particularly White parents, do not understand the importance of hair and other physical markers to their child's ability to negotiate racial borders.

2.   PATROLLING LINGUISTICS

Individuals who think that they can tell who is an "authentic" member of their race and who is not often listen intently to the use of language. Multiracial children are patrolled for their ability to "speak the language." For instance, a young multiracial student was granted acceptance by his Black peers only after he proved that he could play the dozens (or snaps, e.g., "Yo mama is so big . . ."). Once he could show that he understood the nuances of the language as it defines racial groups, then he was more accepted. Multiracial children are often bilingual; that is, they have the ability to comfortably converse as an insider with more than one racial group. Unfortunately, multiracial children who engage in bilingual practices are criticized as being wishy-washy and fake. Parents and teachers sometimes reinforce this idea by advising the child to "be yourself" thus implying that strong, certain, and clear-headed people speak only one way regardless of audience. In short, the message is that bilingualism is not acceptable and the child should choose a side. Such advice can be hurtful to a multiracial child for whom the ability to switch gears may be part of being her or himself.

3. PATROLLING INTERACTION WITH MEMBERS OF THE OUT-GROUP

Here the border patrollers demand a denial of all connections to, or affections for, the racial out-group. While this most often occurs around the issue of dating and friendship circles, multiracial children are even pressured, at times, to deny their parents and relatives. Most multiracial children have been in conversations in which White people are portrayed as universally evil. In these instances, if the child says, "But my father and my grandparents are White, and they are not evil," her loyalties will be called into question; she risks becoming an outsider. Moreover, multiracial children who appear White are assumed by Whites to be an insider and are often subjected to White racist conversation. Multiracial children who speak out in these situations sometimes face the racist compliment, "Oh, we don't think of you as Puerto Rican, you're different, we think of you as White." In this case, the child is devalued, and those Whites giving the "compliment" assume White to be something highly valued and that they have the right to bestow an identity on another human being. The children expend much energy deciding how to respond to the patrolling and discrimination.

4. PATROLLING GEOGRAPHIES

Here, I am using geographies to address the physical spaces individuals occupy in their lives. Because of the segregation in society, racial groups are often geographically defined. Children have little control over where they live, and yet they are held responsible by border patrollers for a street address that might place them on the wrong side of the race line. In addition, other geographies are patrolled including what school a child attends, choice of classes, choice of lunchroom table, and how leisure time is spent. Multiracial children who might be comfortable sitting at several different (and racially defined) lunchroom tables may be reprimanded, "You are either one of us or you are not, you need to decide." A multiracial woman who attended high school in Manhattan recalled that White, Black, Latino, and Asian students each exited the school from different doors. Each day she left the school she was made aware that her choice of exit was being noted by others. In short, because all social spaces are raced, the spaces multiracial children occupy throughout the day carry messages to others about the child's loyalty to a particular side.

5. PATROLLING OF CULTURAL CAPITAL

Cultural capital is the resources individuals can draw upon to give them status and credibility in society. Given racial divisions in society, cultural capital is used by all sides to determine who is a loyal and credible insider. The cultural capital important among children as they become aware of racial categories includes taste in music, television programs, sports, and magazines. A multiracial man who grew up in the Bronx reported that in high school he loved the music of Barry Manilow but that he always hid the tapes and listened to that music when he was alone. His enjoyment of that music marked him "too White," and his Latino friends would have shunned him. Another Black-White multiracial young man remembered the difficulty he had with his Black friends when he joined the high school hockey team. He was given the label "White boy" for playing.

All children face patrolling; however, multiracial children face racial border patrolling in addition to the usual demands children place on each other for conformity. Some children are given (or assigned to) one racial group by parents and teachers and expected to comply. Unfortunately, too often parents and teachers dismiss border patrolling by invoking "colorblind" language. The children are told to avoid labeling themselves and that they are part of the human race. In many cases, however, teachers and some parents just ignore race altogether. In the silence, the children are left to fend for themselves. Fortunately, most multiracial children do successfully negotiate border patrolling; however, if parents and teachers were more aware of the unique forms of discrimination these children face, they might be able to reduce the burden.

While all sides patrol and police the boundaries of their racial communities, the reason for and consequence of the patrolling vary. Everyone who has learned about race, U.S. style, looks for clues about how to racially categorize others. Some White people need to take this step before they feel comfortable interacting with new people. They may sense that the color line is shifting and fear losing their racial status. Thus, until they can categorize others, they feel vague and uneasy about their own racial status and identity. For people of color, the desire to make distinctions may concern a quest for allegiance and unity, a means to determine who is "us" and who is "them" politically, socially, and culturally. Individuals who comfortably claim one racial identity or think that race is something that can be observed or uncovered with enough clues may feel confusion, anger, skepticism, concern, pity, hostility, curiosity, or superiority when they meet someone who does not seem to fit neatly into a preset racial category. These feelings play out through the course of interaction, and a multiracial person, regardless of how he or she identifies, must contend with the response of these individuals. For instance, Kimberly, a multiracial woman living in Manhattan, grew up being chastised by her parents and grandparents for not speaking "proper" English; in school Kimberly was taunted by Black students who insisted that she was trying to be White. As a person with racially ambiguous features, she receives many comments and stares from strangers. She is tired of hearing the same questions and comments and has also grown tired of defending herself:

> People come up to me and they'll say, "Do you get confused between being Black and White?" I say, "Well, yeah, you know, some mornings I wake up with this craving for fried chicken, and other mornings I just can't get the beat, I start dancing and can't get the beat." I want them to see how narrow-minded they're being. What do you think? One day I like fried chicken and the next I don't? It's not like that.

Kimberly points to the thinking that underlies the unique discrimination faced by multiracial people. If it is believed that race is inherent to an individual and that race is a way to group people into discrete categories, then it stands to reason that multiracial people must have separate races compartmentalized within them. Depending on the mix, multiracial people are assumed to have a genetically programmed way of being that can cause, at the extreme, an "internal war." Responding to people the way she does, Kimberly externalizes the problem of race and, at the same time, gives others the opportunity to think about race in a more sophisticated manner.

Given the history of race politics in the U.S., multiracial people have been largely ignored and more generally subsumed under communities of color for statistical and research purposes. Thus, until recently, multiracial people have not had a collective voice and have had to negotiate border patrolling individually. The explosion of writings since the early 1990s has begun the process of documenting and creating a voice for multiracial people and their families. While multiracial children have many more resources available today than they did a generation ago, they still face a society that assumes and demands that people comply with racial codes of conduct—codes that have historically denied the existence of multiracial people.

CONCLUSION

In this chapter I have addressed a brief history of and social context for the discrimination faced by multiracial people in the United States. I have identified those who discriminate against multiracial people as "border patrollers." While the majority of this chapter addresses the individual outcomes of this discrimination, it is important to note that institutional forms of discrimination against multiracials maintain the framework in which border patrolling takes place. For instance, in the United States we have a segregated housing market and thus segregated schools. Stable, racially-mixed areas are few and far between. Thus, multiracial children often find themselves in situations in which they are the "only one" or one of a few. If their families live in predominantly White areas, then they will be the child of color in a White environment. If they are in an area that is predominantly of color, depending upon their own background and the background of the neighborhood, they will be labeled as different. Patrolling takes place on an individual level, the level of daily experience, the level that children are most likely to name and articulate. However, the fact is that border patrolling is the outcome of a larger system of racial injustice and segregation. Parents and teachers should be aware of the unique forms of discrimination faced by multiracial children and the White supremacist system in which that discrimination flourishes.

16

Selected Reports

National Network for Immigrant and Refugee Rights

INJUSTICE FOR ALL: THE RISE OF THE U.S. IMMIGRATION POLICING REGIME

HURRICANE's 2009–2010 report, *Injustice for All: The Rise of the Immigration Policing Regime*, finds that the U.S. government has put into place a brutal system of immigration control and policing that criminalizes immigration status, normalizes the forcible separation of families, destabilizes communities and workplaces, and fuels widespread civil rights violations. This "immigration control policing regime" is also contributing to and tolerating an upsurge in racial discrimination and hate violence against immigrants and those perceived to be foreign born or "illegal."

Based on over 100 stories of abuse reported, collected and documented by volunteers, staff and members of NNIRR's initiative, HURRICANE: The Human Rights Immigrant Community Action Network, *Injustice for All* shows how a new dimension of immigration control, ICE-police collaboration and border security, are hurting communities from the rural areas of New Mexico and North Carolina to New York City and the suburbs of Chicago.

. . .

Over the last ten years, the U.S. has built a policing regime that uses immigration status to segregate people, thereby scapegoating people of color in a new way for the worsening fiscal crisis. Public officials and corporations collaborate to cut and/or privatize public services, including using for-profit private prisons to incarcerate people for immigration charges, destroying civil and labor rights. Immigration status is also being used to deny Indigenous people their right to identity, land and community.

The results are ominous. Congress and the Obama Administration have institutionalized this immigration policing, intensifying criminalization through immigration-police collaboration and other policies and programs. The U.S. has expanded workplace immigration policing, enhancing employer sanctions through the E-verify program to detect and force "unauthorized" workers out of certain kinds of work. In fiscal year 2010, ICE reported more than 2,200 audits, up from 1,400 in 2009, issuing 240 fines totaling $6.9 million, up from 52 fines totaling about $1 million in 2009. And the prospects that Congress or the Obama Administration will reverse policies or restrain policing are unlikely, as dozens of states, local, and county governments and federal agencies are considering similar policies and legislation, egged on by a reactionary nativist movement. Since 2000, some 107 towns, cities and counties have passed anti-immigrant ordinances affecting access to services, housing and employment.

THE RISE OF AN IMMIGRATION POLICING REGIME

In 2003, the majority of U.S. immigration service and policing responsibilities were transferred from the former Immigration and Naturalization Service to the then newly-formed Department of Homeland Security (DHS). In the wake of the September 11th terrorist attacks, the U.S. created the DHS as an umbrella agency that directly incorporated immigration affairs with national security policies. DHS also launched Operation Endgame, a 10-year strategic detention and deportation plan designed to build the capacity to "remove all removable aliens." (11.1 million undocumented immigrants are currently estimated to reside in the United States.)

Operation Endgame represents a significant turning point in U.S. immigration policy. Endgame has built a new "immigration policing regime" that attempts to connect the dots between disparate issues—including immigration, citizenship, the "war on terror," border control, national security, crime, law enforcement, and the economy—all under the guise of "protecting the homeland." This approach to immigration control and enforcement consists of four pillars:

Relentless criminalization of immigration status and the use of incarceration through U.S. laws, policies, measures and practices—weakening and even eliminating constitutional rights, particularly due process rights, and labor protections for noncitizens.

Persistent linking of immigration to the politics of national security and engaging in policing tactics that rely upon racial, ethnic/nationality and religious profiling.

Escalating militarization of immigration control and border communities; reinforcing policies and strategies that deliberately "funnel" migrants, forcing them to cross through the most dangerous segments of the U.S.-Mexico border and compromise the rights and safety of border residents.

Scapegoating immigrants for the economic crisis and leveraging anti-immigrant sentiment to push federal, state, county and local laws and policies that cut and/or eliminate public services, and roll back civil rights, environmental, labor and other social protections. These policies contribute to corporate profit-making and are integral to "free" trade and other economic development programs that displace communities and force individuals around the world into involuntary migration.

. . .

In reports from California, Arizona, New Mexico, Illinois, North Carolina, and New York, different forms of immigration-police collaboration are impacting communities, youth, women, workers, Indigenous people and people of color. Immigration policing is taking different forms along the border (local police and the Border Patrol, for example) than in the interior (driver's license and DUI checkpoints) but the impacts are just as devastating. Immigration-police collaboration creates more problems in all communities:

- Police collusion with ICE undermines community safety. Residents will not report crimes and fires if they fear detection and deportation.
- Women are less likely to report domestic violence if they or their partners have immigration status. Batterers are also more likely to threaten their partners with turning them over to ICE to stop them from reporting an abusive relationship.
- Equally troubling, local law enforcement is not trained in immigration law and requires substantial amounts of time and money to reach a satisfactory level of expertise. As a result, local police departments, already strapped on resources and manpower, cut back other vital community services, affecting community safety.
- Police cooperation with ICE encourages racial profiling, already illegal, resulting in civil rights violations and abuses against immigrant and refugee communities. Even where police departments have worked to end racial profiling, such collaboration undermines the credibility of police departments to effectively serve all communities.

. . .

IMMIGRATION-POLICE COLLABORATION GOES VIRAL

In the past year, dozens of states and other local and county governments have been spurred to create copycat Arizona-style laws. And there is an undeniable economic angle to such immigration policing. For example, Arizona's SB1070 was developed by lawmakers in collaboration with corporations that build private jails to incarcerate immigrants; these companies stand to earn considerable profits from the growing trend of detaining immigrants for enforcement and deterrence. Indeed, some two-thirds of persons imprisoned for immigration charges are held in local jails. In southern California alone, DHS is set to pay almost $57 million to 13 jails.

Other state and local governments are also looking at ways to use the "illegal immigration problem" as a means to solve their fiscal crises. From Virginia to Oregon and Pennsylvania, ICE offers governments immigration jails as a job creation and revenue source strategy. ICE has approached different localities to build and, in some cases, run public-private immigrant jails, where investors will reap millions in profits and governments will boost their revenues. Localities also fear losing an ICE detention center; Etowah

County in Alabama faces a ruinous fiscal crisis because ICE is planning to end its contract that pays the county $14,000 a day to jail immigrants. Additionally, SB1070 is costing Arizona huge losses in revenues.

. . .

RECORD YEAR OF REPRESSION

Fiscal year 2010 was a record year of repression: the U.S. government deported a total of 392,862 immigrant workers, students, women, and youth—many of whom were long-time residents of the United States. Beyond these individuals, untold numbers of family members were separated, children left hopeless, and neighborhoods and workplaces diminished by the absence of hardworking individuals who contributed significantly to the social, economic, and political fabric of our country.

2010 was also a record year for the detention of immigrants, subjected by ICE to inhumane treatment and conditions. Since 2003, at least 104 deaths have been documented of persons in ICE immigrant detention centers and jails.

ICE has some 32,000 jail beds exclusively for persons charged with immigration violations or in deportation proceedings. The DHS runs or contracts with some 350 public and private jails and prisons across the country to detain immigrants who have been arrested for status violations and are awaiting deportation. Many of these facilities are located in remote areas where there is little or no access to qualified, low-cost immigration legal service providers (there is no guaranteed right to counsel for immigrant detainees as in the criminal justice context). Moreover, the DHS frequently transfers immigrant detainees to new facilities without providing notice to their attorneys or family members. There is little accountability for guaranteeing a prison's minimal conditions and basic human rights protections for detained immigrants, including access to medical treatment, recreation, and the freedom to worship. The DHS also uses semi-secret court proceedings to judge, try, and summarily deport immigrants accused of minor immigration offenses, in gross violation of constitutional rights and due process.

Women, who make up over half of all migrants to the United States, have been particularly impacted by the new immigration policing regime. HURRICANE'S database is filled with documentation of abuses committed against immigrant women. (In most instances, women are HURRICANE'S principal monitors and reporters of rights abuses.)

In addition to the rights violations and abuses male migrants face, women in migration are subjected to sexual harassment, assault and rape during the arduous border-crossing journey, at work and in ICE detention. For example, ICE jailed over 10,000 immigrant women in 2008; after routine testing, 965 of the women (nearly 10%), tested pregnant; many of these women reported being raped during the border crossing.

In deportation proceedings, ICE and the courts mete out severe punishment and treatment to women who are mothers and workers, especially, if they are undocumented and Indigenous. In some areas, various U.S. public agencies have taken away and placed into adoption the children of undocumented and Indigenous women. HURRICANE also received reports of immigration jail guards sexually assaulting women detained at the Hutto detention facility.

. . .

Another alarming example of impact of the current immigration policing regime is the growing human rights crisis at the U.S.-Mexico border. In 2010, a record number of migrants died in the border crossing: the remains of 253 migrants were recovered in the Arizona border alone. (See Coalición de Derechos Humanos report in *Injustice for All*.)

Human rights groups that work on the border to uphold the rights of migrants report that for every migrant dead recovered in the border at least ten others are believed to have disappeared. An average of two migrant deaths are recorded every day; border groups estimate that from 5,000 to 8,000 migrant deaths have occurred since this border control strategy was implemented in 1994.

. . .

RECOMMENDATIONS

The 2009–2010 HURRICANE report urges the U.S. government to undertake a major shift in immigration policies, to address the patterns of human and civil rights violations, harm and traumatization of immigrants and their communities, and to provide access to the adjustment of immigration status, a process long held at bay by a lack of political will and action at the federal level. Without such a shift, millions of men, women and children residing in this country will continue to face lives of fear, uncertainty and economic insecurity.

There are significant steps that the Obama Administration can authorize, including:

- The restoration of due process rights and other Constitutional protections, including an expansion of access to the courts;
- The suspension of detentions and deportations, other enforcement operations and high profile raids; undertake a high-level investigation and hearings with impacted communities;
- An end to the policy and practice of jailing persons solely for immigration status offenses, except in cases where there is a high risk to public safety;
- The prohibition of ICE and local, county, state and federal law enforcement from using all forms of racial, ethnic/nationality and religious profiling;
- A thorough investigation of complaints of abuses in public and private corporate detention centers and jails housing immigrants; a moratorium on the expansion of detention centers and privately run prisons;
- An end to all inter-agency and immigration-police collaboration programs;
- Prohibit local, county, and state governments from legislating immigration enforcement, such as Arizona's SB1070;
- The roll back and end to the militarization of immigration control and border communities; end Operation Stonegarden, a federal program for police collaboration with Border Patrol, and Operation Streamline that violates due process, making unauthorized entry a felony with automatic sentencing.

We are disturbed by the lack of congressional action to enact fair immigration policies, and we call on our elected officials in the House and Senate to:

- Hold field hearings with members of interior and border communities to document the impacts and abuses caused by U.S. immigration enforcement and border security policies, measures and practices;
- Repeal employer sanctions and stop all E-Verify programs; protect and expand the labor rights of all workers, native and foreign-born; and increase Department of Labor inspectors;
- Repeal the 287(g), "Secure Communities" initiatives;
- Provide and expand options to legal migration, including access to legal permanent residency and citizenship;

- Institute routine programs, including legalization, to adjust the immigration status and provide "green cards" to immigrants, to ensure civil and labor rights, keep families together and reinforce healthy communities.

Finally, we call upon the Administration and members of Congress:

- To address the root causes of displacement and involuntary migration, by promoting and implementing fair trade and sustainable community development policies;
- To help lead a nationwide condemnation of racial intolerance and xenophobia in keeping with our country's legal and moral commitment to equality for all.

We further urge the United States to respect and uphold international human and labor rights standards, including the ratification and implementation of the U.N. International Convention for the Protection of the Rights of All Migrant Workers and Members of Their Families and the U.N. Declaration on the Rights of Indigenous People.

. . .

NEW AFRICANS IN OLD AMERICA

Nunu Kidane

Following New York, California has the highest number of immigrants from Africa. Estimated conservatively at 145,453 (American Community Survey 2006–08), the African immigrant community is one of the most undercounted.

PAN's recent mobilization activities for the 2010 Census exposed the complexities involved in counting African community members that are unlike any other. African immigrants organize themselves largely along their national or ethnic identities (as opposed to the assumed continental "African") and therefore remain in clusters of small groups, fragmented and excluded from traditional mainstream institutions.

PAN estimates that the actual size of the African community is at least three times this number. After Los Angeles, the Bay Area in particular is home to a high number of African immigrants. A recent study had an estimate of African immigrants in the Bay Area at 2% of the population; no doubt this figure will increase significantly over the coming years.

CLIMATE OF FEAR AND "TRIPLE JEOPARDY"

For the growing population of immigrants from Africa, the recent anti-immigrant raids and attacks have had unexpected impacts, both direct and indirect. Whether or not directly targeted by enforcement agencies, the climate of fear has permeated every association without exception. Prevailing assumptions about African immigrants is that they largely "blend" into existing African American communities and, on the basis of skin color at least, are less likely to be targeted by immigration law enforcement. This is considered, ironically, as one of the few instances where there's a positive factor on being Black in America.

The facts, however, are that African immigrants face the double threat of being Black and immigrant. They are twice as likely to be racially profiled, first on the basis of their skin color and additionally on their status as immigrants. Then, an added factor of *"triple jeopardy"* comes into play for the large numbers of African immigrants who are also Muslim.

. . .

The recent immigration raids in homes and workplaces largely exposed in the Spanish-speaking and other Latin American-origin communities set off a wave of fear in the African immigrant community. Less known and less visible, the sense of fear that reverberated across African immigrant communities left them with no access to information or resources. Consequently, new Africans whose status may be questionable are less likely to be engaged in civic activism or join in community organizing for fear of "not returning home." Individuals have expressed being paralyzed with the fear of being picked up by ICE while out on a casual errand, and separated from their children or families.

RACIAL AND RELIGIOUS PROFILING

Still, the most common experience of negative encounters with police is of African men who report being constantly stopped for "driving while Black." Incidents of being stopped (usually for no reason or weak reasons) have been mentioned on more occasions than can be counted. Many are professionals who work in corporate offices and commute long distances and are likely to experience this multiple times. This fits the standard practice of racial profiling commonly experienced by African American men. The new African immigrant, however, does not have the advantage of contextualizing the experience in the history of race and racism in this country. Many express a sense of feeling targeted, frustrated and at odds with what they consider to be violations of principles of fairness, which they expect from this country.

Additionally, once police stop and question them, their foreign accents identify them as immigrants, leaving them vulnerable to detention if they are unable to prove their "legal" status.

Other shared stories include Somali women in the Santa Clara County, where the largest concentration of Somali communities resides in the San Francisco Bay Area. Highly visible in their traditional veils, the women express a sense of fear in the way they are regarded daily. They are asked to present documents of their status when registering their children at schools or receiving treatments in hospital/clinic.

. . .

Nunu Kidane is the coordinator for Priority Africa Network (PAN), an Africa-promoting/African immigrant community mobilizing grassroots organization based in the San Francisco Bay Area.

SOUTH ASIAN WORKERS ORGANIZE FOR THEIR RIGHTS
AGAINST ABUSIVE EMPLOYERS IN NEW YORK

Ayesha Mahmooda

The South Asian community has the second largest number of undocumented people in New York City after Latinos. At DRUM—Desis Rising Up & Moving, South Asian retail, restaurant, construction, and domestic workers along with taxi drivers are organizing to end abuses they face every day and win better working conditions for all immigrant workers. . . . The worker leaders build alliances with Latino worker centers, labor unions, the NY State Department of Labor's new Wage Watch program, and attorneys who file wage claims.

C
O
N
T
E
X
T

Through a series of meetings, surveys and community research, DRUM'S worker members identified common issues in local industries and reported the following abuses:

- Working long hours without overtime pay;
- Substandard low wages, violating minimum wage protections;
- Employer mistreatment of workers, including unsafe worksite conditions, undermining their health and safety; and
- Employers and owners blacklisting workers who speak out in the industries.

. . .

FATIMA'S STORY

At an early morning DRUM Worker Committee meeting, a Bangladeshi retail store worker named Fatima (not her real name) spoke out about the exploitative conditions at the Jackson Heights clothing stores where she worked. She described how the bosses paid low wages or no back wages, made them work long hours, and harassed them constantly. The store owners instilled fear in the workers, making it hard for her and her co-workers to speak up who were afraid of losing their jobs. She spoke about how difficult it felt for her and her co-workers to stand up for their rights because they are undocumented women.

One day in December 2009, Fatima's boss ordered her to get supplies from his other store across the street. As he rushed her out the door, he began to yell at her to hurry up as she crossed the busy street. Scared and pressured, Fatima got hit by an oncoming car and was thrown 15 feet away. She lay on the cold sidewalk in severe pain, unable to move her shoulder. With the help of some bystanders, Fatima managed to walk back to her store to call 911 for an ambulance and to file a police report. But her boss immediately threatened her as well as all her co-workers in the store, saying that if they called 911, he would get in trouble for having undocumented workers and they would get deported. He also threatened to fire anyone who tried to call 911. After some bystanders and customers persuaded the boss, he allowed Fatima to call a cab and go to the hospital.

At the hospital, doctors told Fatima that she would need surgery to get her shoulder working properly again. Since Fatima had no insurance to pay for the surgery, the hospital advised her to file a police report against the driver and receive some money to pay for her medical expenses.

The next day at work, Fatima's employer threatened to fire her again if she reported the incident to police. She went to the local police station anyway; police told her she could not file a report without the license plate number of the vehicle that hit her, which she did not have.

. . .

The following day she went to the police station again to ask for a report, but police again told her that they could not do anything without the license plate number. When she asked again if they could look at the security cameras near the area where she was hit, they rudely refused, telling her that she should go back to her country if she did not like it.

. . .

Later that same day, the boss fired Fatima. She was never able to file the police report and never received the surgery. Unfortunately, thousands of undocumented immigrant workers in Jackson Heights and New York City face similar abuses and exploitation by their employers coupled with active neglect by law enforcement who fail to protect their rights.

Fatima became a leader and founding member of DRUM Workers' Committee and has reached out to dozens of other workers in similar situations. . . .

FIRE AND ICE: THE RETURN OF WORKPLACE IMMIGRATION RAIDS

At the end of February immigration agents descended on a handful of Japanese and Chinese restaurants in the suburbs of Jackson, Mississippi, and in nearby Meridian. Fifty-five immigrant cooks, dishwashers, servers and bussers were loaded into vans and taken to a detention center about 160 miles away in Jena, Louisiana.

Their arrests and subsequent treatment did more than provoke outrage among Jackson's immigrant rights activists. Labor advocates in California also took note of the incident, fearing that it marked the beginning of a new wave of immigrant raids and enforcement actions in workplaces. In response, California legislators have written a bill providing legal protections for workers, to keep the Mississippi experience from being duplicated in the Golden State.

Once the Mississippi restaurant workers had been arrested, they essentially fell off the radar screen for several days. Jackson lawyer Jeremy Litton, who represented three Guatemalan workers picked up in the raid, could not get the government to schedule hearing dates for them. He was unable to verify that the other detained immigrants were being held in the same center, or even who they were.

The Geo Corporation, formerly known as the Wackenhut Corporation, operates the LaSalle Detention Facility in Jena. Geo's roots go back to the Pinkerton Detective Agency, which became notorious in the nineteenth and first half of the 20th century for violent assaults on unions and strikers.

Today Geo operates 16 immigrant detention centers around the country, according to its 2015 annual report. It runs privatized prisons as well, some of which have been investigated by the federal government after allegations of bad conditions and understaffing. The LaSalle facility has 1,160 beds. Litton says it is normally full, so taking in an additional 55 detainees would result in severe overcrowding.

The use of Jena's immigrant jail to hold workers detained in workplace raids has a bitter history in Mississippi. In 2008 481 workers were arrested at a Howard Industries electrical equipment factory, in Laurel, Mississippi, in the middle of union negotiations. They, too, were taken to the LaSalle detention center. There they were fed peanut butter sandwiches at mealtimes, and according to Patricia Ice, attorney for the Mississippi Immigrant Rights Alliance (MIRA), "There weren't even enough beds and people were sleeping on the floor." Eight workers detained in that raid were charged with aggravated identity theft in federal court, for having given a false Social Security number to the employer when they were hired.

"This latest raid is causing a lot of fear in our community," says MIRA director Bill Chandler. "There's fear everywhere now because of the threats from Trump, but here in Mississippi our history of racism makes fear even stronger."

UNDOCUBLACK AND NILC SEEK TO UNCOVER THE TRUTH BEHIND TRUMP ADMINISTRATION TPS DECISION

WASHINGTON — Days before the Trump Administration announces whether it will re-authorize Temporary Protected Status (TPS) for Haitian migrants, civil rights and social justice leaders emphasized the importance of the program for Haitians in the United States and in Haiti, as well as for the national interests of both countries.

The call for reauthorization of TPS for Haitians comes after the Associated Press last week exposed leaked emails from high-ranking DHS officials requesting data on Haitian nationals' use of public benefits and crime rates. Although DHS officials have denied any connection between these requests and the timing of their decision, the news sent shockwaves through the Haitian community.

UndocuBlack and NILC filed a Freedom of Information Act (FOIA) request with the agencies involved in the adjudication process to uncover the administration's decision-making. Those agencies are the Department of State, the Department of Homeland Security (DHS), and the DHS sub agencies U.S. Immigration and Customs Enforcement (ICE) and U.S. Citizenship and Immigration Services (USCIS).

On a conference call with reporters Wednesday, representatives for the National Immigration Law Center, the UndocuBlack Network, the Black Alliance for Just Immigration (BAJI), and the Center for Law and Social Policy (CLASP) urged the administration to extend the program beyond its current July 22 expiration, noting that recovery efforts following the devastating 2010 earthquake and, more recently, Hurricane Matthew in 2016, have been uneven.

Lys Isma, a student who works in a Biology Genetics lab at her University in Florida, described the consequences of the 2010 earthquake for her and her family and what could happen to them if TPS for Haiti is not renewed. Isma is a member of UndocuBlack who has lived in the United States since she was nine months old.

"It shouldn't be an easy decision to send somebody to the poorest country in this half of the world, where they don't have any memories and where they can hardly speak the language," Isma said. "Where you live should never determine if you live."

TPS gives individuals from designated countries temporary permission to live and work in the United States on humanitarian grounds if they are here at times of great natural disaster or civil strife in their home country. Thirteen countries, including Haiti, are currently designated for TPS.

According to media reports, 58,000 Haitians stand to lose TPS and would be forced to return to their ravaged homeland if the designation is withdrawn. The Trump administration has until May 23, 2017, to announce its decision.

Tia Oso, National Organizer at the Black Alliance for Just Immigration (BAJI), said:

> "TPS for Haiti is a vital program, not just for the Haitian community, but for everyone that lives and works alongside them in Boston, Miami, Brooklyn and beyond. The Black Alliance for Just Immigration is calling on everyone to stand with the Haitian diaspora in the U.S. and fight for TPS, and condemn the Trump administration's racist, xenophobic witch-hunt against Haitian TPS holders and other immigrants." . . .

Alvaro Huerta, Staff Attorney at the National Immigration Law Center, said:

> "TPS has been an economic lifeline to Haitians both here in the United States and in Haiti. Haitian-Americans have built economic and social ties to this country, and they have friends and family here. These ties would be severed if these individuals

lost TPS designation, and the economic ripple effects would extend far beyond TPS holders themselves. We are deeply concerned that the rules for TPS may be shifting for Haitians, and we want to know why."

Jonathan Jayes-Green, Co-Creator and National Coordinator of the Undocublack Network, said:

"Renewing TPS is about maintaining the dignity of human lives and protecting their choice to migrate to avoid extreme circumstances in Haiti and live. We've seen the extraordinary measures and the discriminatory factors the administration is taking into consideration while weighing this decision. As Black immigrant communities, we are very aware of how agencies, organizations and institutions have sought to equate Blackness and poverty with criminality, and used that mantle to deny our communities of our human rights. That's why today we took the unprecedented step of filing this FOIA Request, our first as an organization."

C
O
N
T
E
X
T

17

Finding My Eye-dentity

Olivia Chung

I watched the spoken-word group I Was Born With Two Tongues perform and was inspired by their style of reflecting on personal experiences. This piece flowed from my desire for self-expression and hopes of challenging other Asian American girls to question their definition of beauty. I am a second-generation Korean American, born and raised in a loving family in Silver Spring, Maryland. Currently, I'm a sophomore at the University of Pennsylvania, pursuing interests in activism, writing, and hip-hop. My ultimate goal is to keep it real and selflessly live for the Lord.

Olivia, you wanna get *sang ka pul?*

I'm driving my mother to work, when she randomly brings up the eyelid question. The question that almost every Korean monoeyelidded girl has had to face in her life. The question that could change the future of my naturally noncreased eyelids, making them crease with the cut of a cosmetic surgeon's knife.

You know your aunt? She used to have beany eyes just like you! She used to put on white and black eyeliner every morning to make them look BIG. Then she went to Korea and got the surgery done. Now look! She looks so much better! Don't you want it done? I would do it . . .

I think this is about the 346,983,476th time she has brought this topic up. Using the exact same words. You would look so much more prettier with bigger eyes! she says. *You know, because they look kind of squinty and on top of that you have an underbite, so you look really mean . . .* She explains while narrowing her eyes and jutting out her jaw in emphasis of her point.

A couple of years ago, I would have taken her suggestion seriously. I remember reading a section of *Seventeen* magazine, where the once-did-funky-makeup-for-100-anorexic-white-girls-on-runways beauty expert revealed the secret to applying eye makeup. As a desperate preteen girl seeking beauty advice, I remember it perfectly. Put dark shadow right over the eyelashes, light powder all over, medium shadow over the edge of the crease of your eyelid. That's where I always tripped up. Crease? Umm . . . excuse me? These so-called beauty experts never gave me enough expertise to figure out how to put makeup on my face without looking like a character in a kabuki play. I tried to follow the beauty experts' advice. But I decided it wasn't working when people asked me if I had gotten a black eye.

My friends suggested training my eyelids to fold with tape. *My mother did that and now she has a real crease, one of my friends told me.* I, however, never learned the magic behind that, and always felt too embarrassed to ask. Another friend once excitedly showed me how she had bought a bottle of make-your-own-eye-crease glue from Korea. I let her try it on me too. I could barely open my eyes, thanks to the fierce stinging sensation resulting from the glue that got on my eyeball. And when I finally did take a quick glimpse of myself in the mirror, I saw a stranger with uneven eyelids.

The first time I remember being insulted was when I was little. . . .

In kindergarten, I believe. Oh, it was classic. A little blond kid pulled the edges of his eyes out, yelling, *Ching chong chinaman!* I, being new to this game, could only make a weak comeback. *I'm not Chinese. . . . I'm KOREAN.* I remember feeling a confused hurt, realizing that I looked different and not understanding why being different was bad.

Couldn't we all just get along? I had learned that God loves people as they are, as different as they are. I learned that He looks at the heart, and that it really doesn't matter how a person looks. I think my belief in this, combined with my fear of a sharp object cutting the skin above my eye, kept me away from the *sang ka pul* surgery. Yet, I continued to receive comments on my "chinky" eyes, and I always emerged from these situations feeling confused and angry . . . without ever really knowing why. Why couldn't I be accepted with my so-called chinky eyes? Why in the world were they even called "chinky" eyes? If they meant to insult Chinese, all the Chinese people I knew had huge eyes. With the crease.

As I grew older, the childish "ching chong"s came with less frequency. Still, the magazines continue to give me unhelpful directions on how to apply makeup. Still, I witness my own friends getting the surgery done in an effort to be "more beautiful." Still, my mother continuously confronts me with the dreaded eyelid question. *You wanna get* sang ka pul? I always answer her with an *are-you-crazy?* but simple *no.* All the things I wish I could have told her come flowing on this page with my pen. . . .

Umma, my mother, don't you see that my noncreased eyes are beautiful? Asian eyes are beautiful. Your eyes are beautiful. My eyes are beautiful. Asian is beautiful. After all these years of wanting to open up my eyes with tape and glue and surgery, I have opened up my eyes to a different definition of beauty. A broader definition of beauty, one that embraces differences and includes every girl, who can hold her head up, *sang ka pul*-less and chinky-eyed, because being *Asian is beautiful.*

18

Identification Pleas

Eric Gansworth

So it's the summer of 2002, . . . in the town of Del Rio, Texas, perhaps one of the last places on earth I thought I would be engaged in an identity crisis. . . . I am here with a friend, Donnie, who has a piece of land in this small border town. . . . He asks me if I want to cross the border into Acuña, as it is right there. Though the temperature is over a hundred degrees, we walk across the bridge above the Rio Grande into Mexico. On the exact border, large metal pegs mar the full surface of the pavement, gleam in the heat, and announce the change of country in full-size versions of that dotted line one sees on maps.

Here, trucks pull up, from the United States' end of the bridge, and stop, right on the dotted line. Other trucks meet them on the Mexican side. The drivers descend from their cabs and carry large boxes from the cargo areas of the United States trucks to those of the Mexican trucks. The border guards sit disinterested, watch this transaction under the bright sun, so I take a cue from them that this activity is nothing worth noting, and move on.

. . .

While it was an unpleasantly hot walk across, I see little justification for a bus to make the trip, and again Donnie clarifies that sometimes it is less of a hassle for Mexicans to cross the border if they use the bus instead of walking the bridge.

We leave Mexico a few minutes later, on the bridge's north-bound sidewalk, again stepping on the hot metal pegs, delineating one place from another. Below us, the Rio Grande seems more like the Rio Average, a muddy stream surrounded by dense growth of cane, and above the sidewalk overlooking the river, heavy-gauge steel mesh curves inward on sturdy beams nearly encircling us overhead. This architectural feature is designed to dissuade jumpers from making the five-story leap into the river or thick brush below. Donnie mentions that people have made the attempt and that random surveillance cameras are mounted in the cane—all of this to keep people from entering the United States in inappropriate fashion. . . .

We arrive at the [immigration] office and are both relieved that it is air-conditioned. Donnie shows his license to the officer, who waves him on, and I reach into my pocket, pull out my wallet, and wonder how many minutes it will take for Donnie's truck cab to cool down.

Opening the fold, I am momentarily confused by the version of my face staring back at me from the plastic card in the easiest access slot. I am almost ten years younger, wearing enormous late-eighties glasses, my hair is long, wavy, and pulled back, and behind me the lush foliage of a reservation road fills the rest of the image. It is my tribal identification card, documenting my name, birth date, clan, tribe, reservation address, blood quantum, and the signature of the man on the reservation who officiates on such matters, next to my own signature. Mine is a little more complicated than some, but not unfathomably so. I am a member of the Onondaga Nation, ... The back of the card lists several agreements with the United States, asserting the sovereignty of the Haudenosaunee, the league of six nations to which both the Onondaga and Tuscarora nations belong, known in the United States as "the Iroquois."

The card itself is not confusing to me, of course, but it usually rests in my wallet behind a document I tend to need much more frequently: my driver's license. My license is nowhere to be found within the wallet, and then I suddenly can see the card in my mind, can picture its exact location, and thus can confirm it is not on my body. . . .

Since September 2001, . . . the most consistent change has been nearly relentless requests for my identification from airport personnel. To make things easier on myself and on those asking, I have gotten a "flight wallet" the size of an airline ticket, and in this I keep my boarding pass, frequent flyer card, and, yes, while I am traveling, my driver's license. The flight wallet, at the moment I approach the immigration officer, sits approximately a hundred yards away, in Donnie's truck, across the road, but more important, across the border.

"Identification?" the officer asks, and I hand him my Native American Identification Card. He looks at it, tosses it down, and looks at me, smirking. "Now," he says, ...

"Now," he repeats, snapping the card on his desk this time, perhaps for emphasis, as if he had gotten an ace in a game of solitaire, "do you have any real ID?"

I am what you might call ethnically ambiguous in appearance. Over the years the odd looks, vague frowns, and unasked questions have become the routine. It has been kind of interesting, existing as a walking, breathing Rorschach test for others' perceptions and stereotype templates.

I have been mistaken for Italian, Armenian, Middle Eastern, Hawaiian, Russian, Polish, German, Portuguese, and Jewish, but I am most often wrongly assumed to be Latino. The first time it happened was in a men's room at a concert, when a drunken patron at the next urinal insisted I was a member of Los Lobos, the band whose set had finished about a half hour before. . . . The less glamorous mistake with my ethnicity happens nearly every time I am in the Southwest. This stands to reason, as Mexicans are Indians across the border, in essence, and we are the same in that we had very different, unique cultures before colonialism came along and divided us up with those stainless steel rivets in the bridge.

I was born and raised on a reservation in western New York State, a small place, home to fewer than two thousand people. Many of those people claim full-blood status, though some are blond, some have blue eyes. . . . My complexion is slightly dark, and deepens easily in the summer, so that by the end of June, even with minimal exposure, I usually sport what used to be called "a savage tan." My eyes are dark brown as well, and my hair appears to be black most of the year, but by late summer dark red highlights have burned into it. My body also reveals other telltale signs that prevent me from claiming full-blood status. I have genetic qualities that allow me to grow a beard and a mustache, and I have chosen to cultivate those traits.

. . . My hair was long a fair amount of my childhood and through adolescence—though not the long, straight Lakota hair all Indians are *supposed* to have. It seems many eastern Indians have a rougher textured hair, and mine falls into this category. No matter how much I might brush my hair out every morning, invariably I looked less like any Indians in Edward Curtis photographs and more like Jerry Garcia from the Grateful Dead, ...

On the reservation, as in many other places, hair is a political statement. I learned this reality early. One of my brothers, Lee, . . . began growing his hair long in the late 1960s, before he burned his draft card but after our oldest brother had been shipped out to Vietnam. Lee was suspended from high school a number of times for having his hair too long, until one time my mother grew tired of his forced removals, took him to school herself, grabbed an idle white kid in the hallway whose hair was longer than my brother's, and dragged them both into the office to confront the principal with this discrepancy. My brother was reinstated, but one of his instructors insisted he had missed too much time in his suspensions to graduate, so he went to summer school, but he did it in long hair and graduated in August.

He is not the first member of my family to have an educational institution concern itself with his hair. In the early part of the twentieth century, the Dawes Act was in full swing, and my grandfather's parents were persuaded by government agents to allow their son the great privilege of attending one of the Indian boarding schools. They claimed that he would have a much better chance of surviving in the world if he could learn a trade in the broader culture. He learned to play a western instrument, the piccolo, I believe, and eventually remembered nothing about water drums but was well versed in snare and bass. . . .

Through college I had kept my hair in various stages of long, but it always looked wild, ... In graduate school I got rid of it all and kept a reasonably short style through that period, until I graduated and got past my first set of job interviews. As I began teaching at the college a few miles from the reservation where I grew up, my hair was still fairly short, appropriate for the era, the early 1990s, but as soon as I signed the contract I let it grow back out, and in 1998 my braid was about a foot and a half long, when I decided to get rid of it.

. . .

Other, strangely resonant events occurred in the few months following that, and I finally decided that while I could not stop the perpetuation of this stereotype, I did not have to be a contributing member. Tying off both ends of my braid, I cut it off in 1999, reduced my hair to a flattop, and grew my mustache to join the goatee at the same time. The braid is in my top-right desk drawer, where I keep it to remind me of where I have been.

. . .

Here, at the border, I am suddenly in Los Lobos land again, and my tribal identification is not good enough. National identification papers, it seems, are good enough documentation for the United States from every other nation except those housed within its borders. Haudenosaunee law stipulates we are not citizens of the United States, regardless of any federal laws on Indian citizenship. I am still not sure what the full dynamics are here. Perhaps it is not that our ID cards are not legitimate enough, but instead that braidless and hairy, I am not legitimate enough for my ID. This officer, I see, stares at me, is certain my name is Pedro, Hector, Jesus, and as a result of this perception he wears his illegal alien

Polaroid sunglasses. Regardless of what might or might not be in my pocket, he has decided it is all right to treat me with disdain because I have been forward enough to attempt crossing borders without swimming my way in, and am merely getting what I deserve.

. . .

My faculty ID card looks promising. It is contemporary and formal, professionally laminated, and even has a bar code on it . . . . I hand this over and the officer looks at it. He rapid-fires questions at me. Suddenly I am taking a pop quiz on the academic calendar where I teach—when were finals, when was graduation, when does the school year begin, how many courses do I teach, and then it comes: What in Acuña, Mexico could possibly interest a college professor from New York? This question is so odd, so full of his emptiness, that no answer I can give short of "cheap dentistry," "stuffed armadillos," or "controlled substances" would be satisfactory. Back to the wallet.

My driving license convictions card surfaces next. This has my New York State license number on it, and a spotless driving record, I might add, the entire convictions section blank. The officer rejects this offer as well, observing it has no photograph. I suggest he can match the names from this to my other documents, and he merely raises his right eyebrow in a knowing way. . . .

Finally I remember that the attendants at the gym where I work out insist on picture ID, in addition to their own issued membership card, every time I enter. . . . We solved the dual ID show by photocopying my license and taping it to the gym card. I rifle back through the less-convincing documents in my wallet and find the card, my shoddily photocopied license taped to it, and I am in luck; the numbers are visible, and more important, they match the numbers on my convictions record. I feel like a lotto winner as we compare numbers, the officer and I, and he is satisfied enough to run them through his international-criminal-driver's-license database and see, indeed, that I do live in western New York, or at least that someone who looks remarkably like me does. He gathers my variety pack of ID cards, hands them to me, and tells me, reluctantly, that I am free to go.

My braid is seventeen hundred miles from where I am as I leave the air-conditioned building and head out into the West Texas sun, and the fact that I can now slide my license back into my wallet and become someone I am not—a citizen of New York State, and thus a citizen of the United States of America as well—is no great comfort.

19

American Hijab

Why My Scarf Is A Sociopolitical Statement, Not A Symbol Of My Religiosity

Mariam Gomaa

I remember donning the hijab for the first time three years ago. I say it was the first time, but really it was one of many times that I had slipped it on, standing in front of the mirror and adjusting the folds of fabric around my face. Yet this time was different. Rather than take it off after prayer or a visit to the local masjid (mosque), I was hoping to wear it regularly.

It was sometime in winter during my freshman year of college at Northwestern, and I had spent my first three months of college searching for my place among thousands of students. Like any freshmen, I had several identifying factors that felt true, things that I felt could not go unmentioned as I sought out the people who would become my closest friends. These included everything from my taste in books and music to my leftist political stance, but also my religion.

As a Muslim growing up in a post 9/11 world, I was accustomed to misconceptions about my religion, my race, and my identity. I was acutely aware of the way I navigated the world as a brown body, and how experiences of hate and injustice only magnified themselves when my mother (wearing hijab) or my sister (darker with characteristic African hair) accompanied me places. My body, in spite of its brown shade, was still in the liminal world of racial ambiguity, a place where I could pass into whiteness when it seemed convenient. There were few markers of my race and my religion. In spite of this, however, I had often felt that my religion was not something to be shed or stifled and hidden for the sake of others, for the sake of their comfort. I did not shy away from my heritage, my deeply Egyptian roots, the pride I felt for Africa and Arabia and Islam. They were the places that made me a blank-American, someone different.

That day in winter, as a lonely and homesick freshman, I remembered that being different was far from wanting or choosing to be different. That in fact, I was not in control of my narrative so long as I still sought the acceptance of those who might never want to understand me. My desire to wear hijab increased in that moment. Hijab became a symbol of my rejection of white-passing (or at the very least racial ambiguity), a privilege I was distinctly aware I had, and that I knew was not afforded to many of my fellow non-white Americans.

While hijab has historically had a reputation of being a number of things to "the West," rebellion has rarely been one of them. Certainly among many Muslims and in many Muslim nations it is often considered a sign of piety, or at the very least culture and respect. Yet rebellion, or perhaps a better word is resistance, is one of the many reasons many Muslims wear hijab.

In fact, in the 1970s and '80s, after a period of secularism, many Muslim majority countries were undergoing an Islamic revival, where the society (not the political regimes) responded to its conditions by adopting religion again. It was a reversal of the Westernisation approach, undermining the belief of my grandparents' generation that the West was strengthening Muslim nations. My mother describes choosing the hijab in college during the '80s, a little after this revival. Her parents, the previous generation, rejected her decision; theirs was an era where few women wore hijab, where much of the traditional clothing was left behind in favor of western attire . . .

Many American Muslims wear hijab much like the women of the Islamic revival, as a response to the changing times and a rejection of Western influence. While it seems counter-intuitive to wear hijab in a world that increasingly has a negative perception of Muslims, particularly when the consensus among many American Muslims is that one can be religious with or without it, there is a significant presence of American Muslim women wearing the hijab as a strong sense of identity. As one of these women, I know and have insight into a representation of hijab that is rarely portrayed—a representation that I call the American hijab, the antithesis and retaliation to whiteness and the American media, and a nod of solidarity to other people of color.

In this sense, hijab, rather than strictly being a religious decision, is also a sociopolitical choice and representation. In spite of, or rather in response to the negative portrayal of Muslims by those (Muslims and non-Muslims) who seek to define our narrative as one of barbaric killing and atrocity, women choose hijab—a piece of cloth that declares their identity as Muslims while simultaneously expressing their individual identity as smart, driven, successful, and independent. A simple yet powerful message. A way in which Muslim women can reclaim their narrative.

In choosing to wear the hijab, American Muslim women reconstruct the narrative of Islam in America. More importantly, they define American Islam and celebrate its rich cultural treasures: Islamic songs by Cat Stevens after his conversion, legendary icons like Malcolm X, Muhammad Ali and Kareem Abdul Jabbar, a deep sense of community that transcends immigrant heritage to become a new national heritage of its own, a style of hijab and clothing developed to bring together Islamic tradition from across the globe.

This American Islam has blossomed in many forms: the Mipsters (Muslim hipsters), Muppies (Muslim Urban Professionals), IMAN (Inner-city Muslim Action Network), and many more coalitions of young Muslim Americans who bring together their cross-cultural heritage—their America and their Islam—and share it with the world on a daily basis, through creative productions, concerts, health clinics and activist movements. While each coalition and organization has its own goals, they share a young, vibrant population of men and women alike with a common religious ideology, but also a sociopolitical identity. . . .

In their defiance of social convention, American Muslim women wearing hijab have paved the way for others and developed a sense of social consciousness and social justice among themselves.

While this story of resistance may seem new, it is not unique to Muslim women. It is a story that rings true for many individuals of color, whether it manifests itself as choosing to don an afro or to participate in the traditions of our non-American ancestors. It is the story of rejecting social pressure, of rejecting the influence of western media and the western world, and of choosing to openly and clearly declare our difference in a society that readily rejects us as part of its narrative.

The choice is embracing that difference and declaring it before anyone else can. This often means representing entire worlds, but it also means liberation from the pressures that society imposes with respect to beauty, identity, race, and culture. At the end of the day when I have fears about continuing to represent my faith without trepidation, I remember that I wear my hijab for the empowerment it grants me in declaring where I stand in a world that—more often than not—is in opposition to all that I am.

20

My Tongue Is Divided into Two

Quique Aviles

. . . As far back as I can remember, the promise of English was part of my life.

. . . In 1969, when I was four, my mother borrowed money from her mother to travel to the United States as a tourist. Her real intention was to stay in the States, get a good job, and offer her children a better life. She made a promise to bring us, her four children, one by one—starting with the oldest and ending with the youngest, which was me. . . .

My tongue is divided into two
by virtue, coincidence or heaven

V
O
I
C
E
S

words jumping out of my mouth
stepping on each other
enjoying being a voice for the message
expecting conclusions . . .

I've learned English in three different phases.

PHASE ONE: CURIOSITY AND WONDER

Having a mother who was in the United States meant that my brothers, my sister, and I got American gifts with words in English each time she came home. . . . I would sit with a dictionary and struggle to make out a few words so I could know more about my mother's new world.

In the mid-1970s, the Salvadoran Education Department brought "Televisión Educativa" to schools across the country. With it, came televised English classes . . . .

my tongue is divided into two
into heavy accent bits of confusion
into miracles and accidents
saying things that hurt the heart
drowning in a language that lives, jumps, translates . . .

Like most kids anywhere in the world, American music and television were also my English teachers. . . . My family was only the second family in our whole town to own a television. . . . I would watch *Kojak, Mission Impossible*, and *Starsky and Hutch*—swallowing up English, aspiring to be cool, and knowing that my mother had my ticket on layaway.

In late 1978, I had a political awakening. My country was ruled by the military and their martial law against ideas. I was 13 years old and joined the student movement. We demanded books, chalk, better teachers, and cleaner bathrooms. In the revolutionary fervor of those days, the coolness of English was ruined by Marx and Lenin. The language that fed my wonder and curiosity was now, according to my comrades, the language of the enemy of Yankee Imperialism. It was no longer cool. The next thing I knew, I was on a plane to the United States to save me from the death squads.

My tongue is divided by nature
by our crazy desire to triumph and conquer
this tongue is cut up into equal pieces
one wants to curse and sing out loud
the other one simply wants to ask for water . . .

PHASE TWO: FRUSTRATION AND NEED (HOW ENGLISH BECAME MY IMPERIAL LIBERATOR)

In the fall of 1980, I started 9th grade at Francis Junior High in Washington, D.C. Kids from Central America were coming into the school in droves every week. We were thrown into English as a Second Language (ESL) classes where Mrs. Padrino taught us . . . to say,

"Hello, how are you today? I am fine, thank you," in crisp English. On weekends, I went to rallies and protests—ESL classes for leftists. There, I got to repeat "No draft, no war/US out of El Salvador!" . . . .

By this time, I was beginning to understand that English was not just one language. At school, I became friends with Pichi, a chubby white Puerto Rican who . . . spoke three languages: Puerto Rican Spanish (which I barely understood), formal English (which I was beginning to understand), and Black English (which I now understood I needed to learn in order to survive). Pichi became my real ESL teacher:

> tongue
> English of the funny sounds
> tongue
> funny sounds in English
> tongue
> sounds funny in English
> tongue
> in funny English sounds

It was Pichi who gave me a copy of *Puerto Rican Obituary*, a poetry book by Pedro Pietri, one of the first and most influential of the Nuyorican poets of the 1970s. I had been writing poetry since I was ten years old, mainly rhyming, cheesy love poems. This book changed my life. . . . It introduced me to the possibility of words as a weapon. I started mixing my anger, my Spanish, and my limited English into poetry. . . . But English began to feel good. I began to feel that it was something I could use as revenge.

When it was time for me to start high school, I decided to audition for the Theater Department at the Duke Ellington School of the Arts. With my angry, broken English, I made an impression and got in. My first year was very hard. I was the only Latino in the whole school of more than 400 students. Rosemary Walsh, my acting teacher, would tell me, "You're a good actor, but I can't understand what the fuck you're saying. We're gonna work on you." . . . My second year at Ellington, I was assigned to speech classes. We studied phonetics and the anatomy of our sound-making factory: the mouth, the throat, the vocal chords, and the diaphram. These classes consisted of repetitive speech exercises, such as:

"Theophilus thistle, the unsuccessful thistle sifter, while sifting a sieve of unsifted thistles thrusts three thousand thistles through the thick of his thumb . . ." "Unique New York, Unique New York, Unique New York . . ."

. . .

So, here I was, thinking that I was making so much progress with my English, I could move to New York or L.A. and make it big.

> my tongue is divided into two
> a border patrol runs through the middle
> frisking words
> asking for proper identification
> checking for pronunciation . . .

By my senior year I had become a punk rocker, a combat-boot wearing rebel. I realized that there were no parts for me in traditional theater, that if I wanted to be an actor, I would have to write my own parts. With that realization, I began a deeper, artistic relationship with the English language. My new teachers became Nikki Giovanni, June Jordan, Lucille Clifton, and Alice Walker—black writers who were using language to say that we are beautiful, that we deserve things. I began to write monologues for characters that came from my life. As I began to develop my own voice, English became my imperial liberator.

PHASE THREE: SUBTLETY AND PAYBACK

I am still learning English. *El inglés.* . . .

Since the mid-1980s I have been writing and performing one-person shows that weave together poetry and monologues in English. Latinos often ask me, "Why don't you do more in Spanish?" I often respond, "Because you all don't pay my rent." But the real answer is: payback. I use English to challenge English speakers to question their assumptions about us Latinos, about each other, and, in these xenophobic times, about immigrants in general. I use it to poke, prod, question, and make people feel uncomfortable. I always read my poems from a music stand (I have very few of them memorized), and whenever I leave my house for a gig, carrying my music stand to the car, I always feel that I am carrying my *machete*. Words are my weapon.

They are also the way I build alliances. I have learned that building trust with someone who is different from you in this country is all about mastering their own version of the English language. Most of my work in D.C. has been with black kids. I go into classrooms and use theater improvisation as a tool for encouraging kids to write about their lives. Most kids want to do improvs about drugs and guns, the thug life. I challenge them by asking, "Does your momma love you? Do you smile? Do you laugh? Are there tender moments in your life?" For the majority of kids, the answer is yes. So I challenge them to create skits about those soft and tender moments and then to write poetry about it. I challenge them not to fulfill society's expectations of poor kids by being drug dealers and thugs. And I always tell them, "Ain't nobody gonna sing our song, so we might as well sing it ourselves."

For me, learning English has been about learning to sing my own song.

> my tongue is divided into two
> my tongue is divided into two
> I like my tongue
> it says what feels right
> I like my tongue
> it says what feels right

21

Letter to My Son

Ta-Nehisi Coates

Son,

Last Sunday the host of a popular news show asked me what it meant to lose my body.
. . .

But by now I am accustomed to intelligent people asking about the condition of my body without realizing the nature of their request. Specifically, the host wished to know why I felt that white America's progress, or rather the progress of those Americans who believe that they are white, was built on looting and violence. Hearing this, I felt an old and indistinct sadness well up in me. The answer to this question is the record of the believers themselves. The answer is American history. . . .

Democracy is a forgiving God and America's heresies—torture, theft, enslavement—are specimens of sin, so common among individuals and nations that none can declare themselves immune. In fact, Americans, in a real sense, have never betrayed their God. . . . At the onset of the Civil War, the United States of America had one of the highest rates of suffrage in the world. The question is not whether Lincoln truly meant "government of the people" but what our country has, throughout its history, taken the political term people to actually mean. In 1863 it did not mean your mother or your grandmother, and it did not mean you and me. As for now, it must be said that the elevation of the belief in being white was not achieved through wine tastings and ice-cream socials, but rather through the pillaging of life, liberty, labor, and land.

That Sunday, on that news show, I tried to explain this as best I could within the time allotted. But at the end of the segment, the host flashed a widely shared picture of a 12-year-old black boy tearfully hugging a white police officer. Then she asked me about "hope." And I knew then that I had failed. And I remembered that I had expected to fail. . . . When the journalist asked me about my body, it was like she was asking me to awaken her from the most gorgeous dream. I have seen that dream all my life. It is perfect houses with nice lawns. It is Memorial Day cookouts, block associations, and driveways. The Dream is tree houses and the Cub Scouts. And for so long I have wanted to escape into the Dream, to fold my country over my head like a blanket. But this has never been an option, because the Dream rests on our backs, the bedding made from our bodies. And knowing this, knowing that the Dream persists by warring with the known world, I was sad for the host, I was sad for all those families, I was sad for my country, but above all, in that moment, I was sad for you.

That was the week you learned that the killers of Michael Brown would go free. The men who had left his body in the street would never be punished. It was not my expectation that anyone would ever be punished. But you were young and still believed. You stayed up till 11 p.m. that night, waiting for the announcement of an indictment, and when instead it was announced that there was none you said, "I've got to go," and you went into your room, and I heard you crying. I came in five minutes after, and I didn't hug you, and I didn't comfort you, because I thought it would be wrong to comfort you. I did not tell you that it would be okay, because I have never believed it would be okay. What I told you is what your grandparents tried to tell me: that this is your country, that this is your world, that this is your body, and you must find some way to live within the all of it.

I write you in your 15th year. I am writing you because this was the year you saw Eric Garner choked to death for selling cigarettes; because you know now that Renisha McBride was shot for seeking help, that John Crawford was shot down for browsing in a department store. And you have seen men in uniform drive by and murder Tamir Rice, a 12-year-old child whom they were oath-bound to protect. And you know now, if you did not before, that the police departments of your country have been endowed with the authority to destroy your body. It does not matter if the destruction is the result of an unfortunate overreaction. It does not matter if it originates in a misunderstanding. It does not matter if the destruction springs from a foolish policy. Sell cigarettes without the proper authority and your body can be destroyed. Turn into a dark stairwell and your body can be destroyed. The destroyers will rarely be held accountable. Mostly they will receive pensions.

There is nothing uniquely evil in these destroyers or even in this moment. The destroyers are merely men enforcing the whims of our country, correctly interpreting its heritage and legacy. This legacy aspires to the shackling of black bodies. It is hard to face this. But all our phrasing—*race relations, racial chasm, racial justice, racial profiling, white privilege,* even *white supremacy*—serves to obscure that racism is a visceral experience, that it dislodges brains, blocks airways, rips muscle, extracts organs, cracks bones, breaks teeth. You must never look away from this. You must always remember that the sociology, the history, the economics, the graphs, the charts, the regressions all land, with great violence, upon the body. And should one live in such a body? What should be our aim beyond meager survival of constant, generational, ongoing battery and assault? I have asked this question all my life. I have sought the answer through my reading and writings, through the music of my youth, through arguments with your grandfather, with your mother. I have searched for answers in nationalist myth, in classrooms, out on the streets, and on other continents. The question is unanswerable, which is not to say futile. The greatest reward of this constant interrogation, of confrontation with the brutality of my country, is that it has freed me from ghosts and myths.

And yet I am still afraid. I feel the fear most acutely whenever you leave me. But I was afraid long before you, and in this I was unoriginal. When I was your age the only people I knew were black, and all of them were powerfully, adamantly, dangerously afraid. It was always right in front of me. The fear was there in the extravagant boys of my West Baltimore neighborhood, in their large rings and medallions, their big puffy coats and full-length fur-collared leathers, which was their armor against their world. They would stand on the corner of Gwynn Oak and Liberty, or Cold Spring and Park Heights, or outside Mondawmin Mall, with their hands dipped in Russell sweats. I think back on those boys now and all I see is fear, and all I see is them girding themselves against the ghosts of the bad old days when the Mississippi mob gathered 'round their grandfathers so that the branches of the black body might be torched, then cut away. The fear lived on in their practiced bop, their slouching denim, their big T-shirts, the calculated angle of their baseball caps, a catalog of behaviors and garments enlisted to inspire the belief that these boys were in firm possession of everything they desired. . . .

My father was so very afraid. I felt it in the sting of his black leather belt, which he applied with more anxiety than anger, my father who beat me as if someone might steal me away, because that is exactly what was happening all around us. Everyone had lost a child, somehow, to the streets, to jail, to drugs, to guns. It was said that these lost girls were sweet as honey and would not hurt a fly. It was said that these lost boys had just received a GED and had begun to turn their lives around. And now they were gone, and their legacy was a great fear.

When I was 6, Ma and Dad took me to a local park. I slipped from their gaze and found a playground. Your grandparents spent anxious minutes looking for me. When they found me, Dad did what every parent I knew would have done—he reached for his belt. I remember watching him in a kind of daze, awed at the distance between punishment and offense. Later, I would hear it in Dad's voice—"Either I can beat him, or the police." Maybe that saved me. Maybe it didn't. All I know is, the violence rose from the fear like smoke from a fire, and I cannot say whether that violence, even administered in fear and love, sounded the alarm or choked us at the exit. What I know is that fathers who slammed their teenage boys for sass would then release them to streets where their boys employed, and were subject to, the same justice. And I knew mothers who belted their girls, but the belt could not save these girls from drug dealers twice their age.

To be black in the Baltimore of my youth was to be naked before the elements of the world, before all the guns, fists, knives, crack, rape, and disease. The law did not protect us. And now, in your time, the law has become an excuse for stopping and frisking you, which is to say, for furthering the assault on your body. But a society that protects some people through a safety net of schools, government backed home loans, and ancestral wealth but can protect you only with the club of criminal justice has either failed at enforcing its good intentions or succeeded at something much darker. . . .

Somewhere out there beyond the firmament, past the asteroid belt, there were other worlds where children did not regularly fear for their bodies. I knew this because there was a large television in my living room. In the evenings I would sit before this television bearing witness to the dispatches from this other world. There were little white boys with complete collections of football cards, their only want was a popular girlfriend and their only worry was poison oak. That other world was suburban and endless, organized around pot roasts, blueberry pies, fireworks, ice-cream sundaes, immaculate bathrooms, and small toy trucks that were loosed in wooded backyards with streams and endless lawns. Comparing these dispatches with the facts of my native world, I came to understand that my country was a galaxy, and this galaxy stretched from the pandemonium of West Baltimore to the happy hunting grounds of Mr. Belvedere. I obsessed over the distance between that other sector of space and my own. I knew that my portion of the American galaxy, where bodies were enslaved by a tenacious gravity, was black and that the other, liberated portion was not. I knew that some inscrutable energy preserved the breach. I felt, but did not yet understand, the relation between that other world and me. And I felt in this a cosmic injustice, a profound cruelty, which infused an abiding, irrepressible desire to unshackle my body and achieve the velocity of escape.

The culture of the streets was essential—there was no alternative. I could not retreat into the church and its mysteries. My parents rejected all dogmas. We spurned the holidays marketed by the people who wanted to be white. We would not stand for their anthems. We would not kneel before their God. "The meek shall inherit the earth" meant nothing to me. The meek were battered in West Baltimore, stomped out at Walbrook Junction, bashed up on Park Heights, and raped in the showers of the city jail. My understanding of the universe was physical, and its moral arc bent toward chaos then concluded in a box. . . . Fear ruled everything around me, and I knew, as all black people do, that this fear was connected to the world out there, to the unworried boys, to pie and pot roast, to the white fences and green lawns nightly beamed into our television sets.

Every February my classmates and I were herded into assemblies for a ritual review of the civil-rights movement. Our teachers urged us toward the example of freedom marchers, Freedom Riders, and Freedom Summers, and it seemed that the month could not pass without a series of films dedicated to the glories of being beaten on camera. *Why are they showing this to us?* Why were only our heroes nonviolent? Back then all I could do was measure these freedom-lovers by what I knew. Which is to say, I measured them against children pulling out in the 7-Eleven parking lot, against parents wielding extension cords, and the threatening intonations of armed black gangs saying, "Yeah, nigger, what's up now?" I judged them against the country I knew, which had acquired the land through murder and tamed it under slavery, against the country whose armies fanned out across the world to extend their dominion. The world, the real one, was civilization secured and ruled by savage means. How could the schools valorize men and women whose values society actively scorned? How could they send us out into the streets of Baltimore, knowing all that they were, and then speak of nonviolence?

Some things were clear to me: The violence that undergirded the country, so flagrantly on display during Black History Month, and the intimate violence of the streets were not unrelated. And this violence was not magical, but was of a piece and by design. But what exactly was the design? And why? I must know. I must get out ... but into what? I saw the design in those boys on the corner, in "the babies having babies." The design explained everything, from our cracked-out fathers to HIV to the bleached skin of Michael Jackson.

I felt this but I could not explain it. . . . I was haunted by the bodily sacrifice of Malcolm. I was haunted because I believed that we had left ourselves back there, and now in the crack era all we had was a great fear. Perhaps I must go back. That was what I heard in the rapper's call to "keep it real." Perhaps we should return to ourselves, to our own primordial streets, to our own ruggedness, to our own rude hair. Perhaps we should return to Mecca. . . .

Now, the heirs of slaveholders could never directly acknowledge our beauty or reckon with its power. And so the beauty of the black body was never celebrated in movies, on television shows, or in the textbooks I'd seen as a child. Everyone of any import, from Jesus to George Washington, was white. This was why your grandparents banned Tarzan and the Lone Ranger and toys with white faces from the house. They were rebelling against the history books that spoke of black people only as sentimental "firsts"—first black four-star general, first black congressman, first black mayor—always presented in the bemused manner of a category of Trivial Pursuit. Serious history was the West, and the West was white. This was all distilled for me in a quote I once read, from the novelist Saul Bellow. I can't remember where I read it, or when—only that I was already at Howard. "Who is the Tolstoy of the Zulus?," Bellow quipped. Tolstoy was "white," I understood him to say, and so Tolstoy "mattered," like everything else that was white "mattered." And this view of things was connected to the fear that passed through the generations, to the sense of dispossession. We were black, beyond the visible spectrum, beyond civilization. Our history was inferior because we were inferior, which is to say our bodies were inferior. And our inferior bodies could not possibly be accorded the same respect as those that built the West. Would it not be better, then, if our bodies were civilized, improved, and put to some legitimate Christian use? . . .

"White America" is a syndicate arrayed to protect its exclusive power to dominate and control our bodies. Sometimes this power is direct (lynching), and sometimes it is insidious (redlining). But however it appears, the power of domination and exclusion is central to the belief in being white, and without it, "white people" would cease to exist for want of reasons. There will surely always be people with straight hair and blue eyes, as there have been for all of history. But some of these straight-haired people with blue eyes have been "black," and this points to the great difference between their world and ours. We did not choose our fences. They were imposed on us by Virginia planters obsessed with enslaving as many Americans as possible. Now I saw that we had made something down here, in slavery, in Jim Crow, in ghettoes. . . . They made us into a race. We made ourselves into a people.

And what did that mean for the Dreamers I'd seen as a child? Could I ever want to get into the world they made? No. I was born among a people, Samori, and in that realization I knew that I was out of something. It was the psychosis of questioning myself, of constantly wondering if I could measure up. But the whole theory was wrong, their whole notion of race was wrong. And apprehending that, I felt my first measure of freedom.

This realization was important but intellectual. It could not save my body. Indeed, it made me understand what the loss of all our black bodies really meant. No one of us were "black people." We were individuals, a one of one, and when we died there was nothing. Always remember that Trayvon Martin was a boy, that Tamir Rice was a particular boy, that Jordan Davis was a boy, like you. When you hear these names think of all the wealth poured into them. Think of the gasoline expended, the treads worn carting him to football games, basketball tournaments, and Little League. Think of the time spent regulating sleepovers. Think of the surprise birthday parties, the day care, and the reference checks on babysitters. Think of checks written for family photos. Think of soccer balls, science kits, chemistry sets, racetracks, and model trains. Think of all the embraces, all the private jokes, customs, greetings, names, dreams, all the shared knowledge and capacity of a black family injected into that vessel of flesh and bone. And think of how that vessel was taken, shattered on the concrete, and all its holy contents, all that had gone into each of them, was sent flowing back to the earth. It is terrible to truly see our particular beauty, Samori, because then you see the scope of the loss. But you must push even further. You must see that this loss is mandated by the history of your country, by the Dream of living white. . . .

But American reunion was built on a comfortable narrative that made enslavement into benevolence, white knights of body snatchers, and the mass slaughter of the war into a kind of sport in which one could conclude that both sides conducted their affairs with courage, honor, and élan. . . . Historians conjured the Dream. Hollywood fortified the Dream. The Dream was gilded by novels and adventure stories. John Carter flees the broken Confederacy for Mars. We are not supposed to ask what, precisely, he was running from. I, like every kid I knew, loved *The Dukes of Hazzard.* But I would have done well to think more about why two outlaws, driving a car named the General Lee, must necessarily be portrayed as "just some good ole boys, never meanin' no harm"—a mantra for the Dreamers if there ever was one. But what one "means" is neither important nor relevant. It is not necessary that you believe that the officer who choked Eric Garner set out that day to destroy a body. All you need to understand is that the officer carries with him the power of the American state and the weight of an American legacy, and they necessitate that of the bodies destroyed every year, some wild and disproportionate number of them will be black.

Here is what I would like for you to know: In America, it is traditional to destroy the black body—it is heritage. Enslavement was not merely the antiseptic borrowing of labor—it is not so easy to get a human being to commit their body against its own elemental interest. And so enslavement must be casual wrath and random manglings, the gashing of heads and brains blown out over the river as the body seeks to escape. It must be rape so regular as to be industrial. There is no uplifting way to say this. I have no praise anthems, nor old Negro spirituals. The spirit and soul are the body and brain, which are destructible—that is precisely why they are so precious. And the soul did not escape. The spirit did not steal away on gospel wings. The soul was the body that fed the tobacco, and the spirit was the blood that watered the cotton, and these created the first fruits of the American garden. And the fruits were secured through the bashing of children with stovewood, through hot iron peeling skin away like husk from corn.

It had to be blood. It had to be the thrashing of kitchen hands for the crime of churning butter at a leisurely clip. It had to be some woman "chear'd ... with thirty lashes a Saturday last and as many more a Tuesday again." It could only be the employment of carriage whips, tongs, iron pokers, handsaws, stones, paperweights, or whatever might be handy to break the black body, the black family, the black community, the black nation. The bodies were pulverized into stock and marked with insurance. And the bodies were an aspiration, lucrative as Indian land, a veranda, a beautiful wife, or a summer home in the mountains. For the men who needed to believe themselves white, the bodies were the key to a social club, and the right to break the bodies was the mark of civilization. "The two great divisions of society are not the rich and poor, but white and black," said the great South Carolina senator John C. Calhoun. "And all the former, the poor as well as the rich, belong to the upper class, and are respected and treated as equals." And there it is—the right to break the black body as the meaning of their sacred equality. And that right has always given them meaning, has always meant that there was someone down in the valley because a mountain is not a mountain if there is nothing below.

You and I, my son, are that "below." That was true in 1776. It is true today. There is no them without you, and without the right to break you they must necessarily fall from the mountain, lose their divinity, and tumble out of the Dream. And then they would have to determine how to build their suburbs on something other than human bones, how to angle their jails toward something other than a human stockyard, how to erect a democracy independent of cannibalism. I would like to tell you that such a day approaches when the people who believe themselves to be white renounce this demon religion and begin to think of themselves as human. But I can see no real promise of such a day. We are captured, brother, surrounded by the majoritarian bandits of America. And this has happened here, in our only home, and the terrible truth is that we cannot will ourselves to an escape on our own. . . .

I think now of the old rule that held that should a boy be set upon in someone else's chancy hood, his friends must stand with him, and they must all take their beating together. I now know that within this edict lay the key to all living. None of us were promised to end the fight on our feet, fists raised to the sky. We could not control our enemies' number, strength, or weaponry. Sometimes you just caught a bad one. But whether you fought or ran, you did it together, because that is the part that was in our control. What we must never do is willingly hand over our own bodies or the bodies of our friends. That was the wisdom: We knew we did not lay down the direction of the street, but despite that, we could—and must—fashion the way of our walk. And that is the deeper meaning of your name—that the struggle, in and of itself, has meaning.

That wisdom is not unique to our people, but I think it has special meaning to those of us born out of mass rape, whose ancestors were carried off and divided up into policies and stocks. I have raised you to respect every human being as singular, and you must extend that same respect into the past. Slavery is not an indefinable mass of flesh. It is a particular, specific enslaved woman, whose mind is as active as your own, whose range of feeling is as vast as your own; who prefers the way the light falls in one particular spot in the woods, who enjoys fishing where the water eddies in a nearby stream, who loves her mother in her own complicated way, thinks her sister talks too loud, has a favorite cousin, a favorite season, who excels at dressmaking and knows, inside herself, that she is as intelligent and capable as anyone. "Slavery" is this same woman born in a world that loudly proclaims its love of freedom and inscribes this love in its essential texts, a world in which these same professors hold this woman a slave, hold her mother a slave, her father a slave, her daughter a slave, and when this woman peers back into the generations all she sees is the enslaved. She can hope for more. She can imagine some future for her grandchildren. But when she dies, the world—which is really the only world she can ever know—ends. For this woman, enslavement is not a parable. It is damnation. It is the never-ending night. And the length of that night is most of our history. Never forget that we were enslaved in this country longer than we have been free. Never forget that for 250 years black people were born into chains—whole generations followed by more generations who knew nothing but chains.

You must struggle to truly remember this past. You must resist the common urge toward the comforting narrative of divine law, toward fairy tales that imply some irrepressible justice. The enslaved were not bricks in your road, and their lives were not chapters in your redemptive history. They were people turned to fuel for the American machine. Enslavement was not destined to end, and it is wrong to claim our present circumstance—no matter how improved—as the redemption for the lives of people who never asked for the posthumous, untouchable glory of dying for their children. Our triumphs can never redeem this. Perhaps our triumphs are not even the point. Perhaps struggle is all we have. So you must wake up every morning knowing that no natural promise is unbreakable, least of all the promise of waking up at all. This is not despair. These are the preferences of the universe itself: verbs over nouns, actions over states, struggle over hope.

The birth of a better world is not ultimately up to you, though I know, each day, there are grown men and women who tell you otherwise. I am not a cynic. I love you, and I love the world, and I love it more with every new inch I discover. But you are a black boy, and you must be responsible for your body in a way that other boys cannot know. Indeed, you must be responsible for the worst actions of other black bodies, which, somehow, will always be assigned to you. And you must be responsible for the bodies of the powerful—the policeman who cracks you with a nightstick will quickly find his excuse in your furtive movements. You have to make your peace with the chaos, but you cannot lie. You cannot forget how much they took from us and how they transfigured our very bodies into sugar, tobacco, cotton, and gold. . . .

But you are human and you will make mistakes. You will misjudge. You will yell. You will drink too much. You will hang out with people whom you shouldn't. Not all of us can always be Jackie Robinson—not even Jackie Robinson was always Jackie Robinson. But the price of error is higher for you than it is for your countrymen, and so that America might justify itself, the story of a black body's destruction must always begin with his or her error, real or imagined—with Eric Garner's anger, with Trayvon Martin's mythical words ("You are gonna die tonight"), with Sean Bell's mistake of running with the wrong crowd. . . .

I am sorry that I cannot make it okay. I am sorry that I cannot save you—but not that sorry. Part of me thinks that your very vulnerability brings you closer to the meaning of life, just as for others, the quest to believe oneself white divides them from it. The fact is that despite their dreams, their lives are also not inviolable. When their own vulnerability becomes real—when the police decide that tactics intended for the ghetto should enjoy wider usage, when their armed society shoots down their children, when nature sends hurricanes against their cities—they are shocked by the rages of logic and the natural world in a way that those of us who were born and bred to understand cause and effect can never be. And I would not have you live like them. You have been cast into a race in which the wind is always at your face and the hounds are always at your heels. And to varying degrees this is true of all life. The difference is that you do not have the privilege of living in ignorance of this essential fact.

I am speaking to you as I always have—treating you as the sober and serious man I have always wanted you to be, who does not apologize for his human feelings, who does not make excuses for his height, his long arms, his beautiful smile. You are growing into consciousness, and my wish for you is that you feel no need to constrict yourself to make other people comfortable. None of that can change the math anyway. I never wanted you to be twice as good as them, so much as I have always wanted you to attack every day of your brief bright life determined to struggle. The people who must believe they are white can never be your measuring stick. I would not have you descend into your own dream. I would have you be a conscious citizen of this terrible and beautiful world.

22

My Class Didn't Trump My Race

Using Oppression to Face Privilege

Robin J. DiAngelo

I grew up poor and White. Although my class oppression has been relatively visible to me, my race privilege has not. In my efforts to uncover how race has shaped my life, I have gained deeper insight by placing race in the center of my analysis and asking how each of my other group locations have socialized me to collude with racism. In so doing, I have been able to address in greater depth my multiple locations and how they function together to hold racism in place. Thus my exploration of what it means to be White starts with what it means to be poor, for my understanding of race is inextricably entwined with my class background. I now make the distinction that I grew up poor *and* White, for my experience of poverty would have been different had I not been White. For Whites that experience oppression in other areas of our lives (such as class, gender, religion, or sexual orientation), it can be difficult to center a location through which we experience privilege. When leading discussions in multicultural education courses, I find that White students often resist centering racism in their analysis, feeling that to do so invalidates their oppressions. These students also feel that these oppressions make them "less" racially privileged. However, rather than ameliorating my race privilege, my oppressed class location was a primary avenue through which I came to understand what being White meant. As I work to unravel my internalized racial dominance, I have found two key questions useful:

1.   How does internalized dominance function collectively for Whites, regardless of our other social locations?
2.   How did I learn racism *specifically through my class (or rather) oppression*?

I was born to working class parents; my father was a construction worker and my mother was a switchboard operator. When I was 2, my parents divorced and my mother began to raise us on her own; at that point we entered into poverty. I have never understood people who say, "we were poor but we didn't know it because we had lots of love." Poverty hurts. It isn't romantic, or some form of "living simply." Poor people are not innocent and child-like. The lack of medical and dental care, the hunger, and the ostracization, are concrete. The stress of poverty made my household much more chaotic than loving.

We were evicted frequently, and moved four to five times a year. There were periods when oatmeal was the only food in our house. I had no health or dental care during my childhood, and today all of my front teeth are filled because by the time I was 10 they were rotten. If we got sick, my mother would beat us, screaming that we could not get sick because she could not afford to take us to the doctor. We occasionally had to live in our car and I was left with relatives for 8 months while my mother tried to secure housing for us. My teacher once held my hands up to my fourth-grade class as an example of poor hygiene and with the class as her audience, told me to go home and tell my mother to wash me.

I used to stare at the girls in my class and ache to be like them; to have a father, to wear pretty clothes, to go to camp, to be clean and get to sit with them. I knew we didn't have enough money and that meant that I couldn't join them in school or go to their houses or have the same things they had. But the moment the real meaning of poverty crystallized for me came when we were visiting another family. As we were leaving I heard one of their daughters ask her mother, "What is wrong with them?" I stopped, riveted. I too, wanted to know. Her mother held her finger to her lips and whispered, "Shhh, they're *poor*." This was a revelatory moment for me. The shock came not just in the knowledge that we were poor, but that it was exposed. There was something wrong with us, indeed, and it was something that was obvious to others and that we couldn't hide, something shameful that could be seen but should not be named. It took me many years to gain a structural analysis of class that would help shift this sense of shame.

I begin this narrative with my class background because it so deeply informs my understanding of race. From an early age I had the sense of being an outsider; I was acutely aware that I was poor, that I was dirty, that I was not normal, and that there was something "wrong" with me. But I also knew that I was *not* Black. We were at the lower rungs of society, but there was always someone on the periphery, just below us. I knew that "colored" people existed and that they should be avoided. I can remember many occasions when I reached for candy or uneaten food laying on the street and was admonished by my grandmother not to touch it because a "colored person" may have touched it. The message was clear to me; if a colored person touched something it became dirty. The irony here is that the marks of poverty were clearly visible on me: poor hygiene, torn clothes, homelessness, hunger. Yet through comments such as my grandmother's, a racial Other was formed in my consciousness, an Other through whom I became clean. Race was the one identity that aligned me with the other girls in my school.

I left home as a teenager and struggled to survive. As I looked at what lay ahead, I could see no path out of poverty other than education. The decision to take that path was frightening for me; I had never gotten the message that I was smart and academia was a completely foreign social context. But once I was in academia, I understood that a college degree is not conferred upon those who are smarter or who try harder than others, it comes through a complex web of intersecting systems of privileges that include internal expectations as well as external resources. In academia, racism, a key system that I benefit from, helped to mediate my class-based disadvantages.

Upon graduation, with my degree in sociology and a background in adult education, I answered a call for diversity trainers from a state department that had lost a civil rights lawsuit and been mandated to provide 16 hr of diversity training to all their employees. They needed 40 diversity trainers to train 3,000 people. Looking back from where I am now, I see how naïve I was when I started that contract. I thought that being "liberal" qualified me because after all, racists were people who didn't have an open mind. I had an open mind and was thus not a racist, my reasoning went; these employees just needed help opening their minds too. As happens all too often, those in the position to hire me (primarily other White people) did not have the ability to assess the qualifications of someone leading discussions on race, and I was hired, along with 39 other people from a range of backgrounds.

I was completely unprepared for the depth of hostility and the disconnection from racial realities that I encountered from White people in these trainings. It was unnerving to be in a room composed exclusively of White employees and hear them bitterly complain that because of Affirmative Action, White people could no longer get jobs. That White employees would feel free to express this hostility to my coleader of color (who was racially isolated in the room) was another piece of the puzzle I was yet to put together. Even more significantly, the training teams were always interracial, and the very dynamics that I sought to enlighten my participants on were actively manifesting between my cotrainers and myself. Over time, I began to see racial dynamics more clearly, and after many years in the field, along with much personal work and some very patient mentors, I became more grounded in the dynamics of racialized knowledge construction. These trainings provided an extraordinary opportunity to observe first hand the processes by which a White racial identity is socially constructed and privileged, and the mechanisms by which White people receive and protect that privilege. I also reflected on my own responses to the ways in which I was being racially challenged, for unlike the middle class culture of academia that I found foreign, the culture of Whiteness was so normalized for me that it was barely visible. I had my experience of marginalization to draw from in understanding racism, which helped tremendously, but as I became more conversant in the workings of racism I came to understand that the oppression I experienced growing up poor didn't protect me from learning my place in the racial hierarchy.

Since those early days, I have led dialogues on race with police officers, social workers, teachers, and in both the private and government sectors. I recently completed my dissertation on how White student teachers reproduce racism in interracial dialogues about race. As I look at the world now, I see racism as ever-present and multidimensional. I realize that poor and working class White people don't necessarily have any less racism than middle or upper class White people, our racism is just conveyed in different ways and we enact it from a different social location than the middle or upper classes.

As I reflect back on the early messages I received about being poor and being White, I now realize that my grandmother and I *needed* people of color to cleanse and realign us with the dominant White culture that our poverty had separated us from. I now ask myself how the classist messages I internalized growing up lead me to collude in racism. For example, as a child who grew up in poverty, I received constant reminders that I was stupid, lazy, dirty, and a drain on the resources of hardworking people. I internalized these messages, and they work to silence me. Unless I work to uproot them, I am less likely to trust my own perceptions or feel like I have a "right" to speak up. I may not attempt to interrupt racism because the social context in which it is occurring intimidates me. My fear on these occasions may be coming from a place of internalized class inferiority, but in practice my silence colludes with racism and ultimately benefits me by protecting my White privilege and maintaining racial solidarity with other White people. This solidarity connects and realigns me with White people across other lines of difference, such as the very class locations that have silenced me in the first place. I am also prone to use others to elevate me, as in the example with my grandmother. So although my specific class background mediated the way I learned racism and how I enact it, in the end it still socialized me to collude with the overall structure.

It is my observation that class dictates proximity between Whites and people of color. Poor Whites are most often in closest proximity to people of color because they tend to share poverty. I hear the term "White trash" frequently. It is not without significance that this is one of the few expressions in which race is named for Whites. I think the proximity of the people labelled as White trash to people of color is why; race becomes marked or "exposed" by virtue of a closeness to people of color. In a racist society, this closeness both highlights and pollutes Whiteness. Owning class people also have people of color near them because people of color are often their domestics and gardeners—their servants. But they do not interact socially with people of color in the same way that poor Whites do. Middle class Whites are generally the furthest away from people of color. They are the most likely to say that, "there were no people of color in my neighbourhood or school. I didn't meet a Black person until I went to college" (often adding, "so I was lucky because I didn't learn anything about racism"). Looking specifically at how class shaped my racial identity has been very helpful to me in attempting to unravel the specific way I manifest my internalized racial superiority.

I am no longer poor. Although I still carry the marks of poverty, those marks are now only internal. But these marks limit me in more than what I believe I deserve or where I think I belong; they also interfere with my ability to stand up against injustice, for as long as I believe that I am not as smart or as valuable as other White people, I won't challenge racism. I believe that in order for Whites to unravel our internalized racial dominance, we have two interwoven tasks. One is to work on our own internalized oppression—the ways in which we impose limitations on ourselves based on the societal messages we receive about the inferiority of the lower status groups we belong to. The other task is to face the internalized dominance that results from being socialized in a racist society—the ways in which we consciously or unconsciously believe that we are more important, more valuable, more intelligent, and more deserving than people of color. I cannot address the interwoven complexity of other White people's social locations. However, after years facilitating dialogues on race with thousands of White people from a range of class positions (as well as varied gender, sexual orientation, religious, and ability positions), and bearing witness to countless stories and challenges from people of color about my own racism and that of other Whites, I have come to see some very common patterns of internalized dominance. These patterns are shared across other social positions due to the bottom line nature of racism: Regardless of one's other locations, White people know on some level that being White in this society is "better" than being a person of color, and this, along with the very real doors Whiteness opens, serves to mediate the oppression experienced in those other social locations. In the next section of this article, I will identify several of these patterns of internalized dominance that are generally shared among Whites.

WE LIVE SEGREGATED LIVES

Growing up in segregated environments (schools, workplaces, neighborhoods, media images, historical perspectives, etc.), we are given the message that our experiences and perspectives are the only ones that matter. We receive this message day in and day out, and it is not limited to a single moment, it is a *relentless experience*. Virtually all of our teachers, history books, role models, movie and book characters, are White like us. Further, as White people, we are taught not to feel any loss about the absence of people of color in our lives. In fact, the absence of people of color is what defines our schools and neighborhoods as "good." And we get this message regardless of where we are oppressed in other areas of our lives. Because we live primarily segregated lives in a White-dominated society, we receive little or no authentic information about racism and are thus unprepared to think critically or complexly about it. Although segregation is often mediated somewhat for poor urban (and other) Whites who may live near and have friendships with people of color on the microlevel, segregation is still operating on the macrolevel and informing our collective perspectives and what is deemed the most valuable of "official" knowledge.

Whites from the lower classes who may have more integrated lives on the micro level still receive the message that achievement means moving out of poverty and away from the neighborhoods and schools that define us. Upward mobility is the great class goal in the United States, and the social environment gets tangibly Whiter the higher up one goes, whether it be in academia or management. Whiter environments, in turn, are marked as the most socially and economically valuable. Reaching towards the most valuable places in society thus entails leaving people of color behind.

WE ARE TAUGHT IN OUR CULTURE TO SEE OUR EXPERIENCE AS OBJECTIVE AND REPRESENTATIVE OF REALITY

The belief in objectivity, coupled with setting White people up as *outside of culture* and thus the norms for humanity, allows us to see ourselves as universal humans who can represent all of human experience. People of color can only represent their own racialized experience—that is, Robert Altman is a film director whose work is expected to relate to everyone, Spike Lee is a Black film director whose films are from "the Black" perspective. But there is no objective, neutral reality. Human objectivity is not actually possible, but as long as we construct the world as if it is, and then ascribe it only to ourselves, we keep White experience and people centered and people of color in the margins.

WE ARE RAISED TO VALUE THE INDIVIDUAL AND TO SEE OURSELVES AS INDIVIDUALS, RATHER THAN AS PART OF A SOCIALIZED GROUP

Individuality allows us to present ourselves as having "just arrived on the scene," unique and original, outside of socialization and unaffected by the relentless racial messages we receive. This also allows us to distance ourselves from the actions of our group and demand that we be granted the benefit of the doubt (because we are individuals) in all cases. Thus we get very irate when we are "accused" of racism, because as individuals, we are "different" from other White people and expect to be seen as such. We find intolerable any suggestion that our behaviour or perspectives are typical of our group as a whole, and this ensures that we cannot deepen our understanding of racism.

Seeing ourselves as individuals erases our history and hides the way in which wealth has accumulated over generations and benefits us, *as a group*, today. Further, being an individual is a privilege only afforded to White people. By focusing on ourselves as individuals, Whites are able to conceptualize the racist patterns in our behavior as "just our personality" and not connected to intergroup dynamics. For example, I might be an extrovert and cut people off when I am engaged in a discussion. I can say, "that is just my personality, I do that to everyone. That is how we talked at the dinner table in my family." But the moment I cut off a person of color, it becomes racism because the history and the impact of that behavior for both of us is different. The freedom to remain oblivious to that fact, with no sense that this obliviousness has any consequences of importance, is White privilege (racism).

If we use the line of reasoning that we are all individuals and social categories such as race, class, and gender don't matter and are just "labels" that stereotype us, then it follows that we all end up in our own "natural" places. Those at the top are merely a collection of individuals who rose under their own individual merits, and those at the bottom are there due to individual lack. Group membership is thereby rendered inoperative and racial disparities are seen as essential rather than structural. Thus the discourse of individuality is not only connected to the discourse of meritocracy, but also with the Darwinism of the "bell curve." It behooves those of us oppressed in other places of individuality to understand group membership, for the discourse of individuality may benefit us in terms of racial privilege but ultimately holds all of our oppressions in place.

IN OUR DOMINANT POSITIONS WE ARE ALMOST ALWAYS RACIALLY COMFORTABLE AND EXPECT TO REMAIN SO

We can often choose if and when we will put ourselves into racially uncomfortable situations, and most of our lives have been advised not to do it because it is "dangerous." Thus racial comfort becomes not only an expectation, but something to which we feel entitled. If racism is brought up and we become uncomfortable, then something is "wrong" and we blame the person who triggered our discomfort (usually a person of color). Because racism is necessarily uncomfortable, insisting that we remain comfortable guarantees we will never really face it or engage in authentic dialogue with others about it.

Whites often confuse comfort with safety and state that we don't feel safe when what we really mean is that we don't feel comfortable. This trivializes our history of savage brutality towards people of color and perverts the reality of that history. Because we don't think complexly about racism, we don't ask ourselves what safety means from a position of dominance, or the impact on people of color for Whites to complain about their safety when merely *talking* about racism.

WE FEEL THAT WE SHOULD BE JUDGED BY OUR INTENTIONS RATHER THAN THE EFFECTS OF OUR BEHAVIOR

A common White reasoning is that as long as we didn't intend to perpetuate racism, then our actions don't count as racism. We focus on our intentions and discount the impact, thereby invalidating people of color's experiences and communicating that the effects of our behavior on them are unimportant. We then spend great energy explaining to people of color why our behavior is not racism at all. This invalidates their perspectives while enabling us to deny responsibility for making the effort to understand enough about racism to see our behavior's impact in both the immediate interaction and the broader, historical context.

WE BELIEVE THAT IF WE CAN'T FEEL OUR SOCIAL POWER, THEN WE DON'T HAVE ANY

White social power is so normalized that it is outside of our conscious awareness. Yet we often expect that power is something that one can feel, rather than something one takes for granted. The issue of social power is where a lower class location often becomes confused with a lack of racial privilege. For example, in discussions on race I often hear White working class men protest that they don't have any social power. They work long and gruelling hours, often in jobs in which they have no long-term security, and come home feeling beaten and quite disempowered. These men can often not relate to the concept of holding social power. But if being able to feel racial privilege is required before Whites can acknowledge its reality, we will not be able to see (and thus change) it. The key to recognizing power is in recognizing normalcy—what is not attended to or in need of constant navigation. These men are indeed struggling against social and economic barriers, but race is simply not one of them; in fact, race is a major social current running in their direction and not only moving them along, but helping them navigate their other social struggles. Not feeling power is not necessarily aligned with how others perceive or respond to us, or our relationship to social and institutional networks.

WE THINK IT IS IMPORTANT NOT TO NOTICE RACE

The underlying assumption of a colorblind discourse is that race is a defect and it is best to pretend that we don't notice it. But if we pretend we don't notice race, we cannot notice racism. If we don't notice racism, we can't understand or interrupt it in ourselves or others. We have to start being honest about the fact that we do notice race (when it isn't White) and then pay attention to what race means in our everyday lives. White people and people of color do not have the same racial experience, and this has profound and tangible consequences that need to be understood if we want to stop colluding with racism.

WE CONFUSE NOT UNDERSTANDING WITH NOT AGREEING

Because of the factors discussed previously, there is much about racism that Whites don't understand. Yet in our racial arrogance, we have no compunction about debating the knowledge of people who have lived, breathed, and studied these issues for many years. We feel free to dismiss these informed perspectives rather than have the humility to acknowledge that they are unfamiliar to us, reflect further on them, or seek more knowledge. We trivialize others' intelligence and expertise and counter with simplistic platitudes that often begin with, "People just need to . . . "

People from the lower classes often have the opportunity to learn more about the perspectives of people of color through their more likely proximity to them. Yet the conflicting messages we receive within our own families and the myriad messages we receive from the larger culture contradict these perspectives and do not support us in either seeking out, or valuing, them.

WE WILL BE THE JUDGE OF WHETHER OR NOT RACISM HAS OCCURRED

Because of our social, economic, and political power within a White supremacist culture, we are in the position to legitimize people of color's assertions of racism. Yet we are the least likely to see, understand, or be invested in validating those assertions and being honest about their consequences. We construct racism as specific acts that individuals either do or don't do, and think we can simply look at a specific incident and decide if "it" happened. But racism is infused in every part of our society, our beings, and our perspectives. It is reinforced everyday in countless and often subliminal ways. It cannot be pulled out into specific moments, and our inability to think complexly about racism, as well as our investment in its benefits makes us the least qualified to assess its manifestations.

RACISM HAS BEEN CONSTRUCTED AS BELONGING TO EXTREMISTS AND BEING VERY BAD

Racism is a deeply embedded, multidimensional, and internalized system that all members of this society are shaped by. Yet dominant culture constructs racism as primarily in the past and only currently occurring as isolated acts relegated to individual bad people (usually living somewhere in the South, or "old"). Although many White people today sincerely believe that racism is a bad thing, our abhorrence of racism coupled with a superficial conceptualization of it causes us to be highly defensive about any suggestion that we perpetuate it. Many Whites (and liberal Whites in particular) think that we can deal with racism in our heads (and without ever interacting with people of color) by deciding that we have not been affected because we don't want to have been affected.

A superficial understanding of racism coupled with a desire to distance ourselves from being perceived as "bad" is further complicated by resentments we may feel about places in our lives where we suffer from other forms of social injustice. It is often very difficult for Whites who have not been validated for the oppression they experience elsewhere to keep their attention on a form of oppression from which they benefit. But I have found that when I explore how classism and other oppressions I experience set me up to participate in racism, I am more able to interrupt the manifestation of both in my life. By placing racism in the center of my analysis, I have been able to begin to unravel my other group socializations and how they work together to support social hierarchies.

INTERRUPTING INTERNALIZED DOMINANCE

I have found that a key to interrupting my internalized racial dominance is to defer to the knowledge of people whom I have been taught, in countless ways, are less knowledgeable

V
O
I
C
E
S

and less valuable than I am. I must reach for humility and be willing to *not know*. I may never fully understand the workings of racism, as I have been trained my entire life to perpetuate racism while denying its reality. I do not have to understand racism for it to be real, and my expectation that I could is part of my internalized dominance. Reaching for racial humility as a White person is not the same for me as being mired in class shame.

My class position is only one social location from which I learned to collude with racism. For example, I have also asked myself how I learned to collude with racism as a Catholic and a woman. How did it shape my sense of racial belonging, of racial *correctness*, to be presented with God, the ultimate and universal authority, as White? How did the active erasure of Jesus' race and ethnicity shape my racial consciousness? How did the universalization of Catholicism as the true religion for all peoples of the world engender racial superiority within me when all the authorities within that religion were White like myself? At the same time, how did my conditioning under Catholicism not to question authority lead me to silently collude with the racism of other Whites?

As a White woman, how did I internalize racial superiority through the culture's representation of White women as the embodiment of ultimate beauty? What has it meant for me to have a key signifier of female perfection—Whiteness—available to me? How have images of White women in the careers deemed valuable for woman shaped my goals? How has mainstream feminism's articulation of White women's issues as universal women's issues shaped what I care about? At the same time, what has it meant to live under patriarchy and to be taught that as a woman I am less intelligent, that I should not speak up, that I should defer to others, and at all times be nice and polite? How have all of these messages ultimately set me up to collude in the oppression of people of color? By asking questions such as these I have been able to gain a much deeper and more useful analysis of racism, and rather than finding that centering racism denies my other oppressions, I find that centering racism has been a profound way to address the complexity of all my social locations.

23

Women, Race, and Racism

A Dialogue in Black and White

Andrea Ayvazian and Beverly Daniel Tatum

Beverly Daniel Tatum: . . .

Jean Baker Miller has written eloquently about the constructive power of relational connections and the potentially destructive force of relational disconnections and violations. This theme of connections, disconnections, and violations is certainly central to our thinking about how we can connect across racial lines. What happens when our experience is validated by another in a mutually empathic relationship? We feel a strong sense of connection. But when we have experiences that are not validated, for example, when I as a black woman encounter racism and I am unable to talk about that experience with white colleagues, I may feel a sense of disconnection from them. Or should I choose to share those experiences and in fact find them invalidated by my colleagues, I may question my own perceptions. Without validation from others, I may choose to deny my own perceptions in order to avoid the isolation that comes from disconnection. Repeatedly separating myself from my own experience in order to stay in relationship with others ultimately results in a psychological state of violation. Negotiating the choices involved in maintaining connections across racial lines is a central focus of our dialogue . . . .

Andrea Ayvazian: . . . Beverly and I are venturing into new territory by offering an analysis of our own relationship as a case study of women connecting across racial lines. We want to speak very personally . . . [I]n traveling and doing speaking with Beverly, white women often stop me in hallways and restrooms and at the coffee machine and say, "You two seem so close. How did you create that bond?" . . . We are going to focus on the following three areas, which we call the critical junctures in our relationship: how the relationship was established, the theme of mutuality in our relationship, and difficult periods we have faced. A thread that is also woven into our talk is what we call "common differences," areas where there is sameness between us, where we have similar feelings, viewpoints, even experiences, and yet these similarities are expressed in different ways in our lives. We will close by talking about our friendship as a work in progress. . . .

CRITICAL JUNCTURES

Ayvazian: . . .

In many ways, my kinship with Beverly is *very* easy. Deep affection and admiration flows between us and the friendship is strong, nourishing, and treasured. However, it is also fair to say that nowadays any adult relationship that crosses racial lines is "not easy." If the friends are conscious of the social, political, and economic realities in this country today, their "kinship," . . . will inevitably have times that are "not easy." And we have faced those times.

. . . Beverly and I do not live in the same neighborhood, although we live in the same town, and we do not work in the same place. Our children do not attend the same schools.

We were brought together by an agency that does antiracism education, paired up as a biracial team to do some antiracism training at a college in the Boston area. We were brought together initially on a professional basis and immediately had the experience of preparing to work together as a team. . . . Beverly and I call that first professional collaboration, during which our relationship was formed, our "trial by fire." The group of college students with whom we were working proved to be a very challenging group. . . . Yet, this adversarial experience actually pulled us together as a twosome. Going into what turned out to be a hostile environment forced us to really scrutinize the material that we were presenting to the group.

Consequently, Beverly and I had the experience of talking very deeply about painful issues around race and racism very early in our professional/personal relationship. We had potentially difficult conversations analyzing racial inequity because we had to scrutinize the material we were presenting to this challenging group. These conversations in the first days of our relationship, we have discovered, are of the sort that biracial friendships sometimes avoid for months or years. Looking back on it now, we believe that this process was a bonding experience.

We also found that our rides to and from Boston were opportunities to talk not only about our work but about our personal lives. We discovered some common ground as women, as mothers, and as professionals in our community. Early on, Beverly was very helpful to me as I was going through a difficult period with my then 1-year-old son. We forged close personal ties through what was initially a professional connection.

Tatum: . . . As Andrea has told you, we don't live in the same neighborhood, our children don't go to the same school, and we don't worship in the same places; our lives are separate in many ways. Even though we frequently work together and certainly spend leisure time together now that our friendship has developed, our paths would not likely have crossed in other ways. Given the reality of social segregation, work does provide one of the few places where women of color and white women may come together across racial lines. So, it is not an accident that it was our work together that laid the groundwork for a friendship to develop.

. . . [O]ne of the things that has been very important is that at the beginning of our relationship there was an examination of our values as they related to the work that we did. We were forced to talk at a deeper level—not the superficial chitchat that you might engage with someone over the coffee machine—regarding what we thought about a very significant issue, in this case race relations in the United States. The mutuality that evolved in that relationship was very much in keeping with what Jean Baker Miller calls the "five good things." When a relationship is in fact mutually reinforcing, it gives you a feeling of increased zest, a sense of empowerment, greater self-knowledge, increased self-worth, and—most important in the context of a friendship—a desire for more connection (Miller, 1988). . . .

But as in all relationships, conflict arises. There certainly has been some conflict in our relationship, which we want to talk about, too, because it is also an important part of how one negotiates relationships that are going to be genuinely mutual. The most significant conflict, a real test of mutuality in our relationship, occurred when Andrea and I were conducting a workshop in St. Louis about 3 years ago. At that time, we were facilitating a workshop with a group of clergy on racism and, as we often do, we made reference to other "isms," including heterosexism. This topic . . . triggered a rather heated discussion about homosexuality in which a range of religious viewpoints were expressed. As we struggled to deal with this issue . . . Andrea and I became aware of the fact that we had differing strategies for interacting with our participants on this issue. While we were able to deal with that difference productively in the context of the workshop, as we were processing the event on the flight home we had a conversation that led to a real test of the mutuality in our relationship.

As background information for this incident, . . . I had just joined a church, which was a very important and significant step in my personal life, and as we talked about the controversy that had arisen in our workshop, we talked about the positions that our own religious communities had regarding homosexuality and heterosexism in the church. I am a member of a Presbyterian church. At this writing, that denomination is in the midst of a struggle around whether or not to ordain gay men and lesbian women. Andrea is a Quaker and belongs to a Meeting that is openly gay affirming and sanctions and supports same-sex commitment ceremonies. So our two worship communities have very different positions.

Andrea said to me that she didn't understand how I could be a part of a religious community that was exclusionary in the way that the Presbyterian church currently is, and in fact suggested that I should find another church. When she first said it, I was taken aback by the comment but had some trouble figuring out exactly what it was about it that bothered me. In fact, I shared her concern about the heterosexism in my denomination and in my local church. I have raised, and continue to raise, questions about this issue with my pastor and with fellow parishioners. On the other hand, my local congregation is a relatively progressive, predominantly black, Afrocentric congregation that is very affirming of my racial and spiritual identity . . . . I experienced Andrea's suggestion that I should leave this congregation as an affront. . . .

It occurred to me that there was really a lot of white privilege in her statement. As a black woman living in a predominantly white community, there are not many opportunities for me or my children to be part of a community where our African American heritage is explicitly affirmed. Consequently our Sunday worship experience in a congregation that defines itself as "unashamedly black and unapologetically Christian" is extremely valuable to me. I did feel that her statement that I should withdraw from this community was a statement of her white privilege. In fact, she was taking for granted the many churches or worship communities that she can choose from because almost all of them are predominantly white and will affirm her racial identity. . . . Her statement to me was a failure to recognize that privilege.

I felt that I had to say something to her about this. At the same time, I hesitated because this relationship was important to me and I did not want to alienate our friendship. Yet, it was a real juncture in terms of this issue of connections, disconnections and violations, because I could feel myself disconnecting. . . . In order for us to be able to maintain the growth and development of our relationship, certainly being able to talk about my spiritual journey and my worship community was an important point of connection that I needed to be able to maintain. I decided to share my perspective with Andrea, and I am happy to report that she responded in a very validating way. She simply listened to what I had to say and then said, "You're right."

Ayvazian: I want to speak to this because a potentially serious "disconnection" threatened our relationship—a relationship that had developed strong bonds, one that had become mutually important. When Beverly raised her feelings and concerns with me, two things went through my mind—two things that I knew she and I had said specifically to white people many times in the past! One was that when a person of color tells you something you have said or done is racist or reveals your inattention to white privilege, take a deep breath and begin by assuming she/he is correct until proven otherwise. The other point is that as white people strive to be strong white allies, we do not have to hold ourselves to a standard of perfection. It is impossible, given our socialization, our background, the struggle, the sensitivity, and the pain surrounding these issues, that we can be perfect white allies. I try to remember that I am not called to be perfect. I am called to be faithful and consistent on these issues. Beverly was exactly right. . . . I tried to follow the very advice that I had given to others. . . . That was an important juncture: a disconnection threatened, but we managed to talk it through.

There was another time that a disconnection threatened but was overcome by both of us being aware of what was going on in the relationship. This happened around the time of the Rodney King beating and the Simi Valley verdict in which the four Los Angeles police officers were acquitted. . . . In our shock and grief following the Simi Valley verdict, we essentially separated for a period of time and turned to different communities for comfort and support. Bev talked about her reactions to the events primarily with other African Americans. . . . In my own state of pain, shock, and anger, I found myself talking to two white men who I specifically called and met with, two men who identify as white allies. Meeting with them was the appropriate place for me to take my grief and do some healing and action planning in order to move forward.

. . .

Following the Simi Valley verdict it was appropriate for Beverly and me to separate for a while and immerse ourselves in our own groups to work on these issues. . . . This is an important point because white people can feel a loss, and even a sense of personal rejection, when this happens. . . . Beverly and I see these as normal, necessary, and even predictable after racial trauma. The bridges that have been built may be perfectly strong, but there still may be a need to separate for a time.

Tatum: I want to add just a few comments to what Andrea has said. In fact, the weekend when the events following the Simi Valley verdict were unfolding, I was at a small women's conference, a gathering of about 20 women, to which I had been invited. The only person I knew in the group was the woman who had invited me, and I was the only woman of color there. As we were arriving, everyone was very much aware of the riots that were unfolding in Los Angeles following the acquittal, and what struck me was the reluctance among the group to talk in any serious way about what was going on in Los Angeles. A few people expressed a need to talk about what was happening and what it meant for the country and for their own particular communities, but generally speaking the majority of the participants seemed to disregard these events as someone else's problem, not of concern to us as a group. I felt very alienated by that response, I have to say. Perhaps because I was with white women I didn't know, it did not feel like a safe place for me to completely engage. I was quite concerned about what was happening in communities of color in Los Angeles and in other parts of the country in response to this verdict. Yet I felt that my concern, a part of who I was, a part of my own perspective as an African American woman, could not be safely brought to this meeting. I certainly experienced that as very disconnecting, and in fact I went home early from the conference and declined the invitation to attend the following year.

Ayvazian: . . . White people often say to me, "It sounds like you two work together on issues of racism and talk about them very openly in your friendship, but are you, Andrea, always in the position of learner?" Beverly and I want to take a moment to remind all of us that each individual has multiple social identities. We feel this point is important because there are ways that Beverly and I are, in some areas of systematic oppression, both in the dominant category. We both receive the privilege or advantage, and we support each other in being strong allies. I am not always in the position of being dominant, and Beverly is not always in the position of being targeted. In the area of race inequity and racism—in that form of systematic oppression—I am clearly dominant. I receive the privilege, the unearned advantage and benefit of being white, and Beverly is targeted.

But there are other areas where Beverly and I are both targeted and areas where we are both dominant. We're both targeted as women, and we're both dominant as Christians, as heterosexuals, as able-bodied, as middle class. We felt it was useful to remember that as women we both feel targeted in groups of men where we are negotiating around money, for example. We are both disadvantaged systematically in a society that overvalues male attributes and characteristics. . . . The fact that we are both practicing Christians and women of faith and identify very strongly and publicly in that way means we are both

N E X T

S T E P S

dominant. We are not Jewish or Muslim. We are both able-bodied, both heterosexual, both middle-class women, and we offer each other support in remembering that we have a responsibility to interrupt anti-Semitism, to interrupt homophobia and heterosexism, to interrupt classism, and so on. . . .

. . .

COMMON DIFFERENCES

Ayvazian: . . .

We are two mothers with school-age children who have many similarities but who have made some different choices, we believe, because of our racial difference. In particular, we have made different choices about the schooling for our sons and the environments we feel they need in order to thrive. My son is in a public school in our town and fits in well in his kindergarten class and in his school. During a parent–teacher conference this past spring, his teacher said to me, "Andrea, your son is just like a thousand other rambunctious, big-for-his-age 6-year-old boys that I have had in my teaching career." And I thought to myself, "I'm sure he is. I'm sure he doesn't stand out in very many ways. He's like a thousand other children that this woman has had in her long career of teaching kindergarten." In our predominantly white community, the same could not be said about Beverly's sons. . . .

Tatum: . . . Like many of the black families I interviewed and wrote about in my book, *Assimilation Blues: Black Families in a White Community* (Tatum, 1987), I have worried about how my children will be responded to by what has been to date an entirely white teaching staff (with the exception of an occasional student teacher of color). Though it may only be an illusion, I believe I have been able to exercise more control over my children's classroom experiences as a result of enrolling them in private schools. There have been times when I have felt that racial issues were present in both peer and teacher interactions, and both my husband and I have been actively involved in negotiating those issues with the school and our children.

The task of raising young African American children, especially boys, in contemporary society is not an easy one. My children are also big for their ages, but unlike for white boys for whom physical maturity is often a social advantage, being black and big for your age places you at some psychological risk: 7-year-old black boys may be thought of as cute; 14-year-old black boys are often perceived as dangerous. The larger you are, the sooner you must learn to deal with other people's negative stereotypes, and you may not yet be cognitively and emotionally mature enough to do so effectively. The smallness of their private school environment, where I can easily make myself known as a parent and where my children may be seen as individuals rather than representatives of a racial group, may offer some small margin of protection for them. They will need all the margin they can get. Though I am a product of public schools myself and I support quality public education, I have not regretted our decision to send our children to private schools.

. . .

CHOOSING THE MARGIN

The last point that we want to talk about as another example of common differences is what Beverly and I have come to call from "margin to center" or from "center to margin." Both of us have been influenced by the works of bell hooks, particularly *Feminist Theory:*

NEXT STEPS

From Margin to Center (1984), and Audre Lorde's work, *Sister Outsider*. . . . Beverly and I have remarkably similar political views. We share very similar progressive politics, but again in this area of common differences we have expressed our personal politics in different ways. . . . As a white, middle-class, heterosexual, able-bodied person, I receive considerable privilege in society. (I'm in so many dominant groups.) I start at the center where social, political, and economic power rests. Consequently, bell hooks's book, *Feminist Theory: From Margin to Center*, speaks to me, but in the reverse. I recognize that I start at the center and I feel called to move to the margin.

As I move to the margin, I try to take other progressive people, specifically in my case well-intentioned white people, with me into more progressive politics, living a more progressive agenda, choosing the margin. To accomplish this, I have made decisions like choosing, since 1981, to be a war tax resister, which means I don't pay a portion of my federal income tax every April; I make a public protest, objecting to the priorities reflected in the military portion of our federal budget and our ongoing preparation for and involvement in war. Also in my journey from center to margin, my life partner (who is male) and I have chosen not to sanctify our union and our love of each other in a formal wedding. Instead we had a ceremony of commitment that could be replicated exactly for same-sex couples. We made this decision so that we can advocate as allies to gay, lesbian, and bisexuals as a couple that has chosen in one small way not to accept heterosexual privilege. Because I start with so much privilege—so clearly at the center—these are two ways that I can move to the margin, stir up good trouble, and invite other people like me to question their politics and live their commitments to the principles they hold dear. . . . There are ways that because of my privilege I've had the luxury to step out of the center, to do what is unexpected and in some ways unacceptable. But I have not during the last 5 years suggested that Beverly make the same choices. . . . I recognize that my daily life is more advantaged and more comfortable than hers because of my color. Consequently, I do not advocate that she should choose war tax resistance. She expresses her political convictions in other ways. The same is true around formal marriage and same-sex unions. It has not been an issue for me and it has not been a source of disconnection for us that Beverly has made different choices for her behavior as a strong ally to gay men and lesbians. Her allied behavior is evident in other ways. . . .

Tatum: As Andrea said, this idea, from margin to center, has been important and I'd like to refer to a reading that I found very helpful from Letty M. Russell's book, *Church in the Round: Feminist Interpretation of the Church* (1993). She refers to the work of Audre Lorde and bell hooks, and uses this idea to make the following point. She says, "We make choices about moving from margin toward center or from center toward margin according to where we find ourselves in relation to the center of power and resources and the cultural and linguistic dominance in any particular social structure. Our connection to the margin is always related to where we are standing in regard to social privilege, and from that particular position we have at least three choices, not to choose, to choose the center, or to choose the margins" (p. 192).

As Russell points out, our first choice is not to choose. If we make this choice, if we choose not to choose, we are essentially saying that those of us who are marginalized by gender, race, sexual orientation, class, or disability have the possibility of doing nothing. But, as she says, in so doing we internalize the oppression. I think that if we consider not choosing, if we think about internalizing our oppression and allowing ourselves to be defined as marginal, then we have in effect been psychologically violated. . . . because it forces us to disconnect from our own experience, to try to ignore and not name the particular alienation that we are exposed to in our society.

Our second choice . . . is to choose the center. She says, "those on the margin choosing the center do so by emulating the oppressors and doing everything to pass or to be like those who are dominant and be accepted by them" (p. 192). Whenever we make this choice we are choosing disconnection in the sense that we are saying, "Yes I want to be in relationship with you. If I have to deny certain aspects of my experience to do so, then I will. I will disconnect from that part of my experience in order to maintain my connection with you." . . .

Our third choice is for the margin. Here Russell says, "Those on the margin claim the margin by working in solidarity with others from the margin as they move toward the center. They seek a transformed society of justice where they will be empowered to share the center and no one will need to be marginalized" (p. 193). As I reflect on this choice, it seems to me this is the choice of connection. This is the choice of saying, "I will be connected to those who are able to acknowledge and affirm my experience in the world, who are able to stand on the margin with me." . . . Society can be transformed by those on the margin only if we "choose" the margin. Otherwise we collude in our own oppression and the oppression of others.

I choose to stand on the margin as someone who is defined by society as marginal in terms of my race and in terms of my gender. I also recognize that there are places where I am in the center and need to choose the margin because, as Andrea has already pointed out, there are places where I am dominant. But the primary point here is that those of us on the margin—or in the center—claim the margin by working in solidarity with others from the margin as they move toward the center. It is in this context that I can warmly embrace Andrea as my friend, as someone who has chosen to stand on the margin with me. . . .

Ayvazian: . . . We have forged a relationship that is not based on the false goal of color blindness. We recognize the differences in our life experiences and the difference that race makes in a relationship, and we have built a sturdy bridge across that divide.

In closing I want to share with you two lines of a Pat Parker poem called "For the White Person Who Wants to Know How to Be My Friend." The first two lines are as follows: "The first thing you do is forget that I'm black. Second, you must never forget that I'm black." Do I forget that Beverly is black? Sure I do. She is a dear friend with whom I spend time. Love, admiration, and affection flow between us. . . . But do I really forget that Beverly is black? Yes and no. . . . That is who she is in the world, and yes it is forgotten, and no it is not actually ever forgotten. But in the end, I have discovered that the issue . . . for me is, how I have come to understand social, political, and economic power and my unearned advantage and privilege as a white woman in a racist society. . . . It is my understanding of my own whiteness, not my response to her blackness, that allows me to interact with Beverly in a way that continues to foster mutuality, connection, and trust. . . . Beverly calls us "partners in justice": shoulder to shoulder we move toward our goal. . . .

24

Forging El Mundo Zurdo

Changing Ourselves, Changing the World

AnaLouise Keating

When I first read *This Bridge*, over ten years ago, I was struck by contributors' repeated attempts to forge alliances and coalitions that do not ignore differences among women (and in many instances men) but instead use difference as a catalyst for personal and social transformation. Entering into the "unimaginable gulfs of difference" between self and other, they make visible the previously "invisible edges, frames, [and] frontiers" that divide us. Their willingness to actively engage in open conversations about differences enables them to insist on commonalities without assuming that their experiences, histories, ideas, or traits are *identical* with those of others. Instead, commonalities indicate complex points of connection that negotiate among sameness, similarity, and difference—a potent mixture brewed from all three.

This negotiation represents a radical departure from conventional practices. We've been trained to define differences oppositionally—as deviations from what Audre Lorde terms the "*mythical norm*, which . . . [i]n america . . . is usually defined as white, thin, male, young, heterosexual, christian, and financially secure" and to regard these differences as shameful marks of inferiority. Driven by our fear of difference-as-deviation, we ignore, deny, and misname the differences among us. We hide our differences beneath a facade of sameness and erect rigid boundaries between self and other. But these differences don't go away just because we reject them. They grow stronger as we seek refuge behind stereotypes, monolithic labels, and false assumptions of sameness. . . .

This quest for commonalities culminates in Gloria E. Anzaldúa's concept of El Mundo Zurdo, the "Left-Handed World," a visionary place where people from diverse backgrounds with diverse needs and concerns co-exist and work together to bring about revolutionary change. As she asserts in "La Prieta": "We are the queer groups, the people that don't belong anywhere, not in the dominant world nor completely within our own respective cultures. Combined we cover so many oppressions. But the overwhelming oppression is the collective fact that we do not fit, and because we do not fit, *we are a threat*." Anzaldúa replaces the oppositional definitions of difference I referred to above with a relational approach. She acknowledges that inhabitants of El Mundo Zurdo are not all alike; their specific oppressions, solutions, and beliefs are different, yet she insists that "these different affinities are not opposed to each other. In El Mundo Zurdo I with my own affinities and my people with theirs can live together and transform the planet." Joined by their rejection of the status quo and their so-called deviation from the dominant culture, inhabitants of El Mundo Zurdo use their sense of difference to forge new alliances. . . .

N
E
X
T

S
T
E
P
S

CHANGING MYSELF, CHANGING THE WORLD?

. . . I believe that by changing ourselves we change the world, that traveling El Mundo Zurdo path is the path of a two-way movement—a going deep into the self and an expanding out into the world, a simultaneous recreation of the self and reconstruction of society. . . . Like Anzaldúa, I believe that it entails a simultaneous two-way movement, that by changing ourselves (by changing myself), we/I can change the world.

. . . I can't offer pronouncements on how we can transform the world, or even how you can transform yourself. But I can tell you about my own efforts to engage in this two-way movement. I am a mother, a writer, a teacher. These relational identities give me specific locations where I can begin working for change—today . . . in my home, in the written word, in the classroom. I've developed the following promises, which I attempt to embody throughout my life.

1. . . . *I've used this metaphysics of interconnectedness to design my own form of spiritual activism.* . . . I believe that we're all interconnected—materially and spiritually. As Iaés Hernández-Ávila states . . . "We are related to all that lives." This radical interrelatedness gives us—gives me—a responsibility to meet those I encounter with a sense of openness: my protective boundaries between self and other become permeable, begin breaking down.

Exploring the differences between us, I seek commonalities between your experiences and mine. Empathy—the willingness to imaginatively enter your life through reading, through conversation, through storytelling—is crucial to this search. When "I" empathize with "you," I enact a relational form of thinking, a back-and-forth movement. Immersing myself in your stories. I listen without judging, I listen with open heart and open mind. I travel into your emotions, desires, and experiences, then return to my own. But in the return, I am changed by my encounter with you, and I begin recognizing the commonalities we share.

2. *Language has tremendous psychic and material power.* Like Antony Appiah, I believe that "[S]ticks and stones may break our bones, but words—words that evoke structures of oppression, exploitation, and brute physical threat—can break souls," and so I choose my words with great care. . . . The words we use shape what we perceive, which in turn shapes how we act. Language's creative power requires that I think carefully and thoroughly about the possible effects my words might have and the effects I desire. Since my goal is to awaken a sense of our radical interconnectedness, I try to use words that energize this perception. Whenever appropriate, I use inclusionary language and, as I'll demonstrate below, I do not identify people by categories unless the categories are relevant to the conversation.

3. *Categories and labels, although sometimes necessary, can prevent us from recognizing our interconnectedness with others.* As Andrea Canaan notes, "The enemy is brownness and whiteness, maleness and femaleness. The enemy is our urgent need to stereotype and close off people, places, and events into isolated categories . . . We close off avenues of communication and vision so that individual and communal trust, responsibility, loving, and knowing are impossible." Whether we identify as "of color" or "white," we have *all* been trained to evaluate ourselves and each other according to existing identity categories. However, when we automatically label people by color or gender (or sexuality or religion or any other politically-changed characteristics and/or assumed differences, for that matter), we build walls and isolate ourselves from those we've labelled "different." These categories distort our perceptions, creating arbitrary divisions among us and an oppositional "us" against "them" mentality that prevents us from recognizing potential commonalities. . . .

4. *Out of all the categories we today employ, "race" is the most destructive.* "Race" is, for sure, one of the "master's tools," one of the most insidious tools of all. We've been trained to classify and evaluate ourselves and those we meet according to racialized appearances: we look at a person's body, classify her, insert him into a category, make generalizations, and base our interactions on these racialized assumptions. These assumptions rely on and reinforce monolithic, divisive stereotypes that erase the incredible diversity within each individual and within each so-called "race." But racial categories are not—and never have been—benign; rather, they were developed by those in power (generally property-owning men of Northern European descent) to create a hierarchy that grants privilege and power to specific groups of people while simultaneously oppressing and excluding others. Racialized categories originated in histories of oppression, exclusion, land theft, body theft, soul theft, physical/psychic murder, and other crimes against specific groups of human beings. These categories were motivated by economics and politics, by insecurity and greed—not by innate biological or divinely-created differences. When we refer to "race" or to specific "races" we are drawing on and therefore reinforcing this violent history as well as the "white" supremacism buttressing the entire system.

5. *"Race" and racism are inextricably related.* We can't talk about one without also talking about the other. "Race" is built on and out of the oppressive history referred to above, and this fact must be acknowledged whenever I talk, write, or teach about "race." . . .

My daughter, Jamitrice, was born in 1995 into a highly racialized world. Like the rest of us, she will encounter many messages designed to reinforce the oppressive belief in natural, god-given "races." While I can't prevent her from receiving these messages, I can invite

N
E
X
T

S
T
E
P
S

N
E
X
T

S
T
E
P
S

her to question them and to recognize their tremendous limitations. At this point she's only five, not old enough to understand this racialized system. As Marguerite A. Wright explains, "Young children are developmentally inclined to treat people based on their character, as revealed by their actions, rather than on the color of their skin. As they grow older, this wonderful quality is lost to many of them as they learn some of the racial bigotry of previous generations." Jamitrice still exists in this preracialized space, but I know the day will come when she'll leave it and enter—with her "new awareness (more accurately, acquired illusions)" the "racial bigotry" we all inherit from our teachers, our classmates, the books we read, the TV shows we watch. In a few years she'll ask me, "Mama, what am I?"—meaning "What's my 'race'?" Drawing on my belief in language's power to shape perception, I'll choose my words with great care and tell her our family stories—her grandparents and great-grandparents from Africa, China, England, Ireland, and Spain. Because she needs to understand the systemic role racism plays in restricting our lives, as I tell her these stories I'll subtly point out the differences: Our ancestors from Africa, China, and (to a lesser degree) Ireland experienced greater hardships because of their appearances and nationalities than those who immigrated from England and Spain. . . .

At a larger level, I attempt to instruct my daughter into what I'm calling a metaphysics of interconnectedness. She has not yet created self-enclosed boundaries, and I try to nurture her intuitive sense of interrelatedness by demonstrating the many ways we're connected to others—not just to other humans (even those who don't look like us) but to everything around as, to animals, to the trees, to the water we drink. I use storytelling to encourage her to make imaginative leaps and draw parallels between her own emotions, experiences, desires and those of others.

As a writer, I try to shake—and sometimes even smash—the categories, demonstrating the limitations in the labels. I write about topics like this one, I challenge my readers (like I'm challenging you) to educate themselves about the history of racism and "race." I work on anthologies like the one you're reading right now. I put "race," "whiteness," and "white" (and sometimes also "black") in quotation marks to underscore their artificial nature. Simultaneously, I attempt to expose the "white" supremacy, as well as the economic causes and effects, behind and beneath racial labels. I emphasize the limitations in categorizing people by "race," and I interrogate recent developments in "whiteness" studies, especially the calls for positive "white" identities. Because "whiteness" and the concept of "white" people plays a crucial role in generating and maintaining a hierarchical, racist worldview, the construction of positive "white" identities inadvertently but inevitably supports this already-existing system. As Ian F. Haney López asserts, "Whiteness exists as the lynchpin for the systems of racial meaning in the United States. Whiteness is the norm around which other races are constructed; its existence depends upon the mythologies and material inequalities that sustain the current racial system . . . Its continuation also requires the preservation of the social inequalities that every day testify to White superiority." . . .

TAKING RISKS, TRANSFORMING WALLS INTO THRESHOLDS

. . . We're living in a place/time of nepantha: exiting from the old worldview, we have not yet entered or created new ones to replace it. We're questioning the barriers that divide us, and yet even as we acknowledge their limitations we cling to the labels and claim the power of self-naming in the face of erasure. In this essay I've shared my belief that a recognition of our radical interconnectedness offers one way to negotiate the divisions between "us" and "them," between "self" and "other."

Lest I be misunderstood, let me emphasize: this focus on spiritual activism, on a metaphysics of interconnectedness, must not be conflated with escapism. The spiritual components of life *cannot* be divorced from politics, sexuality, writing, or daily living. As Anzaldúa states in her introduction to "El Mundo Zurdo: The Vision," *Bridge*'s final section, "The vision of our spirituality provides us with no trap door solution, no escape hatch tempting us to 'transcend' our struggle. We must act in the everyday world. Words are not enough. We must perform visible and public acts that might make us more vulnerable to the very oppressions we are fighting against. But, our vulnerability *can* be the source of our power—if we use it."

In part, this vulnerability requires that we let down our guard, relax some of the many defenses we've erected to shore up our fragile sense of self and protect ourselves from harm. We've been battered, in very different ways, by racism, sexism, classism, homophobia, and other forms of physical/psychic oppression and abuse. Identity politics has been extremely useful: we've invented and found specific names and labels that affirm us, give us self-confidence, agency, a sense of belonging, a place to call "home." But at some point—no matter how effective these labels seem to be—they will fail us. They will be walls rather than doorways.

Vulnerability—the willingness to occasionally let go of the labels—transforms these walls into thresholds. Differences don't go away . . . nor should they. But if we posit a shared factor of identity (call it "Spirit," call it "Soul," call it what you will), we can be open to the differences among us. Through conversation, through exchanging stories, through exploring our differences without defensiveness or shame, we can learn from each other, share each other's words. As we do so, we'll begin forging commonalities. Perhaps we'll even say, with Susan Guerra, "*I am because we are*. Without expecting *sameness*."

Sure, we'll make mistakes. Hell, I'll bet I've made some in this essay. But to learn about each other, to grow closer, to create El Mundo Zurdo, we must take this risk.

25

The Personal Is Political

Richard (Chip) Smith

Being involved in the struggle against white supremacy is, first, a personal decision. But how to connect one's everyday activities to the large-scale plan of action proposed in this book is not always clear. Doing so is essential, however, to building a movement—person by person, in a widening circle of activity and commitment.

Here are ten ways people can jump into things right where they are—wherever that might be—and, if already involved, how they can deepen that engagement:

1. **Become aware of privilege and internalized oppression.** Peggy McIntosh has a well-regarded exercise, "White Privilege: Unpacking the Invisible Knapsack," which helps European Americans understand how they are privileged by being white. McIntosh points out that people can be aware that others are worse off than they are; but these same people remain unaware—and the culture keeps them unaware—of how this situation translates into their benefiting from privileges themselves.

"White privilege is like an invisible weightless knapsack of special provisions, maps, passports, codebooks, visas, clothes, tools and blank checks," comments McIntosh. She asks people to take stock of what they have in their own personal knapsacks and offers more than 25 examples—such as, "I can arrange to protect my children most of the time from people who might not like them," or "I am never asked to speak for all the people of my racial group." McIntosh notes that some items everyone in a decent society should be entitled to—things like "the expectation that neighbors will be decent to you, or that your race will not count against you in court." Other privileges confer power, like "My skin color [is] an asset for any move I . . . want to make," or white people are "morally neutral, normative, and average, and also ideal, so that when we work to benefit others, this is seen as work which will allow 'them' to be more like 'us.'"

A similar exercise can be conducted by men, non-working class people, and heterosexuals to get at the specifics of male, class and hetero privileges. Coming from the opposite side, popular education methods developed by the Brazilian educator Paolo Freire, such as *Pedagogy of the Oppressed*, can help oppressed people gain insights into the social system where they live. Anger at oppressive conditions—which may be deeply internalized or bubbling near the surface—can turn into positive energy to transform society. Regardless of color or nationality, the common objective of these exercises is clarity—an awareness of social reality as it is and one's place in it. Without this kind of clarity, people's attempts to bring about change will likely remain unfocused and only occasionally effective.

2. **Build intentional relationships based on equality . . . .**
   A key element for these relationships to be beneficial for everyone is that they be based on equality. The burden here is on those with privilege to be primarily in a learning mode—being willing to examine the reality of their privilege together with others in the relationship. Ultimately the goal is to turn privilege—be it in education, social access, or material wealth—to everyone's advantage by making it available for use by the social justice movement.
   . . .
   Privilege also affects relationships through the deeply internalized feelings of confidence that people with privilege have—and which other very competent people sometimes lack. Important to building up this sense of confidence is the actual experience of struggle—fighting back, taking leadership—as well as coming to understand the historical and social roots of powerlessness.

3. **Study and discuss the history of peoples of color, as well as of white working class people.** . . . Developing personal relationships is essential; but there is also an obligation to learn other folks' history—and to do it on one's own time, so to speak, and not expect to be spoon-fed by friends.
   All these considerations apply to questions of class and gender as well. One goal . . . has been to approach these varied aspects of people in an intersectional way. . . . The movement is only beginning to create a common history of struggle that people of all nationalities can identify with. Learning each other's histories, and drawing on all our varied experiences, is essential to creating a collective memory appropriate to the emerging society the movement hopes to build.

4. **Question, talk about, and challenge the evidence of white supremacy all around us.** Simply putting into words an observation or a question can help people see more clearly what is going on—the composition of a meeting, people's body language, or who is interrupting whom. Questions are good because they leave the answer open and allow folks to respond freely. At the same time, when someone asks a question back, there is the opportunity to "tell it like it is"—or at least as it appears to you—simply and directly.

Resistance or non-cooperation are options when other people voice a snide comment about a certain part of town, a put-down of a particular class of people, or a color-coded joke. Ted Allen suggested one way to respond in this situation: "Oh, you must think I'm white?" Another is to point to a personal relationship with the targeted group—"Just so you know, my wife is a Chinese immigrant." And however one responds, the goal can be more than just silencing the speaker. Most desirable is being able to turn the conversation into a straightforward discussion of race and its role in society. Tim Wise gives an example from a conversation in a bar, when working to defeat David Duke in his campaign for governor of Louisiana in 1991, and concludes: "There are ways to talk to people, even truly tough cases, and make some headway, break down some defenses, get people to at least begin to question the things they have always taken for granted precisely because they have *never been challenged before* by anyone who looked like them." Finally Noel Ignatiev calls for people to become "race traitors."

. . .

In this spirit, one can be proactive by crossing the color line to hear a speaker, attend a holiday celebration, volunteer one's time, go to church, or take part in a discussion. At the same time, it is important to be sensitive about spaces that people of color reserve for themselves—but not jumping to such a conclusion based on little or no information. Discovering what is possible, and what is not, can feel a little risky, but being willing to step out of one's comfort zone is necessary to break down the social barriers that divide people. Still, the invasion and domination of other people's spaces is a real concern—and verges over into the larger issues of gentrification of neighborhoods and cultural appropriation.

Finally, the direct rejection of privilege can make sense at appropriate times—usually combined with organizing others to do the same. Examples include 1) a group of workers who turn down a raise aimed at undercutting their support for a union contract; or 2) the officers in the Civil War movie *Glory* refusing their pay until black soldiers received the same wages as the white soldiers.

5. **Take a good look at your home.** Paul Kivel, in *Uprooting Racism*, notes that people's homes are their most intimate spaces and they reflect who we are. One useful exercise is to look around and see what our home tells us about ourselves. The pictures on the walls, the books or magazines lying around—or their absence; the sound of conversations, TV shows, or music; the traffic in and out of children, friends, or activists; the smells of food, coffee or farmland—all these aspects of people's homes say something about who we are. There is no pre-judgment implied here, because homes depend in part on how much money folks have, their ages, and whether they live in the city, the suburbs, or the country. The point is, however, that if people profess to be against white supremacy, yet everything in their home reflects a white culture, then there is a disconnect. At the same time, there can be a downside here, too, in collecting—or appropriating as commodities—others' cultures. Consciously altering the home environment, however, can reflect movement in a new direction—and can reinforce efforts to be consistent in one's values and to identify with a shared history of struggle. As Kivel notes, engaging children in this project can make it a learning experience for the next generation, too.

6. **Challenge white supremacy (sexism, homophobia) in family life.** A lot of emotional energy goes into maintaining the structure of relationships in a family. Raising questions about the internal culture—the humor, the assumptions about peoples of other races, or who does what tasks around the house—can stir up people's defenses. The challenge is to find ways to address these topics while still maintaining a connection with folks. For white people who become anti-racist activists—and in doing so

NEXT STEPS

break with their families to varying degrees—facing up to this responsibility is often difficult.

Two women from the South who broke with the white supremacist environment in which they grew up make this point. Mab Segrest, in *Memoirs of a Race Traitor*, tells how she came to accept her obligation to her family at the urging of African American mentors in North Carolina. Anne Braden, in *The Wall Between*, reflects on her own struggles with family members and the slow, almost imperceptible changes she saw in her father's attitudes over decades of loving struggle. Neither woman regrets her rejection of the dominant Southern ways and their values; and each sees her personal transformation as a necessary and liberating step forward. At the same time, by re-engaging with their families, both women were able to understand better the social sources of their parents' prejudices—and, in doing so, come to accept their folks' humanity, while continuing to hold up a mirror to offensive words and practices. Just as the family has a powerful ability to shape and contain a person, so too, once free from its negative influences, one can bring that same power to bear to reshape the family culture. The lessons learned in this most intimate struggle—and the sense of personal wholeness achieved—can radiate outward in relationships with friends, coworkers, and other activists.

7. **Take an inventory of activism in the community.** It can be helpful to look around to see who the grassroots activists are in the community—and then plug into what is going on. By being supportive, putting in the time, and establishing ties on the basis of joint work, people can learn the skills needed to bring about change. Building relationships with folks from different oppressed nationalities helps foster understanding and unity. And if of European descent, orienting oneself in this way helps ground a person's activism—providing a base from which to reach out and organize other white people.

If the community is homogeneous—as is the case with many white people, who overall tend to live in segregated communities—the basic approach can still be the same: seek out those who are active in a progressive way and then link up with them. The problem, however, is that when organizations are racially isolated—as in white suburbia or small-town rural areas—they can drift in directions that end up setting people against other grassroots folks. Efforts to improve suburban schools can pit people against the needs of oppressed nationality children in a nearby city. Or the children of immigrant farmworkers can be viewed as a drain on the state's education resources, rather than the asset they actually are to the community. For white organizers who do not have oppressed nationality people to orient themselves to, the challenge to stay ideologically grounded increases. Under such conditions, seeking out activists and movements of color—even if at some distance from where a person lives—can be important to keeping one's bearings.

8. **Be intentional about building a base for activism at the workplace.** For most people who want to be active, it has to be right where they happen to be at that moment in their lives. For others, especially students or youth who are not already tied to a job or a community, there can be an element of freedom to shape where they spend their working life. One possibility is to select a workplace based on its potential as an organizing site—by considering the make-up of the workforce, its history of struggle, and the degree to which the workers share connections to a particular town or neighborhood. Then, rather than getting a job, say, as a union staffperson—where the relationships with workers are less direct—one can hire on as a rank-and-file worker for the long haul. On this basis of equality with others, an organizer can then build ties with coworkers over time in a way that fits with the strategic front against white supremacy. . . .

9. **Examine other aspects of life to see if changes would favor increased activism.**

    - **Where you live:** perhaps a house or apartment in a different community would enable the building of intentional relationships and a social base for activism.
    - **The church, synagogue, sangha, or other religious institution you might attend:** possibilities for increased social engagement might flow from proposing a project or, where necessary, by making a change to a different gathering.
    - **The amount of TV watched:** maybe a different pattern of activity would free up some time for activism, for a progressive book club, or for a class at the local community college.
    - **One's physical condition:** working out, a basketball league, karate or other activity can help keep a person physically fit and more prepared to take on the challenges of an activist's life. Also, the older a person gets, the more important such activity is so that one can bring all the accumulated wisdom of a lifetime to bear for social change.
    - **Where and with whom one socializes:** one of the most segregated spaces in the United States—along with people's religious activities—is where folks relax and enjoy leisure activities. Perhaps other options are available—new places to visit, or new friends to go out with or have over.
    - **Learning a new language:** with the increase of immigrants of color in the United States, learning a second language like Spanish, Tagalog, or Haitian Creole is nearly a necessity for anyone who wants to be effective in opposing white supremacy.

    Generally, the idea is to look at all the ways one might free up time and develop the ability to be more intentionally engaged with others. Having an overarching political perspective is important, too, since it can help a person see the link between everyday activities and the long-term goal of social transformation. The challenge is for people to take responsibility for their lives, be aware of how they spend their time, and make the best use of whatever freedom—or privilege—they may have.

10. **Finally, what if people are just too busy or overwhelmed by trying to hold everything together?** What if they feel they can't change anything, that they will never be effective as a change agent, or that everyone out there is already doing about what they can anyway? The key here is probably not to "do" anything, but just to be open—to people's history, to really seeing what is going on in one's life, to new relationships, and to new kinds of conversation. This society being the way it is, just about everything a person does is tied in somehow with color, class, and gender. A starting point is to keep one's eyes and ears open—along with one's heart and mind—and see what happens.

N
E
X
T

S
T
E
P
S

See Chapter 7 in *Teaching for Diversity and Social Justice* for corresponding teaching materials.

SECTION 3

CLASSISM

Introduction

Maurianne Adams, Larissa E. Hopkins, and Davey Shlasko

INTRODUCTION: ECONOMIC INEQUALITY IN THE AFTERMATH
OF RECENT RECESSION

Before the great recession that started in December 2007, many people felt uncomfortable talking about classism and uncertain about their specific class locations. But now, since the uneven economic recovery benefitted some while leaving others far behind (Fry & Taylor, 2013; Kochhar, 2012; Tatum, 2017), attention to class inequality is out in the open. Town meetings, rallies, and debates during the 2016 national election focused upon the glaring inequities of wealth and income that the recession and its aftermath exacerbated and highlighted. One major candidate on the left, along with his supporters, openly identified with socialism and argued for greater economic equality, raising topics that had been taboo for a generation; the successful candidate on the right made populist appeals to working people who had been left behind by the economy and felt ignored and forgotten by the major political parties.

Unfortunately, public discussion of economic inequality conducted by sound bites in the heat of electioneering is not as nuanced or accurate as one might hope. Much of the political rhetoric evokes ill-defined, one-dimensional class categories – "working class" or "middle class" – without examining what those categories actually mean. Another strain of political rhetoric paints sharp distinctions between the wealthiest 1% and everyone else, as in the Occupy Wall Street slogan "We are the 99%" (selection 40), which glosses over significant differences within the 99% majority. Within the US, the understanding of class categories has been conflated with race, national origins, dialect or accent, immigrant status, generational expectations, and occupation, such that economic status is not a stand-alone class marker (Pew, 2015). This complexity stands in contrast to the simplifications of political rhetoric, and demonstrates that only an intersectional analysis can make sense of our inherited class identities and positions.

For example, the downturn of 2008 had disproportionately negative and long-term consequences for families of color. After decades of being denied mortgages for home investments, they were targeted for high interest subprime home mortgages, so that the bursting of the subprime financial bubble had disastrous consequences for them especially. Latino families lost $75–98 billion in home-value wealth and black families $71–92 billion, the "greatest loss of wealth for people of color in modern U.S. history" according to United for a Fair Economy (Tatum, 2017, pp. 12–13). As for the recovery, the white unemployment rate fell to 4.4% by 2016 while black unemployment remained stuck at 8.5% (Tatum, 2017, p. 13). The disproportionate loss of home equity among families of color cost their college-age children the ability to absorb college costs – thus shifting the subprime mortgage debt to student debt, another financial bonanza and one that could well be the next banking bubble to burst.

The impact and aftermath of the recession in which roughly 8.7 million jobs were lost between February 2008 and February 2010 led to profound changes for many Americans in both economic status and expectations for the future. Even during the "recovery" period of 2009–2014, the proportion of US people living in poverty continued to increase, hovering between 14% and 16% until 2015. Of those almost 20 million, 6.1% of the population, were living in "deep poverty," defined as having incomes of less than half of the (already very low) federal poverty limit (which was $11,770 for a single person and $24,250 for a family of four, in 2015). In 2015, roughly a fifth of all Americans and over 40% of American children received some kind of means-tested government aid (such as Medicaid, SNAP/food stamps, or TANF/welfare), marking a slight increase since the end of the recession ("2015 Poverty Guidelines," 2015; Bishaw, 2013; DeNavas-Walt & Proctor, 2015; Proctor, Semega, & Kollar, 2016; "What is deep poverty?" 2016).

The "recovery" was different for the top 1% of earners, whose income rose 27% while that of the remaining 99% grew only 4% (Saez, 2016). US economic mobility had become restricted, so that 62% of Americans born into families with income in the top fifth stayed in the top two-fifths, while 65% raised in the bottom fifth stayed in the bottom two-fifths (DeParle, 2012). These disparities in wealth and income were accelerated by the recession and its recovery, but the public began to see that they were the consequences of long-term economic patterns. There were many factors in this pattern: job loss and wage decline resulting from increasing automation, outsourcing for cheaper labor overseas, and the declining power of organized labor. Meanwhile, the wealthiest benefitted when corporations moved offshore and international financial mergers reduced US tax obligations, further widening the wealth gap. These ongoing trends assured huge corporate profits, largely through the manipulation of global financial markets. They remain reason for concern.

The downward mobility experienced by many Americans who had thought of themselves as "middle class" contradicted prevalent US assumptions about shared prosperity and upward mobility. Many people whose families had experienced relative prosperity in the post-World War II industrial boom were now struggling to understand their loss of jobs, homes, social status, and self-respect in light of their belief that their hard work would bring financial success. In the search for explanations of their deteriorating economic status, they found scapegoats such as affirmative action programs, social safety net spending, and the immigrant workforce.

In the 2016 election cycle, both major parties capitalized on the growing awareness of and discontent with economic inequality. Populist rhetoric promised greater opportunity for "regular folks" and a return to better times, although with very different strategies for getting there. Stark ideological differences about the role of government in meeting basic human needs such as healthcare, food, and a living wage were juxtaposed with broadly shared suspicion of international economic entanglements and treaties that favor corporate profits at the expense of American workers. Nativist, racist, and sexist sentiments echoed those heard in previous economic crises of the 18th, 19th and 20th centuries, when immigrants, people of color and women workers were blamed for economic hardships impacting all but the wealthiest white men. At the start of a new administration, whose presidential campaign was based on populist rhetoric, we are given a cabinet consisting of billionaires whose wealth comes from the privatization of public resources and the elimination of social services, consumer protections, banking and finance regulations, environmental protections, and economic safety nets (Lipton & Eder, 2017).

We note similar trends globally, as populism combined with nationalism gains traction in Europe, South America, and elsewhere. Immigrants are unfairly scapegoated for economic insecurity, while global finance is met with justified suspicion, but in simplistic ways that fail to analyze the root of the problem. Hardship brought on by volatile financial markets leads to economic and political upheavals, which in turn create local and regional instability, reversing earlier steps toward equality and renewing the marginalization of women, children, elders, people with disabilities, and other vulnerable populations. Outcries against corruption and money in politics are growing, but with little tangible improvement in accountability of governmental and economic elites.

SOCIAL JUSTICE APPROACH TO CLASSISM

This section takes a social justice approach, as do the other sections in this volume. To get the most out of the reading selections in this section, readers need to understand the Social Justice approach presented in Section 1. The Section 1 readings explain the role of identity and socialization in maintaining inequalities (Tatum, selection 1; Kirk & Okazawa-Rey, selection 2); the socialization process by which the social construction of classism plays out (Johnson, selection 3; Harro, selection 5; Sue, selection 4); the levels at which advantage and disadvantage take place in social systems (Bell, Adams, & Zúñiga, selection 6); the manifestations of oppression represented by the "five faces of oppression" (Young, selection 7); and the intersections between classism and other forms of social oppression (selection 8). These concepts are foundational to the approach taken by the Introduction and Reading Selections throughout this section on *Classism*.

MERITOCRACY, DEMOCRACY, AND CAPITALISM

The broadening public conversation about economic inequality has begun to deflate persistent class myths that had made it difficult to discuss classism. For example, *the myth of meritocracy*, which is the belief that hard work and talent are inevitably rewarded by economic success and upward social mobility (McNamee & Miller, 2004), leads to the assumption that those living in poverty have not worked hard enough or are unintelligent, in effect blaming the victims of what is increasingly referred to (not inaccurately) as a "rigged" economic system. Being left out of the post-recession recovery led many formerly middle-class people to question whether our economic system is indeed meritocratic (Alvarado, 2010; McNamee & Miller, 2004). At the same time, chronically low-income communities have long understood, with or without a recession, that economic opportunities follow self-perpetuating cycles of race- and class-based advantage and disadvantage and that the myth of meritocracy rarely applies to them.

A second myth that inhibits discussions of class and classism is the conflation of *democracy* (political equality) with *capitalism* (equality of economic opportunity). The democratic myth that anyone can grow up to be president has been conflated with the capitalist, meritocratic myth that anyone can become rich through hard work and talent. *Democracy* has characterized the US from its constitutional beginnings, although limited at first to the white, male, land-owning colonial elite. Democracy is a *political* system characterized by basic freedoms and a representative (although not an egalitarian) system of governance. *Capitalism*, on the other hand, is an *economic* system based on private ownership of the means of production (agriculture, industry and technology) in which owners' profits derive from the labor of people who receive fixed wages rather than a share of profits. The ownership elites control access to capital (loans, investments), to resources (land, materials) and to labor (through their control of wages). Economic growth, benefiting mainly owners, is in theory driven by a marketplace in which fair competition plays out to everyone's advantage in the absence of regulation (by government or by the organizing efforts of labor unions) (Adams, Hopkins, & Shlasko, 2016). This, too, is a myth.

The *political* processes within a democracy often lead to regulatory laws and policies enacted to protect workers, provide safety, maintain fair labor and banking practices, and fund social safety net programs – as they did in the Progressive Era and in the New Deal. Protective regulations that emerge out of democratic political processes are often described by economic elites as unfair restrictions on the capitalist marketplace. There is a chronic political tension between the beneficiaries of a capitalist system and those harmed by it, who use the democratic political process to seek regulation. But the recent acceleration of money in politics, facilitated by the Supreme Court decision *Citizens United*, has enabled powerful financial and corporate interests to roll back these regulations and safety nets; cut welfare, food stamps, and Medicaid; and roll back environmental protections for clean air and water. The role of money in politics undermines democratic efforts to balance the excesses of capitalism with the people's health and well-being. Even when laws protect individual rights, a capitalist economic system by its very nature creates and reproduces class inequality because of the different ways in which owners and workers can and cannot accumulate wealth.

US HISTORICAL CONTEXT

The history of the US has been one of political and economic struggle. We celebrate the *political struggles* that expanded voting rights to create a representative democracy, but remain relatively silent about *economic struggles* in which tenant farmers and manual and industrial workers resisted economic exploitation. This history of economic exploitation and resistance has been well documented but is not generally well known (Loewen, 1995; Nicholson, 2004; Steinberg, 1989; Zinn, 1995).

The wealth of colonial landowners was built by the labor of unpaid slaves in both the North and South, in a legal system that prevented black slaves and white indentured servants from forming an alliance. Although poor Whites often lived in deprived conditions similar to those of skilled slaves and free Blacks, poor Whites were hired before free Blacks and earned more per hour for the same jobs. This race-based two-tiered labor system became the basis for racialized labor union movements which in turn helped to create a white middle class in the mid-20th century.

US economic growth depended upon the export of cotton grown on slave plantations and on white settler agriculture on fertile lands made available by the forced resettlements of Native peoples. Economic racism continued as immigrants of color (including Sikhs, Chinese, and then Japanese) and Mexicans were shunted into menial labor, the men on farms, factories, mines, and railroads, and the women in farming and domestic labor. The legacy of this racialized and gendered class system appears today in the racially tiered workforce wherein peoples of color are still relegated to low-paid labor in service roles and agriculture, marginalized into criminalized work in the sex trade and drug trade, and literally locked into prison labor jobs that pay pennies an hour (selections 33 and 37). Meanwhile, the wealthy elite from colonial times onward profited from a system of economic and political advantages that maintained their wealth and power through their primary control of and benefit from land speculation, mining, trade, and financial markets (Steinberg, 1989; Takaki, 1993; Zinn, 1995).

Immigrants arrived to a country where a racialized class system already prevailed, starting with colonial landowners and political elites who legalized slavery, eradicated Native communities, and enforced white indentured servitude. Kidnapped Africans were in effect an involuntary immigrant population – millions bought in the transatlantic slave trade and sold throughout the Americas for use as a racially marked workforce in the labor-intensive export crops of sugar and cotton. Later immigrants from Europe, Asia, Arabia, and the Americas arrived and took their places within an already racially tiered workforce to build the infrastructure and provide the domestic labor that allowed the US to expand westward and the owning class to make immense fortunes, while the workers and their children largely remained poor. By 1920, 36 million Americans, more than a third of the population, were immigrant families, the majority from Southern and Eastern Europe with smaller numbers from China, Japan, India, and elsewhere (Daniels, 2002).

Although white European immigrants constituted an exploited, ethnically marked working class whose poverty and desperation left them vulnerable to wage exploitation, their "whiteness" strengthened the "upper" tier of the working class (Roediger, 1991). Irish women displaced black domestic laborers, and worked alongside Italian and Jewish women in textile mills and sweatshops that didn't hire Blacks. A successful but racist labor union movement in the early 20th century provided generational upward mobility for Irish, Italians, Jews, and other white ethnic workers, but not Blacks, Latino/as, or other workers of color who were excluded from most unions. The process by which white ethnics moved from the upper tier of the working class into a "middle class" of "skilled" laborers and small business owners, while most Blacks, Latino/as, and Chinese remained in the lower tier, is part of today's complex racial and economic legacy (Foner, 1998; Roediger, 1991; Steinberg, 1989; Zinn, 1995).

The story of class opportunity still taught in K-12 schools largely ignores the stories of working-class organizing, from the revolts of indentured servants and tenant farmers in the early colonies, to labor organizing by mainly immigrants who improved wages and working conditions across whole industries (Loewen, 1995; Takaki, 1993; Zinn, 1995). Most students know little about the achievements of the labor union movement which include the 40-hour work week and two-day weekend, the right to meal breaks, and protection from wage theft. Nor are they likely to learn about the important exceptions: most labor protections still do not apply to farm workers, domestic workers, incarcerated workers and people who do criminalized work such as in the sex industry (selections 33, 35, and 37).

ECONOMIC, SOCIAL, AND CULTURAL DIMENSIONS OF CLASS: WEALTH AND INCOME, SOCIAL AND CULTURAL CAPITAL

To provide consistency and clarity in discussing the various dimensions of *class* and *classism*, we propose Leondar-Wright and Yeskel's (2007) definition of *class* as "a relative social ranking based on income, wealth, education, status, and power" and their definition of *classism* as "the institutional, cultural, and individual set of practices and beliefs that assign differential value to people according to their socioeconomic class," in a system characterized by economic inequality (Leondar-Wright & Yeskel, 2007, p. 314; see also Fiske & Markus, 2012; Lareau & Conley, 2008).

Class as "a relative social ranking" has a variety of indicators, some material and others relational. Individuals internalize stereotypes about different class positions, often based on misinformation, and these misunderstandings define their relationships to others within a class hierarchy. Thus, *classism* implicates all participants in a social system in which the class categories are nuanced and opaque, and in which relative advantage and disadvantage are reproduced through the interaction of social, institutional, cultural, and interpersonal relationships. In addition to examining a variety of *class indicators*, we consider the cultures and identities that form around shared *class location*.

The material, quantifiable indicators of class are economic capital – *wealth and income*. *Wealth* consists of what one owns (investments, homes, land or businesses) minus what one owes (credit card or school debt, home mortgages), while *income* refers to the periodic inflow of resources from wages, investments, government benefits, or other sources. Non-material indicators of class include *class culture, cultural capital, social capital,* as well as political power (Fiske & Markus, 2012).

Class culture describes the norms, values, and ways of life shared by people with a similar class position, as intersecting also with ethnic culture. Class cultures develop in response to economic realities as well as other dimensions of experience, and can be thought of as those aspects of culture that help people to survive and/or thrive in, and make sense of their roles in, the economic system (Shlasko & Kramer, 2011; Williams, 2012). One's class culture is not shaped only by one's membership in a general class category, but also by a more specific location defined by context and by other social identities (Matos, 2011; Yosso, 1996). The normalization of dominant class cultures and the devaluation of others is an aspect of *classism*.

Cultural capital refers to sets of culturally specific knowledge, skills, language, and self-presentation that act as markers of class, and that can allow someone to successfully navigate social institutions such as education, courts, politics, and healthcare. People often use *cultural capital* to refer specifically to facility with the cultural markers of the more privileged classes, but in our view, all class cultures have their own forms of cultural capital, though these are valued and ranked differently by the broader society. For example, familiarity and comfort with the norms of interaction in a working-class community may help a person to navigate that social environment successfully and lead to work opportunities, access to aid from the community, and so on. However, different groups' cultural capital are neither interchangeable nor equivalent in terms of the potential economic benefits they provide.

Whereas *cultural capital* refers to "what one knows about," *social capital* refers to "who one knows" – that is, the social networks one is part of and to which one has ready access. As with cultural capital, *social capital* is sometimes used in ways specific to privileged class groups, to describe connections to elite social networks that provide access to private schooling, professional advancement, political power, and other forms of class advantage (Allan, Ozga, & Smith, 2009; Mohr & DiMaggio, 1995). *Social capital* also refers to family and neighborhood networks that poor and working-class people rely on for resources like child care, job leads, hand-me-downs, rides, and housing.

As we consider how these multi-faceted class indicators interact, it becomes clear that the category of "class" is multidimensional: a person may have advantages linked to one indicator and disadvantages resulting from another. For example, a woman with greater income than another (because she's a professional athlete or has just won the lottery) may have lower status in terms of her cultural capital (because she is less educated or has less "sophisticated" manners). This nuanced view of class also allows us to examine the mechanisms of *class privilege*, meaning advantages and resources accorded to some groups of people and not others (often at the expense of others) based on relative class ranking.

Visible class indicators intersect with other visible identities. For example, men often appear more prosperous and successful than women, whereas people of color are often assumed to be poor, as are people with noticeable disabilities. Norms of "professionalism" are one mechanism by which intersectional class inequalities are reproduced, because they are culturally specific in terms of class culture as well as ethnic and linguistic cultures, and are gendered, so that anyone who is not both gender-conforming and at home in the dominant white, middle-class culture may be seen as unprofessional and lose status as a result. The interconnections of economic, social, and cultural forms of capital are important for an analysis of *class* and *classism*.

An especially problematic class indicator, not always visible relative to class status, is the ballooning student debt, which cuts across the class spectrum, impacting almost everyone who goes to college except for the few whose families have the income or wealth to cover all college costs. The role of loan companies and banks mirrors their role during the mortgage debt crisis that led to the recession of 2008. The costs of higher education have soared, partly due to reductions in state support to public universities at the same time that federally funded loans and grants to students have been cut drastically. The result has been the accumulation of more than $1.4 trillion in student debt in 2017, with 70% of all students in debt, and debt totals averaging $37,172 per student with some students owing more than $100,000 (Student Loan Hero, 2017). This debt represents a crisis for the current generation of college graduates and indebted dropouts, a burden as they enter the job market and start families that affects the kinds of jobs they need to find, their ability to afford housing, and their choices about when to have children. The challenges many people face in repaying student debt have led to aggressive pursuit by student-loan debt collectors (selection 31; Cowley & Silver-Greenberg, 2017). Student debt undermines the belief that higher education leads to upward mobility (NCES, 2016) and complicates current and future class status for recent graduates as well as those who attend some college but do not finish a degree.

READING SELECTIONS IN THIS SECTION

The first nine selections in this section present *Contexts* for understanding the role of social institutions in maintaining and reproducing class-based inequality. In selection 26, "Class in America," Mantsios punctures the myth of classlessness with portraits that juxtapose upper- and middle-class opportunities with working-poor constraints. Mantsios's thumbnail sketches of class difference dramatize the advantages and disadvantages described throughout these selections.

Smith and Redington (selection 27) describe how long-standing systematic classist bias gives rise to persistent and harmful classist microaggressions. These microaggressions include name-calling and labeling (lazy, dumb, irresponsible, promiscuous, welfare queen) that stereotype poor and working-class people in a manner simultaneously classist and ableist (and often racist and sexist), as being prone to cognitive deficits, educational failure, criminal behavior, and dysfunctional relationships. The authors show how seemingly minor insults, in the context of structural inequality, have a cumulative, damaging impact.

Oliver and Shapiro (selection 28) explain the intergenerational transmission of racialized wealth inequality. The authors describe historical moments in which federal policies intentionally established the structural basis for white opportunity on one hand, and for perpetuating black poverty on the other – for example, the availability of the 1950s GI Bill education grants and Fair Housing Administration loans for Whites only. While the emphasis in this selection is on the role of specific laws and policies in shaping white/black disparities in wealth, this kind of exploration offers a template for identifying obstacles that restrict the economic and social mobility of other US communities of color as well.

Selection 44 consists of several charts that visualize various quantifiable manifestations of economic inequality. Some of the charts show how the distribution of income and wealth has shifted over time in the US while others focus on income inequality across race and gender.

"What's Debt Got to Do with It?" and "Is the Near-Trillion-Dollar Student Loan Bubble About to Pop?" (selections 29 and 31) are vivid portraits of the consequences of debt overload on individuals and families. "What's Debt Got to Do with It?" looks at the $5 billion-a-year poverty debt market, in which international chains of financial services profit through the deceptive practices of pawnshops, rent-to-own stores, and high-interest loans. These poverty-exploiting storefronts advertise "easy" financial services that seem like good deals, but charge exorbitant fees and interest rates that leave customers deeper in debt. "Is the Near-Trillion-Dollar Student Loan Bubble About to Pop?" provides insight into the college student debt burden, a "bubble" ready to burst with dangers to society comparable to the mortgage bubble that precipitated the 2008 recession.

The ease of access for well-to-do "legacy" applicants (selection 30) and the debt burden on economically strapped disadvantaged students (selection 31) dramatizes ways in which access to higher education has become "classed." As costs skyrocket, federal Pell grants are cut, and funding for higher education becomes predominantly loan based, college graduates are left with huge debts and few job opportunities lucrative enough to pay them off. The financial struggles experienced by college students from middle- and low-income families are compounded for students with disabilities (selection 32). Further, many students with disabilities struggle with costs for needed healthcare services and assistive devices, the lack of which negatively affects academic achievement and workforce success.

In "'Free' Labor: Past and Present Forms of Prison Labor" (selection 33) Whitney Benns explains the variety of contemporary prison labor practices in the US. Benns draws connections between incarcerated labor in the Reconstruction era South and today's prison labor system, both of which reproduce the structures of slavery while driving down wages for non-incarcerated workers. This selection highlights an important intersection of racism, classism, and ableism, since people with intellectual, psychological, and physical disabilities are disproportionately incarcerated (Dolan & Carr, 2015).

The Pew report on wealth inequality (selection 34) highlights the racial wealth gaps that have increased since the 2008 recession. It illustrates the explanation of historically constructed wealth inequality (Oliver & Shapiro, selection 28) and enhances the portraits of advantage and disadvantage (Mantsios, selection 26). Other recent Pew studies show the loss of homeownership for Blacks and for young adults, despite a recovering economy (Fry & Brown, 2016), a disproportionate impact noted by Tatum (2017) as explained above.

Five selections in *Voices* speak from contexts of privileged as well as disadvantaged class positions. African American and immigrant women of color in domestic service describe their experiences of exploitation and powerlessness (selection 35), including isolation and race- and class-based insults as part of the reality of their devalued, gendered household labor. In selection 36, bell hooks explores the nuanced intersection of race and class through memories of her rural Southern small town childhood. She recounts how class position sometimes complicated the expected differences between Blacks and Whites, so that poor Whites clung to their racial advantage even while wealthier Whites and Blacks scorned the white poor.

Collins writes as a 1%er (see selection 38) whose experience living among the 99% exposed him to a radically new perspective on his inherited wealth and motivated him to take action. His decision to give away his financial cushion brought him into an experience of community and solidarity that he would never have known if he had not chosen to prioritize a life lived in cross-class coalitions and in solidarity with poor communities working toward social change.

There are clear implications throughout this section for positive social change. Different forms of class exploitation require remedies at different levels – legal, institutional, cultural, and interpersonal. Rounding out the *Voices* section, and also applicable to *Next Steps*, Juno Mac explores the spectrum of legal approaches to a particularly stigmatized labor force – sex workers. As a sex worker activist, Mac outlines the pros and cons of four different approaches. She draws parallels and comparisons across industries, always returning to the question of how each approach impacts the workers themselves.

The *Next Steps* selections in this chapter focus on political, community, and classroom efforts to correct class injustice and create greater class equity. The first selection, "How Occupy Wall Street Changes Everything" (selection 40) lives up to its title. The Occupy Wall Street movement started in 2011 and largely disappeared from the mainstream news cycle by 2013. But many of the activist projects initiated during Occupy continue, and its powerful messaging, such as the slogan "We are the 99%," transformed the way people in the US talk about class and economic inequality. Collins in selection 38 tellingly identifies himself as a member of the 1%, and we hear Occupy's echoes in messaging from the 2016 election season and beyond. The key issues that Occupy raised, such as risky manipulation of financial markets that benefit few at the expense of many, continue to threaten the economic and social stability of society as a whole.

This section's emphasis on cross-class coalition building points to the importance of class awareness, especially among middle and owning class people who have not thought about their everyday class assumptions, in order to coordinate efforts with less privileged organizing partners. Selection 41 quotes personal examples of the everyday, unintentional classism that often interferes with effective cross-class organizing. Selection 42, "Deep Thoughts About Class Privilege," written by Resource Generation, an organization of young people with wealth who are dedicated to acting ethically from their position of privilege, challenges readers to explore their own examples of internalized class privilege. Readers interested in delving further into their own experiences of class privilege should go to the resources at Resource Generation's website.

The excerpts from *Home Economics* (43) detail the plight of domestic workers, also reflected in the narratives in selection 35. At the intersection of gender, race, immigration, and class differences, those who work in others' homes providing childcare, cleaning, home healthcare, and other services have been mostly invisible in US labor politics. This selection presents recommendations for creating safe and healthy workplace norms for domestic workers, together with broader changes in how domestic work and all low-wage work must be understood in order to meet the needs presented by shifting demographics and economies.

Further *Next Steps* relevant to classism are found in other sections of this book and can be located by reviewing "Classism" in the Table of Intersections. All selections in this and other sections raise questions, challenges, and possibilities for change that go well beyond the limits of *class* and *classism* alone. We encourage all readers to turn to the website for questions they might ask themselves and each other based on these readings, as well as related discussion questions, and links to relevant videos and classroom activities.

References

2015 poverty guidelines. (2015, September). Office of the Assistant Secretary for Planning and Evaluation, U.S. Department of Health and Human Services. Retrieved from https://aspe.hhs.gov/2015-poverty-guidelines.

Adams, M., Hopkins, L., & Shlasko, D. (2016). Classism curriculum design. In Adams, M., Bell, L. A., Griffin, P., & Joshi, K. (Eds.), *Teaching for diversity and social justice*, 3rd edition. New York: Routledge.

Allan, J., Ozga, J., & Smith, G. (Eds.). (2009). *Social capital, professionalism and diversity*. Rotterdam, The Netherlands: Sense Publishers.

Alvarado, L. A. (2010). Dispelling the meritocracy myth: Lessons for higher education and student affairs educators. *The Vermont Connection*, 31: 10–20.

Bishaw, A. (2013, September). Poverty: 2000–2012. American Community Survey Briefs. U.S. Census Bureau.

Cowley, S. & Silver-Greenberg, J. (2017, April 10). Suit says lender duped students to fuel growth. *New York Times*.

Daniels, R. (2002). *Coming to America: A history of immigration and ethnicity in American life*, 2nd edition. New York: Harper Perennial.

DeNavas-Walt, C. & Proctor, B. D. (2015, September). Income and poverty in the United States: 2014. Current Population Reports. U.S. Census Bureau.

DeParle, J. (2012, January 5). Harder for Americans to rise from economy's lower rungs. *New York Times*.

Dolan, K. & Carr, J. (2015). *The poor get prison: The alarming spread of the criminalization of poverty*. Washington, DC: Institute for Policy Studies.

Fiske, S., and Markus, H. R. (Eds.). (2012). *Facing social class: How societal rank influences interaction*. New York: Russell Sage Foundation.

Foner, E. (1998). *The story of American freedom*. New York: Norton.

Fry, R. & Brown, A. (2016, December 15). In a recovering market, homeownership rates are down sharply for Blacks, young adults: Most renders say they would like to own in the future, but financial constraints are an obstacle. Pew Research Center Social & Demographic Trends.

Fry, R. & Taylor, P. (2013, April 23). A rise in wealth for the wealthy; declines for the lower 93%: An uneven recovery, 2009–2011. Pew Research Center Social & Demographic Trends.

Kochhar, R. (2012, September 12). A recovery no better than the recession: Median household income, 2007–2011. Pew Research Center Social & Demographic Trends.

Lareau, A. & Conley, D. (Eds.). (2008). *Social class: How does it work?* New York: Russell Sage Foundation.

Leondar-Wright, B. & Yeskel, F. (2007). Classism curriculum design. In Adams, M., Bell, L. A., & Griffin, P. (Eds.), *Teaching for diversity and social justice*, 2nd edition (pp. 308–333). New York: Routledge. Appendix C on CD. (See chapter website for these materials.)

Lipton, E. & Eder, S. (2017, January 6). Trump nominees' filings threaten to overwhelm federal ethics office. *New York Times*. https://nyti.ms/2i2pixX

Loewen, J. W. (1995). The land of opportunity. In *Lies my teacher told me: Everything your American history textbook got wrong* (pp. 200–213). New York: Simon & Schuster.

Matos, J. M. D. (2011). *Fulfilling their dreams: Latina/o college student narratives on the impact of parental involvement on their academic engagement.* Doctoral Dissertations available from Proquest. Paper AAI3465047.

McNamee, S. J. & Miller, R. K., Jr. (2004). *The meritocracy myth.* Lanham, MD: Rowman & Littlefield.

Mohr, J. & DiMaggio, P. (1995). The intergenerational transmission of cultural capital. *Research in Social Stratification and Mobility,* 14, 169–200.

NCES National Center for Educational Statistics. (2016). Employment rates of college graduates. https://nces.ed.gov/fastfacts/display.asp?id=561.

Nicholson, P. Y. (2004). *Labor's story in the United States.* Philadelphia, PA: Temple University Press.

Pew. (2015, December 9). The American middle-class is losing ground: No longer the majority and falling behind financially. Pew Research Center Social & Demographic Trends.

Proctor, B. D., Semega, J. L. & Kollar, M. A. (2016, September). Income and poverty in the United States: 2015. Current Population Reports. U.S. Census Bureau.

Roediger, D. R. (1991). *The wages of whiteness,* revised edition. London: Verso.

Saez, E. (2016, June 30). Striking it richer: The evolution of top incomes in the United States (updated with 2015 preliminary estimates). Retrieved from https://eml.berkeley.edu/~saez/saez-UStopincomes-2015.pdf.

Shlasko, D. & Kramer, T. (2011). Class culture and classism in campus and community organizing. Presentation at *Pedagogies of Privilege Conference,* University of Denver.

Steinberg, S. (1989). *The ethnic myth: Race, ethnicity, and class in America,* updated edition. Boston, MA: Beacon Press.

Student Loan Hero. (2017). A look at the shocking student loan debt statistics for 2017. https://studentloanhero.com/student-loan-debt-statistics/.

Takaki, R. (1993). *A different mirror: A history of multicultural America.* Boston, MA: Little, Brown, & Co.

Tatum, B. D. (2017). Prologue to *"Why are all the Black kids still sitting together in the cafeteria" and other conversations about race in the 21st century?* 2nd edition. Boston, MA: Beacon.

"What is deep poverty?" (2016). Center for Poverty Research at University of CA, Davis. Retrieved from http://poverty.ucdavis.edu/faq/what-deep-poverty.

Williams, J. C. (2012). The class culture gap. In S. T. Fiske & H. R. Markus (Eds.), *Facing social class: How societal rank influences interaction* (pp. 39–58). New York: Russell Sage Foundation.

Yosso, T. (1996). Whose culture has capital? A critical race theory discussion of community cultural wealth. In A. Dixson & C. Rousseau (Eds.), *Critical race theory in education: All God's children got a song.* New York: Routledge.

Zinn, H. (1995). *A people's history of the United States,* revised and updated edition. New York: Harper & Row.

26

Class in America

Gregory Mantsios

Americans, in general, don't like to talk about class. Or so it would seem. We don't speak about class privileges, or class oppression, or the class nature of society. . . . Phrases like "working class," "upper class," "capitalist class," and "ruling class" are rarely uttered by Americans.

For the most part, avoidance of class-laden vocabulary crosses class boundaries. There are few among the poor who speak of themselves as lower class; instead, they refer to their race, ethnic group, or geographic location. Workers are more likely to identify with their employer, industry, or occupational group than with other workers, or with the working class. Neither are those at the upper end of the economic spectrum likely to use the word "class." In her study of 38 wealthy and socially prominent women, Susan Ostrander asked participants if they considered themselves members of the upper class. One participant responded, "I hate to use the word 'class.' We are responsible, fortunate people, old families, the people who have something." Another said, "I hate [the term] upper class. It is so non-upper class to use it. I just call it 'all of us'—those who are well-born."

It is not that Americans, rich or poor, aren't keenly aware of class differences—those quoted above obviously are; it is that class is usually not in the domain of public conversation. Class is not discussed or debated in public because class identity has been stripped from popular culture. . . . There are, however, two notable exceptions to this phenomenon. First, it is acceptable in the United States to talk about "the middle class." Interestingly enough, the term middle class appears to be acceptable precisely because it mutes class differences. References to the middle class by politicians, for example, are designed to encompass and attract the broadest possible constituency. Not only do references to the middle class gloss over differences, but they also avoid any suggestion of conflict or injustice.

This leads us to a second exception to the class-avoidance phenomenon. We are, on occasion, presented with glimpses of the upper class and the lower class (the language used is "the wealthy" and "the poor"). In the media, these presentations are designed to satisfy some real or imagined voyeuristic need of "the ordinary person." As curiosities, the ground-level view of street life and trailer parks and the inside look at the rich and the famous serve as unique models, one to avoid and one to emulate. . . .

We are left with one of two possible explanations for why Americans usually don't talk about class: Either class distinctions are not relevant to U.S. society, or we mistakenly hold a set of beliefs that obscure the reality of class differences and their impact on people's lives.

Let's look at four common, albeit contradictory, beliefs about class in America that have persisted over time.

Myth 1: We are a middle-class nation. Despite some variations in economic status, most Americans have achieved relative affluence in what is widely recognized as a consumer society.

Myth 2: Class really doesn't matter in the United States. Whatever differences do exist in economic standing, they are—for the most part—irrelevant. Our democracy provides for all regardless of economic class: Rich or poor, we are all equal in the eyes of the law.

Myth 3: We live in a land of upward mobility. The American public as a whole is steadily moving up the economic ladder and each generation propels itself to greater economic well-being.

Myth 4: Everyone has an equal chance to succeed. Success in the United States requires no more than hard work, sacrifice, and perseverance: "In America, anyone can become a billionaire; it's just a matter of being in the right place at the right time."

In trying to assess the legitimacy of these beliefs, we want to ask several important questions. Are there significant class differences among Americans? If these differences do exist, are they getting bigger or smaller? Do class differences have a significant impact on the way we live? How much upward mobility is there in the United States? Finally, does everyone in the United States really have an equal opportunity to succeed and an equal voice in our democracy?

THE ECONOMIC SPECTRUM

For starters, let's look at difference. An examination of available data reveals that variations in economic well-being are, in fact, dramatic. Consider the following:

- The richest 20 percent of Americans hold nearly 90 percent of the total household wealth in the country. The wealthiest 1 percent of the American population holds 36 percent of the total national wealth. That is, the top 1 percent own over one-third of all the consumer durables (such as houses, cars, televisions, and computers) and financial assets (such as stocks, bonds, property, and bank savings).
- There are 323,067 Americans—approximately 1 percent of the adult population—who earn more than $1 million annually. There are over 1,000 billionaires in the United States today, more than 70 of them worth over $10 billion each. It would take the typical American earning $49,445 (the median income in the United States)—and spending absolutely nothing at all —a total of 202,240 years (or over 2,500 lifetimes) to earn $10 billion.

Affluence and prosperity are clearly alive and well in certain segments of the U.S. population. However, this abundance is in sharp contrast to the poverty that persists in America. At the other end of the spectrum:

- More than 15 percent of the American population —that is, 1 of every 7 people in this country—live below the official poverty line (calculated at $11,139 for an individual and $22,314 for a family of four). In 2010, there were 42 million poor people in the United States—the largest number since the Census Bureau began publishing poverty statistics more than 50 years ago.
- An estimated 3.5 million people—of whom nearly 1.4 million are children—are homeless.
- The 2010 U.S. Census reported that more than 1 out of every 5 children under the age of 18 lives in poverty.

Reality 1: The contrast between rich and poor is sharp, and with one-third of the American population living at one extreme or the other. It is difficult to argue that we live in a classless society.

While those at the bottom of the economic ladder have fared poorly relative to those at the top, so too have those in the middle—and their standing relative to the top has been declining as well.

- The middle fifth of the population holds less than 4 percent of the national *wealth*.
- The share of wealth held by the middle fifth 30 years ago was 5.2 percent of the total. Today's share held by the middle sector is 23 percent less than what it was 3 decades ago.

Reality 2: The middle class in the United States holds a very small share of the nation's wealth and that share has declined steadily.

The gap between rich and poor—and between the rich and the middle class—leaves the vast majority of the American population at a distinct disadvantage.

- Eighty percent of the population—that is, four out of every five Americans, is left sharing a little more than 10 percent of the nation's wealth.
- The income gap between the very rich (top 1 percent) and everyone else (the 99 percent) more than tripled over the past 3 decades, creating the greatest concentration of income since 1928. . . .

The numbers and percentages associated with economic inequality are difficult to fully comprehend. To help his students visualize the distribution of income, the well-known economist Paul Samuelson asked them to picture an income pyramid made of children's blocks, with each layer of blocks representing $1,000. If we were to construct Samuelson's pyramid today, the peak of the pyramid would be much higher than the Eiffel Tower, yet almost all of us would be within 6 feet of the ground. In other words, a small minority of families takes the lion's share of the national income, and the remaining income is distributed among the vast majority of middle-income and low-income families. Keep in mind that Samuelson's pyramid represents the distribution of income, not wealth (accumulated resources). The distribution of wealth is skewed even further. Ten billion dollars of wealth would reach more than 1,000 times the height of the Eiffel Tower.

Reality 3: Middle- and lower-income earners—what many in other parts of the world would refer to as the working class—share a miniscule portion of the nation's wealth. For the most part, the real class divide in the United States is between the very wealthy and everyone else—and it is a divide that is staggering.

AMERICAN LIFESTYLES

The late political theorist/activist Michael Harrington once commented, "America has the best-dressed poverty the world has ever known." Clothing disguises much of the poverty in the United States, and this may explain, in part, the country's middle-class image. With increased mass marketing of "designer" clothing and with shifts in the nation's economy from blue-collar (and often better-paying) manufacturing jobs to white-collar and pink-collar jobs in the service sector, it is becoming increasingly difficult to distinguish class differences based on appearance. The dress-down environment prevalent in the high-tech industry (what American Studies scholar Andrew Ross refers to as the "no-collar movement") has reduced superficial distinctions even further.

Beneath the surface, there is another reality. Let's look at some "typical" and not-so-typical lifestyles.

C
O
N
T
E
X
T

American Profile

Name:	Harold S. Browning
Father:	Manufacturer, industrialist
Mother:	Prominent social figure in the community
Principal child-rearer:	Governess
Primary education:	An exclusive private school on Manhattan's Upper East Side *Note*: A small, well-respected primary school where teachers and administrators have a reputation for nurturing student creativity and for providing the finest educational preparation *Ambition*: "To become President"
Supplemental tutoring:	Tutors in French and mathematics
Summer camp:	Sleep-away camp in northern Connecticut *Note*: Camp provides instruction in the creative arts, athletics, and the natural sciences
Secondary education:	A prestigious preparatory school in Westchester Country Note: Classmates included the sons of ambassadors, doctors, attorneys, television personalities, and well-known business leaders *Supplemental education*: Private SAT tutor *After-school activities*: Private riding lessons *Ambition*: "To take over my father's business" *High-school graduation gift*: BMW
Family activities:	Theater, recitals, museums, summer vacations in Europe, occasional winter trips to the Caribbean Note: As members of and donors to the local art museum, the Brownings and their children attend private receptions and exhibit openings at the invitation of the museum director
Higher education:	An Ivy League liberal arts college in Massachusetts *Major*: Economics and political science *After-class activities*: Debating club, college newspaper, swim team *Ambition* : "To become a leader in business"
First full-time job (age 23):	Assistant manager of operations, Browning Tool and Die, Inc. (family enterprise)
Subsequent employment:	3 years—Executive assistant to the president, Browning Tool and Die *Responsibilties included*: Purchasing (materials and equipment), personnel, and distribution networks 4 years—Advertising manager, Lackheed Manufacturing (home appliances) 3 years—Director of marketing and sales, Comerex, Inc, (business machines)
Current employment (age 38):	Executive vice president, SmithBond and Co.(digital instruments) *Typical daily activities*: Review financial reports and computer printouts, dictate memoranda, lunch with clients, initiate conference calls, meet with assistants, plan business trips, meet with associates *Transportation to and from work*: Chauffeured company limousine *Annual salary*: $324,000 *Ambition*: "To become the executive officer of the firm, or one like it, within the next five to ten years"
Current residence:	Eighteenth-floor condominium on Manhattan's Upper West Side, eleven rooms, including five spacious bedrooms and terrace overlooking river *Interior*: Professionally decorated and accented with elegant furnishings, valuable antiques, and expensive artwork *Note*: Building management provides doorman and elevator attendant: family employs au pair for children and maid for other domestic chores
Second residence:	Farm in northwestern Connecticut, used for weekend retreats and for horse breeding (investment/ hobby) *Note*: To maintain the farm and cater to the family when they are there, the Brownings employ a part-time maid, groundskeeper, and horse breeder

Harold Browning was born into a world of nurses, maids, and governess. His world today is one of airplanes and limousines, five-star restaurants, and luxurious living accommodations. The life and lifestyle of Harold Browning is in sharp contrast to that of Bob Farrell.

American Profile

Name:	Bob Farrell
Father:	Machinist
Mother:	Retail clerk
Principal child-rearer:	Mother and sister
Primary education:	A medium-size public school in Queens, New York, characterized by large class size, outmoded physical facilities, and an educational philosophy emphasizing basic skills and student discipline *Ambition*: "To become President"
Supplemental tutoring:	None
Summer camp:	YMCA day camp. *Note*: Emphasis on team sports, arts and crafts
Secondary education:	Large regional high school in Queens *Note*: Classmates included the sons and daughters of carpenters, postal clerks, teachers, nurses, shopkeepers, mechanics, bus drivers, police officers, salespersons *Supplemental education*: SAT prep course offered by national chain *After-school activities*: Basketball and handball in school park *Ambition*: "To make it through college" *High-school graduation gift*: $500 savings bond
Family activities:	Family gatherings around television set, softball, an occasional trip to the movie theatre, summer Sundays at the public beach
Higher education:	A two-year community college with a technical orientation *Major*: Electrical technology *After-school activities*: Employed as a part-time bagger in local supermarket *Ambition*: "To become an electrical engineer"
First full-time job(age 19):	Service-station attendant Note: Continued to take college classes in the evening
Subsequent employment:	Mail clerk at large insurance firm; manager trainee, large retail chain
Present employment (age 38):	Assistant sales manager, building supply firm *Typical daily activities*: Demonstrate products, write up product orders, handle customer complaints, check inventory *Transportation to and from work*: City subway *Annual salary*: $45,261 *Additional income*: $6,100 in commissions from evening and weekend work as salesman in local men's clothing store *Ambition*: "To open up my own business"
Current residence:	The Farrells own their own home in a working class neighborhood in Queens, New York

Bob Farrell and Harold Browning live very differently: One is very privileged, the other much less so. The differences are class differences, which have a profound impact on the way they live. They are differences between playing a game of handball in the park and taking riding lessons at a private stable; watching a movie on television and going to the theatre; and taking the subway to work and being driven in a limousine. More important, the difference in class determines where they live, who their friends are, how well they are educated, what they do for a living, and what they come to expect from life.

Yet, as dissimilar as their lifestyles are, Harold Browning and Bob Farrell have some things in common: they live in the same city, they work long hours, and they are highly motivated. More importantly, they are both white males.

Let's look at someone else who works long and hard and is highly motivated. This person, however, is black and female.

C
O
N
T
E
X
T

American Profile

Name:	Cheryl Mitchell
Father:	Janitor
Mother:	Waitress
Principal child-rearer:	Grandmother
Primary education:	Large public school in Ocean Hill Brownsville, Brooklyn, New York *Note*: Rote teaching of basic skills and emphasis on conveying the importance of good attendance, good manners, and good work habits; school patrolled by security guards *Ambition*: "To be a teacher"
Supplemental tutoring:	None
Summer camp:	None
Secondary education:	Large public school in Ocean Hill-Brownsville *Note*: Classmates included sons and daughters of hairdressers, groundskeepers, painters, dressmakers, dishwashers, domestics *Supplemental education*: None *After-school activities*: Domestic chores, part-time employment as babysitter and housekeeper *Ambition*: "To be a social worker" *High-school graduation gift*: Corsage
Family activities:	Church-sponsored socials
Higher education:	One semester of local community college *Note*: Dropped out of school for financial reasons
First full-time job (age 17):	Counter clerk, local bakery
Subsequent employment:	File clerk with temporary-service agency, supermarket checker
Current employment (age 38):	Nurse's aide at a municipal hospital *Typical daily activities*: Make up hospital beds, clean out bedpans, weigh patients and assist them to the bathroom, take temperature readings, pass out and collect food trays, feed patients who need help, bathe patients, and change dressings *Annual salary*: $17,850 *Ambition*: "To get out of the ghetto"
Current residence:	Three-room apartment in the South Bronx, needs painting, has poor ventilation, is in a high-crime area *Note*: Cheryl Mitchell lives with her four-year old son and her elderly mother

When we look at Cheryl Mitchell, Bob Farrell, and Harold Browning, we see three very different lifestyles. We are not looking, however, at economic extremes. Cheryl Mitchell's income as a nurse's aide puts her above the government's official poverty line. Below her on the income pyramid are 42 million poverty-stricken Americans. Far from being poor, Bob Farrell has an annual income ($51,361) as an assistant sales manager that puts him above the median income level—that is, more than 50 percent of the U.S. population earns less money than Bob Farrell. And while Harold Browning's income puts him in a high-income bracket, he stands only a fraction of the way up Samuelson's income pyramid. Well above him are the 323,067 Americans whose annual incomes exceed $1 million. Yet Harold Browning spends more money on his horses than Cheryl Mitchell earns in a year.

Reality 4: Even ignoring the extreme poles of the economic spectrum, we find enormous class differences in the lifestyles among the haves, the have-nots, and the have-littles.

Class affects more than lifestyle and material well-being. It has significant impact on our physical and mental well-being as well. Researchers have found an inverse relationship between social class and health. Lower–class standing is correlated with higher rates of infant mortality, eye and ear disease, arthritis, physical disability, diabetes, nutritional deficiency, respiratory disease, mental illness, and heart disease. In all areas of health, poor people do not share the same life chances as those in the social class above them. Furthermore, low income correlates with a lower quality of treatment for illness and disease. The results of poor health and poor treatment are borne out in the life expectancy rates within each class. Researchers have found that the higher one's class standing is, the higher one's life expectancy is. Conversely they have also found that within each age group, the lower one's class standing, the higher the death rate; in some age groups, the figures are as much as two and three times higher.

It's not just physical and mental health that is so largely determined by class. The lower a person's class standing is, the more difficult it is to secure housing; the more time is spent on the routine tasks of everyday life; the greater is the percentage of income that goes to pay for food, health care (which accounts for 23 percent of spending for low-income families) and other basic necessities; and the greater is the likelihood of crime victimization.

CLASS AND EDUCATIONAL ATTAINMENT

School performance (grades and test scores) and educational attainment (level of schooling completed) also correlate strongly with economic class. Furthermore, despite some efforts to make testing fairer and schooling more accessible, current data suggest that the level of inequity is staying the same or getting worse. . . .

Average Combined Scores by Income (400 to 1600 scale)	
Family Income	Median Score
More than $200,000	1721
$160,000 to $200,000	1636
$140,000 to $160,000	1619
$120,000 to $140,000	1594
$100,000 to $120,000	1580
$80,000 to $100,000	1545
$60,000 to $80,000	1503
$40,000 to $60,000	1461
$20,000 to $40,000	1398
less than $20,000	1323

These figures are based on the test results of 1,647,123 SAT takers in 2010–2011

. . . Students from upper-class families were twice as likely to obtain training beyond high school and four times as likely to attain a postgraduate degree. . . . Today, the pattern persists. There are, however, two significant changes. On the one hand, the odds of getting into college have improved for the bottom quartile of the population, although they still remain relatively low compared to the top. On the other hand, the chances of completing a 4-year college degree for those who are poor are extraordinarily low compared to the chances for those who are rich. Researchers estimate college completion is 10 times more likely for the top 25 percent of the population than it is for the bottom 25 percent.

Reality 5: From cradle to grave, class position has a significant impact on our well-being. Class accurately predicts chances for survival, educational achievement, and economic success. . . .

Several recent studies have shown that there is less class mobility in the United States than in most industrialized democracies in the world. One such study placed the United States in a virtual tie for last place. Why does the United States occupy such a low position on the mobility scale? Several explanations have been offered: The gap between rich and poor in the United States is greater; the poor are poorer in the United States and have farther to go to get out of poverty; and the United States has a lower rate of unionization than other industrialized nations.

The bottom line is that very affluent families transmit their advantages to the next generation and poor families stay trapped. For those whose annual income is in six figures, economic success is due in large part to the wealth and privileges bestowed on them at birth. Over 66 percent of the consumer units with incomes of $100,000 or more have inherited assets. Of these units, over 86 percent reported that inheritances constituted a substantial portion of their total assets. . . .

Reality 6: All Americans do not have an equal opportunity to succeed, and class mobility in the United States is lower than that of the rest of the industrialized world. Inheritance laws provide built-in privileges to the offspring of the wealthy and add to the likelihood of their economic success while handicapping the chances for everyone else.

One would think that increases in worker productivity or a booming economy would reduce the level of inequality and increase class mobility. While the wages of workers *may* increase during good times—that is, relative to what they were in the past—the economic advantages of higher productivity and a booming economy go disproportionately to the wealthy, a factor that adds still further to the level of inequality. For example, during the period 2001 to 2007, the U.S. economy expanded and productivity (output per hours worked) increased by more than 15 percent. During that same period, however, the top 1 percent of U.S. households took two-thirds of the nation's income gains, their inflation-adjusted income grew more than ten times faster than the income of the bottom 90 percent, and their share of the national income reached its highest peak. At the same time, the inflation-adjusted weekly salary of the average American during that 6-year economic expansion declined by 2.3 percent. Observing similar patterns in U.S. economic history, one prominent economist described economic growth in the United States as a "spectator sport for the majority of American families." Economic decline, on the other hand, is much more "participatory," with layoffs and cuts in public services hitting middle and lower-income families hardest—families that rely on public services (e.g., public schools, transportation) and have fewer resources to fall back on during difficult economic times.

Reality 7: Inequality in the United States is persistent in good times and bad. While most Americans rely on their wages or salaries to make ends meet, the rich derive most of their wealth from such income-producing assets as stocks, bonds, business equity, and non-home real estate. This type of wealth is even more highly concentrated than wealth in general. Over 89 percent of all stocks in the U.S., for example, are owned by the wealthiest 10 percent of Americans. . . . Putting aside illegal manipulation of the financial system, the drive to maximize corporate profit has led to job destruction (as companies seek cheaper labor in other parts of the world and transfer investments off shore); deregulation (e.g., so environmental protections don't inhibit corporate profit); and changes in tax policy that favour corporations (through loopholes) and those who rely on corporate profit for their wealth (by taxing their capital gains at lower rates).

Reality 8: The privileges that accrue to the wealthy are tied to the worlds of capital and finance—worlds whose good fortune are often the misfortune of the rest of the population. . . . It is not just that economic resources are concentrated in the hands of a few; so too are political resources. And it is the connection between wealth and political power that allows economic inequality to persist and grow. Moreover, as the costs of political influence rise, so does the influence of the "monied" class. Running for public office has always been an expensive proposition, but it's become increasingly so: It now costs, on average, $1.4 million in campaign funds to win a seat in the House of Representatives and $7 million to win a seat in the U.S. Senate. Most politicians rely on wealthy donors to finance their campaigns. Alternatively, wealthy individuals who want to make public policy often underwrite their own campaigns. The average wealth of U.S. senators, for example, is $12.6 million.

High-priced lobbyists also ensure that the interests of the wealthy and of corporate America are well represented in the halls of government. Not surprisingly, organizations that track the connection between political contributions and votes cast by public officials find a strong correlation between money and voting. It's not that the power of the economic elite is absolute; it's not. The power of the wealthy is often mitigated by social movements and by grassroots organizations that advocate on behalf of the poor and working class. The Occupy Wall Street movement—like movements that came before it—changed not only the public debate, but led to policy reforms as well. The power of the rich, however, remains so disproportionate that it severely undermines our democracy. . . .

Reality 9: Wealth and power are closely linked. The economic elite have a grossly disproportionate amount of political power—more than enough power to ensure that the system that provides them such extraordinary privileges perpetuates itself.

SPHERES OF POWER AND OPPRESSION

When we look at society and try to determine what it is that keeps most people down—what holds them back from realizing their potential as healthy, creative, productive individuals—we find institutional forces that are largely beyond individual control. Class domination is one of these forces. People do not choose to be poor or working class; instead, they are limited and confined by the opportunities afforded or denied them by a social and economic system. The class structure in the United States is a function of its economic system: capitalism, a system that is based on private rather than public ownership and control of commercial enterprises. Under capitalism, these enterprises are governed by the need to produce a profit for the owners, rather than to fulfill societal needs. Class divisions arise from the differences between those who own and control corporate enterprise and those who do not.

Racial and gender domination are other forces that hold people down. Although there are significant differences in the way capitalism, racism, and sexism affect our lives, there are also a multitude of parallels. And although class, race, and gender act independently of each other, they are at the same time very much interrelated.

On the one hand, issues of race and gender cut across class lines. Women experience the effects of sexism whether they are well-paid professionals or poorly paid clerks. As women, they are not only subjected to stereotyping and sexual harassment, they face discrimination and are denied opportunities and privileges that men have. Similarly, a wealthy black man faces racial oppression, is subjected to racial slurs, and is denied opportunities because of his color. Regardless of their class standing, women and members of minority races are constantly dealing with institutional forces that hold them down precisely because of their gender, the color of their skin, or both.

On the other hand, the experiences of women and minorities are differentiated along class lines. Although they are in subordinate positions vis-a-vis white men, the particular issues that confront women and people of color may be quite different, depending on their position in the class structure.

Power is incremental and class privileges can accrue to individual women and to individual members of a racial minority. While power is incremental, oppression is cumulative, and those who are poor, black, and female are often subject to all of the forces of class, race, and gender discrimination simultaneously. This cumulative situation is what is sometimes referred to as the double and triple jeopardy of women and people of color.

Chances of Being Poor in America					
White male/ female	White female head*	Hispanic male/female	Hispanic female head*	Black male/ female	Black female head*
1 in 14	1 in 4	1 in 4	1 in 2	1 in 4	1 in 2

*Persons in families with female householder, no husband present.

Furthermore, oppression in one sphere is related to the likelihood of oppression in another. If you are black and female, for example, you are much more likely to be poor or working class than you would be as a white male. Census figures show that the incidence of poverty varies greatly by race and gender.

In other words, being female and being nonwhite are attributes in our society that increase the chances of poverty and of lower-class standing.

Reality 10: Racism and sexism significantly compound the effects of class in society.

None of this makes for a very pretty picture of our country. Despite what we like to think about ourselves as a nation, the truth is that the qualities of our lives and the opportunities for success are highly circumscribed by our race, our gender, and the class we are born into. As individuals, we feel hurt and angry when someone is treating us unfairly, yet as a society we tolerate unconscionable injustice. A more just society will require a radical redistribution of wealth and power. We can start by reversing the current trends that polarize us as a people and adapt policies and practices that narrow the gaps in income, wealth, power, and privilege. That will only come about with pressure from below: strong organizations and mass movements advocating for a more just and equitable society.

27

Class Dismissed

Laura Smith and Rebecca M. Redington

Everyday life and ordinary language abound with class-based indignities and affronts. These incidents are directly analogous to other forms of racial and cultural microaggressions—the derogatory verbal, behavioural, and environmental messages that are routinely experienced by members of marginalized groups. These classist microaggressions expose and reinforce a status quo that devalues poor and working-class people based on their social class and that undermines the psychological well-being of people who hold these class memberships. Moreover, classism intersects with other forms of bias to produce situations of double jeopardy for poor women, poor people of color, and members of other oppressed groups, with the result that our understanding of the microaggressions experienced by these groups will be deepened when we add class to the analysis. . . .

CLASSIST MICROAGGRESSIONS: HIDING IN PLAIN SIGHT

Societal trends depict a state of diminished access to resources and opportunities for people at the bottom of the economic spectrum and research findings document the corresponding existence of prejudicial attitudes toward poor and working-class people. These circumstances point to the existence of systematic classist bias that could theoretically give rise to corresponding classist microaggressions. . . .

These microaggressions occur at three levels. First, *microassaults* are explicit derogations that can be verbal or non-verbal and are intended to hurt the victim through name-calling, avoidant behavior, or discriminatory actions. They are largely conscious and deliberate but may not be completely so. A *microinsult* is more subtle and is characterized by verbal or nonverbal communications that demean a person's heritage or identity. Perpetrators of microinsults are frequently unaware of the insulting implications of their behavior, as when Black individuals are congratulated by Whites on their articulate speech. *Microinvalidations* include communications that exclude, negate, or nullify a person's thoughts, feelings, or experiential reality. . . .

CLASSIST MICROASSAULTS

Outright classist labeling and name-calling goes almost unchecked in American culture. Labeling includes the use of overtly class-referenced words as modifiers to indicate favourable or unfavourable evaluations, such as describing an object or a person as "classy," "high-class," or a "class act" in a complimentary fashion or describing it as "low-class" or "low-rent" to discredit it. . . .

Although these examples suggest that the use of *low-rent* crosses racial boundaries as a modifier, other forms of classist name-calling refer to specific intersections with different identities, such as the name-calling directed toward poor White Americans, known variously as *White trash, rednecks,* or *hillbillies.* Although generally derogatory, *redneck* is a label that poor or rural Whites may nevertheless embrace to convey a defiant attitude, as exemplified by Gretchen Wilson in her country music hit "Redneck Woman": "Some people look down on me, but I don't give a rip/I'll stand barefooted in my own front yard with a baby on my hip/'Cause I'm a redneck woman/ . . . Let me get a big 'hell yeah' from the redneck girls like me." *White trash,* on the other hand, is a label that corresponds to the social bottom of the class spectrum and conveys disgust and contempt; the commonly heard adjective *trashy* is derived from this term. *Hillbilly* has regional connotations and encompasses the poignant complexity of Appalachian Mountain heritage: distinct traditions of music, food, art, and love of the land, frequently experienced against a backdrop of abject poverty and social isolation. Used in microassaults, it refers to characteristics such as laziness, superstitiousness, lack of intelligence, and illiteracy in its targets, which are often portrayed to comic effect, as in the 1960s television program *The Beverly Hillbillies.* . . .

CLASSIST MICROINSULTS

Through classist microinsults, poor and working-class people receive communications that are more subtle than name-calling but that convey demeaning messages just the same, although their impact may be outside the awareness of the perpetrators. . . . The peers of a rural student found many ways to express their low regard for the circumstances of her upbringing: explaining to her that she could not join them for tennis because she did not have the right clothes, resetting the silverware after she left the room, refusing to eat the foods that she cooked, and offering to give her their hand-me-downs. . . .

Although some of her college friends may have been aware of looking down on working-class culture, others likely were not and may have even felt that they were being helpful to her in explaining to her what "right" clothes and the "right" foods were. This is one of the hallmarks of a microaggressive event: Although people on the receiving end may immediately perceive the message as demeaning, the experience can be confusing in that the perpetrator may simultaneously be perceived as not intending any harm, leaving victims to wonder what actually happened and whether they are entitled to their feelings. The situation is further complicated by the fact that people in marginalized groups have internalized the very same biased messages about themselves that privileged people have learned; in other words, they have internalized their own oppression. . . .

As formal education has become a marker of intelligence among people with class privilege, working-class individuals who have pursued higher education may struggle to understand the meaning of their own advanced degrees (and the congratulations that come with them). Reflecting upon the attainment of her master's degree, Joanna Kadi (1996) described the contradictory feelings that can be experienced by working-class people in higher education:

> Working-class people traverse the minefield of academia and end up with initials after our names. We get confused. Very confused, because those initials symbolize the separation between rich and poor. Rich people need these degrees to feel smart, to remind themselves they are not a lowly janitor sweeping halls, a lowly cook slopping out lousy cafeteria food . . . but somehow we end up with them. We get confused. Are we announcing we're smart? But working-class people can't be smart. . . .

CLASSIST MICROINVALIDATIONS

Powerful perpetrations of classist microinvalidations—or communications that broadly negate or demean the lived experiences of poor and working-class people—stream into popular culture daily via the media's focus on middle-class and wealthy people. Fashion and lifestyle programming spot-lights the wardrobes, dinner parties, and daily activities of wealthy people; issues relevant to them and to middle-class individuals, such as the stock market, comprise the entire programming schedules of cable networks. Simultaneously, we are fed images and narratives evoking our sense that anything is possible and that in this winner-take-all society, we have as good a chance of taking it all as anyone and should be trying to do so. These narratives appear in news magazine television programs, magazine articles, and reality shows like *American Idol*, *The Apprentice*, and *Top Chef*, which have popularized the notion that anyone can become a star. Collins and Yeskel (2005) asserted that many Americans are so indoctrinated in "rags-to-riches" ways of thinking that they are willing to accept large-scale poverty in exchange for the belief they may one day make it into the tiny, exclusive percentile of the very wealthy. . . .

The feminist scholar and social critic bell hooks wrote about the invalidating race-class assumptions that she detected among her affluent, predominantly White neighbors. Although, as hooks observed, her neighbors were socially liberal people who valued multiculturalism and who had "at least one Black, Asian, or Hispanic friend," when it came to who actually moved into their neighborhood, another set of attitudes came into play:

[W]hen it comes to money and class, they want to protect what they have, to perpetuate and reproduce it—they want to have more. . . . They really believe that all Black people are poor, no matter how many times they laugh at Bill Cosby, salute Colin Powell, mimic Will Smith, dance to Brandy and Whitney Houston, or cheer on Michael Jordan. Yet when the rick Black people come to live where they live, they worry that class does not matter enough, for those Black folks might have some poor relatives, and there goes the neighborhood.

These assumptions reveal a multi-layered microinvalidation in that living near Black people is perceived negatively (at least in part) because living near poor people is perceived negatively, and Blackness and poverty are intertwined in mainstream consciousness. Poor people are thus tacitly affirmed as worthy of avoidance, and the existence of Black individuals across the economic spectrum is negated.

Similarly complex microinvalidations are present in cultural representations of working-class people. In an analysis of televised portrayals of the working class from 1946 to 1990, Butsch (2003) concluded that "the working class is not only underrepresented; the few men who are portrayed are buffoons. They are dumb, immature, irresponsible, or lacking in common sense." Working-class female characters, such as the one played by comedian Roseanne Barr in her 1990s television program, may be cited for breaking with stereotyped portrayals of women, but it is often by being sloppy and loud mouthed. Working-class people may be cast in a particularly unfavourable light when they come together to advocate for themselves via labor unions. Union members are often characterized negatively in the media; many times, racism intertwines with these representations. . . .

Classist microinvalidations against working-class people function to support us in looking the other way as the only vehicle by which working people can sit at the table during workplace negotiations is steadily eroded. Workers without the opportunity to organize have none of the resources that command attention from the rest of us and so must live with whatever conditions come their way. They do not own property or control resources, they do not have a voice. They are simply left to do the work that carries the nation along. We depend upon working-class wage earners all around us; without them, our lives would come to a standstill. Their silencing in the workplace does not seem to be in keeping with democratic ideals that include the belief in an even playing field.

28

Race, Wealth, and Equality

Melvin L. Oliver and Thomas M. Shapiro

Over a hundred years after the end of slavery, more than thirty years after the passage of major civil rights legislation, and following a concerted but prematurely curtailed War on Poverty, we harvest today a mixed legacy of racial progress. We celebrate the advancement of many blacks to middle-class status. . . . An official end to "de jure" housing segregation has even opened the door to neighborhoods and suburban residences previously off-limits to black residents. Nonetheless, many blacks have fallen by the wayside in their march toward economic equality. A growing number have not been able to take advantage of the opportunities now open to some. They suffer from educational deficiencies that make find-ing a foothold in an emerging technological economy near to impossible. Unable to move from deteriorated inner-city and older suburban communities, they entrust their children to school systems that are rarely able to provide them with the educational foundation they need to take the first steps up a racially skewed economic ladder. Trapped in communities of despair, they face increasing economic and social isolation from both their middle-class counterparts and white Americans.

. . .

Disparities in wealth between blacks and whites are not the product of haphazard events, inborn traits, isolated incidents, or solely contemporary individual accomplishments. Rather, wealth inequality has been structured over many generations through the same systemic barriers that have hampered blacks throughout their history in American society: slavery, Jim Crow, so-called de jure discrimination, and institutionalized racism. How these factors have affected the ability of blacks to accumulate wealth, however, has often been ignored or incompletely sketched. By briefly recalling three scenarios in American history that produced structured inequalities, we illustrate the significance of these barriers and their role in creating the wealth gap between blacks and whites.

RECONSTRUCTION: FROM SLAVERY TO FREEDOM WITHOUT A MATERIAL BASE

. . .

The close of the Civil War transformed four million former slaves from chattel to freed-men. Emerging from a legacy of two and a half centuries of legalized oppression, the new freedmen entered Southern society with little or no material assets. . . . The slave's often-cited demand of "forty acres and a mule" fueled great anticipation of a new begin-ning based on land ownership and a transfer of skills developed under slavery into the new economy of the South. Whereas slave muscle and skills had cleared the wilderness and made the land productive and profitable for plantation owners, the new vision saw the freedmen's hard work and skill generating income and resources for the former slaves themselves. W. E. B. Du Bois, in his *Black Reconstruction in America*, called this prospect America's chance to be a modern democracy.

Initially it appeared that massive land redistribution from the Confederates to the freed-men would indeed become a reality. . . . Real access to land for the freedman had to await the passage of the Southern Homestead Act in 1866, which provided a legal basis and mechanism to promote black landownership. In this legislation public land already designated in the 1862 Homestead Act, which applied only to non-Confederate whites but not blacks, was now opened up to settlement by former slaves in the tradition of home-steading that had helped settle the West. . . .

This social and economic transformation never occurred. . . . First, instead of disqualifying former Confederate supporters as the previous act had done, the 1866 legislation allowed all persons who applied for land to swear that they had not taken up arms against the Union or given aid and comfort to the enemies. This opened the door to massive white applications for land. One estimate suggests that over three-quarters (77.1 percent) of the land applicants under the act were white. In addition, much of the land was poor swampland and it was dif-ficult for black or white applicants to meet the necessary home-steading requirements because they could not make a decent living off the land. What is more important, blacks had to face the extra burden of racial prejudice and discrimination along with the charging of illegal fees, expressly discriminatory court challenges and court decisions, and land speculators. . . .

THE SUBURBANIZATION OF AMERICA: THE MAKING OF THE GHETTO

. . .

The suburbanization of America was principally financed and encouraged by actions of the federal government, which supported suburban growth from the 1930s through the 1960s by way of taxation, transportation, and housing policy. . . . As a consequence, employment opportunities steadily rose in the suburban rings of the nation's major metropolitan areas. In addition, transportation policy encouraged freeway construction and subsidized cheap fuel and mass-produced automobiles. These factors made living on the outer edges of cities both affordable and relatively convenient. However, the most important government policies encouraging and subsidizing suburbanization focused on housing. In particular, the incentives that government programs gave for the acquisition of single-family detached housing spurred both the development and financing of the tract home, which became the hallmark of suburban living. While these governmental policies collectively enabled over thirty-five million families between 1933 and 1978 to participate in homeowner equity accumulation, they also had the adverse effect of constraining black Americans' residential opportunities to central-city ghettos of major U.S. metropolitan communities and denying them access to one of the most successful generators of wealth in American history—the suburban tract home.

This story begins with the government's initial entry into home financing. . . . Charged with the task of determining the "useful or productive life of housing" they considered to finance, government agents methodically included in their procedures the evaluation of the racial composition or potential racial composition of the community. Communities that were changing racially or were already black were deemed undesirable and placed in the lowest category. The categories, assigned various colors on a map ranging from green for the most desirable, which included new, all-white housing that was always in demand, to red, which included already racially mixed or all-black, old, and undesirable areas, subsequently were used by Federal Housing Authority (FHA) loan officers who made loans on the basis of these designations.

Established in 1934, the FHA aimed to bolster the economy and increase employment by aiding the ailing construction industry. The FHA ushered in the modern mortgage system that enabled people to buy homes on small down payments and at reasonable interest rates, with lengthy repayment periods and full loan amortization. The FHA's success was remarkable: housing starts jumped from 332,000 in 1936 to 619,000 in 1941. . . .

This growth in access to housing was confined, however, for the most part to suburban areas. The administrative dictates outlined in the original act, while containing no anti-urban bias, functioned in practice to the neglect of central cities. Three reasons can be cited: first, a bias toward the financing of single-family detached homes over multifamily projects favored open areas outside of the central city that had yet to be developed over congested central-city areas; second, a bias toward new purchases over repair of existing homes prompted people to move out of the city rather than upgrade or improve their existing residences; and third, the continued use of the "unbiased professional estimate" that made older homes and communities in which blacks or undesirables were located less likely to receive approval for loans encouraged purchases in communities where race was not an issue.

. . . [T]he FHA . . . provided more precise guidance to its appraisers in its *Underwriting Manual*. The most basic sentiment underlying the FHA's concern was its fear that property values would decline if a rigid black and white segregation was not maintained. The *Underwriting Manual* openly stated that "if a neighborhood is to retain stability, it is necessary that properties shall continue to be occupied by the same social and racial classes" and further recommended that "subdivision regulations and suitable restrictive covenants" are the best way to ensure such neighborhood stability. The FHA's recommended use of restrictive covenants continued until 1949, when, responding to the Supreme Court's outlawing of such covenants in 1948 (*Shelly v. Kraemer*), it announced that "as of February 15, 1950, it would not insure mortgages on real estate subject to covenants."

. . .

The FHA's actions have had a lasting impact on the wealth portfolios of black Americans. Locked out of the greatest mass-based opportunity for wealth accumulation in American history, African Americans who desired and were able to afford home ownership found themselves consigned to central-city communities where their investments were affected by the "self-fulfilling prophecies" of the FHA appraisers: cut off from sources of new investment their homes and communities deteriorated and lost value in comparison to those homes and communities that FHA appraisers deemed desirable. One infamous housing development of the period—Levittown—provides a classic illustration of the way blacks missed out on this asset-accumulating opportunity. Levittown was built on a mass scale, and housing there was eminently affordable, thanks to the FHA's and VHA's accessible financing, yet as late as 1960 "not a single one of the Long Island Levittown's 82,000 residents was black."

CONTEMPORARY INSTITUTIONAL RACISM: ACCESS TO MORTGAGE MONEY AND REDLINING

. . .

In May of 1988 the issue of banking discrimination and redlining exploded onto the front pages of the *Atlanta Journal and Constitution*. This Pulitzer Prize-winning series, "The Color of Money," described the wide disparity in mortgage-lending practices in black and white neighborhoods of Atlanta, finding black applicants rejected at a greater rate than whites, even when economic situations were comparable. . . .

A 1991 Federal Reserve study of 6.4 million home mortgage applications by race and income confirmed suspicions of bias in lending by reporting a widespread and systemic pattern of institutional discrimination in the nation's banking system. This study disclosed that commercial banks rejected black applicants twice as often as whites nationwide. In some cities, like Boston, Philadelphia, Chicago, and Minneapolis, it reported a more pronounced pattern of minority loan rejections, with blacks being rejected three times more often than whites.

The argument that financial considerations—not discrimination—are the reason minorities get fewer loans appears to be totally refuted by the Federal Reserve study. The poorest white applicant, according to this report, was more likely to get a mortgage loan approved than a black in the highest income bracket. In Boston, for example, blacks in the highest income levels faced loan rejections three times more often than whites. . . .

The problem goes beyond redlining. Not only were banks reluctant to lend in minority communities, but the Federal Reserve study indicates that discrimination follows blacks no matter where they want to live and no matter how much they earn. A 1993 *Washington Post* series highlighted banks' reluctance to lend even in the wealthiest black neighborhoods. . . .

These findings gave credence to the allegations of housing and community activists that banks have been strip-mining minority neighborhoods of housing equity through unscrupulous backdoor loans for home repairs. Homes bought during the 1960s and 1970s in low-income areas had acquired some equity but were also in need of repair. Mainstream banks refused to approve such loans at "normal" rates, but finance companies made loans that, according to activists, preyed on minority communities by charging exorbitant, pawn-shop-style interest rates with unfavorable conditions. Rates of 34 percent and huge balloon payments were not uncommon. . . .

In Boston more than one-half of the families who relied on these kinds of high-interest loans lost their homes through foreclosure. One study charted every loan between 1984 and mid-1991 made by two high-interest lenders. Families lost their homes or were facing foreclosure in over three-quarters of the cases. Only 55 of the 406 families still possessed their homes and did not face foreclosure. The study also showed that the maps of redlined areas and high-interest loans overlapped.

. . .

Even briefly recalled, the three historical moments evoked in the pages above illustrate the powerful dynamics generating structured inequality in America. Several common threads link the three scenarios. First, whether it be a question of homesteading, suburbanization, or redlining, we have seen how governmental, institutional, and private-sector discrimination enhances the ability of different segments of the population to accumulate and build on their wealth assets and resources, thereby raising their standard of living and securing a better future for themselves and their children. The use of land grants and mass low-priced sales of government lands created massive and unparalleled opportunities for Americans in the nineteenth century to secure title to land in the westward expansion. Likewise, government backing of millions of low-interest loans to returning soldiers and low-income families enabled American cities to suburbanize and their inhabitants to see tremendous home value growth after World War II. Quite clearly, black Americans for the most part were unable to secure the same degree of benefits from these government programs as whites were. Indeed, in many of these programs the government made explicit efforts to exclude blacks from participating in them, or to limit their participation in ways that deeply affected their ability to gain the maximum benefits. . . .

Second, disparities in access to housing created differential opportunities for blacks and whites to take advantage of new and more lucrative opportunities to secure the good life. White families who were able to secure title to land in the nineteenth century were much more likely to finance education for their children, provide resources for their own or their children's self-employment, or secure their political rights through political lobbies and the electoral process. Blocked from low-interest government-backed loans, redlined out by financial institutions, or barred from home ownership by banks, black families have been denied the benefits of housing inflation and the subsequent vast increase in home equity assets. Black Americans who failed to secure this economic base were much less likely to be able to provide educational access for their children, secure the necessary financial resources for self-employment, or participate effectively in the political process.

. . .

RACIAL INEQUALITY IN CONTEXT

. . .

The most visible advances for blacks since the 1960s have taken place in the political arena. As a result of the civil rights movement, the percentage of Southern blacks registered to vote rose dramatically. The number of black elected officials increased and the black vote became a crucial and courted electoral block. Yet, in 1993, blacks still accounted for less than 2 percent of all elected officials. . . .

Since the 1960s blacks have also made gains in education. By the late 1980s the proportion of blacks and whites graduating from high school was about equal, reversing the

late-1950s black disadvantage of two to one. The percentage of blacks and whites attending college in 1977 was virtually identical, again reversing a tremendous black disadvantage. Since 1976, however, black college enrollments and completion rates have declined,
threatening to wipe out the gains of the 1960s and 1970s. The trends in the political and
education areas indicate qualified improvements for blacks.

Full equality, however, is still far from being achieved. Alongside the evidence of
advancement in some areas and the concerted political mobilization for civil rights, the
past two decades also saw an economic degeneration for millions of blacks, and this constitutes the crux of a troubling dilemma. Poor education, high joblessness, low incomes,
and the subsequent hardships of poverty, family and community instability, and welfare
dependency plague many African Americans. Most evident is the continuing large economic gap between blacks and whites. Median income figures show blacks earning only
about 55 percent of the amount made by whites. The greatest economic gains for blacks
occurred in the 1940s and 1960s. Since the early 1970s, the economic status of blacks
compared to that of whites has, on average, stagnated or deteriorated. Black unemployment rates are more than twice those of whites. Black youths also have more than twice
the jobless rate as white youths. Nearly one out of three blacks lives in poverty, compared
with fewer than one in ten whites. Residential segregation remains a persistent problem
today, with blacks being more likely than whites with similar incomes to live in over-
crowded and substandard housing. Nearly one in four blacks remains outside private
health insurance or Medicaid coverage. Infant mortality rates have dropped steadily since
1940 for all Americans, but the odds of dying shortly after birth are consistently twice as
high for blacks as for whites. Close to half (43 percent) of all black children officially lived
in poor households in 1986. A majority of black children live in families that include their
mother but not their father. . . . A recent major accounting of race relations summarized
it like this: "the status of black America today can be characterized as a glass that is half
full—if measured by progress since 1939—or a glass that is half empty—if measured by
the persisting disparities between black and white Americans."

. . .

DWINDLING ECONOMIC GROWTH AND RISING INEQUALITY

The standard of living of American households is in serious trouble. For two decades
the United States has been evolving into an increasingly unequal society. After improving
steadily since World War II, the real (adjusted-for-inflation) weekly wage of the average
American worker peaked in 1973. During the twenty-seven-year postwar boom the average worker's wages outpaced inflation every year by 2.5 to 3 percent. The standard of
living of most Americans improved greatly, as many people bought cars, homes, appliances, televisions, and other big-ticket consumer goods for the first time. The link between
growth and mobility was readily apparent. Between the end of World War II and the early
to mid-1970s, the economy created a steady stream of jobs that permitted workers and
their families to escape poverty and become part of a growing and vibrant middle class.
The economy could absorb millions of new workers and a growing part of the population
found middle-class life within reach. . . .

Since 1973, however, a far bleaker story has unfolded. Real wages have been falling or
stagnating for most families. The 1986 average wage in the United States bought nearly
14 percent less than it had thirteen years earlier. Also beginning in the mid-1970s, after a
long period of movement toward greater equality and stability, the distribution of annual
wages and salaries became increasingly unequal. . . .

These changes have profoundly affected blacks. Plant closings and deindustrialization more often occur in industries employing large concentrations of blacks, such as the steel, rubber, and automobile sectors. Black men, especially young black men, are more likely than whites to lose their jobs as a result of economic restructuring. One study of deindustrialization in the Great Lakes region found that black male production workers were hardest hit by the industrial slump of the early 1980s. From 1979 to 1984 one-half of black males in durable-goods manufacturing in five Great Lakes cities lost their jobs.

. . .

The underlying weakness of the economy in the 1990s is increasingly apparent. Debt and global competition pose enormous challenges to stable economic growth and vitality. The larger economic context for the analysis of contemporary race relations is dominated by slow or stagnant growth, deindustrialization, a two-tiered job and earning structure, cuts in the social programs that assist those at the bottom, budget deficits, increasing economic inequality, a reconcentration of wealth, a growing gap in incomes between whites and blacks, and a much-diminished American Dream, however one wishes to define or gauge it.

. . .

WHY STUDY WEALTH?

. . .

Although related, income and wealth have different meanings. *Wealth* is the total extent, at a given moment, of an individual's accumulated assets and access to resources, and it refers to the net value of assets (e.g., ownership of stocks, money in the bank, real estate, business ownership, etc.) less debt held at one time. Wealth is anything of economic value bought, sold, stocked for future disposition, or invested to bring an economic return. *Income* refers to a flow of dollars (salaries, wages, and payments periodically received as returns from an occupation, investment, or government transfer, etc.) over a set period, typically one year.

. . .

Most people use income for day-to-day necessities. Substantial wealth, by contrast, often brings income, power, and independence. Significant wealth relieves individuals from dependence on others for an income, freeing them from the authority structures associated with occupational differentiation that constitute an important aspect of the stratification system in the United States. If money derived from wealth is used to purchase significant ownership of the means of production, it can bring authority to the holder of such wealth. Substantial wealth is important also because it is directly transferable from generation to generation, thus assuring that position and opportunity remain in the same families' hands.

Command over resources inevitably anchors a conception of life chances. While resources theoretically imply both income and wealth, the reality for most families is that income supplies the necessities of life, while wealth represents a kind of "surplus" resource available for improving life chances, providing further opportunities, securing prestige, passing status along to one's family, and influencing the political process.

In view of the limitations of relying on income as well as the significance of wealth, a consideration of racially marked wealth disparities should importantly complement existing income data. An investigation of wealth will also help us formulate a more detailed picture of racial differences in well-being. Most studies of economic well-being focus solely on income, but if wealth differences are even greater than those of income, then these studies will seriously underestimate racial inequality, and policies that seek to narrow differences will fail to close the gap.

29

What's Debt Got to Do with It?

Brett Williams

. . .

"THEY WILL GLADLY TAKE A CHECK"

. . . America's Cash Express . . . is a plain, grim storefront, staffed by one woman behind ceiling-high Plexiglas, offering pagers for $80, laser tear gas for $10, and myriad one-stop financial services. Customers can apply for a telephone calling card or a secured credit card for a $25 processing fee and a $300 deposit (to be charged against) in First Deposit National Bank in New Hampshire. The annual fee is $35 and the annual percentage rate is 19.8 percent. You can wire a moneygram to pay a bill (for 10 percent of the total and a 10 percent discount on Greyhound) or "wire money in minutes worldwide" through an American Express moneygram. (In some places American Express charges as much as 24 percent of the amount wired.)

You can file a tax return and receive a refund anticipation loan ("After all . . . it's *your* money!" beams the promotional material). If you want ACE to prepare your return, that costs about $30. You can pay gas, water, telephone, and electric bills; play the lottery ("We've got your ticket!"); and purchase money orders with the cash you receive when you cash your payroll, government, insurance, or tax refund check. Some call these outlets "welfare banks" because of their heavy traffic in public assistance checks, and sometimes the government sends checks and food stamps directly there.

. . . For the most routine checks, the outlet charges 2 percent of the total, but this varies quite a bit depending on the amount and type of the check and whether or not you have ID. It can cost as much as 6 percent to cash a payroll check and 12 percent to cash a personal one. The most outrageous, expensive, and quasi-legal transactions are called "payday loans," advances secured by a postdated personal check. These loans can charge interest from 20 to 35 percent of the amount advanced; a typical transaction would offer the customer $200 for a $260 check. . . .

Despite the shame, expense, and tedium of the process, many residents of this neighborhood conduct all their bankless business at places like America's Cash Express. Citizens in poor urban neighborhoods find it increasingly difficult to get to a bank. Even if there is a local bank, residents often cannot afford its minimum balance requirements, fees for checks, or high bounced-check penalties. They may not have enough money in their account at the end of the month to cash a paycheck to pay their bills. They may need immediate cash to deliver to the phone company in person. Some residents do not have the major credit card that is to serve as a second major ID; some cannot manage a bank's restricted hours. Some cannot open checking or saving accounts because of even minor problems with their credit or immigration histories. . . .

Using check-cashing outlets further impoverishes and disenfranchises residents, leaving them with no records or proof of payment, no ongoing relationship to build up a credit history, and in greater personal danger from carrying cash (itself in jeopardy from fire, theft, or loss). From where they stand, residents may find it hard to connect the storefronts to the larger financial system or to the injustices they endure. . . . Atlanta snack-food salesman Ronald Hayes . . . makes a weekly visit to cash his $400 paycheck and buy a money order to pay a bill per week. The total cost to Hayes is $15 a week. . . . He fails to recognize that he is probably paying ten times more than a bank would charge. Even if some poor residents recognize the cost, others bow to hand-to-mouth demands for immediacy, safety, or convenience. One homeless man, coping successfully with the dangers of carrying cash, purchases a money order made out to himself each month, cashes it repeatedly at a 2 percent rate, and then buys another money order to carry the balance. He carries his money more safely, but at a huge cost. Hudson interviewed two men in Manassas, Virginia, who paid $270 to cash a $4,500 insurance check because they didn't have time to wait for the check to clear. At the Eagle Outlet, where they cashed their check, owner Victor Daigle claimed that his customers "would rather pay a little bit more to us and have their convenience. They go to McDonald's because they want their hamburger right now. . . . They can come to us and get their money right now."

. . .

"THAT'S WHY THEY'RE MY CUSTOMERS"

Another, more venerable fringe bank is the pawnshop, a familiar sight in cities for many years. . . . These have proliferated in Washington, D.C., and throughout the nation, doubling during the 1980s to number 10,091 in 1994 and certainly many more today. They have changed in other ways as well, to become centralized and chain-operated, backed by upscale marketing, ruthless acquisitions, and persistent pressure on local governments to raise usury rates. Like check-cashing outlets, they displace small businesses, family-owned pawnshops, and local chains, offering young residents of urban neighborhoods downscale, minimum-wage, no-benefits financial services jobs.

For example, Cash America, founded in 1983, operates hundreds of shops. One of five chains to be publicly traded, it boasts NYSE: PWN (for "pawn") as its symbol, turns lush profits for investors, and has tried to upgrade the pawnshop image as it eyes markets all over the world. If you multiply its monthly rate by twelve, its average annual percentage rate (APR) hovers at around 200 percent, not unusual in an industry that often charges 240 percent, and it recorded $5 million in net income from lending activities in the last quarter of 2000, up 17 percent from the year before. In Washington, D.C., Famous Pawn has been enormously successful by gobbling up mom-and-pop stores including pawn shops in poor neighborhoods.

. . . The store is stuffed with former collateral for these expensive secured loans: from gold chains, wedding bands, and watches to baseball cards, leather jackets, computers, VCRs, television sets, compact discs, cameras, pianos, guitars, saxophones, power tools, and lawnmowers. . . .

Customers pawn these items for 10 percent interest each month, a relatively low rate set by Maryland and the District. A borrower would receive $100 for a pawned item and redeem it in thirty days for $110. One customer complains: "They don't give you nothing' for it. But when they sell it, that's when they mark it up." If a customer is unable to redeem it after thirty days, the shop will keep it on hold for as long as he or she can pay each month's interest. Often, pawnshops' profits lie in nurturing these long-term relationships with borrowers, who come in to pay their "dues" on the first of each month but eventually give up and let their treasures go. Their misfortune allows Famous Pawn to bulge out of its space, overflowing with pawns, featuring a long line of borrowers every day, and swallowing its neighboring establishments. Secondary buyers cruise through periodically, buying up items in bulk and boosting profits in the retail side of the business, long less profitable than the interest-collecting side.

. . .

[T]he vast majority of borrowers are poor, with incomes between $9,000 and $17,000 a year, according to fringe-bank researcher John Caskey. They are young, in and out of work, and disproportionately of color. Cash America's *Annual Report* describes them this way: "The cash-only individual makes up the backbone of America. He's [*sic*] the hard-working next door neighbor, the guy at the corner service station, or the lady who works as a checker at the local supermarket." Caskey quotes Jack Daugherty of Cash America to somewhat different effect: "I could take my customers and put them on a bus and drive them down to a bank and the bank would laugh at them. That's why they're my customers."

"AND YOU DON'T NEED CREDIT TO GET IT"

. . .

By redefining what they are doing as "renting," rent-to-own stores have emerged to evade usury laws that limit the interest paid by people who buy appliances and furniture on credit. Profits in this $3.7 billion-a-year business stem from astounding markups, as customers often pay five times what they would for retail. By the mid-1990s rent-to-own stores had tripled in number, so that by 1994 there were some seventy-five hundred rent-to-own outlets nationwide. Like check-cashing outlets and pawnshops, they increasingly come in corporate chain sizes.

The Rent-A-Center chain boasts twelve hundred stores, a large share of this market. But another patriotic chain, RentAmerica, dominates the Washington, D.C., area. Mostly located in two poorer suburbs (including Jenkins's) and southeast D.C., RentAmerica is a temple to consumption. To walk in is to discover a lush cornucopia of household consumer goods: florid bedroom furniture; leather couches; brightly colored, blaring television sets; giant, gleaming refrigerators; and shimmering gold jewelry. The store offers impoverished customers a shot at the postwar American dream.

But the American-flag sign that soars from the parking lot, the giddy interior, the slick brochures, and the "convenience" (or urgency?) of instant purchases and free delivery belie RentAmerica's harsh and greedy terms. . . . The terms explain that the baby-bear TV requires seventy-eight weekly payments of $9.99, or $779.22 (plus tax); the twenty-seven-inch TV costs seventy-eight weekly payments of $15.99, or $1,247.22 (plus tax); and the thirty-two-inch TV will not be yours until you have paid in full: 104 weekly payments of $24.99, or $2,598.96 (plus tax). Retail prices are much lower. RentAmerica has the good sense *not* to mention either the alleged or actual prices for gold jewelry, refrigerators, freezers, the "bedroom suite," or the "living-room group." The brochure recommends: "Ask for Details!"

. . .

To understand their excesses, it might be helpful to contrast rent-to-own terms and interest rates to the consumer credit available to residents of wealthier neighborhoods, who can receive a 10 percent discount on a purchase up to $300 at Woodward and Lothrop, for example, just by applying for a store card—though if they do not pay on time and in full, they owe 21 percent interest. Or at CompUSA, a computer store in the Maryland/ Virginia suburbs, approved customers can charge a computer and pay no interest for six months; they pay accumulated interest, however, if they do not pay in full at that time. Seeing RentAmerica helps put these admittedly harsh, austere, and misleading terms into perspective.

A FESTIVAL OF DEBT

. . .

Poor neighborhoods in Washington, D.C., are plagued by finance companies peddling loans, to consolidate debt or to make home repairs, to people who are financially desperate or credit starved. These firms target minority, fixed- or low-income, low-wage, and Social Security-dependent households who often hold substantial equity in their homes as their sole resource. Not surprisingly, the finance companies charge high interest: from 36 to 50 percent. They tack on worthless, expensive "credit insurance." They offer shoddy work and pursue ruthless, haranguing collection policies. Sometimes they refinance these loans several times, piling on fees along the way: prepayment penalty fees, more credit insurance, and loan origination fees. They front for some of the country's largest financial institutions: NationsBank (after it acquired ChryslerFirst), Ford Financial Services (whose Associated Services division may keep it afloat), Chemical Bank, ITT, Fleet Financial Services, BankAmerica (through its Security Pacific division), General Motors, General Electric, Westinghouse, and Citicorp. These large lenders front money through lines of credit to finance companies, then buy up and bundle the loans and sell them on Wall Street via secondary securities markets. The customer may be left with shoddy repair work, a huge debt, the threat of foreclosure, and nobody to hold responsible.

. . .

While the poor have developed many creative strategies to provide the essentials of life, such as doubling up, working under the table, managing collective living, and negotiating ongoing exchanges with friends and kin, they are increasingly vulnerable in the current economic climate. When intergenerational network flows, employment, and government assistance fail them, when relatives can no longer provide small loans between checks or the exchange of food stamps for cash, poor people develop strategies to work the fringe banking system: pawning televisions and VCRs when between checks, redeeming them when they can; cashing their checks at America's Cash Express; paying their bills with money orders and moneygrams they purchase at ACE; using the poor person's telephone, the pager; and "renting" their grossly overpriced furniture and appliances for as long as they can.

. . . The same developers who refused to maintain or build low-cost urban housing have gone bust on overpriced condominiums, unnecessary office space, and underutilized shopping centers in the suburbs. The same lenders who disinvested in cities, jobs, workers, and infrastructure squandered their money on junk bonds and takeovers. Now they're back, extending credit to fringe banks for loans of last resort and thus passing on high-cost debt to the poor.

30

At the Elite Colleges

Peter Schmidt

Autumn and a new academic year are upon us, which means that selective colleges are engaged in the annual ritual of singing the praises of their new freshman classes. Surf the websites of such institutions and you will find press releases boasting that they have increased their black and Hispanic enrollments, admitted bumper crops of National Merit scholars or became the destination of choice for hordes of high school valedictorians. Many are bragging about the large share of applicants they rejected, as a way of conveying to the world just how popular and selective they are.

What they almost never say is that many of the applicants who were rejected were far more qualified than those accepted. Moreover, contrary to popular belief, it was not the black and Hispanic beneficiaries of affirmative action, but the rich white kids with cash and connections who elbowed most of the worthier applicants aside.

Researchers with access to closely guarded college admissions data have found that, on the whole, about 15 percent of freshmen enrolled at America's highly selective colleges are white teens who failed to meet their institutions' minimum admissions standards. Five years ago, two researchers working for the Educational Testing Service, Anthony Carnevale and Stephen Rose, took the academic profiles of students admitted into 146 colleges in the top two tiers of Barron's college guide and matched them up against the institutions' advertised requirements in terms of high school grade point average, SAT or ACT scores, letters of recommendation, and records of involvement in extracurricular activities. White students who failed to make the grade on all counts were nearly twice as prevalent on such campuses as black and Hispanic students who received an admissions break based on their ethnicity or race.

Who are these mediocre white students getting into institutions such as Harvard, Wellesley, Notre Dame, Duke, and the University of Virginia? A sizable number are recruited athletes who, research has shown, will perform worse on average than other students with similar academic profiles, mainly as a result of the demands their coaches will place on them. A larger share, however, are students who gained admission through their ties to people the institution wanted to keep happy, with alumni, donors, faculty members, administrators, and politicians topping the list.

Applicants who stood no chance of gaining admission without connections are only the most blatant beneficiaries of such admissions preferences. Except perhaps at the very summit of the applicant pile—that lofty place occupied by young people too brilliant for anyone in their right mind to turn down—colleges routinely favor those who have connections over those who don't. While some applicants gain admission by legitimately beating out their peers, many others get into exclusive colleges the same way people get into trendy night clubs, by knowing the management or flashing cash at the person manning the velvet rope.

Leaders at many selective colleges say they have no choice but to instruct their admissions offices to reward those who financially support their institutions, because keeping donors happy is the only way they can keep the place afloat. They also say that the money they take in through such admissions preferences helps them provide financial aid to students in need. But many of the colleges granting such preferences are already well-financed, with huge endowments. And, in many cases, little of the money they take in goes toward serving the less-advantaged.

A few years ago, *The Chronicle of Higher Education* looked at colleges with more than $500 million in their endowments and found that most served disproportionately few students from families with incomes low enough to qualify for federal Pell Grants. A separate study of flagship state universities conducted by the Education Trust found that those universities' enrollments of Pell Grant recipients had been shrinking, even as the number of students qualifying for such grants had gone up. Just 40 percent of the financial aid money being distributed by public colleges is going to students with documented financial need. Most such money is being used to offer merit-based scholarships or tuition discounts to potential recruits who can enhance a college's reputation, or appear likely to cover the rest of their tuition tab and to donate down the road.

Given such trends, is it any wonder that young people from the wealthiest fourth of society are about 25 times as likely as those from the bottom fourth to enroll in a selective college, or that, over the past two decades, the middle class has been steadily getting squeezed out of such institutions by those with more money?

A degree from a selective college can open many doors for a talented young person from a humble background. But rather than promoting social mobility, our nation's selective colleges appear to be thwarting it, by turning away applicants who have excelled given their circumstances and offering second chances to wealthy and connected young people who have squandered many of the advantages life has offered them.

When social mobility goes away, at least two dangerous things can happen. The privileged class that produces most of our nation's leaders can become complacent enough to foster mediocrity, and less-fortunate segments of our society can become resigned to the notion that hard work will not get them anywhere.

. . .

31

Is the Near-Trillion-Dollar Student Loan Bubble About to Pop?

Sarah Jaffe

. . .

Tarah Toney worked two full-time jobs to put herself through college, at McMurry University in Abilene, Texas, and still has $75,000 in debt. She graduated in six years with a Bachelor's in English and wanted to go on to teach high school.

"Right about the time I graduated, Texas severely cut funding to our education system—thanks, Perry—and school districts across the state stopped hiring and started firing. It became abundantly clear that there was no job for me in the Texas public school system," she told me. "After two months of job searching I got a temporary position in a real estate office."

She continued, "In August my post-graduation grace period was up and all of the payments on my student loans amount to $500/month. Adding that expense to my monthly bills puts me at $2,100 per month. If I don't make my payments they will revoke my real estate license, which I need in order to do my job."

Max Parker (not his real name) enrolled at Texas A&M in College Station, Texas to get a BA in economics and a BS in physics. His freshman year was great—his parents had saved some money to help pay the bills, and after that he was able to get "more generous" student loans. He took a job to help cover the fees and bills that his student loans wouldn't cover, and worked about 35 hours a week during his sophomore year while taking 15 hours of classes—but found that his grades dropped with his workload. . . . He adjusted his course load, but in the spring of his junior year, a family emergency led him to withdraw midway through the semester, taking incompletes in his courses.

"I am 25 years old now, and shacking up in my parents' guest bedroom," he told me. "I have successfully made four payments on my student loans in the past three and a half years. I have over $48,000 dollars of student loan debt, and absolutely nothing to show for it. No degrees. No certificates. No qualifications. I have continued my education to the best of my ability since leaving A&M, but always at community colleges and always paying for everything out of pocket. As you can imagine, since I'm not 'qualified' for a decent paying job, my savings for school piles up very slowly, and then disappears when August and January roll around. I haven't been back to school in about a year now, and I currently work at Subway, making sandwiches. I don't make my loan payments."

He's about to join the military because he sees it as his only option. "I am depressed at the idea of signing my life away for four years so I can fight someone else's wars. I am angry beyond belief that it's come to this" he said.

Kate Sternwood (not her real name) was recently laid off from a job at a nonprofit organization where she was making $55,000 a year. She has $40,000 in debt from the University of Massachusetts. "When I called my repayment program to tell them I was losing my job, they told me my payment would go from $400 a month to $384 a month because making $55K a year I already qualified for the 'hardship' rate."

The agency in question is Van Ru, a collection agency that takes loans from the Dept. of Education if they go into default. Sternwood said they can't even tell her what the rate will be when she's paid enough to get out of default because they don't know which bank will end up with her loans.

. . .

The story is the same around the country. The economy is stagnant, the job market terrible, and graduates who used to believe their degrees would lead to good jobs are struggling. Meanwhile, the unforgiving student loan system continues to penalize them for their inability to pay.

THE BUBBLE

Since the beginning of the recession, most types of credit have gone down. The only exception to that rule has been student loans.

A recent piece in *The Atlantic* noted that student debt has grown by 511 percent since 1999. At that time, only $90 billion in student loans were outstanding—by the second quarter of 2011, that balance was up to $550 billion, according to the New York Fed. And the Department of Education estimates that outstanding loans total closer to $805 billion—and that number will pass $1 trillion soon.

As student loans rise, so has delinquency. Phil Izzo at the *Wall Street Journal* reported that 11.2 percent of student loans were more than 90 days past due and that rate was steadily going up. "Only credit cards had a higher rate of delinquency—12.2 percent—but those numbers have been on a steady decline for the past four quarters," he noted.

It shouldn't be surprising to anyone that student loan defaults are going up as young workers especially are struggling in the current economy. Izzo reported, "Workers between 20 and 24 years old have a 14.6 percent unemployment rate, compared to the national average of 9.1 percent recorded in July. That comes even as the share of 20- to 24-year-olds who are working or looking for a job is at the lowest level since the 1970s, before women entered the labor force en masse."

In his *Huffington Post* blog, Michigan Democratic Representative Hansen Clarke noted, "This year, the average borrower graduating from a four-year college left school with roughly $24,000 of student debt, despite the grim statistic that—according to a Rutgers University study—only 56 percent of 2010 graduates were able to find work following completion of their studies."

. . .

How did student loans go from "good debt" that could be expected to pay off—Pew found that an adult with a bachelor's degree earns about $650,000 more during their career than a typical high school graduate—to a bubble that threatens the economy?

According to the National Center for Education Statistics, college enrollment skyrocketed 38 percent, from 14.8 million to 20.4 million, between 1999 and 2009. (The previous decade it had only gone up 9 percent.) This should be a good thing—except it was not accompanied by measures to make tuition affordable for working families who wanted to send their kids to school. Combined with the decline in the type of union manufacturing jobs that used to allow workers to be comfortably middle-class without a college degree, we've wound up with working-class families taking on debt to send their kids to college, which they are told will help those kids make more money.

. . .

As student loans are relatively easy to come by, both from the government and from private lenders increasingly getting into the game, universities have been able to keep hiking tuition without seeing a drop in enrollment. Students are still advised that student debt is "good debt," as noted above, and that they will be able to pay it off—but the costs are rising far more rapidly than average incomes.

The *Philadelphia Inquirer* reported that Temple University has raised tuition every year since 1995—it's gone up 9.9 percent for in-state students. At the University of Pennsylvania (an Ivy League private university—Temple is the state school) tuition went up 3.9 percent to $42,098 a year. "Throw in a dormitory bed, meals and books, and the price reaches $57,360," wrote *Inquirer* reporter Jeff Gammage.

. . .

All of these factors have combined to send student loan debt into the stratosphere. . . . [S]tudent debt has far outpaced the growth of all other household debt over the past 10 years—including increasing twice as fast as housing debt. . . . [T]he same banks that broke the economy by creating that housing bubble are responsible for the student debt crisis—as well as the federal government, which issues student loans.

. . .

Student loans are not really comparable to housing loans, though: if you default on your student loans, there's nothing to repossess. Instead, you'll face a drop in your credit rating, and constant pressure from . . . collection agencies. . . . They can garnish your wages, and even if you declare bankruptcy, your student loans don't go away. . . . [M]iss a payment, and your interest rate goes up, creating a punitive spiral of debt there's no way to escape from.

Even if mass default isn't likely to happen the same way mortgage defaults did, . . . the cost of college and debt is already slowing the economy. . . . [A]ll the money going into colleges and the pockets of lenders in the form of interest is being funneled away from other places it could be spent.

. . .

THE SOLUTIONS

. . . [J]ust last year in his State of the Union, President Obama proclaimed, "No one should go broke because they chose to go to college." He called for student loans to be forgiven after 20 years—10 for those who go into public service—and a $10,000 tax credit for families paying for a four-year college.

But that's not a solution for people like Parker, who was unable to finish school because of the cost, or Toney, who wanted to go into public service but saw that door shut in her face with state budget cuts. They're in debt now, not in 20 years, and $10,000 doesn't begin to cover their debt. . . . As tuition goes up thousands of dollars a year, a $10,000 tax credit looks pretty measly—and the chances of getting even that through the current Congress are slim to none.

The *Philadelphia Inquirer* reported that New Jersey's state legislature has a bill under consideration that would ban state colleges from raising tuition more than 2 percent a year. Keeping tuition down is certainly part of the solution—tuition growing faster than wages is a recipe for defaults as students struggle to pay back their loans. In addition, just as housing prices going way up wound up pricing many people out of home-buying, increases in tuition will price students out of an education—particularly if the benefits of that education become less clear, as jobs remain hard to come by.

. . .

An idea that's been getting a lot of traction lately—including an online petition pushed by MoveOn member Robert Applebaum that has 320,000 signatures as of this writing—is student loan forgiveness as economic stimulus.

Rep. Hansen Clarke introduced a resolution in Congress, co-sponsored by 12 other members, that includes student loan forgiveness in its suggestions for bringing down the U.S.'s "true debt burden."

In his *Huffington Post* blog, Clarke wrote:

> Congress is now completely focused on reducing debt. This would be a positive development, if not for one detail: it's focused on the wrong kind of debt.
>
> With over a quarter of all American homeowners "underwater"—owing more on their homes than their homes are worth—and total student loans slated to exceed $1 trillion this year, it is household debt, not government debt, that is constraining spending, undermining confidence, and precluding sustainable long-term growth.

Clarke is right. For years, credit was a substitute for real wage growth in the U.S. And now as that debt burden has grown unsustainable, working families are barely able to keep up with payments, let alone spend enough to get the economy back on its feet. And student debt, as we've shown, is on the least sustainable trajectory of all.

. . .

Student debt forgiveness would put $400 a month back into Sternwood's pockets. . . . Even just forgiving the government loans would probably allow Parker to finish his degree instead of going to war.

Of course the resolution is unlikely to pass Speaker John Boehner's Congress, and even if it does, it's just a resolution. But the instant popularity of Applebaum's petition shows something: Americans realize that student debt at the current levels is completely untenable, and something must be done soon.

Republicans love to talk about the debt we're leaving our children with. But saddling them with record levels of student debt and no jobs with which to earn money to pay it back hurts young people much, much more than government budget deficits.

. . .

32

Students with Disabilities

Financial Aid Policy Issues

Thomas R. Wolanin

About nine percent of all undergraduate students in the United States reported having a disability in 2000. This amounts to approximately 1.3 million students. . . . Students with disabilities generally have lower incomes than their peers without disabilities. Thirty-seven percent of students with disabilities in high school came from families with household incomes below $25,000, compared to only 20% of their peers. At the college level, students from the lowest-income quartile have the highest rate of disability, especially independent students. . . .

Low-income students with disabilities, like other low-income students, need financial assistance in order to afford the costs of higher education. However, being disproportionately low-income, students with disabilities have an even greater need for financial assistance than other students. Thus, the financial barriers to higher education opportunities faced by students from low-income families are also even more widespread for students with disabilities . . . .

HAVING A DISABILITY IS EXPENSIVE

In addition to the problems faced by all low-income students, students with disabilities from low-income families face particular financial barriers to higher education not faced by other students. To meet their special needs, persons with disabilities often receive services from a variety of professionals. These may include counselors, doctors, psychologists, and therapists of all kinds, who must be visited in their respective offices, clinics, and hospitals. For persons with disabilities, insurance payments and support from public and private agencies rarely cover the entire cost of the treatments and services they receive. The difference is made up out-of-pocket.

Having a disability also involves incidental costs such as special foods to meet dietary restrictions, cab fares to the doctor, wheelchair maintenance, dog food and veterinary bills for a guide dog, over-the-counter medications, and higher utility bills from running computers and assistive devices. . . . For a low-income student with a disability, in theory at least, all of these additional costs of having a disability can be met through student financial aid sources. . . . Unfortunately, the system does not live up to its ideals, and faces difficulties in practice. . . . Students with disabilities must document to the financial aid administrator the expenses related to their disabilities that are not provided for by another source. This requires self-confidence and self-advocacy skills that often have not been well developed in students with disabilities. These students must undertake the difficult and complex task of cataloging and documenting all of the expenses related to their disabilities and reducing that amount by support received from elsewhere, such as Vocational Rehabilitation (VR). This is a formidable challenge that would test the skills of anyone and is sometimes unreasonable for students with disabilities.

. . .

Currently, fully meeting the needs of students with disabilities would require diverting resources from other low-income students. This would not be a just or desirable result. The most important policy change required to meet the financial needs of low-income students with disabilities is to expand the amount of financial aid available for all low-income students. Otherwise, the process becomes a matter of rationing and redistributing limited financial aid dollars among various groups of financially needy students, including those with disabilities.

HAVING A DISABILITY IS TIME CONSUMING

Generally, students with disabilities in higher education can attain the same academic levels as their peers without disabilities; however, students with disabilities cannot do it as quickly. Students with disabilities may have conditions that slow them down in general. For example, it takes longer to walk from point A to point B when one's energy and stamina are sapped by chronic illness. A person in a wheelchair or with cerebral palsy needs more time to bathe, dress, shop, and accomplish other self-care tasks. Students with disabilities have multiple demands on their time for the treatments and services required to meet their needs apart from their studies. Trips to doctors, therapists, counselors, and administrators take time. It also takes time to acquire, set up, learn how to use, and maintain auxiliary learning aids such as electronic readers or videotext displays. Software bugs and computer crashes are not just inconveniences for a student with a disability, who must have electronic aids to study—these technical glitches bring a halt to learning.

Further, students with disabilities often take longer to perform academic tasks. Many disabilities, particularly learning disabilities, increase the time needed to process information, which is the central task of most academic work. A student with dyslexia needs more time to read and understand a given amount of written text compared with a student without this disability. The speed at which an aide reads text to a blind student is slower than the reading speed of sighted students. Listening to a lecture over again on tape takes longer than reviewing notes taken in the classroom.

. . .

Given the time demands faced by students with disabilities, it follows that the time to degree completion for students with disabilities is longer than for their peers without disabilities. . . . The longer time that students with disabilities need to complete their studies increases their costs of higher education. Their forgone income is greater than that of their peers without disabilities. Most importantly, even if students with disabilities are taking a reduced or part-time course load, they still have to live full time. They face additional years of room and board costs, semester fees, and the extra costs associated with their disability to make the same academic progress that their peers without disabilities make in a shorter time. They may also be charged more per credit hour or per course if they are taking less than the standard full-time course load.

. . .

In sum, low-income students with disabilities generally have a greater need for financial aid than their peers without disabilities. But, they face additional obstacles in assembling the package of resources to pay for college. A larger burden is placed on students with disabilities who may have less capacity to bear it.

. . .

33

"Free" Labor

Past and Present Forms of Prison Labor

Whitney Benns

Incarcerated labor has its roots in the Reconstruction south. In the late 19th and early 20th centuries, Southern states ran prisons populated mostly by Black men. Some of these prisons operated as profit-making enterprises internally, like at Parchman Farm (discussed below), while other prisons leased out their "convicts" to private landowners or businesses to do annual labor, ranging from farming to mining. Businesses benefited from these programs by having access to a nearly free work force, paying only for costs of food and housing for the workers and a payment to the state "leasing" the captive laborers. From 1866-1896 the State of Tennessee widely adopted a system of convict leasing, aiming to make prisons "self supporting" and to provide the state with additional revenue. The practice was an effective money making scheme for the state and for businesses.

Tennessee's convict labor practice also helped Tennessee Coal and Iron Company (TCI) to keep their other labor costs low, as Tennessee's convict leasing system gave TCI "an effective club to hold over the head of free labor." In the late 19th century, the practice was at the center of a dramatic industrial-labor battle. Organized labor campaigned hard to stamp out convict leasing because it was used to bust unions and drive down the cost of labor. In July of 1891, after two decades of minor labor uprisings, free white miners who were on strike launched a series of attacks on Anderson Country, Tennessee. Three hundred miners took charge of forty prisoners and their overseer/prison guards, and "marched them and their guards five miles to Coal Creek, sealed them in box cars and shipped them to Knoxville." Then, they called on Tennessee Governor James Buchanan to negotiate new labor protections. In 1893, after the miners had repeated their attacks multiple times, "the general assembly of the state passed legislation to abolish convict leasing at the end of the lease contract in 1896."

In addition to convict leasing, some prisons operated for-profit operations internally using incarcerated labor. Parchman Farm, now called Mississippi State Penitentiary is the antecedent of the in-house varieties of prison labor that we see in prisons today. Parchman Farm was part of "a movement to restore white supremacy and ensure a source of cheap free labor to replace slave labor." Parchman Farm, which opened in 1903, was in the words of then Mississippi Governor James K. Vardaman, "run 'like an efficient slave plantation' that provided young black men with the 'proper discipline, strong work habits, and respect for white authority.'"

These institutions and practices represent the ancestral roots of prison labor in the United States. While there is more history that might be examined this piece will jump forward a few decades to take a look at incarcerated labor's modern iterations.

PRISON LABOR WORK SYSTEMS

Prisons are organized in a variety of ways. Public prisons are operated by the federal government or a state government, or prisons are operated by a private company under contract with the federal or local government. Currently, the most prominent private prison companies are Correction Corporation of America (CCA), GEO Group, and the Management and Training Corporation (MTC). Each of these institutions uses prison labor. . . .

PUBLIC PRISONS

All individuals incarcerated in a federal prison who have been medically cleared are required to work. Failure to do so results in punitive recourse, including solitary confinement. They will either be given a prison maintenance assignment or assigned to a Federal Prison Industries detail. Incarcerated workers have no right to a particular job assignment. . . .

Federal Prison Industries, Inc. (FPI or otherwise known by the trade name UNICOR) is a "wholly-owned government corporation," which is "authorized to operate industries in federal penal and correctional institutions and disciplinary barracks" under federal law. FPI has industrial and service operations at 78 factories located at 62 prison facilities, employing

16 percent of federally incarcerated workers as of September 30, 2014. FPI work assignments pay from $0.23 to $1.15 per hour, however incarcerated workers working for FPI who have financial obligations, including "cost of incarceration fees" commonly assessed against incarcerated people for prison room and board, are required to pay 50 percent of their earnings to the Inmate Financial Responsibility Program. Under law, FPI is restricted to selling its products to the Federal Government. The U.S. Department of Defense is its principal customer.

Incarcerated workers in public prisons produce products like license plates, mattresses and bedding, brooms, office furniture, prison cell accessories, and gun containers and handcuff cases for police officers. Most of these products end up in government facilities, state universities, and education institutions. . . .

PRISON INDUSTRIES IN PUBLIC AND PRIVATE PRISONS

In many public and private prisons, work systems produce materials for third party private companies. This type of work system is often called "prison industry." Prison work crews sew lingerie for companies like Victoria's Secret, as well as U.S. military uniforms. Prisoners also work as farm laborers, as software shrinkwrapers, on construction crews, and in call centers. . . .

PRIVATE DETENTION CENTERS

In U.S. immigration detention centers, detained persons are also subjected to compulsory labor by the public or private entity that operates their facility. These imprisoned workers labor in mostly prison maintenance jobs, and estimates of the number of immigrants laboring in detention centers in 2013 range between 60,000 and 135,000. Detainees work for free, are paid with sodas or candy bars, or are paid less than $1 per hour depending on the facility. According to the *New York Times*, this "cheap labor....saves the government and the private companies $40 million or more a year by allowing them to avoid paying outside contractors the $7.25 federal minimum wage."

In summary, modern incarcerated labor takes a variety of forms. While different institutions profit from incarcerated labor, one thing is clear: incarcerated individuals continue to hold traditional jobs, but are paid at wages far below those mandated for other classes of workers.

34

Wealth Inequality Has Widened Along Racial, Ethnic Lines Since End of Great Recession

Pew Research Center

The Great Recession, fueled by the crises in the housing and financial markets, was universally hard on the net worth of American families. But even as the economic recovery has begun to mend asset prices, not all households have benefited alike, and wealth inequality has widened along racial and ethnic lines.

Racial, Ethnic Wealth Gaps Have Grown Since Great Recession

Median net worth of households, in 2013 dollars

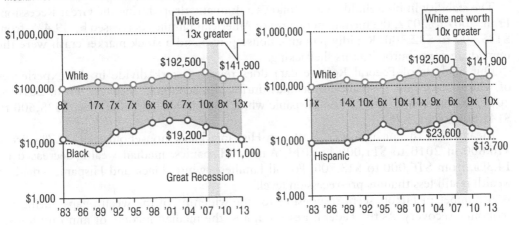

Source: Pew Research Center tabulations of Survey of Consumer Finances public-use data

Notes: Blacks and whites include only non-Hispanics. Hispanics are of any race. Chart scale is logarithmic; each gridline is ten times greater than the gridline below it. Great Recession began Dec. '07 and ended June '09.

The wealth of white households was 13 times the median wealth of black households in 2013, compared with eight times the wealth in 2010, according to a new Pew Research Center analysis of data from the Federal Reserve's Survey of Consumer finances. Likewise, the wealth of white households is now more than 10 times the wealth of Hispanic households, compared with nine times the wealth in 2010.

The current gap between blacks and whites has reached its highest point since 1989, when whites had 17 times the wealth of black households. The current white-to-Hispanic wealth ratio has reached a level not seen since 2001. (Asians and other racial groups are not separately identified in the public-use versions of the Fed's survey.)

Leaving aside race and ethnicity, the net worth of American families overall—the difference between the values of their assets and liabilities—held steady during the economic recovery. The typical household had a net worth of $81,400 in 2013, according to the

Wealth Inequality by Race and Ethnicity Has Grown Since 2007

Median wealth ratios

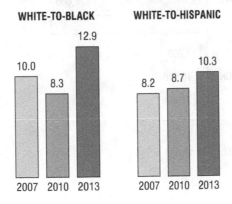

Source: Pew Research Center tabulations of Survey of Consumer Finances public-use data

Notes: Blacks and whites include only non-Hispanics. Hispanics are of any race.

C
O
N
T
E
X
T

Fed's survey—almost the same as what it was in 2010, when the median net worth of U.S. households was $82,300 (values expressed in 2013 dollars).

The stability in household wealth follows a dramatic drop during the Great Recession. From 2007 to 2012, the median net worth of American families decreased by 39.4%, from $135,700 to $82,300. Rapidly plunging house prices and a stock market crash were the immediate contributors to this shellacking.

Our analysis of Federal Reserve data does reveal a stark divide in the experiences of white, black and Hispanic households during the economic recovery. From 2010 to 2013, the median wealth of non-Hispanic white households increased from $138,600 to $141,900, or by 2.4%.

Meanwhile, the median wealth of non-Hispanic black households fell 33.7%, from $16,600 in 2010 to $11,000 in 2013. Among Hispanics, median wealth decreased by 14.3%, from $16,000 to $13,700. For all families—white, black and Hispanic—median wealth is still less than its pre-recession level.

A number of factors seem responsible for the widening of the wealth gaps during the economic recovery. As the Federal Reserve notes, the median income of minority households (blacks, Hispanics and other Non-whites combined) fell 9% from its 2010 to 2013 surveys, compared with a decrease of 1% for non-Hispanic white households. Thus, minority households may not have replenished their savings as much as white households or they may have had to draw down their savings even more during the recovery.

Also, financial assets, such as stocks, have recovered in value more quickly than housing since the recession ended. White households are much more likely than minority households to own stocks directly or indirectly through retirement accounts. Thus, they were in better position to benefit from the recovery in financial markets.

Wealth by Race and Ethnicity, 2007–13

Median net worth of households, in 2013 dollars

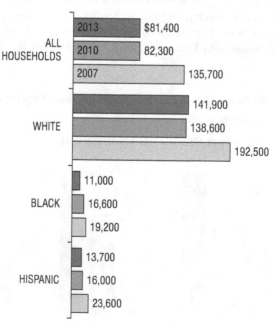

Notes: Blacks and whites include only non-Hispanics. Hispanics are of any race.

Source: Pew Research Center tabulations of Survey of Consumer Finances public-use data

All American households since the recovery have started to reduce their ownership of key assets, such as homes, stocks and business equity. But the decrease in asset ownership tended to be proportionally greater among minority households. For example, the home-ownership rate for non-Hispanic white households fell from 75.3% in 2010 to 73.9%, a percentage drop of 2%. Meanwhile, the homeownership rate among minority households decreased from 50.6% in 2010 to 47.4% in 2013, a slippage of 6.5%.

While the current wealth gaps are higher than at the beginning of the recession, they are not at their highest level as recorded by the Fed's survey. Peak values for the wealth ratios were recorded in the 1989 survey—17 for the white-to-black ratio and 14 for the white-to-Hispanic ratio. But those values of the ratios may be anomalies driven by fluctuations in the wealth of the poorest—those with net worth less than $500. Otherwise, the racial and ethnic wealth gaps in 2013 are at or about their highest levels observed in the 30 years for which we have data.

35

Bonds of Sisterhood—Bonds of Oppression

Mary Romero

. . .

Domestic service reveals the contradiction in a feminism that pushed for women's involvement outside the home, yet failed to make men take responsibility for household labor. Employed middle- and upper-middle class women escaped the double day syndrome by hiring poor women of color to perform housework and child care, and this was characterized as progress. Some feminists defined domestic service as progressive because traditional women's work moved into the labor market and became paid work. However, this definition neglects the inescapable fact that when women hire other women at low wages to do housework, both employees and employers remain women. As employers, women continued to accept responsibility for housework even if they supervised domestics who performed the actual labor. . . .

Although the system of gender domination places the burden of housework on women, middle-class women have financial resources to escape the drudgery of housework by paying someone else to do their work. . . . Thus, middle-class American women aim to "liberate" themselves by exploiting women of color—particularly immigrants—in the underground economy, for long hours at relatively low wages, with no benefits.

. . .

PHYSICAL LABOR

On the surface, the idea of hiring another person to perform the housewife's physical labor appears fairly straightforward. However, it is complicated by the fact that employers hire persons to replace labor at once considered demeaning and closely identified with family roles of mothers and wives. As employers, housewives decide what aspects of their physical labor they no longer want to perform, and in doing so they determine the employee's work. The needs fulfilled through domestics' physical labor structure the work: thus some employers choose to include tasks that they feel are demeaning, others add new tasks and methods of housekeeping that they themselves never engage in, and still others are more interested in having their status affirmed and enhanced than in having their floors scrubbed. . . . The list of physical labor reported by household workers included housecleaning, laundry, sewing, gardening, babysitting, and cooking. . . .

In their efforts to escape the diffuse duties of their housewife roles, employers do not acknowledge work boundaries. Even when the worker's tasks were agreed upon in a verbal contract, employees frequently reported that employers requested additional duties. For instance, household workers commonly complained that employers did not differentiate between housework and child care. In her interviews with women hired to do child care in New York City, Kathy Dobie found that "many of the women are hired as nannies and then asked if they wouldn't mind straightening up a bit. They are asked if they wouldn't clean, then shop, then do the laundry, then, etc." One child care worker told Dobie:

I give her coffee. I take care of Stephen. I do the laundry. I go out and do the shopping. I buy her birth control tablets. I couldn't believe that. . . . Even the light bulbs in the ceiling, I change. Even her panties, I pick them up when she drops them on the floor.

. . . One of the most common experiences reported by women of color in reference to different standards was the request to scrub floors on their hands and knees rather than simply mopping. Maggie Holmes summed up the feelings of most women of color: "They [white women employers] don't get on their knees, but they don't think nothin' about askin' a black woman." . . .

EMOTIONAL LABOR

. . . Domestics are hired not only for their physical labor but to do emotional labor. . . . One clue to the importance emotional labor has for the employer can be found in accounts showing the lack of concern over the *amount* of housework completed. . . .

When I went there they told me, "We're not paying you to scrub floors, but paying you just to take care of the woman, be a companion-like"; but I would do it all. If she was sick, I would stay nights. In the summer *we* would rent a summer cottage and I went there for five years with her.

. . .

One Chicana I interviewed explained why she continued working for a seventy-eight-year-old employer who lived a long distance from her, regardless of the low wages: "I guess you can say she needs companionship. I feel sorry for her, you know, she is one of my farthest ones [employers]. I go once a month to her house. I like to go early so I can sit and talk to her."

Domestics almost invariably found themselves counseling and consoling their employers. Mrs. Okamura described the following work situation to Glenn:

I'd been working for a lady for two hours a week for a long time, but she didn't even give me a chance to work. Upon my arrival, she kept talking and going on and on. For me, housework was much easier because even though I didn't understand English well, I still had to say, "Is that so?" "no" and "yes." . . . They just wanted to complain about their son or their son's wife.

. . .

Gift-giving is domestic workers' almost universal experience and stands as the most obvious symbol of employers' maternalism. Structurally, gift-giving occupies an important place within the underground economy, whereby working-class women are often given presents by middle-class employers in lieu of higher wages and benefits. Chicanas reported that Christmas gifts to them or their children were more common than annual raises. Unlike gift-giving in other work settings, gifts frequently replace higher wages, raises, or other benefits. The following quote from a domestic describes conditions under which the gift occurs: "I'm trying to show you they would do something nice for you when they really felt you needed it. But they wouldn't pay you nothing but these menial wages. Nobody else paid more, and nobody wanted to break the standard." . . .

Employers in domestic service commonly redefine as gifts items that would have gone to the Salvation Army or the trash. Glenn found that old clothes and other discarded items

V O I C E S

were the most common gifts given to Japanese American domestics. I found a similar case among Chicana domestics. Judith Warner and Helen Henderson reported that sixty percent of the 200 Mexican immigrant women surveyed in Laredo received used clothes from their employers. This practice of giving old clothes within a work setting is unique to domestic service. It is almost inconceivable that the same woman would consider offering her old linen jacket to her secretary.

. . .

PURCHASING STATUS BY HIRING A WOMAN OF COLOR

. . .

Taking an innovative research tack of analyzing family photographs, [one researcher] observed the importance of race and ethnicity in affirming employers' class and racial status in their communities. In her analysis of employers' family albums, she observed that "an attractive, well-dressed black domestic signified the family's membership in 'the better class' in the community." In subsequent interviews with domestics, [she] asked about their inclusion in the employers' family portraits. These African American women confirmed that "whites 'liked to dress blacks up' and sought to show that they had 'good-looking servants.'"

The physical appearances of household workers can be further manipulated to function as visible signs of the hierarchical status distinguishing domestics from employers. . . . White uniforms are used to distinguish the maid from families and friends, particularly when employers fear that others might mistake the reason for her presence. . . . "The maid puts on a uniform when there's company"; otherwise she is allowed to wear jeans. Most private household workers report that employers request a uniform to be worn on particular occasions, such as serving a special dinner or party or when accompanying the family on vacation. Mrs. Nishi expressed her opinion of the employer's request to Glenn: "I had to dress up in the maid's outfit when they had dinner parties. It was all part of it about how phoney these people were that I worked for." . . .

PURCHASING DEFERENCE

Confirmation of the employer's status is not always accomplished by the mere physical presence of women of color or white uniforms; it frequently requires daily practices of deferential behavior that continually affirm and enhance the domestic's inferiority. . . .

She [employer] would make me feel like I was nothing or like I was doing this [domestic service] because I was so poor or because I was a Mexican. One day she said that Mexican people are all very poor. They weren't educated. And that did it! I dropped what I was doing. I left it there and I said, "here, take this and shove it. I don't have to take this abuse from you or from anybody. I'm Mexican, yes, but I'm proud of what I am and I'm working." I says, "Everybody has a job and I have this as my job and if you felt this way, you didn't have to hire me." . . .

Another common and almost universal practice was to address domestics by their first names and employers by their last names. Employer Elinor Birney revealed the significance of the practice to Susan Tucker when she expressed her concern over her daughter's refusal to follow the custom: "The servant calls the woman Mary and Mary calls the servant by her name. Now, I think your employer-employee relationship sometimes could get very sticky if you don't have some separation." West Indian domestics reported that employers in New York used their first names but expected to be addressed formally. Laurino remarked on the irony of the practice because a domestic was in the position of knowing "the personal details of the employer's life, yet will most likely address her as Miss or Mrs.—and in return, she'll be called by her first name."

. . .

Several Chicana domestics similarly reported that employers refused to pronounce their names correctly and eventually Anglicized them. On the basis of the stereotype that all Mexican women are named Maria, white employers in the Southwest frequently refer to all Latina domestics as "Maria."

. . .

Deferential behavior is also constructed through eating arrangements. Rarely did domestics eat in the dining room or in the presence of mistresses' husbands. Mrs. Garcia remembered an employer who told her: "If you brought your lunch you wait out in your car or in the patio or out in the street or wherever." West Indians in New York City employed as live-in workers faced the archetypal situation of the domestic eating alone in the kitchen. As one woman described, "I couldn't eat with them at the table. . . . I have to eat after they finish eating. . . . And then I eat in the kitchen." Aware of the status hierarchy produced from acts of deference, the woman quoted above also commented that "there are people who do that because they want us to know that we are not equal." Another West Indian woman described the purpose of deferential eating arrangements as a way to create symbols of her inferiority: "The first day I got there [the employer] took out a fork and a plate and told me that this was mine to always use. They gave me the impression that I wasn't clean enough."

. . .

Household-labor negotiations frequently occur within the underground economy; they involve few government regulations. Consequently, employers have enormous leeway to determine the working conditions by setting wages, establishing job descriptions, and determining the work structure. . . . Employers decide whether to give raises, and they usually decide whether social security or benefits are obtained. Domestics have little influence over working conditions outside the choice to accept a job or to quit. Given the power that employers exert over working conditions, domestics—more than other workers—feel dependent on and at the mercy of their employers. Since the majority of household workers are not unionized, the struggle to improve working conditions remains an individual struggle.

. . .

The system of gifts and obligations in domestic service tends to shape the personalism in the employee-employer relationship into a strategy of oppression. Redefining work obligations as family or friendship obligations assures employers access to both the emotional and the physical labor of their employees. Personalism camouflages work conditions which become distorted and unintelligible within the context of the interpersonal relationships between domestics and employers. Employers' refusal to relate to domestics' concerns as workers' rights distorts the real conditions of their interaction.

JUST LIKE ONE OF THE FAMILY

Alice Childress testified to the way that personal relationships distort working conditions in her essay on the family analogy in *Like One of the Family: Conversations From a Domestic's Life*. The domestic's view of the employer's attempt to redefine her as "one of the family" rather than as a domestic was presented in an exchange between the two. Mildred, the domestic, overheard the employer tell a friend:

> "We just love her! She's *like* one of the family and she *just adores* our little Carol! We don't know *what* we'd do without her! We don't think of her as a servant!"

Mildred responded later to the employer's characterization by listing the ways her interaction with the family distinguished her as a nonmember, an outsider with inferior status.

> The family eats in the dining room and I eat in the kitchen. Your mama borrows your lace table cloth for her company and your son entertains his friends in your parlor, your daughter takes her afternoon nap on the living room couch and the puppy sleeps on your satin spread . . . and whenever your husband gets tired of something you are talkin' about he says, "Oh, for Pete's sake, forget it. . . ." So you can see I am not *just* like the family.
>
> . . .

Although the phrase "one of the family" represents "the epitome of the personalized employer-employee association," domestics' use of the family analogy points to aspects of the emotional labor that some workers are willing to accept and those that they reject. On the one hand, this analogy suggests that domestics are engaged in the emotional labor involved in nurturing and caring; on the other hand, it suggests that domestics are treated with respect and are not forced into doing the emotional labor required to create deference.

. . .

THE BUSINESSLIKE RELATIONSHIP

. . .

Establishing and maintaining a businesslike relationship is difficult in many respects. Virtually all contemporary jobs are structured to include breaks. However, regular morning and afternoon breaks are aspects of work culture absent from domestic service. . . .

> One of the biggest problems with household work is that the employers work you too hard. They want you to do everything in one day. They aren't sensitive to you even taking a half hour lunch break.

Structuring breaks and time off is a particularly serious problem for live-in domestics because the hours, tasks and obligations of the job are constantly redefined. Furthermore, live-in workers even find it difficult to guarantee their days off. . . .

> Thursday was my day off. But every Thursday morning, she would get up as she did every other morning and give me something to do. And usually she would say you can leave after you do so and so. Well, often by the time I finished the task, or giving the children lunch it was usually after 2 o'clock and I had no real day off.

. . .

Like other employers who hire workers in the underground economy, middle-class housewives seldom structure a regular routine for raises. The Chicanas who were interviewed in Denver rarely found employers who offered raises annually or on any regular basis. Domestics generally feel that domestic service is like any other type of job and that employers should thus understand that raises are part of hiring workers. . . .

In their accounts of requesting raises, some domestics expressed a need to force employers to recognize that domestic service is "real work." . . .

So one day I say to her, I say, "Miz Brown," I said, "things is high now." I say, "And what you pay for meat and bread," I say, "that's what I have to pay, too." I say, "I been working here for a long time." I say, "I'd like a raise."

. . .

Wages are the tip of the iceberg. Benefits assumed in other working environments: overtime, vacation, sick pay, a health care plan, and any procedures for redress of grievances, are rarely if ever found in domestic service. At the same time, negative sanctions against employees are common, domestics report that employers expect breakage costs to be borne by the workers. Consider the following account by one of the Chicanas whom I interviewed. After waxing the kitchen floor, Mrs. Tafoya left an open can of floor wax on the dining room table. While she was upstairs vacuuming, her employer opened the sliding doors next to the dining room table to let a breeze in. The curtains flew up, tipped the can, and spilled floor wax onto the table. Mrs. Tafoya was held financially responsible for half of the cost of the repair. . . .

DISCUSSION

Descriptive accounts offered by women of color challenge many perceptions about the function of domestic service in American society today. Even though employers state that they hire domestics to escape the drudgery of housework and to gain freedom to engage in other activities, descriptions of working conditions reveal a more complex set of needs. Interviews with employers and employees alike indicate that domestic service still performs important functions in enhancing the status of middle-class housewives and their families. Moreover, the analysis of the structure of paid housework reveals that the work includes both physical and emotional labor, much of it as shadow work and unpaid labor.

The daily rituals and practices of domestic service reproduce the systems of gender, class, and race domination. All of the gender-specific aspects of unpaid housework—identified in the housewife experience—are also present in domestic service. Even though domestics are paid workers, they do not escape the sexism attached to housework but rather carry the burden for their middle-class women employers. The never-ending job described by housewives is trans-ferred to workers employed by women who treat domestic service as an opportunity to "hire a wife." Employers frequently disregard the contractual or informal labor arrangement made with employees, constantly increasing the work load and incorporating more of their own homemaking duties and obligations. Household workers are faced with tasks that both exceed their job descriptions and are as emotionally and physically burdensome as those completed by housewives. The most common violation of the original labor agreement is the practice of adding child care to general housecleaning instead of keeping the two jobs separate.

. . .

Paid housework that is structured to replicate the unpaid domestic work of the house-wife includes practices affirming women's inferiority. The sexist division of labor that exists in employers' homes, assigning mothers and wives the duty of waiting on and serving their husbands and children, is passed on to the domestics. Middle-class women employers who expect women household workers to "pick up" after their husbands and children reproduce the demeaning and sexist aspects of housework. Rejection of such sexist prac-tices is reflected throughout the service sector when workers refuse to "pick up" after others by saying, "I am not your mother." In the same vein, domestics resist practices that structure paid housework to affirm sexist cultural values by requiring the employer to confront her children and husband about leaving their clothes and wet towels on the floor, leaving dishes and glasses throughout the house, and not throwing trash into the garbage.

However, many women employers simply perpetuate the sexist division of labor by passing on the most devalued work in their lives to another woman—generally a woman of color. Thus, white middle-class women escape the stigma of "women's work" by laying the burden on working-class women of color.

. . .

36

White Poverty

The Politics of Invisibility

bell hooks

In the southern world of racial apartheid I grew up in, no racialized class division was as intense or as fraught with bitter conflict as the one between poor whites and black folks. All black people knew that white skin gave any southern "cracker or peckerwood" (ethnic slurs reserved for the white poor) more power and privilege than even the wealthiest of black folks. However, these slurs were not the product of black vernacular slang, they were the terms white folks with class privilege invented to separate themselves from what they called poor "white trash." On the surface, at least, it made the lives of racist poor white people better to have a group they could lord it over, and the only group they could lord it over were black people. Assailed and assaulted by privileged white folks, they transferred their rage and class hatred onto the bodies of black people.

Unlike the stereotypes projected by the dominant culture about poor black folks, class stereotypes claimed poor whites were supposedly easily spotted by skin ailments, bad dental hygiene, and hair texture. All these things are affected by diet. While poor southern black folks often had no money, they usually had homegrown food to eat. Poor whites often suffered from malnutrition. Living under racial apartheid, black children learned to fear poor whites more than other whites simply because they were known to express their racism by cruel and brutal acts of violence. And even when white folks with class privilege condemned this violence, they could never openly oppose it, for to do so they would have had to take the word of black folks over those of white folks, thus being disloyal to white supremacy. A white person of privilege opposing violence against blacks perpetuated by poor whites might easily ruin their reputation and risk being seen as a "nigger lover."

When I was a small child we lived in the hills without neighbors nearby. Our closest neighbors were "white trash," as distinct from poor whites. White trash were different because they flaunted their poverty, reveled in it, and were not ashamed. Poor whites, like poor blacks, were committed to trying to find work and lay claim to respectability—they were law abiding and patriotic. White trash saw themselves as above the law and as a consequence they were dangerous. White trash were folks who, as our neighbors were fond of saying, "did not give a good goddamn." They were not afraid to take the Lord's name in vain. Most poor white folks did not want to live anywhere near black folks. White trash lived anywhere. . . .

Our "hillbilly white trash" neighbors lived by their own codes and rules. We did not call them names, because we knew the pain of slurs. Mama made it clear that they were people just like us and were to be shown respect. While they did not bother us and we did not bother them, we feared them. I never felt that they feared us. They were always encouraging us to come over, to play and party with them. To most respectable black people, poor whites and white trash were the lowest of the low. Even when they were nice, black folks felt it was important to keep a distance. I remember being whipped for being overly friendly with poor white neighbors. At that time I did not understand, nor did our parents make it clear, that if anything had happened to us in their homes, as black folks we would just have been seen as in the wrong; that was the nature of Jim Crow justice. While we were encouraged to keep a distance from all white children no matter their class, it was clear that black people pitied and often felt contempt toward the white poor.

Desegregation led to the closing of all black schools. Busing took us out of our all-black neighborhoods into worlds of whiteness we did not know. It was in high school that I first began to understand class separation between whites. Poor white kids kept to themselves. And many of their well-to-do white peers would rather be seen talking to a black person than speaking to the white poor, or worse, to white trash. There was no danger that the black person they were talking to would want to come and hang out at their home or go to a movie. Racial lines were not crossed outside school. There could be no expectation of a reciprocal friendship. A privileged white person might confuse the issue if they showed attention to an underprivileged white peer. Class boundaries had to remain intact so that no one got the wrong idea. Between black and white there was no chance of a wrong idea: the two simply did not meet or mix.

Since some folks saw mama's family as backwoods, as black hillbillies, she was always quick to punish any act of aggression on our part toward an underdog group. We were not allowed to ridicule poor whites—not even if they were taunting us. When we began to ride the bus across town to the white school, it was a shock to my sensibilities to interact with black children who were scornful of the misfortune of others. . . .

To this day I have sad memories of the way Wilma, the white girl who was in my class, was treated by aggressive black children on the bus. Their daily taunts reminded her that she was poor white trash, the lowest of the low, that she smelled bad, that she wore the same dress day after day. In loud mean talk they warned her not to sit next to them. She often stood when there was an empty seat. A big girl with dark hair and unusually fair skin, she endured all the taunts with a knowing smirk. When she was pushed too far she fought back. She knew that with the exception of her ten minutes on that predominately black bus, white power ruled the day. And no matter how poor she was, she would always be white.

. . .

The white poor make up the vast majority of the poor in this society. Whereas mass migration of poor blacks from southern states to northern cities created a huge urban poor population, the white poor continue to live in isolated rural and suburban areas. Now and then they live hidden in the midst of white affluence. From their invention to the present day, the world of trailer park homes has been the territory of the white poor. While marking class boundaries, trailer park communities do not carry the stigma of degradation and deprivation commonly associated with the "ghetto"—a term first used to identify poor white urban immigrant communities. Indeed, in the not so distant past the psychological and economic self-esteem of the white working class and the white poor has been significantly bolstered by the class politics of white supremacy. Currently, we are witnessing a resurgence of white supremacist thinking among disenfranchised classes of white people. These extremist groups respond to misinformation circulated by privileged whites that suggests that black people are getting ahead financially because of government policies like affirmative action, and they are taught to blame black folks for their plight.

While anti-black racism has intensified among whites of all classes in recent years as part of civil rights backlash, overall the white underprivileged are . . . far more likely to see immigrants as the group taking needed jobs. Their racism toward non-white immigrants who are perceived to be taking jobs by virtue of their willingness to work for less mirrors that of black workers who blame immigrants. More and more the white and black poor recognize that ruling class greed ensures their continued exploitation and oppression.

. .

More and more Americans of all colors are entering the ranks of the poor. And that includes white Americans. The evidence is in the numbers. In the essay "Trash-O-Nomics," Doug Henwood states what should be obvious but often is not: "Of course, the average white person is better off than the average non-white person, those of Asian origin excepted, and black people are disproportionally poor. But that sort of formula hides as much as it reveals: most officially poor people are white, and these days, a white household should consider itself lucky if its income is only stagnant rather than in outright decline." It serves white supremacist capitalist patriarchal ruling class interests to mask this reality. Hence, the almost invisibility of the white poor in mass media.

Today, most folks who comment on class acknowledge that poverty is seen as having a black face, but they rarely point to the fact that this representation has been created and sustained by mass media. Concurrently, reports using statistics that show a huge percentage of black folks in the ranks of the poor compared to a small percentage of whites make it seem that blacks are the majority group in the ranks of the poor. Rarely do these reports emphasize that these percentages are based on population size. The reality they mask is that blacks are a small percentage of the population. While black folks disproportionate to our numbers are among the poor, the vast majority of the poor continue to be white. The hidden face of poverty in the United States is the untold stories of millions of poor white people.

Better to have poor and working-class white folks believe white supremacy is still giving them a meaningful edge than to broadcast the reality that the poor of any race no longer have an edge in this society, or that downsizing daily drags previously economically sound white households into the ranks of the poor. . . . Undue media focus on poor nonwhites deflects attention away from the reality of white poverty.

. . .

No doubt ruling class groups will succeed in new efforts to divide and conquer, but the white poor will no longer direct its class rage solely at black people, for the white poor is divided within its ranks. Just as there are many poor whites who are racist, there are a substantial group of poor whites who refuse to buy into white supremacist politics, who understand the economic forces that are crippling the American working class. Progressive white poor and working-class people understand the dynamics of capitalism. All over the United States class unrest is mounting. . . .

Ending welfare will mean that more white women than ever before in our nation's history will enter the ranks of the underclass. Like their black counterparts, many of them will be young. Workfare programs, which pay subsistence wages without the backdrop of free housing, will not enhance their lives. As the future "poorest of the poor" they are far less likely to be duped into believing their enemies are other economically disadvantaged groups than their predecessors. . . .

Given that today's culture is one where the white and black working class and poor have more to say to one another, there is a context for building solidarity that did not exist in the past. That solidarity cannot be expressed solely through shared critique of the privileged. It must be rooted in a politics of resistance that is fundamentally anti-racist, one that recognizes that the experiences of underprivileged white folks are as important as those of people of color. The class segregation that historically divided the white poor from their more privileged counterparts did not exist in predominately black communities. And while generations of white families have historically remained poor, a host of black folks pulled themselves out of poverty into privilege. In solidarity these folks have historically been strong advocates for the black poor even though that too is changing. More often than not they did not encourage solidarity with the white poor because of persistent anti-black racism. Now they must become advocates for the white and black poor, overcoming their anti-white prejudices. Concurrently, the black and white poor must do the work of building solidarity by learning more about one another, about what brings them together and what tears them apart. We need to hear more from all of us who have bridged the gap between white and black poor and working-class experience.

When I left the segregated world of my poor and working-class home environment to attend privileged-class schools, I found I often had more in common with white students who shared a similar class background than with privileged class black students who had no experience of what it might mean to lack the funds to do anything they wanted to do. No matter our color, students from poor and working-class backgrounds had common experiences history had not taught us how to sufficiently name or theoretically articulate. While it was definitely easier for folks from poor white backgrounds to assimilate visually, we all experienced estrangement from our class origin as well as the fear of losing touch with the worlds we had most intimately known. The bonds we forged in solidarity were and are not documented. There is no record of our conversations or how these solidarities shaped our future politics. Many of us used this bonding through class across the boundary of race as a groundwork for a politics of solidarity that has stood the test of time.

While racism remains an integral fact of our culture, it too has changed. Xenophobia more so than racial hatred often characterizes where white citizens stand on race. The utterly segregated black neighborhoods of my upbringing are no more. The white poor in need of shelter move into places where once no white face was ever seen. This contact does not mean an absence of racism. But it does mean that the criteria and the expression of racism has changed. It also means that there is more of a concrete basis for positive interaction between poor black and white folks. When I walk in these communities created by class division, I see grown white and black folks refusing to interact with each other even as I see more interaction than in the past. And I see white and black children freely crossing the boundaries of race to meet at that class juncture which brings them together in a common landscape they call home.

These bonds may mean little given the fact that there are so many more race-segregated white working-class and poor communities. Even in the places where white and black do not meet, there are more diverse opinions about class and race. Nothing is as simple as it was in the past when the needs of the white poor were pitted against the needs of the black poor. Today, poverty is both gendered and racialized. It is impossible to truly understand class in the United States today without understanding the politics of race and gender. Ultimately, more than any previous movement for social justice, the struggle to end poverty could easily become the civil rights issue with the broadest appeal—uniting groups that have never before taken a stand together to support their common hope of living in a more democratic and just world—a world where basic necessities of life are available to everyone, to each according to their need.

V
O
I
C
E
S

37

The Laws That Sex Workers Really Want (TED Talk)

Juno Mac

I want to talk about sex for money. I'm not like most of the people you'll have heard speaking about prostitution before. I'm not a police officer or a social worker. I'm not an academic, a journalist or a politician. I'm not a nun, either.

Most of those people would tell you that selling sex is degrading; that no one would ever choose to do it; that it's dangerous; women get abused and killed. In fact, most of those people would say, "There should be a law against it!" Maybe that sounds reasonable to you. It sounded reasonable to me until the closing months of 2009, when I was working two dead-end, minimum wage jobs. Every month my wages would just replenish my overdraft. I was exhausted and my life was going nowhere. Like many others before me, I decided sex for money was a better option. Now don't get me wrong—I would have loved to have won the lottery instead. But it wasn't going to happen anytime soon, and my rent needed paying. So I signed up for my first shift in a brothel.

In the years that have passed, I've had a lot of time to think. I've reconsidered the ideas I once had about prostitution. I've given a lot of thought to consent and the nature of work under capitalism. I've thought about gender inequality and the sexual and reproductive labor of women. I've experienced exploitation and violence at work. I've thought about what's needed to protect other sex workers from these things. Maybe you've thought about them, too. In this talk, I'll take you through the four main legal approaches applied to sex work throughout the world, and explain why they don't work; why prohibiting the sex industry actually exacerbates every harm that sex workers are vulnerable to. Then I'm going tell you about what we, as sex workers, actually want.

The first approach is full criminalization. Half the world, including Russia, South Africa and most of the US, regulates sex work by criminalizing everyone involved. So that's seller, buyer and third parties. Lawmakers in these countries apparently hope that the fear of getting arrested will deter people from selling sex. But if you're forced to choose between obeying the law and feeding yourself or your family, you're going to do the work anyway, and take the risk.

Criminalization is a trap. It's hard to get a conventional job when you have a criminal record. Potential employers won't hire you. Assuming you still need money, you'll stay in the more flexible, informal economy. The law forces you to keep selling sex, which is the exact opposite of its intended effect. Being criminalized leaves you exposed to mistreatment by the state itself. In many places you may be coerced into paying a bribe or even into having sex with a police officer to avoid arrest. Police and prison guards in Cambodia, for example, have been documented subjecting sex workers to what can only be described as torture: threats at gunpoint, beatings, electric shocks, rape and denial of food.

Another worrying thing: if you're selling sex in places like Kenya, South Africa or New York, a police officer can arrest you if you're caught carrying condoms, because condoms can legally be used as evidence that you're selling sex. Obviously, this increases HIV risk. Imagine knowing if you're busted carrying condoms, it'll be used against you. It's a pretty strong incentive to leave them at home, right? Sex workers working in these places are forced to make a tough choice between risking arrest or having risky sex. What would you choose? Would you pack condoms to go to work? How about if you're worried the police officer would rape you when he got you in the van?

The second approach to regulating sex work seen in these countries is partial criminalization, where the buying and selling of sex are legal, but surrounding activities, like brothel-keeping or soliciting on the street, are banned. Laws like these—we have them in the UK and in France—essentially say to us sex workers, "Hey, we don't mind you selling sex, just make sure it's done behind closed doors and all alone." And brothel-keeping, by the way, is defined as just two or more sex workers working together. Making that illegal means that many of us work alone, which obviously makes us vulnerable to violent offenders. . . . Let me tell you about Mariana Popa who worked in Redbridge, East London. The street workers on her patch would normally wait for clients in groups for safety in numbers and to warn each other about how to avoid dangerous guys. But during a police crackdown on sex workers and their clients, she was forced to work alone to avoid being arrested. She was stabbed to death in the early hours of October 29, 2013. She had been working later than usual to try to pay off a fine she had received for soliciting.

So if criminalizing sex workers hurts them, why not just criminalize the people who buy sex? This is the aim of the third approach I want to talk about—the Swedish or Nordic model of sex-work law. The idea behind this law is that selling sex is intrinsically harmful and so you're, in fact, helping sex workers by removing the option. Despite growing support for what's often described as the "end demand" approach, there's no evidence that it works. There's just as much prostitution in Sweden as there was before. Why might that be? It's because people selling sex often don't have other options for income. If you need that money, the only effect that a drop in business is going have is to force you to lower your prices or offer more risky sexual services. If you need to find more clients, you might seek the help of a manager. So you see, rather than putting a stop to what's often described as pimping, a law like this actually gives oxygen to potentially abusive third parties. . . .

Something I'm often hearing is, "Prostitution would be fine if we made it legal and regulated it." We call that approach legalization, and it's used by countries like the Netherlands, Germany and Nevada in the U.S. But it's not a great model for human rights. And in state-controlled prostitution, commercial sex can only happen in certain legally-designated areas or venues, and sex workers are made to comply with special restrictions, like registration and forced health checks. Regulation sounds great on paper, but politicians deliberately make regulation around the sex industry expensive and difficult to comply with. It creates a two-tiered system: legal and illegal work. We sometimes call it "backdoor criminalization." Rich, well-connected brothel owners can comply with the regulations, but more marginalized people find those hoops impossible to jump through. . . . In this two-tiered system, the most vulnerable people are forced to work illegally, so they're still exposed to all the dangers of criminalization I mentioned earlier.

So, it's looking like all attempts to control or prevent sex work from happening makes things more dangerous for people selling sex. . . .

These laws also reinforce stigma and hatred against sex workers. . . . If prohibition is this harmful, you might ask, why it so popular?

Firstly, sex work is and always has been a survival strategy for all kinds of unpopular minority groups: people of color, migrants, people with disabilities, LGBTQ people, particularly trans women. These are the groups most heavily profiled and punished through prohibitionist law. I don't think this is an accident. These laws have political support precisely because they target people that voters don't want to see or know about.

Why else might people support prohibition? Well, lots of people have understandable fears about trafficking. Folks think that foreign women kidnapped and sold into sexual slavery can be saved by shutting a whole industry down. Forced labor does occur in many industries, especially those where the workers are migrants or otherwise vulnerable, and this needs to be addressed. But it's best addressed with legislation targeting those specific abuses, not an entire industry. . . . The solution is clearly to give workers more legal protections, allowing them to resist abuse and report it to authorities without fear of arrest. . . .

As a feminist, I know that the sex industry is a site of deeply entrenched social inequality. It's a fact that most buyers of sex are men with money, and most sellers are women without. You can agree with all that—I do—and still think prohibition is a terrible policy. In a better, more equal world, maybe there would be far fewer people selling sex to survive, but you can't simply legislate a better world into existence. If someone needs to sell sex because they're poor or because they're homeless or because they're undocumented and they can't find legal work, taking away that option doesn't make them any less poor or house them or change their immigration status. . . .

So we've looked at full criminalization, partial criminalization, the Swedish or Nordic Model and legalization, and how they all cause harm. Something I never hear asked is: "What do sex workers want?" After all, we're the ones most affected by these laws.

New Zealand decriminalized sex work in 2003. It's crucial to remember that decriminalization and legalization are not the same thing. Decriminalization means the removal of laws that punitively target the sex industry, instead treating sex work much like any other kind of work. In New Zealand, people can work together for safety, and employers of sex workers are accountable to the state. A sex worker can refuse to see a client at any time, for any reason, and 96 percent of street workers report that they feel the law protects their rights. New Zealand hasn't actually seen an increase in the amount of people doing sex work, but decriminalizing it has made it a lot safer. But the lesson from New Zealand isn't just that its particular legislation is good, but that crucially, it was written in collaboration with sex workers; namely, the New Zealand Prostitutes' Collective. When it came to making sex work safer, they were ready to hear it straight from sex workers themselves. . . .

But we need more allies. If you care about gender equality or poverty or migration or public health, then sex workers' rights matter to you. Make space for us in your movements. That means not only listening to sex workers when we speak but amplifying our voices. Resist those who silence us, those who say that a prostitute is either too victimized, too damaged to know what's best for herself, or else too privileged and too removed from real hardship, not representative of the millions of voiceless victims. This distinction between victim and empowered is imaginary. It exists purely to discredit sex workers and make it easy to ignore us.

No doubt many of you work for a living. Well, sex work is work, too. Just like you, some of us like our jobs, some of us hate them. Ultimately, most of us have mixed feelings. But how we feel about our work isn't the point. And how others feel about our work certainly isn't. What's important is that we have the right to work safely and on our own terms.

Sex workers are real people. We've had complicated experiences and complicated responses to those experiences. But our demands are not complicated. . . . We want full decriminalization and labor rights as workers.

38

Born on Third Base

Chuck Collins

Have you ever lived in a mobile home? Not me. Until the age of 24, I had never set foot in one. But two years later, I'd been inside hundreds. My first job out of college was to work with mobile home owners who rented their homesites in private parks around

New England. The goal was to help them organize and buy their parks as resident-owned cooperatives.

On an April day in 1986, I was sitting at the kitchen table of a spacious double-wide owned by Harlan and Mary Parro in Bernardston, a small town in Western Massachusetts. We were joined by seven other leaders from their thirty-unit park.

At 26, I still had distressing acne that made me feel quite self-conscious. People regularly assumed I was 17 years old, which compounded my insecurity in situations like this one. The tenant group leaders were all looking at me—this kid with bad skin—waiting to hear my assessment about the fate of their mobile home park.

They were understandably anxious. An unknown buyer had made an offer to purchase their park from its current owner. Some buyers around the region were jacking up rents, knowing the residents were basically hostages. And with land values rising, some developers were buying up parks, kicking out the mobile homes, and building subdivisions and condominiums.

Thanks to a state tenant protection law, the Bernardston tenants had forty-five days to match the offer and buy the park themselves. The clock was ticking.

One of the first things I learned on the job is that mobile homes are not so mobile. Moving a home can risk damaging it and diminishing its value. And it presumes you have a piece of land or another park to relocate to. Across New England, local towns were passing snob zoning laws to prohibit new mobile homes.

Equally important, people in mobile home parks put down roots and build tight-knit communities. They construct additions, add carports and garages, put skirts around the base of their homes, landscape and plant trees and gardens. Harlan and Mary proudly showed me the day's vegetable harvest from their garden plot. All this would be wiped out if the park sold and closed, scattering the residents.

I was in agony, sitting at that kitchen table.

You see, I knew all their secrets. I had confidentially surveyed every member of the community about their personal finances. I knew how much each of them could pay toward rent (and a future mortgage) and how much savings they could apply toward the purchase of their share price in the cooperative. If enough residents could buy their shares outright, we would have the estimated $150,000 required for a down payment.

From my survey, I knew that a third of the residents had no savings and barely enough income to pay current rents. Most residents had low-wage jobs or were living on Social Security. Only a dozen had any savings of more than $5,000, including the retirees. These were people with very low incomes with little to fall back on.

Because I had determined that they didn't have the money to buy the park, I was distraught. In my analysis, they were about $35,000 short of what the association needed for the down payment, a sizable sum. I was going to have to break them the bad news.

I was also in agony, however, because I had a secret. I was wealthy. I was born on third base, having inherited a substantial sum a few years earlier.

I could write a check for $35,000 and make it possible for these thirty families to buy the park. And I was seriously thinking about doing just that. Contributing $35,000 would have had a negligible impact on my personal finances.

I broke the bad news to the assembled leaders. There was a quiet pall in the room. And then an extraordinary thing happened.

First, one of the residents named Reggie said he could buy his share and put another $5,000 toward the purchase. Now I happened to know, because of my confidential survey, that this was all the money that Reggie had.

Then a retired couple, Donald and Rita, pledged an additional $8,000. Ms. Dundorf would put in $7,000. Again, I knew that this was all the money they had.

Harlan and Mary said they would buy their full share and put in another $15,000. This was their entire nest egg, saved while Harlan had worked at Greenfield Tap and Die for thirty-five years. "We'd like to buy Ms. Rivas's share on the condition that she must never find out, in order to protect her dignity," Harlan said.

Before I knew it, they had come up with $30,000. Mary and Harlan's daughter, who arrived late for the meeting, pledged the last $5,000, as she worked at a bank.

The group cheered and immediately started writing out personal checks and handing them to me to take to the bank and deposit.

I was physically shaken by what I had seen. These people were *all in*. They were willing to risk everything they had to buy this park. I wiped away tears as I drove to the bank.

And they succeeded. They bought the park. On the day of the closing, all the men had cigars like proud parents. Harlan told the local newspaper, "We are hostages no more. We bought the land from Pharaoh."

Mary approached me after the closing to thank me for my work. "You're a smart young man, you could get a job on Wall Street. You don't need to hang around with a bunch of old fogies like us."

"Oh, that's not how I feel," I replied. "There is nowhere I'd rather be."

Then Mary leaned confidentially toward me and whispered, "Have you ever tried Noxzema? You know, for your skin."

The Bernardston tenants—now owners—had taught me something about solidarity, about the power of community.

I did not have to write a check that day. But sitting there had opened the door to a thinking process. Why not? What would happen if I gave the money away to meet some of the urgent needs around me? I was beginning to understand the rather remarkable privileges that had flowed my way.

At the age of 26, I had three or four times as much money as all the residents of the Bernardston mobile home park combined. There is no rationale I could find that could justify this disparity.

So I decided to give away the wealth. I wrote my parents a letter thanking them for the tremendous opportunities this wealth made possible. And I explained that while having the money was a boost in helping pay for my education, it was now a barrier to my making my own way in the world. I intended to "pass the wealth on."

My father immediately called me when he got the letter. He flew out from Michigan to Massachusetts to meet with me. We talked for a day, and during that time he lovingly asked me a dozen what-if questions. "You're young and single. But over the course of a lifetime, bad things can happen," he said. "What if you get married and your spouse becomes ill? Wouldn't this money make life easier? What if you have a child and that child has a special need, wouldn't you wish you had this money?"

I had thought about many of these scenarios and more. And my response to my father was, "Well, then I would be in the same boat as 99 percent of the people I know, and I would have to ask for help."

"Without this money, you might have to fall back on the government," my father warned. "And that's a terrible system."

"Well, then I'll have a stake in making that system better," I replied, appreciating his parental concern.

"That's pretty idealistic," said my father. But after a day of walking and talking, he was reassured that I had not been possessed by an alien cult.

A few months later I drove to the National Bank of Detroit and signed the paperwork to transfer all the funds in my name to four grant-making foundations.

My trustee at the bank was an African American woman named Glenda whom I'd had very little contact with. We talked briefly about my decision. She looked at me at one point and said, "Are you going to be all right?"

"Yeah, I think I'm going to be all right," I replied. But I didn't know for sure.

Nor did I fully understand the tall mountain of privilege I still had. I was a white college-educated male in the United States, with a debt-free education and an extended family and social network. At the time, if felt like I was taking a leap of faith. I had my father's what-if questions in my head, and an awareness of the fragility of life.

A few months later, something bad did happen. The top floor of the house I was living in burned down. No one was injured, but I lost everything I owned. What wasn't burned was destroyed by the hundreds of gallons of water that had been dumped into the house.

The next morning, the sun came out and shone down on the sooty mess that was our house. My housemate Greg was sifting through piles, recovering little fragments of photographs.

Four cars pulled up to our house. Out climbed a dozen people from the Bernardston mobile home park. They had casseroles and shovels and trash bags. They had come to help.

At that moment, I thought, "I'm going to be okay."

39

Gentrification Will Drive My Uncle Out of His Neighborhood, and I Will Have Helped

Eric Rodriguez

My *tio* Pedro lives behind a trendy bar on Sunset Boulevard in Los Angeles's Echo Park. The apartment owners told him the other day that the price of rent would be going up—again. He is one of many who will be pushed out by rising prices, and I am one of the very people pushing him out.

Since moving back here in July 2014, I've had one foot in my former community and the other in this new place I call "home"—while slowly robbing my uncle of his own. I don't know what the right thing to do is. I did what he and moms told me to do to avoid the gangs and violence: I got an education, and I earn more money than the rest of my family. I made it out of the neighborhood. Now, moving back feels wrong.

When I was a kid you could buy tacos at the park for a dollar. The vendors upped their prices the moment different people came into the neighborhood and were willing to pay more. Now many of the *mamis* with their thin eyebrows and big hooped earrings can't afford living here, nor can many of the shaved headed homies in white t-shirts and tattoos. They're disappearing. As are those random *tiendas* at the center of commerce on Sunset Boulevard which close every other week, only to be replaced by a new coffee shop.

My *tio* works in construction so money is not, well, flowing. Not in the way it does to the developers who buy up charming bungalows in the neighborhood and then demolish them to build mid-rise monstrosities. It's "modern" and makes money, the developers say. You don't get it, they tell me, despite having lived in one in New York City and being an alumnus of a Wall Street investment bank. I get it, I just don't agree with it. *Tío* Pedro could not afford to live in one; he actually thinks they're hideous too. And so he laments the former neighborhood, its charm and character and affordability, minus the gangs and violence, of course.

Violence was common back in the 1990s around here. The park was off-limits at night because of the drug dealing and gang fights. It's different now; the park is safer than ever. I took a girl there for a walk around the lake in the evening the other day and saw the bust of José Marti, the Cuban revolutionary whose writings and philosophy led to Cuba's independence from Spain, and smiled at the thought of how Echo Park itself had wrestled its independence from the crime and violence it was once chained to.

But there are bizarre things happening now.

The other day a few friends and I smoked a joint near the boathouse and no one—not even the cops—cared much to stop and check things out. Back in the day it didn't go down like that at all. Don't take my word for it either, look at Frank Romero's "Arrest of the Paleteros." Even selling ice cream those days was a crime for people of color.

One day my cousin, Echo Park Pete, was walking with me around the lake and he said, referring to the drug use: "Man, I went to jail for this shit and now people do it all the time and the cops don't give a shit." I thought about offering a plausible explanation, you know, invoking my Ivy League education, but it felt forced. It is what it is: discrimination. I kept my stupid mouth shut.

This is the *new* neighborhood. A place where coffee shops and trendy bars are popping up, and drug use at the park goes unchecked because the new people using look different than the ones previously using. One group of people is moving in and another is being moved out. Call it gentrification; call it what you want, but it's happening. I see it happening—because I'm part of it.

40

How Occupy Wall Street Changes Everything

Sarah van Gelder

. . .

Something happened in September 2011 so unexpected that no politician or pundit saw it coming.

Inspired by the Arab Spring and uprisings in Europe, sparked by a challenge from *Adbusters* magazine to show up at Wall Street on September 17 and "bring a tent," and encouraged by veteran New York activists, a few thousand people gathered in the financial district of New York City. At the end of the day, some of them set up camp in Zuccotti Park and started what became a national—and now international—movement.

The Occupy movement, as it has come to be called, named the source of the crises of our time: Wall Street banks, big corporations, and others among the 1% are claiming the world's wealth for themselves at the expense of the 99% and having their way with our governments. This is a truth that political insiders and the media had avoided, even while the assets of the top 1% reached levels not seen since the 1920s. But now that this genie is out of the bottle, it can't easily be put back in.

Without offices, paid staff, or a bank account, Occupy Wall Street quickly spread beyond New York. People gathered in Boston, Chicago, Los Angeles, Portland, Atlanta, San Diego, and hundreds of other cities around the United States and claimed the right of *we the people* to create a world that works for the 99%. In a matter of weeks, the occupations and protests had spread worldwide, to over 1,500 cities, from Madrid to Cape Town and from Buenos Aires to Hong Kong, involving hundreds of thousands of people.

The Occupy Wall Street movement is not just demanding change. It is also transforming how we, the 99%, see ourselves. The shame many of us felt when we couldn't find a job, pay down our debts, or keep our home is being replaced by a political awakening. Millions now recognize that we are not to blame for a weak economy, for a subprime mortgage meltdown, or for a tax system that favors the wealthy but bankrupts the government. The 99% are coming to see that we are collateral damage in an all-out effort by the super-rich to get even richer.

. . .

By naming the issue, the movement has changed the political discourse. No longer can the interests of the 99% be ignored. The movement has unleashed the political power of millions and issued an open invitation to everyone to be part of creating a new world.

Historians may look back at September 2011 as the time when the 99% awoke, named our crisis, and faced the reality that none of our leaders are going to solve it. This is the moment when we realized we would have to act for ourselves.

THE TRUTH IS OUT: THE SYSTEM IS RIGGED IN FAVOR OF THE WEALTHY

One of the signs at the Occupy Seattle protest reads: "Dear 1%. We were asleep. Now we've woken up. Signed, the 99%."

This sign captures the feeling of many in the Occupy movement. We are seeing our ways of life, our aspirations, and our security slip away—not because we have been lazy or undisciplined, or lacked intelligence and motivation, but because the wealthiest among us have rigged the system to enhance their own power and wealth at the expense of everyone else.

. . .

The government actively facilitates this concentration of wealth through tax breaks for corporations and the wealthy, and bailouts for giant banks and corporations. These entities also benefit from mining rights, logging rights, airwave rights, and countless other licenses to use common assets for private profit. Corporations shift the costs of environmental damage to the public and pocket the profits. Taxpayers bear the risk of global financial speculation while the payoffs go to those most effective at gaming the system. Instead of investing profits to provide jobs and produce needed goods and services, the 1% put their wealth into mergers, acquisitions, and more speculation.

The list of government interventions on behalf of the 1% goes on and on: Tax breaks favor the wealthy, global trade agreements encourage offshoring jobs, agricultural subsidies favor agribusiness over family farms, corporate media get sanctioned monopolies while independent media gets squeezed.

. . .

This lopsided division of wealth corrupts government. Few among the 99% now believe government works for their benefit—and for good reason. With the 1% commanding an army of lobbyists and doling out money from multimillion-dollar campaign war chests, government has become a source of protection and subsidies for Wall Street. No wonder there isn't enough money left over for education, repairing roads and bridges, taking care of veterans and retirees, much less for the critical transition we need to make to a clean energy future.

The system is broken in so many ways that it's dizzying to try to name them all. This is part of the reason why the Occupy movement hasn't created a list of demands. The problem is everywhere and looks different from every point of view. The one thing the protesters all seem to agree on is that the middle-class way of life is moving out of reach. Talk to people at any of the Occupy sites and you'll hear stories of people who play by the rules, work long hours, study hard, and then find only low-wage jobs, often without health care coverage or prospects for a secure future.

And many can find no job at all. In the United States, twenty-five million people are unemployed, underemployed or have given up looking for work. Forty-five percent of those without jobs have been unemployed for more than twenty-seven weeks. Some employers won't hire anyone who is currently unemployed. Meanwhile, the cost of health care, education, rent, food, and energy continues to rise; the only thing that's falling is the value of homes and retirement funds.

Behind these statistics are real people. Since the Occupy movement began, some who identify themselves as part of the 99% have been posting their stories at wearethe99percent. tumblr.com. Here's one: "I am a lucky one. I have enough money to eat three of four weeks of the month. I have been paying student loans for fifteen years and still no dent. My husband lost his job . . . Last year I took a 10 percent pay cut to 'do my share' and keep layoffs at bay. I lost my house. I went bankrupt. I still am paying over one thousand dollars in student loans for myself and my husband and that is just interest. We will not have children. How could we when we can't even feed ourselves? I am the 99%."

Another personal story, by a sixty-year-old, reads, "Got laid off. Moved two thousand miles for new job. Pays 40 percent less than old job. Sold home at a loss. Filed Chapter Eleven. Owe IRS fifty thousand dollars. Fifteen thousand dollar per year debt for son's tuition at state university. Seventy-five percent of retirement funds shifted to the 1%! I am the 99%!"

The Web site contains thousands of stories like these.

Now that we know we are not alone, we are less likely to blame ourselves when things are hard. And now that we are seeing the ways the system is rigged against us, we can join with others to demand changes that will allow everyone to thrive.

. . .

Hundreds of thousands have participated in the protests and occupations, millions support the occupations, and tens of millions more support their key issues. Polls show that jobs continues to be the issue that most concerns us, yet the national dialogue has been dominated by obsession with debt. While just 27 percent of Americans responding to an October 2011 *Time Magazine* poll held a favorable view of the Tea Party, for example, 54 percent held a favorable view of the Occupy Wall Street movement. Of those familiar with the protests, large majorities share their concerns: 86 percent agreed that Wall Street and lobbyists have too much power in Washington, DC, 68 percent thought the rich should pay more taxes, and 79 percent believe the gap between rich and poor has grown too large.

The movement has been criticized for its diversity of people and grievances, but in that diversity lies its strength. Among the 99% are recent graduates and veterans who can't find work, elderly who fear losing their pensions, the long-term unemployed, the homeless, peace activists, people with a day job in a corporate office who show up after work, members of the military, and off-duty police. Those involved cannot be pigeonholed. They are as diverse as the people of this country and this world.

The movement has also been criticized for its failure to issue a list of demands. In fact, it is easy to see what the movement is demanding: quite simply, a world that works for the 99%. The hand-lettered protest signs show the range of concerns: excessive student debt; banks that took taxpayer bailouts, then refused to help homeowners stay in their homes; cuts in government funding for essential services; Federal Reserve policies; the lack of jobs.

A list of specific demands would make it easier to manage, criticize, co-opt, and divide the movement. Instead, Occupy Wall Street is setting its own agenda on its own terms and developing consensus statements at its own pace. It's doing this in spaces that it controls—some in parks and other public spaces, others in union halls, libraries, churches, and community centers. On the Internet, the movement issues statements and calls to action through Twitter, Facebook, and its own Web sites. From the start it was clear that the movement would not rely on a mainstream media corrupted by corporate interests.

The Occupy Wall Street movement does not treat power as something to request—something that others can either grant or withhold. *We the people* are the sovereigns under the Constitution. The Occupy Wall Street movement has become a space where a multitude of leaders are learning to work together, think independently, and define the world we want to live in.

Those leaders will be stirring things up for years to come.

. . .

NEXT STEPS

WHAT NEXT?

The organizers of the September 17 occupation say they weren't planning for an occupation that would go on week after week. It just hadn't occurred to them. And no one can say where things will go from here. Harsh weather could drive people away. Other hazards could undercut the movement. Police violence could frighten away would-be protesters, or it could galvanize the movement, as did the pepper spraying of unarmed women in Manhattan and police violence against occupiers in Oakland.

. . .

But the movement has important strengths that add to its resilience. It is radically decentralized, so a disaster at any one occupation will not bring down the others; in fact, the others can take action in support. There is no single leader who could be co-opted or assassinated. Instead, leadership is broadly shared, and leadership skills are being taught and learned constantly.

. . .

New support is flowing in, some from unexpected sources. A group of Marine veterans has formed OccupyMARINES, which will work to recruit police and members of other branches of the military to support the occupations, and to nonviolently protect protesters from police assaults. The Marines also plan to help the occupations sustain themselves through cold weather. The group was inspired by a viral video showing Marine Sergeant Shamar Thomas dressing down the police for brutalizing protesters. "There is no honor in this," he shouted at the police. The wounding of Marine veteran Scott Olsen, who at twenty-four years old had already served two tours in Iraq, has further fired up fellow Marines. Olsen was critically injured by a police-fired projectile in an Oakland police action against occupiers.

Police, though often shown cracking down on occupations, have also expressed sympathy with the movement. In Albany, New York, state and city police declined to follow orders from the mayor to arrest and remove peaceful protesters. "We don't have those resources, and these people were not causing trouble," an official with the state patrol told the *Times Union* newspaper.

Will there come a time when there is no one willing to enforce orders to evict members of the 99% from occupation encampments—or from their homes, for that matter? And if popular support grows, will elected officials look to ally themselves with the movement, rather than suppress it? The fact that these are even questions shows how radically things have changed since a few hundred people occupied Zuccotti Park on September 17, 2011.

Whatever happens next, Occupy Wall Street has already accomplished something that changes everything. It has fundamentally altered the national conversation.

. . .

Now that millions recognize the injustice resulting from the power of Wall Street and giant corporations, that issue will not go away. The central question now is this: Will we build a society to benefit everyone? Or just the 1%?

10 WAYS THE OCCUPY MOVEMENT CHANGES EVERYTHING

Sarah Van Gelder, David Korten, and Steve Piersanin

Many question whether this movement can really make a difference. The truth is that it is already changing everything. Here's how.

1. **It names the source of the crisis.**
   The problems of the 99% are caused by Wall Street greed, perverse financial incentives, and a corporate take-over of the political system.
2. **It provides a vision of the world we want.**
   We can create a world that works for everyone, not just the wealthiest 1%.
3. **It sets a new standard for public debate.**
   Those advocating policies and proposals must now demonstrate that their ideas will benefit the 99%. Serving only the 1% is no longer sufficient.

4. **It presents a new narrative.**
   The solution is no longer to starve government, but to free society and government from corporate dominance.
5. **It creates a big tent.**
   We, the 99%, are made up of people of all ages, races, occupations, and political beliefs, and we are learning to work together with respect.
6. **It offers everyone a chance to create change.**
   No one is in charge. Anyone can get involved and make things happen.
7. **It is a movement, not a list of demands.**
   The call for transformative structural change, not temporary fixes and single-issue reforms, is the movement's sustaining power.
8. **It combines the local and the global.**
   People are setting their own local agendas, tactics, and aims. But we also share solidarity, communication, and vision at the global level.
9. **It offers an ethic and practice of deep democracy and community.**
   Patient decision-making translates into wisdom and common commitment when every voice is heard. Occupy sites are communities where anyone can discuss grievances, hopes, and dreams in an atmosphere of mutual support.
10. **We have reclaimed our power.**
    Instead of looking to politicians and leaders to bring about change, we can see now that the power rests with us. Instead of being victims of the forces upending our lives, we are claiming our sovereign right to remake the world.

41

"Classism From Our Mouths" and "Tips From Working-Class Activists"

Betsy Leondar-Wright

We've all learned classist prejudices, and none of us has completely eradicated them from our minds.

. . .

And we all make mistakes. There's not a middle-class person alive who hasn't said dumb, insensitive things that step on working-class toes. Hiding our classist mistakes or defending ourselves ("I didn't mean it that way") doesn't do any good. The only thing to do is to 'fess up, apologize, laugh at ourselves, and commit to learning how do better in the future.

As we talk, working-class people notice how oblivious or how aware of class issues we seem, and make decisions about how much to collaborate with us based on those evaluations, among other factors. The goal of reducing the classism in our speech is not to keep ourselves out of trouble by avoiding angering working-class people, and it's not to reach some kind of perfect non-classist purity. The goal is to make ourselves more trustworthy and to alienate working-class people less so that we can work together for economic justice and other common goals.

N E X T   S T E P S

TOP THESE! A FEW CLASSIST THINGS I'VE SAID
(IF I CAN ADMIT MINE, YOU CAN ADMIT YOURS)

- I came back from college and bumped into a working-class guy I'd known in high school. I asked what he was doing. "Bagging groceries at the supermarket." I said, "Oh, is it interesting?" He just looked at me like I was an idiot.
- In college, I was going door-to-door in the dorms signing people up for an Oxfam fast in which we would all skip eating for a day and donate the money for famine relief. One guy said, "No, this isn't for me; I'm working my way through college. This is for people whose parents pay their tuition." I told him, "No, this is for everyone!" I wouldn't take no for an answer. He actually opened a drawer and showed me those little packages of peanut butter crackers he was eating for meals, and still I badgered him to contribute.
- My friend with an Associates degree said, "I am *so* tired of teaching dental hygiene." I said, "Well, why don't you try teaching something else?" She looked at me like I was clueless and said, "Because I don't know anything else."

WHAT'S THE MOST CLASSIST THING YOU'VE HEARD AN ACTIVIST SAY?

Five interviewees' answers to this question – and mine:

> Recently I was facilitating a discussion for an organization that was trying to decide how much severance pay to give a staff person leaving because the organization couldn't afford to keep them full-time. Someone said, "Let's give them a huge party and show them we love them, and they'll remember that a lot longer than any money we give them."
>
> —Paul Kivel

> Most of the Homeowners Associations wanted in an icky way to "color up" with racial diversity. They were happy to have people of color at the table as long as they were in the minority and didn't get to make any decisions. At one meeting, this one white homeowner was complaining about "why Latinos won't come to our meetings" and she suggested that maybe people should bring their maids! It was too gross!
>
> —Roxana Tynan

Find the Invisible Working-Class People in These Statements

- Women still have to choose between career success and children.
- I bought some land in Vail and built my dream house.
- Everybody got burned in the stock market crash.
- I run an institute at the university.
- When I was a girl, every family had a cook.

—blw

> There was a fund-raising event that cost $50 and I heard comments about how "anyone can afford that."
>
> —Pam McMichael

Several times I've heard social welfare professionals say about poor mothers, "We have to speak for them because they can't speak for themselves."

—Theresa Funiciello

There was one guy I worked with, he thought he was the smartest organizer, and he would say things to me like "Can you turn out 500 people for this meeting and then we'll go and do the negotiations for them?" He thought of working-class people as props and their voices as sound bites.

I've heard people patronize, tokenize, and fetishize, like "Let's hear from the welfare recipient now! Isn't she smart?"

—Gilda Haas

A new friend said, "My neighbor wanted to put up a 15-foot fence that would block my view. He's real redneck low-life trailer trash." I told her I was offended by that, and we had a big argument that lasted all day.

—blw

. . .

In many organizations I've been part of, decision-making is hard. Middle-class people with more education are just faster and more articulate. Others are silenced because they can't keep up with the style of arguing.

—Barbara Willer

. . .

HANG IN

Low-income folks believe that middle-class folks won't stick around. When the going gets tough, they'll leave. It's a vicious cycle: it happens so much that there's no trust, so middle-class people wonder why they should stick around if they're not trusted. The key is to stick with it even if pushed away. You'll be tested. Like when [civil rights pioneer] Septima Clark sent me as a white person to a black church meeting, and I came back saying they didn't want me there. She asked "What did you expect? Now, next time you go . . ." She kept sending me back to that group until I had built trust.

I really value middle-class activists when they're willing to stick it through hard times—and I say that coming out of an area where doing this work meant Klan harassment and threats.

—Linda Stout

. . .

SUPPORT WORKING-CLASS ISSUES

. . .

Want to be an ally? Honor boycotts, buy union, use union printers, don't cross picket lines, pay a living wage, and give family leave and good benefits.

—Felice Yeskel

N
E
X
T

S
T
E
P
S

In the 1980s in my city, the Nuclear Freeze campaign put a referendum on the ballot, and 60 percent of the voters supported a freeze on nuclear weapons. Then Jobs with Peace proposed a followup referendum calling for more jobs through peace conversion, which had the potential for even more public and labor support. But most of the Freeze people just faded away, uninterested.

I was asked to speak at a statewide Freeze convention, and I made a strong pitch for reaching out to labor and working-class people. Afterwards, in the hallway, a number of working-class people came up to me and said it made a big difference to them; they hadn't had the nerve to raise it themselves.

Sometimes peace activists kind of raise their noses, as if it's more pure to be against war for idealistic reasons, as if it's a bit tawdry to be concerned with jobs and self-interest.

—George Lakey

USE YOUR PRIVILEGE

If you have privilege, have a conversation with low-income leaders about how you could use it strategically. If you have a country house, maybe we could have a retreat there. It's not just your money, it's who you know, what you know, how you talk.

We were organizing a conference on homelessness, and members of our group who were homeless were going to speak. There was a woman who had a lot of classism. She said, "How are you going to find homeless people to ask to speak? Would they know enough? How could you find homeless people who can talk well enough?" I was going to debate someone on the Governor's Council, and she said, "Do you know how to debate? Do you know enough information to debate? Would you be able to keep up with him?" I asked my owning-class coworker to talk with her, and she persuaded her. Now this woman points out classism when it happens. That's the fastest turn-around I've seen. My coworker was able because of her similar background to explain how things sounded. It was a strategic use of privilege.

—Lisa Richards

People with more privilege need to figure out how to equalize things, which doesn't mean to empty out their bank accounts. But it's the responsibility of activists to be generous and to figure out how to support things they care about materially if they possibly can.

—Barbara Smith

I resent people who try to pass as someone like me. I met an upper-middle-class woman who said, "I'm on welfare so I can be a full-time activist with youth." That's not what welfare's there for. I hate it when people hide their privilege and don't acknowledge it.

—Rachel Rybaczuk

If grassroots people have attitudes of racism or anti immigrant prejudice, a negative approach isn't productive. Nobody likes to be told they are wrong, especially by a more privileged person. Instead, ask questions and help someone learn. Hold fast to principles, but let go of ideology. Equity is a principle, but "only one way to get there" is ideology.

—Barbara Willer

LET GO OF CONTROL

I've seen this pattern over and over. A cross-class alliance is formed to deal with a problem. A group with resources offers to sponsor it. They staff it, they control the funding, they control the information . . . . Next thing you know, we have our own class divide internally. We build power just to give it away, without knowing it's been given away until it's gone.

—Sam Grant

I helped start a community development corporation that created affordable housing. The board was all professionals, and all of us in the houses were neighborhood people. There was so much tension over decision-making and who had the control. We argued over what color paint to use. The middle-class folks didn't get the concerns about power and why the working-class folks were so frustrated. We had no language for it, because everyone was white, so weren't we all the same?

—Barbara Willer

RECOGNIZE WORKING-CLASS PEOPLE'S CONSTRAINTS

I remember going to a national women's group conference. They wanted low-income people and people of color there, so we said sure, Piedmont Peace Project would bring a group of folks in. First, they didn't do a sliding scale, which was shocking enough. But the worst thing was, we came with kids in tow, and we got there and there was no childcare. We had to turn around and go home. We were so used to providing childcare, we assumed there would be childcare.

Some groups have meetings in the middle of the day, and then wonder why no working people come. Ridiculous! We used to plan meetings taking people's work hours into consideration. In farm communities, we'd meet after dark. With millworkers, we'd have meetings in shifts, one in the morning and one at 6 P.M. You've got to know your constituency.

—Linda Stout

42

Deep Thoughts About Class Privilege

Karen Pittelman and Resource Generation

CLASS PRIVILEGE AFFECTS OUR FINANCIAL FUTURE

A job interview is only one of many situations where class privilege affects our financial future. Every time we walk into a bank for a loan, into a real estate broker's office for a home, even into an important meeting at work, being a young person with wealth gives us an unspoken advantage.

Another advantage comes from the fact that class privilege can place us in some very powerful networks. Networks are one of the main ways people find out about things like jobs, housing and business opportunities. Class privilege gives us access to exclusive formal associations like alumni groups and prestigious clubs, as well as informal webs of influential neighbors, family and friends.

These connections don't just tell us about possible opportunities, they can also help us act on them. When someone "in the know" puts in a good word for us, it transforms us from an anonymous name into a friendly face—and that can often make all the difference.

THIS DOESN'T MEAN WE DON'T WORK HARD

Thinking about the impact of class privilege on our lives can be unsettling, especially if we grew up wealthy and don't have any other class experience to compare it to. We want to say that our successes happen because we deserve them—because we worked hard, because we studied and sacrificed, because we were committed to our goals. We want to say that maybe we had that privilege, but we chose not to use it, that we didn't need it, that we could make it on our own merits.

The problem is that privilege isn't something that can be turned on or off. While money can be laid aside unused, privilege is deeply embedded in our lives. It's a part of the experiences that make us who we are, that shape how we see the world and the way the world sees us. Class privilege even becomes a part of our bodies, from straight teeth to a "firm" handshake.

Acknowledging how class privilege impacts our lives doesn't have to mean abandoning pride in ourselves. Our hard work is still hard work. Our fabulousness is still fabulous. It just means that, as young people with wealth, the story of where we are and how we got there is more complicated than a list of our merits. There's a lot more there to uncover.

DEEP THOUGHTS ABOUT CLASS PRIVILEGE

Here are some seriously heavy questions about the impact of class privilege in our lives. Woo hoo! Yeah!

Okay, maybe that's a little overzealous. It'd probably be much more fun to watch *MacGyver* reruns and eat Funyuns. But even though it isn't easy, understanding our privilege has the potential to change our lives and our relationships in some amazing ways. Plus, the more we understand, the better we'll be at using our privilege for social change. . . . And, obviously, depending on your background and what's up for you right now in your life, some of these questions will be more or less relevant. Feel free to skip anything that doesn't pertain . . .

BIG DECISIONS

- Think about a big decision you've made recently. Were there ways that having class privilege factored into that decision?
- Has having class privilege ever affected the way you've been able to cope with a difficult or painful time in your life? How so?
- What's one of the biggest risks you've taken—or wish you could have taken—in your life? Were there resources of your own or family resources that you could have fallen back on if it didn't work out? Did that affect your choice to take the risk?

WORK AND SCHOOL

- Has having class privilege affected your education? How so? Has it had an effect on your choices about schools? About what to study?
- Has having class privilege had an effect on your decisions about work? Has it had an impact on your salary, income or level of prestige associated with your work?

WHERE YOU LIVE

- Has having class privilege played a role in your housing decisions? Has it affected where you've lived in the past? Where you live now? The way other people involved, like brokers, realtors and landlords, treated you? Whether you rent or own? If you own, did it impact the way you paid for your home?

DISCRIMINATION

- Are there ways that class privilege *hasn't* made any difference for you in dealing with discrimination? How so?
- Are there ways that class privilege *has* made a difference for you in dealing with discrimination? How so?
- How have your experiences with discrimination impacted the way you understand class privilege?

OTHER KINDS OF PRIVILEGE

- Do you have other kinds of privilege in addition to class privilege? How does that affect the way you look at your experiences with class privilege?
- Has there ever been a time when having privilege made it harder to hear what someone was trying to say to you?

If you grew up with wealth . . .

- Were there ways that class privilege had an impact on your daily life? How so?
- Did having class privilege ever affect the way people treated you? How?
- Did having class privilege affect the way you saw your own potential and your role in the world? How?

If wealth is a more recent thing in your life . . .

- Are there ways that having class privilege has changed your daily life?
- Are there ways that having class privilege has changed the way people treat you?
- Has having class privilege affected your sense of what's possible in your life and your hopes for the future? How so?

SOCIAL SITUATIONS

- Have you ever been in a situation where you knew the "right" way to act because of your class privilege? Or the "right" way to speak? Or where you got a joke or a reference to something that you understood because you had class privilege?

NEXT STEPS

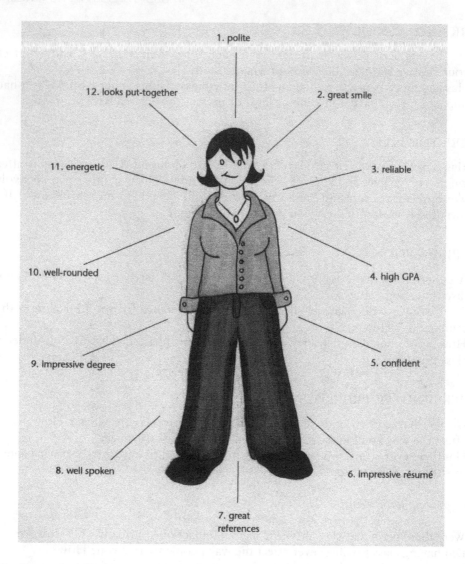

N E X T   S T E P S

FINANCIAL STATUS

- Does having class privilege affect your current income and expenses? Do you have loans? Car payments? Mortgage payments? Do you have a financial safety net or family resources you can fall back on?
- Does having class privilege affect the way you are treated at the bank? How?

HEALTH

- Does having class privilege impact the kind of healthcare you receive? The quality of your doctors? Dental work? Therapy?
- If you've had to deal with a major illness or injury, either your own or a family member's, did having class privilege have an impact on your choices about treatments and options?

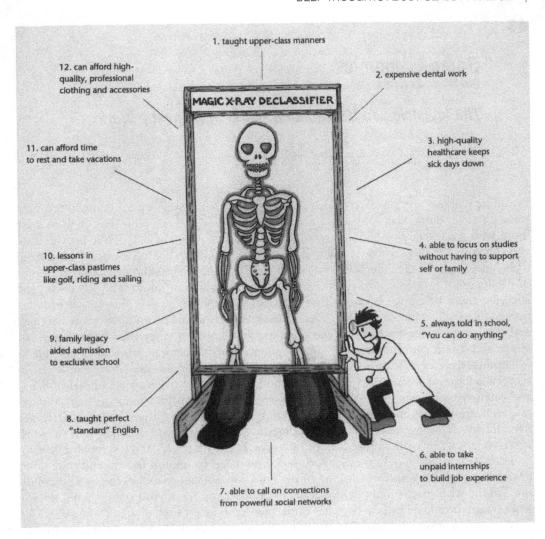

1. taught upper-class manners

2. expensive dental work

3. high-quality healthcare keeps sick days down

4. able to focus on studies without having to support self or family

5. always told in school, "You can do anything"

6. able to take unpaid internships to build job experience

7. able to call on connections from powerful social networks

8. taught perfect "standard" English

9. family legacy aided admission to exclusive school

10. lessons in upper-class pastimes like golf, riding and sailing

11. can afford time to rest and take vacations

12. can afford high-quality, professional clothing and accessories

MAGIC X-RAY DECLASSIFIER

N E X T   S T E P S

LEGAL SYSTEM

- If you've had to deal with the police or the legal system, did having class privilege affect your options and the outcome of the experience? How?

In boarding school, I remember being told, "You guys are the cream of the cream. The education you are receiving here is preparing you to be leaders in the world." I realized that the other young people in my class weren't necessarily that special. They were nice, but they weren't so great. It just made me wonder why these people get to be the leaders. Why do I get to be the leader? There's no real reason for that. It's the luck of the draw.

—Christian

43

Home Economics

The Invisible and Unregulated World of Domestic Work

National Domestic Workers Alliance

Domestic workers are critical to the US economy. They help families meet many of the most basic physical, emotional, and social needs of the young and the old. They help to raise those who are learning to be fully contributing members of our society. They provide care and company for those whose working days are done, and who deserve ease and comfort in their older years. While their contributions may go unnoticed and uncalculated by measures of productivity, domestic workers free the time and attention of millions of other workers, allowing them to engage in the widest range of socially productive pursuits with undistracted focus and commitment. The lives of these workers would be infinitely more complex and burdened absent the labor of the domestic workers who enter their home each day. Household labor, paid and unpaid, is indeed the work that makes all other work possible.

Despite their central role in the economy, domestic workers are often employed in substandard jobs. Working behind closed doors, beyond the reach of personnel policies, and often without employment contracts, they are subject to the whims of their employers. Some employers are terrific, generous, and understanding. Others, unfortunately, are demanding, exploitative, and abusive. Domestic workers often face issues in their work environment alone, without the benefit of co-workers who could lend a sympathetic ear.

The social isolation of domestic work is compounded by limited federal and state labor protections for this workforce. Many of the laws and policies that govern pay and conditions in the workplace simply do not apply to domestic workers. And even when domestic workers are protected by law, they have little power to assert their rights.

Domestic workers' vulnerability to exploitation and abuse is deeply rooted in historical, social, and economic trends. Domestic work is largely women's work. It carries the long legacy of the devaluation of women's labor in the household. Domestic work in the US also carries the legacy of slavery with its divisions of labor along lines of both race and gender. The women who perform domestic work today are, in substantial measure, immigrant workers, many of whom are undocumented, and women of racial and ethnic minorities. These workers enter the labor force bearing multiple disadvantages.

Home Economics: The Invisible and Unregulated World of Domestic Work presents the results of the first national survey of domestic workers in the US. It breaks new ground by providing an empirically based and representative picture of domestic employment in 21st century America. We asked a sample of domestic workers a standardized set of questions focusing on four aspects of the industry:

- pay rates, benefits, and their impact on the lives of workers and their families;
- employment arrangements and employers' compliance with employment agreements;
- workplace conditions, on-the-job injuries, and access to health care;
- abuse at work and the ability to remedy substandard conditions.

We surveyed 2,086 nannies, caregivers, and housecleaners in 14 metropolitan areas. The survey was conducted in nine languages. Domestic workers from 71 countries were interviewed. The study employed a participatory methodology in which 190 domestic workers and organizers from 34 community organizations collaborated in survey design, the fielding of the survey, and the preliminary analysis of the data.

SUMMARY OF FINDINGS

The survey revealed that substandard working conditions are pervasive in the domestic work industry. Wage rates are low, the work is often hazardous, and workers rarely have effective recourse to improve substandard conditions.

- Low pay is a systemic problem in the domestic work industry.
  - o 23 percent of workers surveyed are paid below the state minimum wage.
  - o 70 percent are paid less than $13 an hour.
  - o 67 percent of live-in workers are paid below the state minimum wage, and the median hourly wage of these workers is $6.15.
  - o Using a conservative measure of income adequacy, 48 percent of workers are paid an hourly wage in their primary job that is below the level needed to adequately support a family.

- Domestic workers rarely receive employment benefits.
  - o Less than 2 percent receive retirement or pension benefits from their primary employer.
  - o Less than 9 percent work for employers who pay into Social Security.
  - o 65 percent do not have health insurance, and only 4 percent receive employer-provided insurance.

- Domestic workers experience acute financial hardships. Many indicate that their most basic needs go unmet.
  - o 60 percent spend more than half of their income on rent or mortgage payments.
  - o 37 percent of workers paid their rent or mortgage late during the year prior to being interviewed.
  - o 40 percent paid some of their other essential bills late during the same time period.
  - o 20 percent report that there were times in the previous month when there was no food to eat in their homes because there was no money to buy any.

- Domestic workers have little control over their working conditions. Employment is usually arranged without the benefit of a formal contract.
  - o Key provisions in standard employment agreements are often absent for domestic workers.
  - o 35 percent of domestic workers report that they worked long hours without breaks in the prior 12 months.
  - o 25 percent of live-in workers had responsibilities that prevented them from getting at least five hours of uninterrupted sleep at night during the week prior to being interviewed.
  - o 30 percent of workers who have a written contract or other agreement report that their employers disregarded at least one of the provision in the prior 12 months.
  - o Among workers who are fired from a domestic work job, 23 percent are fired for complaining about working conditions, and 18 percent are fired for protesting violations of their contract or agreement.

NEXT STEPS

- Domestic work can be hazardous. Workers risk long-term exposure to toxic chemicals and a range of workplace injuries.
  - 38 percent of workers suffered from work-related wrist, shoulder, elbow, or hip pain in the past 12 months.
  - 31 percent suffered from other soreness and pain in the same period.
  - 29 percent of housecleaners suffered from skin irritation, and 20 percent had trouble breathing in the prior 12 months.
  - 36 percent of nannies contracted an illness while at work in the prior 12 months.
  - 29 percent of caregivers suffered a back injury in the prior 12 months.
- Domestic workers experience disrespect and abuse on the job.
  - Interviews with domestic workers reveal that they often endure verbal, psychological, and physical abuse on the job—without recourse. Domestic workers, who are unprotected by contracts and laws available to other workers, fear employer retaliation.
  - 91 percent of workers who encountered problems with their working conditions in the prior 12 months did not complain because they were afraid they would lose their job.
  - 85 percent of undocumented immigrants who encountered problems with their working conditions in the prior 12 months did not complain because they feared their immigration status would be used against them.

RECOMMENDATIONS—TOWARDS A CARING ECONOMY

. . . Transforming the conditions outlined in this report requires action on several fronts. We must enact and enforce policies that address the exclusion from employment and labor protections that are specific to domestic workers; hold employers accountable to fair labor standards; create a more equitable economic environment for all low-wage workers; and support families in managing their caregiving responsibilities.

Policy makers, employers, workers' rights organizers and advocates, the philanthropic community, and domestic workers themselves all have essential roles to play in ensuring that domestic workers enjoy a full range of labor and employment rights and protections.

THE ROLE OF PUBLIC POLICY

Many of the laws and policies that govern pay and conditions in the workplace simply do not apply to domestic workers. Domestic workers, when hired directly by their employers, find no remedies in federal law for employment discrimination, unsafe working conditions, or constraints on their right to organize and bargain collectively. The absence of institutional protections leaves domestic workers particularly susceptible to employer exploitation and abuse.

At a minimum, public policy should provide domestic workers with:

- The **right to associate freely**, join organizations that advocate for workers' rights, choose representatives, and create frameworks to bargain collectively.

N E X T S T E P S

- **Inclusion in the minimum wage standards** in all states where domestic workers are currently excluded.
- **Equal rights to state and federal overtime pay** that other workers enjoy.
- **Equal rights to the meal breaks, rest breaks, and rest days** to which other workers in their states are entitled.
- **The right to adequate hours of uninterrupted sleep** for live-in domestic workers.
- **Inclusion in all state-level workers' compensation and unemployment** insurance programs.
- **Protection from discrimination, abuse, and harassment** under all state and federal anti-discrimination laws.
- **Inclusion in state and federal health and safety protections.**

In addition to these minimum workforce protections, policies are required to assure benefits, such as paid vacation and holidays, and notice of termination, that are difficult for domestic workers to negotiate with their employers.

EMPLOYERS CAN CATALYZE CHANGE

Employers have an extremely important role to play in improving the conditions in which domestic workers labor. Well into the 21st century, too many employers are still burdened with 19th century notions of service and subservience. Employers can create better relations with their employees, and improve workplace conditions by clarifying the terms of the employer-employee relationship, and educating themselves about fair labor standards.

There are many things employers can do to improve working conditions for domestic workers:

- Negotiate the terms of employment and provide a clear written agreement or contract.
- Keep accurate records of hours worked, pay, and other employment-related information required by law.
- Pay proper wages including overtime pay, annual raises, and payment when work is cancelled on short notice.
- Provide meal breaks, rest breaks, days off, and, for live-in workers, adequate time to sleep.
- Provide health coverage to full-time employees through either employer-provided insurance or a wage supplement.
- Pay into Social Security or an alternative retirement plan, workers' compensation, and unemployment insurance.
- Provide full-time employees with paid sick and/or personal days, paid maternity leave, paid holidays, and at least two weeks of paid vacation days.
- Respect the right to privacy, including allowing private means of communication for live-in workers.
- Provide advance notice of termination, and pay severance in accordance with the number of years worked.
- Provide employees with protective gear and the option of using nontoxic cleaning supplies.
- Practice respectful communication at all times.

NEXT STEPS

IMPROVED CONDITIONS FOR ALL LOW-WAGES WORKERS

It is difficult to advocate for the rights of domestic workers in an economic and political environment in which the rights of low-wage workers more broadly are so badly frayed. Public policies that raise standards across the low-wage labor market, and improve the working conditions and lives of low-wage workers, will positively affect the lives of domestic workers.

All low-wage workers, including domestic workers, would benefit from public policies that:

- **Increase the federal minimum wage** to a standard that better reflects the cost of maintaining an adequate, healthy standard of living.
- Provide **access to affordable medical care.**
- Strengthen the **enforcement** of wage and hour, health and safety, and other **workplace protections.**
- Ensure **access to** paid sick leave, family leave, maternity and parental leave, holidays, and vacation time.
- **Enact comprehensive immigration reform** to ensure that immigrant workers receive equal protection and status in the workplace.
- Create **pathways to career advancement.**
- Protect Social Security and ensure that all workers **have retirement income** to meet their basic needs.
- Create **pathways to citizenship** for immigrant workers.
- Protect workers who exercise their **right to organize** from employer retaliation.

. . . Domestic workers are an essential part of the solution. Their household labor is a lynchpin connecting the economics of the home and the economics of the workplace. By committing to improving their conditions of work, policy makers and employers—and indeed society as a whole—commit to building an economy based on dignity and care.

CONCLUSION

. . . Domestic workers are mobilizing creative ways to improve their position in the industry. Despite the legal and structural constraints on collective bargaining, they have developed organizations and alliances to amass collective power for change. Both in the US and globally, a domestic workers' movement for rights and respect has been steadily gaining strength. In 2011, the International Labour Organization adopted Convention No. 189, establishing, for the first time, global labor standards for the treatment of domestic workers.

In the US, the very first piece of legislation to provide for domestic workers' basic labor rights was passed by the New York State Legislature in 2010, after a game-changing, unprecedented six-year campaign led by a coalition of grassroots, member-led, domestic worker organizations. The New York Domestic Worker Bill of Rights sets enforceable standards for overtime pay, rest days, paid day off, and other worker protections. . . .

The opportunity is at hand to repair historic wrongs, respect the dignity of all honest labor, and improve, materially and substantially, the conditions of work for a critical sector of our society. Domestic workers, through their organizing, are pointing the way forward. It is past time for both employers and policy makers to take heed.

44

Charts from United for a Fair Economy

FEDERAL TAX RATES FOR TOP AND MEDIAN INCOME EARNERS

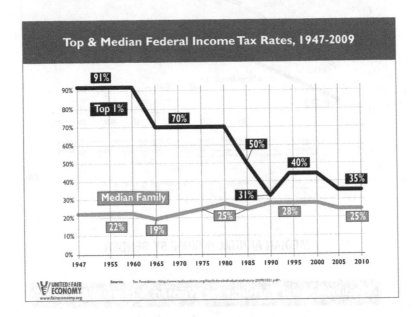

INCOME AND PRODUCTIVITY

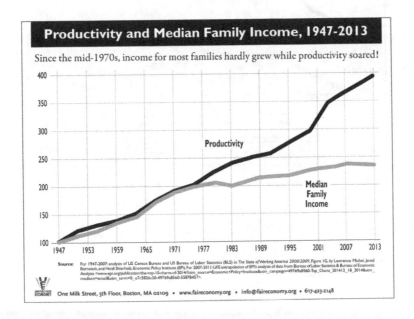

MEDIAN INCOME BY RACE

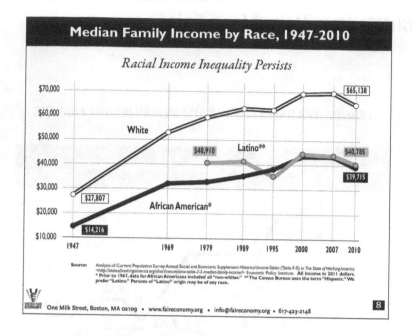

MEDIAN ANNUAL INCOME BY GENDER

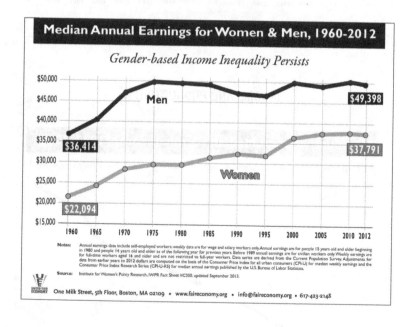

INCOME GROWTH BY QUINTILE

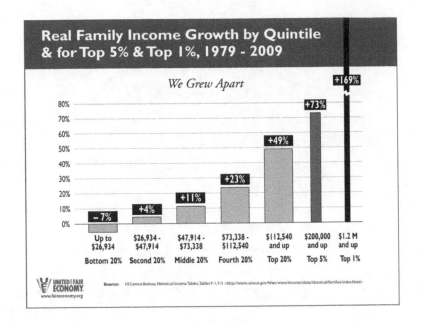

N E X T   S T E P S

See Chapter 8 in *Teaching for Diversity and Social Justice* for corresponding teaching materials.

SECTION 4

RELIGIOUS OPPRESSION

Introduction

Maurianne Adams and Christopher MacDonald-Dennis

PART I: OVERVIEW OF RELIGIOUS OPPRESSION

RELIGIOUS OPPRESSION INTERNATIONALLY AND IN THE UNITED STATES

The current efforts in the United States to ban Muslim immigrants because they are Muslims, because Muslims are stereotyped as terrorists, or because immigrants are themselves unwelcome, is not "new" to US history nor is it unique to the United States. In European countries, extreme measures are being considered in the wake of terrorist attacks and in an effort to draw firm boundaries around national identities deeply interwoven with Christian religious beliefs and practices. For Western-identified nations built on Christian traditions within or exported from Europe, today's influx of North-African, Arab and Asian immigrants who observe different religious faith traditions is felt to threaten a strongly felt religious, cultural, and national identity. The threat is intensified by the fear and the reality of terror attacks. The fear attached to this religious threat to national identity is part of a deeply rooted history in Europe and in the United States.

Christian nationalism is nothing new (Wills, 2002). Non-Protestant immigrants (Irish Catholics, Jews, Buddhists, Hindus, Muslims) became unwelcome in the United States once they began arriving in large numbers in the mid-19th century (Adams and Joshi, 2016; Kivel, 2013). In the United States, the connection of Christianity to national religious identity is expressed through today's Islamophobia and antisemitism (ADL, 2016; Potok, 2016). Christianity shapes the stereotyped religious prejudices that generations of European immigrants brought to the United States in their cultural luggage. It shapes homophobia, opposition to same-sex marriage, misogyny and feminist backlash, dismissal of Native people's tribal rights, based on the foundational belief that the United States is a Christian nation, an idea fundamentally at odds with the belief (also foundational) that the United States is a pluralistic nation based on the separation of "church" from "state."

This idea – which we will explain below as *Christian hegemony* – is a social justice issue that intersects with other forms of oppression. The "faces" of oppression (Young, selection 7) can be seen in the "faces" of religious oppression (Blumenfeld, selection 47). The selections in this section explore the many faces of Christian hegemony as a social justice issue, its intersections with other social justice issues, and the challenges it poses to the future of the United States as a pluralistic nation founded on generations of immigrants going all the way back to the "founding fathers," who (we often forget) themselves were immigrants.

These discussions are not easy to have in classrooms or workshops or communities or among friends and neighbors. Discussions that touch on religious identities and beliefs are fraught with emotion and tension, especially if framed as individual instances of "my" religious identity and convictions versus "yours" or others. But putting aside our personal convictions, it is possible to understand religion as a powerful societal force that affects local, national, and global politics and struggles. We see this in conflicts between nationalist Hindus and Muslims in India; Sunni or Shi'a (Islamic) struggles throughout the Middle East; Protestants and Catholics for control in Northern Ireland; Israelis and Palestinians for the same land and water in their homelands. In all these cases, religions have shaped national identity, justified conflicts, and also obscured powerful political, economic, and military forces also at work under the guise of religion.

Our focus in this section will be on the United States. The international examples are cited to illustrate how political, economic, and cultural inequality within the United States also can be concealed by the veneer of religious identity so that other dynamics of oppression and inequality are obscured and rationalized.

A SOCIAL JUSTICE APPROACH TO RELIGIOUS OPPRESSION

To understand the role of historic and systemic religious oppression in the United States, we need to examine religious oppression as a *social justice issue* similar in its workings to other social justice issues examined in this book. The "Getting Started: Core Concepts" introductory section in this volume presents frameworks for understanding how social group identity and advantage are socialized, internalized, enacted, and reproduced, from one generation to the next (Tatum, selection 1; Kirk and Okazawa-Rey, selection 2; Harro, selection 5). Social group identity privilege or marginalization take place at all levels of society – the personal, institutional, societal (Bell, selection 6; Adams and Zúñiga, selection 6; Young, selection 7). So when we take a social justice approach to different levels of religious oppression, we might notice the following. *On the individual and interpersonal level*: A Jewish woman hesitates to wear her Star of David on dates with a non-Jew; a mixed-religious couple struggle with religious pressures in the naming of a new-born child. *On the institutional level*: Sports team members engage in pre-game Christian prayer, unaware that they have excluded their Jewish or Muslim or atheist teammates and alienated their teamwork. *On the societal level*, we notice the increased frequency of Islamophobic or antisemitic harassment and violence that appear to be "individual" but have been enabled by increased acceptance of Islamophobia and antisemitism (Lichtblau, 2016) which are practiced by Christian nationalist organizations that have become increasingly visible within US political, nationalist, and religious culture (Foderaro, 2016; Lizza, 2016).

A social justice approach to religious oppressions asks that we understand individual social identity in relation to the social structures that perpetuate advantage and disadvantage (Tatum, selection 1; Kirk and Okazawa-Rey, selection 2; Johnson, selection 3) and apply that understanding to the distinction (at the societal level) between dominant and marginalized religious institutions and faith (or non-faith) systems (Adams and Joshi, 2016; Bayoumi, selection 48; Kivel, selection 61; Sue, selection 4). This approach calls attention to religious advantage and disadvantage based on stereotypes and misinformation about the religious "other" and to intersections with economic, political, and legal advantage or disadvantage (Kaye/Kantrowitz, selection 56; Ahmad and Zawam, selection 57).

Some definitions are needed for this section. In the 21st century, Protestants and Catholics are named by the umbrella term "Christianity," despite their different US and European sectarian histories. Most US colonists and settlers were members of different Protestant sects, often as violently opposed to Catholics as they were to Hindus, Jews, or Muslims, and sometimes each other. Many of the founders of the United States, although nominally Protestants, held "free-thinking" Enlightenment views that in later US history became identified with "godless atheism" (Green, 2015; Jacoby, 2004). Thus, when writing about specific phases of US religious oppression, we need to distinguish between Protestants and Catholics, freethinkers and atheists; but when looking at the current meanings of these terms today, we speak more generally about Christians or about secular thinkers (including atheists).

We use the term *Christian hegemony* to refer to cultural assumptions, norms, and beliefs that have Protestant origins and remain embedded in the normative practices of everyday life. *Christian hegemony* thus refers to the societal or institutional assumptions that "Christians" are somehow "normal" US citizens. The reproduction of hegemony on the individual level is referred to as *Christian privilege* (Killermann, selection 46) whereas on the institutional or societal level, it is more often referred to as *hegemony* (Blumenfeld, selection 47). These and other social justice concepts are clarified in Section 1, and we urge you to read them before turning to this section on religious oppression, so that you can understand our approach.

DIVERSITY WITHIN RELIGIONS AND STEREOTYPES ABOUT RELIGIONS

One of the key issues to remember when considering the relationship of religion to national culture, norms, and assumptions in the United States or globally, is that there is as much diversity within any one given religion as there is between different religions (Pew, selection 45). Religious traditions and practices as well as secular, pluralistic, or atheistic perspectives are not uniform, but diverge widely *within religions* between orthodox fundamentalisms (a literal interpretation of religious texts) and the pluralistic openness to the legitimacy of other faith traditions. There are differences within Christianity between Protestant fundamentalism or Catholic orthodoxy and more free-thinking denominations, as between Orthodox and Conservative, Reform, Reconstructionist, or Secular Humanist forms of Judaism (Armstrong, 2000). There are equally significant distinctions within Hinduism, Islam, and other organized religions whose moderate adherents may feel more alienated or threatened by orthodox or politically active extremist co-religionists than they feel from outsiders (ISIS poses such a threat to moderate Muslims in North Africa and the Middle East; there are struggles in Israel between orthodox and secular attitudes toward legal definitions of who is a Jew). Theological or cultural religious communities have different beliefs and practices which evolved in different historical, ethnic, or political contexts, which might differentiate US or Egyptian Sunni Muslims; European (Ashkenazi), Sephardic (Spanish diaspora) or Mizrachi (Middle Eastern) Jews; Sunni or Shi'a Muslims, Sufis and Sikhs, wherever they may live.

It is important to remember these intra-religious differences because too often one hears blanket generalizations about faith traditions that are do not hold true for all members, such as "Buddhists are nonviolent," "Christians oppose abortion," "Atheists think that religion is ridiculous," stereotyped misunderstandings that ignore the different perspectives held within different religious or non-religious traditions.

PART II: HISTORICAL OVERVIEW OF US RELIGIOUS OPPRESSION

REFUGEES AND IMMIGRATION

These distinctions described above challenge current US anti-Muslim stereotypes used to justify barring immigrants from majority-Muslim countries. The politics behind current religious US xenophobia is not surprising (Bayoumi, selection 48), given the media's broad-brush stereotyping of non-Christian faith traditions and the religious "illiteracy" of many Americans (Moore, 2007). With the election of the first black president (whose father was a Kenyan-born Muslim) and changes in the racial and religious demographics of the United States, many consider white American national and Christian identity to be under religious and racial assault.

This national/religious protectionism recycles the backlash that occurred during other periods of high immigration to the United States earlier in our history. In the early 1800s, over half the US population and 85% of Protestants were evangelical (Emerson and Smith, 2000; Green, 2015), and the total number of immigrants was low (143,000 in the 1820s) and mainly Protestant and white. But between 1870 and 1920, immigration had radically transformed the United States. More than a third of the total US population of 105 million Americans were non-Protestant immigrants, such as Roman Catholics, Greek Orthodox, Jews, Muslims, and Sikhs (Daniels, 2002).

Given the earlier demographics, the linkage between Protestantism and US national identity is not surprising. But, the immigration from the 1840s through the 1920s challenged the previously homogeneous, racialized, Protestant US national identity, resulting in a nativist backlash against all immigrants (not "native born" Americans). There were citizenship (naturalization) challenges based on race and religion in US courts (Bayoumi, 2015; Haney Lopez, 1996) followed by a 1924 Immigration Act that restricted immigration to the largely northern Europeans based on an earlier census and restricted Catholic and Jewish immigration, Asians having been cut off by earlier restrictions. These immigration restrictions were largely in place until 1965, preventing most Jewish refugees from the Holocaust from entering the United States. (This history is treated in greater detail by Adams and Joshi, 2016.)

This historical pattern resurfaces in today's nativist scapegoating of refugee Muslims for US crime, popular misconceptions that all Muslims are alike, and an immigration ban on Muslims that assumes they are terrorists in refugee disguise (Bayoumi, selection 48; Gallup, 2016; Walther, 2015). Similar to the nativist opposition to Buddhist, Catholic, Hindu, Jewish, or Muslim immigration more than a century ago, today's proponents of a Christian national identity who fear and oppose pluralistic or inclusive understandings of identity have seized upon political opportunism to shape US policy in the image of a previous America (Eck, selection 51; Prothero, 2006).

INTERSECTIONS OF RACE AND RELIGION: THE RACIALIZATION OF US RELIGIONS

Protestantism in the United States was historically racialized, so that a theme in more recent US religious oppression is the gradual *racialization* of the religions held by peoples of color (Bayoumi, selection 48; Kaye/Kantrowitz, selection 56; Joshi, 2006). In colonial times, the US Protestant *white* settlers and landowners had justified their violence against Native American Indians and maintenance of African race-based slavery on their conviction of *Christian* superiority, although gradually the pseudo-scientific ideology of white *racial* superiority became intertwined with beliefs about religious superiority (Echo-Hawk, selection 52).

European colonialism was a worldwide enterprise in which Christian missions to the "natives" (largely in the Americas and in Africa) became the advance-guard for land seizure and economic exploitation, as Christianity domesticated native peoples thought to be uncultured heathens and Christian domination over the religious "other" justified European colonizing projects throughout Africa, Asia, and the Americas (Echo-Hawk, selection 52).

Contemporary Islamophobia as well as antisemitism are rooted in European conflations of religious with racial difference that isolated and delegitimized the Jew and the Muslim as the infidel "Other" during centuries of Christian nation-building in Europe. Crusades and military conflicts drove Muslims from the borders of Europe and genocidal attacks on ancient Jewish communities in Europe sent Jews into global diaspora in centuries well before the 20th century Holocaust (Hilberg, selection 49; Kaye/Kantrowitz, selection 56; Bayoumi, selection 48; Adams and Joshi, 2016). The expulsions of Jews during the pogroms of Eastern Europe (mid-19th and early 20th century) and the Turkish genocidal expulsion of Armenians during World War I, were concurrent historically with the expulsion of Native peoples from their lands in the

United States and relocation to unproductive land on reservations. The historical parallels between ethnic, racial, and religious cleansing in Europe and in the United States are striking, when one looks at these phenomena globally instead of locally.

The success of European and US racialized and religious "cleansing" set in motion an interwoven white *racial* and Christian *religious* national identity in the United States by which *Christian*, *English*, *free*, and *white* provided intersecting advantages for those who could claim such identities, based on the co-construction of religion, race, and national origins (Goldschmidt and McAlister, 2004; Singh, 2003; Takaki, 1993). Colonial settlers had interpreted divine purposes behind the malarial and influenza epidemics that "cleansed" Native Indian populations from land desired by settlers (Loewen, 1995; Mann, 2005) and the ensuing tribal displacements and cultural genocide of Native American peoples were justified by Protestant certainty of divinely-sanctioned victory over heathens and of Western civilization over primitive savagery (Echo-Hawk, selection 52). In later periods of US history, biblical texts justified race-based segregation between white and black congregations within the same Protestant denominations (Emerson and Smith, 2000) as well as the economical exploitation and residential exclusion of Buddhist, Hindu, Muslim, and Sikh workers and families (all peoples of color). Today's racialized religious profiling is similarly based on the presumption that religious "others" are terrorists or undocumented migrants, and local resistance to building Muslim mosques and Sikh *gurdwaras* in local neighborhoods has similar nativist roots (Bayoumi, selection 48; Eck, selection 51; Williams, selection 54; Dwyer, 2017). In the contemporary United States, this racialization of religion continues in a process whereby the *religions* of brown peoples who observe Islam, Hinduism, and Sikhism are identified with their presumed *ethnic/racial identity* (Arab or South Asian) so that phenotypes alone indicate marginalized religions (Joshi, 2006). Bayoumi widens the parameters for Islamophobia to include the role of politics in the racialization of brown-skinned Muslims (Bayoumi, 2008, 2015).

CHRISTIANITY IN US HISTORY AND LAW: SEPARATION OF CHURCH AND STATE

US history textbooks (Green, 2015; Loewen, 1995) emphasize the religious freedom sought by Pilgrims and Puritans who fled sectarian religious persecution in England and established a safe "New World" haven for themselves and their co-religionists. However, religious freedom meant freedom to practice *their* orthodoxies without persecution, but not freedom for "heretic" nonconformists such as Anne Hutchinson, Roger Williams, and Quakers driven out of the colony (Green, 2015).

Given this historical retrospect, Puritanism becomes the first of many Protestant sectarian orthodoxies planted on US soil whose religious certainties dehumanized Native American religious traditions, came into conflict with Roman Catholic missions, and competed with other Protestant sectarian colonies until they forged a nation from disparate religious colonies, unified by a single Constitution but religiously protected by the First Amendment.

What ultimately became hegemonic Christianity was based on sectarian accommodation among the colonies. On the one hand, Protestants differed from each other and from Catholics; on the other hand, *Christianity* became a convenient umbrella term for Protestants and Catholics whose suspicions over time turned outwards against Buddhist, Hindu, Jewish, and Muslim religious traditions as well as those outside traditional Protestantism, such as the Church of Jesus Christ of Latter-Day Saints (the Mormons), Seventh-Day Adventists, and Jehovah's Witnesses. As Christianity became the umbrella identity, atheists also became suspect and the free-thinking tradition of the country's founders was undermined by fears of the "godless Communism" of 19th century secular socialists and the Cold War furor of the 1950s (Christina, selection 59; Nowicki, selection 58; Jacoby, 2004).

The colonies required a "separation of church and state" if they were to become a nation under constitutional law rather than distinct religious communities ruled by sectarian traditions. But the 17th and 18th century experiences of European sectarian persecution remained too fresh for colonies not to fear the emergence of a new religious domination. Their agreement not to do so was written into the First Amendment to the US Constitution (1791), which stipulates that "Congress shall make no law respecting an establishment of religion, or prohibiting the free exercise thereof" and provides, in effect, a religious mutual assurance pact to prevent any single denomination from becoming the federally established religion. The First Amendment also guarantees *Free Exercise* of religion ("Congress shall make no law . . . prohibiting the free exercise thereof") whose net effect has been to support religious exercise claims brought by Christian groups but to restrict religious practice claims of non-Christian groups, such as Native Americans and Jews (Echo-Hawke, selection 52; Eck, selection 51).

These First Amendment protections succeeded in preventing the *political establishment* of a single mandated religion but could not prevent *culturally hegemonic Christian* repudiation of non-Christian religious practices. Culturally hegemonic assumptions led to Supreme Court decisions that rejected religious *practices* that went against Christian norms, such as Mormon polygamy or Muslim and Jewish head-coverage or Native people's worship in ancient sacred sites (Eck, selection 51; Echo-Hawk, selection 52; discussed in Adams and Joshi, 2016; Feldman, 2005).

Whereas freedom of religious *belief* remained unchallenged because of its close linkage to freedom of speech (also a First Amendment right), cases dealing with religious *worship*, *practice*, *behavior*, *expression*, or *action* were tested against the legal concept of *compelling state interests* which involved broadly assumed Christian norms. The Court generally looked more favorably upon "free exercise" claims brought by Christian-identified groups, such as Seventh-Day Adventists and Amish (*Wisconsin* v. *Yoder*, 1972), but parallel "free exercise" claims brought by non-Christians often failed in the courts (Eck, selection 51; Echo-Hawk, selection 52). For example, the Supreme Court found that Cherokee and Navajo plaintiffs were not justified in claiming "free exercise" relief from federal policies that prevented their religious practice in ancestral sacred sites in federal lands that were designated for public uses (Eck, selection 51; Echo-Hawk, selection 52; Feldman, 2005; Long, 2000). Unlike the Court's findings in cases concerning the Amish or Seventh-Day Adventists, the Court did not believe that Native American peoples similarly practiced ancient recognized religions or that they, like the Amish, held their beliefs sincerely.

If one were to apply a test of consistency to these and other Supreme Court First Amendment decisions on free religious exercise, one would be puzzled by why they failed, since they met the criteria affirmed by the Court in claims brought by Christian sects. The Court had failed to acknowledge (for example) that in Orthodox Judaism (as in other orthodox religions) head-covering was a religious requirement, not a matter of personal preference (*Goldman* v. *Weinberger*, 1986) and head-covering for Muslim women or Sikh men remains highly charged to this day.

At the same time, the Supreme Court upheld the everyday use of politically charged Christian speech, ritual, and symbols, rationalized and framed as US "civil religion." The phrase "In God We Trust" was added to the US currency in 1864 and Congress made Christmas a national holiday in 1865, both during the Civil War. This Christian norm of naming the deity ("In God We Trust") would be unthinkable for orthodox Jews who must not write or utter the divine name and excludes Muslims (who invoke Allah) and Hindus and other faith traditions who invoke the divine in different ways. "In God We Trust" also excludes freethinkers, agnostics, and atheists from the hegemonic Christian identity ("we") assumed by this phrase. So does the wording of the separation of "church" and state. When challenged, Supreme Court decisions between 1890 and 1930 stated that the United States "is one of the 'Christian countries'," a "Christian nation," "a Christian people," although in 1952 the phrasing became more ecumenical: "We are a religious people whose institutions presuppose a Supreme Being" (Feldman, 2005; Murray, 2008).

The courts also became sites of contestations over "establishment" and "free exercise" in their (sometimes contradictory) decisions concerning school prayer, school vouchers paid for by public taxes, conflicts between teaching science (evolution) and Christianity (creationism), disputes over definitions of end-of-life and beginning-of-life (euthanasia, abortion, stem cell research), "the right to decide" versus "the right to life," and "free exercise" as a justification for business owners to refuse services or health benefits to anyone whose life choices on gender, sexuality, or marriage challenged their religious beliefs. These cases continue in the Courts today.

PART III: CHRISTIANITY IN CURRENT-DAY LAW, EDUCATION, AND POLICY

THE POLITICAL AND LEGAL VISIBILITY OF CONSERVATIVE CHRISTIANITY

The political force known as "the religious Right" has become increasingly visible in the past half-century, with differing coalitions of fundamentalist Protestants and conservative Catholics collaborating to repeal women's choice for abortion, to deny marriage equality for same-sex couples, or to use publicly funded vouchers for religious schooling (Armstrong, 2000; Jacoby, 2004). Fundamentalist and orthodox religious leaders have come together to oppose pluralism and change that pose threats to traditional religious convictions.

Since the rise of the Moral Majority and the Reagan presidency, political conservatives and fundamentalist Christians whose religious beliefs require traditional views on gender, sexuality, marriage, and procreation have been particularly effective in accomplishing their political agenda. Politically conservative Christianity has also been responsible for much of the anti-LGBT vitriol in private settings as well as institutional policies, state and federal law (Dallas, selection 53). State laws banning same-sex marriage remained in place until they were declared unconstitutional by the Supreme Court in *Obergefell* v. *Hodges* (2015), although politicians continue to attack pro-LGBT legislation such as the Employment Non-Discrimination Act, the repeal of *Don't Ask, Don't Tell* (Williams, 2012, p. 268) and the legislation confining bathroom choice to gender assignment at birth (North Carolina, Texas) on the basis of religious authority. Conservative religious coalitions pose direct challenges to law and policy based on human rights, pluralism and inclusiveness. These conflicts involve groups whose workers, clientele, and advertisers affirm everyday rights for gay, lesbian, bisexual, and transgender people, as in the positions taken by the National Football League (www.newsobserver.com/news/politics-government/state-politics/article134476919.html). Similarly, the denial of public business services to same-sex couples has become a constitutional conflict between the First Amendment ("free exercise") and the Fourteenth Amendment ("equal protection"). In 2014, the Supreme Court ruled in *Burwell* v. *Hobby Lobby* that "closely held" corporations could not be forced to engage in practices that the owners claimed were against their religious beliefs.

These constitutional issues are far from settled, with the possibility that *Roe* v. *Wade* (a woman's right to make abortion decisions) and *Obergefell* v. *Hodges* (same-sex marriage ruled a fundamental right based on the Due Process and the Equal Protection clauses of the Fourteenth Amendment) could eventually be overturned by a religiously conservative Supreme Court. Though white evangelicals were uncomfortable with many aspects of the 2016 presidential campaign, many were swayed by the promise that a Trump administration would nominate like-minded Supreme Court justices to overturn abortion and marriage equality decisions and to reverse case law regarding "free exercise" to justify the denial of public services to non-conforming GLBT people (www.businessinsider.com/r-with-trump-pick-aboard-top-us-court-tackles-religious-rights-2017-4). In these political and legal conflicts, it becomes difficult to disentangle political ideology, opportunism, and fundamentalist Christian precepts.

Public education is another domain in which conservative Christian groups continue to exert influence, as in the teaching of creationism as an alternative to evolution in science classes. In the landmark case *Kitzmiller* v. *Dover Area School District* (2005), the Supreme Court ruled that teaching "Intelligent Design," a euphemism for creationism used by some Christian public school boards, violated the establishment clause of the First Amendment by bringing religion into the public school classrooms (www.politicalresearch.org/tag/intelligent-design/#sthash.uZJv3LZ3. dpbs). Currently, Secretary of Education Betsy DeVos and Vice President Mike Pence advocate the teaching of creationism in schools (www.propublica.org/article/devos-education-nominees-code-words-for-creationism-offshoot-raise-concerns). Another First Amendment struggle involves a West Virginia mother's 2017 lawsuit to prevent the teaching of Bible classes to elementary and middle school students (http://bigstory.ap.org/article/ec4a4cec48eb49e7878bcab5d18ed2cb/mother-sues-stop-bible-classes-west-virginia-schools).

Homeschooling has been one of the alternative trends whose growth reflects religious education outside public schools. Sixty-four percent of respondents in a 2012 Department of Education survey cited "a desire to provide religious instruction" and 77% "a desire to provide moral instruction" as reasons to homeschool their children (https://nces.ed.gov/pubs2016/2016096rev.pdf). There are disturbing tales of religious-political indoctrination written by people who experienced conservative Christian-based homeschooling (Darkwater, 2017).

OPPORTUNITIES AND CHALLENGES IN ACHIEVING A RELIGIOUS PLURALISM

It is important to recognize the positive role of organized Christianity working with other religions to foster coalitions for lasting social change. Examples include the historical role of churches and synagogues in the anti-slavery and abolition movements and in the Civil Rights movement. Christian Liberation Theology made enormous contributions to social justice movements in the Americas and Africa. Current efforts to provide "sanctuary" for undocumented immigrants were created more than 30 years ago to support undocumented immigrants from deportation and based on the concept of the church as a "sanctuary" or safe space, now revitalized into an international movement by which hundreds of churches, synagogues, and mosques as well as secular organizations and whole communities have identified themselves as sanctuaries for oppressed groups in times of need (Markoe, 2016). Moreover, many religious and non-religious individuals and organizations are participating in a growing interfaith dialogue and action movement focused on justice and the common good (Edwards, selection 62).

For oppressed communities, religion can be an anchor in times of political crisis. Williams (selection 54) describes the importance of Buddhist solidarity during Japanese internment and Edwards (selection 62) notes the strength of coalitions across religious and secular communities to foster cooperation and change. There are numerous examples of historical and contemporary organized resistance to oppression and maintenance of group solidarity through the Black Church, and activist communities within and between Hindu temples, Jewish synagogues, Muslim mosques, and Sikh gurdwaras (Borquaye, 2016; Mendoza, 2017).

Today there are many opportunities to practice US religious pluralism and include different forms of religious workshop and practice in our schools, communities and through interfaith organizations. Many schools misinterpret the First Amendment as requiring the elimination of all religion from public spaces, but the Supreme Court has vigorously said otherwise and affirms teaching "about" religions (but not teaching "of" religions). The concern about religion in public schools is a holdover from earlier times when public schools held daily Protestant Bible readings and prayer to provide Protestant moral authority for immigrants whose religious, linguistic, and cultural diversity seemed to require Protestant assimilation in order to become "American" (Fraser, 1999). People are unaware that the parochial (parish-based) schools emerged to protect Catholic children from the Protestant public school system and Catholics as well as Jews actively challenged the constitutionality of sectarian prayer and teaching in public schools.

As public education became a major legal battleground for these issues, several Supreme Court decisions ruled against sectarian teaching and practice from public schools, while maintaining that study *about* religions in the nation's public schools was both legal and desirable: "It might well be said that one's education is not complete without a study of comparative religions or the history of religion and its relationship to the advancement of civilization . . . [when] presented objectively as part of a secular program of education" (*School District of Abington Township, Pennsylvania, et al.* v. *Schempp et al.*, 1963). On this explicit legal foundation, the American Academy of Religion (AARK, 2010), the Tanenbaum Center (2012), and the First Amendment Center (Haynes, Chaltain, Ferguson, Hudson, and Thomas, 2003) have published guidelines for teaching *about* religion in public schools (Jones and Sheffield, 2009) and suggestions for framing difficult discussions for students at different educational levels and levels of understanding about religion (see Adams and Joshi, 2016; Cornille, 2008; Moore, 2007).

Venues for interreligious dialogue have expanded greatly (Edwards, selection 62; Edwards, 2016). Cross-sectarian coalitions date back to the abolitionist movement, worker and liberation theology movements, settlement and social reform movements, and the Civil Rights movement. Today, peace and environmental activists and interfaith communities work together to achieve understanding and achieve social justice goals by bridging their sectarian, spiritual, secular, or atheist differences (Goodstein, 2016; Markoe, 2016; Patel and Scorer, 2012; Stedman, 2012). Marginalized religions have formed advocacy organizations and published guidelines and curricula to assist in the range of challenging and productive interfaith collaborations (Cornille, 2008; Edwards, 2016; Patel, 2007, 2012; Patel and Scorer, 2012; Tanenbaum Center, 2012).

INTERSECTIONS OF RELIGIOUS OPPRESSION WITH OTHER FORMS OF OPPRESSION

Many of the selections in this chapter offer opportunities for readers to disentangle *religious* dimensions of conflicts and hostilities from political, ideological, or cultural dimensions. These are cases in which *religion* justifies, inflames, or draws attention away from underlying historical, cultural, ethnic, racial, gender, or class antagonisms. For many centuries, religion has shaped how people understand gender, sexuality, ethnicity, race, class, culture, and national identity. These dimensions of identity intersect in everyday life and must be disentangled to understand their interactions. Only an intersectional analysis will prevent our simplifying social justice issues into "either/or" – "either/or" either exaggerates or diminishes one dimension of conflict (religion) at the expense of others (economic class or political advantage) as well as vice versa. These intersectional challenges will be clear in the selections that follow.

OVERVIEW OF SELECTIONS IN THIS SECTION

The first selection in "Context" comes from a 2015 Pew Research Center study of "America's Changing Religious Landscape" (selection 45) that explores the formal affiliation especially of millennial-generation Americans with established Protestant or Catholic congregations. This study is available in its entirely online, as are other Pew studies of interfaith families and the increasing number of "nones" ("none of the above") responding to religious affiliation studies.[1] Killermann (selection 46) looks at Christian privilege as an umbrella term for people from Christian backgrounds (whether or not they are currently practicing Christians) and lists the societal "privileges" that people from Christian backgrounds often don't even know that they possess. On the other side of the coin of Christian privilege, Blumenfeld (selection 47) draws on Young's "Five Faces of Oppression" (selection 7) to describe multiple, intersecting examples of *powerlessness*, *exploitation*, *marginalization*, *cultural imperialism*, and *violence* experienced by peoples of marginalized, devalued faith traditions throughout US history.

Bayoumi (selection 48) details the complex intersections of US racism with religious oppression, especially in cases where both are worsened by political factors and he uses the incarceration of Japanese during World War II as another instance of interconnections of racism, religion, and politics, thus linking this selection to Williams (selection 54). Bayoumi's entire chapter on "Racing Religion" (2015) provides valuable context and background for the issues highlighted in these and other selections. In a different context and for a differently racialized religious people, Hilberg (selection 49) examines antisemitism in Europe by comparing Christian-based exclusionary decrees (Canonical law) from as early as the 4th century CE with Nazi antisemitic measures of the 20th century. Against the background of Hilberg's juxtaposition of examples from different eras of European antisemitism, Gilbert's maps (selection 50) enable readers to visualize 2,000 years of Jewish life in Europe, maintained despite violent expulsions and persecutions. Both Hilberg and Gilbert document the centuries of European antisemitism that pre-dated the concentration camps and Holocaust, which the Nazis created to provide a "final solution to the Jewish question."

Eck (selection 51) shifts our focus back to the United States, with examples of religious discrimination in the workplace and the efforts of Muslims and Sikhs to seek legal recourse under the First Amendment to wear their head-coverings or to find a safe place for daily prayer. She explores the protections offered by the First Amendment with illustrative case law in court cases, some of which are also reviewed, although from different historical and cultural perspective, by Echo-Hawk (selection 52), who juxtaposes early instances of violence against Native Americans with the judicial violence posed by the failure of constitutional protections to assure tribal access to sacred sites.

Dallas (selection 53) shifts the focus to the challenges that face religious coalitions who support lesbian, gay, bisexual, and transgender rights. These efforts take place at all levels – for LGBT rights of worship within religious communities who would otherwise exclude them, and to dismantle discriminatory policies at all institutional and societal levels.

Williams (selection 54) describes the importance of Buddhism for Japanese who were incarcerated in US concentration camps during World War II, although some had been loyal US citizens for generations. (German Americans, mainly Christians although also "the enemy" in World War II, were not incarcerated.) Buddhism provided resiliency and strength for the Japanese in the camps at the same time that many of their youth fought in US forces abroad and Buddhists tried to "Americanize" their religious organizations by renaming them "the Buddhist Churches of America." There are clear parallels between Japanese Buddhists, wrongfully considered "enemy aliens" during World War II, and Arab or Asian Muslims, stereotyped and incarcerated as "terrorists" today.

Semple (selection 55) describes the complications of religious, ethnic, generational, and workplace conflicts between Somali Muslim and Latino Christian meatpackers over "fair" breaks for daily worship (the Muslims) measured against long weekends for Christian holidays. It is daunting to disentangle the multiple factors in conflict within the larger racialized, Christian hegemonic United States to which Latinos and Somalis had immigrated to find work – factors that include economic competition; generationally-rooted immigrants versus newcomers; racial, ethnic, cultural, and religious differences; and the specific "fairness" question (as reflected in hourly pay) concerning the balance between daily prayer breaks for Muslims versus longer Christmas or Easter days off for Christians.

The selections thus far provide *Context* for the following *Voices* that focus on self-reflection upon personal experiences. Kaye/Kantrowitz (selection 56) speaks as an antiracist lesbian Jewish activist reflecting on intersections within her personal experience of white privilege complicated by religious and homophobic stigma. She ponders intersectional questions, such as what are "racialized" markers for Jews? In what national or economic contexts might they be persecuted as Jews or privileged as Whites (or brown if Mizrachi)? Are Jews members of a religion (excluding secular or atheist or Buddhist Jews) or are Jews simply an ancient people in diaspora who share a history? These are similar to questions asked by two young Muslims, Adam Fattah and Hagar Omram (selection 57), about their experiences in school or with families and friends.

Nowicki (selection 58) quotes experiences of people who identify as atheists, their resistance to hegemonic Christianity, and their journeys toward an atheist world-view. Christina (selection 58) is more vehement about her 99 reasons why atheists are so angry, only several of which are included here, along with "Some answers to the questions I know I'll get asked."

The pride, pain, and outrage expressed throughout the *Voices* segment lead readers to ask, *What can I do? How might we do it?* Of the many opportunities for individual or coalitional efforts to achieve social justice, the *Next Steps* segment in this section presents only three, although they can be augmented by *Next Steps* in other sections and the final section of this volume, "Working for Social Justice." In this chapter, Nasir and Al-Amin (selection 60) draw portraits of two Muslim students, one an African-American convert and the other a US-born Muslim of Pakistani parentage – to illuminate their college experiences of risk and of safety. It concludes with acts of recognition and kindness that were meaningful for the recipients – acknowledgment of Ramadan by the college, personal compliments on wearing *hijab*, professors knowledgeable about Islam, safe spaces for prayer, *halal* meals, all of which add up to the experience of acceptance for Muslim students on college campuses. This piece further illustrates how Muslim religious identity (like all other identities) gets complicated by racial, gender, language, and national identities. As if in answer to the question, *Where might I or we begin,* Kivel (selection 61) lists numerous ways for Christians to become allies for people of targeted, stereotyped, and devalued religious faiths.

Edwards (selection 62) discusses social justice approaches to interfaith works and notes the importance of addressing systemic oppression and highlighting marginalized identities. In this, he notes what is necessary for a socially just and inclusive interfaith movement.

Note

1 www.pewforum.org/2015/05/12/americas-changing-religious-landscape/pf_15-05-05_rls2_1_310px/. Readers might want to look at four other Pew studies: "One-in-five U.S. adults were raised in interfaith homes: A closer look at religious mixing in American families" (Pew Research Center *Religion & Public Life*, October 26, 2016); "U.S. public becoming less religious: Modest drop in overall rate of belief and practice, but religiously affiliated Americans are as observant as before" (Pew Research Center *Religion & Public Life*, November 3, 2015); "A closer look at America's rapidly growing religious 'nones'" (Pew Research Center *Religion & Public Life*, May 13, 2015); "How Americans feel about religious groups: Jews, Catholics rated warmly, atheists and Muslims more coldly" (Pew Research Center *Religion & Public Life*, July 16, 2014).

References

AARK (American Academy of Religion) (2010). *Guidelines for teaching about religion in K-12 public schools in the United States*.

Adams, M. and Joshi, K. (2016). Religious oppression. In Adams, M. and Bell, L.A. with Goodman, D.J. and Joshi, K.Y. (Eds.) *Teaching for diversity and social justice,* 3rd edition, pp. 255–297. New York: Routledge.

ADL (Anti-Defamation League) (2016). *ADL audit: Anti-semitic assaults rise dramatically across the country in 2015: Anti-semitic incidents on American college campuses nearly doubled*. New York: ADL.

Armstrong, K. (2000). *The battle for God: A history of fundamentalism*. New York: Ballantine, Random House.

Bayoumi, M. (2008). *How does it feel to be a problem? Being you and Arab in America*. New York: Penguin Books.

Bayoumi, M. (2015). Racing religion. In *This Muslim American life: Dispatches from the War on Terror,* pp. 48-72. New York: New York University Press.

Borquaye, A. (November 30, 2016). *The Black Church is the home of black activism*. http://m.huffpost.com/us/entry/8660586.

Cornille, C. (2008). *The im-possibility of interreligious dialogue*. New York: Crossroad Publishing Co.

Daniels, R. (2002). *Coming to America: A history of immigration and ethnicity in American life*, 2nd edition. Princeton, NJ: HarperPerennial.

Darkwater, K. (January 26, 2017). I was trained for the culture wars in home school, awaiting someone like Mike Pence as Messiah. www.autostraddle.com/i-was-trained-for-the-culture-wars-in-home-school-awaiting-someone-like-mike-pence-as-a-messiah-367057/.

Dwyer, J. (May 24, 2017). A New Jersey township wielded its zoning rules as a barrier to Islam. *New York Times*.

Edwards, S. (2016). *Critical conversations about religion: Promises and pitfalls of a social justice approach to interfaith dialogue*. Charlotte, NC: Information Age Publishing.

Emerson, M.O., and Smith, C. (2000). *Divided by faith: Evangelical religion and the problem of race in America*. New York: Oxford University Press.

Feldman, N. (2005). *Divided by God: America's church and state problem – and what we should do about it.* New York: Farrar, Straus and Giroux.

Fedoraro, I. W. (November 20, 2016). The mosque next door: City law vs. houses of worship. *New York Times.*

Fraser, J.W. (1999). *Between church and state: Religion & public education in multicultural America.* New York: St. Martin's Press.

Gallup (2016). *Islamophobia: Understanding anti-Muslim sentiment in the West.* www.gallup.com/poll/157082/islamophobia-understanding-anti-muslim-sentiment-west.aspx.

Goldschmidt, H., and McAlister, E.A. (2004). *Race, nation, and religion in the Americas.* Oxford and New York: Oxford University Press.

Goodstein, L. (December 6, 2016). Both feeling threatened, American Muslims and Jews join hands. *New York Times.*

Green, S.K. (2015). *Inventing a Christian America: The myth of the religious founding.* New York: Oxford University Press.

Haney Lopez, I. (1996). *White by law.* New York: New York University Press.

Haynes, C.C., Chaltain, S., Ferguson, J.E., Hudson, D.L., and Thomas, O. (2003). *The First Amendment in Schools: A guide from the First Amendment Center.* Alexandria, VA: AACD; Nashville, TN: First Amendment Center.

Jacoby, S. (2004). *Freethinkers: A history of American secularism.* New York: Owl Books, Holt and Company.

Jones, S.P., and Sheffield, E.C. (Eds.) (2009). *The role of religion in 21st-century public schools.* New York: Peter Lang.

Joshi, K.Y. (2006). The racialization of religion in the United States. *Equity and Excellence in Education, 39*(3), 211-226.

Kivel, P. (2013). *Living in the shadow of the cross: Understanding and resisting the power and privilege of Christian hegemony.* Gabriola Island, BC: New Society.

Lichtblau, E. (November 15, 2016). Attacks against Muslim Americans fueled rise in hate crime, F.B.I. says. *New York Times.*

Lizza, R. (October 19, 2016). Twitter's anti-semitism problem. *The New Yorker.*

Loewen, J.W. (1995). *Lies my teacher told me: Everything your American history textbook got wrong.* New York: New Press, distributed by Norton.

Long, C.N. (2000). *Religious freedom and Indian rights: The case of Oregon v. Smith.* Lawrence, KA: University Press of Kansas.

Mann, C.C. (2005). *1491: New revelations of the Americas before Columbus,* 1st edition. New York: Knopf.

Markoe, L. (November 14, 2016). Jewish-Muslim alliance formed against anti-semitism, Islamophobia. *Religion News Service.* http://religionnews.com/2016/11/14/jewish-muslim-alliance-formed-against-anti-semitism-islamophobia/.

Mendoza, S. (April 25, 2017). California's Muslims stand up for action against Trump's policies. www.middleeasteye.net/news/californias-muslims-stand-action-against-trumps-policies-2090326735.

Moore, D.L. (2007). *Overcoming religious illiteracy: A cultural studies approach to the study of religion in secondary education.* New York: Palgrave.

Murray, B.T. (2008). *Religious liberty in America: The First Amendment in historical and contemporary perspective.* Amherst, MA: University of Massachusetts Press.

Patel, E. (2007). *Acts of faith: The struggle of an American Muslim, the struggle for the soul of a generation.* Boston, MA: Beacon Press.

Patel, E. (2012). *Sacred ground: Pluralism, prejudice, and the promise of America.* Boston, MA: Beacon Press.

Patel, E., with Scorer, T. (2012). *Embracing interfaith cooperation: Eboo Patel on coming together to change the world: A 5-session study.* Denver, CO: Morehouse Education Resources.

Potok, M. (November 14, 2016). Anti-Muslim hate crimes surged last year, fueled by hateful campaign. SPLC Southern Poverty Law Center. www.splcenter.org/2016/11/14/Anti-Muslim Hate Crimes Surged Last Year, Fueled by Hateful Campaign _ Southern Poverty Law Center.htm.

Prothero, S. (Ed.) (2006). *A nation of religions: The politics of pluralism in multireligious America.* Chapel Hill, NC: University of North Carolina Press.

Singh, J. (2003). The racialization of minoritized religious identity: Constructing sacred sites at the intersection of white and Christian supremacy. In Iwamura, J.N. and Spickard, P. (Eds.) *Revealing the sacred in Asian and Pacific America,* pp. 87-106. New York: Routledge.

Stedman, C. (2012). *Faitheist: How an atheist found common ground with the religious.* Boston, MA: Beacon Press.

Takaki, R. (1993). *A different mirror: A history of multicultural America.* Boston, MA: Little, Brown and Company.

Tanenbaum Center (2012). *Religions in my neighborhood: Teaching curiosity and respect about religious differences.* By Adams, M., Bode, P. and Hardman, R. New York: Tanenbaum Center for Interreligious Understanding.

Walther, K. (November 17, 2015). Islamophobia is an American tradition. *HNN History News Network.*

Williams, D.K. (2012). *God's own party: The making of the Christian right.* New York: Oxford University Press.

Wills, D.W. (2002). *Christianity in the United States: A historical survey and interpretation.* Notre Dame, IN: University of Notre Dame Press.

45

America's Changing Religious Landscape

Pew Research Center

The Christian share of the U.S. population is declining, while the number of U.S. adults who do not identify with any organized religion is growing, according to an extensive new survey by the Pew Research Center. Moreover, these changes are taking place across the religious landscape, affecting all regions of the country and many demographic groups. While the drop in Christian affiliation is particularly pronounced among young adults, it is occurring among Americans of all ages. The same trends are seen among whites, blacks and Latinos; among both college graduates and adults with only a high school education; and among women as well as men. (Explore the data with our interactive database tool.)

To be sure, the United States remains home to more Christians than any other country in the world, and a large majority of Americans—roughly seven-in-ten—continue to identify with some branch of the Christian faith. But the major new survey of more than 35,000 Americans by the Pew Research Center finds that the percentage of adults (ages 18 and older) who describe themselves as Christians has dropped by nearly eight percentage points in just seven years, from 78.4% in 2007 to 70.6% in 2014. Over the same period, the percentage of Americans who are religiously unaffiliated—describing themselves as atheist,

Changing U.S. Religious Landscape

*Between 2007 and 2014, the Christian share of the population
fell from 78.4% to 70.6%, driven mainly by declines among mainline
Protestants and Catholics. The unaffiliated experienced the most growth,
and the share of Americans who belong to non-Christian faiths also increased.*

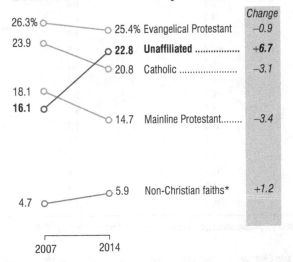

	Change
26.3% → 25.4% Evangelical Protestant	−0.9
23.9 → 22.8 Unaffiliated	+6.7
→ 20.8 Catholic	−3.1
18.1	
16.1	
→ 14.7 Mainline Protestant........	−3.4
4.7 → 5.9 Non-Christian faiths*	+1.2

2007   2014

*Includes Jews, Muslims, Buddhists, Hindus, other world religions and other faiths. Those who did not answer the religious identity question, as well as groups whose share of the populations did not change significantly, including the historically black Protestant tradition, Mormons and others, are not shown.

Source: 2014 Religious Landscape Study, conducted June 4-Sept. 30, 2014 agnostic or "nothing in particular"—has jumped more than six points, from 16.1% to 22.8%. And the share of Americans who identify with non-Christian faiths also has inched up, rising 1.2 percentage points, from 4.7% in 2007 to 5.9% in 2014. Growth has been especially great among Muslims and Hindus, albeit from a very low base.

The drop in the Christian share of the population has been driven mainly by declines among mainline Protestants and Catholics. Each of those large religious traditions has shrunk by approximately three percentage points since 2007. The evangelical Protestant share of the U.S. population also has dipped, but at a slower rate, falling by about one percentage point since 2007.

Even as their numbers decline, American Christians—like the U.S. population as a whole—are becoming more racially and ethnically diverse. Non-Hispanic whites now account for smaller shares of evangelical Protestants, mainline Protestants and Catholics than they did seven years earlier, while Hispanics have grown as a share of all three religious groups. Racial and ethnic minorities now make up 41% of Catholics (up from 35% in 2007), 24% of evangelical Protestants (up from 19%) and 14% of mainline Protestants (up from 9%).

Religious intermarriage also appears to be on the rise: Among Americans who have gotten married since 2010, nearly four-in-ten (39%) report that they are in religiously

Christians Decline as Share of U.S. Populations; Other Faiths and the Unaffiliated Are Growing

	2007 %	2014 %	Change* %
Christian	78.4	70.6	−7.8
Protestant	51.3	46.5	−4.8
Evangelical	26.3	25.4	−0.9
Mainline	18.1	14.7	−3.4
Historically black	6.9	6.5	–
Catholic	23.9	20.8	−3.1
Orthodox Christian	0.6	0.5	–
Mormon	1.7	1.6	–
Jehovah's Witness	0.7	0.8	–
Other Christian	0.3	0.4	
Non-Christian faiths	4.7	5.9	+1.2
Jewish	1.7	1.9	–
Muslim	0.4	0.9	+0.5
Buddhist	0.7	0.7	–
Hindu	0.4	0.7	+0.3
Other world religions**	<0.3	0.3	–
Other faiths**	1.2	1.5	+0.3
Unaffiliated	16.1	22.8	+6.7
Atheist	1.6	3.1	+1.5
Agnostic	2.4	4.0	+1.6
Nothing in particular	12.1	15.8	+3.7
Don't know/refused	0.8	0.6	−0.2
	100.0	100.0	

*The "change" column displays only statistically significant changes; blank cells indicate that the difference between 2007 and 2014 is within the margin of error.

**The "other world religions" category includes Sikhs, Baha 'is, Taoists, Jains and a variety of other world religions. The "other faiths" category includes Unitarians, New Age religions, Native Americans religions and a number of other non-Christian faiths.

Source: 2014 Religious Landscape Study, conducted June 4-Sept. 30, 2014. Figures may not add to 100% and nested figures may not add to subtotals indicated due to rounding.

mixed marriages, compared with 19% among those who got married before 1960. The rise in intermarriage appears to be linked with the growth of the religiously unaffiliated population. Nearly one-in-five people surveyed who got married since 2010 are either religiously unaffiliated respondents who married a Christian spouse or Christians who married an unaffiliated spouse. By contrast, just 5% of people who got married before 1960 fit this profile.

While many U.S. religious groups are aging, the unaffiliated are comparatively young—and getting *younger*, on average, over time. As a rising cohort of highly unaffiliated Millennials reaches adulthood, the median age of unaffiliated adults has dropped to 36, down from 38 in 2007 and far lower than the general (adult) population's median age of 46. By contrast, the median age of mainline Protestant adults in the new survey is 52 (up from 50 in 2007), and the median age of Catholic adults is 49 (up from 45 seven years earlier).

Because the U.S. census does not ask Americans about their religion, there are no official government statistics on the religious composition of the U.S. public. Some Christian denominations and other religious bodies keep their own rolls, but they use widely differing criteria for membership. The Religious Landscape Studies were designed to fill the gap. . . .

A NOTE ON DEFINING RELIGIOUS AFFILIATION AND THE STUDY'S TERMINOLOGY

In this study, respondents' religious affiliation (also sometimes referred to as "religious indentity") is based on self reports. Catholics, for instance, are defined as all respondents who say they are Catholics, regardless of their specific beliefs and whether or not they attend Mass regularly.

The terms "unaffiliated" and "religious 'nones'" are used interchangeably throughout this report. This group includes self-identified atheists and agnostics as well as those who describe their religion as "nothing in particular."

The unaffiliated are generally less religiously observant than people who identify with religion. But not all religious "nones" are nonbelievers. In fact, many people who are unaffiliated with a religion believe in God, pray at least occasionally and think of themselves as spiritual people. Forthcoming reports will describe the Religious Landscape Study's findings about the religious beliefs and practices of "nones" and other groups.

For more details on the exact questions used to measure religious identity, see the survey topline.

In 2007, there were 227 million adults in the United States, and a little more than 78% of them—or roughly 178 million—identified as Christians. Between 2007 and 2014, the overall size of the U.S. adult population grew by about 18 million people, to nearly 245 million. But the share of adults who identify as Christians fell to just under 71%, or approximately 173 million Americans, a net decline of about 5 million. Of the major subgroups within American Christianity, mainline Protestantism appears to have experienced the greatest drop in absolute numbers. In 2007, there were an estimated 41 million mainline Protestant adults in the United States. As of 2014, there are roughly 36 million, a decline of 5 million. By contrast, the size of the historically black Protestant tradition has remained relatively stable in recent years, at nearly 16 million adults. And evangelical Protestants, while declining slightly as a percentage of the U.S. public, probably have grown in absolute numbers as the overall U.S. population has continued to expand.

The new survey indicates that churches in the evangelical Protestant tradition now have a total of about 62 million adult adherents. That is an increase of roughly 2 million since 2007. Like mainline Protestants, Catholics appear to be declining both as a percentage of the population and in absolute numbers. The new survey indicates there are about 51 million Catholic adults in the U.S. today, roughly 3 million fewer than in 2007. And, unlike Protestants, who have been decreasing as a share of the U.S. public for several decades, the Catholic share of the population has been relatively stable over the long term. Meanwhile, the number of religiously unaffiliated adults has increased by roughly 19 million since 2007. There are now approximately 56 million religiously unaffiliated adults in the U.S., and this group—sometimes called religious "nones"—is more numerous than either Catholics or mainline Protestants, according to the new survey. Indeed, the unaffiliated are now second in size only to evangelical Protestants among major religious groups in the U.S.

FACTORS BEHIND THE CHANGES IN AMERICANS' RELIGIOUS IDENTIFICATION

One of the most important factors in the declining share of Christians and the growth of the "nones" is generational replacement. As the Millennial generation enters adulthood, its members display much lower levels of religious affiliation, including less connection with Christian churches, than older generations. . . .

In addition, people in older generations are increasingly disavowing association with organized religion. About a third of older Millennials (adults currently in their late 20s and early 30s) now say they have no religion, up nine percentage points among this cohort since 2007, when the same group was between ages 18 and 26. Nearly a quarter of Generation Xers now say they have no particular religion or describe themselves as atheists or agnostics, up four points in seven years. Baby Boomers also have become slightly but noticeably more likely to identify as religious "nones" in recent years.

As the shifting religious profiles of these generational cohorts suggest, switching religion is a common occurrence in the United States. If all Protestants were treated as a single religious group, then fully 34% of American adults currently have a religious identity different from the one in which they were raised. If switching among the three Protestant traditions (e.g., from mainline Protestantism to the evangelical tradition, or from evangelicalism to a historically black Protestant denomination) is added to the total, then the share of Americans who currently have a different religion than they did in childhood rises to 42%.

Unaffiliated Make Up Growing Share Across Generations

% of each generation that identifies current religion as atheist, agnostic or nothing in particular

	2007	2014	Change
Silent generation (b.1928–1945)	9	11	+2
Baby Boomers (b. 1946–1964)	14	17	+3
Generation X (b. 1965–1980)	19	23	+4
Older Millennials (b.1981–1989)	25	34	+9
Younger Millennials (b. 1990–1996)	n/a	36	n/a

By a wide margin, religious "nones" have experienced larger gains through religious switching than any other group. Nearly one-in-five U.S. adults (18%) were raised in a religious faith and now identify with no religion. Some switching also has occurred in the other direction: 9% of American adults say they were raised with no religious affiliation, and almost half of them (4.3% of all U.S. adults) now identify with some religion. But for every person who has joined a religion after having been raised unaffiliated, there are more than four people who have become religious "nones" after having been raised in some religion. This 1:4 ratio is an important factor in the growth of the unaffiliated population. . . . Other highlights in this report include:

- The Christian share of the population is declining and the religiously unaffiliated share is growing in all four major geographic regions of the country. Religious "nones" now constitute 19% of the adult population in the South (up from 13% in 2007), 22% of the population in the Midwest (up from 16%), 25% of the population in the Northeast (up from 16%) and 28% of the population in the West (up from 21%). In the West, the religiously unaffiliated are more numerous than Catholics (23%), evangelicals (22%) and every other religious group.
- Whites continue to be more likely than both blacks and Hispanics to identify as religiously unaffiliated; 24% of whites say they have no religion, compared with 20% of Hispanics and 18% of blacks.
- The percentage of college graduates who identify with Christianity has declined by nine percentage points since 2007 (from 73% to 64%). Religious "nones" now constitute 24% of all college graduates (up from 17%) and 22% of those with less than a college degree (up from 16%).
- More than a quarter of men (27%) now describe themselves as religiously unaffiliated, up from 20% in 2007. Nearly one-in-five women (19%) now describe themselves as religiously unaffiliated, up from 13% in 2007. . . .
- As the ranks of the religiously unaffiliated continue to grow, they also describe themselves in increasingly secular terms. In 2007, 25% of the "nones" called themselves atheists or agnostics; 39% identified their religion as "nothing in particular" and also said that religion is "not too" or "not at all" important in their lives; and 36% identified their religion as "nothing in particular" while nevertheless saying that religion is either "very important" or "somewhat important" in their lives. The new survey finds that the atheist and agnostic share of the "nones" has grown to 31%. Those identifying as "nothing in particular" and describing religion as unimportant in their lives continue to account for 39% of all "nones." But the share identifying as "nothing in particular" while also affirming that religion is either "very" or "somewhat" important to them has fallen to 30% of all "nones."
- While the mainline Protestant share of the population is significantly smaller today than it was in 2007, the evangelical Protestant share of the population has remained comparatively stable (ticking downward slightly from 26.3% to 25.4% of the population). As a result, evangelicals now constitute a clear majority (55%) of all U.S. Protestants. In 2007, roughly half of Protestants (51%) identified with evangelical churches. . . .
- The share of the public identifying with religions other than Christianity has grown from 4.7% in 2007 to 5.9% in 2014. Gains were most pronounced among Muslims (who accounted for 0.4% of respondents in the 2007 Religious Landscape Study and 0.9% in 2014) and Hindus (0.4% in 2007 vs. 0.7% in 2014).
- Roughly one-in-seven participants in the new survey (15%) were born outside the U.S., and two-thirds of those immigrants are Christians, including 39% who are Catholic. More than one-in-ten immigrants identify with a non-Christian faith, such as Islam or Hinduism.
- Hindus and Jews continue to be the most highly educated religious traditions. Fully 77% of Hindus are college graduates, as are 59% of Jews (compared with 27% of all U.S. adults). These groups also have above-average household incomes. Fully 44% of Jews and 36% of Hindus say their annual family income exceeds $100,000, compared with 19% of the public overall. . . .

Notes

1 For more information on religion and the U.S. Census, see Appendix 3 in the 2007 Religious Landscape Study, "A Brief History of Religion and the U.S. Census."
2 The estimate that there were 227 million adults in the U.S. in 2007 comes from the U.S. Census Bureau's National Intercensal Estimates (2000–2010). The estimate that there were nearly 245 million adults in the U.S. in 2014 comes from Pew Research Center extrapolations of the U.S. Census Bureau's estimates of the monthly postcensal resident population.

46

Examples of Christian Privilege

Sam Killermann

Following is a list of privileges granted to people in the U.S. (and many western nations) for being Christian. If you identify as Christian, there's a good chance you've never thought about these things.

1. You can expect to have time off work to celebrate religious holidays.
2. Music and television programs pertaining to your religion's holidays are readily accessible.
3. It is easy to find stores that carry items that enable you to practice your faith and celebrate religious holidays.
4. You aren't pressured to celebrate holidays from another faith that may conflict with your religious values.
5. Holidays celebrating your faith are so widely supported you can often forget they are limited to your faith (e.g. wish someone a "Merry Christmas" or "Happy Easter" without considering their faith).
6. You can worship freely, without fear of violence or threats.
7. A bumper sticker supporting your religion won't likely lead to your car being vandalized.
8. You can practice your religious customs without being questioned, mocked, or inhibited.
9. If you are being tried in court, you can assume that the jury of "your peers" will share your faith and not hold that against you in weighing decisions.
10. When swearing an oath, you will place your hand on a religious scripture pertaining to your faith.
11. Positive references to your faith are seen dozens a time a day by everyone, regardless of their faith.
12. Politicians responsible for your governance are probably members of your faith.
13. Politicians can make decisions citing your faith without being labeled as heretics or extremists.
14. It is easy for you to find your faith accurately depicted in television, movies, books, and other media.
15. You can reasonably assume that anyone you encounter will have a decent understanding of your beliefs. . . .
16. You can travel to any part of the country and know your religion will be accepted, safe, and you will have access to religious spaces to practice your faith.
17. Your faith can be an aspect of your identity without being a defining aspect (e.g. people won't think of you as their "Christian" friend).

18. You can be polite, gentle, or peaceful, and not be considered an "exception" to those practicing your faith.
19. Fundraising to support congregations of your faith will not be investigated as potentially threatening or terrorist behavior.
20. Construction of spaces of worship will not likely be halted due to your faith.
21. You are never asked to speak on behalf of all the members of your faith. . . .
22. Without special effort, your children will have a multitude of teachers who share your faith.
23. Without special effort, your children will have a multitude of friends who share your faith.
24. Disclosing your faith to an adoption agency will not likely prevent you from being able to adopt children.
25. In the event of a divorce, the judge won't immediately grant custody of your children to your ex because of your faith. . . .
26. You can complain about your religion being under attack without it being perceived as an attack on another religion.
27. You can dismiss the idea that identifying with your faith bears certain privileges.

47

Christian Privilege and the Promotion of "Secular" and Not-So "Secular" Mainline Christianity in Public Schooling and in the Larger Society

Warren J. Blumenfeld

. . .

THE "FACES" OF [RELIGIOUS] OPPRESSION

Many overt forms of oppression are obvious when a dominant religious group tyrannizes a subordinated group, as in the mass slaughter of Jews and other stigmatized minorities in Nazi Germany, and the merciless killing of Jews and Muslims during the Christian "Crusades." Other forms of religious oppression are not as apparent, especially to members of dominant groups. Oppression in its fullest sense also refers to structural/systemic constraints imposed on groups even within constitutional democracies, and "[i]ts causes are embedded in unquestioned norms, habits, and symbols, in the assumptions underlying institutional rules and the collective consequences of following those rules." Young places these forms of oppression and privilege under five overarching categories or "faces" of powerlessness, exploitation, marginalization, cultural imperialism, and violence. The following sections adapt Young's taxonomy to investigate the concept of Christian privilege and religious oppression in the United States [see selection 7 in this volume].

POWERLESSNESS

Subordinated groups have less access to social power than members of dominant groups to engage in the decision-making processes that affect the course of their lives or that name the terms of their existence. "[T]he powerless are situated so that they must take orders and rarely have the right to give them . . . and they rarely command respect" [see selection 7 in this volume].

Historical foundations of religious powerlessness in the colonial period. The spiritual beliefs and identity that were foundational to the Native peoples originally inhabiting the vast territories now known as the United States were violently confronted with the advent of Christian European expansionism to North America. The Pilgrims, for example, who left England for Massachusetts in 1620 believed that they were a divinely chosen people, and soon established "a biblical commonwealth" considered superior to "heathen," "infidel" Native peoples. Massachusetts Puritans crafted their own form of Christianity in which "the church and the state were to support and protect each other."

Over the decades after the Puritans first landed on the shores of North America, other Christian, primarily Protestant "settlers" from Europe included Presbyterians, Methodists, Lutherans, Dutch Reformed, Congregationalist Puritans, and Baptists. In their attempts to assure religious freedom for themselves, under the leadership of William Penn, Quakers founded the colony of Pennsylvania, and Roman Catholics founded Maryland in the 1640s. In the following decades, however, Protestants established political power in Maryland, and in 1704, Protestant legislators passed anti-Catholic legislation unequivocally titled "An Act to Prevent the Growth of Popery within This Province" banishing Jesuits from the territory.

The pattern of Protestant domination and powerless subordinated religious groups continued from the colonial period throughout U.S. history. As recently as the middle-20th century, shortly after the U.S.'s entry into World War II, the government, in a mass relocation effort, interned over 112,000 Japanese Americans, many of them Buddhist, in concentration camps located far from their homes. Many of these incarcerated Japanese were U.S. citizens, born and living in this country for years. Officials used government policy to confiscate the homes, stores, and other property of the politically powerless Japanese Buddhists and to suspend their rights.

EXPLOITATION

Young views the "face" of exploitation as "a steady process of the transfer of the results of the labor of one social group to benefit another" . . . .

Religious justifications for exploitation. In colonial America, as private farms grew larger and farmers needed more cheap laborers to cultivate the land and tend the crops, many white landowners turned increasingly to the slave trade for their labor. Race and religion were intertwined as justifications for slavery in the Americas where "heathen" black Africans were stolen from their homelands and forced into slavery for the remainder of their lives. They were carried by slave ships, some of which were named the "Jesus," the "Grace of God," the "Angel," the "Liberty," and the "Justice," many with Christian ministers on board to help oversee the passage. In fact, Protestant churches offered scriptural justifications for slavery.

Conflicts between biblical justifications for slavery and biblical arguments for abolition split many Protestant congregations. The issue of slavery became a lightning rod in the 1840s among members of The Baptist General Convention, to organize a separate Southern Baptist Convention on a pro-slavery plank. One-hundred and fifty years later, the Southern Baptist Convention officially apologized to African Americans for its support and collusion with the institution of slavery, and also apologized for its rejection of civil rights initiatives of the 1950s and 1960s.

The expansion of the republic and movement west was in part justified by "Manifest Destiny": the belief that God intended the U.S. to extend its holdings and power across North America over native Indian tribes from east to west. The doctrine of "Manifest Destiny" also assumed Anglo-Saxon superiority. "This continent," a congressman declared, "was intended by Providence as a vast theatre on which to work out the grand experiment of Republican government, under the auspices of the Anglo-Saxon race."

During the early years of the new republic, with its increasing population and desire for land, political leaders, such as George Washington and Thomas Jefferson, advocated that Indian lands be obtained through treaties and purchase. President Jefferson in 1803 wrote a letter to then Tennessee political leader, Andrew Jackson, advising him to convince Indians to sell their "useless" forests to the U.S. government and become farmers. Jefferson and other government leaders overlooked the fact that this style of individualized farming was contrary to Indian communitarian spiritual/cultural traditions.

MARGINALIZATION

Marginalization is the "face" of oppression whereby entire categories of people—in the following examples, non-Protestant Christians—are restricted from meaningful involvement in the social life of the community and nation, and thus subjected to acute economic deprivation and even annihilation. Young defines *marginals* as "people the system of labor cannot or will not use" [see selection 7 in this volume].

Marginalization in the schools and society. The media constitute a major societal and institutional means of transmitting religious norms and beliefs, while maintaining the marginalization of the "other." Beaman describes the marginalization of new religious movements, "cults," Muslims, and indigenous Native peoples (2003, 315):

> New religious movements attract media attention for apocalyptic views and actions, and remain "cults" in public discourse. Muslims are the subject of biased media reports that seem to result in attacks on mosques and anti-Muslim sentiment. Aboriginals, for whom daily life and the physical world are inseparable from spirituality, are constructed as "problematic" because of their demands for equality and restitution.

Schools are another institutional means by which social norms are maintained and reproduced. Norms of Christian privilege and marginalization of members of other faith communities and non-believers in the schools are conveyed by curricular materials (curricular *hegemony*), which focus upon heroes, holidays, traditions, accomplishments, and importance of a European-heritage, Christian experience. Students who are Hindu, Muslim, Sikh, Jewish, and of other faiths, and non-believers, for example, see few, if any, people who look like them, who believe as they believe, or who adhere to the cultural expressions that they adhere to introduced and discussed in their classroom lessons.

In addition, the school calendar is organized to meet the needs of Christian faith communities, while marginalizing others. Examples include Jewish students who are compelled to request an excuse from school to attend religious services for their "High Holy Days" on and between Rosh Hashanah and Yom Kippur, which usually fall during the beginning of the academic year. In addition, Jehovah's Witnesses, who do not celebrate holidays—religious or otherwise—must also seek permission to be excused from the observance of holidays in school. (Jehovah's Witnesses, while a Christian denomination, are often marginalized within Christianity, and not accorded the same degree of Christian privilege as members of other so-called "mainstream" Christian faith communities.)

Muslim students, faculty, and staff often are not accorded the opportunity to have a safe prayer space on campus to perform the *salat* (prayer), as required by the Five Pillars of Islam. A case in point involved a 17-year-old high school junior in Ohio who was barred by school administrators from praying in an empty classroom at lunch and before and after class hours. Though a 1963 U.S. Supreme Court case ruled unconstitutional any *mandatory* prayers or Bible readings at public schools, subsequent rulings declared the constitutionality of many forms of personal religious expression on school campuses. In this case, the Council on American-Islamic Relations (CAIR) stepped in on the student's behalf, and convinced the school district to reverse its policy.

CULTURAL IMPERIALISM

Young states that "[c]ultural imperialism involves the universalization of a dominant group's experiences and culture, and its establishment as the norm" [see selection 7 in this volume].

Christian cultural imperialism and privilege. The manifestations of Christian privilege as cultural imperialism are numerous. First, the federal and school calendars are scheduled around Christian holidays and celebrations. In fact, the Christian holiday of Christmas has been declared a *national* holiday in which most businesses and government offices are closed and services suspended.

Society marks time through a Christian lens. Even the language we use in reference to the mainstream calendar reflects Christian assumptions. Not long ago we heard and read of the coming of the "21st Century," and the dawning of "*The* new millennium." Let us not forget, however, that the year 2000 is calculated with reference to the birth of Jesus, and it is, therefore, the beginning of the next *Christian* millennium. In fact, the dictionary definition of "millennium" notes "the thousand years mentioned in Revelation 20 during which holiness is to prevail and Christ is to reign on earth." This fact is apparent when someone mentions the date followed by "in the year of our Lord, Jesus Christ." The century markers B.C. (before Christ) and A.D. (*anno Domini*) are clearly Christian in origin. Therefore, the year 2000 is *one* important milepost, though, for many religious traditions, it also marks a heightening of their invisibility. Even recent attempts to decenter Christian hegemony in the marking of time by replacing B.C. with B.C.E. (before the common era) and A.D. with C.E. (common era), do not in actuality affect the marking of time before and after a "common" (Christian) era.

The workweek is structured to allow Christians the opportunity to worship on Sundays without conflicting with their Monday to Friday work schedules. For most of our history, state and local "Blue Laws" restrict sales, business operations, recreational activities, and governmental services on Sunday, the Sabbath for most Christian denominations. "Blue Laws" date back to colonial times when Sunday church attendance was mandatory. In 1816, a Jewish man named Abraham Wolf was convicted in Pennsylvania of the "crime" of "having done and performed worldly employment on the Lord's day" (Sunday). He appealed his sentence but lost.

In the schools, children or their parents or caretakers of other faiths must take responsibility to request accommodations from school officials either to be excused from ongoing school activities or to be absent to practice their religious traditions. For example, a Muslim elementary school student in central Iowa requested permission to attend the school library or to remain in her classroom for the duration of her lunch period during the Muslim holy month of Ramadan in which it was her practice to fast from sunrise to sunset. The school, however, had a *written* policy mandating that students must be present in the cafeteria during their lunch breaks. After repeated discussions with the school principal, the mother of the student convinced him to allow her daughter to go to an alternate space during the month of Ramadan while the student's classmates were at lunch.

Other examples of Christian cultural imperialism are numerous: the promotion of music, especially Christmas, by radio stations, and Christmas specials played on TV throughout November and December each year; Christmas decorations (often hung at taxpayer expense) in the public square throughout the United States; and the widespread availability of Christian holiday decorations, greeting cards, food, and other items during Christian (and Easter) holiday seasons.

Further examples of Christian cultural imperialism include the phrase "under God" in the Pledge of Allegiance or "In God We Trust" on U.S. currency and *Annuit Coeptis* (He [God] (or Providence) has favored our undertakings) on the Great Seal of the United States and printed on the back of the one-dollar bill, or the teaching of "Intelligent Design." The phrase "under God" was added to the school Pledge of Allegiance in 1954 during the Cold War in reaction to what many saw as a godless Soviet Union attempting to impose its economic and political system throughout the world. The phrase "In God We Trust" was added to U.S. coins during the American Civil War by Abraham Lincoln, and to paper currency in the 1950s during the Cold War.

Deculturalization and schooling of native peoples. In an attempt to add further dimensions and elaborations of Young's concept of cultural imperialism, I employ Spring's discussions of "cultural genocide" defined as "the attempt to destroy other cultures" through forced acquiescence and assimilation to majority rule and Christian cultural and religious standards. This cultural genocide works through the process of "deculturalization," which Joel Spring (2004) describes as an educational process that destroys a people's culture and replaces it with a new culture.

An example of "cultural genocide" and "deculturalization" can be seen in the case of Christian European American domination over Native American Indians, whom European Americans viewed as "uncivilized," "godless heathens," "barbarians," and "devil worshipers."

White Christian European Americans deculturalized indigenous peoples through many means: confiscation of land, forced relocation, undermining of their languages, cultures, and identities, forced conversion to Christianity, and forced removal of Native children to Christian day schools and off-reservation boarding schools far away from their people.

The first of many off-reservation Indian boarding schools was established in Carlisle, Pennsylvania in 1879 and run primarily by white Christian teachers, administered by Richard Pratt, a former cavalry commander in the Indian Territories. At the school, Indian children were stripped of their culture: the males' hair was cut short, they were forced to wear Western-style clothing, they were prohibited from conversing in their native languages and English was compulsory, all their cultural and spiritual symbols were destroyed, and Christianity was imposed.

"Civilizing" Indians became a euphemism for Christian conversion. Christian missionaries throughout the United States worked vigorously to convert Indians. A mid-19th century missionary wrote: "As tribes and nationals the Indians must perish and live only as men, [and should] fall in with Christian civilization that is destined to cover the earth."

VIOLENCE

A number of groups live with the constant fear of random and unprovoked systematic violence directed against them simply on account of their social identities. The intent of this xenophobic (fear and hatred of anyone or anything seeming "foreign") violence is to harm, humiliate, and destroy the "other."

During colonial times, religious dissension was violently repressed. For example, the Pilgrims "warned out of town" a Sephardic Jewish merchant, and banished Quaker missionaries. Later, as Quakers kept coming, the Puritans enacted harsher penalties, for example, cutting off their ears, or using hot irons to bore holes through their tongues. Then between 1659 to 1661, Puritans executed four Quakers on the gallows on Boston Common.

Recent examples of religious violence. Violence against Muslims, Sikhs, Hindus, and Jews has escalated in the United States since September 11, 2001. The Council on American Islamic Relations (CAIR), an American Muslim civil and human rights organization, in their 2005 annual report listed a total of 1,522 civil rights violations against American Muslims, 114 of which were violent hate crimes. This was a 49% increase in total incidents from just one year before. The report included incidents of violence, as well as harassment and discriminatory treatment, including "unreasonable arrests, detentions, searches/seizures, and detentions." The CAIR report included an incident in which a Muslim woman wearing a *hijab* (the garment many Muslim women wear in public) was taking her baby for a walk in a stroller, and a man driving a truck nearly ran them over. The woman cried out that, "You almost killed my baby!," and the man responded, "It wouldn't have been a big loss."

Nearly one-quarter of all reported civil rights violations against American Muslims involve unwarranted arrests and searches. Law enforcement agencies routinely "profile" Muslims of apparent Middle Eastern heritage in airports or simply while driving in their cars for interrogation and invasive and aggressive searches. In addition, governmental agencies, such as the IRS and FBI, continue to enter individuals' homes and mosques and make unreasonable arrests and detentions. Anti-Muslim hate crimes also occur on college and university campuses across the United States.

Sikhs have been the targets of increasing numbers of hate crimes as well. Since 2002, the Sikh Coalition organization listed 62 hate crimes directed against Sikh citizens of the United States. Many of the attacks committed against Sikhs are classified under the category of "personal attacks" or assaults as well as vandalism and arson. One incident involved a Sikh student at the University of North Carolina who was assaulted by three local teenagers. National attention focused on the severe beating of Rajinder Singh Shalsa in New York City, and the fatal shooting of Sikh gas station owner Balbir Singh Sodhi in Mesa, Arizona. It is widely assumed that Sikhs are targeted because they wear turbans, which the public imagination equates with terrorism.

Hindus have likewise been targeted. In June 2003, for example, Saurabh Bhalerao, a 24-year-old Indian graduate student studying in Massachusetts, was robbed, burned with cigarettes, beaten, stuffed in a truck, and twice stabbed before his assailants dumped him along the road. The attackers allegedly misidentified this Hindu student for a Muslim because during the assault, the perpetrators yelled at him, "Go back to Iraq."

Each year the Anti-Defamation League, a Jewish social advocacy organization, documents incidents of anti-Jewish hate crimes. They reported over 1,500 such incidents in 2004 alone, including verbal and physical assault, harassment, vandalism, property damage, and other acts of hate. These included the burning of a Holocaust museum in Indiana, and the spray-painting of swastikas and epithets on the walls and driveway of a Jewish community center near Phoenix, Arizona. This latter incident occurred on my campus, Iowa State University, in 2005. Among the swastikas, the vandals also spray-painted anti-Muslim, racist, misogynist, and homophobic epithets.

"MULTI-FACETED" PRIVILEGE AND OPPRESSION: IMMIGRATION BATTLES

The history of the 19th-century anti-immigration battles illustrates the intersections and interactions among Young's five faces of powerlessness, exploitation, marginalization, cultural imperialism, and violence, by which non-Christian religious status interacted with subordinated racial(ized) status. Throughout the 19th and into the 20th centuries, nativist exclusionist movements gained momentum within the United States. "Nativist" refers to an anti-immigrant ideology by U.S.-born, European-heritage Protestants, directed especially against non-Protestants such as Italian or Irish Catholics, Eastern European Jews, Asian Hindus, Muslims, Sikhs, and Buddhists. In some cases, non-white, non-Protestant ethnic and religious groups were *socially constructed* as lower "racial" forms by the mainline Protestant power structure as a justification for exclusion, exploitation, marginalization, cultural imperialism, and violence. Subsequently, religion was itself "racialized."

Strong "nativist" currents against Asian Muslim, Sikh, and Buddhist immigrants led the United States Congress to bar Chinese immigrants in 1882, and also made it illegal for Chinese to marry white or black Americans. The exclusionist sentiment regarding the Chinese held by many U.S. citizens was summarized by the editor of the newspaper in Butte, Montana: "The Chinaman's life is not our life, *his religion is not our religion*. . . . He belongs not in Butte." The Immigration Act of 1917 further prohibited immigration from Asian countries from the "barred zone," including parts of China, India, Siam, Burma, Asiatic Russian, Polynesian Islands, and parts of Afghanistan.

This "nativist" anti-immigration fever culminated in 1924 with the National Origins Act, which set restrictive quotas of immigrants from *Eastern* and *Southern* Europe, that is, mainly on Catholics and Jews (the latter referred to as members of the so-called "Hebrew race"). The law, however, permitted large allocations of immigrants from Great Britain and Germany in order to "protect our values . . . [as] a Western Christian civilization." Jews were considered racial as well as religious undesirables by the 19th century scientific community as a lower "racial" type, with essential immutable biological characteristics—a trend that increased markedly into the early 20th century C.E. Once seen as largely a religious, ethnic, or political group, Jews were viewed by "nativists," who valued American racial and religious "purity," as a "mixed race" (a so-called "mongrel" or "bastard race"), a people who had crossed racial barriers by interbreeding with black Africans during the Jewish Diaspora.

These restrictions on immigration based on "national origins" were not lifted until The Immigration and Nationality Act of 1965. This legislation resulted in dramatic increases in immigration from both Asian and Latin American countries of many religious backgrounds including Islamic, Hindu, Buddhist, Jain, Sikh, Zoroastrian, varying forms of Catholicism, and African, and Afro-Caribbean religious traditions. The 1965 law allowed for 170,000 immigrants from the Eastern Hemisphere and 120,000 from the Western Hemisphere with 20,000 immigrants per Eastern Hemisphere country. Partly as a result of the removal of restrictions on immigration that were specifically race-based and implicitly religion-based between 1882 until the 1960s—an effort to create an U.S.-American culture that was Protestant as well as northern European—the United States today stands as the most religiously diverse country in the world. This diversity poses great challenges as well as opportunities.

48

Racing Religion

Moustafa Bayoumi

Late in 1942, as World War II raged overseas, a Yemeni Muslim immigrant named Ahmed Hassan quietly appeared one day in front of a US district court judge. . . . Although Hassan was one of the first Arab Muslims to petition for American naturalization, his case was far from unique. Beginning in 1790 and until 1952, the Naturalization Act had limited citizenship to "free white persons" but without exactly defining what makes a person white. Thus, many people, primarily of Asian descent, had appeared in front of the courts before Hassan to argue that they were "white by law", to borrow a phrase from Ian Haney Lopez's book of the same name. The immigration laws had changed over the years . . . and in 1940 language was added to include "races indigenous to the Western Hemisphere." Nonetheless, certain Asians, beginning with the Chinese, had been excluded from American citizenship since 1878. In 1882, Congress passed the first Chinese Exclusion Act, and in 1917, most immigration from Asia was further curtailed with the establishment of what Congress called the "Asiatic Barred Zone." The reasoning here was that the country should not admit people who had no chance of naturalization. Despite all these changes, it was still far from clear just what race Hassan was, especially with Yemen sitting squarely on the Arabian Peninsula in Asia.

Hassan certainly knew he had a fight ahead of him and was aware that the battle would be about his group membership and not his individual qualifications. He understood that the court would want to know if Arabs were white or yellow, European or Asian, Western or Eastern. He probably knew that the court would wonder if Arabs, as a people, could assimilate into the white Christian culture of the United States or if they were, by nature, unsuited to adapt to the republic where they now lived. . . .

We know that Hassan was aware of the impending questions and the legal history of immigration by the fact that he came to court that day armed with affidavits stating that his coloring "is typical of the majority of the Arabians from the region from which he comes, which [in] fact is attributed to the intense heat and the blazing sun of that area." Under his arm were other affidavits, claims by unnamed ethnologists declaring that "the Arabs are remote descendants of and therefore members of the Caucasian or white race, and that [Hassan] is therefore eligible for citizenship." He had done his homework. He had hope.

Whatever optimism he may have had, however, was soon dashed. Hassan's petition was denied. In his three-page decision dated December 14, 1942, Judge Arthur J. Tuttle straightforwardly started that "Arabs are not white persons within the meaning of the [Nationality] Act." Interestingly, Tuttle based his determination of Hassan's whiteness not principally on the color of his skin but primarily on the fact that he was an Arab and Islam is the dominant religion among the Arabs. "Apart from the dark skin of the Arabs," explained the judge, "it is well known that they are a part of the Mohammedan world and that a wide gulf separates their culture from that of the predominately Christian peoples of Europe. It cannot be expected that as a class they would readily intermarry with our population and be assimilated into our civilization."

Religion determines race. At least in 1942 it did, and so Arabs were not considered white people by statute because they were (unassimilable) Muslims. But by 1944, a mere seventeen months later, things changed radically. At that time, another Arab Muslim would petition the government for citizenship. His name was Mohamed Mohriez, and he was "an Arab born in Sanhy, Badan, Arabia," who came to the United States on January 15, 1921. Unlike Hassan, however, Mohriez would succeed in his petition. District Judge Charles E. Wyzanski, who ruled in Mohriez's favour, made a point of explaining in his brief decision (delivered on April 13, 1944) that the global political leadership of the United States requires its adherence to the principles of equality that it espouses. Why? Wyzanski explained that his decision was necessary "to promote friendlier relations between the United States and other nations and so as to fulfil the promise that we shall treat all men as created equal." If in *Hassan* religion produces race, then in *Mohriez*, politics directly sways legal racial determination.

. . . But half a century after the *Hassan* decision, and following the terrorist attacks of September 11, Arabs and Muslims have again been repeatedly forced to undergo state scrutiny and official state definition simply because of their group membership and not because of their individual qualifications. Reminiscent of the earlier racial prerequisite cases, today's post September 11 state policies also teeter uncomfortably on race, religion, and contemporary politics, and the result has been mass exclusions and deportations of Arab and Muslim men from the United States in a strategy that, I argue, can properly be described as deliberate and racist.

Specifically, I am talking about the policy known as "special registration," a program of the Bush administration's War on Terror that drew on the history of the racial prerequisite cases for its authority and its practice. . . .Through special registration the government, in effect, turned a religion, namely Islam, into a race. The program was formally ended by the Obama administration on April 28, 2011. . . .

What exactly was special registration? It was a government mandated system of recording and surveillance that required all non-immigrant males in the United States over the age of sixteen who were citizens and nationals from select countries to be interviewed under oath, fingerprinted, and photographed by a Department of Justice official. Until December 2, 2003, this also applied to those already in the country (what the Department of Justice termed "call-in" registration). All those who were required to register had to provide proof of their legal status to remain in the United States, proof of study or employment (in the form of school enrollment forms or employment pay stubs), and proof of residential address (such as a lease or utility bill). . . . Not a single charge of terrorism was levied as a result of special registration.

Just what was going on here? If special registration was meant to be a program to net terrorists, as the government claims, then it was clearly a colossal and expensive failure. . . . But the criterion for "closer monitoring" of certain people was based almost exclusively on a single fact: national origin. . . .

Initially focused on citizens and nationals from five states (Iran, Iraq, Libya, Sudan, and Syria), the list of targeted nations requiring registration ballooned to twenty-five countries, some in North and East Africa (Egypt, Tunisia, Algeria, Morocco, Somalia, Eritrea), others in West Asia (Yemen, Kuwait, Saudi Arabia, United Arab Emirates, Qatar, Oman, Bahrain, Lebanon, Jordan), South Asia (Pakistan, Bangladesh, Afghanistan), Southeast Asia (Indonesia), and East Asia (North Korea). Six of these countries are listed by the State Department among the seven state sponsors of terrorism. The vast majority of the rest are allies of the United States. This fact alone—that the overwhelming number of men who were subject to special registration came from friendly countries—is significant, for it proves that something else other than enemy nationality was operative here. . . .

One should also note that little unites the disparate group of special registration countries but that they are all Muslim majority nations. . . . It reinscribed, through a legal mechanism, the cultural assumption that a terrorist is foreign-born, an alien in the United States, and a Muslim, and that all Muslim men who fit this profile are potentially terrorists. Through its legal procedures, special registration was a political and bureaucratic policy that created a race out of a religion.

RACING RELIGION

How does special registration "race" Islam? To begin answering this question, we need to understand how both racial and religious difference can be exploited in ways that are racist by definition. Racism is, of course, a complex social phenomenon that is difficult to sum up in just a few words. George Fredrickson, however, offers a useful definition in his book-length essay on the topic: racism "exists when one ethnic group or historical collectivity dominates, excludes, or seeks to eliminate another on the basis of differences that it believes to be hereditary and unalterable." While racism may at times appear similar to religious clashes, Fredrickson sees them as, in fact, quite distinct for the important reason that in religiously based systems or conflicts, the opportunities for conversion have always been present as a way to defeat one's own marginal status. In a religious conflict, it is not who you are but what you believe that is important. Under a racist regime, there is no escape from who you are (or are perceived to be by those in power). . . .

With its broad-brush focus on national origin, special registration juridically excluded thousands of Muslims by category and created a vast, new legal geography of suspicion for the US government. . . . But special registration again did more. In requiring that citizens and nationals of those countries suffer through its burdens, special registration collapsed citizenship, ethnicity, and religion into race. . . . The reason why this in particular is troubling is that, considering the broad geography of special registration, it makes descent or inheritability of Islam (and gender) the defining criterion. . . . And that inheritability has nothing to do with enemy nationality since most of the listed nations are considered allies of the United States. Nor has it anything to do with belief or political affiliation since it says nothing about each individual's worldview. Rather, it is only about one's blood relationship to Islam. Through that blood relationship, legal barriers have been established to exclude as many Muslims as possible, and that fact consequently turns Islam into a racial category. . . .

While we may be accustomed to thinking of racial definition as being determined by the color of one's skin, what we observe here is that religion in general, and Islam in particular, plays a role in adjudicating the race of immigrants seeking naturalization in the United States. The various immigration acts that constitute the body of racial exclusion laws did not explicitly place religion inside a logic of race, but the courts did repeatedly note the religion of an applicant, and that in itself was often a deciding (if not the deciding) factor in determining the race of the petitioner. Although the physical attributes of the applicants were often discussed, the main question surrounding many of these cases was actually about the ability to assimilate to the dominant, Christian culture. . . .

The first time a Syrian is denied naturalization because of his race occurs with Ex parte *Dow*, in 1914, . . . when the court here construed "free white person" to mean "inhabitants of Europe and their descendants.". . .

All of the Syrians to come before the court during the racial exclusion era were Christian, and the court often found it important to underline this fact in every instance it could. "The applicant is a Syrian native of the province of Palestine, and a Maronite. . . . It may be said, further, that he was reared a Catholic, and is still of that faith." . . .

Regrettably, Haney Lopez in his otherwise fine book also fails to account adequately for the role of politics in racial formation. He reaches the conclusion that "the incremental retreat from a 'Whites only' conception of citizenship made the arbitrariness of U.S. naturalization law obvious". But there is nothing arbitrary about the racial shift from *Hassan* to *Mohriez*, or the creation of Islam as a post–September 11 racial category. These are clearly political decisions that have calculated consequences.

. . . The concept of race incorporates, and arguably partially arose out of, cultural prejudice. Instead of a sustained investigation into the politics of whiteness and the whiteness of politics, what we get from Haney Lopez is an appeal for whites to "relinquish the privilege of Whiteness," thus making it clear that, for him, race making in the law is less a system of rational domination by the state than a problem of individual white identity (which he explicitly labels "white race consciousness").

But politics matters a great deal, and it always has. . . . The point is to recognize how labor or civil unrest or, especially for our purpose, war aids in producing citizenship and inclusion, which in the history of the United States functions through political power and along the definitional axis of race.

One of the most painful examples of race in flux during American history must be Japanese internment during World War II. The signing of Executive Order 9066 resulted not only in the internment of over 110,000 people of Japanese ancestry, but also in the removal of the protections of citizenship, at the stroke of a pen, for over 70,000 of them. Race trumped nationality. If you were born in the United States to Japanese parents prior to February 18, 1942, for example, you were an American citizen. But on February 19, you were born an enemy alien. . . .

Special registration is not necessarily a nefarious plot to racialize Islam, but it is a bureaucratic and cultural response to political turmoil. This is not say that religious bigotry no longer exists. If we consider the words of deputy undersecretary for defense, Lieutenant General William Boykin, who claims that "my God [is] a real God," and a Muslim's God is "an idol," and that the United States must attack radical Islamists "in the name of Jesus," we find that his statements participate not in racializing Islam but in older traditions of religious prejudice that, sadly, are still with us. Moreover, we should not exonerate special registration from the charge of being a legal method of racial formation, even if it does not subject all Muslims to its procedures and despite the fact that not every Muslim majority country is included on its list. In fact, what special registration accomplishes is the production of a typology of Muslim for the War on Terror, and by defining one type, it colors the whole population. What it produces is a kind of racial anxiety among Muslims, non-Muslims from Muslim countries, and those who are perceived to be Muslim. Every immigrant male in these groups must disidentify from the Muslim-as-terrorist figure, sometimes officially (as with special registration) or unofficially, as political policy and cultural attitudes bleed into each other. Suspicion is coded into law through race.

In fact, like Operation TIPS (Terrorist Information and Prevention System) (which asked us to spy on our neighbours), special registration is best understood as a form of political theatre. It allows a new bureaucracy (homeland security) to parade itself as being hard at work. The public is both the cast and the audience in this play. While it is acted out, we are propelled into living in an increasingly militarized and surveyed society. And when government actions impact Muslim populations so visibly, the public understands what is politically acceptable (even if critically prosecutable) behavor. Meanwhile, the government bureaucracy can mobilize statistics and bodies to prove that it is cleansing the country of a terrorist threat, all at the expense of Muslims in the United States.

What was particularly disheartening, however, was the academic silence around special registration while it proceeded apace. Without outspoken critique, special registration continued to race Muslims and to bind whiteness in the United States with political exigency and with notions of culture and Christianity. However, as Arendt says, "Neither violence nor power is a natural phenomenon . . . they belong to the political realm of human affairs whose essentially human quality is guaranteed by man's faculty of action, the ability to begin something new." From the beginning of its inception, special registration, in its continuation of this country's past of racial formation and rule through racial ways of thinking, was in fact begging us to begin something new.

49

Precedents

The Destruction of the European Jews

Raul Hilberg

. . .

Anti-Jewish policies and actions did not have their beginning in 1933. For many centuries, and in many countries, the Jews had been victims of destructive action. . . . The first anti-Jewish policy started in the fourth century after Christ in Rome. Early in the fourth century, during the reign of Constantine, the Christian Church gained power in Rome, and Christianity became the state religion. From this period, the state carried out Church policy. For the next twelve centuries, the Catholic Church prescribed the measures that were to be taken with respect to the Jews. Unlike the pre-Christian Romans, who claimed no monopoly on religion and faith, the Christian Church insisted on acceptance of Christian doctrine.

For an understanding of Christian policy toward Jewry, it is essential to realize that the Church pursued conversion not so much for the sake of aggrandizing its power (the Jews have always been few in number), but because of the conviction that it was the duty of true believers to save unbelievers from the doom of eternal hellfire. Zealousness in the pursuit of conversion was an indication of the depth of faith. The Christian religion was not one of many religions, but the true religion, the only one. Those who were not in its fold were either ignorant or in error. The Jews could not accept Christianity.

In the very early stages of the Christian faith, many Jews regarded Christians as members of a Jewish sect. The first Christians, after all, still observed the Jewish law. They had merely added a few nonessential practices, such as baptism, to their religious life. But their view was changed abruptly when Christ was elevated to Godhood. The Jews have only one God. This God is indivisible. He is a jealous God and admits of no other gods. He is not Christ, and Christ is not He. Christianity and Judaism have since been irreconcilable. An acceptance of Christianity has since signified an abandonment of Judaism.

In antiquity and in the Middle Ages, Jews did not abandon Judaism lightly. With patience and persistence the Church attempted *to convert* obstinate Jewry, and for twelve hundred years the theological argument was fought without interruption. The Jews were not convinced. Gradually the Church began to back its words with force. . . . Step by step, but with ever widening effect, the Church adopted "defensive" measures against its passive victims. Christians were "protected" from the "harmful" consequences of intercourse with Jews by rigid laws against intermarriage, by prohibitions of discussions about religious issues, by laws against domicile in common abodes. The Church "protected" its Christians from the "harmful" Jewish teachings by burning the Talmud and by barring Jews from public office.

. . .

Expulsion is the second anti-Jewish policy in history. In its origin, this policy presented itself only as an alternative—moreover, as an alternative that was left to the Jews. But long after the separation of church and state, long after the state had ceased to carry out church policy, expulsion and exclusion remained the goal of anti-Jewish activity.

. . .

The expulsion and exclusion policy was adopted by the Nazis and remained the goal of all anti-Jewish activity until 1941. That year marks a turning point in anti-Jewish history. In 1941 the Nazis found themselves in the midst of a total war. Several million Jews were incarcerated in ghettos. Emigration was impossible. A last-minute project to ship the Jews to the African island of Madagascar had fallen through. The "Jewish problem" had to be "solved" in some other way. At this crucial time, the idea of a "territorial solution" emerged in Nazi minds. The "territorial solution," or "the final solution of the Jewish question in Europe," as it became known, envisaged the *death* of European Jewry. The European Jews were to be killed. This was the third anti-Jewish policy in history.

To summarize. Since the fourth century after Christ there have been three anti-Jewish policies: *conversion, expulsion,* and *annihilation*. The second appeared as an alternative to the first, and the third emerged as an alternative to the second.

The destruction of the European Jews between 1933 and 1945 appears to us now as an unprecedented event in history. Indeed, in its dimensions and total configuration, nothing like it had ever happened before. As a result of an organized undertaking, five million

Table 49.1 Canonical and Nazi Anti-Jewish Measures

Canonical Law	Nazi Measure
Prohibition of intermarriage and of sexual intercourse between Christians and Jews, Synod of Elvira, 306	Law for the Protection of German Blood and Honor, September 15, 1935
Jews and Christians not permitted to eat together, Synod of Elvira, 306	Jews barred from dining cars (Transport Minister to Interior Minister, December 30, 1939)
Jews not allowed to hold public office, Synod of Clermont, 535 . . .	Law for the Re-establishment of the Professional Civil Service, April 7, 1933 . . .
Jews not permitted to show themselves in the streets during Passion Week, 3d Synod of Orléans, 538	Decree authorizing local authorities to bar Jews from the streets on certain days (i.e., Nazi holidays), December 3, 1938
Burning of the Talmud and other books, 12th Synod of Toledo, 681 . . .	Book burnings in Nazi Germany . . .
Jews obliged to pay taxes for support of the Church to the same extent as Christians, Synod of Gerona, 1078 . . .	The "Sozialausgleichsabgabe" which provided that Jews pay a special income tax in lieu of donations for Party purposes imposed on Nazis, December 24, 1940
Jews not permitted to be plaintiffs, or witnesses against Christians in the Courts, 3d Lateran Council, 1179, Canon 26 . . .	Proposal by the Party Chancellery that Jews not be permitted to institute civil suits, September 9, 1942 (Bormann to Justice Ministry, September 9, 1942) . . .
The marking of Jewish clothes with a badge, 4th Lateran Council, 1215, Canon 68 (Copied from the legislation by Caliph Omar II [634–644], who had decreed that Christians wear blue belts and Jews, yellow belts)	Decree of September 1, 1941 (Jews must [wear the] yellow star of David)
Construction of new synagogues prohibited, Council of Oxford, 1222	Destruction of synagogues in entire Reich, November 10, 1938 (Heydrich to Göring, November 11, 1938)
Christians not permitted to attend Jewish ceremonies, Synod of Vienna, 1267 . . .	Friendly relations with Jews prohibited, October 24, 1941 (Gestapo directive)
Compulsory ghettos, Synod of Breslau, 1267	[Compulsory ghettos] by order by Heydrich, September 21, 1939
Christians not permitted to sell or rent real estate to Jews, Synod of Ofen, 1279 . . .	Decree providing for compulsory sale of Jewish real estate, December 3, 1938 . . .
Jews not permitted to act as agents in the conclusion of contracts, especially marriage contracts, between Christians, Council of Basel, 1434, Sessio XIX	Decree of July 6, 1938, providing for liquidation of Jewish real estate agencies, brokerage agencies, and marriage agencies catering to non-Jews
Jews not permitted to obtain academic degrees, Council of Basel, 1434, Sessio XIX	Law against Overcrowding of German Schools and Universities, April 25, 1933

. . .

people were killed in the short space of a few years. The operation was over before anyone could grasp its enormity, let alone its implications for the future.

Yet, if we analyze this singularly massive upheaval, we discover that most of what happened in those twelve years had already happened before. The Nazi destruction process did not come out of a void; it was the culmination of a cyclical trend. One may observe the trend in the three successive goals of anti-Jewish administrators. The missionaries of Christianity had said in effect: *You have no right to live among us as Jews.* The secular rulers who followed had proclaimed: *You have no right to live among us.* The German Nazis at last decreed: *You have no right to live.*

These progressively more drastic goals brought in their wake a slow and steady growth of anti-Jewish action and anti-Jewish thinking. The process began with the attempt to drive the Jews into Christianity. The development was continued in order to force the victims into exile. It was finished when the Jews were driven to their deaths. The German Nazis, then, did not discard the past; they built upon it. . . .

The significance of the historical precedents will most easily be understood in the administrative sphere. The destruction of the Jews was an administrative process, and the annihilation of Jewry required the implementation of systematic administrative measures in successive steps. There are not many ways in which a modern society can, in short order, kill a large number of people living in its midst. This is an efficiency problem of the greatest dimensions, one which poses uncounted difficulties and innumerable obstacles. Yet, in reviewing the documentary record of the destruction of the Jews, one is almost immediately impressed with the fact that the German administration knew what it was doing. With an unfailing sense of direction and with an uncanny path-finding ability, the German bureaucracy found the shortest road to the final goal. . . . Necessity is said to be the mother of invention, but if precedents have already been formed, if a guide has already been constructed, invention is no longer a necessity. The German bureaucracy could draw upon such precedents and follow such a guide, for the German bureaucrats could dip into a vast reservoir of administrative experience, a reservoir that church and state had filled in fifteen hundred years of destructive activity.

In the course of its attempt to convert the Jews, the Catholic Church had taken many measures against the Jewish population. These measures were designed to "protect" the Christian community from Jewish teachings and, not incidentally, to weaken the Jews in their "obstinacy." It is characteristic that as soon as Christianity became the state religion of Rome, in the fourth century A.D., Jewish equality of citizenship was ended. "The Church and the Christian state, concilium decisions and imperial laws, henceforth worked hand in hand to persecute the Jews." Although most of these enactments did not cover all of Catholic Europe from the moment of their conception, they became precedents for the Nazi era. Table 49.1 compares the basic anti-Jewish measures of the Catholic Church and the modern counterparts enacted by the Nazi regime.

50

Maps—History of Anti-Semitism

Sir Martin Gilbert

The maps are shown on the following pages.

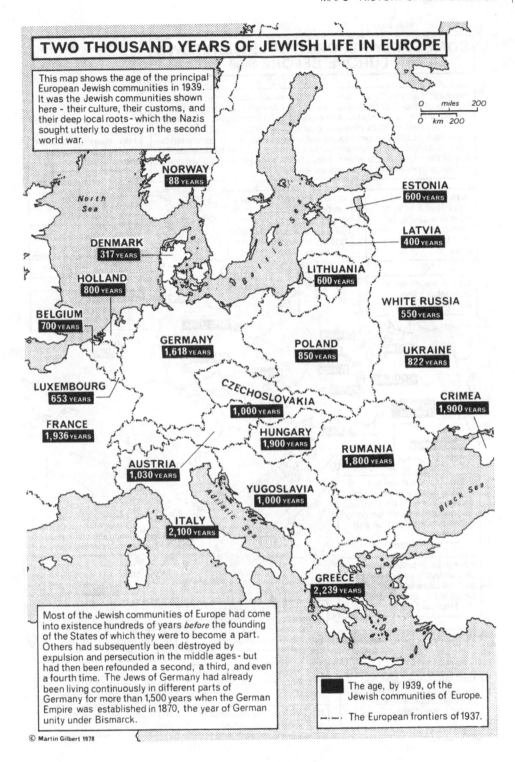

TWO THOUSAND YEARS OF JEWISH LIFE IN EUROPE

This map shows the age of the principal European Jewish communities in 1939. It was the Jewish communities shown here - their culture, their customs, and their deep local roots - which the Nazis sought utterly to destroy in the second world war.

0   miles   200
0   km   200

NORTH Sea

NORWAY 88 YEARS

ESTONIA 600 YEARS

LATVIA 400 YEARS

DENMARK 317 YEARS

Baltic Sea

LITHUANIA 600 YEARS

HOLLAND 800 YEARS

WHITE RUSSIA 550 YEARS

BELGIUM 700 YEARS

GERMANY 1,618 YEARS

POLAND 850 YEARS

UKRAINE 822 YEARS

LUXEMBOURG 653 YEARS

CZECHOSLOVAKIA 1,000 YEARS

CRIMEA 1,900 YEARS

FRANCE 1,936 YEARS

HUNGARY 1,900 YEARS

RUMANIA 1,800 YEARS

AUSTRIA 1,030 YEARS

Adriatic Sea

YUGOSLAVIA 1,000 YEARS

Black Sea

ITALY 2,100 YEARS

GREECE 2,239 YEARS

Most of the Jewish communities of Europe had come into existence hundreds of years *before* the founding of the States of which they were to become a part. Others had subsequently been destroyed by expulsion and persecution in the middle ages - but had then been refounded a second, a third, and even a fourth time. The Jews of Germany had already been living continuously in different parts of Germany for more than 1,500 years when the German Empire was established in 1870, the year of German unity under Bismarck.

The age, by 1939, of the Jewish communities of Europe.

–·–· The European frontiers of 1937.

© Martin Gilbert 1978

C
O
N
T
E
X
T

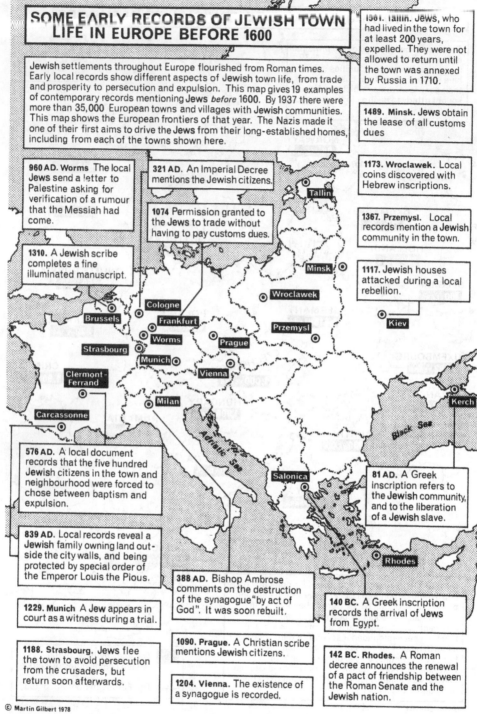

SOME EARLY RECORDS OF JEWISH TOWN LIFE IN EUROPE BEFORE 1600

Jewish settlements throughout Europe flourished from Roman times. Early local records show different aspects of Jewish town life, from trade and prosperity to persecution and expulsion. This map gives 19 examples of contemporary records mentioning Jews *before* 1600. By 1937 there were more than 35,000 European towns and villages with Jewish communities. This map shows the European frontiers of that year. The Nazis made it one of their first aims to drive the Jews from their long-established homes, including from each of the towns shown here.

1561. Tallin. Jews, who had lived in the town for at least 200 years, expelled. They were not allowed to return until the town was annexed by Russia in 1710.

1489. Minsk. Jews obtain the lease of all customs dues

960 AD. Worms The local Jews send a letter to Palestine asking for verification of a rumour that the Messiah had come.

321 AD. An Imperial Decree mentions the Jewish citizens.

1074 Permission granted to the Jews to trade without having to pay customs dues.

1173. Wroclawek. Local coins discovered with Hebrew inscriptions.

1367. Przemysl. Local records mention a Jewish community in the town.

1310. A Jewish scribe completes a fine illuminated manuscript.

1117. Jewish houses attacked during a local rebellion.

576 AD. A local document records that the five hundred Jewish citizens in the town and neighbourhood were forced to chose between baptism and expulsion.

81 AD. A Greek inscription refers to the Jewish community, and to the liberation of a Jewish slave.

839 AD. Local records reveal a Jewish family owning land outside the city walls, and being protected by special order of the Emperor Louis the Pious.

388 AD. Bishop Ambrose comments on the destruction of the synagogue "by act of God". It was soon rebuilt.

140 BC. A Greek inscription records the arrival of Jews from Egypt.

1229. Munich A Jew appears in court as a witness during a trial.

1090. Prague. A Christian scribe mentions Jewish citizens.

1188. Strasbourg. Jews flee the town to avoid persecution from the crusaders, but return soon afterwards.

1204. Vienna. The existence of a synagogue is recorded.

142 BC. Rhodes. A Roman decree announces the renewal of a pact of friendship between the Roman Senate and the Jewish nation.

© Martin Gilbert 1978

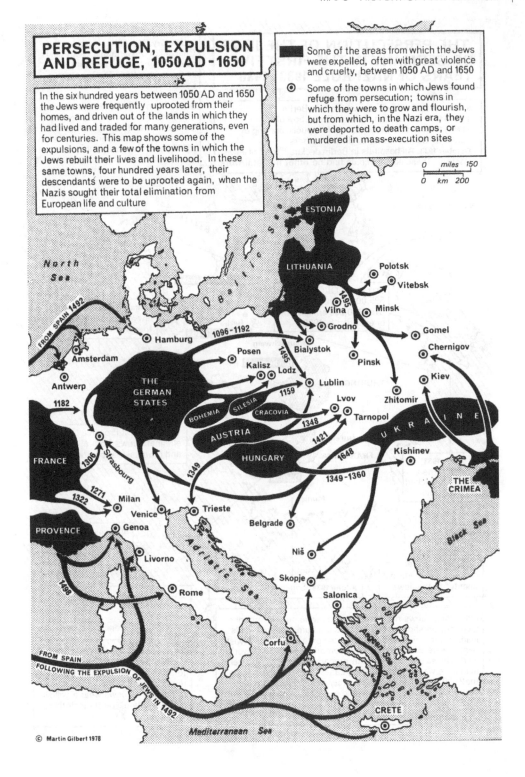

PERSECUTION, EXPULSION AND REFUGE, 1050 AD - 1650

In the six hundred years between 1050 AD and 1650 the Jews were frequently uprooted from their homes, and driven out of the lands in which they had lived and traded for many generations, even for centuries. This map shows some of the expulsions, and a few of the towns in which the Jews rebuilt their lives and livelihood. In these same towns, four hundred years later, their descendants were to be uprooted again, when the Nazis sought their total elimination from European life and culture

▮ Some of the areas from which the Jews were expelled, often with great violence and cruelty, between 1050 AD and 1650

⊙ Some of the towns in which Jews found refuge from persecution; towns in which they were to grow and flourish, but from which, in the Nazi era, they were deported to death camps, or murdered in mass-execution sites

0 __ miles __ 150
0 __ km __ 200

CONTEXT

North Sea

ESTONIA

LITHUANIA

Polotsk
Vitebsk
1495
Vilna
Minsk
Grodno
Gomel
Hamburg
1096 - 1192
1495
Bialystok
Pinsk
Chernigov
Amsterdam
Posen
Kalisz
Lodz
Lublin
Kiev
Antwerp
THE GERMAN STATES
1159
Lvov
Zhitomir
1182
BOHEMIA
SILESIA
CRACOVIA
1348
Tarnopol
UKRAINE
1306
Strasbourg
AUSTRIA
1421
FRANCE
HUNGARY
1648
Kishinev
1349
1349 - 1360
THE CRIMEA
1271
Milan
1322
Venice
Trieste
Belgrade
Black Sea
PROVENCE
Genoa
Livorno
Niš
Adriatic Sea
1498
Skopje
Rome
Salonica
FROM SPAIN FOLLOWING THE EXPULSION OF JEWS IN 1492
Corfu
Aegean Sea
CRETE
Mediterranean Sea

© Martin Gilbert 1978

FROM SPAIN 1492
Baltic Sea

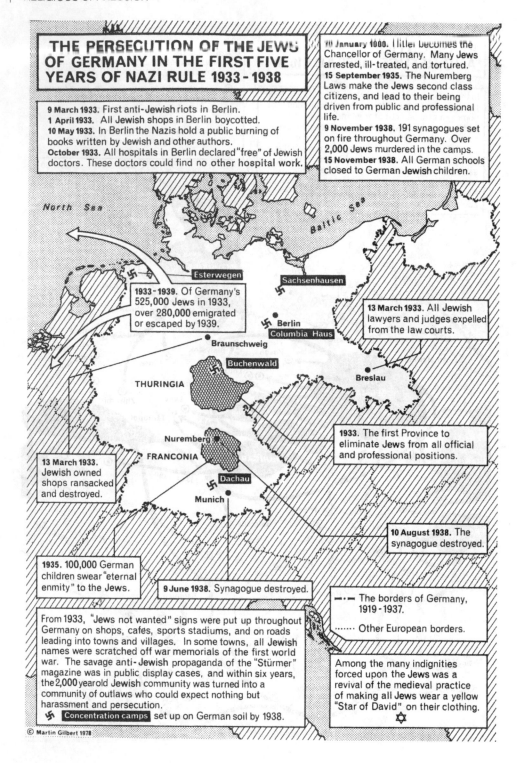

THE PERSECUTION OF THE JEWS OF GERMANY IN THE FIRST FIVE YEARS OF NAZI RULE 1933 - 1938

9 March 1933. First anti-Jewish riots in Berlin.
1 April 1933. All Jewish shops in Berlin boycotted.
10 May 1933. In Berlin the Nazis hold a public burning of books written by Jewish and other authors.
October 1933. All hospitals in Berlin declared "free" of Jewish doctors. These doctors could find no other hospital work.

10 January 1933. Hitler becomes the Chancellor of Germany. Many Jews arrested, ill-treated, and tortured.
15 September 1935. The Nuremberg Laws make the Jews second class citizens, and lead to their being driven from public and professional life.
9 November 1938. 191 synagogues set on fire throughout Germany. Over 2,000 Jews murdered in the camps.
15 November 1938. All German schools closed to German Jewish children.

North Sea

Baltic Sea

Esterwegen

Sachsenhausen

1933 - 1939. Of Germany's 525,000 Jews in 1933, over 280,000 emigrated or escaped by 1939.

Berlin
Columbia Haus

Braunschweig

13 March 1933. All Jewish lawyers and judges expelled from the law courts.

Buchenwald

THURINGIA

Breslau

1933. The first Province to eliminate Jews from all official and professional positions.

Nuremberg

FRANCONIA

13 March 1933. Jewish owned shops ransacked and destroyed.

Dachau

Munich

10 August 1938. The synagogue destroyed.

1935. 100,000 German children swear "eternal enmity" to the Jews.

9 June 1938. Synagogue destroyed.

— · — The borders of Germany, 1919 - 1937.

······· Other European borders.

From 1933, "Jews not wanted" signs were put up throughout Germany on shops, cafes, sports stadiums, and on roads leading into towns and villages. In some towns, all Jewish names were scratched off war memorials of the first world war. The savage anti-Jewish propaganda of the "Stürmer" magazine was in public display cases, and within six years, the 2,000 year old Jewish community was turned into a community of outlaws who could expect nothing but harassment and persecution.

Concentration camps set up on German soil by 1938.

Among the many indignities forced upon the Jews was a revival of the medieval practice of making all Jews wear a yellow "Star of David" on their clothing.

✡

© Martin Gilbert 1978

GERMAN OFFICIAL PLANS FOR THE "FINAL SOLUTION", 20 JANUARY 1942

The number of Jews mentioned at the Wannsee Conference, country by country and area by area, for eventual deportation, and subsequent death. More than 14 million people were thus marked out for death.

One of the macabre features of the numerical list of the Jews submitted to the Wannsee Conference was the fact that no figure was given for the Jews of Estonia, merely a brief note that Estonia was 'Free of Jews'. This was true; the 1,000 Estonian Jews who had come under German rule in October 1941 had all been murdered during the three months before the Wannsee Conference.

NORWAY 1,300
ESTONIA "Free of Jews"
USSR 5 million
DENMARK 5,600
LATVIA 3,500
HOLLAND 160,800
BIALYSTOK DISTRICT 400,000
LITHUANIA 34,000
BELGIUM 43,000
WHITE RUSSIA 446,484
Wannsee Berlin
GERMANY 131,800
Chelmno
GENERAL GOVERNM^T. 2,284,000
420,000
EASTERN TERRITORIES
FRANCE OCCUPIED ZONE 165,000
BOHEMIA AND MORAVIA 74,200
88,000
UKRAINE 2,994,684
SLOVAKIA
AUSTRIA
HUNGARY 742,800
FRANCE UNOCCUPIED ZONE 700,000
43,700
CROATIA 40,000
10,000
SERBIA
RUMANIA 342,000
ITALY 58,000
ALBANIA 200
BULGARIA
48,000
GREECE 69,600

In December 1941, a month *before* the Wannsee Conference, the first Nazi extermination camp had already come into operation, at Chelmno, responsible for the mass-murder of Jews, Gypsies, and Soviet prisoners-of-war. After passing through corridors marked 'To the showers' and 'To the doctor', the victims were forced into a large truck which was in fact a gas-chamber, where they were killed within a few minutes. By the end of 1944 more than 360,000 Jews had been murdered in Chelmno alone.

The Wannsee Conference also specified the number of Jews in *unconquered* countries for eventual destruction, including 330,000 from Britain, 18,000 from Switzerland, 6,000 from Spain and 4,000 from Ireland.

© Martin Gilbert 1978

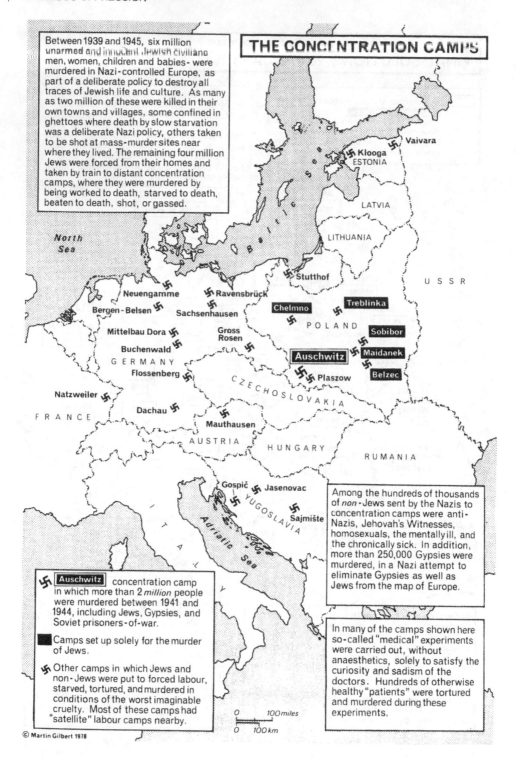

THE CONCENTRATION CAMPS

Between 1939 and 1945, six million unarmed and innocent Jewish civilians – men, women, children and babies – were murdered in Nazi-controlled Europe, as part of a deliberate policy to destroy all traces of Jewish life and culture. As many as two million of these were killed in their own towns and villages, some confined in ghettoes where death by slow starvation was a deliberate Nazi policy, others taken to be shot at mass-murder sites near where they lived. The remaining four million Jews were forced from their homes and taken by train to distant concentration camps, where they were murdered by being worked to death, starved to death, beaten to death, shot, or gassed.

Among the hundreds of thousands of *non*-Jews sent by the Nazis to concentration camps were anti-Nazis, Jehovah's Witnesses, homosexuals, the mentally ill, and the chronically sick. In addition, more than 250,000 Gypsies were murdered, in a Nazi attempt to eliminate Gypsies as well as Jews from the map of Europe.

Auschwitz concentration camp in which more than 2 *million* people were murdered between 1941 and 1944, including Jews, Gypsies, and Soviet prisoners-of-war.

Camps set up solely for the murder of Jews.

Other camps in which Jews and non-Jews were put to forced labour, starved, tortured, and murdered in conditions of the worst imaginable cruelty. Most of these camps had "satellite" labour camps nearby.

In many of the camps shown here so-called "medical" experiments were carried out, without anaesthetics, solely to satisfy the curiosity and sadism of the doctors. Hundreds of otherwise healthy "patients" were tortured and murdered during these experiments.

© Martin Gilbert 1978

0   100 miles
0   100 km

CONTEXT

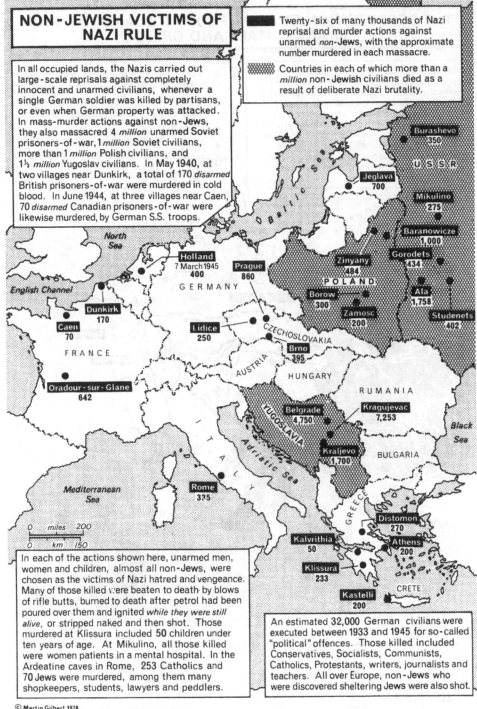

NON-JEWISH VICTIMS OF NAZI RULE

In all occupied lands, the Nazis carried out large-scale reprisals against completely innocent and unarmed civilians, whenever a single German soldier was killed by partisans, or even when German property was attacked. In mass-murder actions against non-Jews, they also massacred 4 *million* unarmed Soviet prisoners-of-war, 1 *million* Soviet civilians, more than 1 *million* Polish civilians, and 1½ *million* Yugoslav civilians. In May 1940, at two villages near Dunkirk, a total of 170 *disarmed* British prisoners-of-war were murdered in cold blood. In June 1944, at three villages near Caen, 70 *disarmed* Canadian prisoners-of-war were likewise murdered, by German S.S. troops.

■ Twenty-six of many thousands of Nazi reprisal and murder actions against unarmed *non*-Jews, with the approximate number murdered in each massacre.

▨ Countries in each of which more than a *million* non-Jewish civilians died as a result of deliberate Nazi brutality.

Burashevo 350
U.S.S.R.
Jeglava 700
Mikulino 275
Baranowicze 1,000
Gorodets 434
Zinyany 484
Holland 7 March 1945 400
Prague 860
POLAND
Borow 300
Ala 1,758
Zamosc 200
Studenets 402
GERMANY
Dunkirk 170
Caen 70
Lidice 250
CZECHOSLOVAKIA
Brno 395
FRANCE
AUSTRIA
HUNGARY
Oradour-sur-Glane 642
RUMANIA
YUGOSLAVIA
Belgrade 4,750
Kragujevac 7,253
Black Sea
Kraljevo 1,700
BULGARIA
ITALY
Rome 335
Mediterranean Sea

0 miles 200
0 km 150

GREECE
Distomon 270
Kalvrithia 50
Athens 200
Klissura 233
Kastelli 200
CRETE

In each of the actions shown here, unarmed men, women and children, almost all non-Jews, were chosen as the victims of Nazi hatred and vengeance. Many of those killed were beaten to death by blows of rifle butts, burned to death after petrol had been poured over them and ignited *while they were still alive,* or stripped naked and then shot. Those murdered at Klissura included 50 children under ten years of age. At Mikulino, all those killed were women patients in a mental hospital. In the Ardeatine caves in Rome, 253 Catholics and 70 Jews were murdered, among them many shopkeepers, students, lawyers and peddlers.

An estimated 32,000 German civilians were executed between 1933 and 1945 for so-called "political" offences. Those killed included Conservatives, Socialists, Communists, Catholics, Protestants, writers, journalists and teachers. All over Europe, non-Jews who were discovered sheltering Jews were also shot.

© Martin Gilbert 1978

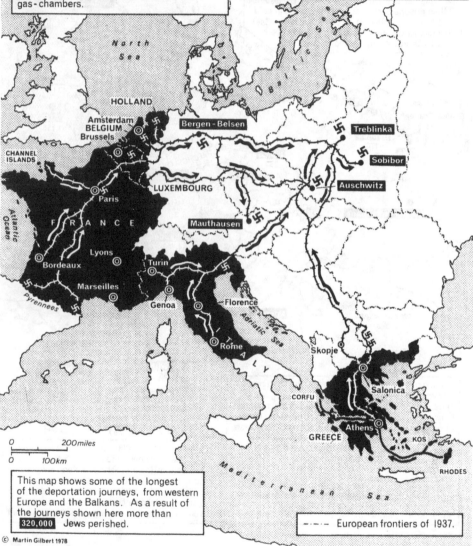

THE DEPORTATION OF JEWS FROM HOLLAND, BELGIUM, FRANCE, ITALY AND GREECE

Driven from their homes and deprived of their possessions, more than four million of the six million Jews of Europe who were murdered by the Nazis were sent in cattle trucks to Nazi death camps in the east. Up to a thousand people were forced into each train, deprived of food or water, and shunted eastwards. Many died during the journey. On arrival at the death camps, the majority, weakened, sick and bewildered, were sent straight to the gas-chambers.

⊚ Some of the principal towns from which Jews were deported from the countries shown here.

卐 Some of the deportation centres, in which Jews were confined before deportation.

↗ Main deportation routes, mostly operating between July 1942 and August 1944.

卐 Death camps.

This map shows some of the longest of the deportation journeys, from western Europe and the Balkans. As a result of the journeys shown here more than **320,000** Jews perished.

© Martin Gilbert 1978

—·—·— European frontiers of 1937.

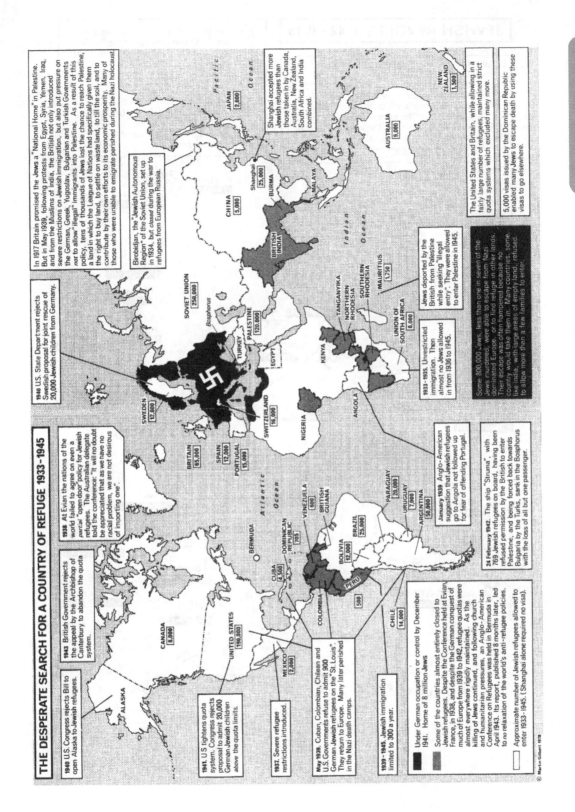

THE DESPERATE SEARCH FOR A COUNTRY OF REFUGE 1933–1945

JEWISH REVOLTS 1942-1945

Despite the overwhelming military strength of the German forces, many Jews, while weakened by hunger and terrorised by Nazi brutality, nevertheless rose in revolt against their fate, not only in many of the Ghettoes in which they were forcibly confined, but even in the concentration camps themselves, snatching from the very gates of death the slender possibility of survival.

 Ghettoes in which Jews rose up in revolt against the Germans, with dates. Many of those who revolted were able to escape to the woods, and to join Jewish, Polish or Soviet partisan groups.

Death camps in which the Jews revolted, with date of the revolt. In almost every instance, those who revolted were later caught and murdered.

This map shows twenty of the Ghettoes and five of the death camps in which Jews joined together and sought, often almost unarmed, to strike back at their tormentors. These twenty-five uprisings are among the most noble and courageous episodes not only of Jewish, but of world history.

© Martin Gilbert 1978

CONTEXT

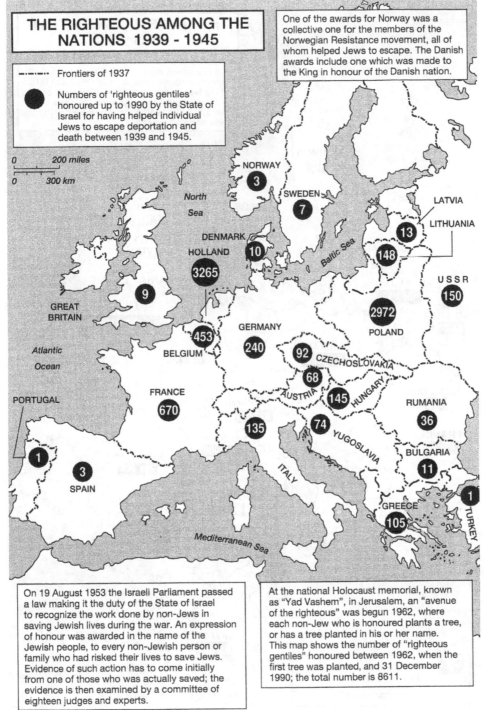

THE RIGHTEOUS AMONG THE NATIONS 1939 - 1945

One of the awards for Norway was a collective one for the members of the Norwegian Resistance movement, all of whom helped Jews to escape. The Danish awards include one which was made to the King in honour of the Danish nation.

—··—··— Frontiers of 1937

● Numbers of 'righteous gentiles' honoured up to 1990 by the State of Israel for having helped individual Jews to escape deportation and death between 1939 and 1945.

0   200 miles
0   300 km

NORWAY 3

SWEDEN 7

North Sea

LATVIA

LITHUANIA

DENMARK 10
HOLLAND 3265

Baltic Sea

13
148

USSR 150

GREAT BRITAIN 9

GERMANY 240

POLAND 2972

Atlantic Ocean

BELGIUM 453

CZECHOSLOVAKIA 92

AUSTRIA 68

HUNGARY 145

RUMANIA 36

PORTUGAL

FRANCE 670

135

YUGOSLAVIA 74

BULGARIA 11

1
SPAIN 3

ITALY

1

GREECE 105

TURKEY

Mediterranean Sea

On 19 August 1953 the Israeli Parliament passed a law making it the duty of the State of Israel to recognize the work done by non-Jews in saving Jewish lives during the war. An expression of honour was awarded in the name of the Jewish people, to every non-Jewish person or family who had risked their lives to save Jews. Evidence of such action has to come initially from one of those who was actually saved; the evidence is then examined by a committee of eighteen judges and experts.

At the national Holocaust memorial, known as "Yad Vashem", in Jerusalem, an "avenue of the righteous" was begun 1962, where each non-Jew who is honoured plants a tree, or has a tree planted in his or her name. This map shows the number of "righteous gentiles" honoured between 1962, when the first tree was planted, and 31 December 1990; the total number is 8611.

© Martin Gilbert 1978

CONTEXT

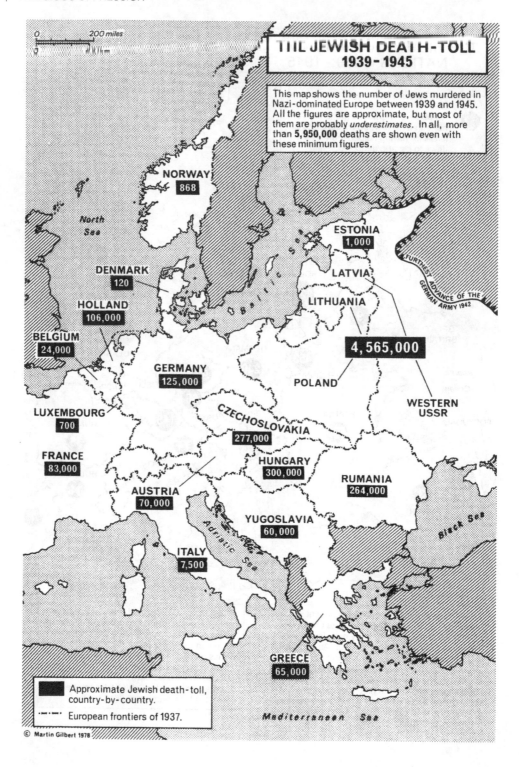

THE JEWISH DEATH-TOLL
1939-1945

This map shows the number of Jews murdered in Nazi-dominated Europe between 1939 and 1945. All the figures are approximate, but most of them are probably *underestimates*. In all, more than **5,950,000** deaths are shown even with these minimum figures.

NORWAY
868

North Sea

ESTONIA
1,000

LATVIA

DENMARK
120

LITHUANIA

HOLLAND
106,000

BELGIUM
24,000

4,565,000

GERMANY
125,000

POLAND

WESTERN USSR

LUXEMBOURG
700

CZECHOSLOVAKIA
277,000

FRANCE
83,000

HUNGARY
300,000

RUMANIA
264,000

AUSTRIA
70,000

YUGOSLAVIA
60,000

Black Sea

ITALY
7,500

GREECE
65,000

Approximate Jewish death-toll, country-by-country.

European frontiers of 1937.

Mediterranean Sea

© Martin Gilbert 1978

51

Working it Out

Diana Eck

One of the places we most commonly encounter religious difference in America today is the workplace. What religious attire may one wear? A cross? Yarmulke? Head scarf? Turban? Where and when is it appropriate to pray? What facilities do employers need to provide, and what policies do they need to implement? Religious difference is a question not just for theological schools and religious institutions but increasingly for businesses and corporations, offices and factories. These are the places where "we the people" most frequently meet, and how we manage our encounters here might be far more important than how we cope with imaginary encounters in the realm of theologies and beliefs.

The most common workplace issues have traditionally concerned working on the Sabbath, which is Saturday for Jews and Seventh-Day Adventists. Consider the case of a computer operator at a hospital in Fort Smith, Arkansas. Although he is a Seventh-Day Adventist and asked not to work on Saturdays, he was placed on call on Saturdays. When he refused to make himself available on his Sabbath, the hospital fired him. Title VII of the Civil Rights Act of 1964 prohibits discrimination on the basis of race, color, religion, national origin, or sex. In interpreting the act in relation to the religious practices of workers, the employer must try to make "reasonable accommodation" of religious practice, at least as long as it does not impose an "undue hardship" on the employer. In this case, the court ruled that the hospital was in violation of the Civil Rights Act. But just what constitutes "reasonable accommodation" and "undue hardship" is the thorny issue as each case comes forward.

In the past ten years the Equal Employment Opportunity Commission (EEOC), which considers workplace complaints that may violate the Civil Rights Act, has reported a 31 percent rise in complaints of religious discrimination in the workplace. This is not surprising given the number of new immigrants in the workforce and the range of questions their attire, their holidays, and their religious life bring to the workplace environment. We have already looked at the incivility and prejudice Muslim women wearing the *hijab* may encounter. But sometimes incivility slides up the scale toward discrimination. For example, in 1996 Rose Hamid, a twelve-year veteran flight attendant with U.S. Air, became increasingly serious about her faith in the wake of some health problems and made the decision to wear a head scarf. Her first day at work, she was ordered to take it off because it was not part of the uniform of a flight attendant, and when she refused she was put on unpaid leave. Rose filed a complaint with the Equal Employment Opportunity Commission. What is reasonable accommodation in Rose's case? Rose had modeled different ways in which the colors of her uniform would be duplicated in her scarf, and some would argue that reasonable accommodation would mean allowing some flexibility in the uniform as long as it was readily recognizable. But U.S. Air moved Rose to a job that did not require a uniform and hence put her out of public visibility. . . .

Hair and beards have also raised workplace issues. In 1987 a Sikh immigrant, Prabhjot Kohli, who had managed a pharmaceutical company in India before coming to the U.S., was turned down for a job at Domino's Pizza in Baltimore because of his religiously mandated beard. "Domino's wants clean-shaven people," he recalls being told, "and you've got a beard." In this case, wearing the baseball cap was not enough. For Domino's it was a business decision: people prefer to be served pizza by clean-shaven employees. The case went to the Maryland Human Relations Commission and was resolved only after a twelve-year lawsuit. In January 2000 the pizza chain dropped its no-beard policy. In California, Manjit Singh Bhatia, a machinist, was removed from his job at Chevron company because new safety requirements mandated the shaving of facial hair. His beard might prevent him from having an airtight seal when he wore a respirator. Chevron moved him to a different job that did not require a respirator and promised to reinstall him as a machinist if a respirator were developed that he could safely use. For the courts, this was "reasonable accommodation."

Some Muslim men, though not all, choose to keep a neatly trimmed beard, considering it part of their customary religious observance. A discrimination case went to court in New Jersey where members of the Newark police force sued for the right to wear a beard for religious reasons. In a 1999 ruling (*Fraternal Order of Police v. City of Newark*) the U.S. Court of Appeals upheld the right of Muslim members of the Newark police force to wear beards on the job. As we have seen from the Sikh experience however, workplace decisions on beards have varied. And so too with Muslim men. A bus driver for a New York transit company can now wear a beard, but an employee of one of the major airlines cannot.

Prayer in the workplace is another issue that has gained complexity with the new immigration. A Christian group might gather at 7:15 to pray together before work. A Buddhist meditation group might spend part of its lunch hour in sitting practice. In the spring of 1998 I received a CAIR bulletin with information on three similar cases of workplace prayer accommodation in manufacturing plants around Nashville. Whirlpool Corporation reportedly had refused to allow Muslim employees to offer obligatory prayers on the job. One Muslim employee quit, and the others continued to perform their obligatory midday prayer secretly during bathroom breaks. When CAIR intervened, contacted the managers, and began a dialogue, together they envisioned a solution: the Muslim employees could perhaps customize their coffee breaks so that they could fit an Islamic prayer schedule. Today, Muslim organizations, including CAIR, are taking the initiative in providing the kind of information that might head off the endless round of discrimination cases. They have published a booklet called *An Employer's Guide to Islamic Religious Practices*, detailing what employers might need to know about the obligations of Muslim workers.

Employers today are encountering workplace issues most of us have never even thought about. For example, where do Muslim cab drivers who work the airport routes pray during the long days in line at the airport? In Minneapolis, at last word, they stand outside in a lot, according to Salina Khan of *USA Today*. She wrote, on June 25, 1999,

> Taxi driver Farhad Nezami rolls out his prayer rug, removes his shoes and raises his hands to begin the early afternoon prayer. Nezami's not worshipping in a mosque. He's standing in a lot near the Minneapolis-St. Paul International Airport that about 300 Muslim cab drivers turn into a makeshift prayer hall several times a day. They pray there in rain, snow and sleet because the Metropolitan Airports Commission has repeatedly denied their request for a room for four years.

The case is not clear-cut, and it probably falls more in the realm of civility than legality. But Denver handled a similar case differently. A hundred Muslim cab drivers there put the question to the Denver Airport authority and received a positive response. Jillian Lloyd of the *Christian Science Monitor* reported, "When the city of Denver moved a glass shelter to its international airport this winter, giving Muslim cabbies a warm place to pray to Allah, it did not merely show government goodwill toward a religious minority. The move highlighted the growing willingness of American employers to provide for their workers' religious needs."

At the federal level, the White House has addressed the complexity that our new religious texture has brought to the workplace. In 1997 it released *Guidelines on Religious Exercise and Religious Expression in the Federal Workplace.* They provide a pathway through some of the issues, generally following one principle: "Agencies shall not restrict personal religious expression by employees in the Federal workplace except where the employee's interest in expression is outweighed by the government's interest in the efficient provision of public services or where the expression intrudes upon the legitimate rights of other employees or creates the appearance, to a reasonable observer, of an official endorsement of religion." For example, employees can keep a Bible or Koran in their desk and read it during breaks. Employees can speak about religion with other employees, just as they may speak about sports or politics. Employees may display religious messages on items of clothing to the same extent as they are permitted to display other messages. A supervisor can post an announcement about an Easter musical service on a bulletin board or can invite co-workers to a daughter's bat mitzvah as long as there is no indication of expectation that the employee will attend. There is a veritable thicket of examples in this nine-page document. It is the first herald of a new day in the workplace.

. . .

51 (CONTINUED)

See You in Court

Diana Eck

The American Constitution guarantees that there will be "no establishment" of religion and that the "free exercise" of religion will be protected. As we have seen, these twin principles have guided church-state relations in the United States for the past two hundred years. But the issues have become increasingly complex in a multireligious America, where the church in question may now be the mosque, the Buddhist temple, the Hindu temple, or the Sikh gurdwara. Every religious tradition has its own questions. Can a Muslim schoolteacher wear her head covering on the job as a public school teacher? Can a Sikh student wear the *kirpan*, the symbolic knife required of all initiated Sikhs, to school, or a Sikh worker wear a turban on a hard-hat job, in apparent violation of safety regulations? Should a crèche be displayed in the Christmas season on public property? Can the sanctity of Native lands be protected from road building? Should the taking of peyote by Native Americans be protected as the free exercise of religion? Can a city council pass an ordinance prohibiting the sacrifice of animals by the adherents of the Santería faith?

These difficult questions make clear that one vital arena of America's new pluralism is the courts. Since about 1960, church-state issues in America have been increasingly on court agendas. Just as the "church" is not a single entity in multireligious America, the "state" is multiple too, with zoning boards, city councils, state governments, and the federal government. At all levels, courts hear disputes and offer interpretations of laws and regulations and the constitutional principles that undergird them.

The First Amendment principles of nonestablishment of religion and the free exercise of religion sometimes almost seem to be in tension: the free exercise of religion calling for the protection of religious groups, while the nonestablishment of religion prohibiting any such special treatment. On the "no establishment" side, a landmark Supreme Court decision was made in the case of *Everson v. Board of Education* (1947) in which a school busing program in New Jersey was ruled to be accessible to students going to parochial schools. The Supreme Court's decision was clearly and narrowly defined: the busing program was a "generally available benefit" that should not be denied to children simply because their destination was a religious school. While the court has consistently ruled against state support of private religious schools, in this case, the benefit in question was not to the schools, but to the children. Justice Black wrote, "[T]he First Amendment requires the state to be neutral in its relations with groups of religious believers and non-believers; it does not require the state to be their adversary. State power is no more to be used so as to handicap religions than it is to favor them." The extended logic of this decision was that religious communities should have "equal access" to those benefits that are available to nonreligious communities. In other words, if a high school gymnasium in Bethesda, Maryland, can be used by the Girl Scouts or the Garden Club, its use cannot be denied to a Hindu temple community for its annual fall Diwali festival.

In "free exercise" cases, the *Sherbert v. Verner* decision in 1963 set a precedent that guided religious liberty cases for thirty years. In South Carolina, Adell Sherbert, a Seventh-Day Adventist, was fired from her job because she refused to accept a schedule requiring her to work on Saturday, her Sabbath, and was then refused state unemployment compensation. In her case, the Supreme Court articulated three questions to guide its decision: Has the religious freedom of a person been infringed or burdened by some government action? If so, is there a "compelling state interest" that would nonetheless justify the government action? Finally, is there any other way the government interest can be satisfied without restricting religious liberty? In sum, religious liberty is the rule; any exception to the rule can be justified only by a "compelling state interest." This form of reasoning came to be called the "balancing test"—balancing state interest against the religious freedom of the individual.

In the Sherbert case, the court ruled that there was no state interest compelling enough to warrant the burden placed upon Sherbert's religious freedom. Similarly, when an Amish community in Wisconsin insisted on withdrawing its children from public schools after the eighth grade and the State of Wisconsin insisted the children comply with compulsory education laws, the Supreme Court applied the three-pronged test and ruled that the religious freedom of the Amish outweighed the state's interest in four years' more compulsory education (*Wisconsin v. Yoder*, 1972).

Beginning in the 1980s, however, a series of Supreme Court rulings gradually weakened the force of the Sherbert balancing test and, in the view of many, weakened the constitutional guarantee of the free exercise of religion. These rulings began to raise disturbing questions about the religious rights of minorities. In the case of *Lyng v. The Northwest Indian Cemetery Protective Association* (1988), the issue was whether the Native Americans' right to preserve intact their sacred sites outweighed the government's right to build roads through Forest Service land. The Yurok, Karok, and Tolowa Indians argued that building a logging road through the land would have "devastating effects" on their religious ways. A lower court acted to prevent the Forest Service from building the road, but the Forest Service appealed to the Supreme Court. In this case, the Supreme Court supported the Forest Service, saying,

> Incidental effects of government programs which may make it more difficult to practice certain religions, but which have no tendency to coerce individuals into acting contrary to their religious beliefs [do not] require government to bring forward a compelling justification for its otherwise lawful actions. . . . However much we might wish that it were otherwise, government simply could not operate if it were required

to satisfy every citizen's religious needs and desires. . . . Whatever rights the Indians may have to the use of the area, however, those rights do not divest the government of its right to use what is, after all, its land.

Here, the balance tipped precipitously in favor of the government, whose policies, just incidentally, compromised Native religious practice.

For the Indians, one of the issues in this and other cases is whether the government recognizes the deeply held religious importance of preserving particular sacred sites undisturbed. A Hopi and Navajo case (*Wilson v. Block*, 1983) questioned whether a ski area could be built on a sacred mountain. The court ruled that the Forest Service had not infringed the religious rights of the Indians because it had not denied them access to the mountain. But the Navajo and Hopi argued that the mountain, the home of the Kachinas—divine messengers—would be desecrated by its commercial development. The court seemed to give little weight to the fact that the Native peoples considered the mountain to be inherently sacred, the very locus of the Divine, and not simply the place where they pray to the Divine. Here, the very nature of Native religious claims for the sanctity of the land seemed to be undermined, or perhaps not even understood, by the court's reasoning.

These and other cases led many to see an increasingly restrictive interpretation of the scope of religious freedom by the Supreme Court. In each case, the government did not have to demonstrate a "compelling interest" in order to restrict religious freedom. And in each case, the government did not have to alter its basic procedures to accommodate a specific religious claim. For example, an Abnaki Indian asked that his daughter, Little Bird of the Snow, be exempt from having to have a Social Security number in order to receive the benefits from the Aid to Families with Dependent Children program (*Bowen v. Roy*, 1986). The father insisted that to assign a number to his daughter would "rob her of her spirit" and interfere with her spiritual growth by making her a number, regulated by the federal government. The court ruled that the First Amendment could not be interpreted to require the government to alter its procedures in this way. Little Bird of the Snow would have to have a Social Security number.

Altering government procedures to accommodate various religious practices was also at stake in the case of *Goldman v. Weinberger* (1986). Dr. Goldman, an Orthodox Jewish psychiatrist serving in the U.S. Air Force, insisted on his right to wear his yarmulke on duty in the hospital, even though Air Force regulations prohibited a uniformed officer from wearing a head covering inside. The Air Force insisted that its code of military discipline requires that it not be continually making exceptions. The court said it would defer to the Air Force's judgment in this matter, which was to say: no yarmulkes.

Friday prayer for a Muslim prisoner was decided along similar lines in the case of *O'Lone v. Estate of Shabazz* (1987). Here, a Muslim prison inmate wanted to return from the work gang at noon for Friday prayers with other Muslims. He was turned down because officials insisted that it would require extra prison security at the work site and the gate in order to bring him back, and the court upheld the prison system's refusal to alter prison practices. In making this ruling, the court also said that a restrictive institution like the prison system had security needs and regulations that would necessarily mean that constitutional rights would not be as broad as those of ordinary citizens.

These increasingly restrictive interpretations of the guarantees of the First Amendment culminated in the controversial 1990 Supreme Court decision about peyote use. In this case (*Employment Division, Department of Human Resources of Oregon v. Smith*, 1990) two members of the Native American church ingested peyote, as is common in the ceremonial life of the church, and were subsequently fired from their jobs for "misconduct." The state of Oregon denied them unemployment compensation because they had been dismissed for the use of peyote, which was classified as an illegal drug. The Supreme Court upheld Oregon's decision, arguing that the state had a "generally applicable" law against drug use. The law did not specifically target the Native American church or any other group, and carving out exceptions to such laws would be impracticable, according to the 5–4 majority of the court. Justice Antonin Scalia argued that to require the government to demonstrate a "compelling state interest" in enforcing generally applicable laws would be "courting anarchy."

The Smith decision thus reversed many years of court precedent, which presumed that religious freedom would be the rule, with any infringement requiring the demonstration of a compelling state interest. Many critics insisted that for the court to refuse to apply the balancing test to "generally applicable laws" would seriously damage the first-amendment protection of religious freedom. The Smith decision, critics argued, would be especially hard on minority religions, since generally applicable laws are passed by the majority. Freedom of religion, on the other hand, is not subject to majority rule. The purpose of the Bill of Rights was precisely to limit the power of the majority in areas of fundamental rights, such as the freedom of conscience and speech.

The Santería Church of the Lukumi Babalu Aye in Hialeah, Florida, was a minority group in danger of losing its freedom of religious practice due to its unpopular and widely misunderstood practice of animal sacrifice. An estimated fifty thousand practitioners of the Afro-Caribbean Santería religion now live in South Florida, and their ceremonial life includes the sacrifice of chickens, pigeons, or other small animals to the *orisha*, their gods. The case that came to the Supreme Court (*Church of the Lukumi Babalu Aye v. City of Hialeah*, 1993) began in 1987 when Ernesto Pichardo, a priest of the Santería religion, purchased a building and a former used car lot to open a place of worship. The city council of Hialeah met to consider the matter, and many voices hostile to Santería were raised. The council passed three ordinances that effectively prohibited animal sacrifice within the city limits. As the city attorney explained, "This community will not tolerate religious practices which are abhorrent to its citizens."

Ernesto Pichardo and his community protested, insisting that the ordinances specifically targeted Santería, as they did not prohibit the killing of animals within city limits for secular reasons but only for religious ones and only, seemingly, for those of the Santería religion. Indeed, the ordinances specifically excluded Jewish kosher slaughter practices. Animals could be killed in butcher shops and restaurants but not in the religious context of Santería. Many quipped that the Church of Lukumi Babalu Aye was being persecuted for killing a few chickens with a prayer, while Frank Perdue and Colonel Sanders kill tens of thousands without one. The question before the Supreme Court was whether the three ordinances passed by the city council were constitutional or whether they violated the constitutional rights of the practitioners of Santería by specifically legislating against their religious practices. The judges unanimously struck down the ordinances, stating that they were not generally applicable laws at all but specifically aimed at the Santería religion. As Justice Anthony M. Kennedy wrote, "Although the practice of animal sacrifice may seem abhorrent to some, 'religious beliefs need not be acceptable, logical, consistent, or comprehensible to others in order to merit First Amendment protection.'"

The Santería case was an easy one, resting on the principle that "government may not enact laws that suppress religious belief or practice." However, many people, including Justice David Souter, were still disquieted about the merits and the precedent of the Smith decision. By this time, legislation called the Religious Freedom Restoration Act had been introduced in Congress precisely to restore the religious freedom many people in public life felt had been eroded with the Smith decision. This act, passed in 1995, stated simply, "The government cannot burden a person's free exercise of religion, even if the burden results from a rule of general applicability, unless the burden is essential to further a compelling governmental interest and is the least restrictive means of furthering that interest." In effect, it reinstituted the balancing test of the Sherbert case, this time in law. The legislation was eventually ruled unconstitutional by the Supreme Court in 1997, in part because it was a legislative maneuver to reestablish a form of judicial reasoning. This, the court believed, was the prerogative of the judiciary.

Questions of religious freedom lie at the heart of some of America's most hotly contested cases. The courts are one site of the encounter and disputation that are endemic to America's new pluralism. They represent the difficult places where we the people do not seem to be able to resolve our differences on our own. Cases involving America's newer religious communities have gradually made their way into the court system and into case law. The willingness to take advantage of access to the courts is itself a signal of the Americanization process.

In California's Livingstone School District, for instance, the schools and the Sikh community arrived at a stand-off on the question of whether three young Khalsa-initiated students would be permitted to attend school wearing the symbolic *kirpan*, a ceremonial dagger that is one of the five sacred symbols of the Sikh faith and is worn by all initiated Sikhs. In 1994 classmates of an eleven-year-old Sikh youngster had spotted his *kirpan* when his shirt slid up on the playground and reported this to the teacher. From the standpoint of the school, policy prohibited carrying weapons, including knives, on the school premises. From the standpoint of the Sikh youngster and his two siblings, the *kirpan* was part of their religious life, a symbol of their historic willingness to stand up for justice, and being required to take it off amounted to an infringement of their religious freedom. The U.S. District court barred the three youngsters from wearing the *kirpan*, and their parents kept them home from school. But when the case came to the Ninth U.S. Circuit Court of Appeals, the court overturned the ruling and required the Livingstone School District to make "all reasonable efforts" to accommodate the religious beliefs and practices of the three Sikh youngsters. According to the ruling, as long as the *kirpans* are small, sewn in the sheath, and not a threat to the safety of other students, the Sikh students must be allowed to wear them to school. Here, the courts were an avenue for working out a genuine dilemma that schools had not before encountered.

In New Jersey the Indo-American Cultural Society also found the court system necessary in order to resolve a community dispute having to do with its annual festival of Navaratri, the "Nine Nights" of the Goddess, observed on a series of weekend nights on the grounds of the Raritan Convention Center in Edison. This fall festival attracted as many as twelve thousand celebrants, and though it was arguably well out of earshot of residential areas, a group of citizens tried to block the festival. A 1995 meeting with the Township Council of Edison revealed a level of overt prejudice that was shocking to the representatives of the Indo-American Cultural Society. The chair of the society wrote to the township council following the meeting,

> We wonder if there is any awareness in Edison of freedoms of assembly and religion. We are immigrants to a democracy that provided the model for the constitution India adopted less than fifty years ago. We wonder how the folk who inspired our struggle against colonialism can arbitrarily dismiss our rights.

The council passed an ordinance aimed at restricting the hours of the festival, permits for the festival were delayed, and the Indo-American Cultural Society responded by seeking an injunction against what it considered the township's unfair ordinance.

Eventually, in July of 1996, a district judge upheld the rights of the Indo-American Cultural Society. But all this required the willingness of the Hindus to use the court system. Reflecting on the whole affair, Vivodh Z. J. Anand, a New Jersey human rights advocate, wrote,

> As a New Jersey State Civil Rights Commissioner, I have, since my immigration in 1963 at the height of the American Civil Rights movement, personally struggled for equity. I can report that the courts seem to be the only venue available to resolve vexing communal conflicts. While advocacy groups for a wide spectrum of social issues exist, the onus of resolving issues of religious freedom and rights, and in this case the more complex conflation of religious and racial "otherness," seems to rest only on those who are wronged and whose rights have been compromised.

Anand went on to report that during the entire struggle of the Indian community in New Jersey not a single religious group or community leader reached out to support the Indo-American Cultural Society in its well-publicized case. "In our democracy there is a paucity of institutions to study, educate, arbitrate, and promote the credence of the religious 'other.' Yet for a democracy to flourish, it is imperative that both individuals and groups be enabled to recognize that their own stories may be found in the stories and lives of fellow citizens who may appear dissimilar to themselves."

52

Native American Religious Liberty

Five Hundred Years After Columbus

Walter R. Echo-Hawk

. . .

HISTORICAL SUPPRESSION OF NATIVE RELIGION

Christopher Columbus's baggage included Europe's long heritage of religious intolerance. In 1492 Spain—fresh from centuries of religious crusades against the infidels for possession of holy places in the Middle East— . . . the Spanish Inquisition was in full force and effect. The King expelled the Jews from Spain on August 2, and, on January 4, military unification as a Christian nation was achieved with the Moorish defeat, which led to the expulsion of the Moslems.

. . .

On 12 October 1492, Columbus wrote this about the native inhabitants he encountered on his arrival in the Western Hemisphere:

They ought to be good servants and of good intelligence . . . . I believe that they would easily be made Christians because it seemed to me that they had no religion. Our Lord pleasing, I will carry off six of them at my departure to Your Highnesses, in order that they may learn to speak.

. . .

Old World attitudes of religious intolerance became ingrained in the United States government's Indian policies from the very inception of this nation. . . . A basic goal of federal Indian policy was to convert the "savage" Indians into Christian citizens and separate them from their traditional ways of life. President Jackson's Indian removal policy was justified in the name of converting and civilizing the Indians. During this removal period, Supreme Court decisions that upheld the government's taking of Indian lands and the reduction of tribal sovereignty from independent nation to "domestic dependent nation" status under discovery and conquest principles of international law referred to Indians as "heathen" savages.

Christian missionaries, hired as government Indian agents, were an integral part of federal Indian policy for over one hundred years. The government placed entire reservations and Indian nations under the administrative control of different denominations to convert the Indians and separate them from their traditions. A number of federal laws, still on the books today, authorize the secretary of the interior to give Indian lands to missionary religious groups for "religious or educational work among the Indians," 25 U.S.C. 348. In *Quick Bear v. Leupp*, 210 U.S. 50, 81–82 (1908), the Supreme Court upheld the use of federal funds to establish a Catholic school on the Rosebud Indian Reservation despite a claim that this government support of religion violated the Establishment Clause of the First Amendment.

. . .

Despite the government's goal to supplant tribal culture with Christianity, many Indians clung to their beliefs and practices even after they were confined on reservations. Chief Walking Buffalo's remarks show defiant native resistance to government-enforced proselytization:

> You whites assumed we were savages. You didn't understand our prayers. You didn't try to understand. When we sang our praises to the sun or moon or wind, you said we were worshipping idols. Without understanding, you condemned us as lost souls just because our form of worship was different than yours.
>
> We saw the Great Spirit's work in almost everything: sun, moon, trees, wind, and mountains. Sometimes we approached him through these things. Was that so bad? I think we have a true belief in the supreme being, a stronger faith than that of most of the whites who have called us pagans . . . . Indians living close to nature and nature's ruler are not living in darkness.

Consequently, in the 1890s, federal authorities became more belligerent toward Indian religion. In that decade, United States troops were called in to quell the Ghost Dance, a widely practiced tribal religion that impeded government assimilation policies. In 1890, more than one hundred Lakota Ghost Dance worshipers were massacred at Wounded Knee, South Dakota. In 1892, Pawnee Ghost Dance leaders were arrested in Oklahoma. In the same year, the BIA [Bureau of Indian Affairs] outlawed the Sun Dance religion and banned other ceremonies that were declared "Indian offenses" and made punishable by withholding of rations or thirty days' imprisonment. Facing the threat of military intervention, arrest, and starvation, many Indians stopped practicing the Ghost Dance and took other rituals underground.

Formal government rules suppressing tribal religions continued well into the 1900s. In 1904, the BIA promulgated regulations for its Court of Indian Offenses, including "offenses" that banned Indian religious leaders and ceremonies:

> . . . The "sun dance," and all other similar dances and so-called religious ceremonies, shall be considered "Indian offenses," and any Indian found guilty of being a participant in any one or more of these offenses shall . . . be punished . . . .

> The usual practices of so-called "medicine men" shall be considered "Indian offenses" . . . and whenever it shall be proven . . . he shall be adjudged guilty of an Indian offense, and upon conviction . . . shall be confined in the agency guardhouse . . . .

Even though this ban was lifted in 1934, serious government infringements on native religious freedom continued into the 1970s. Tribes witnessed governmental suppression of their religious practices in numerous ways: arrests of traditional Indians for possession of tribal sacred objects such as eagle feathers; criminal prosecutions for the religious use of peyote; denial of access to sacred sites located on federal lands; actual destruction of sacred sites; and interference with religious ceremonies at sacred sites. . . .

The treatment of native worship by the Supreme Court in the recent *Lyng* and *Smith* decisions, analyzed below, is especially troubling when considered in the context of the above history. Given the long history of government suppression of tribal religions, it is highly doubtful that these unique and irreplaceable indigenous religions can continue to survive without any American legal protection.

THE LYNG DECISION: NEED FOR FEDERAL SACRED SITES LEGISLATION

. . .

Worship at sacred sites is a basic attribute of religion itself. Since the inception of the major world religions, control over holy places in the Middle East has always been of deep international concern. Beginning around A.D. 1000, the Christian world engaged in a number of military/religious crusades, spanning several centuries, to wrest control of its holy places from the non-Christian world. Following the Crusades, Christian nations resorted to numerous treaties with countries in control of the Holy Land to preserve sacred sites and protect freedom of worship there. The Crimean War between France and Russia was fought over control of Christian holy places.

However, when most Americans think of holy places, they think only of well-known Middle Eastern sites familiar to the Judeo-Christian tradition, such as the Church of the Holy Sepulcher (Grave of Christ) and Basilica of the Nativity in Jerusalem and Bethlehem; Mecca; the Wailing Wall; or Mount Sinai. . . .

Traditional Native American religious sites—some of which rank among the most beautiful and breathtaking natural wonders left in America—serve a variety of important roles in tribal religion, which should be readily understandable to most people. However, in truly understanding and protecting Native American holy places, society may have to confront and modify basic values first implanted in this hemisphere by Columbus, because native sacred sites are natural, not man-made, sites. . . . It is undoubtedly difficult for a culture with an inherent fear of "wilderness" and a fundamental belief in the "religious domination" of humans over animals to envision that certain aspects of nature can be sacred. . . .

[H]owever, federal agencies such as the Forest Service and the National Park Service have repeatedly destroyed irreplaceable native sacred sites. The courts have consistently been unwilling to find any protections for Indians under the First Amendment or any statute. The struggle in the courts culminated in 1988, when the Supreme Court ruled in *Lyng* that Indians stand outside the purview of the First Amendment entirely when it comes to protecting tribal religious areas on federal lands for worship purposes.

In *Lyng*, a sharply divided Court denied First Amendment protection to tribal worship at a sacred site in northern California that would admittedly be destroyed by a proposed Forest Service logging road. The frightening aspect of the Court's refusal to protect worship at this ancient holy area was that the Court withheld protection, knowing that "the threat to the efficacy of at least some religious practices is extremely grave." . . .

In short, government may destroy an entire Indian religion under *Lyng* with constitutional impunity, unless it also goes further and punishes the Indians or forces them to violate their religion. The Court reached this result by an unprecedented narrow construction of the Free Exercise Clause. It held that Free Exercise protections arise *only* in those rare instances when government *punishes* a person for practicing religion or *coerces* one into violating his religion. Because it is hard to imagine rare instances in which that will happen, the Court's narrow interpretation renders the Free Exercise Clause a virtual nullity. This crabbed reading of the Bill of Rights is one that should deeply concern all citizens who cherish religious freedom principles, because, under *Lyng*, United States law guarantees less religious freedom than most other democracies and some nondemocratic nations.

As to the Indians in *Lyng*, the Court disclaimed judicial responsibility to safeguard religious freedom from government infringement, stating that any protection for them "is for the legislatures and other institutions." Former Justice Brennan's dissent noted the "cruelly surreal result" produced by the majority decision:

> [G]overnmental action that will virtually destroy a religion is nevertheless deemed not to "burden" that religion.

. . .

As a result of *Lyng*, there are no legal safeguards for native worship at sacred sites under the United States Constitution and laws, laying bare a basic attribute of religion itself. This legal anomaly has frightening implications for remaining tribal religions struggling to survive. . . .

From a policy standpoint, no religious group should be stripped of First Amendment protections in a democratic society so that its ability to worship is made wholly dependent on administrative whim. This is especially true for unpopular or despised minority religious groups, such as American Indians, who have suffered a long history of government religious suppression.

The failure of American law to protect holy places illustrates a larger failure of law to incorporate indigenous needs into a legal system otherwise intended to protect all citizens. Certainly, if this country contained holy ground considered important to the Judeo-Christian tradition, American law and social policy would undoubtedly accord stringent protections. Because important Judeo-Christian sites are located in other nations, it is understandable that, as American law developed in the United States, it never addressed this aspect of religious freedom. Thus, when native religious practitioners—who are the only ones with religious ties to holy ground located in this country—petitioned the courts, they found that the law was ill equipped to protect their religious liberty. However, if the purpose of law is to fairly protect all fundamental interests of our diverse and pluralistic society, then it must someday address indigenous needs, so that all basic human rights are fairly and equally protected.

. . .

53

Religious Freedom Advocates Are Divided Over How to Address LGBT Rights

Kelsey Dallas

Major players in the ongoing battle over religious freedom and LGBT rights are discussing conscience rights, LGBT protections and legislation needed to balance those competing interests.

Faith leaders and LGBT activists aren't the only ones is search of consensus since the Supreme Court legalized same-sex marriage. They are responding to in-fighting within the community of scholars, lawyers and policymakers who once worked together as religious freedom advocates.

"We all think . . . the view that non-discrimination protections must crowd out every other value is wrong, but we have different visions of the right," said Robin Fretwell Wilson, director of the family law and policy program at the University of Illinois College of Law and one of the meeting's organizers.

Wilson is a leader of what has been labelled the "Fairness for All" camp, working with lawmakers across the country to enact laws, like the Utah Compromise, that balance sexual orientation and gender identity, or SOGI, anti-discrimination laws with exemptions to protect the conscience rights of faith communities and religious business owners.

The other side, populated by prominent scholars and traditional marriage supporters like Robert George of Princeton University and Russell Moore of the Southern Baptist Convention's Ethics & Religious Liberty Commission, rejects SOGI protections, calling for stronger religious freedom laws rather than Fairness for All legislation.

The latter group of religious leaders recently outlined their arguments in a public letter titled "Preserve Freedom, Reject Coercion (http://www.colsoncenter.org/freedom)." . . .

It was the most public acknowledgment yet of the gridlock that's taken hold in compromise efforts that have involved LGBT activists, national corporations, religiously affiliated colleges, small-business owners and other groups with a stake in the LGBT rights.

Conflict is inevitable, especially when SOGI law supporters and detractors can make meaningful arguments to support their view, said Tim Schultz, president of the 1st Amendment Partnership.

But he, like other religious freedom advocates, is hoping to keep war at bay. . . .

RELIGIOUS FREEDOM TODAY

In recent years, the tone and politics of religious freedom debates has changed dramatically. Conscience rights were once a premier bipartisan cause—the Religious Freedom Restoration Act of 1993 fell three votes shy of passing unanimously in both houses of Congress—but has now become a partisan litmus test that carries the divisive labels of bigot and sinner.

Growing tension stems from many sources, including the nature of media coverage, business boycotts and the interference of national advocacy group in local politics, according to Schultz and others.

For example, controversy erupted in 2015 when Indiana passed a law offering typical state-level RFRA protections and also expanding on them. . . . Critics took to news sites, social media pages and blogs to decry it, and the governors of states like Connecticut and New York banned administrative travel to the state.

National businesses threatened boycotts, upping the stakes of the debate in Indiana and jeopardizing future efforts to craft conscience rights protections. . . .

The risk of business interference and negative media coverage has increased interest in Fairness for All legislation, similar to what passed the Utah Legislature in 2015. However, those behind the Utah Compromise say even a more balanced approach isn't immune from high-profile scrutiny.

"As we went through the process (of drafting the bill), people on the LGBT rights side would have to check with organizations like the Human Rights Campaign and the ACLU. And at the same time, we were running it by religious freedom scholars and attorneys inside and outside of the state," said Utah State Sen. Stuart Adams. . . .

Passed in March 2015, Utah's law protected members of the LGBT community from discrimination in housing and employment, while also ensuring the rights of faith groups and government officials with deeply held religious beliefs. It succeeded with the support of the dominant Church of Jesus Christ of Latter-day Saints and other religious stakeholders in the state, as well as representatives of local and national LGBT rights groups.

STUMBLING BLOCK

Adams now partners with Wilson to educate lawmakers and community leaders about the Utah Compromise, correcting false perceptions and combatting the increasingly polarized political climate. . . .

Ryan Anderson, a senior fellow at the Heritage Foundation who signed the December letter, is one of the most prominent SOGI critics. He disagrees with the logic of Fairness for All legislation, arguing that now is not the time to turn sexual orientation and gender identity into protected categories under the law.

Instead, policymakers should prioritize passing laws that ensure the rights of traditional marriage supporters, Anderson said. . . .

Even when SOGI laws include religious exemptions, as Utah's did, they cast belief in traditional marriage in a negative light, Anderson said.

Fairness for All legislation defines discriminations as a refusal to hire, house or serve people from the LGBT community or participate in a same-sex wedding ceremony, and then exempts the actions of some religious groups.

"The concern here is that, over time, the rule will swallow the exemption," he said, citing a 2014 Washington, D.C., City Council decision to remove carve-outs for religious schools from a previously passed SOGI law.

Recent research shows religious objectors fare better in court when they can point to faith-based exemptions to statutory protections instead of just the First Amendment.

Wilson, the Illinois law professor, acknowledged that the legislative landscape of SOGI laws sometimes put religious freedom at risk. . . .

However, Wilson and Schultz both said a spotty SOGI record in the past shouldn't put the brakes on future Fairness for All work.

DEEPER ENGAGEMENT

The arguments for both sides have developed over more than a decade of studying local, state and federal laws, attending conferences and writing books and papers. And their viewpoints continue to evolve. . . .

As they've worked to draw others into their camps, religious liberty experts have tried to pass on this same measured approach, providing context and history rather than a brief stump speech. . . .

The National Association of Evangelicals and the Council for Christian Colleges & Universities saw the value of exploring efforts to balance LGBT nondiscrimination measures and religious liberty. . . .

"The goal was to solicit input from and the wisdom of these leaders. We wanted to hear their thoughts and concerns and offer support," said Shapri LoMaglio, CCCU's vice president for government and external relations. . . .

ON THE HORIZON

Few people would have predicted that Utah would emerge as a groundbreaker in Fairness for All legislation. In addition to public urging by leaders of the LDS Church, policymakers were pushed to address the divisive issue because of the rapid spread of nondiscrimination ordinances at the municipal level, which had created confusion for statewide business. . . .

This situation is becoming more common across the country, as LGBT rights advocates move the needle in their favour at the local level, Schaerr said.

"Most opponents of Fairness for All legislation ignore the reality that the LGBT community has succeeded and continues to succeed in enacting strong LGBT protections in large and small cities throughout the nation," he said.

These SOGI statutes often pass without religious exemptions, Wilson said. Additionally, they create discrepancies from city to city that are hard for business owners to sort out.

Another reason for the recent surge in interest in SOGI laws and Fairness for All legislation is the election of Donald Trump. Some argue that he and a Republican-controlled Congress will be able to reassert religious freedom as a core priority. . . .

In the face of growing polarization, religious freedom scholars on both side of the SOGI debate said they're committed to keeping the lines of communication open.

Both camps find common ground in mutual dissatisfaction with the recent US Commission on Civil Rights report about conflict between religious freedom and SOGI protections. Commissioners sided with LGBT protections over conscience rights, painting a bleak picture of efforts to find compromise.

For Wilson, the report was as frustrating as the December letter from SOGI opponents. They both reject the notion of peaceful coexistence.

"If people from the deep left and deep right descend on a state and both say the other deserves no protection, this isn't going to work," she said. "The reasonable people in the middle get drowned out."

54

From Pearl Harbor to 9/11

Lessons from the Internment of Japanese American Buddhists

Duncan Ryûken Williams

Buddhist priests, classified by the Federal Bureau of Investigation (FBI) as potentially the most dangerous Japanese aliens, were among the first groups arrested by government officials following the bombing of Pearl Harbor on December 7, 1941. . . . Unlike Japanese American Christian priests and ministers, Buddhist priests were closely associated with Japan and thus with potentially subversive activity. . . . This perception that Buddhists (in contrast to Christians) were more Japanese than American was held not only by the FBI and the Wartime Relocation Authority (WRA) but also by the public at large, including some members of the Japanese American community. The history of Japanese American Buddhism during World War II, in fact, centers on this question of identity, both ethnic and religious.

. . .

The first Japanese Buddhist priests arrived in Hawaii and the U.S. mainland in the 1890s to minister to the first-generation issei. Most issei were Buddhists who had initially immigrated to Hawaii to work on plantations and to the mainland as contract laborers for railroad, lumber, mining, and cannery companies as well as on farms. In 1900, the Japanese immigrant population had risen to 24,326, most of them transient men. In 1930, however, the Japanese American population had grown to 138,834 and increasingly was composed of families with stable jobs and even small businesses. By the eve of the war, Buddhist temples functioned as both religious and community centers in all areas where Japanese Americans were concentrated, especially in California. . . . The FBI's decision to target Buddhist priests can be traced primarily to the conflation of Buddhism with state Shinto, which emphasized worship of the emperor as a deity and loyalty to the Japanese imperial empire. Not until the postwar period would Americans see Japanese Buddhism as a distinct tradition.

Newspaper editors and members of Congress accused all Japanese, including Japanese American children, of being loyal to the Japanese government and called for their removal from the West Coast. After their priests were taken away to "enemy alien" camps, the remaining members of Buddhist temples tried their best to continue religious services as well as community affairs. For example, the wives of priests and nonordained temple leaders took on duties that priests previously had performed exclusively.

By February 1942, the U.S. government set in motion the large-scale incarceration of the broader Japanese American community. On February 19, 1942, President Roosevelt issued Executive Order 9066, which ultimately led to the designation of restricted military zones on the West Coast and the subsequent removal of all persons of Japanese ancestry from those areas. In the ensuing months, the atmosphere in the community was one of anxiety, uncertainty, and fear. . . .

During this period of war hysteria, some Buddhists converted to Christianity, while others burned Japanese-language books and other personal Japanese cultural artifacts in an attempt to destroy, literally and symbolically, their Japaneseness while simultaneously demonstrating their Americanness. Mary Nagatomi, for example, remembers her parents telling her to go to the wood stove used for the family bath to burn everything in the household with "Made in Japan" on it, including her favorite traditional Japanese doll set. The one item the family members could not bring themselves to burn was a set of Buddhist sutras, which the father buried after wrapping the scriptures in kimono cloth, placing them in a metal rice-cracker box, and using a backhoe to dig a hole for them on the family farm. These sacred texts remain buried somewhere in central California, a silent testimony to the enduring Buddhist identity of one family, testimony that could not be completely obliterated despite the seeming necessity of doing so.

. . .

Japanese American Buddhists faced a crisis of identity and faith as they endured a harsh journey to the internment camps and the realities of the desert heat, coupled with the knowledge that they were prisoners in their own land. Within the camps, surrounded by barbed wire and armed guards, arose the question of what it means to be simultaneously American and Buddhist. What is an American Buddhist?

Buddhist life in the camps revolved around the barrack "churches," which held religious services and education classes (in some cases in mess halls and recreation buildings), especially on Sundays. According to the Reverend Arthur Takemoto, a young man during the internment period, Buddhist teachings such as those on suffering and patience helped alleviate the pain and confusion that many residents faced: "Understanding the basic tenets of Buddhism orients people to understand the reality of life, that things don't go the way we want them to go. This becomes *dukkha*, suffering and pain. To be able to accept a situation as it is means we could tolerate it more."

. . .

In this way, Buddhism not only provided a spiritual refuge for internees but also served the social function of maintaining family and communal cohesion through ancestral and life-cycle rituals and traditional Japanese festivals and ceremonies.

While Buddhism was, in this sense, a repository of Japanese traditions, it was also forced to operate in the context of an Americanization program promoted by the WRA. This program was organized to assimilate the Japanese and allow them to demonstrate loyalty to the United States. According to the *Investigation of Un-American Propaganda Activities in the United States* (1943) prepared by the Subcommittee of the U.S. House of Representatives Special Committee on Un-American Activities, camp administrators should promote recreational activities such as baseball and basketball as well as encourage internees to join groups such as the Boy and Girl Scouts and the YMCA/YWCA. Being Buddhist obviously was not listed as a method of demonstrating loyalty, but Buddhist groups made their own attempts at Americanization.

In May 1944, the name of the largest Buddhist organization in the Topaz Camp was changed from the Buddhist Mission of North America (BMNA) to the Buddhist Churches of America (BCA) to give the organization a more Christian-sounding name. The camp experience, however, only accelerated an assimilation process that had already begun prior to the war. The swastika symbol, often used on Buddhist temple stationery or on temple equipment prior to the internment, disappeared and was replaced almost universally by the dharma wheel. . . . By singing *gathas* as hymns, including Dorothy Hunt's "Onward Buddhist Soldiers" . . . Buddhists within the camp created a new medium for Americanizing Buddhism. They did so, however, in a way that honored their Buddhist traditions while simultaneously demonstrating loyalty to the United States. The young members of the community, having studied the Buddhist "Junior Catechism," for example, used a Christian medium to maintain Buddhist identity. Many of these elements constitute what might be called the Protestantization of Buddhism. . . .

As Buddhists attempted to find a place in mainstream American society, the English-speaking nisei also worked to gain a place for American Buddhism in the public sphere.

They organized two closely related campaigns to remember the lives and sacrifices made by the many nisei servicemen who had served in the 100th/442nd in Europe or as translators and intelligence gatherers in the Pacific Theater's Military Intelligence Service. A war veteran and devout Buddhist, Tad Hirota, led a *B* for Buddhism campaign to have the army officially recognize Buddhists in the armed services by creating a *B* designation on dog tags. (During World War II, the military had only three official preferences: *P* for Protestant, *C* for Catholic, and *H* for Hebrew.) . . . After some deliberation, a compromise was reached in 1949 that designated *X* to be used on dog tags for anyone not of the existing three religious preferences. Furthermore, an additional dog tag could be supplied by the soldier's church or temple that would positively identify his religion. The National Young Buddhist Coordinating Council subsequently campaigned for a Buddhist symbol to be placed on the headstones of Buddhist veterans at national cemeteries. After petitions were sent to Secretary of Defense, Louis Johnson, the army agreed late in 1949 to inscribe the "Buddhist emblem" for American soldiers of the Buddhist faith. These two campaigns represent an important legacy of the camps, testing both Japanese American Buddhist loyalty to America and America's loyalty to its Buddhist citizens.

. . .

While the long history of the Japanese American Buddhist experience obviously holds lessons for more recent Asian American immigrant Buddhist groups, one wonders if the war and incarceration experience cannot also inform and illuminate the recent unfolding of a "new religious America," as Diana Eck puts it. In particular, one wonders whether the targeting and harassment of Muslim Americans, Arab Americans, and those who may look like those who were responsible for the 9/11 attacks (such as Sikhs and other south Asians) parallels the Japanese American experience following Pearl Harbor.

According to the Council on American-Islamic Relations, which was tracking anti-Muslim incidents long before 9/11, cases of discrimination and attacks have soared since that event. Ethnic and religious profiling at airports and workplaces as well as physical violence (including the shooting of Balbir Singh Sodhi, a Sikh gas station owner in Mesa, Arizona) recall the hate crimes and discrimination faced by Japanese Americans after Pearl Harbor. Just as Japanese American Buddhist temples were vandalized and ancient Buddhist symbols, such as the swastikas (manji) that hung at temple doors, were riddled with shotgun fire by angry white neighbors, one saw an angry mob of three hundred people chanting "U.S.A., U.S.A." and marching on a mosque in Bridgeview, Illinois, right after 9/11. Whether it was the vandalizing of a Muslim bookstore in Alexandria, Virginia, on September 12, or someone shooting into a Dallas-area mosque, the Islamic Center of Irving, Islamic symbols quickly became targets for those caught up in war hysteria. "Visible religion," whether in dress or looks, combined with ethnic profiling has once again proved to be a factor in how American religious pluralism and tolerance are defined.

Just as hundreds of Buddhist priests were picked up by the FBI and hysterical claims were made that Buddhist bells were going to send Morse code message to the Japanese navy, the post-9/11 period has seen its share of indiscriminate arrests of thousands of young Muslim "enemy aliens" as well as the targeting of Muslim charitable organizations accused of having terrorist links. Many have developed the same kind of loyalty strategies as Japanese Americans did following Pearl Harbor: calls by organizations such as the American Muslim Council to cooperate with the FBI and support the president or drives to donate blood for the victims of the World Trade Center. While the rush to conversion, a strategy followed by some Japanese American Buddhists, is not an option for many Muslims, not only Muslims but also Sikhs and Hindus have sought ways of demonstrating loyalty to America, such as flying American flags or toning down religious or ethnic differences.

. . .

In the sixty years since Pearl Harbor, America has changed dramatically for Japanese Americans. In a June 2000 White House ceremony, President Bill Clinton bestowed the military's highest award, the Medal of Honor, on twenty-two Asian American war veterans. Japanese American veterans of the 442nd Regimental Combat Unit and the 100th Battalion, such as Senator Daniel Inoue (D-Hawaii), were honored for their valor in war. This action clearly signaled that Japanese Americans are no longer seen as foreigners. . . . Japanese American and Buddhist occupation of such high-profile public positions demonstrates a significant shift in America's religious, social, and political life. . . .

While the camp experience appears to have accelerated these types of post-war assimilationist tendencies—wanting to belong and to appear loyal—a lingering suspicion of mass incarceration and the denial of civil liberties for Muslim Americans remains strong among Japanese Americans, especially after the FBI brought in five thousand men, primarily of Arab and south Asian descent, for questioning in the domestic "war on terror." Within two and a half weeks of 9/11, two *New York Times* articles, "War on Terrorism Stirs Memory of Internment" and "Recalling Internment and Saying 'Never Again,'" chronicled what many Japanese Americans felt was a special responsibility to guard against ethnic scapegoating. Proclaiming that "we need to do everything that we wish good Americans had done 59 years ago," the executive director of the San Francisco Japanese American Cultural and Community Center, Paul Osaki, was one of many community leaders speaking out against violence and discrimination against Muslim Americans. On September 19, Japanese American leaders coordinated an unprecedented gathering of ethnic and religious leaders, including those from the American-Arab Anti-Discrimination Committee, the American Muslim Council, and the Council on American-Islamic Relations, to meet at the National Japanese American Memorial in Washington, D.C., and call for law enforcement officers and others to adequately address hate violence against religious and ethnic minorities.

. . .

Many Japanese Americans took on the conflicted identity of being a Japanese American Buddhist in the crucible of war. One wonders if 9/11 will also turn out to be similarly significant for Muslim Americans as they struggle with Americanization and resistance to it in their ethnic and religious identity formation.

55

A Somali Influx Unsettles Latino Meatpackers

Kirk Semple

Grand Island, Neb.—Like many workers at the meatpacking plant here, Raul A. Garcia, a Mexican-American, has watched with some discomfort as hundreds of Somali immigrants have moved to town in the past couple of years, many of them to fill jobs once held by Latino workers taken away in *immigration* raids.

Mr. Garcia has been particularly troubled by the Somalis' demand that they be allowed special breaks for prayers that are obligatory for devout Muslims. The breaks, he said, would inconvenience everyone else. "The Latino is very humble," said Mr. Garcia, 73, who has worked at the plant, owned by JBS U.S.A. Inc., since 1994. "But they are arrogant," he said of the Somali workers. "They act like the United States owes them."

Mr. Garcia was among more than 1,000 Latino and other workers who protested a decision last month by the plant's management to cut their work day—and their pay—by 15 minutes to give scores of Somali workers time for evening prayers. After several days of strikes and disruptions, the plant's management abandoned the plan. But the dispute peeled back a layer of civility in this southern Nebraska city of 47,000, revealing slow-burning racial and ethnic tensions that have been an unexpected aftermath of the enforcement raids at workplaces by federal immigration authorities.

Grand Island is among a half dozen or so cities where discord has arisen with the arrival of Somali workers, many of whom were recruited by employers from elsewhere in the United States after immigration raids sharply reduced their Latino work forces. The Somalis are by and large in this country legally as political refugees and therefore are not singled out by immigration authorities.

In some of these places, including Grand Island, this newest wave of immigrant workers has had the effect of unifying the other ethnic populations against the Somalis and has also diverted some of the longstanding hostility toward Latino immigrants among some native-born residents. "Every wave of immigrants has had to struggle to get assimilated," said Margaret Hornady, the mayor of Grand Island and a longtime resident of Nebraska. "Right now, it's so volatile."

The federal immigration crackdown has hit meat- and poultry-packing plants particularly hard, with more than 2,000 immigrant workers in at least nine places detained since 2006 in major raids, most on immigration violations. Struggling to fill the grueling low-wage jobs that attract few American workers, the plants have placed advertisements in immigrant newspapers and circulated fliers in immigrant neighborhoods.

Some companies, like Swift & Company, which owned the plant in Grand Island until being bought up by the Brazilian conglomerate JBS last year, have made a particular pitch for Somalis because of their legal status. Tens of thousands of Somali refugees fleeing civil war have settled in the United States since the 1990s, with the largest concentration in Minnesota. But the companies are learning that in trying to solve one problem they have created another.

Early last month, about 220 Somali Muslims walked off the job at a JBS meatpacking plant in Greeley, Colo., saying the company had prevented them from observing their prayer schedule. (More than 100 of the workers were later fired.) Days later, a poultry company in Minnesota agreed to allow Muslim workers prayer breaks and the right to refuse handling pork products, settling a lawsuit filed by nine Somali workers. In August, the management of a Tyson chicken plant in Shelbyville, Tenn., designated a Muslim holy day as a paid holiday, acceding to a demand by Somali workers. The plant had originally agreed to substitute the Muslim holy day for *Labor Day*, but reinstated Labor Day after a barrage of criticism from non-Muslims.

. . .

Nationwide, employment discrimination complaints by Muslim workers have more than doubled in the past decade, to 607 in the 2007 fiscal year, from 285 in the 1998 fiscal year, according to the federal *Equal Employment Opportunity Commission*, which has sent representatives to Grand Island to interview Somali workers. The Civil Rights Act of 1964 forbids employers to discriminate based on religion and says that employers must "reasonably accommodate" religious practices. But the act offers some exceptions, including instances when adjustments would cause "undue hardship" on the company's business interests.

The new tensions here extend well beyond the walls of the plant. Scratch beneath Grand Island's surface and there is resentment, discomfort and mistrust everywhere, some residents say—between the white community and the various immigrant communities; between the older immigrant communities, like the Latinos, and the newer ones, namely the Somalis and the Sudanese, another refugee community that has grown here in recent years; and between the Somalis, who are largely Muslim, and the Sudanese, who are largely Christian.

In dozens of interviews here, white, Latino and other residents seemed mostly bewildered, if not downright suspicious, of the Somalis, very few of whom speak English. "I kind of admire all the effort they make to follow that religion, but sometimes you have to adapt to the workplace," said Fidencio Sandoval, a plant worker born in Mexico who has become an American citizen. "A new culture comes in with their demands and says, 'This is what we want.' This is kind of new for me."

. . .

For their part, the Somalis say they feel aggrieved and not particularly welcome. "A lot of people look at you weird—they judge you," said Abdisamad Jama, 22, a Somali who moved to Grand Island two years ago to work as an interpreter at the plant and now freelances. "Or sometimes they will say, 'Go back to your country.'"

Founded in the mid-19th century by German immigrants, Grand Island gradually became more diverse in the mid- and late-20th century with the arrival of Latino workers, mainly Mexicans. The Latinos came at first to work in the agricultural fields; later arrivals found employment in the meatpacking plant. Refugees from Laos and, in the past few years, Sudan followed, and many of them also found work in the plant, which is now the city's largest employer, with about 2,700 workers.

In December 2006, in an event that would deeply affect the city and alter its uneasy balance of ethnicities, immigration authorities raided the plant and took away more than 200 illegal Latino workers. Another 200 or so workers quit soon afterward. The raid was one of six sweeps by federal agents at plants owned by Swift, gutting the company of about 1,200 workers in one day and forcing the plants to slow their operations.

Many of the Somalis who eventually arrived to fill those jobs were practicing Muslims and their faith obliges them to pray at five fixed times every day. In Grand Island, the workers would grab prayer time whenever they could, during scheduled rest periods or on restroom breaks. But during the holy month of *Ramadan*, Muslims fast in daylight hours and break their fast in a ritualistic ceremony at sundown. A more formal accommodation of their needs was necessary, the Somali workers said.

Last year, the Somalis here demanded time off for the Ramadan ceremony. The company refused, saying it could not afford to let so many workers step away from the production line at one time. Dozens of Somalis quit, though they eventually returned to work. The situation repeated itself last month. Dennis Sydow, the plant's vice president and general manager, said a delegation of Somali workers approached him on Sept. 10 about allowing them to take their dinner break at 7:30 p.m., near sundown, rather than at the normal time of 8 to 8:30.

Mr. Sydow rejected the request, saying the production line would slow to a crawl and the Somalis' co-workers would unfairly have to take up the slack. The Somalis said their co-workers did not offer a lot of support. "Latinos were sometimes saying, 'Don't pray, don't pray,'" said Abdifatah Warsame, 21.

After the Somalis went out on strike on Sept. 15, the plant's management and the union brokered a deal the next day that would have shifted the dinner break to 7:45 p.m., close enough to sundown to satisfy the Somalis. Because of the plant's complex scheduling rules, the new dinner break would have also required an earlier end to the shift, potentially cutting the work day by 15 minutes.

In a counterprotest on Sept. 17, more than 1,000 Latino and Sudanese workers lined up alongside white workers in opposition to the concessions to the Somalis. . . . The union and the plant management backed down, reverting to the original dinner schedule. More than 70 Somalis, including Mr. Warsame, stormed out of the plant and did not return; they either quit or were fired.

Since then, Ramadan has ended and work has returned to normal at the plant, but most everyone—management, the union and the employees—says the root causes of the disturbances have not been fully addressed. A sizeable Somali contingent remains employed at the factory—Somali leaders say the number is about 100; the union puts the figure at more than 300, making similar disruptions possible next year.

. . .

Xawa Ahmed, 48, a Somali, moved to Grand Island from Minnesota last month to help organize the Somali community. A big part of her work, Ms. Ahmed said, will be to help demystify the Somalis who remain. "We're trying to make people understand why we do these things, why we practice this religion, why we live in America," she said. "There's a lot of misunderstanding."

56

Jews in the U.S.

The Rising Costs of Whiteness

Melanie Kaye/Kantrowitz

BEFORE AMERICA NO ONE WAS WHITE

In 1990 I had returned to New York City to do antiracist work with other Jews, when a friend sent me an essay by James Baldwin. "No one was white before he/she came to America," Baldwin had written:

> It took generations, and a vast amount of coercion, before this became a white country. . . . It is probable that it is the Jewish community—or more accurately, perhaps, its remnants—that in America has paid the highest and most extraordinary price for becoming white. For the Jews came here from countries where they were not white, and they came here in part because they were not white, and incontestably—in the eyes of the Black American (and not only in those eyes) American Jews have opted to become white. . . .

Everything I think about Jews, whiteness, racism, and contemporary U.S. society begins with this passage. What does it mean: *Jews opted to become white*. Did we opt? Did it work? Was it an illusion? Could we have opted otherwise? Can we still?

Rachel Rubin, a college student who's been interning at Jews for Racial and Economic Justice, where I'm the director, casually mentions: when she was eight, a cross was burned on her lawn in Athens, Georgia. I remember the house I moved into in Down East Maine in 1979. On the bedroom door someone had painted a swastika in what looked like blood. I think about any cross-country drive I've ever taken, radio droning hymn after Christian hymn, 2000 miles of heartland.

On the other hand, I remember the last time I was stopped by cops. It was in San Francisco. I was getting a ride home after a conference on Jews and multiculturalism. In the car with me were two other white Jews. My heart flew into my throat, as always, but they took a quick look at the three of us and waved us on—*We're looking for a car like this, sorry*. I remember all the stories I've heard from friends, people of color, in which a quick look is not followed by a friendly wave and an apology. Some of these stories are about life and death.

Liberals and even progressives kneejerk to simplistic racial—black/white—terms, evade the continuing significance of race, and confound it with class. Race becomes an increasingly complex muddle. Growing numbers of bi- and multiracial children. *Hispanic*—not a racial identity, but a cultural/linguistic category conflating Spain with its former colonies. No one was *Asian* before they came to America, either; the term masks cultures diverse and polychromatic as anything Europe has to offer; yet *Asian American* has emerged as a critical and powerful identity. In the academy, obligatory nods to issues of race/class/gender result in language so specialized it's incomprehensible to most people, including those most pressured by these biases, and students tell me, "When Jews are mentioned in class, there's an awkward silence."

Where is *Jewish* in the race/class/gender grid? Does it belong? Is it irrelevant? Where do those crosses and swastikas fit in?

RACE OR RELIGION?

"Race or religion?" is how the question is usually posed, as though this doublet exhausts the possibilities. Christians—religiously observant or not—usually operate from the common self-definition of Christianity, a religion any individual can embrace through belief, detached from race, peoplehood, and culture.

But I have come to understand this detachment as false. Do white Christians feel kinship with African-American Christians? White slaveowners, for example, with their slaves? White Klansmen with their black neighbors? Do white Christians feel akin to Christians converted by colonialists all over the globe? Doesn't Christianity really, for most white Christians, imply *white*? And for those white Christians, does *white* really include *Jewish*? Think of the massive Christian evasion of a simple fact: Jesus Christ was not, was never, a Christian. He was a Jew. What did he look like, Jesus of Nazareth, 2000 years ago? Blond, blue-eyed?

Of course Jewish is not a race, for Jews come in all races. Though white-identified Jews may skirt the issue, Jews are a multiracial people. There are Ethiopian, Indian, Chinese Jews. And there are people of every race who choose Judaism, or were adopted or born into it from mixed parents. The dominant conception of Jewish—European, Yiddish-speaking—is in fact a subset, Ashkenazi. Estimated at 85–97 percent of Jews in the U.S. today, Ashkenazi Jews are those whose religious practice and diaspora path can be traced through Germany. The huge wave of Jewish immigration from Eastern Europe was Ashkenazi (as was the earlier, much smaller, highly assimilated community of German Jews, who looked with dread upon the arrival of—from their perspective—an impoverished, Yiddish-babbling, superstitious horde). Ashkenazi Jews also migrated to the far points of the globe—to South America, Australia, Africa, Asia. They may be very fair or very dark.

Sephardic Jews are those whose mother tongue is/was Ladino (Judeo-Español) and whose religious practice and diaspora path can be traced at some point through the Iberian Peninsula (Spain and Portugal), where they flourished, unghettoized, contributing along with Muslims to Spanish culture, until the Inquisition (read: *torture*) forced conversion or expulsion from Spain of all non-Christians. Sephardim migrated to—and lived for generations and even centuries—in Holland, Germany, Italy, France, Greece, the Middle East, and the Americas. The first Jews in the New World were Sephardim: 1492 marks not only Columbus's voyage but also the expulsion of the Jews from Spain. Some Sephardim consider themselves the aristocrats of the Jews, and look with contempt upon the Ashkenazi history of ghettoization and persecution. They may also be quite fair or quite dark.

Mizrachi Jews are those who lived in the Arab world and Turkey (basically, what was once the Ottoman Empire), as minorities in Muslim rather than Christian culture. Their mother tongue often is/was Judeo-Arabic. *Mizrachi* means "Eastern," commonly translated as "Oriental," and is used by and about Israelis, often interchangeably with *Sephardim*. The Spanish Sephardim sometimes resent the blurring of distinctions between themselves and the Mizrachim, reacting with pride in their history and with Eurocentric bias against non-Europeans, referring to themselves as "true" or "pure" Sephardim. The confusion between the categories is only partly due to Ashkenazi ignorance/arrogance, lumping all non-Ashkenazi together. Partly, it's the result of Jewish history: some Jews never left the Middle East, and some returned after expulsion from Spain, including to Palestine. Some kept Ladino, some did not. I imagine there was intermarriage. Mizrachim, though they may also range from fair to dark, are usually defined as "people of color."

The point is, categories of white and color don't correspond neatly to Jewish reality. (What does correspond is Ashkenazi cultural hegemony—in the U.S., where they are dominant by numbers, and in Israel, where Sephardi/Mizrachi Jews make up about two-thirds of the Jewish population and strongly contest this hegemony.) Jewish wanderings have created a people whose experience eludes conventional categories of race, nationality, ethnicity, geography, language—even religion. Cataclysm and assimilation have depleted our store of common knowledge.

No, Jews are not a single race. Yet there is confusion here, and subtext. Confusion because we have so often been racialized, hated *as if* we were a race. Ethnic studies scholars have labored to document the process of racialization, the fact that race is not biological, but a sociohistorically specific phenomenon. Observing Jewish history, Nancy Ordover has noted, offers an opportunity to break down this process of racialization, because by leaving Europe, Jews changed our "race," even as our skin pigment remained the same.

For the Jews came here from countries where they were not white, and they came here in part because they were not white. . . .

Confusion, too, because to say someone *looks Jewish* is to say something both absurd (Jews look a million different ways) and commonsense communicative.

When I was growing up in Flatbush, Brooklyn, every girl with a certain kind of nose—sometimes named explicitly as a Jewish nose, sometimes only as "too big"—wanted a nose job, and if her parents could pay for it, often she got one. I want to be graphic about the euphemism *nose job*. A nose job breaks the nose, bruises the face and eye area like a grotesque beating. It hurts. It takes weeks to heal.

What was wrong with the original nose, the Jewish one? Noses were discussed ardently in Flatbush, this or that friend looking forward to her day of transformation. My aunts lavished on me the following exquisite praise: *Look at her—a nose like a shiksa* (gentile woman). This hurt my feelings. Before I knew what a *shiksa* was, I knew I wasn't it, and, with that fabulous integrity of children, I wanted to look like who I was. But later I learned my nose's value, and would tell gentiles this story so they'd notice my nose.

A Jewish nose, I conclude, identifies its owner as a Jew. Nose jobs are performed so that a Jewish woman does not look like a Jew.

Tell me again Jewish is just a religion.

Yet Nazi racial definitions have an "only a religion" response. Even earlier, the lure of emancipation (in Europe) and assimilation (in the U.S.) led Jews to define Judaism as narrowly as possible, as religion only: "a Jew at home, a man in the streets," a private matter, taken care of behind closed doors, like bathing.

Judaism, the religion, does provide continuity and connection to Jews around the globe. There is something powerful even for atheists about entering a synagogue across the continent or the ocean, and hearing the familiar service.

But to be a Jew one need not follow religious practice; one need not believe in god—not even to become a rabbi (an element of Judaism of which I am especially fond). Religion is only one strand of being Jewish. It is ironic that it is precisely this century's depletion of Jews and of Jewish identity, with profound linguistic and cultural losses—continuing as Yiddish and Ladino speakers age and die—that makes imaginable a Jewishness that is *only a religion*—only now, when so much else has been lost. But to reduce *Jewishness* to *Judaism* is to forget the complex indivisible swirl of religion, culture, language, history that *was* Jewishness until, in the eighteenth century, Emancipation began to offer some Jews the possibility of escaping from a linguistically/culturally/economically isolated ghetto into the European "Enlightenment." To equate Jewishness with religion is to forget how even the contemporary, often attenuated version of this Jewish cultural swirl is passed down *in the family*, almost like genetic code.

Confusion and subtext. *Jewish* is often trivialized as something you choose, a preference, like tea over coffee. In contrast with visible racial identity, presumptions of choice—as with gayness—are seen as minimizing one's claim to attention, sympathy, and remedy. As a counter to bigotry, *I was born like this* strategically asserts a kind of victim-status, modeled on race, gender, and disability: If you can't help yourself, maybe you're entitled to some help from others. . . .

What happens if, instead, I assert my right to choose and not suffer for it. To say, *I choose*—my lesbianism and my Jewishness. Choose to come out, be visible, embrace both. I could live loveless or sexless or in the closet. I could have kept the name *Kaye*, and never once at Christmas—in response to the interminable "What are you doing for . . . ? Have you finished your shopping?"—answer, "I don't celebrate Christmas. I'm a Jew." I could lie about my lover's gender. I could wear skirts uncomfortably. I could bleach my hair again, as I did when I was fifteen. I could monitor my speech, weeding out the offensive accent, as I was taught at City College, along with all the other first and second generation immigrants' children in the four speech classes required for graduation, to teach us not to sound like ourselves. I could remain silent when queer or anti-Semitic jokes are told, or when someone says, "You know how *they* are." I could endure the pain in the gut, the hot shame. I could scrunch up much, much smaller.

In the U.S., *Christian*, like *white*, is an unmarked category in need of marking. Christianness, a majority, dominant culture, is not about religious practice and belief, any more than Jewishness is. As *racism* names the system that normalizes, honors, and rewards whiteness, we need a word for what normalizes, honors and rewards Christianity. Jews designate the assumption of Christianity-as-norm, the erasure of Jews, as *anti-Semitic*. In fact, the erasure and marginalization of non-Christians is not just denigrating to Jews. We need a catchier term than *Christian hegemony* to help make visible the cultural war against all non-Christians.

Christianism? Awkward, stark, and kind of crude—maybe a sign that something's being pushed; *sexism* once sounded stark and kind of crude. Such a term would help contextual-ize Jewish experience as an experience of marginality shared with other non-Christians. Especially in this time of rising Christian fundamentalism, as school prayer attracts support from "moderates," this contextualization is critical for progressive Jews, compelling us to seek allies among Muslims and other religious minorities.

I also want to contextualize Jews in a theoretical framework outside the usual bipolar frame of black/white—to go beyond dualism; to distinguish race from class, and both from culture; to understand whiteness as the gleaming conferral of normality, success, even survival; to acknowledge who owns what, and in whose neighborhood; to witness how money does and does not "whiten."

> *For in the eyes of the Black American (and not only in those eyes) American Jews have opted to become white. . . .*

To begin to break out of a polarity that has no place for Jews, I survey the range of color in the United States. People of color, a unity sought and sometimes forged, include a vast diversity of culture and history, forms of oppression and persecution. Contemporary white supremacists hate them all, but define some as shrewd, evil, inscrutable, sexually exotic, and perverse, and others as intellectually inferior, immoral, bestial, violent, and sexually rapacious. If it is possible to generalize, we can say that the peoples defined as shrewd and evil tend to be better off economically—or at least *perceived* as better off economically—than those defined as inferior and violent, who tend to remain in large numbers stuck at the bottom of the economic ladder (and are assumed by the dominant culture to be stuck there), denied access to decent jobs and opportunities, systematically disadvantaged and excluded by the educational system.

In other words, among the creeping fearsome dark ones are, on the one hand, those who exploit, cheat, and hoard money they don't deserve, and, on the other, those (usually darker) who, not having money, threaten to rob and pillage hard-working tax-paying white Christians. In this construct, welfare fits as a form of robbery, the women's form; the men are busy mugging. Immigrant bashing—whether street violence or political movements like "English-only" and California's overwhelming passage of Proposition 187—becomes a "natural" response to "robbery."

It is easier now to see where Jews fit: we are so good with money. Our "darkness" may not show, and this ability to pass confers protection and a host of privileges. But we are the model money-grubbing money-hoarding scapegoats for an increasingly punitive economic system. Jews, Japanese, Koreans, Arabs, Indians, and Pakistanis—let's face it: *interlopers*—are blamed for economic disaster; for controlling the economy or making money on the backs of the poor; for raising the price of oil; for stealing or eliminating jobs by importing goods or exporting production.

At the same time, those defined as inferior and violent are blamed for urban crime and chaos, for drugs, for the skyrocketing costs and failures of social programs. This blame then justifies the oppression and impoverishment of those brought here in chains and the peoples indigenous to this continent. Add in the darker, poorer immigrants from Latin America and the Caribbean, and recent immigrants from China and Southeast Asia. Media codes like "inner-city crime" and "teen gangs" distort and condense a vast canvas of poverty, vulnerability, and exploitation into an echoing story of some young men's violent response to these conditions. Thus those who are significantly endangered come to be defined as inherently dangerous.

That is, one group is blamed for capitalism's crimes; the other for capitalism's fallout. Do I need to point out who escapes all blame?

When a community is scapegoated, members of that community are most conscious of how they feel humiliated, alienated, and endangered. But the other function of scapegoating is at least as pernicious. It is to protect the problem which scapegoats are drafted to conceal: the vicious system of profit and exploitation, of plenty and scarcity existing side by side.

THE COST OF WHITENESS

Aryan ideology aside, Jews are often defined as white, though this wipes out the many Jews who are by anyone's definition people of color, and neglects the role of context: many Jews who look white in New York City look quite the opposite in the South and Midwest. Radicals often exclude the category *Jewish* from discussion, or subsume us into *white*, unless we are by *their* definition also people of color, in which case they subsume us as *people of color*.

The truth is, Jews complicate things. *Jewish* is both a distinct category and an overlapping one. Just as homophobia is distinct from sexism yet has everything to do with sexism, anti-Semitism in this country is distinct from racism yet has everything to do with racism. It's not that a Jew like myself should "count" as a person of color, though I think sometimes Jews do argue this because the alternative seems to be erasure. But that means we need another alternative. The problem is a polarization of white and color that excludes us. We need a more complex vision of the structure of racism, one that attends to the sick logic of white supremacists. We need a more complex understanding of the process of "whitening."

57

Oral History of Adam Fattah

Amna Ahmad

I used to wear a little charm around my neck that said *Allah* in Arabic, so naturally people in my school would identify me as Muslim. The Muslim population at my school is also definitely significant, so it's not very difficult to point us out.

. . .

I had a government teacher who used to talk about religion in my class. He used to speak about how all religions—though he focused mainly on talking about Judaism, Islam, and Christianity—can be considered very similar. He used to put the words "Judaism," "Islam," and "Christianity" on the board and write all the characteristics they had in common, such as prayer and the concept of fasting. He actually made sense in the way he approached the idea of likening one religion to another and definitely inspired an interest in me in the topic. . . .

While many of my teachers seem to approach the topic of Islam respectfully, as was the case with my government class teacher, the administration at my high school has made it inconvenient for me to practice my religion. Unfortunately they don't allow students a place to pray during school. Once I had actually gone to my guidance counselor to set up my schedule for the following term and asked her to switch my last period class, which was gym, with my lunch period so that I would have been able to leave school early enough to go to the mosque and pray. My guidance counselor simply would not allow that. As a result of her obvious indifference, I missed an entire term of going to the mosque on Fridays for Jummah prayer. I viewed myself as being at a huge disadvantage and was really upset about the situation. . . .

Sometimes, it seems as though Islamic practices are barely tolerable for administrators. Every so often I feel like I'm being penalized for putting religion before education. This year especially, I'm taking very difficult classes and to take off for three days because of the Eid is hard because I have to miss three days of very difficult work. I can usually only take off for one day of those three because otherwise I would miss more work than I could possibly make up. I often spend entire weekends just focusing on making up the work that I miss. That puts me very far behind. The Islamic holiday season becomes very stressful, and stress is something I really don't need in my life right now. Every time I have to take off for a Muslim holiday I end up having to explain to a teacher or fight with a teacher who argues, "There's no NYC Board of Ed law recognizing it as a holiday. You can't take off on Muslim holidays." . . .

Every so often, I feel as though it is more difficult to be the parent of a Muslim child than a Muslim student when dealing with the complications of the world of academia. A few years ago, my mother went to a parent-teacher conference for my brother, Muhamad. . . . I remember my mother's facial expression when she got home and I was immediately affected by the clear discontentment she expressed following the brief visit. My mother took the seat in front of Muhammad's math teacher when her turn had come. The math teacher was being very condescending and she looked down on my mother because she was wearing the veil, which is a key aspect of Islamic culture. She assumed right away that my mother didn't speak very good English. She spoke to her in language that was choppy, with a face that was uninviting to someone who was meeting her for the first time. With little concern for making a good first impression on a parent, she seemed to presume that my mother wasn't very well educated. When my mother started speaking to her after keeping silent for the first few minutes, it became clear to the teacher that she had been wrong. The math teacher was surprised by the fact that my mother was very well educated and spoke perfect English once she was given a chance. My mother has a bachelor's degree and two master's degrees. She herself is a teacher and was so affected by this feeling of being belittled by a stranger. She knew that she would never approach a parent in a way that communicates such degradation and disrespect. I don't think I would have thought the teacher's approach was motivated by prejudice had I not seen it in the red of my mother's eyes when she returned home to tell the story.

I would never have put too much consideration into connecting my Muslim identity with the more adverse experiences I have had in my life had I not seen it in the eyes of the woman who was prevented from attending school by immigrant parents who didn't know better; the woman who went back to college after raising three boys into maturity.

57 (CONTINUED)

Oral History of Hagar Omran

Hoda Zawam

I identify myself as an Arab American. That's what I am because I was born here. I'm an American, but I'm not like every other American. I spice up the average American by being an Arab American because I have merged both cultures together. It's just like adding rainbow sprinkles on vanilla ice cream.

I am Egyptian and so are both of my parents. Even though I was born and raised here, my parents really stick to Egyptian culture. We eat a lot of Egyptian food. We listen to Arabic music and are very family oriented. . . .

I started wearing the hijab when I was a 6th grader. It wasn't hard for me because it doesn't really matter how I look—I'm still the same person from the inside. . . . My friends were cool and they all wore hijab and they made hijab look good, fun, and easy. Hijab makes me feel proud and it makes me stand out because everyone knows that I'm Muslim. Hijab is not a burden on me, rather it's a pleasure.

I'm an 11th grader in high school. My school is nice and it's pretty cool. But it's not fair that our holidays are not considered government holidays and we don't get time off, just like the Christians get off for Christmas, and the Jews get off for Hanukah. Now that we're a big population in America and we are not a minority anymore, we should get our rights. Another problem is the absence of halal food in schools. So, I don't feel that Muslims are treated equally in this country. . . .

I will never forget the day after September 11th when I went back to school. All of my friends said, "It couldn't be you guys. You guys are really good." My friends reacted this way because they know me, my personality and my family.

But then it was different with strangers after September 11th. We got stereotyped, like when this one guy that came up to me and said, "You immigrant! Go back to your country. You freakin' Arab terrorist!" I was in shock. The first thing I said to him was, "This is my country. I was born and raised here. I'm not an immigrant and neither am I a terrorist!" He was stupefied that I was able to speak such good English and at the fact that I am an American. His reaction was a result of ignorance because he automatically assumed that if you're wearing the hijab that you're an immigrant and you can't speak English. I really don't understand why when one person does something wrong, the whole Muslim community and religion gets blamed for it.

I hate when people assume things about me and believe all the stereotypes that they hear. They believe stereotypes like all Arabs are terrorists and all the girls that wear the hijab are oppressed and forced to wear it. I think all these stereotypes are wrong and they come from ignorance. If you inform the public about these wrong assumptions they'll change their minds about the Muslim community on the whole. I think that Muslims are not depicted correctly here in America, especially through the media.

One story I experienced dealing with stereotypes was with one of my teachers who brought in a cartoon called "The Veil." He then asked the class, "What do you guys think about that?" All the responses were around the same line: oppression, suppression, no women's rights, Taliban, sexism, forced, and sympathy. Since I was the only hijabi in my class my teacher asked me, "What do you think about this cartoon?" I responded by explaining that what everyone thinks are stereotypes, and that none of it was true. I told them how the veil is supposed to protect women, keep them modest, keep them focused, help them respect themselves and others, and keep them pure of heart and soul. Islam values women and it treats them as jewels to be protected. I explained to them that the hijab brings out your personality not your looks. Women are not supposed to be talked to because of their looks or how big their boobs are or their butt or something. It's supposed to be about your personality. When you wear the hijab, it's not like a guy is going to check you out, look you up and down. He's going to talk to you because of your personality, not the way you look. Hijab makes me proud that I'm Muslim and it makes me respect my own body, myself, and it also makes other people respect me.

So as you can see I'm not weird and bizarre, even if I'm not the norm. I am different and unique. I can do fun things like going to beaches, pools, ice skating, skiing, paintballing, biking, and rollerblading. And, I do swim, believe or not, with my hijab. I have fun because I am a normal human being like you are, but I can do it all while I'm fully covered. I also have a life, a family that loves me, a God that cares for me, and a God that I pray to five times a day. I mean what more can you want from life when you are loved, know where your right path is? I want to finish school, get a good education, and get a good career. I want to represent the Muslim community as intelligent, educated, and civilized. I want to take part in raising the standards of the Muslim Ummah and benefiting them.

58

Modesto-Area Atheists Speak Up, Seek Tolerance

Sue Nowicki

It's difficult at times being a person of faith, but it can be even harder to be an atheist, someone who believes there is no God.

. . .

According to a recent, large-scale Pew Forum report, 92 percent of U.S. residents believe in God or a universal spirit. The Pew report and 50 years of Gallup surveys found that atheism in the United States has remained stable over the years, coming in at about

4 percent of the population when lumped with agnostics, who believe it is impossible to know if God exists.

. . .

[I]t's clear that atheists are an overwhelming minority, and atheists say there are several misconceptions about their beliefs. Several strongly make the point that they are not satanists, immoral or dumb. Those who spoke . . . range in age from 20s to 60s and from business owners to blue-collar workers. They'd like faith groups, especially Christians, to be more tolerant of their views.

Here are excerpts of what they had to say:

. . .

Mary Brush, a Modesto resident and teacher, 53, traces her atheist roots to her childhood in a Catholic home. "I went to catechism classes, but I gave my mother so much grief, I didn't take confirmation in eighth grade. The nuns frightened me. They really made me afraid of dying. I thought I'd go to hell."

Biblical accounts added to her doubts. "The stories sounded a little too fantastical to me," she said. "It didn't seem to go with reality. Over the many years, I've had (religious) friends and have gone to church and tried to pray. It just didn't work for me. I'm more of a scientist at heart; science works for me."

. . .

Brush wants people of faith to know: "I'm a good person. Just because you don't have a belief in God doesn't mean you're not a good person. I'd like a little more tolerance."

. . .

Jason Gale, a 57-year-old business manager, said, "As a child, my mom was religious, so I kind of came along for the ride." But when he was 25, someone told him his religion "was a belief in magic. That caused me to start thinking about removing magical things from my thinking."

Gale fell into agnosticism for a while—"someone who says God can neither be proved or disproved"—but didn't like being a "fence-sitter." So he turned to atheism. "It is a belief; not something you can prove, but it seems to be better supported by empirical observations around you than religion," he said. "In religion, you need to have a leap of faith."

Gale said his wife is a Christian and returned to church about three years ago after a 20-year hiatus. He supports her, but admitted, "I knew she believed in God, but I never thought she'd become active."

. . .

He said he "backs way off" when others talk emotionally about their faith or his. But he wants people to know, 'I'm not an evil person because I'm a nonbeliever. I don't torture dogs and cats just because I don't believe in God."

And he gives this advice to believers: . . . "'Keep it on the positive side.' Help people, like the Peace Corps. Do what Jesus said, visit the sick and the people in prison. Do all the good works and stay away from weapons."

. . .

Susan Robinson, 50, said, "I always had the feeling from childhood that (religious) things I was told were not right."

As she matured, Robinson said she "kept looking for something to believe in. I explored other churches—Presbyterian, Mormon. I even started reading the Koran. I could never find a god I considered to be moral.

"Very often, there are different rules for God than for people. Like the flood—I'm sorry; I made a mistake. Let's wipe everyone out except for one family and start all over again. Or when Jesus was born, every child up to two years old was killed. That's a huge price for a savior."

For many years, she said, "I was afraid to tell people I was an atheist because of their reaction. I've read of a poll that says people view atheists less good than Muslims, including terrorists out there, and homosexuals. I read about things happening to people—losing friends, losing family members, losing marriages."

She's still cautious, but not as fearful. And she'd like to tell believers "not to be afraid of atheists. They're usually striving to make the world a better place. And please, please keep religion out of government. Any time God is put into government or someone wants to be treated like a god, it's really bad news for all the people."

. . .

Peggy Gardiner, 62 and a business owner, said her only childhood religious experience was when her grandparents took her to a small church in south Modesto.

"The Sunday school teacher told a Bible story and asked if there were any questions. I raised my hand and said, 'How did God get here?' I was about 5 or 6 years old. She said, 'God has always been here.' That pretty well settled it for me."

. . .

Despite her views, Gardiner doesn't make a scene around believers, she said. "I have a sister and a brother-in-law, and when we go out, they like to say a prayer before a meal. I have no problem with bowing my head with them. To be agnostic or atheist, you have to be pretty open-minded."

She'd like to tell people of faith "that while they all think they have the answer, it's not the only answer. . . . If people would spend as much time trying to improve the world as they do proselytizing, we'd probably have a better world."

. . .

Chris Muir is a 51-year-old Modestan who works as a part-time secretary.

"I grew up in a religious, Mormon household in a little farm town in southeast Idaho. It was pretty much an all-Mormon town."

When he was 8 years old, "I started having doubts. One of the things they said is that when you were baptized, you'd be receiving the gifts of the Holy Ghost. I believed it, but when I was baptized, I didn't feel any different. Then I started finding discrepancies that didn't fit. By the time I was 14, I'd pretty much decided this was baloney."

Over the years, he said, he's studied "the tenets of other religions. Being a skeptic, I find the flaws in those religions, too. Basically, religion appears to be what people want to believe. If it comforts them and helps them cope in life, I'm not going to try to dissuade them. It might be cruel to take (religion) away from them. It may be a false hope, but it's still hope."

He said he remains on good terms with his devout family but is "quite happy without having to give donations and tithes to maintain the church anymore."

And he does have his own beliefs. "I get asked a lot, 'Is there anything you do believe in?' I have to say yeah. I believe the world does exist as we see it."

. . .

59

Why Are You Atheists So Angry?

Greta Christina

There are serious, deep-rooted problems with the way religion plays out, in the United States and around the world. There are ways that religion plays out—extremely common ways—that lead to abuse, injustice, mistreatment, misery, disempowerment, even violence and death. It makes perfect sense to be angry about them. In fact, when people *aren't* angry about them, I'm baffled.

I'm a happy person most of the time. . . . I mean, it's not like I'm running around smashing plates and going "Rrrr! Rrrr! Rrrr!" all the time. (I hardly ever do that.)

But far too many people ask, "Why are you atheists so angry?"—without even considering the possibility that we're angry because we have legitimate things to be angry about.

So I want to try to answer this question: "Why are you atheists so angry?" Or rather, since I don't presume to speak for the atheists: Why am I so angry?

- I'm angry that according to a recent Gallup poll, 53 percent of Americans would not vote for an atheist for President—even for a qualified candidate from the voter's own party—solely because of their atheism.
- I'm angry that atheists in the United States are often denied custody of their children, explicitly because of their atheism.
- I'm angry that it took until 1961 for atheists to be guaranteed the rights to serve on juries, testify in court, or hold public office in every state in the country.
- I'm angry that atheist soldiers—in the U.S. armed forces—have had atheist meetings broken up by Christian superior officers, in direct violation of the First Amendment. I'm angry that evangelical Christian groups are being given exclusive access to proselytize on military bases—again in the U.S. armed forces, again in direct violation of the First Amendment. . . .
- I'm angry at preachers who tell women in their flock to submit to their husbands because it's the will of God, even when their husbands are beating them within an inch of their lives.
- I'm angry that so many parents and religious leaders terrorize children with vivid, traumatizing stories of eternal burning and torture, to ensure that they'll be too frightened to even question religion. . . .
- I'm angry at priests who rape children and tell them it's God's will. No, angry isn't a strong enough word. I am enraged. I am revolted. I am trembling with fury at the very thought of it.
- And I'm enraged that the Catholic Church consciously, deliberately, repeatedly, for years, acted to protect priests who raped children, and deliberately acted to keep it a secret. I'm enraged that they shuttled child-raping priests from town to town, failed to inform law enforcement officers and in many cases flat-out stonewalled them, deliberately dumped the child rapists in remote, impoverished villages. . . .
- And I'm angry that, after 9/11 happened, people of Middle Eastern descent were attacked and their businesses vandalized, because they were Muslims, or because people assumed they were Muslims even if they weren't, and they blamed all Muslims for the attacks.
- And I'm angry that Jerry Falwell blamed 9/11 on pagans, abortionists, feminist, gays and lesbians, the ACLU, and the People For the American Way. I'm angry that this theology of a wrathful god exacting revenge against pagans and abortionists was a theology held by a powerful, wealthy, widely-respected religious leader with millions of followers. . . .
- I'm angry that almost half of Americans believe in creationism. Not a broad, theistic evolution, "God had a hand in evolution" version of creationism, but a strict, young-Earth, "God created man in his present form at one time within the last 10,000 years" creationism.

I should clarify this one, as people often misunderstand it. When atheists say that we're angry about how many creationists there are in the U.S., a common response is, "What business is that of yours? Don't they have the right to believe whatever they want? You're just as intolerant of their beliefs as they are of yours!"

So let me explain. If creationists are trying to get their religious beliefs taught in the public schools—paid for by everyone's taxes, forced on children whose families don't share those beliefs, in direct violation of the First Amendment—then it isn't just their own business, and I have a right to be angry about it.

But if they're not trying to do any of that—if they're just ordinary people trying to get by, working two jobs to pay the bills, and they're leaving their school boards alone—then I'm not angry at them.

I'm angry for them.

I'm angry that they're been taught to fear and scorn one of the most profound, powerful truths about the world, and to embrace a lie that flatly contradicts an overwhelming body of evidence. I'm angry that they've been taught that loving their god means rejecting the reality of the Universe he supposedly created. I'm angry that they're been taught that scientists—people who care so much about the Universe they devote their lives to painstakingly figuring out how it works—are wicked and evil. I'm angry that they're been taught that virtuous religious faith demands that they disconnect themselves from the march of human knowledge.

I'm not angry at them. I'm angry on their behalf. . . .

- And, in a similar vein: I'm angry that science teachers in the U.S. public schools often don't teach evolution, or give it only a cursory mention, even when teaching it is sanctioned and indeed required—because they're afraid of sparking controversy and having to deal with angry fundamentalist parents. Evolution is the foundation of the science of biology—biology literally doesn't make sense without it—and kids who aren't being taught about evolution are being deprived of one of the most fundamental ways we have of understanding ourselves and the world.

- I'm angry that right-wing Christians in the United States are actively campaigning against anti-bullying laws in elementary and high schools, on the grounds that religious freedom includes the right to harass, threaten, and intimidate gay kids.

- I'm angry that, in public, taxpayer-paid high schools around the country, atheist students who are trying to organize clubs—something they're legally allowed to do—are routinely getting stonewalled by school administrators. I'm angry that the Secular Student Alliance has to push high school administrators on a regular basis, and in some cases they're even had to be sued, simply to get them to obey the law.

- I'm angry about what happened to Jessica Ahlquist. I'm angry that, in a public, taxpayer-paid high school in Rhode Island, a banner with an official school prayer was prominently posted in the school auditorium—in direct violation of the Constitution and of clear, well-established legal precedent. I'm angry that when Ahlquist asked her high school to take down the banner, her request was rejected, and she had to go to court to get her school to comply with the law. And I'm angry that, when she won her lawsuit—in an entirely unsurprising, no-controversial ruling—she was targeted with a barrage of brutal threats, including threats of beating, rape, and death.

- I'm angry about what happened to Damon Fowler. I'm angry that when he asked his public, taxpayer-paid high school to stop a school-sponsored prayer at his graduation, he was hounded, pilloried, and ostracized by his community, publicly demeaned by one of his own teachers, targeted with threats of violence and death, and kicked out of his house by his parents.

- And I'm angry that what happened to Jessica Ahlquist and Damon Fowler are not isolated incidents. I'm angry that things like this are happening around the United States, and all around the world. I'm angry that, even when the law clearly states that the government can't endorse religion or force it on its citizens, people are often too intimidated to insist on their legal rights . . . because they're afraid they'll be bullied, ostracized, and threatened with violence by their classmates, their co-workers, their communities, their friends, even their families. I'm angry that this doesn't just happen to atheists: It happens to Jews, Muslims, Buddhists, Wiccans, religious minorities of all varieties. And I'm angry because these people aren't wrong to be afraid.

- And I'm angry that people hear stories like this . . . and still insist that atheists don't suffer from discrimination and should stop complaining about it, because we have protection under the law. I get angry when people blithely ignore the fact that legal protection doesn't do much good if people are intimidated out of demanding it. . . .

- I get angry when religious believers make arguments against atheism—and make accusations against atheists—without having bothered to talk to any atheists, or read any atheist writing. I get angry when they trot out the same old crap about how "atheism is a nihilistic philosophy, with no joy or meaning to life and no basis for morality or ethics" . . . when if they spent ten minutes in the atheist blogosphere, they would discover countless atheists who experience great joy and meaning in our lives, and are intensely concerned about right and wrong.

- I get angry when believers glorify religious faith—i.e., believing in a supernatural world with no good evidence supporting that belief—as a positive virtue, a character trait that makes people good and noble. I get angry they base their entire philosophy of life on what is, at best, a hunch; when they ignore or reject or rationalize any evidence that contradicts that hunch or calls it into question. And I get angry when they do this . . . and then accuse atheists of being close-minded and ignoring the truth.

- I get angry when believers say they can know the truth—the greatest truth of all about the nature of the Universe, namely the source of all existence—simply by sitting quietly and listening to their hearts . . . and then accuse atheists of being arrogant. And this attitude isn't just arrogant towards atheists. It's arrogant towards people of other religions who have sat just as quietly, listened to their hearts with just as much sincerity, and come to completely opposite conclusions about God and the soul and the Universe.

- And I get angry when believers say that the entire unimaginable hugeness of the Universe was made specifically for the human race—when atheists, by contrast, say that humanity is a microscopic dot on a microscopic dot, an infinitesimal eyeblink in the vastness of time and space—and then, once again, believers accuse atheists of being arrogant.

    I want to take a moment and explain why I get so angry about believers making bad arguments for religion. I get angry because they're not arguing in good faith. I get angry because they're refusing to see their privilege. I get angry because so many of these bad arguments for religion end up perpetuating misinformation and bigotry against atheists. . . .

- I get angry when believers treat any criticism of their religion—i.e., pointing out that their religion is a hypothesis about the world, and asking it to stand on its own in the marketplace of ideas—as insulting and intolerant. I get angry when believers accuse atheists of being intolerant for saying things like, "I don't agree with you," "I think you're mistaken about that," and "What evidence do you have to support that?"

- I'm angry that Christians in the United States—members of the single most powerful and influential religious group in the country, in the wealthiest and most powerful country in the world—act like beleaguered victims, martyrs being thrown to the lions all over again, whenever anyone criticizes them or they don't get their way. . . .

- I'm angry that huge swaths of public policy in this country—about same-sex marriage, birth control, abortion, stem-cell research, physician-assisted suicide, sex education in schools—are being based, not on evidence of which policies do and don't work and what is and isn't true about the world, but on religious texts written hundreds or thousands of years ago, and on believers' personal feelings about how those texts should be interpreted, with no supporting evidence whatsoever . . . and no apparent concept of why any evidence should be needed. . . .

60

Creating Identity-Safe Spaces on College Campuses for Muslim Students

Na'ilah Suad Nasir and Jasiyah Al-Amin

. . .

The current national political context has brought Islam (as both a practice and an identity) into the media forefront. The events of 9/11 and the resulting war in Iraq have sparked renewed interest in the religion of Islam and the life of Muslims. One only has to visit any chain bookstore to notice an explosion of books on Islam, terrorism, and Islamic extremists. Unfortunately, this attention has been largely negative, and Muslim communities across the nation are increasingly fearful of discrimination and even violence. This context has made the discussion that we undertake in this article of the issues faced by Muslim college students at once more difficult and more important.

In this brief commentary, we explore some issues that arise for Muslim students on college campuses, drawing on both our own personal experiences and discussions and interviews with Muslim students from a wide range of college campuses. . . .

We begin with the stories of two students from different backgrounds and with very different experiences on their respective campuses.

RASHID

Rashid is a tall, African-American young man with a ready smile and playful eyes, who carries himself with dignity and humility. In our interview he wore an indigo-blue African-style long dashiki and loose pants. He grew up in a medium-sized Northern California city in a family that has struggled through economic and other woes. He won a full basketball scholarship to a well-known institution in another (but still liberal) state. Like many students, college was his first experience living out of the state, and the transition, while exciting, was a bit unsettling. But he adjusted to his new environment well and enjoyed a central role on the basketball team and a good relationship with his coach and teammates. Although he was raised a Christian, he started reading about Islam his freshman year and converted during his sophomore year. He describes this as the turning point in his life on campus.

Rashid's conversion shifted, first and foremost, his relationship with his coach, who was suspicious of Islam. He accused Rashid of becoming a black nationalist, of hating whites, and of being racist. After his junior year, he asked Rashid not to return to the team. Rashid then became active in the largely international Muslim student group on campus and declared Islamic studies as a second major. Here he encountered another obstacle—a non-Muslim Islamic-studies professor who was openly hostile to him and derogatory about Islam.

FATIMA

Fatima is a soft-spoken (almost shy) young woman, with a bit of hesitancy in her voice that lessens as she gets more passionate about her topic. At our interview she wore jeans and a college sweatshirt with a white scarf over her hair, pinned under her chin. Although her father is from Pakistan, Fatima grew up in the same state where she attends college, but in a different region. She says the Muslim community wasn't her first priority in choosing a college, although she knew it was important, partly because her oldest brother (who was already in college and active in the Muslim Student Association in another state when she was choosing a college) told her so.

Her experience as a Muslim on her liberal college campus has been a positive one. She reported no instances of prejudice, and she said she feels involved with both the Muslim community and the broader community on campus. About a month before we spoke with her, Fatima had made a decision, which for her was a step in the practice of her faith—to wear *hijab*. Her biggest problem on campus was finding a place to pray and make *wudu* (a special way of washing up for prayer). She expressed concern about how she is perceived and about stereotypes of "oppressed" foreign Muslim women.

These two stories illustrate some of the variation in Muslim students' experiences on college campuses, which have to do both with characteristics of the student (including class, race, gender, and types of support needed) and characteristics of the campuses and their surrounding communities (including how "liberal" the campus is, the presence of Islamic student groups on campus, and the existence and constitution of the Islamic studies faculty). However, there are also important convergences in their accounts. Below we consider several core issues that these stories illustrate (and that others' experiences corroborate).

THE BURDEN OF MANAGING A POTENTIALLY "RISKY" IDENTITY

All of the students we talked to described (in one way or another) the burden of constantly feeling that others were judging them in terms of negative stereotypes about Islam, such as "Muslim terrorist" or "oppressed Muslim woman." Interestingly, this fear has much more to do with a perception of potential threat than any actual acts of prejudice or discrimination....

For the students we interviewed, this threat became particularly salient in moments of practicing Islam (such as praying while on campus), where they felt vulnerable and highly visible. Since Muslim students need to pray five times a day, they constantly have to search out places to do so, such as an empty classroom. One student noted, "You have to find a place to pray, so you look like you are sneaking, then you find a room, and people are thinking, what is she doing in there?" This student revealed her anxiety that others may judge her as sneaky or strange.

. . .

AN IDENTITY-THREATENING ENVIRONMENT AND
LOWERED ACADEMIC ACHIEVEMENT

This anxiety about the stereotypes that the Muslim identity might trigger also affects students' academic performance.... While our sample was not systematic or representative, we did observe that students who reported more discrimination and contention tended to perform more poorly academically. For instance, while Fatima, a biology major, is in excellent academic standing, Rashid left his university several units short of graduating, returning several years later to complete his degree. Most students we talked to had not been actively denigrated, but they felt taxed by the need to constantly manage others'

N E X T   S T E P S

impressions of them. This identity-management process required energy and time that could have been devoted to their studies.

A hostile environment also made students want to distance themselves emotionally, and such distancing sometimes resulted in a disconnection not just from that particular campus community but from school in general. In some cases, Muslim students reported that the experience of prejudice (at worst) and lack of understanding (at best) on the part of their professors affected their academic performance more directly. For example, Rashid's contentious relationship with the Islamic-studies professor resulted in his refusal to do some of the readings for the course (because he felt that they misrepresented the Muslim experience) and contributed to his low grades in the several courses with that professor that he needed to take for his second major.

AN IDENTITY-SAFE ENVIRONMENT AND WELL-BEING

While academic performance is certainly an important effect of a welcoming campus environment, students' feelings of well-being are perhaps equally significant. That is, students should feel positive about life and grow as people during their college years. They should feel whole and healthy. Our conversations made it clear that students who found their university environment supportive of their practice of Islam, who felt that they were accepted as Muslims and as students and who didn't feel penalized or ostracized, were able to grow in the practice of their faith at their own pace and with full confidence.

For instance, two of the female students we interviewed (both of whom were raised Muslim) spoke of deciding during their college careers to begin wearing *hijab* on campus. They reported the relief and acceptance they felt at receiving compliments on how they looked with the scarf on from both Muslims and non-Muslims. The first day Fatima wore *hijab* on campus, one of her professors told her that she looked beautiful. This remark made her feel good about this step in her faith.

. . .

CONFLUENCE OF GENDER, RACE, RELIGION, AND CLASS

Our two stories illustrate another important point about negotiating Islam on college campuses: Islamic identity interacts with other identities to color both how a student is perceived by others and how he responds to such perceptions. It is significant that Rashid is Muslim, male, African-American, and physically imposing (he is tall and muscular), as he noted in our conversation with him. It may also be significant that he is a first-generation college student from a working-class family, since his resources for surviving college are fewer than those of more affluent or system-savvy students. We might note that the response of the basketball coach to his becoming Muslim was a largely racialized response—the coach objected to what he judged as a black-nationalist political philosophy and feared that Islam would make Rashid too radical regarding race and politics.

We see in Rashid's story that negative reactions to him were compounded by the fact that he belongs to multiple stigmatized groups. He not only has to negotiate being Muslim on a largely non-Muslim campus but also being African-American on a largely white campus, as well as a student athlete (which makes him highly visible and subject to scrutiny). He was explicitly told that he couldn't be both a black male athlete and a serious student activist, but that he had to choose between the two. Then, once his identity as a Muslim caused him to be released from the basketball team and he turned to his school work more seriously, he encountered resistance from others as he attempted to take up a "serious-student" identity.

In other work we have named these sets of identities "identity constellations" to capture the idea that people have not just one but multiple, sometimes conflicting, identities. The opportunity to reorganize these sets is more or less available in different contexts. Indeed in some environments, students are asked to choose among the various identities within these constellations, as Rashid's story shows. He (and other African-American students) talked about the feeling that they must decide whether to affiliate with the Muslim or the African-American campus community. A female student joked that before she began wearing *hijab*, the Muslims on campus didn't speak to her, but once she began covering, the African-American students stopped speaking to her. Such forced choices make students feel as though they have to privilege one aspect of their identities to the detriment of other equally important parts of themselves.

SMALL COMFORTS AND ACTS OF KINDNESS

Our final point is a brief one, but it is critically important. When we asked students about what made their experiences as Muslims positive, they invariably mentioned incidents that seemed to us quite trivial—for instance, professors who acknowledged Ramadan or who complimented them on wearing *hijab*. One student noted with great fondness the special dinner and breakfast packets the dining hall provided during Ramadan. These small acts of kindness were highly valued by students and made a huge difference to their sense that both they and the practice of their religion belonged on campus.

Other things that make campuses more identity-safe for Muslim students include:

- A strong, diverse, and supportive Muslim student group on campus;
- Professors who are knowledgeable about Islam and positive towards it (this especially includes the Islamic-studies professors, since this program is where students often go in order to learn about themselves and to feel connected and supported);
- The presence of a broader student community that is accepting of Islam and its practices;
- Access to physical spaces that facilitate the practice of Islam without ridicule or judgment (for instance, having a private place to pray and wash up for prayer);
- Access to *halal* meals (foods that don't contain pork and for which meats are slaughtered in a particular way) and the accommodation of the special meal times (before sunrise and after sundown) during the month of Ramadan.

CONCLUDING THOUGHTS

While this article has focused on Muslim students, we'd like to conclude with a more global perspective on the important work of supporting all students' religious practices and identities (as well as other dimensions of difference) on college campuses. . . . The idea that it benefits the larger organization to encourage the development of individuals in their respective communities is reflected in the experience of the students whose stories appear here. . . .

61

Guidelines for Christian Allies

Paul Kivel

It is not upon you to complete the task.
Neither are you free to desist from it.

—RABBI TARFON

- If you are Christian or were raised Christian, there are many concrete things you can do to counter Christian hegemony:
- Learn the history of Christianity, its impact on other peoples and the history of the denomination you belong to and/or grew up in.
- Notice the operation of Christian dominance in your everyday life. Consider how Christian concepts affect the way you think.
- Examine how you may have internalized judgements about yourself based on Christian teachings. Have you cut yourself off from your body, from natural expressions of your sexuality or spirituality or from connections to the natural world?
- Examine how you may have internalized feelings of superiority or negative judgement of others, especially those from marginalized or non-Christian groups.
- Understand and acknowledge the benefits you gain from being Christian in the United States.
- Use your privilege to support the struggles of non-Christian peoples throughout the world for land, autonomy, reparations and justice.
- Notice how organizational and institutional policies perpetuate Christian hegemony. Get together with others to change them.
- Respect other people's sacred places, rituals, sacred objects and culture; don't assume you can appropriate them.
- Work for religious pluralism, and support the separation of church and state.
- Analyze public policy through the lens of Christian hegemony.
- Avoid assuming other people you meet are Christian—or should be, and challenge missionary programs.
- Understand and respect non-Christian religions and cultures on their own terms. Avoid universalizing about religion, or assuming all religions are essentially the same, worship the same god under different names or are comparable to Christianity.
- Avoid excusing hurtful behaviour or policies because of the good intent of their perpetrators. Work with others to respectfully hold people accountable for their behaviour.
- Embrace diversity and complexity and avoid reducing things to an artificial either/or dynamic.
- Begin to practice discussing these topics with other Christians in private conversations, when there are public exhibitions of Christianity and in organizational settings.

62

Critical Reflections on the Interfaith Movement

A Social Justice Perspective

Sachi Edwards

. . . There is a growing movement to incorporate education about religious diversity and interfaith dialogue into our higher education curricula and institutional priorities. There are varying motivations for this, however. The . . . primary argument supporting this movement found in existing scholarship [which this article focuses on is] . . . the need to broaden the discourse on diversity and multiculturalism. . . .

BROADENING THE DISCOURSE ON DIVERSITY AND SOCIAL JUSTICE

A . . . reason for engaging students in interfaith dialogue is the need to include religious identity into our discourse on diversity and social justice. In the United States, education (particularly higher education) has attempted to address social inequalities by establishing policies and initiatives that seek to foster diversity on campus and increase social justice for disadvantaged groups. Yet, such efforts have not been made to the same extent for religious minorities. . . .

CURRENT TRENDS IN INTERFAITH STUDENT PROGRAMMING

. . . I have identified three general trends in current models of interfaith student programming based on my own involvement with campus-based interfaith programming over the last five years, conversations with colleagues doing similar work at other institutions, observations from relevant presentations at academic conferences, a review of the available scholarly literature on this topic, and a survey of institutional and organizational websites describing their interfaith initiatives: (a) interfaith community service programs, (b) multifaith spirituality centers, and (c) facilitated dialogues between religiously diverse students.

INTERFAITH COMMUNITY SERVICE PROGRAMS

The predominant form of interfaith engagement found on college campuses attempts to create opportunities for students to have positive interactions with peers from other religious groups through service projects and other extra or cocurricular activities. In the rhetoric surrounding this model of interfaith programming, the term "interfaith dialogue" is often used, with the claim that through bringing students from different religions together in this fashion, interfaith dialogue occurs organically. However, formal dialogue is not emphasized in these programs (so, I choose not to label them as dialogues at all). Instead, interfaith community service programs attempt to help students build interfaith relationships (thus, presumably reducing their fear or bias toward religious others), by engaging religiously diverse students in collaborative projects that highlight their shared value (religious or otherwise) of helping others. . . .

MULTIFAITH SPIRITUALITY CENTERS

Another approach to interfaith programming that is common on college campuses is to create multifaith spirituality centers—also called interfaith centers, interfaith prayer rooms, and meditation rooms, among other names. These centers typically host events such as multifaith panel discussions, religious festival celebrations, or interfaith prayers. In this way, campus-based interfaith centers often serve as a space for students to explore their spirituality through learning about their own and other religious traditions. At Wellesley College, for instance, the Multifaith Center (attached to the campus chapel) is home to their Religious and Spiritual Life Program. This program is guided by a team of chaplains and religious advisors, as well as a multifaith student council, that assists in developing campus-wide campaigns to inspire students, staff, and faculty members to engage in interfaith dialogue and increase their appreciation of religious diversity. The emphasis at Wellesley is on celebrating the traditions of all religious groups on campus, and by doing so, educating the campus community about the different religious identities that make up their college. Additionally, they staff chaplains from a range of religious traditions and facilitate opportunities for students to receive pastoral counselling if they so desire. . . .

FACILITATED INTERFAITH DIALOGUES

Formalized, facilitated interfaith dialogues represent a final version of interfaith programming found in colleges and universities in the United States. These range from less structured to highly structured, but all bring together students from different religious backgrounds to discuss their respective beliefs, traditions, and/or experiences. A less structured approach to facilitated interfaith dialogue includes the types . . . such as "pop-up conversations" (creating a space for people to drop in for a brief interfaith conversation) or "speedfaithing" (like speed-dating, where participants spend a few minutes talking one-on-one with each other person in the group) events. In dialogues like these, students show up voluntarily and exchange information about themselves to a peer(s) with a different religious identity. These casual conversations, guided by students' own interests, curiosities, and comfort levels, allow students to gain exposure to other religious beliefs/traditions and to ask questions about religion they may not feel comfortable doing elsewhere. . . .

A CRITICAL SOCIAL JUSTICE APPROACH

While all of the approaches to interfaith programming described above certainly seem like positive steps toward interfaith harmony, there are some potential negative consequences that become apparent when analyzing them through a critical social justice

NEXT STEPS

N
E
X
T

S
T
E
P
S

lens. The critical social justice perspective asserts that an examination of power and privilege are important in any dialogue about identity (religious or otherwise) to prevent the further marginalization of subordinate identity participants. Many of the interfaith initiatives described above fail to do so. This is not to say that they should not be utilized at all, or that they all must be changed to strictly adhere to a critical social justice agenda. However, considering certain possible areas of weakness that a critical social justice perspective elucidates would help practitioners within the campus interfaith movement be more mindful of the ways religious minority participants may be affected by the initiatives they pursue. . . .

Discussing religious identity with a critical social justice orientation requires careful consideration of the historical, social, political, and legal power imbalance between religious groups. Just as White and male hegemony have hindered people of color and women, so too has Christian hegemony in the United States caused the social and institutional oppression of religious minorities—including internalized oppression, whereby subordinate group members view themselves as inferior due to the normalization of the dominant group. While it may be easiest to think about incidents of interpersonal discrimination toward religious minorities as the primary manifestation of religious oppression, critical theory reminds us that "invisible systems conferring unsought social dominance" of one group over another is far more prevalent and detrimental to marginalized groups than individual acts of meanness. Thus, a critical social justice approach to philosophical analyses of religious identity and oppression contextualizes experiences of religious identity within the historical backdrop of Christian cultural domination.

A common opinion about religious identity is that individuals can choose and change that aspect of themselves at any time. Yet, as many scholars have explained, the religion that one adheres to, is most familiar with, and/or is most comfortable with is largely a matter of the way that individual is socialized. In that way, religious identity is not simply about personal choice. . . .

This perspective—that religion is largely cultural and that affiliation with a religious culture has little to do with one's individual beliefs—aligns with characterizations of religion put forth by prominent scholars in the field of religious studies. Indeed, Durkheim (1912/1995) warned us against defining religion (or religious affiliation, or religious identify) according to beliefs alone, because some religions do not even espouse a specific set of beliefs. He admitted that it may be tempting for those from religious traditions that do emphasize belief to define religion in that way, but warns that doing so would be reflective of their own biases and preconceptions about what religion is in the first place. Echoing this sentiment, Smith suggested that what we think of as religion should be separated into two things: an historical cumulative tradition, and the personal faith of men and women which is similar to the separation between religion and spirituality I make above. One's personal faith (or, spirituality) may change over time, even day-to-day. One's socialization into an historical, cumulative tradition (or, religious identity), however, has implications for culture and worldview that are separate from belief. After all, even "the modern man who feels and claims that he is nonreligious still retains a large stock of camouflaged myths and degenerated rituals" reminiscent of their religious culture.

Combining the emphasis on historical inequity and political power imbalance with the understanding that religious identity is culturally and socially constructed, a critical social justice approach calls for interfaith practitioners to acknowledge religious socialization and examine systemic religious oppression. Applying this approach to our work within the interfaith movement can help us think about how interfaith programming can increase equity for oppressed religious groups, and when there may be the potential for just the opposite.

CRITICAL REFLECTIONS ON THE INTERFAITH MOVEMENT

Reflecting on the interfaith movement in U.S. higher education from a critical social justice perspective raises a number of concerns about how the movement may be alienating or even further marginalizing individuals from minority religious traditions. While there are undoubtedly good intentions motivating most campus interfaith practitioners, and there are surely many positive aspects of existing interfaith initiatives, there are elements of the movement that fail to address key issues related to religious conflict, prejudice, and oppression. Interfaith programs that overlook Christian privilege and religious oppression might make participants, particularly those from the dominant group (i.e., Christians), feel gratified by the experience, but may not make any substantive steps toward social justice for religious minorities. Three primary critiques of this movement from a critical social justice perspective are (a) a lack of explicit examinations of Christian privilege, (b) a tendency to overlook the socioculture nature of religious identity, and (c) the frequent exclusion of non-Abrahamic religious groups/individuals.

RECOGNIZING AND CHALLENGING CHRISTIAN PRIVILEGE

An essential component of critical theory is the recognition and examination of power and privilege. Thus, acknowledging and purposefully challenging Christian privilege is a necessity for critical social justice oriented interfaith dialogues, just as critical dialogues about race should examine White privilege and critical dialogues about gender should examine male privilege. To this point, however, the interfaith movement in higher education has not prioritized examining Christian privilege. In part, this may be because Christian privilege itself is a fairly new concept. In 2002, Clark and her colleagues introduced the idea, relating Christian privilege to the concepts of White privilege and male privilege made famous by Peggy McIntosh (1988, 1998). They adopted McIntosh's (1988) famous list of White privileges to relate specifically to religious identity. . . .

However, there are still many scholars who overlook, are sceptical of, or even deny the existence of Christian privilege. For instance, Kimmel and Ferber's (2010) *Privilege: A Reader*, which included sections on male, White, heterosexual, and class privilege, did not address Christian privilege at all. There is a mention of anti-Semitism in one chapter (Sacks, 2010), but primarily in the context of racial, non-Nordic prejudice rather than as a discussion of religious oppression. Others, such as Nelson (2010), are expressly uncomfortable with the full list of Christian privileges, and assert that Christians are also oppressed . . . claiming that Christians are also marginalized by the media and secular public. Still others flat out reject the idea of Christian privilege, suggesting that what some think is Christian privilege, is really just White privilege. Stewart and Lozano (2009), for example, argued that people of color who are Christian do not benefit from Christian privilege because they often do not fit in with White Christian congregations, a claim that disregards the experiences of non-Christians altogether.

That the legitimacy of Christian privilege is debated, even by those who are self-proclaimed social justice scholars, has likely limited the development of a critical social justice perspective in our discourse about campus-based interfaith initiatives. Unfortunately, this may be preventing the interfaith movement from addressing the bigotry and oppression that religious minorities are experiencing on the very campuses they are operating from. Recently, the nationwide Campus Religious and Spiritual Climate survey found that religious minorities are more acutely aware of religious conflict at their schools than Christian students, and experience more negative interactions with, and feelings of coercion from, peers with different religious identities. Still, most of the interfaith programming in U.S. higher education that is described in peer-reviewed journals, at academic conferences, and on institutional websites does not directly question, address, or analyze the religious stratification at the root of these conflicts and differences in perspective.

A critical social justice approach to interfaith engagement contends that without adequately acknowledging and managing the drastic power imbalance between different religious groups, educational programming that deals with religion and religious identity can be damaging to religious minority students who may perceive the initiatives as hollow attempts to assuage them, while not actually addressing their marginalization. Thus, interfaith programs aiming to be social justice oriented should overtly insert activities, lessons, and other curricular or pedagogical tools demonstrating the existence of Christian privilege. Moreover, they should attempt to inspire positive social action toward rectifying the imbalance and injustice created by the historical and political Christian hegemony in this country. While there is a dearth of literature (both theoretical and practical) that discusses how to successfully pursue or facilitate this type of interfaith dialogue, models of social justice oriented race and gender dialogues, such as Intergroup Dialogue, can be adopted for this purpose. Strategies like ensuring substantial participation by non-Christians, having a Christian and a non-Christian cofacilitate the dialogue, and training facilitators to recognize manifestations of Christian privilege during the dialogue process can all be used to promote a critical social justice agenda through interfaith dialogue.

Indeed, there are some colleges and universities that are pursuing interfaith engagement from a critical social justice perspective (or, at least attempting to). Those that are not, however, may not recognize the ways their religious minority participants might be further marginalized through their programs. For example, if Christian participants are dominating the conversation (in essence, exhibiting their Christian privilege) and facilitators fail to intervene and make space for non-Christian participants to speak uninterrupted, religious minorities may come away from the dialogue feeling disregarded and unappreciated. Similarly, if Christian participants suggest that they are oppressed—either by claiming that Christians are oppressed, or by changing the subject to discuss a different identity for which they are oppressed—and facilitators do not step in to ensure that Christian privilege and religious oppression are validated and recognized, non-Christian participants may interpret that their oppression as religious minorities does not matter. Of course, the goal should not be to silence Christian participants; rather, discussions should be reframed to help all participants recognize the historical context and reality of Christian domination. Failure to do so, despite good intentions, may put an interfaith program at risk of reinforcing Christian hegemony without realizing it. Unfortunately, when it comes to conversations about culture and power, good intentions are often not enough.

Some interfaith programs even claim social justice as a tenet, yet still do not align with a critical social justice perspective on religion or religious identity. . . . [For example,] bringing a religiously diverse group of students together to build houses for economically disadvantaged families or raise awareness of gun violence is critically informed work toward social justice. These are not, however, forms of social justice work that specifically help religious minorities. Recognizing which form of oppression to target is an important aspect of a critical social justice approach to interfaith engagement. As such, attention to religious identity oppression and Christian privilege specially is invaluable for the interfaith movement.

NEXT STEPS

ACKNOWLEDGING AND REFLECTING ON THE SOCIOCULTURAL NATURE
OF RELIGIOUS IDENTITY

Beyond recognizing and challenging privilege, another important aspect of the critical social justice approach is acknowledging and reflecting on the socially constructed nature of identity. However, in current manifestations of the interfaith movement, religious identity is often spoken about as a personal set of beliefs, where individuals are identified according to their own self-chosen religious label. While self-identification is certainly a strongly held value in critical identity paradigms, carte blanch self-identification can also prove problematic when attempting to address identity oppression. For instance, when Rachel Dolezol, a White woman born to two White parents, identified herself as Black, critical scholars descried her chosen identity label as racial appropriation and a hindrance to the social justice efforts of the Black community. Thus, as explained above, from a critical social justice perspective, one's upbringing and identity socialization needs to be recognized as a part of their identity label—whether the individual wants to admit it or not.

It is for this reason that interfaith dialogue (or interfaith programming in general) seeking to adopt a critical social justice approach should focus not on individual belief, but on the societal role of religion characterized by religious domination and subordination. While social justice oriented interfaith dialogue may (or may not) share and compare participants, beliefs, traditions, or values, it should certainly ask students to reflect on their own religious socialization, how it is shaped by Christian hegemony, and how it affects their lived experiences. It is possible that an interfaith dialogue of this sort may not actually spend any time at all discussing individual participants' spiritual beliefs or the beliefs espoused by the religious tradition with which they were raised. After all, enjoying school closures on your religious culture's holidays (or, conversely, having to choose between school and your religious holidays) does not require you to personally believe anything in particular. In other words, experiences of privilege or oppression often have more to do with the way Christianity shapes societal norms, assumptions, and routines than the specific details of people's spiritual beliefs.

Asking participants to examine their own religious socialization often means that those who prefer to label themselves as atheist or agnostic will have to acknowledge the way they are culturally affiliated with a religious tradition—that is, acknowledge their sociocultural religious identity. For instance if a participant was raised in a Christian family and in a Christian social environment, and thereby was taught to see the world through a Christian lens, he or she should be asked to recognize and learn about their Christian privilege, even if they no longer believe in the tenets of Christianity and no longer chose to call him- or herself a Christian. Similarly, if a participant was raised as a Muslim, has an entirely Muslim family, and attended a religious Muslim school all of their lives, he or she should be encouraged to reflect on the way their Muslim cultural identity has shaped, and continues to shape, life experiences, even if he or she has recently adopted a new set of beliefs. Two atheist participants, then, if one was raised as a Christian and the other as a Muslim, have entirely different levels of religious privilege/oppression and, therefore, have entirely different perspectives to offer in an interfaith discussion. An interfaith program focused solely on participants' individual beliefs overlooks this reality and misses an opportunity to examine how Christians (even those who are only Christian by culture) are afforded privileges that religious minorities are not.

Critically examining the sociocultural aspects of religion is important to do, not just in theory or in rhetoric, but in practice as well. Research has shown that even programs following the overtly critical University of Michigan Intergroup Dialogue model may stray

N
E
X
T

S
T
E
P
S

from its social justice mission if/when facilitators and students do not adequately understand the critical perspective on religion and religious identity. When this happens, it becomes possible that interfaith dialogue can, unfortunately, perpetuate the marginalization of religious minorities and further embed their internalized oppression. A critical social justice framework encourages us to consider how power imbalances between religious groups might affect the way religious minorities experience these programs. So, when programs ask participants to explain their religion to others, as speedfaithing events or pop-up conversations might do, it is important to recognize that doing so may place disproportionate pressure on participants from lesser-known and lesser-understood religious traditions to articulate (and sometimes defend) their religion to their peers. Hindus, for instance, may find themselves in a position where they have to rationalize the concept of reincarnation or the existence of multiple deities, while their Christian peers are not likely to encounter such bewilderment at the idea of a single lifetime or god. Likewise, when programs organize educational lectures or panels of religious leaders, they run the risk of leaving audience members exposed to only a single interpretation of a given religion—a risk that threatens minority religions more than larger, more common religious groups. That the vast majority of Americans are Christian makes the diversity within the Christian tradition more widely acknowledged, a privilege that is not afforded to most minority religions whose adherents are often assumed to hold a singular belief system or practice. Furthermore, when programs are run by chaplains and in campus chapels (even if they are labeled as interfaith or multifaith spaces), partner with local houses of worship, involve religious ritual (such as an interfaith prayer), or are centered on personal religious exploration, the entire experience is foregrounded in a context of religious belief, and may exclude those who do not believe in a higher power. It is equally important, however, for atheists and agnostics to engage in interfaith dialogue and to learn about how embedded Christian hegemony is in our society, especially because many of them may still have a cultural worldview and identity rooted in the religious tradition of their upbringing.

To be sure, belief is a big part of the way most people understand religion, despite some of the foremost authorities on religious studies explaining that religion and religious identity is much more complex than that. Focusing solely on belief in an interfaith dialogue makes it possible for culturally Christian atheists to ignore their Christian privilege and the way they benefit from a system that oppresses religious minorities by presenting themselves as separate from the dominant culture. Additionally, it centers conversations about religious minorities on their beliefs rather than their subordination. A dialogue of this sort does not align with the priorities of the critical social justice paradigm.

RELIGIOUS IDENTITY INCLUSION BEYOND THE DOMINANT ABRAHAMIC TRADITIONS

Another aspect of interfaith programming that can be perceived as hollow or insincere to some religious minority students is the bias toward Christianity or the three dominant Abrahamic religions (Judaism, Christianity, and Islam) in much of the existing discourse and practice. Again, this may be a result, in part, of the lack of education research and literature addressing non-Abrahamic religious groups. Much of the existing scholarship intended to help student affairs professionals address issues related to religion or spirituality with students is written from a Christian perspective [or a] categorical definition aligned with mainstream Christianity. The influential faith development theory, for instance, which claims to separate faith and religion, defines and describes students' spiritual development from a Christian perspective (James Fowler was, notably, a Christian minister and theologian). To address this problem, Watt, Fairchild, and Goodman (2009), organized a special issue of the journal *New Directions for Student Services* to help push the field beyond its Christian orientation. However, in this special issue they attend only to Jewish, Muslim, and atheist students; no other religious identity is represented or discussed. In fact, in the introduction to the special issue, the editors list only Islam, Judaism, or atheism as nondominant belief systems. . . . Non-Abrahamic religious identities are completely missing from this model. Where would a student who practices Native Hawaiian religion fit? A Jain? A Taoist? In explaining her choice to put Jews and Muslims in the second tier of religious privilege, what about those who do not believe in the God of Abraham at all? Small complicates her own model by suggesting that Evangelical Christians often face oppression because of their religious identity and thus, are at once both privileged and oppressed. Yet, she does not question the way various denominations of Judaism or Islam are privileged/oppressed differently. . . .

Slowly, academic publications are beginning to acknowledge the existence of non-Abrahamic religious identities. However, in many cases (not all), these acknowledgments come in the form of a brief comment, much like a footnote, whereas the bulk of the discussion and description covers issues pertinent to the three main Abrahamic religions primarily. Also, while some religious traditions are recognized (Budhism, Hinduism, Sikhism, and Native American religions are most often mentioned) others are still largely untouched; for example, Jainism, Taoism, Confucianism, Shinto, Paganism, Wicca, Voodoo, and many others. To be sure, the smaller number of Americans who identify with these religions contributes to the lack of data U.S. researchers are able to produce relevant to these identities. Nonetheless, it is necessary to call attention to the more privileged positions that religious traditions more well-known by the general U.S. population enjoy in this country so as not to simply pay lip service to religious diversity, but to make a genuine effort to incorporate all religious identities into this discussion.

A critical social justice approach to interfaith dialogue reminds us that it is important to include individuals (both participants and facilitators) and perspectives from non-Abrahamic traditions—not as a token, in the form of a single participants, but as well represented and valued religious groups. At the most basic level, an interfaith program that only involves or acknowledges Jews, Christians, and Muslims is an affront to the very existence of other religious groups. It should come as no surprise, then, that many students felt extremely offended when the University of Maryland embarked on its Tree of Life interfaith needlepoint project and only invited participants from the three dominant Abrahamic traditions. Their rationale was that the Tree of Life was a central symbol in Judaism, Christianity, and Islam—neglecting to mention that the Tree of Life is also a theme in Buddhism, Hinduism, and virtually all indigenous religions.

On a more systemic level, excluding non-Abrahamic perspectives limits participants' exposure to different religious traditions, which may lead to a false sense that all or most religions share certain ideas and principles found primarily in the Abrahamic traditions (monotheism, a sacred text, weekly rituals that take place in a particular holy building, among countless others). Perpetuating this myth reinforces the Abrahamic yardstick as a measure of religiosity, or even a determinant of what constitutes a religion (as opposed to merely a form of spirituality, as some might suggest). Participants from non-Abrahamic religions may be forced, then, to justify their tradition as an actual religion—a struggle that indigenous peoples, Buddhists, and others often face. From a critical social justice standpoint, this exemplar of Christian (maybe even Abrahamic) hegemony should be challenged in an interfaith dialogue. Doing so requires substantial participation by individuals with non-Abrahamic religious identities—not to teach others about their traditions, but to broaden the conversation beyond Judeo-Christian-Islamic normative themes. Indeed, asserting a marginalized, misunderstood perspective can be daunting when one is alone, or in the extreme minority. For that reason, it is crucial that non-Abrahamic religions are well represented in an interfaith discussion or event.

NEXT STEPS

To be sure, organizing an interfaith dialogue (or other interfaith initiative) with adequate participation from a wider range of religious identity groups can be a difficult task, but it is important nonetheless. A commitment to social justice often means spending more time and effort recruiting participants from underrepresented identity groups, and an interfaith dialogue is no different. What the critical social justice framework helps us understand, in this case, is that simply including two or three religious identity groups in an interfaith dialogue is not enough to truly combat systemic religious oppression; that it is also necessary to include, in a considerable way, those outside the three dominant Abrahamic religions. Of course, there may be reasons for limiting interfaith dialogue to just two or three specific groups—for instance, when the goal is to address the unique historical tensions between those groups. However, programs attempting to reduce prejudice toward, and promote inclusion of, religious minorities more generally, should avoid such a lack of diversity.

THE FUTURE OF INTERFAITH ENGAGEMENT IN HIGHER EDUCATION: A CRITICAL SOCIAL JUSTICE VISION

Despite the critiques of the interfaith movement I present above, I do see great potential in campus-based interfaith initiatives as a means for reducing interfaith tension and prejudice—not only on college campuses, but in our society as a whole. My hope, however, is that a critical social justice framework becomes further embedded into the discourse and practice of interfaith work, to ensure that religious minorities are not further marginalized by these programs. This vision for the future of interfaith engagement in U.S. higher education includes five specific recommendations, all designed to orient the interfaith movement toward positive social change.

First, when an interfaith program endeavors to be social justice oriented, all participants (students, staff, and faculty members alike) should clearly understand, from the start of the process, exactly what that means; in other words, they should expect Christian privilege and religious oppression to be central themes of their discussions. Second, interfaith initiatives should help participants understand the difference between religious identity (one's sociocultural, group identity) and religious/spiritual belief (one's individual faith), and why discussing religious identity is more important when the end goal is justice for religious minorities. Third, if social justice is a stated priority, participants should commit to discussing structural power dynamics and sharing lived experiences as members of their sociocultural religious group, rather than using the dialogue to debate spiritual, theological, or philosophical matters. Fourth, facilitators, coordinators, and anyone else in charge of guiding an interfaith program should be critically self-aware of their own religious identity (and their associated privilege/oppression); this includes being familiar with the ways power imbalances between religious groups manifest both interpersonally and in society at large. Lastly, participant demographics in interfaith initiatives should reflect diversity across multiple (although not necessarily all) non-Christian and non-Abrahamic religions, where no one participant is left to represent their religious group alone.

This last recommendation is certainly the most difficult to follow. Given the sheer number of distinct religious traditions that exist (in the world, in the United States, and on most college campuses), it would be impossible to have every one of them represented at any given event. Additionally, because facilitating meaningful interaction among participants can get complicated when the group is too large, trying to construct an appropriately diverse group that is also appropriately sized can be quite challenging. I do not claim to know the perfect solution to this predicament. Perhaps further research and theoretical contemplation can help shed more light on this issue. For now, I simply urge that we think

N E X T

S T E P S

critically and deliberately about the composition of our interfaith dialogues (or other inter-faith initiatives), keeping in mind that (a) religious minorities may be unfairly burdened if they are the only participant with their religious background, and (b) individuals with non-Abrahamic religious identities (Dharmic religions, indigenous religions, etc.) often have worldviews and experiences with marginalization that differ greatly from religious minorities from the Abrahamic traditions.

Undeniably, social justice work is difficult, and requires constant reflection and reevalu-ation. My intention here is not to reprimand or ridicule any of the programs or institutions mentioned throughout this article. Instead, my goal is to inspire those committed to social justice to analyze their own processes, critically consider how religious minorities are affected by them, and find ways to improve the initiatives they are involved with as needed. I believe that the interfaith movement in higher education has the ability to shape the future of interfaith relations in this country. Beyond current models, however, we need a nationwide paradigm shift that places our greatest attention on the least recognized and understood religious groups. An interfaith movement with a critical social justice approach quite possibly may turn the tide of interfaith relations away from violence and intolerance, toward acceptance and harmony.

N
E
X
T

S
T
E
P
S

See Chapter 6 in *Teaching for Diversity and Social Justice* for corresponding teaching materials.

SECTION 5

SEXISM, HETEROSEXISM, AND TRANS* OPPRESSION

Introduction

*D. Chase J. Catalano, Warren J. Blumenfeld,
and Heather W. Hackman*

The fourth edition of this book emerges in the latter half of a decade of tumult with respect to the issues represented in this section on sexism, heterosexism, and trans* oppression.[1] At the close of 2017, considerable attention in the United States spotlighted historical and contemporary sexual harassment and violence throughout many institutions (most notably media and politics). The heightened visibility drew attention to the ways sexual violence and harassment are weapons of power directed at people of all genders. Movements such as #metoo shattered the silence that shrouded histories of women and young girls (sexism). Further, those complicit via their silence or willful ignorance, must reconcile how their lack of engagement keeps systems of misogyny, patriarchy, and domination operate with impunity. Legal and political contestation regarding the civil rights of trans* people, the increased assault on women's bodies and the power to control them, the violence enacted toward queer folks in nightclubs and public policy, and an overall retrenchment of masculinity and its concomitant rigidly constructed gender role(s) all have rendered this new edition timely. This is not to say that these issues have been absent or less toxic in the last century of U.S. history and national policy, but instead points out that in a period of presumed "post-race," "post-gender," and "post-anything social justice," our nation's public discourse demonstrates that we are living in anything but that.

In previous editions of this book the three major content areas within this section were presented separately. In the late 1990s, during increased attention to identity politics, distinguishing between sexism, heterosexism, and trans* oppression, this subdivision was perhaps a reasonable way to organize the content since it mirrored the prevailing narratives regarding sexism, lesbian, gay and bisexual (LGB) issues, and trans* issues. In the context of this new updated edition, however, there is a far more complicated conversation (academic and activist alike) about gender, sexuality, queerness, and the ways these lived experiences overlap. As a result, the "siloing" of these areas of study and activism no longer works, and in fact would actually undermine the liberatory ideas and progressive activism that this more complicated and overlapping lens has fomented.

Having said that, however, we also choose not to collapse all three distinct forms of oppression into a singular form because to do so ignores the historics of different social movements that shaped them. Thus, we acknowledge the overlap and interconnection between the social movements and simultaneously want their histories to be viewed in their own context and in relation to other social movements. A combined section allows for a more specific focus on the shared root power structures, the parallel ways these forms of oppression reinforce each other, and the possibilities for deep social change when holding all three of these issues in a connected way. Much like a prism that shows both the separate wavelengths of light *and* their combined illuminating effect, this section offers readings that are both specific to each of these three forms of identity and the corresponding oppression, and intersectional with respect to the connections between these forms of oppression. As such, we ask that the reader hold these individual pieces up to the light and observe the way each article speaks to the larger and more profound dynamics in play.

Oppression directed against all women (sexism), LGB people (heterosexism), and trans* people (trans* oppression) are both distinctive and interlocking because we all have multiple identities that are salient at different times and for different reasons. What connects these forms of oppression is the socially constructed and ruthlessly enforced binary systems of gender and sexuality that divide people along strictly demarcated boundaries into either/or categories (men/women, heterosexual/queer, gender normative/gender subversive) that are then used to rigidly define societal norms. When these socially constructed binary oppositions are then connected to societal power, they serve to establish and maintain hierarchical borders of power and oppression that privilege groups and individuals constructed as "dominant" while marginalizing and disempowering groups and individuals constructed as "subordinate." The borders establish a polarity of exclusion in various degrees on one side and inclusion on the other. This structure is established and enforced on the societal, institutional, and individual/interpersonal levels (Bell, 2016; Hardiman & Jackson, 1997). The most extreme and overt forms of oppression are directed against those who most challenge, confound, or contest these binary frames established within societal norms in their presentation of self and in their attempts to obliterate the very boundaries from which hierarchies of domination and subordination stem.

What then is the complexity we are attempting to capture in this section? Gender is fluid, sexuality is fluid, identities don't matter when it comes to trying to "pin someone down," *and* identities deeply matter when it comes to framing the personal as political and in helping the larger society shift in ways that are ever-more just and inclusive of the variation in the lived human experience. For a long time the emphasis in the social justice literature addressing sexuality was around seemingly separate L-G-B identities and the desire for political equality. Emphases were placed on coming out, legal equality like marriage, options of whether to serve in the military, and fair representation in the media, and those ideas were oftentimes viewed as distinct from gender, race, (dis)ability, and other social identities. In this section we are offering a view that requires us to consider how all of our social identities interact to influence how we understand social justice. Our efforts in this section seek to avoid the trappings that have hindered single identity movements for justice. Instead, we emphasize the overlap in lived experiences for these three communities while capturing the incredible possibility for change when working in coalition and solidarity.

LANGUAGE

Language is complicated, imprecise, and implies conformity of experience (Catalano, 2017), since it is influenced by time, context, interpersonal dynamics, intention, and many other variables. In an effort to develop a shared understanding of identities, we attempt to approach terminology with as much contemporary accuracy as possible. At the same time, we acknowledge that inevitably some of the terminology and definitions we use in this section may be accepted by some people and contested by others. Also, what was "popular" or most often used at the time of the first three editions, and even in this updated version, may seem obsolete or inaccurate by the time of publication. As identity categories are unstable, forever changing, evolving, and progressing, so too is the language defining these categories. Each person will make different meanings and develop internal and external language to describe and define their own multiple social identities. Defining oneself is an essential element of liberation, and thus our offering of some shared language below is not meant to dismiss how each person views their experience, but is simply meant to help readers of this section engage more fully with its contents.

HETEROSEXISM

Heterosexism is the institutionalization of a heterosexual norm or standard, which establishes and perpetuates the notion that all people are or should be heterosexual, thereby privileging hetero-sexuals and heterosexuality, and excluding the needs, concerns, cultures, and life experiences of lesbians, gay males, bisexuals, pansexuals, asexuals, intersex, and trans* people. Put simply, heterosexism is at times overt, and at times subtle, through mechanisms of neglect, omission, era-sure, and distortion. Related concepts include heteronormativity (Warner, 1991) and compulsory heterosexuality (Rich, 1980), which establishes the normalization and privileging of heterosexuality on the personal/interpersonal, institutional, and societal levels. An example of heterosexism is how adults automatically expect that young people will enter a heterosexual marriage at some future date, and that they will produce and rear children within this union. Blumenfeld (selection 69) offers connections between historical and contemporary linkages to the persistence of heterosexism.

Heterosexism also takes the form of pity, when the dominant group looks upon lesbian, gay, bisexual, pansexual, asexual, intersex, and queer people as unfortunate human beings who "can't help being the way they are." Heterosexism forces lesbian, gay, bisexual, pansexual, asexual, intersex, and queer people to struggle constantly against their own invisibility, and makes it much more difficult for them to integrate a positive sexual identity. Heterosexism's occasional subtlety, like all forms of oppression, makes it somehow even more harmful and challenging because it is often harder to define and combat. The dynamics of heterosexism has led to various iterations of language, such as the more commonly used language of queer. Queer might seem unsettling to some, which is the precise reason for its use within gender and sexuality social movements. The term queer is "a positionality that is not restricted to lesbians and gay men but is in fact available to anyone who is or who feels marginalized because of her or his sexual practices" (Halperin, 1995, p. 62). The use of queer (as explored later in queer theory) is to expand potentiality and resist constructions that align with normative categories (Halperin, 1995).

Heterosexism's more active, and at times more visible component, called "homophobia," is oppression by intent, purpose, and design. Derived from the Greek terms *homos*, meaning "same," and *phobikos*, meaning "having a fear of and/or an aversion toward," the word "homophobia" was coined by George Weinberg (1972). Homophobia can be defined as the fear and hatred of those who love and are attracted emotionally and sexually to those of the same sex. Homophobia includes prejudice, discrimination, harassment, and acts of violence brought on by that fear and hatred (Blumenfeld, 2013). Related concepts include "lesbophobia" or "lesbiphobia," which can be defined as the fear and hatred and discrimination and acts of violence stemming from this fear and hatred against women who love women, "biphobia," which is fear, hatred, and oppression directed against bisexuals: people who love and are emotionally and sexually attracted to people of other sexes (Airen, selection 75); and "asexual oppression" is oppression against asexual people.

Increasingly the term "homophobia" is no longer used in preference to the use of "heterosexism" as a more inclusive term by expanding its traditional definition. A "phobia" is commonly known from psychology as an "irrational" or "unreasonable" fear. For example, some people have irrational fears of insects (arachnophobia), or fear of open spaces, or being in crowded public places like shopping malls (agoraphobia). On the other hand, some fears (and forms of prejudice) are *taught* between individuals and within societies and cultures. Homophobia falls within this latter category. Rather than existing as "irrational" or "unreasonable" attitudes and behaviors per se, they exist within the realm of *learned* responses. Therefore, for purposes of discussion throughout this book and in this section, though we sometimes use the terms "homophobia" and "biphobia," we are also employing the term "heterosexism" in its expanded and more inclusive form.

SEXISM

Said most simply, sexism is the use of structural, institutional, and cultural power by cisgender men (and to a lesser degree trans* men) to deny resources to and extract resources from cisgender women and trans* women for the sole benefit of men as a group. "Cisgender is an adjective describing a person whose gender identity is congruent with their gender assigned at birth" (Catalano & Griffin, 2016, p. 185). The resources in question can be material (employment, housing, education, and legal) or non-material (safety, respect, voice, and representation), and participation in this system by men can be conscious or unconscious. And while the action of sexism on individual and interpersonal levels is what tends to be most discussed in mainstream media, for example, reducing systems of oppression to these levels leaves the structural and institutional levels unexamined and therefore unchanged. One byproduct of this overemphasis on individual and interpersonal levels is that it can "seem" like women have made great strides because there is a woman astronaut or another who is a CEO, but when we move back and take the picture in more fully, the incredible and long-standing systemic disparities with respect to gender in the most important areas of power in this country can be seen. For example, it is an important advancement that some cities finally have women as mayors, but when we look at the representation of women in the US Senate, we find that the political system is still substantially skewed. In 2017 women comprised 21% of the US Senate and 19% of the House of Representatives. Those suggesting that change takes time will need to explain why we are approaching a full century of suffrage for women and this is as far as we have gotten. Thus, when restricting the view of oppression on the individual or interpersonal levels, the much more influential level of institutional and structural power is obscured and society mistakenly thinks that women have come farther than they actually have.

The arc of sexism across the globe and in countless societies throughout history is long, and thus the United States is not unique in its lack of full equality and equity for women. Importantly, however, the United States emphatically claims to be a nation where everyone has a set of basic rights that cannot be abrogated by any external force. As with People of Color and Native peoples regarding racism and poor/working class communities with respect to classism, those "inalienable" rights for women are constantly contested, diminished, and undermined by systemic and systematic sexism within every aspect of our society. Throughout the section various selections (Lorber, selection 63; Kimmel, selection 70; Spade, selection 81; and Serano, selection 83) speak to the way gender is socially constructed, making the difference between men and women seem inherent or at least deeply rooted and thus immutable, thereby setting the stage for sexism to operate structurally and institutionally while seeming "normal" and "just the way it is." The action of the system based on these gender narratives can be seen in the ways women's bodies are objectified (West, selection 79), how women are assumed to be inferior (Solnit, selection 80), and the multiple ways women's lives are impacted by violence (Katz, selection 82). Terms that connect to sexism such as misogyny (the hatred of women and the feminine form), patriarchy (the system of power controlled by men), and androcentrism (the placing of the male experience at the center of discourse) can also be found throughout the section and at their core refer to this overall system of male power, privilege, and supremacy that targets women throughout US society.

TRANS* OPPRESSION

For last 20 years or so, there have been a variety of terms used by and for trans* people, as well as terms that pre-date popular culture and academic attention, for both self-determination and administrative enforcement (Spade, 2011). The limitation of trying to pin down trans* identity to a singular definition means that we have the unintended consequence of oversimplifying trans*ness and assuming coherence where there may not be any (Catalano, 2017). Yet, in order for us to try to move forward together, we will attempt to provide a working definition of trans* identity and ways to understand the impact of trans* oppression.

The range of potential gender identities mean there are a limitless number of iterations of trans*ness for those who resist, reject, and reimagine their gender apart from the categories of sex and gender assigned at birth (Feinberg, 1996; Stryker, 2008). As previously mentioned, we use the language of cisgender instead of non-trans* to be affirming of trans* identities (Catalano & Griffin, 2016; Enke, 2012; Serano, 2009; Stryker, 2008). To elaborate, "cisgender individuals are not necessarily gender-conforming in terms of their gender expression" (Catalano & Griffin, 2016, p. 185). The confusion and conflation of gender, sex, and sexuality, as previously mentioned within this introduction, makes us believe that sex dictates gender and gender influences sexual, romantic, and intimate relationships. In reality, however, these identities are independent variables and fluid within their own right, resulting in a complex lived reality that cannot be contained by simple classifications.

Trans* oppression is most easily understood as the marginalization and exclusion for those who do not identify within the category of man or woman; trans*ness in this sense is rejection of the expectation that there are only men who are biologically male and express masculinity and there are only women who are biologically women and express femininity (Bornstein, 1994). Through the lens of the oppressive structure, anyone who transgresses the boundaries of gender, sex, and gender expression is in some way doing their gender wrong (Butler, 1990; West & Zimmerman, 1987; Westbrook & Schilt, 2014). Trans* people experience threats and acts of violence as fueled by the conscious and unconscious fear of those who disrupt gender norms, which is a price too high for anyone to pay to live their authentic lives.[2]

Violence experienced by trans* people is not as simple as individual, but rather as a systemic and institutionally-supported view that trans*ness is "something" to be eradicated. As a result of pervasive violence against trans* people, activists have created International Trans Day of Remembrance (https://tdor.info/), and Chestnut (selection 91) explores and complicates how Trans Day of Remembrance should encapsulate an intersectional focus on the disproportional violence impacting trans* women of color. Further, Ware (selection 77) provides insights into how queer, trans*, and gender non-conforming youth intersect with age, race, and the juvenile justice system.

Misrecognition is a constant psychological stress for those who are misgendered based on how they look, how they are perceived, and the limitations of how they can identify (Snorton, 2009). Even those trans* people who biomedically transition using various hormonal, surgical, and social methods to align with more "recognizable" gender norms carry a history of their gendered pasts through such things such as financial documents, and medical records. While some trans* people go "stealth" (making their trans*ness as invisible as possible for safety), some trans* people openly refuse to disregard, hide, or reject the complexity of their gendered past for others' comfort. In Spade (selection 81) and Serano (selection 83), each offer their experiences with navigating various forms of trans* oppression, and Schulman (selection 68) offers insights into the experience of trans* collegians. Of course, coalition building is integral to understanding how social justice moves forward. Chess, Kafer, Quizar, and Richardson (selection 93) demonstrate how gender-inclusive restrooms are something that is of benefit to everyone.

THEORETICAL AND CONCEPTUAL FRAMEWORK

Today, the reality of gender and sexuality is that none of the previously used frameworks are enough, not just with respect to inclusivity, but especially in terms of what liberation and justice for all axes of identity look and feel like. In attempting to explain this larger, liberatory view, and thus the contours of this section, we want to introduce a few key conceptual organizers: Critical Trans* Politics (CTP), Queer Theory, Intersectionality, and Feminisms. We introduce these conceptual and theoretical frameworks as a way to consider the complexities of genders and sexualities, and to situate the readings that follow. We start with CTP as a means of entry into queer theory, discuss the potentiality of intersectionality, and conclude with feminisms.

CRITICAL TRANS* POLITICS

In the past few years, we have seen an increase in national media attention on the lives and experiences of some trans* people. Popular culture has seen trans* visibility through the work of writer, television host, and advocate Janet Mock, activist and actress Laverne Cox, and former professional athlete and reality television star Caitlyn Jenner. Mock's book, *Redefining realness* (2014) debuted on the *New York Times* bestseller list. Cox has been featured on the cover of *Time* magazine (Steimetz, 2014) and is one of the stars on the *Netflix* show *Orange is the New Black*. Cox has been an outspoken LGBT advocate and did a public interview with bell hooks about intersectionality and feminism (www.youtube.com/watch?v=9oMmZlJijgY). Jenner's reality television show (*I am Cait*) brought up some difficult questions about sports, celebrity, and conservative politics. At the same time, we have seen increased political backlash through state legislation called "trans bathroom bills" that seek to limit and prevent trans* people from accessing public restrooms through the false guise of "protecting" young people and women by labeling trans* people as "sexual predators." There has also been an increased awareness in the number of trans* people murdered through media outlets such as *The Advocate*, *LGBTQ Nation*, and the *Huffington Post*. In effect, the public discourse around trans* identities has been about pronouns, transition related surgeries, restroom access, and murders. None of which we would characterize as liberatory.

Now, to be sure, the current public attention on trans* lives does not acknowledge the long histories of trans* communities. Trans* people have existed throughout histories (Feinberg, 1996; Stryker, 2008). For example, Stryker (selection 76) recounts the history of the Compton's Cafeteria Riot of 1966, which is still relatively unknown, and historically situates trans* people as part of intersectional social justice movements. The invisibility of trans* histories is also addressed in this volume through Meyerowitz (selection 72), who offers historical roots of trans* oppression through medical discourse. It is not surprising that histories of trans* lives are invisible when shadowed by dominant narratives of cisgender conformity and expectations that trans* people's needs are aligned with LGB needs. Yet, trans* people have repeatedly been cast aside by LGB political organizations because they are not politically viable to the current rights agenda (see ENDA, initial repeal efforts of "Don't Ask, Don't Tell," and other examples) (Spade, 2011). Often the refrain has been, "We'll come back for you," but that time never comes because the political climate makes trans* inclusion too difficult and complex. In fact, Critical Trans* Politics (CTP) seeks a "transformation that is more than symbolic and that reaches those facing the most violent manifestations of transphobia, we must move beyond the politics of recognition and inclusion" (Spade, 2011, p. 28).

CTP specifically offers ways to explore ideas of solidarity as a form of dismantling and resisting oppression. We assert that it is imperative to examine how sex, gender, and sexuality manifest (and get reproduced) through oppression, which are best understood in relationship to each other (Catalano & Griffin, 2016). "Power is not a matter of one dominant individual or institution, but instead manifests in interconnected, contradictory sites where regimes of knowledge and practice circulate and take hold" (Spade, 2011, p. 22). Spade (2011) shapes CTP as a way to consider the limits of the law and instead consider the impact of how administrative norms (bureaucracy and regulations) are purportedly neutral, but actually reinforce normativity. "Law reform tactics can have a role in mobilization-focused strategies, but law reform must never constitute the sole demand of trans politics" (p. 28). CTP offers (and demands) an examination of inclusion; Spade argues inclusion only serves to force the most vulnerable into the normative boundaries already determined by institutions like marriage and family.

Spade's suggestion is to do social justice work focused on the most vulnerable, "centering the belief that social justice trickles up, not down" (p. 23). Further, Spade (2011) names how the legal processes of inclusion (hate crime legislation and employment anti-discrimination laws) are flawed and failed attempts for equality. Instead, these legal methods only force

> trans* populations to claim and embrace a kind of recognition that not only fails to offer respite from the brutalities of poverty and criminalization, but also threatens to reduce our struggle to another justification for and site of expansion of the structures that produce the very conditions that shorten our lives.
>
> (Spade, 2011, p. 223)

As with all forms of oppression, looking in isolation at the interpersonal, institutional, or cultural manifestations or a singular identity manifestation will only replicate oppression (Bell, 2016).

QUEER THEORY

Within academic and activist areas, a greater emphasis and discussion is centered on what has come to be called "queer studies" and an area of critical theory called "queer theory." As a theoretical approach, queer theory encourages an analysis that challenges current notions and categorizations of what is considered as repressive binary frames of sexuality and gender constructions. At the heart of queer theory is the principle that "identities" are neither fixed nor inflexible, and they are not biologically determined, but that instead identities are socially determined. Queer theorists have insisted that identities comprise many and varied components, and that it is inaccurate and misleading to collectively categorize people on the basis of one single element (for example, as "lesbian," "gay," "bisexual," "heterosexual," or as "woman," "man," and others).

According to author and theorist David Halperin:

> Queer is by definition whatever is at odds with the normal, the legitimate, the dominant. *There is nothing in particular to which it necessarily refers*. It is an identity without an essence. "Queer" then, demarcates not a positivity but a positionality *vis-à-vis* the normative.
>
> (1995, p. 62, original emphasis)

The resistance to alignment with normativity means that queerness is potentially for transgressive and liminal spaces, places, and subjectivities.

Monique Wittig (1980), for example, asserted that the terms "woman" and "man" constituted *political* rather than eternal or essentialized categories. Pre-eminent scholar and social theorist Judith Butler (1990) addressed what she refers to as the "performativety of gender" in which "gender" is basically an involuntary reiteration or re-enactment of established norms of expression, an act that one performs as an actor performs a script that was created before the actor ever took the stage. The continued transmission of gender requires actors to play their roles so that they become actualized and reproduced in the guise of reality, and in the guise of the "natural" and the "normal."

> The act that one does, the act that one performs, is, in a sense, an act that has been going on before one arrived on the scene. Hence, gender is an act, which has been rehearsed, much as a script survives the particular actors who make use of it, but which requires individual actors in order to be actualized and reproduced as reality once again.
>
> (Butler, 1990, p. 272)

"Gender," therefore, is a taught and learned response, and sustained in the service of maintaining positions of domination and subordination. Not only are the categorical binary frames man/woman, heterosexual/homosexual and bisexual, and gender conforming/gender non-conforming inaccurate, but they also leave no space for those who do not fit within these neat and oppositional categories. For example, "intersex[3] is a general term used for a variety of factors in which a person is born with a reproductive or sexual anatomy that doesn't seem to fit the typical definitions of female or male" (Intersex Society of North America, n.d.). The binary frames make their existence rendered invisible, even an impossibility. Similarly, trans* people resist, reject, and often confound gender norms and sex categories, and thus they experience violence, marginalization, and other manifestations of oppression as a result of measures to maintain the dominance of cisgender and normative notions of gender (gender normativity).

In the case of gender, the binary imperatives actually lock all people into rigid gender-based roles that inhibit creativity and self-expression, and therefore, we all have a vested interest in challenging and eventually obliterating the binaries. The existence of dominance aligns with patriarchy (male dominance), heterosexual privilege, and gender normativity. Within a patriarchal system of male domination, some cisgender heterosexual male bodies matter more, while "othered" bodies matter less. These "othered" bodies (including female, trans*, and intersex bodies) violate the "rules" for the assumed reproduction and maintenance of the dominant patriarchal system. Of course, in this system, people with disabilities, people of color, and other identities are also deemed as "other" to be misaligned with normativity aimed to serve patriarchy.

Butler (1993) reminds us that the term "abjection" is taken from the Latin, *ab-jicere*, meaning to cast off, away, or out. On a social level, abjection signifies someone who is degraded, stigmatized, or cast out. Butler (1990) states that "we regularly punish those who fail to do their gender right," (pp. 139–140) and similarly punish those who fail to do their "race" right. *Doing* one's "race" right often depends on *doing* one's socioeconomic class right. The regulatory regimes and categories of "sex," "sexuality," "gender," "ability," "race," and "class" are connected, and these connections are maintained by systems of oppression.

INTERSECTIONALITY

A third key area of the theoretical framework informing this section is what is called "intersectionality." The term is most often attributed to Dr. Kimberle Crenshaw's (1991) article, but it is likely that Dr. Crenshaw's articulation represented a formalizing of what was a long-standing understanding in feminist, queer, and communities of color. Audre Lorde (1984) regularly spoke to the ways that both the impacts of systems of oppression cross over each other and often compound their effects on the lives of individuals and groups, as well as the shared roots of systems of oppression and how they serve to reinforce each other at a core level. Examples include the intensified oppression of trans* women of color versus white trans* women (Kacere, selection 74), or how abortion and family planning resources are accessed more by women of color than white women of all economic backgrounds (Sherman, 2016).

Focusing on the dynamics of three forms of oppression can add complexity to the work of reading and teaching this section, it also better prepares those engaging with this section how these issues play out in the "real world." No one is merely their gender or their sexuality. Rather, these identities and their concomitant dynamics are constantly in play, and thus an intersectional approach helps ground the reader's experience in a "lived" manner, effectively speaking an even deeper truth to power and offering a more sophisticated pathway to liberation and social justice.

Our theoretical framework allows us to consider how sexism, heterosexism, and trans* oppression interlock and support each other. The necessity of utilizing intersectionality as a theoretical framework is because it reflects an ongoing intellectual and social justice mission that seeks to (1) reformulate the world of ideas so that it incorporates the many contradictory and overlapping ways that human life is experienced; (2) convey this knowledge by rethinking curricula and promoting institutional change in higher education institutions; (3) apply the knowledge in an effort to create a society in which all voices are heard; and (4) advocate for public policies that are responsive to multiple voices.

(Dill & Zambrana, 2009, p. 2)

Our section utilizes this framework to highlight how all forms of oppression support the existence of each other, do not manifest in the same way for people of similar identities (context matters), and marginalized identities disrupt the "naturalizing" assumptions of "normal" (Bell, 2016; Crenshaw, 1995; Johnson, 2006; Young, 1990).

The framework of intersectionality attends to identity while not focusing on the individual (Collins, 2009). Our aim of utilizing intersectionality is to allow for a more complex and nuanced understanding of how systems of oppression operate, moving beyond the individual focus. "Intersectionality attends to identity by placing it within a macro-level analysis that ties individual experience to a person's membership in social groups, during a particular social and historical period, and within larger, interlocking systems of advantage and access" (Wijeyesinghe & Jones, 2014, p. 11). In this way, we can utilize a metaphor of an array of mirrors as a way to communicate the complexity of intersectionality and multiple identities.

Imagine an octagonal room (eight sides) and each wall is covered by a mirror. If you were to stand in the center of the room, then you would have eight images of the singular self; realistically speaking, if you had sight, you would need to choose which mirrors to face since there is a practical limit of how many images you can face at a time (one to three, depending on the size of the room). If each mirror represents one of our social identities, then you would be examining either a singular identity or a few identities. At the same time, you would also be able to see other images of yourself that show up "behind" the image in front of you, which are images projected from the mirrors that surround you. For us, this is a way to think about an individual's multiple identities, since conceptually it is difficult to simultaneously think of them all at any given time. The mirror we face represents a salience of identity, and our experience of salience might be related to various dynamics such as context, time, and location.

Our image is how we might understand ourselves as an individual, which is shaped by how we were taught to view ourselves. The mirror metaphor is more complex than an individual understanding of identity. The construct of a mirror is a way to recognize how the culture influences how we understand and shape the images we make of ourselves, and the walls are the institutions that support those images.

"Intersectionality frames all identities as being mutually constituted, meaning that social identities are not discrete entities that are isolated from the influences of all others" (Wijeyesinghe & Jones, 2014, p. 15). In this way, the constructions of our social identities are shaped by the presences of each other's in how we are constituted by culture, time, history, and context. Our efforts toward liberation are not singular social movements, and our aim is to open up the possibilities of locating the role of systems that influence our inability to move toward social justice.

The work of intersectionality reminds us that it "becomes less about locating oneself within an intersectional framework and more so about using intersectionality to understand the experiences of others and the social structures that perpetuate privilege and oppression" (Wijeyesinghe & Jones, 2014, pp. 16–17). Thus, its values in using intersectionality in the formation of this section are threefold. First, it avoids "oppression Olympics" that so often arise from a siloed approach to social justice work. Too often we end up in interpersonal dynamics of oppression in the attempt to determine "who has it worse," especially when it came to getting access to sparse resources. Second, intersectionality connects this section more effectively to the other sections of this book. We are able to understand how existence and maintenance of sexism serves to support the existence of racism and classism, for example, when we assume that it was "liberating" for women to have the opportunity to work when women of color and poor women of all races had always needed to work to survive. Third, intersectionality sets right long-standing histories where the lack of intersectionality wrought incredible harm on already marginalized populations.

Intersectionality allows the reader to see more easily the connections of this section to other sections, and thereby gain an even better sense of what is happening in our entire society. Knowing parts of the whole is helpful, but seeing how all those parts fit together to make the whole what it is, is the only way that we can collectively and substantially achieve social justice. As such, the connections between sexual oppression, gender oppression, and racial oppression, economic oppression, ableism, and the other sections in this book should be clearer in this edition of the book than any other. The emphasis on intersectionality with respect to the three areas addressed in this section serves as amends for all the failings of movements (i.e., the first two waves of the "women's movement" with respect to women of color), the narrow views of theorists (i.e., trans* academic theory being largely white in its early iterations and somewhat disconnected from activist and everyday roots in the ivory towers), and the biased leadership around specific issues (e.g., the fact that "marriage" was largely a political imperative for professional middle class queer folks and had little relevance to those who are poor and working class).

It is deeply false to act as if intersectionality is a "new" theory. Instead it needs to be framed as an "it's about time" move in the field and in this section. To this end, however, the greatest power of intersectionality is in its capacity to envision a very new world – a world in which folks are liberated along all lines of identity and where systems of oppression and privilege do not thwart the best of our human capacity. We hope the reader will see that liberatory horizon in the intersectional voices in this section and follow their leadership as we collectively organize for social justice.

FEMINISMS

The implications of the above intersectional framing can be seen quite powerfully when considering what the term "feminism" means and what the "feminist" movement is and has been in the United States for over 150 years. The readings by Angela Davis (selection 78) and bell hooks (selection 64) speak clearly to a complicated, multi-identity understanding of feminism that maximizes its liberatory potential. Unfortunately, and much to its own detriment, feminism has not always been framed in a complex and varied manner. In order to get the clearest sense of why this is so, and therefore why not all women and trans* folks align with mainstream feminism, an exploration of the history of US feminist movements is necessary.

The first "wave" of feminism began in the first third of the 19th century, culminating at its best at the Seneca Falls Women's Convention in Seneca Falls, NY. We say "at its best" because the platform at that convention had an intersectional focus (issues of race and class were included) and spoke to the needs of many different women. In the 72 years between that convention and the passage of the 19th Amendment, however, the movement succumbed to external forces. For example, white southern support of suffrage existed so long as racist and supremacist racial lines were upheld. As a result, suffrage movements abandoned their commitment to racial justice and economic justice for all women, resulting in the 19th Amendment providing the vote for white women, but not women of color. While gradualists said this was a victory toward more global women's rights, those who were yet again relegated to the margins found the 19th Amendment a reinforcement of the ravages of racism and white supremacy in the United States.

Forty-three years later, Betty Friedan published *The feminine mystique* (1963), and the second wave of the women's movement took concrete form, albeit again along privileged lines of race and class and, therefore, largely serving women who were white, middle class, and heterosexual. Trying to take this movement mainstream, thereby pulling in a broader base, "Feminism is the radical notion that women are people" and other such pithy slogans emerged as the public face of the movement in the 1960s and 1970s. A radical, engaged, and vocal faction of this movement including women of color, lesbians, and poor women could not as easily be eclipsed this time around, and despite itself, this movement served to advance a broader and more powerful agenda regarding the inherent rights of all women than did the first wave. And still, the seduction of privilege and power left the mainstream movement as one that largely served middle-class white women. In similar fashion, more recent liberal feminism has brandwashed the notion of women "leaning in" rather than changing the systems of white supremacist heteropatriarchy (hooks, 2015; Smith, 2016) in the corporate sphere and elsewhere. Out of the tension and resistance to mainstream ideas of feminism, more specific forms of feminism such as Black and Women of Color, radical, lesbian-separatist, eco-, and Marxist, just to name a few, have arisen. None of these have occupied the center with respect to feminist organizing or even feminism in the academy, but their contributions have been and continue to be critical to the process of de-centering privileged identities within feminism and pushing for greater inclusion and deeper analysis.

Learning from history can be painful and fruitful all at once. Starting in the 1990s and leading to today, a more complicated, inclusive, and therefore challenging "third wave" of feminism has emerged with demands that are at once reaching across identity spectra, focused on systems change, and speaking deep truth to the harm that socially constructed gender roles do in our society. This third wave is largely led by women of color, focuses on intersectionality, and has strong ties to grassroots activism. Rinku Sen's piece (selection 94) in this section is an example of the nature of this third wave feminism and the challenges of organizing it, while also positing the hope that lies within it for coalition building with trans* activists, with advocates for economic justice, with climate justice and environmental activists, and with those who seek racial justice in this country. Organizers and leaders like Winona LaDuke, and the late Wangari Maathai do not see feminism as separate from other social justice issues, but rather as a tapestry wherein all the challenges of our lives can be woven in, seen, understood, and strengthened by our shared human bonds. As such, contemporary feminism is deeper than just the radical notion that women are people; it is the even more radical notion that oppression is anathema to our humanity, and that it is deeply possible, perhaps even probable, that human society can and will live without oppression and thrive in a shared commitment to freedom.

CONCLUSION

The readings we have selected for the fourth edition are largely US focused in legal, ideological, and geographical contexts, and we openly acknowledge that our US-centric selections are a limitation. This drawback might be quite apparent given that we live in an increasingly global community where the issues covered in this section vary greatly as evidenced by the fact that norms, values, laws, policies, and other factors vary significantly by country and even by region within the same country. In some countries around the world, people have fought long and difficult battles to win rights to marriage, to employment access and security, to live where they choose and can afford, to inherit property, to define and choose family, to access affordable healthcare, to serve in the military, to conceive, adopt, and raise children, to experience a workplace free of sexual harassment, to attend school with measures put in place to limit bullying and rape culture, and many other benefits those with various forms of gender and sexual privilege take for granted. We offer Gessen's (selection 87) analysis of the conditions for LGBTQ people in the Russian Federation.

We hope this intersectional section, along with this entire book, can counter historical and contemporary troubling realities and serve as a lamp on the path to substantive and intersectional social change. We invite you to view the readings in this section with curiosity and a willingness to approach the complicated and compelling content herein. The complicated nature of the interplay between trans* oppression, sexism, and heterosexism cannot possibly be captured in a section of this size given that entire university departments are individually devoted to each area. Therefore, this introduction and the readings in this section are designed to offer an initial framework that can serve as an effective template for understanding and for taking action. As mentioned above, all three of these overlapping and still distinct communities are under fire, and thus we hope this section does more than heighten analysis. Our efforts here are meant to inspire ongoing, substantial, and sustainable action. As Jamie Utt shares (selection 95), everyone's liberation is bound up in everyone else's. Therefore we believe it is in the best interests of all marginalized communities to take action and dismantle these systems of oppression so we move into a future of possibilities, change, and hope.

Notes

1 We use trans* as a method of consistency with *Teaching for Diversity and Social Justice* (3rd edition). Although there are conflicting opinions within and across trans* communities about the use of the asterisk, we use it to signal complexity and variation of self and collective definitions, and draw attention to trans communities (Tompkins, 2014).
2 According to the National Center for Transgender Equality (2017), "Transgender people face extraordinary levels of physical and sexual violence, whether on the streets, at school or work, at home, or at the hands of government officials. More than one in four trans people has faced a bias-driven assault, and rates are higher for trans women and trans people of color."
3 Though many experts estimate the number of intersex people at between 1 in 1500 to 1 in 2000 births, since there are many factors in defining who may be considered intersex, no precise estimate can be determined (Intersex Society of North America: www.isna.org/faq/frequency).

References

Bell, L. A. (2016). Theoretical foundations for social justice education. In M. Adams and L. A. Bell (Eds.), *Teaching for diversity and social justice* (3rd edition, pp. 3–26). New York: Routledge.

Blumenfeld, W. J. (2013). Introduction: Heterosexism. In M. Adams, W. J. Blumenfeld, C. Castaneda, H. W. Hackman, M. L. Peters, & X. Zuniga, *Readings for diversity and social justice* (3rd edition, pp. 373–379). New York: Routledge.

Bornstein, K. (1994). *Gender outlaw: On men, women, and the rest of us*. New York: First Vintage Books.

Butler, J. (1990). *Gender trouble: Feminism and the subversion of identity*. New York: Routledge.

Butler, J. (1993). *Bodies that matter: On the discursive limits of sex*. New York: Routledge.

Catalano, D. C. J. (2017). Resistence coherence: Trans men's experiences and the use of grounded theory methods. *International Journal of Qualitative Studies in Education*, 30(3), 234–244.

Catalano, D. C. J. & Griffin, P. (2016). Sexism, heterosexism, and trans* oppression: An integrated perspective. In M. Adams, L. A. Bell, D. J. Goodman, & K. Y. Joshi (Eds.), *Teaching for diversity and social justice* (3rd edition, pp. 183–211). New York: Routledge.

Collins, P. H. (2009). Foreword: Emerging intersections – building knowledge and transforming institutions. In B. T. Dill & R. E. Zambrana (Eds.), *Emerging intersections: Race, class, and gender in theory, policy, and practice* (pp. vii–xiii). New Brunswick, NJ: Rutgers University Press.

Crenshaw, K. (1991). Mapping the margins: Intersectionality, identity politics, and violence against women of color. *Stanford Law Review*, 43, 1241–1299.

Crenshaw, K. W. (1995). Race, reform, and retrenchment: Transformation and legitimation in anti-discrimination law. In K. Crenshaw, N. Gotanda, G. Peller, & K. Thomas (Eds.), *Critical race theory: The key writings that formed the movement* (pp. 103–122). New York: The New Press.

Dill, B. T. & Zambrana, R. E. (2009). Critical thinking about inequality: An emerging lens. In B. T. Dill & R. E. Zambrana (Eds.), *Emerging intersections: Race, class, and gender in theory, policy, and practice* (pp. 1–21). New Brunswick, NJ: Rutgers University Press.

Enke, A. F. (2012). The education of little cis: Cisgender and the discipline of opposing bodies. In A. F. Enke (Ed.), *Transfeminist perspectives in and beyond transgender and gender studies* (pp. 60–77). Philadelphia, PA: Temple University Press.

Feinberg, L. (1996). *Transgender warriors: Making history from Joan of Arc to Dennis Rodman*. Boston, MA: Beacon Press.

Friedan, B. (1963). *The feminine mystique*. New York: W.W. Norton & Company.

Halperin, D. (1995). *Saint Foucault: Towards a gay hagiography*. New York: Oxford University Press.

Hardiman, R. & Jackson, B. W. (1997). Conceptual foundations for social justice courses. In M. Adams, L. Bell, & P. Griffin (Eds.), *Teaching for diversity and social justice: A sourcebook* (pp. 16–29). New York: Routledge.

hooks, b. (2015). *Feminism is for everybody: Passionate politics*. New York: Routledge.

Intersex Society of North America. (n.d.). How common is intersex? www.isna.org/faq/frequency.

Johnson, A. G. (2006). *Privilege, power and difference*. New York: McGraw-Hill.

Lorde, A. (1984). *Sister outsider: Essays and speeches*. Berkeley, CA: Crossings Press.

Mock, J. (2014). *Redefining realness: My path to womanhood, identity, love & so much more*. New York: Atria.

National Center for Transgender Equality. (2017). Anti-violence. www.transequality.org/issues/anti-violence.

Rich, A. (1980). *Compulsory heterosexuality and lesbian existence*. London: Onlywomen Press.

Serano, J. (2009). *Whipping girl: A transsexual woman on sexism and the scapegoating of femininity*. Berkeley, CA: Seal Press.

Sherman, R. B. (2016). What the war on reproductive rights has to do with poverty and race. *Yes! Magazine*. www.yesmagazine.org/peace-justice/what-the-war-on-reproductive-rights-has-to-do-with-poverty-and-race-20160525.

Smith, A. (2016). Heteropatriarchy and the 3 pillars of White supremacy: Rethinking Women of Color organizing. In INCITE! Women of Color Organizing (Eds.), *The color of violence: The INCITE! anthology* (pp. 66–73). Durham, NC: Duke University Press.

Snorton, C. R. (2009). "A new hope": The psychic life of passing. *Hypathia, 24*(3), 77–92.

Spade, D. (2011). *Normal life: Administrative violence, critical trans politics, and the limits of the law*. Brooklyn, NY: South End Press.

Steimetz, K. (2014, June 9). The transgender tipping point: America's next civil rights frontier. *Time, 22*(183), 38–46.

Stryker, S. (2008). *Transgender history*. Berkeley, CA: Seal Press.

Tompkins, A. (2014). Asterisk. *TSQ: Transgender Studies Quarterly, 1*(1/2), 26–27.

Warner, M. (1991). Fear of a queer planet. *Social Text, 29*, 3–17.

Weinberg, G. (1972). *Society and the healthy homosexual*. New York: St. Martin's Press.

West, C. & Zimmerman, D. (1987). Doing gender. *Gender & Society, 1*, 125–151.

Westbrook, L. & Schilt, K. (2014). Doing gender, determining gender: Transgender people, gender panics, and the maintenance of the sex/gender/sexuality system. *Gender & Society, 28*(1), 32–57.

Wijeyesinghe, C. L. & Jones, S. R. (2014). Intersectionality, identity, and systems of power and inequality. In D. M. Miller (Ed.), *Intersectionality and higher education: Theory, research, and praxis* (pp. 9–19). New York: Peter Lang.

Wittig, M. (1980). "On ne naît pas femme" [One is not born a woman]. *Questions Féministes, 8*, 75–84.

Young, I. M. (1990). *Justice and the politics of difference*. Princeton, NJ: Princeton University Press.

63

"Night to His Day"

The Social Construction of Gender

Judith Lorber

Talking about gender for most people is the equivalent of fish talking about water. Gender is so much the routine ground of everyday activities that questioning its taken-for-granted assumptions and presuppositions is like thinking about whether the sun will come up. Gender is so pervasive that in our society we assume it is bred into our genes. Most people find it hard to believe that gender is constantly created and re-created out of human inter-action, out of social life, and is the texture and order of that social life. Yet gender, like culture, is a human production that depends on everyone constantly "doing gender."

And everyone "does gender" without thinking about it. Today, on the subway, I saw a well-dressed man with a year-old child in a stroller. Yesterday, on a bus, I saw a man with a tiny baby in a carrier on his chest. Seeing men taking care of small children in public is increasingly common—at least in New York City. But both men were quite obviously stared at—and smiled at, approvingly. Everyone was doing gender—the men who were changing the role of fathers and the other passengers, who were applauding them silently. But there was more gendering going on that probably fewer people noticed. The baby was wearing a white crocheted cap and white clothes. You couldn't tell if it was a boy or a girl. The child in the stroller was wearing a dark blue T-shirt and dark print pants. As they started to leave the train, the father put a Yankee baseball cap on the child's head. Ah, a boy, I thought. Then I noticed the gleam of tiny earrings in the child's ears, and as they got off, I saw the little flowered sneakers and lace-trimmed socks. Not a boy after all. Gender done.

Gender is such a familiar part of daily life that it usually takes a deliberate disruption of our expectations of how women and men are supposed to act to pay attention to how it is produced. Gender signs and signals are so ubiquitous that we usually fail to note them—unless they are missing or ambiguous. Then we are uncomfortable until we have successfully placed the other person in a gender status; otherwise, we feel socially dislocated. . . .

For the individual, gender construction starts with assignment to a sex category on the basis of what the genitalia look like at birth. Then babies are dressed or adorned in a way that displays the category because parents don't want to be constantly asked whether their baby is a girl or a boy. A sex category becomes a gender status through naming, dress, and the use of other gender markers. Once a child's gender is evident, others treat those in one gender differently from those in the other, and the children respond to the different treatment by feeling different and behaving differently. As soon as they can talk, they start to refer to themselves as members of their gender. Sex doesn't come into play again until puberty, but by that time, sexual feelings and desires and practices have been shaped by gendered norms and expectations. Adolescent boys and girls approach and avoid each other in an elaborately scripted and gendered mating dance. Parenting is gendered, with different expectations for mothers and for fathers, and people of different genders work at different kinds of jobs. The work adults do as mothers and fathers and as low-level workers and high-level bosses, shapes women's and men's life experiences, and these experiences produce different feelings, consciousness, relationships, skills—ways of being that we call feminine or masculine. All of these processes constitute the social construction of gender.

Gendered roles change—today fathers are taking care of little children, girls and boys are wearing unisex clothing and getting the same education, women and men are working at the same jobs. Although many traditional social groups are quite strict about maintaining gender differences, in other social groups they seem to be blurring. Then why the one-year-old's earrings? Why is it still so important to mark a child as a girl or a boy, to make sure she is not taken for a boy or he for a girl? What would happen if they were? They would, quite literally, have changed places in their social world.

To explain why gendering is done from birth, constantly and by everyone, we have to look not only at the way individuals experience gender but at gender as a social institution. As a social institution, gender is one of the major ways that human beings organize their lives. Human society depends on a predictable division of labor, a designated allocation of scarce goods, assigned responsibility for children and others who cannot care for themselves, common values and their systematic transmission to new members, legitimate leadership, music, art, stories, games, and other symbolic productions. One way of choosing people for the different tasks of society is on the basis of their talents, motivations, and competence—their demonstrated achievements. The other way is on the basis of gender, race, ethnicity—ascribed membership in a category of people. . . .

Western society's values legitimate gendering by claiming that it all comes from physiology—female and male procreative differences. But gender and sex are not equivalent, and gender as a social construction does not flow automatically from genitalia and reproductive organs, the main physiological differences of females and males. In the construction of ascribed social statuses, physiological differences such as sex, stage of development, color of skin, and size are crude markers. They are not the source of the social statuses of gender, age grade, and race. Social statuses are carefully constructed through prescribed processes of teaching, learning, emulation, and enforcement. Whatever genes, hormones, and biological evolution contribute to human social institutions is materially as well as qualitatively transformed by social practices. . . . Thus, . . . gender cannot be equated with biological and physiological differences between human females and males. The building blocks of gender are *socially constructed statuses.* . . .

FOR INDIVIDUALS, GENDER MEANS SAMENESS

Although the possible combinations of genitalia, body shapes, clothing, mannerisms, sexuality, and roles could produce infinite varieties in human beings, the social institution of gender depends on the production and maintenance of a limited number of gender statuses and of making the members of these statuses similar to each other. Individuals are born sexed but not gendered, and they have to be taught to be masculine or feminine. As Simone de Beauvoir said: "One is not born, but rather becomes, a woman . . . ; it is civilization as a whole that produces this creature . . . which is described as feminine."

. . .

Many cultures go beyond clothing, gestures, and demeanor in gendering children. They inscribe gender directly into bodies. . . . In Western societies, women augment their breast size with silicone and reconstruct their faces with cosmetic surgery to conform to cultural ideals of feminine beauty. Hanna Papanek notes that these practices reinforce the sense of superiority or inferiority in the adults who carry them out as well as in the children on whom they are done. . . .

Sandra Bem argues that because gender is a powerful "schema" that orders the cognitive world, one must wage a constant, active battle for a child not to fall into typical gendered attitudes and behavior. In 1972, *Ms. Magazine* published Lois Gould's fantasy of how to raise a child free of gender-typing. The experiment calls for hiding the child's anatomy from all eyes except the parents' and treating the child as neither a girl nor a boy. The child, called X, gets to do all the things boys *and* girls do. The experiment is so successful that all the children in X's class at school want to look and behave like X. At the end of the story, the creators of the experiment are asked what will happen when X grows up. The scientists' answer is that by then it will be quite clear what X is, implying that its hormones will kick in and it will be revealed as a female or male. That ambiguous, and somewhat contradictory, ending lets Gould off the hook; neither she nor we have any idea what someone brought up totally androgynously would be like sexually or socially as an adult. The hormonal input will not create gender or sexuality but will only establish secondary sex characteristics; breasts, beards, and menstruation alone do not produce social manhood or womanhood. Indeed, it is at puberty, when sex characteristics become evident, that most societies put pubescent children through their most important rites of passage, the rituals that officially mark them as fully gendered—that is, ready to marry and become adults.

Most parents create a gendered world for their newborn by naming, birth announcements, and dress. Children's relationships with same-gendered and different-gendered caretakers structure their self-identifications and personalities. Through cognitive development, children extract and apply to their own actions the appropriate behavior for those who belong in their own gender, as well as race, religion, ethnic group, and social class, rejecting what is not appropriate. If their social categories are highly valued, they value themselves highly; if their social categories are low status, they lose self-esteem. Many feminist parents who want to raise androgynous children soon lose their children to the pull of gendered norms. My son attended a carefully nonsexist elementary school, which didn't even have girls' and boys' bathrooms. When he was seven or eight years old, I attended a class play about "squares" and "circles" and their need for each other and noticed that all the girl squares and circles wore makeup, but none of the boy squares and circles did. I asked the teacher about it after the play, and she said, "Bobby said he was not going to wear makeup, and he is a powerful child, so none of the boys would either." In a long discussion about conformity, my son confronted me with the question of who the conformists were, the boys who followed their leader or the girls who listened to the woman teacher. In actuality, they both were, because they both followed same-gender leaders and acted in gender-appropriate ways. (Actors may wear makeup, but real boys don't.)

For human beings there is no essential femaleness or maleness, femininity or masculinity, womanhood or manhood, but once gender is ascribed, the social order constructs and holds individuals to strongly gendered norms and expectations. Individuals may vary on many of the components of gender and may shift genders temporarily or permanently, but they must fit into the limited number of gender statuses their society recognizes. In the process, they re-create their society's version of women and men: "If we do gender appropriately, we simultaneously sustain, reproduce, and render legitimate the institutional arrangements. . . . If we fail to do gender appropriately, we as individuals—not the institutional arrangements—may be called to account (for our character, motives, and predispositions)" (West and Zimmerman 1987).

The gendered practices of everyday life reproduce a society's view of how women and men should act. Gendered social arrangements are justified by religion and cultural productions and backed by law, but the most powerful means of sustaining the moral hegemony of the dominant gender ideology is that the process is made invisible; any possible alternatives are virtually unthinkable.

FOR SOCIETY, GENDER MEANS DIFFERENCE

The pervasiveness of gender as a way of structuring social life demands that gender statuses be clearly differentiated. Varied talents, sexual preferences, identities, personalities, interests, and ways of interacting fragment the individual's bodily and social experiences. Nonetheless, these are organized in Western cultures into two and only two socially and legally recognized gender statuses, "man" and "woman." In the social construction of gender, it does not matter what men and women actually do; it does not even matter if they do exactly the same thing. The social institution of gender insists only that what they do is *perceived* as different.

If men and women are doing the same tasks, they are usually spatially segregated to maintain gender separation, and often the tasks are given different job titles as well, such as executive secretary and administrative assistant. If the differences between women and men begin to blur, society's "sameness taboo" goes into action. At a rock and roll dance at West Point in 1976, the year women were admitted to the prestigious military academy for the first time, the school's administrators "were reportedly perturbed by the sight of mirror-image couples dancing in short hair and dress gray trousers," and a rule was established that women cadets could dance at these events only if they wore skirts. Women recruits in the U.S. Marine Corps are required to wear makeup—at a minimum, lipstick and eye shadow—and they have to take classes in makeup, hair care, poise, and etiquette. This feminization is part of a deliberate policy of making them clearly distinguishable from men Marines. Christine Williams quotes a twenty-five-year-old woman drill instructor as saying: "A lot of the recruits who come here don't wear makeup; they're tomboyish or athletic. A lot of them have the preconceived idea that going into the military means they can still be a tomboy. They don't realize that you are a *Woman* Marine" (1989).

If gender differences were genetic, physiological, or hormonal, gender bending and gender ambiguity would occur only in . . . [those] who are born with chromosomes and genitalia that are not clearly female or male. Since gender differences are socially constructed, all men and all women can enact the behavior of the other, because they know the other's social script: "'Man' and 'woman' are at once empty and overflowing categories. Empty because they have no ultimate, transcendental meaning. Overflowing because even when they appear to be fixed, they still contain within them alternative, denied, or suppressed definitions" (J.W. Scott 1988). Nonetheless, though individuals may be able to shift gender statuses, the gender boundaries have to hold, or the whole gendered social order will come crashing down.

. . .

GENDER AS PROCESS, STRATIFICATION, AND STRUCTURE

As a social institution, gender is a process of creating distinguishable social statuses for the assignment of rights and responsibilities. As part of a stratification system that ranks these statuses unequally, gender is a major building block in the social structures built on these unequal statuses.

As a *process*, gender creates the social differences that define "woman" and "man." In social interaction throughout their lives, individuals learn what is expected, see what is expected, act and react in expected ways, and thus simultaneously construct and maintain the gender order: "The very injunction to be a given gender takes place through discursive routes: to be a good mother, to be a heterosexually desirable object, to be a fit worker, in sum, to signify a multiplicity of guarantees in response to a variety of different demands all at once" (J. Butler 1990). Members of a social group neither make up gender as they go along nor exactly replicate in rote fashion what was done before. In almost every encounter, human beings produce gender, behaving in the ways they learned were appropriate for their gender status, or resisting or rebelling against these norms. Resistance and rebellion have altered gender norms, but so far they have rarely eroded the statuses.

Gendered patterns of interaction acquire additional layers of gendered sexuality, parenting, and work behaviors in childhood, adolescence, and adulthood. Gendered norms and expectations are enforced through informal sanctions of gender-inappropriate behavior by peers and by formal punishment or threat of punishment by those in authority should behavior deviate too far from socially imposed standards for women and men.

Everyday gendered interactions build gender into the family, the work process, and other organizations and institutions, which in turn reinforce gender expectations for individuals. Because gender is a process, there is room not only for modification and variation by individuals and small groups but also for institutionalized change.

As part of a *stratification* system, gender ranks men above women of the same race and class. Women and men could be different but equal. In practice, the process of creating difference depends to a great extent on differential evaluation. As Nancy Jay (1981) says: "That which is defined, separated out, isolated from all else is A and pure. Not-A is necessarily impure, a random catchall, to which nothing is external except A and the principle of order that separates it from Not-A." From the individual's point of view, whichever gender is A, the other is Not-A; gender boundaries tell the individual who is like him or her and all the rest are unlike. From society's point of view, however, one gender is usually the touchstone, the normal, the dominant, and the other is different, deviant, and subordinate. In Western society, "man" is A, "wo-man" is Not-A. (Consider what a society would be like where woman was A and man Not-A.) . . . The dominant categories are the hegemonic ideals, taken so for granted as the way things should be that, . . . [t]he characteristics of these categories define the Other as that which lacks the valuable qualities the dominants exhibit.

. . .

Societies vary in the extent of the inequality in social status of their women and men members, but where there is inequality, the status "woman" (and its attendant behavior and role allocations) is usually held in lesser esteem than the status "man." Since gender is also intertwined with a society's other constructed statuses of differential evaluation—race, religion, occupation, class, country of origin, and so on—men and women members of the favored groups command more power, more prestige, and more property than the members of the disfavored groups. Within many social groups, however, men are advantaged over women. The more economic resources, such as education and job opportunities, are available to a group, the more they tend to be monopolized by men. In poorer groups that have few resources (such as working-class African Americans in the United States), women and men are more nearly equal, and the women may even outstrip the men in education and occupational status.

As a *structure*, gender divides work in the home and in economic production, legitimates those in authority, and organizes sexuality and emotional life. As primary parents, women significantly influence children's psychological development and emotional attachments, in the process reproducing gender. Emergent sexuality is shaped by heterosexual, homosexual, bisexual, and sadomasochistic patterns that are gendered—different for girls and boys, and for women and men—so that sexual statuses reflect gender statuses.

When gender is a major component of structured inequality, the devalued genders have less power, prestige, and economic rewards than the valued genders. In countries that discourage gender discrimination, many major roles are still gendered; women still do most of the domestic labor and child rearing, even while doing full-time paid work; women and men are segregated on the job and each does work considered "appropriate"; women's work is usually paid less than men's work. Men dominate the positions of authority and leadership in government, the military, and the law; cultural productions, religions, and sports reflect men's interests. . . .

Gender inequality—the devaluation of "women" and the social domination of "men"—has social functions and a social history. It is not the result of sex, procreation, physiology, anatomy, hormones, or genetic predispositions. It is produced and maintained by identifiable social processes and built into the general social structure and individual identities deliberately and purposefully. The social order as we know it in Western societies is organized around racial, ethnic, class, and gender inequality. I contend, therefore, that the continuing purpose of gender as a modern social institution is to construct women as a group to be the subordinates of men as a group. The life of everyone placed in the status "woman" is "night to his day—that has forever been the fantasy. Black to his white. Shut out of his system's space, she is the repressed that ensures the system's functioning."

. . .

There is no core or bedrock human nature below these endlessly looping processes of the social production of sex and gender, self and other, identity and psyche, each of which is a "complex cultural construction." *For humans, the social is the natural.* Therefore, "in its feminist senses, gender cannot mean simply the cultural appropriation of biological sexual difference. Sexual difference is itself a fundamental—and scientifically contested—construction. Both 'sex' and 'gender' are woven of multiple, asymmetrical strands of difference, charged with multifaceted dramatic narratives of domination and struggle" (Haraway 1990).

64

Feminism

A Movement to End Sexist Oppression

bell hooks

A central problem within feminist discourse has been our inability to either arrive at a consensus of opinion about what feminism is or accept definition(s) that could serve as points of unification. Without agreed upon definition(s), we lack a sound foundation on which to construct theory or engage in overall meaningful praxis. Expressing her frustrations with the absence of clear definitions in a recent essay, "Towards A Revolutionary Ethics," Carmen Vasquez comments:

> We can't even agree on what a "Feminist" is, never mind what she would believe in and how she defines the principles that constitute honor among us. In key with the American capitalist obsession for individualism and anything goes so long as it gets you what you want. Feminism in American has come to mean anything you like, honey. There are as many definitions of Feminism as there are feminists, some of my sisters say, with a chuckle. I don't think it's funny.

It is not funny. It indicates a growing disinterest in feminism as a radical political movement. It is a despairing gesture expressive of the belief that solidarity between women is not possible. It is a sign that the political naïveté which has traditionally characterized woman's lot in male-dominated culture abounds.

Most people in the United States think of feminism or the more commonly used term "women's lib" as a movement that aims to make women the social equals of men. This broad definition, popularized by the media and mainstream segments of the movement, raises problematic questions. Since men are not equals in white supremacist, capitalist, patriarchal class structure, which men do women want to be equal to? Do women share a common vision of what equality means? Implicit in this simplistic definition of women's liberation is a dismissal of race and class as factors that, in conjunction with sexism, determine the extent to which an individual will be discriminated against, exploited, or oppressed. Bourgeois white women interested in women's rights issues have been satisfied with simple definitions for obvious reasons. Rhetorically placing themselves in the same social category as oppressed women, they were not anxious to call attention to race and class privilege.

Women in lower class and poor groups, particularly those who are non-white, would not have defined women's liberation as women gaining social equality with men since they are continually reminded in their everyday lives that all women do not share a common social status. Concurrently, they know that many males in their social groups are exploited and oppressed. Knowing that men in their groups do not have social, political, and economic power, they would not deem it liberatory to share their social status. While they are aware that sexism enables men in their respective groups to have privileges denied them, they are more likely to see exaggerated expressions of male chauvinism among their peers as stemming from the male's sense of himself as powerless and ineffectual in relation to ruling male groups, rather than an expression of an overall privileged social status. From the very onset of the women's liberation movement, these women were suspicious of feminism precisely because they recognized the limitations inherent in its definition. They recognized the possibility that feminism defined as social equality with men might easily become a movement that would primarily affect the social standing of white women in middle and upper class groups while affecting only in a very marginal way the social status of working class and poor women.

. . .

In a recent article in a San Francisco newspaper, "Sisters—Under the Skin," columnist Bob Greene commented on the aversion many women apparently have to the term feminism. Greene finds it curious that many women "who obviously believe in everything that proud feminists believe in dismiss the term "feminist" as something unpleasant; something with which they do not wish to be associated." Even though such women often acknowledge that they have benefited from feminist-generated reform measures which have improved the social status of specific groups of women, they do not wish to be seen as participants in feminist movement:

> There is no getting around it. After all this time, the term "feminist" makes many bright, ambitious, intelligent women embarrassed and uncomfortable. They simply don't want to be associated with it.
>
> It's as if it has an unpleasant connotation that they want no connection with. Chances are if you were to present them with every mainstream feminist belief, they would go along with the beliefs to the letter—and even if they consider themselves feminists, they hasten to say no.

Many women are reluctant to advocate feminism because they are uncertain about the meaning of the term. Other women from exploited and oppressed ethnic groups dismiss the term because they do not wish to be perceived as supporting a racist movement; feminism is often equated with white women's rights effort. Large numbers of women see feminism as synonymous with lesbianism; their homophobia leads them to reject association with any group identified as pro-lesbian. Some women fear the word "feminism" because they shun identification with any political movement, especially one perceived as radical. Of course there are women who do not wish to be associated with the women's rights movement in any form so they reject and oppose the feminist movement. Most women are more familiar with negative perspectives on "women's lib" than the positive significations of feminism. It is this term's positive political significance and power that we must now struggle to recover and maintain.

Currently feminism seems to be a term without any clear significance. The "anything goes" approach to the definition of the word has rendered it practically meaningless. What is meant by "anything goes" is usually that any woman who wants social equality with men regardless of her political perspective (she can be a conservative right-winger or a nationalist communist) can label herself feminist. Most attempts at defining feminism reflect the class nature of the movement. Definitions are usually liberal in origin and focus on the individual woman's right to freedom and self-determination. . . .

This definition of feminism is almost apolitical in tone; yet it is the type of definition many liberal women find appealing. It evokes a very romantic notion of personal freedom which is more acceptable than a definition that emphasizes radical political action.

. . . Feminism is a struggle to end sexist oppression. Therefore, it is necessarily a struggle to eradicate the ideology of domination that permeates Western culture on various levels as well as a commitment to reorganizing society so that the self-development of people can take precedence over imperialism, economic expansion, and material desires. Defined in this way, it is unlikely that women would join the feminist movement simply because we are biologically the same. A commitment to feminism so defined would demand that each individual participant acquire a critical political consciousness based on ideas and beliefs.

. . .

Feminism defined in political terms that stress collective as well as individual experience challenges women to enter a new domain—to leave behind the apolitical stance sexism decrees is our lot and develop political consciousness. . . . By repudiating the popular notion that the focus of the feminist movement should be social equality of the sexes and emphasizing eradicating the cultural basis of group oppression, our own analysis would require an exploration of all aspects of women's political reality. This would mean that race and class oppression would be recognized as feminist issues with as much relevance as sexism.

When feminism is defined in such a way that it calls attention to the diversity of women's social and political reality, it centralizes the experiences of all women, especially the women whose social conditions have been least written about, studied, or changed by political movements. When we cease to focus on the simplistic stance "men are the enemy," we are compelled to examine systems of domination and our role in their maintenance and perpetuation. . . .

Feminism is the struggle to end sexist oppression. Its aim is not to benefit solely any specific group of women, any particular race or class of women. It does not privilege women over men. It has the power to transform in a meaningful way all our lives. . . .

Feminism as a movement to end sexist oppression directs our attention to systems of domination and the inter-relatedness of sex, race, and class oppression. Therefore, it compels us to centralize the experiences and the social predicaments of women who bear the brunt of sexist oppression as a way to understand the collective social status of women in the United States. Defining feminism as a movement to end sexist oppression is crucial for the development of theory because it is a starting point indicating the direction of exploration and analysis.

The foundation of future feminist struggle must be solidly based on a recognition of the need to eradicate the underlying cultural basis and causes of sexism and other forms of group oppression. Without challenging and changing these philosophical structures, no feminist reforms will have a long range impact. Consequently, it is now necessary for advocates of feminism to collectively acknowledge that our struggle cannot be defined as a movement to gain social equality with men; that terms like "liberal feminist" and "bourgeois feminist" represent contradictions that must be resolved so that feminism will not be continually co-opted to serve the opportunistic ends of special interest groups.

65

Patriarchy, the System

An It, Not a He, a Them, Or an Us

Allan G. Johnson

"When you say patriarchy," a man complained from the rear of the audience, "I know what you *really* mean—me!" A lot of people hear "men" whenever someone says "patriarchy," so that criticism of gender oppression is taken to mean that all men—each and every one of them—are oppressive people. Not surprisingly, many men take it personally if someone merely mentions patriarchy or the oppression of women, bristling at what they often see as a way to make them feel guilty. And some women feel free to blame individual men for patriarchy simply because they're men. Some of the time, men feel defensive because they identify with patriarchy and its values and don't want to face the consequences these produce or the prospect of giving up male privilege. But defensiveness more often reflects a common confusion about the difference between patriarchy as a kind of society and the people who participate in it. If we're ever going to work toward real change, it's a confusion we'll have to clear up.

To do this, we have to realize that we're stuck in a model of social life that views everything as beginning and ending with individuals. Looking at things in this way, we tend to think that if evil exists in the world, it's only because there are evil people who have entered into an evil conspiracy. Racism exists, for example, simply because white people are racist bigots who hate members of racial and ethnic minorities and want to do them harm. There is gender oppression because men want and like to dominate women and act out hostility toward them. There is poverty and class oppression because people in the upper classes are greedy, heartless, and cruel. The flip side of this individualistic model of guilt and blame is that race, gender, and class oppression are actually not oppression at all, but merely the sum of individual failings on the part of blacks, women, and the poor, who lack the right stuff to compete successfully with whites, men, and others who know how to make something of themselves.

What this kind of thinking ignores is that we are all participating in something larger than ourselves or any collection of us. On some level, most people are familiar with the idea that social life involves us in something larger than ourselves, but few seem to know what to do with that idea. . . . How, for example, do we participate in patriarchy, and how does that link us to the consequences it produces? How is what we think of as "normal" life related to male dominance, women's oppression, and the hierarchical, control-obsessed world in which they, and our lives, are embedded?

Without asking such questions we can't understand gender fully and we avoid taking responsibility either for ourselves or for patriarchy. Instead, "the system" serves as a vague, unarticulated catch-all, a dumping ground for social problems, a scapegoat that can never be held to account and that, for all the power we think it has, can't talk back or actually *do* anything. . . .

If we see patriarchy as nothing more than men's and women's individual personalities, motivations, and behavior, for example, then it probably won't even occur to us to ask about larger contexts—such as institutions like the family, religion, and the economy—and how people's lives are shaped in relation to them. From this kind of individualistic perspective, we might ask why a particular man raped, harassed, or beat a woman. We wouldn't ask, however, what kind of society would promote persistent *patterns* of such behavior in everyday life, from wife-beating jokes to the routine inclusion of sexual coercion and violence in mainstream movies. . . .

If the goal is to change the world, this won't help us. We need to see and deal with the social roots that generate and nurture the social problems that are reflected in the behavior of individuals. We can't do this without realizing that we all participate in something larger than ourselves, something we didn't create but that we have the power to affect through the choices we make about *how* to participate.

That something larger is patriarchy, which is more than a collection of individuals (such as "men"). It is a system, which means it can't be reduced to the people who participate in it. . . .

[P]atriarchy [is] a kind of society that is more than a collection of women and men and can't be understood simply by understanding them. *We are not patriarchy*, no more than people who believe in Allah *are* Islam or Canadians *are* Canada. Patriarchy is a kind of society organized around certain kinds of social relationships and ideas. As individuals, we participate in it. Paradoxically, our participation both shapes our lives and gives us the opportunity to be part of changing or perpetuating it. But *we are not it*, which means that patriarchy can exist without men having "oppressive personalities" or actively conspiring with one another to defend male privilege. To demonstrate that gender oppression exists, we don't have to show that men are villains, that women are good-hearted victims, that women don't participate in their own oppression, or that men never oppose it. If a society is oppressive, then people who grow up and live in it will tend to accept, identify with, and participate in it as "normal" and unremarkable life. That's the path of least resistance in any system. It's hard not to follow it, given how we depend on society and its rewards and punishments that hinge on going along with the status quo. When oppression is woven into the fabric of everyday life, we don't need to go out of our way to be overly oppressive in order for an oppressive system to produce oppressive consequences. As the saying goes, what evil requires is simply that ordinary people do nothing.

. . .

The crucial thing to understand about patriarchy or any other kind of social system is that it's something people participate in. It's an arrangement of shared understandings and relationships that connect people to one another and something larger than themselves. . . .

PATRIARCHY

The key to understanding any system is to identify its various parts and how they're arranged to form a whole. . . . Patriarchy's defining elements are its male-dominated, male-identified, and male-centered character, but this is just the beginning. At its core, patriarchy is a set of symbols and ideas that make up a culture embodied by everything from the content of everyday conversation to literature and film. Patriarchal culture includes ideas about the nature of things, including men, women, and humanity, with manhood and masculinity most closely associated with being human and womanhood and femininity relegated to the marginal position of "other." It's about how social life is and how it's supposed to be; about what's expected of people and about how they feel. It's about standards of feminine beauty and masculine toughness, images of feminine vulnerability and masculine protectiveness, of older men coupled with young women, of elderly women alone. It's about defining women and men as opposites, about the "naturalness" of male aggression, competition, and dominance and of female caring, cooperation, and subordination. It's about the valuing of masculinity and maleness and the devaluing of femininity and femaleness. It's about the primary importance of a husband's career and the secondary status of a wife's, about child care as a priority in women's lives and its secondary importance in men's. It's about the social acceptability of anger, rage, and toughness in men but not in women, and of caring, tenderness, and vulnerability in women but not in men.

Above all, patriarchal culture is about the core value of control and domination in almost every area of human existence. From the expression of emotion to economics to the natural environment, gaining and exercising control is a continuing goal of great importance. Because of this, the concept of power takes on a narrow definition in terms of "power over"—the ability to control others, events, resources, or oneself in spite of resistance—rather than alternatives such as the ability to cooperate with others, to give freely of oneself, or to feel and act in harmony with nature. To have power over and to be prepared to use it are defined culturally as good and desirable (and characteristically "masculine"), and to lack such power or to be reluctant to use it is seen as weak if not contemptible (and characteristically "feminine").

. . .

Going deeper into patriarchal culture, we find a complex web of ideas that define reality and what's considered good and desirable. To see the world through patriarchal eyes is to believe that women and men are profoundly different in their basic natures, that hierarchy is the only alternative to chaos, and that men were made in the image of a masculine God with whom they enjoy a special relationship. It is to take as obvious the idea that there are two and only two distinct genders; that patriarchal heterosexuality is "natural" and same-sex attraction is not; that because men neither bear nor breast-feed children, they cannot feel a compelling bodily connection to them; that on some level every woman, whether heterosexual or lesbian, wants a "real man" who knows how to "take charge of things," including her; that females can't be trusted, especially when they're menstruating or accusing men of sexual misconduct. To embrace patriarchy is to believe that mothers should stay home and that fathers should work out of the home, regardless of men's and women's actual abilities or needs. It is to buy into the notion that women are weak and men are strong, that women and children need men to support and protect them, all in spite of the fact that in many ways men are not the physically stronger sex, that women perform a huge share of hard physical labor in many societies (often larger than men's), that women's physical endurance tends to be greater than men's over the long haul, that women tend to be more capable of enduring pain and emotional stress. And yet such evidence means little in the face of a patriarchal culture that dictates how things *ought* to be . . .

To live in a patriarchal culture is to learn what's expected of us as men and women, the rules that regulate punishment and reward based on how we behave and appear. These rules range from laws that require men to fight in wars not of their own choosing to customary expectations that mothers will provide child care, or that when a woman shows sexual interest in a man or merely smiles or acts friendly, she gives up her right to say no and control her own body. And to live under patriarchy is to take into ourselves shared ways of feeling—the hostile contempt for femaleness that forms the core of misogyny and presumptions of male superiority, the ridicule men direct at other men who show signs of vulnerability or weakness, or the fear and insecurity that every woman must deal with when she exercises the right to move freely in the world, especially at night and by herself. Such ideas make up the symbolic sea we swim in and the air we breathe. They are the primary well from which springs how we think about ourselves, other people, and the world. As such, they provide a taken-for-granted everyday reality, the setting for our interactions with other people that continually fashion and refashion a shared sense of what the world is about and who we are in relation to it. This doesn't mean that the ideas underlying patriarchy determine what we think, feel, and do, but it does mean they define what we'll have to *deal with* as we participate in it.

The prominent place of misogyny in patriarchal culture, for example, doesn't mean that every man and woman consciously hates all things female. But it does mean that to the extent that we don't feel such hatred, it's *in spite of* paths of least resistance contained in our culture. Complete freedom from such feelings and judgments is all but impossible. It is certainly possible for heterosexual men to love women without mentally fragmenting them into breasts, buttocks, genitals, and other variously desirable parts. It is possible for women to feel good about their bodies, to not judge themselves as being too fat, to not abuse themselves to one degree or another in pursuit of impossible male-identified standards of beauty and sexual attractiveness. All of this is possible; but to live in patriarchy is to breathe in misogynist images of women as objectified sexual property valued primarily for their usefulness to men. This finds its way into everyone who grows up breathing and swimming in it, and once inside us it remains, however unaware of it we may be. So, when we hear or express sexist jokes and other forms of misogyny we may not recognize it, and even if we do, say nothing rather than risk other people thinking we're "too sensitive" or, especially in the case of men, "not one of the guys." In either case, we are involved, if only by our silence.

The symbols and ideas that make up patriarchal culture are important to understand because they have such powerful effects on the structure of social life. By "structure," I mean the ways that gender privilege and oppression are organized through social relationships and unequal distributions of rewards, opportunities, and resources. This appears in countless patterns of everyday life in family and work, religion and politics, community and education. It is found in family divisions of labor that exempt fathers from most domestic work even when both parents work outside the home, and in the concentration of women in lower-level pink-collar jobs and male predominance almost everywhere else. It is in the unequal distribution of income and all that goes with it, from access to health care to the availability of leisure time. It is in patterns of male violence and harassment that can turn a simple walk in the park or a typical day at work or a lovers' quarrel into a life-threatening nightmare. More than anything, the structure of patriarchy is found in the unequal distribution of power that makes oppression possible, in patterns of male dominance in every facet of human life, from everyday conversation to global politics. By its nature, patriarchy puts issues of power, dominance, and control at the center of human existence, not only in relationships between men and women, but among men as they compete and struggle to gain status, maintain control, and protect themselves from what other men might do to them.

. . .

THE SYSTEM IN US IN THE SYSTEM

One of the most difficult things to accept about patriarchy is that we're involved in it, which means we're also involved in its consequences. This is especially hard for men who refuse to believe they benefit from women's oppression, because they can't see how this could happen without their being personally oppressive in their intentions, feelings, and behavior. For many men, being told they're *involved* in oppression can only mean they *are* oppressive.

A common defense against this is to attribute everything to "society" as something external and autonomous, with wants, needs, interests, and the power to control people by making them into one sort of person or another. . . .

Societies don't exist without people participating in them, which means that we can't understand patriarchy unless we also ask how people are connected to it and how this connection varies, depending on social characteristics such as race, gender, ethnicity, age, and class. . . .

From this perspective, *who* we and other people think we are has a lot to do with *where* we are in relation to social systems and all the positions that people occupy. We wouldn't exist as social beings if it weren't for our participation in one social system or another. It's hard to imagine just who we'd be and what our existence would consist of if we took away all of our connections to the symbols, ideas, and relationships that make up social systems. . . .

In this sense, like all social systems, patriarchy exists only through people's lives. Through this, patriarchy's various aspects are there for us to see over and over again. This has two important implications for how we understand patriarchy. First, to some extent people experience patriarchy as external to them; but this doesn't mean that it's a distinct and separate thing, like a house in which we live. Instead, by participating in patriarchy we are *of* patriarchy and it is *of* us. Both exist *through* the other and neither can exist without the other. Second, patriarchy isn't static; it's an ongoing *process* that's continuously shaped and reshaped. Since the thing we're participating in is patriarchal, we tend to behave in ways that create a patriarchal world from one moment to the next. But we have some freedom to break the rules and construct everyday life in different ways, which means that the paths we choose to follow can do as much to change patriarchy as they can to perpetuate it.

We're involved in patriarchy and its consequences because we occupy social positions in it, which is all it takes. Since gender oppression is, by definition, a system of inequality organized around gender categories, we can no more avoid being involved in it than we can avoid being female or male. *All* men and *all* women are therefore involved in this oppressive system, and none us can control *whether* we participate, only *how*. . . .

Because privilege is conferred by social systems, people don't have to feel privileged in order to *be* privileged. When I do public presentations, for example, I usually come away feeling pretty good about what happened and, therefore, about myself. If anyone were to ask me to explain why things went so well, I'd probably mention my abilities, my years of experience in public speaking, the quality of my ideas, and so on, as well as the interest and contributions of the audience. The last thing that would occur to me, however, would be that my success was aided by my gender, that if I'd performed in exactly the same way but happened to be a woman, research shows quite clearly that I'd have been taken less seriously, been evaluated less positively, and attributed less of my success to my own efforts and ability. The difference between the two outcomes is a measure of my gender privilege, and there is little I can do to get rid of it, because its authority doesn't rest in me but in society itself, especially in cultural images of gender. The audience doesn't know it's conferring gender privilege on me, and I may not be aware that I'm receiving it. But the privilege is there, nonetheless, whether we intend or want it. That all this may feel "natural" and nonprivileged only deepens the system's hold on all who are involved in it.

Since we're born into patriarchy, and since participating in social life is what makes us who we are, we can't escape growing up sexist to some degree. This means that the question we have to ask ourselves isn't whether sexism is part of who we are, but how broadly and deeply it is ingrained in us, how it appears in our experience and behavior, and what we can do about it. No one wants to think of themselves as involved in social oppression, but being involved doesn't mean we're bad or to blame for oppression, for people can and do participate in systems that produce horrible, immoral consequences without being horrible and immoral people. None of us is responsible or to blame for the world we were born into or the inevitable way in which we took it into ourselves. But—and this "but" is crucial—the ongoing reconstruction of that society is shaped by how people like us choose to participate in it once we're here. We are involved; we are part of the problem; the question is whether we'll choose to also be part of the solution.

66

Privilege

Devon W. Carbado

. . . This essay is part of a larger intellectual project to encourage a shift in—or at least a broadening of—our conceptualization of discrimination. My aim is to expand our notion of what it means to be a perpetrator of discrimination. Typically, we define a perpetrator of discrimination as someone who acts intentionally to bring about some discriminatory result. This is a narrow and politically palatable conception; it applies to very few of us. In this essay I suggest that those of us who unquestionably accept the racial, gender, and heterosexual privileges we have—those of us who fail to acknowledge our victimless status with respect to racism, sexism, and homophobia—are also perpetrators of discrimination.

Informing this privileged-centered understanding of discrimination is the notion that taking identity privileges for granted helps to legitimize problematic assumptions about identity and entitlement, assumptions that make it difficult for us to challenge the starting points of many of our most controversial conversations about equality. We simply assume, for example, that men should be able to fight for their country (the question is whether women should be entitled to this privilege); that heterosexuals should be able to get married (the question is whether the privilege should be extended to gays and lesbians); that white men should be able to compete for all the slots in a university's entering class (the question is whether people of color should be entitled to the privilege of "preferential treatment").

While a privileged-centered conception of discrimination usefully reveals the bi-directional effects of discrimination—namely, that discrimination allocates both burdens and benefits—the conception may prove entirely too much. After all, all of us enjoy some degree of privilege. Are all of us perpetrators of discrimination? The answer may depend on what we do with, and to, the privileges we have. Each of us makes personal and private choices with our privileges that entrench a variety of social practices, institutional arrangements, and laws that disadvantage other(ed) people....

Others of us have racially monolithic social encounters, live in de facto white only (or predominantly white) neighborhoods, or send our kids to white only (or predominantly white) schools. Still others of us have "straight only" associations—that is, our friends are all heterosexuals and our children's friends all have mommies and daddies. These choices are not just personal; they are political. And their cumulative effect is to entrench the very social practices—racism, sexism, classism, and homophobia—we profess to abhor.

In other words, there is a link between identity privileges, and our negotiation of them, on the one hand, and discrimination, on the other. Our identities are reflective and constitutive of systems of oppression. Racism requires white privilege. Sexism requires male privilege. Homophobia requires heterosexual privilege. The very intelligibility of our identities is their association, or lack thereof, with privilege. This creates an obligation on the part of those of us with privileged identities to expose and to challenge them.

Significantly, this obligation exists not only as a matter of morality and responsibility. The obligation exists for a pragmatic reason as well. We cannot change the macro-effects of discrimination without ameliorating the power effects of our identities. Nor can our political commitments have traction unless we apply them to the seemingly "just personal" privileged aspects of our lives. Resistance to identity privileges may be futile, we cannot know for sure. However, to the extent that we do nothing, this much is clear: we perpetuate the systems of discrimination out of which our identities are forged.

But precisely what constitutes an identity privilege? Further, how do we identify them? And, finally, what acts are necessary to deprivilege our identities and to disrupt their association with power. These questions drive this essay. . . .

HETEROSEXUAL PRIVILEGES

Like maleness, heterosexuality should be critically examined. Like maleness, heterosexuality operates as an identity norm, the "what is" or "what is supposed to be" of sexuality. This is illustrated, for example, by the nature versus nurture debate. The question about the cause of sexuality is almost always formulated in terms of whether homosexuality is or is not biologically determined rather than whether sexual orientation, which includes heterosexuality, is or is not biologically determined. Scientists are searching for a gay, not a heterosexual or sexual orientation, gene. Like female identity, then, homosexuality signifies "difference"—more specifically, sexual identity distinctiveness. The normativity of heterosexuality requires that homosexuality be specified, pointed out. Heterosexuality is always already presumed.

Heterosexuals should challenge the normativity and normalization of heterosexuality. They should challenge the heterosexual presumption. But heterosexuals might be reluctant to do so to the extent that they perceive such challenges to call into question their (hetero)sexual orientation. As Lee Edelman observes in a related context, there "is a deeply rooted concern on the part of . . . heterosexual males about the possible meanings of [men subverting gender roles]" (1990, 50). According to Edelman, heterosexual men consider certain gender role inversions to be potentially dangerous because they portend not only a "[male] feminization that would destabilize or question gender" but also a "feminization that would challenge one's (hetero)sexuality" (1990, 50). Edelman's observations suggest that straight men may want to preserve what I am calling the "heterosexual presumption." Their investment in this presumption is less a function of what heterosexuality signifies in a positive sense and more a function of what it signifies in the negative—*not* being homosexual.

And there are racial dimensions to male investment in heterosexuality. For example, straight black male strategies to avoid homosexual suspicion could relate to the racial aspects of male privileges: heterosexual privilege is one of the few privileges that some black men have. These black men may want to take comfort in the fact that whatever else is going on in their lives, they are not, finally, "sissies," "punks," "faggots." By this I do not mean to suggest that black male heterosexuality has the normative standing of white male heterosexuality. It does not. Straight black men continue to be perceived as heterosexually deviant (overly sexual; potential rapists) and heterosexually irresponsible (jobless fathers of children out of wedlock). Still, black male heterosexuality is closer to white male heterosexual normalcy and normativity than is black gay sexuality. Consequently, some straight (or closeted) black men will want to avoid the "black gay [male] . . . triple negation" to which Marlon Riggs refers in the following quote: "Because of my sexuality I cannot be Black. A strong, proud, 'Afrocentric' black man is resolutely heterosexual, not even bisexual. . . . Hence I remain a sissy, punk, faggot. I cannot be a black gay man because, by the tenets of black macho, a black gay man is a triple negation" (1999, 307) . . .

Keith Boykin, former director of the Black Gay and Lesbian Leadership Forum, maintains that "heterosexual sexual orientation has become so ingrained in our social custom, so destigmatized of our fears about sex, that we often fail to make any connection between heterosexuality and sex" (1997). Boykin is only half right. The socially constructed normalcy of heterosexuality is not due solely to the desexualization of heterosexuality in mainstream political and popular culture. It is due also to the sexualization of heterosexuality as normative and to the gender-norm presumptions about heterosexuality—that it is the normal way sexually to express one's gender.

Moreover, it is not simply that homosexuality is sexed that motivates or stimulates homophobic fears about gay and lesbian relationships. These fears also relate to the fact that homosexuality is stigmatized and is perceived to be an abnormal way sexually to express one's gender. The disparate social meanings that attach to gay and lesbian identities on the one hand and straight identities on the other make individual acts of heterosexual signification a cause for concern.

Recently, I participated in a workshop where one of the presenters "came out" as a heterosexual in the context of giving his talk. This sexual identity disclosure engendered a certain amount of whispering in the back row. Up until that moment, I think many people had assumed the presenter was gay. After all, he was sitting on a panel discussing sexual orientation and had participated in the Gay and Lesbian section of the American Association of Law Schools. There were three other heterosexuals on the panel, but everyone knew they were not gay because everyone *knew* them; they had all been in teaching for a while, two were very senior, and everyone knew of their spouses or partners. Everyone also knew that there was a lesbian on the panel. She, too, had been in teaching for some time and had been out for many years. Apparently, few of the workshop participants knew very much about the presenter who "came out." Because "there is a widespread assumption in both gay and straight communities that any man who says something supportive about issues of concern to lesbian or gay communities must be gay himself," there was, at the very least, a question about his sexuality. Whatever his intentions were for "coming out," whatever his motivations, his assertion of heterosexuality removed the question. . . .

I became sensitized to the politics of heterosexuals "coming out" in the context of reading about James Baldwin. Try to find a piece written about Baldwin and count the number of lines before the author comes out as heterosexual. Usually, it is not more than a couple of paragraphs, so the game ends fast. The following introduction from a 1994 essay about Baldwin is one example of what I am talking about: "The last time I saw James Baldwin was late autumn of 1985, when my wife and I attended a sumptuous book party" (Forrest 1994, 267). In this case, the game ends immediately. Independent of any question of intentionality on the author's part, the mention of the wife functions as an identity signifier to subtextually "out" his heterosexuality. We *read* "wife," we *think* heterosexual. My point here is not to suggest that the essay's overall tone is heterosexually defensive; I simply find it suspicious when heterosexuals speak of their spouses so quickly (in this case the very first sentence of the essay) when a subject (a topic or a personality—here, James Baldwin) implicates homosexuality. . . . The author engages in what I call "the politics of the 3Ds"—disassociation, disidentification, and differentiation. The author is "different" from Baldwin (the author sleeps with women), and this difference, based as it is on sexual identity, compels the author to disassociate himself from and disidentify with that which makes Baldwin "different" (Baldwin sleeps with men).

Heterosexual significations need not always reflect the politics of the 3Ds. In other words, the possibility exists for heterosexuals to point out their heterosexuality without reauthenticating heterosexuality. Consider, for example, the heterosexual privilege list that I give below. While each item on the list explicitly names—outs—heterosexuality, in none of the items does heterosexuality remain unproblematically normative.

As a prelude to the list, I should be clear that the list is incomplete. Nor do the privileges reflected in it represent the experiences of all heterosexuals. As Bruce Ryder observes: "Male heterosexual privilege has different effects on men of, for example, different races and classes. . . . In our society, the dominant or 'hegemonic' form of masculinity to which other masculinities are subordinated is white, middle class, and heterosexual. This means that the heterosexual privilege of, say, straight black men takes a very different shape in their lives than it does for straight white men" (1991, 292). My goal in presenting this list, then, is not to represent every heterosexual man. Instead, the purpose is to intervene in the normalization of heterosexual privileges. With this intervention, I hope to challenge the pervasive tendency of heterosexuals to see homophobia as something that puts others at a disadvantage and not something that actually advantages them.

HETEROSEXUAL PRIVILEGES: A LIST

1. Whether on television or in the movies, (white) heterosexuality is always affirmed as healthy and/or normal (black heterosexuality and family arrangements are still, to some degree, perceived to be deviant).
2. Without making a special effort, heterosexuals are surrounded by other heterosexuals every day.
3. A husband and wife can comfortably express affection in any social setting, even a predominantly gay one.
4. The children of a heterosexual couple will not have to explain why their parents have different genders—that is, why they have a mummy and a daddy.
5. (White) heterosexuals are not blamed for creating and spreading the AIDS virus (though Africans—as a collective group—are blamed).
6. Heterosexuals do not have to worry about people trying to "cure" their sexual orientation (though black people have to worry about people trying to "cure" black "racial pathologies").
7. Black heterosexual males did not have to worry about whether they would be accepted at the Million Man March.
8. Rarely, if ever, will a doctor, on learning that her patient is heterosexual, inquire as to whether the patient has ever taken an AIDS test and if so, how recently.
9. Medical service will never be denied to heterosexuals because they are heterosexuals (though medical services may not be recommended to black people because they are black).
10. Friends of heterosexuals generally do not refer to heterosexuals as their "straight friends" (though nonblack people often to refer to black people as their "black friends").

11. A heterosexual couple can enter a restaurant on their anniversary and be fairly confident that staff and fellow diners will warmly congratulate them if an announcement is made (though the extent of the congratulation and the nature of the welcome might depend on the racial identities of the couple).
12. White heterosexuals do not have to worry about whether a fictional film villain who is heterosexual will reflect negatively on their heterosexuality (though blacks may always have to worry about their racial representation in films).
13. Heterosexuals are entitled to legal recognition of their marriages throughout the United States and the world. [Since 2015, same-sex couples earned this legal right.]
14. Within the black community, black male heterosexuality does not engender comments like "what a waste," "there goes another good black man," or "if they're not in jail, they're faggots."
15. Heterosexuals can take jobs with most companies without worrying about whether their spouses will be included in the benefits package.
16. Child molestation by heterosexuals does not confirm the deviance of heterosexuality (though if the alleged molester is black, the alleged molestation becomes evidence of the deviance of black [hetero]sexuality).
17. Black rap artists do not make songs suggesting that heterosexuals should be shot or beaten up because they are heterosexuals.
18. Black male heterosexuality does not undermine a black heterosexual male's ability to be a role model for black boys.
19. Heterosexuals [could always] join the military without concealing their sexual identity.
20. Children will be taught in school, explicitly or implicitly, about the naturalness of heterosexuality (they will also be taught to internalize the notion of white normativity).
21. Conversations on black liberation will always include concerns about heterosexual men.
22. Heterosexuals can adopt children without being perceived as selfish and without anyone questioning their motives.
23. Heterosexuals are not denied custody or visitation rights of their children because they are heterosexuals.
24. Heterosexual men [have always been] welcomed as leaders of Boy Scout troops.
25. Heterosexuals can visit their parents and family as who they are, and take their spouses, partners, or dates with them to family functions.
26. Heterosexuals can talk matter-of-factly about their relationships with their partners without people commenting that they are "flaunting" their sexuality.
27. A black heterosexual couple would be welcomed as members of any black church.
28. Heterosexual couples do not have to worry about whether kissing each other in public or holding hands in public will render them vulnerable to violence.
29. Heterosexuals do not have to struggle with "coming out" or worry about being "outed."
30. The parents of heterosexuals do not love them "in spite of" their sexual orientation, and parents do not blame themselves for their children's heterosexuality.
31. Heterosexuality is affirmed in most religious traditions.
32. Heterosexuals can introduce their spouses to colleagues and not worry about whether the decision will have a detrimental impact on their careers.
33. A black heterosexual male does not have to choose between being black and being heterosexual.
34. Heterosexuals can prominently display their spouses' photographs at work without causing office gossip or hostility.
35. (White) heterosexuals do not have to worry about "positively" representing heterosexuality.

36. Few will take pity on a heterosexual on hearing that she is straight, or feel the need to say, "That's okay" (though it is not uncommon for a black person to hear, "It's okay that you're black" or "We don't care that you're black" or "When we look at you, we don't see a black person").

37. (Male) heterosexuality is not considered to be symptomatic of the "pathology" of the black family.

38. Heterosexuality is never mistaken as the only aspect of one's lifestyle, but is perceived instead as merely one more component of one's personal identity.

39. (White) heterosexuals do not have to worry over the impact their sexuality will have personally on their children's lives, particularly as it relates to their social lives (though black families of all identity configurations do have to worry about how race and racism will affect their children's well-being).

40. Heterosexuals do not have to worry about being "bashed" after leaving a social event with other heterosexuals (though black people of all sexual orientations do have to worry about being "racially bashed" on any given day).

41. Every day is (white) "Heterosexual Pride Day."

CONCLUSION: RESISTING PRIVILEGES

I have argued that one of the ways to contest gender and sexual orientation hierarchy is for heterosexual men to detail their social experiences on the privileged side of gender and sexual orientation. In advancing this argument, I do not mean to suggest that the role of these men is to legitimize "untrustworthy" and "self-interested" victim-centered accounts of discrimination. There is a tendency on the part of dominant groups (e.g., males and heterosexuals) to discount the experiences of subordinate groups (e.g., straight women, lesbians, and gays) unless those experiences are authenticated or legitimized by a member of the dominant group. For example, it is one thing for me, a black man, to say I experienced discrimination in a particular social setting; it is quite another for my white male colleague to say he witnessed that discrimination. My telling of the story is suspect because I am black (racially interested). My white colleague's telling of the story is not suspect because he is white (racially disinterested). The racial transparency of whiteness—its "perspectivelessness"—renders my colleague's account "objective." . . .

Assuming that the identification/listing of privileges methodology I have described avoids the problem of authentication, one still might wonder whether the project is sufficiently radical to dismantle gender and sexual orientation hierarchies. Certainly the lists I have presented do not go far enough. They represent the very early stages in a more complicated process to end gender and sexual orientation discrimination.

The lists, nevertheless, are politically valuable. . . .

None of this is to say that awareness and acknowledgement of privilege is enough. Resistance is needed as well. But how does one resist? And what counts as resistance? At the very least, resistance to identity privilege would seem to require "critical acquiescence": criticizing, if not rejecting, aspects of our life that are directly linked to our privilege.

In the end, critical acquiescence might not go far enough. It might even be a cop out. Still, it is a useful and politically manageable place to begin.

References

Boykin, K. (1997). *One More River to Cross: Black and Gay in America*. New York: Doubleday.

Edelman, L. (1990). "Redeeming the Phallus: Wallace Stevens, Frank Lentricchia, and the Politics of (Hetero)sexuality." In J. A. Boone and M. Cadden (eds.), *Engendering Men: The Question of Male Feminist Criticism*. New York: Routledge.

Forrest, L. (1994). "Evidences of Jimmy Baldwin." In L. Forrest (ed.), *Relocations of the Spirit*. Emeryville, CA: Asphodel Press/Moyer Ball.

Riggs, M. T. (1999). "Black Macho Revisited: Reflections of a SNAP! Queen." In D. W. Carbado (ed.), *Black Men on Race, Gender, and Sexuality: A Critical Reader*. New York: New York University Press.

Ryder, B. (1991). "Straight Talk: Male Heterosexual Privilege." *Queen's Law Journal*, 16, 287–303.

CONTEXT

67

He Works, She Works, But What Different Impressions They Make

Gwyn Kirk and Margo Okazawa-Rey

Have you ever found yourself up against the old double standard at work? Then you know how annoying it can be and how alone you can feel. Supervisors and coworkers still judge us by old stereotypes that say women are emotional, disorganized, and inefficient. Here are some of the most glaring examples of the typical office double standard.

The family picture is on HIS desk: Ah, a solid, responsible family man	The family picture is on HER desk: Hmm, her family will come before her career
HIS desk is cluttered: He's obviously a hard worker and busy man	HER desk is cluttered: She's obviously a disorganized scatterbrain
HE'S talking with coworkers: He must be discussing the latest deal	SHE'S talking with coworkers: She must be gossiping
HE'S not at his desk: He must be at a meeting	SHE'S not at her desk: She must be in the ladies' room
HE'S having lunch with the boss: He's on his way up	SHE'S having lunch with the boss: They must be having an affair
HE'S getting married. He'll get more settled	SHE'S getting married: She'll get pregnant and leave
HE'S having a baby: He'll need a raise	SHE'S having a baby: She'll cost the company money in maternity benefits
HE'S leaving for a better job: HE recognizes a good opportunity	SHE'S leaving for a better job: Women are undependable
HE'S aggressive	SHE'S pushy
HE'S careful	SHE'S picky
HE loses his temper	SHE'S bitchy
HE'S depressed	SHE'S moody
HE follows through	SHE doesn't know when to quit
HE'S firm	SHE'S stubborn

HE makes wise judgments	SHE reveals her prejudices
HE is a man of the world	SHE's been around
HE isn't afraid to say what he thinks	SHE'S opinionated
HE exercises authority	SHE'S tyrannical
HE'S discreet	SHE'S secretive
HE'S a stern taskmaster	SHE'S difficult to work for

68

Generation LGBTQIA

Michael Schulman

Stephen Ira, a junior at Sarah Lawrence College, uploaded a video last March on We Happy Trans, a site that shares "positive perspectives" on being transgender.

In the breakneck six-and-a-half-minute monologue—hair tousled, sitting in a wood-paneled dorm room—Stephen exuberantly declared himself "a queer, a nerd fighter, a writer, an artist and a guy who needs a haircut," and held forth on everything from his style icon (Truman Capote and "any male-identified person who wears thigh-highs or garters") to his toy zebra.

Because Stephen, who was born Kathlyn, is the 21-year-old child of Warren Beatty and Annette Bening, the video went viral, garnering nearly half a million views. But that was not the only reason for its appeal. With its adrenalized, freewheeling eloquence, the video seemed like a battle cry for a new generation of post-gay gender activists, for whom Stephen represents a rare public face.

Armed with the millennial generation's defining traits—Web savvy, boundless confidence and social networks that extend online and off—Stephen and his peers are forging a political identify all their own, often at odds with mainstream gay culture.

If the gay-rights movement today seems to revolve around same-sex marriage, this generation is seeking something more radical: an upending of gender roles beyond the binary of male/female. The core question isn't whom they love, but who they are—that is, identity as distinct from sexual orientation.

But what to call this movement? Whereas "gay and lesbian" was once used to lump together various sexual minorities—and more recently "L.G.B.T" to include bisexual and transgender—the new vanguard wants a broader, more inclusive abbreviation. "Youth today do not define themselves on the spectrum of L.G.B.T.," said Shane Windmeyer, a founder of Campus Pride, a national student advocacy group based in Charlotte, N.C.

Part of the solution has been to add more letters, and in recent years the post-post-post-gay-rights banner has gotten significantly longer, some might say unwieldy. The emerging rubric is "L.G.B.T.Q.I.A," which stands for different things, depending on whom you ask.

"Q" can mean "questioning" or "queer," an umbrella term itself, formerly derogatory before it was appropriated by gay activists in the 1990s. "I" is for "intersex," someone whose anatomy is not exclusively male or female. And "A" stands for "ally" (a friend of the cause) or "asexual," characterized by the absence of sexual attraction.

It may be a mouthful, but it's catching on, especially on liberal-arts campuses.

The University of Missouri, Kansas City, for example, has an L.G.B.T.Q.I.A. Resource Center that, among other things, helps student locate "gender-neutral" restrooms on campus. Vassar College offers an L.G.B.T.Q.I.A. Discussion Group on Thursday afternoons, Lehigh University will be hosting its second annual L.G.B.T.Q.I.A. Intercollegiate Conference next month, followed by a Queer Prom. Amherst College even has an L.G.B.T.Q.Q.I.A.A. center, where every group gets its own letter.

The term is also gaining traction on social media sites like Twitter and Tumblr, where posts tagged with "lgbtqia" suggest a younger, more progressive outlook than posts that are merely labelled "lgbt".

"There's a different generation of people coming of age, with completely different conceptions of gender and sexuality," said Jack Halberstam (formerly Judith), a transgender professor at the University of Southern California and the author, most recently, of "Gaga Feminism: Sex, Gender, and the End of Normal."

"When you see terms like L.G.B.T.Q.I.A.," Professor Halberstam added, "It's because people are seeing all the things that fall out of the binary, and demanding that a name come into being."

And with a plethora of ever-expanding categories like " genderqueer" and "androgyne" to choose from, each with an online subculture, piecing together a gender identity can be as D.I.Y. as making a Pinterest board.

BUT sometimes L.G.B.T.Q.I.A. is not enough. At the University of Pennsylvania last fall, eight freshmen united in the frustration that no campus group represented them.

Sure, Penn already has some two dozen gay student groups, including Queer People of Color, Lambda Alliance and J-Bagel, which bills itself as the university's "Jewish L.G.B.T.Q.I.A. Community." But none focused on gender identity (the closest, Trans Penn, mostly catered to faculty members and graduate students).

Richard Parsons, an 18-year-old transgender male, discovered that when he attended a student mixer called the Gay Affair, sponsored by Penn's L.G.B.T. center. "I left thoroughly disappointed," said Richard, a garrulous freshman with close-cropped hair, wire-framed glasses and preppy clothes, who added, "This is the L.G.B.T. center, and it's all gay guys."

Through Facebook, Richard and others started a group called Penn Non-Cis, which is short for "non-cisgender." For those not fluent in gender-studies speak, "cis" means "on the same side as" and "cisgender" denotes someone whose gender identify matches his or her biology, which describes most of the student body. The group seeks to represent everyone else. "This is a freshman uprising," Richard said.

On a brisk Tuesday night in November, about 40 students crowded into the L.G.B.T. center, a converted 19th-century carriage house, for the group's inaugural open mike. The organizers had lured students by handing out fliers on campus while barking: "Free condoms! Free ChapStick!"

"There's a really vibrant L.G.B.T. scene," Kate Campbell, one of the M.C.'s, began. "However, that mostly encompasses the L.G.B. and not too much of the T. So we're aiming to change that."

Students read poems and diary entries, and sang guitar ballads. Then Britt Gilbert—a punky-looking freshman with a blond bob, chunky glasses and a rock band T-shirt—took the stage. She wanted to talk about the concept of "bi-gender."

"Does anyone want to share what they think it is?"

Silence.

She explained that being bi-gender is like manifesting both masculine and feminine personas, almost as if one had a "detachable penis." "Some days I wake up and think, 'why am I in this body?'" she said. "Most days I wake up and think, 'What was I thinking yesterday?'"

Britt's grunginess belies a warm matter-of-factness, at least when describing her journey. As she elaborated afterward, she first heard the term "bi-gender" from Kate, who found it on Tumblr. The two met at freshman orientation and bonded. In high school, Kate identified as "agender" and used the singular pronoun "they"; she now sees her gender as an "amorphous blob."

By contrast, Britt's evolution was more linear. She grew up in suburban Pennsylvania and never took to gender norms. As a child, she worshiped Cher and thought boy bands were icky. Playing video games, she dreaded having to choose male or female avatars.

In middle school, she started calling herself bisexual and dated boys. By 10th grade, she had come out as a lesbian. Her parents thought it was a phase—until she brought home a girlfriend, Ash. But she still wasn't settled.

"While I definitely knew that I liked girls, I didn't know that I was one," Britt said. Sometimes she would leave the house in a dress and feel uncomfortable, as if she were wearing a Halloween costume. Other days, she felt fine. She wasn't "trapped in the wrong body," as the cliché has it—she just didn't know which body she wanted.

When Kate told her about the term "bi-gender," it clicked instantly. "I knew what it was, before I knew what it was," Britt said, adding that it is more fluid than "transgender" but less vague than "genderqueer"—a catchall term for nontraditional gender identities.

At first, the only person she told was Ash, who responded, "It took you this long to figure it out?" For others, the concept was not so easy to grasp. Coming out as a lesbian had been relatively simple, Britt said, "since people know what that is." But when she got to Penn, she was relieved to find a small community of freshmen who had gone through similar awakenings.

Among them was Richard Parsons, the group's most politically lucid member. Raised female, Richard grew up in Orlando, Fla., and realized he was transgender in high school. One summer, he wanted to room with a transgender friend at camp, but his mother objected. "She's like, 'Well, if you say that he's a guy, then I don't want you rooming with a guy,'" he recalled. "We were in a car and I basically blurted out, 'I think I might be a guy, too!'"

After much door-slamming and tears, Richard and his mother reconciled. But when she asked what to call him, he had no idea. He chose "Richard" on a whim, and later added a middle name, Mathew, because it means "gift of God."

By the time he got to Penn, he had been binding his breasts for more than two years and had developed back pain. At the open mike, he told a harrowing story about visiting the university health center for numbness and having a panic attack when he was escorted into a women's changing room.

Nevertheless, he praised the university for offering gender-neutral housing. The college's medical program also covers sexual reassignment surgery, which, he added "has heavily influenced my decision to probably go under the Penn insurance plan next year."

Penn has not always been so forward-thinking; a decade ago, the L.G.B.T. Center (nestled amid fraternity houses) was barely used. But in 2010, the university began reaching out to applicants whose essays raised gay themes. Last year, the gay newsmagazine

The Advocate ranked Penn among the top 10 trans-friendly universities, alongside liberal standbys like New York University.

More and more colleges, mostly in the Northeast, are catering to gender-nonconforming students. According to a survey by Campus Pride, at least 203 campuses now allow transgender students to room with their preferred gender; 49 have a process to change one's name and gender in university records; and 57 cover hormone therapy. In December, the University of Iowa became the first to add a "transgender" checkbox to its college application.

"I wrote about an experience I had with a drag queen as my application essay for all the Ivy Leagues I applied to," said Santiago Cortes, one of the Penn students. "And I got into a few of the Ivy Leagues—Dartmouth, Columbia and Penn. Strangely not Brown."

But even these measures cannot keep pace with the demands of incoming students, who are challenging the curriculum much as gay activists did in the '80s and '90s. Rather than protest the lack of gay studies classes, they are critiquing existing ones for being too narrow.

Several members of Penn Non-Cis had been complaining among themselves about a writing seminar they were taking called "Beyond 'Will & Grace,'" which examined gay characters on shows like "Ellen," "Glee" and "Modern Family." The professor, Gail Shister, who is a lesbian, had criticized several students for using "L.G.B.T.Q." in their essays, saying it was clunky, and proposed using "queer" instead. Some students found the suggestion offensive, including Britt Gilbert, who described Ms. Shister as "unaccepting of things that she doesn't understand."

Ms. Shister, reached by phone, said the criticism was strictly grammatical. "I am all about economy of expression," she said. "L.G.B.T.Q. doesn't exactly flow off the tongue. So I tell the students, 'Don't put in an acronym with five or six letters.'"

One thing is clear. Ms. Shister, who is 60 and in 1979 became *The Philadelphia Inquirer's* first female sportswriter, is of a different generation, a fact she acknowledges freely, even gratefully. "Frankly, I'm both proud and envious that these young people are growing up in an age where they're free to love who they want," she said.

If history is any guide, the age gap won't be so easy to overcome. As liberated gay men in the 1970s once baffled their pre-Stonewall forebears, the new gender outlaws, to borrow a phrase from the transgender writer Kate Bornstein, may soon be running ideological circles around their elders.

Still, the alphabet soup of L.G.B.T.Q.I.A. may be difficult to sustain. "In the next 10 or 20 years, the various categories heaped under the umbrella of L.G.B.T will become quite quotidian," Professor Halberstam said.

Even at the open mike, as students picked at potato chips and pineapple slices, the bounds of identity polities were spilling over and becoming blurry.

At one point, Santiago, a curly-haired freshman from Colombia, stood before the crowd. He and a friend had been pondering the limits of what he calls "L.G.B.T.Q. plus."

"Why do only certain letters get to be in the full acronym?" he asked.

Then he rattled off a list of gender identities, many culled from Wikipedia. "We have our lesbians, our gays," he said, before adding, "bisexual, transsexual, queer, homosexual, asexual." He took a breath and continued. "Pansexual. Omnisexual. Trisexual. Agender. Bi-gender. Third gender. Transgender. Transvestite. Intersexual. Two-spirit. Hijra. Polyamorous."

By now, the list had turned into free verse. He ended. "Undecided. Questioning. Other. Human."

The room burst into applause.

69

Women & LGBT People Under Attack

1930s & Now

Warren J. Blumenfeld

In my continuing quest to understand and make meaning of current political, economic, and social realities, I constantly glance back into historical eras looking for similarities and parallels from which I can draw conclusions and possibly learn from past mistakes we as humans have made. While each era unquestionably poses unique conditions and challenges in many respects, I believe history has enumerable lessons to teach if we are willing to learn.

Though I rarely offer comparisons between events transpiring before and during the ascension to power of the German Third Reich with resemblances to contemporary United States – since to do so could result in trivializing one of the most horrific episodes in human history – nonetheless, I am haunted by certain parallels that demand expression.

I am troubled by multiple similarities between that time not so very long ago with the discourses expressed and events transpiring today, though I want to highlight, in particular, the parallels I see in Nazi portrayals and understandings of sex, sexuality, gender, and gender expression: a divisive and brutal program that was anti-feminist, anti-women's equality, anti-women's reproductive freedoms (anti-family planning, anti-contraception, anti-abortion), anti-lesbian, anti-gay, anti-bisexual, anti-transgender, anti-gender nonconforming, anti-sexuality education in schools.

ON WOMEN

Alfred Rosenberg, one of the Nazi's chief ideologues, directed his misogynist outrage against women: "The emancipation of women *from* the women's emancipation movement is the first demand of a female generation trying to rescue nation and race, the eternally unconscious, the foundation of all civilization, from decline. . . . A woman should have every opportunity to realize her potential, but one thing must be made clear: Only a man must be and remain judge, soldier, and politician."

Englebert Huber, a Nazi propagandist, dictated the "proper" place of women in the Third Reich, figuratively (and literally as well) beneath men: "In the ideology of National Socialism, there is no room for the political woman. . . . [Our] movement places woman in her natural sphere of the family and stresses her duties as wife and mother. The political, that post-war creature, who rarely 'cut a good figure' in parliamentary debates, represents the denigration of women. The German uprising is a male phenomenon."

The Nazis added Paragraph 218 of the German Penal Code to outlaw abortions and establish a national file on women who had undergone and doctors who had performed abortions.

ON "INDECENCY"

In their increasing obsession with "purifying" the social sphere, Nazi leadership enacted the "Decree for Combating Public Indecency," which included such provisions as working to eliminate prostitution; closing all bars and clubs that "are misused for the furtherance of public indecency" including "public houses solely or mainly frequented by persons engaging in unnatural sex acts" (a.k.a. homosexuals); closing kiosks and magazine stands in libraries and bookshops "whether because they include nude illustrations or because of their title or contents, are liable to produce erotic effects in the beholder."

Though Pope Pius XII maintained a position of neutrality and rarely spoke out against the atrocities perpetrated by the Nazi regime, of which he was roundly criticized in some circles, The Vatican, on April 3, 1933, praised the Reich on this policy:

"The Vatican welcomes the struggle of National Germany against obscene material. The strong measures that Prussia's Minister of the Interior Göring has ordered for the combating of obscene writings and pictures . . . have received serious attention in Vatican circles. It will be recalled that Pius XII, in his recent encyclicals, has repeatedly and vigorously stressed that defensive actions against obscene material are of fundamental importance for the bodily and spiritual health of family and nation, and he most warmly welcomes the type and manner . . . with which this struggle has been undertaken in the new Germany."

ON HOMOSEXUALITY

The Nazis acted on and eventually extended Paragraph 175, the section of the German Penal Code dating back to 1871 with the unification of Germany:

"Unnatural vice committed by two persons of the male sex or by people with animals is to be punished by imprisonment; the verdict may also include the loss of civil rights."

Nazi ideology rested on the assessment that homosexual (males) lowered the German birth rate; they endangered, recruited, enticed, and corrupted youth; that a possible homosexual epidemic could spread; that homosexuals are "potential oppositionists" and enemies of respectable society; and that sexual relations between people of the same sex impairs their "sense of shame" and undermines morality, which inevitably will bring about the "decline of social community."

Even before taking power, appearing in their daily newspaper, *Völkischer Beobachter* 14 May 1928, Heinrich Himmler for the Nazi party argued:

"Anyone who thinks of homosexual love is our enemy. We reject anything which emasculates our people and makes it a plaything for our enemies, for we know that life is a fight, and it is madness to think that men will ever embrace fraternally. Natural history teaches us the opposite. Might makes right. The strong will always win over the weak. Let us see to it that we once again become the strong. But this we can achieve only in one way—the German people must once again learn how to exercise discipline. We, therefore, reject any sexual deviation, particularly between man and man, because it robs us of the last possibility of freeing our people from the slave-chains in which it is now forced to toil."

While Nazi ideology and practice rejected lesbianism as well, they did not criminalize same sex sexuality between women, as they had in Germany's Paragraph 175 of the Penal Code, because they believed that so-called "Aryan" lesbians could produce children for the "New Germany."

On the other hand, Heinrich Himmler, Gestapo head and chief architect of the Reich's anti-homosexual campaign, justified his actions by arguing that male homosexuals were "like women" and therefore, could not fight in any German war effort. Subsequently, he conducted surveillance operations on an estimated 90,000 suspected homosexuals, arrested approximately 50,000, and transported somewhere between 10,000 and 15,000 to a number of concentration camps throughout the Nazi dominion. Very few survived.

Upon coming to power in 1933, under their Youth Leader, Baldur von Shirach, the Nazis took over all youth groups converting them into Hitler Youth groups. One action taken following consolidation was to eliminate all signs of "homosexual corrosion," because it allegedly posed a threat to state control by "fostering political conspiracies." Nazi leaders purged all boys suspected of "homosexual tendencies." They tried and convicted an estimated 6,000 youth under Paragraph 175 between 1933 and 1943.

Hitler also proposed eliminating all sexuality education from the German school system and encouraged parents to take on the primary responsibilities for sexuality instruction within the home.

While the Catholic Church then and today publicly rejected same-sex sexuality, their own policies actually boomeranged and hit them in their own faces. Used primarily to silence any potential resistance from the Church, the Nazis conducted their so-called "Cloister Trials" in which they dissolved Catholic youth fraternities, arrested and incarcerated a large number of priests, religious brothers, and Catholic laity in prisons and concentration camps accusing them of being "threats to the state" on fabricated charges of homosexuality. For example, prison guards at Dachau concentration camp murdered Catholic priest, Fr. Alois Abdritzki, one of a number of fatalities from the "Cloister Trials."

THE PATRIARCHAL CONNECTING STRAND

The Nazi regime connected multiple forms of oppression when Heinrich Himmler reorganized the Reich Criminal Police Bureau to centralize operations by creating a national file on male homosexuals, transgender people, what they referred to as "wage abortionists" (women and their doctors), and to monitor the production and ban the use of contraceptives to "Aryan" women. Within this Bureau, they established The Reich Office for Combatting Homosexuality and Abortion, which in the single year of 1938 alone, conducted 28,366 arrests for abortion, and 28, 882 arrests of male homosexuals.

The common thread running through Nazi ideology regarding gender, gender expression, and sexuality was their intense campaign to control individuals' bodies and the bodies of members of entire communities in the attempt to control their minds.

Throughout history, examples abound of patriarchal domination over the rights and lives of women and LGBT people. Men denied women the right to join political organizations and the vote until women fought hard and demanded the rights of political enfranchisement; strictly enforced gender-based social roles mandated without choice that women's only option was to remain in the home to undertake housekeeping and childcare duties; women and LGBT people were and continue to be by far the primary target of harassment, abuse, and physical assault; women and LGBT people were and continue to be locked out of many professions; rules required that women teachers relinquish their jobs after marriage; in fact, the institution of marriage itself was structured on a foundation of male domination with men serving as the so-called "head of the household" and taking on sole ownership of all property, thereby taking away these rights from women.

In other words, women and LGBT people have been constructed as second-class and even third-class citizens not merely in Nazi Germany, but today as the current political discourse indicates. But women and LGBT are certainly not victims because through it all, women and LGBT people as individuals and as groups have resisted and challenged the inequities and have pushed back against patriarchal constraints.

I hope, though, that we as a society can learn from the tyranny of the past.

70

Masculinity as Homophobia

Fear, Shame, and Silence in the Construction of Gender Identity

Michael S. Kimmel

We think of manhood as eternal, a timeless essence that resides deep in the heart of every man. We think of manhood as a thing, a quality that one either has or doesn't have. We think of manhood as innate, residing in the particular biological composition of the human male, the result of androgens or the possession of a penis. We think of manhood as a transcendent tangible property that each man must manifest in the world, the reward presented with great ceremony to a young novice by his elders for having successfully completed an arduous initiation ritual. . . .

I view masculinity as a constantly changing collection of meanings that we construct through our relationships with ourselves, with each other, and with our world. Manhood is neither static nor timeless; it is historical. Manhood is not the manifestation of an inner essence; it is socially constructed. Manhood does not bubble up to consciousness from our biological makeup; it is created in culture. Manhood means different things at different times to different people. We come to know what it means to be a man in our culture by setting our definitions in opposition to a set of "others"— racial minorities, sexual minorities, and, above all, women.

. . .

This idea that manhood is socially constructed and historically shifting should not be understood as a loss, that something is being taken away from men. In fact, it gives us something extraordinarily valuable—agency, the capacity to act. It gives us a sense of historical possibilities to replace the despondent resignation that invariably attends timeless, ahistorical essentialisms. Our behaviors are not simply "just human nature," because "boys will be boys." From the materials we find around us in our culture—other people, ideas, objects—we actively create our worlds, our identities. Men, both individually and collectively, can change.

MASCULINITY AS A HOMOSOCIAL ENACTMENT

Other men: We are under the constant careful scrutiny of other men. Other men watch us, rank us, grant our acceptance into the realm of manhood. Manhood is demonstrated for other men's approval. It is other men who evaluate the performance. Literary critic David Leverenz argues that "ideologies of manhood have functioned primarily in relation to the gaze of male peers and male authority." Think of how men boast to one another of their accomplishments—from their latest sexual conquest to the size of the fish they caught—and how we constantly parade the markers of manhood—wealth, power, status, sexy women—in front of other men, desperate for their approval.

That men prove their manhood in the eyes of other men is both a consequence of sexism and one of its chief props. "Women have, in men's minds, such a low place on the social ladder of this country that it's useless to define yourself in terms of a woman," noted playwright David Mamet. "What men need is men's approval." Women become a kind of currency that men use to improve their ranking on the masculine social scale. (Even those moments of heroic conquest of women carry, I believe, a current of homosocial evaluation.) Masculinity is a *homosocial* enactment. We test ourselves, perform heroic feats, take enormous risks, all because we want other men to grant us our manhood.

Masculinity as a homosocial enactment is fraught with danger, with the risk of failure, and with intense relentless competition. "Every man you meet has a rating or an estimate of himself which he never loses or forgets," wrote Kenneth Wayne in his popular turn-of-the-century advice book. "A man has his own rating, and instantly he lays it alongside of the other man." Almost a century later, another man remarked to psychologist Sam Osherson that "[b]y the time you're an adult, it's easy to think you're always in competition with men, for the attention of women, in sports, at work."

MASCULINITY AS HOMOPHOBIA

. . .

Homophobia is a central organizing principle of our cultural definition of manhood. Homophobia is more than the irrational fear of gay men, more than the fear that we might be perceived as gay. "The word 'faggot' has nothing to do with homosexual experience or even with fears of homosexuals," writes David Leverenz. "It comes out of the depths of manhood: a label of ultimate contempt for anyone who seems sissy, untough, uncool." Homophobia is the fear that other men will unmask us, emasculate us, reveal to us and the world that we do not measure up, that we are not real men. We are afraid to let other men see that fear. Fear makes us ashamed, because the recognition of fear in ourselves is proof to ourselves that we are not as manly as we pretend, that we are, like the young man in a poem by Yeats, "one that ruffles in a manly pose for all his timid heart." Our fear is the fear of humiliation. We are ashamed to be afraid.

Shame leads to silence—the silences that keep other people believing that we actually approve of the things that are done to women, to minorities, to gays and lesbians in our culture. The frightened silence as we scurry past a woman being hassled by men on the street. That furtive silence when men make sexist or racist jokes in a bar. That clammy-handed silence when guys in the office make gay-bashing jokes. Our fears are the sources of our silences, and men's silence is what keeps the system running. This might help to explain why women often complain that their male friends or partners are often so understanding when they are alone and yet laugh at sexist jokes or even make those jokes themselves when they are out with a group.

The fear of being seen as a sissy dominates the cultural definitions of manhood. It starts so early. "Boys among boys are ashamed to be unmanly," wrote one educator in 1871. I have a standing bet with a friend that I can walk onto any playground in America where 6-year-old boys are happily playing and by asking one question, I can provoke a fight. That question is simple: "Who's a sissy around here?" Once posed, the challenge is made. One of two things is likely to happen. One boy will accuse another of being a sissy, to which that boy will respond that he is not a sissy, that the first boy is. They may have to fight it out to see who's lying. Or a whole group of boys will surround one boy and all shout "He is! He is!" That boy will either burst into tears and run home crying, disgraced, or he will have to take on several boys at once, to prove that he's not a sissy. (And what will his father or older brothers tell him if he chooses to run home crying?) It will be some time before he regains any sense of self-respect.

Violence is often the single most evident marker of manhood. Rather it is the willingness to fight, the desire to fight. The origin of our expression that one has a chip on one's shoulder lies in the practice of an adolescent boy in the country or small town at the turn of the century, who would literally walk around with a chip of wood balanced on his shoulder—a signal of his readiness to fight with anyone who would take the initiative of knocking the chip off.

As adolescents, we learn that our peers are a kind of gender police, constantly threatening to unmask us as feminine, as sissies. One of the favorite tricks when I was an adolescent was to ask a boy to look at his fingernails. If he held his palm toward his face and curled his fingers back to see them, he passed the test. He'd looked at his nails "like a man." But if he held the back of his hand away from his face, and looked at his fingernails with arm outstretched, he was immediately ridiculed as a sissy.

As young men we are constantly riding those gender boundaries, checking the fences we have constructed on the perimeter, making sure that nothing even remotely feminine might show through. The possibilities of being unmasked are everywhere. Even the most seemingly insignificant thing can pose a threat or activate that haunting terror. On the day the students in my course "Sociology of Men and Masculinities" were scheduled to discuss homophobia and male-male friendships, one student provided a touching illustration. Noting that it was a beautiful day, the first day of spring after a brutal northeast winter, he decided to wear shorts to class. "I had this really nice pair of new Madras shorts," he commented. "But then I thought to myself, these shorts have lavender and pink in them. Today's class topic is homophobia. Maybe today is not the best day to wear these shorts."

Our efforts to maintain a manly front cover everything we do. What we wear. How we talk. How we walk. What we eat. Every mannerism, every movement contains a coded gender language. Think, for example, of how you would answer the question: How do you "know" if a man is homosexual? When I ask this question in classes or workshops, respondents invariably provide a pretty standard list of stereotypically effeminate behaviors. He walks a certain way, talks a certain way, acts a certain way. He's very emotional; he shows his feelings. One woman commented that she "knows" a man is gay if he really cares about her; another said she knows he's gay if he shows no interest in her, if he leaves her alone.

Now alter the question and imagine what heterosexual men do to make sure no one could possibly get the "wrong idea" about them. Responses typically refer to the original stereotypes, this time as a set of negative rules about behavior. Never dress that way. Never talk or walk that way. Never show your feelings or get emotional. Always be prepared to demonstrate sexual interest in women that you meet, so it is impossible for any woman to get the wrong idea about you. In this sense, homophobia, the fear of being perceived as gay, as not a real man, keeps men exaggerating all the traditional rules of masculinity, including sexual predation with women. Homophobia and sexism go hand in hand.

The stakes of perceived sissydom are enormous—sometimes matters of life and death. We take enormous risks to prove our manhood, exposing ourselves disproportionately to health risks, workplace hazards, and stress-related illnesses. Men commit suicide three times as often as women. . . .

In one survey, women and men were asked what they were most afraid of. Women responded that they were most afraid of being raped and murdered. Men responded that they were most afraid of being laughed at.

HOMOPHOBIA AS A CAUSE OF SEXISM, HETEROSEXISM, AND RACISM

Homophobia is intimately interwoven with both sexism and racism. The fear—sometimes conscious, sometimes not—that others might perceive us as homosexual propels men to enact all manner of exaggerated masculine behaviors and attitudes to make sure that no one could possibly get the wrong idea about us. One of the centerpieces of that exaggerated masculinity is putting women down, both by excluding them from the public sphere and by the quotidian put-downs in speech and behaviors that organize the daily life of the American man. Women and gay men become the "other" against which heterosexual men project their identities, against whom they stack the decks so as to compete in a situation in which they will always win, so that by suppressing them, men can stake a claim for their own manhood. Women threaten emasculation by representing the home, workplace, and familial responsibility, the negation of fun. Gay men have historically played the role of the consummate sissy in the American popular mind because homosexuality is seen as an inversion of normal gender development. There have been other "others." Through American history, various groups have represented the sissy, the non-men against whom American men played out their definitions of manhood, often with vicious results. In fact, these changing groups provide an interesting lesson in American historical development.

At the turn of the 19th century, it was Europeans and children who provided the contrast for American men. The "true American was vigorous, manly, and direct, not effete and corrupt like the supposed Europeans," writes Rupert Wilkinson. . . . By the middle of the century, black slaves had replaced the effete nobleman. Slaves were seen as dependent, helpless men, incapable of defending their women and children, and therefore less than manly. Native Americans were cast as foolish and naive children, so they could be infantilized as the "Red Children of the Great White Father" and therefore excluded from full manhood.

By the end of the century, new European immigrants were also added to the list of the unreal men, especially the Irish and Italians, who were seen as too passionate and emotionally volatile to remain controlled sturdy oaks, and Jews, who were seen as too bookishly effete and too physically puny to truly measure up. In the mid-20th century, it was also Asians—first the Japanese during the Second World War, and more recently, the Vietnamese during the Vietnam War—who have served as unmanly templates against which American men have hurled their gendered rage. Asian men were seen as small, soft, and effeminate—hardly men at all.

Such a list of "hyphenated" Americans . . . composes the majority of American men. So manhood is only possible for a distinct minority, and the definition has been constructed to prevent the others from achieving it. Interestingly, this emasculation of one's enemies has a flip side—and one that is equally gendered. These very groups that have historically been cast as less than manly were also, often simultaneously, cast as hypermasculine, as sexually aggressive, violent rapacious beasts, against whom "civilized" men must take a decisive stand and thereby rescue civilization. . . . But whether one saw these groups as effeminate sissies or as brutal uncivilized savages, the terms with which they were perceived were gendered. These groups become the "others," the screens against which traditional conceptions of manhood were developed.

Being seen as unmanly is a fear that propels American men to deny manhood to others, as a way of proving the unprovable—that one is fully manly. Masculinity becomes a defense against the perceived threat of humiliation in the eyes of other men, enacted through a "sequence of postures"—things we might say, or do, or even think, that, if we thought carefully about them, would make us ashamed of ourselves. After all, how many of us have made homophobic or sexist remarks, or told racist jokes, or made lewd comments to women on the street? How many of us have translated those ideas and those words into actions, by physically attacking gay men, or forcing or cajoling a woman to have sex even though she didn't really want to because it was important to score?

POWER AND POWERLESSNESS IN THE LIVES OF MEN

I have argued that homophobia, men's fear of other men, is the animating condition of the dominant definition of masculinity in America, that the reigning definition of masculinity is a defensive effort to prevent being emasculated. In our efforts to suppress or overcome those fears, the dominant culture exacts a tremendous price from those deemed less than fully manly: women, gay men, nonnative-born men, men of color. This perspective may help clarify a paradox in men's lives, a paradox in which men have virtually all the power and yet do not feel powerful.

Manhood is equated with power—over women, over other men. Everywhere we look, we see the institutional expression of that power—in state and national legislatures, on the boards of directors of every major U.S. corporation or law firm, and in every school and hospital administration. Women have long understood this, and feminist women have spent the past three decades challenging both the public and the private expressions of men's power and acknowledging their fear of men. Feminism as a set of theories both explains women's fear of men and empowers women to confront it both publicly and privately. Feminist women have theorized that masculinity is about the drive for domination, the drive for power, for conquest.

This feminist definition of masculinity as the drive for power is theorized from women's point of view. It is how women experience masculinity. But it assumes a symmetry between the public and the private that does not conform to men's experiences. Feminists observe that women, as a group, do not hold power in our society. They also observe that individually, they, as women, do not feel powerful. They feel afraid, vulnerable. Their observation of the social reality and their individual experiences are therefore symmetrical. Feminism also observes that men, as a group, *are* in power. Thus, with the same symmetry, feminism has tended to assume that individually men must feel powerful.

This is why the feminist critique of masculinity often falls on deaf ears with men. When confronted with the analysis that men have all the power, many men react incredulously. "What do you mean, men have all the power?" they ask. "What are you talking about? My wife bosses me around. My kids boss me around. My boss bosses me around. I have no power at all! I'm completely powerless!"

Men's feelings are not the feelings of the powerful, but of those who see themselves as powerless. These are the feelings that come inevitably from the discontinuity between the social and the psychological, between the aggregate analysis that reveals how men are in power as a group and the psychological fact that they do not feel powerful as individuals. They are the feelings of men who were raised to believe themselves entitled to feel that power, but do not feel it. No wonder many men are frustrated and angry.

. . .

The dimension of power is now reinserted into men's experience not only as the product of individual experience but also as the product of relations with other men. In this sense, men's experience of powerlessness is *real*—the men actually feel it and certainly act on it—but it is not *true*, that is, it does not accurately describe their condition. In contrast to women's lives, men's lives are structured around relationships of power and men's differential access to power, as well as the differential access to that power of men as a group. Our imperfect analysis of our own situation leads us to believe that we men need *more* power, rather than leading us to support feminists' efforts to rearrange power relationships along more equitable lines.

. . .

Why, then, do American men feel so powerless? Part of the answer is because we've constructed the rules of manhood so that only the tiniest fraction of men come to believe that they are the biggest of wheels, the sturdiest of oaks, the most virulent repudiators of femininity, the most daring and aggressive. We've managed to disempower the overwhelming majority of American men by other means—such as discriminating on the basis of race, class, ethnicity, age, or sexual preference.

. . .

Others still rehearse the politics of exclusion, as if by clearing away the playing field of secure gender identity of any that we deem less than manly—women, gay men, nonnative-born men, men of color—middle-class, straight, white men can reground their sense of themselves without those haunting fears and that deep shame that they are unmanly and will be exposed by other men. This is the manhood of racism, of sexism, of homophobia. It is the manhood that is so chronically insecure that it trembles at the idea of lifting the ban on gays in the military, that is so threatened by women in the workplace that women become the targets of sexual harassment, that is so deeply frightened of equality that it must ensure that the playing field of male competition remains stacked against all newcomers to the game.

Exclusion and escape have been the dominant methods American men have used to keep their fears of humiliation at bay. The fear of emasculation by other men, of being humiliated, of being seen as a sissy, is the leitmotif in my reading of the history of American manhood. Masculinity has become a relentless test by which we prove to other men, to women, and ultimately to ourselves, that we have successfully mastered the part. The restlessness that men feel today is nothing new in American history; we have been anxious and restless for almost two centuries. Neither exclusion nor escape has ever brought us the relief we've sought, and there is no reason to think that either will solve our problems now. Peace of mind, relief from gender struggle, will come only from a politics of inclusion, not exclusion, from standing up for equality and justice, and not by running away.

71

Overcompensation Nation

It's Time to Admit That Toxic Masculinity Drives Gun Violence

Amanda Marcotte

In the wake of the horrific shooting in Orlando that left 50 dead, a political struggle is forming on whether to define this act as an anti-gay crime or an act of radical Islamic terrorism.

The answer, it's quickly starting to seem, is both of these, and more. A picture is quickly starting to form of who Omar Mateen, the shooter, was. His ex-wife describes a man who was controlling and abusive. A colleague says he was always using racial and sexual slurs and "talked about killing people all the time." Both his ex-wife and his father describe him as homophobic, with his father saying he spun into a rage at the sight of two men kissing. He was clearly fond of guns, having not one, but two concealed carry licenses. He worked at a security firm, a career that can be attractive to men with dominance and control issues. He was investigated by the FBI in 2013 for making threats to a coworker.

There is a common theme here: Toxic masculinity.

Every time feminists talk about toxic masculinity, there is a chorus of whiny dudes who will immediately assume — or pretend to assume — that feminists are condemning *all* masculinity, even though the modifier "toxic" inherently suggests that there are forms of masculinity that are not toxic.

So, to be excruciatingly clear, toxic masculinity is a specific model of manhood, geared towards dominance and control. It's a manhood that views women and LGBT people as inferior, sees sex as an act not of affection but domination, and which valorizes violence as the way to prove one's self to the world.

For obvious political reasons, conservatives are hustling as fast as they can to make this about "radical Islam," which is to say they are trying to imply that there's something inherent to Islam and not Christianity that causes such violence. This, of course, is hoary nonsense, as there is a long and ignoble history of Christian-identified men, caught up in the cult of toxic masculinity, sowing discord and causing violence in our country: The gun-toting militiamen that caused a showdown in Oregon, the self-appointed border patrol called the Minutemen that recently made news again as their founder was convicted of child molestation, men who attack abortion clinics and providers.

Toxic masculinity aspires to toughness but is, in fact, an ideology of living in fear: The fear of ever seeming soft, tender, weak, or somehow less than manly. This insecurity is perhaps the most stalwart defining feature of toxic masculinity.

The examples are endless: Donald Trump flipping out when someone teases him about his small fingers. (Or about anything, really.) The ludicrously long and shaggy beards on "Duck Dynasty," meant to stave off any association with the dreaded feminine with a thicket of hair. The emergence of the term "cuckservative," flung around by hardline right wingers to suggest that insufficient racism is somehow emasculating. Conservatives absolutely are melting down about an Obamacare ad that suggested that, gasp, *sometimes men wear pajamas.*

(This ad traumatized them so much that many conservative pundits are still freaking out, years after the fact, that the Obama administration dared suggest the emasculating fabric of flannel pajamas ever touched the skin of the American male. Indeed, it's probably emasculating to suggest men have skin at all, since "skin" is such a ladified concept in our culture, what with the moisturizers and stuff.)

If toxic masculinity was just about men posturing around each other in a comical fashion, that would be one thing, but this persistent pressure to constantly be proving manhood and warding off anything considered feminine or emasculating is the main reason why we have so many damn shootings in the United States. Whether it's Islamic terrorism or Columbine-style shootings or, as is the case with some of the most common but least covered mass shootings, an act of domestic violence by a man who would rather kill his family than lose control, the common theme is this toxic masculinity, a desire on the part of the shooter to show off how much power and control he has, to take male dominance to the level of exerting control over life and death itself.

Toxic masculinity is also the reason it's so easy for men with major issues to get a hold of the high-powered weaponry necessary to commit these crimes. Sure, the pro-gun movement in this country likes to roll out a bunch of half-baked pseudo-arguments pretending at rationality to justify the lack of gun control in this country, but really, the emotional selling point of guns is that they feed the cult of toxic masculinity. Being able to stockpile weapons and have ever bigger and scarier-looking guns is straightforward and undeniable overcompensation for insecure men, trying to prove what manly men they are.

That's why any attempt to discuss putting even the smallest, most commonsensical restrictions on guns turns into a bunch of right wing dudes squealing about how the liberals are coming to take their guns. This isn't a discussion being held on the plane of rationality, but is a psychological drama about these men's fears of emasculation, represented in an unsubtle way over their attachment to guns and their fear that liberals, stereotyped as effeminate in their imagination, are coming to steal the guns away.

And, of course, in the Orlando situation, we have the added problem of homophobia, which is called a "phobia" for a reason, since it's so often rooted in toxic masculinity and the terror of anything even remotely feminine.

What is particularly frustrating about all this is that, even though toxic masculinity is clearly the problem here, you have a bunch of conservatives running around and pushing toxic masculinity as the *solution,* as if all we need to end violence and terrorism is a bunch of silly posturing about who is the biggest man of all the menfolk out there.

Trump, of course, was leading the pack on this, posturing about how we need "toughness," which he appears to define as a willingness to tweet ignorant, belligerent nonsense. Posturing a lot, in general, is the preferred strategy of the toxic masculinity crowd in response to terrorism. Lots of chatter about how Democrats refuse to say "radical Islam," supposedly out of cowardice, and how the bravest and manliest of men will say it and the sheer force of the bravery demonstrated by the words they use will somehow be the magic ticket to ending the problem.

72

Introduction—How Sex Changed

A History of Transsexuality in the United States

Joanne Meyerowitz

On December 1, 1952, the *New York Daily News* announced the "sex change" surgery of Christine Jorgensen. The front-page headline read: "Ex-GI Becomes Blonde Beauty: Operations Transform Bronx Youth," and the story told how Jorgensen had traveled to Denmark for "a rare and complicated treatment." For years, Jorgensen, born and reared as a boy, had struggled with what she later described as an ineffable, inexorable, and increasingly unbearable yearning to live her life as a woman. In 1950 she sailed to Europe in search of a doctor who would alter her bodily sex. Within months she found an endocrinologist who agreed to administer hormones if she would in return cooperate with his research. Over the next two years she took massive doses of estrogen and underwent two major surgeries to transform her genitals. At the end of 1952 the *New York Daily News* transformed her obscure personal triumph into mass media sensation.

. . .

Jorgensen was more than a media sensation, a stage act, or a cult figure. Her story opened debate on the visibility and mutability of sex. It raised questions that resonated with force in the 1950s and engage us still today. How do we determine who is male and who is female, and why do we care? Can humans actually change sex? Is sex less apparent than it seems? As a narrative of boundary transgression, the Jorgensen story fascinated readers and elicited their surprise, and as an unusual variant on a familiar tale of striving and success, it inspired them. It opened possibilities for those who questioned their own sex and offered an exoticized travelogue for armchair tourists who had never imagined that one could take a journey across the sex divide. In the post-World War II era, with heightened concerns about science and sex, the Jorgensen story compelled some readers to spell out their own versions of the boundaries of sex, and it convinced others to reconsider the categories they thought they already knew. In response, American doctors and scientists began to explore the process of defining sex.

. . .

At the start of the twenty-first century, we routinely distinguish sex, gender, and sexuality, but we cannot, it seems, seal off the borders. Scientists, their popularizers, and their critics still debate whether sex-linked genes or prenatal sex hormones or specific sites of the brain determine the behaviors associated with masculinity and femininity and with hetero- and homosexuality. In much of the popular culture, sex still seems to dictate particular forms of gender, which in turn dictates particular forms of sexuality. In this default logic, a female is naturally and normally a feminine person who desires men; a male is naturally and normally a masculine person who desires women. All other permutations of sex, gender, and sexuality still appear, if they appear at all, as pathologically anomalous or socially strange. . . . [T]he categories of sex, gender, and sexuality—now analytically distinct—remain insistently intertwined in American science and culture.

Jorgensen was not the first transsexual, nor was the publicity accorded her the first media coverage of sex-change surgery. Cross-gender identification, the sense of being the other sex, and the desire to live as the other sex all existed in various forms in earlier centuries and other cultures. The historical record includes countless examples of males who dressed or lived as women and females who dressed or lived as men. Transsexuality, the quest to transform the bodily characteristics of sex via hormones and surgery, originated in the early twentieth century. By the 1910s European scientists had begun to publicize their attempts to transform the sex of animals, and by the 1920s a few doctors, mostly in Germany, had agreed to alter the bodies of a few patients who longed to change their sex.

. . .

The sex-change experiments in Europe reached the United States through the popular culture. From the 1930s on, American newspapers and magazines—and later radio, television, and film—broadcast stories on sex change. . . .

Only after World War II did American doctors and scientists seriously address the issue of sex change. . . . From the start, the doctors and scientists fought among themselves about the explanatory powers of biology and psychology, the use and abuse of medical technology, and the merits of sex-change operations.

In the point and counterpoint of debate, the doctors and scientists gradually shifted their focus from concepts of biological sex to concepts of what they came to call gender. When they tried to explain the desire to change sex, they less often referred to conditions of mixed bodily sex and more frequently wrote of "psychological sex," and later "gender identity," a sense of the sexed self that was both separate from the sex of the body and, some claimed, harder to change than the body itself. The sex of the body, they now asserted, had multiple components—hormones, chromosomes, genitals, and more—some of which could be altered. A few of them began to emphasize the immutability of adult gender identity and to acknowledge the despair of those patients who wanted the sex of their bodies to match their unshakable sense of self. This new understanding of gender was forged and refined in the discourse on transsexuality. With it, more American doctors gradually began to endorse and perform "sex reassignment surgery."

From the doctors' and scientists' point of view, medical examinations and psychological tests could determine a person's sex and verify a person's gender identity. From the point of view of their patients, sex and gender were usually matters of self-knowledge. They had studied themselves, and sometimes they had also read widely in the medical literature. Like the doctors, many of them distinguished between the sex of the visible body and the firm sense of sex that came from an inner sense of self. They had determined for themselves what they were and what they wanted to become. After Christine Jorgensen made the news, hundreds of them approached doctors in order to convince them to recommend or perform surgery. But they ran into constant conflicts with doctors who insisted on their own authority to define sex and gender, diagnose the condition, and recommend the treatment.

. . . After Jorgensen made the news, American doctors and scientists took up the taxonomic process of sorting out a tangled thicket of varied conditions of sex, gender, and sexuality. On the ground, those who identified as transsexuals, transvestites, lesbians, and gay men sorted themselves out in a parallel social process. Amidst a multiplicity of variations, some of them came to define their conditions not only in contradistinction to the mainstream norm—the heterosexual masculine male or heterosexual feminine female— but also with regard to others on the margins. In everyday life, especially in the cities, they gravitated toward each other, schooled each other in the customs and language of particular subcultures, and developed their own vernacular that delineated finer gradations of gender variance than the language used by doctors.

In the 1960s the complicated process of redefining sex took place within a culture increasingly preoccupied by a "sexual revolution," by more liberal attitudes toward individual choice, and by revitalized human rights movements that insisted on social change in the name of justice. In this climate the doctors and scientists who studied transsexuality began to organize programs, clinics, conferences, and associations to promote study of and treatment for transsexuals, and self-identified transsexuals began to organize to demand their own rights.

. . .

[T]he birth of a new identity evolved socially and politically into the birth of a new minority. Self-identified transsexuals distinguished themselves from other "deviants" and saw themselves as members of a distinct social group. In the late 1960s and early 1970s a few transsexuals began to challenge the doctors' authority and to reject the medical model that cast them primarily as patients. They observed and sometimes joined the 1960s movements for civil rights, feminism, and gay liberation, and they began to organize collectively and demand the right to quality medical care and also the right to live, free from harassment, with whatever presentation of gender they chose to express. By the century's end the push for transsexual rights had blossomed into a vocal social movement with local, national, and international organizations and with a new scholarship that sought again to clarify the contested meanings of sex.

. . .

As this thumbnail sketch suggests, the history of transsexuality engages a number of key trends of the twentieth century. It demonstrates the growing authority of science and medicine, and it points to the impact of sensational journalism. It illustrates the rise of a new concept of the modern self that placed a heightened value on self-expression, self-improvement, and self-transformation. It highlights the proliferation of sexual identities, and it offers a new angle of vision into the breakdown of traditional norms of gender. In the 1970s and 1980s the women's and gay liberation movements eclipsed transsexuality as the sites of public debate over sex, gender, and sexuality. But the history of transsexuality had already laid the definitional groundwork and helps explain the peculiar configuration that sex, gender, and sexuality had already assumed in American popular culture, medicine, and law.

. . .

73

The InterSEXion

A Vision for a Queer Progressive Agenda

Deepali Gokhale

This vision is based on the fact that the queer community is a microcosm of humanity, intersecting through the common experiences of the oppression of gender identity and sexual identity, the observation that oppression is rooted in greed and perpetuated by the fear of scarcity, the assertion that no oppression can end without removing the systems that perpetuate it, the recognition that oppression and exploitation are the bases on which current power structures and economies rely, and the observation that because queer liberation requires the end of all forms of oppression and exploitation, the liberation of queer people can be seen as the key to the liberation of humanity itself.

THE ROOT OF QUEER OPPRESSION

Heterosexism is the belief that there are only two genders, and that a sexual relationship between a man and a woman is compulsory for full acceptance into society. It would seem that the root of queer oppression is heterosexism, and so queer folks should work against heterosexism. In order to get into any sort of depth in this work, we would need to know why heterosexism exists in the first place, and we would find that the reason for heterosexism is because it enforces patriarchy, which could lead us to join forces with the women's movement and oppose patriarchy. That venture would expose the fact that the reason patriarchy needs enforcement is because it is essential to capitalism, and that capitalism at its essence relies on greed. Therefore, the root of queer oppression, and in fact, the root of all systemic oppression as it exists in the world today, is unbridled greed.

Capitalism is based in greed, and as it exists today, cannot exist without exploiting labor. One person cannot make a disproportionately large share of profits unless somewhere in the process, another person is making a disproportionately small one. The most basic example of this is in the patriarchal nuclear family, where the man makes profits at the expense of a woman's (and children's) free labor. The people who most benefit from this unbridled greed are the ones who came up with capitalism to begin with: wealthy white men. This is true worldwide; every oppression that is in place exists to ultimately support white male power, and the United States is the clear leader and greatest benefactor of this system.

The main tools used to make an oppressive system work are a defined norm, economic power, and violence. In her book entitled *Homophobia: A Weapon of Sexism*, Suzanne Pharr explains it this way:

> To understand the connection among the oppressions, we must examine their common elements. The first is a defined norm, a standard of rightness and often righteousness wherein all others are judged in relation to it. This norm must be backed up with institutional power, economic power, and both institutional and individual

violence . . . . In the United States, that norm is male, white, heterosexual, Christian, temporarily able bodied, youthful, and has access to wealth and resources . . . .

In order for these institutions to be controlled by a single group of people, there must be economic power . . . . Once economic control is in the hands of the few, all others can be controlled through limiting access to resources, limiting mobility, limiting employment options. People are pitted against one another through the perpetuation of the myth of scarcity which suggests that our resources are limited and blames the poor for using up too much of what little there is to go around . . . . The maintenance of societal and individual power and control requires the use of violence and the threat of violence. Institutional violence is sanctioned through the criminal justice system and the threat of the military—for quelling individual or group uprisings.

(1988, 53–56)

The patriarchal nuclear family, living in a single-family house in the suburbs, serves as the building block for capitalism. As the arbitrarily defined norm, it provides the perfect conditions for the oppression of women. Since men earn wage labor, they can easily control women's access to resources, and can easily accuse women of "spending too much" of "their" hard-earned money. By isolating women from each other, the nuclear family provides a safe haven for men to be violent towards women and thus enforce their power.

In relation to institutional power, the isolated nuclear family unit makes it easy for mass media to be the only source of information citizens receive, since people are no longer talking to their neighbors, and ideally, by isolating the male in the household as the only breadwinner, the nuclear family can easily be moved around for the convenience of those who need wage labor. Because each family needs a house, a car, and their own household items, the nuclear family also promotes the wasteful unending consumerism and environmental exploitation required for "economic progress." Irrespective of whether the nuclear family is actually the "norm," as long as this belief is widespread, other types of families can be judged by whether they conform to that structure.

Everyone strives to conform to the nuclear family model, and a false sense of pride and righteousness is evident in those who "make it." That many poor people, people of color, and immigrants do not fit into that kind of family is considered "their fault," and not the result of those in power limiting access to the resources it takes to sustain a nuclear family. When this shame and blame is internalized, those who don't fit the norm fight amongst themselves about why another oppressed group is the "problem with society."

It is not just gender oppression that keeps capitalism in place. It requires the exploitation of the labor of anyone outside the "norm": the white, wealthy, young, temporarily-abled, English-speaking Christian American male citizen. Racism exists to exploit the work of people of color, sexism exists to exploit women's work, xenophobia exists to exploit the "third world," and ageism/ableism devalues those who are assumed "less productive." Many of us experience more than one of these oppressions. In addition to the myth of the nuclear family, patriotism, the illusion of a meritocracy, and religious oppression are the tools used to brainwash one group to look down on another and trust that the system is working for the "believers." The illusion of scarcity and fear of our neighbors keeps us isolated from and fighting with each other. Divide and conquer is the rule. Meanwhile, those in power continue to reap the rewards.

A VISION FOR LIBERATION: THE INTERSEXION

It is because the queer community categorically rejects this setup, simply by being who we are, that we are such a threat to those in power. When they call gay marriage a threat to human civilization as we know it, they are referring to the fact that gender oppression in the form of heterosexism is the weapon that keeps them in power, and if those gender "norms" weren't considered essential, there would be no way to enforce that oppression. It is precisely because we live outside the basic unit of the very nuclear family structure that would otherwise permit capitalism to continue unchallenged, and because our community experiences not only queer oppression but all oppressions, that we are most capable of creating an alternative culture outside of the culture of exploitation, resolving it for ourselves so that it can be expanded for those outside of our community.

A defining characteristic of the queer community is that within it is reflected all of the oppressions and privileges in our surrounding geography, and that these oppressions and privileges play out in similar proportions and methods. It is the intersection of every oppression and privilege, and the wholeness of the queer community is its power. There is no better place to understand the intersection of oppressions and figure out how to achieve liberation for all forms of life. Because we are an intersection based on gender identity and sexual identity, we can call ourselves the "interSEXion."

We can start by building a real sense of wholeness within the queer community. While our oppressors would like us to remain separate and at odds with each other, we can use our queer oppression to bind us into making connections and understanding the nature of oppression itself. We can begin by socializing with each other. We can each individually learn about our own oppressions so that we know what we need. We can also learn about our privileges, and use them to end the oppression of others. We can end racism, classism, sexism, and any other oppression within our community. We can create a safety net for ourselves so that we are not reliant on the systems of oppression used against us for our basic needs. We can pass the values of liberation that we create from one generation to the next, without the sense of ownership that is inherited with blood relations, and instead allowing each generation to use its own experience and creativity in the struggle. In this way, we will keep intact within our community what is being used to divide and conquer us elsewhere.

Once we have this safer community, non-reliant on the systems of oppression that keep us divided, we can break the systems of oppression for everyone else. We can use our wholeness as an advantage outside the queer community. As whole people with multiple identities, we can use our non-queer identities as bridges to other oppressed communities. Although it may be true that any oppressed community can build bridges, the queer community is particularly fortunate to have representatives from the actual communities surrounding it. Because the queer identity can many times be made invisible, queer people can have access to those communities in ways that no other oppressed community can.

Currently, the progressive community seems to operate in isolated spaces, divided by our issues and oppressions, with no one group to bind it together. We could use our wholeness and reflection of our geography to ensure our policy would most likely be beneficial for all progressive communities around us, and we can be the glue that binds it together and moves it forward. In many cases, we are leading those "other" progressive movements anyway.

The queer community could have a central "policy group" that would be informed by and be informative to any number of affinity groups. The responsibility of the policy group would be to take in the information from the affinity groups, get resources and create infrastructure to support the groups, and to create an overall policy/strategy/direction for achieving our goal of ending exploitation and oppression. This policy group would be accountable not only to the affinity groups, but also to individuals in the community, and we can hold community forums to keep a dialogue going with those individuals who may not belong to any group.

Our affinity groups could organize by whatever affinity they chose (geography, race, ethnicity, religion, class, gender, sexuality, age, campaign, cause, . . .), they could be groups that already exist (like AIDS Survival Project, ZAMI, Trikone Atlanta), and they could dissolve if/when they were no longer necessary, like if they were organized around a campaign. The groups could provide safe spaces for people to talk about particular oppressions or issues. People could belong to as many affinity groups as they wanted. The goals for each group for now could be: figuring out the most important issues for a particular affinity group, building a coalition to support the group, and figuring out a proactive strategy to address the group's issues in order to inform the policy group.

If the affinity groups and the queer community make up an "inner circle" around our interSEXion, our allies could form a second circle around the first. Issue or campaign-based affinity groups can access our allies to form coalitions when needed. Our allies would benefit because through the interSEXion, we could be the quickest connection between allies that would form a coalition. Our allies could create connections even further outside our intersection, and reach people who would never associate themselves with a queer agenda, but would work on a particular issue or campaign through our allies.

Positioning our queer community as the interSEXion would not only ensure that we remain at the center of our own liberation, but it would also require us to leave no one behind. Being the interSEXion implies our community's wholeness, and it requires us to be no less than a full human rights movement. It requires us to honor and celebrate the wholeness of each individual in it, and restricts some of us from achieving our goal of liberation unless everyone in our community is free from oppression. It requires us to identify which parts of our community are underrepresented and to nurture those who are most wounded. It means we cannot even start towards a path of liberation until we are on equal footing within our own community. It requires us to walk our talk and liberate ourselves in order to liberate the world around us, and it is the reason why our interSEXion may be the key to the end of exploitation.

Reference

Pharr, S. (1988). *Homophobia: A Weapon of Sexism*. Little Rock, AR: Chardon Press.

74

Transmisogyny 101

What It Is and What Can We Do About It

Laura Kacere

Let's talk about transmisogyny. This word describes so much of what we see in the cultural and systemic treatment of trans women in our culture and ties in so clearly with feminism, and yet **it's not a word that many people know about or understand.** You may have heard of transphobia: the discrimination of and negative attitudes toward transgender people based on their gender expression. And you've likely heard of misogyny: the hatred and denigration of women and characteristics deemed feminine. **Transmisogyny, then, is the**

confluence of these – the negative attitudes, expressed through cultural hate, individual and state violence, and discrimination directed toward trans women and trans and gender non-conforming people on the feminine end of the gender spectrum.

WHO IS VICITIMIZED BY TRANSMISOGYNY?

Transmisogyny targets transgender and transsexual women – people who were assigned male at birth, but who identify as women. But transgender women are not the only people who experience transmisogyny. Trans and gender non-conforming people who do not necessarily identify as women, but who present feminine characteristics and/or identify along the feminine end of the gender spectrum are also on the receiving end of transmisogyny.

Transmisogyny is *all* about the hatred of the feminine, and it is not limited toward only those who identify as women. It includes transfeminine and feminine-identified gender-queer people, as well as many others who are feminine-of-center but were not assigned female at birth.

So for the purpose of simplicity and brevity in this article, I will use the term trans women to refer to all people victimized by transmigogyny.

WHY DOES TRANSMISOGYNY EXIST?

Transmisogyny is based in the assumption that femininity is inferior to masculinity. It relies on an understanding of all those qualities that are associated with "femaleness" and devaluing them, viewing them as less than those qualities associated with "maleness" and therefore as deserving of hatred, mockery, and violence. This sounds a whole lot like sexism, doesn't it?

Why should there be a specific word used to describe the experience of trans people who are specifically feminine? How is this different from sexism and transphobia?

Trans women experience a particular kind of sexist marginalization based in their unique position of overlapping oppressions – they are both trans and feminine. They are devalued by society on both accounts. Trans people experience transphobia, or cissexism, due to a cultural and systemic obsession with the gender binary: the idea that there are two types of people – men and women – who are born, raised, and naturally associate with that gender and its accompanying characteristics. Our cultural and political institutions are based on this premise. Thus, trans women are not always easily categorized, and for people and institutions whose understanding of gender relies deeply in the repressive gender binary, this is confusing, transgressive, and for some, worthy of hate. The response to the existence of those who challenge the social understanding of gender, then, is extreme oppression and marginalization of trans people of all gender expressions.

TRANS-FEMININITY AND SEXISM

Our society is steeped in the notion that women and characteristics coded as feminine are inferior to men and those qualities coded as masculine. In our sexist society, being a woman automatically places you in a position of less value. But to give up one's "important" position as a man, choosing (as trans people are perceived to do) to be a woman and to be feminine, in a way, poses a fundamental threat to male superiority and may be seen as a rejection of the "superior male identity."

Trans women, therefore, are not only a reminder to society that gender categories are not fixed, but also that womanhood and feminine gender expression is not something to be ashamed of. In this way, understanding transmisogyny is absolutely imperative to our work as feminists, and makes clear just how integral trans issues and rights are to our work around gender. Not only is transmisogyny steeped in sexism, but the resulting oppression is parallel to what cisgender *(those who identify with the gender of which they were assigned at birth)* women face: physical objectification, over-sexualization, stereotyping, policing of bodies, a discrimination on all levels of society, and individual and systemic acts of violence.

THE VIOLENCE OF TRANSMISOGYNY

Transmisogyny rears its ugly head in many ways and on all levels of society. We see it, for instance, in violence on an individual level. Hate crimes against trans people are disproportionately and tragically high, and the majority of this violence victimizes trans women. In fact, over half of all anti-LGBTQIA+ homicides were perpetrated against transgender women (NCAVP, 2013). And while we're talking statistics, it's important to note that nearly three-quarters of those homicides targeted people of Color.

WE SEE TRANSMISOGYNY IN STATE VIOLENCE AS WELL

1 in 5 transgender women (21%) has been incarcerated at some point in her life. This is far above the general population, and is even higher (47%) for Black transgender people. According to the National Center for Transgender Equality, trans people experience disproportionately high rates of poverty and homelessness caused by discrimination in jobs and housing, but they also experience greater incarceration rates, largely due to gender profiling by the police. Gender is policed, quite literally by police officers who target, arrest, and often harass trans women for looking "different" and therefore, "disorderly." Trans women of Color, in particular, tend to be perceived by police through racialized and gender stereotypes framing them as highly sexual and as criminal. Trans women are consistently targeted and arrested for being involved in sex work, even if they have no association with this work. For example, there have been many instances where trans women, most often trans women of Color, have been arrested for carrying condoms. In New York, where having a condom on you can be used as evidence of involvement in sex work, trans women are being profiled, searched, and arrested for being a trans woman at the wrong place at the wrong time.

There's also direct violence at the hands of police: A 2012 study by the National Coalition of Anti-Violence Programs found that transgender people across the U.S. experience three times more police violence than cisgender people. And nearly half of trans people who reported hate crimes to the police experienced mistreatment from them while asking for help. Trans women experience abuse after being arrested as well, when they are most often forced to reside in men's prison facilities, experiencing extremely high rates of sexual and physical violence – a study by the Department of Justice found that 1 in 3 are sexually assaulted in prison. In response, many prisons place trans women in solitary confinement for extended periods of time "for their own protection." (Meanwhile, solitary confinement is considered a form of torture.)

IN THE MEDIA

While trans men are generally ignored and made invisible by American media, trans women are exoticized, their existence perceived as shocking and newsworthy. They are mocked, over-sexualized, and fetishized. Trans women are given an extremely two-dimensional portrayal in the news, where they are most often reported on in association with a hate crime. In these reports, their gender is consistently portrayed as confusing and illegitimate, appearing in countless headlines like this one: "Man Dressed as Woman Found Dead." Additionally, our media portrays trans women in archetypes – as the weak victim of a crime, or as the evil villain; as the mentally unstable character, or as the manipulative one. They are often pathologized and sexualized, portrayed as someone manipulatively hiding their transgender identity to trick a man into engaging with them sexually or romantically. And, reinforcing the assumptions by police mentioned above, they play countless television roles as sex workers.

More generally, they are shown as unattractive; they are the butt of jokes, their desire to be feminine mocked, and their motives for transitioning questioned. And while it is difficult to find complex and honest portrayals of trans women characters on television, it is even more rare to find an authentic and respectful portrayal of a trans woman of Color (though we have seen a few recently, like the great Laverne Cox in *Orange is the New Black*).

IN QUEER AND WOMEN'S SPACES

Sadly, transmisogyny is also very present in LGBTQIA+ spaces, where trans women, particularly trans women of Color, are marginalized within an already marginalized group. The mainstream LGBTQIA+ movement has been called out many times for excluding trans people, and there is a pervasive sexism in the movement as well as in social spaces, that promotes transmisogyny and a denigration of feminine qualities. Masculine privilege, like white privilege, does not disappear once one is in a queer space. So when trans women share their experiences, queer cis male leaders have too many times dismissed them and accused them of "hurting the LGBTQ movement" due to the visible transgression of many of society's norms involved in being a trans woman.

And although it should be the last place where transmisogyny is present, sadly, we see it often in cis women's spaces. Trans women are excluded from many domestic violence shelters and other crisis spaces that exist in response to violence against women in our society.

Trans women continue to be excluded from many women-only spaces and feminist events, while some "feminists" continue to speak out against the very existence of trans women, arguing that they are not "authentic" women and that they are "hurting the movement." Trans women have called these groups and spaces out, creating inclusive spaces in the meantime, citing that they experience sexism and homophobia in very real and concrete ways, and yet are excluded from the spaces which were created in response to these oppressions.

WHAT CAN WE DO?

Transmisogyny, like sexism, is pervasive and structural, but it also exists in our everyday experiences. Once you understand it, you begin to notice it in personal interactions, on television, and in social movements and political campaigns. *Call it out!* Name it for what it is. Transmisogyny, like sexism, goes unnoticed too often because it is so entrenched in our sociocultural and political understanding of gender. Educate others about this issue. And most importantly, don't be afraid to call out other feminists or gay rights advocates for transmisoginistic words and actions. These are the spaces we need to make more inclusive. It is so important that we work together to find a solution to the problem of transmisogyny's existence in our movements and that we always act in solidarity with our trans sisters. If our movements seek to eradicate transphobia, homophobia, and sexism, then we must address transmisogyny, located at the intersection of these oppressions, and make it a priority in our fight.

75

Pansexual Visibility & Undoing Heteronormativity

Cameron Airen

Pride was bittersweet this year. We are still devastated and grieving over the Orlando shooting of 50 people at Pulse, an LGBTQ night club, AND we continue to proudly celebrate who we are. The celebration of LGBTQ [people and identities] feels even more important with the violence that recently happened. Though greater strides have been made towards the acceptance of gay and queer people, we still have a long way towards changing perceptions, beliefs, and the safety of LGBTQ people. I want to acknowledge the intersections like race, gender, and disability that many gay or queer people experience. Thus, the fight towards more acceptance and safety of being queer or gay is also a fight to end all social oppressions.

In this post, I specifically want to talk about pansexualtity and heteronormativity. I'm focusing on pansexuality because I am a pansexual, and pansexuals are hardly acknowledged and represented. Today, being pansexual has a wider understanding than it did eleven years ago when I was first identifying as one. I'm thrilled to see how much of the awareness and acceptance of pansexuality has evolved though we still have a long way to go. Pansexuality is hugely underrepresented in the media, and it's still not taken seriously enough in society at large. We need greater pansexual visibility and awareness of heteronormativity.

WHAT IS PANSEXUALITY?

First, I want to share what pansexuality means to me. Each pansexual can define what their sexuality means, and I do not claim to speak for all pansexuals. For me, I define pansexual as being attracted to multiple genders and/or being attracted to/fall in love with someone(s) irrespective of gender. When I first heard the term *pansexual*, I heard it described as falling in love with the person, not the gender, which resonated with me deeply.

To me, pansexuality differs from bisexuality because of "bi" meaning *two*, as in two genders. I prefer to use pansexual because it acknowledges more than two genders that I could be attracted to. I do want to acknowledge that not all bisexuals only define their sexuality within the binary, but for my love of deconstructing language, I prefer to use pansexual. Sometimes, when my sexuality pops up in conversation with someone who doesn't seem to have an awareness of pansexuality, then I usually identify as bisexual. I'm fine with bisexual, but it doesn't feel like the whole truth. Also, I don't feel like I am attracted to both women and men because I'm not. I'm not attracted to one *being* a woman or a man. I'm attracted to the person underneath. It may sound like an ideal fantasy, but it's true; my genuine attraction stems from the inside first and the outside second.

HETERONORMATIVITY ERASES PANSEXUALITY

A big part of the fight to foster greater acceptance of and to keep LGBTQ folks alive is to dismantle heteronormativity. Heteronormativity is deep seated in our society and we encounter its presence in our everyday lives. In order to help end oppression and violence against queer people, we must face the heteronormativity that we perpetuate. A huge part of this work involves awareness, education, and action.

People are assumed to be heterosexual unless their perceived gender has people believing otherwise. I don't identify as "femme" but, sometimes, I present as more "femme," and thus am assumed to be heterosexual. Heteronormativity assumes that when I am with a man, I am straight; it assumes heterosexual until proven otherwise. I'm not with a man because of my heterosexual "nature." I'm with him because I fell in love with a human being who happens to "be" a man. I'm not going to walk around with a sign on my forehead that states "Pansexual," thus the heterosexual assumption is important to change.

Heteronormativity treats pan, gay, or bi sexuality as a spectacle. When my ex-girlfriend and I would take neighborhood walks holding hands, people would drive or walk by staring and smiling at us. Granted, we were a cute couple, but after a while, I started to feel like a spectacle. This is twofold. On one hand, it was beautiful that people were responding positively to our love. But, on the other hand, my relationship was not on display for other people's pleasure (or disgust). We lived in an open-minded neighborhood, so we rarely, if ever, encountered disgust or negative reactions to displaying our affection for one another in public. But, *because* we lived in an open-minded neighborhood, I was surprised that people were reacting (even though positive) to us at all. If women being romantic with one another is normalized, then there wouldn't be a reaction from others at all.

No one blinks an eye when they see a couple they perceive to be heterosexual walking down the street (at least in relation to sexuality/gender; racism, disability and other identities can still be a factor). This is heteronormativity and heterosexual privilege. Not being aware of heterosexual privilege perpetuates heteronormativity. When we perceive a couple to be heterosexual, we are engaging in heteronormativity. We don't actually know if the couple we perceive to be heterosexual is actually heterosexual. We perceive a heterosexual couple to consist of a "woman" and a "man," but what if the woman or man is bisexual or pansexual? When we perceive people as heterosexual, we are projecting our own social conditioning onto them because of heteronormativity.

Also, heteronormativity tends to assume that if you're pansexual, then you're automatically polyamorous. Polyamorous or monogamous, it doesn't matter. You don't need to be with both a woman and a man at the same time to prove you're pansexual. Being monogamous with a man does not erase pansexuality either, but society treats it that way. A pansexual woman being in relationship with a man does not all of a sudden make her heterosexual.

As a culture and society, we need to do a better job of unpacking heteronormativity. We can unlearn the assumptions we make about other people's sexuality based upon their physical appearance. As pansexuals, we will not be erased. We are here; we are queer, and we're not going anywhere.

THE LACK OF PANSEXUAL REPRESENTATION ONSCREEN

Pansexuals are hugely underrepresented in film and television, which isn't a surprise since society is still catching up in understanding what pansexuality is, and even being introduced to the term. Heteronormativity allows for writers and directors to create heterosexual characters without questioning why they are creating a heterosexual character. Heteronormativity allows most, if not all, of the characters in a film to be heterosexual and have its one token gay character. If we didn't live in a heteronormative world, then there wouldn't be such a disparity, heterosexual would not be the norm.

Pansexual and bisexual representation onscreen is rare. While we have more lesbian and gay people onscreen than ever before, pansexuals and bisexuals pale in comparison. . . Can we say that TV is doing a better job at queer representation? No doubt, we can. Films need to step up to the plate! But, both television and film needs to greatly improve their representation of pansexuals and bisexuals. The more we see pansexuals onscreen, the more pansexual will be normalized as a sexual orientation. But, we can't wait for the media to change, we need to start now. It starts with deconstructing heteronormativity in our everyday lives. Notice the next time you make a judgment (whether it's in your own head or out loud) about someone's sexuality . . .

76

Transgender Liberation

Susan Stryker

. . .

THE COMPTON'S CAFETERIA RIOT OF 1966

By the middle of the 1960s life in the United States was being transformed by several large-scale social movements. . . . The most militant phase of the transgender movement for social change, from 1966 to 1969, was part of this massive social upheaval.

The 1966 Compton's Cafeteria Riot in San Francisco's seedy Tenderloin neighborhood was similar to earlier incidents at Cooper's [in Los Angeles in 1959] and Dewey's [in

Philadelphia in 1965]. For the first time, however, direct action in the streets by transgender people resulted in lasting institutional change. One weekend night in August—the precise date is unknown—Compton's, a twenty-four-hour cafeteria at the corner of Turk and Taylor streets, was buzzing with its usual late-night crowd of drag queens, hustlers, slummers, cruisers, runaway teens, and down-and-out neighborhood regulars. The restaurant's management became annoyed by a noisy young crowd of queens at one table who seemed be spending a lot of time without spending a lot of money, and it called in the police to roust them—as it had been doing with increasing frequency throughout the summer. A surly police officer, accustomed to manhandling Compton's clientele with impunity, grabbed the arm of one of the queens and tried to drag her away. She unexpectedly threw her coffee in his face, however, and a melee erupted: Plates, trays, cups, and silverware flew through the air at the startled police officers, who ran outside and called for backup. Compton's customers turned over the tables and smashed the plateglass windows and then poured out of the restaurant and into the streets. The paddy wagons arrived, and street fighting broke out in Compton's vicinity, all around the corner of Turk and Taylor. Drag queens beat the police with their heavy purses and kicked them with their high-heeled shoes. A police car was vandalized, a newspaper stand was burned to the ground, and—in the words of the best available source on what happened that night, a retrospective account by gay liberation activist Reverend Raymond Broshears, published in the program of San Francisco's first Gay Pride march in 1972—"general havoc was raised in the Tenderloin." The small restaurant had been packed when the fighting broke out, so the riot probably involved fifty or sixty patrons, plus police officers and any neighborhood residents or late-night passersby who jumped into the fray.

CONTEXTUALIZING COMPTON'S

Although the exact date of the riot remains a mystery . . . its underlying causes are reasonably clear. Understanding why the riot happened where and when it did reveals a great deal about the issues that have historically motivated the transgender social justice struggle and helps us understand similar dynamics at work today.

The location of the riot was by no means random. San Francisco's downtown Tenderloin neighborhood had been a sex-work district since the early 1900s. . . .

Much of the so-called vice trade in the neighborhood was supported by nonresidents of one sort or another. . . . But the neighborhood's resident population tended to be those who could least afford to live elsewhere, or who were prevented from doing so: released convicts and parolees, old-timers on small pensions, recent immigrants, pimps, prostitutes, drug addicts, alcoholics—and transgender women.

Housing and employment discrimination against transgender people are still legal in most places in the United States, and this discrimination was even more common in the past than it is now. In the 1960s, more so than today, a person who looked transgendered would be less likely to be rented to and would have a great deal of trouble finding work. As a result, a great many transgender women lived in the Tenderloin in cheap residential hotels, many of them along Turk Street near Compton's. To meet their basic survival needs they often worked as prostitutes or as maids in the hotels and bars where their friends sold sex. While most people who participated in the Tenderloin's illicit economy of sex, drugs, and after-hours entertainment were free to come and go, the neighborhood functioned as more of an involuntary containment zone for transgender women. Police actually helped concentrate a population of transgender women in the Tenderloin by directing them to go there when they were picked up in other parts of the city.

The police could be especially vicious to "street queens," whom they considered bottom-of-the-barrel sex workers, and who were the least able to complain about mistreatment. Transgender women working the streets were often arrested on suspicion of prostitution even if they were just going to the corner store or talking with friends; they might be driven around in squad cars for hours, forced to perform oral sex, strip-searched, or, after arriving at the jail, humiliated in front of other prisoners. Transgender women in jail often would have their heads forcibly shaved, or if they resisted, be placed in solitary confinement in "the hole." And because they were legally men (with male genitalia in spite of their social lives as women, and often in spite of having breasts and no facial hair) they would be placed in the men's jail, where their femininity made them especially vulnerable to sexual assault, rape, and murder.

This chronically bad situation became even worse in the mid-1960s, when U.S. involvement in the war in Vietnam escalated. Wartime is typically a time of heightened surveillance of commercial sexual activity in cities where large numbers of troops are being mobilized for deployment. . . . There were wartime crackdowns on prostitution in San Francisco during the Spanish-American War in the Philippines in the 1890s, during World War II in the 1940s, and during the Korean conflict in the 1950s. Among the hardest-hit establishments in San Francisco during the crackdown associated with the 1964–66 escalation of U.S. troops in Vietnam were the gay and drag bars, which even then catered to the "Don't ask, don't tell" military crowd.

Yet another factor that changed an already grim situation from bad to worse for transgender women in the Tenderloin was the effect of urban renewal and redevelopment. Their increasingly serious plight was directly related to very broad-scale social and economic changes. . . .

In response to the massive social dislocations of urban renewal and redevelopment, Tenderloin residents launched a grassroots campaign for economic justice in 1965. . . . Their immediate goal was to establish needed social services by qualifying the neighborhood for federal antipoverty funding. . . . The Tenderloin organizers not only had to document economic need in their neighborhood; they also had to persuade poor communities of color that adding an additional antipoverty target zone predominately populated by white people would be the right thing to do, even if that meant the already existing zones got a smaller slice of a fixed amount of money. Compounding matters even further, most of the white people were queer, and most of the people of color were straight. The eventual establishment of the Central City Anti-Poverty Program thus represented a singular accomplishment in the history of U.S. progressive politics: the first successful multiracial gay/straight alliance for economic justice.

Tenderloin activists involved in the antipoverty organizing campaign were striving to create conditions in which people could truly participate in structuring the society they lived in instead of just reacting to changes created by others. One unexpected consequence of neighborhood mobilization was the formation of Vanguard, an organization made up mostly of young gay hustlers and transgender people. Vanguard, which formed in the summer of 1966, is the earliest known queer youth organization in the United States. . . .

Vanguard described itself as "an organization of, by, and for the kids on the streets." Its goals were to promote a sense of self-worth among its members, to offer mutual support and companionship, to bring youth issues to the attention of older people, and to assert its presence in the neighborhood. One of the group's early flyers urged people to think past racial divisions and focus instead on shared living conditions: "You've heard about Black Power and White Power," the flyer said, before telling its readers to "get ready for Street Power." . . . Vanguard's first major political action . . . was to confront the management of Compton's Cafeteria over its poor treatment of transgender women. Compton's Cafeteria functioned as a chill-out lounge for the whole neighborhood; for young people who often had no homes, families, or legal employment, who were marginalized by their gender or sexuality, it provided an especially vital resource.

Vanguard held its meetings at Compton's, and during the course of the summer of 1966, tensions there had been on the rise. As the restaurant's customers increasingly claimed its turf as their own, the management asserted its property rights and business interests more and more strongly. It instituted a "service charge" for each customer to make up for income lost to tables of young people "camping out" and not buying any food, but it applied the charge in a discriminatory manner. It hired security guards to harass the street kids and shoo them outside, particularly the transgender youth. And with greater and greater frequency, it called the cops. In July, Vanguard worked with ministers from Glide [Glide Memorial United Methodist Church] and with older members of San Francisco's homophile organizations to set up a picket line protesting the mistreatment of its members, much as the customers and gay activists in Philadelphia had done at Dewey's. In San Francisco, however, the restaurant's management turned a deaf ear to the complaints. Soon after the picket failed to produce any results, frustration boiled over into militant resistance.

. . .

Looking back, it's easy to see how the Compton's Cafeteria riot in 1966 was related to very large-scale political, social, and economic developments and was not just an isolated little incident unrelated to other things that were going on in the world. The circumstances that created the conditions for the riot in the first place continue to be relevant in the transgender movement today: discriminatory policing practices in minority communities, harmful urban land-use policies, the unsettling domestic consequences of U.S. foreign wars, access to healthcare, civil rights activism aiming to expand individual liberties and social tolerance on matters of sexuality and gender, and political coalition building around the structural injustices that affect many different communities. The violent resistance to the oppression of transgender people at Compton's Cafeteria did not solve the problems that transgender people in the Tenderloin faced daily. It did, however, create a space in which it became possible for the city of San Francisco to begin relating differently to its transgender citizens—to begin treating them, in fact, as citizens with legitimate needs instead of simply as a problem to get rid of. That shift in awareness was a crucial step for the contemporary transgender social justice movement—the beginning of a new relationship to state power and social legitimacy. It would not have happened the way that it did without direct action in the streets on the part of transgender women who were fighting for their own survival.

. . .

77

The Impact of Juvenile Court on Queer and Trans/Gender-Non-Conforming Youth

Wesley Ware

. . .

Working with queer and trans/gender-non-conforming youth in the Deep South, I hear stories of state and personal violence from a wide range of people. There was the 16-year-old, black self-identified "stud" in detention after her mom referred her to family court for bringing girls to the house. Then there was the incarcerated white 16-year-old trans youth from a rural town of 642, whose access to transgender healthcare resided in the hands of one juvenile judge. I was told of a black trans feminine youth in New Orleans who was threatened with contempt for wearing feminine clothing to her court hearing. There was also the 12-year-old boy, perceived to be gay by his mother, who was brought into judge's chambers without his attorney and questioned about being gay before he was sentenced for contempt after being found "ungovernable." There was the public defender who refused to represent his gay client because the lawyer believed him to be "sick" and in need of the "services" offered by prison. And there was the black lesbian arrested over and over again for any crime where witnesses described the perpetrator as an African American "boyish-looking" girl. Nowhere is the literal regulation and policing of gender and sexuality, particularly of low-income queer and trans youth of color, so apparent than in juvenile courts and in the juvenile justice system in the South.

Understanding how the juvenile justice system operates and impacts queer and trans/gender-non-conforming youth requires a critical look at the history of youth rights and the inception of juvenile court. During the Industrial Revolution (1800–1840s), poor youth worked in factories, received no public education and were often arrested for the crime of poverty. These youth, some as young as 7 years old, were incarcerated with adults and placed in prisons until they were 21. Inspired by the belief that young people who committed crimes could be rehabilitated and shocked by the horrific treatment of white children in adult prisons, the juvenile justice system was developed. This new system was based on *parens patriae*, the idea that the role of the system was to place youth in the state's custody when their parents were unable to care for them. Later, in 1899, the first juvenile court was established, designed to "cure" children and provide treatments for them rather than sentences. Still rooted in a Puritan ideology, white young women were often sent to institutions "to protect them from sexual immorality."

Black children, however, who were viewed as incapable of rehabilitation, continued to be sent to adult prisons or were sent to racially segregated institutions. In Louisiana, black youth were sent to work the fields at Angola State Penitentiary, a former slave plantation, until 1948 when the State Industrial School for Colored Youth opened. The facilities were not desegregated until the United States District Court ordered desegregation of juvenile facilities in 1969. More recently, the goal of juvenile justice reform has been to keep youth in their homes and in their communities whenever possible while providing appropriate treatment services to youth and their families.

However, with the juvenile justice system's intent to provide "treatment" to young people, many queer/trans youth inherit the ideology that they are "wrong" or in need of "curing," as evidenced by their stories. As sexual and gender transgressions have been deemed both illegal and pathological, queer and trans youth, who are some of the most vulnerable to "treatments," are not only subjected to incarceration but also to harassment by staff, conversion therapy, and physical violence. . . .

Worse than just providing damaging outcomes for youth once they are incarcerated, this rehabilitative system funnels queer and trans/gender-non-conforming youth into the front doors of the system. Non-accepting parents and guardians can refer their children to family court for arbitrary and subjective behaviors, such as being "ungovernable." Police can bring youth in for status offenses, offenses for which adults cannot be charged, which often become contributing factors to the criminalization of youth. Charges can range from truancy to curfew violations to running away from home. Like in the adult criminal justice system, queer and trans youth can be profiled by the police and brought in for survival crimes like prostitution or theft. Youth may be referred for self-defense arising from conflict with hostile family members or public displays of affection in schools that selectively enforce policies only against queer and trans youth.

. . .

Further aggravated by the public's fear of youth sexuality and our desire to control young people and their bodies, juvenile court presents a unique opportunity to destroy the lives of queer and trans/gender-non-conforming youth. The agenda of juvenile court then, for queer and trans youth at least, often becomes to "rehabilitate" youth into fitting heteronormative and gender-typical molds. Guised under the "best interest of the child," the goal often becomes to "protect" the child—or perhaps society—from gender-variant or non-heterosexual behavior.

While not as explicit as the sumptuary laws (laws requiring people to wear at least three items of gender-appropriate clothing) or sodomy laws of the past that led to the Compton's Riots and Stonewall Rebellion, the policing of sexuality and state regulation of gender has continued to exist in practice—perhaps nowhere more than in juvenile courts. In many ways, the system still mirrors the adult criminal justice system, whose roots can be traced to slavery, the commodification of bodies as free labor, institutionalized racism, and state regulation of low-income people of color, immigrants, and anyone deemed otherwise "deviant" or a threat to the political norm. Combined with the Puritan beliefs that helped spark the creation of juvenile courts, it becomes clear that, borrowing the words of Audre Lorde, queer and trans youth of color "were never meant to survive."

. . .

Once locked up, queer and trans youth experience the same horrors that their adult counterparts in the system do, but magnified by a system designed to control, regulate, and pathologize their very existence. In Louisiana's youth prisons, queer and trans youth have been subjected to "sexual-identity confusion counseling," accused of using "gender identity issues" to detract from their rehabilitation, and disciplined for expressing any gender-non-conforming behaviors or actions. Youth are put on lock-down for having hair that is too long or wearing state-issued clothing that is too tight. They are instructed how to walk, talk, and act in their dorms and are prohibited from communicating with other queer youth lest they become too "flamboyant" and cause a disturbance. They are excessively punished for consensual same-sex behavior and spend much of their time in protective custody or in isolation cells. In meetings with representatives from the Juvenile Justice Project of Louisiana, directors of youth jails have referred to non-heterosexual identities as "symptoms" and have conflated youth adjudicated for sex offenses with youth who are queer. In addition, when advocates asked what the biggest problem was at a youth prison in Baker, Louisiana, guards replied, "the lesbians."

. . .

While protections afforded to youth in the juvenile justice system like a greater right to confidentiality are extremely important for youth, they can also be another strike against queer and trans youth seeking to access resources or support networks while inside. Like queer and trans adults in the criminal justice system who have difficulty receiving information that "promotes homosexuality," youth are unable to access affirming information during a particularly formative time in their lives, which can already be plagued with confusion and questioning. The right to confidentiality for youth in prison can result in their being prohibited from communicating with pen pals or seeking services from community organizations. Other rights are afforded to adults but not to minors, such as accessing legal counsel to challenge the conditions of their confinement. Youth under 18 must rely on their guardians to assist with filing a civil complaint, despite the fact that many queer and trans youth have had difficulty with their families prior to their incarceration—and that those family members may have contributed to their entering into the system in the first place. This barrier also holds true for transgender youth who are minors and seeking healthcare or hormones. . . .

Meanwhile, as state institutions are placing queer and trans/gender-non-conforming youth behind bars and effectively silencing their voices, prominent gay activists are fighting for inclusion in the very systems that criminalize youth of color (such as increased sentencing for hate crimes) under the banner of "we're just like everybody else." A far stray from the radicalism of the early gay rights movement, mainstream "gay issues" have become focused on the right to marry and "don't ask, don't tell" policies in the military, despite the fact that queer youth of color have consistently ranked these at the bottom of their list of priorities of issues that impact their lives. Likewise, the public "face of gay" as white, middle-class men has become a further detriment to queer and trans youth in prison. . . . [J]uvenile justice stakeholders . . . assume that any concern for these youth to be coming from white advocates who believe that queer and trans youth have been funneled into a system made for "poor black children;" in other words, into a system that is "OK for some children, but not for others." We must be clear about why we do this work—it is not because *some* children belong locked away at night and others do not—it is because *no* child should be behind bars.

Further, the data tells us that queer and trans youth in detention are equally distributed across race and ethnicity, and comprise 15 percent of youth in detention centers. So far, the data has been consistent among youth in different regions in the United States, including the rural South. Since queer and trans youth are overrepresented in nearly all popular feeders into the juvenile justice system—homelessness, difficulty in school, substance abuse, and difficulty with mental health—the same societal ills, which disproportionately affect youth of color—it should not be surprising that they may be overrepresented in youth prisons and jails as well.

Since incarcerated youth have so few opportunities to speak out, it is critically important for individuals and organizations doing this work to keep a political analysis of the failings of the system at the forefront of the work—particularly the inherent racial disparities in the system—while highlighting the voices of those youth who are most affected and providing vehicles through which they can share their stories.

Despite the targeting and subsequent silencing of queer and trans/gender-non-conforming youth in youth prisons and jails across Louisiana, young people have developed creative acts of resistance and mechanisms for self-preservation and survival. By failing to recognize the ways that young people demonstrate their own agency and affirm each other, we risk perpetuating the idea of vulnerable youth with little agency; victims rather than survivors and active resisters of a brutal system.

. . .

Although prohibited from even speaking publicly with other queer youth in prison, queer and trans youth have formed community across three youth prisons in the state, whispered through fences, and passed messages through sympathetic staff. They have made matching bracelets and necklaces for one another, gotten each other's initials tattooed on their bodies, and written letters to each other's mothers. They have supported each other by alerting advocates when one of them was on lock-down or in trouble and unable to call.

Trans-feminine youth have gone to lockdown instead of cutting their hair and used their bed sheets to design curtains for their cells once they got there. They have smuggled in Kool-Aid to dye their hair, secretly shaved their legs, colored their fingernails with markers, and used crayons for eye shadow. When a lawyer asked her trans-masculine client to dress more "feminine" for court, knowing that the judge was increasingly hostile toward gender-non-conforming youth, her client drew the line at the skirt, fearlessly and proudly demanding that she receive her sentence in baggy pants instead.

Queer and trans/gender-non-conforming youth have made us question the very purpose of the juvenile justice system and holding them behind bars in jails and prisons made for kids. By listening to their voices it becomes apparent that until we dismantle state systems designed to criminalize and police young people and variant expressions of gender and sexuality, none of us will be free. . . .

78

Feminism and Abolition

Theories and Practices for the Twenty-First Century

Angela Y. Davis

Speech delivered at the Center for the Study of Race, Politics, and Culture Annual Public Lecture, in collaboration with the Center for the Study of Gender and Sexuality at the University of Chicago (May 4, 2013).

Let me say, this is the first time in many years that I have spent an extended period of time in Chicago, that is to say, four days—four whole days . . . .

And it is wonderful to be here . . . This amazing city has such a history of struggle. It's the city of the Haymarket Martyrs, the city of radical labor unions, the city of resistance to the police assassinations of Fred Hampton and Mark Clark. It's the city of Puerto Rican activism against colonialism. It's the city of immigrant rights activists. And of course it is the city of the Chicago Teachers Union . . .

And this is a good way to stage out discussion of feminism and abolition, which I consider to be essential theories and practices for the twenty-first century. Assata Shakur exemplifies within feminist struggles and theories the way Black women's representations and their involvement in revolutionary struggles militated against prevailing ideological assumptions about women.

In fact, during the latter twentieth century, there were numerous debates about how to define the category "woman." There were numerous struggles over who got included and who was excluded from that category. And these struggles, I think, are key to understanding why there was some measure of resistance from women of color, and also poor and working-class white women, to identity with the emergent feminist movement. Many of us considered that movement at that time to be too white and especially too middle class, too bourgeois.

And in some sense the struggle for women's rights was ideologically defined as a struggle for white middle-class women's rights, pushing out working-class and poor women, pushing out Black women, Latinas, and other women of color from the discursive field covered by the category "woman." The many contestations over this category helped to produce what we came to call "radical women-of-color feminist theories and practices."

At the very time these questions were being raised, these questions about the universality of the category "woman," similar concerns about the category "human" were being debated, especially in relation to the underlying individualism of human rights discourses. How could this category be rethought? Not only to embrace Africans, indigenous people, other non-Europeans, but how it might apply to groups and communities as well, not only to individuals. And then of course the slogan "Women's Rights Are Human Rights" began to emerge in the aftermath of an amazing conference that took place in 1985 in Nairobi, Kenya. . . .

At the conference, for the very first time, there was a very large delegation of US women of color. And I think it was the first time that US women of color became active in an international arena. The problem was that many of us then thought that what we needed to do was to expand the category "woman" so that it could embrace Black women, Latina women, Native American women, and so forth. We thought that by doing that we would have effectively addressed the problem of the exclusivity of the category. What we didn't realize then was that we would have to rewrite the whole category, rather than simply assimilate more women into an unchanged category of what counts as "women."

Now a few years earlier, 1979, a white woman by the name of Sandy Stone was working at a feminist recording company Olivia Records. Some of you may remember Olivia Records. This woman was broadly attacked by some self-defined lesbian feminists for not really being a woman, and for bringing masculine energy into women's spaces. As it turns out, Sandy Stone was a trans woman, who later wrote some of the germinal texts in the development of transgender studies. This woman was not considered a woman because she was assigned the gender designation of "male" at birth. But this did not prevent her from later asserting a very different gender identity.

So let me fast-forward to the present, when scholars and activists are engaging with questions of prison abolition and gender non-conformity, and have produced some of the most interesting theories, some of the most interesting ideas and approaches to activism. . . .

Let's visit the San Francisco Bay Area where I live, and an organization that is called Transgender, Gender Variant, Intersex Justice Project. Now, TGI Justice Project is an organization led by women of color, by trans women of color. The executive director is a woman whose name is Miss Major. And, yeah, I'll tell Miss Major that she got a lot of applause in Chicago, and that's especially important because she was raised on the South Side of Chicago, not very far from here. She describes herself as a Black, formerly incarcerated, male-to-female transgender elder, born and raised on the South Side of Chicago, and a veteran activist. She participated in the Stonewall Rebellion in 1969. But she said she was not really politicized until the wake of the Attica Prison Rebellion. I was just talking to her the other day and learned that the person who politicized her is Big Black, one of the Attica defendants and a close friend of mine until his death. Frank Smith was known as Big Black, one of the leaders of the Attica Rebellion, who eventually won a lawsuit against the state of New York in connection with Attica. Miss Major met him in prison. She said that he was not only totally accepting of her gender presentation, but he instructed her on so many issues regarding the relationship between racism, and imperialism, and capitalism.

Now, TGI Justice Project is a grassroots organization that advocates for, defends, and includes primarily trans women and trans women of color. These are women who have to fight to be included within the category "woman" in a way that is not dissimilar from the earlier struggles of Black women and women of color who were assigned the gender female at birth. Moreover, they have worked out what I see as a deeply feminist approach that we would do well to understand and emulate.

Miss Major says she prefers to be called Miss Major, not Ms. Major, because as a trans woman she is not yet liberated. The work of TGIJP is deeply feminist because it is performed at the intersection of race, class, sexuality, and gender, and because it moves from addressing the individual predicaments of the members of their community, who constitute the individuals who are *most* harassed by law enforcement, *most* arrested and incarcerated, to large questions of the prison industrial complex. Trans women of color end up primarily in male prisons—especially if they have not undergone gender reassignment surgery, and many of them don't want to undergo that surgery. And sometimes even if they have undergone the surgery, they end up being placed in men's prisons. After they are imprisoned they often receive more violent treatment by the guards than anyone else, and on top of that, they are marked by the institution as targets of male violence. This is so much the case that cops so easily joke about the sexual fate of trans women in the male prisons where they are usually sent. Male prisons are represented as violent places. But we see, especially by looking at the predicament of trans women, that this violence is often encouraged by the institutions themselves.

Many of you are familiar with the Minneapolis case of CeCe McDonald, who was charged with murder after an encounter with a group that yelled out racist, homophobic, and transphobic slurs all at the same time. She . . . [was sent to] a men's prison in Minnesota, serving a three-and-a-half-year sentence. But on top of this violence, trans women are often denied their hormonal treatments, even if they have valid prescriptions.

The point that I'm trying to make is that we learn a great deal about the reach of the prison system, about the nature of the prison-industrial complex, about the reach of abolition by examining the particular struggles of trans prisoners, and especially trans women. Perhaps most important of all, and this is so central to the development of feminist abolitionist theories and practices: we have to learn how to think and act and struggle against that which is ideologically constituted as "normal." Prisons are constituted as "normal." It takes a lot of work to persuade people to think beyond the bars, and to be able to imagine a world without prisons and to struggle for the abolition of imprisonment as the dominant mode of punishment.

And we can ask ourselves in that context, why are trans women—and especially Black trans women who cannot easily pass—why are they considered so far outside the norm? They are considered outside the norm by almost everyone in the society.

And of course we're learned a great deal about gender over the past decades. I suppose just about everyone who's in the field of feminist studies has read Judith Butler's *Gender Trouble*. But you should also read Beth Richie's most recent book, an amazing book called *Arrested Justice: Black Women, Violence and America's Prison Nation*. And specifically look at her account of the case of the New Jersey Four, of four young Black lesbians who were just walking around having fun in Greenwich Village, but ended up in prison because they defended themselves from male violence. This violence was further consolidated by the fact that they saw themselves represented in the media as "a lesbian wolf pack." We see that here race, gender, sexual nonconformity can lead to racist bestialization! Which is an attack, as one of my students, Eric Stanley, points out in his dissertation, not only against the humans but against the animals as well.

TGI Justice Project is an abolitionist organization. It calls for a dialectic of service provision and abolitionist advocacy. TGIJP thus promotes a kind of feminism that urges us to be flexible, one that warns us not to become too attached to our objects, whether they are objects of study—I say that for the academics in the house—or whether they are objects of our organizing—I say this for the activists in the house.

TGI Justice Project shows us that these objects can become something entirely different as a result of our work. It shows us that the process of trying to assimilate into an existing category in many ways runs counter to efforts to produce radical or revolutionary results. And it shows us that we not only should not try to assimilate trans women into a category that remains the same, but that the category itself has to change so it does not simply reflect normative ideas of who counts as women and who doesn't.

But by extension, there's another lesson: don't even become too attached to the concept of gender. Because, as a matter of fact, the more closely we examine it, the more we discover that it is embedded in a range of social, political, cultural, and ideological formations. It is not one thing. There is not one definition, and certainly gender cannot now be adequately described as a binary structure with "male" being one pole and "female" at the other.

And so, bringing trans women, trans men, intersex, many other forms of gender nonconformity into the concept of gender, it radically undermines the normative assumptions of the very concept of gender . . .

Feminism involves so much more than gender equality. And it involves so much more than gender. Feminism must involve a consciousness of capitalism—I mean, the feminism that I relate to. And there are multiple feminisms, right? It has to involve a consciousness of capitalism, and racism, and colonialism, and postcolonialities, and ability, and more genders than we can even imagine, and more sexualities than we ever thought we could name. Feminism has helped us not only to recognize a range of connections among discourses, and institutions, and identities, and ideologies that we often tend to consider separately. But it has also helped us to develop epistemological and organizing strategies that take us beyond the categories "women" and "gender." And, feminist methodologies impel us to explore connections that are not always apparent. And they drive us to inhabit contradictions and discover what is productive in these contradictions. Feminism insists on methods of thought and action that urge us to think about things together that appear to be separate, and to disaggregate things that appear to naturally belong together.

Now, the assumption has been that because transgender and gender-nonconforming populations are relatively small (for example, within a prison system that in the US constitutes almost 2.5 million people and more than 8 million people in jails and prisons worldwide), therefore, why should they deserve very much attention? But feminist approaches to the understanding of prisons, and indeed the prison-industrial complex, have always insisted that, for example, if we look at imprisoned women, who are also a very small percentage throughout the world, we learn not only about women in prison, but we learn much more about the system as a whole than we would learn if we look exclusively at men. Thus, also, a feminist approach would insist both on what we can learn from, and what we can transform, with respect to trans and gender-nonconforming prisoners, but also it insists on what knowledge and activism tells us about the nature of punishment writ large—about the very apparatus of prison.

It is true that we cannot begin to think about the abolition of prisons outside of an antiracist context. It is also true that antiprison abolition embraces or should embrace the abolition of gender policing. That very process reveals the epistemic violence—and the feminist studies students in here know what I'm talking about—the epistemic violence that is inherent in the gender binary in the larger society.

So bringing feminism within an abolitionist frame, and vice versa, bringing abolition within a feminist frame, means that we take seriously the old feminist adage that "the personal is political." . . .

And it seems to me that people who are working on the front line of the struggle against violence against women should also be on the front line of abolitionist struggles. And people opposed to police crimes, should also be opposed to domestic—what is constructed as domestic—violence. We should understand the connections between public violence and private or privatized violence . . .

We have had to unlearn a great deal over the course of the last few decades. We have had to try to unlearn racism, and I am speaking not only about white people. People of color have had to unlearn the assumption that racism is individual, that it is primarily a question of individual attitudes that can be dealt with through sensitivity training . . .

Prisons are racism incarnate. As Michelle Alexander points out, they constitute the new Jim Crow. But also much more, as the lynchpins of the prison-industrial complex, they represent the increasing profitability of punishment. They represent the increasingly global strategy of dealing with populations of people of color and immigrant populations from the countries of the Global South as surplus population, as disposable populations.

Put them all in a vast garbage bin, add some sophisticated electronic technology to control them, and let them languish there. And in the meantime, create the ideological illusion that the surrounding society is safer and more free because the dangerous Black people and Latinos, and the Native Americans, and the dangerous Asians and the dangerous White people, and of course the dangerous Muslims, are locked up!

And in the meantime, corporations profit and poor communities suffer! Public education suffers! Public education suffers because it is not profitable according to corporate measures. Public health care suffers. If punishment can be profitable, then certainly health care should be profitable, too. This is absolutely outrageous! It is outrageous. . . .

And let me say that I really love the new generations of young students and workers. Two generations removed from my own; they say sometimes revolution skips a generation. But that skipped generation has also worked hard! Those of you who are in your forties, if you hadn't done the work that you did, then it would not be possible for the younger generation to emerge. And what I like most about the younger generation is that they are truly informed by feminism. Even if they don't know it, or even if they don't admit it! They are informed by antiracist struggles. They are not infected with the emotionally damaging homophobia which has been with us for so long. And they are taking the lead in challenging transphobia along with racism and Islamophobia. So I like working with young people because they allow me to imagine what it is like not to be so totally overburdened with decades of oppressive ideology.

Now, I just have a couple of more things to say. I know I'm over my time and I apologize. But I just have one more page of notes. [*Laughter*]

And so let me say that marriage equality is more and more acceptable precisely because of young people. But, many of these young people also remind us that we have to challenge the assimilationist logic of the struggle for marriage equality! We cannot assume that once outsiders are allowed to move into the circle of the bourgeois hetero-patriarchal institution of marriage, the struggle has been won.

Now, the story of the interrelationships between feminism and abolitionism has no appropriate end. And with this conversation we have just begun to explore a few of its dimensions. But if I have not come to the end of the story, I have certainly come to the end of my time. So I want to let Assata Shakur have the last word tonight. "At this moment," she wrote a few years ago:

> I am not so concerned about myself. Everybody has to die sometime, and all I want is to go with dignity. I am more concerned about the growing poverty, the growing despair that is rife in America. I am more concerned about our younger generations, who represent our future. I am more concerned about the rise of the prison-industrial complex that is turning our people into slaves again. I am more concerned about the repression, the police brutality, violence, the rising wave of racism that makes up the political landscape of the US today. Our young people deserve a future, and I consider it the mandate of my ancestors to be a part of the struggle to ensure that they have one.

79

Bones

Lindy West

I've always been a great big person. In the months after I was born, the doctor was so alarmed by the circumference of my head that she insisted my parents bring me back, over and over, to be weighed and measured and held up for scrutiny next to the "normal" babies. My head was "off the charts," she said. Science literally had not produced a chart expansive enough to account for my monster dome. "Off the charts" became a West family joke over the years—I always deflected, saying it was because of my giant brain—but I absorbed the message nonetheless. I was too big, from birth. Abnormally big. Medical-anomaly big. Unchartably big.

There were people-sized people, and then there was me.

So, what do you do when you're too big, in a world where bigness is cast not only as aesthetically objectionable, but also as a moral failing? You fold yourself up like origami, you make yourself smaller in other ways, you take up less space with your personality, since you can't with your body. You diet. You starve, you run till you taste blood in your throat, you count out your almonds, you try to buy back your humanity with pounds of flesh.

I got good at being small early on—socially, if not physically. In public, until I was eight, I would speak only to my mother, and even then, only in whispers, pressing my face into her leg. I retreated into fantasy novels, movies, computer games, and, eventually, comedy— places where I could feel safe, assume any personality, fit into any space. I preferred tracing to drawing. Drawing was too bold an act of creation, too presumptuous.

My dad was friends with Bob Dorough, an old jazz guy who wrote all the songs for *Multiplication Rock*, *Schoolhouse Rock*'s math-themed sibling. He's that breezy, froggy voice on "Three Is a Magic Number"—you'd recognize it. "A man and a woman had a little baby, yes, they did. They had three-ee-ee in the family . . ." Bob signed a vinyl copy of *Multiplication Rock* for me when I was two or three years old. "Dear Lindy," it said, "get big!" I hid that record, as a teenager, afraid that people would see the inscription and think, "She took *that* a little too seriously."

I dislike "big" as a euphemism, maybe because it's the one chosen most often by people who mean well, who love me and are trying to be gentle with my feelings. I don't want the people who love me to avoid the reality of my body. I don't want them to feel uncomfortable with its size and shape, to tacitly endorse the idea that fat is shameful, to pretend I'm something I'm not out of deference to a system that hates me. I don't want to be gentled, like I'm something wild and alarming. (If I'm going to be wild and alarming, I'll do it on my terms.) I don't want them to think that I need a euphemism at all.

"Big" is a word we use to cajole a child: "Be a big girl!" "Act like the big kids!" Having it applied to you as an adult is a cloaked reminder of what people really think, of the way we infantilize and desexualize fat people. (Desexualization is just another form of sexualisation. Telling fat women they're sexless is still putting women in their sexual place.) Fat people are helpless babies enslaved to their most capricious cravings. Fat people do not know what's best for them. Fat people need to be guided and scolded like children. Having that awkward, babyish word dragging on you every day of your life, from childhood into maturity, well, maybe it's no wonder that I prefer hot chocolate to whiskey and substitute Harry Potter audiobooks for therapy.

Every cell in my body would rather be "fat" than "big." Grown-ups speak the truth.

Please don't forget: I am my body. When my body gets smaller, it is still me. When my body gets bigger, it is still me. There is not a thin woman inside me, awaiting excavation. I am one piece. I am also not a uterus riding around in a meat incubator. There is no substantive difference between the repulsive campaign to separate women's bodies from their reproductive systems—perpetuating the lie that abortion and birth control are not healthcare—and the repulsive campaign to convince women that they and their body size are separate, alienated entities. Both say, "Your body is not yours." Both demand, "Beg for your humanity." Both insist, "Your autonomy is conditional." This is why fat is a feminist issue.

All my life people have told me that my body doesn't belong to me.

As a teenager, I was walking down the street in Seattle's International District, when an old woman rushed up to me and pushed a business card into my hand. The card was covered in characters I couldn't read, but at the bottom it was translated: "WEIGHT LOSS/FAT BURN." I tried to hand it back, "Oh, no thank you," but the woman gestured up and down at my body, up and down. "Too fat," she said. "You call."

Over time, the knowledge that I was too big made my life smaller and smaller. I insisted that shoes and accessories were just "my thing," because my friends didn't realize that I couldn't shop for clothes at a regular store and I was too mortified to explain it to them. I backed out of dinner plans if I remembered the restaurant had particularly narrow aisles or rickety chairs. I ordered salad even if everyone else was having fish and chips. I pretended to hate skiing because my giant men's ski pants made me look like a smokestack and I was terrified my bulk would tip me off the chairlift. I stayed home as my friends went hiking, biking, sailing, climbing, diving, exploring—I was sure I couldn't keep up, and what if we got into a scrape? They couldn't boost me up a cliff or lower me down an embankment or squeeze me through a tight fissure or hoist me from the hot jaws of a bear. I never revealed a single crush, convinced that the idea of my disgusting body as a sexual being would send people—even people who loved me—into fits of projectile vomiting (or worse, pity). I didn't go swimming for a fucking decade.

As I imperceptibly rounded the corner into adulthood—fourteen, fifteen, sixteen, seventeen—I watched my friends elongate and arch into these effortless, exquisite things. I waited. I remained a stump. I wasn't jealous, exactly; I loved them, but I felt cheated.

We each get just a few years to be perfect. That's what I'd been sold. To be young and smooth and decorative and collectible. I was missing my window. I could feel it pulling at my navel (my obsessively hidden, hated navel), and I scrabbled, desperate and frantic. Deep down, in my honest places, I knew it was already gone—I had stretch marks and cellulite long before twenty—but they tell you that if you hate yourself hard enough, you can grab just a tail feather or two of perfection. Chasing perfection was your duty and your birthright, as a woman, and I would never know what it was like—this thing, this most important thing for girls.

I missed it, I failed. I wasn't a woman. You only get one life. I missed it.

There is a certain kind of woman. She is graceful. She is slim. Yes, she would like to go kayaking with you. On her frame, angular but soft, a baggy T-shirt is coded as "low-maintenance," not "sloppy"; a ponytail is "sleek," not "tennis ball on top of a mini-fridge." Not only can she pull off ugly clothes, like sports sandals, or "boyfriend jeans," they somehow make her beauty thrum even more clearly. She is thrifted J. Crew. She can put her feet up on a chair and draw her knees to her chest. She can hold an ocean in her clavicle.

People go on and on about boobs and butts and teeny waists, but the clavicle is the true benchmark of female desirability. It is a fetish item. Without visible clavicles you might as well be a meatloaf in the sexual marketplace. And I don't mean Meatloaf the person, who has probably gotten laid lotsa times despite the fact that his clavicle is buried so deep as to be mere urban legend, because our culture does not have a creepy sexual fixation on the bones of meaty men.

Only women. Show us your bones, they say. If only you were nothing but bones.

America's monomaniacal fixation on female thinness isn't a distant abstraction, something to be pulled apart by academics in women's studies classrooms or leveraged for traffic in shallow "body-positive" listicles ("Check Out These Eleven Fat Chicks Who You Somehow Still Kind of Want to Bang—Number Seven Is Like a Regular Woman!")—it is a constant, pervasive taint that warps every single woman's life. And, by extension, it is in the amniotic fluid of every major cultural shift.

Women matter. Women are half of us. When you raise every woman to believe that we are insignificant, that we are broken, that we are sick, that the only cure is starvation and restraint and smallness; when you pit women against one another, keep us shackled by shame and hunger, obsessing over our flaws rather than our power and potential; when you leverage all of that to sap our money and our time—that moves the rudder of the world. It steers humanity toward conservatism and walls and the narrow interests of men, and it keeps us adrift in waters where women's safety and humanity are secondary to men's pleasure and convenience.

I watched my friends become slender and beautiful, I watched them get picked and wear J. Crew and step into small boats without fear, but I also watched them starve and harm themselves, get lost and sink. They were picked by bad people, people who hurt them on purpose, eroded their confidence, and kept them trapped in an endless chase. The real scam is that being bones isn't enough either. The game is rigged. There is no perfection.

I listened to Howard Stern every morning in college. I loved Howard. I still do, though I had to achingly bow out as my feminism solidified. (In a certain light, feminism is just the long, slow realization that the stuff you love hates you.) When I say I used to listen to Stern, a lot of people look at me like I said I used to eat cat meat, but what they don't understand is that *That Howard Stern Show* is on the air for hours and hours every day. Yes, there is gleeful, persistent misogyny, but the bulk of it, back when I was a daily obsessive, at least, was Howard seeking validation for his neuroses; Robin cackling about her runner's diarrhea; Artie detailing the leviathan sandwich he'd eaten yesterday in a heroin stupor, then weeping over his debasement; Howard wheedling truth out of cagey celebrities like a surgeon; Howard buoying the news with supernatural comic timing; a Sagrada Familia of inside jokes and references and memories and love and people's lives willingly gutted and splayed open and dissected every day for the sake of good radio. It was magnificent entertainment. It felt like a family.

Except, for female listeners, membership in that family came at a price. Howard would do this thing (the thing, I think, that most non-listeners associate with the show) where hot chicks could turn up at the studio and he would look them over like a fucking horse vet—running his hand over their withers and flanks, inspecting their bite and the sway of their back, honking their massive horse jugs—and tell them, in intricate detail, what was wrong with their bodies. There was literally always something. If they were 110 pounds, they could stand to be 100. If they were 90, gross. ("Why'd you do that to your body, sweetie?"). If they were a C cup, they'd be hotter as a DD. They should stop working out so much—those legs are too muscular. Their 29-inch waist was subpar—come back when it's a 26.

Then there was me: 225, 40-inch waist, no idea what bra size because I'd never bothered to buy a nice one because who would see it? Frumpy, miserable, cylindrical. The distance between my failure of a body and perfection stretched away beyond the horizon. According to Howard, even girls who were there weren't there.

If you want to be a part of this community that you love, I realized—this family that keeps you sane in a shitty, boring world, this million-dollar enterprise that you fund with your consumer clout, just as much as male listeners do—you have to participate, with a smile, in your own disintegration. You have to swallow, every day, that you are a secondary being whose worth is measured by an arbitrary, impossible standard, administered by men.

When I was twenty-two, and all I wanted was to blend in, that rejection was crushing and hopeless and lonely. Years later, when I was finally ready to stand out, the realization that the mainstream didn't want me was freeing and galvanizing. It gave me something to fight for. It taught me that women are an army.

When I look at photographs of my twenty-two-year-old self, so convinced of her own defectiveness, I see a perfectly normal girl and I think about aliens. If an alien came to earth—a gaseous orb or a polyamorous cat person or whatever—it wouldn't even be able to tell the difference between me and Angelina Jolie, let alone rank us by hotness. It'd be like, "Uh, yeah, so those ones have the under-the-face fat sacks, and the other kind has that dangly pants nose. Fuck, these things are gross. I can't wait to get back to the omnidirectional orgy gardens of Vlaxnoid 7."

The "perfect body" is a lie. I believed in it for a long time, and I let it shape my life, and shrink it—my real life, populated by my real body. Don't let fiction tell you what to do.

In the omnidirectional orgy gardens of Vlaxnoid 7, no one cares about your arm flab.

80

Men Explain Things to Me

Rebecca Solnit

I still don't know why Sallie and I bothered to go to that party in the forest slope above Aspen. The people were all older than us and dull in a distinguished way, old enough that we, at forty-ish, passed as the occasion's young ladies. We were preparing to leave, when our host said, "No, stay a little longer so I can talk to you." He was an imposing man who'd made a lot of money.

He kept us waiting while the other guests drifted out into the summer night, and then sat us down at his authentically grainy wood table and said to me, "So? I hear you've written a couple of books."

I replied, "Several, actually."

He said, in the way you encourage your friend's seven-year-old to describe flute practice, "And what are they about?"

They were actually about quite a few different things, the six or seven out by then, but I began to speak only of the most recent on that summer day in 2003, *River of Shadows: Eadweard Muybridge and the Technological Wild West*, my book on the annihilation of time and space and the industrialization of everyday life.

He cut me off soon after I mentioned Muybridge. "And have you heard about the *very important* Muybridge book that came out this year?"

So caught up was I in my assigned role as ingénue that I was perfectly willing to entertain the possibility that another book on the same subject had come out simultaneously and I'd somehow missed it. He was already telling me about the very important book—with that smug look I know so well in a man holding forth, eyes fixed on the fuzzy far horizon of his own authority.

Here, let me just say that my life is well sprinkled with lovely men, with a long succession of editors who have, since I was young, listened to and encouraged and published me, and with my infinitely generous younger brother. Still, there are these other men, too. So, Mr. Very Important was going on smugly about this book I should have known when Sallie interrupted him, to say, "That's her book." Or tried to interrupt him anyway.

But he just continued on his way. She had to say, "That's her book" three or four times before he finally took it in. And then, as if in a nineteenth-century novel, he went ashen. That I was indeed the author of the very important book it turned out he hadn't read, just read about in the *New York Times Book Review* a few months earlier, so confused the neat categories into which his world was sorted that he was stunned speechless—for a moment, before he began holding forth again. Being women, we were politely out of earshot before we started laughing, and we've never really stopped.

I like incidents of that sort, when forces that are usually so sneaky and hard to point out slither out of the grass and are as obvious as, say, an anaconda that's eaten a cow or an elephant turd on the carpet.

THE SLIPPERY SLOPE OF SILENCINGS

Yes, people of both genders pop up at events to hold forth on irrelevant things and conspiracy theories, but the out-and-out confrontational confidence of the totally ignorant is, in my experience, gendered. Men explain things to me, and other women, whether or not they know what they're talking about. Some men.

Every woman knows what I'm talking about. It's the presumption that makes it hard, at times, for any woman in any field; that keeps women from speaking up and from being heard when they dare; that crushes young women into silence by indicating, the way harassment on the street does, that this is not their world. It trains us in self-doubt and self-limitation just as it exercises men's unsupported overconfidence . . .

This syndrome is a war that nearly every woman faces every day: a war within herself, a belief in her superfluity, and an invitation to silence, one from which a fairly nice career as a writer (with a lot of research and facts correctly deployed) has not entirely freed me. After all, there was a moment there when I was willing to let Mr. Important and his overweening confidence bowl over my more shaky certainty.

Don't forget that I've had a lot more confirmation of my right to think and speak than most women, and I've learned that a certain amount of self-doubt is a good tool for correcting, understanding, listening, and progressing—though too much is paralyzing and total self-confidence produces arrogant idiots. There's a happy medium between these poles to which the genders have been pushed, a warm equatorial belt of give and take where we should all meet.

Credibility is a basic survival tool. When I was very young and just beginning to get what feminism was about and why it was necessary, I had a boyfriend whose uncle was a nuclear physicist. One Christmas, he was telling—as though it were a light and amusing subject— how a neighbor's wife in his suburban bomb-making community had come running out of her house naked in the middle of the night screaming that her husband was trying to kill her. How, I asked, did you know that he wasn't trying to kill her? He explained, patiently, that they were respectable middle-class people. Therefore, her-husband-trying-to-kill-her was simply not a credible explanation for her fleeing the house yelling that her husband was trying to kill her. That she was crazy, on the other hand . . .

Even getting a restraining order—a fairly new legal tool—requires acquiring the credibility to convince the courts that some guy is a menace and then getting the cops to enforce it. Restraining orders often don't work anyway. Violence is one way to silence people, to deny their voice and their credibility, to assert your right to control over their right to exist. About three women a day are murdered by spouses or ex-spouses in this country. It's one of the main causes of death for pregnant women in the United States. At the heart of the struggle of feminism is to give rape, date rape, marital rape, domestic violence, and workplace sexual harassment legal standing as crimes has been the necessity of making women credible and audible.

I tend to believe that women acquired the status of human beings when these kinds of acts started to be taken seriously, when the big things that stop us and kill us were addressed legally from the mid-1970s on; well after, that is, my birth. And for anyone about to argue that workplace sexual intimidation isn't a life-or-death issue, remember that Marine Lance Corporal Maria Lauterback, age twenty, was apparently killed by her higher-ranking colleague one winter's night while she was waiting to testify that he raped her. The burned remains of her pregnant body were found in the fire pit in his backyard.

After my book *Wanderlust* came out in 2000, I found myself better able to resist being bullied out of my own perceptions and interpretations. Having public standing as a writer of history helped me stand my ground, but few women get that boost, and billions of women must be out there on this seven-billion-person planet being told that they are not reliable witnesses to their own lives, that the truth is not their property, now or ever. This goes way beyond Men Explaining Things, but it's part of the same archipelago of arrogance.

Men explain things to me, still. And no man has ever apologized for explaining, wrongly, things that I know and they don't. Not yet, but according to the actuarial tables, I may have another forty-something years to live, more or less, so it could happen. Though I'm not holding my breath.

WOMEN FIGHTING ON TWO FRONTS

A few years after the idiot in Aspen, I was in Berlin giving a talk when the Marxist writer Tariq Ali invited me out to a dinner that included a male writer and translator and three women a little younger than me who would remain deferential and mostly silent throughout the dinner. Tariq was great. Perhaps the translator was peeved that I insisted on playing a modest role in the conversation, but when I said something about how Women Strike for Peace, the extraordinary, little-known antinuclear and antiwar group founded in 1961, helped bring down the communist-hunting House Committee on Un-American Activities, HUAC, Mr. Very Important II sneered at me. "HUAC," he insisted, "didn't exist by the early 1960s and, anyway, no women's group played such a role in HUAC's downfall." His scorn was so withering, his confidence so aggressive, that arguing with him seemed a scary exercise in futility and an invitation to more insult.

I think I was at nine books at that point, including one that drew from primary documents about and interviews with a key member of Women Strike for Peace. But explaining men still assume I am, in some sort of obscene impregnation metaphor, an empty vessel to be filled with their wisdom and knowledge. Back in my hotel room, I searched online a bit and found that Eric Bentley in his definitive history of the House Committee on Un-American Activities credits Women Strike for Peace with "striking the crucial blow in the fall of HUAC's Bastille." In the early 1960s.

So I opened an essay (on Jane Jacobs, Betty Friedan, and Rachel Carson) for the *Nation* with this interchange, in part as a shout-out to one of the more unpleasant men who have explained things to me: Dude, if you're reading this, you're a carbuncle on the face of humanity and an obstacle to civilization. Feel the shame.

. . . Most women fight wars on two fronts, one for whatever the putative topic is and one simply for the right to speak, to have ideas, to be acknowledged to be in possession of facts and truths, to have value, to be a human being. Things have gotten better, but this war won't end in my lifetime. I'm still fighting it, for myself certainly, but also for all those younger women who have something to say, in the hope that they will get to say it.

POSTSCRIPT

One evening over dinner in March 2008, I began to joke, as I often had before, about writing an essay called "Men Explain Things to Me." Every writer has a stable of ideas that never make it to the racetrack, and I'd been trotting this pony out recreationally once in a while. My houseguest, the brilliant theorist and activist Marina Sitrin, insisted that I had to write it down because people like her younger sister Sam needed to read it. Young women, she said, needed to know that being belittled wasn't the result of their own secret failings; it was the boring old gender wars, and it happened to most of us who were female at some point or other.

I wrote it in one sitting early the next morning. When something assembles itself that fast, it's clear it's been composing itself somewhere in the unknowable back of the mind for a long time. It wanted to be written; it was restless for the racetrack; it galloped along once I sat down at the computer. Later that day I sent it to Tom Engelhardt at TomDispatch, who published it online soon after. It spread quickly and has never stopped going around, being reposted and shared and commented upon. It's circulated like nothing else I've done.

It struck a chord. And a nerve.

Some men explained why men explaining things to women wasn't really a gendered phenomenon. Usually, women then pointed out that, in insisting on their right to dismiss the experiences women say they have, men succeeded in explaining in just the way I said they sometimes do.

Other men got it and were cool. This was, after all, written in the era when male feminists had become a more meaningful presence, and feminism was funnier than ever. Not everyone knew they were funny, however. In 2008, I got an email from an older man in Indianapolis, who wrote in to tell me that he had "never personally or professionally shortchanged a woman" and went on to berate me for not hanging out with "more regular guys or least do a little homework first." He then gave me some advice about how to run my life and commented on my "feelings of inferiority." He thought that being patronized was an experience a woman chooses to have, or could choose not to have—and so the fault was all mine.

A website named "Academic Men Explain Things to Me" arose, and hundreds of university women shared their stories of being patronized, belittled, talked over, and more. The term "mansplaining" was coined soon after the piece appeared, and I was sometimes credited with it. In fact, I had nothing to do with its actual creation, though my essay, along with all the men who embodied the idea, apparently inspired it. . . . By 2012, the term "mansplained"—one of the *New York Times*'s words of the year for 2010—was being used in mainstream political journalism.

Alas, this was because it dovetailed pretty well with the times. TomDispatch reposted "Men Explain Things" in August 2012, and fortuitously, more or less simultaneously, Representative Todd Akin (R–Missouri) made his infamous statement that we don't need abortion for women who are raped, because "if it's legitimate rape, the female body has ways to try to shut the whole thing down." That electoral season was peppered by the crazy pro-rape, anti-fact statements of male conservatives. And salted with feminists pointing out why feminism is necessary and why these guys are scary. It was nice to be one of the voices in that conversation; the piece had a big revival.

Chords, nerves: the thing is still circulating as I write. The point of the essay was never to suggest that I think I am notably oppressed. It was to take these conversations as the narrow end of the wedge that opens up space for men and closes it off for women, space to speak, to be heard, to have rights, to participate, to be respected, to be a full and free human being. This is one way that, in polite discourse, power is expressed—the same power that in impolite discourse and in physical acts of intimidation and violence, and very often in how the world is organized—silences and erases and annihilates women, as equals, as participants, as human beings with rights, and far too often as living beings.

The battle for women to be treated like human beings with rights to life, liberty, and pursuit of involvement in cultural and political arenas continues, and it is sometimes a pretty grim battle. I surprised myself when I wrote the essay, which began with an amusing incident and ended with rape and murder. That made clear to me the continuum that stretches from minor social misery to violent silencing and violent death (and I think we would understand misogyny and violence against women even better if we looked at the abuse of power as a whole rather than treating domestic violence separately from rape and murder and harassment and intimidation, online and at home and in the workplace and in the streets; seen together, the pattern is clear).

Having the right to show up and speak are basic to survival, to dignity, and to liberty. I'm grateful that, after an early life of being silenced, sometimes violently, I grew up to have a voice, circumstances that will always bind me to the rights of the voiceless.

VOICES

81

Mutilating Gender

Dean Spade

. . .

This essay examines the relationship between individuals seeking sex reassignment surgery (SRS) and the medical establishments with which they must contend in order to fulfill their goals. . . .

Throughout this essay, I draw on my own experience of attempting to find low-cost or free counseling in order to begin the process of getting a double mastectomy. The choice to use personal narrative in this piece comes from a belief that just such a combination of theoretical work about the relationships of trans people to medical establishments and gender norms and the experience of trans people is too rarely found. Riki Anne Wilchins describes how trans experience has been used by psychiatrists, cultural feminists, anthropologists, and sociologists "travel[ling] through our lives and problems like tourists . . . [p]icnicking on our identities . . . select[ing] the tastiest tidbits with which to illustrate a theory or push a book." In most writing about trans people, our gender performance is put under a microscope to prove theories or build "expertise" while the gender performances of the authors remain unexamined and naturalized. I want to avoid even the appearance of participation in such a tradition, just as I want to use my own experience to illustrate how the requirements for diagnosis and treatment play out on individual bodies. The recent proliferation of academic and activist work on trans issues has created the impression in many people (mostly non-trans) that problems with access to services for trans people are being alleviated, and that the education of many specialists who provide services to trans people has made available sensitive therapeutic environments for trans people living in large metropolitan areas who can avail themselves of such services. My unsuccessful year-long quest for basic low-cost respectful counseling services in Los Angeles, which included seeking services at the Los Angeles Gender Center, the Los Angeles Gay and Lesbian Services Center, and Children's Hospital Los Angeles is a testament to the problems that still remain. This failure suggests the larger problems with the production of the "transsexual" in medical practice, and with the diagnostic and treatment criteria that made it impossible for the professionals from whom I sought care to respectfully engage my request for gender-related body alteration.

I hope that the use of my experience in this paper will provide a grounding illustration of the regulatory effects of the current diagnosis-treatment scheme for GID and resist the traditional framing of transsexual experience which posits trans people as victims or villains, insane or fascinating. Instead, I hope to be part of a project already taken up by Riki Anne Wilchins, Kate Bornstein, Leslie Feinberg, and many others which opens a position for trans people as self-critical, feminist, intellectual subjects of knowledge rather than simply case studies.

I. GOVERNANCE: PASSING AS A TRANSSEXUAL

Here's what I'm after: a surgically constructed male-appearing chest, no hormones (for now—maybe forever), no first-name change, any pronouns (except "it") are okay, although when it comes to gendered generics I happen to really like "Uncle" better than "Aunt," and definitely "Mr. Spade." Hausman writes, "transsexuals must seek and obtain medical treatment in order to be recognized as transsexuals. Their subject position depends upon a necessary relation to the medical establishment and its discourses." I've quickly learned that the converse is also true, in order to obtain the medical intervention I am seeking, I need to prove my membership in the category "transsexual"—prove that I have GID—to the proper authorities. Unfortunately, stating my true objectives is not convincing them.

. . .

II. THE TRANSSEXUAL CHILDHOOD

"When did you first know you were different?" the counselor at the L.A. Free Clinic asked. "Well," I said, "I knew I was poor and on welfare, and that was different from lots of kids at school, and I had a single mom, which was really uncommon there, and we weren't Christian, which is terribly noticeable in the South. Then later I knew I was a foster child, and in high school, I knew I was a feminist and that caused me all kinds of trouble, so I guess I always knew I was different." His facial expression tells me this isn't what he wanted to hear, but why should I engage this idea that my gender performance has been my most important difference in my life? It hasn't, and I can't separate it from the class, race, and parentage variables through which it was mediated. Does this mean I'm not real enough for surgery?

I've worked hard to not engage the gay childhood narrative—I never talk about tomboyish behavior as an antecedent to my lesbian identity, I don't tell stories about cross-dressing or crushes on girls, and I intentionally fuck with the assumption of it by telling people how

I used to be straight and have sex with boys like any sweet trashy rural girl and some of it was fun. I see these narratives as strategic, and I've always rejected the strategy that adopts some theory of innate sexuality and forecloses the possibility that anyone, gender-troubled childhood or not, could transgress sexual and gender norms at any time. I don't want to participate in an idea that only some people have to engage a struggle of learning gender norms in childhood either. So now, faced with these questions, how do I decide whether to look back on my life through the tranny childhood lens, tell the stories about being a boy for Halloween, not playing with dolls: What is the cost of participation in this selective recitation? What is the cost of not participating?

Symptoms of GID in the Diagnostic and Statistical Manual (DSM-IV) describe at length the symptom of childhood participation in stereotypically gender inappropriate behavior. Boys with GID "particularly enjoy playing house, drawing pictures of beautiful girls and princesses, and watching television or videos of their favorite female characters. . . . They avoid rough-and-tumble play and competitive sports and have little interest in cars and trucks." Girls with GID do not want to wear dresses, "prefer boys' clothing and short hair," are interested in "contact sports, [and] rough-and tumble play." Despite the disclaimer in the diagnosis description that this is not to be confused with normal gender non-conformity found in tomboys and sissies, no real line is drawn between "normal" gender non-conformity and gender non-conformity which constitutes GID. The effect is two-fold. First, normative childhood gender is produced—normal kids do the opposite of what kids with GID are doing. Non-GID kids can be expected to: play with children of the own sex, play with gender appropriate toys (trucks for boys, dolls for girls), enjoy fictional characters of their own sex (girls, specifically, might have GID if they like Batman or Superman), play gender appropriate characters in games of "house," etc. Secondly, a regulatory mechanism is put into place. Because gender nonconformity is established as a basis for illness, parents now have a "mill of speech," speculation and diagnosis to feed their children's gender through should it cross the line. As Foucault describes, the invention of a category of deviation, the description of the "ill" behavior that need be resisted or cured, creates not a prohibitive silence about such behavior but an opportunity for increased surveillance and speculation, what he would call "informal-governance."

The Diagnostic Criteria for Gender Identity Disorder names, as a general category of symptom, "[a] strong and persistent cross-gender identification (not merely a desire for any perceived cultural advantages of being the other sex)." This criterion suggests the possibility of a gender categorization not read through the cultural gender hierarchy. This requires an imagination of a child wanting to be a gender different from the one assigned to hir without having that desire stem from a cultural understanding of gender difference defined by the "advantaging" of certain gender behavior and identities over others. To use an illustrative example from the description of childhood GID symptoms, if a child assigned "female" wants to wear pants and hates dresses, and has been told that this is inappropriate for girls, is that decision free from a recognition of cultural advantages associated with gender? Since a diagnosis of GID does not require a child to state the desire to change genders, and the primary indicators are gender inappropriate tastes and behaviors, how can this be separated from cultural understandings of what constitutes gender difference and gender appropriateness? If we start from an understanding that gender behavior is learned, and that children are not born with some innate sense that girls should wear dresses and boys shouldn't like Barbie or anything pink, then how can a desire to transgress an assigned gender category be read outside of cultural meaning? Such a standard does, as Billings and Urban argue, privatize and depoliticize gender role distress. It creates a fictional transsexual who just knows in hir gut what man is and what woman is, and knows that sie is trapped in the wrong body. It produces a naturalized, innate gender difference outside power, a fictional binary that does not privilege one term.

V
O
I
C
E
S

The diagnostic criteria for GID produces a fiction of natural gender, in which normal, non-transsexual people grow up with minimal to no gender trouble or exploration, do not crossdress as children, do not play with the wrong-gendered kids, and do not like the wrong kinds of toys or characters. This story isn't believable, but because medicine produces it not through a description of the norm, but through a generalized account of the transgression, and instructs the doctor/parent/teacher to focus on the transgressive behavior, it establishes a surveillance and regulation effective for keeping both non-transsexuals and transsexuals in adherence to their roles. In order to get authorization for body alteration, this childhood must be produced, and the GID diagnosis accepted, maintaining an idea of two discrete gender categories that normally contain everyone but occasionally are wrongly assigned, requiring correction to reestablish the norm.

It's always been fun to reject the gay childhood story, to tell people I "chose" lesbianism, or to over articulate a straight childhood narrative to suggest that lesbianism could happen to anyone. But not engaging a trans childhood narrative is terrifying—what if it means I'm not "real"? Even though I don't believe in real, it matters if other people see me as real—if not I'm a mutilator, an imitator, and worst of all, I can't access surgery.

Transsexual writer Claudine Griggs' book takes for granted that transsexuality is an illness, an unfortunate predicament, something fortunate, normal people don't have to go through....

This is precisely the approach I want to avoid as I reject the narrative of a gender troubled childhood. My project would be to promote sex reassignment, gender alteration, temporary gender adventure, and the mutilation of gender categories, via surgery, hormones, clothing, political lobbying, civil disobedience, or any other means available. But that political commitment itself, if revealed to the gatekeepers of my surgery, disqualifies me. One therapist said to me, "You're really intellectualizing this, we need to get to the root of why you feel you should get your breasts removed, how long have you felt this way?" Does realness reside in the length of time a desire exists? Are women who seek breast enhancement required to answer these questions? Am I supposed to be able to separate my political convictions about gender, my knowledge of the violence of gender rigidity that has been a part of my life and the lives of everyone I care about, from my real "feelings" about what it means to occupy my gendered body? How could I begin to think about my chest without thinking about cultural advantage?

III. CHOOSING PERSPECTIVE: PASSING "FULL-TIME"

From what I've gathered in my various counseling sessions, in order to be deemed real I need to want to pass as male all the time, and not feel ambivalent about this. I need to be willing to make the commitment to "full-time" maleness, or they can't be sure that I won't regret my surgery. The fact that I don't want to change my first name, that I haven't sought out the use of the pronoun "he," that I don't think that "lesbian" is the wrong word for me, or, worse yet, that I recognize that the use of any word for myself—lesbian, transperson, transgender butch, boy, mister, FTM fag, butch—has always been/will always be strategic is my undoing in their eyes. They are waiting for a better justification of my desire for surgery—something less intellectual, more real.

I'm supposed to be wholly joyous when I get called "sir" or "boy." How could I ever have such an uncomplicated relationship to that moment? Each time I'm sirred I know both that my look is doing what I want it to do, and that the reason people can assign male gender to me easily is because they don't believe women have short hair, and because, as Garber has asserted, the existence of maleness as the generic means that fewer visual clues of maleness are required to achieve male gender attribution. This "therapeutic" process demands of me that I toss out all my feminist misgivings about the ways that gender rigidity informs people's perception of me.

. . .

Perhaps the most overt requirement for transsexual diagnosis is the ability to inhabit and perform "successfully" the new gender category. Through my own interactions with medical professionals, accounts of other trans people, and medical scholarship on transsexuality, I have gathered that the favored indication of such "success" seems to be the gender attribution of non-trans people. Because the ability to be perceived by non-trans people as a non-trans person is valorized, normative expressions of gender within a singular category are mandated.

. . .

IV. MAYBE I'M NOT A TRANSSEXUAL

The counselor at the L.A. Free Clinic decided I wasn't transsexual during the first (and only) session. When I told him what I wanted, and how I was starting counseling because I was trying to get some letter that I could give to a surgeon so that they would alter my chest, he said, "You should just go get breast reduction." Of course, he didn't know that most cosmetic surgeons won't reduce breasts below a C-cup (I wouldn't even qualify for reduction), and that breast reduction is a different procedure than the construction of a male-looking chest. I also suppose that he wasn't thinking about what happens to gender deviants when they end up in the hands of medical professionals who don't have experience with trans people.

> *Some surgeons have strong reactions to transsexual patients, and often, if the surgery is done in a teaching hospital, the surgeon turns out to be a resident or staff member who is offended by the procedure. "In one case, with which I am familiar," writes a doctor, "the patient's massive scars were probably the result of the surgeon's unconscious sadism and wish to scar the patient for 'going against nature.'"*

To this counselor, my failure to conform to the transsexuality he was expecting required my immediate expulsion from that world of meaning at any cost. My desire couldn't be for SRS because I wasn't a transsexual, so it must be for cosmetic surgery, something normal people get.

All my attempts at counseling, and all those experiences of being eyed suspiciously when I suggested that I was trans, or told outright I was not by non-trans counselors, made me expect that I would get a similar reception from trans people in activist or support contexts. This has not been the case. I've found that in trans contexts, a much broader conception of trans experience exists. The trans people I've met have, shockingly, believed what I say about my gender. Some have a self-narrative resembling the medical model of transsexuality, some do not. However, the people I've met share with me what my counselors do not: a commitment to gender self-determination and respect for all expressions of gender. Certainly not all trans people would identify with this principle, but I think it makes better sense as a basis for identity than the ability to pass "full-time" or the amount of cross-dressing one did as a child. Wilchins posits an idea of identity as "an effect of political activism instead of a cause." I see this notion reflected in trans activism, writing, and discussion, despite its absence in the medical institutions through which trans people must negotiate our identities.

Feinberg writes:

> *Once I figured out that "transgendered" was someone who transcended traditional stereotypes of "man" and "woman," I saw that I was such a person. I then began a quest for finding words that described myself, and discovered that while psychiatric jargon dominated the discourse, there were many other words, both older and newer, that addressed these issues. While I accepted the label of "transsexual" in order to obtain access to the hormones and chest surgery necessary to manifest my spirit in the material world, I have always had a profound disagreement with the definition of transsexualism as a psychiatric condition and transsexuals as disordered people.*

V. TELLING STORIES: STRATEGIC DEPLOYMENT OF THE TRANSSEXUAL NARRATIVE

. . .

After attending only three discussion group meetings with other trans people, I am struck by the naiveté with which I approached the search for counseling to get my surgery-authorizing letters. No one at these groups seems to see therapy as the place where they voice their doubts about their transition, where they wrestle with the political implications of their changes, where they speak about fears of losing membership in various communities or in their families. No one trusts the doctors as the place to work things out. When I mention the places I've gone for help, places that are supposed to support queer and trans people, everyone nods knowingly, having heard countless stories like mine about these very places before. Some have suggestions of therapists who are better, but none cost less than $50/hr. Mostly, though, people suggest different ways to get around the requirements. I get names of surgeons who do not always ask for the letters. Someone suggests that since I won't be on hormones, I can go in and pretend I'm a woman with a history of breast cancer in my family and that I want a double mastectomy to prevent it. I have these great, sad, conversations with these people who know all about what it means to lie and cheat their way through the medical roadblocks to get the opportunity to occupy their bodies in the way they want. I understand, now, that the place that is safe to talk about this is in here, with other people who understand the slipperiness of gender and the politics of transition, and who believe me without question when I say what I think I am and how that needs to look.

. . .

VII. CONCLUSION

Personal narrative is always strategically employed. It is always mediated through cultural understandings, through ideology. It is always a function of selective memory and narration. Have I learned that I should lie to obtain surgery, as others have before me? Does that lesson require an acceptance that cannot successfully advocate on behalf of a different approach to my desire for transformation?

An examination of how medicine governs gender variant bodies through the regulation of body alteration by means of the invention of the illness of transsexuality brings up the question of whether illness is the appropriate interpretive model for gender variance. The benefits of such an understanding for trans people are noteworthy. As long as SRS remains a treatment for an illness, the possibility of Medicaid coverage for it remains viable. Similarly, courts examining the question of what qualified a transsexual to have legal membership in the new gender category have relied heavily on the medical model of transsexuality when they have decided favorably for transsexuals. A model premised on a disability- or disease-based understanding of deviant behavior is believed by many to be the best strategy for achieving tolerance by norm-adherent people for those not adhering to norms. Such arguments are present in the realm of illicit drug use and in the quest for biological origins of homosexuality just as they are in the portrayal of transsexuality as an illness or disability.

However, it is vital that the costs of such an approach also be considered. First, the medical approach to gender variance, and the creation of transsexuality, has resulted in a governance of trans bodies that restricts our ability to make gender transitions which do not yield membership in a normative gender role. The self-determination of trans people in crafting our gender expression is compromised by the rigidity of the diagnostic and treatment criteria. At the same time, this criteria and the version of transsexuality that it posits produce and reify a fiction of normal, healthy gender that works as a regulatory measure for the gender expression of all people. To adopt the medical understanding of transsexuality is to agree that SRS is the unfortunate treatment of an unfortunate condition, to accept that gender norm adherence is fortunate and healthy, and to undermine the threat to a dichotomous gender system which trans experience can pose. The reification of the violence of compulsory gender norm adherence, and the submission of trans bodies to a norm-producing medical discipline, is too high a price for a small hope of conditional tolerance.

82

Violence Against Women Is a Men's Issue

Jackson Katz

Most people think violence against women is a women's issue. And why wouldn't they? Just about every woman in this society thinks about it every day. If they are not getting harassed on the street, living in an abusive relationship, recovering from a rape, or in therapy to deal with the sexual abuse they suffered as children, they are ordering their daily lives around the *threat* of men's violence.

But it is a mistake to call *men's* violence a *women's* issue. Take the subject of rape. Many people reflexively consider rape to be a women's issue. But let's take a closer look. What percentage of rape is committed by women? Is it 10 percent, 5 percent? No. *Less than 1 percent of rape is committed by women.* Let's state this another way: over 99 percent of rape is perpetrated by men. Whether the victims are female or male, men are overwhelmingly the perpetrators. But we call it a women's issue? Shouldn't that tell us something?

A major premise of . . . [my work] is that the long-running American tragedy of sexual and domestic violence—including rape, battering, sexual harassment, and the sexual exploitation of women and girls—is arguably more revealing about *men* than it is about women. Men, after all, are the ones committing the vast majority of the violence. Men are the ones doing most of the battering and almost all of the raping. Men are the ones paying the prostitutes (and killing them in video games), going to strip clubs, renting sexually degrading pornography, writing and performing misogynistic music.

When men's role in gender violence is discussed—in newspaper articles, sensational TV news coverage, in everyday conversation—the focus is typically on men as perpetrators or potential perpetrators. These days, you don't have to look far to see evidence of the pain and suffering these men cause. But it is rare to find any in-depth discussion about the culture that's producing these violent men. It's almost like the perpetrators are strange aliens who landed here from another planet. It is rarer still to hear thoughtful discussions about the ways that our culture defines "manhood," and how that definition might be linked to the endless string of stories about husbands killing wives, or groups of young men raping girls (and sometimes videotaping the rape) that we hear about on a regular basis.

Why isn't there more conversation about the underlying social factors that contribute to the pandemic of violence against women? Why aren't men's attitudes and behaviors toward women the focus of more critical scrutiny and coordinated action? These days, the 24/7 news cycle brings us a steady stream of gender-violence tragedies: serial killers on the loose, men abducting young girls, domestic-violence homicides, periodic sexual abuse scandals in powerful institutions like the Catholic Church and the Air Force Academy. You can barely turn on the news these days without coming across another gruesome sex crime—whether it's a group of boys gang-raping a girl in a middle school bathroom or a young pregnant woman who turns up missing, and whose husband emerges a few days later as the primary suspect.

Isn't it about time we had a national conversation about the male causes of this violence, instead of endlessly lingering on its consequences in the lives of women? Thanks to the battered women's and rape crisis movements in the U.S., it is no longer taboo to discuss women's experiences of sexual and domestic violence. This is a significant achievement. To an unprecedented extent, American women today expect to be supported—not condemned—when they disclose what men have done to them (unless the man is popular, wealthy, or well-connected, in which case all bets are off.)

This is all for the good. Victims of violence and abuse—whether they're women or men—should be heard and respected. Their needs come first. But let's not mistake concern for victims with the political will to change the conditions that led to their victimization in the first place. . . . It is one thing to focus on the "against women" part of the phrase; but someone's responsible for doing it, and (almost) everyone knows that it's overwhelmingly men. Why aren't people talking about this? Is it realistic to talk about preventing violence against women if no one even wants to say out loud who's responsible for it?

For the past two decades, I've been part of a growing movement of men, in North America and around the world, whose aim is to reduce violence against women by focusing on those aspects of male culture—especially male-peer culture—that provide active or tacit support for some men's abusive behavior. This movement is racially and ethnically diverse, and it brings together men from both privileged and poor communities, and everyone in between. This is challenging work on many levels, and no one should expect rapid results. For example, there is no way to gloss over some of the race, class, and sexual orientation divisions between and among us men. It is also true that it takes time to change social norms that are so deeply rooted in structures of gender and power. Even so, there is room for optimism. We've had our successes: there are arguably more men today who are actively confronting violence against women than at any time in human history.

Make no mistake. Women blazed the trail that we are riding down. Men are in the position to do this work precisely because of the great leadership of women. The battered women's and rape crisis movements and their allies in local, state, and federal government have accomplished a phenomenal amount over the past generation. Public awareness about violence against women is at an all-time high. The level of services available today for female victims and survivors of men's violence is—while not yet adequate—nonetheless historically unprecedented.

. . .

[I propose] that we adopt a much more ambitious approach. If we are going to bring down dramatically the rates of violence against women—not just at the margins—we will need a far-reaching cultural revolution. At its heart, this revolution must be about changing the sexist social norms in male culture, from the elementary school playground to the common room in retirement communities—and every locker room, pool hall, and board-room in between. For us to have any hope of achieving historic reductions in incidents of violence against women, at a minimum we will need to dream big and act boldly. It almost goes without saying that we will need the help of a lot more men—at all levels of power and influence—than are currently involved. Obviously we have our work cut out for us. As a measure of just how far we have to go, consider that in spite of the misogyny and sexist brutality all around us, millions of non-violent men today fail to see gender violence as their issue. "I'm a good guy," they will say. "This isn't my problem."

For years, women of every conceivable ethnic, racial, and religious background have been trying to get men around them—and men in power—to do more about violence against women. . . . On both a micro and a macro level, women in this era have success-fully broken through the historical silence about violence against women and found their voice—here in the U.S. and around the world.

Yet even with all of these achievements, women continue to face an uphill struggle in trying to make meaningful inroads into male culture. Their goal has not been simply to get men to listen to women's stories and truly hear them—although that is a critical first step. The truly vexing challenge has been getting men to actually go out and *do* something about the problem, in the form of educating and organizing *other men* in numbers great enough to prompt a real cultural shift. Some activist women—even those who have had great faith in men as allies—have been beating their heads against the wall for a long time, and are frankly burned out on the effort. I know this because I have been working with many of these women for a long time. They are my colleagues and friends.

My work is dedicated to getting more men to take on the issue of violence against women, and thus to build on what women have achieved. The area that I focus on is not law enforcement or offender treatment, but the *prevention* of sexual and domestic violence and all their related social pathologies—including violence against children. To do this, I and other men here and around the world have been trying to get our fellow men to see that this problem is not just personal for a small number of men who happen to have been touched by the issue. We try to show them that it is personal for them, too. *For all of us.* We talk about men not only as perpetrators but as victims. We try to show them that violence by men against each other—from simple assaults to gay-bashing—*is* linked to the same structures of gender and power that produce so much men's violence against women.

We also make it clear that these issues are not just personal, to be dealt with as private family matters. They are political as well, with repercussions that reverberate throughout our lives and communities in all sorts of meaningful and disturbing ways. For example, according to a 2003 report by the U.S. Conference of Mayors, domestic violence was a primary cause of homelessness in almost half of the twenty-five cities surveyed. And worldwide, sexual coercion and other abusive behavior by men plays an important role in the transmission of HIV/AIDS.

Nonetheless, convincing other men to make gender violence issues a priority is not an easy sell . . . [and, t]here is no point in being naïve about why women have had such a dif-ficult time convincing men to make violence against women a men's issue. In spite of sig-nificant social change in recent decades, men continue to grow up with, and are socialized into, a deeply misogynistic, male-dominated culture, where violence against women—from the subtle to the homicidal—is disturbingly common. It's *normal*. And precisely because the mistreatment of women is such a pervasive characteristic of our patriarchal culture, most men, to a greater or lesser extent, have played a role in its perpetuation. This gives us a strong incentive to avert our eyes.

Women, of course, have also been socialized into this misogynistic culture. Some of them resist and fight back. In fact, women's ongoing resistance to their subordinate status is one of the most momentous developments in human civilization over the past two centuries. Just the same, plenty of women show little appetite for delving deeply into the cultural roots of sexist violence. It's much less daunting simply to blame "sick" individuals for the problem. You hear women explaining away men's bad behavior as the result of individual pathology all the time: "Oh, he just had a bad childhood," or "He's an angry drunk. The booze gets to him. He's never been able to handle it."

But regardless of how difficult it can be to show some women that violence against women is a social problem that runs deeper than the abusive behavior of individual men, it is still much easier to convince women that dramatic change is in their best interest than it is to convince men. In fact, many people would argue that, since men are the dominant sex and violence serves to reinforce this dominance, it is not in men's best interests to reduce violence against women, and that the very attempt to enlist a critical mass of men in this effort amounts to a fool's errand.

For those of us who reject this line of reasoning, the big question then is how do we reach men? We know we're not going to transform, overnight or over many decades, certain structures of male power and privilege that have developed over thousands of years. Nevertheless, how are we going to bring more men—many more men—into a conversation about sexism and violence against women? And how are we going to do this without turning them off, without berating them, without blaming them for centuries of sexist oppression? Moreover, how are we going to move beyond talk and get substantial numbers of men to partner *with* women in reducing men's violence, instead of working *against* them in some sort of fruitless and counterproductive gender struggle?

. . .

I understand the skepticism of women who for years have been frustrated by men's complacency about something as basic as a woman's right to live free from the threat of violence. But I am convinced that men who are active in gender-violence prevention today speak for a much larger number of men. I would not go so far as to say that a silent majority of men supports everything that gender-violence prevention activists stand for, but an awful lot of men privately cheer us on. I have long felt this way, but now there is a growing body of research—in social norms theory—that confirms it empirically.

Social norms theory begins with the premise that people often misperceive the extent to which their peers hold certain attitudes or participate in certain behaviors. In the absence of accurate knowledge, they are more likely to be influenced by what they *think* people think and do, rather than what they *actually* think and do. . . .

There have been a number of studies in the past several years that demonstrate that significant numbers of men are uncomfortable with the way some of their male peers talk about and treat women. But since few men in our society have dared to talk publicly about such matters, many men think they are the only ones who feel uncomfortable. Because they feel isolated and alone in their discomfort, they do not say anything. Their silence, in turn, simply reinforces the false perception that few men are uncomfortable with sexist attitudes and behaviors. It is a vicious cycle that keeps a lot of caring men silent.

I meet men all the time who thank me—or my fellow activists and colleagues—for publicly taking on the subject of men's violence. I frequently meet men who are receptive to the paradigm-shifting idea that men's violence against women has to be understood as a men's issue, as their issue. These men come from every demographic and geographic category. They include thousands of men who would not fit neatly into simplistic stereotypes about the kind of man who would be involved in "that touchy-feely stuff."

Still, it is an uphill fight. Truly lasting change is only going to happen as new generations of women come of age and demand equal treatment with men in every realm, and new generations of men work with them to reject the sexist attitudes and behaviors of their predecessors. This will take decades, and the outcome is hardly predetermined. But along with tens of thousands of activist women and men who continue to fight the good fight, I believe that it is possible to achieve something much closer to gender equality, and a dramatic reduction in the level of men's violence against women, both here and around the world. And there is a lot at stake. If sexism and violence against women do not subside considerably in the twenty-first century, it will not just be bad news for women. It will also say something truly ugly and tragic about the future of our species.

. . .

83

Trans Woman Manifesto

Julia Serano

This manifesto calls for the end of the scapegoating, deriding, and dehumanizing of trans women everywhere. For the purposes of this manifesto, *trans woman* is defined as any person who was assigned a male sex at birth, but who identifies as and/or lives as a woman. No qualifications should be placed on the term "trans woman" based on a person's ability to "pass" as female, her hormone levels, or the state of her genitals—after all, it is downright sexist to reduce any woman (trans or otherwise) down to her mere body parts or to require her to live up to certain societally dictated ideals regarding appearance.

Perhaps no sexual minority is more maligned or misunderstood than trans women. As a group, we have been systematically pathologized by the medical and psychological establishment, sensationalized and ridiculed by the media, marginalized by mainstream lesbian and gay organizations, dismissed by certain segments of the feminist community, and, in too many instances, been made the victims of violence at the hands of men who feel that we somehow threaten their masculinity and heterosexuality. Rather than being given the opportunity to speak for ourselves on the very issues that affect our own lives, trans women are instead treated more like research subjects: Others place us under their microscopes, dissect our lives, and assign motivations and desires to us that validate their own theories and agendas regarding gender and sexuality.

Trans women are so ridiculed and despised because we are uniquely positioned at the intersection of multiple binary gender-based forms of prejudice: transphobia, cissexism, and misogyny.

Transphobia is an irrational fear of, aversion to, or discrimination against people whose gendered identities, appearances, or behaviors deviate from societal norms. In much the same way that homophobic people are often driven by their own repressed homosexual tendencies, transphobia is first and foremost an expression of one's own insecurity about having to live up to cultural gender ideals. The fact that transphobia is so rampant in our society reflects the reality that we place an extraordinary amount of pressure on individuals to conform to all of the expectations, restrictions, assumptions, and privileges associated with the sex they were assigned at birth.

V O I C E S

While all transgender people experience transphobia, transsexuals additionally experience a related (albeit distinct) form of prejudice: *cissexism*, which is the belief that transsexuals' identified genders are inferior to, or less authentic than, those of *cissexuals* (i.e., people who are not transsexual and who have only ever experienced their subconscious and physical sexes as being aligned). The most common expression of cissexism occurs when people attempt to deny the transsexual the basic privileges that are associated with the trans person's self-identified gender. Common examples include purposeful misuse of pronouns or insisting that the trans person use a different public restroom. The justification for this denial is generally founded on the assumption that the trans person's gender is not authentic because it does not correlate with the sex they were assigned at birth. In making this assumption, cissexists attempt to create an artificial hierarchy. By insisting that the trans person's gender is "fake," they attempt to validate their own gender as "real" or "natural." This sort of thinking is extraordinarily naive, as it denies a basic truth: We make assumptions every day about other people's genders without ever seeing their birth certificates, their chromosomes, their genitals, their reproductive systems, their childhood socialization, or their legal sex. There is no such thing as a "real" gender—there is only the gender we experience ourselves as and the gender we perceive others to be.

While often different in practice, cissexism, transphobia, and homophobia are all rooted in *oppositional sexism*, which is the belief that female and male are rigid, mutually exclusive categories, each possessing a unique and nonoverlapping set of attributes, aptitudes, abilities, and desires. Oppositional sexists attempt to punish or dismiss those of us who fall outside of gender or sexual norms because our existence threatens the idea that women and men are "opposite" sexes. . . .

In addition to the rigid, mutually exclusive gender categories established by oppositional sexism, the other requirement for maintaining a male-centered gender hierarchy is to enforce *traditional sexism*—the belief that maleness and masculinity are superior to femaleness and femininity. Traditional and oppositional sexism work hand in hand to ensure that those who are masculine have power over those who are feminine, and that only those born male will be seen as authentically masculine. For the purposes of this manifesto, the word *misogyny* will be used to describe this tendency to dismiss and deride femaleness and femininity.

Just as all transgender people experience transphobia and cissexism to differing extents (depending on how often, obvious, or out we are as transgender), we experience misogyny to differing extents too. This is most evident in the fact that, while there are many different types of transgender people, our society tends to single out trans women and others on the male-to-female (MTF) spectrum for attention and ridicule. This is not merely because we transgress binary gender norms per se, but because we, by necessity, embrace our own femaleness and femininity. Indeed, more often than not it is our expressions of femininity and our desire to be female that become sensationalized, sexualized, and trivialized by others. While trans people on the female-to-male (FTM) spectrum face discrimination for breaking gender norms (i.e., oppositional sexism), their expressions of maleness or masculinity themselves are not targeted for ridicule—to do so would require one to question masculinity itself.

When a trans person is ridiculed or dismissed not merely for failing to live up to gender norms, but for their expressions of femaleness or femininity, they become the victims of a specific form of discrimination: *trans-misogyny*. When the majority of jokes made at the expense of trans people center on "men wearing dresses" or "men who want their penises cut off," that is not transphobia—it is trans-misogyny. When the majority of violence and sexual assaults committed against trans people is directed at trans women, that is not transphobia—it is trans-misogyny. When it's okay for women to wear "men's" clothing, but when men who wear "women's" clothing can be diagnosed with the psychological disorder transvestic fetishism, that is not transphobia—it is trans-misogyny. When women's or lesbian organizations and events open their doors to trans men but not trans women, that is not transphobia—it is trans-misogyny.

In a male-centered gender hierarchy, where it is assumed that men are better than women and that masculinity is superior to femininity, there is no greater perceived threat than the existence of trans women, who despite being born male and inheriting male privilege "choose" to be female instead. By embracing our own femaleness and femininity, we, in a sense, cast a shadow of doubt over the supposed supremacy of maleness and masculinity. In order to lessen the threat we pose to the male-centered gender hierarchy, our culture (primarily via the media) uses every tactic in its arsenal of traditional sexism to dismiss us:

1 The media hyperfeminizes us by accompanying stories about trans women with pictures of us putting on makeup, dresses, and high-heeled shoes in an attempt to highlight the supposed "frivolous" nature of our femaleness, or by portraying trans women as having derogatory feminine-associated character traits such as being weak, confused, passive, or mousy.

2 The media hypersexualizes us by creating the impression that most trans women are sex workers or sexual deceivers, and by asserting that we transition for primarily sexual reasons (e.g., to prey on innocent straight men or to fulfill some kind of bizarre sex fantasy). Such depictions not only belittle trans women's motives for transitioning, but implicitly suggest that women as a whole have no worth beyond their ability to be sexualized.

3 The media objectifies our bodies by sensationalizing sex reassignment surgery and openly discussing our "man-made vaginas" without any of the discretion that normally accompanies discussions about genitals. Further, those of us who have not had surgery are constantly being reduced to our body parts, whether by the creators of tranny porn who overemphasize and exaggerate our penises (thus distorting trans women into "she-males" and "chicks with dicks") or by other people who have been so brainwashed by phallocentricism that they believe that the mere presence of a penis can trump the femaleness of our identities, our personalities, and the rest of our bodies.

Because anti-trans discrimination is steeped in traditional sexism, it is not simply enough for trans activists to challenge binary gender norms (i.e., oppositional sexism)—we must also challenge the idea that femininity is inferior to masculinity and that femaleness is inferior to maleness. In other words, by necessity, trans activism must be at its core a feminist movement.

. . .

It is no longer enough for feminism to fight solely for the rights of those born female. That strategy has furthered the prospects of many women over the years, but now it bumps up against a glass ceiling that is partly of its own making. Though the movement worked hard to encourage women to enter previously male-dominated areas of life, many feminists have been ambivalent at best, and resistant at worst, to the idea of men expressing or exhibiting feminine traits and moving into certain traditionally female realms. And while we credit previous feminist movements for helping to create a society where most sensible people would agree with the statement "women and men are equals," we lament the fact that we remain light-years away from being able to say that most people believe that femininity is masculinity's equal.

. . .

But it is not enough for us to empower femaleness and femininity. We must also stop pretending that there are essential differences between women and men. This begins with the acknowledgment that there are exceptions to every gender rule and stereotype, and this simply stated fact disproves all gender theories that purport that female and male are mutually exclusive categories. We must move away from pretending that women and men are "opposite" sexes, because when we buy into that myth it establishes a dangerous precedent. For if men are big, then women must be small; and if men are strong then women must be weak. And if being butch is to make yourself rock-solid, then being femme becomes allowing yourself to be malleable; and if being a man means taking control of your own situation, then being a woman becomes living up to other people's expectations. When we buy into the idea that female and male are "opposites," it becomes impossible for us to empower women without either ridiculing men or pulling the rug out from under ourselves.

It is only when we move away from the idea that there are "opposite" sexes, and let go of the culturally derived values that are assigned to expressions of femininity and masculinity, that we may finally approach gender equity. By challenging both oppositional and traditional sexism simultaneously, we can make the world safe for those of us who are queer, those of us who are feminine, and those of us who are female, thus empowering people of all sexualities and genders.

84

Real Men and Pink Suits

Charles M. Blow

New York Times, February 10, 2012

Twitter claims another casualty.

This week, Roland Martin, a bombastic cultural and political commentator was suspended by CNN from his role as a political analyst on the network for Twitter messages published during the Super Bowl.

One message read: "If a dude at your Super Bowl party is hyped about David Beckham's H&M underwear ad, smack the ish out of him! #superbowl." Another read: "Who the hell was that New England Patriot they just showed in a head to toe pink suit? Oh, he needs a visit from #teamwhipdatass."

The Gay and Lesbian Alliance Against Defamation said the messages advocated "violence against gay people" and asked CNN to fire Martin. CNN called the messages "regrettable and offensive" and suspended him "for the time being." Martin issued an apology in which he said that he was just "joking about smacking someone."

There is vigorous debate online about what Martin meant, about GLAAD's reaction, and about CNN's policy on who gets suspended or fired and for what kinds of statements.

Martin and GLAAD have signaled, over Twitter, that they plan to meet and discuss the matter. Maybe something positive will emerge from that.

But whether it does or not, I don't want to let this incident pass without using it as a "teachable moment" for us all about the dangerous way in which we define manhood and masculinity. At the very least, Martin's comments are corrosive on this front.

I follow Martin on Twitter. I know that he likes to joke and tease. I have even joked with him. So I can believe that, in his mind, he may have thought that these were just harmless jokes in which the violence was fictional and funny.

But in the real world—where bullying and violence against gays and lesbians, or even those assumed to be so, is all too real—"jokes" like his hold no humor. There are too many bruised ribs and black eyes and buried bodies for the targets of this violence to just lighten up and laugh.

We all have to understand that effects can operate independent of intent, that subconscious biases can move counter to conscious egalitarianism, and that malice need not be present within the individual to fuel the maliciousness of the society at large.

(This is not to say that Martin has been egalitarian on this front. In fact, a widely cited 2006 post on his Web site suggests otherwise. In it, he criticized the Rev. Al Sharpton for appealing to black churches "to become more accepting and embracing of homosexuality." Martin wrote that gays and lesbians "are engaged, in the eyes of the church, in sinful behavior." Furthermore, he said, "My wife, an ordained Baptist minister for 20 years, has counseled many men and women to walk away from the gay lifestyle, and to live a chaste life." And he compared homosexuals to adulterers, disobedient children, alcoholics and thieves.)

Words have power. And power recklessly exerted has consequences. It's not about being politically correct. It's about being sensitive to the plight of those being singled out. We can't ask the people taking the punches to also take the jokes.

And it's about understanding that masculinity is wide enough and deep enough for all of us to fit in it. But society in general, and male culture in particular, is constantly working to render it narrow and shallow. We have shaved the idea of manhood down to an unrealistic definition that few can fit in it with the whole of who they are, not without severe constriction or self-denial.

The man that we mythologize in the backs of our minds is a cultural concoction, an unattainable ideal, a perfect specimen of muscles and fearlessness and daring. Square-jawed and well-rounded. Potent and passionate. Sensitive but not sentimental. And, above all else, unwaveringly heterosexual and without even a hint of softness.

A vast majority of men will never be able to be all these things all the time, but they shouldn't be made to feel less than a man because of it.

And this narrowed manhood ideal has a truly damaging effect on boys.

In *Boy Culture: An Encyclopedia*, which was published in 2010, the editors point out: "Boys are men in training. As such, most strive to enact and replicate hegemonic masculinity so that they achieve status among male peers, and pre-emptively guard against accusations or perceptions that their masculinity is deficient." The editors went on to quote a 2001 study in which a boy who does not measure up to dominant prescriptions of masculinity is "likely to be punished by his peers in ways which seek to strip him of his mantle of masculinity."

In fact, a 2005 report entitled "From Teasing to Torment: School Climate in America," which was commissioned by the Gay, Lesbian and Straight Education Network, found that a third of all teens said that they are often bullied, called names or harassed at their school because they are, or people think that they are, gay, lesbian or bisexual.

We have created this culture, and we can undo it.

Start with this fact: The truest measure of a man, indeed of a person, is not whom he lies down with but what he stands up for. If we must be judged, let it be in this way. And when we fall short, as we sometimes will, because humanity is fallible, let us greet each other with compassion and encouragement rather than ridicule and resentment.

Whatever was in Martin's heart, what was in his Twitter messages wasn't helpful. They may not lead directly to intimidation or violence, but they may add to a stream of negativity that feeds a culture in which intimidation and violence by some twisted minds is all too real. I don't believe that Martin wanted that.

Let's show the whole of mankind that men can indeed be kind, even to other men who dare to wear pink suits.

85

Mestiza/o Gender

Notes Towards a Transformative Masculinity

Daniel E. Solís y Martínez

... On December 9, 1531, on the sacred hill of Tepeyacac, just outside the recently-conquered city of Tenochitlan, an indigenous man who is now known only as Juan Diego combined the traditional Mexica goddess Tonantzín with the Spaniards' Virgin Mary to create the Virgin of Guadalupe. Juan Diego, a recent convert to Catholicism, was visited on Tepeyacac by an unusually brown-skinned Virgin Mary. This seemingly indigenous Virgin Mary told Juan Diego to visit the Spanish Bishop in Mexico City and to ask him to build a church dedicated to her at Tepeyacac. Juan Diego did as she asked; but the Bishop refused to believe the lowly *indigena* (indigenous person) Juan Diego and demanded proof of this miraculous apparition of the Mother of God. Juan Diego returned to the sacred hill in search of proof and found the Virgin Mary waiting for him. The Virgin Mary instructed him to ascend to the mountain-top of Tepeyacac where he would find a bounty of beautiful flowers miraculously growing out of season that would serve as his proof. Juan Diego gathered the flowers into his cloak and then descended the holy mountain to return to the disbelieving Bishop.

Once again, Juan Diego repeated the Virgin Mary's request for the construction of a church at Tepeyacac. The Bishop again demanded proof. Juan Diego simply replied by unfurling his cloak and dropping the flowers at the feet of the Bishop, immediately filling the room with a tremendous fragrance. It was at that moment that the Bishop saw the divine imprint of the brown-skinned Virgin Mary on Juan Diego's cloak. Being humbled by both the choice of the indigenous Juan Diego as the Virgin Mary's messenger and the brown skin of the Virgin herself, the Bishop agreed to build the church at Tepeyacac.

The acceptance of the brown-skinned Virgin Mary on Juan Diego's cloak by the Spanish Bishop was the beginning of the officially-sanctioned cult of the Virgin of Guadalupe in the Americas. Within the racially-mixed form of the Virgin of Guadalupe, indigenous people like Juan Diego were able to merge their traditional religions with the Catholicism imposed on them by the colonizing Spanish, so as to produce a truly new form of cultural and religious expression. Given their inability to directly confront the more powerful Spanish, the indigenous peoples of Mexico and Central America used the Virgin of Guadalupe to create within the dominance of the Spanish a space of their own. Utilizing the legitimization that the Spanish Catholic Church conferred on the Virgin of Guadalupe, *indigenas* such as Juan Diego forged religious customs that were neither Catholic nor the traditional practices of the Mexica, but that mixed elements from both. The birth of the brown-skinned Virgin of Guadalupe was a powerful event that signaled the beginning, first in Mexico and Central America and then in the United States, of a process of cultural mixing that has given rise to new ethnic and national identities.

The story of Juan Diego, with its unequal marriage of conflicted ideas and practices in the face of powerful forces, is a compelling metaphor for my own life as a Latino gay man attempting to create a way of being queer that is ethical, freeing and true to myself. Like Juan Diego's merging of the repressed indigenous goddess Tonantzín into the ascendant European Virgin Mary, I endeavor to create my own gayness through a blending of two distinct systems of homosexuality: that which my parents brought with them from El Salvador and that which I grew into in the United States. Growing up, my queerness was contained by my family within the traditional homosexuality of El Salvador. In that system, homosexuality is a matter of gender difference that is expressed by both sexual behavior and deviant gender practices. In El Salvador and much of Latin America, homosexual men and boys like me are seen not as women or men but instead occupy an ambiguous place in between. Under this particular system of homosexuality, my parents raised me quite differently from my brothers: I am the only one who was taught by my mother and grandmother how to cook, clean, sew, and even now am responsible for organizing family events such as birthdays, holidays and dinners. As a child, I was allowed to socialize with girls and women, all without my gayness being explicitly named. Within my home, my budding gayness was silently accepted and integrated into the larger fabric of my family so long as it did not threaten the heterosexual status quo. . . .

Throughout Latin America and in El Salvador, homosexuality is understood primarily as a matter of gender. Homosexual behavior—particularly the act of penetration—determines to a large degree whether one is or isn't a man. *Maricónes, culeros,* and *putos* are all words that name the non-maleness of the homosexual in the traditional Latin American conceptualization of homosexuality. Mexican anthropologist Héctor Carrillo describes the traditional operation of this gender-sexuality system in Mexico as creating men through non-men. . . . Carrillo notes the distinction between, ". . . masculine men were *hombres* or *machos,*" and ". . . their counterparts were the effeminate men, the *maricones,* who were perceived as having forfeited their manhood altogether" (Carrillo 2003, 352). Carrillo further explains that *maricones* served to legitimize the masculinity of the *hombres.* As such, normative masculinity in the Latin American context was not possible without *maricones.* . . .

In the traditional understanding of homosexuality in Latin America, homosexual male-bodied individuals are not men at all. Instead, they are seen as another type of gender category altogether, existing in a shifting location between women's femininity and men's bodies. Carrillo's observations of Mexican homosexuality hold true for much of Latin America. In fact, many names for male homosexuals throughout Latin America speak to this in-between gendered status. In most of its Latin American articulations, homosexuality is a matter of gender, not sexual identity.

This in-between homosexual gender is centered on the matter of penetration: he who is penetrated is a homosexual. By being the receptive partner in anal intercourse, Latin American *homosexuales* give up their claim to masculinity. Instead they enter into a gender space that borrows and claims much from femininity but that is decidedly different from woman-ness. This articulation of homosexuality as a different gender, which essentializes it into a biological trait, creates spaces for Latin American *homosexuales* within Latin American societies and families. These spaces are often created not by the overt presence of homophobic discourses, but instead by their silent operation. Queer Puerto Rican sociologist Manolo Guzmán describes ". . . this absence of speech [as] no longer talking about things like marriage, represents a suspension of the assumption of heterosexuality" (Guzmán 2006, 88). It is in those spaces of absent speech in which Latin American homosexuality rests. My own parents' response to my budding gender deviance and homosexuality was shaped by this system of homosexual gender. My family's acceptance of my queer impulses was predicated on its safe containment in the traditional queer gender space of the Latin American family structure. So long as my homosexuality was not explicitly named it did not threaten the traditional supremacy of my father over our family. . . .

My childhood experiences in the vast stretches of Los Angeles were defined by a constant shift between two separate worlds firmly divided by a border made up of language, class, and race. The Salvadoreño culture of my home and neighborhood in the eastern San Fernando Valley was an island in the surrounding sea of Americanness. Moving from the Spanish of my family to the English of my teachers and school forced me from an early age to be constantly aware of the need to shift my way of being depending on where I was. Who I was depended on where I was, who I was with and what language I was speaking. Like many budding homo boys, the need to constantly move back and forth between worlds made me a talented performer from an early age. I quickly became a skilled border-crosser.

At the very core of my role switching was a fundamental clash between the migrant gender-sexuality worldview of my family and the "native" system of the United States. My parents were locked in a battle—internally and externally—to craft a family that was the best of the values and cultural forms they had been raised with, but that at the same time recognized the sheer reality that they were not in El Salvador anymore. This battle was never explicitly named by my parents as the source of their discomfort with my brothers' and my own rapid Americanization, but it quietly informed every action they took. . . . My parents' struggle was centered in our home. Patriarchy was the central axis around which my parents constructed our family. My father worked an inhuman amount of hours as a machine-shop operator to support my family, but his salary was simply not enough to make ends meet. In the rapidly de-industrializing Los Angeles of the 1980s, machine-shop work was on the decline. My father's lack of an American education and legal status exacerbated the dwindling supply of work, resulting in a continuous cycle of migration from one job to the next. This instability finally forced my father to allow my mother's entrance into the working world. Like my grandmother and aunt, she too became a domestic worker for the rich and white of the West San Fernando Valley.

The emergence of my mother as our family's co-supporter led to fierce fights for dominance and power within our home. Quite simply, my mother's departure from her traditional role as homemaker undermined my father's masculinity. The assault on my father's manhood was twofold. Since he couldn't fully provide for all of our family's financial needs, he was failing at his manly obligations. This was compounded by the loss of mental and physical control over my mother. It was perhaps the loss of total control over my mother that most undermined my father's masculine power. With work, my mother gained independence as she learned how to drive and for the first time had money of her own to spend. Implicit in my father's frustration was the fear that her daily sojourns to the outside world would corrupt my mother and render her unfit as both mother and wife. My father's fears would explode in dramatic and often violent outbursts aimed particularly at my mother, but also at my brothers and me. These poverty-driven gendered struggles set the stage for the emergence of my queerness within my family.

As is the case for many homo boys, from an early age my mother was my world. The bond between us was one of sameness; in my mind I was just like her. My mother is fond of reminding me of how as a baby she alone had the power to stop my tears. To this day, she is still one of the few people that can get me to shut up. Given the close affinity between my mother and me, when my parents would fight I would stand at her side ready to battle my father, and often my older brother as well. It wouldn't matter who was wrong or right, but simply that my mother was threatened. Since I saw my mother as not only my role model but as the source from which I had sprung, when she was threatened I was threatened.

Often the fights between my parents were about the bond of affinity between my mother and me. My father accused her of spoiling me, which in our working class home had strong undertones of feminization and emasculation. In claiming that my mother was spoiling me, my father was really saying that she was turning me into a non-boy. His accusations were further complicated by his patronizing of my older brother as his Chosen Son. Subtly undermining my mother's authority over him, my father drew my older brother into his orbit as an ally. As time wore on, those battle lines became entrenched gender lines dividing us into two opposing camps: my father and older brother as the men and my mother and I as the women. It was in those moments of anger, of a family divided along lines of what I can only call queer genders that my own unique place in my family began to emerge.

My queer gender developed out of those fights within my family. While never openly named by either of my parents, they had tacitly agreed that I was to be raised differently from my clearly male-gendered brothers. I was to be the *culerito*. As a child, I was the son taught to cook, clean, listen and nurture. At the never-ending string of quinceañeras, birthday parties, and baptismal celebrations, I was always with the women. I would sit among my mother, grandmother, aunt, godmother, and a host of their friends, listening to them gossip about one another, or lovingly (yet critically) pick at their husbands, their sons, and their daughters. Meanwhile, my brothers would play with other boy-children. My inclusion in these circles of women was never questioned, at least while I was present. If whispered conversations of concern about my affiliation with women happened between my mother and her women friends, I was not aware. . . .

The relative acceptance of my family was matched by the unease I felt towards the world "*out there.*" I don't really remember an exact moment when I became conscious of the fact that my love for girl-child toys and women superheroes was a *private* matter—a matter of the home and family. Somehow I just understood that it was not okay for me to take my dolls out of the home. Whenever I played with the other children in my apartment complex, I never mentioned that my favorite G.I. Joe was Scarlett, the red haired counter-terrorist vixen of the team, and I certainly never dared to bring her out with me to play. Like my constant transitions from English and Spanish between school and home, I also switched my gender performance from home to the outside. The queer child I was inside my home butched it up whenever I crossed the threshold of our door. . . .

My family's tolerance of my gayness was markedly different from the clearly defined homosexuality of the United States that I found first on the playgrounds and in the classrooms of my elementary school, and later on in the queer identity groups I joined as a teenager. The homosexuality I found outside of my family was one of a clearly defined gayness that was accessed through personal identification. In what I call the American system of homosexuality, a person was gay either because they called themselves gay or because others labeled them that way. As I grew older, I discovered communities of queer people in the United States built around a shared sense of identity and personal experience. At the core of these communities was the idea of "coming out"—or publicly naming one's queerness to others. This explicitly named gayness was quite different from the unnamed ambiguous position I held within my family. After I came out, my position in my family changed as I sought to force them to accept American gayness as the basis for how they understood me and my queerness. My efforts led to great conflicts between myself and most of my family members. As I grew increasingly isolated from my family, I realized that American gayness with its emphasis on the individual wasn't sufficient for me or my particular situation. I began to seek a way to construct an empowering queerness that challenged heterosexism but that also didn't isolate me from the people I love so much.

Constructing my queerness solely out of either Latin American homosexuality or American gayness presents great obstacles to the type of queerness I want to embody. Like Juan Diego, my options are seemingly limited. Do I choose the gendered homosexuality I grew up with in my family or the individualistic gayness of the country I was born in? Given the overwhelming power of both types of homosexuality to resist challenges to their oppressive elements, I find myself moving within and between both systems to create the queerness I seek. . . .

At the core of both my journey and this essay is a creative process of reclamation. Rather than simply giving up on both of these homosexualities, I seek to work within them by taking elements from both and combining them together in a new way that can challenge the oppressive components within each. Queer theorist José Esteban Muñoz, in studying the oppositional and creative use of mainstream heterosexual and queer cultures by queer performance artists of color, has articulated a process similar to the one I wish to engage in. Muñoz calls this process disidentification. He describes this as,

> . . . the third mode of dealing with dominant ideology, one that neither opts to assimilate within such a structure nor strictly opposes it; rather, disidentification is a strategy that works on and against dominant ideology . . . this "working on and against" is a strategy that tries to transform a cultural logic from within, always laboring to enact permanent structural change while at the same time valuing the importance of local or everyday struggles of resistance.

(1999, 11–12)

Moving beyond the binary idea that in the face of oppressive forces one can either purely resist or assimilate, Muñoz instead sees disidentification as a means to creatively engage with structures of injustice. Disidentification allows marginalized individuals to take the tools of oppression used against them and use them in new ways that alter their meaning so as to challenge the very oppression from which they are drawn. Muñoz values disidentification because it presents a means to escape the binary of assimilation and counteridentification which both serve to reinforce the dominance of oppressive systems. It is what Muñoz calls "working on and against" that makes disidentification a powerful means of altering the harmful elements of both Latin American homosexuality and American gayness.

I utilize disidentification to blend the two forms of homosexuality so as to construct a third path of queerness that can escape the limitations of both. Through disidentification, I can work against the totalizing power of Latin American homosexuality to trap queers in the gender system of man/woman. A third queerness can also work against a gayness in the United States that is increasingly becoming nothing more than a colorful and non-threatening alternative to heterosexuality. As gayness in the United States becomes more mainstream, it is not only leaving unchallenged dominant ideals of consumerism as citizenship, but in fact it is using those same ideals as the definition of social justice for queers. Since both forms of homosexuality are limiting and perpetuate violent forms of oppression, I must create a queerness through my daily practices that draws from the most transformative in both while challenging the most repressive in each. . . .

With the *mestiza/o gender* I am creating, my queerness moves beyond a matter of sexual identity and becomes an encompassing gender location. I embrace the ambiguous position of the Latin American *puto* and realize that pursuing masculinity is not only futile but it is harmful both to me and others. The *mestiza/o* politics of ambiguity show me that to be a gay man in a unified and stable sense isn't possible. The acts of exclusion that are required in creating a stable identity of gay masculinity, through the *mestiza/o* lens, are exposed as immoral and highly suspect. By buying into the binary gender system, queer men support the oppression of women, transpeople, and other gender deviants. The space that Latin American homosexuals occupy in the gender system can provide queer men with a means to construct identities that alter patriarchy and create coalitions of change with others. The gendered basis of Latin American homosexuality, however, must be tempered by the protection of the individual that American gayness so heavily emphasizes. By ensuring that individuals are allowed to develop and creatively construct their own identities, the gendered articulation of homosexuality in Latin America can become truly emancipatory. This *mestiza/o* combination is what I seek to create by living it everyday.

I recognize the potential dangers of engaging in the selective extraction and mixing of elements from diverse cultures, but I believe that the need for new forms of homosexualities justifies taking those risks. A politics of *mestizaje* can produce an impure queerness that is less about how each individual identifies, but instead focuses on how individuals relate to one another in the pursuit of justice. Claiming common cause with others, that is building a coalitional community of change, is an uneven process that must center not on the identities people wear and own, but instead on the act of relating. Who we relate to and how we relate to them is what should define us as queer. Thinking about queerness as a set of relations moves it from the realm of individual sexual identity towards a way of being. This shift sets queerness in the realm of gender, an all-encompassing script that defines who and what we are. *Mestizaje* opens up the category of gender, which is rightfully seen as a limiting force, into a means to structure the conflicting mixture of privilege and oppression that defines many queer men's masculinities. . . . Like the race mixing that *mestiza/o* has traditionally referred to, I am interested in creating a gayness that is a mixture—imperfect, always in process of becoming, yet resisting with all of its might. It is towards that end, that I write these notes, themselves imperfect and in process of articulation. . . .

References

Carrillo, H. (2003). "Neither Machos nor Maricones: Masculinity and Emerging Male Homosexual Identities in Mexico." In M. C. Gutmann (ed.), *Changing Men and Masculinities in Latin America*. Durham, NC: Duke University Press.

Guzmán, M. (2006). *Gay Hegemony/Latino Homosexualities*. New York: Routledge.

Muñoz, J. E. (1999). *Disidentifications: Queers of Color and the Performance of Politics*. Minneapolis, MN: University of Minnesota Press.

86

Look! No, Don't! The Invisibility Dilemma for Transsexual Men

Jamison Green

. . .

Walking down the street in San Francisco or New York City, Boston, Atlanta, Portland, Seattle, London, Paris, Rome, no one seems to take any special interest in me. I am just another man, invisible, no one special. I remember what it was first like to feel that anonymity as testosterone gradually obliterated the androgyny that for most of my life made others uncomfortable in my presence. It was a great relief . . .

Now . . . people are quite comfortable with my male presentation. My psyche seems to fit nicely into male packaging: I feel better; people around me are less confused, and so am I. So why tell anyone about my past? Why not just live the life of a normal man? Perhaps I could if I were a normal man, but I am not. I am a man, and I am a man who lived for 40 years in a female body. But I was not a woman. I am not a woman who became a man. I am not a woman who lives as a man. I am not, nor was I ever a woman, though I lived in a female body, and certainly tried, whenever I felt up to it, to be a woman. But it was never in me to be a woman. Likewise, I am not a man in the same sense as my younger brother is a man, having been treated as such all his life. I was treated as other than a man most of the time, as a man part of the time, and as a woman only rarely. Certainly I was treated as a little girl when I was young, but even then people occasionally assumed I was a little boy. I always felt like something "other." Can I be just a man now, or must I always be "other"?

. . .

Seeking acceptance within the system of "normal" and denying our transsexual status is an acquiescence to the prevailing binary gender paradigm that will never let us fit in, and will never accept us as equal members of society. Our transsexual status will always be used to threaten and shame us. We will always wear a scarlet T that marks us for treatment as a pretender, as other, as not normal, as trans. But wearing that T proudly—owning the label and carrying it with dignity—can twist that paradigm and free us from our subordinate prison. By using our own bodies and experience as references for our standards, rather than the bodies and experience of non-transsexuals (and non-transgendered people), we can grant our own legitimacy, as have all other groups that have been oppressed because of personal characteristics.

Transgendered people who choose transsexual treatment, who allow themselves to be medicalized, depend on a system of approval that grants them access to treatment. That approval may be seen as relieving them of their responsibility—or guilt—for being outside the norm. They then become either the justification for the treatment by embodying the successful application of "normal" standards; or they become the victims of the treatment when they realize they are still very different in form and substance from non-transsexual people, and they still suffer from the oppression they wished to escape by looking to doctors to make them "normal." By standing up and claiming our identity as men (or women) who are also transpeople, by asserting that our different bodies are just as normal for us as anyone else's is for them, by insisting that our right to modify our bodies and shape our own identities is as inalienable as our right to choose our religion (though not nearly as inexpensive or painless), we claim our humanity and our right to be treated equally under law and within the purviews of morality and culture.

. . .

Look! No, don't! Transsexual men are men. Transsexual men are men who have lived in female bodies. Transsexual men may appear feminine, androgynous or masculine. Any man may appear feminine, androgynous, or masculine. Look! What makes a man a man? His penis? His beard? His receding hairline? His lack of breasts? His sense of himself as a man? Some men have no beard, some have no penis, some never lose their hair, some have breasts. All have a sense of themselves as men.

. . . Look! No, don't! What is true, what is false? What is a "real" man?

I am real; I am an authentic and reliable man. I am also a transsexual man. I am a man who lived for 40 years in the body of a woman, so I have had access to knowledge that most men do not have. Invisibility has been a major issue in my life. Throughout my childhood and young adulthood I—my identity—was, for the most part, invisible. I was always defined by others, categorized either by my lack of femininity, or by my female body, or by the disquieting combination of both. The opportunity to escape the punishing inadequacy imposed on me by self-styled adjudicators of sex role performance was one I could not ignore. I simply will not accept a similar judgement of my masculinity. And I have yet to meet someone who could look me in the face, who could spend any time at all in conversation with me, who would deny my masculinity now the way they would dismiss it before as "just a phase" or "inappropriate behaviour for a girl."

. . . One of the most difficult things for me to reconcile about my own transition was my movement out of a place in lesbian culture and into a white heterosexual embodiment. Let me emphasize: Not all transsexual men have lesbian histories, and not all transsexual men are heterosexual. Nonetheless, my personal politics are quite closely aligned with queer culture, so I am again a different sort of heterosexual man. I am not afraid of homosexuality, though I do not practice it. Many gendered and heterosexist social constructs collapse like cardboard sea-walls against the ocean of my transsexual reality.

. . .

Look! No, don't! It all comes down to attitude. If you accept me—if you can acknowledge that I am a man, even a transsexual man—then you can accept that life has variation, life is rich, you don't control it, you experience it. You can still analyse concepts, you can still have opinions, you can even disagree with me. And if you don't accept me, well, then you don't. But as you go through life categorizing and qualifying, judging and evaluating, remember that there are human beings on the other end of the stick you're shaking, and they might have ideas and feelings and experiences that are different from your own. Maybe they look different from you, maybe they are tall women with large hands, maybe they are men who have given birth to their own children, maybe the categories you've delineated won't work in all cases. Look! No, don't! Transsexual men want to disappear because we are tired of being forced into categories, because we are beyond defending ourselves.

Look! No, don't! Transsexual men are entering the dialogue from more perspectives, more angles, than were ever theorized as being possible for them. Maybe if we are ignored we will go away. Maybe if we are continually not permitted to speak, not allowed to define ourselves, not given any corner of the platform from which to present our realities, then we will disappear and refrain from further complicating all the neat, orderly theories about gender and sex. Maybe if no one looks at us we will be safe.

At first I thought my transition was about not being looked at any longer, about my relief from scrutiny; now I know it is about scrutiny itself, about self-examination, and about losing my own fear of being looked at, not because I can disappear, but because I am able to claim my unique difference at last. What good is safety if the price is shame and fear of discovery? So, go ahead: Look!

87

My Life as an Out Gay Person in Russia

Masha Gessen

We tell our stories to know who we are and to tell each other that we are not alone. Our stories bear the traces of other stories we heard about ourselves. I remember my first ones. As a pre-teen, I read the Penal Code of the USSR, which said that the crime of "man lying with man" was punishable by up to five years in prison. I was not a man, but I had been having fantasies about being one and kissing a woman, a friend of my mother's. Somehow, my 12-year-old brain made the connection and I knew two things: I was not alone, and I was a criminal. A year or so later, this was confirmed when I heard that a famous theatre director was facing prosecution for having sex with a young man.

A friend from Leningrad recalls reading, at the age of 16, a textbook on sexual pathology. It suggested treating the female homosexual with thorazine, an early anti-psychotic medication with long-lasting, debilitating side-effects.

That friend left Leningrad and made a new, thorazine-free story for herself in the United States. I also emigrated, with my parents, as a teenager in 1981, and I did not return to the Soviet Union until 10 years later. In 1993, the sodomy law was quietly repealed, thorazine was, as far as I could tell, retired around the same time, and Russian queers got to the slow work of building identities and communities. For years I was the only publicly out gay person who was not a full-time gay activist: my position as a quasi-foreigner gave me a privileged perch, and my ability to earn money by writing for western publications made me almost impervious to discrimination. Other Russians were not in a hurry to come out.

By the mid-noughties, I found that I was no longer the only openly gay person in every setting. At one point, a couple of Moscow magazine publishers even got the idea that they should actively headhunt gay and lesbian staff. Our stories didn't make it onto the pages of mainstream magazines or newspapers, but at least they were quietly being told. A famous singer and a well-known actress, both women, fell in love and began working and living together; their relationship was an open secret, the talk of Moscow's largely approving high society. They would not acknowledge it publicly, though.

Russia, at the start of the 21st century, at least in its larger cities, very much resembled the United States of the early 1990s: being gay was no longer criminal or shameful, but it was still not a topic for polite conversation or public discussion. Issues such as same-sex marriage or protection from discrimination were not on the table, but then again, Russia was rebuilding itself as a dictatorship, so the political table had been hijacked.

The Kremlin, meanwhile, was telling itself and the world a very different story about Russia. Very few of us realized just how different it was; I certainly did not. Russia was stumbling on its way to becoming the "family values" capital of the world. The country, it felt, was being besieged by enemies who aimed to destroy its traditions and social institutions. LGBT people were the country's biggest threat: the quintessential "foreign agent," the ultimate other. In 2006, legislation banning "homosexual propaganda" – enshrining in law second-class citizenship for non-heterosexuals, making it an offence to claim equality – started winding its way from the smallest Russian cities to the largest. In June of this year, it became federal law.

The Patriarch of the Russian Orthodox Church has called the international trend toward legalizing same-sex marriage "a sign of the coming apocalypse." A popular conservative pundit recorded a series of commentaries for state-owned Channel 1, portraying LGBT people as the antichrist. The Kremlin's Nashi youth movement spread the news that I personally was out to destroy the Orthodox family. An online community calling for my murder appeared.

What scared me a lot more, however, was the promise, made by several prominent politicians, to start removing children from same-sex families. My partner and I and our three children are now leaving Russia. Thousands, possibly tens or hundreds of thousands of other LGBT people, are also looking for a way out of the country. The time when we felt our story was just a decade or two behind that of gays and lesbians in western Europe or the US seems impossibly distant now.

What has happened in Russia has captured the world's, which is to say the western media's, imagination. This is surely attributable, at least in part, to the fact that Russians are white. The TV commentator who has been preaching that LGBT people are "creatures who have declared open war on [Russian society] and want to enslave us" would, in his well-cut suits and with his hipster beard, hardly stand out in a London or New York crowd. The politician who drove the anti-gay campaign in St Petersburg and who told a leading Russian daily that "Americans just want to adopt our orphans and bring them up in perverted families like Masha Gessen's," can say all of this in fluent, articulate English.

But there is something else, too, that has driven the international reaction of unprecedented solidarity and support for Russia's besieged queers: it is the spectacle of history shifting abruptly into reverse. The current generation of Russians, though few of them are publicly out, had constructed comfortable lives in which they were open to their social circles. When your doctor and neighbors and child's schoolteachers know you are gay, there is no closet for you to hide in. That makes the tragedy of Russian LGBT people easy for western gays to identify with. This could be their story, too.

Look at the world map on the website of the International Lesbian, Gay, Bisexual, Trans, and Intersex Association. Same-sex relationships, both male and female, are still against the law in most of Africa and much of Asia. There are more countries in the world that send people to jail for loving someone of the same sex than there are countries that recognize same-sex marriage. In many countries, male same-sex relationships are punishable by 10 years behind bars; in at least two, the penalty is death.

The interactive interviews with people from across the world are their stories, too. I hope that they read Israeli activist Yoav Arad Pinkas's words of warning about the way that Israel is growing increasingly conservative and, in his opinion, potentially dangerous for LGBT people, and realize that history can turn back even in a country perceived as a gay haven. But more than that, I also hope that a young person from Egypt, or Afghanistan, or South Africa knows that these stories – some of which are also of love, happiness, and security – are his stories, too. He is not a criminal, and he is not alone.

88

Grassroots

Introduction

Winona LaDuke

I have spent my entire adult life as what you might call a political activist. I have testified at hearings, demonstrated at countless protests, and been involved in litigation. I've worked in a number of Native communities across the continent, and founded the White Earth Land Recovery Project (WELRP) on my home reservation. With our work here, we've been able to recover more than seventeen hundred acres of our land and create a land trust, while we work toward recovery of more of our own birthright. We also continue to work to protect our wild rice from genetic modification and ecosystems from contamination by pesticides, and to stop clear cuts of the forest. From inside my own house, we roast fair-trade and organic coffee. I have written books about the environment, run for vice president twice (as Ralph Nader's Green Party running mate in 1996 and 2000), and been arrested because I don't think that a thousand-year-old tree should become a phone book.

The perception of me, or of any well-known activist, is probably far from reality. Activists, the thinking goes, must be organized, focused, always working on the next strategy. My real life, the one in which I conduct all of my activism, is, of course, messy. If you came over, you might find my five children, ages four to sixteen, three dogs, fifteen horses, a few cats, several interns from around the country, and many friends who double as coworkers helping with WELRP's work. The 2000 veep campaign was conducted with me breastfeeding my newborn son before and after each stump speech and during many an interview. I still coordinate the sustainable food projects central to the White Earth Land Recovery Project literally from my kitchen table at the same time as I figure out meals for my kids, take coffee orders for Muskrat coffee company, and pop in videos for my youngest to watch on TV. I talk to Native community leaders from across the country as I cook meals and clean up (sort of an endless job). I write books at the same table where I make rawhide ornaments for sale as part of WELRP and help with maple syruping in the spring season, and my house is filled with labels that spell out the Ojibwe words for "bed," "book," "cupboard," and "table" as part of my ongoing commitment to indigenous language and culture preservation. My activism is simply in my life—it has to be, or it couldn't get done.

My own life as an identified activist has made me wonder at the term itself. What separates simple "responsibility" in life—motherhood, for example—from the fine line that one crosses to become an "activist"? I have been surprised and moved by encountering so many other mothers in my years as an activist: mothers in Chiapas breastfeeding their babies like anyone else, but who mask their faces as they speak with me because they can't afford to have their identifies known; Mohawk and Ojibwe mothers who face down General Motors and Potlach Corporation, knowing that if they don't, their kids won't ever know clean water, and generations ahead will have contaminated breast milk.

I have developed longstanding friendships with women who are engaged in struggles of responsibility—for their land, their own community health, and the water their children drink. Are these women feminists? That depends on who defines the term. Many of these women, including myself, are committed to the process of self-determination and believe in our inherent rights, as bestowed by the Creator, to live with dignity, peace, clean air and water, and our duty to pass on this legacy to our children and the generations to follow.

At the United Nations Conference on the Status of Women in Beijing, China, in 1995, I asked women from small countries around the world why they came all this way to participate in what was, in essence, a meeting. "I came because the World Bank is here," explained Victoria Tauli-Corpuz, an Igarok woman from the Philippines whose village is targeted for a Word Bank-funded dam. "I believe that those people at the World Bank and the IMF, those who make the decisions which will transform my life, should see my face." That sentiment applies whether you are an Igarok woman from the Philippines or Sherry Honkala from the Kensington Welfare Rights Union, challenging federal budget cuts to aid for dependent families or tending to the needs of homeless families. The message of self-determining women is the same for all people: *We want control over our lives, and we will challenge those who impose laws on our bodies, our communities, and our future.*

I believe that women move to activism out of sheer necessity. As a group, we are not of privilege—budget cuts devastated our household, the military wreaks havoc on our bodies and our homelands. The National Priorities Project reports that $152.6 billion spent on military aid in 2003 could have provided Head Start for an additional 20,211,205 children, health coverage for an additional 89,780,249 children, affordable housing vouchers for an additional 22,894,974 families, or salaries for 2,673,864 new elementary school teachers. Feminist activism, then, doesn't begin or end with my uterus: this is about my whole body, my life, and the lives of my children. We are women who redefine "Women's Issues," and say all issues are women's issues. I say: *We are the mothers of our nations, and anything that concerns our nations is of concern to us as women.* Those choices and necessities move us to speak out and to be active.

I happen to come from a line of these women who speak out, and I continue this work—our work. Women's work. My grandmother Helen Peskin, a Jewish woman from the Ukraine, recently passed into the Spirit World. Her early years were formed by the reality of war, first the Cossacks who overran her village and then the Nazis. With her life came a sheer determination to not be a victim, to speak for peace, to make a better life, and to demand dignity. Of her ninety years on this earth a good forty were spent as a seamstress: a purse maker, a member of the Pocket Book Makers Union in the garment district in New York, a folk dancer, and a peace activist. *A woman's work is about economic justice, and about quality of life.* My mother, Betty LaDuke, made her own path as a muralist and art professor, one of the first women on the faculty of her college, and like other women, she had to do it better than any man around because it took that much to get recognized. She has done this work in a way that celebrates life, and celebrates the work of other women. And she has done this work by linking with women in Eritrea, Nigeria, and Peru. *A women's work is about creating and celebrating life.* Our parents' struggles become our own, in our own time. We can't escape from that history, nor can we escape from our time in it.

In the lives of women in my family, it was never about just our own selves, it was about the collective dignity and *everyone's* health and rights. This is counter, in many ways, to Americanism. Americanism teaches individualism. My family, and indeed movements for social transformation, are not about anything as limited as the better job or the better advantage for the individual woman. Even the tragic deaths of three of my closest friends, activists all, are lessons in the urgency of change on a broader scale. Marsha Gomez, a gifted artist, was killed by her own son, who lacked the psychiatric medical attention he so desperately needed; Nilak Butler passed from ovarian cancer because she did not have adequate health coverage; and Ingrid Washinawatok El-Issa was assassinated by the FARC, Revolutionary Armed Forces of Colombia, with a gun and a bullet that came from my tax dollars in the second most highly financed recipient of U.S. military aid in the world.

N
E
X
T

S
T
E
P
S

The compelling reason behind activism is that our most personal lives—even the intimacy of death—are actually embroidered in the reality of public policy, foreign policy, military aid, and economics. Each day, then, I, like the women in my family before me, and like so many other women in the world, recommit to continue this struggle for life, and to celebrate its beauty in the process. That struggle and that celebration are who we are as women, as we take responsibility for our destinies.

. . .

89

National Latina Institute for Reproductive Health (NLIRH) Statement on Healthcare for All

National Latina Institute for Reproductive Health

The National Latina Institute for Reproductive Health (NLIRH) supports healthcare reform that will move our current system toward one that will improve the health, and well-being of all Latinas, their families and communities. NLIRH embraces a human rights approach to health care, ensuring that all health services are accessible, available, affordable, and of good quality for everyone. These services should be provided on an equitable basis, free from discrimination or coercion. Healthcare reform can take many paths, and it is important that the needs of all Latinas, including immigrant women, women of color and low-income women, are front and center.

NLIRH supports a system that includes all people, regardless of income, immigration status, or any other limiting factor. The current healthcare system leaves many Latinas falling through the cracks; 38% of Latinas are uninsured, the highest rate amongst all groups of women. Some Latinas may have an income too high to qualify for Medicaid, yet too low to afford private insurance. Many Latinas who would qualify based on income are not eligible. Among the ineligible are undocumented Latinas and legal permanent residents who have been in the United States for less than five years. This lack of access to healthcare contributes heavily to the health disparities that Latinas face, in turn affecting many other aspects of Latinas' quality of life.

It is important that such a system includes a full and comprehensive range of services, including coverage for family planning, abortions, prenatal care and preventive services. Currently Latinas—especially low-income, uninsured and immigrant Latinas—face numerous obstacles to obtaining these services, including cost and lack of access. Under the Hyde Amendment, no federal funds can be used for abortion services, meaning that many women on Medicaid are unable to access a full range of options when facing an unintended pregnancy, and may turn to unsafe terminations if they do not wish to carry the pregnancy to term. This and other obstacles create a disproportionate burden of morbidity and mortality on Latinas.

Moreover, NLIRH supports a system that is not only inclusive of all people and offers a comprehensive range of services, but is also one that emphasizes culturally competent and linguistically appropriate services. Comprehensive care is meaningless unless it is provided in a language with which patients are comfortable and accompanied by physicians and other clinicians that understand the needs of Latinas, immigrant women, and low-income women. Unless Latinas feel free of judgment, coercion and discrimination at our doctors' offices, health disparities will continue regardless of availability and access. Supporting health care reform that incorporates a human rights framework would ensure a holistic approach to the care needed for all Latinas to advance *salud, dignidad y justicia*!

90

Becoming an Ally

A New Examination

Nancy J. Evans and Jamie Washington

What does it mean to be an ally? Students in a graduate program that prepares student affairs professionals in higher education responded to this question with the following reflections:

- Being an ally is being supportive of other people who are different than you. . . . This support should be flexible and elastic so that it does not define a person but rather the person defines the needed support. (gay male)
- Being an ally is being open to learning. It is essential to be open to admitting your ignorance in order to grow. Being an ally also requires a commitment. . . . Being an ally requires an examination of our own privilege. In order to be an ally we have to be able to recognize how our privilege might play a role in the oppression of the very group/identity we want to be an ally to. Being an ally is using your powers for good. (lesbian)
- Being an ally is being aware of your own identities, advocating for the rights of others, supporting a cause, and challenging the oppression that particular populations face. It can mean lending a supportive hand to a peer. Being an ally is recognizing the inequality and inequity that exists in society, persistence, learning and teaching. (heterosexual woman)
- Being an ally is listening to other views and ideas without judgment; putting yourself in someone else's shoes; respecting people for who they are; advocating for resources, respect, equal treatment, laws; challenging your previous personal beliefs and ideas; working with underrepresented populations to better understand them and their unique needs; wanting to learn how to help, even in the little things; using non-discriminating language; [it is] important to the campus climate and overall student development; [it is] difficult and can have backlash. [An ally] must be committed and ready. (heterosexual male)
- An ally looks different to everyone. Sometimes an ally is a listening ear and a shoulder to cry on. Sometimes an ally is a fighter, fighting the powers to see justice done. (heterosexual woman)

NEXT STEPS

- Being an ally is confusion, hard, being yelled at, learning, acceptance, fighting to change, and learning you don't have to be right. . . . An ally can be the scapegoat in the room. Being an ally is knowing that you have privilege and oppressions and you can use both. Sometimes it is being called out and trying to realize you can learn from that. Learning when you can tell a story and learning when you can't explain no matter what and to just shut up. (questioning woman)

As these students suggest, being an ally is a difficult and complex role that can take on many meanings and require a wide variety of actions, many of which are challenging. What it means to be an ally often depends on who one asks and the particular situation and context in which one is involved. In this essay, we examine various definitions of *ally*, explore factors associated with becoming an ally of LGBT individuals, including the importance of recognizing heterosexual privilege, motivations for becoming an ally, the practice of advocacy, what an ally should know, and positive and negative consequences of advocacy. This essay is a revised and updated version of a chapter that appeared in the book, *Beyond Tolerance: Gays, Lesbians and Bisexuals on Campus*.

DEFINITIONS

As most writers and scholars in the area of oppression and multicultural education will concur, our language is imperfect and inherently "ism"-laden or oppressive. Therefore, clarifying the meaning of the term, "ally," is important. According to *Webster's New World Dictionary of the American Language*, an ally is "someone joined with another for a common purpose." This definition serves as a starting point for developing a working definition of *ally* as this term relates to issues of oppression. In our earlier work, we defined ally as "a person who is a member of the 'dominant' or 'majority' group who works to end oppression in his or her personal and professional life through support of, and as an advocate with and for, the oppressed population." More recently, Broido defined allies as "members of dominant social groups (e.g., men, Whites, heterosexuals) who are working to end the system of oppression that gives them greater privilege and power based on their social group membership" (2000). While similar to our earlier definition, Broido highlighted that allies must work at the systemic level, as well as the individual level, and more clearly defined what it means to be a member of a dominant group in terms of access to privilege and power.

Both definitions stress that although an oppressed person can certainly be a supporter and advocate for his or her own group, the impact and effect of such activity are different for the dominant group, and are often more powerful when the supporter is not a member of the oppressed population. Understanding this notion is an important first step toward becoming an ally for any "targeted" or oppressed group. Members of the LGBT community will sometimes argue that they can be allies for other members of the community, since "the community" is an umbrella group that includes many different subgroups, e.g., lesbians, gay males, bisexuals, transgendered individuals, and other populations that might choose to identify with the LGBT community (pansexual, questioning, etc.). We certainly acknowledge that with regard to dimensions of identity *other than* sexual identity, members of oppressed groups can be allies to other oppressed groups. For example, a gay man can be an ally to a lesbian woman with regard to *gender* oppression. With regard to *sexual* identity, however, both are oppressed. Given the definitions noted above, only heterosexual individuals can serve as allies of lesbian, gay, and bisexual people.

HETEROSEXUAL PRIVILEGE

The individual who decides to undertake the ally role must recognize and understand the power and privileges that one receives, accepts, and experiences as a heterosexual person. According to Johnson, who drew on the work of Peggy McIntosh, "privilege exists when one group has something of value that is denied to others simply because of the groups they belong to, rather than because of anything they've done or failed to do" (2006, 21). McIntosh noted that privilege comes in two forms: "unearned advantages and conferred dominance," with the former being things of value freely given to members of one group but arbitrarily denied to another group, and the latter referring to power given to one group over another. Developing awareness of one's privilege is often the most painful part of the process of becoming an ally.

Some of the powers and privileges heterosexuals generally have that gay and lesbian, and in some cases bisexual and transgender, persons do *not* have include:

- Family memberships to health clubs, pools, and other recreational facilities
- The right to legalized marriage
- The ability to purchase property as a couple
- The option to file joint income tax returns
- The ability to adopt children as a couple
- Health insurance for one's life partner
- The right to make decisions on health-related issues as they relate to one's life partner
- The assumption that one is psychologically healthy

In addition to such tangible privileges of the heterosexual population, there are a great many other, not so tangible, privileges. One important intangible privilege is living one's life without fear that people will find out that who one falls in love with, dreams about, or makes love to is someone of the same sex or that they were not always the gender with which they now identify. These fears affect the lives of gay, lesbian, bisexual, and transgender persons from the day they first begin to have "those funny feelings" until the day they die. Although many LGBT persons overcome these fears and turn the fear into a positive component of their lives, they have still been affected, and those wounds, even after healed, can be easily reopened.

Coming to terms with the very fact that "as a heterosexual I do not experience the world in the same way as LGBT people do" is an important step in becoming an ally. This awareness begins to move the heterosexual from being a caring, liberal person who feels that we are all created equal and should be treated as such, toward being an ally who begins to realize that although equality and equity are goals that have not yet been achieved, they can have a role in helping to make these goals realities.

Mohr introduced a model of heterosexual identity development, a process that he saw as related to the development of LGBT-affirmative attitudes. This model focuses on the development of awareness of heterosexual privilege. Mohr suggested that four "working models of sexual orientation" exist. Similar to Helms's contact status of white racial identity development in which individuals see themselves as color-blind, in the first working model proposed by Mohr, *democratic heterosexuality*, heterosexuals "tend to view people of all sexual orientations as essentially the same" (2002, 540–541). Individuals using this model rarely think about sexual identity issues and consider them unimportant. *Compulsory heterosexuality*, the second working model, is underscored by a belief that heterosexuality is the only acceptable form of sexual identity and that individuals who identify as LGBT are sick, perverted, and deserve to be oppressed. Individuals who base their beliefs on the third working model, *politicized heterosexuality*, recognize the privilege associated with heterosexuality and experience the emotions of guilt, sadness, and shame noted earlier that come with this awareness. They may also idealize LGBT people rather than seeing them as individuals who lead complex lives that are not solely centered around their sexual and gender identities. In the fourth working model, *integrative heterosexuality*, individuals are cognizant of the system of oppression that exists related to gender and sexual identity and the ways in which this system affects all people, regardless of their specific identity.

When heterosexual persons first learn that their lesbian, gay, bisexual, or transgender friends are truly mistreated on the basis of sexual or gender identity, they often feel anger toward heterosexuals and guilt toward themselves for being members of the same group. This process can only happen, however, if individuals have progressed at least to Mohr's third working model, when persons have an understanding of sexual and gender identity and do not see it as grounds for discrimination, violence, or abuse. These feelings do not occur when the person still believes that lesbian, gay, bisexual, or transgender persons are sick sinners who either need to have a good sexual relationship with a person of the other sex or see a psychologist or a spiritual leader so that they can be cured. Such persons, who might be classified as being in Mohr's second working model, are not yet ready to start down the ally road.

MOTIVATIONS FOR BECOMING AN ADVOCATE

What motivates heterosexuals to become LGBT rights advocates? There are certainly more popular and less controversial causes with which one can become involved. Goodman noted that support of social justice in general is related to empathy, moral and spiritual values, and self-interest. Since involvement in LGBT rights advocacy is often deemed a moral issue, moral development theory suggests some possible underlying reasons for such activity. Lawrence Kohlberg hypothesized that moral reasoning develops through three levels: preconventional, conventional, and postconventional. At the preconventional level, moral decisions are based on what is good for the individual. Persons functioning at this level may choose to be involved in gay rights issues to protect their own interests or to get something out of such involvement (e.g., if this issue is particularly important to a supervisor whose approval is sought). At the conventional level, Kohlberg indicated that decisions are made that conform to the norms of one's group or society. Individuals at this level may work for LGBT rights if they wish to support friends who are gay, lesbian, bisexual, or transgender or to uphold an existing institutional policy of nondiscrimination. Kohlberg's third level of reasoning involves decision making based on principles of justice. At this level the individual takes an active role to create policies that assure that all people are treated fairly and becomes involved in LGBT rights advocacy because it is the right thing to do.

While Kohlberg focused on justice as the basis of moral decision making, Carol Gilligan used the principle of care as the basis of her model of moral reasoning. Her three levels of reasoning are (1) taking care of oneself, (2) taking care of others, and (3) supporting positions that take into consideration the impact *both* on self and others. Using this model, individuals at the first level become advocates to make themselves look good to others or to protect themselves from criticism for not getting involved. At the second level, individuals reason that they should "take care of" LGBT people. The final perspective leads individuals to believe that equality and respect for differences create a better world for everyone, and that these are worthwhile goals.

One could argue that the latter position in each scheme is the enlightened perspective that any advocate needs to espouse. We should, however, be aware that not every person is functioning at a postconventional level of moral reasoning, and that arguments designed to encourage people to commit themselves to LGBT rights advocacy need to be targeted to the level that the individual can understand and accept. Kohlberg indicated that active involvement in addressing moral issues is an important factor in facilitating moral development along his stages. We can, therefore, expect that as people become involved in LGBT rights issues, their levels of reasoning may move toward a postconventional level.

In some ways paralleling our analysis of the moral reasoning that may be involved in advocacy, Edwards introduced a conceptual model of ally identity development. He suggested that self-interest, altruism, and a desire for social justice can all motivate potential allies. *Aspiring allies for self-interest* would take action when an LGBT person they care about is in danger of being hurt. They act on behalf of specific individuals to stop specific actions that are harmful or discriminatory and do not understand or care about the larger system of oppression that affects LGBT people as a group. Edwards noted that aspiring allies for self-interest often thrive on the feelings of power that come with "rescuing" their friend and being seen as a hero, thus perpetuating the system of oppression that creates the problem in the first place.

Edwards suggested that as individuals become aware of the privilege they experience, they can become motivated to be allies to assuage the guilt they feel. While *aspiring allies for altruism* would see the issues that confront LGBT individuals as a group, they would be likely to place the blame for oppression on other heterosexual individuals rather than seeing that they also benefit from an oppressive system. They would be likely to exhibit a paternalistic attitude as they seek to come to the aid of the oppressed LGBT population and, consciously or unconsciously, expect recognition and praise for the work they do on behalf of this group.

The final type of allies that Edwards discussed is *allies for social justice*. These allies "work *with* those from the oppressed group in collaboration and partnership to end the system of oppression" (2006, 51). They would be aware that acting to end oppression of LGBT people in the end benefits heterosexuals as well. Thus, their goal in working to address the issue of oppression would be to achieve a just society rather than to gain recognition for their efforts.

Edwards acknowledged that individuals may experience each of these motivations for ally work depending on the specific situation in which they find themselves. He also stated that "the Ally for Social Justice status is an aspirational identity one must continuously work towards" (53). He argued that understanding each motivation can lead to the development of more consistent and effective ally behaviors.

ADVOCACY IN ACTION

Advocacy can take a number of different forms and target various audiences. Heterosexual supporters may focus some of their energy toward LGBT individuals themselves. At other times the target may be other heterosexuals, and often strategies developed for college and university campuses are focused on the campus community as a whole.

Advocacy with LGBT people involves acceptance, support, and inclusiveness. Examples of acceptance include listening in a nonjudgmental way and valuing the unique qualities of each individual. Support includes such behaviors as championing the hiring of LGBT staff; providing an atmosphere in which LGBT issues can be discussed in training or programming; or attending events sponsored by LGBT student organizations. Inclusiveness involves activities such as the use of nonexclusionary language; publications, fliers, and handbooks that take into account sexual and gender identity differences; and sensitivity to the possibility that not everyone in a student organization or work setting is heterosexual.

Being an advocate among other heterosexuals is often challenging. Such a position involves modeling advocacy, support, and confronting inappropriate behavior. In this context, heterosexual supporters model nonheterosexist behaviors such as being equally physical with men and women, avoiding joking or teasing someone for nontraditional gender behaviors, and avoiding making a point of being heterosexual. Allies are spokespersons for addressing LGBT issues proactively in program and policy development. Confronting such behaviors as heterosexist joke telling; the exclusion of LGBT people either intentionally or by using language that assumes heterosexuality; discriminatory hiring practices; or the evaluation of staff based on factors related to their sexual or gender identities is also part of the role of the advocate.

Advocacy in the institution involves making sure that issues facing LGBT students and staff are acknowledged and addressed. This goal is accomplished by developing and promoting educational efforts that raise the awareness level and increase the sensitivity of heterosexual students, staff, and faculty on campus. Such activities include inviting speakers to address topics relevant to the LGBT community; developing panel discussions on issues related to sexual and gender identities; including LGBT issues as a topic in resident advisor training programs; promoting plays and movies featuring LGBT themes; and advocating for curricular inclusion across the academic disciplines focusing on LGBT-related issues and themes.

Encouraging LGBT student and staff organizations is also part of institutional advocacy. Such groups need to have access to the same campus resources, funding, and sponsorship as other student and staff organizations. Developing and supporting pro-LGBT policies are also necessary aspects of advocacy. Anti-harassment policies, anti-discriminatory hiring policies, and provisions for gay and lesbian couples to live together in campus housing are arenas that deserve attention.

NEXT STEPS

STEPS TOWARD BECOMING AN ALLY

When dealing with issues of oppression, there are four basic levels of ally involvement. The following examples relate specifically to being an ally to LGBT persons.

- *Awareness* is the first level. It is important to become more aware of who you are and how you are different from and similar to LGBT people. Such awareness can be gained through conversations with LGBT individuals, attending awareness-building workshops, reading about LGBT life, and self-examination.
- *Knowledge/education* is the second level. You must begin to acquire knowledge about sexual and gender identities and the experiences of LGBT people. This step includes learning about laws, policies, and practices and how they affect LGBT people, in addition to educating yourself about LGBT culture and the norms of this community. Contacting local and national LGBT organizations for information can be very helpful.
- *Skills* make up the third level. This area is the one in which people often fall short because of fear, or lack of resources or supports. You must develop skills in communicating the knowledge that you have learned. These skills can be acquired by attending workshops, role-playing certain situations with friends, developing support

connections, or practicing interventions or awareness raising in safe settings—for example, a restaurant or hotel out of your hometown.

- *Action* is the last, but most important, level and is the most frightening step. There are many challenges and liabilities for heterosexuals in taking actions to end the oppression of LGBT people. Some are addressed later in this essay in our discussion of factors that discourage advocacy. Nonetheless, action is, without doubt, the only way that we can effect change in the society as a whole; for if we keep our awareness, knowledge, and skill to ourselves, we deprive the rest of the world of what we have learned, thus keeping them from having the fullest possible life.

In addition to the four levels of ally involvement, there are six additional points to keep in mind:

1. Defining yourself as an ally is somewhat presumptuous. Whether your actions would qualify as those of an ally can best be determined by members of the LGBT population. Certainly, a person can advocate for equity and social justice for LGBT people without the permission of the LGBT community but declaring oneself to be an ally and demanding recognition as such can be off-putting to many LGBT people. Referring again to Edwards's model, such behavior seems more indicative of someone who is motivated by self-interest or altruism rather than by social justice.

2. Have a good understanding of sexual and gender identities and be aware of and comfortable with your own. If you are a person who chooses not to identify with a particular sexual or gender identity, be comfortable with that decision, but recognize that others, particularly LGBT people, may see your stance as a cop-out.

3. Talk with LGBT people and read about the coming-out process. This is a process and experience that is unique to this oppressed group. Few other populations of oppressed persons need to disclose so much to family and close friends in the same way. Because of its uniqueness, this process brings challenges that are often not understood.

4. As any other oppressed group, the LGBT population gets the same messages about homosexuality, bisexuality, and gender expression as everyone else. As such, there is a great deal of internalized heterosexism, homophobia, and transgender oppression. There are LGBT people who believe that what they do in bed is nobody's business, and that being an "out" lesbian, gay, bisexual, or transgender person to them would mean forcing their sexual practices on the general society, something they feel should not be done. It is, therefore, very important not only to be supportive, recognizing that you do not share the same level of personal risk as a lesbian, gay, bisexual, or transgender person, but also to challenge some of the internalized oppressive notions, thus helping to develop a different, more positive, perspective.

5. As with most oppressed groups, there is diversity within the LGBT community. Heterosexism is an area of oppression that cuts across, but is not limited to, race, ethnicity, gender, class, religion, culture, age, and level of physical or mental ability. For all of these categories, there are different challenges. Certainly, LGBT individuals as members of these diverse populations share some common joys and concerns; however, issues often manifest themselves in very different ways in different groups, thus calling for different strategies and interventions.

6. It is difficult to enter into a discussion about heterosexism and homophobia without the topic of AIDS/HIV infection arising. Knowing at least basic information about the illness is necessary for two reasons: (1) to address myths and misinformation related to AIDS and the LGBT community, and (2) to be supportive of the members

N
E
X
T

S
T
E
P
S

of the community affected by this disease. Although we recognize that AIDS is a health issue that has and will continue to affect our entire world, the persons who live in the most fear of this disease and have lost the most members of their community are LGBT individuals. Accepting that reality helps an ally to understand the intense emotions that surround this issue within the community.

These six points and the previously discussed levels of ally involvement provide some guidelines for becoming an effective ally. Although we recognize that these concepts seem fairly reasonable, there are some real challenges or factors that can discourage a potential ally from taking these steps.

FACTORS THAT DISCOURAGE ADVOCACY

Involvement in LGBT rights advocacy can be a scary and unpopular activity. Individuals who wish to take on such a role must be aware of and reconcile themselves to several potentially unpleasant outcomes. Some of these problems involve reactions from other heterosexuals, and some come from members of the LGBT community.

An assumption often is automatically made within the heterosexual community that anyone supporting LGBT rights is automatically gay, lesbian, bisexual, or transgender. Although such an identity is not negative, such labeling can create problems, especially for unmarried heterosexuals who might wish to become involved in a heterosexual romantic relationship. Heterosexuals also often experience derisive comments from other heterosexuals concerning involvement in a cause that is viewed as unimportant, unacceptable, or unpopular. Friends and colleagues who are uncomfortable with the topic may become alienated from the heterosexual supporter of LGBT rights, or may noticeably distance themselves from the individual. Difficulty may arise in social situations if the heterosexual ally is seen in the company of LGBT individuals. Discrimination, either overt or subtle, may also result from getting involved in controversial causes. Such discrimination may take the form of poor evaluations, failure to be appointed to important committees, or encouragement to seek a position at a school "more supportive of your ideas."

The LGBT community may also have trouble accepting the heterosexual ally. Often an assumption is made that such persons are really gay, lesbian, bisexual, or transgender but not yet accepting of their identity. Subtle or not-so-subtle pressure is placed on such people to come out or at least to consider the possibility of a nonheterosexual identity.

The LGBT community is one that has its own language and culture. Heterosexual supporters can feel out of place and awkward in settings populated exclusively or mainly by gay males, lesbians, bisexuals, and transgender people. LGBT people may be exclusionary in their conversations and activities, leaving the heterosexual ally out of the picture.

Since most LGBT people have had mainly negative experiences with heterosexuals in the past, the motives of heterosexuals involved in LGBT rights activities are often questioned. These experiences make it difficult for LGBT people to accept that individuals will involve themselves in a controversial and unpopular cause just because it is "right." Many LGBT individuals also believe that persons who are not members of their community cannot truly understand the issues they face and should therefore leave it to LGBT people to educate and advocate for their own rights. They can become angry and resentful of heterosexuals' involvement in programs, spaces, and activities they believe should be exclusively theirs.

THE BENEFITS OF BEING AN ALLY

Although the factors that discourage individuals from being an ally are very real, there are many benefits of being an ally, including:

1. You open yourself up to the possibility of close relationships with an additional percentage of the world.
2. You become less locked into sex-role stereotypes.
3. You increase your ability to have close and loving relationships with same-sex friends.
4. You have opportunities to learn from, teach, and have an impact on a population with whom you might not otherwise interact.
5. You may be the reason a family member, coworker, or community member finally decides that life is worth something and that dependence on chemicals or other substances might not be the answer.
6. You may make the difference in the lives of adolescents who hear you confront anti-LGBT epithets that make them feel as if they want to drop out of junior high, high school, or college. As a result of your action, they will know they have a friend to turn to.
7. Lastly, you can get invited to some of the most fun parties, have some of the best foods, play some of the best sports, have some of the best intellectual discussions, and experience some of the best music in the world, because everyone knows that LGBT people are good at all these things.

Although the last factor is meant as a joke, there is a great deal of truth concerning the positive experiences to which persons open themselves when they allow themselves to be a part of and include another segment of the population in their world. Imagine what it could be like to have had such close friends as Tennessee Williams, Cole Porter, Bessie Smith, Walt Whitman, Gertrude Stein, Alice Walker, James Baldwin, Virginia Woolf, Joan of Arc (trans). Imagine the world without their contributions. It is possible for gay, lesbian, bisexual, and transgender people, as well as heterosexuals, to make a difference in the way the world is, but we must start by realizing equity in our humanness and life experiences.

References

Broido, E. M. (2000) "The Development of Social Justice Allies during College: A Phenomenological Investigation." *Journal of College Student Development*, 41, 3–18.

Edwards, K. E. (2006). "Aspiring Social Justice Ally Identity Development: A Conceptual Model". *NASPA Journal*, 43 (2), 39–60.

Johnson, A. G. (2006). *Privilege, Power, and Difference* (second edition). Boston, MA: McGraw-Hill.

Mohr, J. J. (2002). "Heterosexual Identity and the Heterosexual Therapist: An Identity Perspective on Sexual Orientation Dynamics in Psychotherapy." *Counseling Psychologist*, 30, 532–566.

NEXT STEPS

91

Transgender Day of Remembrance

A Day to Honor the Dead and the Living

Shelby Chestnut

As we honor our friends and family we have lost to anti-transgender violence on Transgender Day of Remembrance (TDoR), how can we ensure that transgender women of color are leading the LGBTQ anti-violence movement?

The New York City Anti-Violence Project (AVP) knows that transgender people of color face severe and deadly violence at disproportionate rates compared with cisgender white LGBQ people. Multi-year data show us that transgender women of color are facing a violent epidemic.

In 2014 we mourned the tragic deaths of 10 transgender people of color across the U.S., nine of whom were transgender women of color: Kandy Hall, Zoraida Reyes, Yaz'min Shancez, Tiff Edwards, Mia Henderson, an unidentified gender-nonconforming person, Alejandra Leos, Aniya Parker, Tajshon Sherman, and Gizzy Fowler.

However, in response to the severe and deadly violence facing transgender people of color, we also see the tremendous leadership and vision of transgender people of color, especially transgender women of color. This leadership and vision seeks to end violence and shows us that another world is possible, a world in which all LGBTQ people live free of violence and the leadership of transgender women of color is honored and leading the LGBTQ anti-violence movement locally and nationally. To end this violence, we must support the leadership of those thriving and surviving in the face of this violence.

Nationally we see the tremendous leadership of transgender people of color like Bamby Salcedo in Los Angeles, organizing trans Latina women and transgender women of color on a national level; Milan Nicole of BreakOUT in New Orleans, fighting against the criminalization of LGBTQ youth; Brooke Cerda Guzmán in New York City, fighting tirelessly to ensure that the LGBTQ community honors the life of Islan Nettles, a young transgender woman of color who died in 2013 as a result of transphobic violence; Elliott Fukui of the Audre Lorde Project's TransJustice Program in New York City, creating and sustaining a political organizing space for and by trans people of color; LaLa Zannell of the New York City Anti-Violence Project, organizing LGBTQ people around issues of hate violence, sexual violence, intimate-partner violence and police violence; Angelica Ross, CEO of TransTech, a Chicago nonprofit that's providing job and tech training for transgender people; and CeCe McDonald in Minneapolis, speaking nationally about the criminalization of trans people, particularly trans people of color.

These are just a few people of the thousands of trans people of color who are changing the world every day and demanding a world in which transgender people of color are seen no longer as victims of violence but as agents of change who must be recognized and respected as leaders in the LGBTQ anti-violence movement.

Each TDoR we read the names of those who have lost their lives to brutal anti-trans violence. What would shift if, in addition, we read the names of those living and surviving to fight against this violence? If we were able to see justice as trans people of color living and creating a world in which transgender people are free of violence?

Will you join AVP and thousands of transgender people of color on TDoR to speak not just the names of those we lost but the names of those who are leading us toward justice?

92

Unbowed

A Memoir

Wangari Maathai

On the morning of October 8, 2004, I was on my way from Nairobi to my parliamentary constituency, Tetu, for a meeting when my cell phone rang. I moved closer to the window of the van I was traveling in so I could hear better amid the static and the bumps on the road. It was the Norwegian ambassador, asking me to keep the line clear for a phone call from Oslo. After some time, it came. It was Ole Danbolt Mjos, chair of the Norwegian Nobel Committee. His gentle voice came through clearly. "Is this Wangari Maathai?" he inquired.

While I receive calls from all over the world, I may not catch the name of the caller or recognize their voice until the reason for the call has been explained. So I paid attention to the caller for the message. "Yes," I said drawing the phone closer to my ear. He gave me the news. It left me speechless.

. . .

It was clear now why the Norwegian ambassador had called. "I am being informed that I have won the Nobel Peace Prize," I announced to myself and those around me in the car with a smile as I pulled the cell phone away from my ear and reconnected with my fellow passengers. They knew it was not a joke because happiness was written all over my face. But at the same time, tears streamed from my eyes and onto my cheeks as I turned to them. They, too, were by now smiling broadly, some cheering loudly and hugging me as if to both comfort and congratulate me, letting my tears fall on their warm shoulders and hiding my face from some of my staff, whom they felt shouldn't see me cry. But these were tears of great joy at an extraordinary moment!

I thought of the long journey to this time and place. My mind went back and forth over all the difficult years and great effort when I often felt I was involved in a lonely, futile struggle. I didn't know that so many people were listening and that such a moment would come. Meanwhile, the car rambled on to Nyeri's Outspan Hotel, where I often take a break before continuing to my rural Tetu constituency.

. . .

The news spread quickly throughout the hotel and among the guests. The manager and his senior staff were quick to come out to congratulate me. Then the enterprising manager responded to a request to provide a tree seedling and a shovel so that I could celebrate the best way I know how: by planting a tree.

A member of the hotel staff quickly dug a hole as a small crowd of onlookers and journalists gathered to witness and record the planting of a Nandi flame tree. Surrounded by the local and international press, the hotel guests, and workers, I prepared to plant this hardy tree seedling along the edge of the green yard, overlooking the imposing Mt. Kenya to the distant north. I kneeled down, put my hands in the red soil, warm from the sun, settled the tree seedling in the ground. They handed me a bucket of clean water and I watered the tree.

I faced Mt. Kenya, the source of inspiration for me throughout my life, as well as for generations of people before me. I reflected on how appropriate it was that I should be at

N E X T S T E P S

this place at this time and celebrating the historic news facing this mountain. The mountain is known to be rather shy, the summit often cloaked by a veil of clouds. It was hidden that day. Although around me the sun was bright and strong, the mountain was hiding. As I searched for her with my eyes and heart, I recalled the many times I have worried whether she will survive the harm we are doing to her. As I continued to search for her, I believed that the mountain was celebrating with me: The Nobel Committee had also heard the voice of nature, and in a very special way. As I gazed at her, I felt that the mountain too was probably weeping with joy, and hiding her tears behind a veil of white clouds. At that moment I felt I stood on sacred ground.

Trees have been an essential part of my life and have provided me with many lessons. Trees are living symbols of peace and hope. A tree has roots in the soil yet reaches to the sky. It tells us that in order to aspire we need to be grounded, and that no matter how high we go it is from our roots that we draw sustenance. It is a reminder to all of us who have had success that we cannot forget where we came from. It signifies that no matter how powerful we become in government or how many awards we receive, our power and strength and our ability to reach our goals depend on the people, those whose work remains unseen, who are the soil out of which we grow, the shoulders on which we stand.

The Nobel Peace Prize has presented me with extraordinary opportunities to travel, both home and abroad . . . to celebrate, encourage, and empower the huge constituency that felt honored by the prize: the environmental movement, those who work on women's and gender issues, human rights advocates, those advocating for good governance, and peace movements. There continues to be lot of interest among government leaders, academic institutions, development agencies, the corporate sector, and the media.

This interest was partly due to the connection the Norwegian Nobel Committee made between peace, sustainable management of resources, and good governance. This was the first time such a linkage had been forged by the Nobel Committee and it was the first time that the committee had decided to recognize its importance by awarding the Nobel Peace Prize to somebody who had worked in these areas for over three decades. As we had said for many years, humanity needs to rethink peace and security and work toward cultures of peace by governing itself more democratically, respecting the rule of law and human rights, deliberately and consciously promoting justice and equity, and managing resources more responsibly and accountably—not only for the present but also for the future generations.

In trying to explain this linkage, I was inspired by a traditional African stool that has three legs and a basin to sit on. To me, the three legs represent three critical pillars of just and stable societies. The first leg stands for democratic space, where rights are respected, whether they are human rights, women's rights, children's rights, or environmental rights. The second represents sustainable and equitable management of resources. And the third stands for cultures of peace that are deliberately cultivated within communities and nations. The basin, or seat, represents society and its prospects for development. Unless all three legs are in place, supporting the seat, no society can thrive. Neither can its citizens develop their skills and creativity. When one leg is missing, the seat is unstable; when two legs are missing, it is impossible to keep any state alive; and when no legs are available, the state is as good as a failed state. No development can take place in such a state either. Instead, conflict ensues.

These issues of good governance, respect for human rights, equity, and peace are of particular concern in Africa—a continent that is so rich in resources and yet has been so ravaged by war. The big question is, Who will access the resources? Who will be excluded? Can the minority have a say, even if the majority have their way?

. . .

As women and men continue this work of clothing this naked Earth, we are in the company of many others throughout the world who care deeply for this blue planet. We have nowhere else to go. Those of us who witness the degraded state of the environment and the suffering that comes with it cannot afford to be complacent. We continue to be restless. If we really carry the burden, we are driven to action. We cannot tire or give up. We owe it to the present and future generations of all species to rise up and walk!

93

Calling All Restroom Revolutionaries!

Simone Chess, Alison Kafer, Jessi Quizar,
and Mattie Udora Richardson

Everyone needs to use bathrooms, but only some of us have to enter into complicated political and architectural negotiations in order to use them. The fact is, bathrooms are easier to access for some of us than for others, and the people who never think about where and how they can pee have a lot of control over how using restrooms feels for the rest of us. What do we need from bathrooms? What elements are necessary to make a bathroom functional for everyone? To make it safe? To make it a private and respectful space? Whose bodies are excluded from the typical restroom? More important, what kind of bodies are assumed in the design of these bathrooms? Who has the privilege (we call it pee-privilege) of never needing to think about these issues, of always knowing that any given bathroom will meet one's needs? Everyone needs to use the bathroom. But not all of us can.

And that's where People in Search of Safe and Accessible Restrooms (PISSAR) comes in. PISSAR, a coalition of UC-Santa Barbara undergrads, grad students, staff, and community members, recognizes that bathrooms are not always accessible for people with disabilities, or safe for people who transgress gender norms. PISSAR was formed at the 2003 University of California Student of Color Conference, held at UC-Santa Barbara. During the lunch break on the second day of the conference, meetings for the disability caucus and the transgender caucus were scheduled in adjacent rooms. When only a few people showed up for both meetings, we decided to hold a joint session. One of the members of the disability caucus mentioned plans to assess bathroom accessibility on the campus, wondering if there was a similar interest in mapping gender-neutral bathrooms. Everyone in the room suddenly began talking about the possibilities of a genderqueer/disability coalition, and PISSAR was born.

For those of us whose appearance or identity does not quite match the "man" or "woman" signs on the door, bathrooms can be the sites of violence and harassment, making it very difficult for us to use them safely or comfortably. Similarly, PISSAR acknowledges that, although most buildings are required by the Americans with Disabilities Act to provide accessible bathrooms, some restrooms are more compliant than others and accessible bathrooms can often be hard to find. PISSAR's mission, then, is threefold: 1) to raise awareness about what safe and accessible bathrooms are and why they are necessary; 2) to map and verify existing accessible and/or gender-neutral bathrooms on the campus; and 3) to advocate for additional bathrooms. We eventually hope to have both web-based and printed maps of all the bathrooms on campus, with each facility coded as to its accessibility and gender-safety. Beyond this initial campaign, PISSAR plans to advocate for the

NEXT STEPS

construction or conversion of additional safe and accessible bathrooms on campus. To that end, one of our long-term goals is to push for more gender-neutral bathrooms and showers in the dormitories, and to investigate the feasibility of multistall gender-neutral bathrooms across the campus as a whole.

As it turned out, we weren't the only restroom revolutionaries on campus. We soon joined forces with a student-run initiative to stock all campus tampon and pad machines, a group called, appropriately enough, Aunt Flo and the Plug Patrol. Aunt Flo's goal is to use funds garnered from the sale of tampons and pads in campus bathroom dispensers (blood money, if you will) to support student organizations in a time of tremendous budget cuts. We liked their no-euphemism approach to the bathroom and the body and joined their effort to make the campus not only a safer and more accessible place to pee but also to bleed. We also expanded our focus to include issues of childcare, inspired in part by one of our members' experiences as a young mom on campus. PISSAR decided to examine whether campus bathrooms featured changing tables, a move that increased our intersectional analysis of bathroom access and politics.

By specifically including the work of Aunt Flo and concerns about childcare access, PISSAR challenges many of the assumptions that are made about genderqueer and disabled bodies. Why shouldn't every gender-neutral restroom have a tampon/pad machine? Putting tampon/pad machines only in women's rooms, and mounting them high on the wall, restricts the right to menstruate conveniently to those with certain bodies. It suggests that the right to tampons and pads is reserved for people who use gender-specific women's rooms and can reach a lever hanging five feet from the ground. This practice reinscribes ideas about disabled bodies being somehow dysfunctional and asexual (as in, "People in wheelchairs get their periods too?") and perpetuates the idea that genderqueer folks are inherently unbodied (as in, "Only real women need tampons, and you don't look like a real woman").

. . .

From the information garnered in the PISSAR patrols, we are in the process of making a map that will assess the safety and accessibility of all the bathrooms on campus. The map is vital to our project because it offers genderqueer and disabled people a survey of all the restrooms on campus so that they can find what they need without the stigma and frustration of telling a possibly uninformed administrator the details of their peeing needs. For people who have never had to think about bathrooms, the map's detailed information suggests the ways in which our everyday bathrooms are restrictive and dangerous. Thus the map also functions as a consciousness-raising tool, educating users about the need for safe and accessible restrooms.

PISSAR patrols aren't simply about getting information. They're also a way to keep our bodies involved in our project. PISSAR is, after all, a project about bodies: about bodily needs, about the size and shape of our bodies, and about our bodily presentation. The very nature of our bathroom needs necessitates this attention to the body. So it makes sense that when we tried to theorize about what a safe, respectful restroom might look like, we realized we needed to meet in the bathroom. Because the bathroom is our site, and the body in search of a bathroom is our motivation, we recognized early on the need to be concerned with body and theory together. PISSAR's work is an attempt at embodying theory, at theorizing from the body.

. . .

Our concern with body/theory is also evident in our insistence that bathroom accessibility is an important issue for a lot of different people. Everyone should be able to find a bathroom that conforms to the needs of their body. Everyone should be able to use a restroom without being accused of being in the "wrong" place. Everyone should have access to tampon dispensers and facilities for changing diapers, regardless of gender or ability. Homeless folks should have access to clean restrooms free of harassment. Bathroom activism is, from the outset, a multi-identity endeavor. It has the potential to bring together feminists, transfolks, people with disabilities, single parents, and a variety of other people whose bathroom needs frequently go unmet. It creates a much needed space for those of us whose identities are more complicated than can be encompassed in a single-issue movement. Viewed in this light, restroom activism is an ideal platform from which to launch broader coalition work. In PISSAR, we tend to think about "queerness" as encompassing more than just sexual orientation; it includes queer bodies, queer politics, and queer coalitions.

94

Why I Marched on Washington—With Zero Reservations

Rinku Sen

As soon as it was announced, I knew that I would be going to the 2017 Women's March on Washington. I thought that it would be politically important, and I felt no emotional conflict about going. I was lucky to experience positive cross-racial feminist organizing early on, which no doubt made it easier for me to engage.

I was in college when I had my first political experience of a multiracial feminist community. Near the end of a remarkable year of activism at Brown University, women who had led campaigns about issues ranging from nuclear war to racial justice decided to push hard against sexual violence on campus. With only a few days of organizing, 120 White, Black, Asian, Latina, straight, queer, butch, femme, rural and urban women planned a women's speakout just before finals. Some of us were new to feminism; some were already veterans.

We made every decision by consensus, including significant time on whether or not to trample newly planted grass on our march to Wriston Quad, where all of Brown's fraternities are housed. The speakout we planned for one hour lasted more than four. The dusk-to-dawn shuttle service we demanded still exists 30 years later. Shortly after our action, the university revoked the charter of a fraternity. We worked together across race and sexuality, and to some degree across class, and we won. Women of color were there from the very beginning and comprised a significant portion of the steering committee. There was never any question that we would do it this way.

There's a world of difference between an elite college campus and those of communities that are far less sheltered, less privileged. But then, as now, the experience of sexual violence, however varied, brought women together. Among the least discussed possible consequences of the election is the emboldening of sexual predators. We can see heightened racist actions, whose victims are encouraged to report incidents to groups like the Southern Poverty Law Center. But emboldened rapists and abusers do most of their damage in private, and the reporting remains so hard amid media that still treat such crimes as "sex scandals."

Having an admitted predator win the 2016 presidential election and proudly holding up a platform that threatens not just the right to abortion but access to birth control, dismisses any notion that we've reached the end of the fight against intimate violence. In the first week of his presidency, Trump signed an executive order reinstating the Global Gag Rule, which prevents health care providers who are receiving foreign aid funds from the U.S. from even *talking* to their patients about abortion. Federal funding for programs related to the Violence Against Women Act was also on Trump's chopping block.

That such struggles must account for poverty, race, sexuality, physical ability, age, immigration status was well represented by the March platform, speakers and signs. Did all of the White women at the march see women's issues through these many lenses? Of course not, and neither did all the women of color. But I wonder why that should be the standard for an action like this. Frankly, massive, planned and permitted marches are more social and cultural events than political ones. The hard-core political action and protest started to move after the march, such as the "10 actions for 100 days" that the march encouraged. I personally spent the week after working with immigrant organizations around deportations and detention and urged the Senate to take a hard look at Betsy Devos for Secretary of Education, given her utter lack of qualifications.

But there's something to be said for the positive effect of sheer proximity in recruitment and political education, and we could do with more spaces like the Women's March on Washington. I did the march with my sister-friend Soyinka Rahim, and was inspired watching her gracefully handle nice-White-lady attention, of which she received a ton. Soyinka stands at 5 feet 10 inches and dresses regally in caftans and head wraps that she designs herself. On Saturday, she carried her baby djembe drum and wooden flute, which she used to lead chants ("Power to the little girls. Power to the women!") or to bring some peace to the crowd. From the minute we arrived at the Silver Spring Metro station, White ladies wanted to take pictures of and with her. She always agreed if they promised to send her the photos.

When they asked her where she was from—definitely a version of, "Where are you *really* from?"—she'd say, "born and raised in Oakland, California, stolen from Africa." This is how she always answers this question, no matter who is asking. One White woman was so puzzled that Soyinka had to repeat it three times, while the African-American mom and daughter standing next to us chuckled quietly. Being used to this reaction, Soyinka didn't get frustrated—but she did remain insistent on her intro. The White ladies needed a reminder that slavery still shapes Soyinka's life, and they got it in a 20-second interaction that started on their provincial terms, but ended on her expansive ones. Such a conversation with a dozen White women hardly constitutes a deep education, but I bet that interaction will stick with more than one of those nice White ladies; maybe they'll be a bit more thoughtful the next time someone says that the history of slavery still matters in the United States.

The fact that a White woman made the initial call to march did not deter me, possibly because my first experience of organizing with White women was so positive. Not all my subsequent efforts have been so, but the feminist circles I've worked with since have been more often cohesive and productive—and led by women of color—than not.

I've read some excellent, heartrending essays by women of color naming their distrust of the march, and their unwillingness to let White women off the hook for the racism they've actively or tacitly supported, like the excellent piece by Jamilah Lemieux (2017). I respect these boundaries, and I loved Lemieux's list of alternative marches White women should make.

There were definitely some fails. I cringed at the American flag hijab in Shepperd Fairy's poster of the Muslim woman. Several celebrities, (OK, Michael Moore and Madonna), took up inappropriate space and time during a program that ran hours late. In the aftermath, the crowing about "no arrests" has an overtone of smug, clueless assumption that arrests during other protests must be justifiable, gross as Black Lives Matter and Standing Rock reveal the extreme measures law enforcement is willing to use on peaceful protesters of color.

But here we are, talking about why these things are not OK, thereby changing the discourse. If we want to build a big movement, there are going to be a lot more of these failures of judgment, and we need to address them without narrowing the movement. Tricky, I know. The trickiest thing in the world to pull off, in fact.

Where I most disagree with march critics, however, is on the idea that these women of color stepped in to "save" White feminists from creating a hot mess with a predictably myopic, racist, imperial, middle-class version of feminism. To my eye, Linda Sarsour, Carmen Perez and Tamika Mallory grabbed an opportunity to bend the arc of feminism in the direction of racial, economic, environmental and global justice. They bent that arc so hard that they pulled off the largest global protest in history, in the face of an administration that many people fear will end history itself.

They did this at considerable risk to their own well-being. White supremacists especially targeted Sarsour (and continue to do so well after the march), an outspoken Palestinian-American, refugee and advocate for Muslim communities, which sparked the hashtag defense, #IMarchWithLinda. I, on the other hand, risked nothing except a day of my life. The least I could do in this global moment was *actually* march with Linda. Given the density, I didn't get to march much, but I watched a good cross section of people go through the Americans With Disabilities Act area. My unscientific estimate is that about 40 percent of the crowd was Black, Asian, Latina, Middle Eastern or Native.

From my spot near the stage, I saw the entire rally from start to finish. I was particularly moved by 6-year-old Sophie Cruz, already a wise veteran of the culture wars. Standing with her parents and younger sister, Cruz allowed no despair, even amid the likelihood that Trump would seek to deport her parents.

Watching Cruz reminded me of my first political thought ever. In the '70s, when I was an immigrant second grader in Hempstead, New York, we covered our schoolbooks with brown paper bags from the grocery store. One day, I decorated mine with the slogan, "Girls are better than boys." I don't remember what incident motivated this claim, but I do remember the glee I felt while transforming this paper bag book cover. My horrified mother gave me a speech about treating everyone equally and made me replace it with a fresh, blank cover.

The weekend of the March, I felt that same kind of glee. It was a giddiness that came from recognizing myself in a community of girls and women, from revealing our real selves without shame, and from understanding that our power is substantial indeed. Maybe girls aren't better than boys; maybe we're not even all that different except in political positioning. But, as much as I love many people on the masculine end of the gender spectrum, I've never been a woman who "mostly has male friends." I am a woman's woman.

For just one day before what has been and will continue to be years of hard struggle, I needed to be surrounded by my sisters' love, energy and leadership. All over the world on that day, women and girls proclaimed ourselves a source of strength, of pride, of movement—not just for ourselves, but for everyone, and for the Earth, too. Women in Iowa, Alaska, Mississippi. Women in Nigeria, India, Antarctica. It was deeply satisfying to my furious, fearful, female soul to be held in this way. I felt our tenderness, our outrage, our humor, our determination and our ingenuity. I felt us signaling the rise of a global movement against sexists, racists, authoritarians and kleptocrats. Communities of women have been humankind's salvation. It is a "fempire," as one sign noted, and I am in for the strike back.

N
E
X
T

S
T
E
P
S

95

Getting to Why

Reflections on Accountability and Action for Men in Gender Justice Movements

Jamie Utt

A mentor once told me that as a cisgender White man, the moment I decide that I am not part of the problem, I *am* the problem. As often is the case when confronted with truths about one's privileges, I became defensive. How could I be the problem if I am working *for* those who are marginalized and oppressed in our society? How could I be the problem if my intentions are to *help*? I realize now, though, that I was asking the wrong questions.

In this political moment characterized by the most persistent attacks in a generation on the rights of cisgender women and transgender and non-binary people of all identities, more and more men, both cis and trans, are being spurred to action. We feel an urgency to act, and indeed, those of us with privilege of any form *must* act. However, the ways in which we act and how we work for accountability matter tremendously in whether our action furthers movements for justice and collective liberation or do more harm than good. Do our actions for gender justice support and follow the leadership of those who are marginalized and oppressed? Of non-binary folks? Of women, particularly Queer women, disabled women[1], women of Color, poor women, women whose lives are lived at other intersections of oppression? Of women who experience gendered oppression as survivors of sexual violence, survivors of intimate partner violence, because of the violence often bound up in sex work? Have we considered and asked what accountability to women and non-binary people might look like as we act for justice?

Notably, I write from the position of a non-disabled, cisgender White man (among other privileged identities I hold), and as such, I am not in a position to speak to the nuances of accountability that Transgender men might need to take up or the nuances of accountability for men of Color or who are disabled. I cannot and should not speak for men who do not share my identity. However, I hope that these reflections will inspire considerations of accountability and action for all men who understand that we must play a role in movements for gender justice.

Many years after that mentor shared her wisdom with me, she called on me to take accountability for a mistake I had made that caused great harm to women in my community. She reminded me that I ought to take time to reflect so that I do not act in ways that hurt people with whom I strive for solidarity, but I need to also recognize that sometimes I will make mistakes and must apologize and work to be better. When talking through the harm my actions caused, she asked me why exactly I believe that I need to act in solidarity with women. I answered that I feel a need to support the women in my life who face harm I cannot relate to or understand fully.

She pressed me, noting that my answer was based in what I want for others, not why I as an individual am taking up social justice work. I offered a response about the ways I contribute to the oppression of women and how I need to do better. She pressed me further, as I still had not answered her question. We went back and forth this way for a while, and this tremendously patient woman told me that so long as I am acting *for* women in gender justice work, I am inevitably acting from a place of paternalism. "You need to deeply understand your *why*, Jamie, your personal investment in working for justice. Otherwise you will continue to commit harm as you act *on behalf of* others."

This story demonstrates, unfortunately, how too often our learning as people with myriad privileges comes at the expense of oppressed people in our lives. We cause harm and are forced to reckon with the damage in our efforts to be more accountable. Or we choose to never deal with the damage we have caused, and those who we have hurt are left doing emotional labor in addition to what they've already invested to help us learn. When we can't understand and articulate our "why" in acting for justice, we are far more likely to end up furthering paternalism and reifying the very gendered oppression we wish to dismantle.

For many men, our entry into movements for gender justice comes in facing the harm that women we love have experienced at the hands of other men. As a teenager, I was initially brought to the work as I supported and listened to the traumatic truth of a dear friend who was drugged and sexually assaulted. The empathic concern for people who don't share our identities must always be central in the decision of those with privilege to act for justice. Without this empathy, we divorce our work from the needs of those who are primarily experiencing the harms of systems of oppression. However, if our *only* investment lies in concern for others, we risk paternalistic, ephemeral action without true accountability. As a result, we must put in the lifelong work of getting to *why*. Having a clear understanding of our own investment means that we must not only be accountable across identity difference but also to ourselves and to our values.

In hopes that it might help other men reflect on their own investments, below I have articulated a few of my *why*'s, humbly offered knowing that these will likely change, evolve, and grow as I continue my own work.

My investment in beloved community: First and foremost, I work for gender justice because of my deep and abiding love and concern for those who do not share my identity. This concern and love must always be central to my work, as it ensures I prioritize the truths and leadership of women and non-binary people, particularly those at multiple intersections of oppression.

My investment in realizing my own humanity: I understand that masculinity and patriarchy demand that I divorce myself from my own humanity, from my ability to empathize and from my ability to fully express myself, my emotions, my needs, and my vulnerabilities. Many men can relate to how masculinity demands we deny our emotions, but each of us must get in touch with what that means for how we understand gender justice. In systems that privilege me while enacting tremendous violence against those who don't share my identity, my empathy and my connection to my own emotionality pose a danger to that system. As a result, working to realize gender justice means working to realize the fullest extent of my own humanity.

My investment as a survivor of men's violence: Like far too many people I know, I have suffered the impacts of another man's violence. In turn, I have come to understand that the need to end men's violence supports the liberation of women (both trans and cis), trans men, and non-binary people who are disproportionately impacted by this violence. Additionally, though, that work helps me find liberation from the violence I have enacted and the violence I have experienced at the hands of men.

My investment in the possibilities of liberation: I cannot now know or understand what it would look like or feel like to experience collective liberation from the violence of patriarchy. Most every intersectional justice movement has asked that we imagine something beyond equality – these movements ask that we expand our imaginaries

NEXT STEPS

to work for something we cannot know while trusting that community outside of oppressive systems will be transformative and liberatory. Thus, outside of the need to end the material conditions of violence that have harmed me and so many I know, I am invested in realizing a justice that I cannot yet imagine but that I know is not simply possible but is every day being realized by those who work for a different world.

Perhaps these investments are ones to which you can relate. Perhaps your reasons for working for justice are profoundly different than my own. But as men, we must put in the work to deeply understand our own stake in realizing intersectional gender justice as but one part of the work for collective liberation.

Collective liberation. When we consider that term's meaning, there is a profound call for trust building and accountable action. After all, if we balance empathic concern for those across difference with a vital self-interest, we realize that this work has the power for us all to get free. Now, I ought to be clear that liberation for those who benefit from our current systems will not simply be a few feel-good exercises in community. The work of collective liberation necessarily means that those who benefit from oppressive systems must sacrifice that which we receive in the status quo, and much of that sacrifice will be painful. As part of getting to *why*, then, we must also be willing to ask what we are willing to give up in the work for collective liberation. And we must remain accountable to the ways that liberation means something different for those who benefit from patriarchy than for those who primarily experience its violence.

However, our efforts to work for gender justice can indeed benefit us all when done through true accountability to those who do not share our identities. So to all the men who happen upon these words, I challenge you to consider what collective liberation might mean and how your own stake in working for intersectional gender justice might lead to more accountable action on your own trajectory and from your own identity position.

Note

1 Though many choose to use "people-first language" in discussing disability (i.e. students with disabilities) because of how such language necessarily humanizes those so often dehumanized in our society, I choose here to follow the leadership of disabled people in my community who call for me to use the word disabled first because of how it reflects the ways our society sees them first as a disability and then as a person. Doing so also recognizes how disability can sometimes be central to one's experience as a person.

See Chapter 9 in *Teaching for Diversity and Social Justice* for corresponding teaching materials.

SECTION 6

ABLEISM

Introduction

Benjamin Ostiguy-Finneran and Madeline L. Peters

WHAT IS A DISABILITY?

In the United States, the Americans with Disabilities Act (ADA, 1990, amended 2008) defines disability as "a physical or mental impairment that substantially limits one or more major life activities" (ADA, 42 US Code § 12102) such as walking, seeing, hearing, learning, speaking, breathing, standing, lifting, or caring for one's self. The ADA covers both physical and mental impairments such as hearing, visual, speech or language impairments, emotional disabilities, learning disabilities, intellectual disabilities, orthopedic conditions, autism spectrum disorders, traumatic brain injury, attention deficit disorders, learning disabilities, psychological disabilities (such as depression, bi-polar disorder, and schizophrenia), and chronic illnesses (such as diabetes, HIV/AIDS, cancer, chemical sensitivities, and epilepsy) (note: this is not a comprehensive list).

Disability is a human condition that is multifaceted and multidimensional and that may intersect with everyone's life through experiences with a temporary disability and/or relatives, friends, and colleagues with disabilities. Over a billion people, about 15% of the world's population, have some form of disability. Between 110 million and 190 million adults have significant difficulties in functioning (World Health Organization, 2014). In that regard, people with disabilities are the largest minority group in the world.

ABLEISM AND DISABILITY OPPRESSION

Ableism or disability oppression is a term used to describe the all-encompassing system of discrimination and exclusion of people living with disabilities. Similar to other forms of oppression discussed in this book, ableism functions on individual, institutional, and cultural levels to advantage people who are temporarily able-bodied and disadvantage people with disabilities (Griffin, Peters, and Smith, 2007). The different levels of ableism all reinforce each other. On the individual level, people develop discriminatory attitudes and behaviors toward people with disabilities by experiencing the cultural values expressed in the institutions of medicine, education, and media. Collectively, these attitudes reinforce institutional policies and practices regarding people with disabilities.

On an institutional level, the medical system controls how the needs of people with disabilities are perceived and how the educational system decides appropriate methods for educating people with disabilities. Laws such as the Americans with Disabilities Act (ADA) and the Americans with Disabilities Act Amendments (ADAA) have been passed to create equal access for people with disabilities. However, years after passing, equal access for people with disabilities remains unfulfilled. One major hindrance is that creating accessibility for some types of disabilities requires building modification, changes in standard procedures, and a clear idea on how to meet the needs of those with disabilities. Although the Individuals with Disabilities Education Act (IDEA) was passed to ensure students with disabilities receive a fair and equal education, these standards are not adequately monitored. Many cities and towns struggle to fund the services and programs because they have not learned how to integrate the needs of students into their standard curriculum and programs. In higher education, students often do not get their accommodation in a timely manner. The faculty and staff are unaware of their obligations to students with disabilities. Many individuals do not want to take the time to create programs, services, and activities that are accessible because such programs are considered very time-consuming. Many professions do not include adequate education for practitioners in how to accommodate people with disabilities.

The stigma directed toward people with disabilities results from and is perpetuated by stereotypical beliefs, invisibility, lack of inclusiveness, and lack of supports. People with disabilities across the world experience inadequate communication, transportation, education, daily living needs, funding, timely provision of access, and service delivery (World Health Organization, 2014). Currently, access to facilities, services, and daily activities is challenging and may require planning and the understanding by individuals with disabilities that some places are not accessible. The entire process of gaining access can be isolating, disempowering, and discouraging. As a result, people with disabilities are often abused, disrespected, misunderstood, neglected, bullied, and stigmatized (US Department of Justice, 2016). As a society, we must guard against oversimplification of the needs of people with disabilities and recognize that disability is a vast and heterogeneous category that we all need to come to understand.

On a cultural level, ableism is apparent in standards of beauty, values related to strength and intellect, and communication centered on visual and auditory abilities. In the mainstream world, beauty equals flawless perfection. Society celebrates those who are physically strong and intellectually smart and discounts the value of anyone who doesn't meet those standards. Everyday communication is centered on modes that require visual and auditory abilities and people without those abilities are excluded from such communication. All of these values are embedded in mainstream media as "the way people should be," perpetuating discriminatory attitudes in all who consume that media.

HISTORICAL TREATMENT OF PEOPLE WITH DISABILITIES

Historically, disability was perceived through a religious lens and considered an unchangeable condition that resulted from sin (Covey, 1998). In Western societies infants with disabilities were dropped off balconies to their death; children with disabilities were abandoned and left to live on the streets where they had no choice but to beg for food and money to survive. The term *handicapped* emerged in England from people with disabilities who used their cap in hand on street corners to plead for money. Many people with disabilities were placed in jails or asylums where they endured inhumane treatment. By the early eighteenth century, people with disabilities were seen as freaks, monsters, and less than human. In Europe and the United States, curiosity about people with severe disabilities made "freak shows" a very popular form of entertainment. Paradoxically, "freak shows" became one of the few viable ways for people with disabilities to earn a living.

In Western societies, as scientific and medical fields became more powerful, their guidelines began to shape the ways in which disability was perceived and understood. Early Western medical textbooks classified people with disabilities as genetically defective. The medicalization of disability fostered the belief that people with disabilities needed to be monitored and controlled by licensed physicians and medical specialists with authoritarian powers. The medical goal was to "cure" the disability, get rid of a deformity, fix the body, and/or numb the existing pain of the person who was described as the patient. This thinking and methodology resulted in solutions that were invasive—usually involving surgery or drugs—and which required the person with the disability to submit to the authority of the other as expert. The view that disabilities are deficiencies that require medical treatment and repair remains pervasive today.

During the 1880s and 1890s, people with "mental retardation," as well as people who spoke English as a second language, were considered disabled or defective in the United States. For example, "medical imbecility" was attributed to people with mental retardation, as well as to paupers, prostitutes, immigrants, and others unable to express themselves in English (Longmore and Umanski, 2001). The power of the early nineteenth-century Eugenics movement spurred policies to segregate and sterilize people considered to be hopelessly unredeemable because of their disabilities. "Eugenics" as a movement was coined in 1883 in England by Sir Francis Galton, a cousin of Charles Darwin. Eugenics is derived from the Greek word meaning "well born" or "of good origins or breeding," and it became the "science" of supposedly improving qualities of a so-called "race" by controlling human breeding. Eugenics at its most extreme became the "scientific" rationale for Germany's genocidal policies during World War II in which thousands of people with mental or physical disabilities (Gallagher, 1995) (as well as members of supposed "lower races," for example Jews, Poles, and other groups, such as homosexuals) were shot, gassed, or left to starve to death.

Veterans returning with disabilities from World War II spurred medical fields to focus on rehabilitation and the development of devices to help soldiers return to work and live productive lives, rather than be restricted to hospitals or asylums. Although a new focus on rehabilitation emerged, many people with disabilities continued to be segregated and treated as patients who needed supervision and care from others who "knew best." In the 1960s and 1970s, a social movement among people with disabilities and allies began to emerge, leading to the Independent Living Movement. On the heels of other civil rights and justice movements, disability activists organized and powerfully fought for their civil rights. This struggle resulted in the passage of Section 504 of the Rehabilitation Act of 1973, the Education of all Handicapped Children Act (PL 94-142) of 1975, Americans with Disabilities Act (ADA) of 1990, Individuals with Disabilities Education Act (IDEA) of 1990, and Individuals with Disabilities Education Act (IDEA) of 2004—all significant feats protecting the rights of people with disabilities.

On September 25, 2008, the ADA was amended, thereby expanding the definition of disability. The new regulation better defines the term "substantially limits" and expands the definition of "major life activities." For example, learning, reading, concentrating, thinking, communicating, and working are now recognized as major life activities. Also added to the law are major bodily functions, such as functions of the immune system. The amended ADA further states that conditions that are episodic or in remission may be labeled as disabilities when the active impairment can substantially limit a major life activity.

DISABILITY DISCOURSE IN CONTEXT

Ableism plays out in current issues across the world, although little attention is given to the subject by society. Three current examples as this introduction is being written in early summer 2017 are actions in the 2016 US presidential campaign, proposed changes to US health care policy, and accessibility in higher education.

POLITICS

During the run-up to the 2016 US election, disability and ableism surfaced as then-presidential candidate Donald Trump was criticized for apparently openly mocking a journalist with a disability (Carmon, 2016). While Trump denied the accusations, claiming "I didn't know what he looked like. I didn't know he was disabled" (Carmon, 2016, para. 8), video footage shows Trump adopting movements, vocalizations, and insulting people with disabilities. Trump's tactic represents an attempt to leverage negative stereotypes about people with disabilities who are presumed to be less intelligent and incompetent. However, this phenomenon is not exclusive to one ideological side. In an attempt to discredit him, comedians and pundits described Trump as "coo coo for cocoa puffs" "crazy" and an "idiot" (Feldman, 2017) by associating him and his ideas with individuals with psychological disabilities. Unfortunately, critics of ableist tactics are often silent when the target of the oppressive ideology is their political opponent. One impact of both Trump's actions and responses to it is the normalizing of ableist behavior, attitudes, and discourse.

HEALTH CARE

People with disabilities are still disproportionately affected by partisan politics. For example, efforts in 2017 to repeal and replace the Affordable Care Act raised the specter of increased costs and significant losses of coverage for people with pre-existing conditions, including children with disabilities (Qiu, 2017). The alternative proposed in summer 2017, the American Health Care Act (AHCA), includes caps on different types of medical procedures. The AHCA calls for drastic reductions to Medicaid, eliminating programs that provide services for people with disabilities. This attack is often justified by describing current health care as an unfair financial burden imposed upon the "healthy" by people who are less responsible for their own health, but the argument in favor of the Affordable Care Act (ACA) is seldom—if ever—framed as a disability rights matter by the mainstream media.

HIGHER EDUCATION

At an institutional level, higher education does not provide the type of access needed to accommodate the increased number of students with disabilities. Not only in higher education, but throughout our society, an ongoing challenge associated with ableism is the frequent need for structural change to support access and equitable inclusion. The unfortunate reality is that most institutions will wait until there is an access demand before they make expensive and disruptive modifications. This means that the person in need of access must wait while the indicated modifications are considered, funded, and (hopefully) completed. For example, when people with disabilities seek inclusion, there often will be a need to alter standard practices and physical structures (e.g., building ramps, modifying restrooms, converting print material to electronic formats, and purchasing adaptive technologies). While these changes are mandated by law, they frequently require time and financial resources to implement. Universal architectural and instructional design principals have been espoused for decades and offer the promise of destigmatizing disability by proactively addressing virtually all access requirements, but they have yet to be broadly embraced outside of the design of new public spaces. Recent calls for more inclusive research, including the application of universal design principles and critical inquiry methods to postsecondary educational disability experiences, suggest that the inequitable experiences of students with disabilities may begin to receive greater scholarly attention (Gose, 2016; Kimball, Moore, Vaccaro, Troiano and Newman, 2016; Pena, 2014; Vaccaro, Kimball, Wells, and Ostiguy, 2015).

ABLEISM INTERSECTIONS

As mentioned earlier in the introduction, disability is multifaceted and multidimensional. People with disabilities belong to numerous social groups and can thus simultaneously experience ageism, classism, heterosexism, racism, religious oppression, or sexism. In some cases one cannot tell whether they're being discriminated against because of one form of oppression or another, or both. The intersection between one's disability and classism, however, can offer a much more glaring example of how the issues may be intertwined. Low-income people with disabilities face many barriers as the cost of health care, computers, software applications, assistive technology, and digital hearing aids (to name a few) are profoundly expensive, resulting in inadequate health care, limited employment opportunities, and significant learning disadvantages while attending school. On the contrary, people with disabilities who are born into families with greater financial means gain access to expensive medical treatment and diagnostic testing, assistive technology, personal care attendants, and other necessary resources.

Likewise, the intersection between disability and sexism further demonstrates how our complex identities and societal manifestations of oppression are overlapping. Unlike the current chatter about veterans returning from war with post-traumatic stress disorder (PTSD), there continues to be little attention paid to the reality that one out of nine women is diagnosed with PTSD symptoms, most often as a result of experiencing rape, sexual assault, domestic abuse, and/or violence (Anxiety and Depression Association of America, 2016). Sexual assault, for example, has wide reaching effects on women, including an impact on physical and mental health, functionality, issues regarding basic needs, and difficulty reading social cues. With PTSD, a raised hand, a half open door, a pointed object, or phraseology in a conversation can unconsciously set in motion intense reactions and the recreation of the original traumatic incident. The continued cultural and institutional silencing of women being disproportionately and violently targeted, most often by men, perpetuates a cycle of atrocious abuse against women that is significantly tied to numbers of women being diagnosed with disabilities.

Another persistent issue within disability discourse brings our attention to the intersection of ableism with racism via the overrepresentation of students of color in Special Education. As early as 1968, a disproportionate representation of students of color, particularly African Americans, in Special Education raised concern as to the legitimacy of such placement (Dunn, 1968). What we have witnessed since 1968 is a much higher percentage of African Americans in Special Education. The National Research Council (2002) was addressing whether the overrepresentation of African Americans in Special Education was a perceived or real problem and if the impact of poverty played a role in the placement of these students. What is known is that large percentages of students of color are labeled as mentally retarded, learning disabled, and emotionally or behaviorally dysfunctional, resulting in referrals to psychologists and intervention teams. The emphasis is on behavioral conformity rather than academic advancement. According to the US Department of Education, in the late 1990s only 25.5% of students with disabilities graduated with a standard diploma and only 22% graduated who were labeled with emotional issues (US Department of Education, 2000). Rendering a solution requires education reform that will include overhauling educational processes, organizational structures, and stressing effective teacher preparation and professional development in multicultural education.

READINGS IN THIS SECTION

In this section, we have attempted to create a better understanding of the complexities of disability by including a representation of issues, ideas, and experiences of people with disabilities across multiple identities. The readings in this section in no way represent every aspect of disability history, reform, treatment, and social, educational, or international issues and experiences. Rather, we present an overview of the issues that individuals, instructors, students, and others can refer to in their search for greater understanding and strategies regarding disabilities. The selections in this section are as varied as the issues regarding disability.

We begin with Willie Bryan's overview of the disability rights movement as a way of contextualizing the historical issues faced and the types of efforts led by persons with disabilities. We continue the historical analysis with selections from Susan Schweik's chapter from *Ugly Laws* (2009) in which she examines the deep intersections between disability oppression and anti-immigrant sentiments. Schweik describes how these laws were instrumental in the eugenic dehumanization of US immigrants in the early twentieth century. Zanita E. Fenton offers a DisCrit (a blending of Disability Studies and Critical Legal Theories [CLT]) theoretical analysis of the intersectional role of disability in the subordination of other non-dominant social identities. Fenton argues that the exclusion of disability from CLT discourses can produce harmful effects, such as dehumanization, violence, and death.

Focusing on global issues, we include an article that addresses war and disabilities and provides important information about the effects of war on the human body and those with psychiatric casualties. In our selection from Edward Murphy's piece, Iraq War combat veteran Miguel Cyr offers a personal account of his struggles with PTSD, and how this invisible disability impacted relationships with friends and relatives, and his ability to maintain steady employment. Cyr also discusses the difficulty of living with a psychological disability because of the significant stigma attached to such disorders. On the global front, Nirmala Erevelles' article gives us insight into transnational capitalism, (neo)colonial institutions and policies that have influenced the social construction of disability in the Third World and the impact on the lives of women.

The article by Rebecca Vallas brings the reader's attention to the inhumane treatment of the disproportionate number of incarcerated people with disabilities. An estimated 32% of prisoners and 40% of jail inmates reported having at least one disability. Prisoners were nearly three times more likely and jail inmates were more than four times more likely than the general population to report having at least one disability (US Department of Justice, 2016). There is limited (if any) access for inmates using wheelchairs, and, in general, it is difficult for inmates with mobility disabilities to get around. Many need assistance getting dressed, eating, and bathrooming—services that are not available in prison. A second piece related to incarcerated people with disabilities addresses the perspectives of people with learning disabilities. Douglas P. Wilson focuses on experiences of inmates with learning disabilities and how the lack of understanding of their needs leads to abuse and longer prison sentences.

The media often omit discussion on disability and hate crimes, and Lennard Davis draws our attention to this oversight. Davis uses the lack of news coverage of a hate crime in which the murder victim, James Byrd, is described only by his race, ignoring the fact that he was also a person with a disability. Davis asks that we deconstruct hierarchies of oppression by acknowledging intersections and the multiple identities that are targeted by oppression. Further, drawing upon intersections, Sumi Colligan's article explores the parallels between the cultural representation and everyday struggles of intersexed persons with disabilities with a particular focus on the medicalization of intersex/disabled bodies and the construction of asexuality.

Each of the above selections address the oppression of people with disabilities on individual, institutional, and cultural levels. The negative treatment described stems from ignorance and lack of knowledge around issues of disability. In general, institutions of higher education have taken the lead in teaching about oppression and working towards creating a more inclusive environment for members of oppressed groups. For people with disabilities, it is quite the opposite. Allie Grasgreen sheds light on the ignorance, negative attitudes, and behaviors of faculty and members of campus communities which contributes toward the discrimination experienced by students with disabilities. The personal narratives included in this section provide a glimpse into the many ways that people with disabilities, who live across multiple social identities, experience issues of oppression and liberation. Allegra Ringo's article discusses a group of protesters who are Deaf protesting outside a conference selling products and attempting to convince parents their children should be "fixed" via cochlear implants and other medical interventions.

"How to Curse in Sign Language" is an account of a child growing up with a disability. Ashley and Deborah describe how a mother and daughter struggle for educational rights in the public school system, acceptance within a religious institution, and society in general. Jess Watsky describes both the relief about and struggle to understand her diagnosis of Asperger's syndrome in the article, "On the Spectrum, Looking Out." After learning how to navigate the world of academia and other life situations, Watsky shares that the very medical reference she used to understand her life and make great strides is being eliminated from the *DSM-V*. Watsky's compelling story sheds light on how this change might have an enormous impact on her life and her ability to access suitable accommodations. Jason Kingsley reflects on what he would tell his parents and doctors about being born with Down Syndrome. He reminds them not to set limitations on people with Down Syndrome and their ability to learn, have relationships, and participate in all sorts of life activities.

Finally, we offer multiple ways to address the prejudice and discrimination experienced by people with disabilities on individual, institutional, and cultural levels. Thomas Hehir opens this section by offering four suggestions to address ablest practices. Hehir asserts that we must challenge ablest assumptions in educational pursuits and gainful employment. Also included in this section is an article by Heather Oesterreich and Michelle Knight that examines how the intersection of race, class, language, and disability inform the responsibilities of special educators to help students with disabilities. The overrepresentation of working-class students of African, Latino/a, and Native American heritages in special education has been a long-standing issue in special education. Oesterreich and Knight provide "teacher tips" to educators in order to increase the social and cultural capital of students with disabilities to support their prospective college-going and vocational identities. The authors are proponents of universal design and universal instructional design, including the use of assistive technology to meet the diverse access needs of all students. Karen Myers, Jaci Jenkins Lindburg, and Danielle M. Nied provide the core principles and concepts of universal design and universal instructional design in their article "Increasing Awareness: Language, Communication Strategies, and Universally Designed Environments." These principles are necessary for achieving accessibility and inclusion in institutions of higher education. This article is critical for understanding how social conditions affect disability.

Cheryl Howland and Eva Gibavic's article presents a learning disability identity development model that incorporates a discussion of several influential variables from dual diagnosis to support systems. Overall, this model helps individuals come to a greater understanding of the complex stages people with learning disabilities might encounter. Also included are additional influences of other identity development models such as gender, race, and moral identity development. In "Creating a Fragrance-Free Zone," the Invisible Disabilities Advocate alerts us to the growing environmental illness identified as multiple chemical sensitivity. This article provides concrete practices that can be incorporated individually and institutionally to create safe and comfortable environments for all people. Madeline L. Peters, Carmelita (Rosie) Castañeda, Larissa E. Hopkins, and Aquila McCants provide examples of beliefs and practices that are ablest on an individual, cultural, and institutional level followed by the actions people can take to eliminate these discriminatory practices and act as unified allies.

References

Americans with Disabilities Act. (42 USC § 12101–12213).
Anxiety and Depression Association of America. (2016). *Posttraumatic stress disorder*. Retrieved June 22, 2017 from www.adaa.org/understanding-anxiety/posttraumatic-stress-disorder-ptsd.

Carmon, I. (2016). Donald Trump's worst offense? Mocking disabled reporter, poll finds. *NBC News*. Retrieved July 8, 2017 from www.nbcnews.com/politics/2016-election/trump-s-worst-offense-mocking-disabled-reporter-poll-find-n627738.

Covey, H. (1998). *Social perspectives of people with disabilities in history*. Springfield, IL: Charles Thomas.

Dunn, L. M. (1968). Special education for the mildly retarded: Is much of it justified? *Exceptional Children*, 35, 5–22.

Feldman, J. (2017, March 8). CNN's Van Jones: There's a danger when we all start to normalize Trump. www. mediaite.com/tv/cnns-van-jones-theres-a-danger-that-we-all-start-to-become-trump/.

Gallagher, H. (1995). *By trust betrayed: Patients, physicians and the license to kill in the Third Reich*. Arlington, VA: Vandamer.

Gose, B. (2016). Disability experts debate merits of universal design. *The Chronicle of Higher Education*. Retrieved May 16, 2017 from www.chronicle.com.

Griffin, P., Peters, M., and Smith, R. (2007). Ableism curriculum design. In M. Adams, L. Bell, and P. Griffin (Eds.), *Teaching for diversity and social justice*, 2nd edn (pp. 336–358). New York: Routledge.

Kimball, E. W., Moore, A., Vaccaro, A., Troiano, P. F., and Newman, B. M. (2016, September). College students with disabilities redefine activism: Self-advocacy, storytelling, and collective action. *Journal of Diversity in Higher Education*, 9(3), 245–260.

Longmore, P. K. and Umanski, L. (Eds.) (2001). *The new disability history: American perspectives*. New York: New York University Press.

National Research Council. (2002). Minority students in special and gifted education. Committee on Minority Representation in Special Education, M. Suzanne Donovan and Christopher T. Cross, (Eds.), Division of Behavioral and Social Sciences and Education. Washington, DC: National Academy Press.

Pena, E. V. (2014). Marginalization of published scholarship on students with disabilities in higher education journals. *Journal of College Student Development*, 55(1), 30–40.

Qiu, L. (2017, July 3). Five misleading Republican claims about health care. *New York Times*, p. A12.

Schweik, S. (2009). *The ugly laws: Disability in public*. New York: New York University.

US Department of Education. (2000). 22nd Report to Congress on the Implementation of IDEA.

US Department of Justice. (2016). Crimes against people with disabilities 2009–2014 statistical tables. Retrieved June 22, 2017 from www.bjs.gov/content/pub/pdf/capd0914st.pdf.

Vaccaro, A., Kimball, E. W., Wells, R. S., and Ostiguy, B. J. (2015). Researching students with disabilities: The importance of critical perspectives. *New Directions for Institutional Research*, 25–41. doi:10.1002/ir.20084.

World Health Organization. (2014). Summary: World report on disability. Retrieved May 16, 2017 from www. who.int/disabilities/world_report/2011/report/en/.

96

Struggle for Freedom

Disability Rights Movements

Willie V. Bryan

. . .

LACK OF CONCERN

Since World War II, there has been an increasing emphasis on human and civil rights in the United States. Minorities and women have spoken out on their own behalf attempting to gain the privileges, freedoms, and rights guaranteed for all Americans by the Constitution. While legal and social ground has been won and lost throughout the years, many minorities and women now enjoy a somewhat more equal existence in the United States than some fifty years ago. Still, the battle for equality is far from victorious. While other groups continue their struggle, individuals with disabilities have joined forces to end discrimination in their lives and claim a life of equality in the United States.

The Civil Rights Movement of the sixties resulted in legislation designed to bar discrimination based on sex, race, and national origin; however, prohibition of discrimination based on physical and/or mental disabilities was not included. As Thomas D. Schneid reminds us, a bill introduced in Congress in 1971 to amend Title VI of the Civil Rights Act of 1964 to prohibit discrimination based on physical or mental disability died in committee. Similarly, in 1972, another bill introduced in Congress, this time to amend Title VII of the Civil Rights Act to bar discrimination in employment based upon physical or mental disabilities, also died in committee. This may be seen as somewhat of a barometer of the level of concern lawmakers and many other nondisabled Americans had with regard to the civil rights of persons with disabilities.

Perhaps the lack of concern demonstrated by these actions of Congress is more of a reflection of ignorance of the needs and capabilities of persons with disabilities rather than a blatant desire to deny the civil rights of a group of people. At the time, the thought was that employers should not be forced to hire persons who could not adequately perform the required tasks. Persons with disabilities and their friends certainly were not advocating employment of nonqualified persons; they were simply asking that employers be required to look beyond a person's limitation to see abilities and attempt to match them with the required job. Employers also had a number of misconceptions with regard to employing persons with disabilities, such as they would not be able to secure insurance for the person and the company's insurance premiums would increase. Another major misconception was the belief that persons with disabilities were unsafe employees. This erroneous belief was held despite safety records indicating that persons with disabilities had fewer accidents than nondisabled employees. Many employers were aware that by making modifications to the work site and/or its environment, a significant number of jobs could be made accessible to persons with disabilities; however, these same employers harbored the belief that making these accommodations would be too expensive. Again, this belief was held even though the DuPont Company had demonstrated that many changes to a work site could be done inexpensively.

These and other misconceptions were firmly held by employers because persons with disabilities and their advocates did not vigorously dispute them. The lack of opposition to discrimination against persons with disabilities with respect to employment allowed long-held stereotypes and prejudices to continue unchallenged. Activism would be necessary to dramatize the extent of the lack of concern for the rights of persons with disabilities and cause action to be taken to correct the neglect that had become an accepted method of treatment of persons with disabilities.

MINORITY STATUS

The political wheels of American progress appear to turn best when pressure is applied. For example, protests by minorities, particularly African Americans, led to the Civil Rights Act of 1964. Similarly, women's organizations engaged in various activities that placed pressure on state and federal government leaders to enact legislation that required equality of rights for women. One may assume that in a free and open democracy which most of us enjoy in America, there would be available on an equal basis to all citizens, the right to vote, to live wherever one can afford, the right to eat wherever one desires, and the right to be educated at the maximum level of one's abilities. However, it was precisely the denial of these basic rights, rights upon which this country was founded, rights for which thousands of Americans have paid the supreme price, that led multitudes of Americans into the streets to practice civil disobedience, until these and other basic rights were granted.

In the process of securing these rights, the minority groups learned that their minority status was not shameful. In fact, they learned that they were a very important cog in the wheel of American life and by withholding their labor and being selective as to how and where they spent their hard earned money, they could considerably slow down the democratic wheel of progress. These groups also learned that by networking they added strength to their demands.

Until recently, persons with disabilities were not widely considered a minority group. In fact, it was not until the Rehabilitation Act of 1973 that they were considered a "class" of people. Persons with disabilities are members of other groups of people, they are male or female, and they have an ethnic identity; their rights and privileges are associated with whatever cultural and/or gender group they belong. It is ironic that with regard to human rights their disabilities were secondary to their cultural and/or gender identity, but with regard to their rights as citizens, their disabilities were primary, over-shadowing gender and/or cultural identity. Since disability groups were not considered a culture at the time, the person with a disability was viewed as a "disabled member of another class." To be more specific, they were considered to be a disabled female or a disabled American Indian female. Hopefully, the point has been made. It is in part because of this dual and sometimes triple classification that the disability label was not considered a class unto itself.

Another reason for the lack of class status is that there are large numbers of disabilities and each one is considered a separate condition within its own group identity. For example, there are persons who have disabilities resulting from polio, arthritis, visual impairments, hearing impairments, lupus, mental illness, mental retardation, amputations, and paralysis, to mention only a few. In most cases, there was and continues to be associations or foundations which are considered the official representative for all who have a particular condition. This has the effect of segregating disabilities into distinct disease groups, thus causing each disabling condition to stand alone and not be part of a larger whole. This internal segregation combined with society's segregation of persons with disabilities has been devastating to efforts of persons with disabilities to unite and demand their constitutional rights.

Although it would not be until the passage of the Rehabilitation Act of 1973 that persons with disabilities would obtain the classification of minority status and be officially viewed as a class of people, several years before the passage of the act they began to think of themselves as a minority. And more importantly, they began to view their life conditions as having been deprived of their basic human rights similar to other minority groups. They also began to think of themselves as being oppressed and disenfranchised. With this realization, they began to unite and to speak openly about the manner in which they were being excluded from full participation in society's activities. Thinking of themselves as oppressed minorities, they also thought of the manner in which other minority groups had placed their agenda before the American people; thus a "grassroots disability rights movement" began which has resulted in the passage of the ADA in 1990.

GRASSROOTS MOVEMENT

. . .

Despite the concern exhibited by charitable organizations and Congress, the one aspect often missing was the involvement of persons with disabilities. For example, much of the legislation prior to the Rehabilitation Act of 1973 had been developed with little, if any, input from persons with disabilities. Charitable organizations established telethons to raise funds for research and/or provide services without giving much thought to the negative images being projected. This was "business as usual" or stated another way, it was the continuation of the paternalistic attitude that has existed in America for many decades. Perhaps without meaning harm to persons with disabilities, nondisabled persons have treated them as though they are incapable of determining and expressing how they would like to live their lives. Regardless of how well-intended the motivation of a non oppressed person there are some things he/she will either overlook or not understand with regard to the effects of being oppressed. Therefore it is imperative that those effected must be involved in determining the best methods for eliminating the problems created by oppression.

There are undoubtedly many reasons why it took persons with disabilities approximately two centuries before they organized and began to speak out on their own behalf. With "sit-ins," marches, and attempts to integrate previously segregated southern schools, the fifties served as the "staging" years of the Civil Rights movement; then in the sixties the final "assault" years were launched which culminated in victory with the passage of the Civil Rights Act of 1964. Similarly for the Disability Rights Movement, the sixties served as the "staging" years with emphasis on consumerism, self-help, and demedication demands as well as demands for self-care rights and deinstitutionalism. Perhaps then the seventies can be considered the "watershed" years of the movement. The sixties was the decade when persons with disabilities began to view themselves as oppressed minorities and demanded their constitutional rights. Similar to the Civil Rights Movement which culminated in the Civil Rights Act of 1964, the Disability Rights Movement led to what has been called the Civil Rights Act for persons with disabilities: The Americans With Disabilities Act of 1990.

. . .

Activism: . . . In the early seventies, rehabilitation leaders backed by disability rights groups began to push for changes in the legislation to advocate a broader nonvocational role for rehabilitation programs. In 1972, such legislation was passed by Congress and Verville informs us that President Nixon vetoed the legislation because it "strayed too far from the essential vocational objective of the program."

This Act had provisions for Independent Living Centers. It would take six more years before this important concept would become a reality. The veto of the 1972 Rehabilitation

Act is a classic example of not involving those most affected. Perhaps the veto served a useful purpose in that it became an issue around which the grassroots movement could unite. While attempting to get the Independent Living Centers provisions included in future legislation, the disability rights organizations gained considerable experience in politics, coalition building, and lobbying, as well as the act of compromising, thus gaining the respect of lawmakers and the admiration of millions of persons both with and without disabilities.

In the interim, additional legislation was passed with provisions to issue directives that persons with disabilities were not to be discriminated against nor treated as second-class citizens. One such piece of legislation was the Rehabilitation Act of 1973. Included in this legislation was Section 504 which forbade any United States institution that received federal financial assistance in the amount of $2,500 or more and all federal and state agencies from discriminating against persons with disabilities in employment. . . .

INDEPENDENT LIVING MOVEMENT

. . .

The quest for independence by most Americans does not occur by accident, but is a quality that is taught and reinforced to every American youth, both by formal teaching and by example. American history is replete with both fictional and factual persons accomplishing or attempting to accomplish extraordinary deeds to establish or maintain their independence.

Independence is therefore highly valued in American society; it is considered an essential building block in constructing and maintaining a democracy. Freedom, to an extent, is reliant upon its citizens having the independence to build better lives for themselves and in the process of accomplishing their dreams, they lift freedom and democracy to new levels. Conversely, being dependent is devalued in American society and those that are considered so are often assigned lower positions on the social totem pole. To many, the word "dependent" denotes lack of initiative, laziness, and a burden upon society. Although public and private social welfare agencies and organizations including hospitals, clinics, and rehabilitation centers, to mention a few, have been developed to assist persons who by virtue of illness, accident, or birth defects must rely upon assistive services, the recipients are often viewed in a negative light and at best given sympathy instead of empathy and understanding.

Illness or disability often places the individual, and sometimes the family, in a state of dependency. For some it is a permanent situation, but for the majority it is temporary. The degree to which a person becomes dependent is obviously affected by several things, not the least of which are attitudes. [A]ttitudes of family, friends, medical and rehabilitation personnel as well as employers have an impact on the level of dependency of the person with a disability.

Given the value placed on independence by American society, no one should be amazed that persons with disabilities began to recognize and resent the limited role society drafted for them. They correctly perceived that society equated disability with dependency. They also recognized that this perception created a very low ceiling and an almost insurmountable wall around their abilities to function and achieve.

. . .

In the early seventies, persons with disabilities began to realize that to be truly free they must take and maintain control of their lives. This train of thought resulted in the development of Independent Living Centers (ILCs). Dejong provides a brief history of the genesis of Independent Living Centers as he reveals that a small group of persons with disabilities at the University of Illinois and at the University of California at Berkeley moved out of their residential hospital setting into the community and organized their own system for delivery of survival services. The centers established by these students became the blueprint by which future centers would be established. As might be expected, since the inception of these centers, the scope of services has expanded. Even so, the idea of persons with disabilities taking greater control of their lives remains the same. Perhaps Dejong best summarizes the independent living philosophy when he said the dignity of risk is what the independent movement is all about. Without the possibility of failure, a person with a disability is said to lack true independence and the mark of one's humanity: the right to choose for good or evil.

When one considers that the independent living movement was initiated by persons with disabilities, many of whom were persons with severe disabilities such as spinal cord injuries, it became quite apparent that these individuals exhibited courage of the highest magnitude. Although prior to the movement they lived in conditions that made them almost totally dependent upon others, it was however a safe environment; therefore, moving from this safe environment to face the many uncertainties created by a society with many barriers and obstacles certainly qualifies the founding members as pioneers.

. . . Laurie also contributes to our understanding of the goal of independent living centers with these comments:

> Independent living is freedom of choice, to live where and how one chooses and can afford. It is living alone or with a roommate of one's choice. It is deciding one's own pattern of life: scheduling food, entertaining, vices, virtues, leisure and friends. It is freedom to take risks and freedom to make mistakes.

Frieden and Cole define the independent living concept as control over one's life based on the choice of acceptable options that minimize reliance on others in making decisions and in performing everyday activities. This may include managing one's affairs, participating in day-to-day life in the community, fulfilling a range of social roles, and making decisions that lead to self-determination and the minimizing of physical or psychological dependence upon others.

Frieden, Richards, Cole, and Bailey tell us that the independent living movement was based on the premise that with reasonable support services, adults with disabilities could manage their own affairs, and participate as full members of the community in all respects. They continue by speaking to the philosophy of the movement as full participation in community life and point out that the movement also was an advocate for a set of services that would meet the long-term support needs of citizens with disabilities. . . .

MORE THAN WORK

Work is so much a central part of most Americans' lives that it, in part, defines who we are. It is common for Americans to describe someone by identifying their occupation. For example, we may identify someone as Mary Smith the attorney, or John Smith the teacher. Work has been the defining feature in American lives for many years. The Puritan work ethic is a standard by which Americans often judge each other. While we no longer subscribe to the theory of hard work for all, we most certainly subscribe to the idea of work for all. Work provides us with economic power to purchase goods and services which in part by virtue of the amount and types of goods we accumulate determines our social standing in America. Social condemnation is the reward for those that are able to work but do not. Work not only is a means by which we develop, maintain or improve our societal standing in American society, it also is patriotic. In a capitalist society, it is through the production of products that our nation develops its standing in the world as compared to other nations.

Obviously, work has many important meanings to Americans and American society. Considering the position work holds in American life, it is easy to understand why virtually all rehabilitation legislation prior to the 1972 Rehabilitation Act emphasized "vocational rehabilitation." In fact, when we speak of rehabilitating a person with a disability we think the ultimate goal of the rehabilitation process is to make the person ready for a job. There is one thing wrong with this approach: what about the person who is unable to work because of the severity or perhaps type of disability? Unless they and/or their families have sufficient financial resources, they have to rely upon sympathy and charity of others as well as some social welfare assistance from the federal government. Because of the social stigma of not working and receiving charity, these persons' independence, self-dignity, and ability to participate as full American citizens are in jeopardy.

Perhaps these reasons, as well as others, caused the disability rights movement leaders to lobby Congress to deemphasize "vocational" in the Rehabilitation Act of 1972. It is unfortunate that the Nixon Administration did not comprehend what persons with disabilities were saying as they lobbied for removal of "vocational" from the rehabilitation act. In part, what they were saying, and perhaps today we are just beginning to hear, is that a person's worth, self-respect, and dignity should not be measured by employment and moreover measured by whether employed in a job, especially if that person is unable to work. The leaders were wise to note that no person with a disability would be totally free until all persons with disabilities had opportunities to more fully participate in American life. Again it was this type of thinking that led them to push for Independent Living Centers, and the abolishment of the segregation of persons with disabilities so they could not only become more involved in American society, but also make decisions that would affect the quality of their lives. In short, they recognized that to be free, life for a person with a disability meant more than being able to work.

. . .

97

Immigration, Ethnicity, and the Ugly Law

Susan M. Schweik

Massive immigration in the late nineteenth century and early twentieth centuries meant an upsurge in the ranks of people who, as Welke puts it, "had nowhere to turn when they found themselves disabled." A tensely conjoined mixture of ableism, biologized racism, and nativism emerged in American culture, an equation of the unsightly with the alien and the alien with the beggar. New systems of screening for the diseased, maimed, deformed, and mendicant developed at U.S. borders. In 1881 for instance, New York State passed a law requiring "a vigilant inspection" of steamships arriving from abroad "to prevent the landing of mendicants, cripples, criminals, idiots, &c". Although ugly laws tend to be remembered as local (as say, a Chicago problem) or universal (as an example of centuries of disability oppression), their operations were neither that small or that large. They took place within a broad but historically specific natural crisis concerning the effects of immigration and the need for exclusive "anticipatory classification" of undesirables.

. . . The panic over immigration provided an easy—a too-easy—explanation for the existence of the unsightly beggar. Beggars were "visible signs," writes Kenneth Kusmer, "of the breakdown of local control that accompanied the rise of urban industrial society in the nineteenth century. Those who responded most antagonistically . . . sought scapegoats, the most convenient of whom were the waves of immigrants pouring into this country."

. . . The peak years of the unsightly begging ordinance occurred at the same time as intensifying measures for exclusion of undesirable immigrants. In the western states, the rise of ugly laws coincided with the anti-Chinese agitation. In 1872, five years after San Francisco passed its ugly law, California legislators passed a law placing restrictions on the entrance of any immigrant "lunatic, idiot, deaf, blind, cripple or infirm person" who was not a member of an already resident family; the law was targeted against disabled Chinese people. In 1882, only a few months after Chicago passed its unsightly beggar ordinance, the U.S. congressmen acted in quick succession first to ban Chinese immigration and then to ban the entrance of "paupers" and "the insane" into the country. By 1891, federal immigration law required medical officers to certify (and generally to exclude) all immigrants who had a "*loathsome* or dangerous contagious disease," and in the realm of the loathsome (defined, in circular fashion, as "a disease which excites abhorrence in others") immigration law meets the unsightly ordinances' "disgusting object." At Angel or Ellis Island, any immigrant body might be understood as inevitably diseased, infectious, and loathsome, a danger to the entire nation. Visibly disabled immigrants, if they made it past the borders at all, posed a particular threat. Douglas Bayton's important work on the systematic exclusion of disabled people at the point of entrance to the United States demonstrates that American immigration law *was*—in policy and practice—ugly law writ large.

At the same time, other laws including ugly ordinances functioned in part as federal immigration policy writ small. Just as, in Baynton's words, the idea of disability was "instrumental in crafting the image of the undesirable immigrant," so too, the idea of uncontrolled immigration was instrumental in crafting the image of the unsightly beggar. When national border policing failed, officials called for backup local measures. States set up roadblocks and checkpoints to enact their own versions of medicalized nativism. In 1907, Alabama, for instance, passed laws prohibiting entrance into the state "of persons of an anarchistic tendency, of paupers, of persons suffering from contagious or communicable diseases, of cripples without means and unable to perform mental or physical service, of idiots, lunatics, persons of bad character, or of any persons who are likely to become a charge upon the charity of the State, and all such as will not make good and law-abiding citizens." But a great deal of the policing persons originally from abroad who were "likely to become a charge upon charity" took place at the municipal level, through the ugly law and by other means.

. . . Unsightly begging ordinances offered more systematic programs for suppressing monstrous imported mendicancy at the local level than individual court rulings did. The first American ugly law that I know of was in San Francisco, 1867; the last attempt to pass one that I have found was in Los Angeles, 1913; and although there may well have been others earlier and later, this California frame calls attention to the ways in which external as well as internal nomadic subjects—immigrants and cross border migrants as well as vagrants—not only rub shoulders but are created hand in hand with unsightly beggars. Both cities turned to ugly law at times when, as far as city leaders were concerned, too many unemployed foreigners packed the streets.

. . . At times the threatening beggar was simply a foreigner, someone who came from *everyplace* else. Foreign groups, east and west, north and south, often blended indeterminately into one another in middle-class nativist accounts of mendicant outsiders. "The beggar in ninety-nine cases out of a hundred is an importation," wrote G. W. Whippert in 1891, following the assertion with a list of just some of the places where mendicants, including "cripples made to order," came from: "Mafia-ridden Sicily," "squalid . . . Warsaw," "the gutters of Jolly Vienna," "the struggling Ireland." L. K. Friedman's fictional *Autobiography of a Beggar* (1903) derived its coarse humor exactly from the clustering and interactions of various criminal and degraded classes at the scene of begging, with a particularly strong emphasis on confused comedies of disability and immigration. Friedman's beggar narrator, Mollbuzzer, writes his memory for an "anterpologist" who offers him twenty-five dollars for his story. As Mollbuzzer's slapstick picaresque unfolds, his putative ethnography trains its sights on a variety of fellow travelers. Foremost among them are the subjects of ugly law:

> The trade of a beggar is beset with more difficulties than any on earth . . . The absence of one leg, even of two, is a decided aid to his calling; if he be blind, his chances for good pay are still better; if he be deaf, dumb, and blind, crippled and maimed, his chances are of the best. The more crippled he is, the higher he will be paid. To be a successful beggar, then, one must be hungry, be ill-clad to the point of rags; one must have a starving wife and children; one must be ever willing to work, yet never be able to find work and one must be a cripple. There is no royal road to beggary.

Mollbuzzer's dealings with crippled beggars overlap and coincide with a crudely racist set of other encounters: a Duke-and-King-like adventure into "joining de circus," in which a black tramp is coaxed "inter playin' de Honoluler King" in a sideshow; "A Tale Ef A Pigtail" set, like many begging narratives at the turn of a century, in a Chinatown; and a dizzying, culminating plot involving "De Chinee Kid An' De Hand-Organ," in which a "man ef bizness" who supplies beggars with hand-organs, . . .beggar signs, crutches, locations, . . . pencils, . . . shoe-strings," and other accessories trades a Chinese boy for an Italian organ-grinder's monkey. Though this final story's humor depends on a series of cultural suspicions and misunderstandings, its structure emphasizes the interchangeability of "Chinese" and "Italian"; both boy and monkey are literally packed and shipped in the same crate.

Like general anti-immigration discourse, antipathy towards specific immigrant groups mobilized easily around the figure of the unsightly beggar. Ugly law offered a compact package of medicalized and moralized language ("diseased," "disgusting," sometimes "improper") with which, at any given moment and location, to define a particular ethnic and racialized difference, to saturate that difference with significance, and to convert social inequity into seemingly natural occurrence. . . .

98

Disability Does Not Discriminate

Toward a Theory of Multiple Identity Through Coalition

Zanita E. Fenton

A CRITICAL FRAMEWORK

Critical Legal Theories (CLTs), including Critical Race Theory, Critical Race Feminism, Queer Theory, Latino/a Critical Legal Theory (LatCrit), and Economic Critical Legal Analysis (ClassCrit), are a few of the burgeoning critical approaches to legal analyses. Each of these approaches examines various forms of social subordination. Disability studies (DS) articulates a theory and ideological critique of inequitable treatment experienced by persons with disabilities. Both DS and the various CLTs expose parallel social imaginings: one created for those meeting normative social expectations and alternativeness for those who in myriad ways, are not considered as normative. Yet, Disability Studies have been critiqued for assuming Whiteness as an unstated norm. Similarly, CLTs have been critiqued for essentialism and for failing to address multiple aspects of identity, most notably, aspects of disability. However, antisubordination activists have engaged in a form of strategic essentialism as a means of resistance. Mimicking conventional strategies of nonsubordinated power holders, strategic essentialism is a move by members of a subordinated category to simplify group identity and counter normative expectations.

Intersectionality, a concept identified by Crenshaw, exposes the inadequacy of legal doctrine for its "focus on the most privileged group members, [which] marginalizes those who are multiply-burdened and obsures claims that cannot be understood as resulting from discrete sources of discrimination." Critical theorists often use intersectionality to describe the ways in which oppressions (such as racism, transphobia and ableism) are interconnected, mutually consecutive, and cannot therefore be examined separately. Intersectionality is often misunderstood as a subordinated category plus another (for example, race plus gender). Because of the misapplication of intersectionality, even those who are multiply disadvantaged may seek to emphasize a particular aspect of identity that provides the greatest authority in a given context. This practice ultimately serves the dominant group.

Disability is not one-dimensional; neither is race or other socially subordinated identity categories. Identity in all its forms, implicates multiple variables such as language, culture, and religion. Social practices play a significant role in shaping how people think about identities. Thus, the ways in which multiple identities converge is fluid and diffuse, dependent on context and circumstance. Yet, as Erevelles and Minear note, "the omission of disability as a critical category in discussions of intersectionality has disastrous and sometimes deadly consequences."

Because hierarchies always exist both between groups and categories, but also between individuals or subgroups, complexity within the various levels of interrelationships must be anticipated. This complexity includes a dissatisfaction with labels of "multiple consciousness" without meaningful redress, and the additional layer of marginalization intendant from the fracturing and atomizing effects of discrete intersectional identities. One must "properly situate the connection between and among competing forms of oppression to understand their relationship." With this in mind, in the next section, I discuss the social creation of disability, moving between and within multiple communities of oppression.

REPRODUCING NORMS: EUGENICS AND PSEUDOSCIENCE

Legal definitions historically grounded in (pseudo) science further the belief that the categories of identity are stable. Indeed, identities (such as disability, race, sexual orientation) are often considered genetically predetermined rather than socially produced. An emphasis on the physiological nature of difference has been used to justify differential treatment.

Although disability is often viewed as inherent, social forces maintain hierarchies based on able-bodied norms. Society also places heavy burdens on Black and Brown under the guise of biological differences, even though these burdens actually stem from social forces that create and maintain hierarchies.

The field of psychology has a strong history of creating disorders specific to a given subordinated group as a means of ensuring the continuation of that status. "Hysteria," for

CONTEXT

instance, was once referred to as a medical condition particular to women and understood to be caused by disturbances of the uterus. Drapetomania, a supposed mental disorder, was said to cause Black slaves to run away. Until 1974, the American Psychiatric Association (APA) defined homosexuality as a mental illness, and AIDS was originally known as GRID (Gay-Related Immune Deficiency). Until recently transgenderism was listed as a disorder by the APA. Society has a recurring habit of conflating poverty, as well as race and disability, with criminality.

In society's pursuit of the "normative," race destabilizes gender ideals; abject poverty precipitates banishment from Whiteness; disability undermines perceptions of normative gender expression as well as of sexuality. In a negative convergence, disability is more prevalent in contexts marked by poverty and homelessness as well as in so-called "third world" contexts. These intersecting categories help explain why society has gone to such lengths to segregate and eradicate difference.

ELIMINATING/CONTAINING DISABILITY

Once disability, broadly defined, is understood as a foil for the normative ideal and therefore as something to be contained, prevented, or destroyed, reproduction becomes of paramount concern. Gender and race likewise are implicated in concerns over reproducing normative bodies. In fact, the confluence of race and disability was introduced as a consequential aspect of enslavement. According to Nielson, "racist ideologies defined . . . African Americans as fundamentally inferior specimens with deformed bodies and minds who were best confined to slavery." These bodies were mutilated and killed through the auspices of the institution of slavery forcing survivors of this brutal institution into submission. Black minds, further manipulated into submission, were kept ignorant through the denial of education and literacy. Capitalism found profit in racially devalued bodies, including those with physical and psychological impairments, even while the "dominant paradigm conceive[d] of disabled bodies as having little economic value." Slavery not only created disabled bodies, but also originated an ideology that inferred an entitlement to dominant society to control the reproductive capacities of Black, female, poor, and disabled bodies. Further, this ideology was one that promoted a conflation of these categories in terms of reproduction.

During the same period as slavery, "most white woman remained as *feme coverts*—legal nonentities determined unfit for civic life." Women were not able to vote prior to 1920 and therefore, effectively were not full citizens. Coverture erased legal personhood for married women, whereby married women could not enter into legal contracts, could not own property outright, and could not seek state protection from an abusive husband. Moreover, the origins of rape law were constructed such that a father or husband "owned" his daughter or wife. Therefore rape could be seen as an offense against *him*. In fact exemptions for claims of marital rape continued in various states until about 1993. This imagined status of women as property also justified lynching of Black men.

Black women, however, were owned through the institution of slavery, and their marriages were not legally recognized. Thus, "while African American women's sexuality was effectively harnessed for the reproduction of slavery in the service of the colonial state, they were deemed as fit only for a 'dehumanized reproduction.'" The rape of a Black women, both pre- and postemancipation, was not legally cognizable. Both Black women and men were supposed to increase the size of the slave population and thus the economic wealth of their owners. Once the 13th Amendment changed the status of Blacks from property to legal personhood, the social agenda transformed from the reproduction of property to a eugenic one of reduction and elimination—some might say genocide. This rapid shift from a pronatalist to antinatalist position in regard to African American reproduction is reflective of the devaluation of Blackness, consistent with Black people's prior status as property. From this one "disability" of being legally characterized as property (whether through servitude or marriage), practically all other forms of disability emanated. Thus, White women too were also at a social disadvantage regarding their reproductive capacities as a result of legal sterilization. Under the guise of loose category of "feeblemindedness," women were sterilized for having the "disability" of being in poverty, unmarried, and pregnant.

The history of forced sterilization impacted poor White women, as well as women of color. Males were not targeted in the same numbers as females, but they were not immune from being characterized as "feebleminded" or from sterilization. Poor White men were targeted for sterilization, as were Black men. In fact Margaret Sanger and other early birth control advocates generally embraced eugenics, encouraging White middle-class women to reproduce, while discouraging reproduction among nonwhite, immigrant, [poor] and disabled people."

In the United States, nearly 100 eugenic statutes were passed between 1900 and 1970, and 60,000 individuals were sterilized for being "feebleminded." Those labelled as feebleminded were sometimes disabled, but often just poor, Black, and/or female. Sterilization epitomized the use of pseudoscientific findings to marginalize entire subpopulations. By the 1970s and 1980s, many states had repealed sterilization laws, but the effects continued. As Erevelles stated, "It is easy to dismiss eugenics as a relic of a bygone era, except that the continued association of race and disability in deficit ways necessitates that we examine how eugenic ideologies continue to reconstitute social hierarchies in contemporary contexts by deploying the ideology of disability." The use of pseudoscience to justify differential treatment remains a pervasive force in American culture and society, responsible for creating, or at least reifying, pervasive social stereotypes.

The specter of eugenics continues today, for instance, through the use of amniocentesis to detect Down syndrome and other fetal genetic "abnormalities." If a physician detects "defects" during the procedure, the woman will likely be encouraged to terminate her pregnancy. Today, a number of disability cases address reproductive capacity or rights. Many of these cases concern sterilizations or abortion of a fetus resulting from either consensual sexual activity or rape in facilitative care or the right of individuals with perceived disabilities to marry. Pseudoscientific ideology, similar to justifications given for antimiscegenation laws, is likewise used to justify disability-related marriage restrictions. . . .

CONCLUSION

Regrettably, the "social category of disability is prominently missing" from the various CLT analyses, "even though it plays a crucial ideological role in destabilizing normative discourses that construct difference in the first place." CLT scholars have not viewed disability as theoretically useful, sometimes relegating its discussion to a passing mention in the text or in footnotes. This is too often the case even though, in aspiration, the CLTs are a set of "collaborative, interdisciplinary inquiry and a self-conscious cultural critique that interrogates how subjects are multiply interpolated: in other words, how the representational systems of gender, race, ethnicity, ability, sexuality, and class mutually construct, inflect, and contradict one another."

The overlaps, connections, and confluences among social categories are so profound that the routine omission of disability from CLT analyses may stem from a belief that disability is already included. The corresponding regularity with which other socially subordinated categories are omitted from DS may likewise reflect the assumption that disability is already equated with "other" socially subordinated groups. Perhaps these omissions are a result of the stubborn belief that the differences among categories are in fact static and not traversable. Individuals do not experience identity as a fractured reality. If we start instead with this understanding of intersectionality informed by DisCrit, the multivariant nature of experience may be a place for coalition. Asch argues that one promotes social change but also acknowledges that the social consequences emanating from different social categories may not be equated. Regardless of the reasons and realities prompting the disconnect among subordinated communities, similarities in theory, experience, and objectives for transformation point to a more collaborative effort to counteract misunderstandings, mischaracterizations, outright misrepresentations, and stereotypes. Seeking a convergence of relevant dominant interests along with the voices of those with disability is one significant means of achieving this transformation.

DisCrit is a useful framework for envisioning a unifying and comprehensive theory. On its own terms, DS struggles with internal stratification. Already DS is a field that by necessity must engender flexibility because of the range of experiences included under the umbrella of disability. It also has the historical benefit of its relation to other subordinated categories. For example, learning and intellectual disabilities are something that may potentially affect any individual, but the subjective nature of their diagnoses and identification is such that overwhelmingly Black boys are identified with this disability. In this vein, the most important, yet most challenging aspect of antisubordination coalition building is understanding that subordination arises from the same structure, with each subhierarchy reinforcing the others. The lessons learned from the various civil rights struggles are therefore instructive if only because of the overlap among categories. A convergence of interests promotes cohesion within a single group and enables coalition building among disparate groups. However, finding common interest, much less agreeing on form and approach, is challenging. Recognizing that collaboration is neither a single event nor zero-sum game is a helpful starting point.

In a broad sense, this chapter is an attempt to identify multiple layers of converging interests. The point is to further destabilize identity so as to enable activists to find unity of purpose across difference. Such destabilization requires finding common interest within subgroups' internal hierarchy, points of cohesion among subordinated groups as well as important interest points with the overriding power structure.

99

Post-Traumatic Stress Disorder Leaves Scars "on the Inside," Iraq Veteran Says

Edward D. Murphy

Miguel Cyr said it's understandable, but still frustrating, to see friends and family members struggle to comprehend the problems he faces in dealing with post-traumatic stress disorder.

"People say, 'There's nothing wrong with you. You have no scars,' but they're on the inside," said Cyr, who served a year in Iraq with a Maine Army National Guard engineering battalion.

Cyr, who lives in Minot, said he joined the National Guard as a way to pay for college, but his battalion was sent to Iraq for a year in early 2004. The unit was based in Mosul, he said, and was building a road to connect several cities in the area.

As he headed out to the work site in July 2004, Cyr said, his truck was rocked by the explosion of a roadside bomb. Cyr said he had no visible wounds, but doctors later determined he had suffered a brain injury similar to a mild concussion.

His unit was also under mortar attack almost daily, he said, and friends of his were injured in the attacks.

"I had constant anxiety" about attacks while in Iraq, he said, and meanwhile, friends and relatives in the United States were pushing him to stay in closer contact.

"I just felt like I wasn't doing enough—(people asked) why wasn't I writing more?" he said. "I didn't need more from people, I just wanted people to stop needing me so much."

That took its toll on relationships when he came home in March 2005, Cyr said. He broke up with his girlfriend, lost track of friends and felt disconnected from fellow students when he attempted to go to college.

"I was only 19, but I felt like I didn't fit anymore," he said, feeling "a constant sadness and depression."

Cyr said he started to have bad dreams, had difficulty keeping a job and has had trouble finding work for the past few years because employers seemed turned off that he's disabled from his military service.

He felt constantly on edge, spent too much money, drank too much and started smoking marijuana because it was the only thing that seemed to help him keep calm.

Cyr signed up for the Army Reserve but eventually resigned because he had trouble following assignments and didn't feel comfortable around his fellow soldiers. His officers, he said, urged him to get tested for PTSD. He was diagnosed by VA [Veterans Administration] doctors four years ago.

Cyr said he takes medication the VA doctors prescribed, including antidepressants and pills to help him sleep, and goes to psychiatric therapy sessions. The treatment helps, he said, especially when he feels the need to talk about an incident in Iraq that's been bothering him.

"I get so emotional, but I keep it to myself because I feel like I'd be depressing people," he said. "Veterans need someone to relate to without bothering their friends and family."

Cyr has since gotten married and now has two children. He says his wife is "a special person to put up with someone who has panic attacks, can't sleep at night, won't sleep in the bed and just has serious rage sometimes."

On a day-to-day basis, Cyr believes he's functioning better, but said he also realizes there's no "cure" for PTSD, just treatment and strategies for managing it better.

"Things are OK, but every day is really affected by it," he said. "Post-traumatic stress is invisible. It's an injury to your emotions and it's lifelong, forever lasting."

100

Disability in the New World Order

Nirmala Erevelles

. . .

In this chapter, I speak from the critical vantage point of two theoretical perspectives: Third World feminism(s) and disability studies. By deploying the term Third World feminism(s), I am referring to the political constituency of women of African, Caribbean, Asian, and Latin American descent, as well as Native peoples of the United States who constitute an oppositional alliance against the sexist, racist, imperialist, neocolonial structures that shape our lives. When defining Disability Studies, I refer particularly to the social, political, and economic conditions within the category of "disability" which is constituted as "deviant" difference, and the ideological effects that such constructions of "disability" have on the reproduction of racial, gendered, and class oppression. At the same time, my discussion will address the actual conditions and experiences of Third World people's lives when mediated via the oppressive and often violent social relations of race, class, caste, gender, and disability.

The dialectical relationship between poverty and disability has been recognized for some time. Living with a disability adds to the risks of living in poverty, while at the same time, conditions of poverty increase the possibility of becoming disabled. In this essay, I will elaborate on this relationship between poverty and disability in Third World contexts—with a special focus on India—in the wake of sweeping economic reforms implemented by state governments in deference to structural adjustment policies (SAPs) which have been recommended by the World Bank and the IMF. . . .

ENGENDERING ECONOMIC REFORM: IMPLICATIONS FOR DISABILITY

Third World feminists have documented how the effects of (neo)colonial institutions and policies have transformed indigenous patriarchies and consolidated hegemonic middle-class cultures in metropolitan and colonized areas in support of oppressive patriarchal structures, albeit in new forms. This has been especially true in the context of the SAPs, where women and children have become the most vulnerable populations. Critics of the World Bank and the IMF have pointed out that SAPs were instituted to prioritize the efficient management of debt, rather than to transform the abject conditions of poverty in contexts where women and children represent the disproportionate percentage of the world's poor. Programs instituted by the World Bank and the IMF also supposedly sought to include women as active participants in wage labor markets to enable their emancipation from patriarchal oppression.

However, most of the labor activities offered to Third World women are for low-wage work, because these women are considered "cheap" and "pliable" labor in both factory production and the service industry. As a result, this new gendered labor shift has forced men out of jobs, and, as a result, poor Third World women are forced to balance wage labor along with subsistence and domestic production. Because of the sharp fall in the purchasing power of their incomes, Third World women, many of whom are single heads of households, are faced with the sole responsibility of meeting household reproduction costs. In the desperation for employment, poor women are forced to take jobs in the informal and other low-wage sectors while, at the same time, their unpaid labor escalates because they must stretch limited funds to cover the subsistence of their households. Additionally, their health is also affected because of reduced food consumption, stress, and domestic violence—experiences that affect fertility, infant mortality, and disabling conditions in both their children and themselves.

It is this economic context that sets the stage for the social construction of disability. According to Elwan, UNICEF's list of major causes of disability among children in Third World countries includes inadequate nutrition of mothers and children, vitamin deficiencies, abnormal prenatal or perinatal events, infectious diseases, accidents, and various other factors including environmental pollution and lack of adequate sanitation—all of which occur as a result of poverty conditions. Notwithstanding the World Bank's claims that the SAPs would eventually lead to a reduction in poverty, according to UNICEF, there has been a drop of 10% to 25% in average incomes, a 25% reduction in spending per capita on health, and a 50% reduction in spending per capita on education in the poorest countries in the world. Though officials argue that they advise sound macroeconomic policies and strategies that favor investment in basic human capital—primary health care and universal primary education—the implementation of the SAPs belie this claim. Abbasi points out that even though World Bank lending for health services has increased over the years, low-income countries are unable to meet and maintain health service costs and at the same time pay their debts, and have therefore begun to levy a small fee also called a "user charge" to all clients using public health services. In already destitute communities, these user charges have resulted in a decline in access to health services with disastrous consequences to these populations. As a result, according to Andrew Creese, a health economist at the World Health Organization (WHO), increases in maternal mortality and the incidence of communicable diseases such as diphtheria and tuberculosis have been attributed to such policies.

India offers a good case study of these practices. Forced to implement the structural adjustment programs (SAPs) in the early 1990s to meet the deficit in its balance of payments, the Indian state was encouraged to liberalize its economy, which required that it perform three main functions: protect and sustain the functioning of markets; use all policy instruments available to entice foreign capital investment; and undertake certain minimal expenditures so as to ameliorate the excesses perpetrated by the market. The implementation of the SAPs has only exacerbated the relationship between poverty and disability in India. Thus, for example, nearly fifteen thousand children in India under the age of five go blind because of a vitamin A deficiency caused by malnutrition. Additionally, limited access to clean water supplies as well as overcrowding in inadequate and unsanitary living conditions are responsible for the spread of intestinal, infectious, and vector-carrying diseases that also contribute to the onset of disability.

Even health policies actively supported by the international organizations barely address the crux of the problem. For example, the Indian state's investment in "Health for All by 2000," based on the Alma Ata Declaration of 1978, fostered only two major programs—oral rehydration therapy and immunization—instead of providing general health care for everyone. While such programs produced good statistics that claimed a lower rate of infant mortality, malnutrition and morbidity rates increased. And in the current context, as SAPs have mandated the increased privatization of health care and user financed health services, the transfer of resources from its poor clients to the wealthy investors of health care is the main outcome.

Additionally, even the rehabilitation projects, such as community based rehabilitation (CBR) programs (which are actively supported by the World Bank and other international organizations, such as ActionAid), also have served to accentuate inequalities along the axes of gender, class, caste, and disability. The dominant representation of the philosophy of CBR has been to integrate disabled people into the social mainstream. In a context where the resources allocated to rehabilitation programs are low and where there is a shortage of trained personnel to provide these services, CBR has become one of the most cost-efficient means to save on mounting staff costs, waste of labor, and the low efficiency of services. Thus, in an attempt to ensure maximum cost-efficiency, policy makers assume that the primary support for these programs will come from the community, where parents and workers, supervised by health volunteers (a village rehabilitation worker, or VRW, and a multipurpose rehabilitation worker, or MRW), will provide more specialized services to disabled members of the community.

However, the very concept of inclusion becomes exploitative in such contexts. Like the health programs supported by SAPs, CBR only serves to transfer the costs of services to the community. Thus, for example, even one of its advocates, Maya Thomas, director of the disability division ActionAid International-India has admitted that "the trend of progressive impoverishment of rural dwellings and the growing abandonment of extended family systems leave little economic and manpower resources in families that continue to look after the needs of their disabled members." Further, in patriarchal contexts, the provision of rehabilitation services by the family predominantly implies the woman, and so this becomes another burden in the life of the rural housewife caught up in her struggle for day-to-day economic survival. At the same time, most of the rehabilitation aides, who are low down in the occupational hierarchy and who receive pitiably low wages, are once again predominantly poor women from the community. Therefore, what has happened is that these state-initiated policies that have been celebrated for their cost-effectiveness are actually geared to "[mobilize] people's resources for government programs," where the additional costs of these services continue to be absorbed by both the paid and unpaid labor of women.

. . .

101

Disabled Behind Bars

Rebecca Vallas

America's four-decade-long experiment with mass incarceration and overcriminalization is widely recognized as a failure. We lock up a greater share of our citizens than any other developed nation, destroying lives and separating families at an annual cost of more than $80 billion. In addition, we do little to prepare individuals behind bars for their eventual release, yet are surprised when some two thirds return to our jails and prisons.

The crushing impact of the criminal justice system's failure is felt acutely in communities across the United States. Significant and growing research shows how certain populations—including communities of color; residents of high-poverty neighbourhoods; and lesbian, gay, bisexual, and transgender, or LGBT, individuals—have been particularly hard hit. But rarely discussed is the impact of the criminal justice system on Americans with disabilities.

The past six decades have seen widespread closure of state mental hospitals and other institutional facilities that serve people with disabilities—a shift often referred to as dein-stitutionalization. The number of Americans residing in such institutions dropped sharply from nearly 560,000 in 1955 to only about 70,000 in 1994. While widely regarded as a positive development, deinstitutionalization was not accompanied by the public investment necessary to ensure that community-based alternatives were made available. As a result, while people with disabilities—and particularly those with mental health conditions—were no longer living in large numbers in institutions, many began to be swept up into the criminal justice system, often due to minor infractions such as sleeping on the sidewalk. Indeed, federal and state jails and prisons are now home to three times as many people with mental health conditions as state mental hospitals.

People with disabilities are thus dramatically overrepresented in the nation's prison and jails today. According to the Bureau of Justice Statistics, people behind bars in state and federal prisons are nearly three times as likely to report having a disability as the nonincarcerated population, while those in jails are more than four times as likely. Cognitive disabilities—such as Down syndrome, autism, dementia, intellectual disabilities, and learning disorders—are among the most commonly reported: Prison inmates are four times as likely and jail inmates more than six times as likely to report a cognitive disability than the general population. People with mental health conditions comprise a large proportion of those behind bars, as well. The Bureau of Justice Statistics reports that fully 1 in 5 prison inmates have a serious mental illness.

Mass incarceration of people with disabilities is unjust, unethical, and cruel. But it is also penny-wise and pound-foolish, as community-based treatment and prevention services cost far less than housing an individual behind bars. According to a 2014 study of Los Angeles County, the average cost of jailing an individual with serious mental illness exceeds $48,500 per year. By comparison, the price tag for providing Assertive Community Treatment, or ACT, and supportive housing—one of the most intensive, comprehensive, and successful intervention models in use today—amounts to less than $20,500 annually, just two-fifths the cost of jail.

In addition to facing disproportionate rates of incarceration, people with disabilities are also especially likely to be the victims of police violence. Freddie Gray, Eric Garner, Kristiana Coignard, and Robert Ethan Saylor were all individuals with disabilities whose tragic stories of being killed at the hands of police officers garnered significant recent national media attention. They are but four high-profile examples of a widespread, commonplace occurrence. While data on police-involved killings are extremely limited, one study by the Ruderman Family Foundation estimates that people with disabilities comprise a staggering one-third to one-half of all individuals killed by law enforcement. According to an investigation by *The Washington Post*, one-quarter of the individuals shot to death by police officers in 2015 were people with mental health conditions. Countless more have suffered brutality and violent treatment at the hands of police, often stemming from misunderstandings related to mental health conditions and other disabilities. Furthermore, the number of individuals who have acquired disabilities while in police custody is unknown.

While behind bars, people with disabilities are often deprived of necessary medical care, as well as needed supports, services, and accommodations. This is despite long-standing federal disability rights laws that mandate equal access to programs, services, and activities for all people with disabilities in custody. Poor conditions in jails and prisons and inadequate access to health care and mental health treatment can not only exacerbate existing conditions, but also lead to further physical and mental health problems that individuals did not have prior to incarceration. Many inmates with disabilities are held in solitary confinement—reportedly, in many cases, for their own protection, due to lack of appropriate alternative accommodations. A growing array of research reveals that even short stays in solitary confinement can have severe and long-lasting consequences for people with disabilities, and particularly those with mental conditions. Furthermore, many individuals who had not previously lived with mental health conditions experience significant psychological distress following solitary confinement. The tragic but all-too-common case of Kalief Browder brought this to light last year. Browder died by suicide after nearly two years in solitary confinement in Rikers Island on charges, later dismissed, that he had stolen a backpack.

Moreover, while many people with disabilities already face barriers to employment, stable housing, and other necessary elements of economic security, adding a criminal record into the mix can pose additional obstacles that make living with a disability an even greater challenge. Meanwhile, reentry programs for formerly incarcerated individuals often lack necessary accommodations and connections to community services, making them incapable of meeting the needs of participants with disabilities.

This year marks the 17th anniversary of the landmark Supreme Court in *Olmstead v. L.C.*, which held that unjustified segregation of people with disabilities in institutional settings constituted unlawful discrimination in violation of the Americans with Disabilities Act, or ADA. Ending the mass incarceration of people with disabilities will require meaningful investment in the nation's social service and mental health treatment infrastructure to ensure availability and funding for community-based alternatives, so that jails and prisons are no longer forced to serve as social service providers of last resort. But bringing about the change will also require including disability as a key part of the bipartisan conversation on criminal justice reform taking place in Congress, as well as in states and cities across the United States.

This report highlights steps policymakers can take to combat inappropriate and unjust incarceration and criminalization of people with disabilities, as well as steps to ensure appropriate and humane treatment of people with disabilities throughout the justice system, from police practices to courts, conditions in jails and prisons, and reentry.

102

The Silent Victims

Inmates with Learning Disabilities

Douglas P. Wilson

Following the John Geoghan murder at the Souza-Baranowski super-maximum security prison in Shirley, the Massachusetts Department of Corrections (DOC) pledged to modernize its policies and management structure to meet the needs of the 21st century. However, all the public comments made by DOC officials and those currently investigating some of the DOC's most dubious actions have failed to address a segment of the inmate population that has suffered extraordinary indignities on a daily basis as a result of the archaic policies and overly authoritarian management of the department. These silently suffering inmates are afflicted with learning disabilities.

The DOC has shown complete indifference to the special needs of inmates with learning disabilities. The DOC's reaction may be predicated on the recent penal philosophy of punishment instead of rehabilitation, longer prison sentences, and an expectation of more severe treatment while incarcerated. This correctional ideology is often referred to as the "warehousing method" since its implementation has caused prison overcrowding and less inmate supervision post release.

The treatment of inmates with learning disabilities has evaded public attention for a number of reasons. First and foremost, the inmates with learning disabilities have been kept silent by existing DOC policies that prevent them from receiving the technical accommodations that would enable them to communicate their unique difficulties to the public, government agencies, the courts, and even DOC administrators. Another problem is that government agencies, charged with the duty of protecting the disabled, turn a blind eye to claims made by inmates.

Without accommodations, inmates with learning disabilities such as dyslexia are less likely to participate in prison educational programs or remain in contact with family and friends. Studies suggest that even the most basic educational opportunities and community support while incarcerated can lower prisoner recidivism rates. Inmates who lack accommodations often depend on other inmates to provide services like letter-writing for them. This situation humiliates and frustrates disabled inmates. Dependency on other inmates also puts disabled inmates at a greater risk of being victims of violence, extortion, or being forced to perform favors in return.

In 1990, the Americans with Disabilities Act was passed by Congress. This law was designed to move society toward removing the barriers and inequities faced by individuals with disabilities. Disabled inmates who were denied equal treatment or access to activities and programs due to their disabilities filed civil litigation to force correctional institutions to make reasonable accommodations for their disabilities. A number of landmark cases by the US Supreme Court, such as Pennsylvania Dept. of Corrections v. Yeskey, 118 S Ct. 1925 (199B), held that disabled inmates are protected from discriminatory actions under the provisions provided pursuant to the ADA. This was a leap forward for corrections. However, the civil actions brought before the court concerned only physical disabilities. Therefore, correctional institutions made little to no progress toward bringing about changes to benefit inmates with learning disabilities.

The Massachusetts DOC has been particularly aggressive in warding off modernization, denying learning disabled inmates access to accommodations while refusing to provide the medical examinations required to identify learning disabilities. A recent civil action illustrating the above, Wilson v. Matesanz, Norfolk Superior Court, CA No.02-00007, prompted one Superior Court Justice to issue this scalding comment as part of a larger ruling "If we are to have any faith in the rehabilitative power of incarceration, our penal institutions should encourage, or at least not discourage, educational efforts by inmates." (Ed. note. The author is the plaintiff in the fore mentioned civil action, the defendant the Superintendent of Norfolk MCI.)

A recent U.S. Department of Justice survey found that 10% of inmates report having a learning disability, although this figure is likely to be misleading, since many inmates are unaware of their medical conditions given their lower economic state prior to incarceration. Frank Wood, a professor of neurology at Wake Forest University and expert in the field of learning disabilities, asserts that individuals with dyslexia are overrepresented in prison populations. Studies proving that 50-75% of prisoners are functionally illiterateseem to corroborate Dr Wood's claim.

The time is ripe to bring public awareness to the silent victims of the DOC's outdated policies and discriminatory action. Through public support and open scrutiny of the DOC, the institution can be strengthened and guided toward fulfilling its charter of public safety, while offering dignity and hope to numerous inmates. Americans ought to demand a safe, humane, and productive prison environment with the goal of aiding inmates who genuinely seek self-education.

103

Go to the Margins of the Class

Disability and Hate Crimes

Lennard J. Davis

With great ceremony, the press reported the February 1999 conviction of white supremacist John William King for the kidnapping and murder of James Byrd, Jr., who had been chained to a truck in Jasper, Texas, dragged two miles, and dismembered. Likewise, the conviction of coconspirator Lawrence Russell Brewer in September 1999 seemed to imply that justice had been done. If justice in a broader sense is to be served, however, another fact of the case deserves attention. Byrd was not only black and the victim of race hatred; he was also disabled. The press has noted this so casually that few people realize it; those who do, including myself, found out that Byrd was severely arthritic and subject to seizures. This information was ferreted out only after extensive searches of news reports.

Indeed, I myself was uncertain that Byrd was a person with disabilities. I recalled reading, on the day the crime was first reported, that a disabled African American had been brutally murdered. Since I was interested in disability, the article caught my eye. Yet when the story reappeared days, weeks, and months later, Byrd was simply referred to as African American. Almost all the news stories contained this simplification. Indeed, when I decided to write a piece on the subject for *The Nation*, I at first thought I might have made an error in thinking that Byrd was a person with disabilities. When I went to the library to look up the articles on microfilm, I found that the *New York Times* mentioned only twice, in the first two reports, that Byrd was a person with disabilities. Any newspaper story I checked tended to follow that pattern.

. . .

Initially, I wanted to write this story as an op-ed piece for the *New York Times*. An acquaintance who is on the editorial board of the paper read my initial article and responded in a somewhat condescending and negative way. He asked me if I seriously thought that race could be equated with disability, whether the history of lynching and slavery could be meaningfully equated with occasional violence against people with disabilities. The editors for both these progressive journals saw race as the primary category and disability as a poor third cousin of race. Their assumption was that violence toward a person of color with disabilities is primarily the result of the color and much less the result of the disability.

But disability is hardly a minor category. Approximately 16 percent of Americans have a disability and, as such, they comprise a significant minority group with an inordinately high rate of abuse. According to the Center for Women's Policy Studies, disabled women are raped and abused at a rate more than twice that of nondisabled women. The risk of physical assault, robbery, and rape, according to researcher Dick Sobsey, is at least four times as great for adults with disabilities as for the general population. In February 1999, for example, a mentally retarded man in Keansburg, New Jersey, was abducted by a group of young people who tortured, humiliated, and assaulted him. In March 1999, advocates for another mentally retarded man filed a lawsuit against a group of Nassau County, New York, police officers who beat him while he was in custody.

People with disabilities and deaf people report that they are routinely harassed verbally, physically, and sexually in public places. In private institutions or group homes, they are often the prime victims of violence and sexual abuse; in their own homes, they are subjected to sexual abuse, domestic violence, and incest, preyed upon by family members, family "friends," and "caretakers." So the question remains, why is American society largely unaware of or indifferent to the plight of people with disabilities? Is it because as an ableist society, we do not really believe that disability constitutes a serious category of oppression? Whenever race and disability come together, as in the King case, ethnicity tends to be considered so much the "stronger" category that disability disappears altogether.

As a society, we have long been confronted by the existence of discrimination against people of color. Students pore over the subject of race in their textbooks and read the work of multicultural writers in high school and college. Martin Luther King Day and Kwanzaa raise our consciousness, and the heroic tales of people like Rosa Parks inspire us.

But while we may acknowledge we are racist, we barely know we are ableist. Our schools, our textbooks, our media utterly ignore the history of disability; the dominant culture renders invisible the works of disabled and deaf poets, writers, and performance artists. The closest we have come to a national media engagement is the 1998 six-part NPR radio series *Beyond Affliction* and a few references to deafness in the TV series *ER*. Motion pictures still largely romanticize or pathologize disability; there is not much else to make the experience of 16 percent of the population come alive realistically and politically.

Yet 72 percent of people with disabilities are unemployed, and their income is half the national average. Among working-age adults with disabilities, the poverty rate is three times that of those without impairments. One-third of all disabled children live in poverty; and despite the Americans with Disabilities Act, a judicial backlash has been under way ever since its passage in 1990. From 90 to 98 percent of discrimination cases brought under the ADA by people with disabilities have been lost in court. . . .

Anita Silvers notes this fact when she writes: "the courts tend to implement prohibitions against discrimination so as to favor paradigmatic members of the protected class. In doing so, they propel individuals whose experiences diverge from those of the class's prototypes, but who are equally at risk, to the class's margins." Thus when disability meets race, disability is propelled to the margins of the class.

From a legal perspective, one wants to make sure that members of a historically unprotected class receive proper justice and consideration under the law. Thus in America, women and minorities have been the focus of antidiscrimination law. There has been much cultural work done to make it acceptable at the end of the millennium for such groups to have public respect and sympathy. Countless novels, movies, and plays have accomplished this goal over the course of the twentieth century. It is unimaginable that a film could be made now that would present African Americans, Native Americans, or women as members of a deservedly subordinate, disenfranchised group. Thus the courts will, in the most obvious cases, uphold the right of members of such groups to redress wrongs in housing, employment, discrimination, and so on.

However, disability occupies a different place in the culture at this moment. Although considerable effort has been expended on the part of activists, legislators, and scholars, disability is still a largely ignored and marginalized area. Every week, films and television programs are made containing the most egregious stereotypes of people with disabilities, and hardly anyone notices. Legal decisions filled with ableist language and attitudes are handed down without anyone batting an eyelid. . . . Newspapers and magazines barely notice the existence of disability and largely use ableist language and metaphors in their articles. In other words, disability may be the last significant area of discrimination that has not yet been resolved, at least on the judicial, cultural, and ethical levels, in the twentieth and twenty-first centuries. . . .

So when it comes to violence against people with disabilities, several factors intervene. Although many states have statutes that describe disability in a list of categories that are protected under hate crime legislation, the actual enforcement of such policies may be muted by the intersectionality I have been describing. The Violent Crime Control and Law Enforcement Act of 1994 defines a hate crime as one "in which the defendant intentionally selects a victim, or in the case of a property crime, the property that is the object of the crime, because of the actual or perceived race, color, religion, national origin, ethnicity, gender, disability or sexual orientation of any person." . . .

Tellingly, though, a distinction is often made in this legislation. For example, previously under California's hate crime law, a murder committed because of the victim's race, color, religion, ancestry, or national origin could bring the death penalty or life in prison without parole. However, the maximum penalty for a murder based on gender, sexual orientation, or disability was twenty-five years to life in prison. A new bill signed in September 1999 increases the maximum in those latter categories to life in prison without parole. Federal efforts to prevent hate crimes, however, are now restricted to race, color, religion, and national origin.

Several U.S. senators have sponsored legislation to extend protections to gender, disability, and sexual orientation. But this idea ultimately did not pass into law and, even if it had, hate crimes based on disability are unlikely to carry as stringent a penalty as crimes based on hate for race, color, religion, or national origin. . . .

But how do we determine, in any philosophical sense, that one kind of identity is more important than another? Historically, although the United States was founded on a separation of church and state, religion has been seen as a "holy" category certainly higher in status than, for example, one's sexual orientation; race, so embroiled in the nation's history, must be more important than something like disability; and so on—the arguments are based more on ad hoc judgments about the viciousness of different kinds of prejudice than on any principle one can articulate. This seems to be the same unreflective influence that gives priority to race over gender or disability in the intersectionality argument.

We can see this contradiction in another arena. The FBI is required to keep track of hate crimes. It has produced a report that found that of the 8,049 incidents of hate crime reported to police in 1997, 12 were motivated by bias based on disability; of these, 9 were based on the victim's physical condition and 3 were based on the victim's mental condition. These numbers seem shockingly low when compared to other studies such as Dick Sobsey's tabulations. Sobsey also notes that when a person with disabilities is a victim of crime, it tends to be a violent crime rather than a property crime.

. . .

Indeed, I am sure that when it comes time for the FBI to list the report on Byrd, they will file it under racial hate crime rather than a disability-related crime. Also, many of the crimes against people with disabilities will simply be seen as ordinary rather than hate crimes. So the rape or murder of a mentally ill resident of a sheltered facility will be seen as a rape or murder, not as one motivated by the status of the person involved. Indeed, one of the arguments used by opponents of hate crime legislation, particularly as it applies to gender or disability, is that crimes such as rapes will have to be investigated by the FBI, putting an undue burden on that organization. Since such crimes are daily occurrences, and since it could be argued that rape itself is a hate crime against women, the FBI will be taxed to the utmost in trying to detail all these acts of violence.

Intersectionality argues that individuals who fall into the intersection of two categories of oppression will, because of their membership in the weaker class, be sent to the margins of the stronger class. What these statistics suggest is that the category of disability, while a weak one to judges or legislators, is a powerful one to those who seek to victimize. Rather than minimizing an identity, victimizers are drawn to the double or triple categories of race, gender, and disability. Each of these categories enhances the opportunity for hate and the likelihood that the crime will go unnoticed, unreported, or disbelieved. For example, the Center for Women's Policy Studies reports that virtually half of the perpetrators of sexual abuse against women with disabilities gained access to their victims through disability services, and that caregivers commit at least 25 percent of all crimes against women with disabilities. In other words, the dependency of such women, compounded by their lower economic status, ethnicity, and diminished mobility or ability to communicate to authorities, is an enticement to victimizers.

. . .

The point here is that the general climate of ableism makes it comfortable for us to regard systematic violence against people with disabilities as accidental. Could one claim that the university's policy of negligence toward students with disabilities, especially after being forewarned, was a willed act of violence? The consciousness of the general public and the legal system would have to undergo a dramatic change for the truth of such a claim to be obvious.

Likewise, the definition of "hate" has to change as well. One of the reasons there is resistance to calling attacks against people with disabilities "hate" crimes is because the general ideology toward people with disabilities rules out hate as a viable emotion. In our culture, it is permissible to "pity" or even "resent" people with disabilities. . . . Thus the idea that crimes against people with disabilities might be a result of "hate" seems to most people somehow wrong. Who would act violently toward a person using a wheelchair merely because that person could not walk? . . . someone who cannot see a clearly posted sign, cannot walk up unblocked stairs, needs special assistance above what other "normal" citizens need[?] This kind of hatred is one that abhors the possibility that all bodies are not configured the same, that weakness and impairment are the legacy of a cult of perfection and able embodiment. When the law begins to catch on to this level of hatred, justice will be served.

. . .

104

Why the Intersexed Shouldn't Be Fixed

Insights from Queer Theory and Disability Studies

Sumi Colligan

The initiatives the Intersex Society of North America (ISNA) promoted to prevent "corrective" surgery for genitals not clearly identifiable as male or female have recently come to my attention. This discovery has stimulated my own reflections on the parallels between American cultural representations and the everyday struggles of the intersexed and those of people with disabilities. Both groups are subjected to anomalous classification, medical management, silencing, and shame; both groups titillate the projected, and often repressed, fantasies of outsiders; and both intersexed and disabled individuals and organizations are challenging the assumptions that underlie these negative images to reclaim their own impassioned, desirable, and desirous bodies. These activists seek to assert the value of their own presence in the world and to raise questions about a system of cultural ordering that renders them symbolically, if not literally, neutered or "fixed."

David Mitchell and Sharon Snyder point out that while there is an abundance of critical theory on the body, disability remains largely untheorized, often appearing as a natural backdrop for the exploration of already established social issues and themes. They explain: "Within this common critical methodology physical difference exemplifies the evidence of social deviance even as the constructed nature of physicality itself fades from view." Yet opportunities to explore the cultural construction of physicality and its intersections with race, class, gender, and sexuality are abundant, appearing both within the realms of popular and medical culture. These references are often quite explicit and should not require the sensitized lens of disability studies for quick detection. For example, apropos of disability and the trans and/or nebulously gendered, talk show host Jerry Springer is quoted as saying:

> When you think of all the things that could go wrong at birth or at least not be as they ought to be, from blindness to mental retardation to cystic fibrosis to, indeed,

the entire litany of possible birth defects, why do we assume that the one thing that can never be out of sync is our gender identity? And yet, while we are quick to heap our love and compassion and charity on any of these disabilities, if it has something to do with sex suddenly we don't want to hear about it. . . . And so with the same compassion that we are offering to those who are trying to fix other parts of their body that perhaps aren't working as they should, why not a word of understanding to those whose gender seems to be out of whack?

A number of issues here go unquestioned: Why are charity and compassion considered to be a desirable and automatic response to certain kinds of physical variation? Why is there an assumption that disability has nothing to do with sex? Why do genitals and gender identity have to match? Why is being fixed a moral imperative?

It is instructive to begin to explore these intersections and parallels by interrogating the meaning of *fixed*. The dictionary definition of the verb indicates "to set in order," "to repair," "to attach or fasten immovably"; even the noun, *fix*, is defined as "an embarrassing or uncomfortable position." Through the lens of *fixed*, I consider how and why Western cultures have come to disable the intersexed and neuter the disabled, subjecting them to similar disciplines of normalization. . . .

MEDICALIZING INTERSEXED/DISABLED BODIES: RETROFITTING AND REFORM

Michel Foucault has documented the forces that have converged in the last two centuries in Western Europe and the United States that contribute to the medical scrutiny of the flesh and its moral attributes. For example, in *The Birth of a Clinic*, Foucault describes processes by which the bodies of individuals undergoing medical treatment came to be viewed as discrete and docile entities whose hidden recesses contained the secrets to their ailments. Likewise, in *The History of Sexuality*, he addresses a range of professions (demography, pedagogy, medicine, and psychiatry among them) that emerged during this period to shape the contours of modernity. These fields used their professional powers to name, locate, regulate, punish, and remold individuals associated with aberrant corporealities. Foucault referred to these approaches as "bio-power," as they are "techniques that make possible a special alliance between specialized knowledge and institutionalized power in the state's management of life."

However, whereas Foucault draws out the implications of the deployment of these forms of power/knowledge to define and contain illness, madness, and sexuality, historian Henri-Jacques Stiker notes that disability is lacking from Foucault's analysis. I contend that such an analysis should be broadened to include the role that the development of statistics played in turning disability into deviance, a process that included upholding a statistical norm against which all else was rendered abnormal. Moreover, the analysis should consider the manner in which the growth of the rehabilitation industry was catalyzed by a drive to remove the "lack" and restore the disabled body to its "assumed, prior normal state." As we shall see, all these powers collided and collaborated to refashion, retrofit, and reform intersexed and disabled bodies to eradicate their "abnormalities" from our social presence and/or to render them invisible.

In Foucault's introduction to *Herculine Barbin: Being the Recently Discovered Diary of a Nineteenth Century French Hermaphrodite*, he states that by the mid-1800s, medical doctors had concluded that everyone had a "true" sex, which even when masked, could be discerned by the penetrating eye of science. This conviction was also corroborated by Alice Dreger, a researcher of French and British physicians between 1860 and 1915, who remarks that "the history of hermaphroditism is largely the history of struggles over the 'realities' of sex—the nature of 'true' sex, the proper role of the sexes, the question of what sex can, should, or must mean." The medical examination of hermaphrodites rested on the assumption of sexual dimorphism such that one's true sex could only be read as male or female. The sorting out of the sexes was conducted by navigating one's way through "genital geography," deciphering anatomical excesses and deficiencies, and distinguishing "veritable" from "pseudo vulvas." If anatomy alone wasn't quick to release its secrets, doctors would also seek clues in behaviors and aptitudes because of an assumed linear correlation between genitals and gendered attractions and performances (ergo, testicles and ovaries are us). Additionally, parents were interrogated for recollections of maternal impressions and "hereditary antecedents," physical indicators of past parental transgressions. Overall, if bodies and actions didn't conform to medical expectations and social conventions, they were forced to comply to nature's imagined calling by medical declaration and legal protocol.

In the past fifty years, surgery and hormonal therapy have become routine, technical solutions for individuals whose genitals are deemed medically problematic. That normative physicality is being constructed here should be readily apparent and is captured humorously by intersex ("intersex" is in common use now because it doesn't carry the mythical connotations of "hermaphrodite") writer Raphael Carter who defines ambiguous genitalia as "genitalia that refuse to declare their sex to doctors—no doubt on the principle that under interrogation by the enemy you should give only name, rank and serial number." This queering of medical authority serves to underscore the invasive consequences of accepted medical definitions and procedures. Intersex reporter Martha Coventry reveals that according to scientific standards, "girls, if they perceive themselves, or want to be perceived as fully 'feminine,' should have clitorises no longer than $3/8$ inch at birth. Boys, if they hope to grow up 'masculine,' should have penises that are about one inch in stretched length at birth. Girls should have vaginas fit for future intercourse, and boys should have urethra openings at the tip of the penis in order to be able to urinate standing up."

Of course, the irony here is that self-identity has nothing to do with this medical intervention because surgeons now generally perform these reconstructive feats on the intersexed in infancy. Biologist Anne Fausto-Sterling argues that the intersexed excite discomfort in medical professionals because "they possess the irritating ability to live sometimes as one sex and sometimes as the other, and they raise the specter of homosexuality." It is clear, then, that intersexed babies are being fixed, at least in part, as a form of rehabilitation that facilitates their bodily deployment into society according to heteronormative measures. In keeping with the body's truth, doctors, however, contend that their medical tampering is simply a means of restoring the infants to their naturally gendered state, denying the role that culture plays in enforcing this imperative.

In parallel fashion, in the last several centuries, people with disabilities have been subjected to pacification through the medical gaze's fixation on essentialized and internalized bodily truths and to reform through the disciplined practices of sheltered workshops, special education, and physical rehabilitation. The benevolence and charity that have been extended to these individuals rest on their willingness, through medical treatment, physical retraining, and mental acquiescence, to strive to achieve normative standards of bodily appearance and physical, linguistic, and cognitive use. By means of these institutional practices, "the disabled are to be 'raised up,' restored." Indeed, historian Stiker concludes: "rehabilitation marks the appearance of a culture that attempts to complete the act of identification, of making identical."

Alternatively, for those who can't be medically disappeared as with the intersexed, there remains the role of desexualized, childlike, dependents who are destined to institutionalization as they await the promise of cure. As historian Paul Longmore notes, these individuals are extended the benevolent hand of charity because, particularly in the United States, their images help reaffirm the virtue and moral fitness of its nondisabled citizens. Stiker asserts that cure suggests removal and that rehabilitation suggests assimilation. Regardless of an emphasis on cure or rehabilitation, "compassion tends to be channeled into normalizing." And either way, intersexed and disabled persons, viewed as destabilizing physical, sexual, gendered, and classificatory presences, have clearly been the targets of coercive regimes of routinization which have nearly, but not so successfully, extinguished their bodily knowledge and their desires.

FIXING BODIES, EXTINGUISHING DESIRES: CONSTRUCTING ASEXUALITY

. . . Both intersexed and disabled bodies have been construed as threatening, with their imagined excesses and deficiencies. Consequently, these bodies have been stripped of their ability to pleasure and be pleasured through the mechanism of denial, the social erasure of sexuality. From this standpoint, both intersexed and disabled bodies are lurking in the social margins, fluctuating between the overly intrusive and the wispy. In this vein, James Porter notes:

> viewed in itself (an essentializing perspective—but that is part of the point), a disabled body seems somehow too much a body, too real, too corporeal: it is a body that, so to speak, stands in its own way. From another angle, which is no less reductive, a disabled body seems to be lacking something essential, something to make it identifiable and something to identify with; a body that is deficiently itself, not quite a body in the full sense of the word, not real enough.

And as Foucault has aptly demonstrated, societal regulatory regimes have been deployed not only to survey these excesses and deficiencies but to contain them as well.

Medicalization of the intersexed and disabled has profoundly shaped their cultural representations and interpersonal relationships, as well as their phenomenological experiences of and with their own bodies. Whereas historically, the intersexed conjured up erotic associations, more recently, repeated medical diagnosis and intervention and medical jargon bantered about in exclusionary or hushed tones have contributed to shrouding disabled/intersexed bodies with an aura of taboo, secrecy, and shame. Overall, medical and cultural assumptions about sex being reserved for heterosexed, symmetrical, and genitally specific bodies tend to promote the expectation that sex and sexuality are privileges awarded to the "normate" only.

The rigid molding of bodies to conform to conventional standards and allowances clearly exacts a toll in conceiving of alternative means of desiring. For the intersexed, "to grow up in a world in which there is no name, at least no spoken name, for what you are" is frightening and confusing. Fear of rejection undermines sexual choices. For instance, Morgan Holmes, an intersexed bisexual, explains: "I learned then that my desire wasn't necessarily linked to my physical difference. However, even that knowledge could not assuage the fear that my lovers of whatever sex, but particularly female, would know I had a fake 'cunt' and would abandon me." In this way, the expectation that our bodies should be strictly products of nature and not culture (as if any human body occupies space outside of culture), awards sexual gratification and relationships to those whose bodies pass the test of normative authenticity.

The story of a person called Toby who was brought up as a girl, then lived as a boy, eventually adopted the label of neuter, and in 1987, endeavored to form a self-help group for others who similarly self-identified, further illustrates the psychic cost of growing up with a body that the surrounding culture denies is possible. "As Toby conceived it, the group's purpose was to provide a forum for people who think of themselves as neuter and/or asexual to make (nonsexual) connections with others." Toby's hope was that such a group would provide "'a setting free of pressure to define ourselves in terms of maleness or femaleness.'" While asexuality should be respected as a chosen identity and practice, the fact that abstinence is the only acceptable alternative in our society for the unmarried, disabled, or nonheteronormative leaves me wondering why neuter was the one option to fill the interspace. Is this yet one more instance of a presence concealed as an absence because Western binary categories disallow more creative possibilities?

What is perhaps most remarkable in the testimonies of intersex though, particularly those individuals whose bodies have escaped medical tampering, is the sense of contentedness with their own bodies. In the video ISNA produced, "Hermaphrodites Speak," Angela Moreno describes the delight she received from her large clitoris at the age of twelve before doctors insisted on performing a "clitoral reduction" as "time in the pleasure garden before the fall." She asserts that what has been most profoundly removed from the intersexed through medical intervention is a uniquely "hermaphroditic eroticism."

Unfortunately, the idea that our bodies harbor our deepest truths tends to obscure the part that our culture and its naturalizing agents play in imposing these so-called truths upon us. Instead we are cast in the role of deceivers if we don't wear our bodies on our sleeves, for we are said to deprive others of their ability to manage us, anchor us, and fix our meaning. Joshua Gamson suggests that on television talk shows, for example, "any dissonance between genital status and genital identity [is taken] as a sign of inauthenticity." Foucault would, in fact, argue that this compulsion to speak incessantly of our sexualities is a manifestation of modern surveillance techniques rather than an expression of our innermost thoughts. This point would indicate that, as much as discourse may attempt to contain the truth of our bodies, there will inevitably be discontinuities between the stories we tell and our bodies themselves. From this vantage point, there can never be a complete correlation between our genital status and our gender identities, no matter who we are. Moreover, David Halperin further complicates this issue of truth telling by stating that "coming out" has the advantage of "claiming back . . . a certain interpretive authority," but never effectively eliminates the "superior and knowing gaze" of the outside viewer.

On the other hand, those of us who have visible disabilities are often neutralized by external fixations that rob us of the opportunity to speak our own pleasures and desires. Part of the problem is that the larger society simply assumes that sexuality and disability are so antithetical to one another that there is no discussion to be had. Certain British disability theorists assert: "In modern Western societies, sexual agency (that is, potential or actual independent sexual activity) is considered the essential element of full adult personhood, replacing the role formerly taken by paid work: because disabled people are infantalized, and denied the status of active subjects, so consequently their sexuality is undermined." Eli Clare argues further that, because disabled bodies are equated so thoroughly with medical pathology, they are generally denied even the distorted and magnified sexuality attributed to many marginalized people.

The tendency to deny any recognition to the sexuality of people with disabilities also contributes to a blurring of their gender identification such that they share a gender ambiguity not so dissimilar from the intersexed. Disability and queer writer Eli Clare explains: "The construction of gender depends not only on the male and female body, but also on the nondisabled body." This refusal to read disabled bodies correctly may even pose a problem for entry and acceptance into gay, lesbian, bisexual, and transgender subcultures as they, too, rely upon visible markers to signify group membership. Attention to the more culturally loaded, but misunderstood qualities of disabled bodies may cause "their less

CONTEXT

visible identity to be neglected." More generally, visuality and visibility produce complex and contradictory effects for those whose bodies are deemed unnatural because the impulse to stabilize our identities and to mold us into singular subjects is there regardless of the source of our visibility (i.e., by our appearance, our actions, and/or our words). The fact that all of us, in some way, participate in this dynamic suggests that these misreadings are powerful cultural scripts to resist and transform.

. . .

105

Students with Disabilities Frustrated with Ignorance and Lack of Services

Allie Grasgreen

INDIANAPOLIS – New college students with disabilities are often insecure. Navigating a complicated bureaucracy for the first time with far less institutional support than they had in high school, these students often must overcome stigma and ignorance surrounding their disabilities and advocate for themselves, which they're often not used to doing. The alternative: risk not getting the tools they need to succeed academically.

That's difficult enough. But some people make it harder.

"I literally had a professor say, 'Well, I've never had a student of that kind before, so I don't know what to do,'" one college employee said here Tuesday at the American College Personnel Association's annual conference. "But the student was standing right there ready to take their test. It felt so violating."

At a session here exploring what students with physical and psychological disabilities have to say about their collegiate experiences, it was clear that professors have a lot of learning to do.

"I have faculty who are more dismissive of something like bipolar disorder than they would be of something like cerebral palsy," one attendee said. Because the affliction is psychological rather than physical, she said, "they don't see it as being as challenging."

But the student affairs and services staff in the room blamed themselves, in part. One person admitted it's "embarrassing" that his small private college does not offer any disabilities service training to workers in the campus writing center.

The situation is so bad on some campuses that one student said it feels like "a luxury" when professors and staff actually work with them. Other times, students will simply go without the necessary accommodation, whether it's extra time on an exam or keeping a therapy dog in the dorm.

"Learning should be a right, not a luxury," said Jackie Koerner, the Saint Louis University graduate assistant who presented a literature review and some of her own dissertation research at the session. "Many faculty members say they would love to present these options to students, they just don't know what's appropriate."

The siloed, dispersed nature of higher education institutions means getting students with disabilities the accommodations they need can be complicated. So rather than a professor approaching the disabilities services office every time he or she needs, say, a textbook converted to digital, campus staff should work to make sure everything is accessible to everyone. (It's called universal instructional design.)

That way, there will be no more requiring disabled students to move to the front of the classroom when a lecture starts, or asking in front of everyone whether they need email versions of today's lecture (to use two more examples from Tuesday). Just always use a microphone and make sure (as Koerner does) that all the text is on Blackboard already.

It'd be a good way to help those with disabilities, of course, but also might not be a bad idea from the institutional liability perspective. In a settlement with the U.S. Justice Department last year, Louisiana Tech University agreed to stop using and purchasing learning materials that limit access for students with visual disabilities. Experts said the conclusion of the lawsuit, which alleged that the university violated the Americans with Disabilities Act, signaled a broader shift in the extent to which colleges are expected to address accessibility. (The ADA doesn't require that students with disabilities receive accommodations, just that they have equitable access.)

Students with disabilities report having a rough first year academically as they transition to a new learning environment, Koerner said, but also have trouble making social connections with professors, staff members and peers. They worry that others won't – or don't, as the above examples demonstrate – accept their needs as a learner, and often they end up moving closer to home or to another, perhaps two-year, institution.

Two-thirds of college students don't receive accommodations simply because their colleges don't know about their disabilities, according to studies Koerner cited.

Many ACPA attendees were surprised to learn that the law does not require medical documentation of a student's disability in order for the college to provide an accommodation, and speculated that the misconception might contribute to students' unwillingness to disclose.

"You don't just take someone's word for it – the documentation is the interview process for classroom accommodations," one person said. But if the need for accommodation isn't clear through the interview alone, the college may request documentation.

Joint initiatives between offices and departments could help disseminate information more efficiently and effectively, Koerner said. She also suggested creating "safe zones" where students can go to relax and talk to a counselor if they feel overwhelmed. The concept has been popular for gay and lesbian students and those with autism.

"If we just provide the information, they will come," Koerner said – and in turn, lighten the load for the practitioners. "The disability services offices on our campuses are so overwhelmed with accommodation requests, and they are small offices. They cannot possibly support the needs of training the entire campus."

106

Understanding Deafness

Not Everyone Wants to Be "Fixed"

Allegra Ringo

The protesters were rallying against the Listening and Spoken Language Symposium, an annual event put on by the Alexander Graham Bell Association for the Deaf and Hard of Hearing (AGB). The symposium featured speakers, workshops, and product displays centered around the topic of, as you may have guessed, listening and spoken language. Many of the sponsors and exhibitors were affiliated with companies that sell cochlear implants, surgically implanted devices that allow a Deaf or hard-of-hearing person to hear (to varying degrees).

The protesters were angry, but acting peacefully. The majority of them were Deaf. (Yes, with a capital D. In the book *America: Voices from a Culture*, Carol Padden and Tom Humphries explain, "We use the lowercase deaf when referring to the audiological condition of not hearing, and the uppercase Deaf when referring to a particular group of deaf people who share a language – American Sign Language (ASL) – and a culture.")

The AGB has a complicated history with members of Deaf culture. AGB's stated mission is to "[help] families, health care providers and education professionals understand childhood hearing loss and the importance of early diagnosis and intervention." Their preferred methods for doing so emphasize spoken language, and de-emphasize the use of ASL. In practice, this translates to teaching communication methods like lip reading, learning to speak (by imitating breathing patterns and mouth shapes) and, relatively recently, using cochlear implant technology.

AGB's reasons for their oral focus depends who you ask. When reached for comment, Susan Boswell, director of communications and marketing for AGB, told me that AGB "supports the development of spoken language through evidence-based practices focusing on the use of audition and appropriate technologies." When I asked Ruthie Jordan, a Deaf activist who runs Audism Free America and helped organize the rally against AGB, she told me the reason is much more bottom-line. (I spoke with Ruthie and other Deaf people at the rally through my interpreter, Drew Tolson, who was extremely helpful.)

Ruthie's take is that AGB "[Makes] money . . . by miseducating the parents of Deaf children." Like many others at the rally, Ruthie feels that AGB takes advantage of the fact that hearing parents may not understand how a Deaf child can lead a functional, fulfilling life. A hearing parent in this situation may be easily convinced that a cochlear implant and an oral-based approach is the only legitimate option.

AGB's "listening and spoken language"-based approach comes out of the school of oralism, which aims to educate Deaf children through the use of oral speech and lip reading (as opposed to manualism, which advocates for the primary use of ASL in Deaf education). The goals of oralism may not sound controversial to most hearing people, but oralism has a long and problematic history.

In the 1860s, Alexander Graham Bell was a prominent oralist, and to some, an important figure in the spreading of audism — the belief that it is inherently better to be able to speak and hear. Although he surely thought otherwise, Bell had an ugly relationship with the Deaf community. Though his mother and wife were Deaf, he was intent on wiping out "hereditary deafness." He removed Deaf faculty from schools, demanded the same schools stop their use of ASL, and advocated against "deaf intermarriage."

Bell was also involved in the Eugenics movement, serving for a time as chairman of the board of scientific advisers to the Eugenics Record Office.

In 1880, prompted by talks between Bell and other prominent figures in deaf education, 164 delegates met for the Second International Congress on Education of the Deaf. Only one of the delegates was deaf. At the conference, a resolution was passed that banned sign language in schools, in an effort to encourage spoken language skills, and thus "[restore] the deaf-mute to society." Other passages in the resolution urge us to "[consider] the incontestable superiority of speech over signs," and argue that teaching deaf people to speak English will "[give them] a more perfect knowledge of language." After its passage, schools in Europe and the United States ceased all use of sign language.

Given this history, some Deaf people feel that oralism is rooted in audism. Some argue that the sentiment of needing to "restore [Deaf people] to society" still underlies the AGB and companies affiliated with them. In fact, many Deaf people and Deaf allies, like the ones at the rally, strongly oppose the AGB and their affiliates. These people argue that the AGB and its affiliates propagate practices that harm Deaf people, all for the sake of making money. And indeed, AGB has a financial stake in the sales of cochlear implants as well as other "hearing technology."

In addition to running an academy that trains teachers in oral-based educational methods, AGB "provides advertising opportunities to companies seeking to promote their products to individuals who are deaf and hard of hearing." According to AGB's website, one of their "partners in hearing" is Med-El, a large manufacturer of cochlear implants. As I mentioned earlier, the exhibitors and sponsors for their 2013 symposium include a long list of companies who sell or otherwise advocate for cochlear implant technology: Advanced Bionics, Cochlear America, the American Cochlear Implant Alliance, and many others.

Those who oppose the AGB's practices argue that this is a large coalition of companies that stand to benefit from the sale of cochlear implants. This, they argue, is a conflict of interest, and renders any information distributed by these companies untrustworthy. Ruthie Jordan told me she feels that AGB is "miseducating the parents of Deaf children . . . [AGB is] earning their millions by perpetuating misinformation. They are using the ears and the bodies of Deaf people to make themselves rich." She thinks AGB's actions are "only related to spoken language and 'fixing' Deaf people . . . they see Deaf people as sick, disabled, as having a deficit."

Many within Deaf culture feel similarly. They argue that the AGB harms Deaf communities by propagating large amounts of information about oralist methods — including cochlear implants — and treating ASL as "less than" spoken English.

The controversy is sometimes difficult for hearing people to understand. Hearing people often assume that Deaf people would naturally want to take advantage of any method that could lead them to become part of the hearing world — especially cochlear implants, the most advanced hearing technology we have. In reality, that assumption is far from true. To members of Deaf culture, American Sign Language is a cultural cornerstone. Because Deaf children who receive cochlear implants at a young age will likely be educated in the oralist method, they are less likely to learn ASL during their early years, which are the most critical years of language acquisition. For some Deaf parents, that would result in a child who speaks a different language than they do. Understandably, some see this as a loss of culture—one that, in some cases, has been passed down through generations. What may seem to a hearing person like an opportunity may be seen by some Deaf people as a loss.

The debate stems from a fundamental disagreement: one group sees deafness as a disability, and the other group sees it as a culture. The trouble is that the former group holds a disproportionate amount of power, and the latter group are the ones affected.

Jeff DuPree volunteers with Audism Free America, and is a proud sixth-generation Deaf person. I spoke with him through an interpreter at the symposium. Jeff told me, "My whole life I've lived as a Deaf person. I married a Deaf person, I've worked and associated with Deaf people, and I've had no problem in this world. So why are organizations like this trying to take away my right to live the way I want to live, my right to raise my children the way I feel they should be raised?"

It's not an easy question to answer. For their part, AGB maintains that they are simply advocates for the Deaf and hard of hearing. They point to the many people who, they argue, they have helped, by giving them information, grants, or general guidance related to cochlear implants and overall oral-focused education. AGB's website states that they "[Help] to ensure that every child and adult with hearing loss has the opportunity to listen, talk and thrive in mainstream society."

That's not a disingenuous statement. The question is whether the affected people are receiving the full truth about "mainstream society."

107

How to Curse in Sign Language

Ashley and Deborah

. . .

When I arrived at Starbucks, I saw Deborah, sitting alone, not drinking any coffee. She appeared to be in her mid-forties and was wearing tapered jeans and white shoes. She looked like a nurse who was exhausted after working the night shift. Raising a child like Ashley, I thought, she must feel fatigued all the time. She sat in her chair like someone who had been standing for years.

I sat down and introduced myself. There was no small talk. Deborah started right in with her story. She had grown up in a rural setting, in Virginia Beach, in a middle-class Catholic home. The household income was just enough to meet the family's needs. Deborah had a twin brother, and their extended family was large. Family gatherings often included more than seventy-five people, "nudging and talking over each other," she told me. "I loved it."

. . .

The problems continued even after the birth of their son, Chip. Finally, after months of drama and upheaval, Deborah—with the support of an Episcopal minister—filed for divorce, went to court, and eventually got custody of her son.

Ashley came into Deborah's life through an announcement posted at a local United Methodist church not long after she and her young son had moved to Richmond. Deborah was trying to rebuild her life. She was working in computers, a career she had set in motion when she was still a cop, and completed her bachelor's degree in computer science while working full-time. She was also taking an exercise class at the aforementioned church. One day, she arrived early, thirty minutes before her class began. To kill time, she stood around reading various postings on the church bulletin board. The tip of a yellow piece of paper, burled under the rest, caught her eye, and she uncovered an announcement from the United Methodist Family Services. This organization was holding an adoption information program for people who might consider "challenging" adoptions. She decided to attend the session just to "see what the group had to say."

. . .

After the meeting, Deborah signed up for a nine-week training session followed by what is known as a "home study." This training was a prerequisite for going any further in the adoption process. According to Deborah, "the leaders of the training didn't pull any punches and shared the very difficult things involved in the adoption of special-needs or older children." Many of these children would need lifelong care. Many would require advanced medical supervision at home. Many would have emotional problems. But after each session, Deborah "felt even more strongly about adoption as an option." Most people who have gone through the adoption process consider the home study to be the most difficult. It requires the prospective parent to undergo multiple background checks, physical exams, and a financial audit; to obtain three letters of recommendation; to write an autobiography; and to submit to three unannounced home inspections by a social worker. Deborah passed the home study with an almost perfect score, and then, in her words, "the search began."

It lasted over a year and a half. Deborah was looking for a child with physical disabilities, not a child with emotional challenges. Here and there were children who could be a good match, but they always went to another family. "I began to wonder," Deborah said, "if I had read my 'leading' incorrectly." She was on the verge of giving up when she got a call from her social worker about Ashley. Deborah was one of two finalists vetted from a field of eighty-five. "Don't expect much," the social worker said. "Ashley looks different. She is not the cutest baby around."

Ashley had been born to an alcoholic, anorexic mother fourteen weeks prematurely. She weighed just over one and a half pounds, and her medical birth records state that she smelled of alcohol when she was delivered. A liver biopsy was performed right after her birth, and it showed that a tumor was present. She also had a "brain bleed." Even more threatening to Ashley's health was a rare condition she had, called Juvenile Xanthogranulomas, which cause tumors to form all over the body. These tumors, according to Deborah, "formed on Ashley's skin, under her skin, on her eyes and ears, on other vital organs, and on her brain."

Deborah and her social worker drove to Ashley's foster mother's apartment. Deborah was warned again about Ashley's condition. At that point, Ashley was about eighteen months old and had just been through surgery to have her first brain tumor removed. She was a "failure to thrive" baby, which meant she ate nothing and only drank a little milk. The apartment was nice enough, Deborah remembers, but had a hushed feeling.

After the introduction and pleasantries, the foster mother pointed to a crib. The three women walked over together, and Deborah peered down at the baby she was told was not quite normal. But that is not what she saw. "I thought she was beautiful," Deborah recalled. "Her left eye, because of glaucoma, was about twice the size of her right eye. And although that skewed the symmetry of her face, she had a smile that lit up the room! She was not the least bit intimidated by having three extra people in her small space and was quite friendly with everyone. She let everyone hold her, and as we all talked and cooed to her, she explored everyone's face with her hands."

Deborah walked away from the crib and pulled the social worker aside. "I love that baby," she said. "I would very much like her to be a part of my family." . . .

Ashley's early struggle for life was far from over. She had a second brain tumor removed just before she turned two years old. Soon, she also had her gallbladder removed because of a tumor, and there was another one forming between her ears and brain. Ashley also had a seizure disorder. On top of all that, she was deaf and blind. Most of us would have seen Ashley's life as either not worth living or pitiful. Deborah saw something different. Deborah saw her as nothing exceptional, as just a little baby.

. . .

After coffee, I followed Deborah to her house in the burbs. It was a typical suburban house with a slight difference. Out front was a large street sign that said *deaf-blind child area*. Once inside, Deborah gave me the obligatory tour, the dining room, the kids' rooms, and the kitchen, with its linoleum floor and faux wood cabinets. I noted that Deborah had a peaceful, quiet way about her when she wasn't talking about Ashley's struggles. Anger did not have a place in her world. Faith played a huge role in Deborah's life. As we walked through her house she told me that finding a church that was welcoming to Ashley had been nearly impossible. The world—even churches, it seemed—shared my fear of people like Ashley and all of its subtle manifestations.

"When I have tried to take her into the service with me," Deborah said, "I am constantly asked to take her out because of the noises she makes and her overall restless nature. It is always the same old story—Ashley appears and acts different from others in the church. It really saddens me." This actually wasn't surprising. Most of the major religions of the world have a long history of associating disability with sin, evil, or the devil. The Church has often been one of the leading institutions to dehumanize people on the wrong side of normal.

. . .

Ashley had had terrible experiences at her regular public school. Referring to Ashley's school trouble, Deborah said, "You know, they are often afraid of Ashley, some of the kids and the teachers. They treat her sometimes as if she is contagious." I nodded my head, feeling ashamed for understanding their feelings. "They *stare*."

These gazes, according to Deborah, were some of the most painful things that she and her daughter endured together. "Surgeries or any medical procedures are things that hurt, but only for a short while," Deborah continued. "The pain of rejection, the pain of being thought of as somehow a 'broken' or inferior person, the pain of ridicule or derision doesn't go away." These experiences "were ten times as painful as her surgeries."

At the time of my visit, Ashley was attending a wonderful school called the Starling Child Care and Learning Complex. . . .

This institution was also committed to a policy of inclusion. As we walked through the halls, I saw many students with disabilities. Ashley was in a fully inclusive, mixed-age classroom. When Deborah and I arrived, the class was having lunch. "There is my little girl," Deborah said, pointing across the small kids' desks, her face illuminated with the first smile I saw all day. I followed the trajectory of Deborah's outstretched hand and saw a little girl who struck me as strong, not sickly at all. She had a body that looked at least twelve years old. "She's a good eater," Deborah said. "Isn't she beautiful?"

I didn't answer the question. Not because I disagreed with Deborah, but because I really had no way to make sense out of Ashley. I didn't see Ashley as a whole. It was as if all I could take in were parts of her. She was wearing a red dress, and her hair was short and black. Her right eye was smaller than its counterpart and was glassy and colorless. She walked around the lunch table like a spinning top that had lost its centrifugal force. She made strange noises, which ranged in pitch from a low hum to an ear-piercing scream. Ashley heard nothing but felt vibrations.

I hoped Deborah didn't notice, but I was staring at Ashley. Not a genial get-to-know-you kind of glance, but a deeply dehumanizing stare, the kind of look that Deborah had talked about earlier. This is the type of stare that people with physical disabilities are very familiar with. But I didn't know how to stop. I didn't know how to make sense out of Ashley. I am ashamed to write this, but a part of me wondered if Ashley and I belonged to the same species.

Ashley confronted me with my own deep prejudices about what it means to be a valuable human being. I didn't know if I could truly value a body that was so damaged. Ashley also challenged some of my ideas about intelligence. If Ashley couldn't hear, speak, or see, how could she learn? And if Ashley couldn't learn, was she a fully functioning member of the human race?

Unfortunately, my reaction to Ashley is not without historical precedent. The history of the deaf, blind, and the deaf/blind is a story of being seen as less than human. . . .

It was Aristotle's contention that, of all the senses, hearing contributed most to intelligence and knowledge. This led Aristotle to characterize deaf individuals as senseless and incapable of reason. Much of the early marginalization of the deaf had to do with religious mythology. The ability to speak was considered a gift from the breath of God. Without speech, the deaf were denied moral status. Even during the Enlightenment, a period defined by questioning religious beliefs, the deaf were denied full humanity. . . .

As we waited for Ashley, Deborah talked about how her daughter was treated. "My experience has been that people will try to avoid that which they do not understand. So many people look at Ashley, see the physical differences in her, and assume that everything else about her is different, *and inferior*. What they don't see is the warmth and compassion inside her, her ability to forgive and forget all the slights from other people, her drive to experience everything she possibly can, her love of nature, and her gentleness around babies and young children."

. . .

At this point in our day, it was time for Ashley's language instruction, a mix of American Sign Language (ASL), touch sign, and speech therapy. Later, I asked Deborah about sign language and about whether Ashley's blindness prevented her from using it. Deborah reminded me that while Ashley has no vision at all in her left eye, the vision in her right eye is 20/2000. This means she can focus at about one to two inches from her face. Deborah elaborated: "She does her signing directly in front of her body, and if she perceives the person to whom she is signing is not paying attention, she will gently put her hands on both sides of their face and move their face to look at her."

Ashley's language instructor came right up to me and introduced herself. "I'm Theresa," she said as she shook my hand. Theresa was in her late thirties and was a large, joyful woman. She seemed like a natural educator, and had a son with a learning disability who struggled with learning to read and write.

"I think that helps me when I work with Ashley," she said. "You know, a struggle with language is a struggle with language whether you're deaf-blind or not." Theresa then turned her attention to her student, signing something to Ashley who signed back. But because I don't know ASL, I had no idea what was being communicated. "I asked her if she was ready to work," Theresa translated. "What did she say?" I asked. "What would any kid say? No, of course," Theresa reported.

I spent the next twenty minutes watching Theresa, trying to understand what she could see, but I could not. Deborah pointed out that the first thing Theresa did when she saw Ashley was smile. I didn't smile when I first saw Ashley, thinking that Ashley couldn't see my expression. Deborah laughed when I mentioned this to her. "To Ashley, your body can't lie." Ashley could feel a smile even if she couldn't see it. After Theresa smiled at Ashley, she touched her on her arm and then got down close to Ashley's stronger eye. She spoke and signed, "Good afternoon." Then she asked, "How are you?"

Theresa was vigilant about letting Ashley know what was going on in her environment. She signed and told Ashley what was on the floor, what chairs had been moved, what time the bell would ring. According to Deborah, this is essential. "One of the biggest potential sources for stress and frustration for Ashley is not being aware of something, especially something that would impact her. She needs access to the environment."

. . .

But like many deaf children, Ashley has had, at best, limited access to signing classrooms. When Ashley started school at the age of two and a half, she was in a classroom led by a teacher who signed with the other signing children. According to Deborah, after one year the school district abolished all signing classes and reassigned the teachers to classes for children with cochlear implants, which are a huge issue in the deaf community. The National Institutes of Health describes a cochlear implant as "a small electronic device that can help to provide a sense of sound to a person who is profoundly deaf or severely hard-of-hearing. The implant consists of an external portion that sits behind the ear and a second portion that is surgically placed under the skin." Many in the deaf community believe, however, that cochlear implants are a nefarious form of cultural genocide for the deaf. The essence of deaf culture is its language—sign language. Implants threaten to suck the life out of ASL.

Teachers are now told to emphasize speech and not to sign. Lipreading was also actively discouraged or prevented. "Classroom teachers were instructed to cover their mouths when they spoke so the children would not be able to read their lips," Deborah said. "The entire emphasis was on getting the children to adjust to their implants and learn to 'hear' and speak." Children without implants, which are initially painful and not always effective, were moved into segregated classrooms with children who had a myriad of other disabilities. Without signing support, according to Deborah, "the education of those children like Ashley suffered greatly. Many formative years were lost, and I'm not sure they will ever be made up."

. . .

What is the cost of teaching speech versus developing Ashley's mind and communication skills through ASL? Research is unequivocal: Deaf and deaf-blind children who acquire signing early have the best educational outcomes. Without signing, education becomes limited. "The school would like to pigeonhole Ashley as incapable of doing academic work," Deborah said, "Rather, they do things like learning to cook, community trips, and learning to clean up." A policy of emphasizing speech for these children is really a policy of forced assimilation of a unique minority group.

"It has been my experience," said Deborah, "that the school staff expects the children to change and is determined to help 'fix' them. The sad thing in my mind is that these children are not 'broken' and do not need fixing." . . .

Before the end of the language lesson Deborah tapped my shoulder and pointed to Ashley. "Do you see that?" she asked me. I didn't know what she was talking about, so I just shrugged my shoulders. "She's laughing. Take a close look."

I looked to the other side of the room. I watched Ashley's face, not her awkward gait or her colorless eye, but her whole face. Her face looked like a Picasso, a face held together with its own inherently savage beauty. Deborah was right; Ashley was laughing. And so was Theresa. I looked back at Deborah, and she was laughing too. Everyone was in on the joke except me. "What's so funny," I asked. "Oh nothing," Deborah said. I pressed her again. "Well, I don't want you to think less of Ashley, but Ashley just cursed us all out in sign language," said her mother. "She has a problem with that; we're working on it." . . .

I ended my day with Deborah and Ashley back at their home. The plan was to have dinner with the family: Ashley; her brother, Chip; and Deborah. Deborah had invited me to dinner at the beginning of the day, when we sat talking at Starbucks, and I had lied, saying I had somewhere I needed to be. But now I wouldn't have missed a dinner with this family for the world. Deborah and I had some time to kill before the rest of the family got home. So before dinner we sat around and talked about Ashley's experiences, the power of language, and the importance of inclusion. When we got onto the latter topic, Deborah told me a story that she had already shared with me over e-mail and in a phone conversation. In fact, she had already shared this story with me during our day together. It was as if this story was somehow the essence of her and Ashley's struggle.

It was the Christmas season, December 2002. That night, Deborah and the kids piled into their car and headed to the elementary school for the big holiday show. Ashley had been given a part. This was huge. Ashley was educated in a fully segregated special educational room, but on this night she would be on the stage with the rest of the kids. She was given a tiny baby rattle that she was supposed to shake at various times during the performance with the prompting of her aide. That's all the teachers thought she was capable of, but Deborah went along with the plan. At least Ashley would be on the stage.

Deborah and Chip sat in the makeshift auditorium, on steel-blue chairs. She had her camera in hand, just like all the other parents. When the lights went out, Ashley walked on the stage with the rest of the kids. She wobbled a little, but she found her spot. These things matter, Deborah thought. These small moments of inclusion. Sure, it's just a first-grade holiday program. But if Ashley can't be here, what's next? Who gets to draw these lines, and where would they stop? No, this night, this act of inclusion mattered, Deborah thought. She poised her camera and sat on the edge of her seat.

Then it happened. Before the program began, Ashley was placed three feet to the side of the group. Her aide stood next to her, holding her hand. The aide did not know touch sign or American Sign Language, Ashley's primary forms of communication. The only way Ashley would have to communicate would be to grip the aide's hand harder.

The first song was "Frosty the Snowman." Ashley waited for her cue, a slight touch on the hand, to shake the rattle. As the kids sang, she swayed. The aide seemed nervous, but when the time for Ashley's part came, she shook the rattle with force. Deborah was filled with a sense of pride. When the first song was over, there were more songs to come, but not for Ashley. The aide led her off the stage. Deborah wondered why. What was going on? Why was she leaving? Ashley was supposed to stay on stage for the whole night. That had been the plan all along, but someone didn't want Ashley on the stage for the whole performance. As they escorted Ashley off the stage and out of the auditorium, a parent in a fancy coat stopped the aide and, looking right past Ashley, said, "Good job." To the aide.

. . .

Ashley lived in a world without sight or sound, but she had heightened senses of smell, of taste, of touch. As Deborah explained to me, "If Ashley doesn't recognize a particular food on her plate, she smells it first. If she is looking for new clothes, she runs her hands down the fabric first to see if it is something that feels like she wants it to feel." We should not underestimate the power of touch. The philosopher Jean-Jacques Rousseau believed that touch was the essence of an ethical life; touch defined our humanity.

. . .

Before I said my good-byes I asked Deborah if she had anything she could give me to help me remember our day. She left the room and came back holding a photograph of Ashley sitting on the beach. "I just love this picture," she said as she handed it to me. "This is my beautiful little girl. Feeling everything."

That picture was taken in the late summer of 2002 at Virginia Beach. It was a few days before school started. Deborah, who had fond memories of the beach, had saved a little money for a vacation. She got her family a hotel room right on the ocean, so the kids could see the sun rise. On the last day of their holiday, they went out on the beach at sunset. Deborah's twin brother, a photographer, was there. Ashley had been to other bodies of water before—lakes, rivers—but she had never been to the ocean. She stepped onto the sand, wobbled a little, as everyone does on the beach, and started walking toward the ocean. But fifty feet or so from the water, she stopped and put her hands out. Other kids were running around in the sand, whining about the cold, asking to go home and eat ice cream, but not Ashley. She stood there in a world of vibration and taste and touch, "relishing every sensory experience."

After a while, Ashley walked up to the line where the ocean meets the sand and sat down. The reaching palms of the surf touched the tips of her toes and she lifted her hands to feel the wind and salt spray. She sat like that for five minutes on the edge of the world, the sea, a shifting line, its edges never anywhere for long. Ashley pressed her hands out like she was feeling someone's face. When a wave washed up on shore, the spray lifted off the water and the ocean came to her toes and then her shins. She laughed in a pitch somewhere between a scream and a song.

108

On the Spectrum, Looking Out

Jess Watsky

My world was changed for the better by a big, technical book, called *The Diagnostic and Statistical Manual of Mental Disorders*. Looking back, I never expected to be at odds with the very publication that opened my eyes to my mind's inner workings. When I was thirteen, flipping through the pages of my mother's copy of the DSM IV-TR, the name of one "mental disorder" stuck out like a sore thumb, enticing peals of laughter from me and my friends—*Asperger's Syndrome*. Though it shouldn't have been a surprise, coming from a child whose idea of fun with friends was to look through psychology diagnostic manuals, it was both a shock and a comfort to be diagnosed a year later from that very same section of the very same book.

Because "Asperger's" was described, my world was a little more transparent. It unveiled some of the intricacies in my own mind that had seemed unexplained. The clearly defined obsessions, ranging from a six-month flirt with marbles to a three-year binge on molecular gastronomy, now had a name—"repetitive interests and obsessions"—and my childhood propensity for big words and inability to comprehend idioms was no longer simply a foible of my past. Even if I didn't feel like Rain Man, I now had a name for the many quirks to my mannerisms that had plagued me for the last decade and a half. Needing to go to three different grocery stores to make sure I hadn't missed any interesting foods was no longer the end result of anxiety, but a starting point, an issue I had the tools to confront and stop in its tracks before I ran my car out driving to other states in search of unique food.

I know this diagnosis has soothed people's fears as well as my own, and served as a jumping ground to plot their next move, just as it has certainly done for me. My Asperger's diagnosis helped me to learn about boundaries and conversational norms, allowed me to rethink my inner-arguments and has given me time to pause and think about what I say, rather than reverting to a repetitive monopoly of a conversation. Without the diagnosis, it felt as though I had been working with a consistently clever, yet idiosyncratic machine for many years without having even a manual or well-versed technician alongside to help me troubleshoot.

That's not to say that things were immediately easier for me. I still struggled in school, unable to foster interactions with peers. When I explained to many of them that I wasn't just strange and had, in fact, an inability to interact as they did, my confession was met with derision. It is a cruel twist of irony that a disorder centering on a social hindrance would don the incredibly clunky—but for me, helpful—moniker of "Asperger's Syndrome." But now, for its new edition, *The Diagnostic and Statistical Manual of Mental Disorders* plans to eliminate the diagnosis of Asperger's Syndrome as a stand-alone condition, and to merge it into the more generalized description of Autism Spectrum Disorder (ASD). This puts me at odds with the very publication that opened my eyes to my mind's inner workings. Although I have prospered through many hardships both socially and academically as a result of working with my Asperger's Syndrome, the new approach may mean that I may not fit the diagnostic criteria for ASD and will not be eligible for related health insurance coverage needs. In fact, in reviewing the proposed diagnostic standards for ASD, for all intents and purposes I fit only three of the four criteria necessary for a diagnosis. Certainly, that is sufficient evidence of a dysfunction, yet not enough (one must meet all four) to receive a diagnosis of ASD. In the eyes of the American Psychiatric Association, as of May 2013 I will cease to have Asperger's Syndrome or ASD.

With this change, thousands of successfully and well-functioning Asperger's-diagnosed adults, and many, many more undiagnosed children, will lose a diagnosis and a name to put to their unique, curious lives. In May of 2013, I am anxiously anticipating another life-changing event, because in that same month I will be graduating from college with a bachelor's degree in History. Although my mental abilities always foretold a future with college, I'm sure that if I hadn't been diagnosed with Asperger's Syndrome, I wouldn't have excelled so well and taught myself to fluently navigate the turbulent university atmosphere. I wouldn't be writing this, thinking about this, realizing my dreams without this key component of my brain.

The changes in the DSM-IV are only one variable in the complicated equation of what it means to have Asperger's Syndrome. The rest is up to society to read words like mine and listen to the people they interact with and understand them. Meet us at face value without forcing us to make eye contact or expect an immediate adherence to your social customs and understand that we are people with different wiring, but similar desires. It is not solely a dream of the Aspergian to want to live in a world where they are accepted and appreciated for their unique talents. People automatically perceive disabilities to be something automatically visible or detectable from their conceptions of "normal" people. It hurts to be told we blend seamlessly into the world, but that we are shunned because of how we work inside. Capture that feeling and meet us with compassion and know that reaching out to us is important. We are not emotionless robots, nor are we calculating sociopaths as some would believe. Nor should we be pigeonholed into relationships with other Aspergians solely because the rest of the world has overlooked us. We have just as much of a right to coexist in society as anyone else, and have the potential to change the world in amazing ways. Regardless of formal status or legal terminology, there are still thousands of people in this world with Asperger's Syndrome, whose identities have been enhanced and helped with such a diagnosis, and we will not vanish simply because our name has gone away. We cannot disappear. We are people, too.

109

What I'd Tell That Doctor

Jason Kingsley

I am Jason Kingsley. I am now almost twenty-nine years old. Ten years ago I wrote an article for *Count Us In: Growing Up with Down Syndrome*, a book that Mitchell Levitz and I wrote. That article is about a confrontation I would have had with the obstetrician—if I had met him—about what he said years ago to my parents when I was born.

What I would say to the obstetrician is the same as what I would say to the parents of any newborn child who is born with a disability and who is born with Down syndrome.

The things I said ten years ago are true now and even more so.

When I wrote that article, I was still in school. But now I am on my own. I live in a house with two other roommates. We have very little supervision. We do our own cooking; we do our own shopping and cleaning. We do take public transportation. And above all else, our house is accessible to the community and to our work.

All three of us work in the community. I happen to work in the White Plains (New York) Public Library. My roommate Raymond works at PETCO, a pet store, and has been there for six years. And Yaniv works at an Armonk (New York) law firm.

In conclusion, I hope you will look at this article that I wrote ten years ago. Then get *Count Us In: Growing Up with Down Syndrome* and read the whole thing. You will find it very essential, inspiring, and helpful.

Here is my article:

When I was born, the obstetrician said that I cannot learn, never see my mom and dad and never learn anything and send me to an institution. Which I think it was wrong.

Today we were talking about if I could see my obstetrician and talk to him, here are things I would say . . .

I would say, "People with disabilities *can learn*!"

Then I would tell the obstetrician how smart I am. Like learning new languages, going to other foreign nations, going to teen groups and teen parties, going to cast parties, becoming independent, being . . . a lighting board operator, an actor, the backstage crew. I would talk about history, math, English, algebra, business math, global studies. One thing I forgot to tell the obstetrician is I plan to get an academic diploma when I pass my RCTs . . .

I performed in "The Fall Guy" and even wrote this book! He never imagined how I could write a book! I will send him a copy . . . so he'll know.

I will tell him that I play the violin, that I make relationships with other people, I make oil paintings, I play the piano, I can sing, I am competing in sports, in the drama group, that I have many friends, and I have a full life.

So I want the obstetrician will never say that to any parent to have a baby with a disability any more. If you send a baby with a disability to an institution, the baby will miss all the opportunities to grow and to learn . . . and also to receive a diploma. The baby will miss relationships and love and independent living skills. Give a baby with a disability a chance to grow a full life. To experience a half-full glass instead of the half-empty glass. And think of your abilities not your disability.

110

Toward Ending Ableism in Education

Thomas Hehir

There is much that educators, parents, and advocates can do toward ending ableism in education. As is the case with racism and sexism, progress toward equity is dependent first and foremost on the acknowledgment that ableism exists in schools. The examples given here have centered around three disability groups: the deaf, the blind and visually impaired, and the learning disabled. However, I believe that deconstructing dominant educational practices applied to other disability groups can yield similar results. Ableist assumptions and practices are deeply embedded in schooling. Further, the absence of discussion and dearth of scholarly inquiry within mainstream educational circles concerning the effects of ableism is stunning.

Though the lack of attention to ableism in schooling is unfortunate, activists within the disability community have long recognized its impact. Therefore, as more adults with disabilities take on more powerful roles in society and seek to influence schooling, the attention to these issues will hopefully increase. In addition to this political force, the lack of acceptable educational outcomes for large numbers of children with disabilities in an era of standards-based reform should force a reexamination of current practices. Fortunately, there is a foundation in both research and practice upon which to build a better future. Schools can take action now. I offer the following suggestions:

Include disability as part of schools' overall diversity efforts. Schools are increasingly recognizing the need to explicitly address diversity issues as the country becomes more racially and ethnically diverse. Some schools are expanding diversity efforts to include disability. Recently, a local high school student with Down's syndrome, whom I had met at a school assembly devoted to issues of disability rights, addressed one of my classes. She stated, "There are all kinds of kids at my school: Black kids, Puerto Rican kids, gay and lesbian kids. Meagan uses a wheel chair. Matt's deaf, and I have Down's syndrome. It's all diversity." Her high school has done a great job of including disabled kids and has incorporated discussions about disability in its efforts to address diversity issues. Adults with disabilities address student groups and disability is presented in a natural way. Students learn about people with disabilities who have achieved great things as well as those who live ordinary lives. People with disabilities are not presented in a patronizing or stereotypical manner. Deaf people are not "hearing challenged" nor are people with mental retardation "very special." Ableism is not the norm; disability is dealt with in a straightforward manner. In schools like this, students with disabilities learn about their disabilities and learn how to be self-advocates.

Encourage disabled students to develop and use skills and modes of expression that are most effective and efficient for them. This article has sought to demonstrate that the strong preference within society, reflected in school practice, to have disabled students perform in the same way that nondisabled children perform can ultimately be handicapping for some students. This is not to say that it is not desirable for disabled kids to be able to perform in the way nondisabled kids perform. For instance, deaf students who can read lips have a competitive advantage in a hearing world. However, assuming that most deaf children can develop elaborate language through oral methods has been proven false, and employing these methods without allowing for the natural development of language almost assures poor language development. What may appear to be a paradox to some is that a deaf child who has well-developed language through learning ASL from birth may actually have a higher likelihood of reading lips because he simply has a larger vocabulary. The problem is not, therefore, in the natural desire of parents and educators to have children be able to perform in a typical manner, but rather the missed educational opportunities many disabled kids experience because of a lack of regard for what are often disability-specific modes of learning and expression.

. . .

Move away from the current obsession with placement toward an obsession with results. The movement to include greater numbers of students with disabilities, particularly those with significant cognitive disabilities, in regular education classes has had a profound effect on the education of students with disabilities. Over the past decade, more and more students with disabilities are educated for more of the day in regular education classrooms.

The inclusion movement in education has supported the overall disability movement's goal of promoting societal integration, using integration in schooling as a means to achieve this result. In 1977, disability activists took over federal offices in San Francisco for twenty-five days, demanding that regulations for implementing Section 504 of the Rehabilitation Act, the first federal act to broadly ban discrimination based on disability, be released. Of particular concern to the protesters were leaked draft regulations that provided for separate segregated education for disabled students. Judy Heumann, one of these protesters, stated, "We will accept no more segregation." The final rules were revised to encourage integration in schooling, and the newly passed PL 94–142 (later renamed IDEA) incorporated the current requirement that children be educated in the least restrictive environment (i.e., in regular classes as much as is appropriate for the child).

The strong legal preference for placement in regular classes, coupled with the political movement of disability activists and parents, has resulted in significant positive change for students with disabilities, who are moving on to jobs and accessing higher education at unprecedented levels. Virtually every school has had to confront the issue of inclusion as parents seek integration for their children with disabilities. However, like all change movements, inclusion has encountered opposition. Some opposition has reflected deeply held negative attitudes toward people with disabilities similar to that experienced by Joe and Penny Ford when he sought enrollment in first grade. I can recall a principal challenging me in a large public meeting concerning our efforts to promote inclusion in Chicago: "You don't really mean kids who drool in regular classes?" The reaction against the integration of students with significant disabilities into regular schools and classrooms has been so strong that TASH, an advocacy group promoting integration, adopted the slogan, "All means all," which reflects the group's efforts to clarify its goal to promote integration for students with significant disabilities.

Another source of criticism has come from within the disability community. Deaf advocates have expressed concerns over the lack of language development and communication access many deaf children experience in regular classes. Supported by some of the research cited above, advocates for the learning disabled have questioned the ability of regular education classrooms to provide the intensive help these students need for skill development. These criticisms receive support from research. The NLTS documented that many students integrated into regular education classrooms did not receive much in the way of accommodation or support, and that many who were integrated into regular classes failed, thus increasing their likelihood of dropping out. The issue is so controversial within the community that virtually every disability group has developed a position. A review of websites reveals, for example, TASH's strong support for full inclusion and deep reservation on the part of the Learning Disabilities Association of America (see http://tash.org and www.ldanatl.org).

N E X T   S T E P S

The controversy over inclusion within the disability community is ultimately dysfunctional and allows those who would limit the rights of students with disabilities to use this as a wedge issue. Fortunately, the community united during the reauthorization of IDEA in 1997 to help prevent a weakening of the act. However, threats to IDEA's fundamental protections remain. In 2001, Congress considered amendments to the Elementary and Secondary Education Act that would enable schools to fully exclude some students with disabilities. In order to fight these regressive provisions, the community must be united.

I believe the lens of ableism provides a useful perspective through which the inclusion issue can be resolved within the disability community. First, there needs to be a recognition that education plays a central role in the integration of disabled people in all aspects of society both by giving children the education they need to compete and by demonstrating to nondisabled children that disability is a natural aspect of life. Central to this role is the need for students with disabilities to have access to the same curriculum provided to nondisabled children. Further, education plays a vital role in building communities in which disabled children should be included. Therefore, for most children with disabilities, integration into regular classes with appropriate accommodations and support should be the norm.

However, the lens of ableism should lead to the recognition that for some students certain disability-related skills might need attention outside the regular classroom. Learning Braille or ASL or how to use a communication device are typically not in the curriculum and might be more efficiently taught outside the mainstream classroom. The dyslexic high school student who needs intensive help in reading may feel deeply self-conscious if such instruction is conducted in front of his nondisabled friends. The 19-year-old student with a significant cognitive disability may need to spend a good deal of time learning to take public transportation, a skill that will ultimately increase her ability to integrate into the community as an adult. Nondisabled students do not spend time in school learning this skill because they learn this easily on their own. The nature of mental retardation is such that this type of learning does not typically happen incidentally; it must be taught over time and within the context in which the skill will be used. Uniting around the goal of societal integration and recognizing that the difference inherent in disability is a positive one that at times gives rise to disability-specific educational needs may help advocates move away from the fight over placement to one that focuses on educational results.

Promote high standards, not high stakes. An important point to reiterate here is that the most damaging ableist assumption is the belief that disabled people are incapable. Therefore, the movement to include students with disabilities in standards-based reforms holds promise. However, high-stakes testing that prevents students from being promoted or from receiving a diploma based on performance on standardized tests is problematic, given the concerns previously cited about basic access to the curricula and those surrounding the construct validity of the tests. In a very real sense, some students with disabilities will have to become nondisabled in order to be promoted or graduate. This is ableism in the extreme. Thus, a promising movement, standards-based reform, may ultimately reinforce current inequities if performance on high-stakes tests becomes the only means by which disabled students can demonstrate what they know and are able to do. As such, disability advocates should oppose high-stakes testing. It is important to note that disabled students are not the only group for whom high-stakes testing is being questioned. Other groups that have been poorly served by our educational systems, such as children from high-poverty backgrounds and children with limited English proficiency, may be equally harmed by these policies.

. . .

NEXT STEPS

111

Facilitating Transitions to College for Students with Disabilities from Culturally and Linguistically Diverse Backgrounds

Heather A. Oesterreich and Michelle G. Knight

The overrepresentation of working-class African American, Latino/Latina, and Native American students in special education has been well documented and the implications that are raised for identification and intake of students with disabilities has been the focus of special education reform for many years. Even as schools have worked to change how students are identified for special education, special educators continue to see a disproportionate number of working-class African American, Latino/Latina, and Native American students in their caseloads. Disproportionate representation is not a problem because something is inherently wrong with special education; however, placement in special education is linked to a number of negative issues including poor graduation rates, high drop-out rates, and limited access to postsecondary education opportunities. Specifically, the overrepresentation of working-class culturally and linguistically diverse students with disabilities in special education is coupled with an underrepresentation in college attendance. Recent research suggests that disability in combination with other characteristics (e.g., race and class) has a much more powerful effect on educational attainment than any one of these characteristics alone. This article examines how the intersection of race, class, and disability informs the responsibilities of special educators. A diverse set of practices needs to be used with working-class African American, Latino/Latina, and Native American students with disabilities to increase their social and cultural capital and support their prospective college-going identities.

THE LAY OF THE LANDS

Increasing opportunities for educational access to college for underserved populations, including students who are first-generation, working-class, and underrepresented culturally and linguistically diverse students labeled with a disability, is a priority of K–16 educational systems. Frequently, however, the hectic pace and large caseloads for special education teachers require them to focus on the immediacy of high school completion for their students. Recently, demographic shifts in the college freshman population highlight the growing numbers of students with disabilities entering college. In 2000, 6% of full-time, first-time freshmen who were enrolled in 4-year public and private institutions had disabilities. Although this statistic represents an increase of postsecondary students reporting a disability, it obscures the link between the race and class of students with disabilities in high school and their transition to college. The increase in students with disabilities who attend college is most notable in students labeled with a learning disability (LD). They have increased from 16.1% to 40.4% of college students with disabilities in the past 12 years. Notably, this increase represents a Caucasian, upper-middle class increase in postsecondary attendance and attainment.

This race and class divide leads to a differentiation in the academic college preparation that many affluent, Caucasian students with LD receive, as opposed to that provided to poor, culturally and linguistically diverse students. These students often are labeled with more stigmatizing disabilities within special education. They also are underrepresented as a result of their disability in college preparation courses, including advanced placement courses. In addition, they cannot afford and do not have access to private tutoring and other out-of-school services (e.g., SAT preparation). These discrepancies in access to quality education limit culturally and linguistically diverse students' acquisition of social and cultural capital to assist them in developing college-going identities.

BUILDING SOCIAL AND CULTURAL CAPITAL FOR COLLEGE

Students' social and cultural capital creates differences in college-going identities. Social capital for students with disabilities in relation to college includes the availability of information-sharing networks about college. Cultural capital is the value placed on obtaining a college education and the information available about acquiring one. Special educators' ability to influence working-class African American, Latino/Latina, and Native American students with disabilities' college-going identities and their subsequent success in college is directly related to nurturing social and cultural capital in relation to college. This includes addressing social and economic stratification that exists in society in relation to race, class, and disability; understanding the law; and facilitating the selection of a college with resources and demographics that match students' social, economic, and emotional needs.

ADDRESSING SOCIAL AND ECONOMIC STRATIFICATION

In a society where inequities in college access still reflect racism, classism, and ableism, it is useful to assist students in understanding the economic and social stratification that affects college admittance and completion. Helping students to understand that their life possibility may be situated in structures of oppression while at the same time helping them to challenge the belief of society that they are deficient, disinterested, with confused priorities, and responsible for their own failure to enter college provides youth with disabilities a place to understand the lives that they are living. With facilitation by the special education teacher, students can not only critique social structures but can also be encouraged to become active agents in fighting the social structures by viewing themselves as college material.

UNDERSTANDING THE LAW

Special education teachers must provide the cultural capital about the differences in services provided in K–12 and postsecondary schools. Under Section 504 of the Rehabilitation Act of 1973 and the Americans With Disabilities Act (ADA) of 1990, at the postsecondary level, students must self-identify with the ADA office on a college campus. In addition, they are responsible for the documentation verifying their need for accommodation, making specific requests for accommodations, and meeting the same academic requirements of all other students. This differs dramatically from the K–12 setting, where it is the responsibility of the institution to reach out and identify students in need of special education, pay for the documentation to evaluate these students, and provide specialized programming. If special education teachers do not work with students, particularly working-class, African

American, Latino/Latina, and Native American students with disabilities, who are more likely to be first generation college students, in identifying these fundamental differences between postsecondary and K–12 services, the transition between the two systems can leave students frustrated and isolated without the accommodations that they require to meet the academic standards of postsecondary education.

Becoming advocates. In this legal context, students must advocate in relation to their disabilities. Special education teachers need to work with students to be able to name their disability, understand the nature of their learning difficulties, and know strategies that allow them to negotiate their learning difficulties. Students who learn early on how to state their accommodation needs in functional, real-world terms will be able to help postsecondary institutions effectively accommodate their needs.

College visits. In addition to teaching students about the shift in laws between K–12 and postsecondary institutions, when dealing with first-generation college students, part of fortifying their social and cultural capital lies in the necessity and structure of on-campus visits. These visits must include planned meetings at the ADA office and a presentation by the personnel there to create a sense of accessibility.

Community connections. Providing mentors, role models, community leaders, and speakers to motivate students can raise their social capital and sense of advocacy in making the shift between disability laws. Specifically, these adults should reflect the race, class, and disability status of the students. They can help working-class, culturally and linguistically diverse students with disabilities realize that their college attendance is part of a larger community pattern and that they have been preceded by earlier college graduates and will be followed by others following their example.

Addressing economic limitations. Although connecting to campuses and people is important for working-class culturally and linguistically diverse students with disabilities, the economic realities associated with college tuition, student fees, and cost of living are only compounded by economic burdens implicit within the necessary documentation of a disability. Section 504 of the Rehabilitation Act of 1973 and the ADA Act of 1990 places the burden on the student to provide and pay for appropriate testing and evaluation to document disability. Each postsecondary institution has specific requirements for what constitutes viable documentation, but the minimum standards require the certified qualifications of the evaluator, the types of testing, and other background documents that must be provided. In addition, the evaluation must have been conducted within the last 3 to 5 years. This type of testing can cost from $300 to $3,500.

To help defray the costs of the burden of proof of disability, special education teachers should ensure that their working-class students graduate with a complete, up-to-date battery of tests verifying their disabilities so that these tests can be used by the students in their freshman year of college—and perhaps beyond—as verification of the necessity to them of services from the ADA on campus.

SELECTING A COLLEGE

Selecting a college to apply to and attend is important for any student, but it takes on added significance for working-class, African American, Latino/Latina, or Native American students with a disability. Several resources exist to assist teachers, counselors, students, and families in the college selection process, and much has been written about college selection for low-income, culturally and linguistically diverse youth. Rarely, however, is the information combined. Table 111.1 includes questions and strategies that special education teachers should use to help their working-class, culturally and linguistically diverse students with disabilities research their decisions for postsecondary attendance.

Table 111.1 Teacher Tips for Increasing Social and Cultural Capital for Post-Secondary Education

Social and Cultural Capital	Questions to Ask	Teacher Tips
Admissions requirements		
These include requirements such as GPA scores, short essays, and minimum standardized test scores that depend on the institution. Students with disabilities may have nontraditional testing materials as well as documentation that could be essential when they apply	Does the school have a separate admission policy for students with disabilities? Do admission requirements include the recognition of certificates of attendance, GEDs, or high school diplomas? Can other documentation be included to support the student beyond academic achievement?	Review the admissions requirements of the institution(s) with the student Create checklists of admission requirements and follow through with the students to make sure they are taking the right steps to meet those requirements Assist students with applications and study sessions for required admissions tests
Cost		
Tuition costs can be daunting to students and their families. Financial aid is often available for students, but aid alone does not always cover all the costs especially the "hidden" costs of books, living expenses, and accommodations and extra educational supports	Are the cost and opportunities for financial aid consistent with the need of the student? What forms are required for financial aid? How far in advance do students need to start applying for financial aid? Do they have specific disability assistance? Are grants available explicitly for students with disabilities?	Create spreadsheets that compare costs of tuition as well as "hidden" costs that will be important to consider (i.e., additional testing materials to document their disabilities, tutoring, technology, transportation needs) Host a family Free Application for Federal Student Aid (FAFSA) night to assist students and their families with forms. Information for the FAFSA is available at http://www.fafsa.ed.gov Assist students with research of specific financial aid resources for students with disabilities, available in Creating Options: Financial Aid for Individuals with Disabilities at http://www.heath.gwu.edu
Demographics		
Demographics include race/ethnicity, language, gender, and disabilities of the full-time, part-time, nontraditional students, faculty, and staff that create the higher institution environment	What is the representation of students and faculty/staff who are African American, Latino/Latina, or Native American on the campus? How many students and faculty/staff with disabilities does the college serve? Are their academic/social groups in any of these areas? Are there institutionally supported mentor programs in these areas?	Create math assignments in which students chart the racial and disability demographics of institutions they are interested in attending Have students develop an interview protocol to ask students with disabilities about their experiences and any advice they might offer Contact the admissions offices for student/faculty/staff names for students to interview. The interviews can be conducted via phone, Internet (i.e., e-mail, instant messaging), or in person

(continued)

Table 111.1 *(continued)*

Social and Cultural Capital	Questions to Ask	Teacher Tips
Disability office/resources		
Institutions of higher education have offices for student services for students with disabilities, but often students are unfamiliar with these offices and the specific services they provide. This is a particularly important resource because these offices represent advocates for the students and their rights	Do they offer the services (e.g., books on tape, text-to-speech software) that the student requires and is familiar with? What other academic support systems are available? Is there a free writing center on campus or a study skills course offered? What about accessible and free tutoring labs?	Assist students with naming their disabilities, knowing specific tests that are required to verify disabilities, and having lists of accommodations

Use books such as *Peterson's Colleges With Programs for Students With Learning Disabilities or Attention Deficit Disorders* to help students research schools that match their needs

Compile a specific contact list with e-mails and phone numbers of individuals in the student services office |
| **Location** | | |
| Students with disabilities should consider the campus that will best suit them and their specific needs when looking at institutions of higher education | Do students need to live at home to defer costs? Is being close to their family for gatherings a necessity for the student? Does the stimulation of a city or the confines of a small town better appeal to the student? | Coordinate students interested in visiting the same schools together or in small groups for support and to cut on costs of transportation

Assist students in critically analyzing the pros and cons of campuses for their specific needs |
| **Size** | | |
| One size does not fit all in education. Most students coming from the secondary education setting can be thrown off by the 300-person lecture halls they may experience in higher education. Students with disabilities need to know how their classes will be able to accommodate their specific needs regarding attention, identity, and participation in the classroom environment | How large is the university? What is the average class size? What types of interactions with faculty are promoted institutionally? What is the standard format/size of general education courses? What is the student-to-teacher ratio in the college in which the student will be studying? Do the classes get smaller, population-wise, as the course of study continues? | Arrange for students to shadow a freshman on a college campus to experience different types of courses

Acknowledge and discuss with students that some classes may be in a format with which they are not familiar and help them plan accommodations such as tutoring, extra time on tests, and making regular visits to the professor's office |

SUMMARY

A critical challenge facing special educators over time has been the overrepresentation of working-class African American, Latino/Latina, and Native American students in their programs. Although much has been done to curtail this overrepresentation, educators have a long way to go now in terms of making sure that those students who are currently over-represented in special education have the social and cultural capital to envision possibilities for themselves beyond high school. Special educators can be at the forefront of bridging the racial, economic, and ability gaps in college admittance, retention, and graduation by engaging in professional practices that confront the discrimination and bias that may have placed many of those students in special education classrooms. Their intentionality and attention to thinking and promoting college in the future of their students can change the landscape of postsecondary attainment for working-class African American, Latino/Latina, and Native American students with disabilities.

112

Increasing Awareness

Language, Communication Strategies, and Universally Designed Environments

Karen A. Myers, Jaci Jenkins Lindburg, and Danielle M. Nied

Stigmaphobia . . . people scrambling desperately to be included under the umbrella of normal—and scrambling desperately to cast somebody else as abnormal, crazy, abject, or disabled.

Michael Bérubé

"Have you excluded anyone today?" When posed with this question, most professionals would agree they have included people in their daily activities. Most programs, classes, and services are intended to be inclusive and welcoming. Few professionals, if any, would intentionally exclude anyone. However, if this question is given a bit more thought, respondents might deduce that some unintentional exclusionary tactics were demonstrated in their attitudes, perceptions, and behaviors during the past week, day, or hour. Not only as a result of inaccessible physical place are people excluded, but people can also be excluded through unintentional (or possibly intentional) acts of ignoring, talking over their heads, talking about an unfamiliar subject matter, not asking for input, and even micromanaging to a point that input is not welcomed. Even though a place of business complies with the letter of the law and does not discriminate against people with disabilities per Rehabilitation Act of 1973 (Public Law 93−112, 1973), the Americans with Disabilities Act of 1990 (ADA; Public Law 101−336, 1990), and the American with Disabilities Act Amendments

NEXT STEPS

Act of 2008 (Public Law 110–325, 42), have administrators and employees in some way not demonstrated the spirit of the law? For example, although an institution might obey the literal wording of the ADA guidelines (i.e., the letter of the law) by installing 36-inch wide doorways in classrooms for wheelchair access and 60-inch high signage with raised and Braille characters at classroom and office doors, they may not be embracing the intent or spirit of the law by providing equal access and demonstrating inclusive practices to all people with disabilities. The spirit of the law can be shown through language, communication, and responses to various situations, an example of which is universal in design.

This chapter examines ways to increase awareness of people with disabilities using language and communication strategies. Insight regarding best practices for communicating with people with disabilities is addressed. This chapter also introduces and discusses universal instructional design and promotes its implementation both in and outside the classroom on college campuses. This chapter includes affirmative and negative language related to disability, communication strategies for interacting with people with various types of disabilities, and description and examples of universal design, universal instructional design, and universal design for student development.

LANGUAGE OF DISABILITY

"Language empowers". Language is instrumental in expressing feelings, perceptions, and attitudes. How people perceive and relate to others is reflected in language, that is, the words used to make meaning of situations. Disability language itself often offers "a symbolic and linguistic description of how individuals are to be regarded, treated, and integrated into society". It is the perception of the dominant culture that defines disability, stigmatizing, and devaluing the lived experience of people with disabilities. Used as a metaphor by society, people with disabilities "have been presented as socially flawed able-bodied people, not as people with their own identities".

AFFIRMATIVE AND NEGATIVE LANGUAGE

Some words used to describe people with disabilities are offensive, demeaning, derogatory, and outdated. Words such as "handicapped," "vegetable," "cripple," "dumb," "crazy," and "spaz" are labels which emphasize deficit, less than, and second class. "When we use words like 'retarded,' 'lame,' or 'blind'—even if we are referring to acts or ideas and not to people at all—we perpetuate the stigma associated with disability." In an effort to eliminate "hurt" words, recent campaigns such as The "r" Word (http://therword.org/) and Spread the Word to End the Word (http://www.r-word.org) have been launched. These words neither focus on identities nor shed light on particular characteristics, but rather may be interpreted as hurtful and hateful. Outdated and antiquated words such as "handicap" appear in older disability laws (i.e., Rehabilitation Act of 1973; Public Law 94-142, Education of All Handicapped Children Act, 1975), whereas "disability" appears in newer laws such as the ADA, ADAAA, and Individuals with Disabilities Education Act (IDEA), the latter of which is an updated version of PL94-142 and combines a children's bill of rights with federal funding. Using current disability language demonstrates knowledge, awareness, and sensitivity to positive societal changes. Above all, it empowers. Other words or phrases that victimize individuals with disabilities include "suffering from," "afflicted with," "confined to," "stricken with," and "wheelchair bound," and labels such as "epileptic," "learning disabled," "autistic," or "the blind." Using "normal" for people without disabilities implies that a person with a disability is not normal or "abnormal," rather than a person with a specific characteristic or identity. Therefore using the term, "people with disabilities" and "people without disabilities" is more appropriate.

Tregoning addresses the subtleties of language and different meanings conveyed when used in-group and out-group. For example, words such as "gimp," "crip," and "freak," are considered acceptable when used within the disability community, indicating pride and ownership, whereas those same words are considered derogatory when used by people without disabilities. Trendy terms such as "special," "physically challenged," and "handi-capable," are neither descriptive nor accurate and should not be used. As greater number of individuals with disabilities take advantage of the opportunities open to them in business, industry, and travel, it becomes increasingly important to promote an environment that is positive for persons with disabilities.

One of the best and easiest ways is appropriate language use. The recommended manner is known as "person-first" language. This means that the person is emphasized first, the disability second. Positive or affirming language places focus on the person first, then on the person's characteristic or disability. For example, "the woman who is blind" places the focus first on the person, that is, the woman, followed by the person's characteristic or identity, that is, being blind. Some other examples include the student with learning disability, the man with cerebral palsy, the child with Down's Syndrome, the girl who uses a wheelchair, and the boy with diabetes. Various lists of items indicating appropriate (affirmative) language and negative language (i.e., terms to avoid) have been distributed over the years.

In *Claiming Disability*, Linton describes how she progressed from negatively descriptive words of disability purporting the medical model such as handicapped, crippled, and lame to person-first language, focusing on the person first, then addressing the person's disability. Linton used person-first language in her early years of teaching. Years later, while becoming more involved in the disability rights movement, she began to see person first language as avoidance and began describing herself as a "disabled" woman. Linton makes a strong argument that the common terminology used in discussing people with disabilities assigns a deficit identity to the disability population and obstructs societal change:

> *It was around this time, somewhere in the early '90s, that I also began to use the term 'disabled woman' to identify myself. I no longer said, 'I am a woman with a disability'; instead I was likely to describe myself by forefronting disability. 'I am a disabled woman,' I would say, and then might explain to my students, 'That means that I identify as a member of the minority group—disabled people—and that is a strong influence on my cultural make-up, who I am, and the way I think.'*

Disability language varies from person to person and certainly can be based on individual preferences and philosophies. Person-first language is one way to focus on the person instead of the disability, providing an inclusive way to communicate about one of the multiple identities of human beings.

COMMUNICATION STRATEGIES

In addition to using appropriate and affirming language, behavior and non-verbal communication send messages indicating our thoughts, feelings, and perceptions toward people with disabilities. Over the years, various authors and educators have provided recommended techniques for communicating with people with disabilities. Popular publications include those by national associations such as the American Council for the Blind, DEAF Inc., Learning Disabilities Association, the National Autism Association, and other

N
E
X
T

S
T
E
P
S

publications by independent living centers, local non-profit organizations, freelance consultants, and disability services at colleges and universities. Inclusive communication shows respect, comfort, and awareness, that is, treating others as you would like yourself to be treated—treating everyone as first-class citizens. Interacting comfortably with people with and without disabilities is the key to effective communication and understanding. Some recommendations for communicating with people with disabilities include the following:

- Speak directly to a person with a disability. Because an individual has a functional limitation, it does not mean the individual cannot communicate for himself/herself.
- Speak in a regular tone. There is no need to shout at a person with a disability. A physical or cognitive limitation does not mean the person cannot hear you or understand you.
- Use descriptive language indicating direction or size when communicating with people with cognitive and visual disabilities. Instead of saying, "over here," "that way," and "this big," use words to describe the direction, space, length, and size (e.g., "about two feet to your left," "straight ahead," "two inches from the curb," etc.).
- Identify yourself when you meet a person with a visual disability. In groups, identify to whom you are speaking and notify people when it is their turn to speak.
- Describe what is drawn, written, or illustrated during presentations. When you ask people to read it on their own, you are excluding those who are not able to see or read it.
- Treat adults as adults. Having disabilities does not mean people are children or less than. Treat them as you would anyone else.
- Listen attentively to people with speech disabilities. Do not assume you understand or pretend you understand. Ask for clarification as needed.
- It is always appropriate to offer your help; just do not assume the person will need or accept your help.

In disability awareness sessions conducted by the authors of this monograph, people continually ask questions about what to say, how to say it, what to do, what is appropriate, and what is offensive. To answer some of these questions, the authors are including the following "Communication Tips" for interactions with people with visual, hearing, mobility, and cognitive disabilities. Although there are many more suggestions available, these are some of the most common communication strategies recommended for interactions with this population.

COMMUNICATION TIPS

In order to decrease inappropriate and potentially even offensive interactions with people with disabilities, the authors suggest utilizing the following communication tips.

WHEN YOU MEET A PERSON WITH A VISUAL DISABILITY

- It is always appropriate to offer your help; just do not be surprised if the individual would "rather do it myself."
- If you are helping and not sure what to do, ask the person.
- A gentle touch on the elbow will indicate to a person with a visual disability that you are speaking to him/her.
- If you are walking with a person who is blind, do not take that person's arm; rather let that person take your arm.
- Do not shout. "Blind" does not mean hard of hearing.

- If you have a question for the person with a visual disability, ask him/her, not his/her companion. "Blind" does not mean one cannot speak.
- Never pet a guide dog, except when the dog is "off-duty." Even then you should ask the dog's master first.
- Do not worry about substituting words for "see," "look," or even "blind." Do not avoid them where these words fit. You can talk about blindness itself, when you both feel comfortable about it.
- When you meet a person you know with a visual disability, mention your name. It is difficult to recognize voices unless you happen to have a very distinctive one.

WHEN YOU MEET A PERSON WHO IS DEAF OR HARD OF HEARING

- Speak clearly and distinctly, but do not exaggerate. Use normal speed unless asked to slow down.
- Provide a clear view of your mouth. Waving your hands or holding something in front of your lips, thus hiding them, makes lip reading impossible. Do not chew gum.
- Use a normal tone unless you are asked to raise your voice. Shouting will be of no help.
- Speak directly to the person, rather than from the side or back of the person.
- Speak expressively. Because persons who are deaf cannot hear subtle changes in tone, which may indicate sarcasm or seriousness, many will rely on your facial expressions, gestures, and body language to understand you.
- If you are having trouble understanding the speech of a person who is deaf, feel free to ask him/her to repeat. If that does not work, then use a paper and pen.
- If a person who is deaf is with an interpreter, speak directly to the person who is deaf—not to the interpreter.

WHEN YOU MEET A PERSON WITH A MOBILITY DISABILITY

- Offer help, but wait until it is accepted before giving it. Giving help before it is accepted is rude and sometimes can be unsafe.
- Accept the fact that a disability exists. Not acknowledging a disability is similar to ignoring someone's gender or height. But to ask personal questions regarding the disability would be inappropriate until a closer relationship develops in which personal questions are more naturally asked.
- Talk directly to a person with a disability. Because an individual has a functional limitation, it does not mean the individual cannot communicate for himself/herself.
- Do not park your car in a parking place that is specially designed for use by a person with a disability. These are reserved out of necessity, not convenience.
- Treat a person with disability as a healthy person. Because an individual has a functional limitation, it does not mean the individual is sick.
- Keep in your mind that persons with disabilities have the same activities of daily living as you do.

WHEN YOU MEET A PERSON WITH A COGNITIVE DISABILITY

- Use very clear, specific language.
- Condense lengthy directions into steps.
- Use short, concise instructions.
- Present verbal information at a relatively slow pace, with appropriate pauses for processing time and repetition if necessary.
- Provide cues to help with transitions: "In five minutes we'll be going to lunch."

NEXT STEPS

- Reinforce information with pictures or other visual images.
- Use modeling, rehearsing, and role-playing.
- Use concrete rather than abstract language.
- Limit the use of sarcasm or subtle humor.
- If you are not sure what to do or say, just ask the person what he/she needs.

UNIVERSALLY DESIGNED ENVIRONMENTS

Designing accessible environments is essential on college campuses and in the community. People with and without disabilities benefit from accessible buildings, walkways, transportation, programs, and services. By applying universal design principals to campus facilities, college curriculum, and student life, the entire campus community will be able to experience all aspects of the institution.

UNIVERSAL DESIGN

Eliminating barriers, promoting inclusion, and recognizing and appreciating the lived experience of people with disabilities are the essence of the social constructive model of disability. Inclusion of all people means providing access to all people with as few accommodations as possible. Case in point: How do all people access a sidewalk from the street? Whether walking, riding a bike, using a wheelchair, using crutches, pushing a stroller, or pulling a rolling suitcase, all people should be able to move comfortably over a curb. Therefore, architects created the universally designed curb cut, an indentation in a curb with a specified slope that allows all people equal access to both the sidewalk and the street. The architectural term known as "universal design" (UD) was conceptualized by Ronald L. Mace as "the designing of all products and the built environment to be aesthetic and usable to the greatest extent possible by everyone, regardless of their age, ability, or status in life." According to the Center for Universal Design at North Carolina State University, the following seven principles are the foundation of UD: (a) *equitable use*: the design is useful and marketable to people with diverse abilities; (b) *flexibility in use*: the design accommodates a wide range of individual preferences and abilities; (c) *simple and intuitive use*: use of the design is easy to understand, regardless of the user's experience, knowledge, language skills, or current concentration level; (d) *perceptible information*: the design communicates necessary information effectively to the user, regardless of ambient conditions or the user's sensory abilities; (e) *tolerance for error*: the design minimizes hazards and the adverse consequences of accidental or unintended actions; (f) *low physical effort*: the design can be used efficiently, comfortably, and with a minimum of fatigue; and (g) *size and space for approach and use*: appropriate size and space is provided for approach, reach, manipulation, and use, regardless of the user's body size, posture, or mobility.

In addition to the curb cut described above, other common examples of universal design of facilities are the automatic door, closed captioning, and audible streetlights. Traditionally used in airports, grocery stores, and hospitals, automatic doors are now used in many office structures, academic buildings, retail establishments, and day-care facilities. Closed captioning, which provides written text for audible words in movies, television shows, and videos, is a federally mandated accommodation and a standard specification on all analog televisions produced or sold in the United States beginning July 1993 and on all digital televisions as of July 2002. The audible street crossing light is yet another example of UD. In addition to a light that changes color from red to green, the words "walk" and "don't walk" appear together with a picture of a person walking and not walking accompanied by the audible words "Walk"/"Don't Walk" or another audible sound such as a bell chime or chirping bird to indicate when it is appropriate to cross the street.

UNIVERSAL INSTRUCTIONAL DESIGN

Following the concept of universal design of facilities, educators brought UD into the classroom. Over the past 20 years, much has been written about universal design in higher education, also known as "universal instructional design" (UID), "universal design of instruction" (UDI) when applied to instruction, and "universal design for learning" (UDL) when applied to learning. Universal design was applied to education, particularly to higher education, through several federally funded projects at the University of Minnesota, University of Washington, and the University of Connecticut, among others. Each of these institutions conducted research and provided training and development on universal design initiatives in postsecondary education settings. Using the principles of universal design, these projects offered standards for best practice. Fox, Hatfield, and Collins and Johnson and Fox address UD and UID guiding principles based on Chickering and Gamson's best practices for undergraduate education. These principles are as follows: (a) creating respectful welcoming environments; (b) determining the essential components of a course or program; (c) communicating class/program expectations; (d) providing constructive feedback; (e) exploring the use of natural supports for learning, including technology, to enhance opportunities for all learners; (f) designing teaching/instructional methods that consider diverse learning styles, abilities, ways of knowing, and previous experience and background knowledge; (g) creating multiple ways for students/employees to demonstrate their knowledge; and (h) promoting interaction among and between faculty and students, and employers and employees.

The term "Universal Instructional Design" (UID) was originally coined by Silver, Bourke, and Strehorn. Some examples of UID in curriculum include reaching out to students prior to the first day of class; learning students' names; putting syllabi and reading lists online; providing all print materials including websites and emails in readable high-contrast sans serif font; captioning videos; offering study guides and support systems; and creating multiple modes of teaching and learning such as traditional lecture, discussion, and tests mixed with the "flipped classroom" (i.e., online teaching sessions with face-to-face application) and social media activities. UID principles such as respectful, welcoming environments, timely feedback, accessible instructional materials, and comfortable interactions may benefit people with and without disabilities. For students, it eliminates the need to be segregated for accommodation, it addresses the stigma associated with the medical model (i.e., disability as deficiency), it recognizes individual differences among all learners, including learning styles and ways of knowing, and it enables students to use their strengths. For faculty, administrators and staff, using UID practices is cost-effective, time-efficient, enhances students engagements, and reduces the need for last-minute modifications to accommodate students with a variety of needs, including but not limited to students with disabilities. Created initially for individuals with disabilities, UID has been expanded to address access for people whose native language is not English and for people of various cultures, ethnicities, ages, and learning styles. An expanded model of UID, integrated multicultural instructional design (IMID) is under development. "IMID picks up where UID leaves off, adding explorations of what teach to the UID model that already addresses how we teach, how we support learning, and how we assess learning."

NEXT STEPS

UNIVERSAL DESIGN FOR STUDENT DEVELOPMENT

As UID became more widespread both inside and outside of the classroom, Higbee and her colleagues extended UID to student affairs personnel and their functional areas. Coining the phrase, "universal design for student development" (UDSD), Higbee and Goff describe the concept and provide examples for practice in their book, *Pedagogy and Student Services for Institutional Transformation* (PASS IT), and its accompanying guidebooks, produced by a national team of faculty, staff, and administrators via a federally funded project (http://cehd.umn.edu/passit). Checklists are included in the guidebooks to assess for UID and UDSD practices by faculty, student development practitioners, and student leaders. (These checklists are included in the educational materials developed through PASS IT and can also be accessed at http://cte.slu.edu/ui.)

When developing services and planning events and activities, Higbee (2008) recommended posing the following questions:

- *"How can we ensure that everyone who wants to participate will have the opportunity to do so?*
- *What steps can we take to ensure that everyone will feel included?*
- *What do we need to do to ensure that everyone will benefit to the greatest extent possible?"*

Implementing intentional UDSD practices, practitioners and student leaders will provide accessible programs and services.

> *Not only is it important to model best practices of UID in our work as professionals on campus, but it is also important to advise student leaders to incorporate UID within their leadership role in campus groups, organizations, and teams. One way student leaders can immediately have an impact on campus is to promote open access to all other students.*

Examples of such practices included ensuring all activities, events, and meetings are in accessible, welcoming locations; supporting written announcements and materials with online and audio versions; promoting accessible (i.e., screen reader and low vision friendly) websites, online registrations, surveys, and other web-based student information sites; captioning videos; and utilizing high-contrast sans serif font on publications, promotional materials, and other print media.

Commitment from national, regional, and state associations to adopt UD, UID, and UDSD principles is a major step toward acceptance and common practice. One association in particular has demonstrated this commitment. ACPA College Students International has offered UID webinars, programs, workshops, and presentations. Articles on universal design and inclusion have been published in the *Journal of College Student Development* and *About Campus,* both ACPA publications. *Making Good on the Promise: Student Affairs Professionals with Disabilities* is sponsored by the ACPA Standing Committee on Disability and contains articles and first-person accounts from over 20 of its members who are professionals with disabilities and their allies. For three years, the association hosted *Allies for Inclusion: The Ability Exhibit*, a national traveling exhibit that promotes disability awareness and inclusion, including UD, UID, UDSD, person-first language, and communication strategies. The ACPA Governing Board and Foundation Board promote the use of inclusive language and the production of UID-friendly web pages and print media. The association's most recent initiative was a four-part series published in *ACPA Developments*. In "Expanding the Frame: Applying Universal Design in Higher Education," ACPA Standing Committee on Disability members Thompson, Myers, Lind burg, and Higbee describe their personal experiences with UID as an administrator, a faculty member, a disability services provider, and a professional with a disability. The purpose of the series was to provide a standard framework in which to develop learning environments in the association and beyond. ACPA is just one example of an association's commitment to disability education and inclusion. It serves as a model for other associations to emulate.

CONCLUSION

Increasing awareness though language, communication strategies, and universal design principals promotes the inclusion of people with disabilities and provides professionals with the tools to shift the disability paradigm and relearn misinformation. The issue encountered by people with disabilities are not consequences of their disabilities; rather they are "products of interaction between the social and built environment." Recognizing and respecting the identities of others can be demonstrated through respectful communication. Higbee encourages us to avoid labelling people on the basis of a single aspect of their social identity (think "person-first"); ask people what terms they prefer to describe aspects of their social identity; refrain from using "othering" language (e.g., *normal and regular*); and be aware that some identity groups are "reclaiming" language to refer to themselves (e.g., *fag, crip, girl, and trannie*), but "[t]he subtleties of language become more difficult when the same words spoken in-group hold a different meaning when used out-of-group."

Educators are models for inclusion. When addressing language, culture, and climate, ask students to reflect on times when they have been the targets of oppressive language and communication. Discuss potential reactions to oppressive language used by others, including when presented as humor. Use these reflections and discussions to create role-playing activities, and encourage students to follow our lead in being allies in respectful language use, comfortable interactions, and creative universal design techniques, thus becoming allies for inclusion.

113

Learning Disability Identity Development and Social Construct

A Two-Tiered Approach

Cheryl L. Howland and Eva Gibavic

INTRODUCTION: THE LD WALL

Most of the time people with a learning disability (LD) look, act and perform like everyone else. However, when they encounter an experience that puts them face to face with their disability it is very much like hitting a wall at full speed. The LD wall is usually invisible to everyone else, yet when a person with a learning disability hits this "wall" s/he can have a powerful and painful reaction.

NEXT STEPS

So here we have a student with LD having just hit the LD wall. Our student is unable to perform as required, and s/he is also having a reaction to the impact. In addition, all around him/her are family, teachers, and friends who did *not* hit this wall and who cannot perceive that there is a wall. These non-learning-disabled individuals often cannot see or understand that our student is severely impacted by his/her experience and, while our student may have a real desire and need to perform in the prescribed manner, s/he cannot.

In the moment when individuals face their hidden disability, having been impacted by their learning disability "wall," they have to deal with the following: 1. They cannot perform in the prescribed manner. 2. They are hurting from the impact. 3. Their experience is denied and questioned by well meaning parents, peers, teachers and others who do not understand. 4. They MUST perform somehow. 5. If you were that person, how would you react?

RESISTANCE TO ASSISTANCE

Why do some students with learning disabilities resist when teachers and other professionals try to help them? Why are some willing and eager for accommodations one day and reluctant the next? What is at the core of their refusals? Why do some teachers still see some students with learning disabilities as "willful non-learners"?

These questions are ones that are often raised in our consulting work by college students, parents, grade school teachers, college professors, and disability advocates. Even with the best of intentions and most current knowledge, teachers and parents can become frustrated with a student's resistance. Even with the best of intentions, students can feel that there is a failure on the part of many helpers to "get it," to truly walk in their LD shoes. This can lead to a functional collapse in the teaching/learning contract and an inability to positively address the issues faced by people with learning disabilities.

THE HOWLAND/GIBAVIC MODEL OF IDENTITY DEVELOPMENT
IN PERSONS WITH LEARNING DISABILITIES

The kernel of our identity development model was formed by the basic premise that neurodevelopmental differences plus life circumstances impact our sense of who we are, in other words, our identity. Who we become in life begins with our inherent makeup and evolves and changes over our life as a result of our experiences. Our goal was to propose a model that would assist helpers, learners, parents and teachers understand the developmental processes that can impact individuals with a learning disability. As these experiences are multi-faceted, we propose a complex, two-tiered model of identity development. The model is based in the stage theory of development, well grounded in the works of Erikson, Vgotsky, Kohlberg and Gilligan, and Jackson and Hardiman.

At the time we began our work, an extensive literature search revealed no models of identity development for individuals with learning disabilities, but as our work continued two models were published at the University of Massachusetts by Rodis and Pliner. While very helpful, we found the models to be limited in their respective abilities to address the complex yet powerful effects of social influences, the widely varying impacts of different types of learning disabilities, and the ongoing life challenges that routinely occur when the expectations of self and others collide with an individual's learning disabilities. These ongoing collisions with the "LD wall," which can result in grief, relief, and resistance periodically over the course of a lifetime, is central to the recycling and re-adjusting of individual identity. In essence, while adjustment and integration can occur with each run-in with the wall, there is typically another "wall" around the corner. The "walls" associated with learning disabilities present themselves through life's various experiences as does a continuation of identity integration. For a model to provide assistance in understanding the experience of an individual with a learning disability, it needs to have a level of complexity, complexity that is not typically explicit in identity development models. Our two-tiered model speaks to these considerations.

TIER ONE: INFLUENTIAL VARIABLES: SOCIAL SYSTEMS AND TIMING

Support Systems: How a person receives and perceives support from their family, community, and teachers represents perhaps the most significant variable in the development of a positive sense of identity related to a learning disability. Children who receive positive support from their family, school and surrounding community develop a positive self-identity more often than a child who is perceived as deficient and or defective by their family, peers, educators and culture. Families and school structures with less knowledge, resources, and social support can contribute to a negative identity development by labeling and stereotyping the child as stupid or lazy or ill-behaved.

Timing: The timing of when a person becomes aware that they have a learning disability and the particular life stage they are in can have a significant impact on the development of their self-identity. Some children in elementary school receive a sufficient amount of remediation and support so that as they grow up they see their LD as only a small part of their learning portfolio. Conversely, children with poor school services and a lack of support can experience the shame of having an LD that shapes their entire school experience. Children who receive their diagnosis in high school have spent a significant part of their learning experience without an understanding of their learning needs. This can result in an inaccurate series of labels and poor self-beliefs. Individuals who receive diagnosis in college or in later adult years may have developed a number of compensation techniques that have assisted them in living and learning while lacking remediation and accommodation and may have developed a significant and largely inaccurate belief system and defensiveness about their learning. This can often be seen as strong negative resistance to help from helping professionals when it may be a positive coping skill developed by the individual struggling to maintain positive self-worth.

Social Receptivity/Acceptance: In 1994 and 1999, the Emily Hall Tremaine Foundation funded two Roper Starch national opinion surveys looking at the social perception of individuals with learning disabilities. The results of these surveys showed that an "alarming 48% of parents think that in the long run being labeled as learning disabled causes children and adults more trouble than if they struggle privately with their learning problems." Some individuals such as Tri-athlete Bruce Jenner (dyslexia) are spared this stigma due to success in other areas, such as sports.

Dual Diagnosis: Having another diagnosis in addition to a learning disability is not unusual for people with learning disabilities. Co-morbidity rates are high, with many people struggling with emotional/behavioral difficulties, ADHD, as well as mental health and other medical issues. The interplay among these multiple diagnoses can complicate and intensify the self-identity process.

Cause of the Disability: While most often the cause of a learning disability is unclear, if the cause of a specific learning disability can be ascertained it can be a powerful variable in terms of self-understanding.

NEXT STEPS

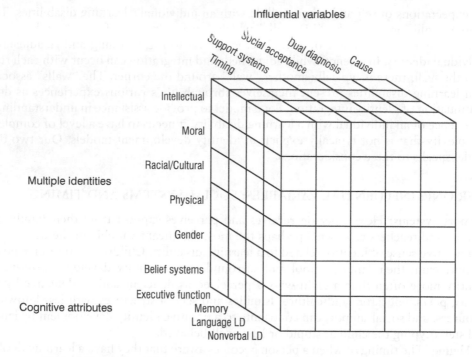

Figure 113.1 Influential variables, multiple identities and cognitive attributes

Multiple Identity Development

Multiple Intelligences: Gardner's theory of Multiple Intelligences posits the existence of eight different forms of intelligence: linguistic, logical mathematical, musical, visual spatial, interpersonal, intrapersonal, natural, and bodily kinesthetic. People with learning disabilities struggle to understand and experience the development of their gifts as positive identities ("I succeed") that are separate from their disability identities ("I struggle"). Those who are able to see themselves from multiple capability perspectives are better able to integrate disability identities than those who are not.

Moral Identity Development: Identity development theory is founded upon theories of moral reasoning and development. Most recognize that children begin with a self-centered approach to the world and, through experiences, develop into beings that interrelate to others in an interdependent, socially-conscious manner. The stages of moral development can influence passage through the stages of learning disability identity development and affect how an individual will respond to his/her learning issues.

Racial/Cultural Identity: In societies where one racial group is unfairly advantaged, people from marginalized cultures and races are impacted by racial oppression, which further influences their racial/cultural identity development. As a student of color struggles to achieve a positive self-identity, the addition of a learning disability and the concurrent stereotyping can further complicate integration, growth, and resolution of one's identity. The interplay between racism and ableism can be seen in the much higher percentages of students of color who are being placed in special education classes (Harry and Klingner 2006).

Gender Identity: Gender oppression continues to be a significant factor influencing how individuals are treated in our society and plays a role in learning disability assessment and intellectual expectations. Boys are diagnosed with an LD more often than are girls. It has been suggested that this is . . . [because boys tend to act out in the classroom more than girls and, as a result, are subjected to more disciplinary action.]

Physical Identity: Physical identity can be experienced positively for some and negatively for others. Peers, as mentioned above, may give an outstanding athlete respect that s/he does not receive academically. Physical attractiveness may have a socially positive effect, whereas individuals with physical challenges or medical co-morbidities may experience negative social reinforcement.

Belief Systems: Individual beliefs can have a profound influence on learning disability identity development and integration. For example, a student of ours was told by a teacher in middle school that individuals with dyslexia have limited brain space and that perhaps her brain was full. She approached all of her learning challenges from that foundation of belief and perspective. The belief acted as a powerful disincentive to achievement.

Cognitive Attributes

Learning Disabilities: Learning disabilities are defined in various ways, but for simplicity in this model we have chosen to delineate four areas, those involved with the auditory/language area, the nonverbal/visual-perceptual area, memory issues and those related to organizational/executive functioning.

Auditory/Language Processing: Included in this would be central auditory processing, receptive and expressive language, including syntax and word retrieval, written language, and phonologically based dyslexia. Also under this broad category we recognize that some math disabilities are verbally based, having to do with math vocabulary and syntax specific to mathematical reasoning.

Nonverbal/Visual-Spatial Processing: Nonverbal communication is believed to represent 60% of all human communication. Individuals who struggle with nonverbal communication fail to accurately perceive and/or express those many and varied nonverbal signals which most of us take for granted. When this happens, they are often socially isolated due to poor social skills development. In addition these people can struggle academically with nonverbal forms of analysis, synthesis and reasoning.

Memory Difficulties: Students who struggle with various memory issues can have their learning impacted by short and long term deficits in verbal, auditory, visual, and/or working memory. Working memory allows the individual to hold the various parts of a problem actively in mind or "on-line."

Executive Functioning: The executive realm involves the ability to initiate tasks, focus and sustain attention for the task, inhibit behaviors unrelated to the task and inhibit preponderant responses, as well as develop appropriate strategies and shift strategies as required to complete the task.

TIER TWO: STAGES OF IDENTITY DEVELOPMENT

Tier Two of our model addresses the following Stages of Identity Development: Problem with the Wrong Name, Diagnosis, Grief and/or Relief, Resistance and/or Alienation, Passing, Redefinition, and Ongoing Resolution Process.

Problem with the Wrong Name: In this stage, the individual and the family has an understanding that there is something different, perhaps something wrong in the learning process, whether it be a problem with behavior, a slower reading rate, an inability to comprehend reading material, and/or difficulty in mathematics, but there is no actual diagnosis. This lack of clarity can often lead to mislabeling, with individuals being called "dumb," "stupid," "lazy," "slacker," or "willful non-learner."

Diagnosis: With diagnosis of a learning disability, a greater understanding of the individual's learning strengths and weaknesses is developed. The individual, if a child, may or

N
E
X
T

S
T
E
P
S

may not be told about the diagnosis and what it means. Many college students come to school with a poor understanding of their learning strengths and struggles.

Grief and/or Relief: Diagnosis typically brings change. These changes may be seen by the individual as positive, leading to a sense of relief, such as an individual who appreciates specialized help. There can also be a sense of grief. Grief may come in the recognition of one's differences and/or due to changes that may be seen as unwanted and negative. A great deal depends on the reaction of the individual's family and teachers, and the nature of the changes.

Resistance and/or Alienation: In this stage, the individual may resent the learning disability itself, resent the consequences of the label, and/or resent the remediation that s/he has received due to the LD. This often co-occurs with the "Passing" stage: the individual may be resistant in classes, while at the same time trying to pass socially.

Passing: The individual downplays the LD, denying it when possible and trying to be like peers. This is a very common stage/place for a student to be in because our society does not easily accept differences and who really wants the disability label?

Redefinition: The individual realizes that passing and resistance doesn't make the LD go away and doesn't make life easier. This re-evaluation may result from some sort of crisis or may grow out of recognition of the value of the individual's strengths as well as different learning needs.

Ongoing Resolution Process: This stage is perhaps the most important to understand. This stage offers the understanding that the whole model is not static, but rather an ever changing launching point as an individual goes through life. It is here that the above-mentioned influences, variables and the actual disability take on a fluidity that forces a person living with a learning disability to re-cycle through an ongoing process.

NEXT STEPS

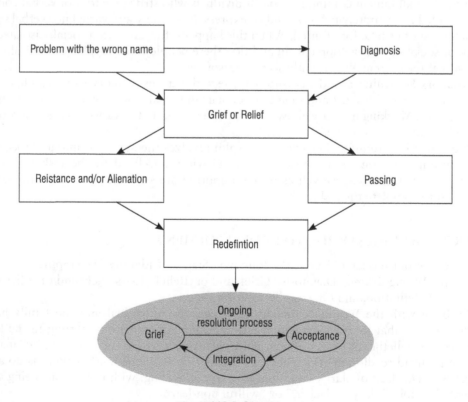

Figure 113.2 Stages

USING THE MODEL

Using these components, including stages and the factors, should guide us to a better understanding of an individual and, therefore, how best to address a variety of issues, including personal, educational and clinical.

CASE STUDY

"David" was a student diagnosed with a significant language-based learning/reading disability with some indication of ADD but with a solid IQ. In the past, he had refused to register with Disability Services. He was seeking readmission to school after failing out two previous times. The admitting Dean required David to sign a contract agreeing to register with Disability Services, meet with me weekly, and achieve a solid 2.0 or better for the semester.

For our first meeting, he was angry, defensive, and independent-minded. He held little hope that anyone including me could or would help him. He came from a working class background where he was the first person in his family to attend college. He'd received little or no help for his disability in high school and (he told me later) expected me to be just another adult who was a harsh judge of his motivation and performance.

David was stuck in the "resistance and alienation" stage of learning disability development and was only willing to attempt school out of love and respect for his mother who was ill. He wanted very much to please her and she had asked him for one Christmas present—a "C" average. He was particularly angry with one professor who had failed him several times and who was unwilling to budge on his grade. Most professionals and adults in David's life saw his struggle as a failure of his character. His anger and resistance reinforced their misunderstanding of David and what he truly wanted and felt about his situation.

In order for us to be helpful to David, we had to allow him to be safe in his resistance and alienation while simultaneously encouraging the part of him that wanted to succeed. Additionally, we had to really help him succeed academically. He was assigned to an Academic Assistant who would work jointly with both of us to help him develop learning strategies that worked for him. We set him up with a schedule that respected his need for physical fun and relaxation but that also made study time more automatic and routine. He met with us every week and soon his resistance faded in the face of his burgeoning academic success. He did not, however, wish anyone including his roommate to know that he was meeting with us and protected his privacy fiercely. He had moved from resistance and alienation to passing. Over the course of our two-year relationship David moved in and out of resistance and alienation, passing, and into the ongoing resolution process. He would sometimes hit his "LD wall" and find himself angry and resistant all over again. But we were able to show that while his learning disability and the frustration associated with it was likely a permanent part of his life, he could and would develop coping skills that would allow him to live a good and successful life. David was able to give his mother her Christmas present that year and for two more Christmases afterward. Most importantly, he took our help and understanding and made it his own. He graduated with a 3.2 GPA.

The Howland/Gibavic model of LD Identity Development allows for a greater understanding of the nature and complex struggles associated with developing a positive LD self-identity, while providing a template that shows the way for individuals and

NEXT STEPS

professionals alike to relate and work positively and effectively with themselves and others with learning disabilities.

114

Creating a Fragrance-Free Zone

A Friendlier Atmosphere for People Living with Environmental Illness

Invisible Disabilities Advocate

Did you know there is a growing number of people who can become ill from simply running an errand in a store, going to work or attending a gathering? Simple tasks that most of us take for granted can cause this group to have mild to severe medical reactions. Even their own homes and work environments can lash out at them.

Why is this happening? "Approximately 12.6% of the population suffers from multiple chemical sensitivity (MCS), a condition in which they experience reactions from exposure to low concentrations of common chemicals . . ."

MCS (also known as Environmental Illness or Toxic Injury) is " . . . marked by *multiple symptoms* in *multiple organ systems* (usually the neurological, immune, respiratory, skin, 'GI,' and/or musculoskeletal) that recur chronically in response to *multiple chemical exposures*. MCS symptoms commonly include difficulty breathing, sleeping and/or concentrating, memory loss, migraines, nausea, abdominal pain, chronic fatigue, aching joints and muscles, and irritated eyes, nose, ears, throat and/or skin. In addition, some with MCS show impaired balance and increased sensitivity not just to odors but also to loud noises, bright lights, touch, extremes of heat and cold, and electromagnetic fields."

The numbers of Americans battling MCS seem to be rising quickly. Most with MCS tell a story of once being healthy and not affected by fragrances. "MCS usually starts with either an acute or chronic toxic exposure, after which this initial sensitivity broadens to include many other chemicals and common irritants . . ." Many experts have found that once a person becomes reactive to a chemical or toxin, their intolerance is rarely reversible.

Furthermore, "In 1998, it was estimated that 26.3 million Americans have been diagnosed with asthma." Asthma is a serious respiratory disorder that can constrict and cause swelling of the airways. "The Institute of Medicine placed fragrance in the same category as second hand smoke in triggering asthma in adults and school age children." What's more, "Up to 72% of asthmatics report their asthma is triggered by fragrance. Asthmatics and others that are negatively impacted by fragrance often have difficulties working, obtaining medical care, and going about activities of daily living because of others' use of scented products."

For those living with asthma and/or MCS, just going to work, a meeting or an activity may expose them to chemicals that could make them ill. These reactions can be very serious and have changed the lives of millions. Because they have to avoid public situations and even having people in their own homes, they can also experience isolation, loneliness, lose their jobs and may even become homebound.

WHAT CHEMICALS?

Most of us are aware that such things as pollution and car exhaust fumes are not good for us. We even realize that sometimes a work environment, like a lab or factory can be hazardous. However, most do not even think twice when entering a building, automobile or even a home that may contain new paint, car smell, carpet or mold, glue, stain, vinyl upholstery, plastic, rubber, smoke, household cleaners, etc.

Moreover, the culprits most of us will never even give a thought to being bothersome are our sweet smelling perfumes, colognes and fragranced products. But aren't these made from natural ingredients like flowers and herbs? Actually, "Perfume formulations changed sometime around the late 70s and early 80s. Today, they are approximately 95–100% synthetic (man-made)." Even seemingly harmless fragrances in our favorite soap, deodorant, lotion, powder, candles, air freshener and laundry products can cause reactions for many.

For the average person, short term exposures to these environmental, everyday household products and perfumes may only seem "bothersome" on occasion. Nevertheless, many people claim they never believed they had an issue until they suddenly or gradually developed their sensitivity or intolerance after normal use of these items.

Author Connie Pitts explained why, "Perfumes, colognes, and many other *scented* products contain an abundance of harmful chemicals, many of which are listed on the EPA's Hazardous Waste List. They also include numerous carcinogenic chemicals, neurotoxins, respiratory irritants, solvents, aldehydes, hundreds of untested and unregulated petrochemicals, phthalates (which can act as hormone disrupters), narcotics, and much more."

WHAT CAN WE DO?

Because many with asthma, MCS and immune disorders risk becoming ill when they go to work, to run errands, to a doctor's office or when attending a gathering, we can all do our part to help.

1) For our own well-being and for the sake of others, we can discontinue the use of products containing VOCs, synthetic fragrances and harmful chemicals.
2) Make meetings and events Fragrance-Free for all to enjoy. This can be done simply by posting this information along with the notices for the event in bulletins, emails, websites and flyers.
3) Office or building management can ask the cleaning crew to start using natural cleaning products like baking soda, vinegar, hydrogen peroxide or environmentally safe products. Moreover, they should not use "air fresheners" in the building or bathrooms. Instead, exhaust fans and air purifiers can do the job.
4) Office or building management can create a list of people who are sensitive to chemicals and fragrances. They would then call people on the list when someone paints the walls, shampoos the carpet, replaces the carpet, gets new furniture or uses glues, insecticides, stains, polishes, etc. In addition, signs should be placed on the doors to notify all employees and customers of the use of these products.
5) Before visiting someone in their home or inviting them to ours, we should ask those living with asthma, chronic illness, immune issues, MCS and/or allergies what fragrances, lotions, soaps, deodorants, candles, air fresheners, detergents, cleaning products, etc. they can and cannot tolerate.
6) For added protection, a Fragrance-Free Zone can be implemented.

NEXT STEPS

CREATING A FRAGRANCE-FREE ZONE

A Fragrance-Free Zone is a smoke, fragrance and chemical free area, designed for those who report mild to serious reactions to these items. Adding a Fragrance-Free Zone can help many in our community work and frequent your establishment in comfort.

At first glance, we may think there are not enough people who struggle with these issues to justify the hassle of providing a Fragrance-Free Zone. However, for every 100 people in America, there is an average of 10 with asthma, 20 with an autoimmune disorder and/or 12.5 with MCS.

Here are basically 3 types of Fragrance-Free Zones that can be implemented in the office or store:

Fragrance-Free Zone #1: Building, Office or Store Policy. Establish a policy of no perfumes or fragrances worn by employees inside the building. In addition, the use of non-toxic cleaning supplies, natural pesticides, etc. can be included. This concept is becoming more and more popular among businesses, doctor's offices and churches, because it makes it possible for many to work in or visit your building. Many medical facilities and religious organizations are also asking patients and congregations not to wear fragrances.

Fragrance-Free Zone #2: Separate Room in Workplace. This is a separate room or floor of a building for employees that provides extra protection from fragrances, as well as paints, glues, formaldehyde, mold, smoke and chemical cleaners. It is sealed off with walls, a door to a direct entrance and exit. It also contains a Fragrance-Free bathroom and a break-room (if space permits).

Fragrance-Free Zone #3: Section in Office. This is a simple and quick way to set up a section in the office. Designate several rows of desks just for those with chemical sensitivities. You can post signs to signify that this section is a perfume, cologne, fragrance and smoke free zone. Put this section in an area where they can have easy access to an outside entrance and away from high traffic areas.

Please note that just creating a "section" within a room is not always a viable answer. Perfumes and fragrances can permeate the air and waft through the area, as well as linger in the hallway, lobby and bathrooms. "Scented products are volatile substances and get into the air quickly. Once in the air, containment to a defined space is impossible. Further, scented products are designed to diffuse into the air and linger."

Finally, "According to the AARDA, approximately 50 million Americans [or] 20 percent of the population . . . suffer from some 80 autoimmune diseases." Thus, for the benefit of all around us, particularly those with immune disorders, when we are sick with a cold or a virus, maybe we should consider staying home. After all, we could infect several more people, who in turn infect several more people—causing them to miss work, activities and maybe even be hospitalized. Consequently, even when we are just "coming down with" a virus or we are "getting over" something, we can still be contagious. If we cannot stay home from work, we should at least steer clear of other people, especially those with immune issues.

Thank you for your cooperation in providing a safer environment, so that millions of people can live better lives, with fewer boundaries! Without everyone's help, going to work or entering a building can put many at risk of having mild to severe reactions that may last several hours or even several weeks. With it, many can live their lives with less risk of exposure.

NEXT STEPS

115

Recognizing Ableist Beliefs and Practices and Taking Action as an Ally

Madeline L. Peters, Carmelita (Rosie) Castañeda,
Larissa E. Hopkins, and Aquila McCants

Ableism is a pervasive form of oppression that tends to be minimally examined and understood by mainstream society. From a young age we learn powerful messages about groups of people, especially those who are perceived to be different than us. These consistent messages are translated into strongly rooted beliefs, stereotypes, and behaviors directed towards other human beings. Our internalization of negative thoughts and subsequent actions has systematically, generation-by-generation, supported the dehumanization and denigration of people with disabilities.

It is vitally important that we begin to question the historical and contemporary patterns and practices that reproduce the discrimination and exclusion of people with intellectual, emotional, and physical disabilities. Challenging ableism truly requires that we recognize how this oppression is manifested on the individual, institutional, and cultural levels of engagement. It is with this recognition that we will be able to replace our harmful language and behaviors with empowering words and actions, and our marginalizing institutional practices with supportive and inclusive practices. By reevaluating our perceptions and stereotypical responses, we can learn to build respectful, dynamic and fulfilling relationships with people living with disabilities. A significant factor necessary for challenging manifestations of oppression is the formation of allies.

An ally is typically a member of advantaged social groups who uses their social power to take a stand against social injustice directed at targeted groups. For example, White people who speak against racism, men who speak out against sexism, and heterosexual people who challenge heterosexism and homophobia. An ally works to be an agent of social change rather than an agent of oppression. While there are many important characteristics of an effective ally, there are a few that we would like to highlight. We believe an ally takes responsibility for learning about his/her own and targeted group heritage, culture and experience, and how oppression works in everyday life. Allies listen to and respect the perspectives and experiences of targeted group members. They acknowledge unearned privileges and work to eliminate or change privileges into rights that targeted group members also enjoy. Allies recognize that unlearning oppressive beliefs and actions is a lifelong process, and welcome each learning opportunity. They are willing to take risks, try new behaviors, and act in spite of their own fear and resistance from other advantaged group members. Allies believe they can make a difference by acting and speaking out against social injustice.

The chart below is designed to provide people with information needed in becoming a stronger, more supportive, and aware ally to people living with disabilities. The left side of the chart organizes perceptions, language, and behaviors about the limiting factors at three levels of engagement: individual, institutional, and societal/cultural levels. The right side of the chart responds to the limiting factors by providing people with examples of supportive ally behaviors and actions. The need for each of us to act as an ally by fostering supportive practices is imperative for the well-being of all people.

N E X T S T E P S

Recognizing Ableist Beliefs and Practices and Taking Action as an Ally

Limiting Factors for People with Disabilities	Supportive Practices for People with Disabilities
Individual	
Denying people with disabilities equal opportunities and seeing him/her as second class citizens. Behaving as if people with disabilities are invisible, a nuisance, disgusting, and should be institutionalized	Recognize the full potential and humanity of people with disabilities in relationships, employment, and cultural, political, social and physical activities in our multicultural world
Assuming that people with disabilities are unaware and unable to make decisions regarding their daily needs. Limiting and/or interfering with their ability to make their own decisions	Accept that a person is more than their disability. They are complex human beings with the ability to make decisions about their daily needs with varying degrees of success and failure like the rest of the population
Not acknowledging people with disabilities: i.e., ignoring, not speaking to, avoiding eye contact, and behaving as if people with disabilities do not exist	Be aware of your body language and avoid staring at people with disabilities. Refrain from talking about the person with a disability in front of them. Establish eye contact and speak directly to the person with a disability
Imposing "help" thereby taking control away from the person: i.e., grabbing the arm of a person who is blind to assist them across the street without asking	Ask the person with a disability if they need assistance, allowing them to have control of the situation. Stay within the boundaries of the stated request for assistance
Not treating people with disabilities as you would treat others: i.e., being afraid to give feedback or advice to person with a disability by being overly concerned about how the person will react to criticism	State ideas and concerns clearly and constructively. Recognize that constructive feedback is meant to help a person grow and learn
Establishing lower expectations for people with disabilities: i.e., a teacher setting lower standards for a student who is deaf or a teacher who inflates the grade of a person with a disability not based on the person's ability but based on the teacher's pity	Lowered expectations are demeaning and a disservice to the person with a disability and only reflect ableist assumptions. Recognize that inflating grades does not benefit people with disabilities. Understand that accommodations can be put in place to allow students to successfully participate and excel in the classroom
Not encouraging people with disabilities to take risks	Encourage people with disabilities to reach their full potential. Encouragement includes praise when one has met a goal and an inquiry about the next goal to be set, suggesting that higher goals are attainable
Discounting the opinions of people with disabilities, except on issues of disabilities	Seek the opinions of people with disabilities for their perspectives on any issue. They may have valuable opinions and may have experience on a breadth of issues
Institutional	
Employing people with disabilities in low-paying occupations or guiding people with disabilities to solely work in jobs geared towards disability services and/or other related specialized fields: i.e., instilling in people with disabilities that the only work available to them is menial tasks	Recognize that people with disabilities can perform essential functions of various jobs. People with disabilities can and do work in every field of employment, from entertainment, science, and technology to philosophy and mathematics, and have strong qualities and attributes like other employees and deserve to earn a livable wage
Assuming all people with disabilities require the same services thereby establishing a uniform system of accommodations	Recognize and provide services on a case by case basis, because all disabilities are manifested differently in each individual
Placing people with disabilities in segregated environments i.e., all students with special needs' classes are held in the basement of the school. Holding segregated events for people with disabilities without the goal and practice of inclusive integration or making all activities accessible	Schedule all activities with accessibility in mind: i.e., space should be wheelchair accessible, bathrooms should be conveniently located; be conscientious of how lighting impacts individuals with disabilities; advocate for a chemically free/fragrance free environment. Mainstream people with disabilities so that they are afforded similar social, cultural and academic experiences. Make inclusive integration the norm (i.e., use multiple teaching methods, make sure all handouts are also printed in Braille and/or on MP3 auditory format; verbally describe all visual aids; welcome sign language interpretation; and provide frequent breaks)

Limiting Factors for People with Disabilities	Supportive Practices for People with Disabilities
Depictions of people with disabilities in mainstream media as different, grotesque, evil, villains, monsters, an alien: i.e., Beauty and the Beast, The Hunchback of Notre Dame, and The Hulk	Recognize that the media has used people with disabilities to incite fear of difference. Be acquainted with positive portrayals of people with disabilities in the media, such as "My Left Foot," etc. Seek out media that portrays people with disabilities as human beings who are living their everyday lives
Maintaining a "hidden" and/or separate set of policies that require people with disabilities to jump through additional hoops in order to prove they need a particular type of service/ accommodation	Institutions need to implement policies that are inclusive of the needs of all people with consideration to the individual needs of people with disabilities. Separate is not equal

Cultural

Assuming that the lives of people with disabilities (i.e., daily living, relationships, choices, passions, emotions, work and lack of work, housing, education, abilities, and civic rights) revolve solely around their disability/ies	Assume that the lives of people with disabilities are full, diverse and complex. People with disabilities make daily decisions, have plans for the future, and enjoy relationships, work and leisure. They also have passions, hobbies, families and friends. The disability is not the essence of who they are in the world
Assuming that people with disabilities do not want a career and prefer to live off of government assistance	Government assistance has never been more than subsistence living. Most people with or without a disability would rather make a meaningful contribution to society than be subject to the stigma of being "lazy" and receiving "a handout." Although many are entitled to disability assistance, they also are searching (despite barriers) to find something more meaningful in their lives, such as good employment, decent shelter, and stimulating recreation
Using limiting language or language with negative connotations to describe people with disabilities: i.e., associating them with terms such as "sick," "bad," "disabled," "broken," "mental," "scary," "stupid," and "sped." For example, "Sam is in Sped, where all the stupid children are"	Recognize that language is a reflection of how people see one another. Use words that locate people with disabilities in a positive and nondestructive manner. Refer to people with disabilities as people first. For example, "Sam is in room 224"
A belief system that people with the same disabilities are the same or share the same experience, not taking their individuality into account	Understand that all people with disabilities are individuals and all individuals have unique qualities. Some wheelchair users are able to walk brief distances, some individuals who are legally blind may be able to see and experience certain sights, and people with learning disabilities may have an Intelligence Quotient in the gifted-to-genius range
Societal belief that people with disabilities are helpless and/or unable to accomplish daily living tasks, thus taking individual power away from the person: i.e., in a restaurant the wait staff asking friends to order for a person with a disability	To think of people as helpless is yet another way of disempowering a group or an individual. All individuals and groups with disabilities lead their daily lives with the same dreams and aspirations as everyone else. There may be accommodations to help them meet their daily goals, but they are not helpless. Helplessness is a learned behavior that can be countered by empowering people to advocate for and do things for themselves as much as is possible
During certain holiday seasons, the gathering of families, the cluttering of aisles, the overcrowded nature of shopping centers, and the added daily responsibilities may result in one's disability becoming more prominent: i.e., increase anxiety, depression, and post traumatic stress syndrome (PTSD)	The holiday seasons are important times to raise one's awareness of the needs of people with disabilities. It is important to be aware of accessibility in your home, and in public spaces, and to be attentive to those who may be left alone. Be supportive and reassuring of the individual's situations
Society's standards of beauty leave people with disabilities invisible: i.e., popular magazines, catalogs, and advertisements do not feature photographs of people with visible disabilities	Society's standards of beauty need to be inclusive of all people from diverse backgrounds, and thus need to include people with disabilities. Recognize that traditional standards of beauty have limited our society's perception of beauty. Standards of beauty are based on the eye of the beholder. Recognize that people with disabilities are beautiful

NEXT STEPS

See Chapter 10 in *Teaching for Diversity and Social Justice* for corresponding teaching materials.

SECTION 7

YOUTH OPPRESSION AND ELDER OPPRESSION

Introduction

Keri "Safire" DeJong and Barbara J. Love *

This section, on youth oppression (also called adultism) and elder oppression (also known as ageism), is concerned with the oppression of young people and elders as age-based social identity groups, and the ways in which access to participation in society and the establishment of relationships of domination and subordination are organized on the basis of age (Hardiman, Jackson, and Griffin, 2007). Chronological age is a physical reality. What is deemed appropriate for people of any age group is societally constructed. The roles, behaviors, and expectations that society has deemed appropriate for any given age group vary across societies and within societies across time, corresponding to the economic and technological developments within that society.

Some social relationships, such as the caretaking of the very young and of elders, are rooted in physical and biological realities. Decisions about power, voice, and decision-making connected to young people and elders are determined by societal expectations and structures rather than biological differences. For example, high-school students have played an important part in organizing and participating in political campaigns but are not permitted to vote until they are eighteen years old. Elders are often subjected to layoffs and may struggle to find employment due to stereotypes about elders even though they are fully capable of meeting the expectations of employers. "Youth" and "elder" are socially constructed identities with related stereotypes and misinformation that impact younger people and older people's ability to exercise power, be listened to and acknowledged, and make decisions that will be supported by the dominant society. Our discussion of youth oppression and elder oppression as issues of social justice acknowledges that, like all other forms of oppression, the oppression of young people and elders exists independent of our ability to observe and acknowledge it.

One strategy to increase our capacity to observe the disempowerment and lack of respect accorded to young people is to examine societal rules and regulations targeted specifically toward young people. Youth escort laws provide one contemporary example. Like sundown laws of the old South requiring black people to get out of town before dark, youth escort laws require young people to be accompanied by an adult over the age of twenty-one or to depart malls before 7 p.m. These laws regulate the presence of members of the subordinant group (young people) to suit the needs and preferences of members of the dominant group (adults). These laws determine when and under what circumstances youth, the target group, can be in the presence of adults, the dominant group, reinforcing and highlighting adult power and the powerlessness of youth. Rooted in the notion that "children are to be seen and not heard," youth escort laws reflect absolute adult power over young people along with societal attitudes of disdain and lack of respect. Another easily observed example takes place daily in schools where young people spend a large portion of their time. Young people in schools must often request and receive adult permission to go to the bathroom though they are legally approved to drive, work, and take care of other young people and elders. Young people may be stopped, detained, and disciplined by any adult in most schools if they leave the classroom without explicit adult permission. Beginning at a very early age, young people learn that they must submit completely to adult authority.

Societal prohibitions against and contempt for growing older are equally pernicious. The advertisements and news lines that are displayed regularly urging us to fight back against aging is an indicator of the negative societal attitude toward growing old. Predatory lending practices and the disproportionate targeting of elders for reverse equity and other mortgage schemes designed to prey on elders with fixed incomes results in elders being forced from their homes, often with devastating results (references to examples and resources are on our section website). Mandatory retirement age, scandalous nursing home conditions, coupled with the prevalence of stereotypes and disparaging humor, all signal loss of power and societal mistreatment of people who are old.

DEFINITIONS AND MANIFESTATIONS OF ELDER AND YOUTH OPPRESSION

One of the first writers on ageism, Robert Butler (1975, p. 12) defines ageism as "A process of systematic stereotyping of and discrimination against people because they are old . . . Old people are categorized as senile, rigid in thought and manner, old fashioned in morality and skills" (p. 35). To Butler's definition, we add a social justice framework that examines the loss of power, voice, and limited access to participation in society from a basis of equity. We define youth oppression as the systematic subordination of younger people as a targeted group, who have relatively little opportunity to exercise power in the United States through restricted access to the goods, services, and privileges of society and restricted access to participation in the economic and political life of the society. This subordination of young people and elders is supported by adult supremacy, which is maintained by a network of laws, rules, policies, procedures, and organizational norms that consistently deny youth access to power, privilege, and opportunity and ensure the continued targeted status of people that are both young and old. For example, a recent Massachusetts law reinforces absolute adult power over young people. The CRA (Child Requiring Assistance) law gives parents and schools the right to ask the court for help when young people do not go along with the "lawful and reasonable commands" of adults in homes and schools (Gershengorn, 2013). Young people and elders are affected by the legal, societal, and institutional norms and practices that marginalize and exclude them and give adults the power to act on and for young people and elders without their agreement. While elders may be revered for their presumed wisdom, they are nevertheless legally excluded from the workplace. While young people may be appreciated for their vigor, energy, and enthusiasm, their participation is likewise restricted.

While adultism and ageism are forms of oppression sharing the identity marker of age, we distinguish between the two, specifically naming *youth oppression* as the oppression of young people by adults and elders, and elder oppression as the oppression of elders by youth and adults (Love and Phillips, 2007). Some writers use the term "ageism" to refer interchangeably to the oppression of elders and young people. Rather than using the same term to refer to both types of oppression, we find it important to distinguish between the two, given the distinctive ways in which these two age-related forms of oppression play out in everyday life.

Our focus in this section is limited to illustrating the ways in which the mistreatment of young people and elders meets our theoretical framework for understanding oppression and providing examples of everyday manifestations of the oppression of young people and elders—that is, examples that are normalized by the culture, rather than examples that are dramatic or horrific. The litany of critical issues in the everyday lives of young people and elders illustrate the long-term consequences of the loss and/or absences of power among members of these two groups. Our focus is on creating a framework for understanding how these experiences illustrate not only mistreatment but oppression as well.

The elements of oppression described in the section on conceptual frameworks (selection 6) are underlying conceptual tools for the analysis of the experience of both young people and elders. For example, it is useful to think about the way schools have become more like prisons. The presence of metal detectors, police in schools, and school buildings without windows emphasize surveillance and indicate that society has accepted a view of young people as a criminal threat. Additionally, vouchers, charter schools, and public funds for private schools result in a massive divestment in public education. Young people with the fewest resources, especially black, brown, and poor youth, are left in public schools. The function of these schools change as they become more clearly an official segment of the school-to-prison pipeline. For example, in 2017, a law went into effect in Missouri mandating that elementary students who fight and injure another student will be charged with a Class E felony and can receive a sentence of up to four years in prison (Einenkel, 2017). These laws in public schools greatly increase the possibility that young people will end up in prison.

The mistreatment of elders takes many forms, including neglect, physical violence, financial abuse and sexual abuse. The Nursing Home Abuse Guide reports that "more than two (2) million cases of elder abuse are reported every year." The 2010 census shows that there are over 40 million elders in the United States, or "more than 13% of the population." "Almost one (1) out of every ten (10) elderly individuals will experience some form of elder abuse" (NursingHomeAbuseGuide.org, n.d.). Furthermore, in an effort to ensure that they continue to receive the income of elder residents, nursing homes have been charged with illegally forcing elders to remain in the institution rather than choosing where they wish to live.

Recognition of the oppression of young people and elders is hampered by the normalization of mistreatment, which renders the oppression invisible. A variety of laws and institutional arrangements make age the sole criteria for determining when an individual can leave school, drive a car, drink alcohol, get married, or join the armed services. Mandatory retirement ages and age-based health-care allocations clearly indicate the denial of power and privilege on the basis of age. Similar to the assertion of a former Harvard University president that biological difference accounted for the limited participation of women in math and science, there will be those who assume that biological and developmental differences justify the differential treatment of young people and elders. As the scientific community was quick to condemn the assertions of that university president, our goal is to increase the consciousness about the oppression of young people and elders so that objection to this oppression can be as clear and unequivocal (Bombardieri, 2005).

INTERNALIZED AGEISM AND ADULTISM

The designation of young people and elders as social identities is so widespread that people of every culture, language, religion, and nationality are sure that their ways of thinking about and responding to these identities are rooted in the rationality of laws, policies, and principles dictated by biology. Across many societies, people are sure that the control of members of these two groups, by those with more power, more resources, more strength, and more size, is justified by that size, strength, power, and possession of those resources. The assumption of the rightness of those with more power and more resources to make decisions about the lives of those with less power and fewer resources is shared not only by those of the dominant group but by those of the target group as well. Both young people and elders have internalized the belief that decisions regarding their lives are appropriately made by members of the dominant group (middle-aged adults). Bonnichsen (2003) contends:

> Very few young people actually feel solidarity with young people as a group . . . [Many young people] spend their entire childhood identifying with the perspective of adults . . . [and] feel that . . . other young people . . . actually deserve to be treated with disrespect . . . [Youth employ a variety of strategies] to dissociate themselves from other young people, trying to shed the negative status of childhood.

(p. 2)

Young people are encouraged and rewarded for practicing youth oppression toward other young people. Similar to the internalized racism that causes some black people to provide greater respect and deference to other black people who look and act more like white people, young people sometimes accord respect on an age-based scale and act out youth oppression on anyone younger, weaker, with fewer resources, and smaller than themselves.

The stereotypes, prejudices, and forms of discrimination against elders, discussed by Butler (selection 119), are practiced not only by middle-aged adults and younger people; they are also practiced and reinforced by elders with each other. "I'm having a senior moment," is a common expression among elders, normalizing the idea that forgetfulness is a condition of aging. This enforcement of the oppression of elders by elders constitutes internalized elder oppression. The depression sometimes associated with isolation, feeling unwanted, and fear of senility can be a manifestation of internalized ageism. Elders internalize feelings of loss, value, being a bother, worthlessness, feeling that they are unworthy of the caretaking of others, and living with the fear of one day being unable to take care of themselves. For both young people and elders, it is the acceptance of these negative stereotypes about themselves that makes it difficult to name their mistreatment as a form of oppression and to effectively organize to change it.

As in the case of elders, the internalization of the oppression by young people has many negative and dysfunctional consequences. One consequence is the enforcement of youth oppression by young people on other young people. For example, young people will often make sure that those younger than them follow the rules at school or in the family or report younger people to authorities when they fail to follow the rules. Another consequence of internalizing adultism is that young people learn how to play the roles of target and agent of oppression. All manifestations of oppression, including racism, sexism, classism, and the like, require people to play the role of target and agent of oppression. Youth oppression prepares young people to play the roles of target and agent, roles that help them function well in the maintenance of systems of oppression (Love, 2017).

Young people are taught to perform the role of subordinant[1] (target). Through that subordination, they learn to desire the role of dominant (agent). Concern about learning appropriate behavior in order to be safe is often the guise under which this socialization takes place. Young people (as subordinants) are taught that adults (as dominants) are entitled to speak for them and to make decisions for them. In turn, they learn not to trust their own thinking, decisions, or feelings. The internalization of the idea that dominants know best what is appropriate for subordinants and are entitled to make decisions for them is a key part of every manifestation of oppression. Learning these ideas of domination and subordination so thoroughly as young people effectively prepares them for future roles when they will be in charge of maintaining systems of oppression (Freire, 2000).

INTERCONNECTION BETWEEN YOUTH AND ELDER OPPRESSION
AND OTHER FORMS OF OPPRESSION

Other forms of oppression converge with elder oppression and youth oppression to produce differential results for members of particular intersecting social identity groups. The interaction between age-based oppression and racism, for instance, means that elders of color are more likely to have lower income than white elders, and that young people of color are more likely to attend underfunded schools with limited curricular offerings, police in the hallways, and metal detectors at the door. Youth of color are less likely to complete high school or college, are more likely to be placed in foster-care settings, and are five to ten times more likely to be imprisoned than white youth who display the same patterns of behavior (Fulbright-Anderson, Lawrence, Sutton, Susi, and Kubisch, 2005). A recent study by Stanford psychologists examining the effect of race on juvenile sentencing reveals that white adults who simply *imagine* youth offenders to be black develop policies that result in harsher treatment of all young people (Donald, 2012). African American youth, and in some cases Latino/a youth, receive fewer primary care, mental health, and asthma services than white youth, even when family income and health insurance are taken into account. Schools spend, on average, nearly $9,000 less per pupil on youth of color than on white youth.

Elder oppression intersects with classism and sexism to produce differences in the distribution of retirement resources for the elderly. Women of all ethnic groups live longer than men and generally have fewer economic or health-care resources than men in their old age. Women, poor and working-class people, and people of color often have lower paying jobs resulting in limited discretionary funds and lower contributions to Social Security. In old age, women of color and poor and working-class women have fewer social security benefits, and are less likely to have pensions from discretionary funds that were invested for retirement (O'Rand, cited by Calasanti and Slevin, 2001). Elder oppression intersects with heterosexism when same-sex partners cannot automatically collect survivor benefits that are restricted to "spouses."

When a young boy plays dress-up with his sisters and is ridiculed or told that his behavior is inappropriate, messages of adultism, sexism, heterosexism, and transgender oppression are conveyed simultaneously. Because the boy in this example could potentially experience name-calling, social isolation, or even violence for dressing, acting like, or simply aligning himself with girls, he is forced to perform a prescribed version of masculinity that clearly distinguishes his gender apart from that of his sisters and simultaneously conveys the ideas that it is shameful to be or act "like a girl." Ridicule and shame are often used to teach the role of dominant and subordinant to young people and is justified to be "for their own good." In their efforts to keep young people safe from potential violence, adults' "that's-just-the-way-it-is" attitude conveys a sense of powerlessness to youth who, as other forms of oppression are experienced, are thereby trained to accept them without questioning, challenging, or fighting back.

Infantilization functions on both the micro and macro levels. Infantilization employs the characteristics ascribed to youth to justify the consolidation of power into the hands of the dominant group. Speaking to elders, people with disabilities and people of color in the same tone that adults use to speak to babies and pets is an example of infantilization and leads to both individual and systematic confusion about appropriate interactions with and support for members of these groups. Describing the indigenous peoples of the Americas, Africa, Australia and other places as childlike was the rhetoric used by Western colonial powers to justify colonial acquisition of their land and resources, removal of power from their government and society, and exercise of cultural and physical genocide. The rhetoric of "developing nations and economies" conveys the image of youth "becoming," justifying the actions of imperial powers which dictate and prescribe how "developing" nations should orient their economic and political policies. Similarly, colonized and formerly colonized populations are seen as dependent (infantile), justifying their treatment as inferior (underdeveloped) and in need of the intervention of imperial (adult/developed) powers (DeJong, 2012).

GLOBAL DIFFERENCES IN THE TREATMENT OF YOUNG PEOPLE AND ELDERS

The treatment of young people and old people varies from one society to another, and within different cultural groups in a given society. For instance, research shows differences between Western and non-Western and between post-industrial and less-industrialized societies in the treatment of both young people and elders (Rogoff, 2003, p. 9). While the focus in this section is on the experience of young people and elders in US society, it is important to recognize the variations among and within cultural and socioeconomic groups globally as well as within the United States.

Different treatment does not connote oppression or the lack of oppression. In many societies, for instance, elders are revered based on the assumption that with age comes increased wisdom. At the same time, there is an assumption in many cultures that age brings inevitable senility and decline. We recognize that both the reverence of elders and youth and the oppression of elders and youth can exist within the same racial/cultural/familial context. Our research shows that this simultaneous revering and enforcement of oppression occurs across societies in Africa, Asia, South and Central America as well as Europe and North America. In addition, it is not limited to rural, urban, industrialized, agrarian, or post-technological contexts.

LIBERATION: ELIMINATING AGEISM AND ADULTISM AND
THE TRANSFORMATION OF SOCIETY

Age-based identities are shared by all humans, across race, gender, class, nationality, sexuality, language, religion, ability, culture, ethnicity, or any other identity, whether target or agent. Their specific meanings will differ in various cultures. Every single human is or has been young. Every human who lives long enough will become an elder. Age-based oppression affects all humans, and so it is in the interest of all humans to work for the elimination of elder and youth oppression. Our purpose in seeking a deeper understanding of oppression is to facilitate liberation, that is, the transformation of society through the elimination of age-based oppression. Here and there, we witness bits and parts of theory and models that contribute to our unfolding vision of a liberatory society.

Contemporary "Western" society has evolved a particular way of thinking about young people and elders that is rooted in structures of domination and subordination. A social justice perspective requires us to envision and develop responses that enable more equitable participation of elders and young people in society. For example, some organizations have young people on their board of directors who are central to making decisions and determining the direction of the organization with their adult colleagues. Groups like the Gray Panthers, whose membership is comprised of elders, are working to challenge ageist attitudes and put pressure on legislative bodies to create policies that protect elders from abuse and support views of elders as productive and important members of a multi-generational, diverse society (Woolf, 2005). Challenging adultist attitudes about young people's role in decision-making can increase the likelihood that young people's needs and perspectives are represented. Challenging ageist attitudes about elders' roles as participants in political and economic life can increase the likelihood that elders' needs and perspectives are represented.

In many parts of the world, young people, elders, and their allies are engaged in research and model-building that result in societal transformation and lead to the creation of a liberatory society. They are developing relationships, organizations, programs, and policies that enable young people and elders to participate in society from a position of equity. As we broaden our understanding of these manifestations of oppression and work toward the elimination of youth and elder oppression, young people and elders can increasingly anticipate living empowered lives with complete dignity and respect. This is a benefit for every single human.

THE SELECTIONS

The selections in the "Context" section address definitions of youth and elder oppression along with individual, institutional, societal, and cultural manifestations of these forms of oppression. Robert Butler (selection 119) defines elder oppression on the basis of attitudes, stereotypes, and behavior patterns that embody the mistreatment and oppression of elders and a discussion of institutional manifestations of ageism. John Bell (selection 116) defines youth oppression and describes common occurrences of adultism. Bell's discussion provides a method for examining individual behavior to determine the extent to which it perpetuates youth oppression. Sheets (selection 120) discusses the experiences of elders with disabilities. Looking at adultism on an institutional level, Giroux (selection 117) and Durkin (selection 118) discuss the ways young people are criminalized in contemporary society, and the increasing role of schools in funneling young people into the prison system.

The selections in "Voices," by Larabee, (selection 123) and Curry (selection 124), describe young people and elders' experience of youth and elder oppression. We note that it was challenging to find descriptions of the experience of youth oppression written by young people, as was locating the voices of elders; most descriptions of the experiences of young people and elders that we found were, more often than not, written by middle-aged adults. We think that this reflects both the oppression and the internalization of powerlessness by young people and elders. (We include some recent resources by young people and elders on the website.)

The selections in "Next Steps" offer strategies to eliminate youth and elder oppression and to move toward liberation. It includes specific suggestions for what allies can do. Jenny Sazama with Boston Area Youth (selection 126) describes strategies to learn about and interrupt youth oppression, and support the empowerment of young people. The BLM Criminalization of Youth Brief (selection 125) describes a vision for ending the criminalization and dehumanization of black youth throughout society. They provide suggestions to stimulate thinking about both individual and systemic and institutional changes that can help in the elimination of both racism and youth oppression. The DeJong and Love selection (129) describes engaging youth oppression as a critical social justice issue to be engaged in transforming all oppression. Gullette (selection 127) examines contemporary cultural assumptions that support elder oppression and encourages the development of coalitions to interrupt and defeat what the author describes as "new ageism." Markee (selection 128) provides a helpful discussion of specific things that allies of elders can do. Marge Larrabee's "Elders' Liberation Draft Policy" (selection 123) provides a good model for examining the oppression of elders from a position of empowerment and with a view toward liberation. In addition to a description of conditions for elders, this statement discusses how elders can work on ending internalized oppression, what they can do to promote their own liberation, and what allies can do to support elders to have good lives.

See companion website for additional resources and material: www.routledge.com/cw/readingsfordiversity.

Notes

* We ask that those who cite this work always acknowledge by name both the authors listed rather than either only citing the first author or using "et al." to indicate coauthors. Both collaborated equally in the conceptualization, development, and writing of this introduction.
1 We prefer the spelling *subordinant* because it parallels the term used to refer to dominants. We do not use the term *dominate* to refer to those in the dominant role. The use of the term *subordinate*, which is a modifying adjective, seems to contribute to the reduction and objectification of members of the group to which this term is applied.

References

Bombardieri, M. (2005, January 17). Summers' remarks on women draw fire. *The Boston Globe*. Retrieved April 8, 2009, from www.boston.com/news/local/articles/2005/01/17/summers_remarks_on_women_draw_fire/.

Bonnichsen, S. (2003). Objections to calling adultism an oppression. Retrieved December 13, 2008 from www.youthlib.com/notepad/archives/2003/12/objections_to_c.html.

Butler, R. N. (1975). *Why survive? Being old in America*. New York: Harper & Row.

Calasanti, T. M., and Slevin, K. F. (2001). *Gender, social inequalities and ageing*. Walnut Creek, CA: AltaMira Press.

DeJong, K. (2012). *On being and becoming: Young people's perspectives on status and power in childhood*. Unpublished manuscript. Amherst, MA: University of Massachusetts.

Donald, B. (2012). Stanford psychologists examine how race affects juvenile sentencing. Retrieved May 30, 2012 from http://news.stanford.edu/news/2012/may/race-juvenile-offenders-052412.html.

Einenkel, W. (2017). Missouri has a new law that makes fights in grade school a felony with up to 4 years of prison time. Retrieved April 27, 2017 from www.dailykos.com/story/2017/4/26/1656572/-Missouri-has-a-new-law-that-makes-fights-in-grade-school-a-felony-with-up-to-4-years-of-prison-time.

Freire, P. (2000). *Pedagogy of the oppressed*. New York: Continuum.

Fulbright-Anderson, K., Lawrence, K., Sutton, S., Susi, G. and Kubisch, A. (2005). *Structural racism and youth development: Issues, challenges, and implications*. Aspen Institute Roundtable on Community Change. Washington, DC: Aspen Institute.

Gershengorn, D. (2013). The Child Requiring Assistance Statute: A step in the right direction. Retrieved October 14, 2017 from https://bostonbarjournal.com/2013/07/10/the-child-requiring-assistance-statute-a-step-in-the-right-direction/.

Hardiman, R., Jackson, B. and Griffin, P. (2007). Conceptual foundations. In M. Adams, L. A. Bell and P. Griffin (eds.), *Teaching for diversity and social justice*, 2nd edition. New York: Routledge.

Love, B. J. (2017). *Understanding and healing the effects of internalized racism*. Seattle, WA: Rational Island Publishers.

Love, B. J. and Phillips, K. J. (2007). Ageism and adultism curriculum design. In M. Adams, L. A. Bell and P. Griffin (eds.), *Teaching for diversity and social justice*, 2nd edition. New York: Routledge.

NursingHomeAbuseGuide.org (n.d.). Nursing home abuse statistics. Retrieved October 12, 2017 from www.nursinghomeabuseguide.org/nursing-home-abuse-statistics/.

Rogoff, B. (2003). *The cultural nature of human development*. Oxford: Oxford University Press.

Woolf, L. (2005). *An in-depth look at ageism*. Retrieved June 30, 2006 from www.webster.edu/-woolflm/ageism.html.

116

Understanding Adultism

A Key to Developing Positive Youth-Adult Relationships

John Bell

Most of us are youth workers because we care about young people. Personally we want to both be effective and have good relationships with young people. . . .

To be successful in our work with young people, we must understand a particular condition of youth: that young people are often mistreated and disrespected simply because they are young. The word *adultism* refers to behaviors and attitudes based on the assumption that adults are better than young people, and entitled to act upon young people without their agreement. This mistreatment is reinforced by social institutions, laws, customs, and attitudes.

. . . [E]xcept for prisoners and a few other institutionalized groups, young people are more controlled than any other group in society. . . . [M]ost young people are told what to eat, what to wear, when to go to bed, when they can talk, that they will go to school, which friends are okay, and when they are to be in the house. . . . [T]he opinions of most young people are not valued; they are punished at the will or whim of adults; their emotions are considered "immature." In addition, adults reserve the right to punish, threaten, hit, take away "privileges," and ostracize young people when such actions are deemed to be instrumental in controlling or disciplining them.

If this were a description of the way a group of adults was treated, we would all agree that their oppression was almost total. However, for the most part, the adult world considers this treatment of young people as acceptable because we were treated in much the same way, and internalized the idea that "that's the way you treat kids." . . .

THE HEART OF IT

. . .

Adults have enormous importance in the lives of almost every young person. This fact may make it difficult to understand what I am calling *adultism*. Not everything the adult world does in relation to young people is *adultist*. It is certainly true that children and young people need love, guidance, rules, discipline, teaching, role modeling, nurturance, protection. Childhood and adolescence are a steady series of developmental stages, each of which has a different set of needs, issues, and difficulties. For example, a three year old needs a different amount of sleep than a 15 year old; or, what works to physically restrain a seven year old will not work with an 18 year old; or, how you explain conception and birth to an inquisitive toddler will be quite different from how you explain these to a sexually active teenager.

Differing cultural, ethnic, gender, class, or religious approaches to these developmental stages can further complicate the identification of *adultism*. For example, what is considered "weak" in one gender, may be considered "strong" in another; or, belching may be considered rude in one culture and an expression of appreciation in another; or, childhood sex play may be condoned in one culture and condemned in another.

The point is that no one act or policy or custom or belief is in itself necessarily *adultist*. Something can be labeled *adultist* if it involves a *consistent* pattern of disrespect and mistreatment that has any or all of the following affects on young people:

- an undermining of self-confidence and self-esteem;
- an increasing sense of worthlessness;
- an increasing feeling of powerlessness;
- a consistent experience of not being taken seriously;
- a diminishing ability to function well in the world;
- a growing negative self-concept;
- increasing destructive acting out;
- increasing self-destructive acting "in" (getting sick frequently, developing health conditions, attempting suicide, depression, etc.);
- feeling unloved or unwanted.

Certainly these serious conditions do not entirely stem from *adultism*. Other factors like sexism, racism, poverty, physical or mental disability, and so on, may also contribute to these results. But systematic disrespect and mistreatment over years simply because of being young are major sources of trouble.

EVIDENCE THAT ADULTISM EXISTS

Other "isms" like racism and sexism are well established and accepted as realities. They each have a huge body of literature and research documenting the effects and history of the oppression. There are novels, movies, media presentations, political organizations, and social movements devoted to illuminating and or eliminating the existence of the "ism."

The concept of *adultism*, the systematic mistreatment and disrespect of young people, is relatively new and has not been widely accepted as a reality. There is certainly much research and literature on children and youth, but very little that concludes that young people are an oppressed group in our society, with parallels to other such groups. Part of my effort in this article is to draw forth enough examples, primarily from the United States, to point to the reality of *adultism*.

COMMON STATEMENTS

Consider how the following comments are essentially disrespectful. What are the assumptions behind each of them? Do you remember having heard any of these as a younger person?

- "You're so smart for fifteen!"
- "When are you going to grow up?"
- "Don't touch that, you'll break it!"
- "As long as you are in my house, you'll do it!"
- "You're being childish."
- "You're so stupid (or clumsy, inconsiderate, etc.)!"
- "Go to your room!"
- "Don't ever yell at your mother like that!" (yelling)

- "She doesn't understand anything." (about a baby)
- "You are too old for that!" or "You're not old enough!"
- "Oh, it's only puppy love."
- "What do you know? You haven't experienced anything!"
- "It's just a stage. You'll outgrow it."

COMMON OCCURRENCES

PHYSICAL AND SEXUAL ABUSE

There are numerous examples of disrespect toward young people. Of course, there is the obvious oppressive treatment: physical and sexual abuse of young people. Official reports of child abuse reached 2.7 million in 1993.

OTHER PUNISHMENT AND THREATS

There is also a whole range of nonphysical punishments or threats: being routinely criticized, yelled at, invalidated, insulted, intimidated, or made to feel guilty with the effect of undermining a child's self-respect; being arbitrarily or unfairly "grounded" or denied "privileges." If young people protest against their mistreatment, they are often subjected to more punishment.

DENIED CONTROL

Young people are denied control and often even influence over most of the decisions that affect their bodies, their space, and their possessions. For example, most adults seem to think they can pick up little children or kiss them or pull their cheeks or touch their hair without asking or without its being mutual. Adults can often be seen grabbing things out of children's hands without asking.

VERBAL INTERACTIONS

Most young people know that in a disagreement with an adult, their word will not be taken over the adult's. Most adults talk down to children, as if children could not understand them. Adults often talk about a young person with the young person present as if he or she were not there. Many adults give young people orders to do things or lay down rules with no explanation. Adults, in general, do not really listen to young people, do not take the concerns of a young person as seriously as they would an adult's, and have a hard time hearing the thinking of young people as worthy of adult respect, let alone on a par with the quality of adult thinking. Yet young people are expected to listen to adults all the time.

COMMUNITY INCIDENTS

Adolescent young people are frequently followed by security guards in stores, passed over by clerks who serve adults in line behind them, chased from parks or gathering places for no good reason by police, assumed by passing adults to "be up to no good." The media often promote negative images and stereotypes of them, especially of urban youth and black youth.

SCHOOL EXAMPLES

Schools subject students to incredible control through the use of hall passes, detention, suspension, expulsion, and other penalties. Any community certainly needs rules to live by, but the rules in most school communities are *imposed* on young people and enforced by the adult staff.

Consider these examples:

- Teachers sometimes yell at students with impunity, but students are disciplined if they yell back at teachers.
- Young people are sometimes punished unfairly because adults feel frustrated.
- Students are forced to accept their "grades" that, over time, cause students to eventually internalize a lifelong view of themselves as "smart" or "average" or "dumb"—with profound impact on many aspects of their lives. However, students do not get to officially "grade" teachers. If a student receives an "F," it is assumed the student failed, not the teacher.
- Young people have no real power in the important decisions that affect their lives in school.

SOCIETAL ADULTISM

LAWS

There is a different set of laws for young people. They do not have the same rights as adults. Of course, some laws specifically protect young people from mistreatment but other laws unduly restrict the life and freedom of young people. Curfew ordinances that exist in many communities apply to young people but not to adults. In divorce cases, until a recent landmark custody case, young people were not even permitted to have a voice in deciding which parent, if either, they wished to live with.

CHILD DEVELOPMENT LITERATURE AND EDUCATION

An institutional example of *adultism* can be found in the literature of child development, which is full of misinformation and unfounded claims about young people that severely underestimates what young people are capable of. For example, in one classic textbook used by many students of child development, *The Magic Years* by Selma Freiberg, the author states that the only reason an infant before six months of age cries is because of physical pain. An infant has no emotional pain before this age, she says, because "an infant's intelligence has not yet developed the cognitive apparatus that gives rise to emotional responses." Many parents, including myself, in observing their own infants closely, know that this is not true. Yet, young child development professionals, often without children, are taught a distorted view of infant functioning as if it were gospel.

THE EFFECT OF CULTURAL PRACTICES: AN INTERESTING EXAMPLE

Generations of young people in western culture have grown up with their development limited by vast cultural biases that consistently underestimate human potential or misunderstand human development. For example, Joseph Chilton Pierce, in his *Crack in the Cosmic Egg*, found that in certain Ugandan cultures, infants reach the milestones of sitting, walking, and talking in half the time it takes for children in the United States. This seems to challenge accepted western norms. Researchers hypothesized two reasons for such seemingly accelerated development:

- From the moment of birth until well into the toddler stage, infants spend most of their time strapped skin to skin next to their mothers. From this vantage point the infants intimately experience the rhythms of body movement and speech, the cues in the environment that their mothers paid attention to, and constant tactile closeness.
- When not being carried, infants and toddlers were given loving massages for long periods every day by their mothers and other women in the community.

Researchers concluded that the combinations of these two practices stimulate complex neurological, motor, and hormonal systems of the infants to speed sitting, walking, and talking compared to what is considered "normal" in the West. The mere existence of such huge differences in the rate of development raises large questions about our assumptions about what is normal.

(The interesting back end of the Ugandan example is that at age five, after this extremely intimate early childhood experience, the children go through a rite of passage that includes being sent alone into the forest for several days, then being forced to leave their mother's home and sent to live with another relative. This shock appears to arrest the earlier rapid development, and maturation slows way down.)

GENERAL ADULT ATTITUDES

Many of us have heard older people say to us or other young people something like, "Growing up is giving up. You'd better get used to it." It is the accumulation of disappointments, losses, smashed dreams, unaccepted love, and other such painful experiences that lead adults to say things like that. This crippling attitude is gradually forced upon young people. It is like a contagion, a virus about aging.

INSTITUTIONAL EXAMPLES

Young people in this country are forced to go to school for 12 years, whether school is an effective learning environment for them or not. They are forced by law and by parents (with the exception of those who exercise the demanding option of home schooling). If their spirit, energy, or learning style does not dovetail with the prevailing teacher, school, or educational philosophy, they begin to "fail," have "special needs," are "tracked," and may eventually be labeled as a "dropout." Throughout the 12 years, students have no voice, no power, no decision-making avenues to make significant changes. A critique of our educational system is beyond the scope of this article. Suffice it to say here that while society's motivation of providing education for all its young people is laudable, the school system as an institution perpetuates *adultism*.

Another institutional example is the absence of socially responsible, productive, and connected roles for young people in most societies. Certainly in the United States, young people find few jobs, no real policy-making roles, no positions of political power, and no high expectations of young people's contributions to society.

On the other hand, the youth market is exploited for profit as the manufacturing and entertainment industries manipulate styles, fads, popularity, and all other aspects of mass culture

A MIRROR

A handy mirror for reflecting what may be *adultist* behavior is to ask oneself questions like the following:

- "Would I treat an adult this way?"
- "Would I talk to an adult in this tone of voice?"
- "Would I grab this out of an adult's hand?"
- "Would I make this decision for an adult?"
- "Would I have this expectation for an adult?"
- "Would I limit an adult's behavior this way?"
- "Would I listen to an adult friend's problem in this same way?"

Sometimes the answer may be "no" for good reason, depending on the circumstance. For example, I insist that my six year old son hold my hand when crossing the street, but not my 18 year old daughter. However, many times there is no justifiable reason for treating a younger person differently except habit and attitude. If your "no" sounds a little hollow, it might be worth re-examining your reasons for doing it.

THE EMOTIONAL LEGACY

I hope this short list of examples begins to put our work with young people in a larger context. Most of the examples I used have been reported to me by young people. They consistently report that the main message they get from the adult world is that they are not as important as adults; they do not feel that they are taken seriously; they have little or no power.

They say that the emotional legacy of years of this kind of treatment is a heavy load, which can include any or all of the following: anger, feelings of powerlessness, insecurity, depression, lack of self-confidence, lack of self-respect, hopelessness, feeling unloved and unwanted.

What are some possible results of such feelings on their behavior, especially as they get into adolescence and early adulthood?

- Some act "out" by bullying, being prone to violence, rebelling against the "norm," leaving home early, and so on.
- Some act "in" by becoming self-destructive: suicide, alcohol and drug abuse, depression, etc.
- Some gain a sense of belonging or safety by joining a gang, a clique, a club, teams.
- Some isolate themselves, being lonely, not asking for help, not having any close relationships, not trusting.

Again, *adultism* is not the only source of such behaviors, but it surely plays a major role.

A LINK TO OTHER FORMS OF OPPRESSION

There is another important reason for understanding and challenging *adultism*. The various ways we were disrespected and mistreated have, over time, robbed us of huge amounts of our human power, access to our feelings, confidence in our thinking and ability to act, and enjoyment of living. The pain we experience as young people helps condition us to play one of two roles as we get older: to accept further mistreatment as women, as people of color, as workers, etc., or to flip to the other side of the relationship and act in oppressive ways toward others who are in relatively less powerful positions than ours.

A simple illustration might help make this clear. Picture this: a sixth grader is humiliated by the teacher in front of the class for not doing the math problem at the board correctly. The recess bell rings. He is fuming. He feels disrespected. He goes outside and picks on someone to get his feelings out. Whom does he pick on? Someone smaller and often someone younger. And so it goes: the 6th grader picks on the 5th grader. The 5th grader turns and knocks down the 3rd grader. The 3rd grader hits the 1st grader. The 1st grader goes home and picks on his little sister. The little sister turns and kicks the cat.

We can observe among a group of children the mistreatment being passed down among them. It is being passed down the line of physical power, bigger to smaller, and often older to younger.

The significance of this early experience becomes clearer when it is generalized to other forms of the abuse of power. Men, for example, who were routinely beaten as little boys, grow up to be wife beaters. This is a clinical truism. Similarly, white people, disrespected as children, turn the same attitude, embellished with misinformation, on people of color.

This is one of the pervasive and lasting effects of the mistreatment of young people. Bullies have been bullied. Abusers have been abused. People who have been put down put others down. If a person had not been disrespected and mistreated over and over again as a child and young person, that person would not willingly accept being treated that way as he got older, nor would he willingly heap disrespect on others.

Adultism, racism, sexism, and other "isms" all reinforce each other. The particular ways young people are treated or mistreated are inseparable from their class, gender, or ethnic background. However, the phenomena of being disrespected simply because of being young holds true across diverse backgrounds.

. . .

117

Terrorizing School Children in the American Police State

Henry A. Giroux

Americans live in an age, to rephrase W.E.B. Dubois, in which violence has become the problem of the twenty-first century. As brutalism comes to shape every public encounter, democratic values and the ethical imagination wither under the weight of neoliberal capitalism and post-racial racism. Giving way to the poisonous logics of self-interest, privatization, and the unfettered drive for wealth, American society reneges on the social contract and assumes the role of a punishing state. Under the regime of a predatory neoliberalism, compassion and respect for the other are viewed increasingly with contempt while the spectacle of violence titillates the multitudes and moves markets. A free-market mentality now drives and corrupts politics, destroys social protections, celebrates a hyper-competitiveness, and deregulates economic activity. As politics is emptied of any sense of social responsibility, the apostles of casino capitalism preach that allegedly amoral economic activity exacts no social costs, and in doing so they accelerate the expanding wasteland of disposable goods and people. One consequence is a vast and growing landscape of human suffering, amplified by a mass-mediated metaphysics of retribution and violence that more and more creeps into every commanding institution of American society, now serving a myriad of functions such as sport, spectacle, entertainment, and punishment. Alain Badiou rightly calls those who run our current political system a "regime of gangsters." These so called gangsters produce a unique form of social violence. According to Badiou, they:

> Privatize everything. Abolish help for the weak, the solitary, the sick and the unem-ployed. Abolish all aid for everyone except the banks. Don't look after the poor; let the elderly die. Reduce the wages of the poor, but reduce the taxes on the rich. Make everyone work until they are ninety. Only teach mathematics to traders, reading to big property-owners and history to on-duty ideologues. And the execution of these commands will in fact ruin the lives of millions of people.

Increasingly, institutions such as schools, prisons, detention centers, and our major economic, cultural and social institutions are being organized around the production of violence. Rather than promote democratic values and a respect for others or embrace civic values, they often function largely to humiliate, punish, and demonize any vestige of social responsibility. Violence both permeates and drives foreign policy, dominates popular culture, and increasingly is used to criminalize a wide range of social behaviors, especially among African-Americans. In part, the totality of violence in American society can be understood in terms of its doubling function. At one level, violence produces its own legitimating aesthetic as part of a broader spectacle of entertainment, offering consumers the pleasure of instant gratification, particularly in the visibility and celebration of extreme violence. This is evident in television series such as Game of Thrones and Hannibal, endless Hollywood films such as Dread (2012), Django (2012), and Mad Max: Fury Road (2015), and video games such as Grand Theft Auto 4 (2008), and Mortal Combat (2011), and Battlefield Hardline (2015).

At another level, violence functions as a brutalizing practice used by the state to squelch dissent, incarcerate poor minorities of class and color, terrorize immigrants, wage a war on minority youth, and menace individuals and groups considered disposable or a threat. Not only does such violence destroy the conditions and institutions necessary to develop a democratic polity, it also accelerates abusive forms of punitiveness and control that extend from the prisons to other institutions such as schools. In this instance, violence becomes the ultimate force propagating what might be called punishment creep. The punishment creep that has moved from prisons to other public spheres now has a firm grip on both schools and the daily rituals of everyday life. Margaret Kimberly captures one instance of the racist underside of punishment creep. She writes: "Black people are punished for driving, for walking down the street, for having children, for putting their children in school, for acting the way children act, and even for having children who are killed by other people. We are punished, in short, because we still exist."

Violence in America has always been defined partly by a poisonous mix of chauvinism, exceptionalism, and terrorism that runs through a history marked by genocidal assaults against indigenous Native Americans, the brutality of slavery, and a persistent racism that extends from the horror of lynchings and chain gangs to a mass incarceration state that criminalizes black behavior and subjects many black youth to the shameful dynamics of the school-to-prison-pipeline and unprecedented levels of police abuse. Violence is the premier signature of what Ta-Nehisi Coates calls "The Dreamers," those individuals and groups who have "signed on, either actively or passively, to complicity in everything from police shootings to real estate redline, which crowds blacks into substandard housing in dangerous neighborhoods . . . The Dream is about the totality of white supremacy in American history and its cumulative weight on African-Americans, and how one attempts to live with that." In part, violence whether produced by the state, corporations, or racist individuals is difficult to abstract from an expression of white supremacy, which functions as an index for demanding "the full privileges of the state."

Police violence against African-Americans has become highly visible and thrust into the national spotlight as a result of individuals recording acts of police abuse with their cell phones and other tools of the new technologies. In the last few years, there has been what seems like a torrent of video footage showing unarmed black people being assaulted by the police. For instance, there is the shocking video of Walter Scott being shot in the back after fleeing from his car; Eric Garner dying as a result of being put in a chokehold by a white policeman who accused him of illegally selling cigarettes; the tragic killing of Freddie Gray who after making eye contact with a police officer was put in a police van and purposely given a jarring ride that resulted in his death; and the needless shooting of 12-year-old Tamir Rice for playing with a pellet gun in the snow in a park, and so it goes. All of these deaths are morally indefensible and are symptomatic of the deep-seated racism and propensity for violence in many police forces in the United States.

Yet, as Jaeah Lee observes, while such crimes have attracted national attention, the "use of force by cops in schools. . . . has drawn far less attention [in spite of the fact that] over the past five years at least 28 students have been seriously injured, and in one case shot to death, by so-called school resource officers—sworn, uniformed police assigned to provide security on k-12 campuses." Increasingly as public schools hand over even routine disciplinary problems to the police, there is a resurgence of cops in schools. There are over 17,000 school resource officers in more than half of the schools in the United States. In spite of the fact that violence in schools has dropped precipitously, school resource officers are the fastest growing segment of law enforcement.

In part, the militarizing of schools and the accompanying surge of police officers are driven by the fear of school shootings, particularly in the aftermath of the Columbine High School tragedy in 1999, and the massacre that took place at Sandy Hook Elementary School in 2013, both of which have been accentuated by the ever present wave of paranoia that followed the terrorist attacks of 9/11. What advocates of putting police in the schools refuse to acknowledge is that the presence of police in schools has done nothing to stop such mass shootings. While the fear of school shootings are overestimated, the fact remains that schools are still one of the safest places for children to be. Caught under the weight of a culture of fear and a rush to violence, many young people in schools are the most recent victims of a punishing state in a society that "remains in a state of permanent, endless war," a war that is waged through militarized policies at home and abroad.

What has become clear is that cops in schools do not make schools safer. Erik Eckholm reporting for the New York Times stated that judges, youth advocates, parents, and other concerned citizens "are raising alarm about what they have seen in the schools where officers are already stationed: a surge in criminal charges against children for misbehavior that many believe is better handled in the principal's office." In Texas, police officers have written "more than 100,000 misdemeanor tickets each year" and many of these students "face hundreds of dollars in fines, community service, and in some cases, a lasting record that could affect applications for jobs or the military." The transformation of disciplinary problems into criminal violations has often resulted in absurd if not tragic results. For instance, in 2009, in Richardson, Texas "a 14-year-old boy with Asperger's syndrome was given a $364 police citation for using an expletive in his classroom." It gets even more ludicrous. "A 12-year-old student in Stuart, Florida, was arrested in November 2008 for 'disrupting a school function.' The 'disruption' was that the student had 'passed gas.'"

Similarly, a number of civil rights groups have reported that the presence of police in schools often "means more suspensions, which disproportionately affect minority students." Many of the young people who end up in court are poor black and brown students, along with students with disabilities. What must be recognized is that schools in general have become combat zones where it is routine for many students to be subjected to metal detectors, surveillance cameras, uniformed security guards, weapons searches, and in some cases SWAT team raids and police dogs sniffing for drugs. Under such circumstances, the purpose of schooling appears to be to contain and punish young people, especially those marginalized by race and class, rather than educate them. What is beyond doubt is that "Arrests and police interactions . . . disproportionately affect low-income schools with large African-American and Latino populations." For the many disadvantaged students being funnelled into the "school-to-prison pipeline," schools ensure that their futures look grim indeed, as their educational experiences acclimatize them to forms of carceral treatment. There is more at work here than a flight from responsibility on the part of educators, parents, and politicians who support and maintain policies that fuel this expanding edifice of law enforcement against the young and disenfranchised. Underlying the repeated decisions to turn away from helping young people is the growing sentiment that youth, particularly minorities of color and class, constitute a threat to adults and the only effective way to deal with them is to subject them to mind-crushing punishment. Students being miseducated, criminalized, and arrested through a form of penal pedagogy in prison-type schools provides a grave reminder of the degree to which the ethos of containment and punishment now creeps into spheres of everyday life that were largely immune in the past from this type of state and institutional violence.

No longer are schools spaces of joy, critical teaching, and support, as too many are now institutions of containment and control that produce pedagogies of conformity and oppression and in the name of teaching to the test serve to kill the imagination. Within such schools, the lesson that young people are learning about themselves is that they can't engage in critical thinking, be trusted, rely on the informed judgments of teachers and administrators, and that their behavior is constantly subject to procedures that amount to both an assault on their dignity and a violation of their civil liberties. Schools have become institutions in which creativity is viewed as a threat, harsh discipline a virtue, and punishment the reward for not conforming to what amounts to the dictates of a police state. How many more images of young school children in handcuffs do we have to witness before it becomes clear that the educational system is broken, reduced largely to a punishing factory defined by a culture of fear and an utter distrust of young people?

According to the Advancement Project, schools have become increasingly intolerant of young people, imposing draconian zero tolerance policies on them by furthering a culture steeped in criminalizing often minor, if not trivial, student behaviors. What is truly alarming is not only the ways in which young people are being ushered into the criminal justice system and treated less as students than as criminals, but the harsh violence to which they are often subjected by school resource officers. According to a report by Mother Jones, Jonathan Hardin, a Louisville Metro Police officer, in 2014 "was fired after his alleged use of force in two incidents at Olmsted Academy North middle school: He was accused of punching a 13-year-old student in the face for cutting the cafeteria line, and a week later of putting another 13-year-old student in a chokehold, allegedly knocking the student unconscious and causing a brain injury." In a second incident that year, "Cesar Suquet, then a 16-year-old high school student in Houston, was being escorted by an officer out of the principal's office after a discussion about Suquet's confiscated cell phone. Following a verbal exchange, police officer Michael Y'Barbo struck Suquet at least 18 times with a police baton, injuring him on his head, neck and elsewhere." Y'Barbo claimed that beating a student with a police baton was "reasonable and necessary" and "remains on regular assignment including patrol." There are have also been incidents where students have been shot, suffered brain injuries, and have been psychologically traumatized. Jaeah Lee cites a young black high school student in Detroit who after a troubling interaction with a school police officer speaks for many young people about the dread and anxiety that many students experience when police occupy their schools. He states that "Many young people today have fear of the police in their communities and schools."

If one important measure of a democracy is how a society treats its children, especially young children who are black, brown, or suffer from disabilities, there can be little doubt that American society is failing. As the United States increasingly models its schools after prisons, students are no longer viewed as a social investment in the future. A deadly mixture of racism and violence in the 21st century has become increasingly evident in the violence being waged against young people in American schools. If students in general are now viewed as a potential threat, black students are regarded increasingly as criminals. One result is that schools increasingly have come to resemble war zones, spaces marked by distrust, fear, and demonization. With more police in the schools than ever before, security has become more important than providing children with a critical education and supportive learning environment. As authority in many of the schools is often handed over to the police and security forces who are now asked to deal with all alleged disciplinary problems, however broadly defined, the power and autonomy of teachers and school administrators are weakened at the expense of the safety of the students. This loss of authority is clear in New York City where school administrators have no control over security forces who report directly to local police departments.

In most cases, the disciplinary problems that take place in schools involve trivial infractions such as violating a dress code, scribbling on a desk, or holding a 2-inch toy gun. The assault on children in the public schools suggest that black and brown children cannot view schools as safe places where they can be given a quality education. Instead, schools have become sites of control, testing, and punishment all too eager to produce pedagogies of repression, and more than willing to erect, once again, what has been called the school-to-prison pipeline, especially for youth of color. Roxane Gay is right in observing that

> Black children are not allowed to be children. They are not allowed to be safe, not at home, not at pool parties, not driving or sitting in cars listening to music, not walking down the street, not in school. For black children, for black people, to exist is to be endangered. Our bodies receive no sanctity or safe harbor.

It is inconceivable that in an alleged democracy poor minorities at all grade levels in the public schools are subjected to shameful criminal practices such as being handcuffed and carted off to jail for minor incidents – and that such draconian practices could take place in a society that views itself as a democracy. Stripped of their public mission as institutions that nurture young people to become informed, critically engaged citizens, schools have become punishing factories all too willing to turn disciplinary authority over to the police and to usher students into the harsh bureaucracy of the criminal justice system.

One recent example of a particularly disturbing incident of police brutality was captured in a series of videos recorded in West Spring High School in South Carolina. Prior to the incident being filmed, a young black student named Shakara took out her cellphone in class. The teacher asked her for it and when she refused to hand it over, she was asked to leave the class. The teacher then called the vice principal. Rather than attempt to defuse the situation, the vice principal called for a School Resource Officer. At this point, Officer Ben Fields enters the classroom. One of Shakara's classmates, Niya Kenny, asked her classmates to start filming because as she put it: "I told them to start filming because we know his reputation—well, I know it." In what follows, as filmed by one of the students, Officer Ben

Fields approaches the young woman, appears to give her no time to stand up and proceeds by grabbing her left arm while placing his right arm around her neck; he then lifts her desk, pulls her out of her seat, slams her to the ground, and drags her across the floor before handcuffing her. The video is difficult to watch given the extreme level of violence used against a high school student. The young woman was arrested as was Kenny, who both filmed the incident and loudly protested the treatment of Shakara. Fields was fired soon afterwards, but incredulously both students are being charged with "disturbing schools, a crime punishable by up to ninety days in jail or a thousand dollar fine."

What has emerged after the incident went viral was information indicating that Fields had a previous reputation for being aggressive with students, and he was viewed as a threat by many students who nicknamed him "Officer Slam." Moreover, he had a previous record of violently assaulting people. The question that should be asked as a result of this shocking act of police violence against a young black girl is not how Fields got a job in a school working with children, but what kind of society believes that police should be in the school in the first place. Whatever happened to teacher and administrator responsibility? Sadly, it was a school administrator who called in the police at Spring Valley High School because the student would not turn over her phone. Even worse, when Sheriff Leon Lott announced his decision to fire Fields, he pointed out that the classroom teacher and administrator supported the actions of the police officer and made it clear that "they also had no problems with the physical part." Both the teacher and administrator should be fired. This incident was in all probability a simple disciplinary problem that should have been handled by responsible educators. Students should not be treated like criminals. It is one thing to not assume responsibility for students, but another to subject them to brutal assaults by the police.

Lawlessness runs deep in American society and has been normalized. Brutal attacks on defenseless children rarely get the attention they deserve and when they do the corporate media refuses to acknowledge that America has become a suicidal society willing even to sacrifice its own children to an expanding punishing state that protects the interests of the corporate and financial elite. How else to explain the shameless defense of such a brutal assault against a young black girl by pundits such as CNN's Harry Houck and Don Lemon, who implied that such violence was warranted because Shakara did not respect the officer, as if the beating of a black child by a police officer, who happens also to be a body-builder, who can lift 300 pounds, justifies such actions. This is a familiar script in which black people are often told that whatever violence they are subject to is legitimate because they acted out of place, did not follow rules that in reality oppress them, or simply refused to fall in line. The other side of this racist script finds expression in those who argue that any critique of the police endangers public safety. In this dangerous discourse, the police are the victims, a line of argument recently voiced in different ways by both President Obama and by James Comey, the director of the Federal Bureau of Investigation. This discourse not only refuses to recognize the growing visibility of police violence, it shores up one of the foundations of the authoritarian state, suggesting that the violence propagated by the police should not be subject to public scrutiny. As an editorial in the New York Times pointed out, this "formulation implies that for the police to do their jobs, they need to have free rein to be abusive. It also implies that the public would be safer if Americans with cellphones never started circulating videos of officers battering suspects in the first place. . . . This trend is straight out of Orwell."

Educators, young people, parents and others concerned about violence in schools need to organize and demand that the police be removed from school. Not only is their presence a waste of taxpayer's money and an interference with children's education, they also pose a threat to student safety. Instead of putting police in schools, money should be spent on more guidance teachers, social workers, teachers, community intervention workers, and other professionals who are educated and trained to provide a safe and supportive environment for young people. It is particularly crucial to support those social services, classroom practices, and policies that work to keep students in schools. Everything possible should be done to dismantle the school-to-prison pipeline and the underlying forces that produce it. At the same time, more profound change must take place on a national level since the violence waged by the police is symptomatic of a society now ruled by a financial elite who trade in cruelty, punishment, and despair. American society is broken, and the violence to which it appears addicted to will continue until the current configurations of power, politics, inequality, and injustice are eliminated.

The increasing visibility of police brutality in schools and in the streets speaks to a larger issue regarding the withering of democracy in the United States and the growing lawlessness that prevails in a society in which violence is both a spectacle and sport–and one of the few resources left to use to address social problems. America is paying a horrible price for turning governance at all levels over to people for whom violence serves as the default register for addressing important social issues. The Spring Valley High School case is part of a larger trend that has turned schools across the country into detention centers and educators into hapless bystanders as classroom management is ceded to the police. What we see in this incident and many others that have not attracted national attention because they are not caught on cellphones are the rudiments of a growing police state. Violence is now a normalized and celebrated ideal for how America defines itself–an ideal that views democracy as an excess or, even worse, a pathology. This is something Americans must acknowledge, interrogate, and resist if they don't want to live under a system of total terror and escalating violence.

118

Police Make Life Hell for Youth of Color

Kathy Durkin

Going to the grocery store, visiting a friend and walking home from work or school are all ordinary, everyday occurrences. But not so for hundreds of thousands of people, mostly from African American and Latin@ communities, who are stopped, questioned, asked for their I.D., searched and often arrested here in New York—and around the country. It happens to many youth and even to children.

At a time when more white people appear to be rejecting racism at the polls, racial profiling by police departments and other state agencies is on the rise. It is systemic and deeply entrenched in the "criminal justice system" nationwide.

Statistics given in new studies and reports starkly bear this out. But the statistics cannot convey the intimidation, anxiety and anger that so many people, especially Black and Latin@ youth, must live with on a daily basis, nor the effect this can have throughout their lives on them and their families.

In the first quarter of this year, New York City police, by their own report, stopped, questioned and/or searched 145,098 people, more than half of them African Americans. At this alarming rate, a record 600,000 people will be stopped this year.

In the last two years, nearly 1 million New Yorkers were harassed by police in this manner. 90 percent of them people of color. That's 1,300 a day. And it's legally allowed.

These operations, just in the past two years, have put more than 1 million innocent people, mostly African American and Latin@, into the huge police database; they are subject to future criminal investigations merely by their inclusion there.

The New York Civil Liberties Union (NYCLU) is challenging the legality of these potentially discriminatory practices and demanding information on the database kept by the NYPD—which the department refuses to turn over. It contains personal information on everyone stopped by police, though the vast majority—90 percent—have not been charged with any crimes.

The NYCLU is also demanding full disclosure from the NYPD about police shootings in this city. The full story of this horror is not known. In addition to the terrible, tragic and totally unjustified killings of unarmed individuals like Sean Bell, Amadou Diallo, Ousmane Zongo and Patrick Dorismund, countless other people of color have been shot. Yet the NYPD refuses to reveal what proportion of those shot over the last 10 years have been members of oppressed nationalities. In the two years prior to that, it was 90 percent (nyclu.org).

Another aspect of the NYPD's racial profiling scheme is the campaign of terror targeting youth for possessing miniscule amounts of marijuana. This, too, usually happens in communities of color, even though social studies show a higher rate of marijuana use among white youth (nyclu.org). In 2007 alone, police arrested more than 100 people per day, or 39,700 in total, for this so-called crime.

The NYCLU has just issued a report entitled, "The Marijuana Arrest Crusade in New York City: Racial Bias in Police Policy 1997–2007," by Prof. Harry G. Levin and Deborah Peterson Small. It describes the NYPD's campaign against oppressed youth. Of the nearly 400,000 people arrested in that 10-year period, 205,000 were African Americans and 122,000 were Latin@s. This represented a tenfold increase over the previous 10-year period.

Since decriminalization in 1977, the possession of a small amount of marijuana has not constituted a "crime" in New York City—as long as it is not shown in public. Possession since then has been merely a "violation," such as speeding and other traffic infractions.

However, the police frequently stop Black and Latin@ youth and then arrest them on the charge of misdemeanor possession—when, most of the time, this is not the case. High school students are kept in jail overnight until they go to court. Then they are pressured into a plea bargain, usually with an overworked, court-appointed attorney representing them.

In a city where police can gun down a young man like Sean Bell just hours before his wedding and get off with not even a slap on the wrist, youth stopped by cops never know what might happen to them.

These youth are then labeled with criminal records, which will follow them for the rest of their lives and can create future obstacles for them in higher education, employment and housing. They're also driven into the "criminal justice" system—their fingerprints and photographs go into the NYPD database—when they've done nothing wrong.

It is well known that there is serious drug abuse in many high-pressure professions in this city, yet the police don't occupy financial centers or carry out random searches in wealthy neighborhoods.

Rafael Mutis, coordinator of 7 Neighborhood Action Partnership Network, which works to repeal the draconian New York State Rockefeller drug laws, explains that "drug use" has become a pretext for stop-and-frisk searches in low-income neighborhoods. "They don't go after people on Wall Street," he said, "where there's a daily snowstorm" of cocaine use (highbridgehorizon.com).

It is no coincidence that police repression has increased even as billionaire Mayor Michael Bloomberg and his Wall Street cronies are trying to make New York City a haven for the super-rich, and the real-estate tycoons are gentrifying working-class neighborhoods as fast as they can. "Law-enforcement" agencies are helping them out by stepping up the intimidation of low-income and oppressed people to suppress opposition and try to drive them further out of the city.

All people need to show solidarity with the oppressed communities, especially the youth, in this struggle against police repression.

119

Ageism

Another Form of Bigotry

Robert N. Butler

Just as racism and sexism are based on ethnicity and gender, ageism is a form of systematic stereotyping and discrimination against people simply because they are old. As a group, older people are categorized as rigid in thought and manner, old-fashioned in morality and skills. They are boring, stingy, cranky, demanding, avaricious, bossy, ugly, dirty, and useless.

An ageist younger generation sees older people as different from itself; it subtly ceases to identify with its elders as human beings. Old men become geezers, old goats, gaffers, fogies, coots, gerries, fossils, and codgers, and old women are gophers and geese. A crone, hag, or witch is a withered old woman.

Ageism takes shape in stereotypes and myths, outright disdain and dislike, sarcasm and scorn, subtle avoidance, and discriminatory practices in housing, employment, pension arrangements, health care, and other services. Older persons are subject to physical, emotional, social, sexual, and financial abuse. They are the focus of prejudice regarding their capacity for work and sexual intimacy, which Freud described as the two most important human activities. Taking away the validation of work or purposeful activities and demeaning the capacity for love are surely the most profound forms of age prejudice.

Historically, older persons have been venerated in most societies and cultures *in word*, although not always in deed. In fact, to be old or disabled was always a liability for practical reasons. Nomadic groups from North Africa to Alaska abandoned their old when the welfare of the entire tribe or group was at stake.

The term *ageism*, which I introduced in 1968, is now part of the English language. It is identical to any other prejudice in its consequences. The older person feels ignored or is not taken seriously and is patronized. Anthropologist Barbara Myerhoff speaks about "death by invisibility" when she describes an older woman who, "unseen," was "accidentally" killed by a bicyclist.

This invisibility extends to emergencies, such as the tragic case of September 11, 2001, in New York City. Animal activists evacuated dogs and cats within twenty-four hours after the World Trade Center was attacked, while disabled or older persons were abandoned in their apartments for up to seven days before ad hoc medical teams arrived to rescue them. Older persons were also invisible in the devastation caused by Hurricane Katrina in New Orleans.

Reminiscent of the great social scientist George Mead's concept of the "looking glass self," older persons may turn ageist prejudice inward, absorbing, accepting, and identifying with the discrimination. Some examples:

- Simone De Beauvoir, author of *The Coming of Age*, described her disgust at growing old, although she wrote lovingly of her own mother's aging in *A Very Easy Death*.
- Comedian George Burns noted the unfortunate tendency of old people to conform to their stereotype—what he called the old person's "act"—by learning to shuffle about and decondition in a kind of identification and collaboration with the ageist society that demeans them.
- Yale psychologist Becca R. Levy reports that constant bombardment of negative stereotypes increases blood pressure. *Ageism can make an older person sick.*

Advertisements and greeting cards depict older persons as forgetful, dependent, child-like, and—perhaps the ultimate insult in our society—sexless. Conversely, older people who continue to have sexual desires are dirty old men and ridiculous old women.

Wrinkles, crow's feet, liver spots, and dull skin are disparaged in our youth-dominated culture and exploited by the cosmetics industry and plastic surgeons. Women who have relied upon their appearance for self-definition and men and women who have depended upon a youthful appearance in their work are up against overwhelming odds. The clock does not stop. When does one cease to be beautiful and start on the journey to being over-the-hill? How many women past fifty can look like model Lauren Hutton or Susan Sarandon? How many men and women can overcome disability with elegance and style?

A study conducted by the American Academy of Facial, Plastic and Reconstructive Surgery revealed that baby boomers have received nearly a quarter of a million face-lifts and other cosmetic surgeries. Most of these patients were over fifty. The Associated Press has quoted Karen Seccombe, a University of Florida sociologist, who said, "The thought of saggy breasts, hair loss or wrinkles doesn't sit well with people who have grown up emphasizing fitness and youth."

The film and television industries help to perpetuate ageism.

- Less than 2 percent of prime-time television characters are sixty-five or older, although this group is 12.7 percent of the population.
- 11 percent of male characters between fifty and sixty-four are categorized as old versus 22 percent of female characters.
- 75 percent of male characters sixty-five and older are characterized as old versus 83 percent of female characters of the same age.
- Only one-third of older characters are women.
- Middle-aged and older white males have joined women and minorities on the side-lines, as white men under forty get most of the jobs writing for television and film. Employment and earning prospects for older writers have declined relative to those for younger writers.
- According to one study, approximately 70 percent of older men and more than 80 percent of older women seen on television are portrayed disrespectfully, treated with little if any courtesy, and often looked at as "bad."
- Although Americans who are forty and over are 42 percent of the American population, more than twice as many roles are cast with actors who are under forty.

But there is some good news, too. By the 1990s, soap operas such as *The Guiding Light* were presenting older characters having more love affairs and not just worrying about their children. In 1994 *New York Magazine* put Paul Newman on the cover, calling him

"The Sexiest (70 year old) Man Alive," and *More* magazine offered women over forty an alternative to those that cater to women in their twenties. Older models began to make their appearance in general women's magazines, too. One widely circulated magazine advertisement in 1994 described "Betty Mettler, age 101, Noxzema user since 1925."

OUR CULTURE'S FEAR OF GROWING OLD

As Tolstoy noted, *"Old age is the most unexpected of all the things that happen to a man."*

The underlying basis of ageism is the dread and fear of growing older, becoming ill and dependent, and approaching death. People are afraid, and that leads to profound ambivalence. The young dread aging, and the old envy youth. Behind ageism is corrosive narcissism, the inability to accept our fate, for indeed we are all in love with our youthful selves, as is reflected in the yearning behind the expression "salad days."

Although undoubtedly universal, ageism in the United States is probably fueled by the worship of youth in a still-young country dominated by the myth of the unending frontier. In 1965, the Who, a British rock group, sang, "I hope I die before I get old," while in America "you never say die." Hollywood veils older actresses with gauzy lens filters. Moreover, age carries less authority.

The powerful imagery of the birth and adoration of the infant Jesus, and the journey of the Magi to see the Christ child, describes a birth of hope. How this contrasts with the final years of life! Children are seen as the future; older people, the past. Grimm's fairy tales depict gnarled and evil old women cursing innocent and beautiful youths with spells and afflictions.

Denial is a close cousin of ageism; in effect, it eliminates aging from consciousness.

One of the striking facts of human life is the intensity with which people avoid aging. Narcissistic preoccupation with our own aging and demise and perhaps, according to Freud, the inability of the unconscious to accept death make it difficult for society as a whole to deal with the challenges of aging. Note our gallows humor at birthdays, the money we spend on cosmetic surgery, and the popularity of anti-aging medicine. This was not always the case. In Europe in generations past, young men in high positions wore wigs they had powdered white in an attempt to appear older and, by implication, wiser. Today, men flock to cosmetic surgeons and colorists to preserve the illusion of youth.

. . .

ELDER ABUSE

Elder abuse is a widespread phenomenon that affects older adults who live in rich and poor nations alike. In the United States alone it is believed that as many as 1.2 million older adults are physically abused or neglected each year. Elder abuse takes many forms, including physical, emotional, financial, and sexual abuse—often by family members. It may involve neglect, such as the failure to provide food, shelter, clothing, medical care, and personal hygiene, as well as narcotic overmedication.

In 2004, UN Secretary General Kofi Annan released a report on the abuse of older persons that mentioned practices such as the ostracism of older women, which occurs in some societies when they are used as scapegoats for natural disasters, epidemics, or other catastrophes. The report stated: "Women have been ostracized, tortured, maimed or even killed if they failed to flee the community."

The World Health Organization (WHO) reported that 36 percent of nursing home staff in the U.S. reported having witnessed at least one incident of physical abuse of an older patient in the previous year, and 10 percent admitted having committed at least one act of physical abuse themselves. This represents sexism as well as ageism, for about 75 percent of nursing home residents are women. Other statistics are equally alarming:

- 1 million to 3 million Americans sixty-five and older have been injured, exploited, or otherwise mistreated by someone on whom they depend for care or protection.
- Estimates of the frequency of elder abuse range from 2 percent to 10 percent.
- Only one out of six incidents of elder abuse, neglect, exploitation, and self-neglect is brought to the attention of authorities.
- Only twenty-one states report that they maintain an elder abuse registry/database on perpetrators of substantiated cases, and less than half of states maintain a central abuse registry.
- It is estimated that each year 5 million older Americans are victims of financial exploitation, but only 4 percent of cases are reported. Many of these cases involve the unauthorized use of an older person's assets and the transferring of power of attorney for an older person's assets without written consent.
- Of the nearly $1 billion National Institute on Aging budget, only $1.7 million goes to NIA elder abuse and neglect research funding.

AGEISM IN HEALTH-CARE SETTINGS

Ageism can be invoked by aesthetic revulsion. Especially when weakened by disease, older persons can be disheveled, unwashed, and appear ugly and decaying. Some older persons "let themselves go" and unwittingly add fuel to the fire. Sphincters loosen, depositing stains and smells. Ear and nose hairs grow more quickly in older bodies, as does the cartilage, causing the nose and ears to enlarge. Some profound and common disorders of old age—mobility problems, dementia, and incontinence—are unattractive and provoke a negative response.

When older men or women are malodorous, scabrous, or disturbing in dress and language, they can scare, disgust, and discomfort younger people. Such older persons become untouchable. (Touch is powerful and therapeutic. Some older persons living alone have not been touched for years.)

Medical schools unwittingly promote the virus of ageism. Fresh out of college, young students are confronted with aging and death and their own personal anxieties about both. They are left to their own devices to insulate themselves from anxiety and pain about disease, disability, disfigurement, and dying. A cadaver that requires dissection is usually the first older person medical students encounter, and they are not ordinarily provided with effective group or individual counseling, either at the time of dissection or later, upon the death of their first patient.

Defense mechanisms like gallows humor, cynicism, denial, the invention of negative language, and facetiousness are common. Long hours in medical training lead to angry exhaustion and feelings of being "put upon."

It was in medical school that I first become conscious of the medical profession's prejudice toward age. For the first time I heard such insulting epithets as "crock," which was used to describe middle-aged women and older patients who were labeled hypochondriacal because they had no apparent organic basis for their complaints, as well as having many symptoms, and "GOMER" (Get Out of My Emergency Room).

The hidden curriculum in medical schools undermines students' idealism and can compromise their education. For example, in some studies up to 35 percent of doctors erroneously consider an increase in blood pressure to be a normal process of aging. In physical diagnosis courses, medical students meet older people who are stripped of their individuality and seen as archives or museums of pathology, rather than as human beings. Men and women in their eighties are particularly valuable in these sessions because they often have a plethora of symptoms and conditions about which the student must learn.

In addition, few medical school graduates will practice geriatrics, and practicing physicians often do not invest the same amount of time dealing with older patients. Medicare expenditures per capita steadily decline as people grow older. In fact, a UCLA study reported that, as people enter their forties, physicians spend less time with them per encounter. Logically, it should be the reverse since medical problems tend to increase as we grow older, and the ramifications are sobering. Sixty percent of adults over sixty-five do not receive recommended preventive services, and 40 percent do not receive vaccines for flu and pneumonia. They receive even less preventive care for high blood pressure and cholesterol.

Some doctors question why they should even bother treating certain problems of the aged; after all, the patients are old. Is it worth treating them? Their problems are irreversible, unexciting, and unprofitable. Their lives are over.

Between 1955 and 1966, Morris Rocklin, a volunteer in the NIMH Human Aging Study, was studied until he turned 101 years of age. Rocklin complained about his painful right knee to his physician, who said, "What do you expect at your age?" To this typical statement by a physician, Rocklin replied indignantly, "So why doesn't my left leg hurt?" The symmetry of the human body offers a good test of the realities of medical ageism. Rocklin's oft-quoted response has been used by many geriatricians to educate medical students on the topic of ageism.

NURSING HOMES: AGEIST SCANDAL

Nursing homes are licensed by the states and must meet federal standards to participate in Medicaid or Medicare. About 95 percent of the nation's sixteen thousand nursing homes (which house 1.5 million men and women) participate in those programs. According to a government study conducted in 2002, nine of ten nursing homes in the United States lack adequate staff, and nurse's aides provide 90 percent of the care. In most nursing homes, the report said, a patient needs an average of 4.1 hours of care each day—2.8 hours from nurse's aides and 1.3 hours from registered nurses or licensed practical nurses.

In 2000, over 91 percent of nursing homes had nurse aide staffing levels that fell below the thresholds identified as minimally necessary to provide the needed care. In response, the Department of Health and Human Services concluded that "it is not currently feasible" for the federal government to require that homes achieve a minimum ratio of nursing staff to patients. Nursing homes would have to hire 77,000 to 137,000 registered nurses, 22,000 to 27,000 licensed practical nurses, and 181,000 to 310,000 nurse's aides. This would take $7.6 billion a year, an 8 percent increase over current spending. The solution given by the Bush administration was to encourage nursing homes to adopt better management techniques so nurse's aides can achieve high productivity and, ultimately, to rely on market forces.

AGE-BASED HEALTH-CARE RATIONING

Medical ageism is prevalent in preventive tests for cancer and treatment of a variety of illnesses, some of them life-threatening. For example:

- Only 10 percent of people sixty-five and over receive appropriate screening tests for bone density, colorectal and prostate cancer, and glaucoma. This despite the fact that the average age of colorectal cancer patients is seventy, that more than 70 percent of prostate cancer is diagnosed in men over sixty-five, and that people over sixty are six times more likely to suffer from glaucoma.
- Chemotherapy is underused in the treatment of breast cancer patients over sixty-five, even though for many of these patients it may improve survival.
- In a cost-cutting effort to reduce supposedly unnecessary medical tests in 1998, the American Cancer Society and government health agencies determined that if an older woman had no abnormalities in a Pap smear for three years in a row, she could be tested less often. Yet over 25 percent of cases of cervical cancer occur in women over sixty-five!
- The pelvic examination is often deferred because many doctors, especially men, do not like to do it. (In both men and women, the rectal examination may meet a similar fate.)
- Although deaths due to ischemic heart disease disproportionately affect persons over sixty-five (85 percent in the United States and 87 percent in France), few national comparisons focus on older people. For example, WHO's MONICA Project—the important international longitudinal study that monitors cross-national trends in cardiovascular disease—focuses on death before sixty-five.
- A patient under the age of seventy-five who is admitted with a heart attack is six times more likely to receive blood clot-dissolving drugs such as streptokinase than a patient over seventy-five, even though data indicate the value of streptokinase in improving the chances for survival of older patients.
- Advanced surgery for Parkinson's disease is less available to older persons.

Unless older people are knowledgeable or have strong advocates, even the more affluent members of our society experience age-determined limits in medical care. Parenthetically, when malpractice suits are won, older persons usually receive lower monetary awards.

. . .

120

Ageing with Disabilities

Ageism and More

Debra J. Sheets

People who are old and who also have disabilities—a growing proportion of the population—find themselves in "double jeopardy" of experiencing prejudice and discrimination, which often leads to difficulty gaining access to needed healthcare and social services. . . .

With older Americans living longer and healthier lives, recent trends suggest that disability is declining and possibly becoming less severe. Still, the combination of large numbers of baby boomers and the increased prevalence of disability accompanying age means that the size of the population with disability will grow rapidly in the next decade. Currently,

32 million people (12.5 percent) living in our communities have a sensory, mental, physical, or other disability that impairs their ability to take care of themselves; more than one in three (38 percent) is age 65 or older. Self-care disability affects 6.7 million people; adults age 65 and older constitute nearly one-half (3.1 million) of this group.

While population aging has received considerable attention, the aging of the "disability population" has gone largely without comment. In the past, people with disabilities often did not survive even into middle age because of complications related to their disability. Now, for the first time in history, an estimated one of every 100 older Americans is aging with a long-term disability such as spinal cord injury, cerebral palsy, multiple sclerosis, post-polio, and intellectual or developmental disabilities. Fifty years ago, the average life expectancy of an individual with spinal cord injury was less than three years after the accident occurred. Today 40 percent of all survivors of such injury are 45 years of age and older, and more than one-half of the estimated 600,000 to one million polio survivors are now age 55 and older. Approximately 526,000 Americans age 60 or older are aging with intellectual or developmental disabilities. Other groups aging with disability include 200,000 people with spinal cord injuries and 600,000 with cerebral palsy.

. . . Many of those with long-term disabilities are experiencing unanticipated health problems (e.g., fatigue, pain) and functional declines (e.g., muscle weakness, mobility limitations) as they reach midlife. These secondary health conditions are related to the effects of aging superimposed on the primary disability. The conditions have been described as "premature aging" because they occur about fifteen to twenty years earlier than would be the case with normal aging. A related problem is that people aging with disabilities may face early and forced retirement as they become physically unable to continue working. In such cases, they often have not had time to plan for how they will address typical retirement issues such as housing, health insurance, transportation, income, and caregiving. Yet they remain too young to qualify for the age-based service system as they shift out of the disability service system, with its strong vocational focus. The resulting gap in services poses a threat to independence and quality of life for people aging with disability.

. . .

TOWARD A SHARED AGENDA TO COMBAT PREJUDICE

The aging and disability service systems have historically developed in parallel but separate tracks, particularly because of different funding sources, despite often overlapping concerns about issues such as affordable housing, public transportation, access to healthcare, long-term-care needs, and economic stability. In the early 1980s, aging and disability advocates began discussing the need to work together to pursue a unified policy agenda that would reflect shared concerns about these issues. In the 1990s several modest attempts to develop a unified agenda were undertaken but to little effect. Efforts between the aging and disability service systems ultimately stalled over disagreements that reflected differences in philosophical perspectives, the definition of problems, and what counted as a solution.

. . .

Recently, economic and political pressures have prompted about two-thirds of all states to consolidate and integrate aging and disability services into a single agency serving both groups—older adults and people with disabilities. Regardless, some advocates remain pessimistic about overcoming the difficulties that keep the aging and disability systems from meaningful collaboration around a shared agenda. However, others are more optimistic and point to a number of state- and local-level initiatives that involve cross-network collaborations and may reflect a coalescing around issues that include improving consumer choice and the quality of longterm care. How this will play out remains to be seen, but there are some promising forces furthering efforts to bring the two service spheres together.

Improvements in the service systems will do much to counter the effects of ageism on older people aging with disabilities. Advocacy efforts by these two groups working together must counter prejudice against elders and those with disability by providing those aging with disability opportunities to maintain their competence, image, and sense of worth within our society. Agencies must replace problem-based approaches with a strengths-based paradigm that focuses on ensuring inclusion and participation in the broader society. In addition, both systems must endorse the self-determination of people aging with disability by adopting a shared focus on consumer choice and the empowerment of individuals to reach their potential. Neither age nor disability should be viewed as a special concern; they should be recognized as issues that are in the interests of our society as a whole.

. . .

121

Black Elderly

Center on Aging Studies, University of Missouri—Kansas City

- *In 1985 approximately 14% of the population, 65 and over, were people of color.* By 2020, 21% are projected to be people of color, and by 2050 this percent is anticipated to increase to 33%. These numbers translate into increasing numbers of black elderly adults in our society. However, despite growing numbers of black elderly adults, most of the programs and services provided to elders of color continue to be based on research and perceptions regarding the majority population. The result is a general lack of ethnic- and culture-specific knowledge.

- *Approximately 33% of black elderly live in poverty.* Black elderly males experience a decline in their longevity. Many black elderly regard themselves as "unretired-retired," since they generally continue to work after retirement. Black elderly retirement is frequently related to subsequent physical or mental disability. Black elderly females who have declining health are frequently sole heads of households, and thus responsible for children or grandchildren. Black elderly underutilize public health services and tend to use emergency room services. Many do not have a regular personal physician, and generally experience problems in accessing all health care systems. In rural areas, nearly one-half of black elderly live at or below the poverty level.

- *Black male elders generally have less personal post-retirement resources and are more dependent on Social Security and Supplemental Security Income.* More than twice as many black males as white males, over the age of 65, are divorced or separated. It is always important to remember that there is cultural diversity within each ethnic group, including differences in values, traditions, educational levels, socioeconomic status, and lifestyles.

. . .

- *Due to life-long patterns of socioeconomic disadvantages (e.g., income, education, access to health care, etc.), and prejudicial treatment, many black elderly don't respond well to service providers of a different race.* In some cases, the elder person may demonstrate a complete lack of trust in the medical and/or mental health system. This can potentially result in fewer attempts to procure care, and low compliance with prescribed interventions. Blacks tend to be institutionalized for mental health reasons more often than whites; their admission to psychiatric institutions are also less likely to be voluntary. In addition, racial and ethnic minorities tend to receive less mental health treatment and are more likely to receive lower quality treatment.
- *Health conditions:* More than half of black elderly in America are in poor health. They also tend to experience higher rates of multiple chronic illnesses than the rest of the population. Hypertension, obesity, and diabetes, in particular, surface as three major diseases which are often found to be related to each other. Left untreated, any one of these diseases can progress into more severe health complications such as stroke, blindness, loss of an extremity, impaired mobility, kidney failure, or heart disease. These three diseases are often associated with a lifetime of poor dietary habits, limited exercise, behavioral responses to discrimination, socioeconomic factors (such as persistent poverty), and poor coping or problem-solving skills—some of which may include the use of sugar, food, alcohol, or drugs, in excess, as a means of minimizing emotional pain and escaping the harsh realities of life. In turn, decreased self-image, self-worth, feelings of helplessness, hopelessness, and frustration often accompany these conditions. Another possible problem is noncompliance with medication instructions and schedules. This problem is often the result of fixed incomes which may not always cover ongoing medication costs. . . .
- *Cancer is found to be a critical problem for black elderly Americans.* For example, as compared to white Americans, black Americans experience significantly higher rates of several types of cancer, with death rates three times higher for esophageal cancer and twice the mortality rate from stomach cancer. In addition, the death rate from lung cancer is 45% higher in black males compared to white males. Black females are also two to three times more likely to die from cervical or uterine cancer than white females.
- *Concerning dementia, research has shown that black females may be at increased risk of multi-infarct dementia due to a higher incidence of obesity and hypertension.* The potential for black males to experience alcoholic dementia before age 50 is also increased due to early age onset of drinking and heavier patterns of consumption. Although the frequency of dementing illness is at least as frequent in the black American community as it is in the general population, black elderly may have lower rates of the Alzheimer's type of dementia. Because of a lack of resources, inefficient doctor-patient relationship, and/or lack of research data applicable to dementias in the black elderly, there is an above-average potential for misdiagnoses.
- *For black Americans, in particular, family is of primary importance.* Family networks provide the main source of needed assistance later in life for many black elderly. In fact, when black elderly live with their children, the possibility of them being institutionalized for disabilities decreases. In general, black elderly do not participate in social or recreational activities that are outside the realm of their individual cultural traditions, backgrounds, or experiences. However, they tend to utilize a more diverse pool of helpers, including both extended family and friends. This network, and its influence, must, in turn, be respected and utilized by outside caregivers and service providers. Increased spirituality, faith in God, and increased participation in religious activities and institutions can also play an important role in providing support for black elderly. Religious beliefs provide a resource for coping with the unexpected or losses (which

naturally increase with age). The church may also serve as a focal point of supportive networks for emotional and material aid.

- *Developing a caregiving relationship:* For someone outside the family to establish and develop a caregiving relationship with a black elder may require special attention and sensitivity to the elder's unique ethnic and cultural experience, history, and family relationships. At a minimum, the service provider must make efforts toward building a trusting relationship—remembering that non-responsiveness or resistance on the part of the elder may represent a means of evaluating providers and their ability to work with the elder effectively. A big step in the right direction is achieved if the provider can meet elders where they are—which means helping the elder determine what will work best, rather than what the provider believes will be best for the elder.

122

From Keystone XL Pipeline to #DAPL

Jasilyn Charger, Water Protector from Cheyenne River Reservation

Amy Goodman and Jasilyn Charger

AMY GOODMAN: At Standing Rock in North Dakota, Native American elders fighting the Dakota Access pipeline have extinguished the Seven Council Fires, which have been burning for months at the main resistance camp, and young Native water protectors have relit a new fire, the All Nations Fire, as part of the continued resistance to the $3.8 billion pipeline. Thousands of water protectors remain at the resistance camps at Standing Rock. Last month, the Department of the Army denied Energy Transfer Partners, the company behind the pipeline, a permit necessary to drill underneath the Missouri River. But the company has vowed to build on.

We're joined here in New York by Jasilyn Charger, a water protector from Cheyenne River Reservation in South Dakota. She's been camping at Sacred Stone Resistance Camp to fight the Dakota Access pipeline since April 3rd, [2016] two days after the camp was launched by LaDonna Brave Bull Allard. Jasilyn founded the International Indigenous Youth Council at Standing Rock. She was also part of the resistance to the Keystone XL pipeline before that.

AMY GOODMAN: How old were you April 3rd? And what exactly did you do?

JASILYN CHARGER: I was 19. I was just part of a delegation of youth that really wanted to help Standing Rock in their fight against this. We know how it feels to have something be pressed upon you that you don't really want, and have the youth voice being drowned out by policies, by political stuff, by money, by greed. And it's—it was devastating to us. I mean, we went to stand with Standing Rock, not only with them, but with their youth, and really encourage them to be active and say this is your future. This is the future that they're destroying. And we really need to stand up and fight for it.

AMY GOODMAN: So, you came up from Cheyenne River. With how many others?

JASILYN CHARGER: With five other people: Joye Braun, Joseph White Eyes, Kili Bald Eagle and Wiyaka Eagleman.

. . .

AMY GOODMAN: Now, you all, as youth, with Standing Rock, some of the members of the Standing Rock Sioux Tribe, really won them over, in the battle against the pipeline. Can you talk about that, your elders supporting you or not supporting you?

JASILYN CHARGER: Well, in the beginning, like nobody really supported us. People really told us that we couldn't change it, that it was going to go through, that it was pointless camping. And we didn't believe that, because we already faced that with the Key XL. They had already faced that, and they won. And they won their respect. They won the points of view of their elders, of the adults, to really make them see where we stand, and really step back and see it through our youth eyes and really know where we come from and why this is so important to us and why it's important to keep us involved in this process, because this is our future that's going to be devastated. And they continue to say that this is for us, and it's up to us to really tell them what we want.

. . .

JASILYN CHARGER: [We ran 500 miles from Cannon Ball, North Dakota, to Omaha, Nebraska] All the tribes that were really going to be directly affected [Yankton, Standing Rock and Cheyenne River and Rosebud] were represented in their youth, which is amazing. The youth came together. And we set the example for the leaders. We said, "Hey, if we can do it, you can, too. We can come together, and we can work together." If the youth can stand there and really work with other youth from different places and not know them personally and do this run and, at the end of the run, become friends, become brothers and sisters and stand together in this fight, the elders, the adults, can do that, too. And they saw that. They said, "Wow! These youth are really taking initiative. And where—where are the adults? Where are the spiritual leaders? Where are the headmen at?" And some men really kind of felt a dent in their ego of "Why are you doing this? The men should be doing this." And it kind of hurt us spiritually that they didn't stand behind us, that they didn't support us. But we just went around and were like, "Well, if you're going to judge us, why don't you run for us? Why aren't you protecting us? Why don't you take that initiative of your responsibility of being a man and protect your women and children?" And we told them, "We aren't going to wait for you to protect us. We have no time." An older woman, Lyota [*phon.*]—Lyota, she really represented the past in that run. She was 62.

. . .

JASILYN CHARGER: The second run we did was from Cannon Ball, North Dakota, to Washington, D.C., which was a 1,200-mile run, and it took us a month to complete.

AMY GOODMAN: So, [you ran into DAPL workers]. What did they say to you?

JASILYN CHARGER: They stopped us at this gas station. And he just strolled up in his diesel truck, and he stepped out of his truck, and he walked up to us. He said, "Why are you doing this?" We explained it to him. And then he's like, "Why? We've been using oil for more than like a hundred years. You guys shouldn't be running. It's a waste of time. You guys should go back to wherever you came from." And, for us, we were like, "What? Is this really happening? Are you going to speak this way to young women and children and elderly?" We felt really disrespected. We felt really angry. And what ended up happening is, a little girl—her name is Wiconi—she really reminded us of why we were there. And her baby sister Leelee [*phon.*] and her older sister Love, they were all like, mind you, four to three weeks old. And it was like, to have that young of youth really represented there was very powerful.

AMY GOODMAN: And what did you respond back to him why you were there?

JASILYN CHARGER: We were all really angry. We were all going to set in our anger. But Wiconi—mind you, she's two years old—she just went up to them. She said, "*Mni wiconi.*" In our language, that means "Water is life." The two-year-old baby could understand the meaning of water and the meaning of why she was running. I don't understand why that DAPL worker couldn't.

AMY GOODMAN: What happened when you got to Washington? Who did you meet with?

JASILYN CHARGER: We met with the Army Corps of Engineers, the two-star general and the Bureau of Indian Affairs and just a delegation that really wanted to hear us. And in that meeting, it was only youth could go in that meeting and meet with them. Our youngest was four years old, and her name was Love, Love Hopkins. She was afraid. But she told them why she was running. She told them that she wanted water, that she didn't want her children to suffer. A four-year-old was speaking about her children, thinking about her children, and telling him that. It was amazing. That little girl was fighting for her younger sister. And her baby sister, mind you, when we started this run, was only three weeks old at the time.

. . .

AMY GOODMAN: Can you talk about the militarization of the Sheriff's Department, of the police, of the National Guard, times when you were on the front line and what you were up against?

JASILYN CHARGER: The strategy of Morton County, they're using fear tactics. They're using strategies that have been used against us for generations, that the government, the police use to keep us on our reservations. Back then, we would have got shot, being off our reservation. We would have got rounded up and sent back to our reservation. For us, we feel the reservation is a prisoner-of-war camp. And just to see the same tactics now, in a different era, is just—it doesn't surprise us, nor does it really faze us.

AMY GOODMAN: Can you talk about the weapons that were used against you?

JASILYN CHARGER: Yeah. They used rubber bullets. They used bean bag guns, flashbangs. They maced us. It was like being at war. It was like we were in battle. There were planes flying over us [and] helicopters that had guns on the side of them. It was so life-changing. It was traumatic. It felt like we were at Iraq.

. . .

AMY GOODMAN: [You have won, for the moment. The Army Corps has not granted the permit.] At this point, the elders at the camp have extinguished the Seven Council Fires. Then young people lit a new fire, the All Nations Fire. Talk about the significance of this.

JASILYN CHARGER: Well, what we feel is that if they want to extinguish the fire in their own hearts and really step back from this fight and really don't want to do that anymore, that's fine. That's OK. But we, as youth, that fire still burns inside of us. That is a representation of our perseverance, of our strength, of our prayer. And that cannot be extinguished, even if you're older than us, even if you tell us to stop, that we aren't going to stop. It's because we feel the power of our ancestors. We feel the power of not giving up. They didn't give up at the Battle of Wounded Knee. They didn't give up when they felt all this oppression of being colonized. They didn't give up. They laid down their very lives so I can be here today. Little children, women, young men, elderly—they all died for me, to make sure that I can have a place in this world whenever they were gone. And we feel, as the youth, we need to make that same type of commitment for our youth. Seven generations ago, our forefathers dreamt about us. They made sure that we had a future here, that we would be here, that we would be able to live peacefully and live on and remember who we are. And that's what they thought about. That's what they strove for. And it's only right of us to think about our seventh generation and really fight for them.

AMY GOODMAN: Jasilyn, what was it like to grow up on the Cheyenne River Reservation in South Dakota?

JASILYN CHARGER: It wasn't easy, especially for youth. It's more about survival. And yeah, we go through all this poverty. We have suicides. We have infestation of meth, of alcoholism. But, for us, we are what grows after that. We are the life that grows after that nuke bomb exploded in the heart of our nation. We're—we carry that within us, but it doesn't define who we are. We really fight. We really say, yeah, all this bad stuff's going on around us, but we don't want that. We don't want to hurt anymore. We don't want to kill ourselves. We don't want to make ourselves sick anymore. What we want is a better future for ourselves. The pain that we go through on the reservation, we don't want our children to go through that pain, because that pain is hereditary. It passes—we pass it down to our children and so on and so forth.

AMY GOODMAN: Do you feel now, after these many months at Standing Rock, a kind of PTSD, post-traumatic stress disorder, after you stand on the front lines? You're taking on the local police, sheriffs, rubber bullets, tear gas, month after month.

JASILYN CHARGER: Yes. I mean, we are experiencing right now—the youth, we feel broken, like from being beaten, from being maced, from—it hurts. It is. I mean, if you go there with no weapons, within prayer, and you stand there, you take that. You take all that hate that is being pushed against you, take that violence, especially as being women and really not doing anything and really putting yourself in that situation of being abused, of really taking that in and being humble and not reacting to it. It is very hard. It is very hard for us to have people hurt us, and really be humble and not do anything back. And, yes, we do have PTSD. But we were born with it, from everything that has happened before us, that we have inherited that from our ancestors, from what happened to us. And that only increased it. That only activated it, like, wow, this is still happening to my people. We are still being beaten down, we are still being oppressed, and we are still being hurt. And it's hard for us, but us, as youth, we are healing. We are—we are moving past it. We're seeing the light at the end of the tunnel. Yeah, we go through all this pain, but, after this, we come out as a better and stronger person and a better leader for our future.

AMY GOODMAN: You're wearing a cap that says "Native pride." What does that mean to you?

JASILYN CHARGER: Native pride is really not having the fear that has been put into us by boarding schools. It's really having pride in where you come from, and remember that where we come from is we come from a very proud nation of where we don't do dishonor. We don't disrespect our elders. We believe all life is sacred. We don't get to choose what life is sacred. Morton County, your life is sacred. The DAPL workers, your life is sacred. Our fight isn't with you personally. Our fight is with this black snake, and we recognize that.

AMY GOODMAN: What do you mean, "black snake"?

JASILYN CHARGER: Black snake, this pipeline. That's what we have referred to it. That's how we see it traditionally. It's a black snake. It's a snake that injects poison into our world, that injects venom into our water. We see that as poison, as a snake really moving through this nation. There are thousands of them everywhere. And, for us, it's really—we remember our pride, remember our honor, our respect, and remember ourselves as warriors. We didn't take lives, we didn't go to war, because we wanted to. We went to war because the warriors sacrificed their heart, their conscience of taking a life. They had to bear that. And we remember that pride of where we come from, not violence, not hate, of pride, of self-respect, of honor. And we remember that. And us, as youth, that's what we want to take into the future, not PTSD, not genocide, not any of that. We want to take the core of our culture, and we want to pass it down to our children.

123

Elder Liberation Draft Policy Statement

Marge Larabee

INTRODUCTION

Everyone is a particular age. Age is universal. One's age is a factor in the life of every person in every country, in every culture. We also deal with change and oppression at any age. However, age is of special importance to elders. We have lived long. In dealing with age oppression in our own lives, we elders also support each person of whatever age, especially young people, whatever country, whatever culture, to move outside the ageist oppression. Elders can be allies for successful aging at any age.

Like people of any age, we elders are: zestful, intelligent, fun-loving, powerful, creative, flexible, sexy human beings. We focus, in present time, on the steps we are now taking and *will* take in the short-term to accomplish our long range goals. We have a future.

. . .

We expect to be seen as unique individuals whose accomplishments and thinking are accepted on their own merit. Whether we choose traditional roles, and/or to "contemplate, reflect and guide," our actions are as valuable as production in the workplace. Any role we select rationally is appropriate for us.

In the world today there are increasing numbers of elders, more and more of whom continue to function as alert human beings as they chronologically reach eighty-five and older. We are a powerful political force. We plan on taking charge of our own activities and policies.

We have a *vision* and perspective on history and the way things can and should be now.

We have coped with much change and can apply what we have learned from those experiences.

Incessant, insidious repetition fosters attitudes that elders have little to offer and can no longer participate in significant work and that any attempt to do so will limit the opportunities for younger people (similar arguments are made to discourage bringing women, people of color, or immigrants into the work force).

Older workers are encouraged to see retirement as a "reward" for years of effort. Retirement years are supposed to be "Golden Years." The facts are different: for many people, retirement is a time of enforced idleness, isolation, loss of self-esteem, and living on a dwindling or absent income.

Gradually, the convention that older persons cannot keep up the pace has been established. It is now widely believed that they cannot be productive, contributing members of society.

LIVING SITUATIONS

In the past it wasn't unusual for elders to live in an extended family in which they were known and had a place, and to which they contributed their wisdom and experience.

Today urbanization and increased geographic mobility have been factors in the breakdown of the extended family unit. As a result elders in nuclear families or alternative living situations experience increased invisibility and isolation.

Eighty-percent of the care of old people is provided by an informal network of family and friends, mostly women. This usually means wives, daughters and daughters-in-law. Many of these women are themselves elders, and they avoid institutionalizing their loved ones at great cost.

We need to examine the difficult role of caregiver. We need to find ways to offer a variety of services that will give help and support to this role.

OLD AGE OPPRESSION AND OTHER OPPRESSIONS

The oppression of ageism intersects with and intensifies other oppressions. Sexism and old-ageism merge blatantly around the artificial standards of beauty for women and the value of women based on their reproductive functions. Older men suffer from stereotypical expectations of work performance and maintaining an ideal virility.

Elders also face intensified classism, racism, and homophobia.

INTERNALIZED . . . AGEISM

What does . . . ageism look like from the inside?

1. We often feel and act inadequate. We act competitive and aggressive or else we withdraw.
2. We sometimes criticize each other, settle for less, and have difficulty rejoicing in our achievements.
3. We act as though we believe the stereotypes and forget how brave, smart and good-looking we are.
4. We are flattered to be thought younger; we long to be youthful.
5. We confuse growing older, aging and ill health.

HOW WE INTERNALIZE . . . AGEISM

Denying old age leads to ignoring, overlooking, minimizing old age oppression. We think to ourselves: "It isn't really a very important oppression." The reality is that old-ageism is important to everybody and affects everybody, throughout their lives.

When young, we internalize stereotypes of disabled, old, sick and dying people. When we think of "old" we call to mind images of an old aunt, grandfather or neighbor we once knew. If they were sick, disabled or dying, these early memories remain as internalized stereotypes of "old."

. . .

MOVING OUT OF THE OPPRESSION

Begin to act. Create good directions and commitments for yourself. Build support groups around you. Put your plans into action.

STEPS

1. Elders and non-elders need to have confident, high expectations of elders. Recognize that we are always learning, growing, and developing, that we have not completed our lives, our contributions, our accomplishments. See elders as able to make changes, to live through many more beginnings. Remember that there are feelings, griefs, fears to be worked through at any age. It is incorrect to assume that elders' distresses are more intractable because we have lived longer.
2. Enlist the support of non-elders as allies; develop a long list and call on them frequently. Other age groups, especially young persons, have challenges in common with elders.
   . . .
3. Know the laws pertaining to older persons and lobby to establish non-ageist policies on employment, housing, health care, etc.
4. Organize with other elders to take leadership for our liberation and the liberation of all other sections of the population. We can lead everything, and from such a position our interests can receive the attention and emphasis they deserve.

5. Form alliances with all other oppressed groups, . . . to support each others' programs. To offer alliances to other liberation groups and request their support is to multiply our effectiveness and our confidence immediately.

. . .

124

People of Color Over Fifty

Dottie Curry

Aging has less stigma in communities of color. There is more respect for age and experience. A lot of the respect for elders is left over from our traditional cultures.

Though grandparents and other older adults are respected and loved within their families, they suffer more from the inhuman treatment of society towards elder citizens than members of the dominant culture. Because of the tradition of segregation and reduced access to opportunities, older people of color are less likely to have good health care, adequate housing and good nutrition. Consequently older people have a lower quality of life and a shortened life span.

Because of the poverty and violence in inner cities, older women in our communities are often taking care of grandchildren or other young people left by the death of the young people's parents. The extended family concept is a good one, but there is very rarely enough money to take care of these children properly. A lot of times the older people are on public assistance for the elderly while at the same time receiving aid for dependent children.

. . . Most of the time, just as with every other issue with people of color, the aging issue is buried under the issues connected with racism, so if there is some difficulty, old-ageism is not looked at. We need for other elders to step outside their fear and encourage older people of color to . . . work on this very important issue. We need younger people to act as our allies and . . . [talk with us about] our internalized oppression (the internalized racism and the internalized ageism).

We need for people . . . to understand that the problems facing all people, and especially people of color, are multiplied when we become elders. This is especially true in such cities as Austin, Texas and Atlanta, Georgia, where the median age is twenty-five. Since people of color have been traditionally denied some jobs (they are currently phasing people over forty out of certain jobs), the employment situation for people of color over fifty is pretty grim.

Older people of color have a lot to offer: we are an asset to any group. Our contribution to the history of this country is immense. We need a chance to share this with the . . . world.

125

An Immediate End to the Criminalization and Dehumanization of Black Youth Across All Areas of Society Including, but Not Limited to, Our Nation's Justice and Education Systems, Social Service Agencies, Media, and Pop Culture

Thena Robinson Mock, Ruth Jeannoel, Rachel Gilmer, Chelsea Fuller, and Marbre Stahly Butts

WHAT IS THE PROBLEM?

- Across the country, Black children attend under-resourced schools where they are often pushed off of an academic track onto a track to prison. Zero-tolerance policies — a combination of exclusionary disciplinary policies and schoolbased arrests — are often the first stop along the school-to-prison pipeline and play a key role in pushing students out of the school system and funneling them into jails and prisons.

- Each year more than three million students are suspended from school — often for vague and subjective infractions such as "willful defiance" and "disrespect" — amounting to countless hours of lost instructional time. As a result, Black students are denied an opportunity to learn and punished for routine child and adolescent behaviors that their white peers are often not disciplined for at all.

- For Black youth, the impact of exclusionary school discipline is far reaching — disengaging them from academic and developmental opportunities and increasing the likelihood that they will be incarcerated later in life. In addition, current research emphasizes the need to examine the unique ways in which Black girls are impacted by punitive zero-tolerance policies. There are higher disciplinary disparities between Black girls and white girls than disciplinary disparities between Black boys and white boys; yet, Black girls have historically been overlooked in the national discourse around youth impacted by the school-to-prison pipeline.

- Black youth are also more likely to experience higher rates of corporal punishment. According to the Office of Civil Rights (OCR) at the U.S. Department of Education, Black students constitute 17.1 percent of the nationwide student population, but 35.6 percent of those paddled. In addition, while girls are paddled less than boys, Black girls are more than twice as likely to be paddled than white girls. In the 13 states that paddle more than 1,000 students per year, Black girls are 2.07 times as likely as white girls to be beaten.

- Outside of schools, young Black people are criminalized in ways that limit their life chances at every point. 2010 data shows that while Black youth comprised 17 percent of all youth, they represented 31 percent of all arrests. These disparities persist even as juvenile "crime" rates have fallen. Among youth arrests, young Black people are more likely to be referred to a juvenile court than their white peers, and are more likely to be processed (and less likely to be diverted). Among those adjudicated delinquent, they are more likely to be sent to solitary confinement. Among those detained, Black youth are more likely to be transferred to adult facilities. The disparities grow at almost every step, stealing the dignity of young Black people and forcing them onto lifelong pathways of criminalization and diminished opportunity.

- For Black girls, the U.S.'s failure to address genderbased violence, which they experience at greater levels than any other group, is paramount to the criminalization they experience. In fact, sexual abuse is one of the primary predictors of girls' entry into the juvenile justice system, with girls often being routed to the system specifically because of their victimization. For instance, girls who are victims of sex trafficking are often arrested on prostitution charges. The punitive nature of this system is ill-equipped to support young girls through the violence and trauma they've experienced, which further subjects them to sexual victimization and a lifelong path of criminalization and abuse.

- There is a critical need for a coordinated strategy in local communities that addresses rampant racial disparities in the application of zero-tolerance policies and criminalization practices that impact Black boys and girls. Fortunately, a powerful grassroots movement, led primarily by youth and parents of color, has taken shape across the country to address these harmful policies — but much more work remains.

- Tens of thousands of youth under the age of 21 are currently incarcerated for offenses ranging from truancy to more serious charges. Every crime bill passed by Congress throughout the 1980s and 1990s included new federal laws against juvenile crimes and increased penalties against children. Similar trends can be seen throughout state legislation. There is mounting research that children under the age of 23 do not have fully developed brains and that the cheapest, most humane, and most cost-effective way to respond to juvenile crime is not incarceration, but programs and investments that strengthen families, increase stability and provide access to educational and employment opportunities. Prosecuting youth with crimes is not only cruel; but it also permanently disadvantages them with a criminal record, which makes completing their education, getting a job, finding housing and growing up to be contributing members of society unfairly difficult.

WHAT DOES THIS SOLUTION DO?

- Advances a grassroots organizing strategy at the local and state level that centers the work of ending the criminalization of Black youth through a racial and gender justice framework — led and informed by youth and parents.

- Addresses state-sanctioned violence that stems from overpoliced schools and the deprivation of resources to public schools.

- Opens resources for alternative practices like restorative justice as a way to train students, parents and staff to deal with interpersonal conflict. Restorative justice practices are used as an alternative to zero-tolerance policies by helping to build stronger school communities through: 1) Developing effective leadership; 2) Building trust, interconnection and deeper relationships amongst students, parents, teachers and staff; 3) Providing methods to address misbehavior in a way that gets to the root cause of conflicts and holds individuals accountable; 4) Repairing harm in a way that maintains the integrity of the community and doesn't further isolate offenders.

- By ending the practice of charging youth with misdemeanors and limiting the ability to charge them with felonies we would save hundreds of millions of dollars annually and provide the opportunity for our children to outlive their mistakes.

NEXT STEPS

FEDERAL ACTION

- Target(s): U.S. Congress and Federal Agencies (Office of Civil Rights, Department of Education, Department of Justice)
- Process: The potential for policy reforms to zero-tolerance and punitive disciplinary practices at the federal level are somewhat limited. In December 2015, the U.S. Senate approved the most recent iteration of the Elementary and Secondary Education Act, also known as "No Child Left Behind." The new law reduces the role of the federal government in education matters and leaves in place punitive highstakes testing requirements that have been a force behind removing students from the classroom and closing schools in Black and Brown communities, creating a "test, punish, push-out" effect. However, there are opportunities to demand greater enforcement of civil rights violations, particularly within federal agencies responsible for enforcing claims of racial disparities involving the administration of school discipline. In January 2014, the Department of Education and Department of Justice issued joint guidance outlining school districts' obligations to ensure that school discipline policies are not administered in a manner that fuels racial disparities. There is strong potential for additional guidance documents around these issues that can be used as a lever for local and statewide organizing efforts — although these documents lack the force to truly push real transformation in schools.
- Target: Legislative
- Process: This would require passage of a bill through both houses of Congress and signed by the President. The Bill would repeal all federal juvenile crimes and amend the Juvenile Justice and Delinquency Prevention Act. It would also provide incentives to states, including the tying of federal prison and policing grants, to adopt statutes that ban the prosecution of children under the age of 23. The bill would also include a mandatory reinvestment strategy where federal and state savings would be captured and reinvested in programs shown to reduce juvenile crime, increase youth educational attainment and support communities where youth incarceration has been most prevalent.

STATE ACTION

- Target: Legislative
- Process: The passage of state law banning exclusionary discipline (suspensions, expulsions, and arrests) for all students pre-K through 12th grade.
- State law banning exclusionary discipline (suspensions, expulsions, arrests) for vague and subjective behaviors including willful defiance, disrespect, insubordination, obnoxious, and disturbing the peace.
- The passage of state law prohibiting the use of corporal punishment in all educational settings.
- State law requiring the use of supportive services for students including fully funding restorative programs and support for students in crisis in educational settings.
- Improve the child welfare system's identification of victims of abuse, implement a gender-responsive approach to victims of abuse, and use Medicaid funds to improve quality care and trauma related services for girls in child welfare.
- Target: Legislative

- Process: This would require passage of a bill through the State legislature. The Bill would repeal all existing juvenile offenses and would also include a mandatory reinvestment strategy where State savings would be captured and reinvested in programs shown to reduce juvenile crime, increase youth educational attainment and support communities where juvenile incarceration has been most prevalent.

LOCAL ACTION

- Passage of local school district policy banning exclusionary discipline (suspensions, expulsions, and arrests) for all students pre-K through 12th grade).
- Passage of local school district policy banning exclusionary discipline (suspensions, expulsions, arrests) for vague and subjective behaviors including willful defiance, disrespect, insubordination, obnoxious, and disturbing the peace.
- Passage of local school district policy prohibiting the use of corporal punishment in all educational settings.
- Passage of local school district policy requiring the use of supportive services for students including fully funding restorative programs and support for students in crisis in educational settings.
- Invest in creating safe and supportive group homes with specialized services for teenage girls.
- Invest in training for students, parents, teachers and staff on restorative justice practices as an alternative to zero-tolerance policies.
- Process: At the local level, reducing the prosecution of juvenile misdemeanors can be accomplished in a variety of ways:
    o Campaigns that target City and County prosecutors and demand that instead of prosecution, youth defendants are diverted to nonpunitive programs.
    o Campaigns that target police, who often have wide discretion in the arrest of misdemeanors, to publically deprioritize the arrest of youth for misdemeanors.

HOW DOES THIS SOLUTION ADDRESS THE SPECIFIC NEEDS OF SOME OF THE MOST MARGINALIZED BLACK PEOPLE?

- These solutions address exclusionary and overly punitive school discipline policies in public schools across the nation that deny Black youth an opportunity to learn. These policies have the greatest impact on queer and trans youth, foster care youth, and girls.
- These solutions will propel Black youth towards graduation, and create a school-to-college pipeline.
- Students will not have minor offenses on their academic records.
- Legislation banning the prosecution of youth for all misdemeanors would have the largest impact on people who are made most vulnerable by incarceration including LGBTQ, undocumented and trans people. It would also reduce the number of incarcerated people significantly. The reinvestment aspect of the legislation would positively impact homeless people by providing increased services.

NEXT STEPS

126

Allies to Young People

Tips and Guidelines on How to Assist Young People to Organize

Jenny Sazama with help from teens in Boston

. . .

THINGS YOU CAN DO TO ASSIST YOUNG PEOPLE

Go to their space and their turf.

- Young people are so often asked to be a part of the adult world.
- Young people feel more empowered and groups build faster if work can be done on their terms and in a space where they feel comfortable.
- This is especially important when there are class and race differences. The unawareness of the "dominant" group is unintentional but strong. Safety needs to be built thoughtfully and carefully.

Build one-on-one relationships.

- This is a good way to get started in figuring out how to be an ally to young people. Choose one or two young people that you are interested in spending special time with. These may be young people that you notice are particularly sharp, or that you think would be good at bringing people together. There are things you are going to be able to accomplish one-on-one that are harder to do in a group.

Form an informal young people's advisory board for yourself.

- Get feedback from them. This will give you information about how to improve your work with young people continually. It will be an amazing growing experience for you, it will bring you closer to them, and it will help them feel that their thinking matters.

. . .

Assist young people to rely on each other and to take themselves and each other seriously.

- Adults cannot completely empower young people. They will not be truly powerful until they can rely on each other, trust each others' thinking and help each other. It's tempting to have the group center around us as adults, but our ultimate goal is for things to run well without us.

- Thoughtfully but firmly interrupt competition and put-downs. Society has told young people that they are not yet full humans and that their thinking is not valuable. They internalize these messages and then take them out on each other.
- Do group feedback. Ask people to give specific positive as well as growth/improvement information to another member of the group, including you. They will learn the most from each other.

Expect to make lots of phone calls and personal contact.

- Because young people are so often told by society that they are not important, adult allies need to make lots of phone calls to personally remind people that meetings are important and that they are wanted.
- They may not call you back. Don't take it personally. Keep calling. Assume you are wanted.
- Remember that in most situations, young people are not taken seriously, and they are told that their struggles don't matter. When you call, you are talking to someone who probably doesn't feel valuable, and thus doesn't remember that the work that she does is valuable. You need to keep reminding her how important she is.

Don't cancel meetings or events.

- It's okay if only a few people show up for things you have planned. Go ahead with them anyway. If you can even get two or three people to get closer to each other or work together on a project, you've come that much closer to the goals of your group.
- Young people have a lot of inconsistency in their lives. It means a lot to them if you can show them that you will follow through with what you say.

. . .

Young people should be a central part of any organization, movement, church group, etc.

NEXT STEPS

- It's necessary for the total health of any movement or organization for young people to be a central part of all facets of the organization. It's great to have a young person chair a youth committee, but also have her chair the outreach committee, or be in charge of the budget. If young people do not have the skills to take on these roles then train them. A young person's perspective is invaluable.
- Make sure that young people are general members to committees and boards, not just occasional representatives.
- Token representation is not helpful in the long term.

In meetings, ask young people to talk first. Never believe that they don't know.

- You may have to ask them to express their ideas at least ten times and you may have to ask in ten different ways.
- They may say they don't know or don't have an opinion. This is what we have all been told as young people many times before.
- They do have thoughts on almost any situation if given enough information, time to think and the expectation that of course they can think.

Ask young people what *they* think should be done in all situations.

- Discuss the goals of the group and how events reflect these goals, but resist the temptation to sway the group in the direction you think it should go.

Insist that young people are represented at every meeting, especially where young people are being discussed.

- It works better if there are at least two young people present.
- Meet with them ahead of time. Get them to share their thinking with you about the meeting topic. Remind them how important their thinking is and encourage them to speak during the meeting.

. . .

Get young people leading quickly.

- It's great for us as adults to begin facilitating and leading meetings. The faster we can turn it over to young people, however, the faster it will grow.

. . .

Appreciate yourself for the many important ways that you have been and continue to be a committed ally to young people.

127

Taking a Stand Against Ageism at All Ages

A Powerful Coalition

Margaret M. Gullette

New ageism is the term I use to describe the current American view of aging-past-youth. Whatever your age, you are likely to be affected by the new ageism—in your job, in your sexual life, in your sense of identity, in your intergenerational relations.

The new ageism has gotten so out of hand that it is culminating in the current Republican war against Social Security, Medicare and Medicaid. The first two are the most beloved and necessary government programs in the history of the Republic. And the third, Medicaid, ought to be another.

Virtually all Americans will eventually need Medicaid if we run out of money and need to be in a nursing home. This looks likelier for many of the so-called "Boomers"—especially the long-lived female Boomers—who lost savings in the ongoing Great Recession, had their pensions and unions taken away or lost their jobs and health insurance.

A person who is over 40 and has been laid off may well be a victim of *middle* ageism, which is discrimination against people over 40. People are suing their employers for midlife job discrimination in greater numbers than ever before; men in their 50s, women 10 years younger. Getting rid of midlife workers is a trend that has been worsening for 30 years, as I describe in my book, *Agewise*.

People under 40 are also immersed in what I call the American "culture of decline"— through the descriptions of later life in the media, if in no other way. Older people rarely appear in movies and never in ads for cool products—nothing but the young, the fit and the air-brushed. Why not airbrush older models?

Much worse: You listen to the radio and hear self-proclaimed "experts" tell about the horrors of longevity—how awful physical aging-into-old age will be personally, or how we on the cusp of retirement will break the bank by needing too much Medicare and Social Security. Some commentators even say that people should choose to die instead. (I call this the duty-to-die campaign.) Younger people overhear this, and it skews their expectations of the future and disheartens them. It alienates them from people older than they and from the selves they will one day become.

PUSHING BACK TERROR AND DENIAL

At the same time, some of us are told that "60 is the new 40" and that "the Boomers will change everything to their liking." These are the twin narratives of age terror and age denial. Parts of these narratives are out-and-out silly, but too much is malevolent.

Even what is positive and true can be true only of individuals or a class of people with access to health care, and the ability to meet other basic needs, rather than of everyone over a certain age. One thing is certain: In nothing do people differ more than in their aging. In short, it makes more sense to fear ageism, not aging.

The war against people over 50 changes everything for the worse. In my state, Massachusetts, my Democratic governor wants to raise the age of retirement for public employees. Unionized "Boomers" in government service are told they are too costly. Uninsured people from 55 to 64 die at a higher rate than any other age group of uninsured. Raising the age of Medicare eligibility would be disastrous. None of this is to *my* liking.

There is, however, a backlash against the cuts aimed at Social Security, Medicare and Medicaid. I think anger is building. And justified anger can lead to activism.

The possibility exists of a nationwide coalition forming in order to try to save all the safety nets: *WIC (Women, Infants and Children)*, Social Security, Medicare, public health—and this coalition includes all of those concerned for the vulnerable. It would add together feminists, union people, AARP (the nonpartisan group formerly known as American Association of Retired People), *OWL (Older Women's League)*, so-called Boomers and Xers, who are alleged to be enemies in a *contrived war*, and people in cohorts not yet named by marketeers, plus people younger than 45 and older than 65.

If that coalition became not only powerful but self-conscious, it would have to declare itself "anti-ageist" in order to show how politically important the no-longer-so-young are. This coalition is concerned with social justice and the right to life in the broadest sense.

In the U.S. such a coalition could then be accompanied, I think, by a revolution in representation, meaning that some in the media would have to look at what topics they ignore and how they treat the issues they choose to cover.

N
E
X
T

S
T
E
P
S

FINDING STRENGTH

For example, in Hurricane Katrina, 64 percent of the dead in New Orleans were over 65, although they were only 12 percent of the population, suggesting that older people were ignored in disaster planning. Most in the media did not notice age or ageism. Prior to a disaster, there have to be decisions about "who comes first and who comes last." . . .

Old, frail and disabled people seem to be the collective target of a new eugenics rhetoric. The "duty-to-die campaign" implies that such people are likely to be a "burden," unworthy of resources. If you are not active, engaged, productive, autonomous, close to the ideal healthy (middle-class) "youthful" person, you should somehow bow out. How? Are we expected to commit suicide? This dismissal can even be explicitly age-graded: older people on dialysis may fall into this useless category, especially if they have some cognitive impairment, but not people on dialysis under 65. If some in our society are unafraid to say such things, I fear for the rest of us. Triage involves split-second decisions, and bias is quickest on the draw. In emergencies the would-be rescuers and society at large have to put the neediest first if humanly possible.

There is an ongoing debate in age studies about whether women and men age differently, and I think they do. Women are aged by culture younger than men. I worry about how forced retirement will undermine my own cohort of working women, because they are like men in one new way: they have gotten a lot of satisfaction out of work and earning. And midlife job discrimination is wearing many people down, whether they know this is a collective problem or not.

But because of the women's movement and feminism, women have at least one big advantage—access to a more generous body of knowledge and a more progressive set of attitudes about growing past youth. Feminists in particular are the first to get the point of my book: to beware of ageism, not aging. More women seem to be liking "natural" looks and finding value in their accumulating experience. They read *Ourselves Growing Older*. They enjoy female company, which is going to be very important in late life.

American women are also turning against plastic surgery. The number of procedures reached a peak in 2004 (at 11,855,000), and has dropped every year since. *In 2010 the total was down* to 9,336,000—a decrease of over 20 percent. But when a *New York Times's blogger* did the annual story, she didn't try to find the trend line; instead she used only the surgical association's latest one-year data and a lead about a rise in one particular surgery (breast enhancement). Much depends on the media.

Journalists and scholars need to be more cautious about using releases or publicity from the uglification industries (surgeons, pharmaceutical companies, fashion magazines, even youth-focused health and fitness magazines) and the dysfunction industries (those selling aids to people supposedly declining from great youth sex). They get rich by peddling anxiety about our deficits. *New evidence* from novels, scholarly studies, and memoirs comes out from time to time suggesting that *sex can actually improve* across the life course. But any good news only gets whispered around because those industries are blaring our defects all the time.

The new longevity, along with Alzheimer's terror, coinciding with Republican deficit hysteria—this historical conjuncture is alarming. If our society can't make anti-ageism and anti-middle ageism into an activist mission, the consequences for American society are disastrous, even lethal. . . . Change will take not only resisting stereotypes but challenging the current dismal politics of midlife employment and old age.

NEXT STEPS

128

What Allies of Elders Can Do

Patricia Markee

It feels like you can ignore ageism until you reach the age when it affects you, but in truth it affects you now. It has affected you ever since you were born. It will affect you much more deeply as you grow older, especially if you keep putting it off, denying reality: your age and the treatment you receive.

Although you must acknowledge this oppression now, you may not have to devote much time to it. You can simply select an elder to support. Remember that what we current elders don't figure out is going to land squarely on your shoulders to figure out (if you're lucky enough to become an elder). Supporting an elder against the oppression is an invest-ment in your own future.

In addition to the above, we ask that our allies:

- Assume that we are potentially brilliant. Do not believe any stupid, slow, or bumbly pattern. These are the effects of distress, not aging.
- Assume that we have long, productive futures. Many elders over sixty-five do not have to work and have more discretionary time to be productive. We are not ready to die nor are we waiting to die. I have seen movies in which the old are expected to be the ones to sacrifice their lives. This colludes with the belief that we no longer have anything to contribute.
- Assume that we have not given up on life. Remember that we have seen several genera-tions of young people pass through their teens, twenties, and thirties, and we have noticed that some things last and some things don't. We may not be interested in everything that comes along not because we are intellectually stagnant or afraid, but, because we may have chosen to place our energy into fewer but more lasting things.
- Assume that we are sexually attractive and that we have in front of us many more years of being sexual.
- Assume that everyone can learn from much of our experience; invite us to share our thinking. . . . Don't give up on us at the first sign of distress. Let's break the cycle of abandonment now.
- Assume that memory loss and physical and mental deterioration may be accumulated distress or ill health, not the process of aging.
  . . .
- Don't assume that you know anything about our physical capacities. We may have trouble sitting in a chair, or we may be able to play basketball.
  . . .
- Interrupt others when they assume we're just being critical. We have a right to speak up for our rights without being dismissed.
- Use the same criteria for us to become leaders as you do for others. Expect us to become leaders, in spite of our individual distress. Don't give up on us at the first sign of distress. . . . It's nice if we're "very alive for a fifty-year-old," spontaneous, can have fun, can tap dance at seventy-eight, or are learning to do cart-wheels. But we are more than a vehicle for contradicting your fears [about aging].

NEXT STEPS

- When we have become effective leaders, remember that we are not the all-loving, all-knowing parent you always wanted. We are human beings like you, struggling to figure out our lives. We may have had the time to figure out a few more things, but we are not gods.
  . . .
- Judy Malinowski has discovered that one's assumptions about elders can best be uncovered by asking the questions, "What surprised you about old people?" Asking the question, "What don't you like about old people?" seems to produce only the response, "I love old people," as in "I love children, Afro-Americans, disabled people, etc."
- Pick an elder leader who is not being supported and support her or him. This is simply an investment in your own aging and you may learn a great deal. Besides, . . . it is the role of leaders from the non-target group; it is the role of white leaders to support people of color leaders; it is the role of owning-class and middle-class leadership to support working-class leadership; and it is the role of younger leaders to support elder leaders.

129

Youth Oppression as a Technology of Colonialism

Conceptual Frameworks and Possibilities for Social Justice Education Praxis

Keri DeJong and Barbara J. Love

. . . SJE has been described as an approach for examining social justice issues and seeing them more clearly, as well as a strategy for transforming and ending oppression. We think that SJE praxis can be expanded and deepened by an examination of youth oppression. Praxis has been defined by Freire as "reflection and action upon the world in order to transform it." A key element of SJE praxis is the support for participants to have as clear an understanding as possible of the situation in need of transformation. Acquiring a liberatory consciousness of the conditions that constitute oppression enable engagement with praxis. In this context, inclusion of youth oppression in any reflection on oppression is a necessary condition for praxis to occur.

YOUTH OPPRESSION AS A GENERATIVE THEME

Awareness and analysis of youth oppression can become a generative theme informing SJE praxis, as part of the "thought-language with which [humans] refer to reality, the levels at which they perceive that reality, and their view of the world." As SJE educators incorporate understanding about adultism into their ongoing reflections about oppression, discussions of strategies for transformation will necessarily change.

Reflection on the concrete realities of youth oppression has the capacity to "awaken critical consciousness," and expand our view of possibilities for societal transformation.

Reflections on youth oppression will radically alter the "culture of silence" that surround the realities of youth oppression in Western society. . . .

ADULTS CANNOT LEAD THE WORK OF ENDING YOUTH OPPRESSION ALONE

The current structures of society place resources and power in the hands of adults. This means that there is a very important role for them to play in ending oppression. Adults as a group are in the position to frame the discourse around youth/adult relations. It is often tempting for adults to try to lead the work of ending youth oppression.

Adults must create spaces where they can follow young people's lead in social justice education work. One way that this can happen is through Youth Participatory Action Research. YPAR engages young people as researchers about social issues and experiences that pertain directly to their own lives. Young researchers (with the support of adult allies) identify a problem, research the problem, develop a plan of action to transform the problem, implement the action plan, and then evaluate the impact of their collective action. Research questions and interventions are developed from young people's standpoints and stand in opposition to other research methods that have been used by adults, ensuring the continued domination of young people. For example, The Collective of Researchers on Educational Disappointment and Desire (CREDD), a group of 12 researchers ages 16-22, focussed their efforts on GED credentials in New York City Schools as a "a gateway to higher education and employment, and as a get away from dehumanizing high schools." Their literature review found that researchers (who were likely adults) "often questioned the value of the GED credential in higher education and employment—but never asked youth why they continue to flock to 'a depleted credential.'" Engaging young people who were working towards their GED, CREDD found:

> Seeking out the lived value helped us see how federal mandates (such as No Child Left Behind) and state-mandated exit exams (like the NY Regents) put pressure on schools to push out students who would not do well on standardized tests. Youth of color and poor youth (many who do not feel like school was made for them anyway) are explicitly and implicitly pushed out and pushed toward the GED. Many youth are misinformed about the GED process and mistakenly think that they will be swapping one set of tests for another without having to attend four years of high school. Our participatory action research has taught us that the value of the GED lies less in it being a gateway to higher education and employment and more in being a get-away from inhospitable high schools.

In this case, young people were able to "challenge mainstream perspectives" and shed light on young people's lived experiences in schools when they participated in constructing the research questions, centered young people's lived experiences in the research, and co-constructed the analysis with adult-ally researchers.

It is clear from this discussion that adults cannot lead the work of ending oppression alone. As former young people, adults must notice where they still carry the internalized limits and feelings of powerlessness installed through youth oppression, alongside a sense of entitlement to the privileges of adulthood. Many adults experience a kind of "historical amnesia" that leads them to forget what it was like being a young person. They lack the information that would enable them to be in effective partnerships with young people that are more liberatory and less oppressive. Through engaging a critical examination of the discourses of childhood and adulthood, adults can become more effective at challenging youth oppression in partnership with young people.

N E X T S T E P S

COLONIAL DISCOURSES IN THE ADULT MIND

Adults in the Western world and those who have been influenced by the West have been socialized with the colonial discourses of Western modern childhood. Most adults experienced eagerness to move into adult roles and leave behind the perceived powerlessness of youth. Memmi theorized that the colonized want to become like the colonizer in an effort to change or distance themselves from the conditions of the oppression. Freire describes the process of playing host to the oppressor. Many adults seem to view the powerlessness of childhood as a rite of passage that must be survived to receive the benefits and privileges of adulthood, which in turn means assuming a position of domination in relationship to young people. For these adults, it may seem that if we change the relationship between young people and adult, it will somehow eliminate, destroy, or invalidate their own experience or diminish their status as an adult. For some, it would be if they endured the powerlessness of childhood for nothing.

Other adults acknowledge that youth oppression exits, but express bewilderment about what to do about it. Whether intentional or not, this bewilderment functions as an avoidance strategy by effectively communicating, "If don't understand adultism, then it's the same as if it doesn't exist." It rarely occurs to these adults that these questions can be most effectively answered only by bringing young people into the center of discussions and analysis.

Adults must recover from the personal and historical amnesia that makes it difficult for them to imagine a liberatory, flexible, and equitable relationship between adults and young people. Creating relationships of equity and parity with young people could serve as a staging ground for their capacity to create the conditions of equity and parity in relationships across race, gender, class, and other social identity-based hierarchical relationships. Settler adults must also develop the ability to see where colonial discourse obscures settler colonial structures in order to support the repatriation of Indigenous land and lives.

YOUNG PEOPLE ENACTING AGENCY

In a recent study examining young people's experiences with status and power, participants noted that this study represented their first experience with an adult listening to them talk about their experiences as a young perpson. These study participants stated that this experience was empowering. SJE praxis can benefit from creating more opportunities for young people to enact their own agency. Observing this process can inform theorizing about how people from other subordinated groups become empowered. SJE praxis must include the creation of spaces where young people can reflect on and talk about experiences related to age. This might be with adults or with young people alone. SJE praxis can include the development of listening practices, such a phenomenological listening, for adults to use in their relationships with young people to support the creation of more authentic and equitable, multi-generational partnerships for societal transformation.

EXPANDING SOCIAL JUSTICE EDUCATION CONCEPTUAL FRAMEWORKS: INCLUDING YOUTH OPPRESSION

SJE conceptual frameworks include extensive discussion and analysis of oppression based on race, class, gender, religion, ability, and sexuality. The field is at the beginning stages of analysis and examination of oppression rooted in age-based identities. In this article, we have examined the role of youth oppression in helping humans learn the attitude, under-standings, and behaviors necessary to occupy the roles of dominant and subordinate and thus effectively participate in and perpetuate other manifestations of oppression. Our con-ceptualizations of how oppression is learned, maintained, perpetuated, and consequently how it can be transformed and ended will be profoundly changed with the inclusion of discussions of youth oppression, shaped by the knowledge and experiences of young people. This means that SJE theorizing about ending all other oppressions must necessarily take into account the pivotal role played by youth oppression in the maintenance of an oppressive society.

NEXT STEPS

WORKING FOR SOCIAL JUSTICE
VISIONS AND STRATEGIES
FOR CHANGE

Introduction

Ximena Zúñiga

It takes courage to interrogate yourself. It takes courage to look in the mirror and see past your reflection to who you really are when you take off the mask, when you're not performing the same old routines and social roles. It takes courage to ask – how did I become so well adjusted to injustice?

Cornel West (2008, p. 9)

To engage in dialogue is one of the simplest ways we can begin as [people], teachers, scholars and critical thinkers to cross boundaries, the barriers that may or may not be erected by race, gender, class, professional standing, and a host of other differences.

bell hooks (1994, p. 75)

Without a minimum of hope, we cannot so much as start the struggle. But without the struggle, hope, as an ontological need, dissipates, loses its bearings, and turns into hopelessness. And hopelessness can become tragic despair. Hence, the need for a kind of education in hope.

Paulo Freire (1994, p. 3)

INTRODUCTION

The goals of a social justice education approach include "awareness and understanding of social oppression and its multiple systemic manifestations, acknowledgement of one's role(s) in these systems (as a privileged and/or disadvantaged social group member) and a commitment to develop the vision, skills, resources and coalitions needed to foster lasting change" (Adams &

Zúñiga, 2016, p. 97). Toward these goals, we have articulated throughout this volume the view that developing critical awareness and knowledge about the pervasive and persistent nature of social oppression is a crucial step toward re-imagining what is possible and working toward social justice. Our understanding of oppression as an overarching social system that maintains and reproduces unequal social structures and supremacist ideologies, as well as our awareness of how we may be implicated in these social dynamics, shape our vision of what a more socially just world might look like and motivate us to work toward realizing this vision. That is why so much of this book focuses on describing and analyzing systems of privilege and oppression from different perspectives and understanding how they impact people's lives. However, learning about social injustices can be overwhelming, especially if we don't believe there is anything we can do to change them, so it is also important to understand what compels people to resist, organize, and create change. Both inside and outside the classroom, and in our workplaces and community centers, we need to find hope, the kind of "critical hope" (Duncan-Andrade, 2009) that will allow us to engage in a committed and active struggle against hopelessness and cheap optimism and to defy socially toxic environments by becoming like "roses that grow in the concrete" (p. 186). Otherwise, our awareness and knowledge may simply become "a prescription for despair" (Tatum, 1992, p. 24).

In this concluding section, we invite our readers to envision and construct new possibilities for social justice and liberatory praxis in multiple contexts. By praxis, we mean a kind of action or practice that values critical consciousness, understanding, connectedness, critical dialogue across differences, accountability, solidarity, organizing for change, and alliances and coalitions as pathways for individual and collective empowerment. This kind of action requires an understanding of how systems of power, privilege, and oppression are connected at the psychological, interpersonal, intergroup, structural/institutional, and global levels and the willingness to work with others to effect change at each of these levels.

While we may not be able to take individual or collective actions against multiple forms of oppression at the same time, we can certainly begin by learning about how we and others may participate in or be affected by injustices, such as youth oppression, ethno-religious oppression, racism and white supremacy, heterosexism, and ableism, and by learning to change specific manifestations of oppression in our own spheres of influence (e.g., within ourselves and in our interpersonal relationships with family, friends, and co-workers). In so doing, we learn more about how dynamics of exclusion, privilege, and oppression come into play in our personal and community lives, how different individuals and groups are affected similarly and differently by these dynamics, and how these issues connect to larger national and global issues and systems. At the same time, we learn more about ourselves and develop the intellectual, relational, and organizational skills needed to create change. Audre Lorde (1984) reminds us that working for change can be painful, but it can also be liberating because our individual actions may lead us to change hearts and minds, foster new connections across differences, and forge meaningful ways of engaging in solidarity work with people with whom we share common goals. These kinds of actions provide us with tools to work within organizations and communities, help us build stronger coalitions to work for social justice, and deepen our commitment to social justice.

One set of tools for creating change includes our own growing awareness, knowledge, commitments, passions, and skills. Forging pathways for personal and collective action, empowerment, and liberation also calls for envisioning new possibilities as well as understanding how change happens. These are necessary but not sufficient ingredients for challenging injustice and transforming our schools, communities, and workplaces. Although change may begin with a critical awareness of social inequality and a vision for a more socially just world, we must also use our awareness, passion, and skills to engage in collective actions that will help us to create the world we envision. For instance, we can begin to effect change by educating ourselves and challenging injustice as illustrated by several of the selections introduced earlier in this book (Katz, selection 82; Chess, Kafer, Quizar, and Richardson, selection 93; Ringo, selection 106); by becoming an ally (Evans and Washington, selection 90; Sazama, 126); by engaging in dialogue across differences (Ayvazian and Tatum, selection 23); or by joining organizations and social movements to create change (Leondar-Wright, selection 41; Smith, selection 25; van Gelder, selection 40; the Black Lives Matter website). Participating in community dialogues about race or xenophobia, participatory action research efforts focusing on police violence and environmental issues, local, national, and global social movements, and coalitions to effect change at school, work, or in the community will expand our spheres of influence and contribute to wider systemic change (see Harro, selection 134).

But working in coalition and collaborating across differences is not easy. It takes personal effort to "get ready" (as Harro describes it, in selection 134) by reading, talking, feeling, healing, and learning with and from people from all walks of life—young and old, urban and rural, privileged and disadvantaged—who have resisted and created change individually or in conjunction with others. This is important because, as hooks (1994) and West (2008) explain in the passages quoted as headnotes to this chapter, we need to find the courage to question and engage in dialogue with others to ensure that our vision and hope for a more inclusive and just democracy is shaped by the perspectives and experiences of all of the people involved. Social action needs to be informed by a shared and collective vision, inspiration, courage, love, and hope. Hence, our individual *and* collective visions of a more just society are what will sustain us and move us to take collaborative action against social injustice.

In closing, it is important to acknowledge that individual and collective actions are powerful forces that inspire and move people and groups to transform society and actively contribute to the development of visions, knowledge, networks, organizations, and tools for creating and sustaining change over the long haul. This is partly why so many of the selections included in this section are from activist writers who have been engaged in civil rights movements, labor movements, feminist movements, lesbian, gay, bisexual, and queer social movements, disability rights movements, and, more recently, in women of color and youth organizing and immigration rights and anti-globalization movements. It is also important to recognize the strengths and limitations of our current visions. For instance, some 20th century activists focused almost exclusively on single issues, such as classism, racism, and sexism, and did not consider the ways that these forms of oppression interact in the lives of many within each of these categories until later scholar activists called for a more intersectional analysis (Adams & Zúñiga, 2016; Collins, 1990). Similarly, much early analysis of oppression in the United States constructed frameworks around the dynamics of race, class, and gender relations in the United States and did not include a more global perspective until Third World activists demanded a wider view (Mohanty, 2006; Moraga & Anzaldúa, 1981). Today, the Black Lives Matter movement reminds us of the power of grassroots organizing and mobilization using an intersectional framework to address issues, such as police brutality, school-to-prison pipeline, under-funded urban schools, health care, violence against black youth, queer and trans* people (Taylor, 2016). We do not know what the primary concerns of emerging and future activists in the coming decades will be, but we do know that they will bring new perspectives, new insights, and new tools for social change. We need both the wisdom and experience of older activists and the ideas and energy of young and emerging activists to create change. Together, we can build a world that is inclusive, democratic, and committed to human liberation and social justice.

READINGS IN THIS SECTION

The authors in our "Context" section outline conceptual frameworks for developing a vision for diversity and social justice and describe methods and practices that support the development of critical consciousness as well as actions and practices for social justice. In the first selection,

Suzanne Pharr (selection 130) reminds us that "a truly democratic society is always in the process of redefining itself" and that struggles for liberation are an essential part of that process. She suggests that liberation requires transforming all forms of discrimination and eliminating barriers that keep large portions of the population from attaining economic and social justice—from participating fully in decisions affecting their lives and from having the rights and responsibilities of living in a free society. In Pharr's view, being aware of the historical and social context of oppression and its manifestations at the cultural, institutional, and personal level is not sufficient. We need to have the ideological commitment to work for social justice and the willingness to engage with our hearts, build and honor relationships across differences, hear other perspectives, lend support where there is pain and loss, develop individual and institutional integrity, and redefine and share power in our daily lives.

In the second selection, Barbara J. Love extends Freire's (1973) concept of liberatory consciousness for envisioning and creating change (selection 131). Love identifies four critical elements for developing such consciousness: awareness, analysis, action, and accountability/ally-ship. In her view, the development of liberatory consciousness is a crucial step because it enables us to live our lives "in oppressive systems and institutions with awareness and intentionality, rather than on the basis of the socialization to which we have been subjected." It also enables us to remain hopeful, connected through ally relationships and not to give up to despair.

In the third selection, Patricia Hill Collins (selection 132) proposes that those who wish to engage in social justice actions with people different from themselves need to learn how to transcend barriers created by their own experiences with race, class, and gender oppression to build the types of coalitions essential for social change. Collins identifies three major challenges: recognizing that differing experiences with oppression create problems in relationships; learning how to build relationships and coalitions around common causes with people of different races, genders, and socio-economic statuses; and developing the capacity for empathy for the experiences of individuals and groups different from ourselves. Probably one of the biggest challenges for people who want to work for social justice is knowing where to begin to take responsibility for changing the systems that produce privilege and oppression. Allan G. Johnson (selection 133) identifies several approaches to help us think about "how to make ourselves part of the solution" as we transform our schools, workplaces, communities, and ourselves and urges us to "make noise, be seen" because systems of oppression feed on silence. He also provides many examples of actions we can take, asking us to "dare to make people feel uncomfortable, beginning with yourself" and to "actively promote change in systems that are organized around privilege," beginning in our own spheres of influence.

The process of becoming more aware and confident in our ability to make a difference involves a life-long process of education, commitment, and empowerment. As Bobbie Harro suggests in "The Cycle of Liberation" (selection 134), this process requires education and building relationships with people "like you" and "different from you" to work for a more socially just future. Reading personal narratives and listening to personal stories from people actively involved in creating change is one of the ways we can begin to break the silence and to learn from each other. The "Voices" section features two authors who have devoted their lives to promoting social justice for all people in distinct but connected areas. Cornel West (selection 135), an African American scholar and civil rights activist, writes about the need to muster the courage to work against the grain, think critically about how history is told to us, and to stand up against injustice. Gloria Anzaldúa (selection 136), a visionary Chicana/woman of color feminist, *maestra*/scholar activist discusses the concept of "allies" and what it takes "to help each other heal," using her own experiences as a Chicana, *mestiza*, Mexican, lesbian, activist, poet, and writer. She argues that when doing alliance work—bridge work, boundary work—we talk about who we are and where we come from, even at the risk of being challenged or betrayed.

The selections in the concluding section, "Next Steps," offer varied approaches, methods, and strategies that people working alone or together can use to organize, build alliances, dialogue across differences, and take actions toward building a more just society. Chip Smith (selection 137) outlines a thought-provoking approach to organizing for social justice, starting with the premise that the systemic character of oppression becomes clearer as groups and organizations gain experience, resources, and influence. Drawing from his experience working against racism, sexism, and classism, Smith recommends merging social movements for national liberation, working-class power, and ending patriarchy. He proposes an approach that centers in self-determination, equity, and international solidarity. In the next selection, Ximena Zúñiga, Gretchen Lopez, and Kristie Ford (selection 138) situate intergroup dialogue, a critical-dialogic practice commonly used in schools, colleges, and communities as a form of social justice pedagogy that brings two or more social identity groups together to engage in examining controversial issues through a sociopolitical lens to foster mutual understanding, relationship building, and dialogic praxis across social divides. Through sustained engagement, these efforts can support singular and intersectional conversations across social divides over a period of weeks or months across race/ethnicity and other forms of group differences. This dialogic approach can increase learning and understanding of some of the roots of intergroup tensions while encouraging new possibilities for coalitional action to address community concerns.

From a feminist decolonial perspective, Chandra Mohanty (selection 139) underscores the importance of solidarity as a practice embodied by people who have chosen to work and struggle together. Drawing from her work on Third World feminism, Mohanty defines solidarity as mutuality, accountability, and the recognition of common interests as the basis for coalescing among diverse communities. We conclude this section with an inspirational selection by Alia Wong (selection 140) on student activism in colleges and universities. This essay describes several examples of student dissent and activism across the United States and is a great reminder of the many strategies and tools available to people who want to become informed, come together, mobilize, express dissent and push for change, including sit-ins, rallies, banner and social media campaigns, and walkouts. As Arundhati Roy (2003), Indian novelist and activist, remarked: "Another world is not only possible, she is on her way. Maybe many of us won't be here to greet her, but on a quiet day, if I listen very carefully, I can hear her breathing" (p. 75).

References

Adams, M., & Zúñiga, X. (2016). Core concepts in social justice education. In M. Adams & L. A. Bell (Eds.), *Teaching for diversity and social justice* (pp. 95–130). New York, NY: Routledge.

Collins, P. H. (1990). *Black feminist thought*. London: HarperCollins.

Duncan-Andrade, J. M. R. (2009). Notes to educators: Hope required when growing roses in the concrete. *Harvard Educational Review, 79*(2), 181–194.

Freire, P. (1973). *Education for critical consciousness*. New York, NY: Continuum.

Freire, P. (1994). *Pedagogy of hope*. New York, NY: Continuum.

hooks, b. (1994). *Teaching to transgress*. New York, NY: Routledge.

Lorde, A. (1984). *Sister outsider*. Freedom, CA: Crossing Press.

Mohanty, C. T. (2006). *Feminism without borders*. Durham, NC: Duke University Press.

Moraga, C., & Anzaldúa, G. (Eds.) (1981). *This bridge called my back: Writings by radical women of color*. Albany, NY: Kitchen Table Press.

Roy, A. (2003). *War talk*. Cambridge, MA: South End Press.

Tatum, B. D. (1992). Talking about race, learning about racism: The application of racial identity development theory in the classroom. *Harvard Educational Review, 62*(1), 1–24.

Taylor, K.-Y. (2016). *From # Black lives matter to Black liberation*. Chicago, IL: Haymarket Books.

West, C. (2008). *Hope on a tightrope*. Carlsbad, CA: Smiley Books, Hay House.

130

Reflections on Liberation

Suzanne Pharr

Liberation politics: seeking social and economic justice for all people; supporting inclusion, autonomy, choice, wholeness; building and honoring relationships; developing individual and institutional integrity, responsibility and accountability; redefining and sharing power.

These political times call for renewed dialogue about and commitment to the politics of liberation. Because a truly democratic society is always in the process of redefining itself, its evolution is fueled by struggles for liberation on the part of everyone wishing to participate in the development of the institutions and policies that govern our lives. Liberation requires a struggle against discrimination based on race, class, gender, sexual identity, ableism and age—those barriers which keep large portions of the population from having access to economic and social justice, from being able to participate fully in the decisions affecting our lives, from having a full share of both the rights and responsibilities of living in a free society.

. . .

This is the challenge for all of us. The work of liberation politics is to change hearts and minds, develop empathy with and sympathy for other people, and help each other discover how we are inextricably linked together for our common good and our survival on this planet.

Like power, liberation cannot be given; it must be created. Liberation politics requires

- helping individuals to fulfill their greatest potential by providing truthful information along with the tools and skills for using it, supporting their autonomy and self-government, and connecting them to life in community with others;
- fostering both individual freedom and mutual responsibility for others;
- recognizing that freedom demands people always be able to make their own choices about their lives;
- creating a politic of shared power rather than power-over;
- learning the non-violent skills of compromise and mediation in the sometimes difficult collective lives of family and community—in organizations, the workplace, and governing bodies;
- developing integrity in relationships through understanding that the same communal values—generosity and fairness, responsibility and freedom, forgiveness and atonement—must be maintained not just in personal relationships but in the workplace, social groups, and governing bodies;
- treating everyone as a valued whole person, not as someone to be used or controlled;
- maintaining civility in our relationships and being accountable for our behavior;
- seeing cultural differences as life-enhancing, as expanding possibilities;
- placing a broad definition of human rights at the center of our values: ensuring that every person has food, shelter, clothing, safety, education, health care, and a livable income.

. . .

We are seeking ways to bring people together to work on common causes across differences. If, indeed, all oppressions are connected, then it follows that the targets of this oppression are connected as well as their solution. This interconnection leads us to the idea of collaborative efforts to create democratic values, discourse and institutions.

We believe that we will succeed when we collectively create a vision that in practice offers a way of life so attractive that people will not be able to resist it. As progressive people across this country we are working to create a multi-issue, multi-racial and multi-cultural liberation movement; we are trying to redefine our work and bring more integrity to it; we are engaged in developing a clearer, more compelling vision, building stronger relationships among justice-seeking people, and including more people in the process of creating a democracy that works for all of us.

. . .

TRANSFORMATIONAL ORGANIZING AND BUILDING COMMUNITY

For whatever reasons, progressive people have not always talked a great deal about the strong moral convictions underlying why we do this work of social justice: *it is because we believe every person counts, has human dignity, and deserves respect, equality and justice.* This morality is the basis for our vision, and when we do our best vision-based organizing (as opposed to response-based or expediency-based), all our work flows from this basic belief.

Ours is a noble history. Because progressive people believe in the inclusion of everyone in the cause of justice and equality, we have struggled for civil rights for people of color, for women, for people with disabilities, and now for lesbians and gay men. We have worked to save the environment, to provide women with autonomy and choice concerning our bodies, to end unjust wars, to end homelessness, hunger, and poverty, to create safe work-places, decent wages and fair labor practices, to honor treaty rights, to eliminate HIV and improve health care, to eliminate biased crime and violence against women and children. We share broad principles of inclusion, fairness, and justice. We must not forget what provides the fire for our work, what connects us in the struggle for freedom and equality.

We are living in a time in which people are crying out for something to believe in, for a moral sense, for purpose, for answers that will bring some calm to the chaos they feel in their lives. As progressive people, we have not always offered up our vision of the world, our activities for justice, as a moral vision. When we have, as during the Civil Rights Movement, people working together for a common good have felt whole.

I believe it is our moral imperative to help each other make connections, to show how everyone is interrelated and belongs in community, or as it is currently expressed, "We all came on different ships but we're in the same boat now." It is at our peril if we do work that increases alienation and robs meaning from life. Today's expressions of violence, hatred, and bigotry are directly related to the level of alienation and disconnection felt by people. For our very survival, we must develop a sense of common humanity.

It may be that our most important political work is figuring out how to make the full human connection, how to engage our hearts as well as our minds, how to heal the injuries we have suffered, how to do organizing that transforms people as well as institutions. With these as goals, we need to re-think our strategies and tactics.

We have to think about our vision of change. Are we involved in a struggle for power that requires forces and resources on each side and a confrontational show-down in which only one side wins? If we are in a shoot-out, then the progressive side has already lost, for certainly there are more resources on the Right at this moment. In other cases where we can organize the most resources, such as the 1992 "No on 9" campaign in Oregon, what is the nature and permanency of the win? The anti-gay and lesbian constitutional amendment was defeated, but in general, people did not have a sense of ecstatic victory. I think there were two primary reasons: 1) the Right immediately announced its intention to take the fight to local rural communities and to build a string of victories in areas where it had developed support—indicating that this is indeed a long struggle for the hearts and souls of Oregonians; and 2) the campaign did not facilitate the building of lasting relationships, of communities, of progressive institutions—because it did not see itself as part of a movement. At the end, I believe people felt a war-like atmosphere had been created, but that the language and tactics of war had failed them. In the months that followed the election victory, people seemed fatigued, wary, often dispirited and in retreat. Rather than being transformed into new politics and relationships by their experience, they seemed battered by it.

Transformational Organizing. There is something to be learned when victory feels like defeat. Somehow, people did not emerge from the Oregon experience with a sense of vitality, of wholeness, of connection. Justice-seeking people must call into question our methods of organizing. Often we have thought that effective organizing is simply being able to move people as a group, sometimes through manipulation, to act in a particular way to achieve a goal. Too often the end has justified the means, and we have failed to follow Ghandi's belief that every step toward liberation must have liberation embedded within it. By concentrating on moving people to action, we have often failed to hear the voice of their spirit, their need for connection and wholeness—not for someday after the goal has been gained, but in the very process of gaining it.

I am not arguing that we should give up direct action, civil disobedience, issue campaigns, political education, confrontation, membership and voter drives, etc. We need to do these things and much more. I am suggesting that we re-think the meaning of social change and learn how to include the long-term work of transforming people as we work for social justice. We must re-define "winning." Our social change has to be more than amassing resources and shifting power from the hands of one group to another; we must seek a true shift in consciousness, one that forges vision, goals, and strategies from belief, not just from expediency, and allows us to become a strong political force.

The definition of transformational politics is fairly simple: it is political work that changes the hearts and minds of people, supports personal and group growth in ways that create healthy, whole people, organizations, and communities, and is based on a vision of a society where people—across lines of race, gender, class and sexuality—are supported by institutions and communities to live their best lives.

Among many possibilities, I want to suggest one way to do transformational work: through building community that is based on our moral vision.

Building Community, Making Connections. Where do we build community? Should it be geographic, consisting of everyone who lives in the same neighborhood? Based on identity, such as one's racial identity, sexual identity? Organizational or work identity? Where are the places that community happens?

It seems to me that community can be created in a vast number of places and ways. What is more important is the *how* of building community. To get to the how, we first have to define what community is. Community is people in any configuration (geographic, identity, etc.) bonded together over time through common interest and concern, through responsibility and accountability to one another, and at its best, through commitment, friendship and love.

To live in authentic community requires a deeper level of caring and interaction than many of us currently exhibit in our drive for individualism and self-fulfillment. That is, it calls for living with communal values. And we face a daunting challenge here because we all live in a culture that glorifies individualism. For example, what the Right calls "traditional family values" actually works against the often-quoted African proverb, "It takes a village to raise a child," which speaks to the communal value of the importance of every child in the life of the community, present and future. Such values point to very different solutions than those currently suggested for the problems of youth alienation, crime, and violence. Rather than increasing police forces and building more jails, with these shared values we would look toward more ways for the community as a whole to be responsible for and accountable to children. We would seek ways to support and nurture their lives. All of us would be teachers, parents and friends for every child.

Creating community requires seeing the whole, not just the parts, and understanding how they interrelate. However, the difficult part is learning how to honor the needs of the individual as well as those of the group, without denying the importance of either. It requires a balance between identity and freedom on the one hand and the collective good and public responsibility on the other. It requires ritual and celebration and collective ways to grieve and show anger; it requires a commitment to resolve conflict.

Most of all, it requires authenticity in relationships between and among whole people. This means that each of us has to be able to bring all of who we are to the relationship, neighbor to neighbor, friend to friend, worker to worker. Bringing all of who we are to community requires working across great differences in culture, in lifestyle, in belief. It demands that we look beyond our own lives to understand the lives of others. It demands that we interact with the lives of others. It requires understanding the connections among people's lives and then seeking comprehensive solutions to multi-issue, multifaceted problems. If we allow only certain parts of people to surface, and if we silence, reject or exclude basic pieces of their essential selves, then we begin designing systems of oppression. Community becomes based on power and non-consensual authority: those who have the most power and privilege dictate the community norms and their enforcement.

One of the goals of every political activity we engage in should be to move beyond superficial interactions to the building of relationships and community. Much of this work is simple, not difficult or complex; it merely requires redefining our values and how we spend our political time. For example, far too often I go to meetings, frequently held in sterile hotel conference rooms, where introductions are limited to people giving their names or, at best, what work they do. Building relationships—whether those of neighbor, friend, lover, work partner—requires that we ask *who are you*? In rural communities in the South and on American Indian reservations, people spend a lot of time talking about who their people are, how they are connected to people and place. Women activists in the housing projects in New Orleans get to know each other by telling their life lines, the major events that shaped them along the way. It is almost ritual for lesbians to get to know each other by telling their coming out stories—when and how they first experienced their lesbianism.

Building connection and relationship requires that we give it time, not just in meetings but in informal opportunities surrounding meetings, structured and unstructured. For instance, when I did political education on oppression issues within the battered women's movement, there was always a dramatic difference in the relationships that were built when we stayed in retreat centers or self-contained places away from distracting outside activities rather than in city hotels. So much of what happened in people's growth and understanding came from living, sleeping, and eating together in an atmosphere that encouraged interaction.

As a way to think about building community, we can ask ourselves these questions:

- In what settings with other people have I felt most whole? What is it that makes me feel known and accepted as who I am?
- What conditions make me most able to work well in partnership with other people? What makes me feel connected rather than alienated?
- What are communal values? What are the practices that support them?
- Where are the places where community is occurring? (For example, in care teams for people living with AIDS, in youth gangs, in certain churches or neighborhoods, in AA groups?) What are the characteristics of these communities?
- Who is being excluded from community? What barriers are there to participation?
- What are the qualities of an inclusive community as opposed to an exclusive community?
- What makes a community democratic?

Our communities are where our moral values are expressed. It is here that we are called upon to share our connection to others, our interdependence, our deepest belief in what it means to be part of the human condition, where people's lives touch one another, for good or for bad. It is here where the rhetoric of belief is forced into the reality of living. It is from this collection of people, holding within it smaller units called families, that we build and live democracy. Or, without care and nurturance, where we detach from one another and destroy our hope for survival.

POLITICAL INTEGRITY AND MULTI-ISSUE POLITICS

It is one thing for us to talk about liberation politics; it is of course another to live them. We lack political integrity when we demand liberation for one cause or one group of people and act out oppression or exploitation toward others. If we do not have an integrated analysis and a commitment to sharing power, it is easy to act out politics that simply reflect a hierarchy of domination.

In our social change organizations in particular we can find ourselves in this dangerous position: where we are demanding, for example, liberation from sexism but within the organization we act out racism, economic injustice, and homophobia. Each is reflected in who is allowed to lead, who makes the highest and lowest salaries, who is allowed to participate in the major decision-making, who decides how the resources are used. If the organization does not have a vision and a strategy that also include the elimination of racism, sexism, economic injustice, and homophobia (as well as oppressions relating to age, physical ability, etc.), then internal conflict is inevitable. People cannot single out just one oppression from their lives to bring to their work for liberation: they bring their whole selves.

Creating a multi-racial, multi-cultural, multi-issue vision of liberation is no easy task. It is much easier to stay within the framework of oppression where our women's organizations' leadership is primarily white, middle-class women, heterosexual or closeted lesbians; our civil rights organizations are male-dominated; our gay/lesbian/bi/transgender organizations are controlled by white gay men and/or white lesbians. And where the agendas for change reflect the values of those who dominate the leadership.

It is easier to talk about "diversity" than about shared power. Or to use a belief in identity politics to justify not including others in a vision for change. I do not believe in either diversity or identity politics as they are currently practiced.

First, diversity politics seem to focus on the necessity for having everyone (across gender, race, class, age, religion, physical ability) present and treated well in any given setting or organization. A core premise is that everyone is oppressed and all oppressions are equal. Since the publication of the report, "Workforce 2000," that predicted the U.S. workforce would be made up of 80% women and people of color by the year 2000, a veritable growth industry of "diversity consultants" has arisen to teach corporations how to "manage" diversity. With integration and productivity as goals, they focus on issues of sensitivity and inclusion—a human relations approach—with acceptance and comfort as high priorities. Popular images of diversity politics show people holding hands around America, singing "We Are the World." People are generally reassured that they do not have to give up anything when they diversify their workplace. They simply have to include other people and become more sensitive to differences.

Because the history of oppression is one of excluding, of silencing, of rendering people invisible, I have great appreciation for the part of diversity work that concentrates on making sure everyone is included. However, our diversity work fails if it does not deal with the power dynamics of difference and go straight to the heart of shifting the balance of power among individuals and within institutions. A danger of diversity politics lies in the possibility that it may become a tool of oppression by creating the illusion of participation when in fact there is no shared power. Having a presence within an organization or institution means very little if one does not have the power of decision-making, an adequate share of the resources, and participation in the development of the workplan or agenda. We as oppressed people must demand much more than acceptance. Tolerance, sympathy and understanding are not enough, though they soften the impact of oppression by making people feel better in the face of it. Our job is not just to soften blows but to make change, fundamental and far-reaching.

Identity politics, on the other hand, rather than trying to include everyone, brings together people who share a single common identity such as sexual orientation, gender, or race. Generally, it focuses on the elimination of a single oppression, the one that is based on the common identity; e.g., homophobia/heterosexism, sexism, racism. However, this can be a limited, hierarchical approach, reducing people of multiple identities to a single identity. Which identity should a lesbian of color choose as a priority—gender, race or sexual identity? And does choosing one necessitate leaving the other two at home? What do we say to bisexual or biracial people? Do we tell them to choose? Our multiple identities allow us to develop a politic that is broad in scope because it is grounded in a wide range of experiences.

There are positive aspects of organizing along identity lines: clarity of single focus in tactics and strategies, self-examination and education apart from the dominant culture, development of solidarity and group bonding. Creating organizations based on identity allows us to have visibility and collective power, to advance concerns that otherwise would never be recognized because of our marginalization within the dominant society.

However, identity politics often suffers from the failure to acknowledge that the same multiplicity of oppressions, a similar imbalance of power, exists within identity groups as within the larger society. People who group together on the basis of their sexual identity still find within these groups sexism and racism that have to be dealt with—or if gathering on the basis of race, there is still sexism and homophobia to be confronted. Whole, not partial, people come to identity groups, carrying several identities. Some of liberation movements' major barriers to building a unified and cohesive strategy, I believe, come from our refusal to work directly on the oppressions—those fundamental issues of power—within our own groups. A successful liberation movement cannot be built on the effort to liberate only a few or only a piece of who we are.

Diversity and identity politics are responses to oppression. In confronting oppressions we must always remember that they mean more than people just not being nice to one another. They are systemic, based in institutions and in general society, where one group of people is allowed to exert power and control over members of another group, denying them fundamental rights. Also, we must remember that oppressions are interconnected, operating in similar ways, and that many people experience more than one oppression.

. . .

The question, as ever, is what to do? I do not believe that either a diversity or identity politics approach will work unless they are changed to incorporate a multi-issue analysis and strategy that combine the politics of inclusion with shared power. But, one might say, it will spread us too thin if we try to work on everyone's issue, and ours will fall by the wayside. In our external work (doing women's anti-violence work, working against police brutality in people of color communities, seeking government funding for AIDS research), we do not have to work on "everybody's issue"—we can be focused. But how can we achieve true social change unless we look at all within our constituency who are affected by our particular issue? People who have AIDS are of every race, class, age, gender, geographic location, but when research and services are sought, it is women, people of color, poor people, who are most overlooked. The HIV virus rages on because those in power think that the people who contract it are dispensable. Are we to be like them? To understand why police brutality is so much more extreme in people of color communities than in white, we have to understand also why, even within these communities, it is even greater against poor people of color, women who are prostitutes, and gay men and lesbians of color. To leave any group out leaves a hole for everyone's freedoms and rights to fall through. It becomes an issue of "acceptable" and "unacceptable" people, deserving and undeserving of rights, legitimate and illegitimate, deserving of recognition as fully human or dismissable as something less.

Identity politics offers a strong, vital place for bonding, for developing political analysis. With each other we struggle to understand our relationship to a world that says that we are no more than our identity, and simultaneously denies there is oppression based on race or gender or sexual identity. Our challenge is to learn how to use the experiences of our many identities to forge an inclusive social change politic. The question that faces us is how to do multi-issue coalition building from an identity base. The hope for a multi-racial, multi-issue movement rests in large part on the answer to this question.

Our linkages can create a movement, and our divisions can destroy us. Each point of linkage is our strongest defense and also holds the most possibility for long-lasting social change.

If our organizations are not committed internally to the inclusion and shared power of all those who share our issue, how can we with any integrity demand inclusion and shared power in society at large? If women, lesbians and gay men are treated as people undeserving of equality within civil rights organizations, how can those organizations demand equality? If women of color and poor women are marginalized in women's rights organizations, how can those organizations argue that women as a class should be moved into full participation in the mainstream? If lesbian and gay organizations are not feminist and anti-racist in all their practices, what hope is there for the elimination of homophobia and heterosexism in a racist, sexist society? It is an issue of integrity.

In the larger social change community our failure to connect issues prevents us from being able to do strong coalition and alliance work with one another. Most frequently, coalitions and alliances are created to meet crisis issues which threaten all of us. Made up of groups that experience injustice, they should have common ground. They most frequently fall apart, I believe, because of failure in relationships. As in all human relationships, it is difficult to solve the issue of the moment without a history of trust, common struggle, and reciprocity. Homophobia, for example, has kept us "quiet" and invisible in our anti-racist work; racism has kept us "quiet" in our lesbian and gay work. We need to be visible in our work on all fronts. Working shoulder to shoulder on each other's issues enables us to get to know each other's humanity, to understand the broad sweep of issues, to build trust and solidarity.

Our separateness, by identity and by issue, prevents the building of a progressive movement. When we grasp the value and interconnectedness of our liberation issues, then we will at last be able to make true coalition and begin building a common agenda that eliminates oppression and brings forth a vision of diversity that shares both power and resources.

. . .

131

Developing a Liberatory Consciousness

Barbara J. Love

All members of society play a role in keeping a "dis-equal" system in place, whether the system works to their benefit or to their disadvantage. Through the socialization process, every member of society learns the attitudes, language, behaviors and skills that are necessary to function effectively in the existing society. This socialization prepares individuals to play roles of dominant or subordinant in systems of oppression.[1] For example, men are assigned the role of dominant and women are assigned the role of subordinant in the system of dis-equality based on gender. Whites are assigned to play the role of dominant and People of Color are assigned the role of subordinant in the system of dis-equality based on race. The socialization process of the society works to insure that each person learns what they need to know to behave in ways that contribute to the maintenance and perpetuation of the existing system, independent of their belief in its fairness or efficacy.

No single human can be charged with the creation of the oppressive systems in operation today. All humans now living have internalized the attitudes, understandings, and patterns of thoughts that allow them to function in and collaborate with these systems of oppression, whether they benefit from them or are placed at a disadvantage by them. The patterns of thought and behaviors that support and help to maintain racism, sexism, classism and other manifestations of oppression are not natural or inherent to any human. They are learned through this socialization process.

Many members of society, both those who benefit from oppression as well as those who are placed at disadvantage, want to work for social change to reduce inequity and bring about greater justice, yet continue to behave in ways that preserve and perpetuate the existing system. This happens because humans are products of their socialization and follow the habits of mind and thought that have been instilled in them. The institutions in which we live reward and reinforce behaviors that perpetuate existing systems and resist efforts toward change.

To be effective as a liberation worker—that is, one who is committed to changing systems and institutions characterized by oppression to create greater equity and social justice—a crucial step is the development of a liberatory consciousness. A liberatory consciousness enables humans to live their lives in oppressive systems and institutions with awareness and intentionality, rather than on the basis of the socialization to which they have been subjected. A liberatory consciousness enables humans to maintain an awareness of the dynamics of oppression characterizing society without giving in to despair and hopelessness about that condition, to maintain an awareness of the role played by each individual in the maintenance of the system without blaming them for the roles they play, and at the same time practice intentionality about changing the systems of oppression. A liberatory consciousness enables humans to live "outside" the patterns of thought and behavior learned through the socialization process that helps to perpetuate oppressive systems.

ELEMENTS OF A LIBERATORY CONSCIOUSNESS

The process for developing a liberatory consciousness has been discussed by many educators working for social change and social justice. Paulo Freire, the Brazilian educator, described it as developing critical consciousness. Carter G. Woodson described it as changing the "miseducation of the Negro." Michael Albert's humanist vision and bell hooks's feminist critical consciousness are examples of other ways that a liberatory consciousness has been discussed.

Four elements in developing a liberatory consciousness are described here. They include awareness, analysis, action, and accountability/ally-ship. The labeling of these four components in the development of a liberatory consciousness is meant to serve as reminders in our daily living that the development and practice of a liberatory consciousness is neither mysterious nor difficult, static nor fixed, or something that some people have and others do not. It is to be continually practiced event by event, each time we are faced with a situation in which oppression or internalized oppression is evident. These labels remind us that every human can acquire the skill to become a liberation worker.

Awareness, the first part of the task, includes practicing awareness or noticing what is happening. The second part includes analyzing what is happening from a stance of awareness along with the possibilities for action. The third part of the task includes deciding on the basis of that analysis what needs to be done, and seeing to it that the action is accomplished. The fourth part may be the most troublesome part for it requires that individuals accept accountability to self and community for the consequences of the action that has been taken or not taken.

With a liberatory consciousness, every person gets a chance to theorize about issues of equity and social justice, to analyze events related to equity and social justice, and to act in responsible ways to transform the society.

AWARENESS

The awareness component of a liberatory consciousness involves developing the capacity to notice, to give our attention to our daily lives, our language, our behaviors, and even our thoughts. It means making the decision to live our lives from a waking position. It means giving up the numbness and dullness with which we have been lulled into going through life. For some, facing life with awareness may at first seem painful. One student, in a class examining oppression, declared with dismay, "You have taken the fun out of going to the movies. Now I can't watch stupid movies and laugh anymore." This student had observed that even while watching "stupid movies" certain attitudes were being instilled in his consciousness. He noticed that some of these were attitudes and ideas that he would reject if he were consciously paying attention.

Living with awareness means noticing what happens in the world around you. If a salesperson reaches around you to serve the person in line behind you, a liberatory consciousness means taking notice of this act rather than ignoring it, pretending that it did not happen, or thinking it is of little consequence. If disparaging remarks about people of a different group are made in your presence, awareness requires taking note that an event has occurred that effects the maintenance or elimination of oppression. It means noticing that the remark was made, and not pretending that the remark is harmless.

ANALYSIS

A liberatory consciousness requires every individual to not only notice what is going on in the world around her or him, but to think about it and theorize about it—that is, to get information and develop his or her own explanation for what is happening, why it is happening, and what needs to be done about it.

The analysis component of a liberatory consciousness includes the activity of thinking about what needs to be done in a given situation. Every human has the capacity to examine any situation in order to determine what seems to be true about that situation. Awareness coupled with analysis of that situation becomes the basis for determining whether change is required, and if it is, the nature of the change needed.

If what we observe to be true about a given situation seems consistent with our values of an equitable society, then the analysis will conclude that the situation is fine exactly as is. If, on the other hand, the observation leads to the conclusion that the situation is unjust, then a conclusion that the situation needs to be changed is reached.

Analysis will reveal a range of possible courses of action. Each possibility will be examined to determine what results are likely to be produced. Some possible activities will produce results that are consistent with our goals of justice and fairness while some will not. Analysis means considering the range of possible activities and the results that each of them is likely to produce.

ACTION

The action component of a liberatory consciousness proceeds from recognition that aware-ness and analysis alone are not enough. There can be no division between those who think and those who put thinking into action. The action component of a liberatory conscious-ness is based on the assumption that the participation of each of us in the liberation project provides the best possibility of gaining liberation for any of us.

The action component of a liberatory consciousness includes deciding what needs to be done, and then seeing to it that action is taken. Sometimes it means taking individual initia-tive to follow a course of action. Sometimes it means encouraging others to take action. Sometimes it means organizing and supporting other people to feel empowered to take the action that the situation requires. And sometimes, locating the resources that empower another person to act with agency is required. In still other cases, reminding others that they are right for the task, and that they know enough and are powerful enough to take on the challenge of seeing that the task is completed will be the action that is required. In any event, the liberatory consciousness requires each human to take some action in every situation when the opportunity to transform the society and move toward a more just world presents itself.

ACCOUNTABILITY/ALLY-SHIP

The socialization to which we have been subjected results in our thinking and behaving in very role-specific ways. We have been socialized into roles of dominant and subordinant. One result is that our vision of possibilities for change is limited by our confinement in the roles to which we have been assigned. Many white people flounder in their efforts to extricate themselves from racist conditioning. They become stuck while working on racism because their socialization to the role of dominant provides very little opportunity to understand what life might be like outside that role. A Person of Color will often have a perspective or "window of understanding" that is unavailable to a white person because of the latter's socialization into whiteness. Left alone in their struggle, some individual white people do eventually figure the difficulty out; many do not. When a Person of Color chooses to share her or his "window of understanding," the growth and development of a white person, away from racist conditioning, can be significantly enhanced and quickened.

Similarly, a Person of Color can become stuck in patterns of internalized racism and left alone to struggle. A white person can hold a perspective that is outside the socialization into racial subordination that, when shared, boosts the efforts of a Person of Color to eliminate patterns of internalized racism. The same holds true for men addressing sexism and for women addressing internalized sexism, as well as for "owning-class" people, those raised poor, and working-class people who are concerned with classism.

People raised on one end of patterns of gender, race, and class subordination or domina-tion can provide a different perspective for people raised on the other end. At the same time, people within role groups can assist other members of their own role group to rec-ognize and eliminate those patterns of thought and behavior that originate in internalized subordination or domination. For example, women, People of Color, those raised poor, and working-class people can help each other better understand the ways that our auto-matic responses help to perpetuate and maintain our own oppression.

The accountability element of a liberatory consciousness is concerned with how we understand and manage this opportunity and possibility for perspective sharing and ally-ship in liberation work. Individuals engaged in liberation work can have confidence that, left to their own struggles, others will eventually figure out what they need to know to disentangle thought and behavior patterns from the internalized oppression, either internalized domination or internalized subordination. But working in connection and collaboration with each other, across and within "role" groups, we can make progress in ways that are not apparent when working in isolation and in separate communities.

In our liberation work, many of us have taken the position that it is not the responsibility of members of the subordinant group to teach or help to educate members of the dominant group. This is a reasonable and essentially "righteous" position. Those people who bear the brunt of the oppression should not be required to also take responsibility for eliminating it. At the same time, it is self-evident that people in the subordinant group can take the lead in setting the world right. For one thing, if people in the dominant group had access to and were able to hold a perspective that allowed them to change systems and patterns of domination, they would have done so already. Members of the subordinant group can wait for members of the dominant group to recognize that their language or behavior is oppressive, or they can share their perspective in every place where it could make a difference, including in the lives of members of the dominant group. In the end, it is in their best interest to do so.

This does not mean that members of groups who have been socialized into roles of subordination should focus their attention outward on the dominant group, or that members of dominant groups should be focused on the subordinant group. It is to suggest that when the perspective of the other group can serve as the critical energy to move things forward, liberation will be hampered if we hold our thinking and perspectives back from each other. Concomitantly, it also suggests that individual members of dominant and subordinant groups offer their perspective to other members of their role group in the effort to move forward.

As liberation workers, it is axiomatic that we will make mistakes. Rather than self-condemnation or blame from others, it will be important to have the opportunity and the openness to hear an analysis from others that allows us to reevaluate problematic behaviors or positions. If a Black person notices another Black person acting out of internalized racism, a liberatory consciousness requires considering the usefulness of sharing a viewpoint that enables that person to explore the implications of internalized racism for their behavior. While we do not take responsibility for another's thinking or behavior, accountability means that we support each other to learn more about the ways that the internalized domination and internalized subordination manifests itself in our lives, and agree with each other that we will act to interrupt it.

Accepting accountability to self and community for the consequences of actions taken or not taken can be an elusive concept for a people steeped in the ideology of individualism. Multiplicities of experiences and points of view contribute to problematizing the concept of accountability as well. None of us can claim for ourselves the right to tell another that her analysis is retrogressive. Recent discussions of "political correctness" can also prove troubling in the effort to grasp the idea of accountability and make it a workable concept.

There will be no easy answers here. The significance of a liberatory consciousness is that we will always question, explore, and interrogate ourselves about possibilities for supporting the efforts of others to come to grips with our conditioning into oppression, and give each other a hand in moving outside of our assigned roles. The accountability element of a liberatory consciousness requires us to develop new agreements regarding our interactions with each other. As a beginning, we get to decide the extent to which we will make ourselves available to interrupt language and behavior patterns that, in our best analysis, originate in an internalization of the ideology of domination and subordination.

SUMMARY

In the end, institutions and systems respond to the initiatives of individuals and groups of individuals. Systems do not perpetuate themselves: they are perpetuated by the actions of people who act automatically on the basis of their socialization. If we all acted on the basis of values and beliefs of our own choosing, systems and institutions would show greater flexibility and propensity for change. As it now stands, most of us act on the basis of values and beliefs instilled in us through the socialization process, designed to prepare us to act in ways that insure the perpetuation of existing systems of oppression.

The development of a liberatory consciousness would allow us the opportunity to reclaim choice in our values and attitudes and consequently, in our response patterns. It would enable us to move from an automatic response system grounded in our socialization, to the capacity to act on a range of responses based on our own awareness, analysis and decision making, and the opportunities we have to learn from our colleagues and others who are themselves embarked on a journey to liberation.

Note

1. I prefer the spelling *subordinant* because: (1) *subordinant* is a noun; *subordinate* is an adjective, modifying the noun; (2) *subordinant* parallels *dominant*, but *subordinate* describes what is done to the *subordinants*; (3) if we were to parallel *subordinate*, then we would need to write *dominate*; and (4) using the modifying adjective to refer to groups of people seems to further objectify and reduce.

132

Toward a New Vision

Race, Class, and Gender

Patricia Hill Collins

How can we transcend the barriers created by our experiences with race, class and gender oppression in order to build the types of coalitions essential for social change?

Reconceptualizing oppression and seeing the barriers created by race, class and gender as interlocking categories of analysis is a vital first step. But we must transcend these barriers by moving toward race, class and gender as categories of connection, by building relationships and coalitions that will bring about social change. What are some of the issues involved in doing this?

1. DIFFERENCES IN POWER AND PRIVILEGE

First, we must recognize that our differing experiences with oppression create problems in the relationships among us. Each of us lives within a system that vests us with varying levels of power and privilege. These differences in power, whether structured along axes of race, class, gender, age or sexual orientation, frame our relationships. African-American writer June Jordan describes her discomfort on a Caribbean vacation with Olive, the Black woman who cleaned her room:

616 | WORKING FOR SOCIAL JUSTICE

... even though both "Olive" and "I" live inside a conflict neither one of us created, and even though both of us therefore hurt inside that conflict, I may be one of the monsters she needs to eliminate from her universe and, in a sense, she may be one of the monsters in mine.

(1985, 47)

Differences in power constrain our ability to connect with one another even when we think we are engaged in dialogue across differences. Let me give you an example. One year, the students in my course "Sociology of the Black Community" got into a heated discussion about the reasons for the upsurge of racial incidents on college campuses. Black students complained vehemently about the apathy and resistance they felt most White students expressed about examining their own racism. Mark, a White male student, found their comments particularly unsettling. After claiming that all the Black people he had ever known had expressed no such beliefs to him, he questioned how representative the viewpoints of his fellow students actually were. When pushed further, Mark revealed that he had participated in conversations over the years with the Black domestic worker employed by his family. Since she had never expressed such strong feelings about White racism, Mark was genuinely shocked by class discussions. Ask yourselves whether that domestic worker was in a position to speak freely. Would it have been wise for her to do so in a situation where the power between the two parties was so unequal?

In extreme cases, members of privileged groups can erase the very presence of the less privileged. When I first moved to Cincinnati, my family and I went on a picnic at a local park. Picnicking next to us was a family of White Appalachians. When I went to push my daughter on the swings, several of the children came over. They had missing, yellowed and broken teeth, they wore old clothing and their poverty was evident. I was shocked. Growing up in a large eastern city, I had never seen such awful poverty among Whites. The segregated neighborhoods in which I grew up made White poverty all but invisible. More importantly, the privileges attached to my newly acquired social class position allowed me to ignore and minimize the poverty among Whites that I did encounter. My reactions to those children made me realize how confining phrases such as "well, at least they're not Black" had become for me. In learning to grant human subjectivity to the Black victims of poverty, I had simultaneously learned to demand White victims of poverty. By applying categories of race to the objective conditions confronting me, I was quantifying and ranking oppressions and missing the very real suffering which, in fact, is the real issue.

One common pattern of relationships across differences in power is one that I label "voyeurism." From the perspective of the privileged, the lives of people of color, of the poor, and of women are interesting for their entertainment value. The privileged become voyeurs, passive onlookers who do not relate to the less powerful, but who are interested in seeing how the "different" live. Over the years, I have heard numerous African-American students complain about professors who never call on them except when a so-called Black issue is being discussed. The students' interest in discussing race or qualifications for doing so appear unimportant to the professor's efforts to use Black students' experiences as stories to make the material come alive for the White student audience. Asking Black students to perform on cue and provide a Black experience for their White classmates can be seen as voyeurism at its worst.

Members of subordinate groups do not willingly participate in such exchanges but often do so because members of dominant groups control the institutional and symbolic apparatuses of oppression. Racial/ethnic groups, women, and the poor have never had the luxury of being voyeurs of the lives of the privileged. Our ability to survive in hostile settings has hinged on our ability to learn intricate details about the behavior and world view of the powerful and adjust our behavior accordingly. I need only point to the difference in perception of those men and women in abusive relationships. Where men can view their girlfriends and wives as sex objects, helpmates and a collection of stereotyped categories of voyeurism—women must be attuned to every nuance of their partners' behavior. Are women "naturally" better in relating to people with more power than themselves, or have circumstances mandated that men and women develop different skills? Another pattern in relationships among people of unequal power concerns a different form of exploitation. In scholarly enterprises, relationships among students and teachers, among researchers and their subjects, and even among us as colleagues in teaching and scholarship can contain elements of academic colonialism. Years ago, a Black co-worker of mine in the Roxbury section of Boston described the academic colonialism he saw among the teachers and scholars in that African-American community:

> The people with notebooks from Harvard come around here and study us. They don't get to know us because they really don't want to and we don't want to let them. They see what they want to see, go back and write their books and get famous off of our problems.

Under academic colonialism, more powerful groups see their subordinates as people that they perceive as subordinate to them, not as entertainment as was the case in voyeurism, but as a resource to be benignly exploited for their own purposes.

The longstanding effort to "colorize" feminist theory by inserting the experiences of women of color represents, at best, genuine efforts to reduce bias in women's studies. But at its worst colorization also contains elements of both voyeurism and academic colonialism. As a result of new technologies and perceived profitability, we can now watch black and white movie classics in color. While the tinted images we are offered may be more palatable to the modern viewer, we are still watching the same old movie that was offered to us before. Movie colorization adds little of substance—its contributions remain cosmetic. Similarly, women of color allegedly can teach White feminists nothing about feminism, but must confine ourselves to "colorizing" preexisting feminist theory. Rather than seeing women of color as fully human individuals, we are treated as the additive sum of our categories.

In the academy, patterns of relationships among those of unequal power such as voyeurism and academic colonialism foster reformist postures toward social change. While reformists may aim to make the movie more fun to watch by colorizing their scholarship and teaching via increased lip service to diversity, reformists typically insist on retaining their power to determine what is seen and by whom. In contrast, transformation involves rethinking these differences in power and privilege via dialogues among individuals from diverse groups.

Coming from a tradition where most relationships across difference are squarely rooted in relations of domination and subordination, we have much less experience relating to people as different but equal. The classroom is potentially one powerful and safe space where dialogues among individuals of unequal power relationships can occur. The relationship between Mark, the student in my class, and the domestic worker is typical of a whole series of relationships that people have when they relate across differences in power and privilege. The relationship among Mark and his classmates represents the power of the classroom to minimize those differences so that people of different levels of power can use race, class and gender as categories of analysis in order to generate meaningful dialogues. In this case, the classroom equalized racial difference so that Black students who normally felt silenced spoke out. White students like Mark, generally unaware of how they had been privileged by their whiteness, lost that privilege in the classroom and thus became open to genuine dialogue.

Reconceptualizing course syllabi represents a comparable process of determining which groups are privileged by our current research and pedagogical techniques and which groups are penalized. Reforming these existing techniques can be a critical first step in moving toward a transformed curriculum reflecting race, class and gender as interlocking categories of analysis. But while reform may be effective as a short term strategy, it is unlikely to bring about fundamental transformation in the long term. To me, social transformations, whether of college curricula or of the communities in which we live and work, require moving outside our areas of specialization and groups of interest in order to build coalitions across differences.

2. COALITIONS AROUND COMMON CAUSES

A second issue in building relationships and coalitions essential for social change concerns knowing the real reasons for coalition. Just what brings people together? One powerful catalyst fostering group solidarity is the presence of a common enemy. African-American, Hispanic, Asian-American, and women's studies all share the common intellectual heritage of challenging what passes for certified knowledge in the academy. But politically expedient relationships and coalitions like these are fragile because, as June Jordan points out:

> It occurs to me that much organizational grief could be avoided if people understood that partnership in misery does not necessarily provide for partnership for change: When we get the monsters off our backs all of us may want to run in very different directions.
>
> (1985, 47)

Sharing a common cause assists individuals and groups in maintaining relationships that transcend their differences. Building effective coalitions involves struggling to hear one another and developing empathy for each other's points of view. The coalitions that I have been involved in that lasted and that worked have been those where commitment to a specific issue mandated collaboration as the best strategy for addressing the issue at hand.

Several years ago, masters degree in hand, I chose to teach in an inner city, parochial school in danger of closing. The money was awful, the conditions were poor, but the need was great. In my job, I had to work with a range of individuals who, on the surface, had very little in common. We had White nuns, Black middle class graduate students, Blacks from the "community," some of whom had been incarcerated and/or were affiliated with a range of federal anti-poverty programs. Parents formed another part of this community, Harvard faculty another, and a few well-meaning White liberals from Colorado were sprinkled in for good measure.

As you might imagine, tension was high. Initially, our differences seemed insurmountable. But as time passed, we found a common bond that we each brought to the school. In spite of profound differences in our personal biographies, differences that in other settings would have hampered our ability to relate to one another, we found that we were all deeply committed to the education of Black children. By learning to value each other's commitment and by recognizing that we each had different skills that were essential to actualizing that commitment, we built an effective coalition around a common cause. Our school was successful, and the children we taught benefitted from the diversity we offered them.

I think that the process of curriculum transformation will require a process comparable to that of political organizing around common causes. None of us alone has a comprehensive vision of how race, class and gender operate as categories of analysis or how they might be used as categories of connection. Our personal biographies offer us partial views. Few of us can manage to study race, class and gender simultaneously. Instead, we each know more about some dimensions of this larger story and less about others. While we each may be committed to an inclusive, transformed curriculum, the task of building one is necessarily a collective effort. Just as the members of the school had special skills to offer to the task of building the school, we have areas of specialization and expertise, whether scholarly, theoretical, pedagogical or within areas of race, class or gender. We do not all have to do the same thing in the same way. Instead, we must support each other's efforts, realizing that they are all part of the larger enterprise of bringing about social change.

CONTEXT

3. BUILDING EMPATHY

A third issue involved in building the types of relationships and coalitions essential for social change concerns the issue of individual accountability. Race, class and gender oppression form the structural backdrop against which we frame our relationship—these are the forces that encourage us to substitute voyeurism and academic colonialism for fully human relationships. But while we may not have created this situation, we are each responsible for making individual, personal choices concerning which elements of race, class and gender oppression we will accept and which we will work to change.

One essential component of this accountability involves developing empathy for the experiences of individuals and groups different than ourselves. Empathy begins with taking an interest in the facts of other people's lives, both as individuals and as groups. If you care about me, you should want to know not only the details of my personal biography but a sense of how race, class and gender as categories of analysis created the institutional and symbolic backdrop for my personal biography. How can you hope to assess my character without knowing the details of the circumstances I face?

Moreover, by taking a theoretical stance that we have all been affected by race, class and gender as categories of analysis that have structured our treatment, we open up possibilities for using those same constructs as categories of connection in building empathy. For example, I have a good White woman friend with whom I share common interests and beliefs. But we know that our racial differences have provided us with different experiences. So we talk about them. We do not assume that because I am Black, race has only affected me and not her or that because I am a Black woman, race neutralizes the effect of gender in my life while accenting it in hers. We take those same categories of analysis that have created cleavages in our lives, in this case, categories of race and gender, and use them as categories of connection in building empathy for each other's experiences.

Finding common causes and building empathy is difficult, no matter which side of privilege we inhabit. Building empathy from the dominant side of privilege is difficult, simply because individuals from privileged backgrounds are not encouraged to do so. For example, in order for those of you who are White to develop empathy for the experiences of people of color, you must grapple with how your white skin has privileged you. This is difficult to do, because it not only entails the intellectual process of seeing how whiteness is elevated in institutions and symbols, but it also involves the often painful process of seeing how your whiteness has shaped your personal biography. Intellectual stances against the institutional and symbolic dimensions of racism are generally easier to maintain than sustained self-reflection about how racism has shaped all of our individual biographies. Were and are your fathers, uncles, and grandfathers really more capable than mine, or can their accomplishments be explained in part by the racism members of my family experienced? Did your mothers stand silently by and watch all this happen? More importantly, how have they passed on the benefits of their whiteness to you?

These are difficult questions, and I have tremendous respect for my colleagues and students who are trying to answer them. Since there is no compelling reason to examine the source and meaning of one's own privilege, I know that those who do so have freely chosen this stance. They are making conscious efforts to root out the piece of the oppressor planted within them. To me, they are entitled to the support of people of color in their efforts. Men who declare themselves feminists, members of the middle class who ally themselves with anti-poverty struggles, heterosexuals who support gays and lesbians, are all trying to grow, and their efforts place them far ahead of the majority who never think of engaging in such important struggles.

Building empathy from the subordinate side of privilege is also difficult, but for different reasons. Members of subordinate groups are understandably reluctant to abandon a basic mistrust of members of powerful groups because this basic mistrust has traditionally been central to their survival. As a Black woman, it would be foolish for me to assume that White women, or Black men, or White men or any other group with a history of exploiting African-American women have my best interests at heart. These groups enjoy varying amounts of privilege over me and therefore I must carefully watch them and be prepared for a relation of domination and subordination.

Like the privileged, members of subordinate groups must also work toward replacing judgments by category with new ways of thinking and acting. Refusing to do so stifles prospects for effective coalition and social change. Let me use another example from my own experiences. When I was an undergraduate, I had little time or patience for the theorizing of the privileged. My initial years at a private, elite institution were difficult, not because the coursework was challenging (it was, but that wasn't what distracted me) or because I had to work while my classmates lived on family allowances (I was used to work). The adjustment was difficult because I was surrounded by so many people who took their privilege for granted. Most of them felt entitled to their wealth. That astounded me.

I remember one incident of watching a White woman down the hall in my dormitory try to pick out which sweater to wear. The sweaters were piled up on her bed in all the colors of the rainbow, sweater after sweater. She asked my advice in a way that let me know that choosing a sweater was one of the most important decisions she had to make on a daily basis. Standing knee-deep in her sweaters, I realized how different our lives were. She did not have to worry about maintaining a solid academic average so that she could receive financial aid. Because she was in the majority, she was not treated as a representative of her race. She did not have to consider how her classroom comments or basic existence on campus contributed to the treatment her group would receive. Her allowance protected her from having to work, so she was free to spend her time studying, partying, or in her case, worrying about which sweater to wear. The degree of inequality in our lives and her unquestioned sense of entitlement concerning that inequality offended me. For a while, I categorized all affluent White women as being superficial, arrogant, overly concerned with material possessions, and part of my problem. But had I continued to classify people in this way, I would have missed out on making some very good friends whose discomfort with their inherited or acquired social class privileges pushed them to examine their position.

. . . As we go forth to the remaining activities of this workshop, and beyond this workshop, we might do well to consider Lorde's perspective:

> Each of us is called upon to take a stand. So in these days ahead, as we examine ourselves and each other, our works, our fears, our differences, our sisterhood and survivals, I urge you to tackle what is most difficult for us all, self-scrutiny of our complacencies, the idea that since each of us believes she is on the side of right, she need not examine her position.

(1985)

I urge you to examine your position.

References

Lorde, Audre. (1985). "Sisterhood and Survival." Keynote address, conference on the Black Woman Writer and the Diaspora, Michigan State University.
Jordan, June. (1985). *On Call: Political Essays*. Boston, MA: South End Press.

133

What Can We Do?

Allan G. Johnson

. . .

The problem of privilege and oppression is deep and wide, and to work with it we have to be able to see it clearly so that we can talk about it in useful ways. To do that, we have to reclaim some difficult language that names what's going on, language that has been so misused and maligned that it generates more heat than light. We can't just stop using words like *racism, sexism, ableism,* and *privilege,* however, because these are tools that focus our awareness on the problem and all the forms it takes. Once we can see and talk about what's going on, we can analyze how it works as a system. We can identify points of leverage where change can begin.

. . .

For several centuries, capitalism has provided the economic context for privilege and oppression. As such, it has been and continues to be a powerful force, especially in relation to class, gender, and race. Its effects are both direct and indirect. Historically, it was the engine that drove the development of modern racism. In a less direct way, it creates conditions of scarcity that set the stage for competition, fear, and antagonism directed across differences of race, ethnicity, and gender. Through the class differences that it creates, it also shapes people's experience of privilege and the lack of it. This is an example of the matrix of domination (or matrix of privilege) through which the various forms of difference and privilege interact and shape one another.

. . .

Although disadvantaged groups take the brunt of the trouble, privileged groups are also affected by it, partly because misery visited on others comes back to haunt those who benefit from it, especially in the form of defensiveness and fear. But trouble also affects privileged groups directly by limiting and shaping the lives of people who have privilege. The trouble also affects entire social systems, from families to corporations and schools to communities, societies, and global political and economic systems.

The greatest barrier to change is that dominant groups . . . don't see the trouble as *their* trouble, which means they don't feel obliged to do something about it. This happens for a variety of reasons—because they don't know the trouble exists in the first place, because they don't *have* to see it as their trouble, because they see it as a personal rather than a systemic problem, because they're reluctant to give up privilege, because they feel angry and deprived and closed to the idea that they have privilege, because they're blinded by prejudice, because they're afraid of what will happen if they acknowledge the reality of privilege and oppression.

. . .

[To] think about the trouble as everyone's responsibility—everybody's "hook"—and nobody's fault . . . is especially useful for members of privileged groups who have a hard time seeing themselves in relation to privilege without feeling guilty. It's easy to fall into this trap because people tend to use an individualistic model of the world that reduces everything to individual intentions and goodness or badness. A powerful and liberating alternative comes from the fact that we're always participating in something larger than ourselves, social systems. To understand privilege and oppression, we have to look at what we're participating in *and* how we participate. . . . This means we can be involved in a society's or organization's troubles without doing anything wrong and without being bad people.

Privilege is created and maintained through social systems that are dominated by, centered on, and identified with privileged groups. A racist society, for example, is white-dominated, white-centered, and white-identified. Since privilege is rooted primarily in systems—such as families, schools, and workplaces—change isn't simply a matter of changing people. The solution also has to include entire systems [that] . . . shape how people feel, think, and behave as individuals, how they see themselves and one another.

. . .

With this approach, we can begin to think about how to make ourselves part of the solution to the problem of privilege and oppression. . . .

It is in small and humble choices that privilege, oppression, and the movement toward something better actually happen.

. . . WHAT CAN WE DO?

. . .

ACKNOWLEDGE THAT PRIVILEGE AND OPPRESSION EXISTS

A key to the continued existence of every system of privilege is unawareness, because privilege contradicts so many basic human values that it invariably arouses opposition when people know about it. . . .

This is why most cultures of privilege mask the reality of oppression by denying its existence, trivializing it, calling it something else, blaming it on those most victimized by it, or diverting attention from it. Instead of treating oppression as a serious problem, we go to war or get embroiled in controversial "issues" such as capital gains tax cuts or "family values" or immigrant workers. There would be far more active opposition to white privilege, for example, if white people lived with an ongoing awareness of how it actually affects the everyday lives of those it oppresses as "not white." . . .

It's one thing to become aware and quite another to stay that way. The greatest challenge when we first become aware of a critical perspective on the world is simply to hang on to it. . . . In some ways, it's harder and more important to pay attention to systems of privilege than it is to people's behavior. . . . [F]or example, the structure of capitalism creates large social patterns of inequality, scarcity, and exploitation that have played and continue to play a major role in the perpetuation of various forms of privilege and oppression. It is probably wishful thinking to suppose we can end privilege without also changing a capitalist system of political economy that allows an elite to control the vast majority of wealth and income and leaves the rest of the population to fight over what's left. But such wishful thinking is, in fact, what we're encouraged to engage in most of the time—to cling to the idea that racism, for example, is just a problem with a few bad whites, rather than seeing how it is connected to a much larger matrix of privilege and oppression.

. . .

By itself, however, changing how we think won't be enough to solve the problem. Privilege will not simply go away as the result of a change in individual consciousness. Ultimately, we'll have to apply our understanding of how systems work to the job of changing systems themselves—economic, political, religious, educational, and familial. . . .

Maintaining a critical consciousness takes commitment and work. Awareness is something that either we maintain in the moment or we don't. And the only way to hang on to an awareness of privilege is to make that awareness an ongoing part of our lives.

PAY ATTENTION

Understanding how privilege and oppression operate and how you participate is where working for change begins. It's easy to have opinions, but it takes work to know what you're talking about. The simplest way to begin is to make reading about privilege part of your life. Unless you have the luxury of a personal teacher, you can't understand this issue without reading. Many people assume they already know what they need to know because it's part of everyday life. But they're usually wrong, because just as the last thing a fish would discover is water, the last thing people discover is society itself and something as pervasive as privilege.

We also have to be open to the idea that what we think we know is, if not wrong, so deeply shaped by systems of privilege that it misses most of the truth. This is why activists talk with one another and spend time reading one another's writing, because seeing things clearly is tricky. This is also why people who are critical of the status quo are so often self-critical as well—they know how complex and elusive the truth really is and what a challenge it is to work toward it. . . .

As you educate yourself, avoid reinventing the wheel. Many people have already done a lot of work that you can learn from. There's no way to get through it all, but you don't have to in order to develop a clear enough sense of how to act in meaningful and informed ways. . . . Men who feel there is no place for them in women's studies might start with books about patriarchy and gender inequality that are written by men. In the same way, whites can begin with writings on race privilege written by other whites. Sooner or later, however, dominant groups will need to turn to what people in subordinate groups have written, because they are the ones who have done most of the work of figuring out how privilege and oppression operate.

Reading is only the beginning. At some point you have to look at yourself and the world to see if you can identify what you're reading about. . . .

[T]aking responsibility means not waiting for others to tell you what to do, to point out what's going on, or to identify alternatives. If dominant groups are going to take their share of responsibility, it's up to them to listen, watch, ask, and listen again, to make it their business to find out for themselves. If they don't, they'll slide down the comfortable blindered path of privilege. And then they'll be *just* part of the problem and they *will* be blamed and they'll have it coming.

LEARN TO LISTEN

Attentive listening is especially difficult for members of dominant groups. If someone confronts you with your own behavior that supports privilege, . . . [d]on't tell them they're too sensitive or need a better sense of humor, and don't try to explain away what you did as something else than what they're telling you it was. Don't say you didn't mean it or that you were only kidding. Don't tell them what a champion of justice you are or how hurt you feel because of what they're telling you. Don't make jokes or try to be cute or charming, since only access to privilege can lead someone to believe these are acceptable responses to something as serious as privilege and oppression. Listen to what's being said. Take it seriously. Assume for the time being that it's true, because . . . it probably is. And then take responsibility to do something about it.

. . .

LITTLE RISKS: DO SOMETHING

. . .

When you *openly* change how you participate in a system, you do more than change your own behavior; you also change how the system happens. When you change how a system happens, you change the social environment that shapes other people's behavior, which, in turn, further changes how the system happens. And when you do that, you also help to change the consequences that come out of the dynamic relationship between systems and individuals, including patterns of privilege and oppression.

. . .

As you become more aware, questions will arise about what goes on at work, in the media, in families, in communities, in religious institutions, in government, on the street, and at school—in short, just about everywhere. The questions don't come all at once (for which we can be grateful), although they sometimes come in a rush that can feel overwhelming. If you remind yourself that it isn't up to you to do it all, however, you can see plenty of situations in which you can make a difference, sometimes in surprisingly simple ways. Consider the following possibilities.

Make noise, be seen. Stand up, volunteer, speak out, write letters, sign petitions, show up. Every oppressive system feeds on silence. Don't collude in it. Breaking the silence is especially important for dominant groups, because it undermines the assumption of solidarity that privilege depends on. If this feels too risky, practice being aware of how silence reflects your investment in solidarity with other dominant-group members. This can be a place to begin working on how you participate in making privilege and oppression happen: "Today I said nothing, colluded in silence, and this is how I benefited from it. Tomorrow I can try something different."

Find little ways to withdraw support from . . . [oppressive systems,] starting with yourself. It can be as simple as not laughing at a racist or heterosexist joke or saying you don't think it's funny, or writing a letter to your senator or representative or the editor of your newspaper, objecting to an instance of sexism in the media. When my local newspaper ran an article whose headline referred to sexual harassment as "earthy behavior," for example, I wrote a letter pointing out that harassment has nothing to do with being "earthy."

The key to withdrawing support is to interrupt the flow of business as usual. You can subvert the assumption that everyone's going along with the status quo by simply not going along. When you do this, you stop the flow, if only for a moment, but in that moment other people can notice and start to think and question. It's a perfect time to suggest the possibility of alternatives, such as humor that isn't at someone else's expense, or of ways to think about discrimination, harassment, and violence that do justice to the reality of what's going on and how it affects people.

. . .

Dare to make people feel uncomfortable, beginning with yourself. At the next local school board meeting, for example, you can ask why principals and other administrators are almost always white and male (unless your system is an exception that proves the rule), while the teachers they supervise and the lower-paid support staff are mostly women and people of color. Or look at the names and mascots used by local sports teams and see if they exploit the heritage and identity of Native Americans. If that's the case, ask principals and coaches and owners about it. Consider asking similar kinds of questions about privilege and difference in your place of worship, workplace, and local government.

It may seem that such actions don't amount to much, until you stop for a moment and feel your resistance to doing them—worrying, for example, about how easily you could make people uncomfortable, including yourself. If you take that resistance to action as a measure of power, then your potential to make a difference is plain to see. The potential for people to feel uncomfortable is a measure of the power for change inherent in such simple acts of not going along with the status quo.

Some will say it isn't "nice" to make people uncomfortable, but systems of privilege do a lot more than make people feel uncomfortable, and there isn't anything "nice" about allowing that to continue. Besides, discomfort is an unavoidable part of any meaningful process of change. You can't grow without being willing to challenge your assumptions and take yourself to the edge of your competencies, where you're bound to feel uncomfortable. If you can't tolerate ambiguity, uncertainty, and discomfort, then you'll never get beneath superficial appearances or learn or change anything of much value, including yourself.

. . .

Openly choose and model alternative paths. [Identifying] . . . alternatives and [following] . . . them openly so that other people can see what we're doing . . . creates tension in a system, which moves toward resolution. . . . We don't have to convince anyone of anything. As Gandhi put it, the work begins with us trying to be the change we want to see happen in the world. If you think this has no effect, watch how people react to the slightest departures from established paths and how much effort they expend trying to ignore or explain away or challenge those who choose alternative paths.

Actively promote change in how systems are organized around privilege. The possibilities here are almost endless, because social life is complicated and privilege is everywhere. You can, for example,

Speak out for equality in the workplace.

Promote awareness and training around issues of privilege.

Support equal pay and promotion practices for everyone.

Oppose the devaluing of women, people of color, and people with disabilities, and the work they do, from dead-end jobs to glass ceilings.

Support the well-being of mothers, children, and people with disabilities, and defend their right to control their bodies and their lives.

Don't support businesses that are inaccessible to people with disabilities, and tell them why you don't.

Don't support businesses that engage in unfair labor practices, including union-busting. Support the formation of unions. Although the U.S. labor movement has a long history of racism, sexism, and ableism, unions are currently one of the few organized efforts dedicated to protecting workers from the excesses of capitalism.

Become aware of how class divisions operate in social systems, from workplaces to schools, and how this results in the oppression of blue- and white-collar workers. Find out, for example, if staff at your college or university are paid a living wage, and speak up if they aren't. There is a great silence in this country around issues of class, in part because the dominant cultural ideology presents the United States as a classless society. Break the silence.

Oppose the increasing concentration of wealth and power in the United States and the global economy. The lower, working, and lower-middle classes are the last to benefit from economic upturns and the first to suffer from economic downturns. Press politicians and candidates for public office to take a stand on issues of class, starting with the acknowledgment that they exist.

. . .

When you witness someone else taking a risk—speaking out, calling attention to privilege and oppression—don't wait until later to tell them in private you're glad they did. Waiting until you're alone makes it safer for you but does the other person little good. Support is most needed when the risk is being taken, not later on, so don't wait. Make your support as visible and public as the courageous behavior that you're supporting.

Support the right of women and men to love whomever they choose. Raise awareness of homophobia and heterosexism. For example, ask school officials and teachers about what's happening to gay and lesbian students in local schools. If they don't know, ask them to find out, since it's a safe bet these students are being harassed, suppressed, and oppressed by others at one of the most vulnerable stages of life. When sexual orientation is discussed, whether in the media or among friends, raise questions about its relation to male privilege. Remember that it isn't necessary to have answers to questions in order to ask them.

Pay attention to how different forms of oppression interact with one another. There has been a great deal of struggle within women's movements, for example, about the relationship between male privilege and privilege in other forms, especially those based on race, social class, and sexual orientation. . . .

One way out of this conflict is to realize that male privilege isn't problematic just because it emphasizes *male* dominance but because it values and promotes dominance and control as ends in themselves. In that sense, all forms of oppression draw support from common roots, and whatever we do that calls attention to those roots undermines *all* forms of privilege. If working against male privilege is seen simply as enabling some women to get a bigger piece of the pie, then some women probably will "succeed" at the expense of others who are disadvantaged by race, class, sexual orientation, and disability status. . . . [I]f we identify the core problem as *any* society organized around principles of domination and privilege, then changing *that* requires us to pay attention to all the forms of privilege those principles promote. Whether we begin with race or gender or disability or class or the capitalist system, if we name the problem correctly we'll wind up going in the same general direction.

Work with other people. This is one of the most important principles of participating in change. From expanding consciousness to taking risks, working with people who support what you're trying to do makes all the difference in the world. . . .

Make contact. Connect to other people engaged in the same work. Do whatever reminds you that you're not alone in this.

It is especially important to form alliances across difference, . . . for whites to listen to people of color, for example—and to give credence to what people say about their own experience. This isn't easy to do, of course, since members of dominant groups may not like what they hear about their privilege from those who are most damaged by it. It is difficult to hear anger and not take it personally, but that is what allies have to be willing to do. It's also difficult for members of privileged groups to realize how mistrusted they are by subordinate groups and to not take that personally as well. . . .

In many ways, the biggest challenge for members of privileged groups is to work with one another on issues of privilege rather than trying to help members of subordinate groups. . . . For members of privileged groups to become allies, they must recall Frederick Douglass's words that "power concedes nothing without a demand" and add their weight to that demand. When dominant groups work against privilege, they do more than add their voices. They also make it more difficult for other members of dominant groups to dismiss calls for change as simply the actions of "special interest groups" trying to better their position.

. . .

Don't keep it to yourself. A corollary of looking for company is not to restrict your focus to the tight little circle of your own life. . . . At some point, taking responsibility means acting in a larger context, even if that means letting just one other person know what you're doing. It makes sense to start with yourself, but it's equally important not to end with yourself.

A good way to convert personal change into something larger is to join an organization dedicated to changing the systems that produce privilege and oppression. . . .

If all this sounds overwhelming, remember again that you don't have to deal with everything. You don't have to set yourself the impossible task of transforming society or even yourself. All you can do is what you can *manage* to do, secure in the knowledge that you're making it easier for other people—now and in the future—to see and do what *they* can do. So, rather than defeat yourself before you start, think small, humble, and doable rather than large, heroic, and impossible. Don't paralyze yourself with impossible expectations. . . .

Don't let other people set the standard for you. Start where you are and work from there. Make lists of all the things you could actually imagine *doing*—from reading another book about privilege to suggesting policy changes at school or work to protesting against capitalism to raising questions about who cleans the bathroom at home—and rank them from the most risky to the least. Start with the least risky and set reasonable goals ("What small risk for change will I take *today?*"). As you get more experienced at taking risks, you can move up your list. You can commit yourself to whatever the next steps are for you, the tolerable risks, the contributions that offer some way—however small it might seem—to help balance the scales. As long as you do something, it counts.

In the end, taking responsibility doesn't have to involve guilt and blame, letting someone off the hook, or being on the hook yourself. It simply means acknowledging an obligation to make a contribution to finding a way out of the trouble we're all in and to finding constructive ways to act on that obligation. You don't have to do anything dramatic or earth-shaking to help change happen. As powerful as systems of privilege are, they cannot stand the strain of lots of people doing something about it, beginning with the simplest act of naming the system out loud.

134

The Cycle of Liberation

Bobbie Harro

As people come to a critical level of understanding of the nature of oppression and their roles in this systemic phenomenon, they seek new paths for creating social change and taking themselves toward empowerment or liberation. In my years as a social justice educator, it became increasingly clear that most socially conscious people truly want to "do something about" the injustices that they see and they recognize that simple, personal-level changes are not enough. They want to know how to make system-level change manageable and within their grasp, and they often become frustrated since so little has been written about the process of liberation.

As more students asked, "How do we make a dent in this thing that seems so big?" I began to think about how we might consciously transform the Cycle of Socialization. The Cycle "teaches" us how to play our roles in oppression, and how to revere the existing systems that shape our thinking, leading us to blame uncontrollable forces, other people, or ourselves for the existence of oppression. If there is an identifiable pattern of events that repeats itself, becomes self-fulfilling, and leads us to a state of unconsciousness about issues of oppression, then there may be another identifiable pattern of events that leads us toward liberation from that thinking. I began to read about and study efforts to eliminate oppression on a systemic level, and discovered that indeed, some paths were successful at actually creating the kind of lasting change that addressed the root cause of the oppression, and people's roles in it, while other paths were not. These paths were not always the same, and certainly were not linear, but they had in common the same cycle-like traits that characterized the socialization process that teaches us our roles in oppression. There were certain skills and processes, certain ways of thinking and acting in the world, certain seemingly necessary ingredients that were present in every successful liberation effort.

I am defining *liberation* as "critical transformation," in the language and thinking of Paulo Freire. By this I mean that one must "name the problem" in terms of *systemic* assumptions, structures, rules, or roles that are flawed. Significant social change cannot happen until we are thinking on a systemic level. Many people who want to overcome oppression do not start in the critical transforming stage, but as they proceed in their efforts, it becomes necessary for them to move to that level for success.

The following model describes patterns of events common to successful liberation efforts. Its purpose is to organize and name a process that may otherwise be elusive, with the goal of supporting people to find their pathway to liberation. It could be characterized as a map of changing terrain where not everyone goes in the same direction or to the same destination or at the same speed, so it should be taken not as a "how to," but rather as a description of what has worked for some.

THE MODEL

The model described in this chapter combines theory, analysis, and practical experience. It describes a cyclical process that seems to occur in most successful social change efforts, leading to some degree of liberation from oppression for those involved, regardless of their roles. It is important to note that one can enter the Cycle at any point, through slow evolution or a critical incident, and will repeat or recycle many times in the process. There is no specific beginning or end point, just as one is never "done" working to end oppression. Although there is not a specific sequence of events in the Cycle, it is somewhat predictable that all of the levels (intrapersonal, interpersonal and systemic) will occur at some point.

WAKING UP

Often liberation begins when a person begins to experience themselves differently in the world than they have in the past. It is marked by an intrapersonal change: a change in the core of someone about what they believe about themself. This may be the result of a critical incident or a long slow evolutionary process that shifts our worldviews. I refer to this phase as the *waking up* phase. We may experience some form of cognitive dissonance, where something that used to make sense to us (or that we never questioned), ceases to make sense. Perhaps a white mother adopts a child who is Puerto Rican and in dealing with her expectations for the child suddenly realizes that she has more deeply based racist attitudes than she thought she did. Perhaps a heterosexual woman who has a gay coworker recognizes that the longer she works with him, the more "ordinary" he becomes to her, and the more she gets angry when people make homophobic remarks. Perhaps a welfare recipient begins to get angry that she is often treated with disrespect by service providers and the general public, and begins to see the disrespect as a pattern of how poorer people are treated in the United States. Any of these examples could mark the beginning of the Cycle of Liberation.

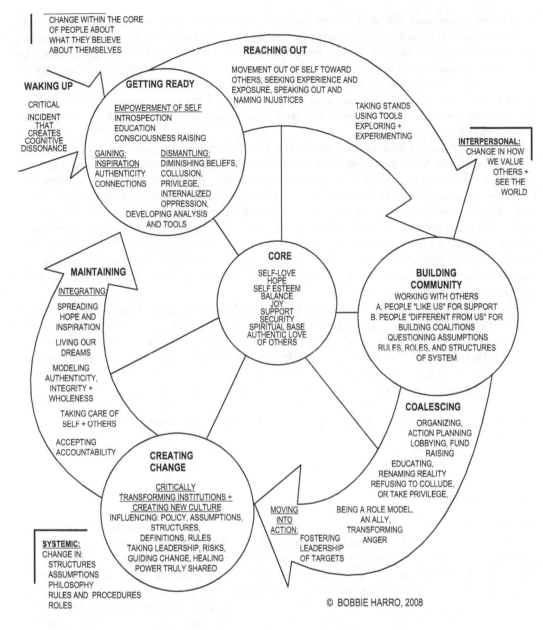

Figure 134.1 The Cycle of Liberation

GETTING READY

Once we know something, we can't *not* know it anymore. The process may not begin immediately, but odds are that it will begin at some point. Often the first part of the process involves a *getting ready* phase. This involves consciously dismantling and building aspects of ourselves and our worldviews based on our new perspectives. Processes that are central to this first part of liberation are introspection, education, and consciousness raising. We become introspective to identify which aspects of our beliefs, attitudes, and behaviors need to be challenged. We tend to pay attention to and inventory thoughts, language, and actions to see if they are consistent with our newly recognized beliefs, or if they need to be dismantled. We may discover that we need to educate ourselves: read more, talk to people, bounce ideas and views around with others, begin listening to the news with new ears, seek expertise. We may begin to "make sense" of our experiences differently and seek out more chances to explore what we thought we knew, and how it compares to the reality. We may start exercising our questioning and challenging skills to expand our conscious understanding of the world.

This *getting ready* phase is composed of dismantling our wrong or diminishing beliefs (stereotypes, ignorance or misinformation), our discriminatory or privileged attitudes (superiority or inferiority), and behaviors that limit ourselves or others (collusion, oppressive language, or resignation). It also involves developing a consistency among what we believe, how we want to live our lives; and the way we actually do it. We move toward gaining authenticity and coherence between our worldview and how we live. We begin to see connections among all of the aspects of our lives and move toward integrity. Part of this phase also includes developing a coherent analysis of oppression and building a repertoire of skills and tools that will serve us throughout the rest of the process. We begin to take steps to empower ourselves.

The mother of the Puerto Rican child might decide to read about Puerto Rican history and cultures, talk to her Puerto Rican coworker, trace the origins of her assumptions and expectations about her child, or begin to catch herself when she makes excuses for her child's behavior. The heterosexual coworker may take a course on the gay rights movement, or pick up a copy of a gay newspaper, or ask her gay coworker to dinner. The woman on welfare may read a book on welfare rights, or start listening to the economic news, or start to keep a list of examples of "corporate welfare" totaling how much money goes from the federal government to large corporations when they are in financial trouble.

REACHING OUT

Almost inevitably, as we are getting ready, it becomes necessary for us to seek experiences outside ourselves in order to check our reality and to expose ourselves to a wider range of difference than we had before. We need to practice using our skills and tools with others, and experiment with expressing our new views, and speaking out when we disagree, instead of staying silent. This *reaching out* phase provides us with feedback about how our new worldviews will be met by others. We may get pressure from some to stop making waves, and accept the status quo (and this may arrest some people's progress for a while), and we may get encouragement and new friends as a result of speaking out on something that we were quiet about before.

The adoptive mother may change social workers so she can talk to a Puerto Rican social worker about her child. She may suggest to her partner that they take a class in Spanish, or attend a local Puerto Rican festival. The heterosexual coworker may disclose in a conversation with friends that she supports the domestic partnership clause in their benefit package, or she may have a talk with her kids about not using the term *gay* to mean something bad. She may invite her gay coworker *and his partner* to dinner, or draw comparisons between her primary relationship and his. The woman on welfare may attend her first welfare rights meeting. She may object assertively when the person behind her in the checkout line treats her with disdain for using food stamps. She may decide to share her list of examples of corporate welfare with two friends also on welfare. All of these actions mark the transition from intrapersonal to interpersonal liberation.

BUILDING COMMUNITY

The interpersonal phase of the liberation process is marked by a change in how we value others and interact with them on a regular basis. It is the phase of *building community,* and consists of two steps: dialoguing with *people who are like us* for support (people who have the same social identities as we do, with regard to this issue of oppression), and dialoguing with *people who are different from us* for gaining understanding and building coalitions. This phase is characterized by the creation of an ongoing dialogue, where views are exchanged, people are listened to and valued, and we begin to view each others' points of view as making sense and having integrity, even if they are very different from our own.

In the first step, building community with people who are like us, we seek out people who may have similar experiences to our own, and talk with them to see how they have made sense of their experiences and what we can learn from them. This often begins happening informally, and even sometimes unconsciously: two mothers with adopted children meet in the pediatrician's waiting room and start comparing notes, or two neighbors who both receive welfare benefits talk in the laundry about their frustrations, or two friends going for a hike begin discussing their experiences working with gay colleagues. With increased knowledge and consciousness, these people might start looking for more organized forms of support discussions. These dialogues serve to prove to people that they are not alone in their situation, that there is a bigger "system" operating, that others have faced and are facing similar situations as our own, and that there are more strategies, ideas, and options than we had initially thought. We feel confirmed, and like we are part of a group that wants to change its role with regard to oppression. Authentic solidarity is crucial.

A large part of this interpersonal step also involves dialoguing about how we see the "other" group (those with power if we are disempowered, or the disempowered if we possess power and/or privilege), and beginning to identify things that we may mutually have in common. We have moved out of stereotyping the "other" and have discovered those "others" who are more like us than different from us. We may begin to see that the "other" is no more to blame for the oppression than we are—that, in fact, we are both victims of a larger system that pushed us into roles. With this realization, a new level of analysis begins, and it becomes inevitable and necessary to expand our dialogue to include "others."

It's important to note that both privileged groups and targeted groups need to find this support step. We can't change *our* roles only; we must address changing the roles of *everyone* involved, as well as the assumptions and structures of the entire system, and we cannot do that alone. Coalitions are a necessity, and dialoguing across differences is the first step to building coalitions. We will never be able to focus on the real challenge—changing the system—until the barriers and boundaries that divide us are minimized. They will not be eliminated, but they can be significantly diminished in potency and clarified through the dialogue process.

This is not to say that creating dialogues about and across differences is easy. An integral part of this dialogue is exploring our differences, clarifying them, erasing assumptions, and replacing them with firsthand contact and good listening. That means that we must talk about our differences on common ground. It is useful, even desirable, to create together some guidelines for how our dialogues across differences will take place, and some principles to guide the process. These are best negotiated by all the parties who will participate.

CONTEXT

Our mission is to question and challenge assumptions, structures and rules of the system of oppression, and to clarify our different needs, perceptions, strengths, resources, and skills in the process. Done well, these dialogues result in a deeper and richer repertoire of options and opportunities for changing the system. We are enhanced in many ways: our energy, our resources, our inspiration, our understanding, our compassion, our empathy, our humanness, and our motivation are all expanded in this process. We discover and are sustained by inspirations that we have not met before. With these new springboards, we move into the coalescing phase.

COALESCING

Having minimized our barriers, joined with allies, and fortified our resolve, we are ready to move into action to interrupt the oppressive system. We may organize, plan actions, lobby, do fund raising, educate and motivate members of the uninvolved public. We coalesce and discover that we have more power as a coalition. This gives us encouragement and confidence. We may find ourselves taking more overt positions, expressing ourselves more assertively, rallying people to support us as we respond to overt oppression. We have begun to "see our reality" differently, and are naming ourselves differently. We are a "we" now, rather than adversaries. We are on the same side as those in our coalition, and that often surprises and confuses the system. We are refusing to "play our roles" and "stay in our places" as we had done before. We are refusing to collude in oppression, and to participate in self-fulfilling prophesies. We are refusing to accept privileges, and we are acting as role models and allies for others. We are interrupting the status quo, by speaking out calmly and with self-confidence. In this process, we have transformed our energy away from anger, frustration, guilt, and mistrust, and toward hope, shared power, trust, and optimism. We begin to see evidence that, working together, and organizing, we can make a difference. This doesn't mean that we will be successful at everything we try, but our likelihood of creating change is greatly enhanced.

CREATING CHANGE

The parameters of this phase of the Cycle of Liberation include using our critical analysis of the assumptions, structures, rules, and roles of the existing system of oppression, and our coalition power, to begin transforming the system. This means creating anew a culture that reflects our coalition's collective identity: new assumptions, new structures, new roles, and new rules consistent with a more socially just and equitable philosophy. It includes operating from a shifted worldview, where the values of a diverse and united community shape the system. It involves forming partnerships across differences to increase shared power. This manifests in influencing structure, policy, and management of organizations and systems of which we are a part. It involves taking initiative, taking risks, and guiding change. We must continue to heal from past differences by sharing power and by redefining power as collective power, power within, and power created through cooperation. In this phase, the very essence of the system is transformed, and nothing can remain the same after the transformation.

People experience this kind of transformation on a personal level, when, for example they or someone in their family is diagnosed with a terminal illness. Priorities shift, and what is important becomes totally different. With regard to oppression, some examples of critical transformation have occurred when psychiatric facilities began to appoint consumers to their boards of directors, or when community funding agencies began to be run by community constituents rather than elected officials. Critical transformation may take place when an organization decides to use only consensus decision making for all policy decisions, or to use a flat collaborative management structure rather than hierarchical.

Critical transformation in our examples might happen like this. The heterosexual coworker and the gay coworker might organize a human rights committee in their workplace; conduct dialogues among employees and a public awareness campaign; design a new domestic partners' benefits amendment and a new policy protecting gay, lesbian, bisexual, and transgendered people from discrimination in the workplace. The person receiving welfare benefits might join a welfare rights coalition that lobbies local legislators, speak at a hearing in the state capital, and propose a referendum that for every dollar spent on "corporate welfare" in their state a dollar must also be spent on domestic welfare. The white mother of the Puerto Rican child might join a local Puerto Rican political action committee working to reform curriculum to include relevant Puerto Rican history, literature, famous people, and current events in her child's school. The committee might also be working to reform policies on bilingual education district-wide, so that her child can study and learn in both Spanish and English.

Efforts to critically transform systems are greatly enhanced by a wide range of resources, perspectives and creativity being brought to bear on a commonly defined problem. If good dialogue has taken place and the coalitions are as inclusive of every perspective as possible, systemic change becomes the logical outcome rather than an unlikely or unattainable goal. Making transformation happen is not, however, the last step. Creative new structures, assumptions, rules and roles must be maintained and nurtured.

MAINTAINING

In order to succeed, change needs to be strengthened, monitored, and integrated into the ritual of daily life. Just like anything new, it needs to be taken care of, learned about, "debugged," and modified as needed. It's rare if not impossible that new structures, assumptions, rules and roles are perfect or all-inclusive. It is imperative that a diverse group of "maintainers" work together to keep the change efforts aimed at their goals, and provided with resources. It's also necessary to celebrate successful change efforts. This process says to the larger world, "Look, this can work. You can change things by dialoguing and working together." It spreads hope and inspiration, and provides a model for others.

When a diverse group of people have worked to understand one another, and have created critical transformation together, we teach the lesson of hope and peace. It becomes increasingly possible that we can live our dream of equality and justice for all people. We become more human, more whole, more authentic, more integrated, and by living this way, we increase the likelihood that the human species will survive.

THE CORE OF THE CYCLE OF LIBERATION

At the core of the Cycle of Liberation is a set of qualities or states of being that hold it together. Some of these are present when people first begin the Cycle, and they are nurtured, elaborated on, filled out, and matured as we proceed through the various phases. They exist and operate on both the individual and collective levels throughout the process of liberation. They are made stronger with each phase and with each human connection we make. Liberation is *the practice of love*. It is developing a sense of self that we can love, and learning to love others with their differences from us. Liberation is *finding balance* in our individual lives and in the agendas of our coalitions. Balance keeps us upright and oriented, moving toward our goals. Liberation is the *development of competence,* the ability to make something happen consistent with a

CONTEXT

goal. It is taking charge of our own destiny and creating the world we want to live in, together with all the others we need to survive. Liberation is the *belief that we can succeed,* a sense of confidence in ourselves and in our collective efforts. Liberation is *joy* at our collective efficacy and at surviving in a world that sometimes tries to kill us. Liberation is the knowledge that *we are not alone.* It is mutual support, encouragement, and trust that others will be there if we fall, and that we need to be there for others. Liberation is *commitment* to the effort of critical transformation, to the people in our community, to the goal of equity and justice, and to love. Liberation is *passion and compassion,* those strong and motivating feelings that we must live by our hearts as well as our minds. Liberation is based in something far bigger than me as an individual, or us as a coalition, or our organization as a community, or any one nation, or any particular world. It's about that force that connects us all to one another as living beings, that force that is defined differently by every spiritual belief system but which binds us by the vision that there can be a better world and we can help to create it.

135

Courage

Cornel West

It takes courage to interrogate yourself.

It takes courage to look in the mirror and see past your reflection to who you really are when you take off the mask, when you're not performing the same old routines and social roles. It takes courage to ask—**how did I become so well-adjusted to injustice?**

It takes courage to cut against the grain and become nonconformist. It takes courage to wake up and stay awake instead of engaging in complacent slumber. It takes courage to shatter conformity and cowardice.

◆

The courage to love truth is one of the preconditions to thinking critically.

◆

Thinking for oneself is based on a particular kind of courage in which you hold truth, wisdom, and honesty in high esteem.

The reason you want to think for yourself is because you understand that people often are not telling you the truth. **When you place a high value on truth, you have to think for yourself.**

◆

If you're unwilling to muster the courage to think critically, then someone will do the thinking for you, offering doublethink and doubletalk relief. People will apply a certain kind of pressure to push you into complacency and maybe even cowardice. It's not long before you rationalize, *This isn't really me. I don't* really *think this way . . . but let's go!*

◆

As crucial and precious as the intellect is, it can become a refuge that hides and conceals emotional underdevelopment, and diminishes your ability to think critically.

What we need at this particular moment is to bring together those who are willing to muster the courage to think critically, look at the basic assumptions of public discourse, and **critique the way our history is told.**

◆

When ordinary people wake up, elites begin to tremble in their boots. They can't get away with their abuse. They can't get away with subjugation. They can't get away with exploitation. They can't get away with domination. **It takes courage for folk to stand up.**

◆

American democracy is great precisely because you have had courageous, compassionate citizens who were willing to sacrifice, to think critically, and connect with others to ensure that the Bill of Rights has had substance, that working people have had dignity, and that people of color have a status that ought to be affirmed. Think of the courage that went into that!

◆

February is a serious month because we start talking about Sojourner Truth, Harriet Tubman, Frederick Douglass, and Martin Luther King, Jr.

And we can't talk about these freedom fighters without acknowledging white brothers like Elijah Parish Lovejoy, an 1834 graduate of the Princeton Theological Seminary. He was shot down like a dog by a pro-slavery mob because of his part in the abolitionist movement, fighting for a free press, and affirming the Bill of Rights.

Lydia Maria Child was a white sister who in 1883 wrote *An Appeal in Favor of that Class of Americans called Africans*, in the same spirit as David Walker's *Great Appeal*.

Asian sisters like Grace Lee Boggs. Jewish brothers like Harry Magdoff. Well-to-do white brothers like Paul Sweezy. Brown sisters like Dolores Huerta. Brown brothers like César Chávez. Red brothers like Russell Means. We can go on and on. This is what makes a democratic tradition strong.

The democratic tradition says what? "Whosoever will, let them come."

◆

It's critical to understand your history, and then be true to oneself in such a way that one's connection to the suffering of others is an integral part of understanding yourself. This is a deep problem these days. To be great in our times too often means to have great material prosperity and no moral magnanimity at all.

◆

If you don't muster the courage to think critically about your situation, you'll end up living a life of conformity and complacency. You'll lose a very rich tradition that has been bequeathed to you by your foremothers and forefathers.

◆

In America, when we talk about a catastrophe, we talk about indigenous people. We talk about slavery. We talk about women coping with patriarchy and domestic violence. We talk about gay brothers and lesbian sisters being taught to hate themselves. We talk about workers crushed by the capitalist elite. **It is a view from the bottom up—through the lens of the cross.**

That view is too often a minority view within the Christian community because it requires too much love, too much courage. Who wants to pay the ultimate cost like Brother Medgar Evers? People are too scared. I understand that. I still love them. I affirm Medgar's courage because he dared to look at the world through the lens of the cross and paid the ultimate price.

Malcolm did it in the Islamic tradition. Martin certainly did it in his tradition. He bore his cross from age 26 until he was assassinated at 39. The American Empire is just so cross-averse.

America denies its night side until it breaks right through. There's no direct reference to slavery in the original U.S. Constitution. That's not just a slight gesture. That's lying.

You can't get away with that. You end up fighting a civil war over an institution not invoked in the Constitution. That's a level of denial that's incredibly deep. You think you're innocent, yet you've created the catastrophe right in your midst. You try to sanitize and sterilize it so expertly that you think the funk is not going to hunt you down. But it never works.

◆

It is unclear whether we're going to make it. I'm not an optimist at all. Brother Barack Obama says he has the audacity to hope. I say, "Well, what price are you willing to pay?"

It's no longer enough to be willing to die. **You have to be willing to live the truth.** Somehow, you have to be able to walk that tightrope.

◆

We have too much cynicism around here. It's too easy. There's too much pessimism. **Pessimism and optimism are the flip sides of the same coin.** We should reject the whole coin.

When you're optimistic, you can stand apart to see how things are going. But **when you're full of hope, you're in the midst of the muck.** You're working it out with love power and a commitment to justice. Your unshakable connection to the story and tradition that shaped you is what sustains you.

We have to expose the social breakdown that produces the conflict that separates human beings from hope and courage and discipline and risk-taking.

. . .

136

Allies

Gloria E. Anzaldúa

Becoming allies means helping each other heal. It can be hard to expose yourself and your wounds to a stranger who could be an ally or an enemy. But if you and I were to do good alliance work together, be good allies to each other, I would have to expose my wounds to you and you would have to expose your wounds to me and then we could start from a place of openness. During our alliance work, doors will close and we'll have to open them up again. People who engage in alliances and are working toward certain goals want to keep their personal feelings out of it, but you can't. You have to work out your personal problems while you are working out the problems of this particular community or this particular culture.

When you are doing alliance work it is very important to say who you are. For example, I am a Chicana, Mexicana, dyke, whatever. I come from a *campesina* background but I have now put one foot into middle-classness. I belong to the *inteligencia*, the intelligence class, the artistic class as an artist, and I am speaking today to you as all these people, but primarily as a Chicana or as a dyke, etc. You must situate yourself and tell what your stance is on particular things, so other allies know exactly where you are coming from. And they can later say, "Oh you say that you are talking from a working-class perspective but you have a house, you have a car, you have these privileges, you are a professor, or a salaried publisher, a privileged writer, etc." Allies might challenge some of your positions as a first step in finding out whether you are a real potential ally. Then you can get a sense of whether you can trust this person or not. And you go with your gut feeling. You go with how you feel, because sometimes they will say all the politically correct rhetoric, but you just know that they are trying to put one over on you.

I have edited three books, *This Bridge Called My Back*, *Haciendo Caras*, and *Signs: Theorizing Lesbian Experience*. In the first two books I consider anthologizing as my way of making alliances with women of color. In *Signs* it was more (or less) white women wanting to make alliances with lesbians of color. Many lesbians of color I asked to submit work didn't, because they didn't trust *Signs* because they know it to be elitist, esoteric and racist.

In the books that other people anthologize me in, some editors are very genuine and want to diversify their community. Then there are the anthologizers that call on me so that dykes of color will not call them and say, "You have one contributor of color and ninety white contributors, this is racist!" So they attempt to tokenize me, or they try to pull a fast one on their readers, by tokenizing in general. Some of my work is hard to assimilate and I consider assimilation in white culture like an amoeba trying to swallow me. But it is hard for them to assimilate me in that manner because of language and because of the way that I write. They can ignore some issues that I bring out, but because of my writing style, there are things they must confront. I don't write like a white person. I don't write like an academic or follow those rules. I break them.

If they can't assimilate my writing what they try and do is assimilate me, by tokenizing me. They bring me into their book, or into their conference, or into their alliance in a way that will acknowledge the easy stuff I raise, but ignore the more dangerous stuff. They try to do this to me all the time, so then I have to respond back, either on the phone or in a letter, and say, why? One anthology that asked for my work was called *Growing Up Latino*. Before I agreed to publish in it, I had this whole dialogue with one of the editors, and talked about naming the book Latino and not Chicano. I asked "How many Chicanos/Chicanas are in your book? How many are Latina and how do they identify themselves?" Once the magazine *New Chicano Writing* asked me to sit on their board. I called and voiced my objections to the editor before I agreed to join: I objected having Chicano writers but not Chicana in the title, and furthermore told them that the groundbreaking writing being done in the Chicano/Chicana community was by women. I also objected to their project only accepting work written in English. So the editor went home and thought about the issues and later called me and said, "I've changed the title of the magazine to New Chicana/Chicano writing, and people can write in Spanish, they can do bilingual, and they can do *Tex Mex*." Then I felt like the editor was open to me, and I agreed to be on their editorial board.

The biggest risk in forming alliances is betrayal. When you are betrayed you feel shitty. When I have been betrayed I have felt stupid, like why did I trust this person and allow this person to stab me in the back, it's all my fault, you know the victim syndrome. Betrayal, especially with Chicanas, betrayal is a big thing, because we were betrayed as women, as Indians, as a *minority* in this country, everything. We have been stabbed in the back by all of these various people. And betrayal makes you feel like less of a person, you feel shame, it reduces your self-esteem. It is politically deadening and dangerous, it's disempowering. When you lose your self-esteem you no longer trust yourself to make value judgments about other people, you lose confidence in yourself and your values. When a whole person is slowly destroyed, and this is what women of color are suffering from, their personhood is destroyed.

At first I felt really good belonging to the lesbian community, even though it was mostly white. It made me feel like where I had no home, I now had a new one. But after two or three or four years, I started looking at power, and who had power and who was trying to define for me what I was as a Chicana lesbian. I realized how my voice was silent and how my history was ignored and that drove me into looking at my roots, my queer roots in my own culture. I had to get a positive sense of being queer from my culture, not just from the white culture. Now I am in a place where I can look at both the white lesbian community and my own culture that is only beginning to have groups of lesbians organizing. *Ellas San Antonio* is a group of Chicana dykes, *Amigas y Que*, in Houston and Austin. But they were not in place when I was coming out. Chicana dyke organizations are just now coming into their power.

Now I look at my culture and white culture and the whole planet. I look at other nationalities and how they deal with their queer people, I'm getting a global perspective on being a queer person. And sometimes I feel very comfortable with a bunch of white dykes and other times I feel totally invisible, ignored. I feel that they only see the queer part of me. They don't see the Chicana part of me or the working class part of me. As long as I leave my class and culture outside the door when I enter a room full of white dykes I am okay, but if I bring in my race or class, then my role as educator starts.

I think that most white dykes really want a community that is diversified. And sometimes they want it so badly that they want to put everybody under this queer umbrella and say we are all in this together and we are all equal. But we are not equal. In their thirst and hunger for this diversity the issues of class and race are issues that they don't even want to examine, because they feel like they're divisive. So they are hungry for being politically correct and having women of color in their organizations, in their syllabi, and as performers, singers, writers and lovers. But a lot of times in order to bring us under the queer umbrella they will ignore or collapse the differences, not really deal with the issues. When it comes down to the numbers of who has power or *how many* dykes of color are getting in this anthology and how many don't—in terms of the real work, they fail. I mean the ideas are good, like the greater numbers/the greater strength kind of thing but they want us to leave our race and our class in the check room when we enter their space.

As a group, I think dykes are more progressively political than any other group because of feminism, and because of being (at least) doubly oppressed. Because they have been oppressed as dykes, I believe white lesbians are more apt to recognize the oppression of women of color. So they have a true wanting of multi-cultural groups. And there are always the false ones of course, there are always the ones that do want it to be white. But there is some honest motivation about wanting to be allies and in this they still have a lot of work to do. For example, one of the things they often don't contend with is the unconscious motivation of doing it out of guilt. But I am very hopeful and I think that I am one of the very few people. I think that most people of my age or younger have been burned out and disillusioned and feel like it's the pits right now. Much younger people than me have no hope, do not see alliances working, do not see white people reaching out or doing their work, and do not see the possibility of white people changing perspectives. Or allowing change to come into their lives, but I do.

137

Social Struggle

Richard (Chip) Smith

. . . As people connect with others actively engaged in struggle—and reach out to new forces in creative ways—the movement grows. Organizations gain experience, resources, and influence. The systematic character of oppression becomes clearer. Social forces join together, work through differences, learn how to challenge for political power and carry through social transformation.

. . . Here we want to suggest an approach to organizing that over time will have the greatest chance of bringing into being a strategic front against white supremacy and racism.

STAY CENTERED ON SELF-DETERMINATION, AFFIRMATIVE ACTION, AND INTERNATIONALISM

Self-determination focuses attention on the central demand for political power by . . . oppressed . . . peoples. Without the fundamental democratic right to political power . . . the system of white supremacy and the racist ideas it generates in people's minds will continue. The struggles to end patriarchy and capitalism also involve questions of power—in personal relations through to the organized power of the working class to reshape society, with leadership centered among the oppressed. . . .

Affirmative action in its broadest sense is simply another way to talk about ending privilege. It emphasizes the historic roots of race and gender privilege and calls for proactive policies to set matters straight—affirmative action on the job, in the home, in popular culture, in the criminal justice system, in politics and throughout society. By orienting to the struggles of people of color at any particular moment, white organizers can distinguish the specific form the struggle is taking at the moment—be it for reparations, Katrina reconstruction, or immigration rights; or for an end to right-to-work laws or male violence.

Internationalism is a third bedrock perspective, because of the imperialist role of the United States in the world. This standpoint allows people to see clearly the underlying forces driving an issue like immigration, for example, or the war in Iraq, the "War against Drugs" in Colombia, and the "War on Terror" generally. It helps one be mindful of the material benefits—and associated racial and national prejudices—that come from living in a superpower in the Global North. Armed with this awareness, one can then—as a simple act of solidarity and with no special recognition due—turn that privilege around and target U.S. imperialism from the inside. The prescription to "Think globally, act locally" is sound—but it can be broadened to "Think globally, act globally," as well. . . .

START WHERE PEOPLE ARE AT

"Starting where people are at" is a truism of organizing—but it has two aspects. The first is the obvious call to listen to what people say without prejudgment and without pushing one's own views on others. In particular, for white people organizing among white workers, it means not leading with a rap on white privilege. The perspective of this book holds that white working class people are oppressed by capitalism. So the first step in organizing is to get a concrete feel for the ways people experience their lives and understand their situation. This listening aspect can help organizers appreciate both the problems people face and the ways they have to resolve them. Some individuals will be more active; others will be more passive—but observing all the while what is going on. And a few may be a source of issues themselves. By sorting out what the concerns are and who is dealing with them in what ways, an organizer can begin to get a sense of which folks to connect up with in a supportive way, and around which key issues.

The second aspect of this approach is less obvious. It comes down to being a true friend to folks you are working with. If the United States is white supremacist; if white folks are privileged simply by virtue of their skin color; and if this privilege has negative consequences for white people themselves, as well as for others—then there is an obligation to share this understanding and discuss it through with people. What makes the conversation possible is the underlying unity established by working together on issues of recognized importance. The overall learning process is two ways—but the main responsibility in connecting with people is the organizer's.

. . .

GO BROADER AND DEEPER

When engaging in struggle, the challenge often is to broaden the ranks of the forces fighting around an issue—take ending the war in Iraq, as one example. Two different approaches are possible for primarily white organizations in this situation: One amounts to activists' asking people of color to "come join our . . ." coalition, demonstration, or organization. As a way to entice a new constituency to take part in a demonstration, for example, the peace group might invite a speaker, include a slogan, or encourage an information table at their event. None of these steps is bad in itself, and the result can be a richer learning experience for the people who attend the demonstration. But the likelihood of large-scale participation by the new constituency is small at best.

A second approach is more long term in its outlook but carries with it the prospect of real unity of action in the future. Here the organizers identify issues of concern to the new constituency—perhaps by first bringing a speaker to the peace group's organizational meeting. The second step is then to offer organizational support to one or several groups within the new constituency that are active—say, around police violence, domestic abuse, or LGBTQ rights. By actually following through on the commitment of support, the original peace group develops new ties with people in the community, learns the kinds of pressures people are experiencing in their lives, and in the course of joint activity gains some first-hand understanding of people's attitudes toward the war. Over time, these relationships generate a new, richer common language of resistance to oppression at home, as well as to the war. The peace folks bring their people out to demonstrations against police abuse. And when the next peace demonstration comes along, new community forces may now decide to be part of the planning process—helping to shape the event in a way that resonates with their community. By actively linking up in this way, primarily white organizations can transform their outlook and put their relative privilege to work—through their personal connections and networks or fundraising skills—to oppose the concrete, material disadvantages being experienced by folks of color.

NEXT STEPS

DEVELOP CONSCIOUSNESS, THEORY, VALUES

People learn best from their own experience. People can hear all the arguments about why gay and lesbian folks are the same as everyone else and should enjoy the same rights. But until heterosexual folks meet and become friends with real human beings, the issue remains abstract. Personal relationships are critical—across the color line, among different oppressed nationality peoples, or with women in positions of leadership.

On becoming socially active, people are often open to new ideas as they search for ways to advance their issues. Engaging in struggle helps a person understand who holds power and what it takes to bring about a favorable result—what arguments work, in what settings, and with how many people mobilized to get the point across. No amount of discussion or study conveys a sense of popular power better than taking part in a campaign—win or lose. But people draw the clearest lessons through evaluating their collective experience together with others.

. . .

THE ROLE OF THEORY

. . . [T]heoretical work is essential to keep a movement on the path toward its goals, while adapting to changing circumstances.

Not paying attention to the deep structure of society and to long-term principles, by contrast, almost always leads people and organizations to conform to the system, even if they start out in militant opposition. . . . A community struggle around a school can turn into a platform for someone to run for city council—OK as far as it goes. But if that person's career becomes the goal instead of empowering the community, the campaign goes off track.

In general, campaigns can be summed up from three standpoints:

- What were the immediate benefits or losses from the struggle?
- To what extent did the broader popular movement gain strength?
- Were forces won to a deeper understanding of society, to the need for revolutionary organization, and to committing for the long haul?

A fourth criterion that overlaps the first two can be drawn out as well: Was there an advance in the battle for the minds of the broader public? Contesting the hegemony of ruling class ideas is critical to developing conditions where a mass movement can take hold and flourish.

By evaluating experience collectively along these dimensions, a movement deepens its theoretical understanding of the system and how to oppose it effectively. Also, individuals' summing up their personal experiences using these criteria can help people stay on course—by gaining insight into their strengths and weaknesses and clarifying how best to contribute to the struggle.

PHILOSOPHICAL OUTLOOK

Carrying the process of social activism and reflection more deeply can bring people to a philosophical outlook that embraces change and the power of ordinary people to transform the world. Seeing oneself in the flow of a constantly changing reality empowers people to relax into their role as change agents. Otherwise their activism can seem exceptional—passivity being the normal state—and required only by temporary difficulties in their lives. . . .

SOCIAL JUSTICE VALUES

The social justice movement embodies a set of values that can be brought to consciousness, validated, and taught to others. These values are secular in origin, emerging out of the concrete conditions of contemporary struggle. At the same time they overlap with the teachings of many religions, without requiring a specific accompanying belief system. Examples of such values are:

- *Solidarity:* realizing that "an injury to one is an injury to all"
- *Confidence in the power of ordinary people:* trusting grassroots people's ability to learn, struggle, and transform both the world and themselves
- *Openness and commitment to learning:* being skilled at listening, putting effort into study, and being willing to examine oneself and one's actions
- *Being active and useful:* being intentional about one's life; taking responsibility to understand the world and one's place in it, and to work to change things for the better
- *Courage:* being willing to take a stand and act on it—not only in relation to the dominant forces in society, but also in relation to one's family, friends, and comrades
- *Being all-sided:* striving to base judgments on the whole picture, while recognizing that all the information is usually not available
- *Commitment to shared effort:* rejecting privileges, and turning those that one must live with—like being white or male—to the advantage of the struggle
- *Being good at uniting:* seeing differences clearly while, at the same time, uniting wherever possible to broaden the movement and increase its impact
- *Reliability:* having one's words and actions be in accord with each other
- *Seeing clearly and acting appropriately:* being able to find one's bearings independently; making proper distinctions between who is a friend and who is not
- *Being principled, yet flexible:* knowing where one stands, while not being rigid
- *Valuing life:* having a sense of oneness with other people and the environment, and a commitment to their protection

. . .

Values should not be the exclusive property of the religious right, as they often seem to be today. The list above points to the powerful ethical system inherent in the revolutionary struggle to transform society. It also foreshadows the standards that are likely to guide behavior in the future—at least until people develop their moral outlook further under the new conditions of social liberation.

NURTURE THE STRATEGIC ALLIANCE WHERE YOU ARE

. . . While each movement has its own strategic configuration, priorities, and plan of action, the target is the same—a single, integral oppressive system that must be transformed . . . .

Being guided by such an awareness has implications for the way activists conduct their organizing work today. While engaging in a particular struggle, one can keep in mind the larger systemic reality of race, gender, and class oppression. By doing so, one can then look for intersections and ways to connect with other strategic forces. . . .

INCREASE TIES AMONG ORGANIZATIONS

. . . [T]here is much to learn to enable people in groups to function effectively together. The points made there about managing differences while uniting to carry out work applies

NEXT STEPS

also to groups of organizations—in the form of coalitions, federations, and fronts. In order for one group to join in united action with another, both groups have to first exist—so the first responsibility is to the health of one's own organization. But once this aspect is taken care of, it is good to find ways to link up with others. Organizations together can magnify each other's impact, deepen understanding of the issues, and learn important lessons on how to keep decision-making power at the base.

The dominant culture works overtime to keep people fragmented—focused solely on their own personal and small group issues. Part of building a movement, and then a movement of movements, is learning how to keep all the many relationships among individuals and organizations working in a positive way—handling differences, allowing space for independence and initiative, and maximizing impact in a way that is flexible and adaptive to changing circumstances.

. . .

In this spirit, initiatives are underway in the United States to "refound the left"—efforts aimed at bringing conscious movement forces into a formation that can contest for power. For our purposes, however, it is the overall outlook activists have in their organizing work that we want to stress. As people engage in social struggles, they can keep in mind the need to bring everything together in an organizational form that can contest for political, economic, and social power. Overcoming white supremacy and racism requires 1) an uncountable number of individual actions every day, 2) a multitude of organizations struggling around the issues that grassroots people deal with daily in their lives, and 3) a wealth of experience flowing out of the specific conditions in every community across the country. It also requires a revolutionary organization—party, alliance, front, or federation—that can concentrate people's vast experience and put it back out to them in a way that keeps the movement growing, struggling, learning, and moving forward together.

Movement activists can strive to embody and represent this outlook in their own lives and organizing work. In doing so, each person becomes a center of initiative. And the old Buddhist saying, "the universe in a grain of sand," becomes "the social justice movement in each individual."

And just as each individual is an integral whole made up of many parts, so too the social justice movement is the same—not just a collection of oppositional trends, tendencies, and competing initiatives, but a movement foreshadowing a different world, a new way of living together.

. . .

138

Intergroup Dialogue

Critical Conversations about Difference and Social Justice

Ximena Zúñiga, Gretchen E. Lopez, and Kristie A. Ford

Numerous efforts have been made in formal and non-formal educational settings to address issue of diversity, inequality, and social justice. While some of these efforts have focused on reducing prejudice or enhancing multicultural understanding, other have emphasized the study of social oppression and its many manifestations, particularly differences in power, status, and access to resources within and across social identity groups. Intergroup dialogue practices in educational settings reflect the third approach, social justice education, which addresses both difference and inequality while seeking to foster the dispositions and skills that may be needed to work together to address social injustices. In this section, we situate intergroup dialogue as social justice education pedagogy and provide an overview of intergroup dialogue principles and practices. Next, we look at several approaches to intergroup dialogue practice that fit within this broader umbrella.

INTERGROUP DIALOGUE AND SOCIAL JUSTICE EDUCATION

Social justice education may be described as an interdisciplinary approach for examining social justice issues and addressing them through education. This approach to transformative education examines and addresses "the enduring and ever-changing aspects of social oppression" that perpetuate social exclusion and social inequities in particular historical periods and social contexts by examining "how 'common sense' knowledge and assumptions make it different to see oppression clearly." Social justice education relies on the development of critical consciousness and transformative pedagogical practices to foster educational change in classrooms, schools, and organizations. As such, it examines the sociopolitical and ideological dimensions of systems of privilege and oppression (e.g., adultism, ableism, sexism, and racism) while accounting for their "historical roots, intergenerational legacies, within-group differences, and local as well as global manifestations."

Social justice educators understand social identity group differences, both within and across groups, as socially and politically constructed, that is, as subjective rather than objective, as fluid rather than static, as specific rather than abstract, and as rooted in particular historical, geographic, and cultural contexts. Because differences are often used to justify inequality on the basis of hegemonic beliefs and explanations, especially when these differences legitimize access to privilege for social groups associated with what is considered "normal," social justice education explicitly links conversations related to group differences to questions related to equity and social justice. Social justice education is important because dominant cultural norms about how people should think, feel, live, or behave are assumed to be universal, when in reality, people from marginalized or disadvantaged groups may not have the same means, experiences, or values as members of dominant or privileged groups and may not conform or subscribe to these beliefs and norms.

In classrooms, social justice educators integrate content knowledge about single and intersecting forms of oppression with a pedagogy that gives careful epistemological and relational considerations to how participants learn/unlearn about issues of oppression and how they consider taking action for individual and collective empowerment, equity, inclusion, and social justice. Such pedagogical considerations are crucial because learners do not live or learn in a vacuum; they are historically, politically, culturally, and subjectively situated as members of social groups (knowingly or unknowingly) that have different social positions and may have a history of conflict with one another. For this reason, social justice education theory and practice strives for a "conscious and reflexive blend of content and process, intended to enhance equity across multiple social identity groups (e.g. race, class, gender, social orientation, and ability) to encourage critical perspectives and social action."

As a form of social justice education, intergroup dialogue seeks to engage difference, social identity, and social justice through an intentional process that attempts to enhance equity across two or more social identity groups with distinct subject positions and statuses in asymmetrical power relations. It does so by addressing some of the intergroup contact conditions outlined by Allport. For example, most intergroup dialogues try to include fairly equal numbers of participants and facilitators from each of the groups participating in the dialogue. In addition, intergroup dialogue, like other forms of social justice education, gives particular attention to the experiences of marginalized groups and makes an effort to enhance equity by amplifying the voices of those who have had to struggle to be heard. Intergroup dialogue also challenges *all* participants to grapple with the interconnected histories and circumstances of their singular or intersecting privileged and disadvantaged social group identities within micro and macro sociopolitical contexts in order to engage and sustain a process in which multiple points of view can be explored and held as valid. Collins argues that honoring multiple perspectives is vital because in dialogue across difference participants bring a partial point of view that stems from their own experience and understanding of that experience: therefore, they need to hear others' partial perspectives to make sense of their own perspective and develop empathy for individuals from different social identity groups. Furthermore, in intergroup dialogue, it is just as important that members of privileged groups understand how they and others have been privileged by systems of advantage and domination as it is for members of less-advantaged groups to understand how they have been affected by systems of disadvantage and subordination. Meaningful dialogue also requires that all participants gain a nuanced and complex understanding of how oppression becomes established and reproduced and how it can be challenged and transformed at the individual, group, community, institutional, and cultural levels. According to Collins, this kind of learning requires developing a critical consciousness—"coming to see how our individual biographies are shaped by and act on our specific historical and social contexts" that can help participants understand how their distinctive group histories reflect power differences, privilege, and oppression. Educators hope that this critical consciousness will help participants develop a clearer understanding of socially constructed social group differences and begin to situate their lived experiences as social actors who have agency and can transform, as hooks states, "the barriers erected by race, gender, class, professional standing, and a host of other differences."

While intergroup dialogues often focus on a single issue (e.g. racial/ethnic relations or gender relations) or forms of oppression (e.g., racism or sexism), the range of possible issues and questions that emerge will vary from group to group. Issues of multiple and intersecting social identities and varied positions of power will inevitably arise in dialogues across differences. Hence seldom are there "fixed boundaries" to a single social category (e.g., race or gender) or relationship (e.g., white people and people of color or men and women). Regardless of the primary focus of the dialogue, the diversity of ideas and experiences brought by the participants will ultimately shape the conversation and the extent to which participants grapple with singular or intersecting privileged and targeted social identities within a particular dialogue.

INTERGROUP DIALOGUE AS CRITICAL DIALOGIC PRAXIS

The practice of intergroup dialogue underscores Freire's definition of education as a practice for freedom by seeking to coordinate the processes of unlearning oppression with learning liberation. Toward this goal, intergroup dialogue seeks to embody the examination and transformation of oppressive social realities (critical praxis) with a socially-situated critical communicative and consciousness raising practice (dialogic praxis). Thus, intergroup dialogue can be conceived of as a critical-dialogic praxis that simultaneously supports *critically* (the capacity to critically examine social hierarchies and dominant beliefs or explanations) and *liberation* (the capacity to free oneself and help support others to free themselves from oppressive scripts and habits through authentic dialogue, problem-posing, and reciprocal and empowered relations). Ultimately, intergroup dialogue may enable the development of

NEXT STEPS

a sense of individual and collective agency for creating social change and more equitable and just relationships across differences in power and perspective.

In considering intergroup dialogue a critical dialogue praxis, it is important to keep in mind Freire's and Collins' recognition that multiple perspectives and unequal power relations are always present among participants and facilitators, learners and teachers, and members of oppressed and oppressor groups. This recognition frames how dialogue processes are conceived, theorized, and structured when diverse groups meet inside and outside of the classroom. In such settings, multiple voices are valued, but not unquestioned. Participants' stories are encouraged as entry points for critical social inquiry to understand why people experience both common and different social realities and why they act in the ways that they do. This level of engagement is not easy. Participants must be willing to engage in difficult conversations that critically examine how differences in perspective, values, and access to cultural and material resources impact social identities and relationships between groups within as well as outside of the group, and facilitators must have the knowledge and skills to help them do this. Moreover, dialogue across status differences may only be possible when people from more advantaged social identity groups are challenged to take responsibility for identifying and reducing "socially determined asymmetries that dictate who gets to speak, what forums and forms of speech are deemed legitimate, whose speech counts and to whom it counts." This challenge requires a structured and intentional process and is addressed somewhat differently in different models of intergroup dialogue practice.

Regardless of the form it takes, however, intergroup dialogue addresses some of the challenges inherent in bringing members of different social groups together by promoting dialogue rather than debate or discussion. Debate aims to convince and to establish the superiority of one point of view over another, while discussion emphasizes "breaking things apart, seeing its elements" rather than "unfolding meaning that comes from the many parts." The goal of dialogue is not to convince, but to critically analyse prevailing ideas and expand what is known in a space where listening, respect, appreciation and inquiry build relationships and understanding. It is a process that engages the heart and the capacity to act, as well as the intellect. Also different from "mere talk" or casual conversation, dialogue is an intentional practice that has a focus and a purpose. Intergroup dialogue challenges participants to be mindful, involved, responsive, and willing to explore contentious issues in a collaborative way. . . .

139

Decolonizing Theory, Practicing Solidarity

Chandra Talpade Mohanty

ON SOLIDARITY, DECOLONIZATION, AND ANTICAPITALIST CRITIQUE

I define solidarity in terms of mutuality, accountability, and the recognition of common interest as the basis for relationships among diverse communities. Rather than assuming an enforced commonality of oppression, the practice of solidarity foregrounds communities of people who have chosen to work and fight together. Diversity and difference are central values here—to be acknowledged and respected, not erased in the building of alliances. Jodi Dean develops a notion of "reflective solidarity" that I find particularly useful. She argues that reflective solidarity is crafted by an interaction involving three persons: "I ask you to stand by me over and against a third." This involves thematizing the third voice "to reconstruct solidarity as an inclusive ideal," rather than as an "us vs. them" notion. Dean's notion of a communicative, in-process understanding of the "we" is useful, given that solidarity is always an achievement, the result of active struggle to construct the universal on the basis of particulars/differences. It is the praxis-oriented, active political struggle embodied in this notion of solidarity that is important to my thinking—and the reason I prefer to focus attention on solidarity rather than on the concept of "sisterhood." Thus, decolonization, anticapitalist critique, and the politics of solidarity are the central themes of this book. Each concept foregrounds my own commitments and emerges as a necessary component of an antiracist and internationalist feminism without borders. In particular, I believe feminist solidarity as defined here constitutes the most principled way to cross border, to decolonize knowledge and practice anticapitalist critique.

In what is one of the classic texts on colonization, Franz Fanon argues that the success of decolonization lies in a "whole social structure being changed from the bottom up"; that this change is "willed, called for, demanded" by the colonized; that it is a historical process that can only be understood in the context of the "movements which give it historical form and content"; that it is marked by violence and never "takes place unnoticed, for it influences individuals and modifies them fundamentally"; and finally that "decolonization is the veritable creation of new men." In other words, decolonization involves profound transformations of self, community, and governance structures. It can only be engaged through active withdrawal of consent and resistance to structures of psychic and social domination. It is a historical and collective process, and as such can only be understood within these contexts. The end result of decolonization is not only the creation of new kinds of self-governance but also "the creation of new men" (and women). While Fanon's theorization is elaborated through masculine metaphors (and his formulation of resistance is also profoundly gendered), the framework of decolonization that Fanon elaborates is useful in formulating a feminist decolonizing project. If processes of sexism, heterosexism, and misogyny are central to the social fabric of the world we live in; if indeed these processes are interwoven with racial, national, and capitalist domination and exploitation such that the lives of women and men, girls and boys, are profoundly affected, then decolonization at all the levels (as described by Fanon) becomes fundamental to a radical feminist transformative project. Decolonization has always been central to the project of Third World feminist theorizing—and much of my own work has been inspired by these particular feminist genealogies.

Jacqui Alexander and I have written about the significance of decolonization of feminist anticolonial, anticapitalist struggle and I want to draw on this analysis here. At that time we defined decolonization as central to the practice of democracy, and to the reenvisioning of democracy outside free-market, procedural conceptions of individual agency and state governance. We discussed the centrality of self-reflexive collective practice in the transformation of the self, reconceptualizations of identity, and political mobilization as necessary elements of the practice of decolonization. Finally, we argued that history, memory, emotion, and affectional ties are significant cognitive elements of the construction of critical, self-reflective, feminist selves and that in the crafting of oppositional selves and identities, "decolonization coupled with emancipatory collective practice leads to a rethinking of patriarchal, heterosexual, colonial, racial, and capitalist legacies in the project of feminism and, thus, toward envisioning democracy and democratic collective practice such that issues of sexual politics in governance are fundamental to thinking through questions of

NEXT STEPS

resistance anchored in the daily lives of women, that these issues are an integral aspect of the epistemology of anticolonial feminist struggle." . . . A formulation of decolonization in which autonomy and self-determination are central to the process of liberation and can only be achieved through "self-reflexive collective practice."

I use the term "anticapitalist critique" for two reasons. First, to draw attention to the specificities of global capitalism and to name and demystify its effects in everyday life—that is, to draw attention to the anticapitalist practices we have to actively engage in within feminist communities. And second, to suggest that capitalism is seriously incompatible with feminist visions of social and economic justice. In many ways, an anticapitalist feminist critique has much in common with earlier formulations of socialist feminism. But this is a racialized socialist feminism, attentive to the specific operations and discourses of contemporary global capitalism: a socialist feminist critique, attentive to nation and sexuality—and to the globalized economic, ideological, and cultural interweaving of masculinities, femininities, and heterosexualities in capital's search for profit, accumulation and domination.

To specify further, an anticapitalist critique fundamentally entails a critique of the operation, discourse, and values of capitalism and of their naturalization through neoliberal ideology and corporate culture. This means demystifying discourses of consumerism, ownership, profit, and privatization—of the collapse of notions of public and private good, and the refashioning of social into consumer identities within corporate culture. It entails an anti-imperialist understanding of feminist praxis, and a critique of the way global capitalism facilitates U.S.- and Eurocentrism as well as nativism and anti-immigrant sentiment. This analysis involves decolonizing and actively combating the naturalization of corporate citizenship such that democratic, socialist, antiracist feminist values of justice, participation, redistribution of wealth and resources, commitment to individual and collective human rights and to public welfare and services, and accountability to and responsibility for the collective (as opposed to merely personal) good become the mainstay of transformed local, national, and transnational culture. In this frame, difference and plurality emerge as genuinely complex and often contradictory, rather than as commodified variations on Eurocentric themes. . . .

140

The Renaissance of Student Activism

Alia Wong

Maybe the campus protests seemed rather isolated at first. Dissatisfaction with the administration. Outrage over bad decisions. A student altercation gone bad.

For example: The protest at Florida State University last fall, when students didn't like the idea of having the Republican state politician John Thrasher as their school's president and launched a campaign—#SlashThrasher—against his candidacy. Citing the lawmaker's corporate ties, various groups staged demonstrations, including some who organized a march to the city center.

Or the protest at the University of Michigan in September, when, amid frustrations over their football team's losses, students rallied at the home of the school's president to demand that he fire the athletic director. They had more on their minds than lost points: The director had neglected to remove the team's quarterback from a football game after he suffered a serious head injury that was later diagnosed as a concussion. (The Florida students' protest failed to change minds at FSU, but Michigan's athletic director was quickly sent packing.)

There was the confederate-flag fiasco at Bryn Mawr, which resulted in a mass demonstration by hundreds of students who, all dressed in black, called for an end to racism on the Pennsylvania campus. A week later, more than 350 students staged a similar protest further north, at New York's Colgate University. That one—dubbed #CanYouHearUsNow—likewise aimed to end bigotry among students and faculty; it was in part prompted by a series of racist Yik Yak posts.

Just as has been happening in communities at large, campus protests against racism and bigotry—along with related types of discrimination—have become commonplace. Students at the University of Chicago hosted a #Liability of the Mind social-media campaign last November to raise awareness about institutional intolerance. A "Hands Up Don't Shoot" walkout was staged the same month by hundreds of Seattle high-schoolers. Roughly 600 Tufts students lay down in the middle of traffic in December for four and a half hours—the amount of time Michael Brown's body was left in the street after behind shot. Students at numerous other colleges did the same.

Of course, there were other common themes, too. Early last fall, Emma Sulkowicz, then a student at Columbia, pledged to carry a mattress on campus daily to protest the school's refusal to expel her alleged rapist. Soon, hundreds of her classmates joined her, as did those at 130 other college campuses nationwide, according to reports. Anti-rape demonstrations became a frequent occurrence as colleges across the country came under scrutiny for their handling of campus sexual-assault cases. There were walkouts and sit-ins, canceled speeches and banner campaigns. Last May, the U.S. Department of Education reported that it was investigating 55 colleges and universities for possible violations of Title IX. As of this January, the number had gone up to 94.

Sulkowicz even carried her mattress—with the help of two classmates—across stage to get her diploma. . . .

These demonstrations were, and are, very far from isolated. "There's a renaissance of political activism going on, and it exists on every major campus," Harold Levy, a former chancellor of New York City's public schools who now oversees the Jack Kent Cooke Foundation, recently told me. Levy attributed this resurgence in part to the growing inequality in educational opportunity in the country, which has contributed to great tensions between institutions and the public they're supposed to serve; even protests that don't explicitly focus on this cause, he said, are byproducts of this friction.

It's happening again—it's like when we were here! It's happening! Levy, 61, was quoting a recent remark made by a friend who's a trustee at Cornell, Levy's alma mater. "He's in a position of authority now, and he didn't know whether to celebrate it or to worry about it," Levy said. "And of course the answer is both: You want kids to be politically active precisely because you want their engagement in the world, and you want to encourage them to be free thinkers." But that activism also threatens the institutions' control.

This resurgence in campus activism necessarily a new phenomenon. After all, *The New York Times* wrote about "The New Student Activism" back in 2012, attributing the trend to the Occupy Movement. But observers say the activism that's since proliferated has a different feel, and this new chapter could trigger significant shifts in the way things are run.

At least 160 student protests took place in the U.S. over the course of the 2014 fall semester alone, according to Angus Johnston, a history professor at the City University of New York who specializes in student activism. "There's certainly something of a movement moment happening right now," he said, pointing in part to the news media, which fuels activism by putting protests on the public's radar. "The campus environment right now has, for the past couple of years, reminded me a lot of the early-to-mid-60s moment, where there was a lot of stuff happening, a lot of energy—but also a tremendous amount of disillusionment and frustration with the way that things were going in the country as a whole and on the campuses themselves." And this sentiment has been taking hold in other parts of the world, too: Thousands of students (and teachers) have been demonstrating in Chile this month in the name of education reform, including two students who were killed last week.

For younger generations, Johnston added, the "belief that you can change the world [hasn't been] beaten out of you yet."

Johnston runs a blog-ish website featuring a resource that's oddly hard to find on the Internet today: a modern timeline of student protests, including color-coded maps illustrating the location and theme of these demonstrations. Perhaps unsurprisingly, the map (which has yet to be updated with data from the spring semester) reveals that most of the recent student uprisings during the fall of 2014 focused on racism and police violence, all but a few of them in the eastern half of the country. Many of these demonstrations used hashtags to mobilize, some of which are still in use today. Meanwhile, according to Johnston's analysis, about half of the 160 protests were evenly split between two main themes: sexism/sexual assault and university governance/student rights. The remainder called for improvements to tuition and funding—about half of them at University of California schools.

But they don't always have to do with issues specific to students. Just take the divestment campaigns, which are becoming a popular form of political activism at college campuses across the country, including Harvard, Boston University, and Princeton. These efforts are aimed at convincing university administrations to drop their investments in controversial industries (such as guns or fossil fuels) or corporations (such as those that side with Israel) and have little to do with on-campus issues.

"A lot of the protests . . . embrace national issues through the lens of campus policies," Johnston said. "The university is big enough to matter but small enough to have an influence on. It becomes a site of organizing because there are opportunities to organize on campus that a lot of times you don't have in an off-campus community."

Young Americans are often characterized as politically apathetic and ignorant. It's true that they vote at exceptionally low rates, but some say that's because they don't believe going to the polls makes much of a difference. Perhaps they see activism as a more effective means of inciting change—particularly when the change they seek has little to do with politics. Just last week, the entire graduate class of 2016 at the University of Southern California's art and design school simply dropped out of the program in protest of faculty and curriculum changes.

Sometimes students demonstrate precisely because they *don't* have political power. A group of Kentucky teens recently spent months campaigning for a state bill that would've given them the opportunity to have a say in the selection of district superintendents. The high-schoolers testified before lawmakers, wrote op-eds, consulted attorneys, and collected piles of research. The legislature didn't pass the bill.

Indeed, despite the uptick in activism, those in power—from lawmakers to school administrators—don't appear to be any more sympathetic student activists. Though graduate-student employees across the country have for years struggled to unionize in pursuit of tuition relief and better wages, for example, only a number of groups have succeeded in that effort.

Perhaps school officials are even less sympathetic now than in the past. According to Johnston, as Occupy spread, student activists were faced with increasingly violent punishment. One of the most egregious examples involved the University of California, Davis, in 2011, when a campus police officer, with the backing of his superiors, pepper-sprayed a

N
E
X
T

S
T
E
P
S

group of seated students involved in an Occupy protest. Though that's an extreme example, Johnson added, "we are seeing a less transparent, less responsive, less democratic university than we've seen in the past."

Recently, a group of students at Tufts refused to eat for five days—more than 120 hours—in protest of the administration's decision to lay off 20 janitors. For health and safety reasons, the students ended the hunger strike without arriving at a deal with the administration. But students have continued to rally, including at commencement.

And earlier this semester, the University of California, Santa Cruz—a school founded during the civil-rights movement that still markets itself as a mecca of radical politics—delivered one-and-a-half year suspensions to a group of students who blocked a major highway in protest of tuition hikes. (The students each face sentences of 30 days in jail and restitution, too.) Critics accused the school of capitulating to community members, who were furious over the gridlock caused by the protesters. Undergraduate tuition at UC schools has more than doubled in the last decade to its current level of $12,192—increasing at an even higher rate than has the national average.

"There has been a real powerful sense among a lot of student activists that the future they were promised has been taken away from them," Johnston said. "One of the thing that ties (the campus movements) all together is a sense that the future doesn't look as rosy as it might have a few years ago."

Permissions Acknowledgments and Citations

Adams, M., Zuniga, X. Core Concepts for Social Justice Education. In M. Adams, W. Blumenfeld, H. Hackman, M. Peters, X. Zuniga (eds), *Readings for Diversity and Social Justice*, 3e (95–115). New York: Routledge.

Ahmad, A. (2008). Oral history of Adam Fattah. In L. Cristillo (ed.), *This is Where I Need To Be: Oral Histories of Muslim Youth in NYC* (pp. 27–30). New York: Student Initiative Press/CPET, Teachers College, Columbia University. Reprinted with permission of the Student Initiative Press.

Airen, C. (2016, July 10). Pansexual visibility & undoing heteronormativity. Available at: http://cameronairen.com/blog/2016/07/10/pansexual-visibility. Reprinted with permission.

Anzaldúa, G. (1999). *La Frontera: The New Mestiza* (2nd edition, pp. 99–120). San Francisco: Aunt Lute Books. Selections of "La Conciencia de la Mestiza: Towards a New Consciousness." From *Borderlands/La Frontera: The New Mestiza.* Copyright © 1987, 1999, 2007 by Gloria Anzaldúa. Reprinted by permission of Aunt Lute Books.

Ashley and Deborah. (2007). How to curse in sign language. In J. Mooney (ed.), *The Short Bus: A Journey Beyond Normal* (pp. 106–122). New York: Henry Holt. Adapted from pages 106–122 "How to curse in sign language" from *The Short Bus: A Journey Beyond Normal* by Jonathan Mooney. Copyright © 2007 by Jonathan Mooney. Reprinted by arrangement with Henry Holt and Company, LLC.

Aviles, Q. (2007). My tongue is divided into two. In R. Suarez, F. McCount, T. Miller (eds), *How I Learned English: 55 Accomplished Lessons in Language and Life* (pp. 175-181). Cambridge, MA: South End Press. By permission of the author.

Ayvazian, A., Tatum, B. D. (2004). Women, race and racism: A dialogue in black and white. In J. V. Jordan, M. Walker, L. M. Hartling (eds), *The Complexity of Connection* (pp. 147–163). New York: The Guilford Press. Reprinted with permission of the publisher.

Bayoumi, M. (2015). Racing religion. In *This Muslim American Life: Dispatches from the War on Terror* (pp. 48–72). New York: New York University Press.

Bell, J. (1995). *Understanding Adultism: A Key to Developing Positive Youth-Adult Relationships.* Available at http://www.freechild.org/bell.htm. Reprinted with permission of John Bell, Youth-Build USA.

Bell, L. A. (2007). Theoretical foundations for social justice education. In M. Adams, W. J. Blumenfeld, R. Castañeda, H. W. Hackman, M. L. Peters, X. Zúñiga (eds), *Readings for Diversity and Social Justice* (3rd edition, pp. 21–26). New York: Routledge. Printed by permission of the author.

Benns, W. (2015). "Free" labor: Past and present forms of prison labor." *On Labor.* Available at: https://onlabor.org/free-labor-past-and-present-forms-of-prison-labor/. Reprinted with permission.

Bilge, S., Collins, P. (2016). *Intersectionality* (pp. 200–204). Malden, MA: Polity Press. Reprinted with permission.

Blow, C. (2012). Real Men and Pink Suits. *The New York Times* (November 2). © 2012 *The New York Times.* All rights reserved. Used by permission and protected by the Copyright Laws of the United States. The printing, copying, redistribution, or retransmission of this Content without express written permission is prohibited.

Blumenfeld, W. (2012). Human & civil rights under attack: 1930s & now. Available at: www.warrenblumenfeld.com/2012/03/12/human-civil-rights-under-attack-1930s-now/. Reprinted with permission.

Bryan, W. V. (2006). Struggle for freedom: Disability rights movements. In W. Bryan (ed.), *In Search of Freedom: How Persons With Disabilities Have Been Disenfranchised from the Mainstream of American Society and How the Search for Freedom Continues* (pp. 31–50). Springfield, IL: Charles

C. Thomas. From Willie V. Bryan, *In Search of Freedom*, 2nd edition, 2006. Courtesy of Charles C. Thomas Publisher, Ltd., Springfield, Illinois.

Butler, R. N. (2008). Ageism: Another form of bigotry. *The Longevity Revolution: The Benefits and Challenges of Living a Long Life* (pp. 40–59). New York: PublicAffairs. From *The Longevity Revolution: The Benefits and Challenges of Living a Long Life* by Robert N. Butler. All rights reserved. Copyright © 2008 by Robert N. Butler, M.D. Reprinted by permission of PublicAffairs, a member of Perseus Books Group.

Carbado, D. W. (2005). Privilege. In E. P. Johnson, M. G. Henderson (eds), *Black Queer Studies: A Critical Anthology* (pp. 190–206). Durham, NC: Duke University Press. Devon W. Carbado, "Privilege," in *Queer Black Studies*, pp. 190–191, 198–206. Copyright © 2005, Duke University Press. All rights reserved. Used by permission of the publisher.

Center on Aging Studies, University of Missouri-Kansas City and University of Missouri Extension. *Black Elderly.* http://cas.umkc.edu/casww/blackeld.htm. Printed with permission of the Center on Aging Studies, University of Missouri–Kansas City and University of Missouri Extension. http://cas.umkc.edu/casww/blackeld.htm.

Chess, S., Kafer, A., Quizar, J., Richardson, M. U. (2008). Calling all restroom revolutionaries! In M. B. Sycamore (ed.), *That's Revolting! Queer Strategies for Resisting Assimilation* (pp. 216–229). Brooklyn: Soft Skull Press. Copyright © 2008 by Mattilda Bernstein Sycamore from *That's Revolting: Queer Strategies for Resisting Assimilation*. Reprinted by permission of Counterpoint.

Chestnut, S. (2014, November 20). Transgender Day of Remembrance: A day to honor the dead and the living. Available at: www.huffingtonpost.com/shelby-chestnut/transgender-day-of-rememb_3_b_6186280.html.

Christina, G. (2012). *Why Are You So Angry? 99 Things That Piss Off the Godless.* Durham, NC: Pitchstone Publishing.

Chung, O. (2001). Finding my eye-dentity. In V. Nam, A. Quil (eds), *YELL-Oh Girls! Emerging Voices Explore Culture, Identity, and Growing Up Asian American* (pp. 137–139). New York: Quill/HarperCollins. "Finding my eye-dentity" by O. Chung, pp. 137–139, from *YELL-Oh Girls!* By Vickie Nam. Copyright © 2001 by Vickie Nam. Reprinted by permission of HarperCollins Publishers.

Coates, Ta-Nehisi (2015). *Letter to My Son. The Atlantic.* Available at: www.theatlantic.com/politics/archive/2015/07/tanehisi-coates-between-the-world-and-me/397619/.

Colligan, S. (2004). Why the intersexed shouldn't be fixed: Insights from queer theory and disability studies. In B. Smith, B. Hutchinson (eds), *Gendering Disability* (pp. 45–58). New Brunswick, NJ: Rutgers University Press. Smith, Bonnie G., and Beth Hutchinson (eds), *Gendering Disability*. Copyright © 2004 by Rutgers, the State University. Reprinted by permission of Rutgers University Press.

Collins, C. (2016). *Born on Third Base* (pp. xiii–xvi). White River Junction, VT: Chelsea Green Publishing. Reprinted from *Born on Third Base*, copyright 2016 by Chuck Collins, used with permission from Chelsea Green Publishing (www.chelseagreen.com).

Collins, P. H. (1993). Toward a new vision: Race, class, and gender as categories of analysis and connection. *Race, Gender, and Class* 1(1), 36–45. Reprinted with permission of the publisher.

Curry, D. (1993). People of color over 50. *Older and Bolder* 5, 31. Copyright © 1993 Rational Island Publishers.

Dallas, K. (2017). Religious freedom advocates are divided over how to address LGBT rights. Available at: http://religionnews.com/2017/01/13/religious-freedom-advocates-are-divided-over-how-to-address-lgbt-rights/. Reprinted with permission.

Dalmage, H. M. (2003). Patrolling racial borders: Discrimination against mixed race people. In M. P. Root, M. Kelley (eds), *Multiracial Child Resource Book: Living Complex Identities* (1st edition, pp. 18–25). Seattle, WA: Mavin Foundation. Reprinted with permission.

Davis, A. (2016). *Freedom is a Constant Struggle: Ferguson, Palestine, and the Foundations of a Movement* (pp. 91–110). Chicago: Haymarket Books.

Davis, L. J. (2000). Go to the margins of the class: Disability and hate crimes. In L. Francis, A. Silvers (eds), *Americans with Disabilities: Exploring Implications of the Law for Individuals and Institutions* (pp. 331–340). New York: Routledge.

DeJong, K., Love, B. J. (August 2015). Youth Oppression as a Technology of Colonialism: Conceptual Frameworks and Possibilities for Social Justice Education Praxis. In *Equity & Excellence in Education* 48 (3), 489–508.

DiAngelo, R. (2006). My class didn't trump my race: Using oppression to face privilege. *Multicultural Perspectives*, 8 (1), pp. 51–56.

Dunbar-Ortiz, R. (2015). *An Indigenous Peoples' History of the United States* (pp. 1–14). New York: Beacon Press.

Durkin, K. (2008). *Police Make Life Hell for Youth of Color*. Available at http://www.workers. org/2008/us/police_OS22/print.php. Copyright © 2008 Workers World. Verbatim copying and distribution of this entire article is permitted in any medium without royalty provided this notice is preserved.

Echo-Hawk, W. R. (1993). Native American religious liberty: Five hundred years after Columbus. *American Indian Culture & Research Journal* 17(3), 33–45. Reprinted from the *American Indian Culture and Research Journal*, volume 17, number 3, by permission of the American Indian Studies Center, UCLA. © 2008 Regents of the University of California.

Eck, D. (2001). *A New Religious America: How a "Christian Country" Has Become the World's Most Religiously Diverse Nation* (pp. 294–321). San Francisco: HarperSanFrancisco. Pages 297–300, 304–06, 316–20, 320–28 [3209 words], as specified, from *A New Religious America* by Diana L. Eck. Copyright © 2001 by Diana L. Eck. Reprinted by permission of HarperCollins Publishers.

Edwards, S. (2016). *Critical Conversations about Religion: Promises and Pitfalls of a Social Justice Approach to Interfaith Dialogue*. Charlotte, NC: Information Age Publishing.

Erevelles, N. (2006). Disability in the new world order. In INCITE! Women of Color against Violence (eds), *Color of Violence: The INCITE! Anthology* (pp. 25–31). Cambridge, MA: South End Press. Reprinted with permission of the publisher.

Evans, N. J., Washington, J. (2009). Becoming an ally: A new examination (updated version). Original (1991) in N. J. Evans, V. A. Wall (eds), *Beyond Tolerance: Gays, Lesbians, and Bisexuals on Campus* (pp.195–204). Alexandria, VA: American College Personnel Association. Reprinted with permission from the American College Personnel Association (ACPA), One Dupont Circle, NW at the Center for Higher Education, Washington, DC 20036.

Fenton, Z. E. (2015). Toward a Theory of Multiple Identity Through Coalition. In D. Connor, B. Ferri, S. Annamma (eds), *DisCrit—Disability Studies and Critical Race Theory in Education* (pp. 203–212). New York: Teachers College Press.

Gansworth, E. (2003). Identification pleas. In M. Moore (ed.), *Genocide of the Mind* (pp. 269–279). New York: Thunder Mouth's Press/Nations Books. From *Genocide of the Mind* by MariJo Moore. Copyright © 2003 Amerinda. Reprinted by permission of Nation Books, a member of Perseus Books Group.

Gessen, M. (2013, November 15). My life as an out gay person in Russia. Retrieved October 16, 2017, from www.theguardian.com/world/2013/nov/15/life-as-out-gay-russia.

Giecek, T. S. with United for a Fair Economy. (2007). *Teaching Economics As If People Mattered: A High School Curriculum Guide to the New Economy*. Boston: United for a Fair Economy. Reprinted with permission of the publisher.

Giroux, H. A. (2015, November 15). Terrorizing Students; The Criminalization of Children in the US Police State. Retrieved from http://www.truth-out.org/opinion/item/33604-terrorizing-students-the-criminalization-of-children-in-the-us-police-state.

Gokhale, D. (2005). The InterSEXion: A vision for a queer progressive agenda. *InterSEXion*. Online journal: http://intersexion.org/?q=node/1. Reprinted with permission of INTERSEXION. ORG, an Online Queer Progressive Community. This essay was written by Deepali Gokhale, with valuable input from many conversations with members of the queer community in Atlanta, GA.

Gomaa, M. (2014). American hijab: Why my scarf is a sociopolitical statement, not a symbol of my religiosity. Available at: http://time.com/3576827/american-hijab-scarf-sociopolitical-statement-religion/.

Goodman, A., Charger, J. From Keystone XL Pipeline to #DAPL: Jasilyn Charger, Water Protector from Cheyenne River Reservation. Retrieved from https://www.democracynow.org/2017/1/4/from_keystone_xl_pipeline_to_dapl.

Grasgreen, A. (2014, April 2). Dropping the Ball on Disabilities. Retrieved February 07, 2018, from https://www.insidehighered.com/news/2014/04/02/students-disabilities-frustrated-ignorance-and-lack-services

Green, J. (1996/1999). Look! No, don't! The invisibility dilemma for transsexual men. In K. More, S. Whittle (eds), *Reclaiming Genders: Transsexual Grammars at the Fin de Siècle* (pp. 117–131). New York: Cassell. By kind permission of Continuum International Publishing Group.

Gullette, Margaret, M. (2011). Taking a stand against ageism at all ages: A powerful coalition. In *On The Issues Magazine: The Progressive Women's Magazine*. Reprinted with permission.

Harro, B. (2016). Updated version of The cycle of socialization (2000). In M. Adams, W. J. Blumenfeld, R. Castañeda, H. W Hackman, M. L. Peters, X. Zúñiga (eds), *Readings for Diversity and Social Justice* (pp. 45–52). New York: Routledge. Printed by permission of the author.

Hehir, T. (2002). Eliminating ableism. *Harvard Educational Review* 72(1), 1–32. Excerpted with permission from Thomas Hehir, "Eliminating ableism in education," *Harvard Educational Review*, Volume 72:1 (Pring 2002), pp. 1–32. Copyright © by the President and Fellows of Harvard College. All rights reserved. For more information, please visit www.harvardeducationalreview.org.

Hilberg, R. (1961/2003). *The Destruction of European Jews* (3rd edition, xi–8). New Haven, CT: Yale University Press. Copyright © 1961, 1985, 2003 by Raul Hilberg.

hooks, b. (2000). *Where We Stand: Class Matters*. New York: Routledge.

Howland, C. L., Gibavic, E. (n.d.). *Learning Disability Identity Development Model and Social Construct: A Two-Tiered Approach*. Unpublished manuscript. University of Massachusetts, Amherst, MA. Reprinted with permission of authors.

Invisible Disabilities Advocate. (2008). *Creating a Fragrance-Free Zone: A Friendlier Atmosphere for People Living With Environmental Illness*. http://www.invisibledisabilities.org/creatingafragrancefreezone. *Creating a Fragrance-Free Zone: A Friendlier Atmosphere for People Living with Environmental Illness*. (2008). The Cleaner Indoor Air Campaign (www.CleanerIndoorAir.org) – Launched by The Invisible Disabilities Advocate (www.InvisibleDisabilities.org). Pamphlet. *Creating a Fragrance-Free Zone: A Friendlier Atmosphere for People Living with Environmental Illness*. Copyright © 2008 The Invisible Disabilities Advocate: www.InvisibleDisabilities.org.

Jaffe, S. (2011, September 28). *Is the Near-Trillion-Dollar Student Loan Bubble About to Pop?* Posted on Alternet Sept 28, 2011. Reprinted with permission.

Johnson, A. G. (2006). What can we do? *Privilege, Power, and Difference* (2nd edition, pp. 17–40, 125–153). New York: McGraw-Hill. Reprinted with Permission of the McGraw-Hill Companies.

Kacere, A. L. (2016, November 13). Transmisogyny 101: What it is and what we can do about it. Retrieved October 16, 2017, from https://everydayfeminism.com/2014/01/transmisogyny/

Kaye/Kantrowitz, M. (1996). Jews in the U.S.: Rising costs of whiteness. In X. Thompson, X. Tyagi (eds), *Names We Call Home*. New York: Routledge.

Keating, A. (2002). Forging El Mundo Zurdo: Changing ourselves, changing the world. In Gloria Anzaldua, AnaLouise Keating (eds), *This Bridge We Call Home: Radical Visions for Transformation*. New York: Routledge.

Killermann, S. (2012). It's pronounced metrosexual. Originally published on http://itspronouncedmetrosexual.com/#sthash.JEwBSpen.dpbs and reprinted here with permission.

Kimmel, M. S. (1994). Masculinity as homophobia: Fear, shame and silence in the construction of gender identity. In H. Brod, M. Kaufman (eds), *Theorizing Masculinities* (pp. 119–141). Thousand Oaks, CA: Sage. Reprinted with permission of the publisher.

Kingsley, J. (2004). What I'd tell that doctor. In S. Klein, J. Kemp (eds), *Reflections from a Different Journey: What Adults With Disabilities Wish All Parents Knew* (pp. 13–14). Blacklick, OH: McGraw-Hill Professional. Excerpt from "Who we are" in *Count On Us: Growing Up With Down Syndrome*, copyright © 1994 by Jason Kingsley and Mitchell Levitz, reprinted by permission of Houghton Mifflin Harcourt Publishing Company.

Kirk, G., Okazawa-Rey, M. (2012). Identities and social locations: Who am I? Who are my people? *Women's Lives: Multicultural Perspectives* (6th edition, pp. 99–108). New York: McGraw-Hill. Reprinted with permission of The McGraw-Hill Companies.

Kivel, P. (2013). *Living in the Shadow of the Cross: Understanding and Resisting the Power and Privilege of Christian Hegemony*. New Society: Gabriola Island, BC V0R 1X0, Canada.

LaDuke, W. (2005). Introduction. In J. Baumgardner, A. Richards (eds), *Grassroots* (pp. xi–xv). New York: Farrar, Straus, and Giroux. Introduction by Winona LaDuke from *Grassroots: A Field Guide to Feminist Activism* by Jennifer Baumgardner and Amy Richars. Introduction copyright © by Winona LaDuke. Reprinted by permission of Farrar, Straus and Giroux, LLC.

Larabee, M. (1993). Elder liberation draft policy statement. *Older and Bolder* 5, 19–24. Copyright © 1993 Rational Island Publishers. Reprinted with permission of the publisher.

Leondar-Wright, B. (2005). *Class Matters: Cross-Class Alliance Building for Middle-Class Activists*. Gabriola, BC [Canada]: New Society. Reprinted with permission of the publisher.

Lipsitz, G. (1998). *The Possessive Investment in Whiteness: From Identity to Politics* (pp. 1–23). Philadelphia, PA: Temple University Press. Materials excerpted from "The possessive investment in whiteness" from *The Possessive Investment in Whiteness: From Identity to Politics* by George Lipsitz. Used by permission of Temple University Press. © 2006 by Temple University. All Rights Reserved.

Lorber, J. (1994). "Night to his day": The social construction of gender. *Paradoxes of Gender* (pp. 13–36). New Haven, CT: Yale University Press. Copyright © 1994 Yale University Press. Reprinted with permission of the publisher.

Love, B. J. (2000). Developing a liberatory consciousness. In M. Adams, W. J. Blumenfeld, R. Castañeda, H. W. Hackman, M. L. Peters, X. Zúñiga (eds), *Readings for Diversity and Social Justice* (pp. 470–474). New York: Routledge. Reprint permission granted by the editors.

Maathai, Wangari. From *Unbowed: A Memoir* by Wangari Muta Maathai, copyright © 2006 by Wangari Muta Maathai. Used by permission of Alfred A. Knopf, a division of Random House, Inc.

Mac, J. (2016). The laws that sex workers really want. Available at: www.ted.com/talks/juno_mac_the_laws_that_sex_workers_really_want?language=en.

Mantsios, G. (2013). Class in America—2012. In P. Rothenberg (ed.), *Race, Class, and Gender in the United States* (9th edition, pp. 182–919). New York: Worth. Reprinted with permission by the author.

Marcotte, A. (2016). Overcompensation nation: It's time to admit that toxic masculinity drives gun violence. (n.d.). Retrieved October 16, 2017, from www.salon.com/2016/06/13/overcompensation_nation_its_time_to_admit_that_toxic_masculinity_drives_gun_violence/.

Markee, P. (1993). What allies of elders can do. *Older and Bolder* 5, 93–94. Copyright © 1993 Rational Island Publishers. Reprinted with permission of the publisher.

Meyerowitz, J. (2002). Introduction. *How Sex Changed: A History of Transsexuality in the United States* (pp. 1–9). Cambridge, MA: Harvard University Press. Reprinted by permission of the publisher from *How Sex Changed: A History of Transsexuality in the United States* by Joanne Meyerowitz, Cambridge, Mass.: Harvard University Press, Copyright © 2002 by Joanne Meyerowitz.

Mohanty, C. T. (2003). *Feminism Without Borders: Decolonizing Theory, Practicing Solidarity* (pp. 1–13). Durham, NC: Duke University Press.

Murphy, E. D. (2011, Nov 27). *Post-traumatic Stress Disorder Leaves Scars on the Inside, Iraq Veteran Says*. McClatchy-Tribune Business News. © McClatchy-Tribune Information Services. All Rights Reserved. Reprinted with permission.

Myers, K. A., Lindburg, J. J., Nied, D. M. (2014). Increasing Awareness: Language, Communication Strategies, and Universally Designed Environments. In *Allies for Inclusion: Disability and Equity in Higher Education* 39 (5), 85–99.

Nasir, N. S., Al-Amin, J. (2006). Creating identity-safe spaces on college campuses for Muslim students. *Change: The Magazine of Higher Learning*, March/April Special Issue, 23–27. Reprinted with permission of the Helen Dwight Reid Educational Foundation. Published by Heldref Publications, 1319 Eighteenth St., NW, Washington, DC 20036–1802. Copyright © 2006.

National Latina Institute for Reproductive Health. (2007). *National Statement on Healthcare For All*. Available at http://www.raisingwomensvoices.net/PDF-docs/JumpstartLinkFiles/2bNLIRH HealthcareforAllstatement-FINAL-2.20.08.pdf. Reprinted with permission of National Latina Institute for Reproductive Health.

National Network for Immigrant and Refugee Rights. (2010). *Injustice for All: The Rise of the U.S. Immigration Policing Regime* by the Human Rights Immigrant Community Action Network, an initiative of the National Network for Immigrant and Refugee Rights. Reprinted with permission.

Nowicki, S. "Modesto-Area Atheists Speak Up, Seek Tolerance." *Modesto Bee* (Aug. 16, 2008). Reprinted with permission.

Oesterreich, H., Knight, M. (2008). Facilitating transitions to college for students with disabilities from culturally and linguistically diverse backgrounds. *Intervention in School and Clinic* 43(5), 300–304. Reprinted with permission of the publisher.

Oliver, M. L., Shapiro, T. M. (2006). Race, wealth, and equality. *Black Wealth/White Wealth: A New Perspective on Racial Inequality* (pp. 11–33). New York: Routledge.

Peters, M., Castañeda, C., Hopkins, L., McCants, A. (2008). *Recognizing Ableist Beliefs and Practices and Taking Action as an Ally*. Unpublished manuscript. University of Massachusetts, Amherst, MA. Printed by permission of the authors.

Pew Research Center: Social & Demographic Trends (2014, December 12). Wealth inequality has widened along racial, ethnic lines since end of Great Recession. www.pewresearch.org/fact-tank/2014/12/12/racial-wealth-gaps-great-recession/. Reprinted with permission.

Pew Research Center (2015, May 12). *America's Changing Religious Landscape*. www.pewforum.org/2015/05/12/americas-changing-religious-landscape/. Reprinted with permission.

Pharr, S. (1996). Reflections on liberation. *In the Time of the Right* (pp. 87–122). Little Rock, AR: Chardon Press. By permission of the author.

Pittelman, K., Resource Generation. (2005). Classified: How To Stop Hiding Your Privilege and Use It For Social Change. Copyright by Karen Pittelman from *Classified*. Reprinted by permission of Counterpoint.

Pittelman, K., Resource Generation. (2005). Deep Thoughts About Class Privilege. Copyright by Karen Pittelman from *Classified*. Reprinted by permission of Counterpoint.

Ringo, A. (2013, August 09). Understanding Deafness: Not Everyone Wants to Be 'Fixed'. Retrieved February 07, 2018, from https://www.theatlantic.com/health/archive/2013/08/understanding-deafness-not-everyone-wants-to-be-fixed/278527/

Rodriguez, Eric (2015). Gentrification will drive my uncle out of his neighborhood, and I will have helped. www.theguardian.com/commentisfree/2015/aug/23/gentrification-drive-uncle-out-i-will-have-helped. Reprinted with permission.

Romero, M. (1992). *Maid in the U.S.A.* New York: Routledge.

Sazama, J. (1994). *Tips and Guidelines: For Allies to Young People*. Somerville, MA: Youth on Board. By permission of Youth on Board 58 Day Street Somerville, MA 02144 info@youthonboard.org (p) 617–741–1242 (f) 617–623–4359.

Schmidt, P. (2007, September 28). At the elite colleges—dim white kids. *The Boston Globe*. © 2007 The Globe Newspaper Company.

Schulman, M. (2013, January 9). Generation LGBTQIA. Retrieved from www.nytimes.com/2013/01/10/fashion/generation-lgbtqia.html.

Schweik, S. M. (2010). Immigration, Ethnicity, and the Ugly Law. *The Ugly Laws: Disability in Public* (pp. 165–182). New York: New York University Press.

Semple, K. (2008, October 16). A Somali influx unsettles Latino meatpackers. *The New York Times*, pp. A1, A21. From the New York Times, October 16, 2008. © 2008 The New York Times. All rights reserved. Used by permission and protected by the Copyright Laws of the United States. The printing, copying, redistribution, or retransmission of the material without express written permission is prohibited.

Sen, R. (2017, January 24). Why I marched on Washington—with zero reservations. Available at: www.colorlines.com/articles/why-i-marched-washington-zero-reservations.

Serano, J. (2007). Trans woman manifesto. *Whipping Girl: A Transsexual Woman on Sexism and the Scapegoating of Femininity* (pp. 11–20). Emeryville, CA: Seal Press. From *Whipping Girl* by Julia Serano. Copyright © 2007 by Julia Serano. Reprinted by permission of Seal Press, a member of Perseus Books Group.

Sheets, D. J. (2005). Ageing with disabilities: Ageism and more. *Generations* 29(3), 37–41. Reprinted with permission from *Aging with Disabilities: Ageism and More*, volume 29, issue 3, pages 37–41. [Fall]. Copyright © 2005. American Society on Aging, San Francisco, California. www.asaging.org.

Smith, A. (2006). Heteropatriarchy and the three pillars of white supremacy: Rethinking women of color organizing. In INCITE (ed.), *The Color of Violence: The INCITE! Anthology* (pp. 66–73). Cambridge, MA: South End Press. Reprinted with permission of the publisher.

Smith, C. (2007). The personal is political. In *The Cost of Privilege* (pp. 374–382). Fayetteville, NC: Camino Press.

Smith, L., Redington, R. (2010). Class dismissed: Making the case for the study of classist microaggressions. In D. W. Sue (ed.), *Microaggressions and Marginalized Groups in Society: Race, Gender, Sexual Orientation, Class, and Religious Manifestations* (pp. 269–286). New York: Wiley.

Solís y Martinez, D. E. (2008). Mestiza/o gender: Notes towards a transformative masculinity. In T. Hoppe (ed.), *Beyond Masculinity: Essays by Queer Men on Gender and Politics*. Available at http://www.beyondmasculinity.com/articles/martinez.php. Reprinted with permission of the author.

Solnit, R. (2015). *Men Explain Things to Me*. New York: Haymarket Books. Reprinted with Permission.

Stryker, S. (2008). Transgender liberation. *Transgender History* (pp. 59–75). Berkeley, CA: Seal Press/Perseus Books Group. From *Transgender History* by Susan Stryker. © 2008 Susan Stryker. Reprinted by permission of Seal Press, a member of Perseus Books Group.

About the Contributors

Maurianne Adams is Professor Emerita of Education at the University of Massachusetts Amherst and a founding member of the graduate faculty in Social Justice Education. She has written on SJE for *The Routledge International Handbook of Social Justice* (2014) and *The Praeger Handbook of Social Justice and Psychology* (2014). She has written for all editions of *Teaching for Diversity and Social Justice* and *Readings for Diversity and Social Justice*.

Warren J. Blumenfeld, former Associate Professor in the School of Education at Iowa State University and current Instructor in the College of Education at the University of Massachusetts Amherst specializes in social justice education and queer studies. His books include *Warren's Words: Smart Commentary on Social Justice* (2012), *Homophobia: How We All Pay the Price* (1992), and *Investigating Christian Privilege and Religious Oppression in the United States* (2009).

D. Chase J. Catalano is an Assistant Professor in the College Student Personnel (CSP) Program at Western Illinois University. He previously served as Director of the LGBT Resource Center at Syracuse University. His research interests are trans* students in higher education, cultural centers in higher education, and social justice praxis.

Sue, D. W. (2010). Introduction. *Microaggressions and Marginality: Manifestation, Dynamics, and Impact*. Hoboken, NJ: John Wiley & Sons, Inc.

Takaki, R. (1993). *A Different Mirror: A History of Multicultural America* (pp. 1–17). Boston, MA: Little, Brown. From *A Different Mirror* by Ronald Takaki. Copyright © 1993 by Ronald Takaki. By Permission of Little, Brown & Company.

Tatum, B. D. (2017). *Why Are All the Black Kids Sitting Together in the Cafeteria? And Other Conversations About Race*. 2nd edition. New York: Basic Books. From *Why Are All the Black Kids Sitting Together in the Cafeteria?* By Beverly Daniel Tatum. Copyright © 2017 Beverly Daniel Tatum, Ph.D. Reprinted with permission from Basic Books, a member of Perseus Books Group.

The Movement for Black Lives (2016). An Immediate End to the Criminalization and Dehumanization of Black Youth Across All Areas of Society Including, but Not Limited to, Our Nation's Justice and Education Systems, Social Service Agencies, Media, and Pop Culture. Retrieved from https://policy.m4bl.org/end-war-on-black-people/.

Utt, J. (2016). Getting to Why: Reflections on Accountability and Action for Men in Gender Justice Movements. Unpublished Article. Reprinted by permission of the author.

Vallas, R. (2016, July 18) Disabled Behind Bars: The Mass Incarceration of People With Disabilities in America's Jails and Prisons. *Center for American Progress*.

van Gelder, S. (2012). How Occupy Wall Street changes everything. In Sarah van Gelder and the editors of *YES! Magazine* (eds), *This Changes Everything: Occupy Wall Street and the 99% Movement* (pp. 1–13). San Francisco: BK Berrett-Koehler Publishers. Reprinted with permission.

Ware, W. (2011). Rounding up the homosexuals: The impact of juvenile court on queer and trans/gender-non-conforming youth. In E. A. Stanley, N. Smith (eds), *Captive Genders: Trans Embodiment and the Prison Industrial Complex* (pp. 77–84). Oakland, CA: AK Press. Reprinted with permission.

Watsky, J. (2012) "On the Spectrum, Looking Out." Unpublished article. Reprinted by permission of the author.

West, Cornel. *Courage*. 1,034 word excerpt from *Hope on a Tightrope: Words and Wisdom* by Cornel West (SmileyBooks, 2009). Reprinted with permission of the publisher.

West, Lindy (2016). *Shrill: Notes from a Loud Woman*. New York: Hachette Books. Reprinted with permission.

Williams, B. (2001). What's debt got to do with it? In J. Goode, J. Maskovsky (eds), *The New Poverty Studies: The Ethnography of Power, Politics, and Impoverished People in the United States* (pp. 79–101). New York: New York University Press. Reprinted with permission of the publisher.

Williams, D. R. (2006). From Pearl Harbor to 9/11: Lessons from the internment of Japanese American Buddhists. In S. Prothero (ed.), *A Nation of Religions: The Politics of Pluralism in Multireligious America* (pp. 63–78). Durham: University of North Carolina Press. From *A Nation of Religions: The Politics of Pluralism in Multireligious America* by Stephen Prothero. Copyright © 2006 by the University of North Carolina Press. Used by permission of the publisher. www.uncpress.unc.edu.

Wilson, D. P. The Silent Victims: Inmates with Learning Disabilities. Criminal Justice Policy Coalition.

Wolanin, T. R. (2005). Students with disabilities: Financial aid policy issues. *NASFFA Journal of Student Financial Aid*, 35 (1), 17–26. Reprinted with permission of the publisher.

Wong, A. (2015, May 21). The Renaissance of Student Activism. Retrieved from https://www.theatlantic.com/education/archive/2015/05/the-renaissance-of-student-activism/393749/.

Young, I. M. (1990). Five face of oppression. *Justice and the Politics of Difference* (pp. 39–65). Princeton, NJ: Princeton University Press. Young, Iris M.; *Justice and the Politics of Difference*. © 1990 Princeton University Press. Reprinted by permission of Princeton University Press.

Zawam, Z. (2008). Oral history of Hagar Omran. In L. Cristillo (ed.), *This is Where I Need to Be: Oral Histories of Muslim Youth in NYC* (pp. 57–60). New York: Student Initiative Press/CPET, Teachers College, Columbia University.

Zuniga, X., Lopez, G. E., Ford, K. A. (2012). Intergroup Dialogue: Critical Conversations About Difference, Social Identities, and Social Justice: Guest Editors' Introduction. *Equity and Excellence in Education* 45(1) (pp. 1–13).

Keri "Safire" DeJong, Ed.D., is a researcher, educator, and consultant focusing on social justice education, intergroup dialogue, technology, and digital citizenship. Her publications focus on centering young people in social justice education praxis, preparing intergroup dialogue facilitators, and developing theory and curricula about youth and elder oppression.

Michael Sean Funk is a Clinical Assistant Professor for the Steinhardt School of Culture, Education, and Human Development, Higher Education and Student Affairs program at New York University. He earned his doctorate from the University of Massachusetts Amherst Social Justice Education program.

Heather W. Hackman was an Associate Professor at St Cloud State University from 2000 to 2012. In 2005 she founded Hackman Consulting Group, and in 2012 resigned to consult full-time. She is a nationally known trainer, consultant, and keynote speaker and has published on a wide array of social justice issues. To learn more please visit www.hackmanconsultinggroup.org.

Larissa E. Hopkins is Assistant Dean for Undergraduate Students at Dartmouth College. She is co-editor of "Ableism" in *Readings for Diversity and Social Justice* (2013) and co-author of "Classism" in *Teaching for Diversity and Social Justice* (2016). Larissa received her B.A. in Women's Studies and Education from Hamilton College; M.Ed. and Ed.D. in Social Justice Education from the University of Massachusetts Amherst.

Barbara J. Love, Ed.D, is Professor Emerita, Social Justice Education, College of Education, UMASS Amherst. Best known for her work on "Developing A Liberatory Consciousness", Dr. Love has written on self-awareness for social justice educators, internalized oppression and teaching about social justice issues including racism, ageism, and adultism. Dr. Love can be reached for comment at info@drbjlove.com.

Christopher MacDonald-Dennis has been a student affairs scholar-practitioner for over 20 years, having served in numerous roles including Assistant Dean/Director of Intercultural Affairs at Bryn Mawr College and most recently as Dean of Multicultural Life at Macalester College. He has begun working with national interfaith and student affairs organizations around developing curriculum to help educate student affairs professionals about interfaith/interworldview engagement and how to engage students in religious/spiritual/meaning-making work. Christopher is an ordained minister in the Christian Church (Disciples of Christ).

Benjamin Ostiguy-Finneran is a doctoral student in higher education and the Associate Director of Operations for Disability Services at the University of Massachusetts Amherst. His inquiry focuses on institutional practices designed to support college students with disabilities. His work has appeared in *New Directions for Institutional Research*.

Madeline L. Peters is the Director of Disability Services at the University of Massachusetts Amherst. She consults nationally on Accommodation Services. She co-wrote "Ableism" for *Teaching for Diversity and Social Justice* (third edition, 2016), co-edited *Readings for Diversity and Social Justice* (2000), and as a disability advocate has won a national lawsuit for the disabled.

Davey Shlasko is an educator and consultant and director of Think Again Training. Davey facilitates group learning about and in the context of social justice movements using creative expression, popular education and practical skills building to help communities and organizations deepen their understanding and practice of social justice principles.

Rani Varghese is Assistant Professor, School of Social Work at Adelphi University. Her clinical training is from Smith College School for Social Work and Ed.D. in Social Justice Education at the University of Massachusetts Amherst. She brings an interdisciplinary approach to her teaching, consulting, practice, and research.

Ximena Zúñiga is Professor of Education and Coordinator of the Social Justice Education Concentration at the University of Massachusetts Amherst. She recently co-authored two books: *Dialogues across Difference: Practice, Theory and Research* (Russell Sage Foundation, 2013), and *Intergroup Dialogue: Engaging Difference, Social Identity and Social Justice* (Routledge, 2014).